PETER CADDICK-ADAMS

SNOW & STEEL

THE BATTLE OF THE BULGE 1944–45

OXFORD
UNIVERSITY PRESS

OXFORD
UNIVERSITY PRESS

Oxford University Press is a department of the
University of Oxford. It furthers the University's objective
of excellence in research, scholarship, and education
by publishing worldwide.

Oxford New York
Auckland Cape Town Dar es Salaam Hong Kong Karachi
Kuala Lumpur Madrid Melbourne Mexico City Nairobi
New Delhi Shanghai Taipei Toronto

With offices in
Argentina Austria Brazil Chile Czech Republic France Greece
Guatemala Hungary Italy Japan Poland Portugal Singapore
South Korea Switzerland Thailand Turkey Ukraine Vietnam

Published in the United States of America by
Oxford University Press
198 Madison Avenue, New York, NY 10016

First issued as an Oxford University Press paperback, 2017

Library of Congress Cataloging-in-Publication Data
Caddick-Adams, Peter, 1960–
Snow and steel : the Battle of the Bulge, 1944–45 / Peter Caddick-Adams.
page cm
Includes bibliographical references and index.
ISBN 978-0-19-933514-5 (hardcover); 978-0-19-062779-9 (paperback)
1. Ardennes, Battle of the, 1944–1945. 2. World War, 1939–1945—
Campaigns—Belgium. 3. World War, 1939–1945—Campaigns—
Luxembourg. I. Title.
D756.5.A7C27 2014
940.54'219348—dc23
2014021570

To Roger Marsh Blomfield
1925–2012
Housemaster and History Teacher
Shrewsbury School

Praise for *Snow and Steel*

"Peter Caddick-Adams's *Snow and Steel* offers readers, at long last, the entirety of the German Ardennes offensive of 1944–5, popularly known as the Battle of the Bulge. Until now the story of the Bulge has been recounted unevenly, in bits and pieces and with emphasis upon pockets of heroism and horror. This book's singular achievement is to offer a balanced view of the strategy and tactics of both sides. Writing with authority yet wearing his scholarship lightly, Caddick-Adams offers an encyclopedic and immersive narrative of the battle that was, in Churchill's words, 'an ever-famous American victory.'"—**Andrew Roberts, author of *The Storm of War: A New History of the Second World War*, and *Napoleon: A Life***

"[Caddick-Adams] has woven the threads together skillfully and written a book which analysis and narrative combine to provide a brilliant anatomy of a modern battle. Above all, and this is what makes the book enjoyable for the general reader as well as the military buff, Caddick-Adams explains the context of the battle and examines the strengths or weaknesses of the antagonists, their leaders, equipment, ideologies, economic resources, and intelligence systems."—***The Times (UK)***

"Peter Caddick-Adams is fast emerging as one of our most authoritative and exciting military historians... Combining deft analysis with anecdote, he never loses sight of the immense human drama, and his empathy for the many combatants and civilians caught up in this brutal battle is profoundly moving. This is a rich, thought-provoking and surely definitive account of one of the most iconic battles of the Second World War."—**James Holland, author of *The Battle of Britain* and *Dam Busters***

"*Snow and Steel* tells the story of the Battle of the Bulge from foxhole to the Fuhrer's Command Headquarters, leaving the reader with a new appreciation for the largest battle America fought in the Second World War. With a soldier's insight into the flow and fog of battle, *Snow and Steel* demonstrates why Peter Caddick-Adams rates highly among the new generation of battlefield historians. A must-have and must-read for students of the European War."—**LTC (Ret) Roger Cirillo, Association of the US Army Institute of Land Warfare**

"Caddick-Adams is probably the best military historian of his generation, and *Snow and Steel*is the definitive account of one of the key punctuation marks in history, when the western Allies thwarted Germany's last attempt to turn the tide of the Second World War."—**Chris Bellamy, University of Greenwich**

"*Snow and Steel* is a fresh re-telling of a widely known story. Throughout the narrative Peter Caddick-Adams transitions smoothly back and forth between the highest strategic and operational echelons, down to the level of the frontline GI and Landser. The result is a rich tapestry of the single largest battle in American history."—**Maj. Gen. David T. Zabecki, U.S. Army (Ret'd)**

"Like its predecessor (*Monte Cassino: Ten Armies in Hell*), *Snow and Steel* brings a fresh and innovative approach to military history-so long restricted to the dry study of generals and operations. By exploring the cultures and motivations of the participant armies, as well as by excavating veterans› accounts of surviving the sharp end, Caddick-Adams suffuses life, spark, and dynamism into his new narrative of the incredible story of the Battle of the Bulge."

—**Alexander Rose, author of *Washington's Spies* (now an AMC series)**

"A gripping account of one of the most important campaigns of the last year of World War Two, *Snow and Steel* deserves attention from anyone interested in the war."
—Jeremy Black, author of *War and Technology*

"Caddick-Adams casts a wide net, delving deep into the background, conduct, consequences and even historiography of this iconic battle, so even experienced military buffs will find plenty to ponder."**—*Kirkus Reviews***

"Caddick-Adams is a master at integrating narrative and analysis, and at balancing personal experiences with descriptions of operations. Broadly conceived, comprehensively researched, clearly written, *Snow and Steel* stands at the forefront among accounts of the Battle of the Bulge."**—Dennis Showalter, Colorado College**

"*Snow and Steel* highlights very effectively a chapter in American military history that has real resonance today. We all have something to learn from reflecting on it."
—General Sir Nick Parker, former Commander, UK Land Forces

"Caddick-Adams knows the battlefield well and tells a gripping tale based on the first hand experiences of those who fought across its snowy landscape, pricking a few myths along the way and re-assessing the fighting reputation of some of the commanders involved."**—Tim Newark, author of *The Mafia at War***

"Most military historians write about command and control, but very few have such powerful command and control themselves to drive such a comprehensive and excellent narrative. This is a complex tale, told in an utterly compelling fashion."
—Paul Moorcraft, Director of the Centre for Foreign Policy Analysis, London

"Packed with fascinating firsthand accounts, authoritative analysis and compelling personal vignettes, *Snow and Steel* is hard to put down. Peter Caddick-Adams, a leading Bulge scholar, has walked the battlefields of the Ardennes and studied the campaign for decades. Only an author of his vast experience could produce such a work of importance and excellence. Even if you have read many books on the Bulge, you will learn more from this one."**—John C. McManus, author of *Alamo in the Ardennes: The Untold Story of the American Soldiers who Made the Defense of Bastogne Possible***

"Superb: an impeccably researched, finely judged reappraisal of a pivotal World War Two battle that still resonates today."**—Saul David, author of *All the King's Men: The British Soldier from the Restoration to Waterloo***

"Peter Caddick-Adam's depth and level of analysis of Adolf Hitler's last great offensive, in a desperate gamble to alter the course of World War II is impressive. Packed with fascinating detail, *Snow and Steel* captures the perspectives of both sides in the epic Battle of the Bulge in a manner that hooks the reader into the unfolding drama. A riveting account, his book spans the generalship of the opposing armies and their grand sweeps of strategy down to the experiences of the frontline soldier at the sharp end. The 1944 German Ardennes offensive has been covered many times before, but this is a classic and gripping examination that stands out."
—Colonel Stuart Tootal DSO OBE,
author of *Danger Close* and *The Manner of Men*

Contents

Glossary

Ia	German chief of staff (at division), or chief of operations (corps and above), sometimes
Ib	German chief quartermaster/supply staff officer
Ic	German chief intelligence staff officer
IIa	German Adjutant for officers
IIb	German Adjutant for non-commissioned personnel
I SS Panzer Corps	Gruppenführer Hermann Priess's 1st SS *Panzerkorps*
II SS Panzer Corps	Obergruppenführer Willi Bittrich's 2nd SS *Panzerkorps*
III Corps (US)	Major-General John B. Millikin's 3rd Corps (Third Army)
4×4	US four-wheel-drive vehicle, usually a ¼-ton jeep or ¾-ton Dodge
V Corps (US)	Major-General Leonard T. Gerow's 5th Army Corps (First Army), headquarters at Eupen

6 × 6	US six-wheeled cargo truck, usually a 2½-ton 'Jimmy'
VI Corps (US)	Major-General Edward H. Brooks' 6th Corps (Seventh Army)
VII Corps (US)	Major-General J. Lawton Collins' 7th Corps (First Army)
VIII Corps (US)	Major-General Troy H. Middleton's 8th Corps, (First, then Third Army), HQ originally Bastogne, then Neufchâteau
88	The 88mm anti-tank/anti-aircraft gun, also widely used by GIs to mean German artillery, assuming that every enemy gun was an '88'
XII Corps (US)	Major-General Manton S. Eddy's 12th Corps (Third Army)
XV Corps (US)	Major-General Wade H. Haislip's 15th Corps (Seventh Army)
XVIII Airborne Corps (US)	Major-General Matthew B. Ridgway's 18th Airborne Corps
XXX Corps (British)	Lieutenant-General Sir Brian Horrocks' British 30th Corps
XXXIX Panzer Corps	Generalleutnant Karl Decker's 39. *Armeekorps*
XLVII Panzer Corps	General Heinrich von Lüttwitz's 47. *Panzerkorps*
LVIII Panzer Corps	General Walther Krüger's 58. *Panzerkorps*
LXVI Corps	General Walther Lucht's 66. *Armeekorps*
LXVII Corps	General Otto Hitzfeld's 67. *Armeekorps*
LXXIV Corps	General Karl Püchler's 74. *Armeekorps*
LXXX Corps	General Franz Beyer's 80. *Armeekorps*
LXXXV Corps	General Baptist Kneiss' 85. *Armeekorps*
150 Panzer Brigade	Special Forces troops commanded by Otto Skorzeny
AAA	Anti-Aircraft Artillery
AAR	After Action Report

Abteilung	German battalion or detachment
Adlerhorst	Eagle's Nest, codename for Hitler's HQ at Ziegenberg
AEF	American Expeditionary Force, First World War US Army in France
AIB	US Armored Infantry Battalion
'All American'	James M. Gavin's US 82nd Airborne Division
Amel	German name for Amblève
AMGOT	Allied Military Government for Occupied Territories
Ami	German slang (abbreviation) for American
Army Group 'B'	Field Marshal Walther Model's *Heeresgruppe* B, with operational command of *Herbstnebel*
Army Group 'G'	*Heeresgruppe* G, south of Model's 'B', led by Hermann Balck (until 24 December 1944), subsequently Johannes Blaskowitz
Army Group 'H'	*Heeresgruppe* H, north of Model's 'B', led by Kurt Student
Aufklärungs	German military term meaning reconnaissance
ASTP	Army Specialised Training Program, GI scholarship programme at universities, terminated 1944
A/T	Anti-Tank
B-17	US four-engined Boeing 'Flying Fortress' bomber
B-24	US four-engined Consolidated 'Liberator' bomber
B-25	US twin-engined North American 'Mitchell' bomber
B-26	US twin-engined Martin 'Marauder' bomber
BAOR	British Army of the Rhine, post-Second World War occupation army
BAR	US Browning Automatic Rifle, 0.30-inch magazine-fed light machine-gun

Baraque/*Baracke*	Belgian/German term for a crossroads with a military checkpoint (from the word for barrack, or military hut)
Battalion, or Bn.	Single-arm unit, usually 500 to 1,000 men in strength and commanded by a lieutenant colonel or a major
battery	Artillery unit of company size, of between four and eight guns
BDM, *Bund Deutscher Mädel*	Nazi youth movement, girls' equivalent of *Hitlerjugend*
'Beetle'	Nickname for Walter Bedell Smith (1895–1961), SHAEF Chief of Staff
Befehlspanzer	Command tank, fitted with extra radios
'Big Red One'	Clarence R. Huebner's US 1st Infantry Division
Black Watch	A kilted Highland regiment from Scotland in XXX Corps
Bletchley Park	Allied code-breaking centre in Buckinghamshire, England
'Bloody Bucket'/ 'Keystone'	Norman D. 'Dutch' Cota's US 28th Infantry Division
Bodenplatte	'Baseplate', German codename for 1 January 1945 air attack
Bofors	Allied 40mm anti-aircraft gun
Bosche	Old French name for German invaders
'Brad'	Nickname for General Omar Nelson Bradley (1893–1981)
Brigadeführer (SS Rank)	Brigadier-General (US one-star)
Bronze Star	US award for valour below Silver Star, established 1944
Browning machine gun	As well as the BAR (q.v.), the US Army operated .30-inch and .50-inch belt-fed machine guns, both manufactured by the Browning Arms Company. The former were used on tripods by infantry units, the latter generally mounted on vehicles

Bundeswehr	Modern German Army, founded in 1955
Burp Gun	US slang for German MP-40 *Schmeisser* machine pistol
C-47	US twin-engined Douglas 'Skytrain' or 'Dakota' (RAF designation) transport aircraft, twenty-eight paratroopers / 6,000 lbs payload, became the post-war DC-3 civil airliner
CCA, B, or R	Combat Command 'A', 'B' or 'R' (for Reserve), temporary combined arms combat groupings of a US armored division
CCS	Combined Chiefs of Staff, Anglo-US supreme military body for strategic direction of the Second World War, established 1942.
'Carpetbagger'	Airborne supply drops to resistance movements, hence specialist 'Carpetbagger' squadrons
Caserne	French/Belgian term for barracks
Cavalry Reconnaissance Squadron	US Cavalry battalion
'Checkerboard'	Walter E. Lauer's US 99th Infantry Division
CG	Commanding General (corresponding to UK term GOC)
Chemical Mortar Battalion	Operated 4.2-inch (107mm) mortars, which fired high explosive, white phosphorus (incendiary) and smoke marker shells up to 4,400 yards (US Army)
Christrose	Initial German codename for *Herbstnebel*
CIC	US Counter-Intelligence Corps, founded 1 January 1942
CIGS	British Chief of the Imperial General Staff (Field Marshal Sir Alan Brooke), senior military adviser to Churchill
Clerf	German name for Clervaux
CO	Commanding Officer

Combined Arms	Usually a combination of infantry, artillery, armour (and sometimes air) assets.
Company, or Co.	Single arm unit composed of two or three platoons, *c.* 200 men, commanded by a captain or major. US companies lettered 'A' to 'D' formed an infantry regiment's 1st Battalion, 'E' to 'H' the 2nd, and 'I', 'K', 'L' and 'M' (there was no 'J'), the 3rd battalion. German companies numbered 1–4 formed their I Battalion, 2–8 the II Battalion and 9–12 the III.
COM-Z	Communications Zone, US area behind front line to logistics ports, commanded by Lieutenant-General J. C. H. Lee
CP	Command Post
C-rations	Assortment of drab-green food tins and packets, plus accessories of gum, cigarettes, matches, toilet paper and tin opener
Das Reich	German 2nd SS Panzer Division
Der Führer	Regiment of *Das Reich* Division
Distinguished Service Cross	America's second highest decoration for valour, established 1918
Division	The smallest standard combined-arms formation, 10,000–15,000 men in strength and usually commanded by a major-general
DR, *Deutsche Reichsbahn*	German Railways
Enigma	German enciphering machine whose secrets were unlocked at Bletchley Park (q.v.)
Ersatzheer	German Replacement Army (Stauffenberg was originally its chief of staff, until 20 July 1944). Afterwards commanded by Heinrich Himmler
ETHINT	Post-Second World War US Army European Theater Historical Interrogations Program

ETO	European Theater of Operations
FA	US Army Field Artillery (FAB = FA Battalion), with twelve 105 or 155mm guns
Fallschirm Division	German parachute division
Fallschirmjäger	German paratrooper
Fallschirmpionier	German parachute engineer
Fahnenjunker	Officer cadet, all German officers had to serve in the ranks before commissioning
Feldwebel	German Army/Luftwaffe rank of Sergeant (senior to *Unteroffizier*)
Fifteenth Army (US)	US Army formation led in 1945 by Gerow, then Patton
Fifth Panzer Army	German formation commanded by General Hasso von Manteuffel
Firefly	Sherman tank mounting British 17-pounder gun
First Army (US)	Formation led by Lieutenant-General Courtney H. Hodges, based in Spa until 18 December, Chaudfontaine until 22 December, then Troyes, headquarters codename 'Master'
Flak	*Fliegerabwehrkanone*, German anti-aircraft gun, or unit
Focke-Wulf	Focke-Wulf 190 single-seat German fighter
Fort Benning, Georgia	US Army infantry school since 1918
Fort Knox, Kentucky	US Army armour school 1918–2012
Fort Leavenworth, Kansas	US Army Command and General Staff College since 1881
Freiherr	German term of nobility, equivalent to Baron
Fronthasen	'Front hare', German slang for veteran soldier
Führerbunker	Hitler's command bunker, latterly in Berlin where he died
Führerbefehl	Order emanating directly from Hitler

Führer-Begleit-Brigade	Hitler's (literally leader's) Escort, German mini-division, commanded by Oberst Otto Remer
Führerhauptquartier	Hitler's personal headquarters
FUSAG	First US Army Group, fictional command, led by Patton
G-1	Personnel officer or department (division level and above)
G-2	Intelligence officer or department (division level and above)
G-3	Operations officer or department (division level and above)
G-4	Supply officer or department (division level and above)
G-5	Civil affairs officer or department (division level and above)
Garand	US M-1 rifle, used .30-06-inch cartridges in an eight-round clip
Gauleiter	Senior Nazi official, presiding over each of the 43 *Gaue* (districts) of Nazi Germany, answerable only to Hitler
Gefreiter	German rank of Lance Corporal
Generalfeldmarschall	German Field Marshal (five-star rank)
Generaloberst	German General (four-star rank)
General der Infanterie, der Panzer, etc.	German Lieutenant-General (three-star rank)
Generalleutnant	German Major-General (two-star rank)
Generalmajor	German Brigadier-General (one-star rank)
Gestapo	Abbreviation of *Geheime Staatspolizei*, Secret State Police
GI	American soldier
GOC	General Officer Commanding (corresponding to US term CG)
'Golden Lions'	Alan W. Jones's US 106th Infantry Division

Graf	German term of nobility, equivalent to Count
Granatwerfer	German mortar (literally 'grenade-thrower')
Grease Gun	US copy of *Schmeisser* machine pistol, .45-inch calibre
Greif	Griffin, German codename for Skorzeny commando operation
Grenade	Allied operation launched with Operation Veritable
Grenadier	German infantryman
GrossDeutschland	Greater Germany/name of elite German division
Gruppe	Group (usually German air force)
Gruppenführer	SS rank equivalent to Major-General
Halifax	RAF four-engined bomber, manufactured by Handley-Page
Hauptquartier	Headquarters
Hauptmann	German army/Luftwaffe Captain
Hauptscharführer	SS rank equivalent to Battalion Sergeant Major
Hauptsturmführer	SS Captain
Heinie	Allied slang for a German (also Jerry, Bosche, Kraut, Hun)
Herbstnebel	'Autumn Mist' (or Fog), final German codename for Ardennes offensive
Hetzer	Small, turretless, 15-ton German tank destroyer, 75mm gun
HIAG	*Hilfsgemeinschaft auf Gegenseitigkeit der Angehörigen der ehemaligen Waffen-SS* (Mutual Help Association of Former Waffen-SS Members), founded in 1951 by former Waffen-SS officers
HJ, *Hitlerjugend*	Hitler Youth, modelled on Boy Scouts, also the 12th SS Panzer Division

I & R	(US Army) Intelligence and Reconnaissance Platoon
IDF	Israeli Defense Forces
Ike	Universal nickname for Dwight D. Eisenhower (1890–1969)
'Indianhead'	Walter M. Robertson's US 2nd Infantry Division
Infatuate	Allied operation to capture Walcheren, November 1944
IPW	Interrogation of Prisoner of War team, attached to each US division
'Ivy'	Raymond O. 'Tubby' Barton's US 4th Infantry Division
Jabo	German abbreviation for *Jagdbomber* (Allied fighter-bomber)
Jagdpanther	German turretless tank destroyer, 88mm gun on Panther (q.v.) suspension
Jagdpanzer IV	German twenty-five-ton tank destroyer with 75mm gun, built onto a Panzer Mark IV suspension
Jagdtiger	Turretless seventy-ton tank destroyer on Tiger II (q.v.) suspension with 128mm gun
Jägeraufmarsch	German fighter plane concentration
JCS	US Joint Chiefs of Staff, military chiefs' committee to coordinate army and naval activities, established 1942
Jeep	US GP (General Purpose, hence Jeep) 4 × 4 vehicle (also known as a Peep in US armour and cavalry units)
Jerry	Allied slang for a German (also Heinie, Bosche, Kraut, Hun)
Jerrycan	Military twenty-litre/five-gallon fuel can, modelled on the German invention

Jimmy	US 6 × 6 cargo truck, mostly manufactured by GMC (hence 'Jimmy') and mainstay of the 'Redball Express'
Junkers-52	German tri-motor transport aircraft, seventeen paratroopers/4,000 lbs payload
Kampfgruppe	(Plural *Kampfgruppen*) German combat group of variable size often a combined arms task force, typically named after its leader
Kampfwert	German military term meaning combat readiness state
Kanonier	German artillery private
King Tiger	Also Royal Tiger, sixty-nine-ton German Tiger II tank, 88mm main gun
K-rations	US individual packaged meal units for breakfast, lunch and supper
Kraut	Allied slang for German soldier
Kriegsakademie	German military staff college in Berlin, two-year course
Kriegsberichter	German war correspondent
Kriegsschule	German army schools for officer and NCO instruction in infantry, artillery, armour, etc. tactics
Kriegsmarine	German war navy
Kriegstagebuch	German war diary
Kübelwagen	German four-wheeled military Jeep made by Volkswagen
Lancaster	RAF four-engined bomber, manufactured by Avro
Landser	German slang for German soldier
Lehr	Panzer Lehr, armoured division formed from instructors at panzer schools, led by Generalleutnant Fritz Bayerlein

Leibstandarte	Hitler's Life Guard, later the 1st SS Panzer Division
Leutnant	German army/Luftwaffe Second Lieutenant
LST	Allied Landing Ship Tank naval vessel
Luftwaffe	German air force, established 26 February 1935
Lüttich	German name for Liège
M-1	Standard US semi-automatic .30-inch calibre Garand rifle Also M-1 carbine, lightweight weapon, chambering special 0.30-inch (short) cartridge from a fifteen-round magazine
M-3	US 0.45-inch light machine-gun, dubbed the 'Grease Gun' from its appearance and copied from the MP-40 *Schmeisser*
M-4	US Sherman medium tank, many variants
M-5	US Stuart high-speed light tank, turreted 37mm main gun
M-7	US Priest, 105mm self-propelled gun
M-8	US Greyhound six-wheeled armoured car, turreted 37mm main gun
M-10	US tank destroyer, three-inch (76.2 mm) gun
M-18	US Hellcat tank destroyer, 76mm gun, used a unique Buick-designed suspension
M-36	US Jackson tank destroyer, 90mm main gun
Magic	Japanese code deciphered at Bletchley Park (q.v.)
Market Garden	Allied airborne operation, 17–25 September 1944
Mauser	German 7.92mm bolt-action five-round rifle, first issued in 1898
Medal of Honor	America's highest award for valour

Messerschmitt	The Messerschmitt 109 and 262 were single-seat German fighter aircraft, the latter a jet
MG-34 or 42	German belt-fed 7.92mm machine-gun, often known as the Spandau or 'Hitler's band-saw'
MIA	Missing in Action
Michelin	French tyre and map-making company
MLR	Main Line of Resistance (US Army term)
Monty	Nickname for Sir Bernard Montgomery (1887–1976)
Mosquito	RAF high-speed, twin-engined aircraft made by De Havilland
MP-40	German *Schmeisser* 9mm machine pistol, the 'Burp Gun'
MP-44	*Sturmgewehr*, German assault rifle, with signature curved magazine, containing thirty 7.92mm (short) rounds
MSR	Main Supply Route (US military logistical term)
NATO	North Atlantic Treaty Organisation, founded 1949
NCO	Non Commissioned Officer
Nebelwerfer	German six-barrelled mortar on two-wheeled trailer
Ninth Army (US)	American formation led by Lieutenant-General William H. Simpson, located at Maastricht, headquarters codename 'Conquer'
Ninth Army (German)	German formation led by Walther Model in Russia
Nordwind	'North Wind', German 1 January 1945 operation south of Ardennes
Null-Tag	Sometimes *O-Tag* (Zero Day), German equivalent of D-Day

OB West	*Oberbefehlshaber West*; Supreme Command of German forces in the West – von Rundstedt or his headquarters
Oberfeldwebel	German Army/Luftwaffe rank of Master Sergeant/WO2
Oberführer	SS rank of Senior Colonel, no exact Allied equivalent
Obergefreiter	German Army/Luftwaffe Corporal
Obergruppenführer	SS rank equivalent to Lieutenant-General
Oberleutnant	German Army/Luftwaffe First Lieutenant
Oberscharführer	SS rank equivalent to Company Sergeant Major
Oberst	German Army/Luftwaffe Colonel
Oberstgruppenführer	SS rank equivalent to Colonel General ('Sepp' Dietrich)
Oberstleutnant	German Army/Luftwaffe Lieutenant-Colonel
Obersturmbannführer	SS rank equivalent to Lieutenant-Colonel
OCMH	Office of the Chief of Military History (US Army)
ODESSA	*Organisation der Ehemaligen SS-Angehörigen*, post-Second World War Nazi bureau that ran secret escape routes out of Europe
Oflag	German *Offizierlager*, officers' POW camp
OKH	*Oberkommando des Heeres* (High Command of the German Army, Chief of OKW Staff, was Guderian in December 1944)
OKL	*Oberkommando der Luftwaffe* (Air Force High Command, established 5 February 1944)
OKW	*Oberkommando der Wehrmacht* (German Armed Forces High Command, Keitel was Chief in December 1944)
OP	Observation Post

OSS	Office of Strategic Services, modelled on British SOE, established 13 June 1942, later became the CIA
Ostfront	Eastern Front
OT, *Organisation Todt*	Nazi Civil Engineering Service, headed by Albert Speer
Overlord	Allied operation to invade Normandy, beginning 6 June 1944
P-38	US twin-engined Lockheed 'Lightning' multi-role fighter
P-47	US single-engined Republic 'Thunderbolt' fighter, usually used in ground attack role
P-51	US singled-engined North American 'Mustang' fighter, used to escort bombers and intercept opposing aircraft
Panther	German Mark V battle tank, forty-five tons, 75mm main gun
panzer	German for armour or tank
Panzer Mark IV	Standard twenty-five-ton German tank of 1943–4, with 75mm main gun
Panzerfaust	'Tank Fist', German throw-away anti-tank weapon
Panzergrenadier	German mechanised infantry soldier or unit
Panzerjager	German anti-tank gun or unit
Panzerschreck	'Tank Terror', German bazooka-like anti-tank weapon
Panzerwaffe	Armoured branch of German armed forces
PFC	Private, First Class
Phantom	British GHQ Liaison Regiment under Montgomery's personal command
PI	Photo Intelligence
Pionier	German military engineer
PIR	Parachute Infantry Regiment

Platoon	infantry unit of 30–50 troops or armour unit of four tanks
POW or PW	Abbreviation for Prisoner of War
Plunder	Anglo-US-Canadian Rhine crossings of 23–24 March 1945
Priest	M-7 self-propelled 105mm artillery piece on tracked Sherman suspension
PTSD	Post Traumatic Stress Disorder
Purple Heart	US medal awarded to those wounded or killed, established 1932, with awards backdated to 1917
RAD, *Reichsarbeitsdienst*	German Labour Service, compulsory for young men prior to military conscription
RAF	Royal Air Force
RB	Rifle Brigade, a British Army battalion
'Railsplitters'	Alexander R. Bolling's US 84th Infantry Division
'Red Ball Express'	US trucking operation from Normandy to the front lines, August–November 1944
REFORGER	Post-Second World War REturn of FORces to GERmany NATO military exercises
Regiment, or Regt.	US or German term for a single-arm unit, consisting of two or three battalions; a typical infantry regiment was 3,000 men and usually commanded by a colonel
Reichsbahn	German state railway network
Reichsführer-SS	Leader of the SS, Heinrich Himmler
Reichskanzlei	Hitler's Reich Chancellery building in central Berlin
Reichsmarschall	Rank above *Generalfeldmarschall*, only used by Göring
Reichswehr	German Army 1921–35
Ritter	German title of nobility, equivalent to Knight ('Sir')

Ritterkreuz	German Knight's Cross of the Iron Cross, worn at the neck
Rollbahn	German march route, assigned to panzer units
Rottenführer	SS rank of Corporal
R and R	Rest and Recuperation, time away from the front
RSO	*Raupenschlepper Ost*, German military truck on caterpillar tracks
RTR	Royal Tank Regiment, British armoured formation
S-1	Personnel officer or section (regiment and below)
S-2	Intelligence officer or section (regiment and below)
S-3	Operations officer or section (regiment and below)
S-4	Supply officer or section (regiment and below)
SA, *Sturmabteilung*	Storm Detachment, pre-Second World War Nazi 'brownshirt' paramilitaries
SACEUR	Supreme Allied Commander Europe, established 2 April 1951, first holder of post was Eisenhower
SAM	Surface to Air Missile
SAS	Special Air Service, British special forces regiment
SCR	US Signal Corps Radio
'Screaming Eagles'	Maxwell D. Taylor's US 101st Airborne Division
Scharführer	SS rank of Staff Sergeant
Schütze	SS rank of Private
Schwere	Heavy, as in *Schwere-Panzer-Abteilung* (heavy tank battalion)

Schwimmwagen	German amphibious jeep, manufactured by VW
Second Army	British formation commanded by General Sir Miles Dempsey
Seventh Army (German)	Formation led by General Erich Brandenberger
Seventh Army (US)	Formation led by General Alexander M. 'Sandy' Patch
SHAEF	Supreme Headquarters Allied Expeditionary Force, in Versailles, codename 'Shellburst'
Sherman	The M-4 standard Allied tank of 1943–5
Siegfried Line	Western frontier defence lines, of dragon's teeth, bunkers and minefields (German *Westwall*)
SIGINT	Signals Intelligence
Silver Star	US award for valour above Bronze Star, below Distinguished Service Cross, established 1918
Sippenhaft	Guilt and punishment extended by the Nazis to families of those accused of treason after 20 July 1944
Sixth Army Group (US)	Formation commanded by General Jacob 'Jake' L. Devers
Sixth Panzer Army	Formation led by Oberstgruppenführer Sepp Dietrich containing mostly SS troops
'Skyline Drive'	GI name for road that ran from St Vith to Diekirch, on high ground west of and parallel to River Our
SLU	Special Liaison Unit, Ultra-cleared liaison officers
SNAFU	Situation Normal, All F***ed Up; in Bastogne, Team SNAFU was formed from stragglers to repel German penetrations

SOE	British Special Operations Executive, special forces organisation which aided partisans and resistance units, established 22 July 1940
SP	Self-propelled (armoured vehicle)
SPECOU	Special Coverage Unit of the US Army Signal Corps
Spitfire	RAF single-engined fighter, made by Supermarine
Spitze	'Point' or vanguard of German *Kampfgruppe*
Squad	smallest military unit of eight to twelve soldiers (corresponds to British army section)
SS, *Schutzstaffel*	Protection Squad, Hitler's original 'blackshirt' bodyguards
Stahlhelm	German steel helmet
Stalag	German *Stammlager*, prisoner of war camp for all ranks
Standartenführer	SS rank equivalent to Colonel
Stars and Stripes	US daily military newspaper, founded 1861
Stösser	German parachute drop behind US lines
StuG, *Sturmgeschütz*	German twenty-five-ton turret-less mini-tank, with 75mm main gun
Sturmbannführer	SS rank equivalent to Major
Sturmgewehr	German MP-44 assault rifle
Sturmmann	SS rank of Lance Corporal, or PFC
T/4	US rank of Technician Fourth Grade with status of Sergeant
TD	US tank destroyer, either a towed 57mm gun or an M-10, M-18 or M-36 tracked armoured vehicle
TF	US Army Task Force
Third Army (US)	George S. Patton's command, based in Nancy, headquarters codename 'Lucky'

Tiger	German tank, the sixty-nine-ton Tiger II was used in the Ardennes. Term was widely used by GIs to denote German tanks, though very few were actually Tiger IIs
Totenkopf	Death's head insignia worn by tank and SS personnel
Tracer	Illuminating ammunition to help correct aim
Twelfth Army Group (US)	Commanded by General Omar Bradley, based in Luxembourg, headquarters codename 'Eagle'
Twenty-First Army Group	Commanded by Field Marshal Bernard Montgomery, based at Zonhoven, Belgium, headquarters codename 'Lion'
Typhoon	RAF single-seat, ground-attack fighter, manufactured by Hawker
Ultra	Codename for process of deciphering German Enigma traffic, hence 'Ultra-classified' documents and 'Ultra-cleared' officers
Unteroffizier	German Army/ Luftwaffe rank of Sergeant
Unterscharführer	SS rank of Sergeant
USAAF	United States Army Air Force, succeeded in 1947 by the USAF
USAEUR	United States Army Europe
USO	United Service Organization, provided live entertainment shows to US troops overseas, established 1941
V-1	'Doodlebug' flying bomb, *Vergeltungswaffe*-1 (Vengeance Weapon)
V-2	Rocket *Vergeltungswaffe*-2 (Vengeance Weapon)
Varsity	Allied airborne operation supporting the Rhine Crossings, 24 March 1945
Vaterland	Fatherland

Veritable	Allied operation to clear the *Reichswald*, February–March 1945
VMI	Virginia Military Institute, US military school attended by Patton, founded 1839
Völkischer Beobachter	Nazi Party daily newspaper widely circulated throughout Germany
VolksArtillerie	Artillery units working with *Volksgrenadier* divisions
Volksdeutsche	Citizens of a non-German country considered by the Nazis to be ethnically German
Volksgerichtshof	People's Court
Volksgrenadier	German People's infantry division organized in late 1944
Volkssturm	People's Militia Home Guard, established 18 October 1944
VolksWerfer	*Nebelwerfer* units working with *Volksgrenadier* divisions
WAC	(US) Women's Army Corps, established 1 July 1943
Wacht am Rhein	Penultimate codename for Ardennes offensive, after the popular nineteenth-century German song (see also *Christrose* and *Herbstnebel*)
Waffen-SS	The 'Fighting SS' (as opposed to other branches)
Wald	Wood or forest, as in *Hürtgenwald*, *Krinkelterwald*, *Reichswald*
Wehrmacht	German Armed Forces (excluding SS)
West Point	US Military Academy for officers, established 1802
Westwall	German Siegfried Line (q.v.)
'*Windhund*'	Greyhound, nickname of 116th Panzer Division (Waldenburg)

Wirbelwind	'Whirlwind', German four-barrelled 20mm anti-aircraft tank
Wolfsschanze	Hitler's headquarters, near Rastenburg in East Prussia
XO	Executive Officer, US term for second in command
Ziegenberg	Location of Hitler's headquarters near the Schloss Kransberg
Zug	German Platoon, hence *Zugführer* – platoon commander

Orders of Battle

Showing principal units only

US Forces in the Bulge on 16 December 1944

TWELFTH ARMY GROUP
Lieutenant General Omar N. Bradley
(Chief of staff: Maj. Gen. Leven C. Allen, HQ: Luxembourg)

US FIRST ARMY
Lt. Gen. Courtney H. Hodges
(Chief of Staff, Maj. Gen. William B. Kean, HQ 16 December: Spa)
Troop B, 125 Cavalry Recon Sqn
5 Belgian Fusilier Bn, 99 Inf Bn (Norwegian-Americans)
526 Armored Inf Bn, 143 and 413 Anti Aircraft Artillery Bns
825 Tank Destroyer Bn (towed), 9 Canadian Forestry Co.
61, 158, 299, 300 and 1278 Engineer Combat Bns

V Corps
Maj. Gen. Leonard T. Gerow, HQ: Eupen
51, 112, 146, 202, 254, 291, 296 Engineer Combat Bns
186 and 941 Field Artillery Bns, 62 Armored FA Bn

102 Cavalry Group, Mechanized (38 and 102 Cavalry Recon Sqns)
78th Infantry Division (Maj. Gen. Edwin P. Parker)
309, 310 and 311 Inf Regts
95 Armored FA Bn, 709 Tank Bn, 893 Tank Destroyer Bn
99th Infantry Division (Maj. Gen. Walter E. Lauer)
393, 394 and 395 Inf Regts
196, 776 and 924 FA Bns, 801 TD Bn (towed)
2nd Infantry Division (Maj. Gen. Walter M. Robertson)
9, 23 and 38 Inf Regts
16 Armored FA Bn, 18, 200, 955 and 987 FA Bns
741 Tank Bn, 644 (M-10) and 612 (towed) TD Bns
CCB, 9th Armored Division (Brig. Gen. William H. Hoge)
27 Armored Inf Bn, 14 Tank Bn, 16 Armored FA Bn

VIII Corps
Maj. Gen. Troy H. Middleton, HQ: Bastogne
35, 44, 159 and 168 Engineer Combat Bns
333, 559, 561, 578, 740, 770, 771, 965 and 969 FA Bns
274 Armored FA Bn
14 Cavalry Group, Mechanized (18 and 32 Cavalry Recon Sqns)
(Col. Mark A. Devine)
106th Infantry Division (Maj. Gen. Alan W. Jones)
422, 423 and 424 Inf Regts
28th Infantry Division (Maj. Gen. Norman D. Cota)
109, 110 and 112 Inf Regts
630 TD Bn (towed), 687 FA Bn, 707 Tank Bn
4th Infantry Division (Maj. Gen. Raymond O. Barton)
8, 12 and 22 Inf Regts, 81 and 174 FA Bns
802 (towed) and 803 (M-10) TD Bns, 70 Tank Bn
CCA and CCR, 9th Armored Division (Maj. Gen. John W. Leonard)
52 & 60 Armored Inf Bns, 2 & 19 Tank Bns, 3 & 73 Armored FA Bns

German Forces in the Bulge on 16 December 1944

OB WEST
Generalfeldmarschall Gerd von Rundstedt
(Chief of Staff: General der Kavallerie Siegfried Westphal)

ARMY GROUP 'B'
Generalfeldmarschall Walther Model
(Chief of Staff: General der Infanterie Hans Krebs)

GERMAN SEVENTH ARMY
General der Panzertruppen Erich Brandenberger
(Chief of Staff: Generalmajor Freiherr Rudolf von Gersdorff)

LXXX Corps
General der Infanterie Franz Beyer
408 VolksArtillerie Korps, 8 VolksWerfer Brigade, 2 and Lehr Werfer Regts
212 Volksgrenadier Division (Generalmajor Franz Sensfuss)
316, 320 and 423 Volksgrenadier Regts
276 Volksgrenadier Division (Genlt Kurt Möhring /Oberst Hugo Dempwolff)
986, 987 and 988 Volksgrenadier Regts
340 Volksgrenadier Division (Oberst Theodor Tolsdorff)
208, 212 and 226 Volksgrenadier Regts

LXXXV Corps
General der Infanterie Baptist Kniess
406 VolksArtillerie Korps, 18 VolksWerfer Brigade
11 Sturmgewehr (StuG) Brigade (Oberstleutnant Georg Hollunder)
5 Fallschirmjäger Division (Oberst Ludwig Heilmann)
13, 14 and 15 Fallschirmjäger Regts
352 Volksgrenadier Division (Oberst Erich Schmidt)
914, 915 and 916 Volksgrenadier Regts
79 Volksgrenadier Division (Oberst Alois Weber)
208, 212 and 226 Volksgrenadier Regts

LIII Corps (committed 22 December)
General der Kavallerie Edwin von Rothkirch und Trach
9 Volksgrenadier Division (Oberst Werner Kolb)
36, 57 and 116 Volksgrenadier Regts
15 Panzergrenadier Division (Oberst Hans-Joachim Deckert)
115 Panzer Bn, 104 and 115 Panzergrenadier Regts
Führer-Grenadier-Brigade (Oberst Hans Joachim Kahler)

GERMAN FIFTH PANZER ARMY
General der Panzertruppen Freiherr Hasso von Manteuffel
(Chief of Staff: Generalmajor Carl Wagener)

LXVI Corps
General der Artillerie Walther Lucht
460 Heavy Artillery Bn, 16 VolksWerfer Brigade
18 Volksgrenadier Division (Oberst Günther Hoffmann-Schönborn)
293, 294 and 295 Volksgrenadier Regts
62 Volksgrenadier Division (Oberst Friedrich Kittel)
164, 193 and 190 Volksgrenadier Regts

XLVII Panzer Corps
General der Panzertruppen Freiherr Heinrich von Lüttwitz
766 VolksArtillerie Korps, 15 VolksWerfer Brigade, 182 Flak Regt
2 Panzer Division (Oberst Meinrad von Lauchert)
3 Panzer Regt, 2 and 304 Panzergrenadier Regts
9 Panzer Division (Generalmajor Harald von Elverfeldt)
33 Panzer Regt, 10 and 11 Panzergrenadier Regts
Panzer Lehr (Generalleutnant Fritz Bayerlein)
130 Panzer Regt, 901 and 902 Panzergrenadier Regts
26 Volksgrenadier Division (Oberst Heinz Kokott)
39 Fusilier, 77 and 78 Volksgrenadier Regts
Fuhrer-Begleit-Brigade (Oberst Otto Remer)

LVIII Panzer Corps
General der Panzertruppen Walther Krüger
401 VolksArtillerie Korps, 7 VolksWerfer Brigade, 1 Flak Regt
116 (Windhund) Panzer Division (Generalmajor Siegfried von Waldenburg)
16 Panzer Regt, 60 and 156 Panzergrenadier Regts
560 Volksgrenadier Division (Oberst Rudolf Langhauser)
1128, 1129 and 1130 Volksgrenadier Regts

XXXIX Panzer Corps (committed end of December)
Generalleutnant Karl Decker
167 Volksgrenadier Division (Generalleutnant Hans-Kurt Höcker)
331, 339 and 387 Volksgrenadier Regts

GERMAN SIXTH PANZER ARMY

Oberstgruppenführer Sepp Dietrich
(Chief of Staff: SS Brigadeführer Fritz Krämer)
Fallschirmjäger Bn (Oberst Freiherr Friedrich-August von der Heydte)
506 Heavy Panzer Bn (Tiger II)
2 Flak Division, 4 Todt Brigade

I SS-Panzer Corps

Gruppenführer Hermann Priess
388 and 402 VolksArtillerie Korps, 4 and 9 VolksWerfer Brigades
1 SS-Leibstandarte Panzer Division (Oberführer Wilhelm Mohnke)
1 SS-Panzer Regt, 1 and 2 SS-Panzergrenadier Regts
12th SS-Hitlerjugend Panzer Division (Standartenführer Hugo Kraas)
12 SS-Panzer Regt, 25 and 26 SS-Panzergrenadier Regts
3 Fallschirmjager Division (Generalmajor Walther Wadehn)
5, 6 and 9 Fallschirmjäger Regts
12 Volksgrenadier Division (Generalmajor Gerhard Engel)
27 Fusilier, 48 and 49 Volksgrenadier Regts
277 Volksgrenadier Division (Oberst Wilhelm Viebig)
289, 990 and 991 Volksgrenadier Regiments
150 Panzer Brigade (Obersturmbannführer Otto Skorzeny)

LXVII Corps

Generalleutnant Otto Hitzfeld
405 VolksArtillerie Korps, 17 VolksWerfer Brigade
3rd Panzergrenadier Division (Generalmajor Walther Denkert)
103 Panzer Bn, 8 and 29 Panzergrenadier Regts
246 Volksgrenadier Division (Oberst Peter Körte)
352, 404 and 689 Volksgrenadier Regts
272 Volksgrenadier Division (Oberst Georg Kosmalla)
980, 981 and 982 Volksgrenadier Regiments
326 Volksgrenadier Division (Oberst Erwin Kaschner)
751, 752 and 753 Volksgrenadier Regts

II SS-Panzer Corps

Obergruppenführer Willi Bittrich
410 VolksArtillerie Korps, 502 SS-Heavy Artillery Bn
2nd SS-Das Reich Panzer Division (Brigadeführer Heinz Lammerding)

2 SS-Panzer Regt, 3 and 4 SS-Panzergrenadier Regts
9th SS-Hohenstaufen Panzer Division (Oberführer Sylvester Stadler)
9 SS-Panzer Regt, 19 and 20 SS-Panzergrenadier Regts

US Forces in the Bulge, 1 January 1945

TWELFTH ARMY GROUP
Lt. Gen. Omar N. Bradley
(Chief of Staff: Maj. Gen. Leven C. Allen, HQ: Luxembourg)

US FIRST ARMY
Lt. Gen. Courtney H. Hodges
(Chief of Staff: Maj. Gen. William B. Kean, HQ: Chaudfontaine / Troyes)

V Corps
Maj. Gen. Leonard T. Gerow, HQ: Eupen
102 Cavalry Group, Mechanized (38 and 102 Cavalry Recon Sqns)

1st Infantry Division (Brig. Gen. Clift Andrus)
16, 18 and 26 Inf Regts, 745 Tank Bn, 634 and 703 TD Bns
2nd Infantry Division (Maj. Gen. Walter M. Robertson)
9, 23 and 38 Inf Regts, 741 Tank Bn, 612 and 644 TD Bns
9th Infantry Division (Maj. Gen. Louis A. Craig)
39, 47 and 60 Inf Regts, 38 Cavalry Recon Sqn (attached), 746 Tank Bn
78th Infantry Division (Maj. Gen. Edwin P. Parker)
309, 310 and 311 Inf Regts, 709 Tank Bn, 628 and 893 TD Bns
CCR, 5th Armored Division (attached), 2nd Ranger Bn (attached)
99th Infantry Division (Maj. Gen. Walter E. Lauer)
393, 394 and 395 Inf Regts, 801 TD Bn

VII Corps
Maj. Gen. J. Lawton Collins
4th Cavalry Group, Mechanized (4th and 24th Cavalry Recon Sqns)
29 Inf Regt, 509 Parachute (Para) Inf Bn
740 Tank Bn, 759 Light Tank Bn, 635 TD Bn

2 Armored Division (Maj. Gen. Ernest N. Harmon)
41 Armored Inf Regt, 66 and 67 Armored Regts
3 Armored Division (Maj. Gen. Maurice Rose)
36 Armored Inf Regt, 32 and 33 Armored Regts
83 Infantry Division (Maj. Gen. Robert C. Macon)
329, 330, and 331 Inf Regts, 774 Tank Bn
84 Infantry Division (Brig. Gen. Alexander R. Bolling)
333, 334, and 335 Inf Regs, 771 Tank Bn

XVIII Airborne Corps
Maj. Gen. Matthew B. Ridgway
14 Cavalry Group, Mechanized (18 and 32 Cavalry Recon Sqns)

7 Armored Division (Brig. Gen. Robert W. Hasbrouck)
23, 38 and 48 Armored Inf Bns, 17, 31, and 40 Tank Bns
434, 440 and 489 Armored FA Bns
30 Infantry Division (Maj. Gen. Leland S. Hobbs)
117, 119 and 120 Inf Regts, 743 Tank Bn, 99th Inf Bn (attached)
517 Para Inf Regt (attached), 526 Armored Inf Bn (attached)
75 Infantry Division (Maj. Gen. Fay B. Prickett)
289, 290 and 29 Inf Regts, 750 Tank Bn
82 Airborne Division (Maj. Gen. James M. Gavin)
504, 505, and 508 Para Inf Regts, 325 Glider Inf Regt
551 Para Inf Bn (attached)

US THIRD ARMY
Lt. Gen. George S. Patton, Jr
Chief of Staff: Brig. Gen. Hobart R. Gay, HQ: Nancy

III Corps
Maj. Gen. John B. Millikin, HQ: Arlon
6 Cavalry Group, Mechanized (6 and 26 Cavalry Recon Sqns)

4 Armored Division (Maj. Gen. Hugh J. Gaffey)
10, 51 and 53 Armored Inf Bns, 8, 35 and 37 Tank Bns
6 Armored Division (Maj. Gen. Robert W. Grow)
9, 44 and 50 Armored Inf Bns, 15, 68 and 69 Tank Bns
26 Infantry Division (Maj. Gen. Willard S. Paul)

101, 104 and 328 Inf Regts, 735 Tank Bn

35 Infantry Division (Maj. Gen. Paul W. Baade)

134, 137 and 320 Inf Regts

90 Infantry Division (Maj. Gen. James A. Van Fleet)

357, 358 and 359 Inf Regts

VIII Corps

Maj. Gen. Troy H. Middleton, HQ: Neufchâteau

9 Armored Division (Maj. Gen. John W. Leonard)

27, 52 and 60 Armored Inf Bns, 2, 14 and 19 Tank Bns

11 Armored Division (Brig. Gen. Charles S. Kilburn)

21, 55 and 63 Armored Inf Bns, 22, 41 and 42 Tank Bns

17 Airborne Division (Maj. Gen. William M. Miley)

507 and 513 Para Inf Regts, 193 and 194 Glider Inf Regts

28 Infantry (Maj. Gen. Norman D. Cota)

109, 110 and 112 Inf Regts, 707 Tank Bn

87 Infantry Division (Brig. Gen. John M. Lentz)

345, 346 and 347 Inf Regts, 761st (Black Panthers) Tank Bn

101 Airborne Division

(Brig. Gen. Anthony C. McAuliffe/Maj. Gen. Maxwell D. Taylor)

501, 502 and 506 Para Inf Regts, 327th Gilder Inf Regt

1 Battalion, 401 Glider Inf Regt

XII Corps

Maj. Gen. Manton S. Eddy

2 Cavalry Group, Mechanized (2 and 42 Cavalry Recon Sqns)

4 Infantry Division (Maj. Gen. Raymond O. Barton)

8, 12 and 22 Inf Regts, 70 Tank Bn

5 Infantry Division (Maj. Gen. S. Leroy Irwin)

2, 10 and 11 Inf Regts, 737 Tank Bn

10 Armored Division (Maj. Gen. William H. H. Morris, Jr)

20, 54 and 61 Armored Inf Bns, 3, 11, and 21 Tank Bns

80 Infantry Division (Maj. Gen. Horace L. McBride)

317, 318 and 319 Inf Regts, 702 Tank Bn

TWENTY-FIRST ARMY GROUP

Field Marshal Sir Bernard L. Montgomery
(Chief of Staff: Maj. Gen. F.W. de Guingand, HQ: Zonhoven)

BRITISH SECOND ARMY

General Sir Miles Dempsey
(Chief of Staff: Brigadier Harold 'Pete' Pyman)

XXX Corps

Lt. Gen. Sir Brian Horrocks
6 Airborne Division (Maj. Gen. Eric L. Bols)
3 and 5 Para Brigades, 6 Air Landing Brigade
51 Highland Division (Maj. Gen. Tom G. Rennie)
152, 153 and 154 Inf Brigades
53 Welsh Division (Maj. Gen. Robert K. Ross)
71, 158 and 160 Inf Brigades
29 Armoured Brigade (Brig. Roscoe B. Harvey)
(3 Royal Tank Regiment, 2 Fife & Forfar Yeomanry, 23 Hussars, 8 Rifle Brigade)
33 Armoured Brigade (Brig. H.B. Scott)
(144 Royal Armoured Corps, 1 Northamptonshire Yeomanry, 1 East Riding Yeomanry)

GERMAN, AMERICAN AND BRITISH COMPARATIVE RANK STRUCTURES 1944–45

Waffen-SS	*Wehrmacht inc. Luftwaffe*	*US Army/ US Air Force*	*British Army*	*Royal Air Force*
Reichsführer (5-star rank)	*Generalfeldmarschall*	*General of the Army*	*Field Marshal*	*Marshal of the RAF*
Oberstgruppenführer (4-star rank)	***General-Oberst***	**General**	**General**	**Air Chief Marshal**
Obergruppenführer (3-star rank)	*General*	Lieutenant General	Lieutenant-General	Air Marshal
Gruppenführer **(2-star rank)**	***Generalleutnant***	**Major General**	**Major-General**	**Air Vice-Marshal**
Brigadeführer (1-star rank)	*Generalmajor*	Brigadier General	Brigadier	Air Commodore
Oberführer	(Senior Colonel – no equivalent)			
Standartenführer	***Oberst***	**Colonel**	**Colonel**	**Group Captain**
Obersturmbannführer	*Oberstleutnant*	*Lieutenant Colonel*	*Lieutenant-Colonel*	*Wing-Commander*
Sturmbannführer	***Major***	**Major**	**Major**	**Squadron Leader**
Hauptsturmführer	*Hauptmann Rittmeister (Captain of Cavalry)*	*Captain*	*Captain*	*Flight Lieutenant*
Obersturmführer	***Oberleutnant***	**1st Lieutenant**	**Lieutenant**	**Flying Officer**
Untersturmführer	*Leutnant*	2nd Lieutenant	2nd Lieutenant	Pilot Officer

Non-Commissioned Officers*

Stabsscharführer	***Hauptfeldwebel***	**Sergeant Major**	**WO1 (RSM)**
Sturmscharführer	*Stabsfeldwebel*	*Sergeant Major*	*WO1 (RSM)*
Standarten-Oberjunker	***Oberfähnrich***	**(Senior Cadet Officer – no equivalent)**	
Hauptscharführer	*Oberfeldwebel*	*Master Sergeant*	*WO2 (CSM)*
Oberscharführer	***Feldwebel***	**Technical Sergeant****	**WO2 (CSM)**
Standartenjunker	*Fähnrich*	*(Cadet Officer – no equivalent)*	
Scharführer	***Unterfeldwebel***	**Staff Sergeant**	**Staff Sergeant**
Unterscharführer	*Unteroffizier*	*Sergeant*	*Sergeant*
Rottenführer	***Obergefreiter***	**Corporal**	**Corporal**
Sturmmann	*Gefreiter*		*Lance Corporal*
Oberschütze	***Obergrenadier***	**Private 1st Class**	
Schütze	*Grenadier*	*Private*	*Private*

*Some of these ranks, particularly at Senior NCO level, do not quite equate because of the different ways that the German Army, Waffen-SS, US Army and British/Canadian armies organised their units; e.g. the Germans had more NCO ranks because they had NCO platoon commanders; other titles reflected a function, rather than a rank. The US Army also altered its NCO ranks after WW2.

**Now Sergeant 1st Class.

Foreword

I AM A creature of the British Army. My father served in the Second World War. My grandfather and his brother commanded battalions in the First World War; their father was an officer in the Militia. My first experience of uniform was joining the cadet battalion of my school in the days when Field Marshal Bernard Montgomery was still alive. Shrewsbury School, which nurtured my love of history, had produced several distinguished leaders of 1914–18 and General Sir Miles Dempsey, commander of the British Second Army in North West Europe during 1944–5. Although my nation's army has educated me, clothed me, fed me and kept me safe from harm, there is no land force I admire more for its adaptability and perseverance than that of the United States, with whom I have soldiered throughout the Balkans, in Iraq and Afghanistan.

Twice in the twentieth century it returned to fight and spill its blood in Europe, despite 18 per cent of Americans being of Germanic descent.[1] Thus, it makes perfect sense to me for, a Briton, to be writing about America's finest hour in Europe. Winston Churchill once observed, 'A nation that forgets its past has no future'. His words could not better describe the purpose of this book. Having walked the woods of the Ardennes for over thirty years with soldiers and civilians, and interviewed hundreds of eyewitnesses, my aim has been not only to remember and commemorate those who fought and died in the Bulge, but also to remind another generation of the debt we owe to our forebears.

In many ways the Ardennes has changed very little since 1945. Cities, with their wealth, recover from battle more quickly. The poorer, rural backwaters get left till last. The Ardennes are now pretty and quaint – and peaceful. The summer months see the landscape swarming with hikers and picnickers. Yet the keen eye will find buildings that still bear the scars of shellfire. Foxholes and craters still litter the forest floors. War photographers of both sides captured this small, intimate battlefield like no other, and today it is possible to match a huge number of their photographs with the same locations. Local farmers were thrifty and repaired their homes and barns, rather than demolishing them and rebuilding. That is what makes the Battle of the Bulge so fascinating to study. Using photographs and eyewitness testimony, the visitor can retrace the footsteps of the generation who fought here, with more ease than in almost any other battlefield in history.

I first became acquainted with the area in the summer of 1978 when I joined some friends who had restored a selection of Second World War military vehicles. We toured the Ardennes battlefields in the company of a dozen veterans of the Bulge campaign. Our jeeps, trucks and half-tracks, correctly painted in olive drab and bearing white stars, in some cases driven by veterans of the Second World War, brought tears to the eyes of the older residents who were transported back immediately thirty-four years.[2]

I practised my schoolboy French on a local Belgian farmer who beckoned us to follow him. Our jeeps laboured up a small forest track. 'Here,' he said dismounting, 'were the American lines.' Sadly there was nothing to see. I kicked idly at a pile of pine needles . . . and stubbed my toe. Not on a stone, but on an entrenching tool. Slowly the forest floor revealed its secrets. A German mess tin mangled by mortar fire, shell cases, cartridges. An American helmet. I reached down to pluck a bullet I could see under some twigs, and found I'd pulled out an entire belt of German machine-gun ammunition. And less welcome, a hand grenade rolled into view. It was as though the battle had finished yesterday. Naturally, this made a big impression on a seventeen-year-old school boy. Ever since, I've tried to capture the memories of those who witnessed the battle – soldiers and civilians. Most of them are no longer with us, and since then I have gone on to become a soldier and experience my own wars.

Each year, military units from the United States, Britain and other NATO countries explore the Ardennes battlefields. This is partly to honour their forebears, but also to study how soldiers and their leaders behave in combat. Such expeditions are highly relevant to any understanding of war. To comprehend how the combatants died, survived and made a difference in 1944–5 is to understand how they will do so in future wars. The weapons may change, but human beings do not. Despite globalisation and the lure of technology, campaigns like the Ardennes remind us that, in most cases, to prosecute war with success, ultimately you must do this on the ground, the way the Roman legions did, by putting your young men (and today, women) in the mud. In this respect, the Battle of the Bulge is the most significant campaign to study, for it was when armies fought not only each other, but the elements. It was when people battled with snow and steel.

Introduction

'An ever famous American victory.'
Winston S. Churchill, 18 January 1945

Nestling deep in the Ardennes, overlooked by hills and woods, Hotton is an unremarkable Belgian town of fewer than 1,500 souls, sitting astride the River Ourthe.[1] It is as close to the centre of the region as it is possible to be, and is really two towns. Divided by the water, it has a few shops, several cafés and its church, dedicated to St Pierre, which sits on the west bank, and is attended mostly by the farmers who make up the local community. This sleepy crossroads settlement, with its stone farmhouses and wooden barns, still bears a close resemblance to the 1940s town, although the number of modern structures, including the church, make it obvious that vicious fighting occurred here.

The road signs point you south to Rendeux and La Roche-en-Ardenne, or westwards, to Rochefort and Marche; beyond lies Dinant on the River Meuse, a mere twenty-four miles from Hotton.

Walk down the main street and you can picture the 5th Panzer Division racing through, on their way to the Meuse during the Saturday afternoon of 11 May 1940. Clattering down the cobbles from the east, young, keen and scenting victory, the black-clad tank men easily captured Hotton's little bridge over the Ourthe, despite attempts by Belgian pioneers to destroy it. At the same hour three miles south, other panzers belonging to an obscure major-general named Erwin Rommel were splashing across a ford, upriver at Beffe.

At 08.30 a.m. on the winter solstice, Thursday, 21 December 1944, the panzers returned, following the same route, aiming again for Hotton's bridge. This time it was men from 116th Panzer Division, called the '*Windhund*' – Greyhound – which is how they saw themselves: fast, sleek and straining at the leash to reach the Meuse. The sturdy wooden two-way bridge at Hotton was new, put in place by US Army engineers to replace one the retreating Germans had destroyed three months earlier. Without warning, and accompanied by sudden mortar and machine-gun fire on their objective, the Greyhounds emerged from the morning mists to surprise a few men of the US 23rd and 51st Combat Engineers, armed with an anti-tank gun, a couple of 40mm Bofors guns from the 440th Anti-Aircraft Artillery Battalion and a few tanks of the 3rd Armored Division. None of these units knew each other or had worked together before. The Greyhounds' morning assault, and another launched in the gloom of evening, narrowly failed to take the crossing from no more than a handful of defending American engineers, clerks and mechanics 'armed with a smattering of bazookas and .50-inch calibre machine-guns', crouching behind hasty barricades of overturned trucks.[2]

Ordinarily the defenders wouldn't have stood a chance but they had been through the Normandy campaign and the Hedgerow War and were combat-hardened and determined, if few in number. They knew the value of their little bridge to the column of impatient panzers, and determined to hold out until reinforcements arrived. The Greyhounds were low on fuel too. Before reaching Hotton, they had captured stocks of food and enough gasoline for the whole division, abandoned by the US 7th Armored in nearby Samrée, but would soon run out again, hampering their ability to manoeuvre around the little town. The defenders noted many Germans wearing GI olive drab. 'We could not tell the difference until we got close enough to see . . . Most of the Germans we killed and captured there were in American uniforms,' recounted LeRoy Hanneman of the 3rd Armored Division.[3]

Private Lee J. Ishmael volunteered to man the little anti-tank gun, firing sixteen rounds in three minutes at a German tank almost on the bridge. One of his shots wedged between the turret and the hull, preventing the panzer's turret from traversing and eventually it was destroyed.[4] Casualties on both sides were heavy, but when the Greyhounds withdrew after two days and headed south for La Roche, they left behind a graveyard of Panther tanks, and realised their hopes of a breakthrough to the River Meuse and beyond was a dream that had become a nightmare.[5]

Soon, other US units joined the fray, such as the 517th Parachute

Infantry Regiment (who won a Presidential Unit Citation there), and the 84th 'Railsplitters' Division. They repelled attacks from the newly arrived 560th *Volksgrenadiers*, who took over the sector once the panzers had departed to find another crossing over the river. The GIs who stopped the Germans at Hotton were men like Indiana-born PFC Melvin E. Biddle of the 517th, ordered forward with his unit to rescue US soldiers trapped in the area. On 23 December, as company scout, he crawled through snow and bushes and spotted and killed three German snipers with his M-1 rifle.

Then Biddle, who had just turned twenty-one, came upon four successive machine-gun nests, which he silenced with gunfire and grenades, killing twelve. Hours later he stalled a German advance, despatching another thirteen grenadiers crossing a field, and brought down artillery fire on two tanks. However, when he found a fourteen-year-old boy in a German uniform roped to a tree – presumably so he couldn't run away – he felt compassion and took him prisoner. In October 1945 the one-man army stood on the White House lawn, as President Harry S. Truman placed the blue ribbon of the Medal of Honor around his neck. 'Then the president whispered into my ear, "People don't believe me when I tell them I'd rather have one of these than be president",' Biddle would recall later.[6]

Equally brave but less fortunate was Second Lieutenant James B. Lawson, Jr, of Sandy Springs, South Carolina. Two days after Biddle's acts of valour, the twenty-one-year-old was leading his platoon of 290th Infantry, US 75th Infantry Division, in an attack through woods a few yards south-east of Hotton. His unit, which had left the USA exactly two months earlier and never seen action before, undertook three vicious assaults to clear La Roumière (Hill 87 on army maps), which dominates the surrounding road network and River Ourthe. In one of the attacks, Lawson was reported as wounded. His family and fiancée had an agonising wait until 5 February 1945 before learning that the young mechanical engineering graduate of Clemson University had died in a fire-fight, on Christmas Day.[7]

One of the soldiers advancing towards Hotton at the same time was Werner Klippel of the Wehrmacht's 1128th Grenadier Regiment. Many of his mates were older garrison guards formerly based in Norway and now sent into combat with little training. Born at Mainz in January 1927, Werner was nineteen days short of his seventeenth birthday when his company hit the outskirts of the town, battling to punch through American lines after the panzer crews had left. Having lost all their motor transport due to aerial attack, Werner's regiment had experienced a tiring few days marching up to the Front on foot through the snow and ice, with little food. Equally scarce was winter clothing: his unit had none. Within hours of reaching Hotton, Grenadier Klippel was caught in a shell blast and evacuated back to an aid post in Grandmenil, where he died, also on Christmas Day.[8]

Damage to the town was significant but not catastrophic; the main square is named after twenty-eight-year-old Philip E. Zulli, a Brooklyn-born-and-raised captain in the 36th Armored Infantry of 3rd Armored Division. He was talking to his friends Captain Anderson and Chaplain John Kraka, and reaching for a pack of cigarettes, when his half-track was hit by shells on the morning of 22 December, killing him instantly.[9]

With shrapnel peppering his church roof, Father Edmond Marquet finished Mass abruptly and handed one of his parishioners a strongbox containing the silver chalices. As in 1940, they were buried in a local garden, along with some of the town's finest bottles of wine.

Nervous of spies and infiltrators, American military policemen and local gendarmes watched the trickle of refugees become a flood; all headed west, weighed down by their possessions, some in horse and cart carrying all they owned, others pushing wheelbarrows containing the elderly. Children, sensing the fear of the adults, cried; a man hauled his suitcase along the ice with ropes like a sleigh. Haunted by memories of Gestapo arrests and deportations to Germany for forced labour, they were devastated by the return of their traditional foes.

Hotton's inhabitants had had no warning of the Germans' arrival, and only just managed to tear down Allied flags and posters of Churchill, Roosevelt and Stalin before their old adversaries saw them. Girls who had doted on GIs fled in panic when they recognised the field grey and guttural accents. Bursting into houses, hungry Wehrmacht troopers demanded information on the American defenders as they emptied kitchen cupboards and carried off sides of bacon. A farmer's wife begged them to leave her family enough to eat over Christmas. 'My men haven't eaten in days. They come first' was the unequivocal reply from a stern, helmeted officer. Civilian casualties were inevitable during the battle; on 21 December, Auguste Collard was killed by shrapnel while fetching straw for his family's bedding in their cellar. Raymond Richel died on the 22nd, killed in his kitchen by a tank round, while the day after Alexandre Lobet was wounded by a mortar shell; despite being rushed by GIs to an aid station, he was beyond help.[10]

Casualties at Hotton would have been much higher had it not been for Allied fighters patrolling overhead – when they could fly. On Christmas Eve, First Lieutenant Charles J. Loring's Thunderbolt was hit by anti-aircraft fire as he made a strafing attack during his fifty-sixth combat mission. His

P-47D crashed outside Hotton, where he was captured by the *Volksgrenadiers*. Via hospital and an interrogation centre, Loring, just turned twenty-six, ended up in the Dulag Luft Prison Camp at Oberursel, near Frankfurt. He was liberated on 6 May 1945, two days before VE-Day, echoing the experience of nearly 24,000 US personnel captured in the Bulge.[11]

Texan Jack B. Warden, a twenty-one-year-old platoon leader with 'B' Company of the 36th Armored Infantry, was far luckier. Though young, he proved a natural soldier, commissioned in the field less than a month earlier. He arrived in Hotton with four tanks on 24 December and found himself defending Raymond Richel's house, battling with German tank-hunting squads who were trying to infiltrate the ruins. Early next morning, at six, he heard shots from an adjacent barn where his men were on watch. He ran down to them: 'They were being attacked by a calf and had to shoot it in self-defence,' he recounted, eyes twinkling. 'Someone else came up with three or four chickens, despatched for the same reason, and we had a nice Christmas Dinner.'[12]

After the war it took years for scrapmen to remove the abandoned armour, weapons and unexploded munitions. From 1945, the dead were gathered into their own national cemeteries: the Americans, like Philip Zulli, to the Henri-Chapelle Cemetery where 7,992 US soldiers lie in fifty-seven acres of neatly kept lawn and trees administered by the American Battle Monuments Commission. James Lawson's parents wanted him home, and he lies in Sandy Spring Methodist Cemetery, Anderson County, South Carolina. Werner Klippel was taken not far away to the German military cemetery at Recogne, outside Bastogne, where he keeps company with 6,806 other soldiers. Auguste Collard, Raymond Richel and Alexandre Lobet were laid to rest within sight of their own homes. The war had even descended on Hotton's graveyard, where headstones are still scarred by the bullets of that dark December.

Just outside the town, along Route N86, and down the appropriately named rue de la Libération, is a small military graveyard maintained by the Commonwealth War Graves Commission. In many ways it sums up Britain's commitment to continental Europe during the Second World War. Among the 666 headstones, several commemorate men who fell in May 1940 but the vast majority date from January 1945, when units tangled with *Volksgrenadiers* in the last stages of the Battle of the Bulge. Most signify United Kingdom nationals, but others honour 88 Canadians, 41 Australians, 10 New Zealanders, a Belgian pilot serving in the RAF, a Pole and 20 who have the misfortune to be unidentified, but soldier no more.

This cemetery reminds the visitor that on New Year's Day 1945 patrols of the British 6th Airborne and 53rd Welsh Divisions arrived in Hotton as reinforcements to help prevent any further breakthroughs. They saw themselves as a 'backstop' to the Bulge created in American lines, and the graves within include those of a forty-one-year-old brigadier, Gwynne Brian Sugden, then commanding 158 Infantry Brigade, who died when his armoured car skated on the icy roads and overturned in a nearby ditch. The Allied strategic bombing campaign casts its long shadow at Hotton, where six of the seven aircrew of an RAF bomber, five of them Australians, lie side by side. Their four-engined Halifax, returning from a raid on Essen, had collided with an RAF Lancaster; only the bomb aimer survived, the rest were gathered up and buried here.

There is an unlucky fifty-three-year-old war correspondent for the *Daily Telegraph* who possessed a gallantry medal from the First World War, and a Member of Parliament.[13] Major Ronnie Cartland, MP, of the 53rd Worcestershire Yeomanry Anti-Tank Regiment, aged thirty-three, had actually been killed in 1940, but was one of Winston Churchill's loyal circle of pre-war anti-appeasers and would no doubt have held high office after the war. Regarded as one of a great 'lost generation', he was mourned ever after by his elder sister, the world-renowned romantic novelist Barbara Cartland. Back in the town, there are now plaques to the 'Dead of the War', the 51st Combat Engineer Battalion and to Belgian parachutists of the SAS, as well as a Sherman 'Firefly' tank turret on a brick plinth commemorating where Grenadier, GI and Tommy traded shots amidst the back gardens and hedges of snow-blanketed Hotton.

Twice invaded and twice liberated during the Second World War, the town – which lies almost at the tip of the German 'Bulge' into US lines – represents the reality of the forty days of the Battle of the Bulge. The population were defenceless and learned to cope as best they could with every colour of uniform until the fighting was over. Much of the wider campaign, as in Hotton, revolved around shortages of fuel, rivers, bridges and road junctions. Some Germans donned GI clothing, often to stay warm but sometimes to deceive: in the inevitable confusion, there were issues of fratricide, on both sides. The fighting at various times took the lives of Belgians and Britons, Germans and Americans, civilians and soldiers, and underlines the fact that the Second World War in Europe was fought by coalitions. In May 1940, it was an Anglo-Franco-Belgian alliance resisting the Germans in this corner of Belgium. By December 1944, the Anglo-American coalition also included military units from Canada, France, Belgium, Holland,

Norway, Luxembourg, Czechoslovakia, Poland and others, fighting under Eisenhower's command. Without this rainbow alliance of committed nations, Western Europe would not have been freed as quickly, if at all.

None of this detracts from the achievement of US forces in the Ardennes campaign, to whom a grateful and admiring Winston Churchill paid tribute: 'Care must be taken in telling our proud tale not to claim for the British Army an undue share of what is undoubtedly the greatest American battle of the war, and will, I believe, be regarded as an ever famous American victory.' He went on to tell the House of Commons on 18 January 1945: 'I have seen it suggested that the terrific battle which has been proceeding since the 16th of December on the American front is an Anglo-American battle. In fact, the United States troops have done almost all the fighting and have suffered almost all the losses. They have suffered losses almost equal to those on both sides in the battle of Gettysburg. Only one British Army corps has been engaged in this action. All the rest of the 30 or more divisions, which have been fighting continuously for the last month, are United States troops. The Americans have engaged 30 or 40 men for every one we have engaged, and they have lost 60 to 80 men for every one of ours.'

By January 1945, the war in Europe had become one of attrition which Germany was losing. As Churchill told his listeners, 'Let the Germans dismiss from their minds any idea that any losses or set-back of the kind we have witnessed will turn us from our purpose. We shall go on to the end, however the storm may beat . . . the decisive breaking of the German offensive in the West is more likely to shorten this war,' he concluded. 'The Germans have made a violent and costly sortie which has been repulsed with heavy slaughter, and have expended in the endeavour forces which they cannot replace.'[14]

The Battle of the Bulge deprived the Third Reich of the ability to launch another major attack in the west or east again. Three years after the offensive, the US War Department issued a definitive list of the nearly 3,000 units which qualified for the Ardennes campaign credit, similar to a British battle honour. It ran to forty pages. They varied in size from military intelligence interpreter teams of a few people, small detachments and companies to twenty infantry, ten armoured and three airborne divisions, the Eighth and Ninth Army Air Forces and Bradley's Twelfth Army Group.[15] In terms of participation, losses and sheer professionalism, the Bulge was without doubt the greatest battle in American military history.

PART ONE

1

In the Eagle's Nest

'Never in my life have I accepted the idea of surrender, and I am one of those men who have worked their way up from nothing. Our present situation, therefore, is nothing new to me. Once upon a time my own situation was entirely different, and far worse. I say this only so that you can grasp why I pursue my goal with such fanaticism and why nothing can wear me down.'

Adolf Hitler, 28 December 1944[1]

On 11 December 1944 Toronto is battered with its worst ever winter storm in a single day, which brings twenty inches of snow in a few hours and causes twenty-one Canadians to freeze to death on its streets. In England, RAF squadron logs read 'missions scrubbed, as the weather is very poor, being overcast all day'.[2] Elsewhere, in the gloom of a German afternoon some senior officers collect in the pretty half-timbered settlement of Ziegenberg, about five miles east of the fashionable spa of Bad Neuheim and twenty-five miles north of Frankfurt am Main. To the casual observer, the only thing distinguishing this farming village from dozens like it in the vicinity is its eighteenth-century fortress, Schloss Kransberg, a small castle atop a cliff. Now the stone edifice houses the staff of the *Oberbefehlshaber West* (Supreme Commander in the West), Field Marshal Gerd von Rundstedt. There is light rain and a chill in the air, no more. Exactly three years earlier, on 11 December 1941, Germany and Italy declared war on the United States; now that struggle was about to enter a new dimension, though not all the august assembly of officers are as yet aware of this.

They have already scratched their signatures across a document offered to them by an SS orderly. It is a pledge of secrecy about the briefing they are to receive. Something, it tells them, to do with an operation called *Herbstnebel* (Autumn Mist), which means nothing to them. The form threatens *Sippenhaft* if they break their oath: in other words, instant execution, but their families will be held to blame also, which would mean arrest, if not a concentration camp. This is the long shadow of the 20 July, when other army officers, led by Oberst Graf von Stauffenberg, chief of staff of the Reserve Army, tried to assassinate Hitler in his East Prussian headquarters, code-named *Wolfsschanze* (Wolf's Lair).

They are ordered to turn over their pistols and briefcases (another ghost of the July 'Valkyrie' plot: Stauffenberg had left his bomb in a briefcase). The lack of trust towards the Wehrmacht is palpable: everywhere it is the SS, Hitler's bodyguards, who are in control. Still wearing their now empty holsters, the officers collect in the rain-splashed courtyard and board a couple of motor coaches, driven by SS troopers. They begin a circuitous tour which thoroughly confuses them as to their destination, exactly as intended. Their journey through the darkness and rain lasts about half an hour but, bizarrely, deposits them barely a mile from Schloss Kransberg. Unbeknownst to Allied military intelligence, a stairway leads down from the stronghold to several traditional country cottages below, each possessing rustic stone walls, thatched roofs and pretty wooden porches decorated with flower baskets.

Designed by Hitler's personal architect, Albert Speer, these are, in fact, gas-proof bunkers with modern communications and three-foot-thick reinforced concrete walls and ceilings. Above and below ground, some rooms are panelled with pine and hung with deer antlers, and tapestries depicting hunting or battle scenes. As construction workers had been brought in from elsewhere, not even the locals know the significance of the base: code-named *Adlerhorst* (Eagle's Nest), and built in 1939–40, the complex was designed to be the *Führerhauptquartier* (Führer headquarters) for the invasion of France, but not used.[3]

Dismounting at the collection of bunkers below the castle, the officers are ushered past a double row of armed SS guards standing rigidly to attention, and guided to the building innocuously labelled 'Haus 2'. They descend deep into an underground conference room, and as they sit around a large square table littered with maps, a stony-faced SS guard

For the Ardennes campaign, some of Rundstedt's *Oberbefehlshaber West* (Supreme Commander in the West) staff occupied Schloss Kransberg, a small castle overlooking the pretty half-timbered settlement of Ziegenberg, north of Frankfurt am Main. Behind the castle in a series of concrete bunkers disguised as country cottages lay Hitler's secret headquarters, code-named *Adlerhorst* (Eagle's Nest). Here, on 11 and 12 December 1944, the Führer addressed all the senior commanders of the forthcoming campaign. Hitler spent his last Christmas at Ziegenberg, and broadcast his final New Year's message to the German people from the *Pressehaus* bunker within the complex. Admitting *Herbstnebel* was over, the Führer finally quit the *Adlerhorst* on 15 January 1945. (Author's collection)

takes position behind each chair, a movement that alarms the generals; Fritz Bayerlein of the Panzer Lehr Division is nervous even to reach for his handkerchief. Again the pervading sense of menace – even to these loyal servants of the Reich who have proved their bravery countless times. At their head sits Field Marshal Wilhelm Keitel, head of the Armed Forces High Command; on his left an empty chair, then General Alfred Jodl, his deputy. Other top brass – Gerd von Rundstedt, Walther Model, another field marshal who commands Army Group 'B', and two of his subordinates, Hasso von Manteuffel of Fifth Panzer Army and Josef 'Sepp' Dietrich, former tank sergeant in the First World War and now an SS general – perch nearby. It is crowded, perhaps fifty in the room.

They witness the arrival of a shuffling figure in field grey, 'a broken man, with an unhealthy colour, a caved-in appearance . . . with trembling hands', who unexpectedly takes his seat between Keitel and Jodl. Then the newcomers realise: it is Hitler. Manteuffel, sitting directly opposite him, is shocked at his demeanour; his left arm is completely limp and he is sitting 'as if the burden of responsibility seemed to oppress him . . . his body seemed more decrepit and he was a man grown old'.

All eyes on him, Hitler suddenly comes to life; he begins by awarding two newly promoted panzer generals – Harald Freiherr von Elverfeldt of the 9th and Siegfried von Waldenburg, commanding 116th Panzer Division – the Knight's Cross. He bedazzles them both with intimate knowledge of their formations, then he surveys Germany's strategic position; in his stride now, he moves on to the weaknesses of the Allies. He reminds those present of his idol, Frederick the Great, who in 1762 was facing a coalition every bit as powerful as the Anglo-US-Russian alliance now ranged against the Third Reich. At Prussia's last gasp, he tells them, Empress Elizabeth of Russia suddenly died and was succeeded by the pro-Prussian Peter. At a stroke, the anti-Prussian coalition collapsed and Frederick's fortunes revived dramatically. Now, Hitler announces he has found a way to make history repeat itself by puncturing the coalition ranged against him. That is why these commanders have been summoned.

The Führer's face has now lit up; the shuffling figure has been replaced by a confident leader who raves for over two hours. Frederick II of Prussia (known to his men as *der Alte Fritz*, Old Fritz), is never far from the monologue. How he led his military forces personally and had six horses shot from under him; that he was one of the greatest tactical geniuses of all time, and had read every conceivable book connected with the art of war. Hitler will emulate and even exceed Frederick's achievements. The coming offensive that will destroy the Allied coalition will have unprecedented air support, fresh divisions, new tanks, additional artillery and plenty of ammunition and fuel. He guarantees it, cracks a joke at Hermann Göring's expense; he realises how they all distrust the Luftwaffe's boasting – if Hermann promises a thousand aircraft, they should expect 800 to turn up. Nervous laughter.

He announces he has even found a way to negate the dreaded Allied air threat – by attacking in the dead of winter when visibility is at its poorest. However, a vigorous defensive struggle will only postpone the inevitable, so there is only one thing to do: play the card of attack. Britain is a dying empire; America will lose heart if the war turns sour for her. Once the west is stabilised with a negotiated peace advantageous to

Germany, we can again turn our attention to Russia. We will master our fate. Manteuffel, who has met Hitler several times, knows that those in the room who have never actually met their Führer before are totally under his spell by the time they leave. These corps and division commanders believe they are the ones who will rescue the Third Reich in five days' time, just as *der Alte Fritz* had saved Prussia in years gone by.[4]

Departing, relieved and forgetting their empty holsters, the carmine-striped breeches and field grey of the generals stride away from the black and silver of the SS. They are more confident of survival than they were on their arrival. As they leave the musty atmosphere of the bunker for fresh, wintry air and their transport, each wonders whose survival they are contemplating, their own or Germany's.

·

The chain of events which led to the Battle of the Bulge began in that long, hot summer, during the closing stages of the battle for Normandy. Although some historians of the Ardennes date the birth of the campaign to a sudden brainwave in Hitler's East Prussian headquarters on 16 September 1944, they are mistaken: the seeds were sown much, much earlier.

The leader of the Third Reich himself was contradictory. He was fascinated by everything to do with war and military operations, but in never having progressed beyond the rank of corporal he did not appreciate the methodology of military staff work necessary to every undertaking. As Major Percy Schramm, the German High Command's official historian and war diarist, recalled, 'He thought that if he had ever learnt to think in the terms of a General Staff officer, at every single step he would have to stop and calculate the impossibility of reaching the next. Consequently, he concluded, he would never have even tried to come to power since on the basis of objective calculations he had no prospect of success in the first place.'[5]

Early luck in his political and military campaigning persuaded Hitler that he was a genius; he read widely, but randomly, on military affairs, while possessing a phenomenal memory for facts and figures. All of this convinced him he had a sound understanding of the logistical needs of his forces. He was neither a genius – nor had any concept of defence logistics – but nevertheless concluded his own intuition was preferable to the plodding of his General Staff. Hitler's service of nearly four years at the Front in the Kaiser's army, with the award of both classes of Iron

Cross, gave him the confidence to enter politics. The army had essentially helped him into power in 1933 to counter Communism, and supported him during the 'Night of the Long Knives' against the rising power of Ernst Röhm's brown-shirted *Sturmabteilung* (the SA), who considered themselves the future defence force of the Third Reich.

The army, with the navy then known as the Reichswehr, were limited by the Versailles Treaty to no more than 100,000 men, whereas the SA numbered over three million. Röhm openly wanted to be Minister of Defence and the threat had manifested itself on 2 October 1933, when he proclaimed, 'I regard the Reichswehr now only as a training school for the German people. The conduct of war, and therefore of mobilisation as well, is the future task of the SA.' The black-shirted *Schutzstaffel* (the SS), led by its thirty-three-year-old Reichsführer, Heinrich Himmler, were lent weapons surreptitiously by the army, which they used on 30 June 1934 to execute as many as 300 senior SA leaders, including Röhm. The Brownshirts were not banned, but their malign influence had been checked and thereafter diminished.

The Reichswehr (and many of the SS) had looked down on the SA, whom both regarded as a rabble – the majority were unemployed, farm labourers, or the unskilled and poorly educated working classes of Germany's urban centres – but it was also the very background from which Hitler had sprung.[6] Unlike most in the ranks of the early SS or Reichswehr, Himmler had neither seen service in 1914–18 nor become an officer, and would have failed the stringent entry requirements of candidates for his organisation. Despite his personal failings, Himmler's subsequent leadership of the *Schutzstaffel* would reflect a desire, like an over-ambitious parent, to thrust his personal, unrequited aspirations on to his children. From this moment, the Reichsführer's much smaller SS eclipsed their rivals within the Party and grew rapidly in size. They had begun in 1921 as a thirty-man security detachment of the SA, by 1929 they numbered only 300, but had risen to 50,000 in 1932 and quadrupled within another year; all were bound by personal loyalty to Hitler. While in 1934 the Reichswehr may have felt that Hitler was 'their' man, ten years later he had outwitted them all and was now their cruel and unsympathetic overlord – perhaps because, deep down and because of his humble origins, the Führer had always felt uncomfortable in the company of army officers, a high proportion of whom were aristocrats.[7]

Hitler had already dismissed one of these loathed, stuffy aristocrats, the *Oberbefehlshaber West* (usually abbreviated to OB West), Field

Marshal Gerd von Rundstedt, Germany's senior serving soldier and nearly fourteen years Hitler's senior, on 2 July 1944. From the distant *Wolfsschanze*, Hitler had countermanded orders issued by Rundstedt, giving permission for units in Normandy to withdraw rather than stay put. Rundstedt contacted Keitel at Hitler's HQ immediately to protest; when asked what alternatives Rundstedt could think of, the latter shouted down the phone, '*Schluss mit dem Krieg, Idioten*!' (literally 'Finish with the war, idiots', but usually interpreted as 'Make peace, you fools!'). Rundstedt was soon packing his bags, sacked on grounds of age and ill-health (the firing was sweetened by two unusual gestures from the *Wolfsschanze*: a cordial letter and the award of Oak Leaves to his Knight's Cross). The field marshal will re-enter the Bulge story, on being re-appointed OB West in September. His immediate replacement was Field Marshal Günther von Kluge, who would soon take on the additional duties of commanding Army Group 'B', in place of Rommel, who had been wounded by an air attack on 17 July.

The Germans were losing the war in the west. By 1 July, the Anglo-Canadians had landed twelve divisions in Normandy and the Americans thirteen – but these achievements were totally dwarfed by developments in the east, for June 1944 was a month of two 'D-Days'. On 22 June 1944 (the third anniversary of the invasion of the Soviet Union), the Red Army had launched their summer offensive in White Russia, which resulted in the complete destruction of Army Group Centre. In Operation Bagration, four Russian army groups with 126 infantry divisions, 6 cavalry divisions, 16 motorised brigades and 45 armoured brigades penetrated almost 200 miles, and by 3 July had liberated Minsk. The German Ninth and Fourth Armies, totalling nearly 400,000 men, or twenty-eight divisions, were surrounded by swift armour envelopments and ceased to exist. This was a military catastrophe double the size of Stalingrad, and in terms of matériel and losses of experienced manpower ranked as the most calamitous setback of the war, one from which the Wehrmacht would never recover.

Then, of course, came the events of Thursday, 20 July, Stauffenberg's completely unforeseen assassination attempt in Hitler's own East Prussian headquarters. Narrowly surviving, Hitler became even more mistrustful of his generals. If the Wehrmacht had any leeway before the assassination attempt, it had none afterwards; no longer would the Führer tolerate any insubordination, for he now saw even disagreement as disloyalty. Heinz Linge, Hitler's SS valet, remembered that after 20 July, 'Only about sixty people, whose names Hitler had listed personally, were permitted access to him without a prior body search. Briefcases and the like had to be left behind. I saw the need for such measures, but they depressed me. Generals, colonels, staff officers, lieutenants, NCOs and simple privates with the highest decorations came – men who had risked their lives for Hitler – and had to be patted down by the RSD (*Reichssicherheitsdienst*, the SS sub-unit responsible for Hitler's security) like convicted thieves.'[8] Hitler interpreted 20 July as a conspiracy of army officers against him, for it included no ordinary soldiers and few from other professions; furthermore, most were old-school aristocrats and members of the General Staff. Thus he took against each group – officers, nobles and the General Staff – but especially those whose background combined elements of all three – which happened to include many of his field commanders and their best staff officers.

The aftermath of the Stauffenberg plot became a witch-hunt against this combination. It amounted to a self-inflicted wound, removing vital talent, groomed through many years of study and experience, from the front lines just when it was needed most, for they were the only ones in the Reich with the necessary skills to counter the Allies. Their Waffen-SS rivals, however talented, were too few in number. The army was collectively humiliated, even its military salute was abolished: forthwith, the correct salutation was the Nazi raised arm and 'Heil Hitler'.[9]

They were forbidden by law to join political parties, even to vote: an historic way of keeping the army out of politics.[10] Thus, after the war, Wehrmacht commanders argued they were set apart and had nothing to do with the political processes of the Reich, whereas in fact they had acquired a convenient moral blind spot. The older officers who had served the state without question under the Kaisers, during the difficult pre-Nazi Weimar era of the Reichswehr, and latterly under Hitler, had devoted their professional and personal loyalty to the Fatherland. Since 2 August 1934 Hitler had made the Wehrmacht swear loyalty to him personally. The oath, which all serving soldiers and new recruits subsequently swore, ran as follows: 'I swear by God this sacred oath that I shall render unconditional obedience to Adolf Hitler, the Führer of the German Reich, supreme commander of the armed forces, and that I shall at all times be prepared, as a brave soldier, to give my life for this oath.' Now he was cashing in, demanding payment on this sacred rite.

For the Wehrmacht, these words were sworn publicly, and both parties – the soldiers and Hitler – were persuaded that deviation from it was treason against the state. Disobeying the Führer was not an option. Thereafter, the Wehrmacht hid behind this oath, with their argument that obedience was everything and they were somehow set apart from politics. The reality was that collectively, German military leadership lacked *Zivilcourage*, moral courage, to overcome their oath, even when military logic demanded they should. After 20 July the officers were persuaded it was their duty to fight on and to inspire their men, by leadership or terror, to do likewise.

Uprising at home, disaster in Normandy. The day following the bomb plot, Kluge, newly appointed to Army Group 'B', had written to Hitler, 'In the face of the total enemy air superiority, we can adopt no tactics to compensate for the annihilating power of air except to retire from the battlefield. I came here with the firm resolve to enforce your command to stand and hold at all cost. The price of that policy is the steady and certain destruction of our troops . . .'[11] Hitler's typical response was to demand, 'The utmost boldness, determination, and imagination must inspire every commander down to the lowest levels.'[12] This was providing, of course, that such boldness and imagination was in accordance with his own wishes. Four days after Kluge's letter, the Americans had launched Operation Cobra to break out of Normandy. Following a massive aerial bombardment on 25 July, units of Lieutenant-General J. Lawton Collins' US VII Corps led an assault which took two days to overcome most organised German resistance and seal off the Cherbourg peninsula. 'Lightning Joe' Collins and his formation would continue to harry the Germans in the Ardennes.

There is evidence that Hitler may have been evaluating commanders for a future offensive as early as 30 July, for on that date he interviewed Freiherr Hasso von Manteuffel, then commanding the elite *GrossDeutschland* Division on the Eastern Front. He was one aristocrat (*Freiherr* translates as Baron) Hitler could stomach because he was known as a brilliant leader of men, who could be relied upon to deliver whatever was asked of him.

By the following day the Normandy front had broken wide open in the vicinity of Avranches, and a desperate Hitler looked for ways of containing the American deluge with mobile counter-attacks. However, after the daily conference on 31 July at the *Wolfsschanze*, Hitler embarked on a Führer monologue that revolved around the idea of 'a final decision happening in the West, where Germany's destiny will be decided', which he would command from somewhere in western Germany – the Black

Forest or Vosges were mentioned. Jodl was tasked to form a small planning staff to enable this, while other fronts might have to be denuded of forces in order to achieve this final, victorious effort.

The notion of a decisive battle in the west dates from even earlier, however, when in a November 1943 Directive Hitler had stated, 'In the East, the vastness of the space will, as a last resort, permit a loss of territory even on a major scale, without suffering a mortal blow to Germany's chance for survival. Not so in the West! If the enemy here succeeds in penetrating our defences on a wide front, consequences of staggering proportions will follow within a short time.' Hitler had anticipated the invasion which arrived in Normandy on 6 June 1944, and ordered the construction of the Atlantic Wall, concluding, 'It would produce the greatest political and strategic impact if it [an invasion] were to succeed . . . I expect that all agencies will make a supreme effort toward utilising every moment of the remaining time in preparing for the decisive battle in the West.'[13]

The moment had passed for his decisive battle to be fought on the landing beaches, but on 31 July 1944 Hitler was still looking for a strategic turnaround in the west, rather than on the Russian Front. With considerable foresight he had ordered the chain of forts and bunkers constructed in 1938–9 along the Franco-German border and known by the Allies as the Siegfried Line, but throughout the Reich as the *Westwall*, to be rearmed. Furthermore, Jodl was told to study the documents relating '*dem Vorbild des Jahres 1940*' – the model of 1940, which can only refer to the Wehrmacht's successful attack through the Ardennes into France. The staff in the *Wolfsschanze* may have been focused on Normandy, but here is evidence of the Führer's 'Plan B' if the French front collapsed.[14] Thus, the seeds which grew into the Battle of the Bulge had been sown personally by Hitler even before the end of the struggle in Normandy.

2

The Machinery of Command

EXPLORING THE POSSIBILITIES of the Führer's 31 July 1944 vision was the responsibility of staff attached to the *Oberkommando der Wehrmacht* (OKW, or Armed Forces High Command). Senior members of OKW, such as its head, Field Marshal Wilhelm Keitel, were based with Hitler, wherever his headquarters was located. Until 20 November, when the Red Army were fifty miles away, the Führer's HQ was at the *Wolfsschanze* in East Prussia, where Stauffenberg had narrowly failed to alter history. Also located within the network of over thirty reinforced bunkers sited in a swamp-ridden forest was a massive communications centre that linked to every military headquarters, and Generaloberst Alfred Jodl. He acted as Keitel's deputy as head of the *Wehrmachtführungsstab*, the Operations Staff of OKW, which translated Hitler's ideas into operations plans and orders.

Keitel was one of Hitler's inner circle, but a sycophant distrusted by the army – and was known behind his back as '*Lakeitel*'. This was a pun on his surname, for 'Lakai' translates as 'lackey', his perceived function. Between them, Keitel and Jodl (who, being respected more, had no nickname) briefed Hitler daily on the military situation and translated his whims into directives for transmission down the chain of command. After its departure from East Prussia in November, the *Führerhauptquartier* decamped to Berlin, then to the *Adlerhorst* at Ziegenberg, where Hitler arrived hours before the 11 December 1944 conference, travelling by his personal train and car.

Only a small proportion of OKW remained with Hitler; the main organisation, staffed by a huge collection of officers running everything from propaganda and personnel to signals and intelligence, were housed at '*Maybach II*', codename for a series of purpose-built bunkers, near Zossen, fifteen miles south of Berlin.[1] For reasons of secrecy, early skeleton plans for the campaign Jodl was scoping for Hitler – modelled on the strategy used over four years earlier – were worked out within the *Wolfsschanze* itself, but later, as the project became more concrete and alternatives explored, the staff at Zossen became involved and forwarded their work to Jodl.

The story of the 1940 invasion of France, which Hitler instructed Jodl to study, was remarkable in two respects. First, Hitler backed an unusual idea, previously rejected by the General Staff. Secondly, the result achieved victory beyond anyone's wildest dreams. The original German strategy, named innocuously *Fall Gelb* (Case Yellow), envisaged a thrust into northern Belgium and Holland, similar to the Schlieffen Plan of 1914. As a result, the Germans correctly anticipated the cream of the Allied forces would be sent into northern Belgium – France's best armoured divisions and the whole of the British Expeditionary Force.

While 'Case Yellow' originated from the General Staff, General Erich von Manstein proposed an alternative. A northern army group should still thrust into Belgium, distracting Allied attention, while in great secrecy a southern force would assemble, then attack through the poorly defended Ardennes, and eventually swing north to surround and destroy their opponents. The Germans were taught to think in terms of vast encircling operations, emulating Hannibal's 216 BC triumph over Rome at Cannae, considered the most perfect of manoeuvres.

Generalleutnant Heinz Guderian, creator of Germany's *Panzerwaffe* (tank arm), contributed to Manstein's plan by suggesting his tanks could slice through the dense Ardennes forests, which he alone considered passable by armour, cross the River Meuse at Sedan and Dinant and execute a swift, deep penetration to the English Channel. He understood the terrain, having attended the German Staff College in 1918, when it was based at Sedan. German pre-1940 doctrine dictated that tanks could not advance without infantry support, but Guderian and Manstein recommended their panzers push on to the coast without waiting for lumbering, horse-drawn infantry units. British military historian Basil Liddell Hart later called the advance into Belgium 'the matador's cloak', simultaneously enticing the Allies into Belgium and distracting them from the real attack further south. The Germans called Manstein's manoeuvre *Sichelschnitt* (the 'cut of the sickle').

Hitler had harboured private doubts about the General Staff's scheme of a main thrust into Belgium, which he considered might bring about another stalemate, as in 1914, and had already been drawn to the Ardennes area as a means of initiating a secondary assault. When in February 1940 Manstein's idea had been brought to his attention, he seized on it as though it were his own, and, overriding the advice of the entire General Staff, ordered all original plans scrapped in favour of Manstein's. It was a bold strategy, and foreshadowed the Führer's interference in military plans that had become routine by 1944.

The strategy of May 1940 was underpinned by the Luftwaffe overhead supporting armour, artillery, engineers and mechanised infantry, all of whom travelled at high speed and fought a thoroughly integrated combined-arms battle. It was only after the defeat of France that the Wehrmacht fully embraced these tactics, subsequently dubbed *Blitzkrieg* ('lightning war'). In retirement Guderian observed that the word 'blitzkrieg' was unknown in pre-war German manuals or training, and did not enter widespread vocabulary until after use in the British and American press to describe the Wehrmacht's successes in Poland and France.

Historians generally accept that there was no coherent doctrine or developed concept of blitzkrieg; rather, it was an evolving notion that is best defined by its characteristics, which revolved around the concept of the *Schwerpunkt*, a centre of gravity or point of maximum effort, where land and air forces were concentrated to achieve penetrations of the Front, exploiting speed to disrupt, disperse and destroy their opponents. Ironically, fast movement was also one of the defining ideas of blitzkrieg and in 1940 the Wehrmacht was not designed for speed: only around 10 per cent of its land forces were mechanised or armoured, the rest using horses. Four years later, the percentages were not much different. By 1944 the Russians and the Western Allies had also learned to apply the principles of blitzkrieg – a classic case of taking a rival doctrine and improving upon it. (As the Official Historian in Iraq, I witnessed a modern version of blitzkrieg being employed by the American and British forces in their invasion of March–April 2003.) To a certain extent, commanders through the centuries had arrived at a similar conclusion, to concentrate combined arms and produce a lightning strike of frightening speed, but the vital 1940s innovation was that of air support – and what would challenge Hitler's 1944 blitzkrieg was his inability to integrate Luftwaffe support.

The incredible triumph of May 1940, achieved in six weeks, was due partly to the adoption of these high-risk concepts, which overwhelmed opponents by the sheer momentum and brutality of the attack, paralysing their command chain, but also because the Franco-Belgian forces chose not to defend nodal points in the Ardennes, their training was very poor, equipment obsolete, decision-making slow at every level and political and military resolve low. Victory had been achieved to everyone's surprise, largely thanks to Manstein and Guderian.[2]

These, then, were the events of four years earlier, narrated in documents, some fire-damaged by bombing, that were retrieved and studied by one of Jodl's trusted circle, a middle-aged former professor of history at the University of Göttingen, one of Germany's most prestigious universities. Major Percy Schramm, Anglophile and distinguished expert on European monarchy, had been appointed the OKW's diarist from 1 January 1943, and was based in the *Führerhauptquartier*.[3] Schramm knew that the Kaiser's army had attacked through the Ardennes, albeit on foot, with great success in 1914, while on 1 September 1870 Sedan had been the scene of another amazing triumph over the French. Field Marshal von Moltke, Wilhelm I and Bismarck had all been present to witness the humiliation of the French, commanded in person by Napoleon III. The Ardennes, Sedan and the River Meuse (known to the Germans and Dutch as the River Maas) were synonymous in most German minds with victories over their traditional enemy. Given the weight of history attached to the region, Schramm also understood three things: the events of 1940 had taken place in May when the weather was glorious, Luftwaffe support had been vital to the achievement of 'Case Yellow', and the Wehrmacht had been able to manoeuvre off-road and bypass any significant roadblocks in the Ardennes. None of these factors would be relevant in the winter of 1944.[4]

The OKW had been established in 1938 as an umbrella headquarters to oversee and coordinate all army, navy and air force plans, exercises and operations. It was the world's first 'joint' headquarters, commonplace and invaluable today but then unique. OKW had a rival organisation, which had been its subordinate, but by 1944 came to be seen as an equal. This was the *Oberkommando des Heeres* (High Command of the Army, or OKH), founded in 1935, which directed all land operations. After the December 1941 defeat outside Moscow, its chief had been dismissed and

Hitler appointed himself its new commander. Under him, OKH was run by successive army chiefs of staff, with responsibility solely for the Russian Front. Meanwhile Keitel and Jodl at OKW directed all land activity elsewhere, while Göring's Luftwaffe and Karl Dönitz of the Kriegsmarine decided they would create their own command chains direct to Hitler.

Sadly, for the efficiency of the German armed forces, the tri-service nature of OKW had succumbed to inter-service bickering and personal rivalries. The air force and navy acted independently, while Himmler and his SS organisations stood apart from OKW and OKH, even though Waffen-SS divisions soldiered alongside the Wehrmacht in the east and west. By 1944, this extraordinary network of conflicting commands made for great inefficiency, duplication, poor decision-making and time-wasting, to the detriment of German military effectiveness in the field – but it removed any domestic military threat to Hitler: he encouraged any potential opponents to compete, rather than unite against him.

At Zossen, OKH in *Maybach I* was located next to OKW in *Maybach II*, but the two headquarters were separated by a physical fence which was also a mental one, serving to underline their ridiculous rivalries. From 21 July 1944 OKH was presided over by the fiery tank commander Guderian, who chose to stay at Zossen as much as possible, rather than tolerate the viper's nest of the *Wolfsschanze*. OKW would direct the forthcoming Ardennes attack, but moving reinforcements away from the Eastern Front in order to build up the necessary reserves in the west required the participation and support of Guderian's OKH.

Meanwhile, what of the real threat, the Allies? With US formations pushing into Brittany and lower Normandy, Hitler concluded the best hope was for a surprise assault to punch through the still narrow American corridor stretching south from Avranches. His first attempt was Operation Lüttich, launched on 7 August and intended to start in the little hilltop town of Mortain, advancing westwards, towards Avranches. For this, Hitler through OKW forced a reluctant Kluge to assemble the remnants of four panzer divisions (1st and 2nd SS, 2nd and 116th, all of whom would serve in the Ardennes) to move against the American flanks like a giant armoured steamroller. From the *Wolfsschanze* he demanded: 'We must strike like lightning. When we reach the sea the American spearheads will be cut off. Obviously they are trying all-out for a major decision here, otherwise they wouldn't have sent in their best general, Patton. He's the most dangerous man they have.' In the event, the entire effort mustered less than 200 tanks, and though all were seasoned veterans of earlier campaigns, it was an unrealistic plan, concocted thousands of miles away in East Prussia, and doomed by their opponents' air power.[5]

The armour needed at Mortain had already been frittered away in the largely successful static defence of the *bocage* – those peculiar Norman hedgerows which dominated the campaign. The attack was contained around Mortain during the first day and although fighting continued for a week, it failed to stop the American advance elsewhere, with Patton's Third Army capturing Le Mans, 65 miles south-east, on 8 August.[6] Even the codename for the Mortain offensive was a clue into Hitler's mind. Lüttich is the German name for the Belgian city of Liège, five miles from Aachen and the Reich's frontier; historically it was considered German, hence its having a Teutonic name. Operation Lüttich was not merely a counter-attack but, in Hitler's mind, retaking that which the Germans considered rightfully their own. Hitler chose the titles of other operations, such as 'Barbarossa' (the invasion of Russia) 'Retribution' (the bombing of Belgrade) or 'Hercules' (the projected invasion of Malta), which likewise conveyed a meaning, often through historical reference; and so, too, for the Ardennes offensive, as we shall discover.

Operation Lüttich had the added disadvantage of being compromised by signals intelligence. Allied code-breakers based at Bletchley Park, a country house in Buckinghamshire, England, had worked out the secrets of the German Enigma enciphering machine and forewarned Allied high command that the Mortain attack was on its way. Subsequently, every attempt at seizing the initiative with mobile armoured attacks failed, owing to the lack of remaining combat power and the withering effect of Allied air power over the battlefield. Although the Reich never realised their strategic secrets were compromised in any way, Allied reliance on Enigma intelligence products, warning them of forthcoming German operations, would become a huge issue with the Ardennes offensive in December.

Early August saw the strategic situation in Normandy alter dramatically. By this time the millionth Allied serviceman (and a few servicewomen, too) had just stepped ashore. On the first of the month, General Omar Nelson Bradley was promoted to lead American Twelfth Army Group, which included US First Army, his old command, now under Lieutenant-General Courtney H. Hodges, and Third Army, the creature of George S. Patton. Bradley was a West Point contemporary of Eisenhower's and both had received accelerated promotion: his two subordinates were somewhat older than him (he was fifty-two; Hodges was fifty-seven and Patton would turn fifty-nine in November), requiring great tact and diplomacy in his direction of the army group.

In addition, from 5 September, units of Lieutenant-General William H. Simpson's US Ninth Army had also begun to arrive in France, eventually taking their place alongside the First and Third. Units from these three armies would comprise America's response to the German Ardennes offensive. Patton's arrival and Bradley's elevation were only revealed by Eisenhower at a press conference on 15 August, the same day that the Allies landed in southern France. This operation, code-named Dragoon, was extremely successful but overshadowed by Overlord in Normandy and consequently is today little known; it saw Lieutenant-General Alexander M. Patch's US Seventh Army and French forces under Général Jean de Lattre de Tassigny rapidly overwhelm Generaloberst Johannes Blaskowitz's Army Group 'G' along the French Riviera. These Allied forces, which included three US and five French divisions, were eventually redesignated the Sixth Army Group from 15 September 1944.

By this point, Hitler was also smarting from the July attempt on his life and had been informed there were grounds to think his field marshal commanding the defence of Normandy was implicated in the Stauffenberg plot. Accordingly, on 17 August, ten days after the failed Mortain attack, Kluge was recalled. Faced with an interview at No. 8 Prinz-Albrecht-Strasse, the most feared address in the Third Reich as the Gestapo's Berlin HQ, Kluge seemed to confirm his guilt by taking poison en route. Hitler had never trusted Kluge but the Führer's SS valet, Heinz Linge, remembered his boss was convinced 'that the English had poisoned him after they had failed to convince the Generalfeldmarschall to come over to their side', for which, it has to be said, there is absolutely no evidence.[7] His replacement was another field marshal, Walther Model, a soldier far more to Hitler's liking.

Although a product of the General Staff, the monocle-wearing Model was no aristocrat, coming from a lower-middle-class, non-military family and therefore closer to the classless ideals of National Socialism. In April 1940 he had been a colonel, and was promoted to *Generalfeldmarschall* exactly four years later, evidence of his sheer ability. In June 1941 he had led 3rd Panzer Division into Russia, yet by January 1942 he was commanding the Ninth Army. Though he asserted that he was a committed Nazi, Model's merciless command style and military effectiveness frequently coincided with Hitler's wishes, and that is not quite the same thing: he was more ruthless fellow-traveller than dedicated Party fanatic.

Model was a hard-driving, aggressive panzer leader, superbly self-confident, abrasive and unpopular with superior and subordinate officers, though feted by his troops, whose lives he did not hesitate to sacrifice if he felt the need. He knew how to handle soldiers and was usually at the front, where his presence was felt to be lucky. Although known as Hitler's *Feuerwehrmann* (fireman) for his ability to retrieve desperate situations, he was not afraid to stand up to his Führer. Early in Model's tenure of Ninth Army, which he led for two years in Russia, Hitler had started to interfere with his dispositions. After a heated debate, Model turned to Hitler, held his gaze and asked simply, 'Who commands the Ninth Army, my Führer; you or I?' His boss wavered, uncharacteristically, and thereafter left him to it, with perhaps a sneaking admiration for his cheek, which very few dared replicate. His deadliest weapon against superiors and subordinates alike was contemptuous silence, while his glance could freeze scalding-hot coffee, Hitler once remarking, 'Did you see those eyes? I wouldn't want to serve under him.'

A more accurate description of Model's particular skill throughout 1943–4 was as a 'frontline patchwork artist of the first order'.[8] Manteuffel's observation to Liddell Hart, made in 1945, that Model was 'not a great strategist, but . . . had a ruthless energy in scraping up reserves from a bare cupboard, and was one of the few generals who dared argue with Hitler', precisely echoes this.[9] Until Rundstedt's return in September, Model would wear the twin hats of OB West as well as commanding Army Group 'B'. His significance for our story was as the operational commander of the Ardennes offensive.

On 19 August, even while his Fifth Panzer and Seventh Armies were encircled within the Falaise Pocket in Normandy and in their final death throes, Hitler again discussed the rearming of the Siegfried Line; he knew it was just a hollow shell, for its weapons had been removed and installed in the Atlantic Wall before D-Day and had now been captured.[10] The *Westwall* was a pet project of Hitler's; he had designed it in the 1930s partly as a propaganda exercise to demonstrate Germany's building abilities, as well as for defence. Comprising more than 18,000 bunkers, it stretched 400 miles from Holland to the Swiss frontier. At a time when the Reich needed to build houses, 20 per cent of annual cement production and 5 per cent of steel output had been diverted to this massive state enterprise. Built by the Inspector-General for Reich Highways, Dr

Building 'dragon's teeth' tank obstacles in front of the *Westwall.* Hitler was unwilling to abandon this defensive line of 18,000 bunkers to the Allies. In August 1944, even before the fall of Normandy, he ordered the *Westwall* refurbished, and from these positions his men poured forth to attack the US Army in December. (Author's collection)

Fritz Todt, between 1936 and 1940, using half a million workers, 25 per cent of the nation's construction industry, it had cost a crippling 3.5 billion Reichsmarks.[11]

In 1944 the Führer was unwilling simply to abandon one of his major pre-war programmes to the Allies, hence diverting attention and resources to the obsolete and largely irrelevant *Westwall.* Taken with his 31 July notion of 'a decision in the west', and reanalysis of the 1940 campaign, it becomes obvious that Hitler was not just thinking in terms of defence, but some sort of decisive counter-attack. He had already realised that Normandy was lost, and that he had almost no means of halting the Allies until they reached the German frontier. The Ardennes was still not mentioned specifically at this stage, though it was implicit, given the requirement to study 1940, while the idea grew through August and into September that any 'change in the situation will have to be brought about by an attack originating from the Westwall'.[12]

By 22 August the Falaise Pocket had been overwhelmed, and more than 70,000 troops had been killed or captured, while perhaps 20,000 with fewer than fifty tanks had escaped – the sad remnants of nineteen experienced divisions which had been deployed to Normandy. Later, the RAF's No. 2 Operational Research Section counted 187 tanks and self-propelled guns, 157 other armoured fighting vehicles, 1,778 lorries, 669 cars and 252 artillery pieces abandoned or destroyed in the area.[13] No count was made of horse-drawn transport, while the stench of uncounted thousands of decaying horses in the hot August weather was so overpowering that investigators had to hurry past; consequently, the region was quarantined for the next sixty days. Normandy is reckoned to have cost the Reich 1,500 panzers, 3,500 guns, 20,000 vehicles and nearly 500,000 men, many of whom could have been pulled back across the Seine to fight another day. Their numbers would be sorely missed in the winter campaign, though the two parent formations, Fifth Panzer and Seventh Armies, would re-emerge in the Ardennes attack. Privately, those who knew referred to the debacle as 'Stalingrad in Normandy'.

The experience of Gefreiter Alfred Becker, a twenty-year-old in the 326th Infantry Division, was typical of most. Somehow, he managed to survive Normandy when most of his comrades did not; his formation was completely annihilated. Always on the move and constantly harassed by Allied artillery and the *Jabos* (from *Jagdbomber*, the German for Allied fighter-bomber), his unit quickly unravelled and separated. They soon lost their supply chain and ran out of ammunition. Water and food they took from French farmers when they could, or butchered livestock. The seriously wounded usually had to be abandoned to their fate as there were no medical supplies, nor the means to convey them. Becker himself was injured, though not through enemy action. Nevertheless, he recalled, that after he had made it back across the Siegfried Line, he was awarded a *Verwundetenabzeichen* (Wound Badge, like a Purple Heart). 'They came in black, silver and gold. Black was the lowest grade, you got it for minor wounds. If you got your legs blown off they would give you a gold one, or if you were wounded lots of times. They gave mine to me in hospital. A guy next to me had tried to fire a *Panzerfaust* and it blew up, killing him. I could barely see because I had gravel blown into my eyes and cuts on my head. When I told the doctor what happened, he said, "No, you are mistaken. An enemy bullet hit the weapon and blew it up. You have an honourable wound". Hah. I wore the medal on the pocket of my new field blouse when I left hospital.'[14]

The victory at Falaise is commonly attributed to the efficacy of Allied airpower against German armour, but after-action surveys of captured panzers revealed that relatively few had been hit by fighter-bombers, while some had even been abandoned intact, with full fuel tanks. Inaccuracy was an issue that plagued both the RAF and USAAF, for all airborne tactical weapons (cannon shells and rockets) were then unguided. Nevertheless, the impression both of panzer crews and OKW was that the Allied air forces were all-powerful. Close air support was also responsible for numerous friendly-fire instances reported in Normandy: 'Wish you would tell the Air Corps we don't want them over here,' an irate staff officer had demanded of his chain of command, following a raid by friendly P-47s on a US artillery battalion which wounded several men.[15] By 1944 tactical air cover over the battlefront was a great psychological weapon against German ground forces, however, regardless of the actual damage it caused.[16] This would remain the case in December – when the planes could fly.

August 1944 was probably the worst month militarily in the history of the Third Reich, for the bad news flooded in from west and east. On the Russian Front, notwithstanding the loss of the 400,000 men of Army Group Centre, 20 August saw the Soviets launch a new attack which resulted in the loss of Romania by the end of the month, and with it the vital Ploesti oilfields, Germany's only source of this basic resource so crucial to her war machine. On 26 August, Bulgaria formally withdrew from the Axis, while in September Finland would also discount herself as one of Hitler's coalition partners, and Hungary began to wobble. It was not just the loss of this political coalition that damaged the Third Reich. The regime had now lost its call on Ukrainian manganese, French bauxite, nickel from Finland, coal, lead, zinc, copper and mercury from Yugoslavia, while Turkish chrome, Portuguese and Spanish mercury, nickel and tungsten, and supplies of high-grade iron ore from Sweden, were in doubt, as neutral countries began to reassess who was likely to win the European war. The loss of steel from France and Belgium cut the Reich's output back by one third. Without tungsten and chrome, for example, factories could not produce armour plate. Collectively, this threatened the Reich's continued capacity to wage war, and in September 1944 it was calculated by Albert Speer's Armaments Ministry that Germany had stockpiled enough raw materials to last only another year of conflict. Hitler realised he now had a time constraint in which to force a military solution in the west.[17]

Back in the *Wolfsschanze* on 24 August, previous discussions about the *Westwall* had translated into a *Führerbefehl* (Hitler Order), calling for the strengthening of its defensive positions by mobilising hundreds of thousands of civilian labourers, directed by local Nazi officials. Away from the combat zone, security and administration of the rear areas was the responsibility of the Commander of the *Ersatzheer* (Reserve Army). Stauffenberg, executed on 20 July, had been its chief of staff, and several of its senior officers in Berlin were part of his plot. In the immediate aftermath, the utterly loyal head of the SS and Gestapo, Reichsführer Heinrich Himmler, took over the Reserve Army, to wield even more dreadful power than hitherto. This was a time when zealous *Gauleiters* (the forty-three regional political leaders of the Reich) and SS officials competed with one another to prove their loyalty to Hitler. Frequently they confused activity with achievement, and very little of practical value had been done along the Siegfried Line by the time the Allies neared the German frontier, whereupon OB West took back responsibility for military defence of the *Westwall* and its vicinity.[18]

On 25 August, tank columns from Général Philippe Leclerc's Free French 2nd Armoured Division had freed Paris, assisting the French Resistance who had risen against the German garrison; this was a sure sign if nothing else that France was lost. The move towards Paris was actually a deviation from Eisenhower's strategy of advancing to Germany as quickly as possible, and liberation of his own capital gave *Général de Brigade* (the rank he held when marooned in Britain in June 1940) Charles de Gaulle the credibility and authority he needed to establish a provisional government, avoiding Eisenhower's planned administration by the ponderous Allied Military Government for Occupied Territories (AMGOT). De Gaulle wisely called on his countrymen to do their 'duty of war' and help the Allies complete the liberation of France, the Benelux countries and invade Germany. Consequently, three days later, on 28 August, the French Resistance was incorporated into his army (already totally reliant on US vehicles, uniforms and weapons). De Gaulle and the politics of ceding recently liberated French territory back to the Germans would become a huge issue during the Ardennes campaign.

Another hint of Hitler's plans came on 1 September, when he promoted the diminutive Hasso von Manteuffel – he was all of five feet four inches – whom the Führer had last met on 30 July, to *General der*

Panzertruppe and gave him the leadership of Fifth Panzer Army, then fighting on the Western Front. Manteuffel had spent the previous two years in the east, and switching a talented commander away from Russia demonstrates that Hitler's attention was now focused elsewhere. This was a huge vote of Hitlerian confidence in the forty-seven-year-old Baron, for he had skipped the intermediate challenge of first commanding an army corps. Straightaway he had a series of defensive battles ahead of him in Lorraine; pushed back over the next few weeks, his army was soon pulled out of the line to refit. His real test would arrive in December when he took Fifth Panzer into the Ardennes.

Also on 1 September, Hitler reappointed Field Marshal von Rundstedt, whom he had sacked two months earlier, as OB West. Percy Schramm, the OKW historian, assessed Rundstedt as 'one of the cleverest operational brains', which was one reason why Hitler had recalled the elderly (he was sixty-nine) marshal to service.[19] Rundstedt arrived in Koblenz on 5 September, allowing Model, who had been dual-hatted with responsibility for Army Group 'B' as well as OB West, to concentrate on the battle for France and Belgium. Generalleutnant Siegfried Westphal was assigned as Rundstedt's chief of staff. The former had been promoted unusually early in his career – at forty-two, he was twenty-seven years younger than his boss – because of his exceptional ability and had previously worked for Kesselring in Italy in the same capacity; he took up his new post on 9 September. Since his dismissal in July, Rundstedt had been forced to serve the Reich in a different capacity. In the wake of the 20 July plot, Hitler ordered the convening of the *Ehrenhof der Wehrmacht* (Armed Forces' Court of Honour), a cynical legalistic device to expel military officers involved in the Stauffenberg plot from the forces, so they could suffer the indignity of a public trial and humiliating death. Rundstedt was forced to head it, with his fellow field marshal, Keitel, and Generaloberst Guderian, appointed head of OKH and the Army General Staff on 21 July.

The Court became an arena for settling old personal grudges or protecting protégés, and not all officers presented to it were expelled. For example, Hans Speidel, Rommel's old chief of staff at Army Group 'B', who was in the plot up to his neck, was removed from his post, but protected and survived to become the post-war head of the Bundeswehr. Speidel's replacement at Army Group 'B' was the monocle-wearing General Hans Krebs, who had previously worked for Field Marshal Model on the Eastern Front, and was brought over to be reunited with his old boss as chief of staff at Army Group 'B'.[20] The removal of these talented officers from the east – Model, Manteuffel and Krebs, among many more – was a sure indication of Hitler's attention turning more and more towards a decision in the west. Meanwhile, the *Ehrenhof* worked hard, cashiering fifty-five officers, including a field marshal and nine generals. None of the accused appeared before it, their guilt being determined by Gestapo reports. Thus ejected from the army, all were handed over to the quasi-legal *Volksgerichtshof* (People's Court), a road to certain death.

The surviving perpetrators of 20 July began to be tried by the People's Court on 7 August and were sentenced to death by hanging. At the Führer's request, depraved movies were made of their slow and agonising deaths, dangling by piano wire from meat hooks at the Plötzensee prison, in north-west Berlin, which he watched with his circle at the *Wolfsschanze.* Hitler's architect-turned-Armaments Minister, Albert Speer, remembered noticing a pile of photographs on a table; 'it was a picture of a hanged man in convict dress . . . One of the SS leaders standing near me remarked in explanation, "That's [Field Marshal] Witzleben. Don't you want to see the others too? These are all photos of the executions".'[21]

Nearly 5,000 were murdered in the wake of 20 July, the regime using the opportunity to execute all critics, even potential political and religious opponents, whether connected to Stauffenberg or not. Many victims were well-connected upper-middle-class intellectuals, which meant that most of Germany's ruling elite knew someone who had disappeared. Among the executed, for example, was a schoolmistress, Elisabeth von Thadden, sister to the wife of Major Percy Schramm. The essential point of all this – the *Sippenhaft* law, the *Ehrenhof* and the People's Court – was that the professional classes running the Third Reich for Hitler, particularly those officers involved in planning and executing the Ardennes attack, had terror breathing down their necks. Just as the Führer intended, they knew that unless they served the Reich with unswerving loyalty and fanaticism, they and their families were doomed.

Whatever his command skills, Rundstedt's re-employment was principally a propaganda exercise, designed to raise the morale of the officer corps after 20 July and steady the German people. It also impressed the Allies (as it was designed to do), who believed him to be more powerful and influential than he was. Rundstedt allowed himself to become a figurehead for the forthcoming offensive. The operational control, however, remained with the energetic and ruthless Field Marshal Model. Such was the state of affairs that Rundstedt probably had no choice in either of his appointments, to the Court of Honour or OB West, as the consequences of refusing the Führer in the autumn of 1944 were too terrible to contemplate. At the time of his reappointment, Rundstedt's job, he was told, was to defend forward of the Siegfried Line for as long as possible, then withdraw as ordered. No more. He was not told of Hitler's intentions for the Ardennes (if they were concrete in the late summer of 1944), but he was told of Hitler's desire for an armoured counter-attack, to wrest back the initiative, possibly from the Vosges region.

The appointments of Manteuffel and Rundstedt are evidence of Hitler assembling the commanders he wished for the coming offensive: one a tactical genius, the other a name to bring reassurance. (The latter would be mortified to learn that Allied newspapers and generals eventually labelled the attack the 'Rundstedt Offensive'.) These twin appointments were complemented on 3 September – the fifth anniversary of the advent of war with Great Britain – by the advancement of General der Panzertruppe Erich Brandenberger to command the Seventh Army. This unfortunate formation had been the sitting tenant in Normandy when the Allies arrived on Tuesday, 6 June, and destroyed in all but name during the subsequent campaign. The steady Eastern Front veteran would be its fourth commander in three months, his predecessor, Heinrich Eberbach, having been captured on 31 August by the British at Amiens. Brandenberger would lead the Seventh to the Bulge in December.

On the day of General der Panzertruppe Eberbach's capture, at the *Wolfsschanze* came another hint of the workings of the Führer's mind – evidence that a decisive offensive was in the offing. Hitler announced to Keitel that he would 'fight on until he had secured a peace which safeguarded the Reich for the next century', which 'above all does not besmirch our honour a second time, as happened in 1918', but he regarded the moment 'not yet right for negotiation' with the Western Allies: 'such moments come only when you are victorious'.[22]

Whether or not Hitler was thinking specifically of a counter-offensive from the Ardennes, he was actively considering ways of regaining the initiative. On 24 August, the newly appointed Model (in office for one week) had proposed concentrating the remaining panzer divisions on a flank of the advancing US First or Third Armies, to strike one of them a deadly blow. Initially events dictated an attack from the Vosges, but from his own appointment in September, Rundstedt saw his main challenge as enabling his forces to retreat in good order, retaining as much of their equipment as possible, rather than standing firm to create an assembly area for an attack, and risking encirclement as they did so. Rundstedt's first directive, issued on 3 September, spoke of the 'heavily worn out German forces and the impossibility of providing quickly adequate reinforcements', and the need to 'gain as much time as possible . . . for the build-up of the Western Position [i.e. the *Westwall*].'[23]

Hitler thought otherwise, and immediately seized on Model's proposals, enlarging them into a grand, strategic counter-blow from the line of retreat, possibly using the Vosges as an assembly area, which became Manteuffel's first task on taking over Fifth Panzer Army. The Wehrmacht, however, was never allowed the luxury of time to assemble and deploy enough tanks and troops, so the decisive strike kept being postponed due to the speed of the Allied advance. This explains Hitler's obsessional desire for a counter-attack throughout late August and into September, even though military circumstances consistently denied him any opportunity; by 14 September there was nowhere else from which to launch a decisive blow except the *Westwall*.

3

I Have Made a Momentous Decision!

THE FIRST OF September, the day of Rundstedt's reappointment as OB West, also witnessed the capture of Dieppe by the Canadians – a poignant moment for they had suffered great casualties there in Operation Jubilee, their ill-fated raid of 19 August 1942, one of the early attempts to test the German defences on the Continent. The day additionally saw the liberation of Brussels, an event perhaps more symbolic than militarily significant, but the third European capital city to be freed after Rome and Paris. Just as the Free French 2nd Armoured Division had rescued their own capital in August, the Piron Brigade, named after its commander and composed entirely of Belgian and Luxembourg nationals, was hurried forward and entered their city on 4 September.

The Dutch Princess Irene Brigade was also readied for the move into their own country, while Eisenhower could also call on Stanisław Maczek's Polish Armoured Division and Major-General Alois Liška's Czechoslovak Armoured Brigade. The Belgian, Dutch and Czech brigades were all self-contained battlegroups of around 3,000 personnel, including infantry, engineers, artillery, transport, signals, medical and armoured car units, and evidence of the political importance Eisenhower attached to a broad alliance of nations liberating Northern Europe. Cumulatively these amounted to a well-trained, sizeable military force of committed soldiers dedicated to destroying any German formation they met. The Belgians immediately raised other battalions from enthusiastic members of the Resistance and one of these, the 5th Fusiliers, was deployed to the Ardennes in November and fought in the subsequent campaign under US command.

The Allies advanced at a tremendous pace, storming Sedan on the River Meuse on 1 September. A captured German diary recorded the moment: 'We reached Sedan again in a very hasty retreat – much faster than our advance four years ago – but there is only one fifth of our regiment left. The rest of the men and vehicles do not exist any longer. It is impossible to describe what happened to us during the last five days . . .'[1]

On the following day, Hodges' US First Army freed Mons, but of strategic importance was Antwerp's liberation on 4 September, the port facilities being captured intact by the local Resistance. This offered great logistical possibilities, providing both German-held banks of the Scheldt estuary, which stretched from the port to the North Sea, could be cleared. By 6 September, the Poles had liberated Ypres, the Flemish city forever associated with 1914–18, and the Americans Liège (Lüttich, as we've seen, to the Germans); US forces reached the Dutch border at Maastricht on the 8th and two days later liberated Luxembourg, the fourth capital city to be freed.

On 6 September, as the German army flooded back to the borders of the Reich, and recognising the overwhelming might of Allied air power, the OKW War Diary noted, 'Führer agrees with the assessment of [Jodl's] planning staff that a large decisive attack in the west is not possible before 1 November, *when the enemy is unable to fly.* [Italics in original.] What matters is to withdraw as many units for refitting, to be operational by then. Meantime, keep the front as far west as possible'.[2] Jodl had concluded that any carefully husbanded reserves would be needed to prevent a further Allied advance, rather than initiate Hitler's planned decisive attack. This would impose a delay until November, by which time the Front might have stabilised, an attacking army could be assembled and the onset of poor weather would remove the Allies' crushing might in the skies. Such was the predominant motivation: to find a way of circumventing Allied control of the skies, which had created such carnage in northern France.

This was a development of Hitler's 31 July/19 and 31 August ideas, fused with extensive calculations from Jodl. Although Keitel, the lackey, was head of OKW, it was the planning genius Jodl who was scoping the counter-offensive. The winter attack was already germinating in Hitler's mind, coupled with the need to avoid destruction from the air. Jodl had calculated that it would need an extra twenty-five divisions, which would require a huge effort, and men would have to be combed out of the other services.[3] Meanwhile, OKW recorded that 211,000 Hitler Youth and RAD (*Reichsarbeitsdienst* – the Reich Labour Service) workers were hard at work strengthening the *Westwall*.[4]

The initial reason for this 6 September discussion at the *Wolfsschanze* was the Allied capture of Antwerp two days earlier, which the Führer realised could solve the Allies' logistical problems and possibly allow them to outflank the *Westwall* in an early attack. As we shall see, Eisenhower and Montgomery did not view the opportunities offered by Antwerp with the same sense of urgency as OKW, where its loss was regarded as a strategic setback 'of the first order'. Also on 6 September, Major-General 'Gee' Gerow's US V Corps began pouring into the lightly defended Ardennes and over the next couple of days pushed across the Ourthe river, reaching St Vith on 10 September, and beginning the US Army's acquaintance with that densely wooded region. Americans commanders seemed not to have realised that for a few days the opportunity existed to push through the *Westwall* and deep into Germany – but it was only a fleeting chance and risky. Small penetrations were also difficult to sustain logistically and liable to be overwhelmed if not quickly reinforced.

At this time, OKW assessed the strength of all its forces in the west (excluding those encircled in ports) as thirteen infantry and three panzer divisions fully combat-effective, with forty-two infantry and thirteen panzer divisions incapable of concentrated action, being scattered and worn out. Model's Army Group 'B' could only field about 100 battle-ready tanks.[5] Moreover, the defenders were in disarray because officious local Nazi Party leaders, working with Himmler's authority, were requisitioning army vehicles and personnel to create 'alert units' in the event of an American breakthrough, while roadblocks and barriers prevented the movement of vital logistics, including ammunition, forward. Local German commanders appealed that 'this nonsense be stopped, otherwise it will be impossible to provide supplies and handle communications in the combat zone'.[6] Such conflicts between the army doing its job and Nazi Party leaders jealously guarding their authority soon became commonplace as the fighting moved into the Reich itself.

Besides a few scattered SS and army battlegroups, the 116th Panzer Division (down to 600 men and eighteen tanks), there were only eight German 'fortress battalions' covering seventy-five miles of the Ardennes front at this stage. It says much for German improvisation and urgency that, by 14 September, a very worried Rundstedt had increased the eight battalions to thirty-two, totalling some 16,000 men. According to Milton

Shulman, an intelligence officer of Ukrainian extraction serving with the First Canadian Army, by late 1944 much of the German defence in the west had come to rely on over 200 of these ad hoc fortress battalions, who comprised veterans and conscripts unfit for combat on account of age or medical impairment, but able to undertake limited military duties, and used to garrison the permanent fortifications of the *Westwall* and elsewhere.

While still in uniform, Shulman was fortunate to interrogate many senior German officers, and used his intelligence reports with the interview material to publish his 1947 bestseller *Defeat in the West.* Decades later, his work holds up well, though he tended to ridicule some aspects of the Wehrmacht, including these fortress battalions. Shulman referred to 'Stomach' and 'Ear' battalions, comprising men afflicted with specific ailments of those organs, who could nevertheless bear arms, noting of the 'Ear' battalions:

> The problems that beset such a formation were practically insurmountable. Verbal orders could only be given by a frantic series of gestures. Inspecting the guard at night was a nerve-racking and hazardous task since the men on duty could not hear anyone approach. Thus when suddenly confronted in the dark they fired first and attempted to find who it was later. In one Ear battalion, two sergeants of the guard had been killed in this way shortly after the unit went into action. Casualties from artillery fire were also inordinately high because the men could not hear the sound of approaching shells and therefore took shelter much too late.[7]

With hindsight it makes an amusing read, but in 1944 Allied troops could be confronted by an opponent whose skills varied between the comically inept, as here, or the deadly, as in almost any Waffen-SS unit. In 1943–4, the fortress troops were gathered together into so-called battalions, a few hundred strong, commanded by a captain or major. Many would be absorbed into new *Volksgrenadier* units and sent into the December battles in the Ardennes, regardless of their infirmities. In no way did these fortress units resemble regular combat battalions in structure, equipment, motivation or capability. Yet, to Hitler's eyes, they represented another pin on the maps in his headquarters. Ranged against them, Eisenhower fielded nearly forty combat-ready divisions, including twenty American, thirteen British, three Canadian, one Polish and one French, never mind numerous independent tank and artillery brigades.

On 8 September, Rundstedt and Model were finally allowed by OKW to withdraw units to man the *Westwall*, there being no more positions forward capable of being defended, which caused one German soldier to record, 'My total estate now fits into my little bag as I have now lost everything else. The words "hot meal" sound like a foreign language. We are gaining ground rapidly but in the wrong direction.'[8]

That same evening, Hitler was ecstatic when the first V-2 rockets were launched successfully and landed on London. Four earlier attempts, from locations at St Vith and Houffalize (both sites soon to be fought over in the Ardennes) were technical failures, but the later missiles were detonated at Epping, north of London, and Chiswick, west of the capital, where a ten-metre crater was gouged out of Staveley Road, killing three, injuring twenty-two and demolishing six houses. The forerunner of modern intercontinental ballistic missiles and designed by Werner von Braun, who later conceived the Saturn V rocket, the projectile's original title was the A-4, but Goebbels renamed it *Vergeltungswaffe-zwei* (Vengeance Weapon 2), or V-2. In all, over 1,300 were to be fired at England, killing 2,724 people; slightly more struck Antwerp and Paris with thousands more casualties, but from these few details it is obvious that the V-2 was a tactical terror weapon, not the strategic war-winning device the Reich expected it to be.[9]

Hitler's mantra throughout 1944 had been that new secret weapons would suddenly change the course of the war. More and more he alluded to them, without explaining what they were, as if relying on a *deus ex machina* fantasy to alter history. Speer, as Armaments Minister, noted that he was asked frequently when they would be arriving, which illustrated how widely such rumours had circulated, encouraged and incited by Goebbels and Hitler.[10] Goebbels eventually ended such false reports, but Hitler believed his own fantasies, gloating, 'Sheer panic will grip the masses and drive them out into the open countryside . . . It will be an avalanche of misery and suffering . . . What parliamentary government can survive that! There will be such a storm of protest and war-weariness that the government will be overthrown'.[11] Yet troops who had been stationed near V-1 'doodlebug' and V-2 rocket launch sites and saw explosions on take-off or premature landings, immediately dubbed, with soldierly humour, the earlier vengeance weapons *Versager-eins* (Failure-1).[12] Neither V-weapon was affected by weather, which grounded the Luftwaffe's aircraft, and throughout the Ardennes offensive troops of both sides observed V-1s flying overhead towards Antwerp's docks and

Brussels, the glow of the tail motor at night and tell-tale drone featuring distinctly in many veterans' memories.

The eleventh of the month witnessed the first hostile troops setting foot on German soil in combat since the days of Napoleon: a patrol from Troop 'B', 85th Reconnaissance Squadron of Major-General Lunsford E. Oliver's US 5th Armored Division waded across the Our river on the Luxembourg–German border, near Vianden – an area that would be the focus of a battle between the local Resistance and the Waffen-SS in November and contested again during the December campaign.[13] Although this was more of a symbolic setback, the scale of German reverses in the west escalated during 12 September when Oberst Eberhard Wildermuth was obliged finally to surrender the port of Le Havre, which his men had meanwhile rendered completely inoperable. This again drew attention in Hitler's mind to the importance of the Allies' logistics and ports. At about this time, one source indicates that the Führer, who had taken to his bed with poor health, sent for Jodl and they spread out maps of Belgium on the bed sheets. It seems that on this informal occasion together they devised the basics of the winter offensive, deciding to strike through the Ardennes and make for Antwerp. At this stage all these rough appreciations were geared towards a start date on 1 November, a time determined by the assumed onset of the poor weather that would clear the skies of hostile marauding aircraft.[14]

A couple of days later, on 14 September, in preparation for, in his words, the '*großen Gegenangriff*' (great shock), Hitler ordered the appointment of staff for a new formation, Sixth Army (renamed Sixth Panzer Army on 8 November), which was to refit armoured units withdrawn from OB West.[15] This was the first mention of the new army to be commanded by his one-time bodyguard, SS-Oberstgruppenführer Josef 'Sepp' Dietrich, and another indication of Jodl's detailed plans for the attack, which were at this stage advancing on a daily basis.[16] Dietrich was the last of the three army commanders featuring in the Bulge to be appointed, following the earlier elevations of Manteuffel and Brandenberger. Yet it would take weeks to find the necessary personnel and support units for the new organisation, so that Sixth Panzer Army was created formally only on 26 October at Bad Salzuflen, Westphalia, a mere seven weeks before its first major commitment.[17] At this stage none of the three new army leaders had even the remotest inkling that Hitler was intending a major offensive with their formations, merely that he had assembled their forces for a defensive campaign.

Josef 'Sepp' Dietrich (1885–1966) was Hitler's bodyguard in the nascent Third Reich, and one of the earliest recruits into the SS. No party ideologue, he was at heart a warrior, having cut his teeth in the First World War as a sergeant-major in Imperial Germany's tank corps. On 14 September 1944, Hitler placed him in charge of the Sixth Army, the first army-level formation entrusted to the Waffen-SS, but by the time of the Ardennes, Dietrich was thoroughly disillusioned with Hitler's leadership of the war. A front-line soldier, he had no talent for paper work and leant heavily on his chief of staff, Fritz Krämer, who gave up his own division to join Dietrich in the Ardennes. (Author's collection)

By 16 September, the Allies had reached and began to besiege Dunkirk, the scene of the British evacuation after the Anglo-French debacle of May 1940. Perhaps the name of another port triggered something in Hitler's mind, for that afternoon in his headquarters events took an unusual turn. Earlier, the Führer had experienced some kind of minor seizure, presumably brought on by stress, and his third in five days, but he recovered to sit through the usual afternoon military conference. Afterwards he asked a chosen few to join him in his study, one of the many camouflaged bunkers within the *Wolfsschanze* complex.

They included Keitel, Jodl, Generaloberst Heinz Guderian of the OKH,

SS-Gruppenführer Hermann Fegelein, Himmler's liaison officer at the *Wolfsschanze*, General Walther Buhle, on the OKW staff, who had been wounded on 20 July, Ambassador Walther Hewel, chief diplomatic liaison official, and Luftwaffe acting chief of staff, General Werner Kreipe, representing Göring – who was at the *Wolfsschanze*, but curiously not present.[18] Of itself, this specific guest list indicated a major strategic gathering rather than a straightforward military briefing, Kreipe noting in his personal diary, 'Führer situation discussion without Göring, very brief. Immediately thereafter special meeting with a small circle.'[19]

At this second assembly, Hitler first asked Jodl to summarise the military situation in the west. It was a sobering brief; the Reich had suffered over a million casualties in the previous three months, half of whom had been lost in the west. Hitler's long-standing vision of a decision in the west was coming to pass: for the first time the loss statistics in France and Belgium had exceeded those of the Eastern Front. The Wehrmacht was being pushed out of southern France, while in the north they were forming defensive lines along waterways in Belgium and Holland or defending old nineteenth-century forts like Metz.

Jodl announced there was one area of concern. The Reich had virtually no defences in the Ardennes, which the Americans had just reached. At the mention of 'Ardennes', Hitler (according to Kreipe, who kept a transcript of the meeting) ordered Jodl to pause, stood up and stabbed at a map. 'I have made a momentous decision! I shall go over to the attack, here, out of the Ardennes'; a rhetorical flourish and another stab at the map: 'objective Antwerp. It will be a new Dunkirk!' he exclaimed.

His whole demeanour had changed, he stood erect, shoulders squared and eyes blazing, as though his recent illnesses, including his seizure of that very morning, kept secret from this audience, had never happened.[20]

We should realise that Hitler's sudden order for an attack out of the Ardennes, with the objective of Antwerp, made in East Prussia on Saturday, 16 September, was no mere spontaneous gesture to his generals. Possibly rehearsed beforehand with Jodl, this was Hitler the actor, ever the political showman. But why all the drama?

Hitherto, historians of the Bulge have interpreted the campaign purely in military terms. We know that Hitler had been looking for opportunities to go over to the offensive ever since Avranches (first the failed Operation Lüttich, then attempts to get Manteuffel to counter-attack from Lorraine). The method and timing of this announcement suggest the fundamental reason for the Ardennes undertaking was political, not military. What was at stake was Hitler's hold on power in Germany. The Führer needed to demonstrate to those who might still pose a threat to him that he was still in control, that he had direction and purpose. The army would always be a threat: it had helped him to power in 1933 and demonstrated in July 1944 that it could remove him. He had been extremely lucky to escape.[21]

As Professor Theodore Hesburgh, one of the foremost scholars of modern leadership, has observed, 'The very essence of leadership is that you have to have a vision. It's got to be a vision you articulate clearly and forcefully on every occasion.'[22] That was exactly the purpose of Hitler's 'dramatic moment' on 16 September, like Saul's on the road to Damascus. Hitler loathed the laborious General Staff method of testing and analysing options. That wasn't his style. A sudden conversion was both more noteworthy and credible – and far more Hitleresque.

He knew he had drifted ever since the shock of 20 July, lost the initiative and now had to demonstrate to the Reich he was back in control, mentally and physically. He chose his audience carefully, for he needed Guderian, Buhle and Kreipe (representing the army and air force), Fegelein (for the SS) and Hewel (of the diplomatic corps) on his side; he understood that if they were convinced, they would sell his plan to their commands. The Ardennes offensive was, in short, Hitler's response to 20 July, far more so than murdering those who had plotted against him. Militarily, it was irrational, counter-intuitive, even suicidal. The concept in Hitler's mind was not merely of a military counter-attack, but a political game-changer that would shatter the coalition ranged against him. It would also restore the power and prestige of the Third Reich and – crucially – of his own person within the regime.

The Third Reich is best envisaged as a series of competing power blocs, rather than Hitler sitting on high, commanding everything. There was Göring, his undisputed second-in-command, chief of the Luftwaffe, who also accumulated great wealth through the number of ministries and industries he ran throughout the Reich. Himmler controlled much of the security apparatus – the police forces, the SS, Gestapo, the camps, and after 20 July, the *Ersatzheer*. Then came the army, less powerful after the Stauffenberg plot, though still numerous. The 'gatekeeper', Martin Bormann, head of the Party Chancellery, a schemer who controlled access to Hitler and kept files on absolutely everyone. Also influential was Bormann's younger brother, Albert, a *Gruppenführer* of the NSKK (the Nazi Motor Corps), another of Hitler's chief adjutants and member of the inner circle; he was considered far more popular and trustworthy by everyone in the *Führerhauptquartier* than his sibling, with whom his relationship was caustic.[23] There were more: Speer with his six million armaments workers; Goebbels the ideologue, who controlled all the media; the *Abwehr* (secret service) and their spies; and the diplomats. Hitler's fortune was that they generally detested one another.

In the chaotic, divisive and toxic environment of the Third Reich, the Führer liked the notion of courtiers and ministers competing with one another, so that in his pseudo-Darwinian world only the strongest emerged; admittedly inefficient, it also kept all of his potential rivals busy, defending their own turf. In an interview after the war, Speer recalled how there was no unanimous handling of state affairs, 'all the big stars of Hitler's government were doing things on their own. Hitler liked this, but there was always some overlapping and this caused natural friction. His aim was to divide and rule. It also was in the interests of Bormann, his secretary, the most powerful man, more powerful than Hitler, because [everyone] had to go via him to Hitler.'[24]

The Führer had absolutely not foreseen the attack from Stauffenberg and realised he was vulnerable to other power blocs within the Third Reich. Hitherto he had stayed in power by playing these conflicting parties off against one another. But what if they were to find their Führer wanting, and united against him?

There was a precedent, for it was almost exactly ten years since the 30 June 1934 'Night of the Long Knives'. At the time, the crackdown was justified by the Nazi media as forestalling an SA coup, led by Röhm against Germany, though Himmler's and possibly Hitler's interpretation was subsequently that of a plot against Hitler himself. Perhaps the Führer may have pondered the fact that so many of his senior colleagues – Göring, Himmler and Goebbels – who frequently attended briefings at the *Wolfsschanze*, had been absent on 20 July 1944, though all subsequently rushed to Rastenburg to be seen offering congratulations at his survival.

Despite Hitler's decree of 29 June 1941 that 'if I should be restricted in my freedom of action, or if I should be otherwise incapacitated, Reichsmarschall Göring is to be my deputy or successor in all offices of State, Party and Wehrmacht', Himmler's subsequent instruction to the Gestapo 'to investigate Göring's connections with the revolt' may have been motivated by opportunism rather than suspicion.[25] The SS leader was certainly heard to remark to Dönitz, head of the Kriegsmarine, that if Hitler had died, 'It is absolutely certain, Herr Großadmiral, that under no circumstances would the Reichsmarschall have become his successor.'[26] Much later on the evening of 20 July, when Hitler broadcast to the Reich announcing the plot and his survival, he invited Dönitz to address the nation after him, and before Göring – the Reichsmarschall's star was no longer in the ascendant, being rapidly eclipsed by Himmler's, with the latter playing his own game.

In this respect, Hitler's decision to initiate the Ardennes offensive was similar to the Argentinian junta in 1982 deciding to invade the Falkland Islands. Although the Malvinas were an attractive prize, it is generally accepted that the Galtieri government's real motivation for the attack was to perpetuate their military rule of Argentina. The method adopted was to unite its population in a patriotic cause – invasion and recovery of the disputed islands – in order to distract attention away from their nation's chronic economic problems, political suppression and human rights violations.

The 16 September announcement, and the dramatic fashion in which it was made, was to demonstrate, even and perhaps especially to loyal servants like the SS, that Hitler was still in control. Fegelein, a thirty-eight-year-old Waffen-SS general, Himmler's eyes and ears in his headquarters, was no fool. A Knight's Cross-wearing, accomplished front-line commander, he had married Eva Braun's sister to advance his own career. Fegelein's master and the *Schutzstaffel* were so powerful, Hitler may have realised, that they could constitute an alternative power base to himself: he had to present *der Führer* as a strong, credible leader, with a viable plan for the future. The Ardennes offensive was the answer: it was both an end in itself, with its military and political objectives, but also the very Machiavellian means to a different end.

Yet the conference drama was a conceit, for Hitler had suffered a seizure that very morning and his health would continue to collapse, although this was hushed up. Other historians have tended to neglect this aspect of the story.

It may have appeared to those present that on 16 September Hitler had suddenly made his 'momentous decision'. But we now know that since 31 July, Jodl's trusted staff, including Major Schramm, had been planning the operation quietly behind the scenes.

4

Adolf Hitler

ALL THE RECORDS agree that on Tuesday, 15 October 1918, a little over a week before the Armistice, Adolf Hitler was blinded by poison gas. A hardened veteran, his four years of service with the 16th Bavarian Reserve Regiment had brought him full circle, almost back to where he first saw action in 1914, advancing on the Flemish city of Ypres. This time, his company was manning the lines at Wervicq-Sud, twelve miles south of Ypres, when a bombardment from the British 30th Division caught them in the early morning. Six were incapacitated, including Gefreiter (Lance Corporal) Hitler, one of the *Meldegänger* (despatch runners), considered by his mates to be lucky until that moment. Reeling from the effects of a mixture of phosgene and chlorine gas, the twenty-nine-year-old recalled later how his 'eyes had turned into glowing coals; it had grown dark around me'.[1] He was evacuated quickly through a series of aid stations and hospitals from the little village on French side of the Lys river which separated France from Belgium. This occurrence allegedly explained his aversion to the military use of poison gas during the Second World War.

According to his medical notes, despite washing out his red, swollen eyes, he stated that he remained totally blind. Travelling by hospital train for several days, his piercing blue eyes, which would one day captivate millions, covered by grubby bandages, Hitler was not to know that the end of the war was days away. His destination was a specialist eye clinic at Pasewalk, in north-eastern Germany near the Polish border, for the diagnosis in his case was most unusual. His continuing blindness was attributed not to injuries suffered in the gas attack, but to hysteria. Doctors from all the belligerent nations were overwhelmed by servicemen suffering from such hysteria, in the same category as shell shock – acute stress, mental rather than physical in origin – that manifested itself in a range of symptoms, which varied from memory loss, insomnia, stutters or mutism, to extreme physical tics, paralysis, deafness or *in extremis*, blindness. In Hitler's case there was no lasting or serious damage to his eyes – they were sore from rubbing, not gas – which suggested that the cause was mental not physical. He could not see because he *believed* he had gone blind. In other words, Hitler, far from being injured in the British attack, had suffered a mental breakdown.[2]

Hitler's case was considered unique by those treating him, for he possessed an excellent combat record; wounded by shellfire in October 1916, he had written to his commanding officer from convalescent leave asking to return to his regiment at the front. As recently as 4 August 1918 he had received the rare award of an Iron Cross, First Class. Although the medal was first instituted in 1813 by Frederick William III of Prussia, it was most commonly issued during the First World War, where almost six million were awarded. While the majority of these (over 5,500,000) were awarded in Second Class, only 220,000 recipients were decorated with the more unique First Class cross, most of whom were officers. Hitler would ever after sport it with great pride on his tunic, and died wearing the cross in the *Führerbunker* on 30 April 1945. The citation for Hitler's 1918 award read:

> As a runner, his coolness and dash in both trench and open warfare have been exemplary, and invariably he has shown himself ready to volunteer for tasks in the most difficult situation and at great danger to himself. Whenever communications have been totally disrupted at a critical moment in a battle, it has been thanks to Hitler's unflagging and devoted efforts that important messages have continued to get through despite every difficulty. Hitler received the Iron Cross Second Class for gallantry on 1 December 1914. [He] fully deserves to be awarded the Iron Cross First Class.[3]

This document alone gave Hitler the ability to face down any general or soldier in the Second World War whom he thought was under-performing. The author of this citation was Hitler's company commander,

Leutnant Hugo Gutmann, whose words make it clear that the award was not for one act of bravery, but several.[4] There is much about Hitler's performance during the Great War that was swathed in mystery and myth by the Nazis. That he was brave and genuinely earned his medals was beyond doubt. That he suffered a mental breakdown and had been awarded the coveted Iron Cross First Class by a Jewish officer had to be concealed. One of Hitler's biographers has noted with irony that 'Gutmann's qualities – bravery, selflessness, resilience, loyalty and education – were those demanded by Hitler from the "tough as leather, hard as Krupp steel" youth of the Third Reich'. Had Gutmann not been Jewish, he would surely have become a National Socialist hero.[5]

What happened next cannot be conclusively proven, but more than one biographer has argued that Hitler's hysterical blindness was self-induced. German scholar Joachim C. Fest suggested this blindness was 'precipitated by the shock he [Hitler] felt at the abrupt change in the course of the war'.[6] A reading of *Mein Kampf* seems to support this; initially Hitler 'was unable to read the papers'. Then 'in the last few days I had been getting along better. The piercing pain in my eye sockets was diminishing; slowly I succeeded in distinguishing the broad outlines of things about me . . . I was on the road to improvement when the monstrous thing happened.' This 'monstrous thing' was Germany's surrender, the fall of the House of Hohenzollern and Communist revolution. Hitler's reaction was extreme: 'I could stand it no longer. It became impossible for me to sit still one minute more. Again everything went black before my eyes; I tottered and groped my way back to the dormitory, threw myself on my bunk and dug my burning head into my blanket and pillow.'[7]

Unguarded comments made to Albert Speer seem to agree with this conclusion. In 1942 Hitler had stated that his eyesight meant nothing if all one could see was a world in which the nation was enslaved; in 1944 when all was sliding downhill, he told Speer gloomily he feared losing his sight once more, 'as had happened towards the end of the First World War'.[8] Certainly at Pasewalk he was recommended for psychiatric treatment by the hospital's consultant neuropsychiatrist, Dr Edmund Forster. Forster's approach was to 'bully' the patient into recovery, based on his conviction that the underlying cause of all combat hysteria was a lack of willpower. In Hitler's extreme case, Forster concluded that his patient 'refused to see because he could not bear to witness the defeat of Germany'. He 'believed himself the victim of a physical, and therefore to his way of thinking, honourable, injury'.[9]

According to this interpretation of Hitler and his visual impairment, Forster assessed his challenging patient for a fortnight and realised that in order to persuade Hitler to regain his sight, he would have to resort to an extreme technique. Essentially lying to his patient, Forster told Hitler that while 'any ordinary individual would be condemned to lifelong blindness by such injuries, there remained the possibility that someone extraordinary, a man of destiny chosen by a higher power for some divine purpose, might overcome an obstacle as great as this'. Forster struck a match in front of his patient's face: 'You must have absolute faith in yourself, then you will stop being blind. You are young, it would be a tragedy if you remained blind. You know that Germany now needs people who have energy and faith in themselves.' Hitler's sight returned gradually, as Forster intoned, 'You have been cured. You have made yourself see. You behaved like a man and you managed to put light into your eyes because of your *willpower*.'[10]

Hitler's version of this in *Mein Kampf* implies a self-cure, without the help of Forster or anyone else: 'And when at length the creeping gas – in the last days of the dreadful struggle – attacked me too, and began to gnaw at my eyes, and beneath the fear of going blind forever, I nearly lost heart for a moment, the voice of conscience thundered at me: miserable wretch, are you going to cry when thousands are a hundred times worse off than you! . . . What was all the pain in my eyes compared to this misery?'[11] *Mein Kampf* doesn't go into the details of how he regained his sight, but the event seems to have been swift and dramatic. The records show that Hitler was discharged on 19 November 1918, fully recovered.[12]

A seasoned biographer and a sharp, incisive contemporary observer, Winston Churchill, in his chapter on Hitler in *The Gathering Storm*, understood the Pasewalk episode as seminal in the Führer's life: 'As he lay sightless and helpless in hospital in the winter of 1918, his own personal failure seemed merged with the disaster of the whole German people. The shock of defeat, the collapse of law and order, the triumph of the French, caused this convalescent regimental orderly an agony which consumed his whole being, and generated those portentous and measureless forces of the spirit which may spell the rescue or doom of mankind.'[13] Published in 1948, the first volume of Churchill's Second World War memoirs was begun within months of the Führer's death when the former Prime Minister had lost the July 1945 general election. Only Churchill could have written such prose, but in identifying the 'measureless forces of the spirit', Hitler's leading British opponent, who himself understood the requirement for immeasurable reserves of inner strength, also hit on the mechanism that drove the Führer.[14]

Willpower is certainly the key to Hitler. The Führer was a great disciple of the Prussian military philosopher Carl von Clausewitz, claiming to have read his famous 1832 treatise *Vom Kriege* (*On War*) several times. Clausewitz is not an easy read and open to misinterpretation, yet Hitler (who read very widely, but selectively, cherry-picking ideas and maxims that suited his own interpretations of life, rather than acquiring a more nuanced understanding) recognised, and perhaps consciously emulated, one of the fundamental Clausewitzian concepts, 'that War therefore is an act of violence to compel our opponent to fulfill our will . . . War is a contest between independent wills . . . and the strength of the will.'[15] Hitler took this quite literally, to an absurd degree. The title (chosen by Hitler himself) of Leni Riefenstahl's memorable movie record of the 1934 Nuremberg Rally tells us so: *Triumph des Willens* (*Triumph of the Will*).

Of Hitler in the 1914–18 war, Alan Bullock observed, 'Those years . . . had hardened him, taught him to be self-reliant, confirmed his belief in himself, toughened the power of his will.'[16] General Friedrich von Mellenthin, later chief of staff to Baron von Manteuffel, remembered Hitler as 'an incredibly clever man, with a memory far beyond the average. He had terrific willpower.'[17] Whether over the people of Germany, its soldiers and generals, or other countries, willpower also answers the question as to specifically why and how the Ardennes attack was launched.

There was nothing inevitable about the Battle of the Bulge. It made no sense at the time, and makes none with hindsight. It was launched simply because of the vision, dogged determination and sheer willpower of one man, who ignored all professional military advice to *not* initiate it. Although it was German military doctrine always to counter-attack, the question was when and where, not if.

After the war, the OKW historian Percy Schramm also saw Hitler's leadership in terms of his self-discipline, recalling one of his boss's monologues in late August 1944: 'My task has been never to lose my nerve under any circumstances. For the past five years I have cut myself off from the other world. I have neither visited the theatre, heard a concert, nor seen a film. I live only for the single task of leading this struggle, because I know if there is not a man who by his very nature has a will of iron, then the struggle cannot be won.'[18] Aside from Hitler's mistruth that he had enjoyed no music and movies during the war, Schramm believed his Führer interpreted all his political and later military activities in terms of never losing his nerve, and ensuring that his will dominated everyone else's.

Jodl concluded the same, observing that Hitler's interference in minor details was 'in order to impose with unbending will . . . that one had to stand or fall, that each voluntary step backwards was an evil in itself'. Guderian noted Hitler's 'compelling willpower was entirely devoted to this thought which dominated him completely: "Never yield and never capitulate!"' While such an attribute is a positive characteristic, and one without which no military leader can succeed, Hitler linked it to his entire mission in the world. Thus in his mind, willpower became rigidity for its own sake, with no room to learn, adapt or compromise. In this way, Schramm felt, for example, that the struggle for Stalingrad was really a contest of Hitler's determination triumphing over that of his generals, with victory over the Russians taking second place.

Albert Speer, his Armaments Minister, interpreted Hitler's use of willpower slightly differently. People around Hitler 'admired his composure in critical situations . . . This self-command was an extraordinary achievement of his will till the end: in spite of his ageing, in spite of illness, in spite of . . . endlessly accumulating burdens. To me his will seemed unbridled and untrammelled like that of a six-year-old child who will not be discouraged or worn out; that was, in part, ludicrous, but it was also impressive.'[19]

Eventually his unbroken will became divorced from military reality, and became toxic. Such was the context for launching the Ardennes assault.

In the wider context we need to understand how unwell Hitler was by the autumn of 1944, a situation exacerbated by the wounds he received on 20 July. His various medical conditions had long been affecting both his decision-making and his ability to process information – crucial factors missed by previous historians of the Bulge campaign. These provoked violent mood swings, and not untypically on 31 August, a week after the defeat in Normandy, he was recorded as laying into Keitel, 'I accuse the General Staff of failing to give the impression of iron determination and . . . affecting the morale of combat officers . . . when the General Staff go up to the front I accuse them of spreading pessimism!'[20]

From the end of 1942, the Führer had been unable to tolerate intense light and wore a cap with a lengthened peak to protect his eyes when outdoors. When travelling by train, he kept the blinds drawn, and this may explain his proclivity to living and working in underground headquarters bunkers. After 20 July, he avoided the open air, afraid of infections and assassins, and although his staff urged him to leave the dusty, depressing concrete rooms, he refused and withdrew ever more into himself. Jodl likened the atmosphere of the *Wolfsschanze* as a cross 'between a concentration camp and a monastery'.[21] Albert Speer recalled how Hitler 'often interrupted a conference because of his gastric pains and withdrew for half an hour or more, or did not return at all'.[22]

A creature of habit, at the *Wolfsschanze* Hitler generally woke at 11 a.m. each morning, dressed to a stopwatch held by his SS valet, Heinz Linge, walked his German Shepherd bitch, Blondi, breakfasted, then attended a military briefing held at midday. Stauffenberg's briefcase bomb had exploded at 12.42 p.m., in the midst of such a conference. These often lasted a couple of hours and were followed by lunch at 14.00 and a siesta. Dinner was at 8 p.m. sharp and he always attended the second daily situation conference at midnight. Thereafter he would work into the small hours, sometimes as late as four or five, meaning that military decisions could only be made during his unusual waking hours.[23] Hitler's hours were not to Himmler's taste, Martin Bormann noting in September 1944 that the SS chief 'is always quite shocked by our unhealthy way of living. He says he has to be in bed by midnight, at least as a rule. And we go on working till four in the morning, though we do stay in bed a little longer.'[24]

On moving to the *Adlerhorst* to oversee the December Ardennes offensive, Hitler's routine remained the same. Part of the personal entourage who accompanied the Führer everywhere was twenty-seven-year-old Oberscharführer Rochus Misch, whom I interviewed twenty years ago in Berlin. Misch was part of Hitler's SS HQ bodyguard detachment, transferred from a combat unit in late 1939 after being wounded in Poland. He had lost his parents at a very young age and worked as a painter before joining the SS in 1937, aged twenty. When not protecting his boss, Misch served as one of Hitler's telephone operators. 'He wasn't a monster, he wasn't an *Übermensch* [superman],' he told me. 'He stood opposite me like a perfectly normal gentleman, and spoke kind words,' and sent his bodyguard a case of champagne on his marriage in 1942. Of the *Adlerhorst*, Misch recalled each day watching the sky full of the contrails of US bomber fleets attacking the Reich, a sight new to him and the *Führerhauptquartier* staff, for this hadn't been seen at the *Wolfsschanze.*[25]

At this time one of his doctors observed that Hitler, then aged fifty-five, 'gave the impression of being prematurely aged . . . worn out and exhausted . . . a man who had to husband his strength; his shoulders sagged, his chest was hollow and his breathing superficial'.[26] Witnesses commented that his skin was white and flaccid and he was hypersensitive to certain tastes and smells. The Stauffenberg plot exacerbated his fears and phobias. He looked awful, with bags under his steel-blue eyes, which had lost their intensity and lustre; he dragged himself along rather than walked and had lost his physical sense of balance, too; 'I always feel as though I'm falling over to the right,' he stated in July 1944, sometimes having to walk with legs stride, 'like a sailor on a pitching ship'. His stature was permanently hunched, indicating scoliosis, and his dark brown, almost black, hair had become flecked with grey.[27] All agree that from the time of Stalingrad his left arm had begun to tremble sometimes uncontrollably, which he had to grip with his right hand, perhaps indicating the onset of Parkinson's disease. The irony may not have escaped Hitler's attention that he was emulating the medical afflictions of Germany's previous autocratic ruler, Kaiser Wilhelm II, who was born with a weak and withered left arm – for the Führer loathed the former emperor, whom he held partly responsible for Germany's humiliation in 1918, and he despised any manifestation of physical infirmity.

The immediate effects of the 20 July bomb were insomnia, a loss of hearing in his right ear and flickering vision in his right eye – he relied heavily on reading glasses, though refused to be photographed wearing them, believing them a sign of weakness.[28] The lack of sleep was exacerbated by builders drilling and hammering to reinforce the *Wolfsschanze* bunkers against further attack. One of those present in the conference room on 20 July was Kapitän zur See Heinz Assmann, a senior naval officer on the OKW Operations Staff, who remembered Hitler's 'handclasp was weak and soft, all his movements were those of a senile man; only his eyes retained their flickering gleam and penetrating look'.[29]

As photographs testify, Stauffenberg's bomb had torn Hitler's clothing to ribbons; 200 tiny wood splinters were removed from his body and he was unable to shave with his right hand for a while. Hitler put his survival down to providence, but the Stauffenberg attempt represented only one of Hitler's several brushes with death, each time reinforcing the dictator's self-belief that he had been chosen by destiny to make Germany great, as an OSS wartime psychoanalysis report on the Führer made plain. Forthwith he began to be more interested in astrology and the supernatural, which he believed would govern his own fate.[30] Goebbels realised that Hitler was not the only one in the Reich pinning their hopes on the stars, and widely distributed fake horoscopes which spoke of 'valleys of darkness' to be passed through, 'imminent surprises' and 'happy final outcomes', by way of influencing public opinion, which had grown tired of gloomy news reports.[31]

In August 1944, at the time of the Allied breakout from Normandy, Hitler complained of violent headaches and sinus pain, for which he was prescribed a 10 per cent cocaine solution, inhaled twice a day.[32] On 12, 14 and 16 September 1944 (latterly, the day of Hitler's dramatic announcement about the Ardennes attack), he appears to have suffered very minor coronaries, brought on by stress. For several days he endured fits of dizziness, intense sweating and stomach cramps before consenting to be X-rayed on 19 September. Dr Erwin Giesing, one of his doctors, felt the cause to be tablets prescribed for wind by his rival, Dr Theodore Morell, which contained very mild doses of two poisons – strychnine and atropine.

There were several doctors, who competed with one another fiercely for Hitler's attention with conflicting prescriptions. Many witnesses remembered the corpulent and bespectacled Morell shuffling protectively around Hitler, to whom he had been introduced by Eva Braun first in 1935.[33] Albert Speer, who felt him to be a repulsive Rasputin-like fraud, observed that 'if Hitler had the faculty for placing others under his spell, in this case the reverse relationship developed: Hitler was completely convinced of his personal physician's genius and soon forbade any criticism of the man'.[34] A secretary remembered, 'Either before or after meals, Linge [the valet] had to give him at least five different pills . . . In addition Professor Morell, grunting and groaning, turned up in person every day to administer his usual miracle-working injections.' Göring once observed with cruel accuracy that Morell was the 'Reich Injection Minister'.[35]

Essentially, Hitler had become by late 1944 a nervous hypochondriac under the spell of several dubious medical consultants who, having wormed their way into the bizarre world of Hitler's court, created a culture of dependency.

A panzer general, who was allowed to visit his Führer on 26 September, remembered that, 'it was a tired, broken man who greeted me, then shuffled over to a chair and asked me to sit down'. General Nikolaus von Vormann, whose Ninth Army had just been destroyed in the east, recalled that Hitler spoke 'so softly and hesitantly that it was hard to understand him. His hands trembled so much he had to grip them between his knees.' Vormann put all of this down to 20 July, because he then observed, 'This was not the same Hitler I had last seen at war conferences on 15 and 18 July, before the murder attempt of the twentieth.'[36] Vormann was not aware that Hitler's health had already been going steadily downhill; Stauffenberg's briefcase had merely accelerated the process.

On 25 September he was diagnosed with jaundice and on 1 October fainted while being treated by Giesing.[37] Of these days, another of his secretaries, Traudl Junge (whose husband had died in Normandy fighting with the Waffen-SS), remembered Hitler 'lying disinterested in his bed looking around with tired eyes . . . his body had suddenly realised how senseless had been all the efforts of brain and will, and had gone on strike'.[38] On 13 November the Führer developed a sore throat, finding it difficult to eat. X-rays revealed a non-malignant laryngeal polyp on his left vocal cord, a common affliction of professional singers.

Hitler's final departure from the Wolf's Lair – he would never return, for the Russian army was within fifty miles of the bunker complex – was for an operation in Berlin to remove it. The procedure to remove this tiny, but irritating anomaly (they are the size of a millet seed) was completed on 22 November, and the Führer was voiceless for a week (a blessed time, apparently, for those in the vicinity), the entire Chancellery adopting whispers in sympathy. He totally withdrew from all aspects of public life while he recovered, apart from a conference on 2 December about the Ardennes, and then left Berlin overnight on 10–11 December, when he journeyed by train then car to the *Adlerhorst* in the lee of the Schloss Kransberg at Ziegenberg.[39]

Thus, in the midst of planning and executing the Ardennes campaign, Hitler's physical and mental faculties were excessively impaired: he slept little, was exhausted and subject to an extraordinary daily cocktail of drugs, which may partly explain the extreme risk-taking that the eventual plan entailed. Whatever the political logic, the Ardennes was not a sane venture and certainly not an operation that Hitler or OKW would have contemplated even a year earlier.

Hitler's diet, mostly potatoes and vegetables – he was a strict vegetarian – was never good, his meals were prepared lukewarm (an intolerance of hot food due allegedly to the physical consequences of his being gassed), and he had a sweet tooth with a weakness for chocolate cake. Newly discovered records of his personal dentist, Brigadeführer Dr Hugo Blaschke, Deputy Chief Dental Surgeon of the SS, who put ten fillings into Hitler's mouth in 1944 alone, also noted at this time his boss frequently complained of pain and had 'terribly bad breath, yellowing teeth, abscesses and gum disease'. Hitler's anxieties can only have increased as he had a personal phobia of the dentist's chair.[40] Göring had been a patient of Blaschke's in 1930, whereupon the latter had joined the SA and the Party, subsequently treating Goebbels, Himmler and Eva Braun. In the competitive inner sanctum of the *Führerhauptquartier*, Himmler like to have his acolytes closely watching everything; Blaschke was one, along with SS-Brigadeführer Dr Karl Brandt, yet another of Hitler's personal physicians for over a decade. Behind the Führer's back and responding to protests from Dr Giesing, his rival Morell was prevailed upon to alter his treatments. Thereupon Hitler's physical condition improved somewhat, perhaps because he was buoyed mentally by plans for the Ardennes attack.[41]

Hitler's illnesses and psychological reactions need to be inserted into our picture of events leading to the Bulge campaign – particularly in the Führer's refusal to listen to advice or alter plans. As General Walter Warlimont, Jodl's deputy in the *Wolfsschanze*, who was himself injured by Stauffenberg's bomb, commented in a post-war interview, 'Hitler controlled everything from the beginning, down to single modifications of weapons. [His] health at that time was not good; he had to bear the consequences of 20th July; he was the initiator of the plan, not OKW. When we had studied the possibilities of reaching Antwerp, we were convinced it was impossible with our forces.'

As we shall discover, various feasible alternatives were proposed, which then and today were considered to have stood a much better chance of success, but as Warlimont observed, his Führer always countered with the statement that 'This operation is unalterable in every detail'.[42] Hitler's leadership, once inspirational, had become poisonous; he was no longer able to assess data unless it corresponded to his own preconceived notions, and blatantly ignored facts he did not like, such as intelligence reports with adverse conclusions.[43]

Some of the Führer's physical ailments – the uncontrollable trembling of his left arm and hand – suggest, as noted earlier, a form of Parkinson's disease, but mentally Hitler's traits put him at least somewhere on the autism or Asperger's spectrum, possibly with extreme pathological demand avoidance (PDA) syndrome, which can develop in childhood. Sufferers typically exhibit obsessive behaviour, a lack of boundaries, avoid everyday work and social demands due to their own high anxiety levels, and feel they are not in control. They often possess great communication skills, but in appearing charming when feeling secure, they lack depth in their understanding of colleagues and intimates, and suffer excessive mood swings, often switching violently with a 'Jekyll and Hyde' tendency, having real problems controlling their temper, which can take the form of prolonged tantrums and violent outbursts. Speer observed these increase in frequency as the war drew on; in one conference at which he presented unwelcome statistics, 'That alone made Hitler nervous and angry. Although he listened, I could see by his expression, by the lively fluttering of his hands, the way he chewed his fingernails, that he was growing increasingly tense . . . When I had finished . . . Hitler was no longer in control of himself. His face flushed deep red; his eyes turned lifeless and fixed. Then he roared at the top of his lungs . . . Abruptly, he terminated the conference, cutting off all further argument.'[44]

Those afflicted by PDA syndrome often have an inability to see the bigger picture and a desire to dominate; they understand the rules of human behaviour, which they nevertheless feel do not apply to themselves. Their ability to avoid decisions can include refusal, distraction, excuse-giving, delay, argument, suggestion of alternatives, or withdrawal into fantasy, and may be supported by temporary physical incapacitation. If pushed to comply, they can become verbally or physically aggressive with severe behavioural outbursts, fashionably described these days as a 'panic attack'.[45]

Schramm likened Hitler's temper and fierce determination but physical exhaustion to 'a poorly serviced locomotive fired up to red heat in order to barely be able to creep into the last station on its route'.[46] It is of course extremely difficult to diagnose Hitler at this distance, but all the evidence points to a high degree of pathological disorder, sustained by the drugs of Morell and others. This emphasises the conclusion that the Ardennes attack was forced through by Hitler despite extreme opposition from his generals.

The Führer's visits to factories or military units had ceased in 1943 and his knowledge of the outside world was based solely on telephone, wireless and written reports. He still met soldiers to whom he awarded

Even when inspecting a parade of Wehrmacht troops, Hitler entrusted his security to the SS, not the army. Two rows of SS men, in the foreground and middle distance, can be seen guarding their Führer – but from whom? Here the tension between the two armed, uniformed organisations of the Third Reich is palpable. (Author's collection)

the Knight's Cross and other high decorations, but such events were heavily stage-managed with no opportunity for unpleasant truths to be told. Thus his first-hand experience of the war and meetings with combat troops had dwindled to nothing: it was uncomfortable and therefore shut out of his world. When Speer presented photographs he had taken of German civilian refugees, in an attempt to draw their plight to Hitler's attention, 'he roughly pushed them aside'.[47] Another bystander noted that Hitler's war was 'an affair of maps and paper, away from the blood and turmoil'. Rastenburg was a setting of 'forests, lakes and woods, a landscape that had nothing in common with the horrors of the war. He saw neither photographs nor films from the front line; nothing must interfere with the decisive power of his genius.'[48] The advent of these self-delusional attributes was advanced by the events of 20 July, and in the aftermath, with unchecked power, his quick temper and a circle of SS acolytes ready to undertake any task, few chose to argue with their Führer.

Psychologically, he had become aloof and lonely, confiding in no one and terminating any conversation abruptly if a disagreeable topic arose.

As the war progressed, he treated generals more as privates, and even those figures in his own headquarters ceased to have the influence with him they possessed formerly. Hitler began increasingly to meddle in the process of directing his field forces, countermanding orders of senior officers and reserving decisions for himself, even in the employment of battalions and brigades numbering a few hundred troops, while working from out-of-date reports and based in the far-distant *Wolfsschanze*.

The freedom of subordinate commanders to exercise their initiative, *Aufstragstaktik* (the doctrine of delegated tactical authority, loosely translated as 'mission command'), which had been a hallmark of German successes during 1914–18 and 1939–42, was removed in favour of direct orders from Hitler. Quite junior officers were dismissed, reduced in rank or – *in extremis* – executed, if they were perceived to have disobeyed a *Führerbefehl*, whether or not such was the case. A typical Führer rebuke to a senior commander at this time was recorded: 'There's no need for you to try to teach me. I've been commanding the German army in the field for five years and during that time I've had more practical experience than any gentlemen of the General Staff could ever hope to have. I've studied Clausewitz and Moltke and read all the Schlieffen papers. I'm more in the picture than you are!'[49]

But, of course, he wasn't.

5

Unconditional Surrender

THE SATURDAY, 16 September, meeting in East Prussia was greeted with immediate consternation, which Hitler probably expected. As General der Flieger Werner Kreipe, the Luftwaffe representative at the *Wolfsschanze*, noted in his diary, 'Objective Antwerp . . . Guderian protests, because of situation in the East. Request by Hitler for 1,500 fighter planes by 1 November! Pointed remarks that offensive should be launched during period of bad weather, when opponent cannot fly either. Von Rundstedt is to take command. Preparations for 1 November. The Führer again summarises his decision in a long discourse. Binds us by obligation to maintain secrecy and asks us to employ few and reliable men. Afterwards brief discussion with Jodl; still have to think it over myself. Briefed Göring, who flies back to Karinhall tonight. I am quite tired, headache.'[1]

Well might Kreipe have suffered from headaches. Such had been Hitler's mania for secrecy that these revelations clearly came as a great surprise to even the inner circle at the *Wolfsschanze.* As events turned out, the November attack would not begin as planned, but on 16 December, exactly three months after the September conference.

The forty-year-old Kreipe found the *Wolfsschanze* a difficult posting, as he was for ever taking the blame for Göring's follies and foibles. Hitler apparently liked Kreipe, a recipient of the rare *Blutorden* (Blood Order), meaning he had been one of several cadets at the Munich Infantry School who marched in support of the November 1923 Nazi Beer Hall *putsch* twenty years before. However, in Hitler's mind, the Luftwaffe was on borrowed time, having made no impact in Normandy or on the daily bombing raids over Germany. Behind his back, Göring was held to blame for every military setback. He responded – through Kreipe, his frontman at the *Wolfsschanze* – that the Luftwaffe was husbanding thousands of aircraft to throw at the Allied bombers on a single day, though this never materialised.

Although the fifty-one-year-old *Reichsmarschall* had been the last commander of Manfred von Richthofen's fighter wing and a decorated flying ace with twenty-two victories, he left the service in 1918 as a lowly *Hauptmann*. His political leap on 1 March 1935 to the rank of General and commander-in-chief of the Luftwaffe (subsequently *Generalfeldmarschall* in 1938 and *Reichsmarschall* in 1940), omitted the valuable years of experience between captain and colonel when a professional officer would have received a thorough grounding in command and staff work. Consequently, Göring had no qualifications whatsoever to run an air force, except a lot of bluster and self-importance, and essentially thought at the level of a fighter pilot, of the next 'kill', rather than possessing any skills in longer-term strategy.

The Ardennes would emphasise these personal shortcomings, with Göring's inability to provide even air parity over the battlefields by day, or mount a modest parachute drop in support. Moreover, his leadership of the Luftwaffe was hampered by his other duties, for he was President of the Reichstag, acting *Reichsstatthalter* (Prime Minister) of Prussia, and *Reichsminister* of three ministries – Economics, responsible for the government's four-year plans, Forestry and Aviation; as Interior Minister of Prussia, he had been the first head of its police force, the infamous Gestapo.

Göring rarely visited East Prussia in person, for relations with his Führer had been strained for some time and were getting worse. He preferred to spend time at his beloved Karinhall estate, north-east of Berlin, hunting game, accumulating plundered art and maintaining his power base, while Kreipe took the heat for his boss's mismanagement of the air force. An acceptable second-in-command of the Luftwaffe might have done much to iron out such problems, but the man who *de facto* performed this role, Field Marshal Erhard Milch, was not a career military man either, being the pre-war head of Lufthansa. Milch was regarded with suspicion by senior Nazis, on account of his Jewish ancestry, though Göring protected him, stating, '*Wer Jude ist, bestimme ich*' ('I decide who is a Jew').

Thus by 1944 the Luftwaffe was a frequent target of attack from Goebbels and Himmler, jealous of Göring's influence and power, which nevertheless remained considerable, if waning.

Göring's stock had been falling since his failure to supply the besieged garrison at Stalingrad by air, while the Luftwaffe's seeming impotency on D-Day and generally over the skies of Europe compounded his sinking reputation. On 5 September there had been a major confrontation between Hitler on one hand and Göring and Kreipe on the other. The latter's diary noted: 'Nothing but reproaches against the Luftwaffe, it is inefficient, for years it has been deteriorating more and more. Complete failure in France, ground organisations and signals communication units had abandoned their aerodromes in wild flight to reach safety instead of helping the army in its fight . . . Hitler and Göring talked alone for an additional ten minutes.'[2]

In this private meeting, faced with Hitler's opprobrium and a brooding Himmler (who was not present) requesting additional manpower for his *Ersatzheer*, Göring agreed to release some of his redundant Luftwaffe personnel into the army for combat duties. The deal done, Göring's mood lightened, as Kreipe recorded: 'Later . . . he was in high spirits . . . said the idea to dissolve the flying maintenance personnel of the Luftwaffe was dead. He promised he would ask Himmler to stop the monitoring of my telephone.' Apparently, Hitler toyed seriously with the idea of disbanding the flying branch of the Luftwaffe altogether, in favour of tripling the Reich's ground-based air defences – principally anti-aircraft guns – while here was evidence of the long shadow of the Reichsführer-SS, whose men tapped every phone line out of the *Führerhauptquartier*.[3] The same disbandment issue had already arisen back in August, when Speer and Adolf Galland, the Luftwaffe's Fighter chief, had a run-in with their Führer, who had lost his temper in a discussion about aircraft production, 'I want no more planes produced at all. The fighter arm is to be dissolved. Stop aircraft production. Stop it at once, understand? Let all the workers produce anti-aircraft guns . . . A programme five times what we have now. We'll shift hundreds of thousands of workers into *Flak* production.' Needless to say, Speer quietly let the matter drop and Hitler soon withdrew his absurd demand.[4]

The Luftwaffe's reputation was also strained because of the delay into service of the Messerschmitt 262 jet fighter. Göring and Galland had wanted this revolutionary aircraft deployed early as a high-speed interceptor and it had shown great promise in its first victory, against an

RAF high-speed Mosquito in July 1944.[5] Hitler demanded it operate as a tactical fighter-bomber and the consequent re-engineering imposed a five-month delay on it coming into service. By the time this excellent plane, also named the *Schwalbe* (swallow), was ready the Luftwaffe had run out of fuel, and pilots. With a top speed of 530mph – about 100mph faster than any of its rivals – and four 30mm cannon, its presence over the Ardennes would have made a significant difference to clearing the skies of Allied aircraft.

The autumn of 1944 had seen Goebbels, Himmler and Speer nudge the Reich into top gear for total war. Himmler provided the manpower, Goebbels the ideological glue and Speer the armaments. From his appointment in February 1942, Hitler's pre-war friend and personal architect, Speer, had been Reich Minister of Armaments and War Production; during his tenure of office, and despite the Allied bombing campaigns, German war production generally increased rather than declined. In 1943 it generated eight million tons of steel, a comfortable two million *more* than the Soviet Union's output of this valuable commodity.

Compared to 1.83 million tons of steel produced in Germany in the first quarter of 1940, the last quarter of 1943 had seen this rise incrementally to 2.37 million tons produced, the first quarter of 1944 witnessed another leap to 2.56 million and the next quarter an increase again to 2.6 million.[6] Coal and aluminium production in 1944 also exceeded that of 1943. Across most sectors, 1944 accounted for the highest growth rates of the war for German industry. The year 1943 had witnessed the unprecedented total of 6,418 Messerschmitt 109 fighters produced, but 1944 saw this more than doubled to 14,152; totals climbed steadily through the year from 932 assembled in January to 1,718 by September. Whereas 12,013 tanks and 35,235 twenty-mm *Flak* gun barrels had been produced in 1943, some 19,002 panzers and 47,729 equivalent guns were manufactured in 1944.[7]

However, the traditional view of the Reich's 'economic miracle' needs revising. While Speer was a talented organiser, he was also able to use millions of slave labourers, who suffered appalling privations in order to raise output. After release from Spandau Prison, and through his 1970 bestselling volume *Inside the Third Reich*, Speer emphasised his undoubted logistical abilities as a way of deflecting attention from his cynical use of the enslaved workforce, and contrasted low output figures from the pre-Speer era to prove how talented he was at improvisation in generating the impressive industrial increase.[8]

There is evidence that Allied bombing actually helped streamline manufacturing processes and forced the Reich's inventors to devise cheaper components for weapons that used fewer vital metals and were quicker to assemble. For example, 10 per cent was successfully shaved off the weight of many parts to save essential raw materials. Hitler was already aware of the differences between German and US industrial manufacturing methods, but had done nothing to implement change; in February 1942 he had observed, 'We've always been hypnotised by the slogan "the craftsmanship of the German worker" . . . we are far behind the Americans [in industrial terms] . . . they build far more lightly than we do. A car of ours that weighs eighteen hundred kilos would weigh only a thousand if made by the Americans.'[9]

Nevertheless, the Wehrmacht's very backwardness constituted a drain on its raw materials: throughout the war its horses and mules (the peak strength in 1943–4 was 1.2 million equines) – it would use more than 50,000 in the Ardennes – required reshoeing with 4.8 million horseshoes ideally every six to seven weeks, the equivalent of 5,000 tons of iron a month or 60,000 tons a year. Illustrative of the Wehrmacht's use of horses was the huge German convoy on the outskirts of Montélimar caught by artillery fire that Sergeant Audie Murphy – the most decorated American soldier of the war – remembered in August 1944 when moving up from southern France with the US 3rd Infantry Division: 'As far as we can see, the road is cluttered with shattered, twisted cars, trucks and wagons . . . Hundreds of horses . . . have been caught in the barrage. They look at us with puzzled, unblaming eyes, whinnying softly as their torn flesh waits for life to drain from it. We are used to the sight of dead and wounded men, but these shuddering animals affect us strangely.'[10]

The ferrous content of steel produced in 1943–4 was also lower than in earlier years, which impacted on quality, sometimes with dire results in combat. Yet some of these austerity measures were needed desperately, as German designers tended to over-engineer their inventions: for example, the sixty-ton Tiger I tank took 300,000 man-hours to manufacture compared to 55,000 for a Panther, 48,000 for a Sherman – and only 10,000 hours for a Russian T-34.[11] Nevertheless, monthly panzer production rose from 1,284 in January 1944, to 1,697 in June and peaked at 1,854 in December.[12]

Under Speer's leadership, war production continued to increase despite the air attacks, which caused less than 1 per cent casualties of his workforce. However, German industry had not been mobilised for total war until 1944, had plenty of spare capacity, and, as noted earlier, Speer was able to replace some of his workforce conscripted into the Wehrmacht with cheap slave labour, some of which comprised skilled factory workers from defeated nations; naturally this boosted production. Additionally, it was only in 1944 that the Wehrmacht standardised much of its weapons and equipment: fewer designs of field gun, anti-aircraft artillery and anti-tank weapons and their associated ammunition, for example, and just three types of tanks – the Mark IV, Panther and Tiger – plus assault guns. Yet there is evidence that some weapons and supplies desperately needed in the Bulge, such as artillery shells, ammunition for the MP-44 and, above all, fuel, *were* disrupted.

For perhaps a three-week period in late August to early September 1944, the Fatherland was laid open and defenceless to her foes. The Wehrmacht was in a shambles. Most of its combat power had been lost in Normandy, and the remainder, disorganised, was hurrying back to the safety of the Reich and the *Westwall* as fast as they could. Their pursuers were not as diligent as they might have been. Partly the Allies were worn out after their heady chase across France; they were also running critically short of fuel and ammunition. There may have been a psychological factor at work as well. They had experienced three weeks of being fêted as liberators by the French and Belgians, with little combat, and perhaps sensed the Wehrmacht was irreparably damaged and the end of the European war nigh. Consequently the necessary sense of urgency was lacking – and within that time frame the Germans made good their escape to the *Westwall*, brought in reinforcements and raised new formations. The moment soon passed.

This was not apparent to the Allies. By the second week in September 1944, the Americans had reached the ancient town of Aachen, beloved of the Romans and Charlemagne, and the first city of the Third Reich to be threatened by the Allies. On the twelfth of the month, they occupied the first pillbox of the nearby *Westwall*. Given the speed of their advance, both Hodges' US First Army and the Germans assumed Aachen would fall straightaway and the local commander, Generalleutnant Gerd Graf von Schwerin, left a letter in the city's telephone exchange, written in his superb English, requesting his opposite number respect the non-combatant status of Aachen's civilian population: 'I stopped the absurd evacuation of this town; therefore, I am responsible for the fate of its inhabitants and I ask you, in the case of an occupation by your troops, to take care of the unfortunate population in a humane way. I am the last German Commanding Officer in the sector of Aachen.'[13] Humanitarian, but hardly controversial; the Count was a secret opponent of the regime, with form to prove it. In January 1939, as Major von Schwerin, he had approached the British Military Attaché in Berlin, Lieutenant-Colonel Kenneth Strong, with a deal. If Chamberlain abandoned his policy of appeasement and opposed Hitler, his friends in the army were willing to mount a coup against the Nazis. Lamentably this excellent opportunity was ignored by the Foreign Office. Meanwhile, by 1944 Strong had become Eisenhower's chief of intelligence.[14]

Supply problems and lack of urgency delayed the final US assault. Meanwhile Schwerin's Aachen letter was retrieved and read by local Nazi officials, brought to Himmler's attention and the Count, then also commanding 116th Panzer Division (the Greyhounds), was sacked on 20 September and threatened with treason for his defeatist letter. Model and Rundstedt managed to fight off Himmler's demands for a trial and had Schwerin posted out of harm's way to Italy, where – off the SS radar – he made good and even rose to corps command. Scion of a high-achieving family of East Prussian nobility, whose ancestors had included a field marshal under Frederick the Great, Schwerin's other relatives included a government minister and another divisional commander, while a cousin was connected closely to the Stauffenberg plot and had been hanged on 8 September. These were days when your surname could get you executed. Fortunately, the Count had friends in the right places: his operations officer in 116th Panzer – the Greyhound Division which would fight at Hotton – was Heinz Günther Guderian, son of the chief of the Army General Staff, who would himself later rise to high rank in the post-war Bundeswehr.[15] As we will see, the Greyhound Panzer Division fought a cleaner war than many in the Bulge, generally following the noble example of their erstwhile commander.

Throughout the autumn of 1944 it was Himmler even more than Hitler who interfered constantly to remove or arrest senior officers whom he considered unreliable. The Count's corps commander, Friedrich Schack, was replaced for no other reason than being Schwerin's superior, while General Franz Beyer, who would lead his formation to the Ardennes in Brandenberger's Seventh Army, was placed under suspicion on the absurd grounds that a report of his had 'lacked optimism'. The day after Schwerin's removal, the very capable Generaloberst Johannes Blaskowitz was also sacked. This was a significant interference, for he was a contemporary of Model's, commanding Army Group 'G', which included the frontier terrain south of Seventh Army. The grounds were that Blaskowitz had failed to mount an armoured counter-attack against the US forces pursuing him, but the real reason dated back to 1940. He had complained through the Army General Staff about atrocities committed in Poland, and the insolent attitude of the SS to the army. This earned him the undying enmity of Himmler and brought about his loss of office four years later. He was replaced on 21 September 1944 by an officer who epitomised military achievement.

In May 1940 Hermann Balck had stormed across the River Meuse at Sedan at the head of his *Panzergrenadier* regiment. It brought him a Knight's Cross and rapid promotion; by November 1943 he had risen to full general. Yet even he did not last long at Army Group 'G', and was replaced at the end of December 1944 in the ever-faster game of musical chairs that the combination of Hitler, Himmler and OKW saw fit to inflict on their commanders.[16] Not even a field marshal could intervene in a colleague's favour: since July 1944, Rundstedt had been sacked once, while Rommel, Kluge and von Witzleben had died as a result of the plot. Even Major Schramm in the *Führerhauptquartier* had been under suspicion and threatened with removal after the execution of his sister-in-law, though Jodl managed to protect him.

Thus, all commanders in the west, but especially those entrusted with leading the Ardennes attack, found themselves fighting while more than occasionally having to glance over their shoulders, just to check that the SS were not about to blacken their name or arrest them on some trumped-up notion of Himmler's. Illustrative of the gap between front soldiers and Nazi functionaries in the rear at this time was the experience of Major Georg Grossjohan, a highly decorated regimental commander on leave from the Vosges front. He was enjoying a cup of coffee in a café when a field security policeman asked to see his leave pass and identification. 'The demeanor with which this officer requested my paybook was extremely close to the line between brevity and insubordination. One could really sense the gratification this armchair warrior enjoyed by bothering the wearer of a German Cross in Gold and Knight's Cross,' remembered Grossjohan. As his paybook did not include confirmation of the award of his *Ritterkreuz*, he was obliged to retrieve the relevant documentation from his lodgings, an hour away. Evidently disappointed, the policeman 'muttered an apology' and reproached Grossjohan for failing to have his latest award annotated in his paybook. 'At the end of my rope with this nonsense, I reminded him that barely seventy-two hours before, at the front, I had problems of quite a different kind than checking the entries in my paybook!'[17]

The revelations about Schwerin angered Hitler who, with the nihilism that characterised his later defence of Berlin, ordered that 'each individual house in Aachen is to be defended exactly the way the Russians defended Stalingrad'. Walther Model's 14 October 'Order of the Day' to his Army Group 'B' reiterated this fanaticism: 'Now we must shield the sacred soil of the Fatherland with tenacity and doggedness.' Defenders had to 'radicalise the fighting to the utmost degree of toughness in the battle zone, employing every physically capable man . . . every bunker, every city block, every village must become a fortress which shatters the enemy. That's what the Führer, the people and our dead comrades expect from us.' This phraseology was not Model's but almost certainly written by Goebbels or a senior propaganda officer: 'The enemy shall know that there is no road into the heart of the Reich except over our dead bodies . . . Whoever retreats without giving battle is a traitor to his people. Soldiers! Our homeland, the lives of our wives and children are at stake! Commanders of all ranks are responsible for making sure this fanaticism is spread amongst the troops and population . . . Anybody who does not do his job by fully committing his own life will be eliminated.'[18]

It was this rhetoric which dominated the fighting from then on, certainly acting as a motivator in the Bulge, and into 1945. It combined the stick of threatened execution with the carrot of revenge for the sufferings of the population and dead comrades. Meanwhile, Himmler had already taken his own steps to counter any notions of defeatism; his 10 September 1944 memorandum was brief and to the point: 'Certain unreliable elements seem to believe that the war will be over for them as soon as they surrender to the enemy. Against this belief it must be pointed out that every deserter will be prosecuted and will find his just punishment. Furthermore, his ignominious behaviour will entail the most severe consequences for his family. Upon examination of the circumstances they will be summarily shot.'[19]

This probably lessened the tendency to desert, but could not stem it altogether, especially for single men faced with a barrage of equally succinct and clever Allied propaganda leaflets. Fashionably called 'information operations' today, propaganda or 'psyops' were regarded as vital to the Allied war effort, and whole RAF and USAAF squadrons were devoted to delivering propaganda leaflets over German-occupied territory. It was calculated that the Allies dropped 1,512,000,000 paper leaflets, usually attempts to get German soldiers to desert, mostly during 1944–5.[20]

A much-damaged Aachen, which was open for the taking at the beginning of September, thus fell only on 21 October after a bitter fight, the acting Commandant of the city, Oberst Gerhard Wilck, having been obliged to fight to the last. Even in the moment of defeat, the long shadows of Hitler, Himmler and Model produced a defiant farewell as his men marched into captivity: 'I have been forced to surrender, as ammunition, food, and water are exhausted. I have seen that further fighting would be useless. I have acted against my orders which directed I should fight to the last man . . . I wish you all the best of health and a quick return to our Fatherland when hostilities have ceased so that you may help in the rebuilding of Germany. The American commander has told me that I cannot give you the "Sieg Heil" or "Heil Hitler" but we can still do it in our hearts.'[21]

Nevertheless, as the man who surrendered the first German city to the Allies, his words did not prevent the Nazis from producing a hostile propaganda leaflet entitled 'Wilck – *Er trägt die Schuld* ("Wilck – he carries the blame"), which encouraged hostility even to distant relatives who bore his surname.'[22] Despite massive artillery and aerial support, Aachen's capture cost each side 5,000 casualties and was the largest urban battle fought by US forces in the European war; the tenacious defence seemed a grim prophecy of things to come and removed all hope of victory before Christmas.

Two other factors induced the Germans to fight on. One was the highly charged political announcement, made by Roosevelt on 24 January 1943, at the end of the ten-day Casablanca 'Symbol' Conference, that the Allies would accept nothing less than the unconditional surrender of the Axis powers, Roosevelt borrowing the term from Ulysses S. Grant (who had demanded it as a pre-condition to ending the American Civil War). In Volume IV of his memoirs, *The Hinge of Fate*, Churchill suggested he was startled by the president's words. Churchill was still uneasy about it when he wrote the relevant volume of his memoirs, published in 1951, and spent seven pages justifying himself:

> It was with some feeling of surprise that I heard the President say at the press conference on 24 January that we would enforce 'unconditional surrender' upon all our enemies. It was natural to suppose that the agreed communiqué had superseded anything said in conversation . . .

> In my speech which followed the President's, I of course supported him and concurred in what he had said. Any divergence between us, even by omission, would on such an occasion and at such a time have been damaging or even dangerous to our war effort. I certainly take my share of the responsibility, together with the British War Cabinet.[23]

The purpose was to keep Soviet forces battling on the Russian Front, thus depleting German munitions and troops, and to prevent Stalin from negotiating a separate peace with the Third Reich.

The news was not universally welcomed; many inside both governments felt the stance too inflexible, removing any opportunity for accommodation with Germany and staving off a Soviet takeover of Eastern Europe. Allen Dulles, the new OSS station chief in Switzerland, soon realised that Goebbels had been handed an extraordinary coup. He later maintained the Casablanca declaration was 'merely a piece of paper to be scrapped without further ado if Germany would sue for peace. Hitler had to go.'

The US military's view was universally hostile, Eisenhower feeling that 'Unconditional Surrender' would do nothing but cost American lives; later, he observed, 'If you were given two choices, one to mount a scaffold, the other to charge twenty bayonets, you might as well charge twenty bayonets'. General Albert C. Wedemeyer, who had attended the Kriegsakademie, said it would 'weld all the Germans together', while Ira C. Eaker, commander of the US Eighth Air Force, was more blunt – 'How stupid can you be?'[24]

As late as 20 November 1944, Eisenhower had again asked the Combined Chiefs of Staff 'for a modification' of the 'Unconditional Surrender' demand, which he felt was preventing an early collapse of German morale in the west – by then he had realised the Germans would be 'able to maintain a strong defensive front for some time, assisted by weather, floods and muddy ground'.[25] But Roosevelt was stubborn, and though military logic dictated otherwise, was determined not to give in to Eisenhower's demands.

The second factor was US Secretary of the Treasury Henry Morgenthau's plan for the post-war Allied occupation of Germany. It advocated destruction of all Germany's industry in any way connected with war-making and the conversion of the Reich 'into a country primarily agricultural and pastoral in its character'. Agreed at the Second Quebec 'Octagon' Conference of 12–16 September 1944, the plan was immediately leaked to the world's press. Even in the US these ideas were unpopular with a public that was heavily Germanic in origin, and *Time magazine* ran an editorial on 2 October 1944, calling it 'The Policy of Hate'.[26] The *Washington Post* argued, 'if the Germans suspect that nothing but complete destruction lies ahead, then they will fight on'.

This is exactly what happened, with banner headlines in the *Völkischer Beobachter* announcing that 'the Jew Morgenthau wishes to convert the Reich into a giant potato patch'. Even in private, Goebbels could not believe his luck: 'we need not add a single word to its publication in order to enflame the spirit of resistance of our people,' he wrote to his aide. Speer observed that it could have been 'made to order for Hitler and the party, insofar as they could point to it for proof that defeat would finally seal the fate of all Germans. Many people were actually influenced by this threat.'[27] Even Roosevelt disowned it when he learned that US troops had to fight so hard to capture Aachen, and complained that 'Morgenthau's ideas were worth thirty divisions to the Germans'.

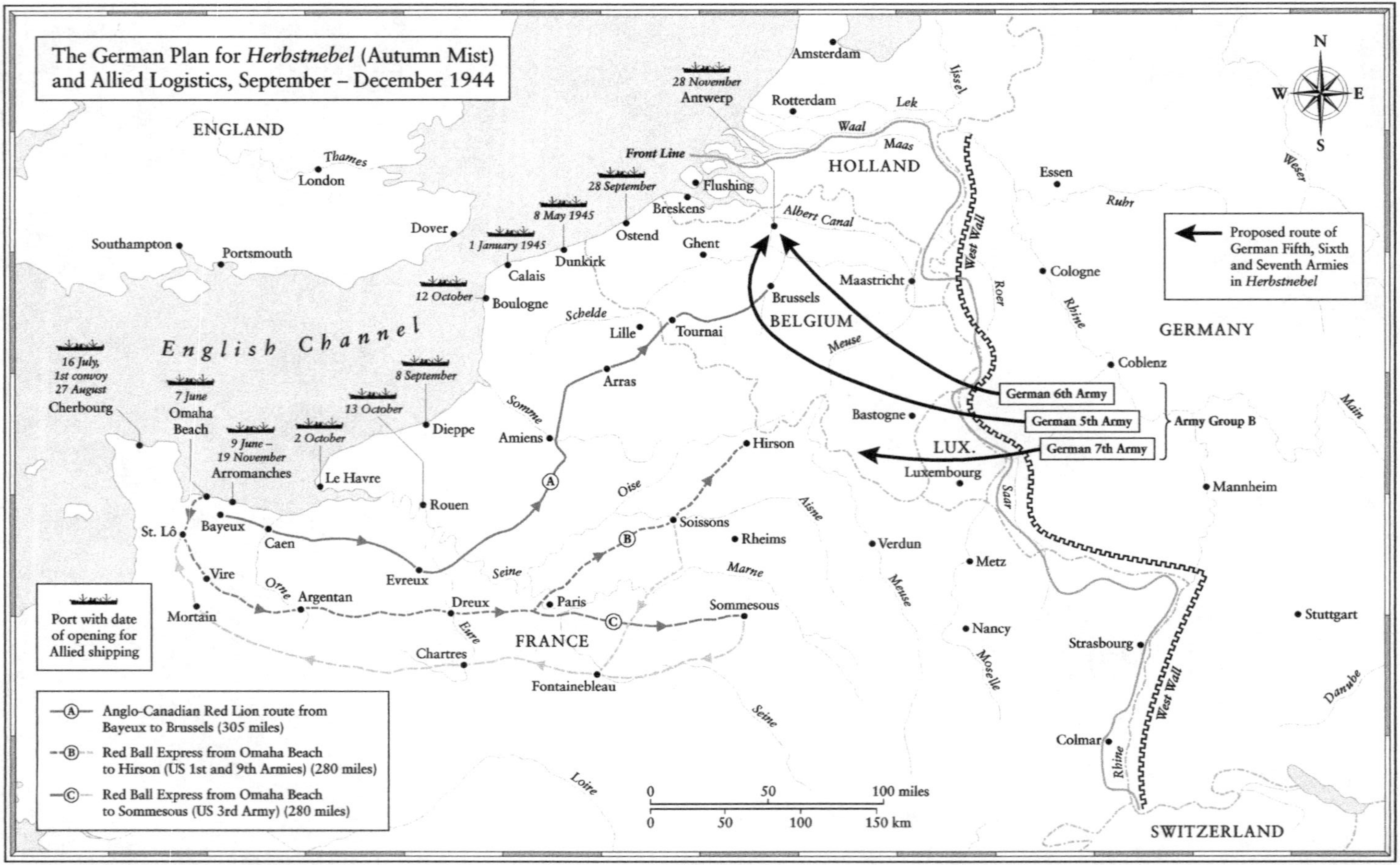
The German Plan for *Herbstnebel* (Autumn Mist) and Allied Logistics, September – December 1944
ENGLAND
Thames
London
Southampton
Portsmouth
Dover
English Channel
16 July, 1st convoy 27 August
Cherbourg
7 June
Omaha Beach
9 June – 19 November
Arromanches
2 October
Le Havre
13 October
Rouen
8 September
Dieppe
12 October
Boulogne
1 January 1945
Calais
8 May 1945
Dunkirk
28 September
Ostend
Front Line
Breskens
Flushing
28 November
Antwerp
Amsterdam
Rotterdam
Lek
Waal
Maas
Ijssel
HOLLAND
Albert Canal
Ghent
Maastricht
Brussels
BELGIUM
Meuse
Schelde
Lille
Tournai
Arras
Somme
Amiens
Bastogne
LUX.
Luxembourg
Hirson
Oise
Soissons
Rheims
Aisne
Verdun
Marne
Meuse
Seine
Paris
Sommesous
Dreux
Eure
FRANCE
Chartres
Fontainebleau
Seine
Loire
St. Lô
Bayeux
Caen
Evreux
Vire
Orne
Argentan
Mortain
Metz
Nancy
Moselle
Saar
West Wall
Roer
Essen
Ruhr
Cologne
Rhine
Coblenz
GERMANY
German 6th Army
German 5th Army
German 7th Army
Army Group B
Mannheim
Main
Stuttgart
Danube
Strasbourg
Colmar
Rhine
West Wall
SWITZERLAND
Weser
N
S
E
W
Proposed route of German Fifth, Sixth and Seventh Armies in *Herbstnebel*
Port with date of opening for Allied shipping
(A) Anglo-Canadian Red Lion route from Bayeux to Brussels (305 miles)
(B) Red Ball Express from Omaha Beach to Hirson (US 1st and 9th Armies) (280 miles)
(C) Red Ball Express from Omaha Beach to Sommesous (US 3rd Army) (280 miles)
0
50
100 miles
0
50
100
150 km

6

A Bridge Too Far

THE STRUGGLE FOR Aachen merged, somewhat inevitably, into a second battle, to control a nearby stretch of dense woodland to the south, the Hürtgen Forest (*Hürtgenwald*). Even while Aachen was besieged, the GIs of Major-General Lewis A. Craig's US 9th Infantry Division first entered the woods on 20 September, determined to prevent their opponents from reinforcing Aachen, less than ten miles to the north. Part of the *Westwall* ran through the fifty-square-mile forest, and German troops defended this part of their frontier with as much determination and skill as did their comrades the streets of Aachen. American tactics overlooked the difficulties of effective artillery and air support in the dense woodland, with narrow and muddy logging trails slowing any advance to a crawl in appalling autumnal weather.

Technical Sergeant George Morgan of the 1st Battalion, 22nd Regiment of US 4th Division, summed up the Hürtgen: 'The forest was a helluva eerie place to fight. You can't get protection. You can't see. You can't get fields of fire. Artillery slashes the trees like a scythe. Everything is tangled. You can scarcely walk. Everybody is cold and wet, and the mixture of cold rain and sleet keeps falling. They jump off [i.e. attack] again, and soon there is only a handful of the old men left.'[1] Another soldier wrote of the area in similar vein: 'Once-proud trees were in ruin; blackened stumps remained where great wooded giants had stood. There were no birds, no sighing winds, no carpeted paths. There was desolation such as one associated with the 1864 Battle of the wilderness. An American general who had fought through one of the battles in the forest offered $5 for every tree his men could find unmarked by shelling and got no takers.'[2] Both men might have been describing the Ardennes just a few weeks later.

The *Hürtgenwald* became a mincing machine for several US and German divisions and the campaign was associated with its very cold and damp weather, and an excessively high number of non-battle casualties caused by pneumonia, trench foot and frostbite. German soldiers in possession of the Russian campaign medal (christened the *Gefrierfleischordnung*, 'Order of the Frozen Meat') had already learned how to cope with such conditions, wearing their jackboots one size too large, lining the gap with straw or newspaper and wrapping their feet in foot-rags rather than socks, to keep their feet dry. Consequently trench foot, which often resulted in the loss of toes, and caused more casualties than bullets in the winter months among US forces, was hardly known in the Wehrmacht.[3]

Leutnant Günther Schmidt of the 272nd *Volksgrenadier* Division was the only officer left in his battalion after the battles in Normandy, who fought through the Hürtgen before getting sucked into the Ardennes. The experience of his battalion marching to the front for the first time must speak for countless other units of *Volksgrenadiers* about to engage in their first combat.

> Shortly thereafter enemy planes appeared and threatened the whole area. Our companies were marching in a long stretched column . . . In the distance we could hear the rumbling of the front very clearly. After marching for a while, we recognized the explosion of every single shell. No one knew what was going to come the next day, and the men were in a depressed and quiet mood. Once in a while we met [German] civilians [from the Eifel area] with all their belongings, some with horse-drawn carts, handcarts and even with baby carriages or bags and backpacks for their most important things only. Their faces expressed what they had to live through, having to leave their home and belongings. The 'front-thunder' was coming closer; we could hear the bursting menace of the exploding shells. Our tension grew when the front came closer. I marched with our commander, Hauptmann Schneider, at the lead of the battalion. At the crossroads at Brück I stopped a truck to ask for the road to Harscheidt. When the truck

> drove on, I saw what it had loaded. The legs and boots of about twenty dead soldiers could be seen under the canvas. Some officers' boots were among them also.[4]

In many ways, the Hürtgen was a dress rehearsal for both sides in the Ardennes, as the impenetrable forest limited the use of tracked weapons and wheeled transport due to the difficult roads and fuel shortages; casualties were magnified by artillery fire showering troops with deadly wood splinters as well as shrapnel, foxholes were difficult to dig in the root-strewn, boggy woodland, while mortars and guns were challenging to deploy, needing stable firing platforms and clearings, of which there were few. After the war, the Seventh Army's chief of staff, Generalmajor Rudolf Freiherr von Gersdorff (who had managed to keep secret his involvement with the Stauffenberg plot) was moved to observe, 'I have engaged in the long campaigns in Russia as well as other fronts and I believe the fighting in the Hürtgen was the heaviest I have ever witnessed.'[5]

The Hürtgen today remains littered with former foxholes, shell craters, even the odd tank track, while rotting military capes and ponchos are commonplace, found underfoot, tangled among the rusting shrapnel and the pine needles.

The Germans managed to contain their opponents, for the Hürtgen lay on the northern flank of the Ardennes start lines and was an assembly area for the attacking troops. American objectives in the forest remained unfulfilled when the Bulge attack began, bringing all offensive action to a close. Essentially both sides had fought each other to a standstill with a combined total of just over 60,000 casualties in this unforgiving battle, the longest fought by US troops in Europe. In the event, whatever lessons were learned in the Hürtgen were not passed on, because the Ardennes followed immediately, and there was no time for any formal, post-battle analysis.

As American troops had been trespassing on German soil since 11 September, the fighting in Aachen prompted Hitler into another move, reflecting the danger to his Reich. On 18 October, he ordered the raising of a national people's militia, the *Volkssturm*, requiring all males between sixteen and sixty not already serving in the armed forces to undertake basic weapon handling. Under Himmler's command while training and Wehrmacht control when in combat, it drew on the traditions of the old *Landsturm* which had contested Prussian terrain with Napoleonic troops in the early nineteenth century – and was scarcely better equipped. These poor militiamen, who carried a motley assortment of museum exhibits for weapons and an armband for uniform, were gathered into battalions of 300–400 each, and frequently sucked into pointless battles in the last months of the war. The *Volkssturm* did not feature in the Ardennes, but their relevance was that in this border region, US troops regarded all civilians as potential fifth columnists, spies and *Volkssturm* loyalists.

It was in late August 1944 that Montgomery had first started to lobby Eisenhower to turn over to him the bulk of *matériel* and allow his Twenty-First Army Group, with American support, to thrust quickly into the Ruhr, capturing the Reich's main supply of coal, iron and steel. This, in turn, Monty argued, would open the road to Berlin, and might end the war by Christmas. The RAF had earlier attacked the region's synthetic oil, coke and steel plants. During March to July 1943, targets like Krupp's armament works at Essen, Nordstern's synthetic-oil plant at Gelsenkirchen, and Rheinmetal's factory in Düsseldorf had all been hit, at a cost of 872 bombers and 5,000 aircrew. The famous Dam Busters raid of 17 May 1943 was part of this wider campaign. In consequence, the Reich had learned to disperse its war-manufacturing capabilities, and Speer's *Organisation Todt* had been mobilised to repair buildings and machinery within hours.

Speer's workforce, often abbreviated to OT, was the Reich's civil engineering organisation, named after its founder, Fritz Todt. Speer succeeded Todt in February 1942 after the latter's death in a plane crash, and by 1944 he was administering around 1.4 million labourers, mostly prisoners of war and conscript workers from occupied countries, all of whom were treated as slaves. Under Speer, and despite Allied bombing raids, the production of weapons had risen, not declined. There is no doubt that the Ruhr was still the key manufacturing centre for the Reich in late 1944, though not the only one, and its main population centre. The Allies assessed that its loss would trigger a total collapse within ninety days.

Montgomery's rival, George S. Patton, who saw himself as waving the banner of US military prowess, was also advocating a thrust into Germany through the Saar, but using his Third Army as the engine of destruction. This was notwithstanding the tough fight he had on his hands at the time, subduing the fortress city of Metz, where of all units the 19th *Volksgrenadier* Division gave a very good account of themselves. Some of their number were officer cadets who, according to a contemporary Reuters report, 'fought the way only fresh SS units would . . . Hardly any prisoners were taken, and the few who were captured would thrash about and bite.'[6] Nevertheless, this was an incredible waste of tactical leaders, for these were former veteran NCOs promoted to second lieutenant days before and sent into combat as officer-only companies. Their sacrifices bought much-needed time for Hitler, however, as Metz resisted until eventually taken on 22 November.

This forced Eisenhower to acknowledge in his 9 September report to the Combined Chiefs of Staff that although the Germans had appeared close to collapse in recent weeks, resistance had become 'somewhat stiffer'.[7] Eisenhower was uneasy, favouring a wide front, to engage the Wehrmacht in all places and prevent it from concentrating in a single area. This also dispersed his own forces, but had the merit of keeping each of his various Allies and their armies occupied. He was, after all, fighting a coalition war and had to recognise the necessity of liberating Allied countries like France, Belgium and Holland, and accordingly held to the 'broad front' strategy agreed to before the Normandy landings. The Supreme Commander thus rejected Monty's proposals as often as the latter presented them. To a certain extent, too, Eisenhower was under pressure from Roosevelt to deliver results quickly. The latter was running for a fourth term in office, and though likely to win in the 7 November elections, he knew that any American battlefield successes in Europe would assist his political campaign.[8]

Eisenhower, who turned fifty-four in October 1944, was hesitant about indulging his two army group commanders, Montgomery and Badley, and allowing either to pursue their own agendas. His own Achilles heel was his personal lack of experience in combat, so he tended to lead by consensus and compromise, aware that, almost without exception, his military and political contemporaries from all nations had seen action in both the First World War and the early years of the Second – even the future President Truman, an unlikely military figure, had seen active service in France between 1917 and 1919 with the Missouri National Guard.

Eisenhower's military credentials are relevant to the Bulge story. He was commissioned into the infantry from the West Point Class of 1915, famous for producing fifty-nine generals out of 164 graduates, including Omar Bradley, but 'Ike', as he was universally known, narrowly missed being posted overseas. His aptitude for staff work was demonstrated in 1926, when he graduated first out of 275 at the US Army's Command and General Staff School, Fort Leavenworth, and again in 1928, when he attended the Army War College. He drew his own conclusions about the First World War in 1929, when as a major he was attached to the American Battle Monuments Commission, and helped write *A Guide to the American Battle Fields in Europe.* The *Guide* was as close to that war as he got, but he was able to make sense of it. He saw particularly the need for a resolute political coalition, overwhelming superiority in men and *matériel*, and thorough training.

Lieutenant-Colonel Eisenhower's career changed course when he attracted the patronage of the US Army's chief of staff, George C. Marshall, in late 1941. After Pearl Harbor, he was appointed brigadier-general to head the Army War Plans Division, and later, as major-general, of the Operations Division in Washington, DC. This concept of a professional staff officer remains anathema to the British, who intersperse staff work with regimental duty – the Germans followed more closely the US model. In June 1942, Marshall promoted him over 366 senior officers to be commander of US troops in Europe, a move which was more than justified but unthinkable in some other armies.

That it worked was due to Eisenhower's personal charm and tact, where a lesser man would have excited envy or bitterness. This personal quality, his superb inner confidence, as well as Marshall's patronage, are surely the keys to Ike's success. He was the ultimate 'team player', able to reconcile different national interests, as well as being a first-class staff officer. Promoted lieutenant-general in November 1942 to command the Operation Torch landings in French North Africa, the US defeat at Kasserine Pass, Tunisia, in February 1943 might have destroyed a lesser man and was, effectively, his first command in war. With necessary ruthlessness, Ike sacked his II Corps commander, replacing him with George Patton.

From his experience of overseeing the landings on Sicily and at Salerno, it is not difficult to see why Eisenhower was appointed to lead SHAEF and the Normandy invasion – though still only a substantive lieutenant-colonel.[9] Crucially, he had the support of military contemporaries and the backing of his political masters.One of Montgomery's first meetings with Ike came in March 1943, and the former confided to Brooke:

'Eisenhower came and stayed a night with me on 31 March. He is a very nice chap. I should say he is probably quite good on the political side. But I can also say, quite definitely, that he knows nothing whatever about how to make war or to fight battles; he should be kept away from all that business if we want to win this war. The American Army will never be any good until we can teach the generals their stuff.'[10] Eisenhower reported back to Marshall of the same encounter that Montgomery was 'excessively cautions'.

Though Ike was never privy to Monty's letter, it illustrated the fundamental friction between the pair, never resolved, and at times he found himself as much keeping the peace between Montgomery, Patton and Bradley as fighting the Germans, which is precisely why he had been selected as Supreme Commander – to manage his team, all of whom were brilliant in their own ways.

Eisenhower's equipment losses were rising, not just from combat but from wear and tear. Major-General Maurice Rose on 18 September reported that his US 3rd Armored Division had but seventy Shermans fit for battle (his authorised strength of these handy tanks was 232).[11] At the same time, Ike was equally conscious of his own casualties and reluctant to allow subordinates to risk soldiers' lives for narrow-front, prestige objectives. He had watched his US battle losses *per month* in Europe climb from 39,367 in June to 51,424 during July, dip slightly between August and October, then reach 62,437 by the end of November. Approximately one in four of these were killed, the rest being wounded, posted missing or captured.[12]

British and Canadian monthly casualties in Twenty-First Army Group had risen dramatically, from 24,464 in June, to 26,075 over July and 26,776 at the close of November, and Monty had already been forced to disband two infantry divisions (50th and 59th), and re-role their anti-artillery and pioneers as infantry, because he had run so short of manpower.[13] For this reason, Monty kept back eight armoured brigades (1,400 tanks), six artillery brigades (700 guns) and six Royal Engineer groups, to provide a reserve of firepower equivalent to six additional divisions. He knew he was likely to run short of manpower, so was prepared to use firepower to compensate for the lack of men. Monty's 'metal not flesh' approach was also to offset personal fears associated with the 1914–18 casualties he and his British-Canadian contemporaries had witnessed, but it laid him open to accusations of 'excessive caution' from US Army leaders, who had experienced fewer months of First

World War combat. By November 1944 these various losses, mostly borne by the infantry, had exceeded the estimated casualty bills for these months; both Marshall and Brooke warned Eisenhower there was no infinite pool of manpower, and that Japan would need to be subdued after Germany.

Ike was cautious too. Although Berlin had been listed as the military goal of the Western Powers in a pre-D-Day plan of May 1944, by mid-September, when Soviet forces had reached Warsaw, he no longer saw the capital city of the Reich as a vital western target. He knew that Roosevelt and Churchill had already agreed (to be confirmed at Yalta) that areas of eastern Germany, including Berlin, would fall under Russian influence, and saw no point in spilling blood to win territory, only to hand it over to the Soviets at the war's end. To him, it was more important to capture the industrial heartlands of the Ruhr and Saar, than Germany's capital city. The Western Allies' advance needed to be coordinated with Russia, he felt, and, possibly reluctant to provoke Stalin, Eisenhower wisely insisted on sticking to his broad-front concept.

Monty not only wanted to lead a spearhead towards Berlin, but felt that someone, preferably himself, should be appointed as overall land commander. On the latter issue, Monty was doctrinally correct. Eisenhower reigned over the Supreme Headquarters of the Allied Expeditionary Force (SHAEF), enacting Anglo-US policy given to him by Roosevelt and Churchill via Marshall and Brooke. He had a British deputy, Air Chief Marshal Sir Arthur Tedder, and under them were the three army group commanders: Monty of the Twenty-First, the Twelfth under Bradley and Jacob L. Devers' Sixth Army Group, which was activated on 15 September.

By the time of the Bulge, the manpower involved was phenomenal – nearly three million men. At the end of August, Eisenhower had some 1,017,817 US Army personnel in Europe, which had increased to 1,353,079 a month later, and risen to 1,921,481 at the close of November. In the same month, British and Canadian forces in Europe had reached 925,664.[14] Monty was right in advocating that all the land forces, together with the air and maritime components, needed further coordination under a single operational commander. He was wrong in suggesting it should be him. Apart from his abrasive personality, an overall commander would have to represent the nation fielding the most troops and resources, and incurring the most casualties.

If such an appointment was to be made, it could not, therefore, be the British Bernard Law Montgomery, inconveniently appointed to the five-star rank of field marshal on 1 September 1944, when Eisenhower, his boss, remained a four-star general. (There was actually no American five-star rank until Congress created one in December 1944 for Marshall, MacArthur, Eisenhower and Arnold.) Without doubt, strategy suffered, and land operations were not sufficiently coordinated – because Eisenhower and Tedder spent their time talking up to their political masters, not down to their operational subordinates. Because prime ministers and presidents will always require extensive attention and mollification, there existed in 1944 a theoretical gap in the Allied command chain, which we would recognise today in the lack of a Combined Joint Task Force Commander, meaning an individual and his staff directing multinational, tri-service military operations below Eisenhower's quasi-political level. However, the need was not understood or identified in 1944–5.

Ironically, in their *Oberbefehlshaber West* (OB West), the Germans created exactly the kind of appointment after which Montgomery was hankering. Although the title Supreme Commander of the German Armed Forces in the West implied the sort of power about which Monty dreamed, as we've seen earlier inter-service rivalries and Hitler had systematically stripped the position of whatever effective power it may ever have possessed, so that Rundstedt, who held the post at the time of the Ardennes, used to joke that the only troops over whom he had authority were those who mounted guard outside his gates.

Notwithstanding the strategy and doctrine debates, the Allies had also run out of steam by late August. Reaching the German frontier so fast meant they had outrun their supplies: for example, units had no adequate maps of the terrain ahead as map-printing trucks, run by army engineers, were too far behind, working to a timetable devised before Normandy and long since overtaken by events. According to the original plan, twelve US divisions were expected to have reached the Seine by 4 September, but on that date sixteen US divisions had already raced 150 miles beyond.[15] By the end of August, Eisenhower's advance had begun to slow for lack of fuel, ammunition, and in fact – everything. On 2 September, two of Hodges' corps, V Corps and XIX Corps, were forced to halt, the latter over four days, for want of a range of supplies. Precisely the same reason forced Second British Army's commander,

General Sir Miles Dempsey, to immobilise his VIII Corps on the Seine for two weeks.

All logistical needs to Montgomery, Patton's Third Army on the Moselle and Hodges' First at Aachen had to be relayed from the artificial harbour at Arromanches and beaches of Normandy, there being no other large port and docking facilities captured and operable. Patton and Hodges at this time were receiving around 3,500 tons each daily, about half their actual needs.[16] This was a self-inflicted problem, as neither Eisenhower nor Montgomery had focused serious attention on developing the port of Antwerp, captured intact on 4 September, as a new logistical hub for the advance. This would have acted as a radical transfusion to the Allies' ability to pursue the Wehrmacht into and through Germany in September 1944. Although the southern French ports of Marseilles and Toulon surrendered on 28 August, both had been sabotaged and the former was only able to receive shipping on 15 September. Accordingly, as each of his divisions required 700–750 tons of supplies every *day*, Eisenhower had to shift focus to the unglamorous world of logistics and concentrate much of the available American trucking capacity.

The vehicles (nearly 6,000 of them), impounded swiftly from any and every US unit, constituted the 'Red Ball Express', which in three months delivered over 412,000 tons of ammunition, food and fuel along a series of one-way major roads from which all other traffic was barred. The whole logistics scheme was a superb improvisation, conceived in a thirty-six-hour brainstorming session. Initially, there were not enough drivers and provisional truck companies were formed of rear-echelon troops who were asked, or ordered, to crew them. Vehicles were identified by painted twelve-inch red discs, hence the name, and operated from 25 August until 16 November. At its peak 132 US transportation companies were operating 24/7, averaging 12,500 tons of supplies ferried by 900 lorries with two-wheeled trailers every day.

This took a heavy toll on men (75 per cent of whom were African Americans) and vehicles, with many accidents caused by poorly maintained trucks and exhausted drivers: Patton's Third Army was 350 miles away and Hodges' First nearly 400, necessitating a round trip of about fifty-four hours, regardless of weather. Master Sergeant David Malachowsky remembered that the ability to drive was secondary. 'All of us assigned on the Red Ball detail had been in some kind of hassle

Operating between 25 August and 16 November 1944, the Red Ball Express eased the Allies' embarrassing logistics shortages and provided a useful rehearsal for moving huge quantities of supplies at very short notice. In December this expertise was used to send everything needed to repel the Germans from the Bulge. Immediately the Ardennes sector was attacked, semi-trailers and these GMC 2½ ton 6 x 6 trucks were filled with men, who were conveyed, standing up, to the front. (NARA)

with the officers . . . I had an argument with the Major two days before the list was posted. We saw the list on the bulletin board, moved out in a truck within one hour and were at Omaha Beach by 02:00–03:00 a.m. We divided up by twos, and mounted up . . . directions were posted on the dashboard . . . Only 5 of the 15 men on the detail list were from the Motor Pool. The rest were litter bearers, corpsmen, even a dental technician.'

In October, Eisenhower wrote them a grateful Order of the Day, concluding, 'To you drivers and mechanics and your officers, who keep the Red Ball vehicles constantly moving, I wish to express my deep appreciation. You are doing an excellent job, but the struggle is not yet won. So the Red Ball Line must continue the battle it is waging so well, with the knowledge that each truckload which goes through to the combat forces cannot help but bring victory closer.'[17]

The Red Ball was possible only because of America's stupendous manufacturing capability. In 1939 the US Quartermaster Corps had standardised its design for a medium 2½-ton 6 × 6 medium truck and by 1940 had tested and approved the prototype submitted by General Motors Corporation (GMC). Civilian vehicle manufacture was banned in the US from June 1942, enabling the production of more than 800,000 2½-ton 6 × 6 trucks during the war, some by Studebaker and International Harvester – who in peacetime made cars and agricultural tractors – but a staggering total of 562,750 by GMC, in Pontiac, Michigan, leading to their inevitable nicknames of 'Jimmies'.[18] By contrast, the Germans never standardised, relying on a huge variety of captured vehicle stocks (a maintenance nightmare) and the Opel Blitz 2½-ton truck, of which perhaps 90,000 examples were produced – but hampered, of course, by their lack of fuel.

Major efforts to reopen the French rail network were also begun, and by the end of August 18,000 men, including 5,000 German prisoners, were engaged in railway repair, the first trains reaching Third Army's rail depot at Le Mans on 17 August. Yet everything still needed to be trucked forward from this railhead, and, to free up transport, Bradley's Twelfth Army Group took a calculated risk in unhitching much of their heavy artillery, freeing additional vehicles and drivers for logistical use. Montgomery's Twenty-First Army Group likewise stripped two divisions of their lorries, loaning four British truck companies to US forces. A lack of spare parts such as vehicle tyres and tank tracks, of which there were almost none left in France by October, further threatened to halt Eisenhower's forces.[19]

Fuel was the chief bugbear and pipelines under the Channel and overland in France were constructed to shorten supply distances, but these took time to build and commission, and could not solve the short-term issue. To keep rolling, infantry divisions – reflecting their generous allocation of vehicles – needed a daily assignment of 150 tons of gasoline, but the thirstier armoured divisions required 350 tons per day. Fuel was supplied for use in five-gallon jerrycans, named after its German original, of which twenty-one million had been issued in Europe alone by 1945. Thus, of all supplies landed in France, fuel comprised around 25 per cent. This did not alleviate the sudden shortage, which became so acute that on 28 August both the US First and Third Armies reported less than a day's worth of fuel in hand for their needs. These two formations had each consumed around 400,000 gallons of fuel per day in their race across France to the German frontier, while the Red Ball Express itself used another 300,000 gallons a day, just trucking supplies to the front.

The shortage was so dire in September that the US 492nd Bomb Group, based at Harrington, a secluded airbase in rural Northamptonshire, was also tasked to airlift fuel forward to Third Army. A Special Operations force nicknamed the 'Carpetbaggers', the Group specialised in the delivery of supplies, agents and propaganda leaflets over occupied Europe, using highly modified, black-painted, B-24 Liberators. After working non-stop to convert their B-24s into flying fuel bowsers, between 21 and 30 September 1944, up to sixty aircraft a day, each carrying 2,000 gallons of fuel, lumbered into the air at Harrington to make the five-hour trip. In ten days they shifted nearly a million gallons of gasoline to three separate airfields in France and Belgium.[20] This illustrated that the Allies controlled the skies sufficiently to risk sending aircraft laden with fuel close to the combat zone, and also how far air transport had come of age by 1944.

By tonnage, artillery ammunition comprised the largest percentage of trucked logistics: in operations around Aachen, US First Army fired 300,000 rounds of 105mm shells (or two Liberty shiploads), and this in a month when their activities were constrained by a shortfall of ammunition. Firepower grew to First World War proportions, with six million shells and two million mortar rounds fired in October. Some historians have alleged that 'winter clothing was sacrificed to make more room for gas and ammunition', but this is nonsense – winter clothing was not ordered or requested from the US because the Allies expected a victory before the winter of 1944–5 arrived. The general supply famine was no one's fault, just a symptom of the original pre-Normandy plan which envisaged a different rate of advance. Unfortunately for the Allies it coincided precisely with the three-week period of late August to early September when Germany was open for the taking.

In September, as increasing numbers of tanks, trucks and aircraft were laid up for maintenance, Eisenhower's chief logistician, Major-General John C. H. Lee, estimated that 100,000 tons of replacement equipment were needed to re-equip the Allied armies and create a small reserve. The Bible-punching Lee was a vital figure to the sustainment of the battle through France and beyond, as chief logistician and commander of the Communications Zone (known as COM-Z, the area behind the combat zone stretching to the coast), but was his own worst enemy. His imperious manner, 'heavy on ceremony, somewhat forbidding in manner and appearance, and occasionally tactless', set him against many of the front-line commanders he was meant to assist, who referred to him, after his initials, as 'Jesus Christ Himself' Lee.

Even the US Official Historian was forced to admit that the fifty-seven-year-old general 'often aroused suspicions and created opposition'. However, Lee was perceptive enough to realise that US segregation policy against African American troops fighting in combat arms deprived the army of much-needed personnel. In December 1944 he appealed to these troops, hitherto confined to driving the Red Ball trucks, to volunteer for assignment 'without regard to color or race to the units where assistance is most needed, [to] give you the opportunity of fighting shoulder to shoulder to bring about victory'. Eventually, 2,253 black Americans fought in thirty-seven rifle platoons at the front.

Having overcome these supply challenges and learned from them, no Anglo-American force had ever been as well equipped and sustained as was Eisenhower's by the time of the Ardennes. This diversion into the world of logistics meant that the Allies were unusually well resourced to contain an attack when it emerged, while their opponents remained critically short of everything. It also meant that, in the coming months, were the Allies suddenly to require men and *matériel* rounded up at very short notice and driven to an obscure part of the front, without plan or rehearsal, to deal with an unexpected German attack, the Red Ball had taught them how to do it.[21]

Other one-way vehicle arteries, meanwhile, had sprung up to emulate the success of the Red Ball, including the Le Havre–Rheims 'White Ball Highway', and the British 'Red Lions Express', which ran from Bayeux to Brussels. All these routes tended to be tree-lined and potholed, twin nightmares for tired drivers of heavily laden trucks at night. The American Red Cross supplied mobile canteens to provide hot coffee and sandwiches to drivers, medics operated aid stations along the route, while massive military police, recovery, repair and rest facilities were set up. Driver John R. Houston recalled, 'We lugged an awful lot of stuff to the front, particularly to Third Army. We ran through summer, fall and winter, through snow, ice and rain. Guys were falling asleep all the time. You couldn't get enough rest. I remember falling asleep on top of a jeep hood when it was raining like hell.'[22] Houston's daughter, the singer Whitney, remained inordinately proud of her father's wartime service. There being no other way to sustain the advance, this amounted to war by internal combustion engine.

*

Meanwhile, Eisenhower, relentlessly badgered by Montgomery, for once lowered his guard and agreed to an ambitious plan to seize a bridgehead over the Lower Rhine at Arnhem and thus outflank the Siegfried Line from the north, which he confirmed in his 13 September 1944 Directive. The objective was not quite Monty's dream of a deep thrust into the industrial heartland of the Ruhr and beyond, but retained the Allied initiative and promised a big psychological leap, with the ability to 'bounce' at will Germany's traditional geographical frontier, the majestic River Rhine. A secondary aim, which originated in Whitehall, was to rid the area of its V-2 rocket launch sites, from which the Luftwaffe had been bombarding London since the previous week. The operation's name, Market Garden, betrayed one of its weaknesses. It was not one plan, but two: 'Market' – the airborne assault – being pulled 'off the shelf' by the RAF and adapted to circumstances, while 'Garden' was conceived hurriedly by planners in Monty's Twenty-First Army Group and XXX Corps. The result was an untidy and hasty marriage.

Thus, while the 16 September conference was taking place in East Prussia, with Hitler exclaiming 'objective Antwerp' and jabbing his map, Lieutenant-General Brian Horrocks, popular commander of British XXX Corps, was briefing his officers on a daring Allied venture to do something similar: drive armoured forces down a sixty-mile corridor deep into the German lines over two days – 'objective Arnhem'. There would be no pause in the advance; 'keep going like hell,' Horrocks told his officers, which was almost certainly what the Führer was saying at a similar hour in the *Wolfsschanze* of his Ardennes plan.

Eisenhower and Monty, in their different ways, were suffering from 'victory fever'. In a 13 September 1944 exchange of letters between Ike and his boss, George C. Marshall, the latter reflected the prevailing mood in writing that 'the termination of the war in Europe might be expected by the end of November 1944'.[23] Marshall was then attending the Quebec Conference (which would produce the Morgenthau Plan with its Carthaginian peace proposal) and this mutual optimism, though unfounded, goes some way to explaining the decision to indulge Monty.

The expectancy was reflected throughout the chain of command; at this time US First Army's Courtney Hodges sent his boss, Bradley, a bronze bust of Hitler his men had just liberated from a house in the Belgian border town of Eupen. It was accompanied by the message that 'given ample ammunition and an extra division, First Army would deliver the original in thirty days'.[24] With his logistics still not secure, so buoyant was Eisenhower that he expected to execute his Market Garden airborne drop, cross the Rhine and only after that to pause, regroup and re-engineer his supply lines. As he wrote to Montgomery on 5 September, once the Saar and Ruhr had been seized, only then would he turn his attention to 'Le Havre and Antwerp'.[25]

Le Havre would fall shortly (though sabotaged), but Eisenhower in this display of unguarded optimism seemed to regard Antwerp as a secondary objective. Likewise, in expecting the Saar and Ruhr to fall into his lap, he was six months ahead of himself. Ike perhaps felt that the German army might be in a state of 'melt-down' similar to that of autumn 1918, and that the shock of a huge airborne assault might accelerate this process, hence his lack of attention towards Antwerp. To be fair to Ike, when Market Garden was first contemplated around 10 September, the Wehrmacht was in serious disarray in the Arnhem area; however, the situation changed rapidly in the days before the ambitious operation was implemented, illustrating the need for frequent and ongoing intelligence assessments.

Operation Market Garden was to give the Germans great hope. On 17 September, this massive drop of the British First and US 82nd and 101st Airborne Divisions, the latter both veterans of Normandy who would return to the Ardennes, began landing on a chain of locations leading to the road bridge at Arnhem. The relevant Ultra intelligence, confirmed by the Dutch resistance, definitely alerted Allied planners beforehand to the presence of Oberführer Walter Harzer's 9th SS *Hohenstaufen* Panzer Division (another unit that would soon reappear in the Bulge) and its sister, the 10th SS, both refitting in the area after being massacred in Normandy.

However, the timing was crucial: this was a mere three weeks after German Fifth and Seventh Armies had been annihilated at Falaise, and to Monty's staff it seemed inconceivable that either SS division, known to be at less than half-strength and possessing few serviceable armoured vehicles, was in any position to pose a significant threat. The Ultra analysts at Bletchley Park in rural Buckinghamshire had provided much important strategic and operational intelligence (such as warning of the impending Operation Lüttich against Mortain), and were good at reporting trends and movements of formations. However, they were less accurate in reporting tactical information. Once the fighting moved into

Germany itself, wireless orders previously intercepted by Ultra were more usually given in person, sent between German headquarters by trusted officer courier or relayed by secure telephone link. From August, Ultra intelligence was given less weight by all Allied commanders and by September, in the instance of Market Garden, Bletchley's reports were deliberately disregarded.

The Allied intelligence failure over Arnhem would precede the much more serious one before the Ardennes, both shortcomings made for exactly the same reason. Due to the prevailing victory fever, which affected all levels of the Allied governments and military chains of command, Montgomery (and Lieutenant-General 'Boy' Browning of the First Airborne Army) displayed a worrying tendency to disregard unwelcome intelligence. Few significant individuals questioned the Market Garden planning, and those who did, including the exiled Crown Prince Bernard of the Netherlands, Major-General Stanisław Sosabowski of the Polish Parachute Brigade and Major Brian Urquhart, Browning's intelligence officer (and later Deputy Secretary-General of the United Nations), were ignored or rebuked, and in Urquhart's case, relieved for alleged battle fatigue, but in reality simply for bearing unpleasant news. This problem would arise again in December, when few questioned the Allied planning and intelligence assumptions.

German intelligence, by contrast, was excellent and respected. Model's Army Group 'B' headquarters had already concluded that an offensive was likely by Monty's formations along an axis of Eindhoven–Nijmegen–Arnhem–Wesel, while at the 16 September conference in the *Wolfsschanze*, Jodl stated an 'expectation of parachute landings in Holland, Denmark and Northern Germany'.[26] On 11 September all units in Holland, including II SS Panzer Corps, were told to expect airborne landings and put on Alert Level II – indicating an enemy attack was considered imminent. This demolishes Montgomery's argument, advanced then – and for long after the war – that 'the enemy was expecting our attack at that point last of all'.[27]

Field Marshal Model was himself staying in the De Tafelberg Hotel, Oosterbeek, a suburb of Arnhem, when gliders and paratroopers descended in the early morning of Sunday, 17 September, to interrupt his breakfast. He decamped immediately to Doetinchem, fifteen miles due east and the HQ of Obergruppenführer Wilhelm Bittrich's II SS Panzer Corps. From there, Model was able to direct personally the initial countermeasures, possessing enviable and precise situational awareness.

(Arnhem would amount to his last victory in the field.) Bittrich's understrength Waffen-SS units and other garrisons in the vicinity subsequently reacted with speed and cunning to surround the British troops at Arnhem, who were hampered by poor communications. The American airborne divisions, however, managed to secure their locations and link up with Horrocks' advancing armour from XXX Corps. With reinforcements delayed by poor weather, after ten days of savage fighting the Allies abandoned their attempt to reach Arnhem, the British First Airborne Division losing all but 2,163 of its 9,000 men; Bittrich paid tribute to his adversaries 'who fought bitterly to the very last', his men generally treating their prisoners with a respect they reserved usually for their own.[28] II SS Panzer Corps and Horrocks' formation would find themselves fighting later in the Bulge.

The effect of repelling this daring Allied assault and incapacitating such large numbers of elite troops (airborne troops were considered as such by all nations) cannot have been lost on Hitler, especially when Market Garden began the day after his formal decision to attack from the Ardennes. Here is the origin of the Führer's decision to mount a large-scale parachute drop in support of the Ardennes attack, something he had eschewed from doing since his *Fallschirmjäger* suffered huge losses at Crete in 1941. Since Crete, he had insisted his parachute arm be used as a land-based 'fire brigade', an emergency counter-attack force to be rushed to critical spots on the Russian Front, and later in Italy at Cassino. Market Garden revived in Hitler's mind the efficacy of parachute forces, and he determined to use them in their traditional role for the forthcoming assault.

Field Marshal Model, who had personally witnessed the airborne forces' arrival, was less jubilant about the German triumph at Arnhem than worried about the evidence of Allied superiority in men and *matériel*, which allowed Eisenhower to undertake such a risky venture. Therein lay the difference between these two late-1944 operations, dominated by tight timetables, armoured corridors, narrow roads, rivers and bridges as they were. Montgomery's Market Garden was a calculated risk; Hitler's Ardennes undertaking was a high-stakes gamble.

Both sides should have analysed Market Garden more than they did. The ability of scantily trained Luftwaffe, army and Kriegsmarine battlegroups, hastily summoned to the Market Garden area to prevail alongside the Waffen-SS, should have warned the Allies what they might expect in the future, for it was precisely this mix of veteran and green, multiservice troops that would emerge out of the Ardennes three months later. For the Germans, if Horrocks' XXX Corps was unable to manage the sixty miles to Arnhem in good weather with air superiority, what hope had the Ardennes venture of reaching Antwerp, 120 miles distant, in poor weather without air cover?

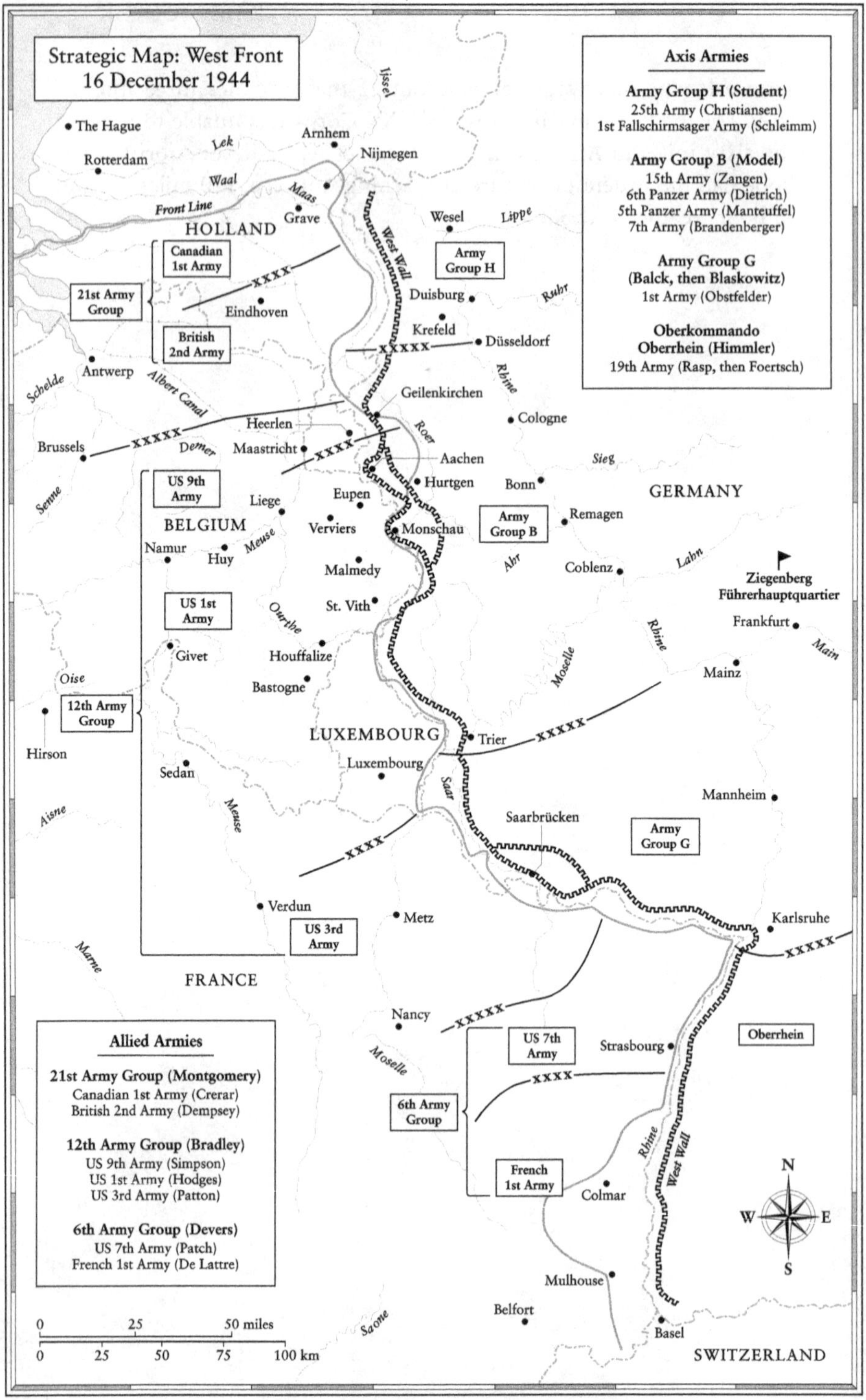
Strategic Map: West Front
16 December 1944
Axis Armies
Army Group H (Student)
25th Army (Christiansen)
1st Fallschirmsager Army (Schleimm)
Army Group B (Model)
15th Army (Zangen)
6th Panzer Army (Dietrich)
5th Panzer Army (Manteuffel)
7th Army (Brandenberger)
Army Group G
(Balck, then Blaskowitz)
1st Army (Obstfelder)
Oberkommando
Oberrhein (Himmler)
19th Army (Rasp, then Foertsch)
Allied Armies
21st Army Group (Montgomery)
Canadian 1st Army (Crerar)
British 2nd Army (Dempsey)
12th Army Group (Bradley)
US 9th Army (Simpson)
US 1st Army (Hodges)
US 3rd Army (Patton)
6th Army Group (Devers)
US 7th Army (Patch)
French 1st Army (De Lattre)
HOLLAND
BELGIUM
LUXEMBOURG
FRANCE
GERMANY
SWITZERLAND
The Hague
Rotterdam
Arnhem
Nijmegen
Grave
Eindhoven
Antwerp
Brussels
Heerlen
Maastricht
Liege
Namur
Huy
Eupen
Verviers
Malmedy
St. Vith
Givet
Houffalize
Bastogne
Hirson
Sedan
Luxembourg
Verdun
Metz
Nancy
Wesel
Duisburg
Krefeld
Düsseldorf
Geilenkirchen
Cologne
Aachen
Hurtgen
Bonn
Monschau
Remagen
Coblenz
Ziegenberg
Führerhauptquartier
Frankfurt
Mainz
Trier
Mannheim
Saarbrücken
Karlsruhe
Strasbourg
Colmar
Mulhouse
Belfort
Basel
Canadian 1st Army
21st Army Group
British 2nd Army
US 9th Army
US 1st Army
12th Army Group
US 3rd Army
US 7th Army
6th Army Group
French 1st Army
Army Group H
Army Group B
Army Group G
Oberhein
Front Line
West Wall
Lek
Waal
Maas
Ijssel
Lippe
Ruhr
Rhine
Roer
Sieg
Ahr
Lahn
Main
Moselle
Saar
Meuse
Ourthe
Schelde
Albert Canal
Demer
Senne
Oise
Aisne
Marne
Saone
N
S
E
W
0 25 50 miles
0 25 50 75 100 km

7

A Port Too Far

MONDAY, 25 SEPTEMBER, was the ninth and final day of Operation Market Garden. Although he should have been buoyed by the news that his troops were prevailing over the Allied elite at Arnhem, Hitler's health was at rock bottom and he was diagnosed with jaundice. He had taken to his bed, and perhaps reaching for a positive tonic in his life dictated his wishes for the Ardennes attack to Jodl. He required, remembering the First World War bombardments he endured, a massive artillery preparation to clear the way for an infantry assault, after which his panzers would roll.

This was a curious reversal of the traditional blitzkrieg tactics that had worked in the Ardennes during May 1940, where tanks preceded infantry, except in river crossings. However, in 1944, panzers were in short supply, and the Führer felt his troops, fuelled with the spirit of National Socialism and thirsting for revenge after the destruction of their cities by American bombers, would triumph easily over their adversaries. 'There was only one thing for me. Either to win with Adolf Hitler or to die for him,' a storm trooper remembered candidly: 'The personality of the Führer had me in its spell.'[1]

Once the initial wave of tanks had seized bridges over the Meuse, a second wave would follow on. Hitler anticipated the new Sixth Panzer Army under SS-Oberstgruppenführer Josef 'Sepp' Dietrich, would administer the *Schwerpunkt* (main effort) of the assault, a desire clearly prompted by the disloyalty of the army on 20 July, but also the recent performance of the Waffen-SS at Arnhem. Of course, Hitler had no knowledge of the intelligence-gathering operation at Bletchley Park, but he was paranoid about security. Very few were 'in' on the plan to begin with, and those close to Hitler and admitted to its secrets, even Manteuffel and Dietrich, had to sign pledges of secrecy, with their threats of *Sippenhaft* (summary execution for next of kin). Hitler's paranoia meant no signals were sent over the air by Enigma encoding device or any other transmitter, and most communication was face-to-face, or conveyed by trusted officer-courier.

With the Ardennes planning at an advanced stage, it was only on 12 October that Hitler drew his Armaments Minister aside and shared the news with him, warning him not to spread the secret. Speer was tasked to organise a special corps of his *Organisation Todt* workers, who were motorised and able to carry out all types of bridge-building. 'Stick to the organisational forms that proved their value in the western campaign of 1940,' Hitler ordered. Speer countered that he was gravely short of transport but was instructed: 'Everything else must be put aside for this, no matter what the consequences. This will be a great blow which must succeed.' The long shadow of 1940 again. In the event, each attacking army would have a brigade of Speer's civil engineers, all expert in bridging, which acknowledged the poverty of the army's own engineering resources at this stage of the war. The move was fine in theory, and his men may have been expert at bridge-building, but few had any military experience, training, uniforms or equipment, and were likely to be under fire at the chosen crossing sites. Later on, Hitler expounded on his fantastical vision to Speer:

> A single breakthrough on the Western Front! You'll see! It will lead to collapse and panic among the Americans. We'll drive right through their middle and take Antwerp. Then they'll have lost their supply port. And a tremendous pocket will encircle the entire English army, with hundreds of thousands of prisoners. As we used to do in Russia![2]

Here was Hitler again reaching for examples of past successes to repeat: whether 1940 or the early days of Barbarossa, but without regard to the changed circumstances of the war. There is no evidence of reality in his pronouncement, no sense of Allied airpower or superior capabilities; no recognition of the Wehrmacht's chronic fuel shortages or the difficulties of fighting in mid-winter. The concept, language and justification for the attack had also shifted in Hitler's mind. From being advertised in the *Wolfsschanze* as a counter-attack to force the Western Allies to agree to a peace with Germany on Hitler's own terms, then shift focus back to Russia, his Ardennes offensive seems here to have become a classic encirclement battle of annihilation, leading to the military defeat of the British and American armies. Or was he hoping that in shattering the Western alliance against him, he could cause such unrest in America that its army would be recalled? History is unclear, probably because Hitler was unclear in his own mind. In a later address to commanders before the attack, the archives recorded his words: 'When we strike a few heavy blows here, then it may happen that at any moment their artificially upheld alliance suddenly collapses with a gigantic thud.'[3] In his mind, the operation had almost taken place already; his demeanour suggested that he could already sense victory. As usual, Hitler had interpreted the coming operation as a struggle of willpower: his against that of the Allies.

Mid-October 1944 also saw another drama from the 20 July plot being played out. Hitler's former favourite, Field Marshal Rommel, since wounded in Normandy, had been implicated. The degree to which he was involved will probably never be conclusively ascertained, but he was likely to have had 'guilty knowledge' of something afoot (Speidel, his chief of staff, was a leading conspirator), even if not directly in league with Stauffenberg's friends. On 14 October, Hitler discreetly sent two generals to his house at Herrlingen, near Ulm, carrying the incriminating evidence, but bearing an offer. The popular field marshal would be spared the humiliation of the *Ehrenhof*, People's Court and a possible death sentence, provided he take the proffered cyanide capsule. He could die with his reputation intact. Rommel's consequent widely reported demise, attributed to wartime injuries, does not necessarily prove his guilt to historians, but the author John Toland recorded that in death his face was apparently 'marked by an expression of colossal contempt'.[4]

Had he survived, the audacious Afrika Korps commander would no doubt have been the leading light of the Ardennes offensive, which he had done so much to inspire through his daring leadership in this exact region four years earlier. Rommel had led his 7th Panzer Division into Belgium at Hemmeres, five miles south of St Vith, advanced via Montleban and Chabrehez on 10 May 1940, to the River Ourthe which he traversed in three places, using a ford at Beffe (just south of Hotton), an engineer bridge at Marcourt and a captured crossing at La Roche on the 11th. Moving through Chéoux and Marche, his tanks had then followed minor roads via Haversin and Ychippe to the Meuse, where his reconnaissance battalion splashed across an old weir between Houx and Leffe (a suburb of Dinant), overnight on 12–13 May. All of these are names and routes that would resurface in the drama of the Bulge.

Rommel would have been the first to point out the difficulty of this terrain, as did Major Percy Schramm, where all the major roads ran north–south, and those few lanes which wound east–west were challenging enough for armoured columns in the fine conditions of May, never mind the snows of December. It was Rommel's 1940 performance here that had brought him a very high profile within the Reich, although he was already known to Hitler, having previously commanded his bodyguard battalion. Rommel's three-day achievement of reaching the Meuse through this very locale in May 1940 directly inspired the Führer and Jodl to replicate the attempt in December 1944.[5]

Still in mid-October 1944, Hitler had learned that Hungary's Regent, Admiral Miklós Horthy, was negotiating in secret with the advancing Red Army. To forestall this, he despatched SS-Lieutenant Colonel Otto Skorzeny to remove Horthy from power. The Führer had come to rely on the tall *Obersturmbannführer*, a fellow Austrian, as a 'fixer' in times of crisis: in September 1943, he had rescued Mussolini from captivity in central Italy, while a year later he had helped crush the 20 July plot in central Berlin. Against a very tight deadline, Skorzeny devised Operation Panzerfaust, in which he lured Horthy's son to a supposed meeting with Soviet mediators, kidnapped him at gunpoint, dramatically rolled him up in a carpet and flew him to Vienna. Resisting the blackmail, Horthy broadcast an armistice with the Russians over national radio, which the pro-Nazi Arrow Cross party immediately countermanded, while Skorzeny surrounded Horthy's HQ with Tiger tanks; the admiral capitulated on 15 October and Hungary remained an Axis partner. Six days later, on the 21st, Hitler sent for his favourite commando (though even he had to sign the obligatory *Sippenhaft* oath of secrecy, which still exists in the files) to offer congratulations and ask him to undertake another special mission.

In the battle for Aachen, which would fall that very day, Hitler recounted to Skorzeny how the Americans had used captured German tanks, still in their national colours, to penetrate the defenders' positions – actually a not uncommon and perfectly straightforward *ruse de guerre.* Could, the Führer wondered, Skorzeny do something similar on a larger scale to precede his Ardennes operation? Perhaps in terms of capturing bridges and spreading confusion? From his recorded conversations, as we shall see, Hitler was also under the spell of the ancient Germanic warrior Arminius, who had created similar mayhem in the Teutoburg Forest against the advancing Roman legions of Varus in AD 9. Skorzeny left the *Wolfsschanze* with a secret brief to raise a unit of American-speaking troops, who would use captured weapons and equipment to achieve Hitler's wishes. His part in the forthcoming offensive had a Wagnerian ring to it – the mission would have a special codename: Operation *Greif* – after the half-lion, part mythical griffin, which bore extremely sharp claws.

Most of Skorzeny's unit, innocuously titled 150 Panzer Brigade, were to talk, behave and appear as GIs, wearing US uniforms. Supplemented by 'normal' SS combat units bearing support weapons, some of Skorzeny's men, travelling in captured tanks and jeeps, would accompany Dietrich's SS panzer columns with a mission to dash ahead and seize three crossings over the Meuse for their Sixth Panzer Army colleagues. Others in the special unit, wearing GI olive drab, were to infiltrate American lines in their jeeps and roam about, creating confusion behind the front, radioing back tactical information to the panzer spearheads, spreading rumours, switching signposts and cutting communications links. Skorzeny later recorded how his men, at their secluded *Amerikanischschule* (American School) training camps at Grafenwöhr and Friedenthal, assumed they were all heading for Paris in an assassination attempt on Eisenhower. This belief, which he did nothing to discourage, and uttered by Skorzeny's men when captured, would eventually produce confusion and fear on a catastrophic scale, far beyond the original intent.

Hitler gave him a *Führerbefehl* to requisition whatever he required in terms of equipment, particularly captured US Army booty – highly prized by the Wehrmacht – and recruit anyone he needed. He eventually assembled 57 jeeps, American rations, documentation, radios, weapons, helmets and uniforms – though some of the latter had to be taken from prisoners or removed from the dead. Even gathering the uniforms proved difficult. Sergeant Michael W. Collins of Kentucky, captured in Tunisia when serving with the 509th Parachute Infantry

Battalion, remembered the authorities in his prison camp, Stalag 3B near Frankfurt, requesting 'American uniforms to clothe a captured GI unit that did not have garments'. Smelling a rat, he and his comrades 'walked to the centre of the barracks and added their American uniforms to the pile. But the day before each prisoner had taken a scissors and slashed his uniform to ribbons.' Their red-faced jailer 'stared at the pile of slashed American uniforms, then turned on his heel and stomped out of the barracks'.[6]

Other vehicles for Skorzeny had to be adapted from German-manufactured stock. He expected a unit of about 2,500 comprising fluent English speakers, but acquired fewer than 1,000 former merchant seamen, bartenders and students who had worked or studied in the States at one stage. Hardly any were fluent, but about 300 might 'get by' if not drawn into a detailed conversation with genuine GIs. Obergefreiter Gries, a radio operator on one of Skorzeny's Trojan tanks, recalled the tensions of having a trained English speaker in his crew. 'The loader was a "speaker" . . . His job included operating a medium-wave radio with an umbrella aerial on the turret [to contact Skorzeny's commandos]. The deployment of "speakers" in panzer crews was controversial as they hadn't any specialist panzer-crew training. We were afraid they would weaken our combat strength by making operational mistakes . . . Leutnant Gertesnschläger was keen to get rid of him at the first opportunity.'[7]

Skorzeny's unit was designed to assist Dietrich's Sixth Panzer Army only: another sign of the favouritism Hitler accorded the Waffen-SS. However, a setback for his clandestine force arrived within days of leaving the *Wolfsschanze* when he encountered a widely circulated notice, issued in the name of Keitel, requesting 'English-speaking officers and men from all three services to volunteer to serve in a special operation'. The leaflet, entitled 'Secret Commando Operations', detailed that 'approximately two battalions' of volunteers were sought for 'use on the Western Front', who were required by 10 November and should report to 'Dienststelle Skorzeny'. The *Obersturmbannführer* went apoplectic at the security breach, complaining directly to the chief SS liaison officer at the *Wolfsschanze*, General Fegelein, that as his mission had been so blatantly compromised it should be cancelled. The latter agreed this was an unfortunate development but suggested the honour of the SS was at stake and ordered Skorzeny to proceed nevertheless – 'surely he must know that his part in the offensive could not be put off unless they went to the Führer about it. And how could they confess such a mistake to Hitler, even if not their fault? The mission must proceed as planned.'[8] Had it not borne Keitel's name, the originator of the leaflet might otherwise have been shot for treason. As Skorzeny feared, a copy, issued by LXXXVI Corps on 30 October, soon fell into the hands of Allied intelligence. They knew precisely who Skorzeny was, but assumed – because of the stupidity of the wide distribution – it was propaganda: German mischief-making at its worst, and that no such unit was intended.[9]

The thirty-six-year-old Skorzeny was very much a protégé of Hitler. An extremely capable charmer, a natural businessman and charismatic leader in his own right, he usually 'got things done', whatever the circumstances, and would remain loyal to his boss and his ideals long after the war. A well-connected bon viveur, he bore a dramatic scar on

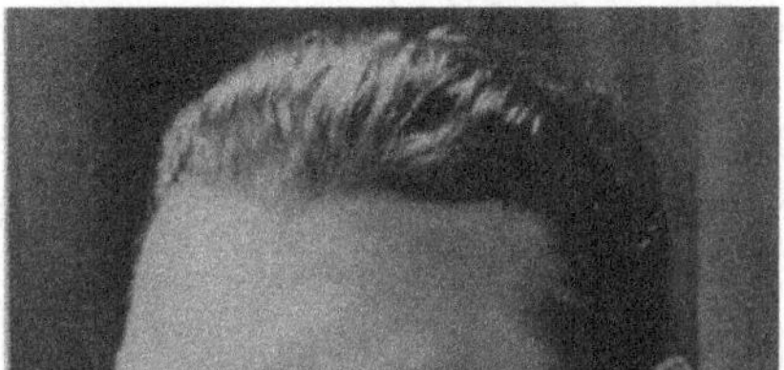

Otto Skorzeny (1908–1975) was an extremely capable charmer, natural businessman and charismatic leader in his own right, Skorzeny usually 'got things done', whatever the circumstances, and would remain loyal to the Führer and his ideals long after the war. (Author's collection)

his left cheek, which was in fact a duelling *Schmiss* – a highly sought-after sign of bravery. That Hitler took to him, seeing the light of a 'true believer' in his eyes, is obvious, because Skorzeny was one of the first to be told of Hitler's plans outside the tight circle of the *Wolfsschanze* – even before the field marshals and army commanders who would eventually launch the attack. Skorzeny was clever enough to check immediately with German lawyers the interpretation under international law of what he was ordered to do. He received assurances that the body of international legal opinion was that only the *use of weapons* was forbidden, but the wearing of a foreign uniform was permitted. Weapons could be fired and conform with international law if the user wore his own uniform underneath and discarded any disguise before opening fire.[10]

In retrospect, given the extensive modern use of Special Forces troops, it is surprising that Germany made little use of Skorzeny-type units. Although the British had developed a wide range of specialist troops in the Special Air Service (SAS), Long Range Desert Group, Parachute Regiment, Commandos and SOE, among others, and the US had their Rangers and OSS, the answer lies in the fact that very few German units had received such specialist training. A tiny number of SS commandos had performed such functions in 1939–40, but by 1944 the Reich were the occupiers, on the defensive, and had not planned on the need for infiltration troops: in this respect, the Germans fought a remarkably 'conventional' war. What is surprising about Skorzeny's mission was that it hadn't been tried before by any side on such a scale, and wasn't practised more extensively in the Ardennes. The sanction of any such deployments was also in the hands of Hitler personally; while he had flashes of battlefield genius, the mind of the First World War *Gefreiter* did not travel in such unconventional directions. He was also acutely nervous of sending German troops behind Allied lines for fear they would desert; the *Greif* commandos came under SS control, and hence their numbers were limited to a controllable quantity.

There was one other use of unconventional forces built into Hitler's plan, prompted by Market Garden and examined in the previous chapter: the decision to use paratroopers in their traditional role for the first time since Crete. Whereas the loyal SS warrior Skorzeny was told of his small part in the big attack even before the generals, the *Fallschirmjäger* commander was not warned of his task until 8 December. This was only eight days before deployment, and perhaps symbolic of the Führer's lack of trust in the Luftwaffe, under whose command Germany's paratroopers fell.

Meanwhile, *Unternehmen Christrose* (Operation Christmas Rose) was the provisional codename for the outline plan that Jodl had submitted to Hitler, which included the minutiae of paratroops, and SS commandos disguised as Americans, seizing bridges across the Meuse and disrupting US reactions to the attack. OKW records also refer more generally to the *Abwehrschlacht im Westen* (Defensive Battle in the West) which had been used to describe the battles around Aachen and early plans for the Ardennes. Perhaps because of its religious associations, but more likely because of Hitler's deep paranoia about security, he immediately altered it from *Christrose* to *Wacht am Rhein* (Watch, or Guard, on the Rhine), after the nineteenth-century popular song which exhorted citizens to defend Germany's western frontier.

Using this name tapped deep into the psyche of the Fatherland. 'The Watch on the Rhine' had become a patriotic favourite in the early days of building the German nation, with huge sales of books, sheet music and picture postcards on the theme of guarding the frontier against the traditional western foe; later German migrants took some of this culture with them to the United States, where the song, in English, was also popular. From the 1870s, the *Kaiserreich*, as we shall see, very deliberately used the imagery of guarding the Rhine to evoke images of collective defence against other adversaries, such as Roman legionaries and Catholic French knights, and so it seemed natural for the Nazis to include the US Army in this category.

An unlikely survivor of post-1945 denazification was the giant Niederwald Monument near Rüdesheim on the Rhine. Commissioned by Kaiser Wilhelm I in 1871 as a national symbol, its central figure is a thirty-foot-tall Germania, holding crown and sword, overlooking the great river. Beneath Germania is a large relief engraved with the '*Wacht am Rhein*' lyrics. Hitler first saw it in 1914 en route to war, and it summed up the Fatherland to him.[11] In the post-First World War occupation of the Rhineland, all the Allied occupation forces (French, Belgian, British and American) twisted the knife by referring to 'their' watch on the Rhine, which only incensed all patriotic Germans.

In the ambiguous history of 'Germany', only united as a single state in 1870, the one common denominator for all German speakers in the west was the Rhine. Apart from being a huge source of trade, since Roman days it delineated the western boundary of the German language. There was no such easy border to the east or south of the Fatherland. Consequently the Rhine represented historical continuity and a sense of nationhood for all Germans, and its symbolism was exploited by the Kaisers after 1870. The Rhine, and the necessity for guarding it, was drummed into all Germans as an essential ingredient of statehood, as was compulsory military service. The majestic river was – and remains – a source of pride for most Germans, and consequently the post-1918 Allied occupation of the Rhineland became a festering sore.

Thus offspring from the union of African American and French colonial Rhineland occupation soldiers with German girls were singled out for particular contempt in *Mein Kampf*, and eventually sterilised under the Third Reich; Hitler described children resulting from such marriages as a contamination of the white race 'by Negro blood on the Rhine in the heart of Europe', which would guide Nazi policy when African American prisoners were taken in December 1944. All of this kept the Rhine in the public eye until Hitler sent his newly created Wehrmacht marching in on 7 March 1936, reuniting this 'lost' province with the rest of Germany: a hugely popular move and his first conquest. Hitler's Ardennes operation is still known by many as 'Wacht am Rhein', perhaps because the title is both clever and memorable, although, as we will discover, technically speaking they are wrong, for its codename was changed again, for a final time, on 2 December.

Meanwhile, a Canadian intelligence officer came across a German propaganda leaflet, aimed at the Wehrmacht, similarly titled 'Watch on the Rhine', which depicted a medieval German knight, equipped with flowing cloak, chain mail and sword, standing guard over the Rhine, with the words:

> Comrade, the enemy means to outflank the *Westwall* at the very point where we are and to cross the Rhine into Germany! Shall our people, shall our families, have suffered five years in vain? Shall they suffer misery and starvation amid the ruins of our cities in a conquered Germany? Do you wish to go to Siberia to work as a slave? *What do you say about it? Never* shall this happen. *Never* shall the heroic sacrifices of our people prove in vain! Therefore everything depends now on your courage! The struggle against an enemy who at the moment is still superior is tremendously hard. But for all of us there is no

> other way than *to fight on with knives if need be.* It is better to die than to accept dishonour and slavery! It is better to be dead than a slave! Therefore – keep the Watch on the Rhine steadfastly and loyally.[12]

The operation's title and devices like this leaflet (which was bound to fall also into Allied hands) deceived Hitler's own Wehrmacht and population as to his intentions: until briefed as to the real nature of the operation, any German commander was likely to think that *Wacht am Rhein* was an operation to husband reserves behind the great river, ready to defend its banks to the last when the Allies attacked, which they surely would. Hitler's move was doubly advantageous, for, unbeknownst to him, it also deceived the Allies who were monitoring and decoding OKW signals traffic at Bletchley Park. They saw exactly what they expected: an operation to prevent the Anglo-US-Canadian crossing of the Rhine. Despite the events of 1940, there was never a hint that an offensive was being planned from the unlikely terrain of the Ardennes. The observation of Général Lanzerac in 1914, that 'If you go into that death-trap of the Ardennes you will never come out', still applied to most military minds.[13]

On 22 October, the day after Hitler's meeting with Skorzeny, the chiefs of staff of OB West (Generalleutnant Siegfried Westphal) and Army Group 'B' (General Hans Krebs), both newly appointed, were summoned to the *Wolfsschanze*, with no foreknowledge of the purpose. They were nervous, due to the fall of Aachen the day before, and anxious to squeeze more reinforcements out of OKW to prevent what seemed like an imminent Allied breakthrough to the Ruhr. Both were surprised at having to surrender their briefcases and sidearms, and sign the pledge of secrecy threatening *Sippenhaft*, in connection with a mysterious operation called *Wacht am Rhein.*

Westphal and Krebs arrived at Rastenburg in time to attend the usual midday situation conference, and were then summoned to a much smaller private meeting where Hitler and Jodl briefed them on a forthcoming operation to be undertaken, much to their astonishment, in the area of Army Group 'B'. By the time Hitler and Jodl had briefed Westphal and Krebs, the Führer's notions had taken concrete form; the planning for *Wacht am Rhein* was firmly in the hands of Jodl and his staff, who had observed that 1 November was too soon and the key dates were moved back to 20 November for the end of all preparations, and 25 November for the beginning of the offensive. The latter date had been selected by the Reich's meteorologists in response to demands for a period of at least ten continuous days of poor flying weather.

The attack was to be made through the Ardennes on a sixty-mile front between Monschau (twenty miles south-east of Aachen) and Echternach (a similar distance north-east of Luxembourg), with an initial object of seizing bridgeheads over the Meuse between Liège and Namur, thereafter aiming for Antwerp. Rundstedt and Westphal both pointed out after the war that there was almost no planning for the phase beyond the Meuse to Antwerp, and none whatsoever following the port's capture.

In order to achieve this, Jodl had recommended a minimum of thirty divisions, including ten armoured, distributed among two attacking formations, Fifth and Sixth Panzer Armies, and two infantry-heavy outfits, Seventh and Fifteenth Armies, which were to guard each flank, all supported by vast numbers of *Flak* (anti-aircraft) regiments from the Luftwaffe, plus a host of artillery corps and *Nebelwerfer* brigades. Göring's Luftwaffe would have to support the operation on an unprecedented scale, and every effort made to achieve operational surprise and maintain a high tempo, while secrecy was vital and the absolute minimum of individuals should be admitted to the plan before *Null-Tag* (D-Day). Hitler assured his visitors of substantial Luftwaffe support (the records are at variance as to whether 1,000, 1,500 or 3,000 aircraft were promised), of which a hundred would be the new Messerschmitt 262s. Keitel, seemingly his only part in the whole drama, promised 17,000 cubic metres (4,250,000 gallons) of fuel and special reserves of ammunition.

All this was presented to them, for transmission to their respective bosses, as a 'done deal'. Westphal remembered, 'Throughout September we kept demanding reinforcements from OKW. On 22 October Hitler told us we would get them at the end of November or beginning of December; he identified twenty infantry and ten armoured divisions and a lot of special troops, and promised three thousand planes. However we would not be allowed to use them to reinforce the front. Hitler said they were a miracle and miracles didn't repeat themselves. Therefore we would use them to attack.' Westphal and Krebs flew back from East Prussia and reported to their bosses, Rundstedt and Model. 'We knew we could only succeed if we were able to cross the River Meuse within two days,' Westphal later observed. He left unsaid 'before the Americans reacted'.[14]

Two days was a tall order indeed, given that in the brilliant conditions of May 1940 it had taken Rommel three days to achieve the same result. Hitler had also ended on the ominous note of anticipating *Nebel, Nacht und Schnee* ('Fog, night and snow'), possibly in a Wagnerian sense, but it seemed certain to threaten Westphal's estimate of two days to reach the Meuse.[15]

Apart from the obvious slight that they had been excluded from the early planning processes, the two field marshals were horrified at the military implications of such a huge undertaking. Rundstedt was forthright about this exclusion. 'I had nothing to do with it. It came to me as an order complete to the last detail . . . When I was first told about the proposed offensive in the Ardennes, I protested against it as vigorously as I could. The forces at our disposal were much, much too weak for such far-reaching objectives.'[16]

Although in September Rundstedt had advised OKW that the 'ultimate objective for all strategy in the West should be a counter-offensive to inflict a decisive defeat on the enemy', by mid-October his sole aim was simply for the front to survive intact; there were no forces available and no logistics to sustain any sort of counter-stroke. The *Wolfsschanze* to them seemed suddenly very out of touch with the reality of life in the west. Rundstedt would observe after the war: 'It was a nonsensical operation, and the most stupid part of it was the setting of Antwerp as the target. If we had reached the Meuse, we should have got down on our knees and thanked God – let alone try to reach Antwerp.'[17]

Behind the scenes, as the Kriegsakademie had taught generations of staff officers to do, Jodl studied other possible options to go over to the offensive, identifying five: a single thrust from Venlo also to Antwerp, and four other double-pronged encirclements of Allied forces at different places along the Western Front. Of these, though less ambitious in its reach, an envelopment launched simultaneously from northern Luxembourg towards Liège and from north of Aachen angled south offered the destruction of US forces in the Aachen salient, and Jodl began to scope this also. Schramm would observe after the war that of all the possibilities to go over to the offensive, Hitler seemed to have unerringly chosen the most promising terrain on the whole Western Front. There then followed a period until 1 November when Jodl at OKW and Model and Rundstedt, all unbeknownst to each other, drew up similar alternative offensive plans to dilute their Führer's ambitions, keeping east of the Meuse, united in their certainty that the forces allocated were far too inadequate to reach all the way to Antwerp.

The port of Antwerp, in Model's view, was beyond their grasp unless substantially more forces were available. His reaction to Krebs' verbal account of Hitler's scheme was succinct and dismissive: 'This plan hasn't got a damned leg to stand on.'[18] Model protested to Hitler via Jodl that 'Antwerp was too far to reach, and beyond our means. The troops around Aachen would be a danger to our advance unless they were wiped out first,' the field marshal argued. Jodl countered after the war that 'Hitler and I believed we could not wipe out the very strong and well-armed Allied forces around Aachen. We thought our only chance was an operation of surprise which would cut the life-line of the Allied forces at Aachen and in that way alone neutralise them.'[19]

Memoirs show that while relations between Rundstedt and Model were 'correct but not cordial', they were nevertheless united in believing that Antwerp was too ambitious and there was no point in attacking beyond the Meuse. Initially their two headquarters produced slightly differing solutions – Rundstedt wanted an envelopment around Aachen, whereas the Army Group 'B' plan, code-named *Herbstnebel* ('Autumn Mist'), called for a single thrust by Fifth and Sixth Panzer Armies, with Seventh Army following as a second wave. Westphal wrote later of Hitler's plan, 'It appeared out of the question that the Seventh Army would be strong enough to protect the southern flank for long. Nor could the Allied troops adjacent to the breakthrough front be expected to stand back politely and make way for the attackers. What would happen if they stood fast, or, as was probable, launched counter-attacks? Even if Antwerp were reached, it would be impossible to hold onto the ground covered by the advance. And it was hardly worth aiming at such an objective if it must be given up almost at once.'[20] This is where Hitler's dreams departed from reality: he left the likely reactions of his opponents out of the equation. He had devised an operation based on what he assumed his Wehrmacht was capable of achieving, even though he was using 1940 as a benchmark, not 1944. The US Army did not feature in his calculations whatsoever.

Without the knowledge of Hitler or OKW, on 27 October in a meeting that lasted several hours, Rundstedt and Model and their staffs debated various alternatives along with Manteuffel, Dietrich and Brandenberger, the commanders of Fifth, Sixth and Seventh Armies. Thereafter, all (very few could be let in on the secret) decided to combine their intellectual horsepower to produce a collective, less ambitious plan, which they hoped would be acceptable to Hitler, still promising maximum damage to the Allies but at greatly reduced risk. All agreed that a range of active deception measures would be vital to ensuring surprise – their greatest weapon – and that (in Rundstedt's post-war analysis), 'all, absolutely all, conditions for the possible success of such an offensive were lacking' in Hitler's plan. The result was the *kleine Lösung* ('Small Solution'), a synthesis of the ideas of both headquarters, proposing an envelopment of the US Army east of the Meuse around Aachen and Liège, which Model's staff drew up on 28 October.[21]

Meanwhile, Jodl and Hitler were having a similar debate in East Prussia. The former, too, had dismissed Antwerp as an objective too far, on the basis of an inadequate number of fresh divisions, and proposed his own *kleine Lösung*, not dissimilar to the Rundstedt–Model concept, an envelopment of US forces east of the Meuse and the seizure of Liège. Hitler, however, refused to budge, or allocate more resources to his own scheme. Only after ten fruitless days of impasse at the *Wolfsschanze* did Jodl bow to the inevitable and issue further operational instructions for Hitler's plan on 1 November, which were delivered to Rundstedt by special courier during the night of 2 November. They contained a covering letter from Jodl warning that 'the venture for the far-flung objective [Antwerp] is unalterable, although from a strictly technical standpoint, it appears to be disproportionate to our available forces. In our present situation, however, we must not shrink from staking everything on one card.'[22]

At least six forthright written protests against Hitler's plan were lodged with the *Wolfsschanze* by Model and Rundstedt in November/December, each time presenting versions of their *kleine Lösung* as more practical. Initially Rundstedt objected on 3 November, but was completely ignored. Hitler's 10 November operations directive specifically forbade any attack by Fifteenth Army, the northern arm of the Rundstedt–Model 'Small Solution' encirclement, on the spurious grounds that 'the enemy must not be warned in advance by secondary attacks'.[23]

Meanwhile, operations in the Hürtgen Forest and at Metz prompted Model to request permission to use troops earmarked for *Wacht am Rhein* against Hodges' US First Army and Patton's Third. With the resources to reach Antwerp diminished further, Rundstedt wrote again to Hitler on 18 November, observing, 'A surprise attack directed against the weakened enemy, after the conclusion of his unsuccessful breakthrough attempts in the greater Aachen area, offers the greatest chance of success.'

On 20 November, Model again protested to Hitler of the plan's inadequacies, and argued for an alternative improvised envelopment, which stood a good chance of destroying the fourteen US divisions belonging to US First and Ninth Armies in the Aachen area. It would, Model observed, certainly offer as much tactical and psychological success as *Wacht am Rhein.* Hitler's unequivocal answer on 22 November stated simply, 'Preparations for an improvisation will not be made'. On 26 November they tried again, only to be told 'There will be absolutely no change in the present intentions'. As Hitler's throat (the polyp) required he move to the capital for an operation and the Russians were in any case nearing the Wolf's Lair, the next conference to discuss *Wacht am Rhein* took place at Wilhelmstraße 77, Berlin – Hitler's *Reichskanzlei* (Reich Chancellery) – on 2 December. Rundstedt absented himself in disgust, and Model, Manteuffel and now Sepp Dietrich, in command of the new Sixth Panzer Army, argued for the smaller offensive, but Hitler was adamant in refusing to concede. Eventually, in Berlin, he did alter two details, allowing minor changes to Manteuffel's method of attack and changing the title from *Wacht am Rhein* to Model's 'Small Solution' codename – *Herbstnebel* – almost an insult, but not quite. That was all.

Originally, *Wacht am Rhein* had envisaged two flanking attacks to support the main thrust: one using Brandenberger's Seventh Army in the south but a second employing General Gustav-Adolf von Zangen's Fifteenth Army to the north. The fifty-two-year-old Zangen had considerable combat experience under his belt from the First World War, Russian and Italian campaigns, had led his formation with enormous energy since 25 August and would be responsible for a successful series of delaying actions that denied use of the port of Antwerp to the Allies in the coming months. Along with the tiny First *Fallschirm-Armee* (Parachute Army), Fifteenth was responsible for most terrain north of Dietrich's Sixth Panzer Army to the Belgian–Dutch coastline.[24] Zangen's assigned mission for *Wacht am Rhein/Herbstnebel* was to protect the northern flank against Allied counter-attacks, but with a qualification. Hitler was aware that US forces had fought hard and paid dearly to gain Aachen and felt that a frontal assault there, if only to support Dietrich's panzer attacks on their left, would be suicidal folly. Therefore, he directed that 'The Fifteenth Army was not to be employed until the Allies had reacted in force to the German attack, and in any case could not be expected to launch a large-scale attack until the Allied front east of Aachen had been drastically denuded of troops.' In fact, a US 2nd Infantry Division assault on the Fifteenth Army's area would fix Zangen's men in place, so none played any significant role in the Ardennes battles.

The squabbles over *Herbstnebel* (as we shall now refer to it) boiled down in the end to a clash of wills, and seems to have had little to do with military logic. In the end, on principle, Hitler's will had to prevail. Compromise was not a word he had ever understood. It was almost as though he perceived his most senior and loyal generals, Jodl, Rundstedt, Model, Westphal, Krebs, Manteuffel, Brandenberger – even Dietrich, his old bodyguard commander from over twenty years before – as the 'enemy', and not the Americans.

Besides, Hitler was obsessed with his Reich retaining the military initiative, which all knew had been surrendered since Normandy; grand, proactive offensives were part of his psyche, as he'd revealed far, far earlier in *Mein Kampf.* There is no doubt that in 1944 he intended to relive the early, heady days of the March 1918 offensive in which he personally took part: 'I had the good fortune to fight in the first two offensives and the last. These became the most tremendous impressions of my life; tremendous because now for the last time, as in 1914, the fight lost the character of defence and assumed that of attack. A sigh of relief passed through the trenches, and the dugouts of the German army when at length, after more than three years' endurance in the enemy hell, the day of retribution came. Once again the victorious battalions cheered . . . Once again the songs of the Fatherland roared to the heavens along the endless marching columns . . .'[25]

With the plan finalised, it was time to admit more participants into the secret and fill in the details: for example, the *Fallschirmjäger* commander needed time to make his preparations. On 8 December, Luftwaffe Generaloberst Kurt Student, himself an ex-paratrooper but by then commanding Army Group 'H', covering Holland with twelve divisions, summoned Oberstleutnant Friedrich Freiherr von der Heydte to his office. The Luftwaffe lieutenant-colonel was to assemble immediately a 1,000-man unit of trained jumpers to be deployed soon on the Eastern or Western Fronts (Student couldn't, or wouldn't, be more specific). With a Knight's Cross swinging at his throat, the thirty-seven-year-old von der Heydte was one of the Reich's most experienced and decorated soldiers, having jumped into Crete in 1941 and seen action in Russia, Tunisia, Italy and Normandy; his *Fallschirmjäger* were some of the toughest combat veterans in the Wehrmacht. Soon he was told his mission, dubbed Operation *Stösser* (named after the penguin-like auk): his men were to jump into the Ardennes forests very early one morning, when it was still dark, and seize road junctions and bridges ahead of Dietrich's Sixth Army. Some had never jumped before, most not since Crete, and very few at night or into woods. Few transport aircraft were available, and none of their aircrew had worked with parachutists before.

By the summer of 1944 Walther Model (1891–1945) had been promoted to *Generalfeldmarschall* in command of Army Group 'B' and was the main driving force behind *Herbstnebel*, though he had no part in its planning. He only learned of it when Hitler revealed the plan to his chief of staff, General Hans Krebs, summoned to the *Wolfsschanze* for the purpose on 22 October 1944. Model's verbal reaction was succinct and dismissive: 'This plan hasn't got a damned leg to stand on'. As late as 12 December, when approached by Colonel von der Heyte to cancel the parachute drop with which he had been tasked, Model confided, 'It is necessary to make the attempt since the entire offensive has no more than a ten percent chance of success'. (Author's collection)

Dispirited by his meagre resources, on 12 December von der Heyte approached Model to suggest his mission be scrubbed. The normally caustic field marshal on this occasion seemed quite fatherly to the younger officer: 'Do you give the parachute drop a ten percent chance of success?' he asked von der Heyte. With an affirmative answer, Model then confided in the astonished Luftwaffe lieutenant-colonel, 'Then it is necessary to make the attempt since the entire offensive has no more than a ten percent chance of success. It must be done, since this offensive is the last remaining chance to conclude the war favourably. If we do not make the most of the ten percent chance, Germany will be faced with certain defeat'.[26]

Did Model really believe the whole offensive stood any chance of success? In the fifty-one days of preparations, since Model first heard of Hitler's ideas via Krebs on 22 October, his own view of it had moved hardly at all. His earlier utterance that 'This plan hasn't got a damned leg to stand on' essentially had not changed with this ringing endorsement on 12 December that it had a 'ten percent chance of success'. By this astonishing testimony (given by von der Heyte to US interviewers in 1948), even Model, Hitler's most loyal of army commanders, had realised the war was lost and the Führer had imprisoned himself in a fantasy world; yet after 20 July, none dare oppose him – perhaps because they already had too much blood on their own hands.

The *Fallschirmjäger* lieutenant-colonel was instructed to discuss the forthcoming operation with Sixth Panzer Army's commander, Dietrich, and his chief of staff, Fritz Krämer, a meeting which did not go smoothly. Neither had worked with parachutists before and they were unsympathetic to von der Heyte's complaints about shortages of trained men, equipment and aircraft. Ordered to drop in advance of Sixth Army's panzers, at night, deep inside US lines, when the paratrooper asked simply where American troops were known to be, Dietrich exploded, 'I am not a prophet. You will learn earlier than I what forces the Americans will employ against you. Besides, behind their lines are only Jewish hoodlums and bank managers.' Von der Heyte asked about communications – even more vital to paratroopers than other formations – and requested carrier pigeons if his radios were broken in the descent, a not unreasonable request. This was too much for the SS commander: 'I am leading my panzer army without pigeons, you should be able to do the same!'

There were three subtexts here. The most senior SS leader after Himmler, Dietrich would have known that von der Heyte's political credentials were highly suspect in the post-20 July world. The paratroop commander was a much-travelled, well-connected aristocrat, who had studied international law in Vienna, The Hague, Munich and Switzerland on an American-funded Carnegie Scholarship, but was tainted chiefly as a cousin of Claus von Stauffenberg. Any hint of a lack of enthusiasm on his part would be interpreted as treason. The writer Patrick Leigh Fermor encountered von der Heydte in Vienna during a trek across Europe made during 1933–4. He remembered him as 'civilised, quiet, thoughtful and amusing, he belonged to a family of Catholic landowners and soldiers in Bavaria, but his style and manner were far removed from what foreigners consider the German military tradition; and with the Nazi movement he had still less in common . . . A few years later he had become a cavalry officer, rather like *ancien régime* Frenchmen, I think, who followed the profession of arms in spite of their hatred of the government.'[27]

Secondly, Dietrich, the former butcher's son and NCO, was a world away in terms of class and background from the languid aristocrat Heydte. Finally, the discord between them underlined how poorly different branches of the German armed forces cooperated. Sixth Army's responses to the Luftwaffe commander betrayed their ignorance of parachute operations, in a way that would be considered laughable today. The antagonism of Dietrich and Krämer also emphasised the arrogance with which the Waffen-SS had come to regard the army and Luftwaffe.

Meanwhile, the *éminence grise* Himmler, Dietrich's immediate boss, lurked in the background, still accumulating power and watching everyone. The army interpreted the creation of Dietrich's Sixth Panzer Army, staffed solely by the Waffen-SS, as a further extension of the SS leader's power. Perhaps the result of lobbying by the Reichsführer himself, Sixth Panzer was the first SS army, and evidence of the ever-growing influence of the *Schutzstaffel*. After one of his tours of the front in the autumn of 1944, Himmler had been tactless and brash enough to sign one of his letters to Rundstedt as 'Supreme Commander in the West', obviously challenging the latter's position as OB West. Westphal noted enigmatically, 'Although we never discovered whether Hitler had in fact appointed him as such for a time, his rival authority was speedily eliminated.'[28] Instead, Himmler, who had never commanded so much as a platoon in training, shortly afterwards had himself appointed Commander of Army Group Rhine by Hitler, who thought his loyal disciple would succeed where his generals had failed.

In 2000, I interviewed a panzer commander who encountered Himmler at this time; Hauptmann Otto Carius told me that he met the SS chief on the latter's personal train, sitting on tracks deep in the Black Forest, far away from the Rhine, and shunted into a nearby tunnel whenever an air raid was sounded. On receiving a Knight's Cross from Himmler's hands, when the two were alone, the Reichsführer apparently asked him, 'Can we really win this war?' Unless this was a clumsy attempt to trap him, Carius felt sure this was an indication that even the SS leader was having private doubts about the war in late 1944.[29] History's verdict is that as commander of an army group Himmler proved remarkably incompetent, issuing 'a deluge of absolutely puerile orders', and when he moved on two months later, Westphal recalled, he 'simply left behind a laundry basket full of unsorted orders and reports'.[30]

Husbanding resources for the planned offensive proved as difficult as deciding its route. Ammunition and fuel reserves for the big assault taxed the Reich's dwindling war economy to the maximum. Generalmajor Alfred Toppe, the *Oberquartermeister*, had managed to scrounge 15,099 tons of artillery ammunition by 13 December for Army Group 'B', which sounded more impressive that it actually was. Model's logisticians reckoned on a daily ammunition consumption of 1,200 tons, but that excluded the planned opening barrage. In other words, there was enough for a maximum of ten days' worth of artillery support, period. Air defence had relatively more at its disposal for the Luftwaffe's III *Flak* Corps, with its sixty-six heavy and seventy-four medium and light batteries. The biggest headache of those final days, and one which would ultimately spell doom for the entire enterprise, can be summarised in one German word: *Benzin.*

Page after page of the relevant OKW, OB West, Army Group 'B' and lower formation war diaries are obsessed with records of urgent discussions as to the whereabouts of promised gasoline. By 16 December, Generalmajor Toppe and *Deutschereichsbahn* (the German state railway) had delivered 4,680,000 gallons, though much of it was still on the eastern banks of the Rhine when the attack started. Every historian of the Bulge pounces on the panzers running out of fuel, but the Germans' challenge could be described more accurately as having the fuel but not being able to get it to the front when and where it was needed. Likewise, an astonishing 2,000 trains (1,502 troop and around 500 supply trains) conveyed men and *matériel* to the assembly areas in the Eifel under the noses of prowling Allied aircraft, without detection. Before 16 December, 144,735 tons of supplies had been unloaded, but, like the *Benzin*, much of it was detrained far away on the eastern banks of the Rhine, and too much would never reach the formations for which it was intended. Concerns of operational security overrode the practicalities of logistics and combined to give the Germans more headaches than were ever necessary.

Poor weather to mask the Ardennes from prowling Allied reconnaissance aircraft was still a vital ingredient of Hitler's plan. In early December, word went out to Admiral Dönitz's U-boats in the North Atlantic that they were to take and transmit meteorological readings, though for what purpose they were not told. Bletchley Park intercepted the requests, but had no context to understand their significance. Foreknowledge of the conditions that *Herbstnebel* needed – heavy sleet and snow showers, with temperatures that would generate fog – was crucial to decide the start day; weather reports from the Western Atlantic, off the North American and Canadian coasts, could provide Berlin with about a week's warning before the same conditions hit Europe.

Null-Tag[31] for the offensive was also tied to the speed with which troops, equipment and combat supplies could be moved and concentrated, the infantry divisions in the Eifel, the armour around Cologne. Most convoys were rail-bound and as Allied bomber fleets continued to strike at railway bridges over the Rhine, marshalling yards and other vulnerable transport hubs (none too specifically so as not to betray the Ultra secret), Hitler's timetable was interrupted, and the start date postponed several times. On 26 November, the Führer decided on 10 December for *Null-Tag*. This date slipped again because of fuel shortages and several units being still en route by rail to their assembly areas. The bombing of railway lines caused delays on 11 and 12 December with the result that *Null-Tag*, which had already been postponed several times, was delayed to 15 December, and finally to the following day; there it rested. Meanwhile, a last protest was made by Rundstedt and Model on 6 December with the final draft of the *Herbstnebel* operations order, which Hitler simply ignored, endorsing his original plan that had changed not one jot since 22 October.

With the dates set and all machinery in motion, there then followed secret briefings to all the divisional and corps commanders, overseen by the SS, held over two consecutive nights, on 11 and 12 December. After the second address on the 12th, when Hitler had departed, the commanders stayed behind to celebrate the seventieth birthday of Generalfeldmarschall von Rundstedt. Two briefings were required simply because there was not enough room for a single gathering in the operations room at the *Adlerhorst* – the new *Führerhauptquartier* – in the shadow of Schloss Kransberg at Ziegenberg, where Rundstedt's OB West had also relocated, and where we began.[32]

8

Heroes of the Woods

THE OFFICIAL US Army Battle of the Bulge historian, Hugh M. Cole, stated in 1965 that 'the precise reasons for the selection of Antwerp as the German objective are none too clear. The city represented the main supply base for British operations and it might be expected that the British public would react adversely to an Allied command responsible for the loss of an area so close to England which could be employed for V-2 attacks at short range. Later, at Nuremberg, Rundstedt would say that the Meuse bridgeheads and Liège actually were the ultimate objectives.'[1] In fact, when we consider why Hitler was drawn specifically to the Ardennes and Antwerp as the setting for his winter offensive, reassessment of old evidence and new factors makes the reasons abundantly clear.

It has been established that there was an element of wishful thinking in hoping to repeat his success of 1940 over the same ground; Hitler's 31 July request for Major Schramm to research the historical documents, his 16 September comment about 'a new Dunkirk' and later conversation with Albert Speer about using organisational data from the western campaign of four years earlier, confirm this. However, there was much more behind his allegedly 'spontaneous' choice of the Ardennes.[2]

In his 16 September meeting, Hitler was partly reacting to the capture of Antwerp, the named objective of his December assault, which General Sir Miles Dempsey's British Second Army had captured twelve days earlier, on 4 September. Hitler could not have known then that Antwerp would remain unusable for the Allies until 28 November, due to the river being mined and both banks of the Scheldt estuary leading from the port to the North Sea remaining in German hands. With the port's modern berthing facilities, a peacetime discharge capability of 80,000 to 100,000 tons of cargo per day, 592 cranes, dry docks and storage capacity for 120 million gallons of fuel, mostly untouched by war, this was a catastrophic oversight on the part of Eisenhower and Montgomery (distracted as they were by the Market Garden operation), to tidy their logistics. That is why all Anglo-US supplies had to be trucked to the front from Normandy – wasteful exercise, tying up valuable transport and consuming much-needed fuel. Unlike the Allies – who seemed not to recognise the importance of the undamaged harbour to their advance at that stage – OKW regarded the loss of Antwerp as an operational catastrophe, knowing the port could dramatically infuse the Allied advance, which they realised was slowing.

In Führer Orders of 4 and 6 September, Hitler ordered that OB West make the port unusable for as long as possible by defending both banks of the Scheldt, and the island of Walcheren as its mouth.[3] It also became the focus of attacks by V-1s and V-2s, even before the Allies opened the harbour. Whatever the tactical shortcomings of his continued battlefield meddling, on this occasion it was the Führer's clear strategic thinking that explains why the Scheldt took so long to clear: it was not merely Monty's seeming indolence, or distraction by Operation Market Garden. Furthermore, the Canadian First Army, under temporary command of Lieutenant-General Guy Simonds, assigned the task of clearing the Scheldt estuary, were also overcommitted in having to subdue or encircle the other Channel ports. These were all designated 'fortresses' by Hitler – to be held to the last man.

Monty and Eisenhower only initiated operations along the Scheldt estuary on 2 October, in revolting autum weather; but it had taken far longer for the importance of Antwerp to occur to the Allied commanders, Eisenhower writing belatedly to Marshall on 23 October, 'the logistical problem had become so acute that all plans had made Antwerp a *sine qua non* to the waging of the final all-out battle'.[4]

Operation Infatuate, the amphibious assault on Walcheren Island between 1 and 8 November, brought the campaign to a close, by which time stout German resistance had caused 12,873 Allied casualties, though 41,043 German prisoners had been taken. De-mining the waters still took until 28 November, when the first convoy entered the port, led by the Liberty Ships *Fort Cataraqui* from Canada and *James B. Weaver* from the USA. They contained, among other crucial supplies, the personnel and equipment necessary to set up a port headquarters, the 268th Port Company and a critical cargo of war correspondents. By this time Hitler had managed to buy nearly three months in which to bolster his *Westwall* defences and plan the Ardennes counter-attack.[5]

Thereafter Antwerp became the focus of V-weapon attacks, with 5,950 falling in the area. Of these, 302 actually fell within the docks, killing or injuring 750, and destroying or damaging 150 ships, two warehouses, twenty berths, a canal lock, and a floating crane sunk by a direct hit from a V-2. Worse was the distraction of endless air raid warnings and rescue and repair details, which diverted personnel away from their unloading duties.[6] This did affect onward supplies by rail to the front during the Bulge, though not excessively so. While a major strike by a lethal area weapon could still have had grave consequences for the Allies even at this stage of the war, the threat of Hitler's secret flying bombs and rockets doing so proved after all to be a damp squib.

Of the other ports that might have alleviated Allied logistics concerns, Cherbourg had fallen in late June, and Brest, Le Havre and Ostend by mid-September, though all were sabotaged and unusable until the end of October. Meanwhile, Boulogne, Calais and Dunkirk remained resolutely in German hands, if surrounded and containing thousands of Wehrmacht personnel desperately needed elsewhere. Of the importance and extent of the Allied logistics squeeze, Hitler seems to have had great insight, perhaps more than many of his generals, but this is not only what drew him to the Ardennes.

The Führer was also partly attracted by the presence of American troops in the densely wooded frontier region, an army whose military abilities he denigrated constantly, in contrast to the soldierly skills of the British whom he admired more. 'I like an Englishman a thousand times better than an American,' he once ventured, but without the faintest idea of either nation.[7] Back in 1941, in declaring war on the United States, Hitler had picked a fight with the world's leading industrial power. Of itself this move made no sense, but in a wider context he assessed the US Army to be tiny and obsolete, and was convinced that Roosevelt was in any case about to side with his Anglo-Saxon friends against the Third Reich.

He also misread the reasons behind American isolationist foreign policy and overestimated potential support from US Nazi sympathizers, especially the German American Bund. His Kriegsmarine had already attacked US warships escorting convoys in the North Atlantic, which resulted in the sinking of the destroyer USS *Reuben James* on 31 October 1941, and the US Navy was consequently attacking his U-boats. In the days after the attack on Pearl Harbor, Hitler was also under huge pressure to support his Axis partner in the Pacific. Believing Japan to be much stronger than it was, and that it could help the Reich defeat Soviet Russia, at 15.30 p.m. (Berlin time) on 11 December 1941, the German chargé d'affaires in Washington, DC, handed Secretary of State Cordell Hull a letter bearing the declaration of war.

In Washington, President Roosevelt told the 77th Congress that the free world must act quickly and decisively against the enemy: 'The forces endeavouring to enslave the entire world now are moving towards this hemisphere. Delay invites danger. Rapid and united efforts by all peoples of the world who are determined to remain free will ensure world victory for the forces of justice and righteousness over the forces of savagery and barbarism.' Resolutions against Germany and Italy were passed without debate. In Congress, the only person who voted against was the pacifist Jeannette Rankin, who had similarly voted against war with Japan; in the Senate the vote was unanimous. Democrats and Republicans agreed to 'adjourn politics' for the duration of the war and focus on national defence; Speaker of the House Sam Rayburn, Vice-President Henry A. Wallace and Roosevelt officially signed the joint resolution of both houses declaring war on Germany at 15.05 p.m. Eastern Standard Time, 11 December 1941.[8]

On the one hand, Hitler admired America's industry and capacity for hard work, in February 1942 observing, 'The great success of the Americans consists essentially in the fact that they produce quantitatively as much as we do with two-thirds less labour . . . It was reading Henry Ford's books that opened my eyes to these matters.'[9] He envied the reach of her national media, enjoyed Hollywood movies and (apparently) Mickey Mouse cartoons, shown nightly in his private cinema at the Berghof, but despised Roosevelt personally for his incessant verbal attacks on National Socialism. Movies apart, Hitler hated most American art and culture, and alongside an instant distaste for anything Jewish, blues, ragtime and jazz came in for special opprobrium and were banned in Germany. 'I don't see much future for the Americans,' he ruminated. 'In my view it's a decayed country. And they have their racial problem and social inequalities. Those were what caused the downfall of Rome.'[10]

This was throwing stones from afar, for unlike Roosevelt Hitler's great weakness was that he spoke no foreign languages and rarely travelled abroad: he simply had no concept of other nations. Displaying an astonishing insecurity, he disliked meeting foreign leaders, whether friends or adversaries, except on his own turf, declining to meet Churchill or Stalin when invited. In early 1933 Hitler turned down Roosevelt's invitation to discuss economic issues in Washington, DC.[11]

Ironically, the Third Reich was more isolationist than the US, sending few officers to study overseas, whereas on graduating from the Command and General Staff School at Fort Leavenworth, the US Army sent Captain A.C. Wedemeyer on the two-year Berlin Kriegsakademie course during 1936–8, where his contemporaries included Claus von Stauffenberg and Ferdinand Jodl, brother of the future Generaloberst at OKW.[12] Wedemeyer soon realised the superiority of what he was being taught there, recognising that the organisation, doctrine, equipment and training of the Wehrmacht would revolutionise the coming battlefield. On returning, Wedemeyer served in the War Plans Division under Marshall and Eisenhower, devising the 1941 Victory Program, and helped to plan the Normandy invasion.[13]

Hitler did have a view of the United States, but it was extraordinarily puerile, arising from a childhood liking for the adventure and travel stories of Karl May, a bestselling north German writer noted mainly for novels set in the American Old West. May's younger years were marked by a propensity to fraud and petty theft, and he spent time in jail and workhouses. After achieving success, May started to claim some of his novels were true-life experiences, but he travelled only once to the United States, after he had written most of his forty volumes. While there he purchased a fake doctorate from a phoney university but failed to visit the Wild West. Embarrassingly, Hitler never lost his admiration for May's works, recommending them to colleagues even while Führer. The upshot was that Hitler's knowledge of the United States was furnished principally from the cowboy novels of a convicted fraudster who had never himself visited any of the locations in which he set his stories.

Before the war, and during it, Hitler looked down on the Land of the Free, calling it a 'mongrel nation' and 'devoid of any military tradition'. 'I'll never believe that an American soldier can fight like a hero,' he exclaimed in January 1942.[14] These bizarre notions both denied the influx of talent from neighbouring European countries into the German states over the years, and overlooked the mass movement of over eight million

Germanic migrants to the United States, mostly in the eighteenth and nineteenth centuries; by 1940, 18 per cent of Americans regarded themselves as of German origin. Scholars of the Revolutionary War would observe that it was the Prussian-born Baron von Steuben who trained the Continental Army at Valley Forge during 1778–9, later serving as a divisional commander and George Washington's chief of staff. In the civil war, over 200,000 German Americans fought under Union banners, about one in ten of the total force, sixteen of whom won Medals of Honor. Many were able to respond only to German words of command, and served in XI Corps, under the popular Major-General Franz Sigel, a refugee from the 1848 uprisings in Germany.

Many of America's greatest military names owed their origins to German political or economic refugees: George Armstrong Custer's ancestors, Paulus and Gertrude Küster, had moved to the US in 1693 from the Rhineland; John Pershing, who commanded the US Army during the First World War, was descended from the Perschings, who left the Fatherland in the late eighteenth century, while the Eisenhauer family had migrated from Karlsbrunn, near Saarbrücken, in 1741. Among Eisenhower's senior contemporaries, Admiral Chester W. Nimitz, descended from a German merchant seaman, commanded the Pacific Fleet, while General Carl A. Spaatz (born Spatz, he added a second 'a' to make his name sound Dutch rather than German) led the Strategic Air Forces in Europe, responsible for reducing the cities of his ancestors to rubble.[15]

OKW's initial assessments of US military ability were coloured by the setbacks at the Kasserine Pass in Tunisia, Gela on Sicily and Salerno, all in 1943, while the destruction of two battalions of elite Rangers at Anzio (January 1944) and the punishment meted out on Omaha Beach perhaps served to reinforce the jaundiced anti-American views of those in the distant *Wolfsschanze*. In September 1944 an intelligence assessment issued by the German Nineteenth Army observed the US Army still 'advanced too hesitantly, focused almost exclusively on security, always attacked at the same time of day, never attacked at night, and never without tank support. Objectives were shallow, leading to frequent failures to exploit opportunities.'[16] This report and others like it formed the basis of interpreting likely American tactics and intentions before the Bulge counteroffensive.

One of the basic reasons for the optimism of the German plan for the Ardennes was this poor estimation of US tactical ability. The

Wehrmacht had been at war constantly since September 1939 and had proven itself one of the world's finest fighting machines: in the eyes of Hitler and OKW, these were combinations which could beat even the industrial might of the United States. However, both these parties had become wilfully blind and failed to recognise how quickly American soldiers had learned and adapted in Tunisia, Sicily, Italy and Normandy – and would do so in the Ardennes.

Even more notable among the reasons which attracted the Führer to the region for his counter-attack was a personal obsession with woods and forests, something other historians of the Bulge campaign have tended to overlook. Many of his wartime headquarters were located in them; for example, the *Wolfsschanze* in East Prussia was hidden in a dense, swampy forest of pine and birch trees, five miles east of Rastenburg (Kętrzyn in modern Poland).

Among the most consistent influences on Hitler throughout his life were the thirteen operas created by Richard Wagner. The latter had an almost religious effect on the former, who idolised this most German of nineteenth-century composers, and to understand Wagner is one of the keys to the Führer's mind. According to the American correspondent William L. Shirer, Hitler used to expound, 'Whoever wants to understand National Socialist Germany must know Wagner'.[17] The composer died six years before Hitler was born, but both men shared a love of animals, were vegetarians, vicious racists and anti-Semites, who craved the devotion of others. Wagner's dragon-slaying warrior culture, his themes of triumph, sacrifice and nationalism precisely anticipate Hitler's Reich, and his works were a subtext to Nazi propaganda newsreels and films. Hitler's Bavarian retreat, the Berghof at Obersalzberg, was adorned by a large bronze bust of Wagner, whose descendants also presented him with pages from the original score of *Lohengrin*.

It was allegedly a performance of Wagner's *Rienzi* in 1905 that inspired Hitler to consider a political career. His boyhood friend August Kubizek later concluded that Wagner's operas provided Hitler with a means for both self-hypnosis and escapist fantasy. Of Hitler's first reaction to *Rienzi*, Kubizek recounted, 'Hitler began to orate. Words burst from him like a backed-up flood breaking through crumbling dams. In grandiose, compelling images, he sketched for me his future and that of his people.' Thirty years later, at Bayreuth, Hitler acknowledged, 'It began at that hour!'[18]

Wagner permeated almost everything to do with National Socialism; the soundtrack of Leni Riefenstahl's 1934 *Triumph of the Will* was peppered with excerpts from Act 3 of *Die Meistersinger*, as was her earlier portrayal of the 1933 Nuremberg Rally, *Der Sieg des Glaubens* (Victory of Faith). Karl Ritter's 1941 propaganda film *Stukas* has a depressed and apathetic bomber pilot cured by listening to a performance of *Götterdämmerung*, which gives him spirit and energy to return and blitz England.[19] A remarkable newsreel of 1942 portrayed *Die Meistersinger*, conducted by Wilhelm Furtwängler, being performed for workers and convalescent soldiers in the austere surroundings of an AEG factory in Berlin.[20]

The Nazi elite saw Wagner's operas as 'redeeming music for the people', which was perhaps not quite how the jazz-deprived population of the Third Reich understood the composer.[21] A highlight of the pre-war Nazi social calendar, almost a religious duty, was to attend performances of Wagner's works in his opera house, completed at Bayreuth in 1874. Hitler's favourites were the four operas of the *Ring des Nibelungen* cycle: *Das Rheingold*, *Die Walküre*, *Siegfried* and *Götterdämmerung*.[22] How ironic, then, that *Die Walküre* was very nearly the end of him; the Stauffenberg plot to kill Hitler utilised a pre-existing contingency plan for the continuity of government, code-named *Unternehmen Walküre* (Operation Valkyrie).

The Führer knew that most of *The Ring*'s thirty-six scenes were set in or near a forest. Since Wagner was aware of the significance of trees in Teutonic culture and its myths, he chose woods as the principal background for nearly all his operas, and one of the most memorable Wagnerian excerpts remains 'Forest Murmurs' from Act 2 of *Siegfried*. Wagner was part of a long thread in the Romantic art movement, which likened Germany's stately conifers to marching soldiers, standing tall and unbowed against the elements.

In 1936 Nazis released the propaganda movie *Ewiger Wald* (Eternal Forest), which alleged that Germanic traditions sprang exclusively from the forests; that the ancient Aryan tribes had lived free among the trees, but their idyllic life was shattered when the Romans and their successors invaded, bringing alien beliefs. In woodland groves, noble tribes had worshipped their gods; early Christian missionaries, however, had felled the ancient oaks dedicated to Nordic deities to favour their substitute religion. Therefore, National Socialist ideology suggested, only in woods could the modern *Volk* tap into their primeval roots (literally and metaphorically) and feel truly free. Forests, then, were fundamental to Nazi views of their own history.[23]

Hitler shared Wagner's passion for ancient Teutonic mythology, where northern Europe's vast swathes of forest were regarded also as magical places, lived in by gods. In the ancient legends, dense forests were usually inhabited by mysterious creatures, symbols of all of the dangers with which young men must contend if they are to become worthy adults.[24] The menace of the forest is also the dominant theme running through the three volumes of *Grimm's Fairy Tales*, published between 1812 and 1822; both Wagner and Hitler were known to have been brought up on the famous German folklore collected by the brothers Grimm, and their many imitators.

All the old myths and stories suggested the outlook for mortals was pretty bleak, the only bright factor being the belief that one should die a courageous, heroic death. Slain warriors qualified for admittance to Valhalla, perceived as a celestial dining hall, festooned with coats of mail, spears and war shields, ruled over by Odin. The brave dead joined others who had died in combat and various legendary Germanic heroes and kings. In this respect, subsequent Western ideals of heroism and heroic deeds in the face of certain death seem to spring from these dark north European legends, and not from sunnier Greek or Roman mythology.

Wagner's version of this was best expressed in *Tristan und Isolde*, an opera Hitler later claimed to have heard over *forty* times during his pre-war days in Vienna. After the hero Tristan was mortally wounded, he is kept alive by the power of devotion until reunited with his lover, Isolde. Wagner portrayed this as the triumph of love in the face of all adversity, which not even death could defeat. Hitler translated this into a requirement to lay down one's life for Germany. The individual was worth nothing, but in dying for the Fatherland one achieved a kind of salvation. Hitler's public utterances were full of this rhetoric: 'We will die, but Germany will live on in you,' he told his *Hitlerjugend* (Hitler Youth) at the 1934 Nuremberg Rally.[25]

Ideals of heroism and fighting to the death against any odds inspired the kind of fanatic loyalty demanded by Goebbels and Himmler, who in turn used propaganda to persuade their followers that this was what an earlier generation had died for in 1914–18. Visitors to German military cemeteries administered today by the *Volksbund Deutsche Kriegsgräberfürsorge* (German War Graves Commission, or VDK) often comment on how gloomy and depressing they appear, with dark granite grave markers and an abundance of pine and oak trees, when compared to their British and American equivalents – but that is precisely their point, echoing the Teutonic ideals of death and sacrifice. Hitler knew the Langemarck German war cemetery near Ypres in Belgium well, because it is where some of his comrades from the Great War had been buried. He visited it again in May 1940 and by 1944 Himmler had named the 27th SS Division '*Langemarck*', perpetuating the Nazi notion of necessary sacrifice.

As with trees, Wagner used frequent references to wolves and their relationship to the gods, guiding their charges wandering the forests, throughout the *Ring* cycle. Perhaps for this very reason, Hitler called himself *Führer* (guide), rather than the more obvious *Leiter* (leader). Wolves were also inseparable from the gods in Nordic mythology, particularly Odin (Wotan), and it is surely significant that Hitler was known in his early life and by close family intimates as 'Wolf', an old German form of Adolf – and from the codenames he gave to his own headquarters, a nickname with which he was clearly comfortable.

Apart from the *Wolfsschanze* in East Prussia, Hitler named his tree-studded HQ on the Franco-Belgium border, from where he oversaw the humiliation of France in 1940, the *Wolfsschlucht* (Wolf's Gorge). Another headquarters, *Werwolf*, more concrete bunkers in woodland, was built in the Ukraine and used in 1942–3. Although it was his Alsatian, Blondi, who famously accompanied her master to their *Götterdämmerung* in the Berlin *Führerbunker* in 1945, it was Hitler's first hound, Wolf, who greeted his owner's return from Landsberg prison in 1924.[26] He liked 'Wolf' because the forest-dwelling lupine was one of the most significant animals of early Teutonic legends, a beast to be both feared and honoured, worshipped and held in awe, which reaffirmed for Hitler his wolf-forest obsession.

Himmler, too, perhaps more than Hitler, fell upon Wagner, subverting the myths into his own nonsense, incorporating them into a pseudo-religion he inculcated into the SS, centred on Wewelsburg Castle in North Rhine-Westphalia. His fantasy castle incorporated a Valhalla-like chamber, decorated with ancient weapons, and another inspired by the Knights of the Round Table, where senior SS officers would gather. He intended his quasi-Nordic cult to replace Christianity, and in homage to Wagner, late in the war, he named his last SS division '*Nibelungen*'. Wagner portrayed the *Nibelungen* as a race of evil dwarves, but he adapted this from earlier Nordic legends where *Nibelungen* were the ominous 'children of the mist, or fog'. Presumably this is how Himmler saw his young SS warriors, emerging out of the dawn mists.[27]

While German army insignia incorporated the usual eagle, swastika and a belt buckle bearing the words *Gott Mitt Uns* ('God With Us'), Himmler's SS insignia incorporated the *Totenkopf* (a skull), further reminding them of the requirement, if necessary, of surrendering life. Himmler reinforced this ideology with his personal award of an engraved silver SS-*Ehrenring* (honour ring), patterned with oak leaves, Nordic runes and a skull, to deserving SS officers. The 15,000 or so rings given were to be returned on the death of the wearer and stored in a special chest at Wewelsburg, symbolising the Wagnerian importance of sacrifice to the continuance of Nazism. Tens of thousands of Waffen-SS troops, many of whom were fanatical believers in Himmler's folklore, were to fight and die in the Bulge for these curious and completely contrived values.

Thus the old legends and Wagner's dramatic presentation of them were key tools of the Nazi Party, but Hitler's warped mind was perhaps also a prisoner of Wagner's vision, not merely to the composer's musical genius. The huge extent to which Wagner influenced the Führer was illustrated on 7 December 1941, when a *Führerbefehl* decreed that anyone 'endangering German security' should suffer '*Nacht und Nebel*' – Night and Fog – at the hands of the SS and Gestapo. The term was a direct quote from Scene 3 of *Rheingold*, where one of the characters cites a spell for invisibility, 'Be like the night and fog. Disappear!' The Reich's euphemism meant that those identified were worked to death or otherwise murdered, and made to 'vanish without trace'; even their graves went unrecorded.[28]

In this context, the final codename chosen for the 1944 Ardennes operation, *Herbstnebel* (Autumn Mist – *Nebel* can also translate as smoke or fog), was actually a term loaded with hidden significance. Any analyst who understood Hitler's mind would have realised that the innocent sounding *Herbstnebel* actually heralded something very sinister. Autumn marks the return of darkness, seasonally and spiritually, while in his operas Wagner used mist as a device to alert his audiences to the presence of the dark side; he was reflecting the Norse interpretation of fog as suffocating light and goodness.

Death and suffering were essential to National Socialism; it is impossible to conceive of the NSDAP without it. An early Nazi hero was Horst Wessel, murdered by Berlin Communists in 1930. His death became a great propaganda event, with 30,000 lining the streets; the 'Horst Wessel Song' became an unofficial national anthem; the Kriegsmarine named a ship in his honour, the Luftwaffe an aircraft wing and the 18th Waffen-SS *Panzergrenadier* Division also adopted his name. Inspired by Wagner, Nazi iconography saw warriors as more valuable in death than life. The Ardennes campaign would develop this idea, that in order to save Germany, Hitler's armies had to be prepared to sacrifice their lives.

To oversee these sacrifices, Hitler created a medieval court, hidden away from public view, which followed him to his various headquarters. His own personal psychology reflected a primeval need to hide away, either at the Berghof, his mountaintop eyrie 6,000 feet up in the Bavarian Alps, from where he could reign like a god, or more usually, underground.[29] His various command centres, usually consisting of a complex of subterranean concrete bunkers secreted in woods, were the equivalent of Wagnerian caves, which Nordic legend understood as a means of communicating with the underworld. Hitler spent much of his life in this kind of environment: dugouts in the trenches of 1914–18; his various headquarters throughout the Second World War (he spent more than 800 days in the *Wolfsschanze*), and of course he ended his days in his own Berlin bunker.

Underground shelters were not obligatory for war leaders, even those with experience of the Great War trenches. Churchill may have had his famous bunker, beneath the Foreign Office in Whitehall, but hated being there, and preferred the risk of living in Downing Street. All the various Allied leaders, for example, preferred to command from simple ground-level headquarters (sometimes relatively primitive caravans), leaving one with the assumption that there was a psychological dimension to Hitler's preference for his troglodyte life, surrounded by walls of concrete.

To Wagner and Hitler, woods were a place of testing, a realm of death holding the secrets of nature, which men must penetrate to find meaning, purpose and achievement. Perhaps because Hitler felt he was shaping the destiny of others, but not his own, he felt safe lurking in caves and forests. As the war drew on, and particularly after his 'miraculous' preservation from death on 20 July 1944, the Führer would lose himself more often in such esoteric nonsense, clutching at straws, to persuade himself that his Germany would survive the war which was his *personal* Wagnerian test.

In the Führer's mind, his beloved Siegfried the dragonslayer (who cropped up even in *Mein Kampf*, written in 1924), translated, in 1944 terms, into crushing the mighty, fire-breathing, winged American reptile in a suitably Wagnerian setting – and where better than the endless, mysterious forests of the Ardennes?

A final significant motivation also drew Hitler to the dense, ancient woods that proliferated throughout Germany. This additional reason, ignored by other historians of the Ardennes campaign, had sunk into obscurity until the summer of 1987, when Major Tony Clunn, a British officer with a passion for Roman archaeology, serving in the Royal Tank Regiment, discovered a scattering of coins and slingshot in the vicinity of Kalkriese, near Osnabrück. Working with local archaeologists, who uncovered significant Roman military detritus, Clunn was able to reconstruct the route taken by the 17th, 18th and 19th Roman Legions under Publius Quinctilius Varus in AD 9, and to determine precisely where they had been ambushed and massacred by tribes led by the Germanic chieftain Arminius. The site of Rome's most famous defeat, where perhaps 20,000 died, originally deep in the Teutoburg Forest (*Teutoburgerwald*), but open farmland by the 1980s, had eluded scholars for hundreds of years.[30]

The details had hitherto been vague, but it was known that Arminius, a trusted senior auxiliary in the service of Varus, learned the Roman techniques of war, turned traitor and lured a huge force of three legions, six auxiliary cohorts and three wings of cavalry into the dense Teutoburg woodlands to die. This was over 10 per cent of the Imperial Army, the Empire stretching from northern England to Egypt amounting to twenty-eight legions at the time. Later Roman units found their bleached bones lying on the ground and skulls nailed to trees. Some colour was added in 1455 with the rediscovery in an obscure monastic library of a book by Tacitus, describing the lands, laws and customs of the Germanic peoples. Written circa AD 98, *Germania* presented the old tribes in a noble light, not as barbarians but ethical, loyal and brave. Their most significant leader, who had forged a coalition to destroy Roman power, was Arminius of the Cherusci, later translated as Hermann the Cheruscan. Martin Luther is thought to have been the first to interpret Hermann (meaning 'army man' or warrior) as the German equivalent of Arminius.[31]

Over the centuries, scholars hijacked Tacitus' Arminius/Hermann as a role model of resistance and an advocate of freedom and independence, in the same way Robert the Bruce or William Wallace was reinterpreted by successive generations of Scots. The alliance of Germanic tribes and their victorious defiance of Rome became a story that could be paralleled to other eras, whether the Protestant northern states opposing the Vatican and Catholicism, or resistance to Napoleon. In the fine arts, Hermann was always associated with an oak tree, a symbol representing the battle, the Teutoburg Forest and Germany itself. Following unification in 1871 under Prussia, the Teutoburg was regarded as the foundation date of the new German empire, a turning point in national destiny, and taught in all schools as such.

In 1875 a 200-foot bronze Hermann Monument was unveiled on a hill overlooking a forest of oaks, near Detmold. The *Hermannsdenkmal*, with a seven-yard sword raised aloft, was originally intended to serve as a reminder of the liberation and unity of Germany but became a symbol of the victory over the arch-enemy France, towards whom his head is angled.[32] A half-size copy was erected shortly afterwards by the Germanophile communities of Minnesota. This dramatic battle of centuries before was thus used to shape national consciousness – and was popularised by numerous novels, plays and historical paintings, on which the young Hitler was groomed.

Hitler first saw this statue in 1914 when wearing the uniform of a Bavarian *Landser*, en route for the battlefields of Flanders, and fell under its spell immediately, accepting as gospel truth all that it stood for.[33] Later, the monument and other images of Arminius were used extensively in National Socialist election and cultural posters; it became a shrine for Nazi organisations (50,000 turned up in 1925), and the forest victory against Rome was presented as a battle for living space (*Lebensraum*) and the right to exist: implicit justification for future wars of the Third Reich. The Nazi newspaper *Völkischer Beobachter* described the January 1933 elections, which would bring Hitler to power, in terms of 'The Second Battle of the Teutoburg Forest . . . Historical memory is awake, which will never disappear so long as tongues speak the German language . . . A monument, a symbol, the statue of Hermann the Liberator in the grey mist of January.'[34] Nazi cinematographers also made a movie about the *Teutoburgerwald* in 1935, ending with the line, 'The people, like the forest, will stand forever'.[35]

The Nazis used Arminius not just as a symbol of victory, but to give the Fatherland a bloodline – he was offered as a blond-haired Nordic military pin-up, a role model oozing racial purity. Hermann was seen also as embracing the Darwinian notions of 'survival of the fittest', in accordance with Nazi ideals of 'conquer or die'. As the 1937 Nazi volume

Das deutsche Führergesicht; 200 Bildnisse deutscher Kämpfer und Wegsucher aus zwei Jahrtausenden (Face of the German Leader: 200 Portraits of German Fighters and Pioneers from Two Millennia) confidently explained, Arminius was the first of a line of German rulers, via Frederick the Great, which ended with Hitler.[36]

This was, of course, rubbish. When the Romans referred to 'Germans', it was a vague term to describe the peoples east of the Rhine (the *Rhenus*), in parts of what we know today as Germany, Holland, Denmark, Switzerland and Poland. As their loyalty and cultural identity was purely tribal, with no sense of national ethnicity, any talk of the Third Reich as their direct descendants was propagandist nonsense. Nevertheless, the Nazis presented Arminius as the birth certificate of the German *Volk*, in their woodland habitat.

Der Spiegel observed in 2009 that 'The country is marking the 2,000th anniversary [of the Teutoburg battle] with restraint . . . In fact, a lot of Germans don't even know about Arminius. Many schools shunned his story after 1945 because he became so contaminated by the militant nationalism that led to Hitler.'[37] That was because, as it turns out, the Führer was as obsessed with the defining battle of AD 9, which stopped a huge army in its tracks, almost as much as he was with Wagner. There are many parallels between the two forested worlds – one mythical, the other real.

Hitler commissioned a series of huge historic tapestries for his Reich Chancellery, the first of which depicted the Teutoburg, completed in August 1939. The participants of the battle were deliberately 'Aryanised', both Romans and Germans becoming symbolic of the martial and nationalistic values of the Reich.[38] In October 1941 he was referring to Arminius as the 'first architect of our liberty, wasn't he a Roman knight . . . Germanic blood constantly regenerated Roman society'.[39] When comparing his Reich with the Americans and British in April 1942, he reminded his lunch guests, 'Our history goes back to the days of Arminius',[40] while his anger at the newly promoted Field Marshal Friedrich Paulus's capitulation at Stalingrad in January 1943 was expressed in terms of the Teutoburg battle: 'The man [Paulus] should shoot himself as generals used to fall upon their swords . . . Even Varus commanded his slave: Kill me now! . . . Life is the nation; the individual must die.'[41]

Most tellingly, in May 1942 over dinner, when his Reich was at the height of its power, Hitler had pontificated,

> To teach a nation the handling of arms is to give it a virile education. If the Romans had not recruited Germans into their armies, the latter would never have had the opportunity of becoming soldiers and, eventually, of annihilating their former instructors. The most striking example is that of Arminius, who became Commander of the Third Roman Legion [sic]. The Romans instructed the Third in the arts of war, and Arminius afterwards used it to defeat his instructors. At the time of the revolt against Rome, the most daring of Arminius' brothers-in-arms were all Germanics who had served some time or other in the Roman legions.[42]

In AD 9 Arminius and his comrades had originally worn Roman military uniform, spoken Latin and studied their opponents closely, before slipping into the woods and unleashing an ambush of terrible ferocity, turning their opponents' own weapons against them, under conditions of complete surprise. Despite getting the legion wrong and confusing Arminius's role in the debacle, this 1942 Führer-monologue betrays Hitler's admiration of Arminius's cunning and tactics. Predating the Ardennes battle by two and a half years, in this remarkable passage we can see perhaps the genesis of Hitler's 1944 idea to use a fifth column, uniformed and talking as Americans, in the woods.

Against this backdrop of Wagner, Arminius and 1940, myth and reality somehow intertwined in Hitler's mind, and it becomes obvious why Hitler was drawn to the timeless, misty Ardennes as the setting for Germany's final test.

9

Who Knew What?

'It is pardonable to be defeated, but never to be surprised.'
Frederick II (the Great), King of Prussia

In terms of intelligence it is clear the Western Allies completely underestimated German capabilities in the autumn of 1944, with the Twelfth Army Group and its subordinate formations failing correctly to understand the threat, or mitigate the risks, of a possible offensive in the Ardennes. When discussing the inability of Ultra to warn him of the Ardennes in his second autobiography, *A General's Life*, Omar N. Bradley noted, 'One major fault on our side was that our intelligence community had come to rely far too heavily on Ultra to the exclusion of other intelligence sources. Ultra had become virtually infallible. But Ultra depended on radio intercepts . . . the German Army had less need of radio communications and more often used secure land lines. Moreover, it apparently did not occur to our intelligence community that the Germans could plan and launch an operation with complete radio and telephone silence imposed.'[1]

Bradley's memoirs (the first volume published in 1951 and the second, after the declassification of the 'Ultra Secret', posthumously in 1983), are misleading, for Ultra had actually begun to decline in importance at Allied headquarters, from being *the* source, to simply one of many. The key to Bradley's opaque vision of his 1944 opponents was partly Allied 'victory fever' which produced a bullish mindset; personality clashes among intelligence chiefs at different levels; but mainly a failure to coordinate and assess intelligence data from multiple sources. In shifting blame to the intelligence community, Bradley was overlooking the tendency of staff at SHAEF (Supreme Headquarters Allied Expeditionary Force) and in his own headquarters to think only in terms of what they could do to the enemy and rarely about what their enemy might do to them. Thus, the intelligence community, rather arrogantly, could not entertain the idea of the Germans managing to hide anything from them, let alone have the capability to attack. Whether Eisenhower was ill served by his own intelligence staff remains to be seen, but they were certainly encouraged to reflect their commander's optimism, rather than dampen it with intelligence estimates of a negative nature. As Ike's overriding policy was to attack all along his front, SHAEF's G-2 department was tuned to justify this strategy. 'This policy required intelligence to report the German army as being incapable of mounting an offensive', according to the Cambridge scholar-turned colonel, Noel Annan, who worked in the SHAEF intelligence office. He sensed institutional pressure on his colleagues, who 'were regarded as defeatist if they did not believe the end of the war was in sight'.[2]

Admittedly, some kinds of signals intelligence (SIGINT in today's military language) had lessened because the Germans were inside the frontiers of the Reich and had no need of wireless transmissions, instead using secure landlines and face-to-face meetings, but much SIGINT still came from two other sources: standard traffic analysis and interception of poorly disciplined radio transmissions from across the front. These were in addition to interceptions and decrypts from Enigma, the patented machine that transmitted enciphered Morse code messages in German, and 'Fish', the *Geheim Fernshreiber* (secret telegraph), which consisted of encoded teletype messages, neither of which diminished in number.

Major Ralph Bennett, a Cambridge don and wartime intelligence officer in Hut 3 at Bletchley Park (perhaps the least appealing example of an English country house one could ever encounter), has left us a description of the process by which Enigma messages were decoded and sent to field commanders.[3] Churchill was sent daily a clutch of the most significant. Mathematical ability to decipher was not enough, as linguistics experts were needed to understand colloquialisms, abbreviations and slang, while proficiency with German orders of battle and equipment was also needed by others to assess the importance of a decrypt. The scale of the Bletchley operation was staggering, with three eight-hour shifts of 4,000 people each passing through its gates every twenty-four hours. The operation was so secret ('Ultra' was the highest level of security classification from which most were excluded) that even at

Bletchley analysis of intercepted data was limited to a chosen few individuals. In order further to protect the whole operation, hardly anyone had an overview of the complete set-up and everyone worked on a 'need-to-know' basis. This was before any of this information was passed on to Allied field commands for them to incorporate into their plans, or not.

While Hut 5 in the grounds of Bletchley Park oversaw similar work for the German navy (mainly U-boat movements), Bennett's office was responsible for the analysis and distribution of air and land forces intercepts, and wrote commentaries to suggest a context and background for each. This was a gargantuan task; for example, between 1 October 1944 and 31 January 1945, of the 11,000-plus messages intercepted, half concerned the Western Front, which amounted to a daily average of forty to fifty Ultra intercepts for Bennett's team to annotate. As the original message texts were little more than meaningless translations of German abbreviations, sent by some of the 100,000 Enigma machines distributed throughout the Third Reich, Hut 3's comments were added to each decoded message and sent onwards by secure radio and teleprinter network to military headquarters in the field.

To maintain tight security of the Bletchley intercept operation, Bennett's team also reworked messages so that each appeared to originate from Agent Boniface, a fictitious British spy with a network of agents inside Germany, wrapping Bletchley Park within a necessary bubble of deception, even for the Allies. The recipients were twenty-eight Special Liaison Officers, trained by Group Captain F. W. F. 'Fred' Winterbotham, and embedded as part of a Special Liaison Unit (SLU) to each Allied army group and army or air force headquarters.[4]

In the field, military intelligence officers went through a similar process of analysis to that of Hut 3, with the difference that they could call on the wide variety of their own intelligence sources, among them patrol reports, tactical radio intercepts, signals traffic analysis, weapons and equipment examination, prisoner-of-war, civilian and refugee interrogations, assessments of captured letters and documents, interpretation of aerial photographs and artillery sound-ranging and flash-spotting. In military command posts this was undertaken by G-2 (intelligence) personnel, linguists, prisoner interrogation teams and, for civilians, by civil affairs officers. Of these sources, aerial photography usually offered the richest pickings, though this opportunity diminished rapidly in the winter months and almost disappeared while the Bulge battles were

The liberation of Paris on 25 August swept these and other German occupation forces from Versailles, where they were replaced by the multitudes of Eisenhower's SHAEF staff, which was so vast that the French drily referred to them as *la Société des Hôteliers Américains en France.* SHAEF itself occupied the Trianon Palace Hôtel, where the 1919 peace conferences had been negotiated, though Ike lived in Rundstedt's former villa at Saint-Germain-en-Laye. (Author's collection)

being fought. Photography was difficult throughout the five days before the offensive, 11–15 December, with all aircraft grounded on the 13th.

The SLUs worked with the intelligence cells in their various headquarters, integrating Bletchley-originated material with locally captured data.[5] Ultra (the codename for the whole process of interception, analysis and distribution of Enigma-derived material) evolved with the war, and was outside Anglo-American military doctrine. Thus the way each SLU was embedded with field commands, and the use made of their skills, varied with different headquarters, and often rested on personalities and politics rather than the importance of the material itself. SLUs had another crucial role, which was to ensure that any operations influenced by Ultra reports were not too obviously linked to Bletchley-originated intelligence.

The first recipient of Bletchley material was SHAEF, Eisenhower's command, first established in London during December 1943. A year later the only place large enough to accommodate its vast acreages of staff officers (the French drily referred to SHAEF as *la Société des Hôteliers Américains en France*) was the sumptuous Trianon Palace Hôtel in

Versailles. Ike actually lived apart from the huge headquarters in his own villa at Saint-Germain-en-Laye (the very dwelling from where Rundstedt had commanded earlier), about ten miles west of Paris and the same distance north of Versailles. At the Trianon, SHAEF's chief of intelligence, British Major-General Kenneth Strong (the Military Attaché in Berlin who had met Count von Schwerin in 1939), had served with Eisenhower since March 1943 and was popular among US staff officers, though relations with Montgomery's Twenty-First Army Group were frosty. Any British close to SHAEF became suspect to members of Monty's headquarters; the latter's own head of intelligence, the thirty-two-year-old Brigadier Edgar 'Bill' Williams, a pre-war German-speaking Oxford history don, later referred to Strong as the 'Chinless Horror'.[6] Fiercely, but not blindly, loyal to his boss, Williams had been a major when Montgomery first encountered him in the desert in 1942, but possessing a fine historian's brain which questioned every fact and supposition, despite his youth, he rose rapidly under Monty's patronage.

Below SHAEF was Bradley's Twelfth Army Group, whose headquarters was established in London on 14 July 1944, activated on 1 August and had migrated to Luxembourg by December 1944. It grew into the largest US ground combat force ever created. For most of its nine months of war, Twelfth Army Group directed Hodges' First Army, Patton's Third and Simpson's Ninth. Its very size made it a complicated command to handle. Indeed, the United States had never deployed an army group before, and there was precious little doctrine or experience of how to run any higher formation. Inside Bradley's HQ, two SLU colonels, called the Estimates and Appreciation Group, operated an 'Ultra room' which received and collated Bletchley material with other sources to provide estimates of German strengths and intentions.[7] Underlining Bletchley's importance, Twelfth Army Group held two daily Ultra briefings, firstly at 09.45 a.m., attended by Bradley, after each morning staff briefing.

So sensitive was the 'Ultra secret' that data provided by Bletchley was forbidden from inclusion in Allied written intelligence reports or summaries unless it could be ascribed truthfully to another source (as opposed to Bletchley and its pseudo-spy ring). All intelligence assessments composed for transmission downwards had to reflect this, so that more junior headquarters would not raise embarrassing questions as to the source of knowledge. Very few officers throughout the Allied armies were cleared for access to Ultra material, and an army (or equivalent air force) headquarters was the last level at which Ultra-cleared officers were permitted to work – corps and divisional staff were not in on the secrets emanating from Bletchley.

In Bradley's Forward HQ ('Eagle Tac'), at No. 2 Place de Metz in the centre of Luxembourg City, Ultra clearance was limited to his chief of staff Major-General Leven C. Allen; principal staff officers; the chief of Intelligence Branch (also known by the name of his branch, G-2), Brigadier-General Edwin L. Sibert; the British Liaison Officer Major Tom Bigland; and the commander and operations officer of the Ninth Air Force.[8] At this stage, Major-General Lewis H. Brereton's Ninth, whose headquarters was also located in Luxembourg City, had become the largest tactical air force ever assembled under one command, comprising 250,000 people with 3,500 aircraft in 1,500 units. The previous twenty-four hours of Ultra-relevant events were reviewed, while Sibert highlighted any new German intentions or capabilities as revealed by all sources. Bradley discussed these in conjunction with his forthcoming operations, inviting debate and contributions from the Ninth Air Force, whose commander was usually present. A second Ultra daily briefing took place at 11.30 a.m., attended by their deputies.[9]

Subordinate to Twelfth Army Group was Bradley's old command, US First Army, in December 1944 stationed at the Hôtel Britannique in the fashionable Ardennes town of Spa, where its Chief G-2, Colonel Benjamin A. ('Monk') Dickson, a blunt, uncompromising Philadelphia reservist and 1918 graduate of West Point with an engineering degree from MIT, recalled to active duty and thrust into intelligence because of his familiarity with French and German, presented the raw Bletchley material personally to Hodges and his chief of staff, Major-General William B. Kean, Jr, twice daily.

Unlike his contemporaries, First Army's SLU Officer, thirty-nine-year-old Princeton graduate and Philadelphia lawyer, Lieutenant-Colonel Adolph G. 'Rosey' Rosengarten Jr, was not granted direct access to Hodges. Instead, 'Monk' Dickson bypassed him, controlling all Ultra data, personally integrating it with other G-2 analysis and presenting it to a smaller circle than at Twelfth Army Group.[10] This included Major-General Elwood R. 'Pete' Quesada, commander of IX Tactical Air Command, who insisted his own SLU officer attend, despite strident objections from Dickson.[11] Rosengarten's frequent reports of frustration make it clear he felt Dickson's role was unnecessarily possessive and 'obstructive' and that 'Ultra had a limited use in the First Army command', where Bletchley's material was often 'poorly presented' by Dickson.

Furthermore, he pointed out, Bletchley Park's valuable insights were 'complicated by the personality of the G-2 at First US Army and his relatively unimportant voice in the Army cabinet'.[12]

In the US Army, as in British and Canadian forces, 'intelligence' was not considered a good career move, thus few senior officers with the necessary experience, skills or clearance were available. The US Army headquarters that deployed into France generally had inadequate information-gathering capabilities, lacking the manpower or equipment to keep accurate and timely situational awareness of subordinate corps and divisions. This improved with time and reflected the desires of the army commander; Patton echoed Montgomery's need for efficient liaison and control, and used his 6th Cavalry Group as his personal eyes and ears in the way that Monty used his 'Phantom' GHQ Liaison Regiment.

Personality matters most in the assembly of a collective intelligence picture and, among others, Dickson clashed with the First Army G-3 (in charge of Operations), Brigadier-General Thurman C. Thorson. In any headquarters the principal relationship among staff officers that has to work well is that between the G-2 and G-3, and under Hodges the two were at loggerheads. But Dickson was inclined to be fractious with his peers. He had been Bradley's chief of intelligence in North Africa, Sicily and Normandy, and hoped to move (and be promoted) with his boss when he took over Twelfth Army Group. Instead, Dickson was left at First Army and Brigadier-General Edwin L. Sibert, a well-connected career artillery officer, son of a general and brother to another, was chosen as Bradley's new G-2 in the higher headquarters, despite the fact that he had no prior experience of intelligence work.[13]

Dickson, who had already shown himself to be a challenging personality (variously described as 'volatile, a pessimist, an alarmist' and 'hard-drinking'), and whose promotion to general rank would have invited controversy, took this very personally. He vowed never to consult Sibert at his headquarters, instead visiting 'Bill' Williams at Monty's Twenty-First Army Group if he needed advice.[14]

Chalk and cheese, thereafter Sibert and Dickson became 'not mortal enemies, but competitive – each one insisting that his information was better than that of the other'. In retrospect, both would claim to have been right and the other wrong about the Ardennes.[15] Furthermore, Dickson had also developed an antipathy to intelligence sources beyond his control, and when presented with Rosengarten made him a member of his G-2 staff, giving him work apart from his Ultra reporting. Dickson's view of any external intelligence agencies seems to have been 'I don't want any spies snooping in my office'.[16]

The First Army was afflicted with other issues, too. Hodges, a Marshall protégé and Deputy Commander of First Army under Bradley, was very different from his predecessor. Bradley was 'modest and gregarious in manner' and 'communicated well with people' which 'served him well in keeping in line the numerous egos within his headquarters'.[17] Hodges, by contrast, who had been commissioned from the ranks in 1909 and won a Distinguished Service Cross (second only in precedence to the Medal of Honor) as a battalion commander in the Meuse–Argonne campaign of 1918, was insecure as a result of his schooling, and was said to lack Bradley's intelligence, communicative skills and energy. He 'preferred to work through a small inner circle; to those outside he was a remote figure' and rarely travelled forward from his headquarters. Shy and inarticulate, his approach to any military situation was to 'follow the book', demonstrating little flair or imagination. By December he was somewhat tired, and by his inclination towards lower-level tactics 'the methodical Hodges often encountered problems in maintaining the broader perspective of an army commander'.[18] Slightly younger than George Patton, at fifty-seven Hodges sometimes seemed almost elderly in comparison.

Bradley noted that Hodges' generals 'trudged ahead with a serious and grim intensity', while Ernest N. Harmon, commander of the 2nd Armored Division, characterised his boss as 'slow, cautious, and without much zip'.[19] If Hodges trusted any subordinate it was the affable 'Lightning Joe' Lawton Collins, but he deferred much authority to his domineering chief of staff, Major-General Kean, an infantryman ten years younger, and, like Dickson, a West Point graduate of 1918. During the Bulge, when Hodges' health broke down, the capable Kean was in day-to-day charge. 'Able, perceptive, and clear-thinking', Kean was also a 'hard taskmaster, efficient, but with little of the human touch', who nevertheless held the staff together in the first few days of the Bulge.[20] Hodges was uncomfortable with allowing subordinates any latitude, expecting his (often vague) oral directions to be followed without question or deviation; his solution to problems was often to blame or sack individuals. In this context, Hodges, the 'by-the-book' commander, and Kean, his efficient deputy, were not particularly open to the imaginative possibilities suggested by Ultra and 'Monk' Dickson, who trod warily.

At Third Army's forward HQ (nicknamed 'Lucky Forward'), the process of using Ultra was evolutionary. Initially, material from Bletchley was passed by the attached SLU officer direct to Colonel W. Koch, the chief G-2; in December 1944 he was based with Patton at the Caserne Molifor in Nancy.[21] Due to Bletchley's success in providing a specific forewarning of the Mortain counter-attack, Ultra was thereafter presented in 09.00 a.m. briefings to Patton and his main staff officers, as in Twelfth Army Group. The SLU officer also kept a situation map posted with Bletchley-derived and open-source information, which Ultra-cleared staff could consult at any time: the opposite approach to Dickson's furtiveness. Bletchley's strategic intelligence outputs were fully integrated into the operational plans of Third Army, though their German Order of Battle intelligence officer was deliberately refused access by Koch, and had to develop his own picture of the Germans without the influence of Bletchley material. Koch then used Ultra as a check on the latter's conclusions, derived from other sources. Every headquarters maintained a German Order of Battle section, whose job was to research and keep an up-to-date picture of their opponents' locations, strengths, capabilities and commanders.

Koch (pronounced Kotch), a career cavalry officer, had been assigned to Patton's 2nd Armored Division in 1940 and followed his boss as senior intelligence officer of II Corps in Tunisia, Seventh Army in Sicily, and, finally, Third Army. Known as 'the spark plug of the Third Army', with 'the most penetrating brain in the United States Army', Koch, forty-seven, was noted for his exceptional situation awareness of his army's battlefield, and was 'snooping all the time', often far beyond Third Army's own area. His area of interest always extended 150 miles beyond Third Army's boundaries, the limit of his tactical air reconnaissance, but also the notional distance of any German motorised reinforcements. One witness remembered his lair as the 'most comprehensive and spectacular in the American, British, and Canadian Armies, which contained a 1:250,000-scale map, showing the situation of the entire Western front down to division-level formations. On the flanks of this centrepiece were two 1:100,000-scale maps, one showing the Eastern front and the other Third Army's zone, depicting units down to battalion level.'[22]

Other data included terrain models, charts, graphs and orders of battle, providing any visitor with up-to-date information at a glance. Koch's techniques were in response to his boss's intelligence requirements, which were beyond the norm of his contemporaries, and many of Patton's pronouncements and his famous insights arguably stemmed from Koch's map room. When, for example, on 25 November Patton observed, 'the

First Army is making a terrible mistake in leaving VIII Corps static [in the Ardennes], it is highly probable that the Germans are building up east of them', his comment was clearly prompted by a glance at Koch's maps. This was in dramatic contrast to First Army, whose 'long-range planning was deficient, corps boundaries [were] often uninspired and reflected a dismaying lack of knowledge of the ground'.[23] With his far-reaching knowledge it is easy to see why the straight-talking Koch started to badger Patton with serious concerns about Ultra-indicated German troop movements towards the Ardennes, confirmed by his other intelligence sources. Koch was less hierarchical than Dickson and persisted in his warnings up the chain of command, even when they were dismissed by Strong at SHAEF and Sibert at Twelfth Army Group, demonstrating a considerable amount of moral courage, which Patton appreciated.

In late October, Koch had produced an Intelligence Estimate noting the German 'withdrawal, though continuing, has not been a rout or mass collapse', that they were 'playing for time' and determined 'to wage a last-ditch struggle in the field at all costs'. Yet, at the same moment, Strong at SHAEF observed that the Germans were losing the equivalent of a division at least every week, surmising 'the dwindling fire brigade is switched with increasing rapidity and increasing wear and tear, from one fire to another'.[24] All these G-2 officers – Strong, Sibert, Dickson and Koch – were bright and capable, but as many have observed, 'these chiefs of intelligence at various levels cooperated very little'.[25]

Apart from Ultra intelligence material, at the time of the Ardennes offensive there were eight US Signal Radio Intelligence Companies deployed along the *Westwall* and one attached to Bradley's headquarters; these were corps and army-level outfits, acting as the ears of SHAEF. Each company included Direction Finding (DF), Wire (to provide communications), Traffic Analysis (TA), Intercept, and Cryptanalysis sub-units, usually working out of trucks and spread over wide areas. Their ranks included mostly college-educated personnel, linguists and technicians, whose job was to build up a picture of the German order of battle, as well as interpret movements and monitor messages. Some would randomly search the frequencies for chatter, while others locked on to particular call signs, recognising the 'fist' of individual German operators.[26] One radio intelligence officer observed: 'In cases of emergency the Germans sometimes resorted to uncoded communications. Such clear text messages were brief and without such clarifiers as articles, prepositions, adjectives, adverbs or punctuation marks. Verbs, pronouns,

nouns and numbers were the usual inventoried (and sometimes abbreviated) contents of tactical messages which took knowledge and imagination to understand.'[27]

Ray Walker was a twenty-nine-year-old lieutenant commanding the direction-finding section of US First Army's Radio Intelligence Company. 'My primary job was to determine where enemy radio transmissions were coming from and what unit was sending them. In early December 1944, we told Eisenhower's headquarters the Germans were moving four or five panzer units into the Eifel Forest and maintaining radio silence,' he recalled.[28] A GI with the Traffic Analysis platoon of the 114th Signal Radio Intelligence Company was monitoring the area in front of US V Corps, a twenty-mile stretch through which the German Sixth Panzer Army formations travelled to their assembly areas. Sergeant Jay C. von Werlhof remembered the German offensive 'came as no surprise' to his unit, which had

> identified several units of the Sixth Panzer Army between 9–14 December. But to not embarrass himself or our company's good reputation in the eyes of Higher Command, our 1st Lieutenant refused to send in our first, and then even our revised, report on the build-up, especially between Monschau and Manderfeld. In spite of identities and five-point DF fixes on eight German divisions . . . our lieutenant compared our data with obsolete reports from First Army, Twelfth Army Group and SHAEF that said there were only four divisions east of the entire [West] Wall between Monschau and Echternach. Several of the units we pinpointed were supposed to be on the Eastern Front fighting the Russians or in R and R. Our lieutenant was a New York social climber who hoped to make captaincy before the war ended.[29]

This was an extreme reaction of a nervous young lieutenant determined not to 'rock the boat', and emphasises the prevailing mindset of the higher formations. It demonstrated that the warning signs were out there and being accumulated, if not (as in this instance) being acted upon. It is at variance with the historian Charles MacDonald's view, among others, that these companies 'discerned absolutely no indication of what was about to happen'.[30]

Additionally, we now know that further intelligence along the front was provided by German-speaking agents of the OSS (Office of Strategic Services)[31] who operated deep-penetration missions behind the lines;

they included exiled Communists and Socialist party members, union activists, anti-Nazi prisoners of war and Jewish refugees. Intended initially to gather intelligence and conduct operations with partisan and resistance groups, they often masqueraded as German officials or pro-Axis civilians. Just as preparations for *Herbstnebel* were stepped up, what had been a torrent of OSS agent information from behind German lines suddenly slowed to a trickle after October 1944, as the Allies left French-speaking areas and advanced into Germany, where there were no resistance movements.

Just as with Ultra, there was no military doctrine written for the use of OSS, consequently relations between it and the various field formations ranged from excellent to terrible. Lieutenant-Colonel William Quinn, G-2 of Patch's Seventh Army, was delighted to have OSS parachutes blossoming behind German lines in the south of France, dropping spies to join the *Maquis* and radio information about defences and troop concentrations, smoothing the way for Seventh Army's tanks. But at this exact moment US First Army was without an OSS field detachment, which had been banished by 'Monk' Dickson in October due to his suspicion of outside agencies, particularly the civilian-dominated OSS.

Under Colonel, later Major-General, William ('Wild Bill') Donovan, OSS culture was very 'unmilitary', which antagonised traditionalist 'West Pointers' and other professional soldiers; its chief European office, on London's Grosvenor Street, was populated by well-connected young men 'fresh from the polo fields of Long Island and Virginia'. The voice of the BBC, writer and MI6 spy Captain Malcolm Muggeridge, remembered the early OSS men 'arriving like *jeunes filles en fleur* straight from a finishing school, all fresh and innocent, to start work in our frowsy old intelligence brothel'. Kim Philby of the British Foreign Office, who knew a thing or two about spying, regarded the new transatlantic arrivals as 'a pain in the neck', but the two nations soon adjusted to their shotgun marriage, with views like Dickson's only hindering their war effort.[32]

The upshot of Dickson's unilateral action against his OSS detachment was that First Army's area had no 'deep' reconnaissance behind the German lines. While Hodge's command may have deprived itself of an extra source of useful intelligence, Patton's Third Army kept theirs, adopting 'all-source' collection and analysis procedures. However, there was no guarantee that one small OSS group would have stumbled on the German secret, verified the accuracy of its discovery and had time to issue an early warning to hundreds of Allied units poised on the

German frontier, let alone been believed, thus altering the course of history.

Just after the war a US Army report into the workings of SHAEF intelligence observed that 'the failure of the United States [beforehand] to establish and maintain a highly developed intelligence organisation, world-wide in scope, resulted initially in the lack of intelligence data, and trained personnel necessary for the conduct of operations in the European Theater'. The result was that 'British influence was predominant in the G-2 Division during the planning phase of the campaign in Europe and continued in only slightly lesser degree throughout the operation on the Continent'.

Without discussing Bletchley Park, whose operations were beyond their security classification, the report concluded, 'the greater portion of the tactical intelligence . . . came from agencies operating in the field' and 'better results would have been obtained from the Office of Strategic Services had this agency been under direct control of the SHAEF Assistant Chief of Staff, G-2 [General Strong], and its efforts been more closely coordinated with those of the military forces'.

The report team, consisting of two colonels and three lieutenant-colonels, was given added weight by the addition of Eisenhower's son, John, then a lowly first lieutenant, to the team, which undoubtedly opened many doors which otherwise would have remained shut. It also concluded that Strong's organisation needed to be able to conduct 'long-range intelligence planning concurrently with military operations' – implying it did not.[33]

Also shaping the intelligence picture was RAF/USAAF tactical air reconnaissance, then called Photo Intelligence (PI), which processed the results of aerial photographic missions every day, supporting and confirming the revelations from Bletchley. Section Officer Jeanne Sowry of the British Women's Auxiliary Air Force (WAAF), who worked at the headquarters of PI, called RAF Medmenham (actually a mansion called Danesfield House), in Buckinghamshire, recalled, 'The work of photographic interpreting was important, secret, demanding and, at times, very exciting. Our requests for photographs came from many sources . . . When you were given the photos, you had no idea what you might see. The missions were flown from RAF Benson nearby and the aircraft that were used were Mosquitos. We watched shipping movements daily, we studied airfields old and new, likewise aircraft, marshalling yards and railways, ports and beaches.'[34] In mid-January 1945 a group of six British and American senior officers was sent to Belgium to discover if there were any institutional flaws in the way the Allied air forces collected and analysed their intelligence. They found that reconnaissance flights had taken place every day before and during the campaign, except 13 December; on occasions flying conditions were so poor that most aircraft were unable to return to their operating base at Benson in Oxfordshire, and landed all over Allied-controlled Europe.

The 10th Photographic Group (Reconnaissance) supporting US First Army had flown 361 sorties beforehand, mostly with P-38 Lightnings and P-51 Mustangs, but had failed to identify anything threatening, except what they interpreted as routine traffic moving through. One of the RAF investigating officers, Wing Commander Douglas Kendall – who had spotted and correctly identified the threat of panzers lurking in the Eifel on 6 May 1940, four days before the first German invasion of the Ardennes – blamed the 'lapse' on the 'failure of the many separate field units to link all the evidence that they had separately gathered'. Kendall was of the opinion that, had everything been passed to a central interpretation unit, the various elements of the puzzle would have been assembled.[35] Kendall was in charge of the RAF's photo interpretation activities, and, significantly, he was the only person at RAF Medmenham cleared for Ultra; his report therefore contained a subtle message to those who knew of Bletchley Park.[36]

The Bletchley Park Director-General, Commander Sir Edward Travis, likewise demanded a post-campaign investigation into the Allied intelligence failure. The confidential Special Report written in January 1945 by Peter Calvocoressi, its head of air intelligence, and the renowned Cambridge classicist F. L. Lucas, then head of research in Hut 3, robustly defended the code-breaking centre and its processes. The authors found that Ultra indicated a 'substantial and offensive' operation was likely, but could not identify a location or time. They identified a concentration of Luftwaffe aircraft and personnel, and movement by rail of divisions and equipment to the Eifel region beforehand, but these indicators were not acted upon, the authors argued.[37] The pair concluded the failure lay with SHAEF (Kenneth Strong), and the Air Ministry, and expected their report would cause 'heads to roll at Eisenhower's HQ but they did no more than wobble'.[38]

Intelligence organisations today try to collate their information more efficiently, but tensions remain between competing agencies. Military intelligence generally tries to follow an intelligence-gathering cycle of five phases. A commander usually states an intelligence requirement in the form of a question. The staff convert the requirement into a collection plan, refining the data needed into 'essential elements of information'. As news arrives from several tasked sources, it is collated into a readily accessible database. Other staff then quiz the resultant data with such key questions as 'What is it? What is it doing? and What does it mean?' Only at this stage is information turned into intelligence. The results are then distilled as a written or verbal brief, or transmitted as a signal with varying degrees of urgency. Intelligence problems nearly always arise at the collation stage, when for reasons of operational security, staff are precluded from access to all the sources and their products or from sharing their work. Intelligence organisations, by their very nature, tend to be furtive and husband, rather than share, their knowledge.

This was the case with Bletchley Park, whose secrets were restricted to very few. Additionally, military-run intelligence organisations are frequently at odds with their civilian counterparts. In wartime France there were rivalries between Communist-inspired resistance groups and right-wing Gaullist ones, which resulted in the withholding or corruption of intelligence, a story repeated in Belgium and elsewhere. Even the British Foreign Office reflected a left/right political split, expressed most obviously by the Cambridge spy ring of Philby, Maclean, Burgess and Blunt (and possibly more), all of whom were found to have been spying for Moscow, motivated by ideology, during the war. There are often issues of intelligence-sharing between nations, and while Anglo-US cooperation generally worked superbly well during the war, this wasn't always the case, and rivalries developed between the American OSS and British SOE, resulting in duplication.

This illustrated neatly the somewhat chaotic processes of Allied intelligence-gathering from multiple sources, which varied between headquarters, and suggests how some of the warning indicators picked up by Bletchley Park came to be overlooked. Very similar clashes between intelligence organisations also led to the unpleasant surprises of the Yom Kippur war for Israel and the September 11th 2001 attacks. The 1944 intelligence failure is also partly explained by the clash between 'top-down' material emanating from Ultra and 'bottom-up' reports filtering up from the combat units via division and corps headquarters, in addition to personality and culture clashes within the Allied intelligence architecture. Be that as it may, the Allies were taken completely by surprise, at every level, on 16 December 1944.

10

The Cloak of Invisibility

WHAT OF THE warnings and indicators that Allied intelligence picked up? Enigma revealed to Bletchley analysts some twenty-nine decoded messages intercepted between 18 September and 15 December concerning preparations for the offensive. Forthwith, Ultra was no longer going to hand over German battle orders on a plate, as it had done at Mortain in August; Allied intelligence officers were going to have to work harder to extract nuances from the Bletchley intercepts. The first Ultra intercept definitely associated with the Ardennes, decoded on 27 September, was of a German message transmitted nine days earlier, on the 18th, which summarised 'SS Operations orders the rest and refit for 1, 2, 9 & 12 SS Panzer Divisions, three heavy panzer battalions, and 1SS Panzer Corps troops. All are assigned to the new 6 Panzer Army, Sepp Dietrich commanding. Assignment of Sepp Dietrich is clear sign of an offensive purpose.'[1]

The time lag of nine days is indicative of the everyday challenges Bletchley staff experienced in finding cipher keys to crack the daily Enigma code for each headquarters. The 18 September message, with its mention of Oberstgruppenführer Josef 'Sepp' Dietrich of the Waffen-SS, was worrying, for his was a name that rang alarm bells throughout the Allied military community. Having established a reputation for being a hard-driving and tenacious division and corps commander in Russia and Normandy, Dietrich's personal reappearance on German orders of battle sent shivers down the collective Allied spine.

Coupled with mention of 'heavy panzer battalions', which was a Wehrmacht euphemism for units of Tiger, or King Tiger tanks, the two were assessed as heralding extremely aggressive military activity.

Deutsche Reichsbahn (German railways) also used a version of the Enigma enciphering machine to coordinate their activities across Europe, which Bletchley analysts first cracked in November, revealing some military movements. For example, on 3 November, intercepts of *Reichsbahn* instructions unveiled two movements for the Fifth Panzer and Seventh Armies, with forty-one trains for the 352nd *Volksgrenadier* Division and twenty-eight trains for another formation identified.[2] Two days later, Army Group 'B' called for fighter protection in an arc over Cologne while important trains were unloaded. These belonged to Sixth Panzer Army and over the next month other similar signals followed, shifting gradually to locations in the Eifel, directly east of the Ardennes.[3]

On 10 November, a *Reichsbahn* message betrayed the rail movement of Sixth Panzer Army HQ and 12th SS Panzer Division to west of the Rhine, while in another the Director General of the Transport Office demanded that Sixth Panzer Army order all its formations to observe strict punctuality in loading trains, reporting that 2nd SS Panzer Division was thirty-six hours late, Panzer Lehr twenty-four hours, and 12th SS Division, twelve hours behind schedule.[4] On 21 November, a message was intercepted, revealing that 9th and 10th SS Divisions, which comprised the same II SS Panzer Corps that had countered the Allies so effectively at Arnhem, had arrived at Euskirchen, a town south-west of Cologne and a mere twenty miles east of US troops along the Belgian border.[5] Illustrating the frustrating nature of Ultra decrypts was the message at the end of November, requiring the allocation of 150 vehicles to *Dienststelle* (Department) *Skorzeny*. Intelligence knew who Skorzeny was, but not what he was up to, so the decode was of no immediate value.[6]

Key air force intercepts included Central Rhineland Luftwaffe Command on 16 November, calling for daily serviceability returns from all airfields for the aircraft involved in the *Jägeraufmarsch* (fighter concentration). The latter was a special Luftwaffe term for the build-up of air strength to support an operation; this was highly significant because the concentration was a reversal of recent policy to strip the Eastern and Western Fronts, creating a huge reserve of fighters over Germany to combat Allied bombers. On 23 November, intercepted Luftwaffe communications discussed the participation of assembled fighter units in 'combat air patrol (CAP) missions for the concurrent rail movements', clearly indicating vital trains that needed escorting to their onward destinations.[7] By 29 November, the Luftwaffe were responding to requests from Army Group 'B' for aerial reconnaissance sorties over the Meuse river crossings, which on 8 December were switched to the much faster Arado 234 jet, whose speed made it almost impossible to intercept, which was of itself an indicator of the importance of the targets.[8] Meanwhile, reports of a conference of almost all Western Front fighter commanders, held in the vicinity of Cologne on 5 December, alerted analysts to an approaching major Luftwaffe effort in the west.[9]

This theme continued on 2 December, when an Army Group 'B' signal requested 'with special urgency' fighter protection for troop movements in the Moselle Valley. The same day a Luftwaffe West HQ transmission referred to twelve formations involved in these movements, including the mechanised *Führer-Begleit-Brigade* (Führer Escort Brigade). Analysis of the sudden appearance of Hitler's expanded personal guard was that it 'had to be for an offensive purpose'. Again, on 2 December, an OKW Order was intercepted, calling for the withdrawal of 1,000 trucks from Italy for use by the Sixth Panzer Army. Analysts pondered where the formation was going that it needed so much extra transport.[10] Finally, on 10 December Bletchley analysts reported preparations for the establishment of radio silence by Sixth Panzer Army, a universally acknowledged indicator of an impending attack.

These messages were just some of the endless stream intercepted daily from *Deutsche Reichsbahn*, Luftwaffe, OKW and other military headquarters transmissions, which referred to thousands of formations, units or trains. Each separate German organisation changed its cipher daily, which diminished Bletchley's ability to decipher messages on some days. Ultra was monitoring as many headquarters throughout the Reich as it could, from which thousands of messages emanated, and Bletchley analysts had no way of knowing which were important until deciphered. In this context, none of these intercepted communications in themselves provided enough information to press a 'panic button' (although the name of 'Dietrich' came close), and illustrated that for the true intelligence picture to emerge, then as now, the right questions had to be asked, with data assembled from multiple intelligence sources, of which Ultra was but one. Consequently, unless the indicators were interpreted correctly, there would be no straightforward directives to alert the Ultra analysts at Bletchley Park to the forthcoming maelstrom.[11]

One of the potential ways to crosscheck information was Magic. Since mid-1941 the United States had been intercepting and decoding Japanese diplomatic traffic, the process code-named 'Magic', sent via cipher machines similar in concept to the German Enigma device. The machine itself, nicknamed 'Purple' by the Americans, was first used in 1940, but never by Japan's military. There remains controversy over 'who knew what before Pearl Harbor in 1941' because there were indicators of the coming attack from the Japanese Foreign Ministry's instructions to its embassy in Washington, DC, to sever diplomatic relations. A similar situation arose in late 1944.

No military *plans* about the Ardennes were leaked by coded wireless signal, but on 4 September Hitler had boasted to the Japanese ambassador to Berlin, Baron Hiroshi Oshima, that 'when the current replenishment of the air forces is completed and when the new army of more than a million men is ready, I intend to combine the new units with others to be withdrawn from all possible areas and open a large-scale offensive in the West. Asked when, Hitler replied, "at the beginning of November".'[12] The baron dutifully reported this to Tokyo two days later, but his intercepted signal was then open to a variety of different interpretations: was this a misunderstanding, an exaggeration, an idle boast or a credible threat?

The baron had a further meeting with German Foreign Minister von Ribbentrop on 15 November, which he summarised for Tokyo five days later: 'Hitler's health has returned and is engaged in operational planning and rebuilding the German air force. Hitler is opposed to defence and war of attrition. There is no change in his intentions to undertake a large-scale offensive as soon as possible. No definite time or method has been decided on.'[13] Hitler was deceiving his ally, for by then he had certainly fixed the method and timescale. However, as time moved on and no offensive was forthcoming, the significance of the two possible Japanese indicators seemed to fade.[14]

On 12 November, four days before the start of a major offensive that was supposed to break through the Hürtgen to the Roer beyond, both General Strong at SHAEF and 'Monk' Dickson at First Army issued estimates that identified a possible German offensive. The SHAEF Weekly Intelligence Summary, No. 64, judged the German military reinforcement (meaning the establishment of strategic and tactical reserves and the strengthening of the *Westwall*) as preparation for the final showdown before the winter set in.[15] In tandem, Dickson's First Army Intelligence

Summary of 12 November echoed the same: 'it's a race against time, can the enemy complete his dispositions for his offensive prior to the launching of our attack? With the approach of winter in the east, it is believed the enemy will stake all on an offensive in the west.'[16] Here is the evidence, derived from all sources, not just Ultra, that Bradley's superior and subordinate formations both felt there was a threat.

While the battle for the Scheldt estuary was still raging, early in the morning of 27 October the 9th Panzer and 15th *Panzergrenadier* Divisions (of Freiherr von Lüttwitz's XLVII Panzer Corps) launched a powerful local assault against thinly held British VIII Corps positions at Meijel in the Peel Marshes, south-east of Eindhoven. The attack actually hit the British–US Army Group boundary on the extreme right of Dempsey's British Second Army. The terrain was difficult, with low-lying marshes criss-crossed with canals, natural streams and drainage ditches. Considered an unlikely venue for an attack, the Germans nonetheless managed to build a bridge over the Deurne canal in daylight to facilitate the venture.

By 28 October Dempsey's troops had swarmed into the battle's northern area, allowing Major-General Lindsay M. Silvester's US 7th Armored Division, attached to Dempsey, to counter-attack the south. In spite of strong Allied fighter-bomber activity on the 29th, the panzers still gained ground at the expense of 7th Armored, with a few Luftwaffe sorties in support. During the morning of 30 October, aided by 140 Luftwaffe sorties, the panzers made more gains, expelling the Americans from their positions, but by afternoon Allied resistance and counter-attacks had grown so powerful that the assault ceased, and XLVII Panzer Corps withdrew back to their line of departure.

The Twenty-First Army Group G-2 (Brigadier 'Bill' Williams) had underestimated German forces in the area, but the spoiling attack managed to push five miles west in two days along a ten-mile front, threatening a narrow salient the Allies had gained during Operation Market Garden over a month earlier. While the real purpose was to deflect Montgomery's attention away from the German Fifteenth Army defending the Scheldt estuary, it managed some temporary success before stalling. For his failure (as much in front of the British, as the Germans, one feels), Silvester was relieved of his command on 30 October and replaced by Brigadier-General Robert W. Hasbrouck.

The significance of this relatively minor action lay in a later Twelfth Army Group G-2 Periodic Report, issued on 17 November, with an annex on the Peel Marshes attack.[17] It concluded: '(a). With the lengthening nights and with limited air observation and photography during the day, the enemy has demonstrated that he can mass a large force – two divisions with up to fifty tanks – in an assembly area close to our lines without any of our sources becoming aware of it. (b). Then taking advantage of the morning fog or haze he can attack and be on us with less than half an hour's notice. These conditions and proximity of the wooded areas greatly increase the necessity for alert OPs, listening posts, air OPs, aggressive patrolling and defensive preparation for a variety of eventualities. Rapid, complete dissemination of each bit of information to the next higher echelon can frequently produce the picture of lurking dangers and avoid disaster . . . . (d). The German selection of the swamps west of the Meuse as a spot to employ two of his best mobile divisions alerts us to the fact that the enemy cannot be trusted always to attack according to the "book". He remains a clever, aggressive foe.'[18]

Here was ample evidence of what the Germans could still achieve in the west: undetected concentration of troops and armour, bridge-building under fire, a surprise attack in the dawn mists, some local air support, and progress despite Allied air cover – which all amounted to the ability to overwhelm a battle-hardened US division – Silvester's 7th Armored had arrived in Normandy during August and covered huge distances under US Third and Ninth Armies. More importantly, this may have been a useful 'trial run' for Lüttwitz and his XLVII Panzer Corps, for although they had yet to be informed, they would appear in the Ardennes within two months under similar circumstances – as would Hasbrouck with his 7th Armored Division.

The intentions of Sixth Panzer Army continued to perplex and concern SHAEF, Twelfth Army Group and US First and Third Armies. In several reports beginning as early as 1 November, Koch at Third Army had highlighted the strength and general location of the Sixth Panzer Army, stating 'this force had a strong offensive capability anywhere in the US zone'. On 21 November, Sibert at Twelfth Army Group published his Intelligence Summary No. 15 for the week ending 18 November; hedging his bets, he wrote:

> So far the enemy has not produced the counter-attack or counter-offensive punch which Sixth Panzer, with perhaps 500 tanks, is capable of delivering . . . The necessity for launching a strong counter-attack to stop an Allied thrust toward Cologne or the Ruhr has not yet arisen.

> On the other hand if the enemy intends to launch a major counter-offensive against any Allied salient East of Aachen, designed to re-establish the Siegfried Line positions, or to cripple American forces in this area, the most opportune time will presumably come when our attacks have spent their forces and our supplies are dwindling. The enemy is thus in the position of holding his punch and awaiting developments . . . He will then be in a position to launch a major counter-offensive or move some or all of the elements of Sixth Panzer Army to Army Group 'G' or to whatever vital area is seriously threatened. However . . . it is unlikely that he will move Sixth Panzer Army from this area.[19]

Meanwhile, the flow of ominous Ultra intercepts caused Strong, who was at Versailles with SHAEF, enough concern to issue an Intelligence Estimate on 7 December which suggested 'the increasingly strong German reserve could be used by the German High Command to rupture Allied lines'. He ventured 'a possible German objective might be to disrupt the overstretched US VIII Corps in the Ardennes'. Was it significant that this also happened to be the third anniversary of Pearl Harbor, when Americans would have been more than usually sensitive to unpleasant military surprises? For a fleeting moment Strong (an Englishman, but serving an American-dominated headquarters) had unwittingly penetrated the murk of German operational security, though he was unaware of it.

The Allied reaction was immediate. The SHAEF chief of staff, Lieutenant-General Walter Bedell 'Beetle' Smith, directed Strong to visit and brief General Bradley on his concerns.[20] On 9 December, Koch (Third Army's G-2) in Nancy briefed Patton on the assembly of forces in the Eifel and the next day published his Intelligence Summary No. 186, stating 'although the Allied offensive is destroying weekly a number of German divisions, nevertheless the enemy has been able to maintain a coherent front without drawing on the full of his infantry and armored reserves, thereby giving him the capability to mount a spoiling offensive in an effort to unhinge the Allied assault on *Festung Deutschland*'.[21] The same day, 10 December, 'Monk' Dickson's First Army Weekly Intelligence Summary No. 37 warned of the possibility of an 'all out counter offensive'.[22]

His document provided the strongest pre-battle indication of a forthcoming offensive, and Dickson for the rest of his life used it to proclaim he was the 'prophet in the wilderness'. He identified the recruitment of

English-speaking personnel for Skorzeny and associated it with an action in the west. 'Von Rundstedt', Dickson wrote, 'has skilfully defended and husbanded his forces and is preparing for his part in the all-out application of every weapon at the focal point and in the correct time to achieve defense of the Reich west of the Rhine by inflicting as great a defeat on the Allies as possible.' Dickson identified the general area of Sixth Panzer Army's concentration and noted that morale among the latest prisoners was at 'a new high', expressed by attempts to escape to 'rejoin the battle for Germany'. However, Dickson wasn't sure whether this 'concentrated counter attack with air, armor, infantry and secret weapons' would take place before or after an American attack across the Roer, on the way to the Rhine, or where; he speculated about a fifty-mile area between Roermond and Schleiden, well north of the Ardennes.

In other words, Dickson had assumed that, if there was an offensive, it would follow the logical military lines of the 'Small Solution', as proposed by Jodl, Rundstedt and Model, aimed at encircling US forces around Aachen and culminating at Liège on the Meuse, but certainly not straying beyond the river. As recent deserters and prisoners had spoken of 'winning back Aachen as a Christmas present for the Führer', Dickson ascribed no specific threat to VIII Corps' thinly held Ardennes sector further south. Nevertheless, the 2nd and Panzer Lehr Divisions were identified as lurking over the border in the Eifel, but Dickson believed they were to counter-attack in the event of an American seizure of the Roer river dams, and did not order an increased G-2 collection effort in the Eifel. Hodges' First Army's attention was focused firmly on their impending attack to take the Roer dams. They knew that the dams held a huge volume of water and, had the Germans released the winter water, the resultant tidal wave would have impeded the Allied advance into the Reich for many weeks and swept away its vanguard.[23]

However, almost immediately the various headquarters began to backtrack, perhaps fearing they were being unduly alarmist before Christmas, and anxious to preserve their reputations if no attack transpired. Sibert – in Luxembourg at Twelfth Army Group – for example, decided to view events more positively. He was anxious not to be cast in the same mould as Dickson, whom he considered an alarmist, tending to pessimism. In complete contrast to his 21 November Intelligence Summary, on 12 December, Sibert's Twelfth Army Group G-2 Summary read in part: 'It is now certain that attrition is steadily sapping the strength of German forces on the Western Front and that the crust of defences is thinner, more brittle and more vulnerable than it appears on our G-2 maps or to the troops in the line.' He wrote of 'the ample evidence that the strength of the infantry divisions that have been in the line on active sectors since the beginning of our offensive has been cut by at least fifty percent and several other divisions are known to have been virtually destroyed'.[24]

He suggested that the Wehrmacht had suffered such horrendous casualties, without replacement, that they were incapable of any mobile or offensive action. Third Army's Koch, however, stuck to his guns, on 13 December estimating the Fifth and Sixth Panzer Armies at fourteen divisions, when Dickson at Spa with First Army had pinned down only eight or nine; his comprehensive understanding of German orders of battle, as displayed in his impressive office, and a sympathetic boss, contributed to his more realistic assessment of the German threat.

Two days later, on 14 December, Strong explained to Bradley in Luxembourg the reasoning behind his 7 December SHAEF Intelligence Estimate, which had spoken of the 'increasingly strong German reserve' that might 'rupture Allied lines', particularly 'the overstretched US VIII Corps in the Ardennes', as he had been instructed to do by Bedell Smith. Being closer to Bletchley in the Ultra paper trail, Strong would have been surer of his sources than Sibert, who was present, the latter repeating and defending his more sanguine Army Group Intelligence Summary of 12 December, which emphasised the attrition of German forces. Bradley, as he had to, stood by his intelligence chief, and went on to say he was 'aware of the danger', and had 'earmarked certain divisions to move into the Ardennes should the enemy attack there'. Bradley's dismissive and unfortunate parting shot to Strong was, 'Let them come!'[25]

The Germans obliged two days later.

Brigadier General Sibert was determined to reinforce the arguments he used in the 14 December meeting with Strong and Bradley, and issued his last Intelligence Estimate before the storm, on 15 December, which read in part:

> It would seem doubtful that the enemy can hold the Aachen area without committing the Sixth Panzer Army . . . [or] The enemy may have to divide the Sixth Panzer Army, thus risking defeat both in the north and in the south, or if he holds Sixth Panzer Army in the north, run a good chance of the US Third and Seventh Armies reaching the Rhine this year in the area of Mainz. Finally, to solve this problem with reinforcements from the Russian front is to invite disaster in the east.[26]

All these G-2 officers and their commanders were looking straight at the strategic picture through logical military eyes, as they assumed Rundstedt was doing, unable to notice the serpents in their peripheral vision. The collective assumption was that Hitler had reappointed his oldest field marshal to run the war for him in the west, while the Führer ran Germany's war in the east. They were all wrong. Rundstedt was merely the figurehead, but his presence fooled the Allies. As we have seen, the Ardennes campaign was Hitler's and his alone: he launched it in defiance of military logic, against Rundstedt's advice, which is why it surprised the Allies. Rundstedt's military dominance was such an obvious military assessment to make, that initially the G-2 reports and newspapers all spoke of the 'Rundstedt offensive'. That wounded the old Prussian gentleman, who never approved of Hitler's reckless gamble.

Autocratic rulers from Mussolini to Nasser and Saddam Hussein have frequently wrong-footed their opponents by defying military logic. So madness prevailed, and Hitler was content to risk disaster in the east in order to spring his Christmas surprise. Brigadier 'Bill' Williams, Monty's G-2 at Twenty-First Army Group, had it right in his 16 December Intelligence Appreciation, when he argued that 'if Hitler were running the war we could expect a surprise action before Christmas. [However]. . . We know that Rundstedt is now running the war and he is a cautious man.' Williams continued:

> The enemy is at present fighting a defensive campaign on all fronts; his situation is such that he cannot stage major offensive operations. Furthermore, at all costs he has to prevent the war from entering a mobile phase; he has not the transport or the petrol that would be necessary for mobile operations, nor could his tanks compete with ours in the mobile battle.[27]

To imply the US Army was adhering to Patton's maxim 'If everybody is thinking alike, then somebody isn't thinking' is untrue. There were a wide range of interpretations at every level as to German capabilities and intentions for late 1944: the presence of Dietrich's Sixth Panzer Army taxed every G-2 mind, but few divined its real purpose. Further down the First Army's chain of command, within Leonard T. Gerow's V Corps sector – on the very northern edge of the future battlefield – Walter E. Lauer's newly arrived 99th 'Checkerboard' Infantry Division was told that German capability was limited to potential 'battalion-sized infiltrations in several locations throughout the division sector'. Assessments of the threat repeatedly read 'no change' and were based solely on terrain analysis with no mention of location, strength or identification.[28]

The 99th Infantry Division were green and had never met 'the enemy' before. Activated at Camp Van Dorn, Mississippi, in November 1942, after training they had landed in France exactly two years later, immediately heading for a quiet area of the front to acclimatise. On D+156, 9 November 1944, with Lauer's HQ in a Belgian villa just behind the front, at Bütgenbach, they first entered battle, mounting patrols in the Ardennes.[29] 'It was a very cold and rainy season, and the roads were basically impassable due to mud, even to 6 × 6 vehicles. We were deployed into different forests to cut pine trees to make logs . . . these were laid side-by-side crossways on the road to create a passageway for the trucks,' recounted one Checkerboarder of this pre-battle time.[30] Most were concerned more with the plunging temperatures than combat; although they suffered 187 killed or wounded in November 1944, four times that number, 822, were hospitalised with trench foot, pneumonia or frostbite.[31]

Cecil R. Palmer was a twenty-two-year-old staff sergeant in the Checkerboard's 394th Infantry Regiment, drawing $96 a month basic pay, plus a 20 per cent Foreign Service Allowance. Cold weather has always since reminded him of those November days in the Ardennes, before the Bulge: 'The Army did not provide us with the proper clothing or boots; so many men got trench foot or froze to death,' he recalled. 'Each time I shave, I cannot help but think of Captain Goodner making the men in our company shave every day, no matter how cold it was, tears freezing in our eyes from the pain of the cold. Other companies were allowed to grow beards but not ours. He did it out of concern for our safety; having a beard would not allow for a good tight seal if we needed to use our gas masks . . . We were given the nickname "Battle Babies" because of our inexperience.'[32]

New Yorker Jerry C. Hrbek was drafted in February 1943 and assigned as a military policeman with 99th Division; on the afternoon of 15 December he was escorting nineteen German prisoners to an old farmhouse near Berg for interrogation. The interrogators, sergeants of the division's G-2 staff, quizzed their captives one by one. On being asked their units, the first four had answered Fifth Panzer Army, but the next one answered he was from the Sixth. Surprised, 'the sergeant behind the table looked up from his writing and asked him again. He got the same answer. Slowly the sergeant stood up and stood there about thirty seconds looking at the man. His open hand shot out and with a thunderous slap he hit the Jerry across the face.' The interrogator thought his prisoner was lying. The twenty-year-old Hrbek, bystanding, complained at the sergeant's behaviour and pointed out, 'We've been getting prisoners from the Sixth Panzer for the last three weeks, one here, two there.' Eventually, six of the nineteen revealed they were from the Sixth Panzer Army, the remainder from the Fifth. The interrogator's reaction was 'it couldn't be, the Sixth Panzers were in Holland', as indeed some of their constituent units had been – once.[33]

Hitler's paranoia about security had forbidden any of the attacking units to venture near the front lines, much less undertake reconnaissance patrols of their future battle terrain, leaving each individual intelligence staff officer (termed the 'Ic') in the dark.

Had they done so, they might have discovered elements of the battle-hardened 2nd Infantry Division lurking on their extreme right flank. Major-General Walter M. Robertson's 'Indianheads' (after their shoulder patch) had landed on Omaha Beach on D+1, fighting through Normandy until arriving in St Vith on 29 September 1944. However, the eyes of his G-2, Lieutenant-Colonel Donald P. Christensen, were elsewhere, for on 11 December two of their three regiments were ordered north to attack and seize the Roer river dams. This left the highly experienced, full-strength 23rd Infantry Regiment on the high ground of the Elsenborn Ridge, whom the Germans mistook for soldiers of the vastly less experienced 99th Division. Among their number, at just twenty-one, was Captain Charles B. MacDonald, commanding 'I' Company, of the 3rd Battalion in 23rd Infantry, who has left us two important accounts encompassing his adventures there and elsewhere.[34]

Gerow's V Corps intelligence staff, led by Lieutenant-Colonel Jack A. Houston and based at the Caserne Antoine in Eupen, recorded vehicular movement south of Düren, while the last tactical reconnaissance reports (on 7 December) observed troop concentrations opposite, but did nothing about them. Aerial reconnaissance patrols – when they could fly (there were no flights on the 13th, as we've noted, due to thick fog) – likewise picked up troop concentrations and camouflaged dumps, but these were assessed as belonging to German units in transit to positions north or south of the Ardennes. On 14 December, Thunderbolt pilot Captain Jack Barensfeld piloted his P-47 over the Eifel Forest – the

German concentration area east of the Our – and encountered a huge amount of anti-aircraft fire coming from what should have been (according to his pre-flight briefing) near-empty woods; it killed one of his wingmen.[35] The 99th's G-2 report, that 'the enemy has only a handful of beaten and demoralised troops in front of us and they are being supported by only two pieces of horse-drawn artillery', lodged firmly in the memory of Captain Charles Pierce Roland, the 3rd Battalion's executive officer (XO) in the same 394th Infantry Regiment as Staff Sergeant Palmer. He and many others were lulled into a false sense of security by the 'fir forests whose cone-shaped evergreens standing in deep snow and sparkling with crystals formed a scene of marvellous beauty'.[36]

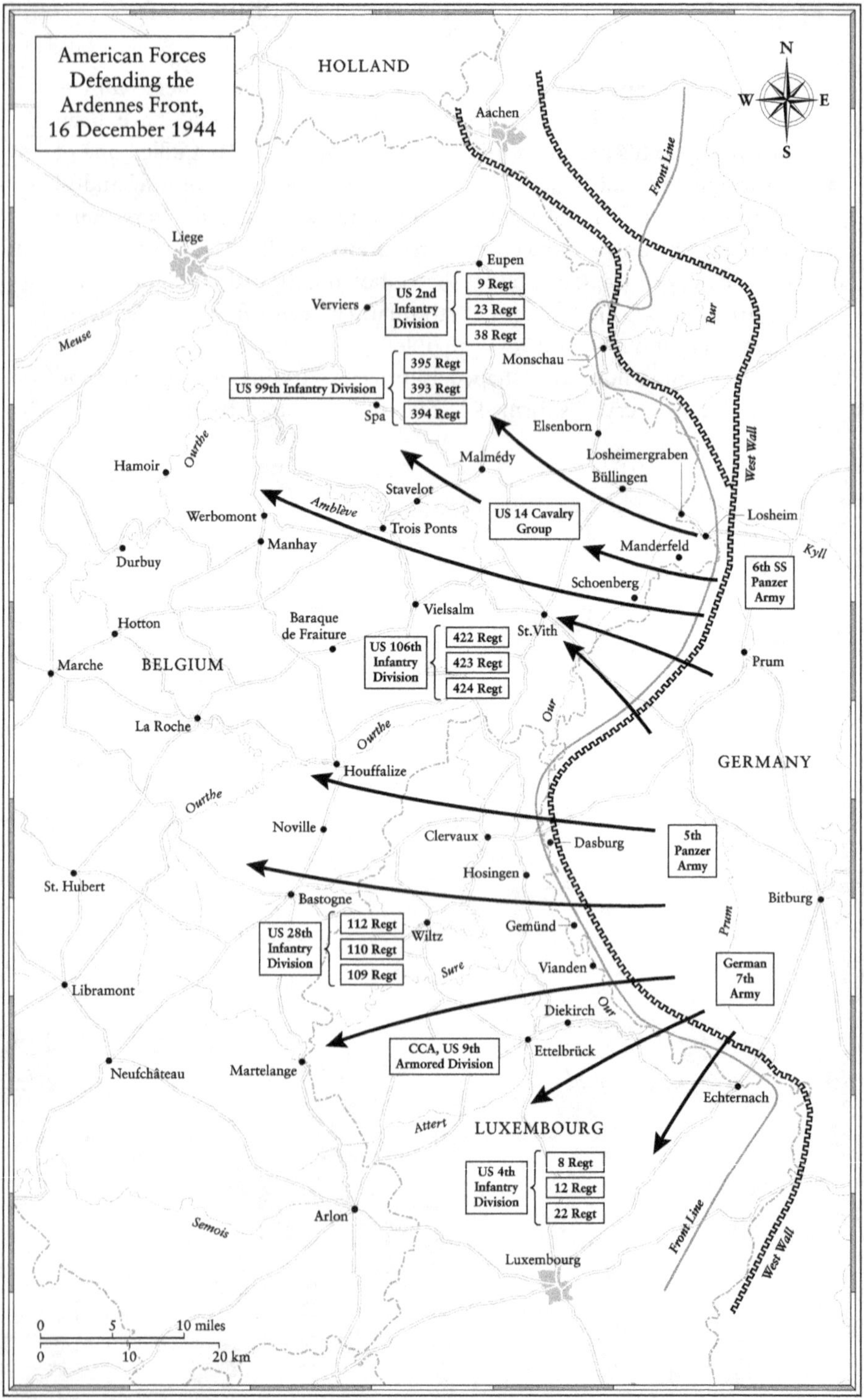
American Forces Defending the Ardennes Front, 16 December 1944
HOLLAND
Aachen
Front Line
Liege
Eupen
US 2nd Infantry Division
9 Regt
23 Regt
38 Regt
Verviers
Meuse
Rur
Monschau
US 99th Infantry Division
395 Regt
393 Regt
394 Regt
Spa
Elsenborn
West Wall
Ourthe
Hamoir
Malmédy
Losheimergraben
Büllingen
Stavelot
Amblève
Werbomont
Trois Ponts
US 14 Cavalry Group
Losheim
Manhay
Manderfeld
Kyll
Durbuy
Schoenberg
6th SS Panzer Army
Vielsalm
Hotton
Baraque de Fraiture
St.Vith
US 106th Infantry Division
422 Regt
423 Regt
424 Regt
Marche
BELGIUM
Prum
La Roche
Our
Ourthe
GERMANY
Houffalize
Ourthe
Noville
Clervaux
Dasburg
5th Panzer Army
Hosingen
St. Hubert
Bastogne
Bitburg
US 28th Infantry Division
112 Regt
110 Regt
109 Regt
Wiltz
Gemünd
Prum
Sure
Vianden
German 7th Army
Libramont
Diekirch
Our
CCA, US 9th Armored Division
Ettelbrück
Neufchâteau
Martelange
Echternach
Attert
LUXEMBOURG
US 4th Infantry Division
8 Regt
12 Regt
22 Regt
Arlon
Semois
Front Line
West Wall
Luxembourg
0 5 10 miles
0 10 20 km
N
W
E
S

11

This is a Quiet Area

JUST AS THE Ardennes offensive was a huge risk for the Germans, its defence was an equal risk for the Allies. On his way from his headquarters to a 7 December conference in Maastricht to decide Allied policy, Eisenhower drove through the Ardennes and immediately noticed how few GIs he encountered en route, a fact he drew to Bradley's attention. The latter justified the thinly held sector by stating he could not reinforce the woodland region without weakening his concentrations in the Roer or Saar. Bradley was gambling on a thin defence of the central Ardennes in order to concentrate Hodges' First Army in the north, ready to punch through to the Roer and the Rhine beyond, at the same time assembling Patton's Third Army to the south, likewise ready to push into the Saar and deep into the Fatherland. It is easy to sympathise with the Twelfth Army Group's commander and difficult to conceive of an alternative policy he might have taken, without jeopardising the two decisive break-in battles to German territory he was about to launch.[1]

The Maastricht policy meeting, held at Simpson's US Ninth Army headquarters, had in fact been demanded by Montgomery who remained unhappy with Allied strategy and was still determined to have his say and push Eisenhower into backing another of his narrow thrusts into Germany, as opposed to Ike's stated broad-front strategy. A Monty 'victory' in realigning Eisenhower's strategy would be at the expense of Bradley's impending Roer attack and that of Patton into the Saar. Thus, there may be merit in the argument advanced by some that Bradley's eyes were so firmly fixed on countering the threat from Montgomery that his gaze was averted from the Ardennes, despite the concerns of Ike and Strong at SHAEF. The resultant 'soggy centre', relatively devoid of GIs, was what Middleton's VIII Corps, with the US 28th Infantry Division to his front, were defending.

Omar Nelson Bradley had turned fifty-one when he was elevated to command 12th US Army Group – as noted earlier, the largest force ever wielded by a US commander. The 'GI's General' (as war correspondent Ernie Pyle dubbed him and he liked to be known) was the epitome of the American dream, being born in a log cabin in Missouri, the only surviving child of a schoolteacher who died when he was fourteen. Bradley entered West Point in 1911 and graduated with his classmate Dwight Eisenhower in 1915; the pair were then obliged (and frustrated) to sit out the First World War in the States. His lucky inter-war career brought him into contact with all the US Army's future leaders. In September 1920 he began a four-year tour of duty as chief weapons instructor at West Point where Douglas MacArthur was Superintendent; he graduated second from the Advanced Infantry Course, behind Leonard Gerow, later V Corps commander; his next appointment, to the Hawaiian Division, brought him into contact with George S. Patton (the divisional G-2) and after Command and General Staff College, Bradley was posted as chief weapons instructor at the Infantry School in 1929, where the Assistant Commandant was George C. Marshall.

Marshall's personal teaching, in part through the informal seminars he conducted for his staff, and the stimulating company of a group of officers devoted to the study of their profession, created a group of future commanders on whom he would come to rely. They included 'Vinegar Joe' Stilwell, Walter Bedell Smith (future SHAEF chief of staff), Matthew Ridgway and J. Lawton Collins. In February 1941, as the US Army was expanding in anticipation of war, Marshall (now army chief of staff) promoted Bradley to brigadier-general (the first of his West Point class to achieve one-star rank), over the heads of many, and sent him to Fort Benning to command the Infantry School. There, Bradley devised the officer candidate school (OCS) model that would serve as a prototype for similar schools across the army. When war came, they would turn out the thousands of platoon commanders needed in an army that eventually fielded eighty-nine divisions; they were known as 'Ninety Day Wonders' after their three-month OCS courses that resulted in a commission.

Two months after Pearl Harbor, Bradley took command of the 82nd Infantry Division. Within four months, at Marshall's behest, he had relinquished the 82nd to Matthew Ridgway (who later converted them to the airborne formation they remain today) and soon found himself in North Africa working for Eisenhower, whom he had occasionally seen but not served with since West Point. This was in the aftermath of the Kasserine Pass debacle, where American units had performed poorly against their more experienced German opponents and received severe criticism from neighbouring British commanders; his task was to serve as Eisenhower's eyes and ears. Ike appointed Bradley as Patton's deputy with the result that when Patton left to plan the Sicily invasion, Bradley took command of II Corps in Tunisia and Sicily.

Afterwards, Ike wrote to Marshall: 'He [Bradley] is in my opinion the best-rounded combat leader I have yet met in our service. He possibly lacks some of the extraordinary and ruthless driving power that Patton can exert at critical moments, [but] he still has such force and determination that even in this characteristic he is among our best.' By this time, Bradley had more combat experience than any other corps commander and this won him command of US First Army for Normandy. On 1 August he assumed command of the twenty-one divisions of US Twelfth Army Group, comprising some 903,000 men, handing First Army to Courtney Hodges but retaining the pick of his First Army staff at his new headquarters.[2]

The bulk of American forces that absorbed the initial German attack comprised Middleton's overstretched VIII Corps of Hodge's First Army. From 4 October, Middleton was based in Bastogne at the Caserne Heintz, built for the Belgian *Chasseurs Ardennais* (the local infantry unit), and subsequently used as barracks for the Hitler Youth. His 68,822 men covered a front of about eighty-five miles, three times the recommended frontage for a corps in 1940s US doctrine. His corps was so extended that he was forced to commit to the front not only his three infantry divisions, but his reconnaissance cavalry and one combat command of 9th Armored, leaving himself with almost no immediate reserves. He had placed the 106th Division, headquartered in St Vith, in the northern part of his front, Major-General Norman 'Dutch' Cota's 28th in the centre, while Combat Command 'A' (the equivalent of a brigade) of the 9th Armored and 'Tubby' Barton's 4th Infantry Division covered the south.

Troy Houston Middleton had turned fifty-five in December 1944,

There was a time in 1944 when nearly every divisional and most corps commanders in Europe had been students of Troy Middleton (1889–1976), the outstanding instructor of his generation at the Command and General Staff School, Fort Leavenworth. One of his star pupils was Eisenhower, who finished first in his year. Middleton had enlisted in the US Army as a private in 1910 and risen via battalion and regimental command to full Colonel in 1918, but quit the military in 1937. Recalled after Pearl Harbor, he was promoted to command VIII Corps in early 1944, taking it to Normandy and the Bulge. Those who had served with him in combat knew him to be tough and unflappable – as his determination to hold on to Bastogne at all costs proved. (NARA)

the same age as Hitler. His seniority, maturity and experience would count for a great deal in the coming days, for he possessed unrivalled combat experience. George C. Marshall described him as 'the outstanding infantry regimental commander on the battlefield in France' of the earlier world war. A Mississippian by birth, Middleton had enlisted in the tiny US Army as a private in 1910 and was selected for officer training two years later. It was his outstanding war record in 1918 that brought him to wide attention; initially he served as a battalion commander with the 4th 'Ivy' Division in the Second Battle of the Marne. Aged twenty-nine, he then commanded a regiment during the

Meuse–Argonne offensive, received a Distinguished Service Medal and was promoted to full colonel. After the war he attended the Command and General Staff School at Fort Leavenworth with fellow classmate George S. Patton; Middleton graduated eighth out of 200, Patton came fourteenth.

Asked to stay on as an instructor, one of Middleton's star students was Eisenhower who, as we have noted, finished first in his year. At one stage in 1944, nearly every divisional and most corps commanders in Europe had been students of his. Middleton progressed on to War College in 1928 and was generally very well liked in the small, almost collegiate, inter-war US Army. However, with the prospects of high command remote and the offer of a lucrative job in the administration of Louisiana State University, he quit the military in 1937. After Pearl Harbor, he was recalled to service in early 1942, commanded the 45th Infantry on Sicily and was promoted to command VIII Corps in early 1944, taking it to Normandy. His steel-rimmed spectacles accentuated the appearance of an elderly college professor, but those who had served with him in combat knew Middleton to be tough and unflappable. He knew all his fellow commanders from previous service and, despite his four years out of the US Army, he was one of the most experienced and well regarded combat leaders it had.[3]

Middleton's corps G-2 in Bastogne, Colonel Andrew Reeves, had actually identified five of the twelve divisions belonging to Fifth and Seventh Armies which were shortly to attack them, including two of the panzer divisions. Sounds of German traffic were reported opposite several division sectors, but the defenders were persuaded that these were incoming units replacing others being moved out. Shallow patrolling, the capture of few prisoners, including several deserters, and repeated entries of 'no change' in divisional G-2 reports confirmed the tendency throughout VIII Corps of passive intelligence collection, accompanied by repeatedly inadequate analysis of the threat. This menace would eventually translate into an eight-to-one advantage in infantry and a four-to-one advantage in tanks for the Germans opposing the US VIII Corps. Middleton's troop strength amounted to the equivalent of roughly one soldier for every two yards of front.[4]

They assumed, but could not prove, their opponents were merely doing what the US Army did – using a quiet area to rest tired formations or bring in new ones, giving them a chance to experience front-line life in a relatively safe zone, before being committed to battle elsewhere.

On 9 December, Reeves circulated his G-2 estimate that their opponents' 'present practice of bringing new divisions to this theatre to receive front line experience and then relieving them out for commitment elsewhere indicates [their] desire to have this sector of the front remain quiet and inactive'.[5] VIII Corps G-2's retained a mental outlook that their opponents did not possess the manpower or material superiority to conduct a major offensive, reflecting the prevailing view, in the words of GI James Madison, that 'the German troops facing us were of low quality and appeared to be of the opinion that if we didn't bother them, they would leave us alone'.[6]

Indeed, it was so relaxed that one night, just before the Bulge began, Private Friedrich Schmäschke of the opposing 352nd *Volksgrenadiers*, found himself with a small squad trying to repair a little generator powered by the waters of the River Our. 'Suddenly we heard voices nearby calling "hello boys!" For a moment we were confused to find Americans facing us. We heard something about "no shooting" but since none of us except the engineer understood English, this meeting with our opposite numbers was extremely brief. After a short chat, we exchanged cigarettes and hastily and mistrustfully parted from each other.' They were so worried about being punished for this fraternisation, Schmäschke remembered, that 'On the advice of one of our men, the cigarettes were taken out of their packs and the empty packs were thrown away or buried.'[7]

Cavalry groups of National Guardsmen were attached to each US Army corps, and Middleton had inserted his into a vulnerable gap on the boundary of V and VIII Corps, the five-mile Losheim Gap. Colonel Mark A. Devine's 14th Cavalry Group comprised the 32nd and 18th Cavalry Reconnaissance Squadrons, each a battalion-sized unit of thirty-eight officers, three warrant officers and 700 enlisted men equipped with M-8 armoured cars and M-5 Stuart light tanks. Devine was a disciplinarian, 'not wholeheartedly accepted by members of his command', who always insisted his men, vehicles and equipment be meticulously clean and, like Montgomery, frowned on anyone smoking in his presence. His place was normally ahead of VIII Corps, providing forward reconnaissance, screening, flank guards, security and liaison. In other words, the Cavalry Group would normally be one of the key sources of intelligence for General Middleton. However, in the Ardennes, due to the widespread shortage of infantry, Devine's Cavalry Group, with 14th Squadron deployed forward and 32nd in reserve, were employed out of their customary role, in defending terrain, and unable to contribute much to the corps G-2 picture. While not exactly veterans, the group had landed in France during September and had seen two months of combat opposite the *Westwall*, from 20 October; however, they had little density of manpower to provide defence in depth, though far greater mobility than ordinary infantry units.

Of Middleton's other formations, the 4th Infantry Division was one of the most experienced in the US Army, having hit Utah Beach at H-Hour on 6 June. Possessing an impressive record from the First World War, the Ivy Division (wordplay on the Roman numerals 'IV' for four) had sailed out of New York on 18 January 1944 for its second European war. For the twenty-one consecutive days after D-Day, the 4th, led by Major-General Raymond 'Tubby' Barton, had pushed inland, capturing Cherbourg but at heavy cost. Breaking out of the beachhead, the 'Ivymen' helped liberate Paris, raced through northern France and Belgium, then moved into the Hürtgen Forest in November, which they soon dubbed the 'Death Factory'. While there, the division again suffered high losses, Colonel Buck Lanham's 22nd Infantry Regiment sustaining a mind-numbing 2,678 casualties in eighteen days – 82 per cent of its authorised strength of 3,257 officers and men. Ernest Hemingway accompanied the 4th, an inspirational figure for the future novelist J. D. Salinger, who at that time was a staff sergeant, responsible for interrogating prisoners. As one of Salinger's comrades recalled, 'The 4th Division anchored the southern hinge of the Bulge in Luxembourg. Its Counter Intelligence Corps (CIC) team numbered about fourteen men, six of whom were located in pairs at each of the three regimental command posts. One of these pairs included Jerry (J. D.) Salinger, who was fluent in French and German.'[8]

'My mental anguish was beyond description,' Lanham wrote of this time just before the Bulge. 'My magnificent command had virtually ceased to exist . . . these men had accomplished miracles . . . my admiration and respect for them was . . . transcendental.'[9] Hemingway, who spent eighteen days under fire in the Hürtgen, later wrote that Lanham was 'the finest and bravest and most intelligent regimental commander I have ever known'. One of Lanham's battalion commanders, Swede Henley, remembered Hemingway: 'He stayed with me in my command post in the front lines in the rain, sleet and snow . . . He carried two canteens – one of schnapps, and the other of cognac.' The writer later fictionalised some of his Hürtgen experiences in his 1950 novel *Across the River and into the Trees.*[10] Hemingway's room-mate and fellow correspondent William Walton published an article on the awfulness of the Hürtgen in *Life* magazine on 1 January 1945, featuring Lanham and Henley, which concluded: 'The only way we can get this thing [the war] over is by killing Krauts.'[11] With many green replacements, Lieutenant George Wilson of Company 'F' in Lanham's regiment worried at how inexperienced his company had become by mid-December – and 'With only four officers and eighty-four men, the company was eighty men short of full strength as well'.[12] The whole of Barton's division was understrength by 2,678 casualties when they deployed to the Ardennes to lick their wounds, taking over positions vacated by the US 83rd Division.

Just before they vacated the area taken over by the 4th Division, Colonel Edwin B. Crabill's 329th Infantry of the 83rd Division in Echternach had a special visitor. She was the former fashion model-turned-acclaimed (and glamorous) war correspondent-photographer Lee Miller, who had followed their war earlier for *Vogue*. Her pen portrait gives us a sense of the oasis of calm in the Ardennes sector: 'The Siegfried Line was just landscape to the unaided eye,' the thirty-seven-year-old Miller wrote in October. 'Through the glasses I could see luscious flat lawns like putting greens. They were the fire areas between the black mushrooms which were gun emplacements – a tank trap accompanied by a gun was at a crossroads and on the horizon was a village which they said was housing two divisions of retreated Huns.' The following day Miller witnessed 'the whole valley echoed with the boom, bark, tattoo and cough of different styles and sizes of weapons' as her companions patrolled the terrain by jeep searching for refugees 'who didn't match the landscape, as they could easily be and often were disguised Krauts'. She later observed, 'Some Tank Destroyer men said they'd been talking and thought it was very good to have me around, as they minded their four-letter language.'[13]

It was only after the Hürtgen, when his unit arrived in Manternach, Luxembourg, on 8 December, that Donald Faulkner in Company 'E' of Lanham's 22nd Infantry took his first bath 'since leaving the USA on 15 September'. It was just a tub in a bombed-out house, fed with hot water from a nearby stove; 'I took off my boots and jumped into the tub, muddy clothes and all.'[14] John H. Kunkel, in Company 'L' of 22nd Infantry, remembered how they all discovered body lice on leaving the forest; the best method to remove the offending creatures was with an old sock dipped into an upturned helmet full of kerosene. By that point, Kunkel recalled, 'we all smelled like Billy goats'.[15] Many of the 4th had been evacuated from sheer combat fatigue to the 622nd Exhaustion Centre near Eupen, where 'they were injected with enough sodium amytal to keep them sleeping for three days, being woken up only for food and in order to carry out their bodily functions. At intervals they were given saline intravenous injections.'[16] Nevertheless, the Hürtgen had taught them much about fighting in wintry woodland against their foes, which would pay off shortly.

Major Frederick T. Kent, the 22nd Regiment's S-4 (logistics and supply officer) had been able to reflect on the lessons of the November battle, and his succinct observations written afterwards betray some of the awful problems his unit had suffered in the forest, '. . . in woods fighting, where artillery and mortar fire is more than normally effective, communications facilities must be reinforced to prevent the possibility of a complete breakdown . . . a unit should be removed from the line when excessive casualties have been suffered, and reinforcements integrated and trained before the unit goes back into combat . . . fragment-proof overhead cover is essential if casualties are to be minimised . . . the effectiveness of armour in woods is greatly reduced . . . the determination of the individual soldier to continue fighting under the worst conditions is the most important factor contributing to success'.[17] Experience like this counted and would save lives in the Ardennes.

Barton had responsibility also for Luxembourg City, where he knew German agents circulated among the German-speaking local population. This offered abundant opportunities for contact with GIs in bars, which the US Counter Intelligence Corps and OSS could do little to prevent.[18] In September the Allies had recaptured the powerful radio transmitters of Radio Luxembourg at Junglinster, which broadcast all over Europe. When they could wrestle airtime away from the US Army ('The Voice of SHAEF') playing forces requests and information messages to loyal civilian listeners, the British Political Warfare Executive (PWE) and Psychological Warfare Branch of the US Office of War Information (OWI) created *Nachtsender* 1212, a 'black' propaganda station. 'Black' referred to a disguised source, in this case the station pretended to be 'Radio Annie', broadcasting from within the Reich. Waveband 1212 proved popular with the Wehrmacht and German civilians alike, transmitting music and news between 02.00 and 06.30 a.m., but interspersing true information reports with false news stories, designed to undermine morale and hasten surrender.[19]

Nevertheless, most daytime programmes from Luxembourg featured Glenn Miller, Perry Como, Nat King Cole, Duke Ellington and Frank Sinatra, but the popular hit tune that third week of December 1944 was 'Don't Fence Me In', sung by Bing Crosby and the Andrews Sisters. The song had come from the motion picture *Hollywood Canteen*, starring Bette Davis, Joan Leslie and Joan Crawford, which was playing to GIs at R and R camps throughout the region. The 115th Anti Aircraft Artillery (AAA) Gun Battalion found themselves protecting the Junglinster site from the Luftwaffe, marvelling at the incongruities of manning their guns one moment, then wining and dining in 'any number of movie houses, cafes, night clubs a fellow could wish to visit. It was incredible . . . In all our travels we had never experienced anything like Luxembourg. It was a beautiful city, relatively untouched by war. Its people were friendly, clean, well dressed and, best of all, many could speak English. It was the closest thing to the States we'd seen.'[20]

Luxembourg itself had military origins. Often known as the 'Gibraltar of the north', from the castle that evolved from Roman days, its name derived from Old German *Lucilinburhuc*, meaning the 'Little Fortress', whose remains still overlook the Alzette river today. The city and other big towns nearby were popular with soldiers, where US-issued cigarettes sold for up to $40 a carton (ten packs) on the black market, or could be traded for other things, principally sex and hard booze. The weekly ration for each soldier was seven packs; he could supplement this by buying more in the PX, at five cents a pack, which he could sell on at $2.40 to $4 on the black market.[21] A five-gallon jerrycan of fuel could fetch 5,000 French francs. Almost anything could be traded, as *Newsweek* reported in January 1945: 'Gasoline trucks are sometimes hijacked (by bands of outlaws) but if the drivers are cooperative they simply drive their trucks into underground garages, sell 1,000 gallons of gasoline for $5,000 or sell the truck as well and pocket another $1,000.'[22] The trucks were then reported as 'stolen' or 'requisitioned by another unit'. Patton's Third Army was notorious for requisitioning fuel (at gunpoint on occasion) from neighbouring friendly forces. The theft of military vehicles reached such proportions that drivers were obliged to remove the rotor arm from the distributor when leaving their vehicles unattended.

Organised crime is clever and never far from a profit: a black market speciality of rotor arms for different military vehicles, principally jeeps and the 6 × 6 'Jimmies' we met on the Red Ball Express developed, where the items sold for $40 apiece.[23] Cigarette theft reached such proportions that in one thirty-day period only eleven million out of seventy-seven million packs of cigarettes destined for US troops in France, Belgium and Luxembourg reached their destination – prompting Eisenhower (himself a chain-smoker on sixty a day) to order an immediate investigation.[24] Cigarettes have remained a hard currency in war, and during the mid-1990s Bosnian war swirling around Sarajevo I witnessed the price of a pack Marlboros climbing to an astronomical $200 on the local black market, presenting many temptations to UN and NATO peacekeeping troops. In 1944 Luxembourg, Staff Sergeant Paul F. Jenkins, a Sherman commander with the 707th Tank Battalion, recalled bribing a waiter, 'you could get all kinds of things: I'd give a bartender two packs of cigarettes (usually Lucky Strikes) and ask, "Where can I get a good steak?" We went back in the kitchen; they had steaks stacked up that high. It was all from horse, but they was steaks. The only thing was, the meat was a little bit coarser than what beef was, but it was good. Anything would be good after C-rations.'[25]

Yet one of the problems was, as Jenkins observed, 'we couldn't tell a German from a Luxembourger'. There were two official languages, German and French, but some locals spoke their own Germanisch dialect, *Letzeburger*. Although the state of Luxembourg, created in 1839 and confirmed as independent in 1867, had remained neutral, it endured invasion and a cruel occupation after May 1940; more than 5,000 of its 300,000 citizens would die in the war. Appropriately, one of the liberators of Luxembourg City on 10 September 1944 was Grand Duke Jean, heir to the Duchy and a tank troop commander in the Irish Guards. He had escaped in 1940, joined the British army as a private, gained a commission and had fought through Normandy. His wartime adventures helped to cement his legitimacy as a future ruler of Luxembourg. The Germans had absorbed the state into the Reich and forcibly conscripted around 5 per cent of the population into the Wehrmacht, hence American concerns. In fact, there was no love lost, for the native language was suppressed, French-sounding names altered, the name Luxembourg ceased to exist, being renamed *Gau Moselland* (Mosel Province), and German law imposed.[26] The Americans assumed there would be a degree of leakage of their own dispositions to the Germans, but this outflow of information went both ways: the neighbourhood *knew* something was afoot. On 14 December, Captain Franklin Anderson of the 4th Division encountered a crowd of agitated civilians over the border, in St Vith; a local explained in English, 'They think the Germans are going to be back here soon . . . [they] always come through the Ardennes. Now there is activity, noise . . . over to the east, and [these people] are worried.'[27]

When on 15 December, at 4th Division headquarters, the G-2, Lieutenant-Colonel Harry F. Hansen, passed on news from VIII Corps of 'large German formations in Bitburg', fearing a raid on Bradley's headquarters in the centre of Luxembourg City, General Barton was savvy enough to order all his men in rest centres back to their posts. This made 4th Division probably the best-prepared US formation before the attack – but even Barton hadn't anticipated a major offensive, and allowed Hansen, his G-2, to depart on a long-planned leave. The following morning, in 4th Division's headquarters log, the entry for 09.00 a.m., 16 December, read 'G-2 left Command Post for a three-day pass to civilisation'. We may speculate as to Hansen's actual destination, but wherever it was, he never got there – for *Herbstnebel* was already under way.[28]

John A. Leonard's 9th Armored Division (the 'Phantom Nine'), were fairly new to France, having shipped over on the *Queen Mary* and landed on 25 September (D+111). The first elements began operations on 23 October, but the entire division would not be committed in their three brigade-sized Combat Commands until the Bulge began. It was only on 10 December that Combat Command 'A' (CCA), including the 60th Armored Infantry Battalion, 19th Tank Battalion and 3rd Field Artillery Battalion, was assigned its own sector of the front, north of 4th Division. Lieutenant-Colonel George Ruhlen, commanding the 3rd FA Battalion, remembered that his guns had 'fired day after day on German transport columns in the Siegfried Line, as well as troop concentrations around Echternach . . . Several times my observers reported the visits of German officers in black leather coats to the bunkers of the Western Wall. We ourselves had picked up three Polish forced labourers and several German runaways who had swum the Sauer to surrender to us. They reported that a gun or tank was hidden under almost every large haystack or barn in the Rhineland, and that fresh German divisions crossed the Rhine almost every night.'[29] Also in CCA was Donald H. Bein, nineteen-year-old PFC who crewed a 57mm gun. In the days before the Bulge, he remembered that every night, between 10.00 and 11.00 p.m., a small

German reconnaissance plane flew over his unit's positions around Luxembourg. Bein reckoned, as the darkened aircraft flew at low altitude, that it was trying to pick out American positions by their lights. 'We called him "Bed Check Charlie".'[30]

Even more recent arrivals into Middleton's VIII Corps were the 'Golden Lions', the nickname adopted by Major-General Alan W. Jones's 106th Division, after their shoulder patch. They were one of the last conscript formations, activated at Fort Jackson, South Carolina, on 15 March 1943, and trained at Camp Atterbury, Indiana, through the spring and summer. Landing on French soil in late November, they deployed straight into the Ardennes from 10 December. Few had ever fired a shot in anger and were even newer to combat than Lauer's greenhorn 99th Division. Some were hopelessly ill-prepared, as a 2nd Division captain recalled when he was asked by a Golden Lions officer for useful combat tips. Noting the Golden Lions GIs toted unloaded rifles, the green officer was told to get ammunition distributed to his men. 'But I don't have orders to distribute any ammunition' was the puzzled response. 'Well, I can tell you from recent experience the soldiers opposite have loaded weapons and know how to use them, whether or not they've been given an order to load,' the veteran replied.[31] With or without ammunition, the 106th would have been heartened as a departing Indianhead of the 2nd Division shouted across to an incoming Golden Lion, 'Lucky guys! You're coming into a rest camp!'[32] Yet, over their first few nights at the front, Jones's outposts reported 'the sound of vehicles all along the front after dark – vehicles, barking dogs, motors', while a wounded prisoner warned of a 'large-scale offensive, employing searchlights against the clouds to simulate moonlight', but in neither case did the 106th's G-2, Lieutenant-Colonel Robert P. Stout, hurry this intelligence up to VIII Corps.[33]

By contrast, General 'Dutch' Cota's 28th, originally Pennsylvania National Guard volunteers, were tough veterans who had arrived in France in July, fought through Normandy at a cost of 2,000 casualties, and – like Barton's 4th – lost far more in the 'Green Hell' of the Hürtgen, for Cota 6,184 during a month. These included 614 killed, 2,605 wounded, 855 missing, 245 captured and 1,865 non-battle losses – more than 750 of which were caused by trench foot. Cota's leadership would prove critical – he himself had been the highest ranking officer on Omaha Beach during D-Day and had rallied many disorganised and scared soldiers and got them off the shingle. His reward was a Distinguished

Service Cross and command of the 28th, replacing Major-General Lloyd D. Brown who had been relieved and demoted for his 'lack of drive'.

December found his formation still recovering from its wounds, absorbing several thousand replacements and defending a twenty-five-mile stretch of the Luxembourg–German border. He put his command post in Wiltz, about twelve miles from the forward lines. As his frontage was too great for a continuous line of resistance, Cota had to place all three of his infantry regiments in the line facing east to the Our river (the actual frontier with Germany). They manned company-sized strongpoints to control the local road network, each based in one of the numerous small villages that dotted the landscape. With so many troops forward, Cota had only a single battalion squirrelled away as his reserve, but putting his men in houses allowed units to rotate soldiers into shelter for rest, minimising exposure to the tough, wintry weather.

Cota's men received much valuable information offered by two plucky Luxembourgers. Marguerite Linden-Meier was one of several civilians seized by a German patrol from US-occupied territory, which had crept over the frontier seeking knowledge of local American dispositions. After questioning by the Wehrmacht and Gestapo about their US Army opponents, then put to work on a German farm, Linden-Meier managed to escape and drift back through the troops gathering for *Herbstnebel*, crossing the lines with the help of the local underground, and reported what she had seen to the American garrison in Vianden. She detailed 'tanks and troops assembled near the border and a German soldier who had proclaimed "By Christmas we'll be in Paris again"'.[34]

More specific intelligence came from another Luxembourg lady, Elise Delé, normally resident in the German-occupied border hamlet of Bivels, but a temporary refugee in US-liberated Vianden, less than two miles to the south. Although the border zone was evacuated and all civilian movement restricted, the front was so thinly held that individuals could freely cross it, especially at night. She had been stopped by the Wehrmacht while crossing the lines to collect clothes from her old home, and taken to Bitburg for questioning. Soon left alone, she simply left town and like Linden-Meier began walking back to the safety of Vianden.

Moving cautiously, she noticed a sharp increase in military traffic, guns and trucks, piles of military equipment under the trees, including 'rows of small boats', and concentrations of troops, some of whom she recognised, from their black collar patches, as belonging to the SS. On the morning of 14 December, two men from the underground rescued her. When she told them what she had seen, they took her straight to Vianden's Hôtel Heintz, where the Intelligence and Reconnaissance (I&R) Platoon of Cota's 109th Infantry Regiment was billeted. Each US infantry regiment maintained an I&R platoon as its eyes and ears; they were a group of twenty-eight men, equipped with seven jeeps crewed by four men each, acting as scouts when in the advance, and intelligence-gathering from a fixed position when static, as in December 1944. The Americans in Vianden showed much interest in Elise Delé's story, and took her to Diekirch for more questioning. From there she was taken to VIII Corps HQ in Bastogne, while a report was transmitted to Dickson's staff at US First Army in Spa. But 'Monk' Dickson was not there – he had departed for a long-delayed visit to Paris.

The night after Elise Delé's arrival in Diekirch, another special guest followed her into town. Ralph Boettcher, a twenty-three-year-old staff sergeant from Illinois, seconded to Civil Affairs in Ettelbrück, was chosen to chauffeur the glamorous arrival around town in a 1939 deluxe model Packard. He drove her to a special party thrown in a Diekirch hotel for men of the 28th Division, and there the sultry Marlene Dietrich and her USO Troupe put on a two-hour Christmas variety show for the boys. During the coming days of battle, Boettcher and his friends would never forget her alluring attire as she sang and danced, flashing her stockinged legs. The following day she was due to perform again for the 99th Division further north in Honsfeld, an appointment that her country of birth managed to cancel.[35]

Many historians have alleged that Colonel 'Monk' Dickson was 'sent', or 'banished' to Paris for a rest, or even 'sidelined, to remove a troublesome character', and allude to a 'hard drinking' habit or 'exhaustion'. The truth was more mundane. Dickson's forty-seventh birthday occurred on 18 December and, having worked solidly at First Army headquarters since landing in France, he was overdue a well-earned break. Unfortunately, electing to head for the French capital shortly after issuing his alarmist 10 December prediction somewhat undermines Dickson's case that he was convinced the Germans were about to attack – he simply wouldn't have left his post at such a vital time. Be that as it may, Linden-Meier's warning appears to have been overlooked, while the report of Elise Delé's adventures was received at the First Army G-2 office just before midnight on 14 December; and there, sadly, it stayed.[36]

Also bound for Paris, and on the same wintry afternoon that found Marlene Dietrich preparing to perform in Diekirch, a single-engined

Noordwyn C-64 Norseman, a small, rugged Canadian-designed aircraft, rose from the ground at RAF Twinwood Farm on the outskirts of Bedford, England. The weather had been deteriorating and the pilot, Flying Officer John R.S. Morgan of the RAF, and his passengers, Lieutenant-Colonel Norman F. Baessell, and a forty-year-old major in the United States Army Air Force who would be awarded a Bronze Star, were in two minds whether to fly or not. A pressing engagement at the Olympia music hall in the French capital persuaded the officers that they ought not to delay and the trio departed in the murk. The major's friend, Don Haynes, waved the trio off from the warmth of his staff car, but the Norseman never arrived for the morale-boosting concert Major Glenn Miller was about to stage for Allied troops. That was the last time anyone saw the world-famous bandleader alive.[37]

Outside the towns and villages, the Ardennes region has changed little since 1944, and this part of the battlefield, overlooking the Our, is no exception. The south-flowing river, shallow and around forty feet wide, is flanked by high-sided banks which were extremely challenging for tank drivers and still make a vehicular approach difficult; there is no natural harbour area along the water's edge. On 13 December, Cota's centre regiment, the 110th Infantry under Colonel Hurley E. Fuller, established their headquarters in the Hôtel Claravallis in Clervaux. Most of his men occupied company-sized positions in the villages that dotted the ridgeline west of the Our, along the ancient north–south road connecting St Vith with Diekirch, dubbed the 'Skyline Drive' (after the famous route built through the Shenandoah National Park by the federally funded Civilian Conservation Corps a decade earlier). To say that Fuller's front was 'extended' would be an understatement: a later observer wrote, 'A man in a jeep could drive along Skyline Drive for *four miles* between strongpoints without encountering any of Fuller's troops'.[38] Yet, it is important to remember that terrain and numbers prevented both sides from maintaining a continuous front line.

This was no reflection on the briar pipe-smoking fifty-year-old colonel, a seasoned veteran of the Argonne who knew his own mind and had a reputation for outspokenness; he was simply making the best of the situation with the forces at his disposal. Overlooking the river itself, each battalion maintained five outposts occupied during daylight hours. In October, Chicagoan Captain Robert E. Merriam was working as a US Army Historian and drove along the Skyline Drive, writing, 'We were riding along the top of a huge ridge, silhouetted in plain view of an enemy no more than eight hundred yards away, guns of the West Wall supposedly bristling behind every bush, and nothing happened . . . We left the ridge road and wound our way into the valley along a narrow secondary road which twisted and turned its way through the thickly wooded hills until it came to a beautiful resort town called Clerf [Clervaux]. There, eight miles behind the so-called front line . . . [was] a rest centre, where the men frolicked, drank beer, flirted with the pretty Luxembourg girls, seduced them when they could, and relaxed from the worries of war.'[39]

Like Rudder's 109th Regiment to the south, many in Fuller's battalions had yet to see a German, or fire a shot in anger, but would soon have to live up to their unit motto '*Cuisque devotis est vis regimenti*' ('The devotion of everyone makes the strength of the regiment'). Pennsylvanian PFC John F. Peters was one of those who already had. Enlisting into the state National Guard in February 1941 before his country was at war, he had started out as a bandsman. When training later on England's Salisbury Plain, the twenty-five-year-old found himself assigned to Company 'E' of the 110th Infantry Regiment, and arrived in time for the Hürtgen campaign. He survived and was jubilant at moving to Clervaux on 13 November, being told this was the tame part of the front; even so, Peters recalled the oddity of seeing no civilians during his time at the front.[40]

To integrate all the replacements, 110th Infantry endeavoured to train while occupying and holding their elongated front. To make matters worse, Fuller was short-handed as his 3rd Battalion had been taken by 'Dutch' Cota as the divisional reserve. Fuller had recently arrived in the 'Bloody Bucket' Division, having had a run-in with his superiors in 2nd Division for speaking his mind and had been relieved. The 110th Infantry was his second chance: even though he knew he was holding the longest front with the fewest resources, but he wasn't going to complain. It was Middleton who had intervened to find another regiment for Fuller. In April 1918 Captain Troy Middleton had taken over his first company in the 4th Ivy Division from a certain Captain Hurley Fuller, 'a cantankerous fellow, but a good fighter' as the future VIII Corps commander remembered of the future 110th Infantry's colonel.[41] Though by all accounts a grouchy character who said exactly what he thought (a trait that not infrequently leads to career suicide), Fuller was a natural pugilist, and pitched right into what was to become one of the Bulge's hottest spots.

Lieutenant-Colonel Daniel B. Strickler, who took over as XO of the regiment on 10 December, remembered, 'I found that the regiment was holding a defensive line of about fifteen miles . . . It was supposed to be a quiet sector as no aggressive fighting by either side had taken place in that area, since the initial push to the German border in September. Most of the officers of the regiment were replacements and likewise the majority of the men were reinforcements having been sent to the regiment after the gruelling battle in the Hürtgen Forest during November'.[42] That awful combat in the forest had battered each of the Bloody Bucket's units: even the Official Historian of the Bulge noted its 'regiments were in pitiable condition' immediately after the campaign.[43]

As Fuller's two infantry battalions, plus regimental staff, totalling perhaps 2,000 would have to contend with the better part of three German divisions, amounting to eighteen battalions, or about 30,000 including other divisional troops, it was thus better that they had no foreknowledge of the coming struggle, faced as they were with well-nigh impossible odds.

Chicagoan Ed Uzemack of the 110th Infantry remembered the third week of December beginning quietly. He watched the Germans opposite his position 'doing pretty much what we were on our side of the river, hanging out personal laundry to dry'.[44] Some noted 'at twilight German women being smuggled into the bunkers and pillboxes of the Siegfried Line for a night of love', while the German observers could watch the GIs queue up in line for chow.[45] The Pennsylvanians of the 28th were focused more on warmth than combat, and generally disinclined to pester the Germans with patrols, hoping their opposite numbers would do the same.[46] In the little town of Hosingen, Lieutenant Thomas J. Flynn, XO of Company 'K' of the 110th, recalled hearing engine noises, 'like the motorcycles used by couriers', from the distant German lines across the River Our. Puzzled, he told his men to 'stay alert'.[47] Some of the more experienced GIs 'sensed' something was wrong. Joe Soya, a company commander in the US 109th Infantry Regiment of Cota's 28th, reported he was 'constantly being hit by reconnaissance patrols and they will not fight . . . they disappear the minute you try to make contact with [i.e. fire at] them'. Furthermore, the same captain observed, 'all night long, the minute it gets dark – they start shooting [to cover] the rumble of heavy equipment – tanks moving around in position and what not . . . something is going on.'

His battalion commander dismissed these concerns with the demeaning retort, 'are you getting nervous?' To this the younger officer responded, 'Look, Colonel, I've been in this damn outfit since St Lô. I've been a rifle company commander in combat in the beachhead . . . so don't tell me I'm getting nervous. I'm just trying to tell you something that should be reported back.' The response – which was echoing from many a higher commander and G-2s across the front – was: 'It can't be, this is a quiet area.'[48]

12

Brandenberger's Grenadiers

TIRED AND UNDERSTRENGTH, Major-General 'Tubby' Barton's US 4th Infantry Division was ordered to garrison the southern Ardennes at the beginning of the month, but it was 13 December by the time they had completed their occupation of positions along a thirty-five-mile stretch of the front. With their left flank adjacent to the 9th Armored Division, only Colonel Robert H. Chance's 12th Infantry Regiment, whose forward line amounted to outposts overlooking the Sauer river, would find itself in the path of the planned offensive. Theirs was the terrain to be attacked by *Volksgrenadiers* of General Erich Brandenberger's Seventh Army, whose aim was to seize and hold ground, then block any US attempt to slice into the southern flank of the panzer armies. However, nowhere else on the Ardennes front was the irrational thinking of Hitler and OKW more in evidence than in their allocation of units to Brandenberger.

His Seventh Army had been reactivated in Stuttgart on 25 August 1939 under General Friedrich Dollmann. Its predecessor had invaded France through Alsace and Lorraine in 1914 and, when most of the Wehrmacht attacked Poland in 1939, Dollmann's Seventh was left manning the *Westwall*. It stayed there in 1940 when Rundstedt, Manstein and Guderian invaded France, belatedly attacking outposts of the Maginot Line just before the Armistice. Seventh was thereafter designated an occupation force, from April 1941 taking responsibility for the defence of Normandy.

The least experienced and most poorly equipped of all German formations by 1944, Seventh's comfortable rear-area life disappeared when the Allies landed on their patch in June 1944. With no experience of any of the blitzkrieg-type invasions of France or Russia, or of fighting the British and Americans in Africa or Italy, and no understanding of the defensive battles in the east, or the threat posed by Allied tactical airpower over the battlefield, Dollmann was rather like his army: out-of-date, ill-trained and unfit for modern war. As Cherbourg fell to the Allies, the sixty-two-year-old Dollmann died from a heart attack on 28 June (although some sources point to suicide, knowing Hitler's wrath at the capture of this key port), after not quite five years in command. Despite the efforts of his successors, SS General Paul Hausser and Panzer General Heinrich Eberbach, most of the Seventh were killed or captured in Normandy, with very few escaping from the Falaise Pocket. After Eberbach's unlucky capture (by a British forward patrol as he was on the point of evacuating his HQ in Amiens), the autumn of 1944 found Seventh Army reinforced, lurking behind the Siegfried Line under a new commander, and designated with a role in the forthcoming winter offensive.

The fifty-two-year-old, bespectacled Brandenberger (actually he wore pince-nez, like President Roosevelt or Heinrich Himmler, which clipped on to his nose) possessed little charisma, but was thoroughly competent, having served with Bavarian artillery units in the First World War and spent most of the inter-war period in staff and training posts. He had been chief of staff of border troops on the *Westwall* in 1939, and had gone on to command 8th Panzer Division with great distinction for two years in Russia, which won him a Knight's Cross and first brought him to Hitler's attention. He progressed to leading two army corps, winning Oak Leaves for his *Ritterkreuz* in November 1943. In Hitler's eyes, his stock was elevated also because he lacked the aristocratic background of so many of his contemporaries. It was his confidential personnel report that won Brandenberger his army command: 'Gifted militarily, full of foresight, and very active, he filled his divisions with action and passion. A very experienced combat leader, even in the worst circumstances he always improvised and mastered the situation. *Excellent National Socialist behaviour*.'[1] Whether true or not, the last four words, one feels, were the most important of the whole assessment.

Nonetheless, Brandenberger irritated his superior, Model, who referred to him as 'the professor, a typical product of the general staff system', but the latter was a harsh taskmaster and fell out with most officers

Appointed to command the Seventh Army on 3 September 1944, Erich Brandenberger (1892–1955) was an old Russia hand, having led armoured divisions and corps on the Eastern Front. A former Kriegsakademie instructor, he was methodical rather than flashy, and earned his army on account of his confidential personnel report which concluded 'a very experienced combat leader, even in the worst circumstances he always improvised and mastered the situation. *Excellent National Socialist behaviour*'. (Author's collection)

during his career. The Army Group 'B' chief saw his job as to deliver, not to be liked. His subordinate Brandenberger was not a flashy army commander, nor inclined to stamp his own personality on his commands, as did Manteuffel on his Fifth Panzer, Montgomery with Britain's Eighth Army or Patton with the US Third. For one thing, he had no time, officially taking over on 3 September, but also he had few troops. To observers, the four divisions plus supporting arms he possessed, totalling perhaps 50,000 men, would constitute merely a corps, scarcely an army. Another challenge for him was that all of his formations were recently raised, meaning none of the new Seventh Army had worked together before; Fifth and Sixth Armies were different, being built around a core of long-established units, with a proven track record.

Field Marshal Model's orders, issued on 27 October to an incredulous Brandenberger and his chief of staff, Oberst Rudolf Freiherr von Gersdorff, were the first hint they had that their formation was going over to the attack. With the focus of *Herbstnebel* weighted to the north, Seventh Army was assigned the role of southern flank protection. For this they were allotted initially two army corps, each of two infantry divisions, with the promise of further support, including panzers. The highly competent, Kriegsakademie-trained Gersdorff was a complicated character. An aristocratic former cavalry officer of the old school, he had won a Knight's Cross for guiding what remained of the Seventh out of the Falaise Pocket that August. He was also part of the Stauffenberg plot, a fact he miraculously managed to keep secret during the era of subsequent repercussions. With what must have been divided loyalty by October 1944 (which side did he really want to win?), Gersdorff set about planning his Army's part in *Herbstnebel.*

Model ordered that Seventh Army was 'to protect the flanks of the operation on the south and south-west . . . It will break through the enemy positions . . . and build up a defensive front . . . Using vanguard units of its *Volksgrenadier* divisions, the right wing will maintain contact with the Fifth Panzer Army.' This immediately gave Brandenberger cause for concern, for how on earth were his *Volksgrenadiers* (only some of whom had bicycles for mobility) to keep up with Manteuffel's much faster panzers?

Model's instructions continued, 'By energetic thrusts to the south and south-west using any favourable opportunities, Seventh Army will gain time and ground to build up a strong defensive front, carrying out intensive destruction and minelaying in front of its lines.' Once the Allies had started to react to *Herbstnebel*, Brandenberger and Gersdorff realised, their formation would become the punchbag of Patton's counter-attacking Third Army. The orders went on: 'The most important task . . . is the destruction of enemy artillery units stationed to the south . . . It will be necessary to provide fully adequate matériel and units for blocking purposes, as well as anti-tank weapons.'[2]

Brandenberger's three years' experience of commanding panzer divisions and corps on the Eastern Front provided him with insights into the problems he would almost immediately encounter in the Ardennes. As he had taught prospective staff officers to do, when an instructor at the Kriegsakademie in 1932–3, he analysed the US Third Army's capabilities and equipment, as well as its aggressive commander. He assessed correctly that Patton would counter-attack very quickly – much faster than OKW anticipated – and was concerned that the Seventh had been allocated no tanks at all with which to halt and drive back any American assaults. Model's requirement of 'units for blocking purposes' was a euphemism for a mobile armoured reserve to counter Patton's tanks, and Seventh possessed none.

On 3 November, at one of the many planning conferences attended by the three army leaders, Brandenberger, Dietrich and Manteuffel, the latter echoed the Seventh Army's concerns; 'I don't think we need anticipate a strong reaction coming from the north, or the east bank of the Meuse, but I am rather worried by the possibility of strong enemy counteraction from the south', meaning, of course, Patton's Third Army. Generaloberst Jodl tried to reassure him that 'General Brandenberger will have six infantry divisions and one of panzers in his Seventh Army to cover the southern and southwestern flanks'. Manteuffel countered wisely, 'Yes, I know, but I have to anticipate strong enemy forces – maybe even the bulk of his [Patton's] forces – in action in the Bastogne area by the evening of the third day of our attack.'

In the event, Manteuffel only slightly overestimated Patton, but it was clear that it was the US Third Army's commander whom the *Herbstnebel* planners considered their greatest threat. General Brandenberger later recalled his conclusion that a southern counter attack 'would probably be commanded by General Patton, who . . . had given proof of his extraordinary skill in armoured warfare, which he conducted according to the fundamental Guderian concept, made it quite likely that the enemy would direct a heavy punch against the deep flank of the German forces . . .'[3] Hitler and Jodl were unruffled at these concerns, partly because they had reasoned the Western Allies would be so off-balance and weighed down with bureaucracy that their decision-making and reactions, in mid-winter just before Christmas, would be slow. Hitler was also convinced the Allies would first deploy reinforcements along the west bank of the Meuse rather than boldly attack either flank.

Sworn to secrecy by *Sippenhaft*, prevented from sharing these plans with all but a trusted few subordinates at this stage, and forbidden to drive forward and make any form of reconnaissance, Brandenberger and Gersdorff conducted map exercises to identify their options. They knew straightaway that climate and terrain were against them: two of the very factors upon which Hitler was counting. The thick fogs of the season, morning mists rising from the rivers and low-lying ground, together with the hills, woods, steep gorges and a difficult road network would play into the hands of the American defenders (however few there were) and make their own going slow. With Seventh's limited engineering resources, 'intensive destruction and minelaying', as well as the provision of 'units for blocking purposes', were considered impossible tasks. They realised also that the fast-flowing Our and Sauer rivers which ran across their front would be swollen in December by rain and the first snowmelt, presenting a particular challenge to their meagre bridging units.

In fact, Seventh Army possessed only one bridge-building battalion and five bridging columns. The former, 900-strong, was trained to construct crossings under fire, while the latter was a 100-man unit of two platoons, equipped with bridging parts and pontoons, that constructed and operated vehicle ferries. By comparison, Sixth Panzer Army in the north deployed six bridging battalions and nine bridging columns. Furthermore, all Seventh Army's potential bridging sites were obvious to their opponents and preregistered by US artillery – hence the emphasis in Model's order to ensure 'destruction of enemy artillery units'. Speer's civilian bridging experts would prove of only limited value under these conditions. Likewise, Brandenberger knew the dangers from the air; whereas Dietrich's Sixth Army had the four regiments of 2nd *Flak* Division (164 anti-aircraft guns), the entire Seventh Army could draw only on the protection of the Luftwaffe's *Flak*-Regiment 15, with sixty AA guns, though around half were the powerful 88mm, equally deadly to Allied tanks and aircraft.[4]

General Brandenberger's main combat power rested on the four infantry divisions he would deploy in his attack. As with so many other aspects of the German army, the 20 July 1944 attempt had acted as a spur for Hitler to reorganise his infantry. Cumulatively, the Wehrmacht had lost 1.8 million killed by 1944, of whom 4.5 per cent were officers. Almost as many again had been posted as missing or were prisoners of war; neither of these totals included the wounded. In June, July and August 1944 alone, the Wehrmacht had been deprived of forty-four divisions with the destruction of Army Group Centre during Operation Bagration in the east, in Italy, and the disaster of Normandy. To these could be added another 200,000 men, whom Hitler had ordered to defend the French ports and Channel Islands, manpower and equipment that were now completely surrounded and impotent.[5] Not only did these lost formations need replacing, but on 6 September Hitler and Jodl had discussed the creation of an *additional* operational reserve of around twenty-five divisions for his Ardennes offensive.

When Himmler seized his chance to control the *Ersatzheer* (Reserve Army) on 21 July 1944, in place of Stauffenberg and his fellow plotters, he also assumed responsibility for raising new army units and training them. This was empire-building on the part of the Reichsführer-SS, for he saw an opportunity to finally 'Nazify' the German army. His partner in this enterprise was propaganda chief Josef Goebbels. Earlier in 1944 the latter had already seen the need to shake Germany into a (belated) mobilisation of all resources for a 'total war' – something his British, Russian and US opponents had done from the outset. On 18 February 1944, in a passionate speech at the Sports Palace in Berlin, Goebbels had advocated the complete devotion of the Reich's economy and society towards the war effort. He argued that if they did not prevail in Russia, then Germany would fall to Bolshevism, and the rest of Europe would follow. 'Two thousand years of Western history are in danger,' he screamed.

Supporting Himmler's recruitment drive, Goebbels now saw his chance to move to a total war footing, shutting theatres and universities, mobilising youth to work in the Red Cross or help with air defence, and – finally going against the Nazi creed – encouraging women to become part of the war effort, too. In July 1944 some 500,000 German women were still working in domestic service, when their Allied counterparts, typified by 'Rosie the Riveter' in the USA, were working in armaments factories. Hitherto their role had been to stay at home and bring up children for the Reich, even encouraged to do so with the award of a 'Mother's Cross' for bearing large families. The army, meanwhile, was forced to identify itself totally with the state, to prevent a repetition of 20 July. Goebbels' Party newspaper, *Völkischer Beobachter*, echoed this on 3 August with an editorial stating 'True marriage between Party and Wehrmacht has today become a living reality . . . The Army that will win this war will be a National Socialist People's Army.'[6]

Between them, Himmler and Goebbels established that all new infantry formations raised after July 1944 were labelled *Volksgrenadier*. The title embraced both the political notion of the *Volk* ('People'), and the older, distinguished notion of the Grenadier, a term that harked back to the days of Frederick the Great. Thus, the concept was designed to appeal to modernists and traditionalists.[7] Nineteen such divisions were created by order on 31 August 1944, another seventeen on 9 October and seven more before the end of the month; a total of forty-three fresh formations must have seemed like a heaven-sent miracle with which to prosecute the war. From where did this manpower suddenly appear?

Himmler, controlling recruitment, had created mobile drafting units, *Heldenklaukommandos* (literally 'hero-snatching units'), press gangs who searched the Reich for manpower. Although there was fierce inter-service rivalry between the German army, navy and air force, the Luftwaffe could no longer justify the 1.9 million personnel on its books in the summer of 1944, nor did the Kriegsmarine have jobs for all the 700,000 men they employed at the same time. Neither organisation, in any case, was prepared to argue with the Reichsführer-SS. Similarly, the *Ersatzheer* was already responsible for some 2.4 million soldiers, a quarter of the Wehrmacht's total strength. The majority were on courses or under some form of education or instruction, so training periods were abbreviated. The Reserve Army also administered the wounded, many of whom were on convalescent leave: they were called back to duty or had their recovery periods shortened. These were all veterans, although in some cases physically or psychologically exhausted.[8] Speer and Goebbels also assessed that 3.2 million men were working in government administration and industry, some of whom could be diverted to the army.

With health and fitness entry requirements for army personnel also relaxed, Himmler's commandos, local party officials and hospitals (which were forced to discharge wounded soldiers earlier than hitherto) filled the new divisions with a mix of older, poorly trained fortress troops withdrawn from garrisons elsewhere; Kriegsmarine sailors who no longer had vessels to crew or maintain; Luftwaffe ground personnel now redundant given the paucity of aircraft; able-bodied civilians 'combed out' of jobs in industry; older men exempted from war service because of large families or their farms; railway workers who were replaced by women; and new age groups, born in 1926–7, mobilised on reaching seventeen or eighteen. Some of the latter, as we saw with Grenadier Werner Klippel at Hotton, were as young as sixteen.

Ethnic German men, the *Volksdeutsche*, were also regarded as fair game for military service and conscripted. These population groups, who lived beyond the borders of the Reich, included Czechs, Slovaks, Danes, Poles, Ukrainians, Hungarians, Romanians, Slovenians from Yugoslavia, and Baltic Germans from Estonia, Latvia and Lithuania, whose ancestry might, once upon a time, conceivably have been German or Austro-Hungarian; they might not even speak German, but looked Germanic, were suspicious of Britain and the United States, and hated

Communism. By 1944, approximately 100,000 *Volksdeutsche*, 10 per cent of whom were Ukrainians, were already working alongside 500,000 Germans in Luftwaffe air defence. From January 1943 *Hitlerjugend* (HJ – Hitler Youth) boys, aged fifteen or over, and from 1944, *Bund Deutscher Mädel* (BDM – 'League of German Girls') girls, could be called up to work as *Flakhelfer*, releasing further manpower for the *Volksgrenadier* divisions.

By this stage of the war, some of these *Volksdeutsche* would also be conscripted into the Waffen-SS divisions that deployed to the Bulge. Several frontier provinces of Belgium, France and Luxembourg were forcibly absorbed into the state, making their citizens German and thus liable for service. In many cases, their reliability would prove questionable, though this could sometimes be offset by good leadership. Such a blend of backgrounds, nationalities, ages and experience hardly made for homogenous units.

By mid-1944, the huge number of *Luftwaffenhelferinnen*, female assistants in the Luftwaffe, and other girls called up to work as *Flakhelfer*, enabled valuable air force manpower to be re-roled as infantry in the *Volksgrenadier* divisions for the coming offensive. (Author's collection)

Training such groups was Obergefreiter (a lance corporal of several years' service) Günter Koschorrek, a wounded and much decorated Eastern Front veteran, who noted in his diary on 9 October, 'the rabble to be trained in our company consists of a mix of older East Europeans of German ethnic descent, most of whom were heads of families, and naval personnel, who because of the shortage of ships are to be retrained as tank infantry. Because of the undisciplined attitude of the sailors, many of whom had served in the Kriegsmarine for years, instructors who were highly decorated combat veterans were preferred because these were the only people the sailors would respect. Even so, it was not always easy for us instructors to find the right tone of voice to use in order to get the message across to this group.'[9]

Whereas the old *Ersatzheer* under Stauffenberg and his boss, Generaloberst Friedrich Fromm, had turned out 60,000 new soldiers a month, by the end of August Himmler had assembled 450,000 new grenadiers.[10] It was a stupendous achievement. Not all became infantrymen, for Himmler created or redesignated other units to become *VolksArtillerie* corps (heavy artillery groups attached to army corps) and *VolksWerfer* brigades, which operated the Wehrmacht's multi-barrelled rocket launchers, known to the Allies as 'screaming minnies' but to the Germans as *Nebelwerfers*.

To lead all these *Volks*-titled organisations, Himmler could draw from a large pool of experienced combat leaders, like Koschorrek, all highly decorated and given accelerated promotion. The posting of officers to the *Volks* units was initially delayed, because Himmler insisted on his own vetting procedure, to ensure his new formations were led by true National Socialist fanatics. Practicality overtook this Himmlerian fantasy and the measure soon lapsed. Throughout the war a very high number of German commanders perished while leading their men in combat, in sharp contrast to the Anglo-American forces where this happened comparatively rarely. Experience of the First World War, which killed many battalion and brigade leaders, persuaded the Allied armies that commanders had a role out of the line of fire, directing the battle, rather than getting their heads blown off. German leadership culture dictated otherwise, as this pre-battle order, issued on 20 November 1944, reminded officers: 'Commanders up to and including divisional commanders should be where they can obtain the best overall view of the battlefield, where they can intervene personally at a moment's notice. They must not only lead their men, but . . . direct the extensive and varied fire of supporting weapons. We still attack too much with our legs and not enough with our weapons.'[11]

This debate, as to where a field commander should be, has still not been resolved, despite many advances in military technology and communications. A battalion CO killed in the British 1982 Falklands campaign was posthumously blamed for leading a failed attack which rendered his battalion leaderless, while another who died in 2009 was similarly criticised for being in the lead vehicle of his battlegroup in Afghanistan, instead of further back. Neither observation constitutes a slur on the reputation of a brave officer, but underlines the tension in all modern armies today as to how far forward a tactical commander should place himself.

Unsurprisingly, given Himmler's obsession with his pagan quasi-religion, Protestant and Catholic chaplains were left out of the *Volksgrenadier* order of battle, while a *Nationalsozialistischer Führungsoffizier*, or Nazi Guidance Officer, effectively a political commissar, was introduced instead. Their job was to deliver morale-building lectures to the troops and furnish independent reports on the loyalty of their commanders. They were inexperienced, zealous and universally resented. Many senior commanders after the war recalled with bitterness the ability of these quite junior Nazis to be able to overrule their decisions.

In 1944, German divisions were frequently commanded by an *Oberst* (colonel); regiments – the equivalent of a British brigade – led by an *Oberstleutnant* (lieutenant-colonel) or a *Major*; battalions by a *Hauptmann* (captain); and companies by a *Leutnant* (lieutenant), in each case a grade or two lower than their Allied opponents. This partly reflected necessity, but also that German combat arms were lean, efficient and needed fewer officers because more weight was thrust onto the shoulders of NCOs, the *Fronthasen* ('front hare') – a euphemism for a veteran soldier. In the German army system every officer migrated through the ranks, serving as a corporal and sergeant first, so the calibre of NCOs was generally very high. In March 1944, General Wilhelm Burgdorf, head of the Army Personnel Office, outlined the Reich's expectations of its leaders: 'The Führer wants soldiers who distinguish themselves by their courage [and] willingness to assume responsibility . . . but the most decisive factor of all is . . . the ability to command; social origins or educational background should not even be taken into consideration . . .'[12]

At the other end of the spectrum, basic training for new recruits had shrunk from sixteen weeks in 1938 to twelve by early 1944. With little ammunition to spare for recruits and time in short supply before the Bulge, such was the requirement for fresh divisions that some *Volksgrenadier* units were raised and sent to the front in *six weeks*. The reality was that those personnel already in the forces, such as re-roled Luftwaffe aircraft mechanics and Kriegsmarine sailors, were lucky if they had a month in which to reskill and learn the basics of fieldcraft before being committed to battle as a *Landser*. This term, used universally throughout the Reich for any soldier, was a corruption of the old German *Landsknecht*, the trooper of the Thirty Years War, and akin to GI Joe, the French *grognard* (literally 'grumbler') or British Tommy Atkins. Although the arrival of all these fresh divisions seemed impressive, on being reappointed to OB West in September 1944 Rundstedt immediately warned OKW that 'the state of training of the newly-arrived *Volksgrenadier* divisions is poor due to insufficient time dedicated to instruction. Greater in-depth training has been disrupted by the constant commitment of . . . weapons schools to the fighting.'[13]

To a certain extent it was all smoke and mirrors for Hitler's benefit, because these new formations did not represent the full-strength units that had previously featured on the Wehrmacht's order of battle. A glance at the map table in the *Wolfsschanze* would be misleading; although the number of units represented might be as high as ever, the combat capability of each was lower. A *Volksgrenadier* division, for example, had a nominal strength of 10,072 men in three regiments of two battalions each. Instead of a reconnaissance battalion with armoured cars and motorcyclists, *Volksgrenadiers* had an *Aufklärungskompanie* (reconnaissance company), equipped with bicycles (quite what they were intended to achieve on a 1944 battlefield is anyone's guess). The main combat power of previous German divisions had rested on their nine infantry battalions; now there were only six. By November 1944, the average divisional strength was 8,761, nearly half of the September 1939 figure of 16,626. For comparison, the average US divisional strength, in January 1945, taking into account casualties, was around 13,400.

However, there was nothing standard about the *Volksgrenadier* order of battle and some divisions, for example the 212th, were lucky to retain a *seventh* infantry battalion, 500- or 600-strong, traditionally used for divisional reconnaissance. This was always called the Fusilier Battalion, and harked back to an older military tradition; but for most divisions this was reduced to a single 200-man Fusilier Company. The use of older military terminology was to suggest strength which simply did not exist. Besides the loss of three battalions, *Volksgrenadier* divisions also suffered a dilution of their remaining six, losing mostly logistics and administrative personnel, although this served to increase the proportion of combat versus service troops to around 80 per cent. In 1939 infantry battalions boasted a theoretical strength of twenty-three officers and 800 NCOs and men; by late 1944 this had shrunk to fifteen officers and 700 NCOs and men, but in practice they were lucky to achieve five officers and 500 NCOs and men.

By way of compensation for their fall in manpower, there was a greater allocation of automatic weapons. The mainstay of this was the arrival into *Volksgrenadier* arsenals of the *Maschinepistole*-44, the world's first modern assault rifle, alternatively known as the *Sturmgewehr.* With its signature curved magazine holding thirty rounds, the MP-44 was the direct ancestor of the famous Kalashnikov AK-47, the US M-16 and all modern self-loading, automatic-fire rifles. Nearly 500,000 MP-44s had been manufactured by the war's end, used predominantly by the *Volksgrenadiers*, its metal stampings and wooden stock making it cheap and quick to assemble. It was designed to replace the standard bolt-action, five-round 7.92mm K-98 Mauser rifle, first introduced to the German soldier in 1898 (and which I witnessed being used by Bosnian Croat soldiers in the mid-1990s).[14]

Each infantry company was meant to possess two platoons' worth (about fifty) of MP-44-equipped grenadiers and one of Mauser-clutching riflemen. Although slightly heavier than the Mauser, the MP-44's main drawback was the same as the 7.92mm MG-42 machine-gun with which the *Volksgrenadiers* were also furnished. 'Their MG-42 machine-guns could fire 1,500 rounds a minute,' remembered 2nd Infantry Division Sergeant Joseph Jan Kiss, Jr. 'It scared the holy hell out of us. It was a vicious, wicked gun. Just went *BBRRRRUUPPP.* We called it "Hitler's saw". Our air-cooled only fired 600 rounds a minute.'[15] Yet the high rate of automatic fire of the MG-42 and MP-44 (500–600 rounds per minute) meant an excessive consumption of ammunition, which was always in short supply. These weapons did, to a certain extent, offset the lack of *Volksgrenadier* numbers (an MP-44 had twenty times the firepower of a Mauser), but they couldn't make up for the lack of combat experience.

All German divisions were graded periodically by their higher commanders as to their readiness and capability, according to a scale of *Kampfwert* (combat performance), from I to IV. It is telling that at the time of *Herbstnebel*, no *Volksgrenadier* division in the west was rated *Kampfwert* I (able to perform an all-out attack); some were *Kampfwert* II (capable of limited offensive actions) most were III (fit for mobile defence) and a few IV (fit only for static defence). This was no slur on their enthusiasm, but a reflection of several factors, revolving around their mobility and equipment. While the panzer and Waffen-SS divisions possessed the lion's share of half-tracks and trucks, all *Volksgrenadier* units relied on horses to tow equipment and supplies across the battlefield. In the summer of 1944 the Wehrmacht had lost 250,000 horses, which greatly affected its mobility. In an effort to restore some degree of mobility, one *Volksgrenadier* battalion in six was bicycle-mounted, a pathetic acknowledgement of how immobile the infantry arm had become. A couple of days into the Bulge, one GI specifically remembered that 'Every fourth or fifth German [we captured] carried about a five-and-a-half inch hose. We wondered why. Then it dawned on me – it was to siphon gas from disabled vehicles; they were short of gas.'[16]

Another way to compensate for the smaller infantry divisions was to attach to their parent army corps a generous quantity of artillery. There were *VolksArtillerie* formations available to the Seventh, but, as with engineers and air defence, Sixth Army in the north had the lion's share. Whereas Dietrich had three corps of 'People's Artillery', totalling 685 gun barrels, 180 of them over 150mm calibre, Seventh were allotted two *VolksArtillerie* corps, comprising 319 guns, of which only 76 were over 150mm. The bigger the calibre, the heavier the shell, and its concomitant destructive power, so here, too, Brandenberger lost out. Seventh's *VolksArtillerie* units included guns, mostly captured in Russia, of no fewer than eight different calibres – a quartermaster's nightmare. Formations obviously work much better with a consistency of weapons and ammunition throughout.[17]

The Wehrmacht was also generally at a disadvantage when it came to communications. The standard army man-pack field radio was in very short supply, heavy and required two men to carry all its components. Issued as a couple of cumbersome steel boxes weighing over forty pounds apiece, the VHF portable field transceiver was developed in 1936–9 and obsolete by 1944. The same held true for tank radios, which in any case were hampered by the screening effect of the trees and geology of the region. All required many components made of raw materials that were in short supply by 1944. The Wehrmacht never had the chance to revisit their pre-war designs and found that US radios were generally lighter, more robust in the field, and, of course, mass-produced. As with many things, the US Army had out-engineered their opponents by 1944, producing field equipment of far superior quality.[18]

Wehrmacht wireless equipment was only issued at company level, while platoons and squads had no direct means of wireless contact. In contrast, every American rifle platoon possessed the superb SCR (Signal Corps Radio)-536: the walkie-talkie, which weighed around five pounds and had a range of one mile. The positive side of the lack of low-level signals equipment was that junior German commanders were required to develop a higher degree of initiative, rather than wait for orders, as was the tendency in the top-down culture of British and American units. Such independence, however, came at the cost of situational awareness. Instead,

The need for real-time direction of artillery and mortar fire was paramount in the Ardennes. German wireless sets were heavy, cumbersome and obsolete by 1944, and they preferred instead to rely on field telephones, connected by miles of cable, which were effective in defence but useless in attack. On the other hand, in the SCR-536, the US Army found a battle-winner. Originally designated the 'handie-talkie', it was more popularly known as the 'walkie-talkie'. Weighing five pounds, its one-mile range was often restricted by the Ardennes terrain to a few hundred feet, but it provided great situational awareness for US infantry squads, platoons and companies. (NARA)

for communications downwards, a *Kompanietrupp* (company headquarters group) had three *Melder* (messengers), mounted on bicycles if necessary, to relay orders to each *Zug* (platoon). This was one of the most dangerous tasks in a battalion, and frankly should not have been necessary in the 1940s era of wireless radios; it was, as we have seen, a role Hitler had performed in 1914–18 for which he won his Iron Crosses.

Wherever possible, German units relied on field telephones, which worked well in static defence but not in the kind of rapid advance envisaged by *Herbstnebel*. This affected forward artillery observers, who were deployed, but not in the quantities used by US forces. Thus, advancing *Volksgrenadiers* could not reply on timely fire support to the extent of their opponents. At short range, they made extensive use of flare pistols, sending up combinations of coloured flares to initiate quick bombardments. An indication of the obsolescence of communications equipment was that their standard means of transport was a horse-drawn signals wagon.

Kanonier Emil Frie of the 18th *Nebelwerfer* Brigade observed that in peacetime his launchers were towed by half-tracks, as here, but by December 1944 his unit had one Opel truck to tow three launchers, and sometimes his chief's *Kübelwagen*, making them look 'like a circus'. (Author's collection)

Seventh Army could also call on the 8th and 18th *VolksWerfer* brigades, which fielded 108 *Nebelwerfers* – those 'screaming minnies' of various calibres, but, again, Dietrich's Sixth Panzer Army in the north had managed to grab three brigades, with 340 of the multi-barrelled rocket launchers.[19] In Seventh Army, seventeen-year-old Kanonier Emil Frie had been drafted into the third battery of the 18th Brigade in April that year and had since learned how to launch and direct his *Nebelwerfer* rockets, which were effective to around four miles. They were fired from a group of five barrels, mounted on a pair of pneumatic tyres. Each 150mm rocket was carried by one man, but the larger 210mm warheads were a four-man lift. Frie recounted how each launcher was pulled by an Opel Blitz truck, which carried the crew of an NCO and five men, their baggage and the rockets. In peacetime the launcher was towed by a half-tracked vehicle but by December 1944 only the faithful Opel was available: 'it often happened that one truck towed three launchers . . . Sometimes the VW *Kübelwagen* used by the chief of the unit was also hitched on behind. The whole train then looked more like a circus and had little in common with a dangerous military unit.'[20] Lack of vehicles and especially petrol hampered the artillery and rocket troops, as well as the tanks.

The cutting edge of both Fifth and Sixth Panzer Armies would rest on the four armoured divisions and several independent battalions of panzers that Manteuffel and Dietrich each possessed, yet Seventh Army owned not a single tank whatsoever. All it had were their divisional *Panzerjäger* (anti-tank) battalions. These included a company of tracked, turretless armoured vehicles – little four-man *Sturmgeschütz* (literally 'assault gun', and abbreviated to StuG) or *Hetzer* ('Baiter') tank destroyers, both carrying a 75mm gun and built on to a tank chassis. This equated to between six and fourteen vehicles per anti-tank battalion.[21] Lightweight compared to tanks (a StuG weighed twenty-nine tons, a *Hetzer* half that), they were effective in defence, but the limited traverse of their main gun, having no turret, made them very vulnerable in attacks of the kind envisaged by *Herbstnebel*. American tank men regarded these as 'an interminable viper slinking across the terrain' by comparison to a 'tyrannosaurus of a King Tiger, which was too big and too dumb to succeed, and sloshed through the mud like a primeval beast'. The StuG 'made a hell of a nice target. Just fire low and you'd hit something . . . Fascinating to look at, but you don't win a war by fascinating the enemy,' wrote one tanker.[22] Another company in the same anti-tank battalion possessed horse-drawn 75mm anti-tank guns.

All *Volksgrenadier* divisions possessed a few tracked, turretless armoured vehicles like this four-man *Sturmgeschütz* (literally 'assault gun', and abbreviated to StuG), armed with a 75mm gun. At only 7 feet tall, its low profile made it easy to conceal and effective in defence, but the limited traverse of the main weapon, having no turret, made it very vulnerable in attacks of the kind envisaged by *Herbstnebel*. Panzer divisions used large numbers of them as substitute tanks, while American tankers regarded the StuG as 'an interminable viper slinking across the terrain'. (NARA)

As we shall see, even a modest allocation of some extra cannon and armour would have aided Brandenberger considerably.

The Seventh Army commander continued to protest about his lack of armour; as noted, he had originally been promised a panzer division by Jodl at OKW; later this was revised to a *Panzergrenadier* formation (mechanised infantry which included some tanks), but they were used elsewhere on the front. In the final days before the offensive, Gersdorff lodged a formal complaint with Model over the famine of tank support and, at the last minute, Seventh Army was allocated some StuGs. This was Oberstleutnant Hollunder's *Fallschirm-Sturmgeschütz-Brigade* 11, a battalion-sized unit of about 500 men and a theoretical thirty StuGs armed with 75mm guns, which had been attempting to halt the tidal wave of General Jake L. Devers' US Sixth Army Group in its romp through southern France. The 11th StuG Brigade entered combat in the vicinity of Nancy and was virtually destroyed in September, withdrawn and remained under-strength when given to Brandenberger in mid-December, at which time it possessed three batteries of six or seven vehicles, totalling about twenty assault guns.[23] Called a 'brigade' for the purposes of deception, the Eleventh was another example of the bizarre, competitive world of the German armed forces. They were Göring's idea, designed originally to support paratroops, who had no tank support of their own, so came under Luftwaffe control: an oddity for armoured crewmen to wear the badges of their air force.

Apart from these vehicles, *Volksgrenadiers* had very few towed anti-tank guns; instead they were lavishly equipped with personal anti-tank weapons, such as the hand-held *Panzerschreck* ('tank terror') and *Panzerfaust* ('tank fist'). Although the former's hollow-charge warhead could penetrate the armour of every Allied tank easily, its range of just 120 yards meant that the two-man crew had to squat in their foxholes and practically wait for opponents to roll on to them. The same applied to the single-shot, throwaway *Panzerfaust*, with its shorter range of 60–100 yards, and issued in the tens of thousands. Unfortunately for their operators, Allied doctrine was to precede any advance with an artillery bombardment, precisely to destroy any such threats with high explosive. Nevertheless, both these anti-tank weapons constituted a cheap, practical way to counter Allied tanks at very short range, if at a high cost in personnel. By the war's end nearly six million *Panzerfausts* had been manufactured – the US 82nd Airborne Division assessed it as even more effective than their own bazookas, and used captured stocks whenever possible in the Ardennes. After the war, of course, Russian designers adapted it into the highly successful RPG (Rocket-Propelled Grenade) family of shoulder-launched anti-armour weapons.

Each *Volksgrenadier* division also had its own firepower in the form of an artillery regiment of four battalions, in theory nine batteries of cannon, totalling fifty-four weapons; however, the allocation of guns had been diluted in 1944, in an effort to equip all the new formations. Previously, divisions had a similar number of guns, but distributed across twelve batteries; the smaller number of these sub-units was an economy measure, designed to trim the number of officers and specialist staff needed. In earlier times, vehicle-drawn batteries possessed modern 150mm howitzers and 105mm guns, designated heavy and light, but by 1944 the *Volksgrenadier* horse-drawn units were mostly equipped with field guns of First World War vintage, 77mm *Feldkanone* re-bored to 75mm, or captured from vanquished nations, such as France, Italy and Russia. These were less accurate, had a shorter range and slower rate of fire than their more modern equivalents.

*

In the Ardennes offensive, Brandenberger's Seventh Army had a front of over twenty miles to cover, initially with just four weak infantry divisions. The extreme left (southern) wing of the attack was the concern of General der Infanterie Dr Franz Beyer's LXXX Corps, which comprised, from south to north, the 212nd and 276th *Volksgrenadier* divisions. Further north, simultaneous attacks would be launched by the LXXXV Corps of General Baptist Kneiss, who likewise possessed two divisions, the 352nd *Volksgrenadiers*, and a miscellany of Luftwaffe personnel swept up into a formation called the 5th *Fallschirmjäger* Division.

Kneiss had commanded his LXXXV Corps since July, but was allowed to take a month's leave beforehand, incredibly returning to active duty on the day *Herbstnebel* began. Of his two commanders, forty-one-year-old Oberst Ludwig Heilmann was the superbly energetic leader of the 5th Luftwaffe Division. He had joined the army as a private in 1921, invaded Poland as an infantryman, volunteered for airborne training and jumped into Crete as a battalion commander in 1941. He had led a regiment fighting British paratroopers on Sicily. However, Heilmann's finest hour was defending Monte Cassino earlier in 1944 which brought him Swords to the previously awarded Knight's Cross and Oak Leaves. Popular with his men but stubborn, he used to refer to his high decorations for bravery as *Blech* (tin) or a 'good cure for throat-ache' (the Knight's Cross being worn around the neck), when joking with the 'stubble hoppers', the veterans in his units. A capable and resourceful commander at regimental level, Heilmann was appointed to his new post on 15 October; the Ardennes would be his first test in charge of a division.

Heilmann's formation, however, was a different matter. Raised in March 1944, destroyed at Falaise and re-formed in October, the 5th *Fallschirmjäger* was airborne in name only; but a fraction of its personnel were trained jumpers, and most of them were the result of Himmler's policy of redirecting unemployed Luftwaffe troops into combat roles. Most had hitherto enjoyed a comfortable war on airbases behind the lines, servicing and maintaining aircraft, carousing with the local female population and returning to clean sheets and mattresses. Unfit, untrained in ground tactics, few had seen action or fired weapons in anger. The only thing they shared with Heilmann was the swooping eagle badge of the Luftwaffe they all wore on their tunics.

Oberst Eric-Otto Schmidt, who possessed a solid record of experience in infantry units, serving in Poland and Russia, had commanded 352nd

Volksgrenadier Division since 6 October, shortly after its activation as a unit in Schleswig-Holstein.[24] He had some help from a sprinkling of seasoned officers and NCOs in his formation, which was created from the remnants of the old 352nd Infantry Division, destroyed in Normandy. The original unit had been stationed behind Omaha Beach on D-Day where it had caused great harm to the US First and Twenty-Ninth Divisions, but was overwhelmed in the subsequent fighting, with very few of its ranks escaping unscathed. For example, only one Normandy veteran was known to have served in the Ardennes with its 916th *Volksgrenadier* Regiment, Leutnant Willi Heller of the 6. Kompanie. Another veteran recalled that 50 per cent were seventeen- or eighteen-year-old Hanoverian conscripts, 20 per cent were Poles classed by the authorities as being of German stock (*Volksdeutsche*), and therefore eligible for combat service, a further 20 per cent came from the recently dissolved Vlassov division of Russian volunteers, and the final 10 per cent were *Ostfront* veterans.[25]

Leading the Seventh Army's other formation, LXXX Corps, was General Dr Franz Beyer, a reliable veteran *Ostfront* hand, who was leading a formation in the attack because he was assessed as being a convinced National Socialist: Himmler had vetted all the senior commanders for their loyalty.[26]

The more experienced of Beyer's two divisional commanders, Franz Sensfuss, had taken over his formation on 17 September 1944 when its sub-units came together for the first time. The *Generalleutnant*'s 212th *Volksgrenadier* Division contained mostly young recruits, including many Bavarians aged seventeen. The 212th had been reconstructed from a destroyed division, as was its twin, Generalmajor Kurt Möhring's 276th *Volksgrenadiers.* Möhring was something of a rising star in the army. At sixteen he had volunteered to serve as a *Fahnenjunker* (officer cadet) in the First World War, doing well enough to be retained in the 1919 slimmed-down Reichswehr. Twenty years later he was an infantry battalion commander; promoted to *Oberst* and given a regiment in 1942, this was followed by the significant command, still in Russia, of the elite *GrossDeutschland* Division for a year. His reward was a Knight's Cross and ultimately the 276th *Volksgrenadiers.* Möhring's experience was unrivalled, having commanded in Poland, France and Russia, reaching the gates of Moscow, and at Kursk, before commencing the Battle of the Bulge. However, 276th proved to be ill prepared for their coming test, which was blamed on inadequate training, just as Rundstedt had warned in September, and too few good leaders to make it a first-class formation. As we shall see, it would perform less well than Senfuss's 212th.

In sum, the Wehrmacht that attacked the Ardennes in December 1944 was an inferior version of its predecessor, which reached the peak of professionalism by mid-1942 and had declined slowly since. Its experienced troops had generally been wounded in the east and sent to Western Europe to convalesce. Many of the 'comb out' from industry were in their late forties, less fit and slower to react in combat; to offset this, most of the youngsters were true disciples, fanatics who believed in *Endsieg*, the final victory, were highly motivated and fit, so fought bravely if carelessly. Generally, though, the *Volksgrenadiers* comprised ill-trained and ill-equipped men held together by the quality of their few officers and experienced NCOs.

Actual bayonet strength – as a head count of riflemen is called – in a *Volksgrenadier* division was at least 1,500 less than in an equivalent US formation, but total divisional firepower was similar. About equal in artillery, German divisions enjoyed a superiority in automatic weapons (if they were issued as planned), and bazooka-type anti-tank guns. American units had a much higher proportion of administrative and logistics personnel, and so experienced none of the headaches of mobility, fuel and ammunition supply that routinely bugged their counterparts.

Unfortunately, the *Volksgrenadier* divisions were essentially devised for defence, not offence. Despite the impressive firepower, without armoured help their manpower was generally inadequate to batter their way through a front line, even thinly held lines in the Ardennes; if they achieved a penetration, units were unable to exploit with a pursuit, for they lacked any mobility. Successful offensive operations have always required manoeuvrability and reserves of manpower to reinforce success quickly. Alas, the *Volksgrenadiers* had neither. They were relatively poorly prepared, too. Secrecy was so paramount that junior officers in all the attacking divisions were only given their individual assignments on 15 December, leaving less than twenty-four hours in which to ready and brief their men.

Friedrich Schmäschke, a seventeen-year-old former sailor and runner with the 352nd *Volksgrenadier* Division, had been manning a concrete blockhouse behind the lines when he and his mates received their orders on 15 December.

> The peaceful silence of the bunker was now replaced by restless muttering. There were even comrades who broke out in wild euphoria . . . Then we had a hot meal which some ghoulishly called our 'hangman's meal'. Our iron rations were distributed and checked. Some of the men turned to the liquor ration to raise their spirits. Everything non essential was left at the bunker. Hand grenades, Panzerfausts and extra small arms ammunition was passed out and we had to lie down and rest while fully dressed . . . It had a numbing effect on us. Our minds were cleared, resulting in a terrible emptiness. No thoughts of home or family . . . The morning of 16 December came inexorably. We were to be awakened at 04:00 am but that didn't prove necessary since nobody slept.[27]

When I first visited the area held by 352nd Division in December 1989, I came across a relic from the fighting. The countryside was still and blanketed by deep virgin snow as it had been in 1944, though it hadn't penetrated the woods where the *Volksgrenadiers* had gathered on 15 December, forty-four years earlier. Their foxholes were still evident, and so were the shell craters caused by retaliatory US artillery fire. It was there I found the helmet. Issued to a grenadier for the coming battle, at some stage damaged by shrapnel, it had been discarded. It was of the traditional German coal-scuttle shape, I noted, but slightly different from the helmets the Wehrmacht usually wore. For this was a steel helmet from the First World War. In equipping all their *Volksgrenadiers* for the coming offensive, the Reich's quartermasters had to have been scraping the very bottom of the barrel in order to issue this 1917-model *Stahlhelm.*

So carried away in their enthusiasm for *Herbstnebel* were the Führer and OKW that they failed to see they were sending their Seventh Army into battle in late 1944 exactly as it had been deployed in 1914: with its infantry marching on foot and horses dragging the same weapons it had used thirty years before.

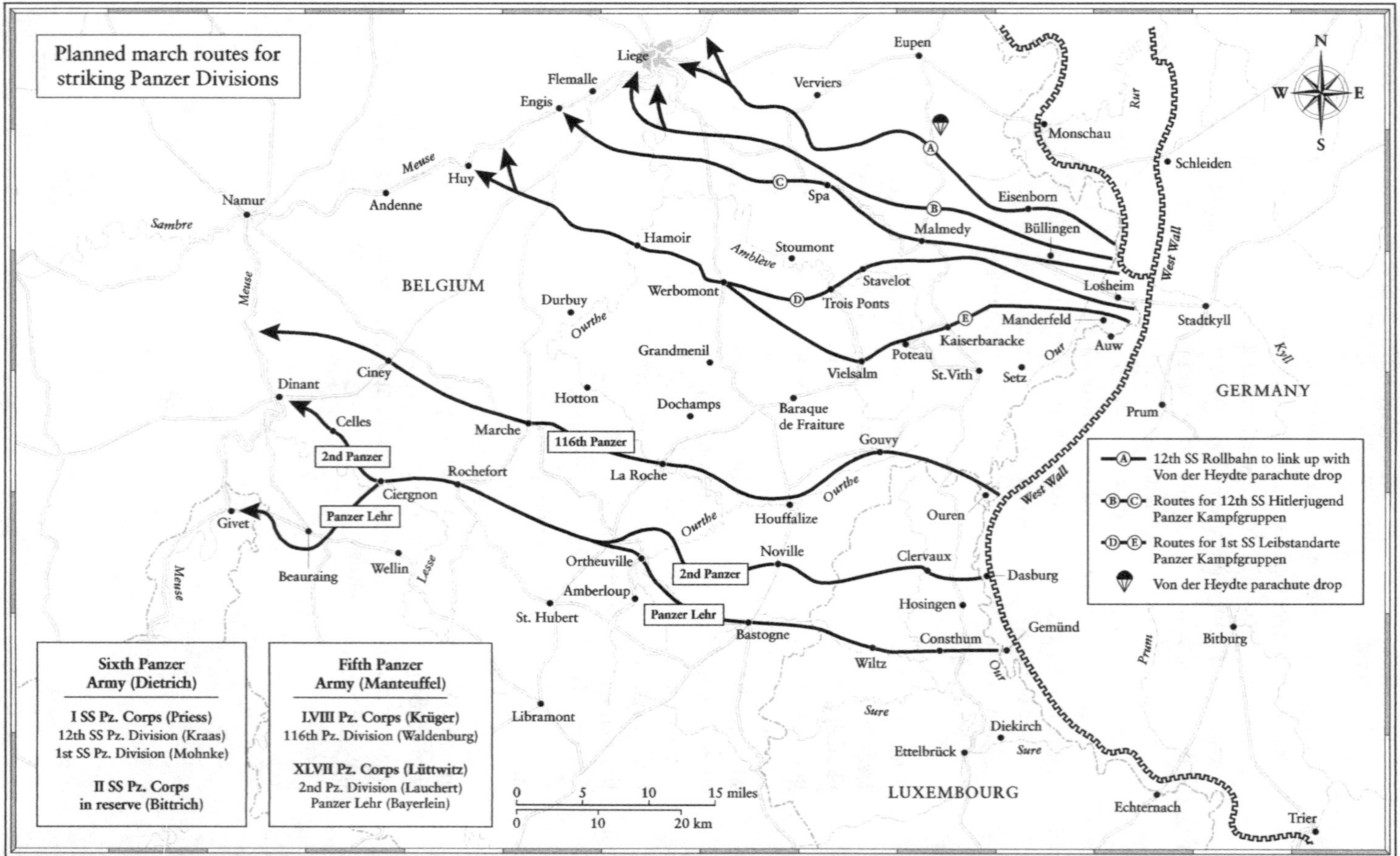
Planned march routes for striking Panzer Divisions
N
E
S
W
Liege
Eupen
Flemalle
Verviers
Engis
Monschau
Rur
Schleiden
Meuse
Huy
Spa
Andenne
Namur
Sambre
Eisenborn
Malmedy
Büllingen
Hamoir
Amblève
Stoumont
Stavelot
BELGIUM
Werbomont
Trois Ponts
Losheim
West Wall
Durbuy
Ourthe
Manderfeld
Stadtkyll
Kaiserbaracke
Auw
Grandmenil
Poteau
Our
Kyll
Vielsalm
St. Vith
Setz
Ciney
Dinant
Hotton
Dochamps
Baraque
de Fraiture
GERMANY
Prum
Celles
Marche
116th Panzer
2nd Panzer
Gouvy
Rochefort
La Roche
Ciergnon
Panzer Lehr
Houffalize
Ouren
Givet
Beauraing
Wellin
Lesse
Ortheuville
Noville
Clervaux
Dasburg
Amberloup
St. Hubert
Bastogne
Hosingen
Gemünd
Wiltz
Consthum
Bitburg
Sure
Diekirch
Libramont
Ettelbrück
LUXEMBOURG
Echternach
Trier
0 5 10 15 miles
0 10 20 km
A 12th SS Rollbahn to link up with Von der Heydte parachute drop
B C Routes for 12th SS Hitlerjugend Panzer Kampfgruppen
D E Routes for 1st SS Leibstandarte Panzer Kampfgruppen
Von der Heydte parachute drop
Sixth Panzer Army (Dietrich)
I SS Pz. Corps (Priess)
12th SS Pz. Division (Kraas)
1st SS Pz. Division (Mohnke)
II SS Pz. Corps in reserve (Bittrich)
Fifth Panzer Army (Manteuffel)
LVIII Pz. Corps (Krüger)
116th Pz. Division (Waldenburg)
XLVII Pz. Corps (Lüttwitz)
2nd Pz. Division (Lauchert)
Panzer Lehr (Bayerlein)

13

The Baron

GIVEN THE CRUSHING weight of air power which had undermined German morale in Normandy, how did the three attacking armies manage to move all the troops, tanks, horses, artillery and supplies they required for *Herbstnebel*? As we have seen from the relevant Ultra decrypts, despite attempts by the Allied bomber fleets, German railways continued to function until the very end of the war. This was because the Fatherland had always put an excessive reliance on its railway infrastructure, the largest in Europe. In the nineteenth century, all main lines had been built with strategy in mind, and ran east–west with plenty of spare capacity, the Army General Staff having a special railway department dealing with this important state asset.

Deutsche Reichsbahn was the largest single public enterprise in the world at the time of its nationalisation in 1937, when its 660,000 employees ran 24,000 locomotives and 20,000 stations, with 40,000 miles of track. It took over the Austrian system in 1938, that of Czechoslovakia in 1939 (who made first-class rolling stock and engines), and during the war the militarised state railway operated a staggering total of 50,000 locomotives and at least three million freight cars, more than double that of the United States. This included those absorbed from conquered nations, but they also manufactured another 15,000 engines and 245,000 wagons to keep pace with losses.[1]

By June 1944, 1.6 million people, including 200,000 women, worked for the German-run railway system across Europe, despatching 29,000

The Third Reich relied on railways rather than motor transport to move and concentrate all its formations for the Ardennes. During the war, *Deutsche Reichbahn* operated over three million pieces of rolling stock and 50,000 locomotives of its own and from conquered countries, like this one, captured from the French state railways, SNCF. (Author's collection)

military trains per day and loading up to a million wagons per week, carrying everything from casualties, reinforcements, horses and prisoners, to munitions, supplies, even entire panzer divisions. Trains had advantages over road transport; they could operate at night and could travel further: German staff calculations worked on the basis of a troop train covering 500 miles per day. Furthermore, they used coal (and occasionally wood), which the Reich possessed in abundance, rather than gasoline that trucks required, which was in critically short supply.

Although stations and marshalling yards were hammered by air attacks each night, the individual lines were difficult to hit. There were spare lengths of rail and wooden sleepers alongside most lines and roving rail repair crews who could, within a few hours, make good the damage wrought by the previous night's bombing. As sabotage was only an issue in occupied countries, not within the Reich, the destruction caused by Allied bombing was a pinprick compared to the railway resources at the disposal of the Fatherland.[2] Thus, the sight of an eagle and swastika-adorned locomotive belching smoke, pulling an endless line of flat car after flat car, each bearing a tank or truck under camouflage netting with a bored soldier scanning the skies for hostile aircraft, was considered neither remarkable nor unusual in early December 1944. It was what the *Reichsbahn* had been doing for the Wehrmacht ever since September 1939, and for the armies of several Kaisers before that.

If Germany's expectations of a final victory relied on her railways then Hitler's hopes for victory in the Ardennes rested firmly on the shoulders of his two panzer armies, the veteran Fifth and the brand-new Sixth. In his own mind he was confident, of course, that the Allies would be unable to react quickly or forcefully until after his armoured forces had reached and crossed the Meuse. Certain that the US Army would initially crumble in the face of adversity, he also anticipated Eisenhower would mount some form of counter-attack against its western bank. Even the sceptical Model, along with many of his subordinate commanders, was of the opinion that German forces could probably get as far as the Meuse before the American reacted in a coordinated way – though all, with the exception of Hitler, seem to have reasoned that any progress beyond that river was unlikely. Yet, as we have seen, under no circumstances was the Führer prepared to switch to a less ambitious goal, or reduce his striking force at the expense of defending his flanks. The meagre allocation of an assault gun brigade to Brandenberger's Seventh Army was about the only compromise he agreed, expressed in his blind refusal to alter his plans in any way from conception to execution.

Encouraged by Himmler, the Führer pinned his personal hopes on Dietrich's Waffen-SS in the Sixth Army triumphing over the Americans in the Ardennes. In fact it would be Manteuffel's Fifth Panzer who did best of all. We have already met its diminutive boss, the forty-seven-year-old General Hasso-Eccard Freiherr von Manteuffel, who in so many ways represented the traditional aristocratic Prussian officer that Hitler loathed. It is a mark of his ability that he succeeded in the Third Reich when the odds were stacked heavily against him. Everything about Manteuffel's background put him at odds with Hitler: born in Potsdam, scion of a Junker family that traced its origins to 1287 (his great-uncle had been a Prussian field marshal); student at the Royal Prussian Cadet School (then considered an academy for the elite); young officer in the famous Zieten Hussars, a regiment that dated back to 1730, founded in the days of Frederick the Great; Olympic pentathlon champion at the 1936 Berlin Olympics, and expert horseman.[3] Reputed to be the shortest officer in the German army, he was extremely tough, wiry, resourceful and athletic. He was the sort of individual one would encounter leading a Special Forces unit today.

Corporal Hitler by contrast, the outsider, technically an Austrian by birth, rose from an uncertain poverty-stricken environment, collected fellow outsiders from equally low backgrounds around him, and was more at home in the beer halls of Munich and Nuremberg than fashionable Berlin; yet somehow he and Manteuffel forged a workable Faustian pact. Perhaps Hitler had heard of his legendary physical courage and habit of leading from the front, which brought him wounds as well as medals, on occasion refusing to leave his command post to receive

Hasso-Eccard, Freiherr (Baron) von Manteuffel (1897–1978) was short, wiry and full of explosive energy. Like George S. Patton, the Baron was an Olympics-level pentathlete (Patton competed at Stockholm in 1912, Manteuffel at the 1936 Berlin Olympics). Despite the striking difference in their backgrounds, Hitler, who generally loathed aristocrats, was greatly impressed by Manteuffel and promoted him straight from a division to command of the Fifth Army on 1 September 1944. Manteuffel's troops achieved the greatest penetrations in the Bulge and had Hitler given him a fraction of the resources allocated to Dietrich's Waffen-SS, the Fifth Army would have undoubtedly reached the Meuse. (Author's collection)

medical treatment; the Führer always admired such examples of sacrifice for the Fatherland.

As Leutnant Freiherr von Manteuffel of the Reichswehr, the future general published a treatise on mounted infantry in 1922 and later taught at the new Wunsdorf Panzer training school under the eye of Guderian from 1935, who tutored this enthusiastic convert to tank warfare. Invading Russia in 1941 as a battalion commander, he swiftly took over a regiment after its colonel had been killed and was rewarded with a division in Tunisia in 1943. The baron soon moved on to command the elite *GrossDeutschland Panzergrenadiers*, a unit of hand-picked warriors of generally tall stature. Manteuffel was easily the shortest man in the division. No matter: by this time he had been awarded a Knight's Cross and Oak Leaves, which is what brought him to Hitler's attention. Promotion straight to command of an army – the Fifth Panzer – followed on 1 September 1944. He took up his appointment on the 12th, and gathering a carefully selected staff around him, who were personally devoted to their little general, he led the Fifth in the Lorraine campaign and struggle for Aachen. Far more than the Seventh's Brandenberger or Dietrich of the Sixth, he stamped his personality on his army and their battle plans and tactics.

Manteuffel had found himself in violent if respectful disagreement with the original plans handed to him by Jodl back in November. In defiance of his orders, he had made a personal reconnaissance of his future battle terrain, disguising himself as a Wehrmacht colonel and visiting front-line units which regularly patrolled into American territory. What they revealed amazed him: the American outposts manned their foxholes from an hour before dawn, but retired to warm buildings after dark: at night their positions were unmanned! At the last planning conference held with Hitler in the Berlin *Reichskanzlei* on 2 December, Manteuffel, in the presence of Model and Sepp Dietrich, wrung from his Führer several tactical alterations, which greatly assisted the initial hours of his assault. This was the last occasion when those present tried to dissuade Hitler from his 'Big Solution' in favour of the more practical 'Small Solution' of encircling the Americans around Aachen. Though Hitler refused to yield on the major part of his plan, perhaps the concessions granted to Manteuffel were a form of compensation for one of his favourite generals. Reflecting Hitler's fire, from his headquarters in Manderscheid, north-east of Bitburg, the baron demanded of his commanders that consideration be given only to the advance; the flanks would have to look after themselves, and above all, the pace must not slacken.

He had been uneasy with Hitler's idea of an opening barrage, beginning at 07.30 a.m., prior to the attack going in at 11.00 a.m. On 2 December, Manteuffel argued wisely that 'all this will do is wake the Americans and they will then have three and a half hours to organise their counter-measures before our assault comes . . . After 4:00 pm it will be dark. So you will have only five hours, after the assault at 11:00 am, in which to achieve the break-through.'[4] It would also use up huge quantities of ammunition, already in short supply. Eventually Hitler conceded a ninety-minute cannonade, starting much earlier, at 05.30 a.m. when the Americans would be groggy. Manteuffel also asked permission to throw small storm detachments forward, at the same hour, under cover of their own fire, to infiltrate their opponents' positions, as the Germans had done in 1917–18, and which both sides did routinely in the east; a good ploy, but it would only be used by Fifth Army. The use of searchlights, bouncing light off the clouds was his idea too.

This bizarre circumstance, that an army commander had to seek permission from his head of state to make such tactical alterations to an operation plan, sums up the impracticality of Hitler's constant interference, down to deciding the hour of attack. He was poorly advised, too, for Manteuffel observed that 'Keitel, Jodl and Warlimont [Jodl's deputy] had never been in the war. At the same time their lack of fighting experience tended to make them underrate the practical difficulties, and encourage Hitler to believe that things could be done that were quite impossible.'[5] The Führer intervened because he could, so he did.

Speaking to the British historian Basil Liddell Hart within a year of the events, in 1945, Manteuffel was highly critical of Jodl at OKW in particular, laying the blame for fuel shortages at his door. 'Jodl had assured us there would be sufficient petrol to develop our full strength and carry our drive through. This assurance proved completely mistaken. Part of the trouble was that OKW worked out a mathematical and stereotyped calculation of the amount of petrol required to move a division for a hundred kilometres. My experience in Russia had taught me that double this scale was really needed under battlefield conditions. Jodl didn't understand this. Taking account of the extra difficulties likely to be met in a winter battle in such difficult country as the Ardennes, I told Hitler that five times the standard scale of petrol ought to be provided. Actually when the offensive was launched, only one and a half times the standard scale had been provided. Worse still, much of it was kept too far back, in large lorry columns on the east bank of the Rhine.'[6]

With high expectations of the baron, his Fifth Army was given three panzer and four infantry divisions with which to prosecute *Herbstnebel*, spread throughout three corps – over 90,000 men, 963 guns and almost 300 tanks and assault guns. Left to get on with his own planning and aided by the able Generalmajor Carl Gustav Wagener, his chief of staff, the pair planned to use General Walter Lucht's LXVI Corps of two *Volksgrenadier* divisions to encircle Alan W. Jones's US 106th Infantry Division on their northern flank.[7] The Americans were deployed along the high ground of the Schnee Eifel, occupying outposts of the Siegfried Line around the villages of Auw, Bleialf and Winterspelt, and known to be newly arrived and inexperienced. The wider Eifel region is, effectively, the Germanic name for the range of high hills, narrow gorges and forests – the best word to describe the landscape is 'rugged' – known further west as the Ardennes. The two are one and the same and, apart from crossing a frontier, a traveller would not be aware of crossing from the Ardennes to the Eifel because they constitute a single geological feature.

In Roman times a huge impenetrable forest of Brothers Grimm proportions, by 1944, as now, a controlled agricultural programme of forestry meant that much of the woodland on the high ground on the Schnee Eifel had been felled, with innumerable clearings, but passage across the upper landscape was slow with reliance on poorly drained logging trails. Movement across the lower ground was channelled by many small stretches of water, where run-off from the heights collected and flowed south into the Our. Small, stone-built villages had evolved at each crossroads or frontier post. It was, and remains, picturesque, a favourite with hikers and hunters, though offering few locations with grandstand panoramas at which to site good observation posts. Few roads were paved, as most of the pre-war traffic was horse-drawn. The confusing array of local hills frequently screened wireless contact, and line-of-sight communications was prevented by trees, which also interrupted fields of fire. This meant the defending troops placed an over-reliance on line communications, particularly field telephones. During the opening barrage on 16 December, this mode of signalling was the first to fold as German shells cut American wire.

Having encircled the Schnee Eifel, Lucht would then move straight on via Schönberg to seize the important town of St Vith, eight miles beyond the frontier, and as vital a route centre in the north of the

Ardennes as Bastogne was further south. Manteuffel ordered St Vith seized by the end of Day One. Thereafter their journey would take them, via Vielsalm, along roads heading west, to the Meuse.[8]

Lucht's two *Volksgrenadier* divisions were both ill-equipped and under-strength, comprising sweepings mostly from the Luftwaffe. Few of Oberst Günther Hoffmann-Schönborn's 18th had campaign ribbons or decorations. According to the division's chief of staff, Oberstleutnant Dietrich Moll, the division, activated on 2 September, was very much the result of Himmler's 'hero-snatching units' and comprised 2,500 Luftwaffe men who had been trounced out of Normandy in August, and 3,000 redundant Luftwaffe and Kriegsmarine personnel acquired in Denmark, where the division first trained. More recruits came from a pool of middle-aged men combed out of industry. Very few were young, and even fewer had seen any action, including the officers: altogether the 18th was extraordinarily inexperienced formation, considering Germany was in her sixth year of war.[9]

By contrast its commander, Hoffmann-Schönborn, holder of the Knight's Cross with Oak Leaves, conformed to Himmler's requirement for highly decorated combat leaders and had served already in Poland, France, Greece and Russia. With such a disparate unit, in November Hoffmann-Schönborn had felt obliged to dish out some National Socialist discipline *pour encourager les autres*. A captured divisional order signed by him read that 'Traitors from our ranks have deserted to the enemy'. After naming them, the divisional commander went on:

> These bastards have given away important military secrets. The result is that for the past few days the Americans have been laying quite accurate artillery fire on your positions, your bunkers, your company and platoon headquarters, your field kitchens and your messenger routes. Deceitful Jewish mud-slingers taunt you with their pamphlets and try to entice you into becoming bastards also. Let them spew their poison! We stand watch over Germany's frontier. Death and destruction to all enemies who tread on Germany's soil. As for the contemptible traitors who have forgotten their honour, rest assured the division will see that they never see home and loved ones again. Their families will have to atone for their treason. The destiny of a people has never depended on traitors and bastards. The true German soldier was and is the best in the world. Unwavering behind him is the Fatherland, and at the end is our Victory. Long live Germany! Heil the Fuhrer![10]

This crude missive, with its coarse language, was clearly *not* written by the divisional commander who in any case had better things to do. It was the work of the divisional *Nationalsozialistischer Führungsoffizier* (Nazi Guidance Officer), one of the loathsome commissar-like creatures inserted by Himmler personally into each staff headquarters, in place of the division's chaplain. From now on the poor old grenadier had vicious enemies behind him as well as in front.

Known as the *die Mondscheindivision* (Moonshine Division), after its insignia, Lucht's other division was the 62nd *Volksgrenadiers*, commanded by Oberst Friedrich Kittel. He had served in the Bavarian army in the First War, and spent most of the Second on the Eastern Front. In contrast to their middle-aged stable-mates of the 18th *Volksgrenadier* Division, on taking over his new formation on 1 November, Kittel found that two of his sub-units contained seventeen-year-old Hitler Youths: 164th *Volksgrenadier* Regiment included *HitlerJugend* from Düsseldorf and its sister 183rd Regiment, youths from nearby Cologne. Both of Lucht's *Volksgrenadier* divisions were to fix Jones's US 106th and prevent them from interfering with the advance of Manteuffel's two panzer corps, further south.

The baron's real achievements would turn on the success or failure of his two panzer corps, whose missions were the same: to use their *Volksgrenadiers* to cross the River Our and overwhelm the forward American defences on the ridge west of the river, thus covering the construction of bridges for his panzers. The Our, then as now, was neither deep nor wide, but the slopes to it were steep, with little room to manoeuvre. Manteuffel wanted this completed by midday in order for the tank divisions, following closely behind, to cross to the west bank by mid-afternoon; they would then take the lead and race beyond by road as quickly as possible, seizing towns and road junctions on the way to the Meuse. In the centre, Manteuffel intended General Walter Krüger's LVIII Panzer Corps to use the 560th *Volksgrenadiers* to cross the river at Ouren and break into the US lines, whereupon Siegfried von Waldenburg's 116th Panzer Division would then exploit the breach and race for the Meuse via Houffalize.[11]

We have already met some of 116th's men at Hotton, and their commander, Waldenburg, being given his Knight's Cross by Hitler at Ziegenberg. Another East Prussian, old-school aristocrat, Waldenburg, forty-six, had served in the exclusive Emperor Alexander Grenadier Guards from 1915, later attending the Kriegsakademie and acting as a staff officer in France and Russia, before commanding panzer units in the east.[12] His *Windhund* (Greyhound) Division had been formed only in March 1944 and was led through the attritional Normandy campaign by Gerhard Graf von Schwerin, whose removal from command Himmler had engineered during the battle for Aachen. The replacement was Waldenburg, appointed on 14 September, ably assisted by his young chief of staff and operations officer (the 'Ia'), Major Heinz-Günther Guderian, son of the founder of the Reich's panzer force. The Greyhounds had already fought at Mortain and Falaise, where they were gradually whittled down to 600 men and twelve tanks.

In readiness for the Ardennes, on 10 December 1944 Waldenburg's Sixteenth Panzer Regiment reported forty-three Panthers in its First Battalion, while its Second Battalion had twenty-six operational Panzer IVs, a divisional total of sixty-nine tanks. Of course, to an opposing US infantry division equipped with few or no tanks, the Greyhound Division was frighteningly powerful, but, in reality, 116th Panzer was a shadow of its former self. This was less than the strength of a German tank battalion: in Normandy, the formation had fielded 157 panzers.[13]

Krüger's *Volksgrenadier* Division was the 560th, raised in Norway on 10 October, and comprised of surplus garrison units – the fortress battalions – of trained soldiers from Denmark and Norway's coastal defences.[14] Led by a former artillery officer, forty-six-year-old Generalmajor Rudolf Bader from 10 November, the division was identified by its badge of Thor's hammer. It was the weakest German division deployed, intended for the Russian Front but sent to the Ardennes at the last minute – many of its soldiers were still en route from Norway on 16 December. Consequently, on the line of departure each regiment was at half-strength, being able to field only a battalion apiece, while the division's anti-tank battalion of tracked assault guns was absent altogether.

The division also started the battle without its commander, who was in hospital; it was led by forty-four-year-old Oberst Rudolf Langhäuser, commander of 1128nd Regiment, until Bader's return on 27 December. Like all the *Volksgrenadier* units, they were totally reliant on horses for mobility, being authorised 3,002, though few units ever acquired this number. In turn, the animals required a veterinary company of 152 officers and men to treat, shoe and look after them. Altogether, *Herbstnebel* would involve over 50,000 horses struggling along the freezing roads – not the usual image we have of the battle.[15] While the Wehrmacht's *Propaganda Kompanie* photographers and cameramen mostly took images of panzers crashing through the Ardennes, the truth is that for every German tank deployed in the winter offensive there were forty horses.

In the case of the 560th *Volksgrenadiers*, only their *Flak* and anti-tank battalions possessed any motorised transport at all, and all units were encouraged to capture and use American vehicles and fuel. However, that the Wehrmacht relied on horses so heavily and had relatively few vehicles produced an interesting, oft-overlooked consequence – that not many German soldiers knew how to drive a motor vehicle. Many had been brought up before the war on the land and understood horses, while their contemporaries in the United States, with the highest car-ownership in the world, were learning to drive automobiles. Comparative figures for 1935 reveal that 1.6 per cent of Germans owned a motor vehicle, compared with 4.5 per cent in Britain, 4.9 per cent in France and a staggering 20.5 per cent in the USA, or one-in-five of the entire population.[16] By contrast, the German army actually awarded a driver's badge to those who could sit behind a steering wheel with proficiency.

Thus, when the *Volksgrenadiers* captured many US vehicles in the

The truth of the Ardennes offensive was that for every German tank deployed, there were forty horses. As so little of the Wehrmacht was motorised, few German soldiers knew how to drive a motor vehicle, with dire consequences when vast numbers of American trucks and jeeps were captured. (Author's collection)

initial days, fuelled up and ready to go, they were not always able to use them, and sometimes compelled GI prisoners of war to drive captured trucks. This was the case even with armoured formations. On 17 December, when the 1st SS-*Leibstandarte* Panzer Division arrived at the Baugnez crossroads outside Malmedy on 17 December, and took more than a hundred GIs prisoner, their first action was to request drivers for captured American vehicles.[17]

Horses pulled all the guns and ammunition wagons of the 560th Division's *VolksArtillerie* regiment in which Kanonier Josef Reusch served. Born in 1927, he was not yet seventeen when he was drafted on 25 March 1944. He grew up in the border village of Bleialf, soon to be the scene of hard fighting, and attended school in St Vith, likewise bitterly contested. Trained as a *Rechner* (tabulator) on a 105mm howitzer and a forward observer, he later learned similar duties on a 75mm anti-tank gun. Reusch was stunned to learn on 15 December that he was going into battle only a few miles north of his home, now occupied by Americans.

To their south, and adjacent to Heilmann's 5th *Fallschirmjäger* of the Seventh Army, lurked General von Lüttwitz's XLVII Panzer Corps, the strongest of Manteuffel's three army corps. It was only on 2 December that Lüttwitz, then fighting the British around Geilenkirchen, received word from Manteuffel that his corps would feature in a forthcoming counter-offensive in the Ardennes. Four days later he had disengaged and relocated closer to Fifth Panzer Army headquarters. This was incredibly short notice for a formation to plan an important operation beginning a few days' hence. He was lucky, however, with the quantity of corps assets he was given for *Herbstnebel*: the 15th *VolksWerfer* Brigade and 766th *VolksArtillerie* Corps, totalling nearly 200 weapons, 600th Army Engineer Battalion, and 182nd *Flak* Regiment, all motorised.

Their mission was for the 26th *Volksgrenadiers* to cross the Our at Gemünd and establish a bridgehead for Panzer Lehr to follow in their wake. Meanwhile, to their north, 2nd Panzer would bridge the same river at Dasburg, climb the opposing banks, seize the lateral road that ran along the high ground (christened the Skyline Drive) and the little fortress town of Clervaux – or Clerf, to the Germans – a distance of seven miles. Thereafter 2nd Panzer was to grind its way through the remaining American lines, seizing Bastogne, a mere eighteen miles further, preferably by the end of the first day.

Today Bastogne is less than an hour's drive from Dasburg, which straddles the Our. In 1944, those same twenty-five miles were narrow, twisting, largely unpaved and particularly muddy; the road network only improved west of Bastogne. Lüttwitz's mission boiled down to one essential: Bastogne had to be taken if the Meuse was to be reached. Should his panzers fail to take the town, the *Volksgrenadiers* were to besiege it, leaving the tanks free to continue their dash to the Meuse, which they were ordered to reach by the end of the second day. With his corps advancing on two axes, Lüttwitz envisaged Panzer Lehr as being able to reinforce or relieve 2nd Panzer, or the 26th *Volksgrenadiers*, and to exploit any opportunity that arose.[18]

An important German figure in the story of the Bulge was General Heinrich Freiherr von Lüttwitz, a baron, like his army commander. This old school aristocrat was yet another example of an individual who epitomised all that Hitler loathed nevertheless doing well in the classless Third Reich. With his monocled right eye, peaked cap and huge Iron Cross swinging from the neck, Lüttwitz looked like the stereotypical German officer from central casting. Looks can be deceptive: he was clever and an instinctive leader. He had been appointed Ensign of a smart Uhlan cavalry squadron in October 1914, served in mounted regiments on the Eastern Front from 1915 to 1917, fronted a reconnaissance battalion in Poland in 1939 where he was wounded, missed the French campaign but recovered in time for Operation Barbarossa in 1941.

Two years later Lüttwitz had risen to command a panzer division, and on 5 September 1944, the bearer of a Knight's Cross and Oak Leaves, he was promoted to lead the XLVII Panzer Corps. On 27 October, as we have seen, he had already caught the British napping in his two-division attack further north, at Meijel in the Peel Marshes, and the lessons of stealth, surprise, speed and momentum in difficult country cannot have been lost on him. Although Lüttwitz turned forty-eight just ten days before he led his formation into the Ardennes, there is evidence that he was physically exhausted, having commanded formations in action almost without a break for nearly three and a half years. Photographs of him at this time show a man looking far older: evidence of the strain of continuous fighting, surely shared by many of Hitler's combat leaders.

Oberst Heinz Kokott's 26th *Volksgrenadier* Division was a 'hollowed out' formation, retaining a few veterans from the Russian and Normandy fronts, but mostly Luftwaffe and Kriegsmarine replacements. Like all

Volksgrenadier units, their mobility was hampered by total reliance on horses, some of which were a tough Russian breed, used to winter. Nevertheless, they were up to strength with an outstanding cadre of sub-unit leaders and experienced troops, on whom the new arrivals could lean for experience. Its *Panzerjäger* (anti-tank) battalion had its full complement of fourteen tracked *Hetzer* tank destroyers, and an impressive forty-two 75mm anti-tank guns, making the 26th one of the best-equipped *Volksgrenadier* units in the Ardennes.

Though protected by the opening bombardment and in the dark, before they even reached the river Kokott's *Volksgrenadiers* had to penetrate hundreds of felled trees, copious barbed wire entanglements and large areas of mines, all left behind by retreating German troops earlier in the year.[19] Next, they had to navigate the fast-flowing Our by rubber assault craft, climb the not inconsiderable far slopes, and overwhelm the forward American lines. Meanwhile, bridging units were to prepare crossing sites for the waiting 2nd Panzer Division. Superbly able and energetic, the bespectacled, buck-toothed Kokott had joined the German army on 1 October 1918 just before the Armistice and had carried on as a career officer, mostly serving in Russia, where he won a Knight's Cross in 1943. An unlikely brother-in-law of SS chief Heinrich Himmler, in late 1945 the distinguished American historian Colonel S.L.A. Marshall found him 'a shy, scholarly and dignified commander who never raises his voice and appears to be temperate in his actions and judgments'.[20]

The 2nd Panzer Division was Lüttwitz's old division, which he had led in Normandy. Raised in Austria by its first commander, Heinz Guderian, in 1935, and known as the *Wiener* (Vienna) Division, it had fought in Poland, France and the Balkans. In Russia its forward units had witnessed the winter sun glinting off the onion domes of the Kremlin on 2 December 1941: the high tide of the Wehrmacht's advance into Russia. Later it was transferred to the west before D-Day in 1944. On the eve of the Normandy invasion, the formation was several hundred men over-strength and reported ninety-four operational Panzer IVs and seventy-three Panthers: a very strong unit.

Fighting at Mortain alongside the 116th Greyhounds, both divisions lost heavily in the *Jabo Rennstrecke* (fighter-bomber racecourse) that was Normandy.[21] By 21 August, they had escaped from the Falaise Pocket with little more than an infantry battalion left; it possessed not a single surviving tank. Although refitted and re-equipped, its War Diary indicates that on 10 December it could boast only 49 Panthers, 26 Panzer IVs and 45 StuG assault guns.[22]

It was still powerful, at 120 tanks and assault guns, but far less so than its peak Normandy strength of 167, and half the size of the US Third Armored Division. Nevertheless, some Panthers were the latest factory-fresh model, equipped with novel infra-red optics for night-fighting. Noteworthy was the high number of turretless assault guns, rather than true tanks, that 2nd Panzer deployed and more evidence of the dilution of its strength. By 1944 German armoured doctrine was to break down into self-contained *Kampfgruppen* (battlegroups) for combat, which comprised tanks, engineers, artillery and mechanised infantry in half-tracks, each named after its senior commander.[23]

Until 14 December, Generalmajor Henning Schönfeld had led 2nd Panzer Division, since taking over from Lüttwitz on the latter's elevation to corps command. However, the fifty-year-old Schönfeld, like many of his contemporaries, felt the resources allocated to him were woefully inadequate to the task and voiced his opinion too vociferously to his superiors, Lüttwitz and Manteuffel. It cost him his division. In the post-20 July atmosphere, where a lack of enthusiasm could be misconstrued in some quarters as treason, Manteuffel felt he had no option but to remove him immediately. A promising young colonel, who had attended a divisional commander's course and recently relinquished leadership of a panzer regiment in Russia, was found and the thirty-nine-year-old Oberst Meinrad von Lauchert found himself the new commander of 2nd Panzer, appointed on the day before the offensive was launched.

The official reason for the departure of Schönfeld, an infantryman by background, was stated to be his lack of experience with armour, but that was clearly nonsense. It underlined the extreme anxiety that was attached to executing Hitler's pet project as well as possible. These were the days anyone could face a firing squad if the Führer or Himmler perceived in them a lack of vigour. Being appointed the day before to lead a division at the spearhead of a major offensive must have been nerve-wracking for Lauchert, but on the other hand that is the nub of the military profession – coping with the unexpected quickly – and he managed well although, as he later complained, he hadn't even time to meet his regimental commanders.[24]

Lüttwitz's other tank unit was the 130th Panzer Division, better known by its designation Panzer Lehr (the 'Panzer Instruction' unit). Its task was to reinforce the advance wherever Lüttwitz saw an opportunity. It had been formed in France that January by combining the staff and instructors of the Wehrmacht's panzer training schools and demonstration units into a combat formation, which made it something of an elite, highly experienced unit from birth. The Lehr had served in Normandy where, like so many armoured formations, it had been almost annihilated, fielding just eleven tanks, no artillery and fewer than 500 men by 1 September. Its commander later described the experience of being under Allied air attack, which underlined how battle-hardened the division was by December 1944. Other veterans fighting in the Ardennes would echo this, where the same punishment was repeated:

> The duration of the bombing created depression and a feeling of helplessness, weakness, and inferiority. Therefore the morale of a great number of men grew so bad that they, feeling the uselessness of fighting, surrendered, deserted to the enemy, or escaped to the rear, [in] as far as they survived the bombing. The shock effect was nearly as strong as the physical effect. For me, who, during this war, was in every theatre committed at the point of the main effort, this was the worst I ever saw. The well-dug-in infantry were smashed by heavy bombs in their foxholes and dugouts or killed and buried by blast. The whole bombed area was transformed into fields covered with craters, in which no human being was alive. Tanks and guns were destroyed and overturned and could not be recovered, because all roads and passages were blocked.[25]

This was the story of Allied air supremacy for the rest of the war – unless the fog of an Ardennes winter could intervene.

Generalleutnant Fritz Bayerlein, as we've seen, was the popular, high-profile commander of Panzer Lehr, both in Normandy and the Ardennes. One of Germany's younger divisional generals at forty-five, he just caught the end of the First World War, being drafted in 1917. After the war he went through officer training in 1921 and was lucky to be one of the 4,000 officers retained in the reduced Reichswehr. The invasion of Poland saw Oberst Bayerlein as chief of staff in Guderian's panzer corps, and he continued as Guderian's right-hand man for the invasion of France the following year, crossing the Meuse at Sedan on 14 May. He had drafted Guderian's corps operations order to undertake that opposed river crossing with three divisions (over 20,000 men) – it came to a succinct two pages. Bayerlein gained a high profile and he was next posted as chief of staff to Rommel's Afrika Korps during 1941–3.

His appointment to Panzer Lehr in 1944 was Guderian's doing; the war required that the Wehrmacht's elite armour training and demonstration units be broken up and drafted into a division. Guderian (as Inspector-General of Armoured Troops) wanted to protect this investment of his finest personnel with a brilliant commander. He chose Bayerlein, who had served in every theatre (east, west and Africa), experienced Allied tactical air power at first hand, and worked as chief of staff to the key exponents of armoured warfare, Guderian and Rommel. Before *Herbstnebel* Bayerlein was concerned at operating with Kokott's 26th *Volksgrenadiers* who were to precede his advance, due to the differential mobility of Panzer Lehr with the almost medieval *Volksgrenadiers*, equipped with horses and bicycles; his anxiety would prove justified. However, as Manteuffel and Lüttwitz soon came to realise, Bayerlein was also exhausted and past his best by December 1944.[26]

Although re-equipped when earmarked in September for the Ardennes, Panzer Lehr was deployed to counter Patton's thrust into the Saar region, and had to be refitted again in early December. Then its tank commander, Oberst Rudolph Gerhardt, reported 23 Panthers, 30 Mark IVs and 14 assault guns operational – a far cry from the 14,699 personnel, 612 half-tracks and 149 panzers of its peak strength in June 1944.[27] In terms of armoured infantry, both *Panzergrenadier* regiments were between 40 and 50 per cent under their authorised strength, though more replacements were 'promised'.[28] As the assault guns came from an attached brigade, this meant that Panzer Lehr was actually at, or below, half-strength and should not have been deployed at all, even though Manteuffel felt all of his three panzer divisions 'very suitable for attack' in mid-December, even if lamentably short of equipment.[29]

From this roll-call of German commanders it becomes clear that a majority of Hitler's panzer commanders seemed to be *Freiherren* (barons), *Ritteren* (knights) or have acquired the suffix 'von' after their name, meaning they or an ancestor owned the terrain after which they took their surname. Hitler may have been suspicious of his aristocrats, but there were a surprising number in the Wehrmacht, and particularly in the *Panzerwaffe* (tank arm). As in most European nations, medieval landowners had ridden into battle, which evolved into their descendants joining cavalry regiments. With the decline of the horse for offensive and shock action (as opposed to logistics), cavalry officers adapted by crewing armoured cars and tanks, hence most German mounted units became part of a panzer division. As many of these officers had been brought up together, were educated as the same schools or interconnected by marriage, such informal familiarity often helped command and control in battle.

All these divisions constituted the 'shock wave' of Manteuffel's Fifth Panzer Army. However, if necessary, the baron could – and, indeed, did – request reserve formations from Army Group 'B' or OKW. Several were committed to combat in the later stages of *Herbstnebel*, though permission to do so had to be granted at the highest level. They included the *Führer-Begleit* (leader's escort)-*Brigade*, an expansion of Hitler's personal bodyguard battalion – not an SS formation, but one filled by the army. In 1939–40 this had been commanded by an obscure colonel named Rommel, but it had gradually been enlarged to become an elite formation which fought on the Eastern Front. When refitting after battling the Soviet steamroller in East Prussia, Hitler had ordered it to head west in early December 1944 to prepare for the Ardennes. We have already seen how Ultra had detected its presence and considered it a combat indicator of 'trouble brewing'. This was because it was really a mini-division rather than a brigade, and comprised just over 6,000 battle-hardened personnel, including 200 officers. A very powerful formation, it included a armoured regiment of two battalions (nearly 100 tanks) and *Panzergrenadier* regiment of three battalions, with around 150 half-tracks, a *Flak* regiment and an artillery battalion.

Fully motorised, it reflected Hitler's bizarre favouritism – showering equipment on some units at the expense of others: the formation had more vehicles than all the *Volksgrenadier* divisions combined. Its presence in the Ardennes was undoubtedly political: Hitler expected another of his favourites – like the Sixth Panzer Army – to shine with National Socialist fervour in the forthcoming battle. In background, experience and equipment it was on a par with Waffen-SS formations, and its presence was also a reward for its commander. Oberst Otto-Ernst Remer was another of Hitler's protégés, who had played a key role in foiling the 20 July 1944 Stauffenberg plot in Berlin. As a result, on 21 July Major Remer had been promoted straight to *Oberst*. With the Knight's Cross and Oak Leaves glinting at his throat, the tall, athletic Remer, thirty-two, was resourceful, highly dangerous and had already proven himself rabidly National Socialist.

It would not be until 4.00 p.m. on 18 December that he was ordered to join the battle and take his *Führer-Begleit-Brigade* to the St Vith front under Lüttwitz's XLVII Panzer Corps; Manteuffel, though glad of its combat power, also felt Remer to be Hitler's personal spy in his camp.[30] Also in OKW reserve was the *Führer-Grenadier-Brigade*, which sprang from similar origins, and likewise was considered an elite and equally unusual formation, very similar in size and capability to its twin, the *Begleit-Brigade*. Not released from OKW until 22 December, this powerful unit was scattered along march routes in traffic jams, when it was ordered south to face the US Third Army.

As we consider Manteuffel's Fifth Army, several themes emerge. All his four infantry divisions, the *Volksgrenadiers*, were new formations which had undertaken little training, and none as divisions. If their leaders were experienced, the vast majority of grenadiers were new to combat. One *Volksgrenadier* commander, Bader, was in hospital and the battle run initially by one of his sub-unit colonels, Langhäuser. If the panzer divisions were formed of veterans, they were hopelessly understrength, and two of the three divisional commanders, Waldenburg and Lauchert, were new. The third, Bayerlein, was tired. We have seen how General Baptist Kneiss, a corps commander in Brandenberger's Seventh Army, took a month's leave and returned the day the offensive began, which hardly seems professional. Perhaps Kneiss was making the same point as the sacked Generalmajor Schönfeld of 2nd Panzer – but in a subtler way – that he, like Field Marshal von Rundstedt, had little faith in the offensive and thus wanted no part in planning it.

All of this put the attacking force at an enormous disadvantage, with little pre-battle training and none at higher formation level. Few of the commanders had worked together, so could not guess their superiors' or subordinates' intentions; combat flows more smoothly when commanders instinctively sense their colleagues' movements, the result of months or years of fighting together.

This was in great contrast to Middleton's VIII Corps. Although many were tired and degraded because of the Hürtgen battles, the Americans had been campaigning together since June in Normandy, and even the newcomers, such as Jones's 106th or Leonard's 9th, had trained together for longer than any of the *Volksgrenadier* units. The US Army – whether experienced but tired, or green and nervous – were vastly better resourced than their Wehrmacht counterparts. Manteuffel's army alone boasted over 15,000 horses, whereas the Americans relied entirely on wheeled and tracked mobility, with unlimited fuel, now that Allied logistics flowed from Antwerp and the Red Ball Express had build up a reserve of combat supplies close to the front.

All the panzer divisions were woefully understrength; many of the anti-tank battalions were deficient in tracked tank destroyers, air defence units reported shortages of *Flak* guns, and ammunition and gasoline were in critically short supply. As Rundstedt admitted to the historian Liddell Hart in 1945, 'there were no adequate reinforcements, no [re] supplies of ammunition, and although the number of armoured divisions was high, their strength in tanks was low – it was largely paper strength'.

The morale of German troops picked up when they saw the extent of resources carefully husbanded and camouflaged all around them. Perhaps they could win, after all? Gefreiter Hans Hejny, with 2nd Panzer Division, mirrored the experience of any soldier who has had to drive with minimal lighting in a convoy at night. It is exhausting on the eyes (the consequence is usually the 'bug-eyed' look tired soldiers exhibit in daylight), for a moment's lapse of concentration can lead to a wrong turning or worse. Hejny remembered a trek to the concentration area, at the head of his armoured engineer battalion: 'Orders were given quietly, and lights were dimmed. Only a thin ray of brightness came from the convoy-light made the lane even barely visible. It was hard to see the roads and we had to concentrate to avoid falling into the trackside ditches. We reached the top of a hill and could see the vague outlines of Luxembourg. The road extended from a forest into a plain and ahead were the tail-lights of another column gliding downwards and disappearing into the woods.'[31]

14

We Accept Death, We Hand Out Death

HITLER ENVISAGED THE star turn of his Ardennes offensive to be the Sixth Panzer Army, an entirely new creation. That it was to be led by the Waffen-SS's senior field commander, and contain four SS panzer divisions, was no accident. This was another of the Führer's responses to 20 July: thereafter the only organisation with which he felt safe, on which he could rely, was Himmler's SS. Heinrich, Graf von Einsiedel, a great-grandson of Otto von Bismarck and a young lieutenant in 1944, observed, 'The generals kept on assuming that the army was the only arms-bearer of the nation. But it was quite clear that another force was being built up that wanted to compete with the army for power'.[1] It was almost as though Hitler built the Ardennes offensive around the capabilities of his Sixth Panzer Army, created expressly for the purpose on 14 September 1944 and bulging with SS troopers, rather than the force being harnessed to Hitler's master plan.

Back in the early 1980s, over dinner one night when stationed in Germany, I exchanged a few civilities with a spry, well-groomed and respectable looking citizen of what was then West Germany, seated at the next table with his wife. Our conversation – for these were the years of the Cold War – turned to the threat posed by the USSR. It soon transpired that he had personal experience of the east, conning a panzer through the endless Russian steppes. Following several schnapps, and after other encounters, his guard lowered, my new-found friend revealed himself as the former Obersturmführer Hans Hennecke, a tank commander who had served in Russia, Normandy and the Ardennes.[2]

Born in August 1920 in the northern spa town of Waren, Hennecke spent his spare time in the *HitlerJugend* while at school, and after six months compulsory service in the *Reichsarbeitsdienst* he volunteered for the Waffen-SS. 'I was lured,' he remembered, 'partly by the snappy black uniform and also by recruiting posters.' The clothing was designed by the fashion consultant Hugo Boss, and the posters were the work of Ottomar Anton, an SS officer who produced pre-war art deco-style travel advertising for the Hamburg-Amerika, Cunard and White Star shipping lines and the Berlin Olympics. By using top designers, the Nazis showed an appreciation of the importance of branding and image, which appealed domestically to millions of Germans like Hennecke, and overseas to many who frankly sympathised with Germany's ideals, at least until war came.

He was immediately accepted, volunteering just as the Waffen-SS had started to expand following the fall of France; with a possible invasion of England looming, they needed to fill their ranks. Pre-war volunteers for the SS had to be perfect physical specimens, to show proof of pure Germanic ancestry back to 1800, while those who became officers had further to demonstrate their ancestry to 1750; all signed on for an initial period of four years, but under wartime conditions all these requirements were gradually relaxed.

'Our training,' Hennecke remembered, 'stressed three points: physical fitness, weapons proficiency and character. Our days began at 06.00 a.m. with a rigorous hour-long physical training session, a pause for a bowl of porridge, then intensive weapons training, followed by target practice on the ranges and unarmed combat lessons. We continued after a hearty lunch with a drill session, followed by cleaning duties and finished off with a run or a couple of hours on the sports field.' He thought it was ironic that he spent relatively little time on drill and more on tactics, because the unit he served with, the *Leibstandarte*, 'originated as Hitler's personal body guard and, spending most of their time on the parade square, had acquired the derisory nickname of *asphaltsoldaten* (asphalt soldiers)'. Nevertheless, thanks to athletics and cross-country running every day, Hennecke and his SS comrades developed levels of fitness and endurance enabling them to cover half a mile in full kit in twenty minutes, which far surpassed the requirements of conscripts in the *Heer*, the German army.

On qualifying as an SS-*Schütze* (private), Hennecke and his class were awarded their SS walking-out daggers during a ceremony at the Feldherrnhalle Memorial in Munich. This annual ritual, steeped in mysticism and intended to reflect the traditions of medieval Teutonic knights, was held each 9 November, the date of the unsuccessful putsch of 1923 (and later, ominously, of *Kristallnacht*). Etched on his dagger's blade, he remembered, was the SS motto, *Meine Ehre Heisst Treue* (My Honour is Loyalty). On 20 April (Hitler's birthday), they had each taken their oath of loyalty to the Führer.

After gruelling service in the ranks in Russia, Hennecke was selected for officer training and sent to a *Junkerschule* in 1943. The Waffen-SS offered advancement to promising candidates regardless of their education or social background, and named their academies *Junkerschulen* (schools for young nobles). 'We were even issued an etiquette manual that included a chapter on table manners,' he recalled. 'In the middle of the war we were being taught "champagne glasses to be parallel to the third tunic button, arm extended at forty-five degrees, white wine to be drunk from tall glasses, red from short". I've never forgotten that . . . In the middle of the war!' Hennecke broke off, shaking his head in mirth. 'Off-duty, officers and men were obliged to address each other with the classless title of "Kamerad", as you would say "mate", or "buddy". We were forbidden padlocks on our lockers to build the mutual trust necessary in a combat unit, whilst unconditional obedience was required at all times. Such obedience was embodied in the term *Führerprinzip* (leader principle), which essentially meant that Hitler's word was above all written law and therefore refusal of orders from him or his delegates was not an option.'

Evening sessions concentrated on Nazi ideology, the evils of Bolshevism, Aryan genealogy and Nordic mythology, all now exposed as bogus. Hennecke observed of those times, 'we lapped it up, knowing nothing else'. They had to study Hitler's book *Mein Kampf*, and he recalled that during his five-month course, one officer candidate in three was rejected for failing the ideology examination. Simultaneously, field exercises were designed to turn Hennecke and his generation into not just leaders, but an elite. Even before the war, SS schools were producing more than 400 officers a year, but by 1942 nearly 700 Waffen-SS officers had been killed in action, and Hennecke remembered fellow officer candidates from several occupied countries. Most foreigners who volunteered for service in the Germanic legions enlisted to fight Communism, but still had to be able to prove Aryan descent for two generations, and to possess a 'good' character, whatever that meant by SS standards.

Leadership training groomed them to notions of individual responsibility and military teamwork. At the heart of Waffen-SS doctrine, reinforced by Russian Front experiences, were combat concepts born of the final year of the Great War, when *Sturmtruppen* (elite storm troop units) were raised and trained for trench raids. Here, the need for speed, shock and surprise was paramount, all of which required strong leadership skills, the ability to employ initiative when circumstances dictated, and exhaustive training to be able to use any weapon, fight at night and cope with being surrounded and cut off. Leaders were trained always to take immediate, aggressive action, counter-attack without thinking and induce fear in the enemy. Such Great War combat was unconventional and necessarily ruthless, employing knuckle-dusters, trench knives and bayonets, grenades and entrenching tools with edges sharpened to razors. Under these circumstances the taking of prisoners was often regarded as an inconvenience.

Hans Hennecke at the beginning of his career in the Waffen-SS. By December 1944 he was a seasoned veteran of the Russian Front, had won the Iron Cross, gained a commission and was commanding a tank platoon in Jochen Peiper's 1st SS Panzer Regiment. (Author's collection)

Though the scale and technology had changed from 1918, such extreme ruthlessness and fitness, when fused with ideology, made the Waffen-SS a lethal opponent. Taught to believe that the Russians were subhuman and that they were embarking on a crusade to save Western civilisation, Hennecke and his colleagues were indoctrinated to achieve victory at whatever cost. On the Eastern Front, Hennecke remembered his battalion's motto, *Wir nehmen Tod, Wir teilen Tod Aus* (We accept death, we hand out death). Nearby in Russia, he reminisced, was a unit (III Battalion of the 2nd SS *Panzergrenadier* Regiment) which acquired the nickname of *der Lötlampe Abteilung* (Blowtorch Battalion) because of the speed with which they burned through Soviet formations and torched villages. Such concepts the Waffen-SS brought to the Western Front and would employ against their American foes in the Ardennes: they knew no other way.

Hennecke could still recite his SS serial number (363530), and proudly recounted that by 1944 he had become a seasoned veteran of the Russian Front, won the Iron Cross, gained a commission and was commanding a tank platoon in the 1st SS Panzer Regiment. He proved very adaptable and served as a platoon leader (*Zugführer*) of tank, anti-aircraft and combat reconnaissance units, which was his role when an *Untersturmführer* in an SS *Kampfgruppe* during the Battle of the Bulge, aged twenty-four.[3]

Hans Hennecke's story was typical of many 'true believers' in the formations which comprised Josef 'Sepp' Dietrich's Sixth Panzer Army. The potential presence of Dietrich, as we have seen, greatly worried Allied intelligence because of the unique reputation he had accrued to this date, for he was no ordinary military commander but one of the original Nazis. In contrast to the younger and immature Himmler, he was a colourful character, said to be 'larger than life' and one of the closest men to Hitler, who had won over many contemporaries with his sheer military competence during the Second World War; Rundstedt called him 'decent but stupid'. His several biographers agree that his rise to prominence was not necessarily due to Nazi fanaticism, acceptance of unsavoury National Socialist racial policies or political beliefs, but from blind, stubborn loyalty, as well as tactical military skill.[4] Perhaps Hitler identified with the mustachioed, stocky, five-foot-six Bavarian ex-sergeant-major, with blue eyes and brown hair, who had a strong, square jaw and spoke with a broad accent. By all accounts, he was extraordinarily brave, had an infectious sense of humour and enjoyed his drink. [5]

Possibly aware he was overpromoted, Dietrich relied heavily on his chief of staff, Fritz Krämer, a former Wehrmacht officer, to run his command on a day-to-day basis, while – ever the sergeant-major – he spent time with his troops, for example visiting tank repair workshops where he distributed Iron Crosses to the mechanics who kept his panzers on the road.[6] Although Dietrich was liked by many non-SS personnel, the panzer staff officer Oberst Bernd Freytag von Loringhoven observed, 'We weren't impressed with his talents as a commander. He had no prior training at all. He'd been a sergeant in the First World War and after that he never had any kind of advanced military training whatsoever.'[7] The Jesuit-educated cavalry officer Oberstleutnant Philipp Freiherr von Boeselanger (who with his brother was part of the Stauffenberg circle of plotters) agreed: 'Dietrich had a strange way of giving orders. I heard several of his during the war. He'd say "You attack this, you that, then sort it out". It wasn't the way we gave orders in the army, with clear aims and limits and so on. His method was simply "Well do it this way. You left, you right".'[8]

The final instructions for *Herbstnebel* issued to Dietrich and Krämer renamed their command the innocuous-sounding *Auffrischungstab 16* (Refurbishment Staff No. 16), in a final attempt at operational deception (Manteuffel's Fifth Army was similarly retitled as the meaningless *Feldjäger-Kommando z.b.v*) – though Bletchley Park saw straight through these half-hearted ruses. Model's orders, issued via Rundstedt's OB West headquarters, were that they should 'break through the American front to the north of the Schnee Eifel, and resolutely thrust forward with their fast-moving units [i.e. panzers] on their right flank, towards the Meuse crossing points between Liège and Huy, in order to capture these in conjunction with Operation *Greif* [Skorzeny's commandos]. Following this, Sixth Panzer Army will drive forward to the Albert Canal between Maastricht and Antwerp . . . As soon as the Sixth Army has secured the Meuse crossings, this defensive flank will be placed under command of Fifteenth Army. Operation *Strösser* will be carried out with 800 paratroopers at 07.45 a.m. on *Null-Tag* . . . should this operation [*Strösser*] not take place because of unfavourable weather conditions, it will take place 24 hours later . . .'[9]

Privately, Dietrich felt the plan was doomed, but his political nose had taught him to keep his reservations to himself and do what he was told. In a famous September 1945 interview with the Canadian intelligence officer Milton Shulman, all Dietrich's tensions about the offensive bubbled to the surface, with Shulman witnessing him flinging out his arms and puffing out his cheeks. He was under investigation at the time for war crimes against murdered GIs; nevertheless Shulman recorded Dietrich's outburst, expressed in the following dramatic terms:

> 'All I had to do was cross a river, capture Brussels and then go on and take the port of Antwerp. And all this in December, January and February, the worst three months of the year; through the Ardennes where snow was waist deep and there wasn't room to deploy four tanks abreast, let alone six armoured divisions; when it didn't get light until eight in the morning and was dark again at four in the afternoon and my tanks can't fight at night; with divisions that had just been reformed and were composed chiefly of raw untrained recruits; and at Christmas time.' The crack in Dietrich's voice when he reached this last obstacle made it sound like the most heartbreaking of all.[10]

We have to take it at face value that these were Dietrich's private thoughts at the time, and there seems no reason to doubt the victor of endless fights under mountains of Russian snow in much worse sub-zero conditions. Hitler's favouritism towards the SS was reflected not only in the strength and equipment of those individual units committed to battle, but in the size of Dietrich's Sixth Panzer Army itself. With five infantry and four panzer divisions distributed over three corps, plus substantial artillery, *Nebelwerfer* and engineer units, the formation was the size of Fifth and Seventh Armies combined, and clearly designed to be the *Schwerpunkt*, or main effort. He had nearly 700 tanks, tracked tank destroyers and assault guns at his disposal, 685 artillery pieces and 340 *Nebelwerfers.*[11]

None of Dietrich's infantry divisions belonged to the SS, although they came under his command for the offensive. In contrast to Manteuffel's approach in the Fifth Panzer Army's sector, of advancing on a wide front on the basis that 'if we knock on ten doors simultaneously, several will open', Dietrich and Krämer proposed to move along narrow attack corridors, echeloned in depth, which the Fifth Army commander felt inappropriate in the treacherous Ardennes region with its poor roads, numerous rivers and challenging terrain.

Manteuffel argued with much logic that such a tactic offered endless opportunities for the ardent defender to slow down his attacker with well-sited roadblocks and ambushes. The baron would prove correct, as did his map appreciation of the *Herbstnebel* battlefront. Sixth Panzer Army, with the most powerful forces, had been allocated the most difficult terrain. It would not matter how much combat power Dietrich possessed; if the Americans chose to block him, there was no power in the Reich that could force a passage through what was termed the 'northern shoulder'. Manteuffel argued with great foresight in December 1944 that just a little of Dietrich's combat power transferred south to Brandenberger (who had no tanks and too few bridging units) and to his own Fifth Army would yield much greater opportunities than being stuck in traffic jams north of the Schnee Eifel. This was not sour grapes; hindsight has proved Manteuffel right.

Dietrich's Sixth Army included three corps, only two of which were staffed by the Waffen-SS. The exception was that of Generalleutnant Otto Hitzfeld, bearer of the Knight's Cross with Oak Leaves, five times wounded and known as the 'Lion of Sevastopol' for his victory there in 1942. He had taught infantry tactics at the Infantry *Kriegsschule* in Dresden alongside Rommel in the 1930s, later commanding units in France and Russia, before being appointed to lead LXVII Corps on 1 November. Then forty-six, Hitzfeld commanded two horse-drawn *Volksgrenadier* divisions, whose appearance was in total contrast to the usual image one might have of an SS panzer army.

Knight's Cross holder and Eastern Front veteran Oberst Georg Kosmalla commanded the 272nd *Volksgrenadiers*, which had been engaged in heavy fighting against the American 78th Division in the Hürtgen Forest.[12] One of his officers, Leutnant Günther Schmidt, a survivor of the original 272nd Division which had been badly mauled in Normandy, returned to Germany as the only officer left in his battalion. His experience of preparing for *Herbstnebel* was like that of so many other junior leaders: 'Every day more newcomers came; many in grey-green *Kriegsmarine* uniforms, or in the blue-grey of the Luftwaffe. Most of them had only short and insufficient training.'[13]

Another Normandy survivor was Obergefreiter Otto Gunkel of the 981st *Volksgrenadier* Regiment, who remembered the replacements, 'well-fed guys equipped as if it was peacetime, and who were not very happy about a duty as infantry. They had first to resign themselves to their fate and then they would become good and loyal infantrymen'.[14] In overall terms, Kosmalla's division, recalled Schmidt, included about 20 per cent skilled infantrymen and the rest were former Kriegsmarine or Luftwaffe personnel. On 30 October they boarded a train in the dark heading westwards; at Cologne they stopped while an air raid was in progress. 'The train stopped between houses, no one was allowed to get out of the train. The *Flak* started to shoot and some bombs fell in the distance.'[15]

Echoing the experience of the US 4th and 28th Divisions, the Hürtgen soon reduced the much-battered 272nd *Volksgrenadiers* to a 'sad little group of tired soldiers, with dirty, unshaved and torn uniforms, one third of our original strength,' remembered Obergefreiter Gunkel. 'Our company HQ detachment had only four men. Both our heavy-machine gun platoons were decreased to squads. The 5th company was wiped out – wounded, dead, or taken prisoner. This was the horrible result of only ten days in the Hürtgen Forest, even higher losses than during the first ten days in Normandy. I walked behind the horse-drawn cart that was loaded with our dead of the day before.'[16] As they withdrew from the Hürtgen to prepare for *Herbstnebel*, Gunkel saw that the woods around Gemünd and all the other small villages were full of soldiers from newly arrived units.

'These men were well equipped with winter camouflage uniforms, winter-boots, fur-hoods, etc. Long convoys of armoured vehicles, assault guns and artillery were standing along the roads. But we did not then know that these troops were preparing for the Ardennes Offensive.'[17] Arriving after the Hürtgen was seventeen year-old Grenadier Andreas Wego, apprenticed to a mason by trade, who was inducted into the Kriegsmarine in July 1944 for three months' basic training. This included 'half-mile forced marches with a sixty-pound pack and combat gear while wearing a gas mask, followed by classroom training back at the barracks'. At the end of September, when he received his last monthly naval pay of 30 Reichsmarks, his whole class was transferred into the army and the 272nd *Volksgrenadiers*. He then had a month at the divisional battle school near Berlin before heading for the front in November.[18]

Many histories of the Ardennes campaign have alleged the Germans were better-equipped and trained than the opposing US forces. Here is evidence which suggests a different overall trend. German infantry divisions in the Bulge were in nearly every case inferior to their American counterparts and some, such as the 272nd *Volksgrenadiers*, had already taken huge casualties in the Hürtgen, with a consequent effect on morale.

General Hitzfeld's other division was the 326th *Volksgrenadiers*, reformed from another formation annihilated in Normandy and partially containing ethnic *Volksdeutsche* from Hungary. It was commanded by Generalmajor Dr Erwin Kaschner, who had been captured by the British in the First World War and served in France and Russia from 1940 to 1943. His division was originally slated for Manteuffel's Fifth Army, but due to its lack of mobility (it was 400 horses short), it was transferred to the Sixth for operations to protect Dietrich's right flank, where there was less call for movement. Both the 272nd and 326th *Volksgrenadiers* had a largely static role, not unlike Brandenberger's Seventh Army in the south, of seizing the high ground of the Elsenborn Ridge and protecting the flanks from counter-attacking US divisions.

Gelinenkirchen-born Josef Reinartz was a twenty-eight-year-old platoon commander with the 326th in the Ardennes. He had been conscripted in 1938, seen action in France where he was wounded, and Russia where he survived the awful 1941–2 winter before being discharged with severe exhaustion and the effects of frostbite (missing toes) in June 1942. Reading between the lines, his discharge may also have been connected with combat stress (PTSD). He worked on the *Deutsche Reichsbahn* as a locomotive engineer until being recalled to the colours in September 1944 under Himmler's recruitment schemes. He was attached to the 753rd *Volksgrenadier* Regiment and moved to the front with his unit on 26 November, being promoted *Unteroffizier* on 1 December. Combat experience like his – Reinartz had been awarded an Iron Cross and Infantry Assault Badge in Russia – would make a huge difference in the coming days.[19]

Another *Landser* in the 326th was Alfred Becker of Köln, a twenty-year-old *Gefreiter*, who still sports a purplish-red letter 'A' tattooed on his left shoulder blade because 'my *Erkennungsmarke* (dog tags) omitted to indicate my blood group, so I had it done on my shoulder'.[20] In the Ardennes, Becker wore 'an overcoat with a *Kopfschutzer* (toque), mittens with a trigger finger and a sweater with a high neck. Some in our division had camouflaged snow suits.' At the front, Becker smoked a pipe, observing, 'pipes were popular with young men back then. They were better for the front lines. You can see a cigarette burning and so they tend to draw bullets to your face. This is not good for your teeth.' Becker carried a carbine and a smoke grenade. 'The smoke grenade was to hide you if you wanted to attack or get away. Later on, when I became the squad leader, I carried a sub-machine-gun.' He remembered of his days in the Ardennes, 'We thought we could beat the English and Americans in a fair fight, but they had more *matériel* than we did, so the fights were very uneven. If you shot at an American infantry unit, they would blow you to bits with bombs or artillery shells. This was very frustrating. The Americans were very spoiled. Lots of good food, good clothing, nice boots. But they were very humane.'[21]

Despite the fact that Hitzfeld's LXVII Corps mission was to help clear the way for the 1st and 12th SS Panzer Divisions, then contain the 'northern shoulder' of the Bulge, his two divisions wholly, or in part, would fail to achieve even that. Due to the unexpected US V Corps (78th and 2nd Divisions) attack to reach the Roer dams on 14 December, some of the 326th *Volksgrenadiers* would be tied down fighting the US Army at Wahlerscheid. At the same time, Kosmalla's 272nd Division, also embroiled in the same battle, were likewise too preoccupied to shift south and take a full part in the Ardennes assault. Both found themselves fighting hard to retain the village of Kesternich because it was a transit point for *Herbstnebel* units heading south for the concentration areas in the Eifel. Though the pressure on the Germans eased on the days after 16 December, when the US V Corps withdrew south to aid their comrades, the damage had been done. Hitzfeld's divisions had been unable to contribute to the start of the Ardennes attack, besides losing badly needed personnel.[22] The failure of Hitzfeld's corps to support Sixth Panzer Army was not his fault, but further evidence that Hitler had thrown together his Ardennes plan without any real reference to what the US Army might do to thwart him.

The forty-three-year-old Gruppenführer Hermann Priess commanded the I SS Corps, formerly Sepp Dietrich's old formation, which contained 1st and 12th Panzer Divisions, totalling around 240 panzers on 16 December. We have seen via Dietrich's career how the *Leibstandarte* expanded from a motorised regiment in 1939 to the largest division in the armed forces by December 1944. Priess himself had joined the nascent SS in 1934 and fought in Poland, France, Russia, where he led the 3rd SS-Panzer Division *Totenkopf* (Death's Head), and in Normandy leading a corps. Agile and clever, he took over his formation on 30 October. Even though an SS panzer corps sounded the very epitome of a ruthless, fully motorised formation that would slice its way through any opponent or terrain in *Herbstnebel*, Priess was allocated three infantry divisions in addition; their job would be to carve their way through American positions to allow the following panzer divisions unimpeded passage.

The infantry included the 277th *Volksgrenadiers* of Oberst Wilhelm Viebig, an artilleryman by background, who had served in Russia on Field Marshal von Manstein's staff, and assumed command of his division on 4 September. Though formed from the pitiful remnants of a formation that had crawled out of Normandy, few of Viebig's headquarters staff, officers or NCOs were battle-hardened. Many of the replacement grenadiers were *Volksdeutsche*, hailing from Croatia, Alsace (whose loyalty was tested, holding French sympathies), and Vienna, then under threat from the Soviets. Their crest (a 'V' crossed with a sword, referring to Viebig) was painted on their few vehicles, but most mobility rested on bicycles and horses. Field Marshal Model, who inspected them on 28 November around Dahlem, was well aware of their deficiencies but insisted they would perform well through 'ardour and spirit'. At only 80 per cent strength, and with one of their eight battalions already committed to defending a portion of the Siegfried Line elsewhere, the 277th's mission was to break through to the Elsenborn Ridge, north of the Losheim gap.

Alongside Viebig was the 12th *Volksgrenadier* Division, under Generalmajor Gerhardt Engel, an impossibly distinguished combat commander and already holder of a Knight's Cross with Oak Leaves, an adjutant on Hitler's staff from 1938 to 1940, and possessing high decorations from Italy, Serbia, Romania and Finland. A high-flying officer, he had taken over his *Volksgrenadiers* on 9 November and received advancement to *Generalmajor* on 15 November, only three months after his promotion to *Oberst*. One of the best *Volksgrenadier* units allocated to *Herbstnebel*, their badge of a shorting bull reflected the aggression and confidence of its commander – which was mirrored throughout the formation; unlike most of the other *Volksgrenadier* divisions, the 12th was highly experienced, efficient and possessed most of its authorised equipment.

Their role was to punch through the American lines along one of the routes assigned to elements of the 12th SS Division, through Büllingen towards Malmedy, working ahead of the panzers. Helmut Stiegeler of the 12th remembered the night of 15 December when he and his mates received a rare hot meal, and a bottle of schnapps each. Then they began to advance through the hills in the darkness. 'The villages through which we marched lay peaceful in the December night. Perhaps a dog barked here and there, or people were talking and looking at the passing soldiers. Out of an imperfectly blacked-out window a vague light shone out. With all these sights, most of our thoughts were of home in our warm houses with our families.'[23]

The third infantry unit under Priess was the 3rd *Fallschirmjäger* Division under the bespectacled forty-eight-year-old Generalmajor Walther Wadehn; this was an old veteran unit that no longer contained any veterans. Completely destroyed in the fighting around St Lô in July and Falaise in August, its numbers had been made up with Luftwaffe ground personnel, like the 5th *Fallschirmjäger* Division further south. Most of the old jump-trained *Fallschirmjägers*, veterans of Crete or Russia, had already been sacrificed in combat and their replacements were relatively unfit with little understanding of ground combat. Photographs of the division in action show most of its men wearing the ordinary coal scuttle-shaped Wehrmacht helmet, rather than the signature cut-down *Fallschirmjäger* version, which indicated a veteran paratrooper and was only worn by the German parachute force.

Johannes Richter was a not untypical platoon commander in the 3rd *Fallschirmjägers.* He had enlisted as a twelve-year army man in 1932, but was transferred to the Luftwaffe at its creation, and served with the Condor Legion in Spain. He spent nearly ten years with a *Fliegerhorst* (aerodrome) Company, responsible for general supply, maintenance and guarding duties, reaching the rank of *Oberfeldwebel.* That easy life ended when he was transferred to a parachute school in September 1944, where his training lasted six weeks (without any parachuting), before being posted to the division on 11 November. Promoted to *Fahnenjunker/Oberfeldwebel* (Senior Cadet Officer/NCO) in the 6th Company, Richter and his regiment were almost immediately pitted against the US 1st Infantry Division in the Hürtgen fighting, where he was wounded twice and his formation suffered 1,658 casualties in two weeks. Some of them were still in combat around Düren when the rest of the division transferred south for the start of *Herbstnebel.*[24]

This is why the Sixth Army chief of staff, Krämer, assessed the 3rd *Fallschirmjägers* 'at only 75 per cent strength' on 16 December, an optimistic rating in itself, given they had no armoured vehicles (StuG assault guns) in their anti-tank battalion. Although Wadehn, its commander, had taken over back in August, his chief of staff was so clueless about land operations that Wadehn had to request his immediate replacement. By *Null-Tag,* only two of the division's three regiments were assembled, with the third disengaging from the fighting in Düren. The *Fallschirmjäger's* task was to dislodge the US 14th Cavalry Group from the Losheim gap, overwhelming it in the towns of Manderfeld and Holzheim, and opening up routes for the 1st SS Panzer Division.

While also controlling four army *Nebelwerfer* and two army artillery regiments attached for fire support, the undoubted mainstay of Preiss's corps were his two crack SS panzer divisions, and the 501st SS Heavy Panzer Battalion (*Schwere-SS-Panzer-Abteilung*) of around thirty monster sixty-nine-ton King Tigers, although only half of the latter were fully operational on 16 December. Despite the ravages of war, 'crack' was still an appropriate word to describe the combat power and efficiency of the men and equipment they contained. The youthful Brigadeführer Wilhelm Mohnke, aged thirty-three, commanded the 1st SS Panzer Division *Leibstandarte.* He had joined the Nazi Party in September 1931 and been one of the original 120 members of Dietrich's SS Watch-Battalion-Berlin, formed to guard Hitler's Chancellery in March 1933. Mohnke saw action in France, Poland and the Balkans, and was eventually given command of a regiment in the 12th SS Panzer Division *Hitlerjugend*.

After leading his regiment through the attritional Normandy campaign, on 20 August Mohnke was awarded his original division, the *Leibstandarte*, which he would take to the Ardennes. Normandy had been in every way a killer for his division, from which no tanks or artillery returned at all; in a typical 1,000-man battalion only fifty escaped to fight again in the Ardennes.[25] Yet, by December, it managed to boast a formidable complement of armoured vehicles and half-tracks. Its panzer regiment, led by Joachim 'Jochen' Peiper (one-time commander of *der Lötlampe Abteilung*, Blowtorch Battalion), a former adjutant of Himmler's and recently recovered from wounds received in Normandy, fielded thirty-eight Panthers and thirty-four Panzer IVs. Along with the King Tigers, Panthers and Panzer IVs, the division's anti-tank battalion boasted ten *Panzerjäger* IVs, a grand total of nearly one hundred tanks and tank destroyers, over 19,000 officers and men and nearly 3,000 vehicles.[26]

It was in the *Leibstandarte*'s panzer regiment that Hans Hennecke served, leading a platoon of tanks from his mount, Panther No. 111, driven by *Rottenführer* Bahnes. 'Peiper was the most dynamic man I ever met. He just got things done,' Hennecke told me. 'He was not much older than me, but seemed to belong to another generation. He was mature, spoke languages, was clever,' Hennecke remembered, still in awe of his former comrade.[27]

In 1944, according to Hans Bernhard, then a twenty-four-year-old *Hauptsturmführer* and Wilhelm Mohnke's 1c (intelligence officer), their men responded to the 'guiding principles of duty, loyalty, honour, Fatherland, comradeship'.[28]

Duty. Honour. The Bulge gave rise to much debate about the brutality of Waffen-SS units towards American prisoners, and one commander consistently close to such accusations was Mohnke. On 28 May 1940, he had led an SS company which murdered eighty British prisoners of war at Wormhout, near Dunkirk. On 8 June 1944 his regiment was implicated in the killing of thirty-five Canadian prisoners in Normandy. We will never know how many Russians had disappeared under similar circumstances in the east. Carl-Heinz Bohnke remembered in Russia 'We saw endless lines of prisoners. We couldn't look after them. The later units did. We couldn't.'[29]

Oberst Bernd Freytag von Loringhoven (an *Ostfront* veteran who would command the Bundeswehr's 19th *PanzerBrigade* in the 1960s) also recalled seeing 'a line of Russian prisoners and a group of SS soldiers getting ready to shoot them. The SS sergeant said, "They're just sub-humans, colonel". And it was absolutely typical of the ideology that leaders in the Waffen-SS had told the simple man, the NCO, that prisoners of war without weapons were simply to be shot whenever necessary.'[30] The Russians themselves were already used to similar treatment from Stalin's own thugs, but the consequences would be vastly different when organised murder met a democracy in war. It was this kind of unrestricted, premeditated horror, practised routinely by Himmler's henchmen in Russia, which the Waffen-SS would bring to the Bulge. In short, murder and mayhem was the business of Mohnke and his men, as we shall discover shortly.

Such Nazi brutality was, and remains, beyond comprehension, except in one area. Ever since the RAF's first thousand-bomber raid on Cologne of 30–31 May 1942, German soldiers and civilians had witnessed the terrible destruction of their own cities with consequential horrendous casualties, from which no one in the Reich was immune – except Hitler, of course, who refused to acknowledge or visit the stricken areas. On 16

Exactly a month before the offensive, on 16 November 1944, RAF bombers attacked the German city of Düren, killing 3,000 and wrecking the town. Amongst those detailed to clear up was the 1st SS Panzer Regiment. On seeing the carnage wrought by Allied bombs, they vowed revenge. (Author's collection)

November 1944 the city of Düren had been attacked by 485 Lancasters and thirteen Pathfinder Mosquitoes of the Royal Air Force. Sirens sounded and residents went down into the cellars. 'When we emerged to clear up the mess, there was no mess to clear up because there was no town. There was just rubble. Düren was no more. The whole thing had taken about forty minutes,' remembered one resident. Of 22,000 inhabitants, over 3,000 were killed and Obersturmbannführer Peiper and some of his men had been among those detailed to help rescue the survivors. After the war, the SS officer recounted how 'the civilians had to be scraped from the walls', and in response he swore he 'would personally castrate the men who did that – with a piece of broken glass – blunt at that'. The *Leibstandarte*'s, and Peiper's, viciousness could never be justified or forgivable, but the suffering of Düren, and other German cities, made it slightly more understandable.[31]

Although Mohnke consistently denied he had issued orders to mistreat or murder captives, a similar pattern of deaths followed his military career wherever he served. In an organisation of thugs and murderers, with such 'form' Mohnke seems to have been near top in terms of nastiness. 'After several years [of war] they were so desensitised,' reflected Gerhard Stiller, a panzer commander with Mohnke's division, 'they didn't even notice it any more. They'd bump someone off just like that. They had to develop humanity again, and that takes time.'[32] Perhaps Mohnke and his crew echoed the conversation that an army officer, Leutnant Freiherr Peter von der Osten-Sacken remembered with some SS officers, 'who more or less told me, yes, things are pretty bad, but we have to win. We have so many bad things on our conscience that we have no choice but to hold out.' Eduard Jahnke of the 2nd SS *Das Reich* Division admitted the same in a different way: 'We were sure, we Waffen-SS men, they'd take no prisoners, just put us up against the wall. So it was "fight to the last bullet".'[33]

The second armoured formation under Priess was Brigadeführer Hugo Kraas's 12th SS-Panzer-Division *HitlerJugend*, which grew out of a cadre of the 1st SS Division in late 1943. Like his compatriot Mohnke, Kraas was born in 1911, joined the Nazi Party in 1934 and the SS the following year. He followed a similar career path in the *Leibstandarte*, fighting through Poland, France, the Balkans and Russia, but was wounded in January 1944 and missed the gruelling Normandy campaign which killed so many of his colleagues – the 12th left Normandy with 300 men, ten tanks and no artillery.[34] It had commenced that campaign with a strength of over 20,000 men, many of them extremely experienced NCOs and veterans of Russia, and 150 tanks. Having recovered and passed a division commander's course, Kraas stepped up to lead the 12th SS on 15 November when its former commander, Fritz Krämer, resigned to head Dietrich's staff.

Assessed at 90 per cent strength in manpower and 80 per cent in equipment, on 10 December its Panzer Regiment included 38 Panthers and 37 Panzer IVs, the anti-tank battalion possessed 22 *Panzerjäger* IVs, while another 28 *Panzerjäger* IVs and 14 *Jagdpanthers* ('hunting panthers') served in attached formations, a total of 139 tracked, armoured vehicles.[35] The forty-five-tonne *Jagdpanther* tank destroyer combined the 88mm gun carried in the Tiger I and King Tiger, with the excellent suspension and sloping armour of the Panther. Army Hauptmann Erwin Kressmann of the 519th *Schwer Panzerjäger-Abteilung* (Heavy Anti-tank Battalion) took his *Jagdpanthers* to the Ardennes, remembering, 'With the enormous penetrating power of the eighty-eight we were able to effectively fight American tanks . . . We were able to let the enemy come fairly close, first of all because of our own armour and because of the strength and impact of the eighty-eight gun.'[36]

Among the *Panzergrenadiers* serving in the 12th SS was Werner Kinnett, of Duisburg, who had turned seventeen in 1944. In April that year, two officers from the 12th *HitlerJugend* Division had arrived at his school and shown a propaganda film depicting various Waffen-SS heroes on the Eastern Front; they followed it with a recruitment talk, ending with 'Raise your hand if you want to join'. They all did, some out of enthusiasm, others probably because of peer pressure. A couple had wanted to join a Wehrmacht unit; the recruiting officer cleverly warned them they must wait a further year, but the Waffen-SS would take them immediately. Werner asked if he should get his father's permission, but the officer again had a ready answer: 'If it's alright by the Führer, then it will be alright by your father'. He joined the division in April 1944, and *eight weeks* later found himself on the Invasion Front at Caen, where he was soon wounded. He remembered that at the front other SS units got beer in rest areas, but the boys of his unit were given only milk. In hospital he was poached by an officer from the *Das Reich* Division and joined its *Aufklärungs Abteilung* (Reconnaissance Battalion), training in the Eifel in readiness for the Ardennes.[37]

The nineteen-year-old *Unterscharführer* Hans Baumann, who would command a *Hitlerjugend* assault gun in the Ardennes, had already experienced combat with the Allies in Normandy. He observed: 'We had already found out about the American army during the invasion. We were impressed by the high numbers of people and amount of *matériel.* We couldn't keep up with that. You could be as brave as you wanted, but no soldier can endure that. We were simply overwhelmed by the vast amount of *matériel.* Even at that point our fight was basically already useless.' [38] Nineteen-year-old Bernard Heisig also fought in its ranks, recalling, 'We didn't like the name *Hitlerjugend* at all, as it made us sound like boys. We wanted to be real soldiers. The youngest ones weren't given cigarettes. They didn't smoke. They were actually given sweets instead.'[39]

Dietrich possessed an even more powerful armoured formation, equipped with around 280 panzers, commanded by the victor of Arnhem, fifty-year-old Willi Bittrich. The history of the latter's II SS Panzer Corps was a short and violent one. It included the 2nd SS Division *Das Reich*, led by Brigadeführer Heinz Lammerding, aged thirty-nine, who took command of his division on 23 October. It, too, was rebuilding after Normandy, where it was recorded as losing all but 450 men, fifteen tanks and six guns.[40] Assessed at 80 per cent strength on 10 December, *Das Reich* fielded 58 Panthers, 28 Panzer IVs and 28 StuGs, with 20 *Jagdpanzer* IVs in the anti-tank battalion, totalling 130 armoured vehicles. Commanding a company of *Das Reich*'s Panthers was Obersturmführer Fritz Langanke, who at twenty-five had already been awarded a Knight's Cross for his leadership in Normandy. He enthused about his mounts: 'The Panther was the most functional and best tank in the world until the very end of the war. This was based on three components: velocity, cross-country mobility and tank protection. The Panther definitely achieved the best results in all three. The Sherman was an easy opponent for us. They could fire at us, but couldn't penetrate our tanks. They had to come close within a few hundred metres to stand a chance.'[41]

Bittrich's second formation was the 9th SS *Hohenstaufen* Division, under the capable Brigadeführer Sylvester Stadler. The title came from a noble dynastic family who produced a number of kings and emperors in the twelfth and thirteenth centuries. The thirty-four-year-old Stadler, an Austrian, was another pre-war SS recruit who had fought in most campaigns prior to the Ardennes. In December 1944, the *Hohenstaufen* possessed 151 tanks and assault guns, distributed throughout the division: an impressive turnaround for a division reduced to 460 men, twenty-five tanks and twenty artillery pieces after Normandy, although it had fought more recently at Arnhem.[42] Both the 2nd and 9th Divisions had followed the bloody trail of combat in Russia and Normandy and their few surviving officers and NCOs were very experienced indeed.

With these two divisions, Bittrich's strong corps was considered the most militarily professional in the Waffen-SS.

Full of young fanatics as all these Waffen-SS divisions were, in December 1944 it would not be correct to call all Dietrich's men 'true believers'. Until 1941 the SS was an entirely voluntary organisation, but after the invasion of Russia the original SS formations began receiving small numbers of *Volksdeutsche* replacements as the supply of German volunteers became exhausted. Serving under Jochen Peiper in the 1st SS Division, for example, was twenty-two-year-old Georg Fleps, tall, blond-haired and known as 'a bit of a hot-head'; he was in fact a Romanian volunteer, and we shall meet him later.

Although Himmler's divisions still had the pick of Germany's manpower, at the same time they began to rely on draftees, in competition with the army. Two of the last prisoners brought into American lines before 16 December were from the 12th SS Division. One had stepped on a mine and caused quite a stir among the US medics treating him, as their first SS casualty. The second, unwounded, prisoner was Polish, recently drafted into the SS from a part of western Poland absorbed into the Third Reich. He and his mate were far from home, had no wish to fight the Americans

The Panzer Mark V 'Panther' was probably the best tank to emerge from the Second World War. It weighed in at 45 tons and although 15 tons heavier than its rival the Sherman, Panthers had excellent cross-country mobility due to their wide tracks. Its sloping frontal armour proved invulnerable to most Allied tanks, while its 75mm gun could kill its opponents at 2,000 yards. For *Herbstnebel*, each German armoured division fielded an under-strength battalion of Panthers (between 35–45 tanks), half the number the same divisions deployed in Normandy. In all, about 400 were committed to battle in the Ardennes. (NARA)

and wished to desert, hence his friend colliding with a *shu-mine* in no man's land at night. Both *Hitlerjugend* Division conscripts recounted a story to the medical staff, delivered via an interpreter, of how their division were assembling opposite for an attack, using searchlights to illuminate their advance, which – sadly – was not relayed to VIII Corps headquarters as the divisional intelligence officer concerned wished to talk personally with the prisoners.[43]

By 1944, it had become commonplace for Luftwaffe and naval personnel to be reassigned to the Waffen-SS, without any say in the matter. Although he did not fight in the Ardennes, the German writer and future Nobel Prize-winner Günter Grass was typical of this latter group, applying to join the submarine force on his seventeenth birthday in 1944, but on rejection was drafted into the 10th SS Panzer Division instead. Among numerous others in *Kampfgruppe Peiper*, for example, Rottenführer Heinz Schwarz, commander of a half-track in the 2nd SS-*Panzergrenadier* Regiment, was one of many in the formation to have been forcibly transferred from the Luftwaffe that summer.[44]

In the Ardennes, out of 150 personnel in one sample company of the *Leibstandarte* (10th Company of 2nd SS-*Panzergrenadier* Regiment), 10 per cent were Normandy veterans, 15 per cent came from the Luftwaffe (aged between eighteen and thirty), and 60 per cent were seventeen-year-old youths, all born in 1927, drawn straight from the *Reichsarbeitsdienst* (RAD), who had received *at most* three weeks of training. The remainder were new recruits from a variety of backgrounds with different levels of training.[45] Himmler's desperate drive for recruits in 1944 – whether into the *Volksgrenadiers* or the Waffen-SS – had completely broken the system for recruitment and training in the Reich. In overall terms, of all the military recruits born in 1928, some 95,000 (17.3 per cent) were drafted into the SS. Few of these had received any meaningful military training, yet they made up the bulk of manpower within the SS divisions in the Ardennes. A GI on the receiving end may have viewed these statistics in a different light – each one would have seemed a potential killer – but youth and enthusiasm alone do not make a soldier.

This analysis is very much at odds with that of Hugh Cole, who in the US Army Official History of 1965, wrote, 'The 1st SS Panzer Division . . . was the strongest fighting unit in the Sixth Panzer Army. Undiluted by any large influx of untrained Luftwaffe or Navy replacements, possessed of most of its T/O&E [Table of Organisation and Equipment], it had an available armored strength on 16 December of about a hundred tanks, equally divided between the Mark IV and the Panther, plus forty-two Tiger tanks belonging to the 501st SS Panzer Detachment.'[46] Cole was writing from the best available data twenty years after the Bulge, but far more detailed information has surfaced since then.

Given that the *Volksgrenadier* infantry divisions were composed of many similar individuals, what set the SS divisions apart? It was the effort made to teach these new recruits, whether volunteers or conscripts, ex-Luftwaffe or Kriegsmarine, that they were an elite. Training times were ludicrously short, and the men themselves were not always as enthusiastic as the earlier, more impressionable youngsters, but veteran soldiers and NCOs were sprinkled at every level in all units, specifically to engender the SS ethos. The cavalry officer Philipp von Boeselanger realised, 'They almost took it for granted that they would die; but they were also brutal in their killing', while Rottenführer Jürgen Girgensohn later mused, 'In retrospect I believe there was a strong *esprit de corps* based on a common attitude. We were convinced it was a just struggle and that we were a master race. We were the best of the master race – that does unite people.'[47]

However, this much is also clear: all the four SS panzer divisions were a shadow of their former selves in terms of personnel and equipment, when compared to the same formations that had fought in Normandy just six months earlier. Himmler had restored their numbers, but the replacements were immature, lacked experience and in some cases had received no meaningful combat training whatsoever. Whatever they were, they certainly weren't superhuman. Some of the Waffen-SS troopers who fought in the Bulge were undoubtedly brainwashed thugs and fanatics, but many were ordinary conscripts, new to war and caught in a brutal system.

In the midst of this system was Hans Hennecke, by his own admission an enthusiastic 'believer', but someone who, I sensed, would have made an efficient leader of men in any army. His combat experience had made him a professional soldier. However, it was not until after his death that I discovered he had been sentenced to be executed in July 1946 for war crimes committed against American soldiers in the Ardennes, something he had never admitted to me in his lifetime.

Interlude

THE COMING BATTLE was not initiated on land, but in the North Atlantic.

The Captain's log read '9 December 1944, 27th Day at Sea. On station, map square AK 5226'. The conditions were appalling. Outside, the green sea boiled like an erupting volcano as the bows emerged – like a knife of dark metal in an unfriendly sea, and then the periscopes, dripping. Next the conning tower pierced the surface at a crazy angle and icy spume cascaded down as the submarine clawed its way to the surface. Mountains of water heaved and flung themselves madly at the sky. The craft rolled uncomfortably as waves pummelled her hull. While *U-1232* wallowed, four crewmen tumbled on to the bridge. Gusts of wind bearing sleet and snow cut into their faces like needles. With smarting eyes, the watch scanned every compass point: torn, menacing clouds, no horizon and little visibility though it was midday. It was unhealthy for a U-boat to remain long on the surface, but aircraft were far from their thoughts. No flyer could survive such a storm.

Since leaving Horten in Norway, *U-1232* had been discreet, running submerged on her silent electric engines and surfacing only at night, using her diesels to recharge the batteries. The swifter, air-breathing diesels would have exhausted the crew's oxygen and were useless underwater, unless they used the snorkel, a device that allowed them to travel submerged – and hidden – while drawing in air to feed the hungry diesels. In such a storm snorkels were redundant. So the Type IXC

U-boat had crawled along on her twin electric motors at five knots, the speed of a man on a bicycle, when she could easily have made fifteen on the surface. After twenty-seven days of no washing, *U-1232*'s crew of fifty welcomed any opportunity for fresh air, even if storm-tossed with cold water streaming through the conning tower hatch every few seconds.

On his way to hunt the waters off Halifax, Nova Scotia, forty-year-old Kapitän zur See Kurt Dobratz had been given an important mission. Although carrying twenty-two torpedoes, he was not after Allied shipping – for the time being. Since the gradual capture of its weather ships, the Third Reich had been weather-blind. For some reason beyond Dobratz's knowledge U-boat *Kontrol* in Berlin was keener than usual on meteorology. His submarine was one of four despatched to send back weather reports from the North Atlantic. Days earlier his admiral, Eberhard Godt, the *Befehlshaber der Unterseeboote* (Commander of Submarines), had radioed him 'weather reports are of the greatest importance for the war on land and in the air'. Another reminder of the following day read 'Importance and seriousness of task demands that all means be used to get messages through'. The Allies intercepted both messages and pondered. Dobratz must have known something was afoot and was anxious not to screw up his first war patrol. Although trained as a naval officer, the already highly decorated officer had spent eight years attached to the Luftwaffe, with eleven combat sorties in bombers under his belt, and understood the importance of accurate climatic returns.

As each broadcast increased the risk of detection by Allied direction-finding, Dobratz crammed as much information as possible into his signal, which consisted of no more than two dozen letters, each representing a certain measurement – barometric pressure, cloud cover, wind strength and direction, visibility, air temperature, and so on. The Allies as well as *Kontrol*, he knew, would be waiting for his report, and use it to hunt him down. Thrown about in the conning tower, doubtless with numb fingers by this point, the watch took the necessary readings quickly and sent them below to the radio operator, who swiftly encoded them using his Enigma machine. Shortly after, a *Wetterkurzschlussel* (short weather signal) of only a few seconds flew across the airwaves via relay stations to Berlin. Knowing that Allied destroyers would now be vectored on to his position, he moved away quickly, ready to report again in twelve hours' time. Job done, *U-1232* slunk beneath the furious waves.

In *Koralle* ('Coral'), codename for the bunker complex of U-boat headquarters at Bernau, five miles north of Berlin, the report was read impatiently. Cloud, fog, driving snow, freezing temperatures were all welcome news. Dobratz's information corresponded to that of the other weather-reporting submarines and the eleven-strong team of Operation Haudegen, a land-based weather station on the Norwegian island of Spitzbergen. A cold weather front of intense severity was moving towards Europe and would arrive within the week. It was just what the Fatherland needed.

In Berlin, Dr Karl Recknagel, the Kriegsmarine's chief meteorologist, analysed these and other reports. Back in November the head of the Luftwaffe's Weather Office, Oberstleutnant Werner Schwerdtfeger and his deputy, Major Dr Schuster, had been summoned and given a well-nigh impossible task:

> two days before the occurrence in the coming month of December, you have to forecast the date of a period of five days or more in which fog or low clouds will continuously cover a wide area of the Rhine River north of the 50° parallel, including the region of the Ardennes and southern England.[1]

Fortunately, Schwerdtfeger had been cataloguing and analysing weather trends of the preceding thirty years and was able to find some patterns that conformed, in part, to the requirements demanded.[2] With due caution, on 11 December he predicted three-to-four days of calm succeeded by poorer weather and fog commencing on 15 December. This corresponded with Recknagel's prediction of two weeks of rain, fog and heavy snow, beginning on 16 December, based on the reports of Dobratz, his fellow submariners and the Spitzbergen weather station.[3] Both Schwerdtfeger and Schuster were promoted one grade for their services, while Crista Schroeder, one of Hitler's secretaries, recalled that his young 'weather prophet' Schwerdtfeger, who had predicted the period of fog before the offensive began, 'received a gold watch in gratitude for his correct forecast'.[4]

Bletchley Park analysts saw a sudden spike in the number of U-boats recording weather and in the quantity of meteorological reports transmitted, but were clueless, until the great attack began, as to why. On 19 December, Kapitän Dobratz in *U-1232* and three other U-boat commanders were radioed thanks from *Koralle* in Bernau, 'Your recent [weather] reports contributed decisively to determining the beginning of our great offensive in the west on 16 December.'[5]

'Weather was a weapon the German army used with success, especially in the Ardennes offensive,' mused Rundstedt in a post-war debrief. Eisenhower would observe later that 'as long as the weather kept our planes on the ground it would be an ally of the enemy, worth many additional divisions'.[6]

Herbstnebel was on!

In planning, Hitler and OKW seemed to have thought of everything: the weather; paratroopers; SS commandos and, of course, the three attacking armies. They had also come up with another – often overlooked – aspect of attacking and distracting the Allies, this time on the soil of England. It was known that many German military prisoners were screened initially for their political sympathies at Camp 23 (Le Marchant Barracks in Devizes, Wiltshire), where they would be graded by a coloured patch sewn on to their uniform. White denoted indifference to National Socialism. Grey meant that the prisoner, although not an ardent Nazi, had no strong feelings either way; dedicated fanatics and true believers wore a black patch, were labelled Category 'A', and posted elsewhere to 'black' camps in remote parts of the United Kingdom.

The screening process was hurried during the autumn of 1944 due to the large volume of prisoners arriving in Britain, which led to some 'blacks' being mixed in camps with the moderates. In early December 1944 the Category 'A' Waffen-SS, U-boat and *Fallschirmjäger* captives housed temporarily at Devizes received orders by means of coded letters from 'relatives' in the Reich. They were to break out in support of the Ardennes offensive, seize weapons including tanks from a nearby army base and march on London.

The plan was betrayed by an anti-Nazi captive, Feldwebel Wolfgang Rosterg, and the ringleaders immediately despatched as far away as possible, to Camp 21 at Cultybraggan, deep in the central highlands of Scotland. Because of an administrative error, Rosterg and another moderate, Unteroffizier Gerhard Rettig, were sent there too – where the Category 'A' Germans retaliated. Rosterg was hanged in the camp latrine and Rettig beaten to death, though seven of their murderers were later executed in north London's Pentonville Prison. The innovative rebellion caused much concern in wartime Britain, where around 600 camps containing 250,000 German prisoners of war were guarded by the merest fraction of that number, often men from the Pioneer Corps or Polish refugees in uniform.

Generally the German captives were an extremely well-behaved lot, for whom British hospitality represented a consistently higher standard of living than their comrades enjoyed in the Third Reich. The same was true of the far greater numbers shipped to the United States and Canada. In all three countries, prisoners worked on the land and befriended local families, while very few indeed proved to be diehard members of the 'escapers club' more frequently seen in the Allied prisoner of war camps of Germany and Poland. Astonishingly, in Britain those captives who undertook farm labouring, construction work or cleared bomb damage were actually paid at current union rates, of between three and six shillings for a forty-eight-hour week.[7]

The march on London was a brilliant concept, if illegal under international law, which came to nothing. Today's military minds would call it asymmetric warfare.

PART TWO

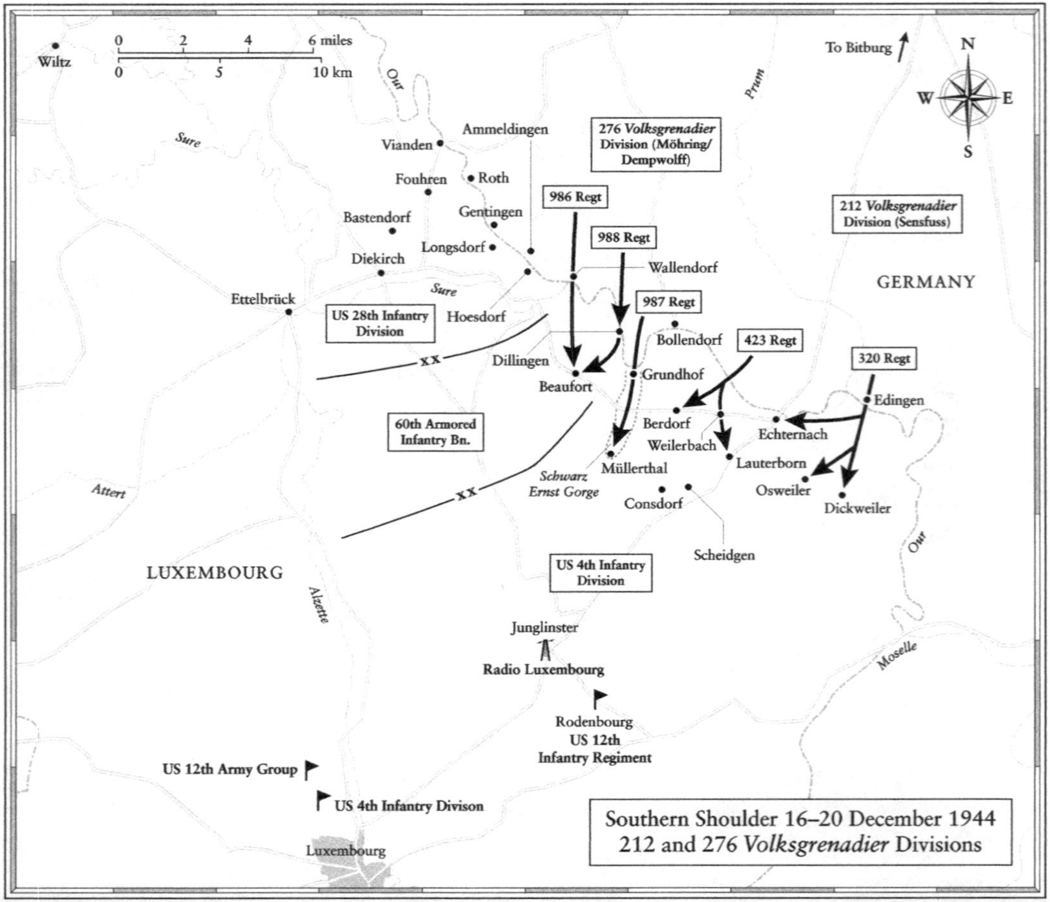

Southern Shoulder 16–20 December 1944
212 and 276 *Volksgrenadier* Divisions

15

Null-Tag

Order of the Day
We attack!
Soldiers of the Western front! Your great hour has come. Strong attacking armies have banded today against the Anglo-Americans. I don't have to add anything to this. You sense it all! We gamble everything! Carry with you the holy duty to give everything and to do superhuman efforts. For our Fatherland and the Führer!
Signed: v. Rundstedt, OB West, Generalfeldmarschall.
Addendum to the Order of the Day
We will not disappoint the faith that the Führer and Fatherland have put in us, which has created the sword of retribution. Let's move on in the spirit of Leuthen! Our slogan remains right now: No soldier in the world must be better than we soldiers of the Eifel and Aachen!
Signed: Model, Army Group 'B', Generalfeldmarschall.[1]

'THE HISTORY OF a battle is not unlike the history of a ball,' famously uttered Arthur Wellesley, 1st Duke of Wellington, in 1815. 'Some individuals may recollect all the little events of which the great result is the battle won or lost, but no individual can recollect the order in which, or the exact moment at which, they occurred, which makes all the difference as to their value or importance.'[2] Wellington was thinking of Waterloo which he had just fought seven weeks earlier, but his quote encapsulates the difficult job of the military historian in trying to piece together a huge jigsaw of combat episodes.

If the swirling mass of troops at Waterloo was complicated, the Bulge was a hundred times more so. The 1944 winter campaign was a vast series of loosely interconnected battles, each fought in separate locales, often in ignorance of other, equally important, skirmishes taking place just down the road. Historical events are slippery and facts frequently burnished to a distracting lustre that alternately dulls or shines as its participants fade.

In order to understand what the Battle of the Bulge was really like, we need to spend a while piecing together the first days, getting to know the terrain. It makes sense to divide the terrain into three sectors, one for each attacking German army, and start on the southern flank of the offensive, with Brandenberger's Seventh Army, and work our way gradually north. Most histories have tended to start – and linger – in the north, which distorts the sheer breadth of the offensive.

At precisely 05.30 a.m., Saturday, 16 December 1944, the misty gloom of the Ardennes was ripped apart by a deafening roar. To those who happened to be watching, the eastern horizon turned white, 'as though a volcano had suddenly erupted or someone had turned a light switch on'.[3] The sudden cacophony rolled from the resort city of Echternach in the south and along eighty-nine miles of front, to the pretty half-timbered town of Monschau in the north. Woods were shredded, the earth trembled and the ground exploded in showers of stones and red-hot metal splinters. GIs cowered in their tree-trunk bunkers and stone houses, while every calibre of shell the Third Reich possessed was hurled at them.

All manner of weapons, from huge railway guns firing 280mm (eleven-inch) and 380mm (fifteen-inch) projectiles to V-1 flying bombs, and V-2 rockets were added to the range of firepower, hurtling their way beyond American lines to Liège, Brussels and Antwerp. At 3.20 p.m. one of the V-2s hit the Rex Cinema in central Antwerp, killing 567 people, including 296 Allied servicemen; they were part of a capacity audience watching *Buffalo Bill*, starring Joel McCrea and Maureen O'Hara. In the Ardennes, hunkering deeper, the US Army wondered what to make of the sudden storm of steel as nearly two thousand guns and rocket launchers made their lives hellish for ninety long minutes.[4]

The American presence in the Ardennes region amounted to around 85,000 GIs in elements of five infantry divisions and part of an armoured division – 242 Sherman tanks, 182 tank destroyers and 394 artillery pieces. Against them, the first wave of Hitler's last great offensive began to march – around 200,000 men, supported by just over 600 tanks in thirteen infantry and five panzer divisions. Both sides would commit many more units to battle in the ensuing days. Such was the cloak of secrecy that all German divisional commanders had been told of their missions only on 9 December, then briefed personally by Hitler on 11 and 12 December at Ziegenberg – there were two briefings because of the number of personnel involved. Regimental commanders were let in on the great secret on 14 December, and their junior officers put in the picture on the 15th, the day before the offensive. These are ludicrously short times in which to plan any military endeavour, made more difficult because, for security reasons, personal reconnaissance of the forward terrain was forbidden and aerial photography in short supply. Never before in modern warfare had such a large force stumbled into combat with such a paltry knowledge of their opponents or the terrain.

In some sectors, to aid the advance of assault detachments in the early morning murk, searchlights were deployed, bouncing their beams off the low lying clouds, bringing an eerie half-light to the proceedings. Charlie Haug of the US 28th Division recalled, 'The Germans had set up about ten or twelve gigantic searchlights on the hills about two or three miles from our positions. They aimed the beams of the lights up

Serving in the 212th *Volksgrenadier* Division, Bavarian Major Ernst Schrotberger had survived severe wounding in Lithuania to be posted to command a battery of six of these 105mm howitzers for *Herbstnebel*. Each gun had a range of 12,000 yards and with their ammunition limbers, were pulled by teams of six horses. (Author's collection)

into the fog and clouds. This caused the lights to reflect down from the fog onto our positions and made it seem almost like moonlight' – it was probably inspired by the British tactic of doing something similar in the closing stages of the Normandy campaign.[5]

Opposite 'Tubby' Barton's US 4th Division in the extreme south, where the terrain was exceptionally difficult, Generalleutnant Franz Sensfuss's 212th *Volksgrenadier* Division was at full strength with a good core of experienced junior leaders. In its ranks were men like Grenadier Georg Jedelhauser, a native of Swabia, assigned to a *Granatwerfer* (mortar) squad. Aged nineteen and a shoemaker in Grösskotz (near Ulm) until conscripted, Georg had been the breadwinner for his mother, sister and younger brother, his father having died in 1930. Like many of his comrades, Jedelhauser was a *Grünschnabel* (literally green beak) and could not call on any previous combat experience, so would rely on the *alte Hasen* (old hares) for guidance.

Grenadier Friedrich 'Fritz' Gabriel provided that kind of experience. Born in West Prussia, and twenty-eight when he was called up in August 1941, Gabriel had served as a Luftwaffe anti-aircraft gunner in Russia before being retrained as a grenadier in December 1944 and joining the 5th Company of 423rd Grenadier Regiment. His was a typical *Volksgrenadier* experience, of a skilled Luftwaffe man being re-roled as infantry. Other experienced soldiers included Grenadier Peter Kelch, who served in the 212th's Fusilier Battalion. In December 1944, Kelch had just turned twenty, but already boasted two years' service in Russia. Although wounded in May 1943, he had returned to duty and was awarded an Iron Cross, Close Combat Badge in Bronze and Infantry Assault Badge between January and May 1944 – evidence of pretty desperate fighting. He was precisely the kind of veteran the new division needed to steady its green recruits as it prepared for battle.[6]

Bavarian Major Ernst Schrotberger was a veteran officer commanding a battery in the division's artillery regiment. He had served in Russia since 1941, where his horses, commandeered in France, all perished in the cold. He recalled reaching Leningrad's suburbs and being based at one stage in the Peterhof Palace. August 1944 saw him fighting in Lithuania, where he was ordered on account of his rank to take command of an infantry battalion – despite his background as a gunner – and lead it in a local counter-attack. Severely wounded in the action, he was evacuated; during his convalescence he was promoted from *Hauptmann* to *Major*, awarded an Iron Cross, but learned that his two fellow battery commanders and artillery CO, all close friends, had been killed. This was part of the collapse of Army Group Centre, from which he was lucky to have escaped. Once recovered from his wounds, Major Schrotberger was posted to command a horse-drawn battery of 105mm howitzers for the Ardennes attack.

The 212th had trained briefly at Schieradz (now Sieradz) in Poland in September–October, then entrained and transferred by rail to the Trier area before commitment to battle. Like most other *Volksgrenadier* units, they possessed virtually no vehicles and far fewer tank destroyers than authorised, starting *Herbstnebel* with five. Because of its confident commander, full strength, lively training and high morale, Brandenberger rated the 212th best of his four divisions. The downside of this was that he withdrew one of Sensfuss's Grenadier regiments for use as his Seventh Army reserve.[7]

Against the Ivy Division's northern sector, the 423rd *Volksgrenadier* Regiment (containing Georg Jedelhauser with his mortar, and Fritz Gabriel) were ordered to take the plateau where the US-occupied village of Berdorf stood. Sensfuss's 320th Regiment was deployed in the south, opposite the bulk of Colonel Chance's US 12th Infantry, while his third regiment was kept in reserve. For security reasons, the *Volksgrenadiers* had been forbidden to pre-register any artillery targets. Yet, with patient flash-spotting and sound-ranging, they had managed to pinpoint on their maps all the outposts of the US 4th Infantry Division and their supporting artillery.[8]

In fact the American positions were obvious, as the US rifle companies from Barton's division simply garrisoned each village and dominated the surrounding terrain with fire. They were mostly quartered indoors, which offered a welcome change from the woodland foxholes filled with icy water. Although tactical measures of preparedness were not neglected, their mental attitude was one of relaxation and long overdue rest. Thanks to the ravages of the Hürtgen Forest campaign – that 'Death Factory' – this was the first time in the combat history of the Ivy Division that its commanding general had to report that his veteran unit was in other than excellent condition.

Reinforcing this 'relaxed' American attitude was an order that had been passed from SHAEF via General Omar Bradley to the First, Third and Ninth Armies back on 21 September, just as the latter formation was entering the line. This was when those forces had run perilously low on supplies, inhibiting their offensive capabilities, and were reliant on the Red Ball Express: 'the First, Third and Ninth US Armies will remain on the defensive for the time being. So that the enemy learns nothing of this, in no case are clearly defensive-appearing manoeuvres to be carried out. These include among others: the construction of defensive positions, fortifications, the laying of anti-personnel and anti-tank mines, barbed wire barriers, road blockades, mine traps, etc.'[9] To what extent this mentality still prevailed in those three armies three months later is debatable, but some commanders would have been aware there had been an edict on minimising tactical defences in the recent past. As General Courtney Hodges, commanding the US First Army, and Patton, of the Third, were both committed to offensives, an argument can be made that those formations in the Ardennes might have been discouraged from anything but cursory defence. This mindset, in conjunction with the intelligence assessments belittling German offensive capability, cannot have been helpful in countering the 16 December attacks.

Franz Sensfuss knew that 'Tubby' Barton's guns would need to be silenced quickly if the *Volksgrenadiers* were to get their own artillery, assault guns and transport safely over the Sauer in the first few hours of the offensive. Perhaps there was some subterfuge also. At the 67th Armored Field Artillery Battalion (US 3rd Armored Division), an entry for 14 December in the S-3 (Operations) Log read:

> Two strange officers reported in the Division area this afternoon asking questions about anti-aircraft defenses, front lines, locations of and communication systems. Descriptions follow: A captain wearing .45 cal. Pistol, height six foot, 1 inch about 210 lbs. Dressed in new trench coat and all new army clothes, a 1st Lieutenant armed with a carbine, height five feet, ten inches, weight about 175lbs., dressed in new clothes, trench coat, olive drab, heavy growth of beard. Story: '*had come from Roer River and were interested in radio equipment*'. Officers had not any transportation in evidence.[10]

They may have been imposters, but as this entry was written two days before Skorzeny's commandos started their mission (after which many such accounts appeared), it thus has a ring of truth about it. Their fate remains unknown.

Ernest Hemingway, an accredited correspondent for *Collier's Magazine* – though, as we have seen, also a self-appointed member of Barton's 4th

Division – sniffing danger, raced to the area, interrupting a riotous sojourn at the Ritz in Paris with his mistress, Mary Welsh. On hearing news of the attack, he equipped himself with GI-issue clothing, a helmet, two white fleece-lined jackets, a .45-inch pistol, boxes of cartridges, a Thompson sub-machine gun and a case of hand grenades. He had already been reprimanded for assembling a small arsenal and 'commanding' a group of resistance fighters in Normandy, dubbed 'Hemingway's Irregulars' – unacceptable practice for a war correspondent – though he claimed that he was only offering advice. Undeterred, he wrote to his brother, Leicester, on 16 December, 'There's been a complete break-through, kid . . . This thing could cost us the works. Their armour is pouring in. They're taking no prisoners.'[11] Then he headed for the front, a witness capturing his departure: 'He kissed Mary heartily, then clad in his two white fleece jackets, strode through the lobby of the Ritz like an overfed polar bear. A little crowd cheered the great author on his way to war again. Outside in the grey dawn, his driver gunned the engine of the Jeep, its exhaust steaming in the icy air. The steel-helmeted policeman with the old-fashioned rifle slung over his shoulder saluted, and Hemingway was off to his last battle.'[12]

To the sheltering GIs, the shock of the opening barrage was all the greater as it had been so quiet beforehand. German artillery fire from, among others, Major Ernst Schrotberger and his horse-drawn howitzers, soon cut many of the lateral communications, giving Chance's 12th Regiment and Barton at the 4th Division's command post in Junglinster (the village which housed the Grand Duchy's most prized possession, Radio Luxembourg) very little situational awareness. They were focused on their own battle, and, assuming initially that this was a local incursion, felt they could deal with these troublesome guests themselves. To the Americans huddled in their shelters the shelling must have seemed random, but the primary targets of artillery positions, battalion and company command posts were chosen carefully and soon all wire communications had been cut. Much of the initial difficulty in assessing and controlling the resultant situation was due to the confusion caused by the destruction of the field telephone network and because a large number of 4th Division's radio sets had been withdrawn, to undergo repair.

Colonel Chance had placed two battalions forward, covering the Sauer, with his third in divisional reserve; forward of them was a line of outposts on high bluffs along the river, with sweeping views. Yet none of the sparsely positioned, sleepy GIs appear to have spotted the pre-dawn crossing of the Sauer by some of the 212th's *Volksgrenadier* Fusilier Battalion, which included the *Ostfront* veteran Peter Kelch. The first intimation of trouble came, as elsewhere, with the heavy and accurate barrage. While Chance's men were taking cover, the first assault troops crossed quickly by rubber boats, any noise drowned by the shelling, and captured the outpost line, then moved on to Osweiler and Dickweiler, two settlements a couple of miles behind the lines. Yet, because other units had some difficulty in crossing the River Sauer, which was wide, fast-flowing and under fire, it was almost 10.00 a.m. before the 320th *Volksgrenadier* Regiment hit the main village positions of Chance's 3rd Battalion. As a US company commander was reporting the assault by telephone to his superior, both were startled by a gruff German voice cutting in to announce, 'We are here'. Strangely enough, the interloper continued to eavesdrop while the CO used the line like a radio link and continued to communicate in code.

Any serving soldier will be aware of the painful time lag as reported information works its way up the chain of command, and the story of Chance's 2nd Battalion, further north, illustrates this well. Lieutenant McConnell of Company 'F' reported seeing a German detachment nearing the small village of Berdorf, two miles behind American lines. At 09.00 a.m. this news reached his battalion HQ, then Chance's regimental command post some forty-five minutes later. By 10.20 a.m. the news had finally reached Barton at 4th Division, a full eighty minutes after the initial sighting. No one was particularly concerned until Lieutenant Feinsilver, also of Company 'F', screeched to a halt outside Barton's HQ with his driver, who had been wounded in five places, slumped and bleeding beside him: they had just driven through a hail of bullets in Berdorf, Feinsilver having dramatically seized the wheel and performed a U-turn. The CO concluded that the area was occupied by a whole *Volksgrenadier* battalion and tasked his executive officer to investigate; it was 2.00 p.m. before he was able to send his assessment back from another nearby company HQ, five hours after the Germans had first been spotted. Only afterwards could Barton plan a response and release appropriate reserves to Chance.

Despite the rain of shells, it was shortly after noon that Colonel Chance and his men of the 12th Infantry realised that the fire-fights forward were more than a troublesome raid. Meanwhile, Barton in his headquarters had already concluded that both his advance battalions were under strong attack, and sent his divisional reserve (a third battalion) to aid Chance's 12th Infantry, and instructed the 70th Tank Battalion to send a detachment to Colonel Chance as well.

Attached to each US infantry division was an independent tank battalion, and ever since H-Hour on D-Day at Utah Beach, Lieutenant-Colonel Henry E. Davidson Jr's 70th Tank Battalion had worked with Barton's 4th Division.[13] However, as soon as both units had left the Hürtgen Forest, the armour had gone into workshops for long overdue maintenance. Consequently 16 December found forty-three of its complement of fifty-four tanks undergoing repair and out of action, thus only eleven of its Shermans were operational and able to help. The battalion had already suffered high casualties and from an average strength of 750 officers and men, they would suffer eventual losses of 166 killed or missing and 530 wounded in action by 1945.[14]

In the workshops everything became a mad scramble, as every spare man made an all-out effort to get each tank, half-track and other armoured vehicle back on the road. Caterpillar tracks and power packs had worn particularly; on the older tanks the Wright R975 radial engines suffered from a perennial problem of spark-plug fouling, created when tanks idled their engines while remaining stationary. They were being replaced by newer M-4A1 models with a Ford V8 water-cooled engine that had overcome the issue, but spare parts were in chronic short supply. There was a good deal of hasty cannibalisation to get a selection of vehicles into combat within hours, and some of the 70th's tanks moving forward were engaged en route by plucky *Panzerfaust*-wielding *Volksgrenadiers.*[15]

Chance's 12th Infantry Regiment was also supported by one of the division's 105mm artillery battalions and two 155mm howitzer battalions from the 422nd Field Artillery Group. The former weapons had a maximum range of about six miles, the latter nine. He could also count on two Tank Destroyer battalions, the 802nd Towed and 803rd Self-propelled for anti-armour support, but their gun barrels and vehicles were tired, too. The latter, under command of Lieutenant-Colonel Charles W. Goodwin, was equipped with thirty-six M-10 Tank Destroyers, basically a three-inch (76.2mm) gun in an open-topped turret, mounted on a Sherman chassis. The M-10's gun proved ineffective against the frontal armour of Tigers and Panthers, but was better suited to engaging the more common tanks, like the Panzer IV, and self-propelled guns. An M-10 looked like a tank, behaved like a tank and had many engine and suspension parts in common with the Sherman; at a distance it was indistinguishable from one. Its open-topped turret theoretically left the crew vulnerable to artillery and mortar fire, especially in wooded areas, and the elements, but brought compensations too. These were much improved communications with accompanying infantry, excellent visibility, and the turret also made escape easier if the vehicle was hit.

Within the 4th Ivy Division itself, many weapons and wireless sets were being reserviced and the shortage of working radios would soon make itself felt. This was the case more generally throughout US First and Third Armies, whose equipment was worn or faulty after nearly six months of combat, and was being repaired as the support organisations caught up with the combat arms, after the heady gallop through France and Belgium of the autumn. The men were worn out too; some had begun to be sent back to R and R centres in Liège, Arlon or Luxembourg City. The latter, which also housed Bradley's HQ, was only twenty miles distant.

On 15 December, Jack Capell, serving in the headquarters of 8th Infantry Regiment, had just arrived in Arlon and enjoyed his first night for ages on a cot with mattress, sheets and blankets. His morale soared with the hot water, clean laundry and good hot food, but on the morning of the 16th he and his friends were ordered back. 'We were shocked and thought there must be a mistake . . . We protested loudly and a major then came on the scene . . . He said there was a problem at the front . . . so we reluctantly complied but complained bitterly.'[16] Likewise, Tom Reid, an officer in the 22nd Infantry, had just stepped out of 'the first hot shower I had enjoyed in over a month' at the US-commandeered Luxembourg Country Club, when he got word of the German attack, dressed hurriedly and dashed back to join his company. In retrospect, he realised, speeding through the gloom in his open-top jeep, he had been lucky not to catch pneumonia in his haste.[17]

By nightfall, Chance's 12th Infantry had lost over a hundred men killed or captured, and another fifty were missing, most of whom would eventually find their way back to friendly lines. His regiment was still holding the five main villages dominating his sector, Dickweiler, Osweiler, Echternach, Lauterborn and Berdorf; these five centres of resistance constituted the initial architecture of his defence, dominating all the routes within the regiment's boundaries. The control of these roads and intersections would prove to be key, not only to the 4th Infantry Division's successful defence of their area, but the model adopted independently by other American units – and one which would ultimately stall the German advance.

Of this, Barton was unaware; all he knew – from other reports now coming into his headquarters – was that he was in the midst of a large, local German attack; the enormity of the offensive was not obvious to many on the American front lines for a couple of days. This is true of the Bulge as a whole; because of the isolation of troops and breakdowns in communications it took a long time for the magnitude of *Herbstnebel* to become apparent on the US front lines. As Lieutenant Cecil E. Roberts of the 14th Tank Battalion observed, 'on 18 December we finally began to realise we were in a situation that was more than a local spoiling attack by the Germans', while another recorded, 'it was 20 December before we found out this was the Battle of the Bulge and we were in it'.[18]

The 12th Infantry's tactic of all-round defended centres of resistance, largely evolutionary and unplanned, but proven to be very effective, negated all German attempts to bypass the villages. The results of 16 December were mixed for both sides. At Dickweiler, the *Volksgrenadiers* overran one outpost and were allowed to advance to a very short range, then hammered with mortars, machine-gun and tank fire which annihilated two infantry companies, surviving prisoners later testifying as to the devastating efficacy of this action. In Lauterborn, one US squad was surrounded, caught totally by surprise; as the *Volksgrenadiers* marched their captives down the road, their colleagues concealed in a stone-built mill opened fire, while the prisoners hit a roadside ditch, eventually escaping to rejoin their unit as the fire-fight erupted around them. An American company remained in defiant occupation of the Parc Hôtel in Berdorf (they would defy all attempts to remove them for five days); another refused to be prised out of Echternach, though the *Volksgrenadiers* moved beyond and captured a dominating hill to the south.

These actions forced Sensfuss's 212th *Volksgrenadiers* into counterattacks of progressively increasing size, but their efforts suffered through having virtually no artillery support. This was no reflection on Major Ernst Schrotberger and his colleagues of the 212th *VolksArtillerie* Regiment, but a result of poor communications, and the fact that the weight of fire support had been shifted to Seventh Army's northern flank. The German advance was checked to such a degree by the 'hedgehog' style defence that it took the 212th three days to reach their initial Day One objectives. In a sense this mattered less to Brandenberger's Seventh Army, which was not part of the German main effort; their mission was only shallow penetration of the American front in order to fix their opponents, and deflect counter-attacks from the *Schwerpunkt* of the two panzer armies, further north.

North of 4th Division lay Combat Command 'A' of John W. Leonard's 9th Armored Division. In creating its armoured units, the US Army had initially designed them to be 'heavy', denoting a preponderance of tanks, but short on infantry. Combat operations forced the realisation that a better-balanced formation was needed, and in September 1943 the 'light' division structure was adopted and applied to most tank divisions. Leonard's 9th, like all apart from the 1–3rd Armored Divisions, was therefore a 'light' formation. Outfits like Leonard's had an authorised strength of 10,670 personnel, and contained three battalions each of tanks, armoured infantry and armoured field artillery as well as a mechanised cavalry squadron for reconnaissance, and armoured engineer, armoured medical and armoured ordnance battalions. They were bolstered by permanently assigned tank destroyer and self-propelled anti-aircraft artillery battalions and other support units. In combat, US armoured divisions were designed to be split down into three roughly equal groupings called Combat Commands, designated 'A', 'B' and 'R' (for Reserve), a response to, and imitation of, the very effective German *Kampfgruppen*.

The mainstay of the division were its 195 M-4 Shermans, seventy-seven light tanks (Stuart M-5s), fifty-four self-propelled artillery pieces (the M-7, incorporating a 105mm howitzer on a Sherman hull) and 466 half-tracks. Raised in 1942, much of the Ninth Armored's personnel had transferred in from the recently deactivated Second Cavalry Division, meaning Leonard's command comprised a high percentage of regulars; Leonard himself had taken over the division in the autumn of 1942, and was a West Pointer, graduating in 1915, thus a classmate of Bradley and Eisenhower. Having only lately arrived in France, the Ninth, acclimatising to European combat, had been split into its separate combat commands to support several divisions in the Ardennes, which was how it would fight during the Bulge. In this sector, responsibility for defence rested with Colonel Thomas L. Harrold's Combat Command 'A', who deployed his armoured infantry battalion, the 60th, forward to overlook the river.

Climate and terrain aided their opponents, Generalmajor Kurt Möhring's 276th Division, of whom two *Volksgrenadier* regiments (four battalions) were ordered to advance against the single defending US armoured infantry battalion. Möhring's *Volksgrenadier* Division had been raised on 4 September 1944 from a predecessor unit which had been wiped out in Normandy; his six infantry battalions contained a high number of young conscripts and veterans recovered from wounds, while his artillery used captured Polish, French and Russian guns of a bewildering variety of calibres. They had gathered and trained at Graudenz (modern Grudziądz) in East Prussia, then in late November the entire division with all its equipment had transferred by rail to the Mosel area. Considered by Brandenberger to be the weakest of his four divisions, they were fortunate to be aided by thick fog.

This enabled the 276th to exploit several wooded ravines and filter through the American outposts, until they stumbled upon the main line of Lieutenant-Colonel Kenneth W. Collins's 60th Armored Infantry Battalion dug in overlooking the confluence of the Our and Sûre rivers, near Wallendorf. The Battalion's After Action Report (AAR) for early December 1944 recounted the quiet before the storm: 'We patrolled actively along our front but nothing took place to change this sector's reputation of being exceptionally quiet . . . Enemy activity for the above mentioned period was confined to very light artillery fire covering the Battalion sector and limited night patrolling.'

Then the blow fell; quartered in Beaufort at his company command post was Captain Roger Shinn, about two miles from the River Sauer and leading Company 'C'. He remembered, 'A thunderclap awakened me abruptly . . . and chunks of plaster and dust rained down from the ceiling of the company's CP. The building trembled, the ground shook. Shells exploded everywhere, such as we had never experienced before. Our senses were no longer capable of reacting reliably for a moment, for we were all so shocked and confused.'[19] As it grew light, Shinn 'saw numerous Jerries on the [far] bank of the river but could not spot a crossing point', but many others were obviously over the water and gaining ground. At this stage it was German artillery that caused the greatest damage, hampering the American response and frightening local civilians, as it was designed to do.

A shell hit his CP and the roof caved in. As they started to evacuate the area, 'we heard this dreadful howling in the air! These were the "screaming minnies" or nebelwerfer shells, whose nerve-numbing screech as they arrived had an even more paralysing effect than the explosion of its shell . . . Although the terrible howling noise frightened all my soldiers, its shrapnel effect was quite meager.' Despite this, Shinn felt his men 'did an excellent job in their first real battle'. This was, he reasoned, because 'they were all very well known to me, since I had commanded and trained the same unit in the USA'.[20] By the end of the day, however, the Germans had advanced as far as Beaufort and pushed Shinn's company out of their defensive positions parallel to the river line, forcing their withdrawal. The escapades of the other forward companies were similar. The crisp, succinct AAR of the 60th Armored Infantry represents the story of many American units caught in the front line that first day.

> At 160630 Dec 44 [05.30 a.m. Wehrmacht time] the Germans attacked our sector following a 1,000 round artillery preparation, consisting chiefly of nebelwerfer and medium caliber artillery. The attacking force was estimated at two Infantry Regiments, one to attack the Battalion and the other to move through and attack positions to our rear. The enemy used infiltration tactics successfully supported by many automatic weapons . . . The success of the infiltration tactics was aided by the heavily wooded terrain of our front line and our thinly held position. Vehicular bridges were established across the Our River at Dillegen, Wallendorf and Grundhof. From the moment the Germans were seen constructing the above mentioned bridges, they were heavily engaged with artillery fire by the 3rd FA Bn[21] and mortar fire . . . During the afternoon of the 16 Dec the enemy infiltration tactics continued with success and the last of the Battalion reserve, the A[nti]/T[ank] platoon of Co[mpany] 'B', employed as riflemen, were dispatched to reinforce the center of our weakened line. [22]

This was the beginning of a very busy month for the 60th Armored Infantry. Having lost eighteen personnel wounded or sick in October and November, December would see the outfit lose 494 officers and men killed, wounded, missing, captured or reporting sick, and twenty-eight vehicles destroyed or captured, though they would acquire 518 prisoners. The previous two months had seen them use no more than 1,500 rounds of machine-gun ammunition and 532 grenades. By the end of December, this had risen to 136,000 machine-gun rounds, 156,000 of rifle and carbine ammunition and 3,605 hand grenades.[23] Its initial story for *Herbstnebel* was very similar to Chance's 12th Infantry Regiment's further south: both US units managed to hold their ground, though the Germans penetrated beyond and around them, but nowhere to a depth of more than two or three miles.

The 60th AIB, 19th Tank and 3rd FA Battalions were the principal elements of Colonel Harrold's Combat Command 'A' (or CCA), whose artillery and tank support would prove vital in bolstering their friends of the armoured infantry. Lieutenant Colonel Ruhlen's 3rd Field Artillery amounted to around 480 men with eighteen tracked M-7 105mm howitzers. He remembered the 'dull rumble' in the early hours of 16 December of artillery and identified them 'from shell fragments as being 105, 150 and 170 mm calibers . . . The intensity of the fire increased, the echoes of the shots resounded down the Sauer valley . . . Nebelwerfer rockets, recognisable by their howl that penetrated to the bone, exploded not far from my dug-out gun positions . . . An advanced observer reported that some sixty Germans were in the process of crossing the Sauer near Dillingen on a narrow footbridge . . . All the phone lines were broken.'[24]

Armored field artillery battalions like Lieutenant Colonel Ruhlen's 3rd AFA in the US 9th Armored Division comprised around 480 men with eighteen M-7 Motor Gun Carriages, which combined a 105mm howitzer mounted on a Sherman chassis. Each US armored division had three battalions of M-7s, whose weapons could reach out to 6 miles, giving them unsurpassed mobile artillery support. Tons of spare ammunition can be seen stacked ready for use, while the wintry conditions underline just how unpleasant was life on the line. (NARA)

This aptly demonstrated how vital communications were to the defenders. In military terms, the American 'centre of gravity' (their key vulnerability) on 16 December was their communication links: without correction, the US artillery could not hope to destroy the Germans' own centre of gravity, their bridging sites. By destroying the US centre of gravity, the *Volksgrenadiers* had protected their own. Generalmajor Kurt Möhring's staff had also done their homework, for by mid-afternoon Lieutenant-Colonel Ruhlen had discovered the gun positions occupied by his predecessors had taken 'about 150 accurately aimed direct hits. Apparently the Germans knew the exact location of our positions all along the Sauer. Fortunately I didn't occupy these positions.'[25]

By this time the *Volksgrenadiers* had infiltrated snipers into the outskirts of many blasted villages, and communication between all US units was proving problematical because of their reliance on field telephones, whose wires were cut. On hearing by radio that a company of the 60th was surrounded in Beaufort with no reserves available to help them, Ruhlen sent his three artillery observation tanks (Shermans equipped for fire-direction, armed with real machine guns but a dummy main gun) to rescue those trapped and bring them out. However, it soon became apparent that this situation prevailed for all the 60th's rifle companies, who were beginning to be pushed back, and Ruhlen's gun positions began to be overlooked by *Volksgrenadier* units seizing higher terrain. He, too, was obliged to withdraw, a move sanctioned by CCA, which recognised the weight of the German attack, and the paucity of local reserves with which to counter it.

By the end of the day, Brandenberger had been so unimpressed by 276th's progress that he demanded they push forward through the night. Meanwhile, the US 60th Armored Infantry called down such effective artillery fire on Möhring's chosen bridging site at Wallendorf that construction had to be completely abandoned, and efforts switched to an alternative site at Bollendorf. However, the Seventh Army was so short of engineering equipment that no replacements were available for the items destroyed. Eventually an irate Brandenberger relieved Generalmajor Möhring for his lack of progress, and his place was taken quickly by Oberst Hugo Dempwolff, one of several officers on standby to take over in just such an eventuality. As the sacked Möhring was being driven away from the front in a captured jeep on the evening of 18 December, he was killed by a burst of machine-gun fire at about 5.00 p.m. Although both the Germans and Americans at the time attributed this to a brave

GI, the truth seems to be that a nervous young *Volksgrenadier* had seen an American vehicle driving at high speed in the gloom through terrain just captured and shot at it. Such incidents of 'friendly fire' were a remarkably common occurrence in the confusion of the Bulge.[26]

Hemingway, meanwhile, had reached 'Tubby' Barton's HQ after dark on the 17th. 'It's a pretty hot show. You'd better come on up!' Barton had told him in Paris. The writer, despite his fleece-lined jackets, had not travelled well in the arctic conditions, and arrived with the symptoms of flu. Colonel Buck Lanham – about to engage the *Volksgrenadiers* – banished Hemingway to sweat it out in bed at his CP, 'a decaying old mill in the tiny hamlet of Rodenbourg', a mile away from Barton's own Junglinster HQ. Settled in the former home of the Abbé Didier, Hemingway adopted his own cure of working his way through the priest's store of communion wine. 'He took a maniacal delight in refilling every bottle with his own urine, re-corking it and labelling the bottles *Schloss Hemingstein 1944*'. The joke backfired one night when he searched in the dark and found a bottle of Hemingstein '44. He was less than impressed by the vintage.[27]

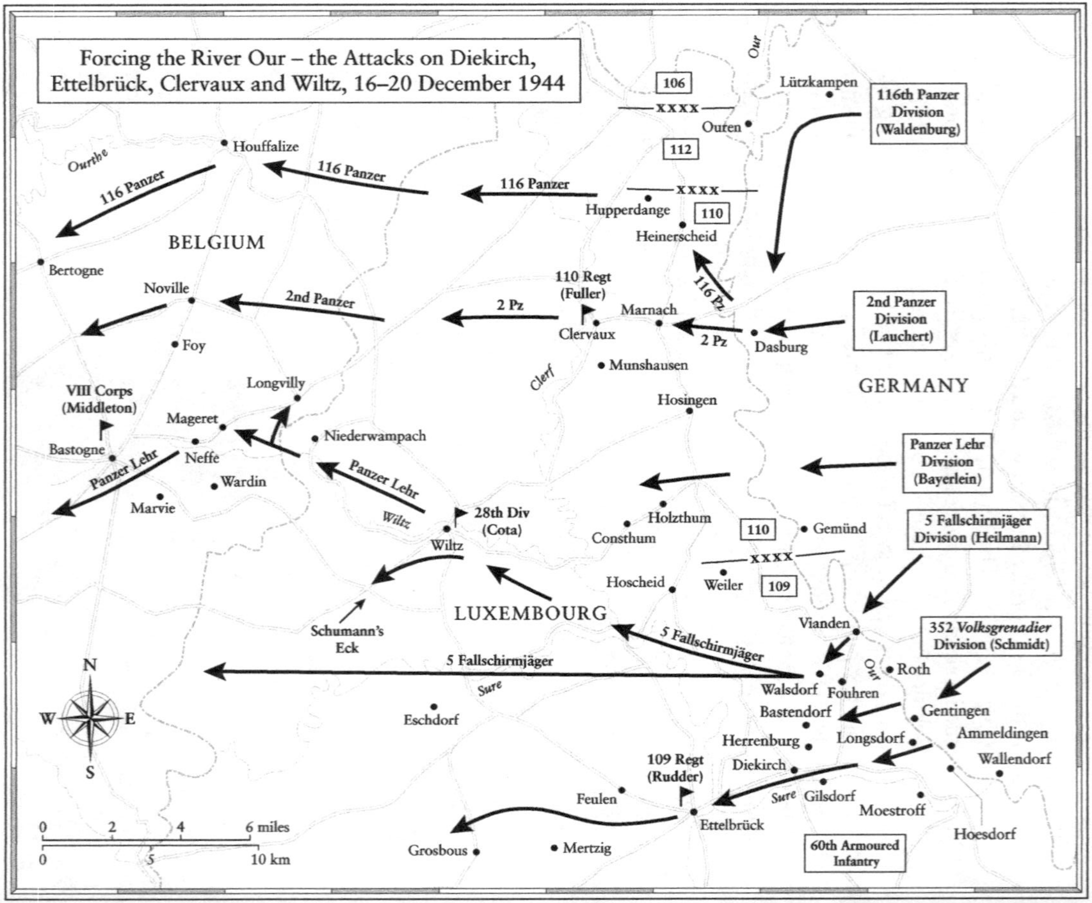

Forcing the River Our – the Attacks on Diekirch, Ettelbrück, Clervaux and Wiltz, 16–20 December 1944
116th Panzer Division (Waldenburg)
2nd Panzer Division (Lauchert)
Panzer Lehr Division (Bayerlein)
5 Fallschirmjäger Division (Heilmann)
352 Volksgrenadier Division (Schmidt)
60th Armoured Infantry
110 Regt (Fuller)
109 Regt (Rudder)
28th Div (Cota)
VIII Corps (Middleton)
106
112
110
110
109
XXXX
XXXX
XXXX
116 Panzer
116 Panzer
116 Panzer
116 Panzer
116 Pz
2nd Panzer
2 Pz
2 Pz
Panzer Lehr
Panzer Lehr
5 Fallschirmjäger
5 Fallschirmjäger
BELGIUM
GERMANY
LUXEMBOURG
Our
Our
Ourthe
Clerf
Wiltz
Sure
Sure
Lützkampen
Ouren
Hupperdange
Heinerscheid
Houffalize
Bertogne
Noville
Foy
Marnach
Clervaux
Dasburg
Munshausen
Hosingen
Longvilly
Mageret
Neffe
Bastogne
Niederwampach
Wardin
Marvie
Holzthum
Consthum
Gemünd
Weiler
Hoscheid
Wiltz
Schumann's Eck
Vianden
Roth
Walsdorf
Fouhren
Bastendorf
Gentingen
Ammeldingen
Herrenburg
Longsdorf
Wallendorf
Diekirch
Gilsdorf
Moestroff
Feulen
Ettelbrück
Hoesdorf
Eschdorf
Grosbous
Mertzig
N
S
E
W
0
2
4
6 miles
0
5
10 km

16

The Bloody Bucket

North of the 60th Armored Infantry Battalion, in Lieutenant-General Middleton's VIII Corps patch of the Ardennes, lay the highly experienced 28th Division. They were the pre-war Pennsylvania National Guard, who wore as their shoulder patch a red keystone badge, Pennsylvania being the 'Keystone State', but in the Hürtgen Forest the Germans had learned to call it the 'Bloody Bucket', on account of the casualties the Pennsylvanians inflicted and the punishment they took.

Major-General 'Dutch' Cota's men, stretched along their wide front in the Ardennes, were best pictured as a very taut longbow. Though far from ideal, the front they had to defend dictated that all of Cota's three regiments were in line, 112th to the north, 110th in the centre and his 109th Regiment in the south. Forward of their positions, following the line of the bow, was a twenty-five-mile stretch of river. The southerly flowing Our river to Cota's front, after joining a smaller tributary called the Sûre, was the same stretch of water that flowed past Leonard's 9th Armored and Barton's 4th Infantry divisions, but there was called the Sauer river. Cota put his headquarters in Wiltz, about a dozen miles behind the front, where the archer might notch his arrow in the bowstring. The same distance again behind Cota was Bastogne, home to his corps commander, Middleton, and one of the key route centres in the whole Ardennes. A glance at any map would have told American and German officers alike that control of Bastogne was vital to all military movement through the Ardennes.

Cota's Bloody Bucket boys were about to receive attacks from both the southern formations in Manteuffel's Fifth Panzer and northern units of Brandenberger's Seventh Army. In Cota's southern sector, his 109th Infantry Regiment would be hit by both divisions of Kneiss's LXXXV Corps. Thus on the morning of 16 December the three battalions comprising the US 109th Infantry were faced with twelve battalions: 352nd *Volksgrenadiers* on their right, Heilmann's 5th *Fallschirmjäger* Division against their left flank, plus the entire weight of the LXXXV Corps' artillery.

The 109th was led by another capable soldier, who, like Cota, had been promoted for his outstanding leadership on D-Day – Lieutenant-Colonel James Earl Rudder. An 'Aggie' – as Texas A&M University graduates were known – and commissioned into the US Army Reserves in 1932, the thirty-four-year-old had commanded the Second Ranger Battalion which scaled the cliffs of the Pointe du Hoc on 6 June. Out of 230 who had made the assault, only seventy Rangers remained unwounded, Rudder himself being hit twice during the course of the fighting.[1] Awarded a Distinguished Service Cross, he then took his battalion to the Hürtgen Forest. On 7 December – nine days, as it turned out, before the German attack – Rudder was promoted to command the 109th Infantry Regiment, his predecessor, Colonel Jesse L. Gibney, being reassigned as Cota's chief of staff.

Rudder may have been fit, highly capable and a born leader, and his new command close to full strength, but in mid-December Rudder's rifle companies were 'hollowed-out'. After sustaining horrendous losses in the Hürtgen Forest – like the whole Fourth Division – their ranks were full of green replacements possessing no combat experience. Rudder had a huge front to cover; with his headquarters in the Hôtel Lieffrig in Ettelbrück, he put two battalions forward, each nursing a frontage of about four miles watching the German fortifications on the eastern bank, and his third some distance back from the river in outposts.

Before Rudder took over the 109th it had experienced more than its fair share of problem soldiers. Not every draftee was cut out for combat and twenty-four-year-old Edward D. Slovik was one such. Since the age of twelve the Detroit native had been in and out of jail until drafted in January 1944. He was one of twelve reinforcements assigned to the 109th Infantry on 20 August, but deserted en route to his unit when he first came under shellfire. After further similar episodes, by November he had been court-martialled, found guilty and sentenced to death; but Slovik wasn't worried as he knew that no US soldier had been executed for desertion since the civil war, eighty years before. In December Slovik wrote what he assumed would be a routine letter to Eisenhower, pleading for clemency. His timing was awful as desertion was increasing; after 16 December, with 'lost' GIs wandering the length and breadth of the Ardennes, Eisenhower felt he needed an example.

As any senior commander will testify, the action of a single soldier in being seen to desert the battlefield at a crucial moment, refuse to fight or neglect to protect his comrades, can undermine the cohesiveness of an entire unit, possibly encouraging others to do likewise. Slovik, with his history of run-ins with authority, was clearly set to continue in his ways, and, given the context of the Bulge, had his plea turned down and sentence confirmed. He was shot by firing squad on 31 January 1945 for the crime of desertion.[2] Given the circumstances, Eddie Slovik's execution was perhaps understandable. What is surprising is that no other US deserters met a similar fate, although 140 GIs (seventy in the European theatre of war) were executed for murder and/or rape between 1942 and 1945.

Meanwhile, on 16 December, one of the indirect causes of Slovik's demise, Heilmann, had ordered his *Fallschirmjäger* to avoid pitched battles for defended positions, push inland and reach Wiltz, the divisional

Major Goswin Wahl had been an airman in the Mediterranean, but on account of his rank was given a battalion of *Fallschirmjäger* Regiment 13 to train in preparation for battle. Three days before the offensive began, he was appointed the regimental commander, with no prior ground combat experience whatsoever. Wahl was brutally criticised by one of his battalion commanders, Hans Frank (front seat, in car) for his wasteful and costly attacks against Foühren on 16 December. 'Our liaison was a complete failure', Frank later complained. (Author's collection)

objective (and Cota's HQ), twelve miles inland, by that first evening. The mission would eventually take three days, due to the resistance of the US Bloody Bucket Division and the woeful inexperience of Heilmann's impressive sounding formation. Major Goswin Wahl had been a Luftwaffe airman in the Mediterranean, eventually retreating from southern France in the autumn of 1944. Purely on account of his rank, he was made one of Heilmann's battalion commanders: 'I became a paratrooper without parachute training,' he wrote later, observing that he had no intermediate commander, only his divisional chief. Around 10 December he was warned to conduct combat drills for his battalion and on the 13th reported to Heilmann, 'Herr Oberst, I am of the opinion that it is probably time for *Fallschirmjäger* Regiment 13 to be assigned a commander'. Heilmann responded, 'You lead the regiment. I cannot wait until they have dug someone out of the drawer at the Reich Air Ministry.' One of his three infantry regiments (which the British would call a brigade), was thus going into battle led by an airman who had never before led ground troops in combat.[3]

As Heilmann himself warned Brandenberger and Model, he assessed his command as only *Kampfwert* IV (fit for static defence). Himmler may have found his recruits, in this case from Luftwaffe ground crews, but he didn't have to lead them in battle. When a dispirited Heilmann asked Model how his division could possibly achieve victory, the field marshal responded in his usual cold fashion, 'with audacity'. To Heilmann this must have seemed a personal insult to his otherwise gilt-edged combat career – but the state of his formation was merely a symptom of the chaos in which the Third Reich found itself by late 1944.[4]

The 5th *Fallschirmjäger's* first task was a quick and unopposed crossing of the Our; like the German divisions further south, their commanders saw river crossings in terms of unwelcome choke points, where pre-registered American artillery could cause havoc. In fact the Our was less than fifty feet wide at the points chosen for the initial assaults, and between 05.30 and 06.00 a.m. Heilmann's assault companies made their way over by rubber craft quickly, bypassing or overwhelming American outposts under cover of the bombardment. As he rightly anticipated, the best results came from the only seasoned units in his division – Oberstleutnant Kurt Gröschke's 15th *Fallschirmjäger* Regiment and the 5th Parachute Engineer Battalion of Major Gerhard Mertins, already a Knight's Cross holder, and Normandy veterans all.

The 15th *Fallschirmjäger* pushed over the Our near Vianden, though during the Engineer Battalion's assault upriver some of their little rubber boats overturned in the fast-flowing winter torrent; the engineers, weighed down with weapons and ammunition, perished immediately. The Parachute Engineers repaired a stone bridge for use in Vianden itself, and another damaged railway bridge, and eventually assembled a pontoon bridge, for wheeled, but not tracked, vehicles, inevitably called *die Brücke Gröschke* (the Gröschke Bridge), after their commander. The paratroops crossed so quickly and quietly in the first few minutes that the US 2nd Battalion's outpost in Vianden castle simply disappeared. Leutnant Hans Prigge led his 4th Parachute Company into the town, overwhelming the I&R (Intelligence and Reconnaissance) Platoon who had first encountered Elise Delé two days earlier. After the successful Our crossing, the paratroopers moved on to Hoscheid, almost halfway to Wiltz, eventually basing their heavy mortars there. In the absence of warnings, it was only at 09.00 a.m. that Lieutenant-Colonel Rudder began to receive reports of German incursions, but by this time his forward lines had been breached and Gröschke's advance was gathering strength and momentum.

Heilmann's other two regiments, comprising the airmen-turned-infantrymen, did much less well, and the construction of a wooden bridge at Roth was held up by mortar fire from Foühren, a mile south of Vianden, which should have been taken straightaway by Major Wahl's men. Throughout the 16th, Rudder gradually committed whatever reserves were available to him, but it was his field artillery support that most slowed the Germans; by nightfall Rudder's lines had held – just. His situation was similar to that of Chance's 12th Regiment and the 60th Armored Infantry; they still controlled their ground, but the Germans had managed to infiltrate beyond and behind. As Heilmann had anticipated, bridge construction was slow in the first few hours because of American artillery fire, which in turn meant less fire support from his own guns and rocket-firing *Nebelwerfer* than he would have liked, stranded as they were on the wrong side of the Our. Much later, when American armour appeared on the scene, Major Wahl would report, 'In this combat it was shown again that troops lacking combat experience are very sensitive on their flanks and act scared and witless when faced with enemy tanks.' [5]

Luftwaffe Major Hans Frank, who commanded the III Battalion in Wahl's *Fallschirmjäger* Regiment, remembered trying to storm Foühren, held by Rudder's Company 'E', on 16 December. Within twenty-five yards of his objective the attack stalled as his company commanders were killed; he crawled forward on his stomach and took personal control. Each runner he sent back with requests for heavy weapons support was shot. 'Then, for two and a half hours, I worked my way back, [moving] by inches on my stomach. What a show for the young boys, making their way over a plain without support of heavy weapons!' Frank explained the situation to Wahl, his regimental commander, and wanted to wait for a forward observation officer before re-attacking. Wahl ordered, 'Get going, take that village; there are only a few troops holding it'. The battalion commander demurred calling another attack 'madness'. 'No, it's an order. Get going, we must capture the village before evening,' Wahl insisted. As Major Frank observed, 'We took the village without any support and scarcely were we in it when our heavy guns began firing into it. I brought out 181 prisoners altogether. I rounded up the last 60 and a salvo of mortar shells fell on them. After 22 hours our own artillery was still firing into the village.'[6]

Meanwhile, holed up in Foühren was Bill Alexander, serving in the 109th with the Intelligence Section of Rudder's Second Battalion. He had fond memories of the kindness of the Luxembourger, who had cooked a roast goose for him and his unit on Thanksgiving Day. Later, he had manned an observation post in Vianden castle, watching the German OP in a sanatorium on the far bank watching him. The afternoon of the sixteenth found him besieged in Foühren with Company 'E', when he noticed the *Volksgrenadiers* collecting for an attack. 'One of the ways the Germans were using to move troops across the open area was by means of stretcher bearers wearing Red Cross armbands. They would move across the road further south with four men carrying the stretcher, and they came back with only two. They were doing this for some time before we brought down artillery fire.'[7]

Also hurrying towards Foühren late that afternoon was one of Rudder's officers, Lieutenant James V. Christy of Company 'B'. He was having difficulty coaxing his platoon of new arrivals to move into battle, even though they were mounted on two Shermans of the 707th Tank Battalion. His men were tired, hungry and had already taken losses. Fearful of Germans lurking with *Panzerfausts*, the tank crews eventually refused to go any further in the dark without the infantry clearing ahead. When Christy ordered his platoon sergeant, Stanislaus Wieszcyk, to get a squad forward, Wieszcyk reflected their reluctance. 'The guys have had more than enough today. They won't go.' There was nothing for it but for Christy himself to set out alone and guide the tanks. He had barely begun to stretch out when the officer made out a figure on his left. It was Wieszcyk. 'OK lieutenant, you made your point.' With him was the platoon's first squad.[8]

Major Frank lamented the *Fallschirmjäger's* lack of experience and training, 'Our liaison was a *complete* failure. Later we had tanks [assault guns] but they were never used in conjunction with the infantry, and were recklessly thrown away. But if there had been a little co-operation, if one or two hours had been allowed for preparation, then it would have been wonderful.'[9] Hans Frank's comments were sharply critical of his superior, Major Wahl, but were made from the safety of a British Prisoner of War camp. His remarks, made to a fellow inmate on his arrival, were picked up by covert surveillance microphones and transcribed by intelligence service operatives. The Files containing these transcripts have only recently been discovered in the UK National Archives.[10]

Once the Germans had moved beyond and pushed US artillery out of range, Foühren fell to the *Fallschirmjäger* and sixty to seventy men of Company 'E' were captured along with some of Rudder's Second Battalion headquarters staff. They had held their opponents at bay for twenty-four hours and surrendered only when their building, home of the Betzen family, was in flames. PFC Kahn, the only Jewish member of Company 'E', was determined not to fall into German hands. He stood silhouetted against the flames, was cut down and killed. Amazingly he was the only one who died. Bill Alexander of the Intelligence Section remembered his captors 'were of a paratroop unit. They treated us well. Most of them very young, they may have been seventeen or eighteen.'[11]

Despite these infantry successes, to best exploit their gains Heilmann needed artillery forward, but his cannon remained out of touch, short on ammunition, and were queuing to cross the river. Like Major Ernst Schrotberger's guns further south, they were horse-drawn but were expected to motorise and advance with captured American vehicles and fuel. Failure to provide heavy bridges quickly removed the possibility of help from the twenty or so 75mm StuGs from the 11th Assault Gun Brigade, which had been attached to his division. As Major Frank observed, they would have made a significant difference early on. Heilmann hoped for extra enthusiasm from the armoured support, for both the assault gun crews and his division wore the emblem of the Luftwaffe. Later that night, the StuGs in fact found an undefended weir by which they crossed the Our, reached the Skyline Drive – the north–south route running along the American front – and turned south along it in the small hours. This would unhinge the American defences around Ettelbrück on the 17th. Ultimately, the first day saw Heilmann's *Fallschirmjäger* firmly lodged on the west bank of the Our, to a depth of two or three miles. Their objective of Wiltz, however, was well beyond reach.

Against Rudder's southern flank, Oberst Erich Schmidt's 352nd *Volksgrenadiers* flung themselves over the Our, via two sets of temporary bridges, towards the route centres of Diekirch and Ettelbrück, small towns five and seven miles from the river respectively. In the pre-campaign report on his new division, which would reflect that of all the *Volksgrenadiers* deploying into the Bulge, Schmidt has observed that while his men's ages averaged between twenty-two and thirty, they were limited in other ways: 'too briefly trained, no experience with terrain or combat, not yet been in action. NCOs: Vary in front experience and level of training. Strength is only 75 percent of what it should be. Officers: vary very much in combat experience and training.'[12]

Schmidt had assessed his two infantry regiments as possessing 'good fighting spirit', amongst whom was Friedrich Schmäschke, a teenager of seventeen when transferred from a naval support unit in Wilhelmshaven to the *Volksgrenadiers*. Receiving three months' condensed infantry training, Schmäschke was luckier than Günter Münnich, a year older, who received no further combat tuition, though was given specialist courses on air defence and on operating a telephone switchboard.[13] The division's artillery reportedly had 'too brief training time; tactically and [was] technically not dependable in directing and adjusting fire and observation'. Of his equipment, Schmidt was concerned that 35 per cent of radios for fire direction were missing, as were 25 per cent of the MP-44s he was authorised.[14] Oberst von Gersdorff, Seventh Army's chief of staff, concluded of the unit: 'Small cadre of veteran lower officers and men. Commanders generally good, lower officers and NCOs only partially suited. A useful division, but suffering from shortages.'[15]

The advance of Schmidt's men was to be coordinated with Heilmann's 5th *Fallschirmjäger* Division, and in turn the pair were to remain on an axis parallel to Manteuffel's Fifth Army. Schmidt's soldiers were luckier than many in that they had been issued with the Wehrmacht's brand-new reversible winter uniform, white on one side, camouflaged on the other. However, as the first waves of *Volksgrenadiers* crested the ridge beyond the river on the American side, they were mown down in the open primarily by fire from Captain Embert A. Fossum's Heavy Weapons outfit (Company 'L'), equipped with eight Browning .30-inch water-cooled machine-guns and six 81mm mortars. Each gun, with its solid tripod and 250-round belts of ammunition, weighed in at a hefty 103 lbs, albeit broken down into a minimum of three man-portable loads. This meant their gun emplacements had to be good, for moving the Brownings in a hurry wasn't an option. Yet on the grenadiers charged, for many their first – and last – time in battle. After three unsuccessful assaults during the first day, incurring almost 400 casualties, the *Volksgrenadiers* abandoned their attempts to take the plateau.

The GIs responsible for the carnage on the plateau above Hoesdorf were amongst three companies from the US 109th Infantry, dug in with their machine-guns and mortars looking east to the river and south-east towards Reisdorf. Accompanying their rude awakening at 05:30 am, Rudder's men had witnessed searchlights bouncing their beams off the low clouds and fog to provide artificial daylight for their foes. At Ammeldingen, directly opposite the American lines, assault companies of 916th *Volksgrenadier* Regiment negotiated the swollen and fast-flowing Our via ingenious footbridges made from lines of farm carts dragged into the river and walkways constructed from house doors nailed to the carts. Some battalion staff were about to follow the assault troops across when a rubber-boat ferry also in use was destroyed by a direct hit from an American shell.

The alternative, as recalled by Günter Münnich of 914th Regiment, evoked images of an African safari, though in a more unpleasant setting: 'we and the battalion staff now had to cross the Our on foot at a shallower place, in ice-cold water up to our chests. Holding all our baggage above our heads, we reached the far shore thoroughly soaked.'[16] Later, Münnich's squad came to the small village of Longsdorf, a mile west of the river: 'the Americans must have been taken completely by surprise; anyway there was an abandoned gun nearby . . . its ammunition had been unpacked and spread out on a tarpaulin, and there were two Jeeps there too'.[17]

At Gentingen, the 915th *Volksgrenadiers* used rubber boats pulled across on cables, and footbridges made from felled trees; in most cases the civilian engineers of Albert Speer's 1st Todt Brigade were doing the work. Schmidt's army pioneers were too short-handed and ill-prepared, since most of their resources had been diverted to Fifth and Sixth Panzer Armies. The regiment included at least one Frenchman; as with all young males from Alsace-Lorraine (which had been forcibly reincorporated into the Reich), Celestin Lejeune was conscripted, in his case into the Kriegsmarine in 1944, not speaking a word of German. When training at Kiel, his job – with fellow conscript Frenchmen – was to collect by hand any unexploded incendiary bombs dropped by British aircraft the previous night. In mid-December his group was suddenly posted to the front, issued ammunition, stick grenades and *Panzerfaust* 'the use of which I did not know. My immediate superior was a *Feldwebel*; I didn't even know the name of the company commander, nor the precise name of the company, but I did know that I belonged to *Volksgrenadier* Regiment 915.' Crossing the Our at Roth, south of Vianden, his first job was picking up dead soldiers and loading them into a truck.[18]

Unteroffizier (Sergeant) Wilhelm Stetter of the 915th was only alerted to the offensive less than forty-eight hours beforehand; of his regiment he recalled that 'most NCOs and officers came from the infantry, but everybody else was Kriegsmarine; there were even volunteers from seventeen to twenty years old'. He remembered being read Rundstedt's Order of the Day (which begins Chapter 15) by his company commander Oberleutnant Schubert, who 'closed with an exhortation [of his own] to fight in the spirit of Frederick the Great, and I had to think of the fact that in the days of "Old Fritz" they had no tanks. Nor did we have any, but the Americans had plenty of them.'[19]

Stetter led his platoon forward all day until that evening when 'A messenger appeared and led us into a patch of woods where almost the whole battalion was waiting. "Dig in" was ordered, but with our short infantry spades we scarcely made a dent on the frozen, root-filled soil . . . Sentries were posted, men checked. There must have been US batteries all around us, for shots were heard constantly from not far away. It was a cold December night, and we stiffened in our holes. Complete silence was ordered. No fires were allowed.'[20] (A few years ago I came across one of the Wehrmacht's tiny entrenching spades, cast aside in an Ardennes pine copse. Somehow its wooden handle had remained intact after fifty years, but the rusting blade had been bent back when its first owner had tried to dig a foxhole in 1944, and lost his battle with a tree root.)

Stetter's experience was mirrored exactly when Oklahoma-born PFC Hubert 'Bill' Cavins of Company 'E' in the 109th told me of the exact same night, in a similar setting. Then twenty years old, he recollected, 'I had no winter clothing, just long underwear, a woollen shirt and pants, my field jacket and a thin woollen overcoat. Overcoats were a thing of the past for most of my buddies, who had thrown theirs away when they had gotten covered with mud, as they were really heavy to wear when wet. We was freezing cold. After running around all day, we kinda got separated and a bunch of us holed up in this forest. It was dark, we could hear gunfire all around, but we was too tired to mount guard and just collapsed on the ground, somehow I fell asleep, my head on a log.

It froze overnight. A gun cracked and I jerked awake so quickly I left a whole patch of my hair frozen to the wood. I was too scared to care.'[21]

Major Günther Stottmeister of the *Volksgrenadier* engineer battalion recalled his men were 95 per cent young former naval personnel, who had received *three weeks'* engineering training; they managed after two days to construct a bridge made of tree trunks, but not before 'a central pier made of lumber failed. The swift current at this point tore the construction apart even before it could be fastened. Since time was short the central pier was dispensed with.'[22] American defensive fire halted construction for two hours and Stottmeister remember the 'wounded were taken by the dozens to Dr Krause at the battalion commander's bunker. Arms and legs were amputated before my eyes.'[23] Some forty-eight hours after the first assaults, trucks, half-tracks and the first *Hetzer* crossed to support the *Volksgrenadiers* who had been pinned down on the American side all the while under intense automatic and mortar fire.

Other troops, however, had managed to thrust two miles beyond the river to the villages of Longsdorf and Bastendorf, in spite of vigorous opposition from the 109th Infantry's rear battalion, badly stretched along their own four-mile front. Stationed in Bastendorf was Dr M. Bedford Davis, one of Rudder's combat surgeons, who had (illegally for a medic) acquired a P-38 pistol from a dead German soldier. 'During the seesawing of the front lines over 16–17 December, I hid it in the coal bin in the cellar of our store three separate times. I guessed if the Germans caught me with one of their pistols they would think I had killed its rightful owner and deserved the same treatment,' Davis recalled. He remembered Bastendorf 'was so small and the battlefield so limited that no one could escape a front line position. It was like watching a football game from the fifty-yard line. The Germans attacked our town time after time, in massed formation . . . We piled them like cord wood in front of our position. Yet, they kept on coming . . . by noon they were piled up several high, just a few yards in front of us.'[24]

Rudder's report of that first day communicates his own *sangfroid*: 'Everyone was holding and I saw no cause for alarm. We were in a good position and had a distinct advantage of terrain. As the attack progressed it became apparent that it was in great strength. We did not consider giving up any ground, and the division order was to hold as long as tenable.'[25] The more than creditable performance of Rudder's men was sometimes matched by Schmidt's unit, full of ex-Kriegsmarine sailors with only a month's training in infantry tactics. However, that night, in trying to spear their way through American lines, Rudder's Third Battalion witnessed some of Schmidt's *Volksgrenadiers*, whether high on alcohol or ideology, charge 'wildly, screaming and firing their weapons until killed or wounded'.[26]

Many of the 916th *Volksgrenadier's* casualties were caused by one of Company 'L's machine-guns, mounted on its heavy tripod and dug in along a wood-line overlooking the Hoesdorf plateau. Some 81mm mortars, of which Company 'L' had six, added to the carnage. These fired fifteen-pound shells up to three thousand yards. Heavy fighting and hand-to-hand combat would continue on this high ground for two days when the exhausted Americans were ordered to withdraw. Today, shallow dips in the ground betray the signatures of shell craters from the opening barrage, and Company 'L's foxholes still dot the landscape, now home to the foxes of Luxembourg. Local children showed me some of the empty cartridges they had dug out of the earth where the machine gun had been. Incredibly, nearby trees still bear GI graffiti, where Elmer Hiott carved his name in 1944 and Paul Zuhlki left his address (51, 11th Av, Chicago).[27] In 2004 a memorial stone was erected on the machine-gun position commemorating those who fought here, both GI and grenadier.

By the evening of 16 December, Rudder's front had been penetrated, and he had German troops behind him, but appeared unworried by the fact and stayed put. At the end of the month, he reported succinctly, 'We learned that if you stay in position and hold your ground, enemy infiltrations behind your front lines can be repelled by small well-organised counter-attacking forces. The men must be taught not to become panicky at the sound of a few burp guns to the rear. When Field Artillery positions are threatened to be over-run by enemy infiltrations, we learned from experience that artillery gun crews can be very effective fighting forces if they do not abandon their guns and attempt to escape . . . One of the Regiment's biggest assets during this operation was having infantry officers trained as forward artillery observers.' After the fighting was over, a GI painted a vivid description of the area in a letter home: 'Everywhere there is the tangle of shell-shot tree trunks, the litter of prolonged fighting at close quarters: bits of broken rifles, bayonets, shattered helmets, unexploded hand grenades, fragments of shell, displaced sandbags, broken stretchers, boots and gloves not quite empty and shreds of uniform and equipment.'[28] December 1944 would turn out to be an expensive month for Rudder's new command, and his report enunciated almost half his pre-battle strength missing – 1,174 casualties killed, wounded, missing or captured, losses of fifty-six vehicles and trailers, ninety-seven mortars and machine guns, with sixty tons of ammunition expended, though fifteen truckloads of Christmas mail had been distributed before 16 December.[29]

Apart from the combat and casualties, most *Landser* had only one thing on their minds – *Futter* (fodder, i.e. food). German military rations at this time were both appalling and in short supply. They included canned meat, which generations of German soldiers referred to as *Alter Mann* ('older man'), as it was reputedly made from the bodies of old men found in Berlin's workhouses. Former grenadiers Ulrich Jonath and Horst Hennig of the 352nd *Volksgrenadiers* remembered part of their incentive to reach the American lines was simply to eat: 'food supplies were unsatisfactory; other than captured American chocolate and some preserves taken from civilian houses, there was nothing. Cooking could be done only in rare cases because of the ever-watchful American Artillery observers.' Not that there was much to cook, although in the same battle Unteroffizier Stetter remembered the cooks in his 3rd Company of the 915th *Volksgrenadier* Regiment issuing him with 'our first warm food in ten days, pea soup on which the fat was swimming, for there was plenty of pork fat in the deserted houses. So we ate, no, we gobbled as much of the fatty broth as we could hold.' Inevitably rich food on empty bellies led to stomach cramps and diarrhoea shortly afterwards.[30]

The US Army used two different kinds of pre-packed meals. C-rations were the mainstay; they came in six combinations of menu arrangements to provide variety: two each for breakfast, lunch and supper. They included – as with modern military rations – packets of crackers, chocolate bars and caramels, with sachets of soluble coffee, lemon or orange-juice powder. This was the origin of modern freeze-dried coffee powder. GIs became quite imaginative in their use of C-rations: Lieutenant Otts of the US 75th Infantry Division recalled a merry evening on 27 December, giving toasts of officer-issue gin mixed with lemonade powder.[31] A particularly vicious GI version, popular among medics, was 'razor swipe', made with orange or lemon powder and surgical spirit or aftershave.[32] A C-ration accessories packet included nine cigarettes; water-purification tablets; a book of matches; toilet paper; chewing gum and an opener for the meat cans.

K-rations were designed for just a few days' use under assault conditions. Adopted for use in 1942, the demands of war meant that GIs often ate them for weeks on end. They were colour-coded, brown for breakfast, green for supper, and blue for lunch, and the packaging dipped in wax to keep the contents waterproof and provide fuel for fire-lighting. PFC

In the Ardennes, GIs subsisted on pre-packaged 'C' and 'K' ration packs. However, the most prized items for both sides were chocolate bars. By 1945 Hershey estimated they had produced and distributed over three billion ration bars like these. The Germans often relied on captured US rations and one prisoner claimed in his interrogation that 80 per cent of his unit's food came from liberated American stocks. (NARA)

Richard D. Courtney of the Twenty-Sixth 'Yankee' Division preferred the chocolate bars, caramels and Milky Ways they contained. He was 'glad to get the little packs of toilet paper (tan coloured)' in his K-rations, but one of his post-war ambitions was to 'find that committee of nutrition specialists that chose the dry, hard crackers for K-rations and force them to eat that stuff for a week'.[33]

For the Germans, captured C-rations more than lived up to their expectations, although many GIs quickly tired of the canned meat and beans, meat and vegetable stew, spaghetti, ham, egg and potato varieties. The most prized item for Germans and GIs was the 'D-bar'. In 1939, Hershey Chocolate responded to a US Army contract to produce a high-energy, heat-resistant, four-ounce chocolate bar intended to provide a soldier with 600 calories, a third of the minimum recommended daily requirement. Initially, the company produced 100,000 units per day but output soon reached twenty-four million Hershey 'D-bars' per week. By 1945 the company estimated they had produced and distributed over three billion Hershey ration bars.

Even today, rusting cans and traces of silver foil from old ration items decorate many an old foxhole; sometimes one can still read the labels: 'Instant Coffee Powder: Empty Contents into ½ Canteen Cup'. At least this was *real* coffee: the Wehrmacht had long had to make do with an ersatz alternative made from acorns or barley. *Volksgrenadiers* more than happily exchanged their issued *Krebstangen* (cancer sticks) for captured Lucky Strikes. Grenadier Friedrich Schmäschke, the seventeen-year-old former sailor introduced earlier, always recalled his first encounter with the 'olive green packs, similar to naval packs, and I searched them curiously. Out came small brown cartons that I had a hard time opening for they were coated with wax. They contained peanut butter, cookies, chocolate, tea, coffee in powdered form, chewing gum, soft drink powder, fruit bars, cigarettes, and other such things.'[34] These were unheard-of delights in the austerity-ridden Fatherland. Feldwebel Hans Griesbach, of the 14th *Fallschirmjäger* Regiment, captured on 2 January 1945, claimed in his interrogation that 80 per cent of his unit's food (and much of their clothing to keep warm) came from captured America stocks.[35]

Capturing an American food and clothing store in a convent located at Bettendorf, Grenadier Herbert Brach, of the 352nd *Volksgrenadiers*, had no complaints: 'Now, for a pleasant change we had enough to eat. Everybody feasted on the tasty US field rations, and nobody asked where our field kitchen was. The grenadiers stuffed their pockets, food bags and assault packs again. In fact, some of them had even rounded up old baby carriages and milk carts and filled them with food . . . That evening, after several days, the field kitchen finally came to supply us with hot food, but nobody was hungry, thanks to the tasty delicacies from much sought-after American rations. The supply chief himself came on the scene and was annoyed to have to take the watery stew away again.' [36]

Despite his concerns over a lack of armoured support, by the end of 16 December Brandenberger could take heart that Sensfuss, Möhring, Schmidt and Heilmann had all made some progress, though nowhere near that required by their ambitious timetable. The 212th had lived up to Brandenberger's high expectations of it, fixing a fair proportion of the US 4th Infantry Division, as ordered, and made shallow penetrations of the American front, even if behind schedule. Among the German casualties of those first few days of vicious fighting was the shoemaker from Grösskotz, Grenadier Georg Jedelhauser. On 21 December, he was caught, ironically, by enemy mortar fire while serving in his own mortar squad of 4th Company, part of the 423rd *Volksgrenadier* Regiment. Severely wounded at Consdorf, near Echternach in Luxembourg, he died later the same day, aged nineteen. Later, his divisional commander, Generalleutnant Sensfuss, took the trouble to write a personal letter to his mother, offering his condolences and telling her that Georg's unit was sending her a gift of 300 Reichsmarks. Perhaps he knew of the family's poverty. Not every grenadier of his rank received such a send-off; a nice touch from a decent man in an inhumane war.[37]

Möhring's 276th Division had the misfortune to come up against the US 60th Armored Infantry Battalion, which could – and did – call on the considerable resources of the rest of Combat Command 'A' of 9th Armored Division. Schmidt's 352nd likewise were evenly matched against half of Rudder's 109th Regiment, but the latter could call on excellent fire and tank support. Heilmann desperately needed his armour across the Our and indeed that evening some of his StuGs made it across an old weir, but he would also start to benefit from the effect of Fifth Panzer Army operating on his right flank, to the north.

Seventh Army's main problem, as Brandenberger and Gersdorff feared, was the time taken to assemble vehicle bridges, meaning all their *Volksgrenadier* attacks had taken place without armour and with minimal artillery support. The infantry had managed to cross via rubber boats or used ferries made from pontoons, but if Seventh could get their artillery and the StuGs from the 11th Assault Gun Brigade forward, then they could still make progress. Barton, Leonard and Cota, on the other hand, had been totally surprised and had desperate fights on their hands. They had held their ground but were being slowly eroded and needed reinforcement. At this stage, not all American reserves could head to the front, for a concern remained that the Germans might break through to Luxembourg City and GIs were held back in readiness to block any such attempt.

Nowhere was there panic among the forward troops, although plenty of eyewitnesses remember the service personnel further back who, never having seen a German except behind the barbed wire of a stockade, had begun to take fright and move westwards, their convoys frequently claiming road space from reinforcements heading the other way. Combat troops and service personnel have always maintained tense relationships: in the Wehrmacht they referred to each other as *Etappenhengste* ('rear echelon stallions') or *Frontschweine* – the 'front swine'.

In considering Rudder's dispositions and the reserves available to him, it is quite apparent that both the attacking divisions of Baptist Kneiss's LXXXV Corps had the advantage of surprise, numbers and – initially – firepower. In depriving Seventh Army of suitable bridging units, adequate artillery or armour, Hitler and Jodl, as the planners of *Herbstnebel*, had thrown away their best opportunity to push through the weakest sector of the American lines.

The Battle of the Bulge is replete with tactical 'what ifs', which are invariably a distraction in considering the campaign, but it is worth observing at this stage that the Germans had a good chance of reaching the Meuse through the Ardennes, though not by following Hitler's plan. The original scheme as enacted saw the main German effort, with all the panzers and majority of bridging units and artillery, weighted to the north. Given the slenderness of 'Dutch' Cota's defences due to the front he had to cover, and the sparsity of Rudder's positions in the south for the same reason, it is not unreasonable to surmise that, suitably reinforced, Brandenberger's Seventh Army could have done much better against Cota's Bloody Bucket Division than it managed.

With far more combat power shifted to Kneiss's Corps, including an allocation of panzers and superior bridging and artillery units, the evening of 16 December might well have seen elements of the resourceful 5th *Fallschirmjäger* Division cascade out of Vianden and reach Wiltz, halfway to Bastogne, as planned. Driving the route today, along the beckoning network of good roads westwards, it is apparent that Heilmann, using captured transport, could then have easily reached Middleton's almost undefended headquarters beyond by the following morning; for Bastogne lies only twelve miles west of Wiltz – as the Messerschmitt flies.

17

The Baron's Blitzkrieg

To the shrill Order of the Day penned by Rundstedt and Model, Freiherr von Manteuffel had attached his own carefully chosen words. They dwelt not on National Socialism, the Führer or Fatherland, but on the army, as befitted a representative of the old values: 'Forward. March, march! In remembrance of our dead comrades, and therefore on their orders, and in remembrance of the tradition of our proud Wehrmacht!'[1]

Opposite Freiherr von Lüttwitz's XLVII Panzer Corps the first signs of trouble pre-empted the mighty roar of the opening barrage early on 16 December by moments. As the seconds ticked towards 05.30 a.m., Company 'K' of Colonel Fuller's 110th Infantry, based at Hosingen, reported that the entire German line was a series of 'pinpoints of light'. Such words betrayed the inexperience of the observation post (OP), for veteran troops would have realised their ominous significance. The 'pinpoints' were shells and soon landing around the OP and every forward position, severing their field telephone links. These did less damage than the Germans hoped – the effect was more psychological than physical – and left the GIs able to call down artillery fire by radio. At the same time, the S-3 (Operations Officer) of the 14th Cavalry Group radioed 106th Division's headquarters: 'I am receiving heavy artillery fire on all, repeat, all my forward units, and my Command Post. No damage reports have come in yet and I will advise you as soon as info is available. What is going on? This is a hell of a lot of artillery for a Ghost Front.'[2]

Across the divide, Gefreiter Hans Hejny, an engineer in 2nd Panzer Pioneer Battalion, remembered the 'sudden flash. Then followed ear-splitting explosions . . . As far as the eye could see there were flashes everywhere, heavy and heavier guns were fired. Everything was lit up as if by day . . . All of us jumped into our vehicles without averting our eyes from the horrible spectacle. Because of the fires the landscape seemed drenched in blood. We had to continue forward, fearful as we watched the awful bombardment over our heads that brought death and destruction. The road ended at a river, whereupon we left our trucks.'[3]

Even before the barrage, Oberst Heinz Kokott's *Volksgrenadiers* in the very south of Manteuffel's Fifth Army's sector had started ferrying assault companies and heavy weapons across the Our from 03.00 am. As Manteuffel later observed, his men 'infiltrated rapidly into the American front – like rain drops'.[4] They knew any US outposts that might have spotted them were withdrawn – due to the manpower and terrain constraints – each day at last light. On 2 December Manteuffel had sought, and been granted, permission by Hitler personally to send in these companies. It aided him considerably and, in retrospect, there was no good reason why the Sixth and Seventh Armies should not have adopted the same tactics, except that in the pre-battle wrangles with Hitler and Jodl, Dietrich and Brandenberger were less vociferous than Manteuffel. Lüttwitz had left Kokott in no doubt as to the need for speed and momentum, and the commander of the 26th *Volksgrenadiers* was aware the clock was ticking if he was to secure the ridgeline as far as the River Clerf, and seize at least Clervaux by nightfall. This in turn meant the villages garrisoned by Fuller's companies along the high ground would have to be bypassed or captured quickly.

Thick fog, the early start and searchlights aided Kokott, and it wasn't until 09.00 a.m. that Fuller was able to warn Major-General 'Dutch' Cota that the Germans had crossed the river in force and were attacking the Skyline Drive. Despite Kokott's orders to press on and avoid costly fights with the US-garrisoned villages, his *Volksgrenadiers* repeatedly blundered into the small settlements, and the day witnessed numerous German attempts to subdue the various American companies. All failed due to US field artillery firing 105mm shells with very short fuses, which meant they detonated almost immediately and decimated the attackers. Companies 'I', 'K' and 'L', in villages of Weiler, Holzthum and Hosingen respectively, atop the ridge, held out using mortars and machine guns to break up the seemingly endless waves of *Volksgrenadiers*.

Surrounded at Weiler, a section of 81mm mortarmen and an anti-tank platoon equipped with 57mm guns repelled rows of attacking Germans, before picking up their rifles to continue the fight when their heavier ammunition was expended. There were no explicit orders to hold on, but Fuller had trained his regiment well enough in the short time available for them to understand the importance of holding their ground. Some of Fuller's men had survived the Hürtgen fighting, which, as we've seen, had severely taxed the Bloody Bucket's leaders. The fact that they hung on, rather than disintegrating during these opening moments of the 16 December attack, can be attributed to their earlier blooding in the Hürtgen and strong leadership. However, by 6.00 p.m. some of the 26th *Volksgrenadier*'s lighter vehicles were crossing a newly completed bridge at Gemünd, and shortly afterwards Company 'I' in Weiler reported being under attack by vehicles with multiple 20mm guns and asked for American artillery fire on their own positions; the vehicles were from Kokott's 26th *VolksFlak* Battalion, which finally persuaded the defenders to abandon Weiler, divide into two groups and head west, trickling cross-country. They had done the best they could.

Kokott later admitted to US Army historians that he had not expected the manner in which 'the remnants of the beaten units of the 28th did not give up the battle. They stayed put and continued to block the road. Fighting a delaying battle . . . individual groups time and time again confronted our assault detachments from dominating heights, defiles, on both sides of gullies, on forest paths.' The whole *Herbstnebel* plan, Kokott realised, had been predicated on a swift advance. There was no alternative plan if the Americans resisted as strongly as they in fact did. 'It became evident,' he went on, 'already during the morning hours [of 16 December] that the enemy, after the initial shock and surprise, was beginning to get hold of himself and was making efforts to delay and stop the German assault with all available means.' [5] What Kokott could not have known was that this resistance was spontaneous, for there was no way of coordinating this kind of response across the front immediately.

At about 4.00 p.m., just before dark, as a pair of sixty-ton bridges capable of bearing the armour of Panzer Lehr had been completed by his engineers at Gemünd, Manteuffel urged his tanks and assault guns across to give the *coup de grâce* to those determined GIs still holding out in the villages against Kokott's grenadiers. They were aided again by more artificial moonlight created by the *Flak*'s searchlights.[6] The bridging had taken far longer than planned because the site chosen was just before the confluence of two rivers, the Irsen and the Our, and two successive structures were needed, something good reconnaissance (forbidden by Hitler) should have revealed. With some vehicles of the Lehr's 130th Panzer Regiment crossing in the late evening, much of the later fighting swirled around Company 'K' in Hosingen, whose continued defence caused traffic jams at the exit from the Gemünd bridges. Yet to defeat the villages, especially at Hosingen, whose successful defence was delaying the panzers, the *Volksgrenadiers* needed armoured support. It was a classic catch-22 situation. By the end of the day, the 26th *Volksgrenadier* Division had crossed the Our by ferry and boat, were working their way through the ridgeline, but had yet to descend the high ground and reach or control the Clerf river crossings. Very few of the Lehr's vehicles were across before dark – only part of the Reconnaissance Battalion, known as *Kampfgruppe von Fallois.*

Back in Wiltz, to where the Bloody Bucket Division's headquarters had first moved on 19 November, all wire communications forwards and to the rear had been severed. Wholly reliant on radio networks, 'Dutch' Cota was beginning to understand this was no local attack and that Troy Middleton, beset with troubles everywhere, had no reserves to offer him. Consequently, Cota dispersed the 707th Tank Battalion, permanently attached to him, sending two tank companies to Hurley Fuller, one to James Rudder and the last to Gustin Nelson's 112th Infantry covering the north.

The 707th were old friends, having trained in England and landed in Normandy on 1 September, then accompanied the division into the Hürtgen campaign, taking their share of casualties. Commanding one of their Sherman tanks was Staff Sergeant Paul F. Jenkins of Platteville, Wisconsin, whom we met in Luxembourg. In the Hürtgen his tank had a hole a foot wide punched in the turret by an anti-tank round, fortunately without casualties, which destroyed his turret-mounted 0.50-inch calibre machine gun, but they'd carried on. Jenkins had learned to carry 'maybe twenty-five cases of C-rations on the back of our tank. We carried them because you'd always run into some infantry men that hadn't eaten for a couple days, and we could feed them. We'd go through the rations and pick out the hash. If they got meat in it then we could trade to the civilians for fresh potatoes, tomatoes, anything.'[7]

When they arrived in the sector in October, key personnel from the 707th had been sent over to the veteran 70th Tank Battalion, attached to the 4th Ivy Division, to benefit from the latter's collective experience, for the 70th had been in Europe since 6 June. Like their colleagues, the 707th were rebuilding when the German attack came in. Jenkins' most hair-raising day was 16 December, when he was summoned to defend one of Fuller's villages. 'They wanted two tanks. They said there's a patrol of eighty men coming, and they want two tanks to go down and check it out. I went with my platoon leader; we went up the hill [from the Clerf river] and could hear the gunfire to our right. The number soon grew from eighty Germans to eight hundred, and I think before the day was over, it was over eight thousand. So we went back down and got near the company, and bivouacked with them for the night. The next morning, we found out we had slept amongst some Germans.' [8]

We have seen how German 'friendly fire' had killed a divisional commander further south; something similar occurred in this sector on the 16th. Just like Jenkins' mission, in the early afternoon a platoon of the 707th's Shermans had been sent to remove some of Kokott's *Volksgrenadiers* known to be occupying the route between Holzthum and Consthum, in the area of Fuller's Companies 'I' and 'L'. On being reassured that there were no friendly troops in the vicinity, the tankers immediately engaged and destroyed one of Company 'I's anti-tank guns. There was then a delay while both sides identified themselves to the other's satisfaction before the tanks rolled on. Wilfrid R. Riley of the 188th Combat Engineer Battalion had a similar encounter, wearing his greatcoat. Deploying with his platoon one night, a voice in the dark suddenly commanded 'the soldier wearing the long coat to move forward'. Riley did as he was instructed, then ordered to halt again. Passwords, questions and answers about American culture flew back and forth, before he was motioned forward and told by a tank crewman 'Soldier, if I was in your shoes I would get rid of that long coat . . . because in it you sure as hell look like a German.'[9] Such is the currency of war, and the majority of such encounters often go unrecorded, but in the confusion of the first week of the Bulge it is estimated that between 5 and 15 per cent of casualties on both sides may have been due to such instances.[10]

To Fuller's exasperation, though correctly, Cota refused to commit his final reserve, the infantry battalion he had withdrawn from Fuller's 110th Regiment earlier. Throughout the day the 707th Tank Battalion managed to fend off the Germans for light losses, dispersed into companies and platoons, as most of their opponents were infantry regiments of *Panzer-* or *Volksgrenadiers*, the feared German armour still waiting to cross the Our once the engineers had performed their magic at the bridging sites.[11]

On Fuller's left flank in the north, Lauchert's 2nd Panzer Division had enormous problems at Dasburg, a frontier hamlet with a customs post and integrated into the Siegfried Line. In September, retreating German engineers had sensibly demolished the bridge over the Our at this point, the east bank being protected by a series of obstacles, like gates, constructed in 1939–40. They had been left in place, for the Germans possessed an unlocking device which enabled the obstacles simply to be moved out of the way. The 2nd Panzer Division's plans were predicated on being able to swing these impediments aside, but at the last moment an embarrassed officer admitted the unlocking key could not be found. The alternative was to spend precious hours waiting for Major Georg Loo's 600th Bridging Battalion to blow the obstacles, which – for reasons of surprise – couldn't happen until after the preliminary bombardment. This is what eventually transpired, after which the 600th Engineers laboured hard to construct a sixty-ton timber trestle bridge capable of bearing the armour of 2nd Panzer (including their forty-five-ton Panthers).

While this was taking place, Gefreiter Hejny of 2nd Panzer's own divisional engineer battalion recalled, 'We engineers had to build a ferry very quickly so the most important vehicles could cross the Our, whilst the blown-up bridge was being replaced. We made this using flotation bags and also constructed a stone pier on the bank for the first ambulances.' Hejny's ferry conveyed wheeled vehicles from 2nd Panzer's Reconnaissance Battalion first, with troops from 304th *Panzergrenadier* Regiment. Next door, the main bridge was completed by 4.00 p.m., just before last light; however, after the first few panzers had rolled across, the eleventh tank misjudged his approach and slipped through a span, crashing into the river below and drowning the driver: repairs to the bridge entailed a further three-hour delay.[12] Nevertheless, the first assault troops had much earlier crossed by rubber boats, and reached Company 'B's position in Marnach as early as 08.00 a.m., halfway to Clervaux. Dasburg, apart from a new bridge built on the site of the old, has hardly changed from 1944 and, given the narrowness of the twisting approach road, it is easy to see why the engineers had such a hard job and how a nervous young panzer driver lost his life and cost his division three hours, when every minute counted.

Some German troops heeded Manteuffel's demand for speed, and rushed beyond Marnach towards Clervaux, though others set to, in an attempt to destroy Marnach's hard-pressed garrison, who fought on. After years of black news, in the initial moments of *Herbstnebel* the attackers were jubilant, as Gefreiter Friedrich Bertenrath, a signaller with the 2nd Panzer Division, recalled. 'We had begun to act like a beaten army. Now, moving forward, the men were extremely happy and filled with enthusiasm. Everywhere there were signs of renewed hope.'[13] Hitler also thought with the brain of the *Gefreiter* he had once been. He understood that what his Wehrmacht needed was a taste of victory again – and he was right; the value to Germany's fighting prowess by the lifting of spirits was incalculable. All armies prefer to be on the offensive, where they retain the initiative and dictate the course of events, than the defensive, where they do not.

Yet even the Wehrmacht's corporals could see the writing on the wall, for Bertenrath perversely concluded, 'I never thought this attack would change the tide of the war. But it was a moment to enjoy.'[14]

After dark, once their bridge at Dasburg was finished, tanks from 2nd Panzer entered the fight at Marnach, but could not overcome the little town that night. To say that this left Lüttwitz and Manteuffel annoyed is an understatement. A series of delays – the missing key to the obstacle, then the accident at Dasburg, the slow process of bridging, determined resistance of the American defenders and tendency of their *Volksgrenadiers* to get sucked into fire-fights – all contributed to shaving a day off their aspirations to reach at least the Clerf river and Clervaux, if not Bastogne.

Billeted in the luxury Villa Prüm on Clervaux's rue Brooch was Sergeant Frank A. LoVuolo, with Battery 'B' of the 107th Field Artillery, who would later play professional football with the New York Giants. He remembered being on guard duty when the German artillery barrage began. 'I could hear shell fragments strike the pavement and nearby buildings and was forced to race for the protection of the villa,' he recalled. 'Crawling and running, I finally reached the front door.' He slammed it shut behind him. 'No one knew at that time what all the German activity really meant. We were completely out of communication with everyone, and stayed put until late morning. At that point in time we heard the clanging and creaking sound of armor coming down the Wiltz road and thought the worst.' The tanks were friendly Shermans and their commander entered LoVuolo's villa and told his group that the Germans had broken through their lines in several places. 'He advised us to get out of Clervaux as quickly and as best we could and to avoid encirclement. Those were the last semblance of orders I was to receive until I rejoined my unit at Christmas. Without hesitation and without packing any of our belongings everyone escaped onto the hillside behind, becoming part of an ever-growing stream of Americans moving west. There was mass confusion and I was a part of it,' admitted LoVuolo.[15]

Meanwhile, in Bastogne General Middleton had recognised the magnitude of the attack he was facing with virtually no reserves, the result of Bradley's gamble. He had no option but to order VIII Corps to 'stand fast' until their positions were 'completely untenable', then withdraw back to a further specified line. Colonel Fuller at his CP, in Clervaux's Hôtel Claravallis, had much better awareness of the situation. Radio reports were flooding in of the German attacks, and he knew Clervaux was not yet in danger. Like Middleton, his main worry was a lack of fresh troops to stem the German tide, and GIs, like LoVuolo and his friends, who had been prematurely ordered to withdraw. However, by the end of the first day Fuller was surprised to discover most of his companies of the 110th Infantry were still in position.

Fuller's main concern was Marnach, through which ran the only good, hard-surface road in the region westwards, via Clervaux, straight into Bastogne. Clearly the Germans wanted to make for Bastogne and this would become their main effort on 17 December. General Cota recognised this too. Somewhat buoyed by Colonel Rudder's positive assessments from the 109th Infantry's sector, at 9.00 p.m. Cota returned Fuller's third rifle battalion back to the 110th Infantry, minus a company to defend Wiltz. With this unit, and as many tanks in the area as he could muster, Fuller hoped to counter-attack Marnach on the morrow. He had no way of knowing he would run slap-bang into Lauchert's 2nd Panzer Division intent on doing the same.

Typical of many GIs cast adrift in those first few days, Sergeant Frank LoVuolo had now begun to make his way cross-country in search of his unit. As he recalled, 'This began an eternity of foraging for food, sleeping in barns, sprinting across open fields, and hiding in deep woods. I decided that as long as I was on my own and under no direct orders, I would strive for three objectives: (1), stay alive; (2), avoid capture and (3), find my artillery unit – in that order. I succeeded in all three.'[16]

North of Fuller and his troubles lay Cota's third regiment, forty-five-year-old Colonel Gustin M. Nelson's 112th Infantry; like the others it was at full strength, though many of the men were post-Hürtgen replacements. Nelson, who described himself as a 'regular army man with no home town', was a West Pointer who graduated in 1921. His father was a senior journalist with the *New York Sun*, which ensured his son, who at one stage led his men in combat waving a malacca cane, always had a good write-up in its pages.[17] His sector, a six-mile stretch of the Our, was also where the Belgian, Luxembourg and German frontiers met. Then, as now, there were few houses or settlements in the area to use for shelter and pine forests made observation difficult. The ground was altogether more challenging and undulating than that which Rudder or Fuller were defending, with fewer creature comforts. It was dominated by heights on the German side, with numerous small draws. It contained no major roads, and most routes were effectively unpaved, muddy logging trails.

Nelson's men had merely a series of squad and platoon posts, incorporating where possible captured Siegfried Line pillboxes on the eastern bank of the Our, though these were mainly built for shelter, not to fight from. As the structures faced the wrong way, companies had to rely on foxholes and barbed wire for protection and defence, as Richard S. Shoemaker remembered. He had grown up in rural Michigan and was drafted in 1942; by 1944 he was a veteran of Company 'E' who had fought through Normandy and the Hürtgen. Though still a PFC, the twenty-four-year-old was acting as squad sergeant, leading patrols. As the weather deteriorated in the Ardennes he remembered the hunt for food in particular: 'One day we found a barn to get out of the weather. We used the wax boxes from our K-rations to start a fire and I supplied the food. Outside I saw a chicken and wanted to get it for dinner. I picked up a frozen apple and hurled it at the chicken breaking its legs. I was lucky to hit it and ran over and picked it up and we had a great dinner. I cleaned it and we put it in an old pot we found in the barn. I put some bouillon cubes in the water and boiled the chicken. That was a good meal.'[18]

He and the rest the 112th were, of course, unaware of the impending attack by the entire muscle of Krüger's LVIII Panzer Corps, comprising Siegfried von Waldenburg's 116th Panzer Division (the Greyhounds), and the 560th *Volksgrenadiers*, under temporary command of Oberst Rudolf Langhäuser, deputising for his hospitalised boss. Both the German formations were for different reasons grossly under-strength. Nevertheless, elements of two Wehrmacht divisions were about to attack three American battalions under conditions of total surprise. Krüger had realised astutely that substantial numbers of Nelson's regiment, including an entire field artillery battalion, occupied the Our's east bank and therefore used intact bridges to negotiate the river and resupply the forward units. Rather than build his own structures, Krüger intended to capture at least four of his opponents'. To the north 116th Panzer would try and seize US bridges at Lützkampen, while barely a mile away the 560th *Volksgrenadiers* were assigned two bridges either side of the tiny village of Ouren.

Among these *Volksgrenadiers* was the young *Kanonier* named Josef Reusch, who had grown up in this frontier neighbourhood. He recalled that his *Panzerjäger* (anti-tank) battery 'consisted of 108 men and had six 75mm PAK-42 guns that were pulled by the *Raupenschlepper Ost* (RSO) which had an Opel engine'. This was essentially a truck on caterpillar trucks designed for Russia, and an indication of the division's original destination, but enormously handy in the muddy conditions of the wintry Eifel. However, and illustrative of the transport variation within 560th's sub-units, he went on, 'Each gun had a crew of six men and the remaining material and supplies were pulled by horse-drawn wagons'. Pausing in the villages Reusch, then merely seventeen, remembered resting while 'the *Pferdeführer* (horse wagon drivers) gathered food in the first few houses. An old lady recognised me because of my dialect and then cursed at me. I felt guilty because I belonged to the robber bands, but what were the wagon drivers to do? The animals would not go further if they did not eat!'[19]

With Nelson and Headquarters Company of the 112th Regiment, spread through a few buildings in Ouren, was PFC Earl T. Chamness, already a veteran of the Hürtgen by the time he moved to the Ardennes. He couldn't help contrasting the quiet of the area with the activity he had known in the 'Green Hell' of the Hürtgen a few weeks before. 'It was quiet now, only occasional artillery and mortar fire disturbed the prevailing peace. Line upon line of (previously humming) pill boxes now seemed lifeless,' he recalled. At 05.30 a.m. on 16 December the German attack found him 'lying on a kitchen floor by my telephone switchboard. Traffic had slowed so we were trying to get some shut-eye. Suddenly, all hell broke loose. Mortars coming in, shells going over head, and many guns firing all over the place. The switchboard rang, I answered, but recognised it was not an American speaking. *Heinie* had captured one of my phones!'[20]

Clarence Blakeslee, with Company 'M' of the 112th, remembered hearing German voices in the pre-dawn darkness. One was calling out for his leader, Karl. 'I found our sentry and used his phone to call the CP . . . The lieutenant said there would be "hell to pay" if I was wrong and he alerted the company. I said it would be much worse if I am right and you don't. He alerted everybody. Someone from Company "K" heard them and emptied his carbine at them. Suddenly they came running toward me.' [21] The barrage had fixed many of Nelson's men and daylight showed the attacking 1130th *Volksgrenadier* Regiment already beyond and behind many of the forward platoons, using the wooded areas to maximum advantage. At Sevenig, they overran a platoon of Nelson's Company 'L' at breakfast, reaching one of their objectives, a stone bridge south of Ouren. US artillery fire managed to blunt much of this assault, so the German troops at the bridge really amounted to the tip of a damaged arrow; by evening a battalion counter-attack had pushed the grenadiers – according to one prisoner, all ex-Luftwaffe personnel with the 560th *Volksgrenadier* Division – back and restored the situation.

Krüger's main effort was Waldenburg's attack; the latter threw his two *Panzergrenadier* regiments forward as the bombardment started and by 06.30 a.m. Nelson was receiving reports of his forward battalions in this sector under assault from Germans who had filtered between his companies on the line. At this stage a captured map revealed how the *Panzergrenadiers* had managed to plot all the American machine-gun positions through careful observation.

After the barrage, Charlie Haug of Company 'B' at Lützkampen remembered there was complete silence from 07.00 to 07.30 a.m. and a few minutes later he and his friends acting as company messengers 'experienced what was perhaps the biggest hair-raising scare of our entire army career. Out of the darkness came the awfullest screaming and yelling you would ever want to hear. The Germans were coming! They were screaming like a bunch of wild Indians. They were less than a hundred yards in front of us. How they ever got so close without us hearing them, we'll never know.'[22] PFC Richard S. Shoemaker in Company 'E' had earned himself a furlough in Paris; he had just returned when the attack came in. 'I did not even have my rifle yet. We were overwhelmed and we had to run. Some men just gave up and sat there. I said "come on guys get moving". I don't know what the Germans did to them.' [23]

Sergeant Lamoine 'Frank' Olsen, commanding a platoon in the 112th that morning, was likewise overtaken by the initial confusion. The Union City, New Jersey, inhabitant had joined the Pennsylvania National Guard in 1941 and three and a half years later found himself forward of most of the Keystone Division, on the east side of the Our. He was checking his unit's positions when the German attack erupted, and was swiftly surrounded as shooting broke out. 'The Germans couldn't distinguish me from their own in the dark so I removed my helmet and tucked it under my arm like a football and ran through them as fast as I could.' Olsen barged into several Germans who fell to the ground as he ran at them in the dark, 'being a prudent man, I kept my mouth shut, got up and continued on my way'. He recalled, as he arrived at the stone farmhouse which housed his platoon command post, that 'all hell was breaking loose' with his men and the Germans were trading shots all around the vicinity. Soon he received a radio message from his company commander to delay their opponents as long as they could. 'We had more men than windows and doors to shoot out, so some crawled up to the attic and poked holes in the straw roof to fire out of.' They held out throughout the day.[24]

Many of Waldenburg's *Panzergrenadiers* were young and new to war. Company 'B' around Lützkampen claimed around 135 killed. 'The remaining thirty or forty Germans decided to call it quits,' remembered Charlie Haug with Company 'B'. 'The oldest was perhaps about eighteen, and they went down to about fourteen years old. This was part of what we had been fighting all morning . . . As soon as we had finished searching the Krauts, they started to ask us questions. The main one seemed to be, "Will we be sent to New York?"'[25]

Just before the daylight began to fade, Waldenburg's panzers had appeared on a knoll overlooking Lützkampen, but could not shift the GIs in the vicinity, who replied with accurate defensive artillery fire. Haug watched through his field glasses, seeing 'hundreds of German tanks, trucks and half-tracks coming down the winding roads', one of which had a flame-thrower. 'It stopped about fifty feet from a foxhole, and as the two kids sat there helplessly, a gigantic stream of roaring fire shot in on them. Their worries were over. They had been burned to a crisp,' Haug recalled. Many men around him 'jumped up from their holes and ran back over the hill', seeking safety in the dense woods behind his position; others, like Haug, wanted to run, but couldn't. Many stood their ground, shaking uncontrollably, crying or praying for deliverance. It came unexpectedly as US anti-tank guns opened up on the fire-breathing dragons. 'From a hillside about a quarter-mile to our left, we heard a series of sharp cracks . . . and we could see the streaks of fire coming from the hillside towards the tanks. The first few shells missed, but the third made a direct hit on the first tank, and it burst into flames. The streaks of fire kept coming from the hillside, and soon the second and third tanks were also in flames. Did we ever have fireworks. Shells exploding in every direction. It was only a matter of seconds and the fourth and fifth tanks were also hit. Their tracks were knocked off and they couldn't move.' [26]

Milton J. Schober, serving with Company 'F' of the 424th Regiment, part of the Golden Lions Division, to the north of the inter-unit boundary, also witnessed this exchange and could remember looking south to 'see the action of German troops moving against Company 'B', 112th Regiment, at the outskirts of Lützkampen and we noticed German artillery landing in the farm fields in front of us, but nothing was landing on us at the time. In the late afternoon of the sixteenth, our company jeep came bouncing down a logging road to bring hot chow to first platoon men. While waiting to be served, there was a loud explosion that I took to be incoming artillery but then realized that 25–35 feet away was a three-inch anti-tank gun of Company 'B', 820th Tank Destroyer Battalion, which was firing toward Lützkampen – a column of German tanks was the target, and what excitement there was in watching those fiery orange balls streaking to and exploding the tanks. Some say there were six tanks, others say five tanks and a truck, but whatever, they all burned furiously. While all of this was going on, one of the cooks dishing out the food said, "Hurry up, you guys – we've got to get out of here". He got no sympathy from us!'[27]

General Krüger was acutely aware of the lack of momentum and time ticking away, and ordered the panzers to sideslip down the river line, using a handy track on the German bank. Despite the 560th *Volksgrenadiers* seizing a destroyed bridge south of Ouren at midday which they reckoned repairable, Krüger's corps engineers could not guarantee a tank-bearing structure constructed on that site for at least twenty-four hours. At least one panzer tried to cross, for Kanonier Reusch remembered, 'The first situation we encountered was a tank that was too heavy for a bridge and it lay in the Our.'[28] The hunt for a crossing site resumed while the Reconnaissance Battalion of the 116th

Panzer Division was despatched to cross over 2nd Panzer's bridge at Dasburg, searching for a suitable bridge as they moved down along the east bank of the Our.

Meanwhile, for PFC Chamness and Colonel Nelson's Headquarters Company, the situation soon degenerated into confusion as he remembered, 'Our head sergeant shouted, "Close up board, let's get out of here!" So we put everything in a jeep and trailer and took off across the snow covered fields. I was in a jeep and we came upon a captured American ammunition convoy. Jerry had just stopped the convoy, so our driver took us across some more snow covered fields till we got out. Later we found our lines, were put in covered trucks and passed through Spa, a resort town. We finally came to Bastogne, and since it was getting late, we were told to bed down in a barn. We were so tired we went right to sleep in the hay.'[29]

The day ended with the 112th Infantry still in its positions east of the Our, less damaged than its southern neighbours but defending a sector alive with German tanks, and possessing none of their own. Haug's Company 'B' had started the day with about 190 men, and by 9.00 p.m. was down to 'one lieutenant and seventeen enlisted men', though the majority of these were lost rather than killed or wounded, a story that echoed throughout 112th Infantry. Krüger, on the other hand, was livid. Hardly any vehicles, let alone a formation of panzers, had crossed the Our. The various German attacks against the front of the US 28th Division nevertheless succeeded in splitting the 112th Infantry apart from the rest of Cota's division. As communications gradually broke down over the next few days between the 112th and Cota, his northern regimental commander, Nelson, had to act very much on his own, and would be eventually pushed back north-westwards to St Vith, where he found himself swept up in the array of units defending this crucial route centre. His defence on 16 December exposed the *Volksgrenadiers'* inexperience and lack of training, and the fault lay entirely at Hitler's feet for committing such an inadequate unit to a major task. In their first day of battle the half-strength 560th *Volksgrenadiers* had suffered nearly 1,000 casualties.

This need not have been so, for many of Nelson's troops were inexperienced replacements too; but they had been better trained and integrated with veterans in the short time available. Several historians and military analysts have argued that all three of Cota's regiments 'collapsed' to varying degrees in the Hürtgen fighting, which is why each regimental commander in the Bulge – Rudder, Fuller and Nelson – was relatively new in post.[30] It was a wise move, for with good training and fresh leadership, despite the intense shelling and psychological shock of panzers grinding about, none of Nelson's men folded. Middleton helped by designating a clear defensive line to hold (the Skyline Drive), which helped orientate the small groups of defenders. But this was just the beginning.

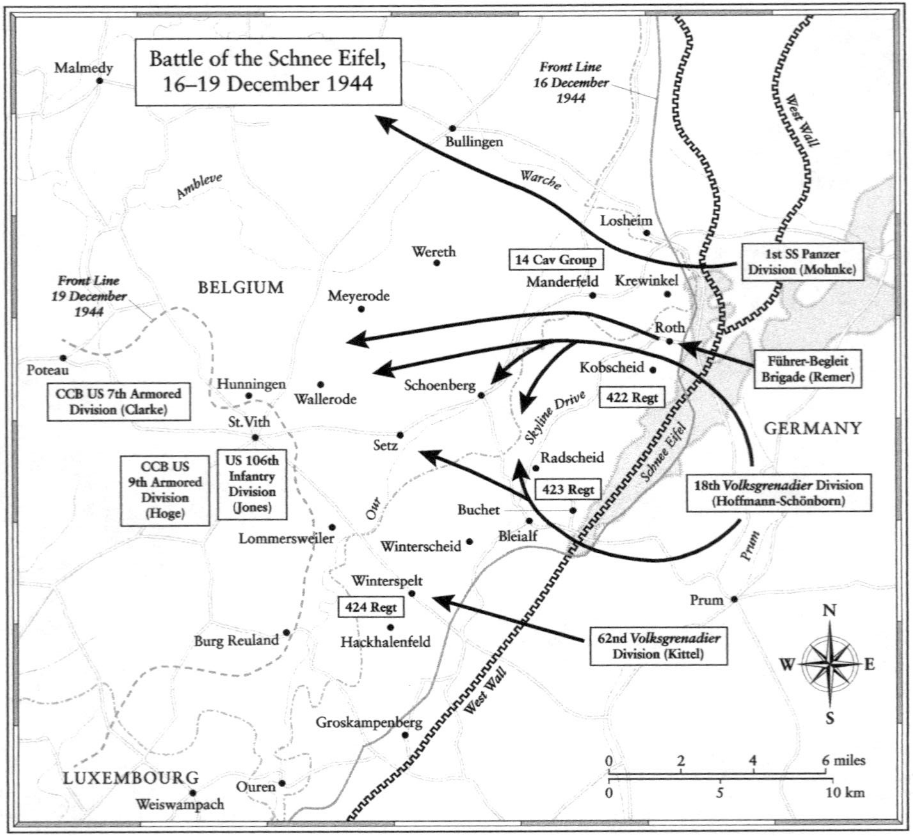

Battle of the Schnee Eifel, 16–19 December 1944
Malmedy
Front Line 16 December 1944
West Wall
Bullingen
Warche
Ambleve
Losheim
Wereth
14 Cav Group
1st SS Panzer Division (Mohnke)
Manderfeld
Krewinkel
Front Line 19 December 1944
BELGIUM
Meyerode
Roth
Poteau
Kobscheid
Führer-Begleit Brigade (Remer)
Hunningen
Wallerode
Schoenberg
422 Regt
CCB US 7th Armored Division (Clarke)
Skyline Drive
St. Vith
GERMANY
Setz
Schnee Eifel
Radscheid
US 106th Infantry Division (Jones)
CCB US 9th Armored Division (Hoge)
423 Regt
18th Volksgrenadier Division (Hoffmann-Schönborn)
Our
Buchet
Lommersweiler
Winterscheid
Bleialf
Prum
Winterspelt
Prum
424 Regt
N
Burg Reuland
Hackhalenfeld
62nd Volksgrenadier Division (Kittel)
W
E
West Wall
S
Groskampenberg
0 2 4 6 miles
LUXEMBOURG
Ouren
0 5 10 km
Weiswampach

18

Golden Lions

Of all the attacks in the Ardennes, one of the most dramatic was on the patch of rolling high ground known as the Schnee (Snow) Eifel where Major-General Alan W. Jones' 106th Golden Lions Division were deployed. Jones, fifty-one, was born in Glendale, Washington, graduated from its university as a chemical engineer and was commissioned in 1917. Although anxious to see action in France, Jones shared the fate of Eisenhower and Bradley in remaining in the USA for the remaining months of the First World War, despite attempts to be sent overseas. Alert-looking, with a fashionable Clark Gable pencil-line moustache, in 1943 Jones raised the new 106th Infantry Division at Camp Jackson, South Carolina, trained it and took it to war. It comprised the usual three infantry regiments, three 105mm artillery battalions, one of heavy 155mm howitzers, and support units.

In the years since the Bulge a degree of 'scapegoating' has been levelled at the leaders of the Golden Lions, with frequent observations along the lines of 'not only did the enlisted men lack any combat experience, but most of its officers did as well. Even General Jones, the division commander, had never heard a shot fired in anger.'[1] Much of what subsequently happened to the Golden Lions was predetermined by events before it left the United States, however. The fact that Jones 'had never heard a shot fired in anger' would have little to do with his command abilities, as Bradley and Eisenhower aptly demonstrated, though other officers and men, scattered through the levels of command *had* seen recent action in the Mediterranean and France. Several had received Bronze and Silver Stars for their valour, when serving with other units, before arrival in Belgium.

Jones was one of a group of officers who had come to George C. Marshall's attention as the future of the US Army, which also included Eisenhower, Bradley, the SHAEF chief of staff Walter Bedell 'Beetle' Smith, J. Lawton Collins and Matthew Ridgway. Considered a high-flyer, he joined the staff of General Lesley J. McNair's Army Ground Forces Command in Washington, DC, and was rapidly promoted to brigadier-general. Soon, he was appointed Assistant Division Commander of the 90th Infantry Division, clearly being groomed for higher things, and gained his own formation in March 1943. Hard training followed until the Golden Lions were considered ready to enter combat. However Jones's formation began to be 'raided' for trained personnel because of higher than expected casualties in the Italian and Normandy campaigns. Several tranches of junior officers and NCOs were transferred out to Europe with the result that, by August 1944, a staggering total of 7,247 men had been removed, among them the sub-unit leaders who would have bonded the division in combat. Training replacements, who knew their men and would command equal respect, would take almost as much time again. As one historian of the campaign noted, 'regardless of how well trained a unit is, it cannot lose over 60 percent of its best and brightest and retain a high level of combat efficiency'.[2] It is impossible to believe that, had the Golden Lions deployed to France in July–August, as originally scheduled, with most of their original personnel, the debacle of December would have happened just the same.

Numbers were made up by reassigning men from coastal artillery, anti-aircraft, and rear-echelon service units; many volunteered to transfer, others had no option. In addition, 1,100 recruits from the Air Corps and 1,200 from the Army Specialised Training Program (ASTP) were redirected to the 106th. By December 1943, the ASTP had enrolled about 150,000 bright young scholars into college courses with the intention of producing highly skilled, qualified young officers for the armed forces. It was also a subtle bit of horse-trading with American universities that were resistant to the lowering of the draft age from twenty to eighteen, which they considered would endanger their institutions. Because of combat casualties, in 1944 the ASTP courses were scaled down and the aspirant officer-scholars absorbed into infantry divisions as enlisted men. Among those who were selected for ASTP courses but were re-employed in combat was future New York City mayor Ed Koch, who fought on the northern flank of the Bulge with 104th Division; Henry Kissinger, who arrived in the Bulge with 84th Division; actor-director Mel Brooks, who likewise served in the Ardennes with 78th Infantry Division; and author Kurt Vonnegut Jr, whom we shall meet shortly with the 106th Division.

With a paper strength of roughly 700 officers, 40 warrant officers and 12,500 enlisted men, Jones's division passed the Statue of Liberty on 21 October 1944, arrived in England six days later and were soon shipped over to France. PFC Frederick Smallwood was with HQ Company of 423rd Infantry Regiment and arrived in Le Havre on 1 December where he received his first 'war currency. It was not real French francs, but GI issue. It looked like play money, different sizes and different colors for each denomination. It was all paper even down to the one franc notes. The exchange rate was about 50 francs to the dollar. I was now getting $65 a month as I had received my PFC stripe and gotten my Good Conduct Medal while we were in England, plus we now received $10 per month extra for overseas pay, less insurance. I bought a money order and sent most of it home for Daddy to put in the bank.'[3]

The division was immediately trucked along the Red Ball Express route to the Ardennes in order to acclimatise to combat and the European weather, completing a relief in place with 2nd Infantry Division by 12 December. The latter were amazed that the Golden Lions were still wearing their neckties in a combat zone. The 'Ghost Front' was a perfectly logical place to put the newly arrived division, as comments from the departing veterans of the 2nd Indianhead Divisions made to the Golden Lions, that they were 'entering a rest camp', illustrated. 'It has been very quiet up here and your men will learn the easy way,' Colonel Boos of the outgoing 38th Infantry Regiment had said to the incoming Golden Lions when the latter took over their twenty-two-mile sector of the line.[4]

'The defensive positions were well-prepared, the product of two months' work,' wrote a 2nd Division officer who had overseen their construction. 'Almost all foxholes had log cover, and the troops had dry sleeping quarters in pillboxes or in squad huts constructed from logs.'[5] PFC Smallwood recalled his log bunker 'half dug in the ground and half-logs above with logs and dirt for a roof and a blanket for a door. We had navy type cots inside and a bottle of gasoline with a rag wick for a light, of course it smoked. We had a two-man OP foxhole, dug chest deep in the ground, with a log roof also to keep the snow off us.

There was snow all over the ground and it kept falling. Being from the south, I was not used to snow or that much cold.'[6]

George R. Kester, from Albia, Iowa, had just finished junior college when his draft notice arrived in January 1943. Following basic training, he was assigned to the 527th Army Engineers Light Pontoon Company and trained to build Bailey bridges. Kester's engineer unit sailed out of New York on 1 September, arriving in Normandy two weeks later. On reaching Belgium by truck convoy it was attached to Middleton's VIII Corps. Kester, twenty-one, spent the next two months on 'engineering tasks such as road maintenance, logging [building corduroy roads made of logs], constructing Bailey bridges and building squad huts for the 2nd and 106th Infantry Divisions' up on the Schnee Eifel. His most valuable weapon was his 'General Purpose Vehicle or Jeep, which was liked by everyone who used it. It was useful as a point vehicle on a motorized march. You could use it as a command car. Throw two or three litters on and it was an ambulance. It was used for a scout car and went ahead of a convoy where it left off road guides at key points. It was a great stand-up bar for eating a can of C-rations or a box of K-rations. Its motor could even warm up the can! Because it was an all-terrain vehicle, it simply went around traffic grid locks.'[7] Armoured and cavalry units called them 'Peeps'.

Snowfalls and a low ceiling added to the sense of a dormant front, where for the previous ten weeks there had been only light patrol activity, just as for the 28th Division to their south. The wintry climate took its toll straightaway – this affected every unit along the front – with cases of sickness and trench foot caused by the icy, driving rain and muddy terrain. Weather apart, the 2,000-feet-high plateau of Schnee Eifel was challenging terrain to defend, and not simply an endless carpet of pine woods covering the gentle, rolling landscape that some historians and movie-makers have suggested.

Sergeant John P. Kline of Glen Ayre, Indiana, was drafted into the army aged eighteen, one week after completing his high school education. Enrolled on an ASTP degree course, he was transferred into the Golden Lions in March 1944 and found himself in Company 'M' of the 423rd Regiment, assigned to positions along a tree-covered ridge on the Schnee Eifel. His heavy weapons company was equipped with 81mm mortars and water-cooled .30-inch calibre machine guns. He remembered of his first night on 12 December, 'I can personally confirm that a snow covered tree stump will actually move. That is, if you stare at it long enough – and if you are a young, nineteen-year-old machine-gun squad leader peering into the darkness towards the enemy through a slit in a machine-gun bunker. Every sound was amplified. Every bush could be an enemy crawling towards you. Your eyes grow bleary from staring into the darkness. You are happy when the relief crew shows up. The next day, you take a good long look at the stump that moved during the night. You take note of all unusual objects, and then things start to settle down.'[8]

When building the *Westwall* in 1938–9, the Germans had found this sector just as challenging when considering where to site a series of worthwhile, interconnected defences. They opted instead for a sparse line of bunkers in which mobile artillery units could shelter, and situated their main positions further east, deeper into Germany, where visible lines of approach were covered by anti-tank ditches and rows of 'dragon's teeth' concrete obstacles – our classic image of the Siegfried Line. Both sides were aware that on Jones's northern flank was the Losheim gap, a five-mile-wide patch of very different terrain where the road network was much improved. It had been used historically as an invasion route into what is today southern Belgium and north-east France. In that sector, Jones placed Colonel Mark A. Devine's 14th Cavalry Group, attached to his division.

They used their mobility to cover the vital roads of this vulnerable sector, a sure bet for an attack – not that one was anticipated. Devine owned the 32nd and 18th Cavalry Reconnaissance Squadrons, each battalion-sized outfit designed for speed, normally equipped with jeeps and M-8 armoured cars, with the latter Squadron in the line. Middleton was nevertheless worried enough about Losheim to site eight battalions of his field artillery, representing most of his corps guns, to cover the sector with pre-registered fire. The gap was doubly vulnerable, as it also represented the boundary of Middleton's VIII Corps and the northern V Corps of Major-General Leonard T. Gerow. Considered 'rock solid' and unflappable, 'Gee' Gerow, who had graduated from the Infantry School with Omar Bradley and the Command and General Staff College with Eisenhower, was the first corps commander ashore on D-Day. If the northern Ardennes needed an unflinching commander, trusted by both Bradley and Ike, then Gerow was the perfect choice.

As Cota had found further south, because of his frontage, Jones was obliged to deploy all three infantry regiments to the front; normal military custom would be to keep one back as a reserve. His chief concern was that two of his forward regiments, the 422nd and 423rd, both in exposed positions on the Schnee Eifel, could be surrounded by attacks to either flank. In the south, a three-mile gap yawned between the Schnee Eifel and the positions of Jones's third outfit, the 424th Infantry. In the gap lay the town of Bleialf. In order to surround the two forward regiments, all the Germans would have to do was control the Schonberg to Bleialf road.

To hold the little town and plug the gap between regiments, like their 2nd Division predecessors, the Golden Lions had to deploy a mix of support units. The 423rd's Anti-tank Company, which fielded nine 57mm guns, and other units, acted as infantry, and occupied the town and immediate vicinity, along with a company from the 820th Tank Destroyer (towed) Battalion. The nearby railway station was held by a troop detached from the 18th Cavalry, with their armoured cars. Regular patrols made contact with the 424th Infantry further south, but they were out of view, half a mile away through heavy forest. The Bleialf garrison made repeated requests for more mines, barbed wire and ammunition of all types to strengthen the defences. More, they were told, would be available on 16 December.

Up on the Schnee Eifel itself, Colonel George L. Descheneaux's 422nd Infantry Regiment occupied the northern sector of the high ground, his southern neighbour being Colonel Charles C. Cavander's 423rd. The tiny Bleialf garrison bridged the gap with Jones's other infantry formation, 424th Regiment, led by Colonel Alexander D. Reid, with his headquarters in Winterspelt. Reid held the front line as far south as Lützkampen, the boundary with Cota's Bloody Bucket division. Delbert P. Berninghaus from West Bend, Iowa, was a newly promoted corporal with Descheneaux's 422nd Infantry. On the Schnee Eifel he was assigned lookout duty in an OP, remembering, 'The forest of oak, beech, and fir trees was behind us, a vast white field of snow spread out before us. The snow clung to the trees and covered the terrain. Occasionally, we would catch sight of one of our scouts, dressed all in white to camouflage their movements, steal across the field. They were called "white cow" patrols.' [9]

In Cavander's regiment, Sergeant John Kline remembered his own company commander had set up his headquarters in 'one of the enormous Siegfried Line bunkers. He had taken a room several flights down. The command bunker was on a crest of a hill. The firing apertures faced west towards Belgium, the backside towards the present German lines.

There were steep slopes on either side, with signs and white caution tape warning of minefields. There was a pistol belt and canteen hanging in one of the trees on the slope. Apparently, some GI had wandered into the minefield.'[10]

At thirty-two, Descheneaux was one of the youngest colonels in the US Army and considered a high-flyer; his HQ was in the village *Gasthaus* at Schlausenbach. Cavander, commanding from the village of Buchet, near Oberlascheid, was a forty-seven-year-old Texan who had served in the Argonne in 1918 as a PFC, subsequently winning a place to West Point; General Jones's only son, Alan W. Jones Jr, was an officer in one of his battalions. Jones Sr put his headquarters in St Vith at the St Josef's Convent, formerly a school that had been used as the local German HQ, about twelve miles from his forward positions, and no more than forty minutes' drive in a jeep, using the road network of the day.

Then numbering around 2,000 souls, St Vith has since quadrupled in size, but remains the hub of six roads. The most important of these ran via Houffalize to Bastogne, nearly thirty miles to the south; another twelve miles north, to Malmedy, while a third stretched a similar distance west to Vielsalm. Additionally, the only railway line along the entire front that crossed from the Reich into Belgium passed through St Vith. Thus for Field Marshal Model, the roads and railway leading to the town represented one of two main supply routes (MSR) for *Herbstnebel*, the other being through Bastogne. Model had hedged his bets in the planning processes, for St Vith lay in the centre of the Fifth and Sixth Armies' thrusts. If necessary, either could incorporate the town into its advance, for both would need to be supplied through it. Manteuffel assessed that the success or failure of *Herbstnebel* would be measured by the speed with which St Vith was captured. Accordingly, St Vith's retention was as vital to the Americans as its capture was to the Germans.

Jones was uneasy about his two forward regiments, as had been his predecessor, Walter M. Robertson. The latter had asked Middleton back in November if he could withdraw his exposed units, and although the VIII Corps commander agreed, Hodges and Bradley refused, citing the argument that these positions represented a penetration of the Siegfried Line.[11] Thus, their men stayed at the front, watching from observation posts by day and sometimes patrolling the terrain at night. Corporal Berninghaus of the 422nd on his first night patrol remembered 'the winter stretched out its fingers touching us with cold. I wore my combat boots, field jacket, and helmet with liner for protection from the elements.

We had no overcoats or overshoes as we stood in the wet snow, stood, watched, listened, then moved on to repeat the cycle in another location. The snow was wet and heavy as it clung to the branches and sides of the trees. I can still see in my mind's eye the night, moonlit, crisp, cold and silent and then I heard a sound. I froze. Hearing the sound again, I called out in German, *Wer ist das*? [Who is that?]. No one answered me. I knew, despite my fear, my ears had not played a trick on me; the sound was real. I held my position; not moving a muscle. It came again. It was then I knew my fear; heavy snow was being pulled from the branches by the force of gravity and dropping to the ground. The footsteps I heard were not those of the enemy, but those of the snow stepping down from the trees. Relieved and thankful I rose from the ground to my feet and again started walking.'[12]

Across the divide, Jones's opponents, Baron von Manteuffel and General Walter Lucht, commanding LXVI Corps, had come to the same conclusion about the Americans' vulnerable positions on the Schnee Eifel. Lucht instructed Oberst Günther Hoffmann-Schönborn of the 18th *Volksgrenadiers* to deploy two of his infantry regiments at either end of the high ground to surround the Americans, then move forward and take St Vith with his third. To the south, Oberst Friedrich Kittel's 62nd *Volksgrenadier* (Moonshine) Division, with his Hitler Youth from Düsseldorf and Cologne, was to seize bridges over the Our at Steinebrück and screen the southern approaches to St Vith, opposite the US 424th Infantry. His attack would be preceded as elsewhere, with a 05.30 a.m. bombardment, followed by infantry assaults.

Though the region was peaceful, at night PFC Smallwood of the 423rd, like the rest of his regiment, 'could hear all kinds of noises. There were sounds drifting across the valley, of wheels turning and grinding, and motors running, which indicated to us lots of activity, but what did we know, we were new to combat and anything we heard sounded ominous. We told the officers what we had heard and they reported this back to Regimental HQ . . . They said it was probably the Germans playing the noises over a PA system to harass us.'[13]

At 05.32 a.m., the S-3 of 423rd Regiment radioed, 'We're receiving another bunch of artillery fire in our sector. We haven't seen this much activity since we've been here. My S-2 [intelligence officer] has been listening in on the division net and tells me others are getting hit. Please keep us advised on what's going on.'[14] Minutes later, at 05.45 a.m., the 14th Cavalry announced the presence of ground troops: 'We are receiving all types of artillery, mortar and rocket fire on our forward positions. Lasting about fifteen minutes, the Command Post of the 18th Cavalry in Manderfeld received approximately 100 rounds of medium and heavy artillery fire. No report of ground attacks so – [changes subject] The 2nd Platoon, Troop 'C' 18th Cavalry in Krewinkel, reports a large enemy column approaching his position. Apparently the enemy doesn't know his unit is there and Lt. Farrens is holding fire until they get within twenty yards.'[15]

Despite losing most of his wire communications to the opening barrage, from radio reports General Jones in St Vith soon realised the *Volksgrenadier* attacks amounted to a general assault along the length of his wafer-thin forward lines. He was not immune from the shelling, experiencing some of the longer range warheads (from railway guns) landing in St Vith itself. The Golden Lions' headquarters at St Josef's Convent had only just established themselves and had yet to settle into a routine before being overwhelmed by multiple reports from nearly every unit within the formation. By 06.00 a.m., the eighth report in the division's signal log in as many minutes was reporting the first ground combat. 'From S-3, 14th Cavalry Group: "Large enemy force is attacking Troop 'A' in Roth and Kobscheid and Troop 'C' in Krewinkel. The enemy troops are pushing hard and both our Troops are engaging with all their weapons at this time. Lt. Farrens, Platoon Leader of 3rd Platoon, Troop 'C' 18th Cavalry in Krewinkel reports they're killing a lot of Germans".'[16] Farrens beat off his attackers but not before one of them shouted in perfect English, 'Take a ten-minute break. We'll be back!' 'We'll be waiting for you, you son-of-a-bitch!' replied Farrens.

All the earliest reports of infantry incursions came from the 14th Cavalry on the northern flank, between Losheim and the Schnee Eifel; most of Hoffmann-Schönborn's 18th *Volksgrenadiers* were moving round to outflank Jones's two forward regiments and there were few grenadiers left to feint or demonstrate against the fronts of the 422nd and 423rd Infantry. The forward troops up on the Schnee Eifel heights saw almost no action throughout 16 December, as most of the combat took place miles off to their flanks, as PFC Smallwood of the 423rd remembered: 'My immediate area was never attacked,' he said. But perhaps some clever opponents infiltrated the lines for later, when he was on guard duty in his observation post, 'a big blond lieutenant came walking down the trail and asked me where Company 'A' was. I told him that I didn't know, which was the truth, so he asked if Company

'C' was farther down the trail. Again I answered him if he wanted to go into Company HQ that they could tell him. He replied "No, he would just go on down the trail". I'm not sure how good his English was or exactly how he sounded but, to me being from Georgia, all the soldiers from "up north" talked funny.'[17]

Middleton's first message to Jones was at 06.32 a.m: 'Enemy ground units are using searchlights, bouncing the light off clouds to provide artificial moonlight. North of the 106th Infantry Division, the 99th Infantry Division is under heavy attack. A patrol the 99th sent to gain contact with 14th Cavalry Group, reported the Losheim Gap was overrun with enemy troops. That was the last report from the patrol and it appears they were killed or captured.'[18]

Meanwhile, at first light, Reid's 424th Regiment in the south reported a long line of German skirmishers to their front. They seemed inexperienced and 'fired their weapons wildly without regard for specific targets. They also appeared to be either drunk or doped.' Some of the 424th were challenged in other ways. PFC Jim D. Forsythe, a former ASTP student and latterly runner with Company 'A' in Reid's regiment, recalled being billeted in the village of Lommersweiller in various houses. He was issued only forty rounds of ammunition for his M-1 Garand rifle; this equated to five eight-round clips, but, as Forsythe observed, 'At this time we did not anticipate a battle and forty rounds appeared to be more than adequate . . . by the evening our forty rounds were gone within a few minutes.' [19]

By contrast an experienced GI recorded of the same time, 'I had thrown away my gas mask, had an ample supply of toilet paper inside my helmet, and my pockets were stuffed with "K" rations, candle stubs, cigarettes, grenades and two 2½-pound blocks of TNT complete with fuse to blow myself a hole in the frozen ground, if necessary. I had my good old M-1 with the regulation belt load of eight clips ball, two clips A[rmour]P[iercing], two extra bandoliers of ammo (each carrying six more clips), bayonet, canteen, first-aid pouch, plus three bazooka rounds.'[20] This equated to 176 rounds of Garand ammunition. After the eight rounds had been fired, the Garand automatically ejected the empty clip with an audible 'ping', and the Ardennes forest floors are still littered with the old clips.

The 424th's opponents were the Hitler Youth from Kittel's 62nd *Volksgrenadier* (Moonshine) Division, led by Leutnant Kurt Schwerdtfeger, who was adjutant of the 164th Grenadier Regiment under the legendary

Found on the body of a dead German, this image was given to the author at St Vith on the 50th anniversary of the opening of the offensive, 16 December 1994, by a former GI from the US 424th Infantry Regiment of the 'Golden Lions' Division. The boys on this *Hitlerjugend* camp were drafted into the 62nd *VolksGrenadier* Division and in their first battle most died, in a hail of artillery fire at Winterspelt. (Author's collection)

thirty-six-year-old Oberst Arthur Jüttner. The latter, already bearer of a Knight's Cross with Oak Leaves, was one of the few to have escaped the collapse of Army Group Centre (he trekked for 300 miles with five soldiers), though nearly all in his old regiment had been killed or captured. I interviewed Schwerdtfeger, also highly decorated, at his home in Biedenkopf in 1994, whence he'd retired after a career as a lawyer in Munich. His background was typical of many junior officers in 1944. After compulsory service in the RAD, he'd joined his father's old infantry regiment and served in Poland as a corporal and in France as a sergeant. Commissioned soon after, he led a platoon into Russia but was badly wounded twice, losing the use of both hands, necessitating extensive hospitalisation until he voluntarily returned to the front in 1944, aged twenty-five.

Schwerdtfeger recalled particularly the fate of his young conscripts: 'they'd had minimal training and were still just boys; some openly cried with fear before this, their first and last battle'. As each wave of his former *Hitlerjugend* were blasted by American artillery, 'our line would waver, but with strong exhortations from my NCOs to "remember the Fatherland", we got them to reform and continue,' he recalled, still visibly distressed by the memory. 'Some of my NCOs resorted to shouting and blowing whistles, which reminded the frightened Hitler Youths of discipline they had learned on their summer camps.' Eventually they continued forward. 'One of my boys had brought along his HJ trumpet, which he played to urge his comrades into battle, until American fire cut him down.'[21]

Harry F. Martin Jr, with Company 'L' of the 424th, witnessed 'hundreds of shadowy heads bobbing up and down, coming over the crest of the hill . . . They acted like they were drunk or on drugs. They came over the hill screaming and shrieking. Their shrill screams went right through my head. I was absolutely terrified. They had already outflanked our company, and now they were coming to finish us off. In the middle of this terrifying battle, I heard a very confident calm voice inside my head say, "squeeze the trigger". I instantly calmed down, took careful aim at one of the charging Germans . . . and squeezed the trigger. He flung his arms over his head and fell down . . . At this moment I was a veteran combat soldier . . . [Eventually] The battle was over. After such intense fighting it was very strange how suddenly the battle ended, how quiet everything had become . . . I had conquered my worst fears and stood to fight the enemy.'[22] These observations of possible German drug use were correct. Since at least May 1940, the Wehrmacht had routinely issued its soldiers with Pervitin tablets (made from methamphetamine, commonly known today as crystal meth). Tested on inmates at Sachsenhausen and Dachau, the pills enabled the Reich's soldiers to fight for longer and without rest.[23] In my interview, the former Leutnant Schwerdtfeger was reluctant to discuss the use of any stimulants by his troops.

An hour later, pressure was evident against the boundary of 423rd and 424th Regiments, as the former's commander, Colonel Cavander, was on the radio:

> Enemy advancing on Bleialf is threatening to cut off Troop 'B', 18th Cavalry and I [pauses] Enemy is now in Bleialf, Repeat, enemy are in Bleialf now! They wiped out one of my platoons defending there and

> I urgently need permission to use my 2nd Battalion so I can launch a counterattack. I fully understand that it is part of the division reserve, but the Bleialf situation is serious and is a threat to the division's defence. Have alerted Service Company and Cannon Company to move to the support of Bleialf. I'll try and do my best with what I have, but if we want to kick those people out, I need my 2nd Battalion released to me now![24]

Since around 06.15 a.m., the Bleialf defenders had been hit from three directions by hundreds of ghostly looking *Volksgrenadiers*, who emerged out of the fog in their white snowsuits. Cavander's seeming panic reflected his awareness that, should the Germans (they were Hoffmann-Schönborn's 293rd *Volksgrenadier* Regiment) manage to push beyond Bleialf, then a good road to St Vith would be open and the GIs on the Schnee Eifel surrounded.

In the north, Descheneaux's 422nd Regiment also reported German troops in white snowsuits, supported by assault guns, attacking Auw and then his headquarters in Schlausenbach. Initially, the division's leaders responded as Jones had trained them, committing units from the division's small reserves to threatened areas, all the while keeping Middleton at VIII Corps in Bastogne abreast of developments. Meanwhile, Jones sent his Assistant Divisional Commander, Brigadier-General Herbert T. Perrin, forward to Winterspelt, near the boundary between 423rd and 424th Regiments, where he was able to exert some calm and control the application of reserves.

This is when Bradley's gamble of using Middleton to garrison almost the entire Ardennes was exposed, for VIII Corps was so thinly spread that it had precious few assets with which to help Jones. At 11.20 a.m., Middleton released a battalion of his corps engineers for use as riflemen, and Brigadier-General William H. Hoge's Combat Command 'B' (CCB) of the 9th Armored Division, to the Golden Lions – but they were to be committed only on Middleton's orders. CCB had originally been slated to assist the 2nd Division in their assault on the Roer dams, hence their presence in the area; their colleagues of CCA had already been sucked into the fighting alongside Barton's 4th Ivy Division, down in Luxembourg.

By 11.45 a.m. Jones had released a battalion to help Colonel Reid's 424th Regiment in the south, and at midday one of the division's engineer companies was deployed as infantry to help reassert control over

Bleialf, two-thirds of which was now in German hands. Around noon, Lieutenant-Colonel Frederick W. Nagle, the 423rd's regimental executive officer, assumed overall command of the vital Bleialf sector. Aided by artillery support, GIs, including the engineers, cooks, clerks and military policemen, counter-attacked their opponents and by mid-afternoon had snatched seventy-five German prisoners from the little town.

The much-battered cavalry troop belonging to Colonel Devine were eventually authorised to withdraw from their lonely outpost in the railway station and support the 424th Regiment near Winterspelt. This still left a two-mile gap about which Jones could do nothing for the time being, unless CCB of the Ninth Armored arrived early. At the same time defensive fire from his field artillery batteries dried up when they came under attack, as Descheneaux of the 422th Regiment in the north reported: 'The 589th and the 592nd Field Artillery Battalions are both under artillery and ground, Repeat, ground attack. The artillerymen are defending their guns and holding, but obviously they can't provide much fire support if they have to defend their firing positions from ground attacks.'[25]

This was disastrous, for the only immediate fire support the Golden Lions could receive was from their own artillery, the 105mm guns having a maximum range of about six miles, and their single battalion of 155s, nine miles. Once on the move, the cannon were silent, and some batteries in any case withdrew beyond range, so as to be out of harm's way from a German ground assault. Their accuracy relied on forward artillery observers and spotter planes – but the latter were unable to fly in the grey weather.

At about this time in 424th's southern sector, an officer from Company 'K' took possession of a map case worn by a wounded German officer. It contained details of Operation *Greif*, the employment of German troops wearing US uniforms, and was rushed back to Jones's headquarters in St Vith, the first confirmation of this ploy. An hour further on and Jones's headquarters had to admit to Middleton at 1.16 p.m., 'Due to the tactical situation in this sector, the 106th Infantry Division no longer has the capability to maintain physical contact with the 99th Infantry Division, or V Corps.'[26] This was a tragic admission that their front had been penetrated successfully and a gap created in the north, which the Germans would not be slow to exploit. Middleton and Jones would be able to do very little about this in the immediate short term, due to their lack of sizeable reserve formations. Jones meanwhile threw in most of the rest of his paltry divisional forces later in the afternoon, as other areas were threatened. The 422nd in the north had committed its own regimental reserve early but requested extra help from the division at 5.00 p.m. Jones was aware that with one breakthrough in the north, all the Germans needed to do was punch through at Bleialf in the south, and two-thirds of his division would be swept away in the ensuing chaos.

By early evening, at 6.05 p.m., the 106th's divisional artillery commander, Brigadier-General L.T. McMahon, had ordered his guns to move back: 'To COs of the 589th and 592th Field Artillery Battalions: "You will, Repeat, will break contact with the enemy and begin displacing as soon as possible. The 589th will go into position three miles south of Schönberg and the 592nd will displace to St Vith".'[27] At the same time, Hoge of Combat Command 'B' arrived at St Vith, whereupon Jones told him to counter-attack and clear the Losheim gap the following morning. In much older age Hoge remembered, 'I was making a reconnaissance at Monschau, I saw an attack come over against the 99th Division . . . Then I got a message to call corps – I was attached to V Corps at that time – as soon as I could. They told me that I had been reassigned to VIII Corps and was to go back to St Vith . . . A new division had just come over, the 106th. Well, that division had lost two of its regiments in the attack [they had yet to lose them at the time Hoge was describing, on the 16th] and was a shambles. But I got there, reported in to the commanding general [Jones]. He was jittery and knew nothing.' [28]

By 8.00 p.m., Middleton had updated Jones on the wider situation: 'Enemy attacking 110th Infantry Regiment just east of Clervaux. Men on R and R [Rest and Relaxation] are being organised for defence of the town. Enemy artillery is falling on Clervaux.'[29] At this stage Middleton in Bastogne told Jones by phone that he was sending him Brigadier-General Robert W. Hasbrouck's entire 7th Armored Division, whom we last met in October, at the Peel Marshes in Holland. They were several long hours' drive away, but the 7th's CCB, under Brigadier-General Bruce C. Clarke, were racing to get to St Vith as soon as possible. With the prospect of these fresh reserves, Jones rethought his orders to Hoge, putting his CCB into Losheim. Instead, he decided to push Hoge's CCB forward to help his 424th Infantry in Winterspelt, and use Hasbrouck's 7th Armored Division to support his two regiments up on the Schnee Eifel. Although Reid's 424th Infantry was in no immediate danger of encirclement, if Winterspelt fell the Germans would have another direct route to St Vith, a risk Jones could not take. He could read a map as well as Manteuffel and knew the Germans needed St Vith in order to break through to the Meuse. At all costs Jones had to stop them.

This in turn prompted Jones to rethink the state of his 422nd and 423rd Regiments, whose flanks were being threatened. If possible he would like to pull them back, off the high ground, to relative safety. A little later, at 8.47 p.m., Jones was logged as speaking to his staff, saying, 'I have decided to call and suggest to General Middleton that I withdraw my forward regiments', meaning the pair on the Schnee Eifel.[30] It was almost an hour before Jones and Middleton were able to speak on a secure but intermittent phone line; their important conversation was pieced together by the author John Toland, who interviewed both men for *Battle*, his work on the Bulge published in 1959. Both commanders spoke hurriedly, but guardedly, aware the Germans might be monitoring their call. The line was often bad and both men sometimes had to shout and repeat, to make themselves understood.

> Jones – I'm worried about some of my people.
> [He was referring to his two regiments on the Schnee Eifel]
> Middleton – I know. How are they?
> J – Not well. And very lonely.
> M – I'm sending up a big friend, 'Workshop' [codeword for Hasbrouck's 7th Armored Division]. It should reach you about 07.00 a.m. tomorrow.
> J – Now about my people. Don't you think I should call them out?
> [Middleton did not hear this last sentence from Jones, as the line momentarily cut out, but said]
> M – You know how things are up there better than I do, but don't you think your troops should be withdrawn?
> [Jones, likewise, failed to hear this sentence of Middleton's, for the same reason, but asked]
> J – I want to know how it looks from where you are. Shall I wait? [31]

Jones already knew about 'Workshop', but realised Middleton's estimate of a 07.00 a.m. arrival, made in all innocence, was grossly optimistic. More importantly, as Toland observed, 'Jones was convinced that Middleton meant him to keep his men on the Schnee Eifel'.[32] The Golden

Lions commander wondered whether he should argue the point with his corps commander, but, being new to battle, was self-conscious and hesitated. Perhaps Middleton knew of other facts that were not in his – Jones's – possession. In the end he thought he should rely on Middleton's experience and judgement, and hung up on an already atrocious line. Another historian put it succinctly: 'Each man thought the other had agreed to just the opposite course of action – Middleton thought Jones was pulling the units back, but Jones believed his corps commander had approved his decision to leave them in place. This disaster was nearly catastrophic for the entire American defence of the Ardennes, for Jones had made the wrong decision.' [33]

By leaving the units in place, Jones had signed the death warrant for two regiments and other units of his division. This is where his inexperience counted, for a more self-confident leader would have contested his superior's decision and discovered the awful mistake. We may observe that, whereas Jones may have been physically brave, it was his moral courage that let him down on this occasion, in failing to pursue the issue with Middleton. The 106th signals log recorded at 9.43 p.m. that Jones explained the situation to Middleton and discussed the advisability of withdrawing the forward units; when the phone call ended, Jones said to one of his artillery staff officers, Colonel Malin Craig, 'Well that's it. Middleton says we should leave them.' [34]

Yet with General Jones's knowledge of the intensity of the struggle for Bleialf, the threat to Winterspelt and the fact that the loss of either would jeopardise his own position in St Vith, it is surprising that the Golden Lions' commander said nothing more to his superior on the subject of his two 'lonely' units, for the two headquarters were still in contact through the night. That Jones's third regiment, Colonel Alexander Reid's 424th, would subsequently launch a valiant blocking and rearguard action, fighting from ridge to ridge back to Vielsalm during 16–22 December, would be overshadowed by the loss of the other two regiments.

Thereafter the situation continued to deteriorate as messages poured into St Josef's Convent. Another situational message from VIII Corps arrived at 10.40 p.m.: 'Enemy has crossed the Our River in the 28th Infantry Division's sector and most units are cut-off and isolated. Clerf [Clervaux] and Marnach are still in friendly hands, but the situation is changing rapidly.' Communications were still open to Middleton in Bastogne, but Jones never thought to question his corps commander subsequently, because, in his own mind, his superior's instructions were quite clear.

Jones would nonetheless have been aware that his losses were heavy. Lieutenant David Millman of Company 'C', 331st Medical Battalion supporting the division, recorded the first battle casualties swamping his aid station around 09.00 a.m., and during the course of the day 'artillery barrages occurred in and around the aid station, injuring many men, including First Lieutenant Bradley, First Battalion Surgeon's Assistant. The attached ambulance made several trips forward, and under fire, evacuated approximately thirty casualties'. By 02.00 a.m. on 17 December the fighting had forced them to shift position rearwards, but during the day Millman's company alone had evacuated 123 serious casualties by ambulance.[35]

The 331st Medical Battalion had only arrived in Rouen by LST on 5 December, and hitherto had been treating a handful of casualties for colds, cuts and bruises. PFC Edward L. Christianson, another former ASTP student and ambulance driver in the same medical unit, recalled receiving casualties very early that first morning. 'Being inexperienced of the "real" war, there was much confusion at first but that didn't last long. Training and good common sense soon put order into our efforts. My main job was to transport the seriously wounded from our level of treatment to the clearing station in St Vith where they would get better treatment. I made several trips to St Vith that day; it sure was an exciting baptism to the real war.' Christianson was twenty years old.[36]

At 11.00 p.m., the First Army Group's Intelligence Summary for 16 December, issued by Brigadier-General Sibert at Bradley's headquarters in Luxembourg, was received. 'The sudden attacks and seemingly overpowering array of six enemy divisions . . . should not be misinterpreted. The quality of divisions involved, the piecemeal efforts . . . and the apparent lack of long-range objectives . . . seem to limit the enemy threat . . . the day's events cannot be regarded as a major long-term threat.'[37] This may also have served to nullify Jones's concerns for his two forward regiments: armoured help was on its way and his army group commander (three levels above him in the chain of command) seemed to downplay any danger. Perhaps, an exhausted Jones may have felt after his first day of combat, he had got it wrong and was overreacting in wanting to call back his two forward regiments. In fact Sibert, Bradley's intelligence chief, had got it terribly wrong.

Later that night, at 11.32 p.m., 106th Division issued their own Intelligence Report. Included were details of 'Fifty-eight enemy prisoners were interrogated. They were members of the 62nd *Volksgrenadier* Division; 116th Panzer Division; and 18th *Volksgrenadier* Division. A prisoner considers the attack a failure since the losses of the Germans were extremely heavy and most objectives were not reached.'[38] A captured copy of Rundstedt's Order of the Day was attached with a translation. Finally, at ten minutes to midnight on 16 December, VIII Corps in Bastogne passed down the following: 'The following was announced over Radio Berlin, "Our troops are again on the march. We shall present the Führer with Antwerp by Christmas".'[39]

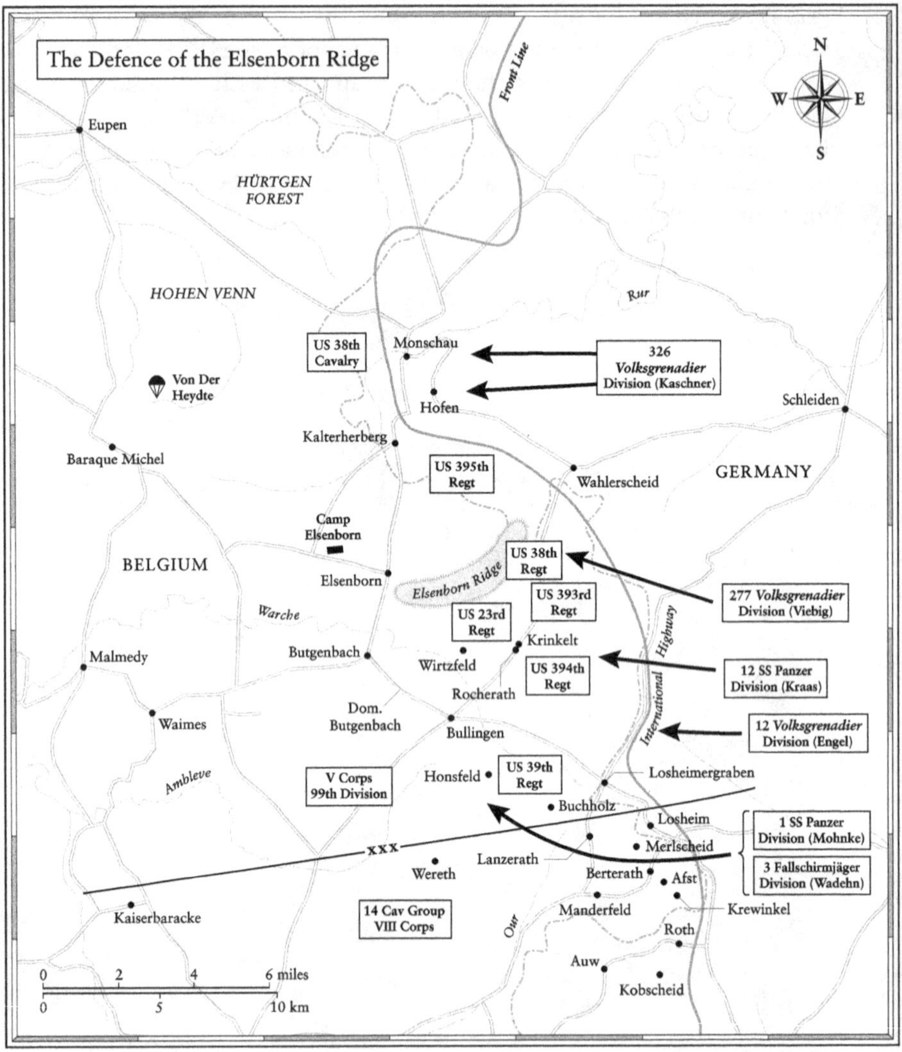
The Defence of the Elsenborn Ridge
N
W
E
S
Front Line
Eupen
HÜRTGEN FOREST
HOHEN VENN
Rur
US 38th Cavalry
Monschau
326 Volksgrenadier Division (Kaschner)
Von Der Heydte
Hofen
Schleiden
Kalterherberg
Baraque Michel
US 395th Regt
Wahlerscheid
GERMANY
Camp Elsenborn
BELGIUM
US 38th Regt
Elsenborn
Elsenborn Ridge
277 Volksgrenadier Division (Viebig)
US 393rd Regt
Warche
US 23rd Regt
Krinkelt
International Highway
Malmedy
Butgenbach
Wirtzfeld
US 394th Regt
12 SS Panzer Division (Kraas)
Rocherath
Waimes
Dom. Butgenbach
Bullingen
12 Volksgrenadier Division (Engel)
Ambleve
V Corps 99th Division
Honsfeld
US 39th Regt
Losheimergraben
Buchholz
Losheim
1 SS Panzer Division (Mohnke)
xxx
Merlscheid
Lanzerath
3 Fallschirmjäger Division (Wadehn)
Wereth
Berterath
Afst
Kaiserbaracke
14 Cav Group VIII Corps
Manderfeld
Krewinkel
Our
Roth
Auw
Kobscheid
0 2 4 6 miles
0 5 10 km

19

They Sure Worked Those Two Horses to Death

HAVING OBSERVED THE reaction to the attacks of Brandenberger's Seventh Army in the south and Manteuffel's Fifth Army in the centre of the Bulge, the drama now swings north.

Opposite the proposed onslaught of Oberstgruppenführer Josef 'Sepp' Dietrich's Sixth Panzer Army lay three US formations. On Dietrich's left, bridging the boundary between General Troy Middleton's VIII Corps and General 'Gee' Gerow's Vth, was Colonel Mark A. Devine's 14th Cavalry Group, stretched out in a static role totally unsuited to their low numbers, and that disdained their high mobility. A few minor sub-units were detached to Major-General Alan W. Jones's Golden Lions Division further south, as we have seen, but the majority were clustered around the villages of the Losheim gap through which the inter-corps boundary ran.

North of the cavalry, and garrisoning the front from the Losheimergraben crossroads up to the twin villages of Krinkelt and Rotherath on the Elsenborn Ridge were the 14,208 men of Major-General Walter E. Lauer's US 99th Division. Beyond them and guarding the rest of the northern flank, to the scenic, half-timbered town of Monschau, were Major-General Walter M. Robertson's veteran Indianheads, the US 2nd Infantry Division. Since 14 December some of the 2nd were already committed to a small offensive to seize the Roer dams along with the US 78th Division, north of the Ardennes area, but would withdraw to aid their comrades, once the threat of *Herbstnebel* had manifested itself.

During the war the US Army created eighty-nine active divisions, of which sixty-one, including the 99th – the Checkerboard Division – served in Northern Europe. The Checkerboarders were almost as new to combat as the Golden Lions. They had arrived in foggy, wet England in six troopships, fresh from training in Texas. LSTs had then conveyed them to France, followed by a 285-mile trek along the Red Ball Express route to Belgium, taking over areas of the front from 9 November. Until they were warned for service in Europe, none of the division knew to which theatre they would be assigned – many feared in the autumn of 1944, when the European war appeared to be drawing to a conclusion, that they would be sent to the jungles of the Pacific – and felt they had experienced quite enough of that heat in Texas. In the Ardennes, from the outgoing troops, they rapidly picked up the nickname of 'Battle Babies', a descriptor they wore with pride.

A wave of depression quickly settled on the 99th when they met grey, overcast skies, icy rain, sleet and snow, mixed with endless forests, drab stone buildings and suspicious locals – many of whom had relatives over the border. Visibility was generally poor with less than eight hours of daylight; it usually grew light from 08.00 a.m. but it was dark by 4.00 p.m. Unlike the natives of Luxembourg further south, the neighbouring Belgians were reserved in their manner towards the American soldiers, fearing a German return. As with the 106th, the Checkerboard Division included 3,000 ASTP scholars-turned infantrymen to replace others previously sent to Europe. Many of these were initially the butt of bullying, jokes and insults from the older Checkerboarders, who derided the college boys with their aspirations to graduate and become officers.

The Brooklyn-born commanding general, Walter Lauer, had seen action in North Africa before taking command of the Checkerboarders in August 1943. December 1944 found him headquartered in a Belgian villa at Bütgenbach, about eight miles behind the front. It was equipped with a grand piano, for Lauer's way of working off stress was to lose himself in music, and attack the keyboard as though nothing else mattered. His staff had no idea what to make of a grand piano *in* their CP.[1] Having led his division for nearly sixteen months, Lauer was not popular with all his officers or soldiers, and several wrote in their memoirs of finding him 'humorless, abrasive, arrogant and disagreeable', yet he proved himself a good commander.[2] His division's front followed the Siegfried Line and was obscured by dense pine woods which removed fields of fire and visibility, but provided plenty of material for log huts, overhead cover for bunkers and trunks for engineer-constructed corduroy roads. They could take heart from the proximity of the seasoned veterans of the US 2nd Division, some of whom were already in combat, attempting to reach the Roer dams, in conjunction with Combat Command 'B' of the 9th Armored Division.

Taking over positions vacated by the US 9th Infantry Division, Lauer placed his three regiments in line – like the Golden Lions and Bloody Bucket divisions to his south, he was stretched thinly, covering a wide sector. Colonel Alexander J. Mackenzie's 395th Regiment covered the northern flank to the boundary with US 2nd Division. In the centre Lauer placed Lieutenant-Colonel Jean D. Scott's 393rd Infantry. In the south, Lauer felt the area around Losheimergraben, which marked his forward lines, to be his most challenging sector. This is where Colonel Don Riley's 394th Infantry Regiment was assigned a five-mile front to garrison. If Lauer was unpopular, so was Riley; several Checkerboarders thought him 'vainglorious and incompetent'. His final pep talk to his men before they headed overseas began, 'War is fun!' He was met with stony silence.[3]

Of all the areas in the Ardennes, that of Riley's regiment covered the most likely, shortest and best movement corridor for an army hurrying from the east towards the Meuse. Initially the route stretched from Losheim, then in German hands, across the Americans' front, where it was known as the International Highway. The favoured road to the Meuse then turned north-west at Losheimergraben and, today called the N632, ran on towards Liège, some fifty-six miles distant – these days a journey of less than two hours.

With his limited resources, Riley, who had taken command on 12 October, focused most of his attention on the triangle of settlements, each a mile apart, of Lanzerath to the south, Losheimergraben to the north and Buchholz railway station to the rear. He put two of his three 860-man battalions along the front, the third he kept in reserve, near Buchholz, while he placed the regiment's I&R (Intelligence and Reconnaissance) Platoon near Lanzerath, in over-watch of the surrounding road network. The I&R Platoon, commanded by First Lieutenant Lyle Bouck, was a set-up similar to the 28th Division's I&R outfit based in Vianden, who had interviewed the Luxembourg civilians escaping the Germans.

Bouck had volunteered for the army before the war, lying about his age, and been commissioned as an officer aged just eighteen.[4] He had managed to scrounge some extra weapons and ammunition for his small unit, which boasted several machine guns and BARs (the 1917 model Browning Automatic Rifle, effectively a squad light machine gun which fired the same .30-06-inch ammunition as the Garand rifle), certainly more firepower than one might have expected for a small detachment; his communications back to the regimental CP were by a network of field telephones. He, the rest of Colonel Riley's three battalions and the 14th Cavalry, would shortly have the misfortune to find themselves under attack by elements of three infantry divisions, the equivalent of eighteen battalions – and that was before a single German tank appeared.

The 99th at least had a month to acclimatise to their new surroundings before the maelstrom descended upon them, but their first few days were depressing. Byron Reburn noted his friends in Company 'L' of the US 394th Infantry 'standing like harnessed draft horses, vapour rising from the irregular columns of young men, humbled by the penetrating cold, the impersonal discipline, and the gods of fate that put us there'.[5] PFC Donald Wallace was also with Company 'L' and vividly remembered the division's unimpressive stay in England before crossing to France. 'It was always raining there, and it was mudsville; sloppy, mushy mudsville. We got one forty-eight-hour pass into London and for the first time witnessed a city in blackout. With overcast skies and complete blackout at night, we couldn't see for any distance.' Soon they crossed the Channel, bound for Belgium, and Wallace observed, 'As we passed through villages, French and Belgian citizens threw apples to us and ran alongside the slow-moving trucks pouring wine and passing it up to us. It was very heart-warming for our cold bodies in those open trucks.' On 11 December, his company moved into divisional reserve at Buchholz station, near the 3rd Battalion's HQ.[6]

Kenneth F. Haas had grown up in the small town of Ellis, Kansas, during the Great Depression of the 1930s. With no job, he volunteered for the army before being drafted in August 1943 and was accepted on to an ASTP course. When the programme closed, he was assigned to the 99th and sailed for England. 'About 1 November,' he recalled, 'we boarded ship at Southampton and docked at Le Havre, the first full division to disembark there since the Germans destroyed the port facilities. We went down rope ladders in full equipment at night and boarded "Red Ball" trucks for the drive across France and Belgium. On 4 November, we started passing "Long Tom" (155mm) artillery firing at the enemy many miles away. After fifteen months, we had arrived at the front.' Haas was soon sent to the anti-tank platoon of Headquarters Company of the 2nd Battalion, 395th Infantry Regiment. Of his first month in Belgium, he recollected, 'We spent a relatively quiet month on line watching the Germans across the way sawing wood, hanging out laundry and occasionally tossing a few mortar shells our way and we returned the favour.'

Haas and his comrades had to support the US 2nd Infantry Division's assault on the Roer dams. His job was to 'carry cases of ammunition, dynamite, and K-rations cross icy streams and snowy hills to the attacking forces. On the return trip, we often carried litters with recent casualties.'[7]

A foot of snow lay on the ground and some of the recently inherited dugouts from the 9th Division were little more than 'a muddy hole with a makeshift roof of shelter halves'.[8] As with the 106th Division, the Checkerboarders set to, by building log cabins behind their fighting positions where they could sleep in relative warmth, with stoves taken from deserted houses. Nevertheless the cold sapped morale, and the clothes they were issued didn't help.

The GI-issue leather footwear let in water and cold to such an extent that in the period until 15 December some 822 of the division had reported sick with cold-related injuries, chiefly trench foot, a problem mirrored throughout the other US divisions. The 99th were wearing their M-43 olive drab four-pocket field jackets, made of water-repellent cotton, which had just replaced the earlier zipper-fronted M-41, produced from thinner wind-resistant cotton cloth and lined with shirting flannel. The latter was totally unsuited to winter conditions and the former not much better. A new high field boot had been designed, but not yet issued, to replace the ankle boots and khaki canvas leggings that GIs had worn to this point. The only concession to winter was a woollen overcoat, which many had discarded because they were too heavy. Some had retained their issue raincoats, which were waterproof but hardly warm. Looking back, one GI recalled how he had arrived as a replacement 'without an overcoat (stolen) and throughout the winter wore long woollen underwear, two sets of olive drabs, a sweater and field jacket, a scarf and (replacement) overcoat, with two pairs of woollen socks under my combat boots and galoshes'.[9] Men were theoretically issued a couple of blankets apiece; sleeping bags, on account of their bulk, were a rarity.[10] (In a small Ardennes *Gasthaus* I visited in 1990, I was astonished to find my bed made up with a US-issue khaki woollen blanket, left behind as my elderly host explained, by a GI forty-five years earlier.)

Even by the standards of the day, this clothing and equipment was totally inadequate for the harsh winter of 1944–5, while no thought, either, had been given to white camouflaged snow gear. The reason was not a lack of care from the top brass, but that US military planning before D-Day had assumed the Allies would be further into Germany, fighting and sheltering in towns and cities. There had even been a vain expectation of victory before the Christmas of 1944, but certainly no prediction of being stuck in the woods along Germany's borders. Nevertheless, Lauer's response was unsympathetic, issuing an order that trench foot was to be regarded as 'in the same category as a self-inflicted wound'.[11] However, as the First World War had already demonstrated, the twin issues of trench foot and troop hygiene on operations boiled down to the good management of soldiers by their junior leaders – NCOs and young officers – not orders issued from on high.

Sergeant Rod Ingraham, a nineteen-year-old squad leader from Anderson, California, was one GI in the 99th who suffered with trench foot. It came about from sharing a snow-covered foxhole with another

Trench foot was a major cause of non-battle casualties during the First World War and resurfaced as a problem during the winter of 1944–45. Up to 20 per cent of some US infantry divisions were bedevilled with this complaint, the result of having to loiter in wet or freezing foxholes, wearing issue boots that were not waterproof. Recommended solutions included the frequent airing of feet and changes of socks, as here, which were almost impossible on the front line. Some commanders were unsympathetic, such as Major General Walter E. Lauer of the 99th Infantry Division, who decreed that trench foot was to be regarded 'in the same category as a self-inflicted wound'. (NARA)

soldier that was seven feet by three feet and about two feet deep. 'We always had two men to a foxhole. At night one person stayed awake while the other slept. We usually had one hour on and one hour off,' Ingraham remembered. As his affliction worsened, he was assigned to work at the regimental headquarters a mile behind the front lines. 'A few days after I left the front lines,' he recalled, 'half of my squad was killed by a machine-gun burst.'[12] Meanwhile, General Lauer had been ordered to support the Roer dams attack, stripping one battalion from the 393rd and two from the 395th to do this, making his front even thinner than it already was. As elsewhere, the division was amazed at the stillness of the sector, though some of the outgoing Ninth Division had briefed William Bray, a former ASTP student and soldier with Company 'L' of the 394th, 'Don't bother the Germans when you have to go on patrol, and they won't bother you. Don't tell the officers, as they know nothing of the agreement.'[13]

That no such arrangement really existed was amply illustrated when Dietrich's guns opened fire at 05.30 a.m. on the 16th. Sergeant Richard Byers of the 371st Field Artillery Battalion remembered the sense of dread as he dived into his foxhole and felt as though he was 'inside an enormous bell while giants pounded it with sledgehammers'.[14] Captain Charles Pierce Roland of the 394th Infantry's 3rd Battalion was woken by the 'thunderclap of massed artillery fire . . . One moment our battalion chaplain and his assistant were kneeling beside their disabled vehicle. The next moment they were headless, decapitated by an exploding shell as if by the stroke of a guillotine.' He immediately recalled the intelligence briefing he had received earlier, that 'The enemy has only a handful of beaten and demoralised troops in front of us and they are being supported by only two pieces of horse-drawn artillery'. Captain Roland felt the entire division was 'in peril of destruction' and mused on the opposing artillery, 'They sure worked those two horses to death'.[15]

South of Lauer's division and Bouck's I&R Platoon, Colonel Devine's 14th Cavalry Group were garrisoning the road networks up to the divisional boundary with the Golden Lions. Just as with everyone else in Middleton's VIII Corps, he was stretched thinly along a sector that far exceeded the doctrine handbook's recommendations. His 9,000-yard front was normally the suggested patch for a division. Instead he had just two battalion-sized cavalry squadrons. The 18th Cavalry Squadron, consisting of just over 800 men under Lieutenant-Colonel William F. Damon, he placed strung out in the various towns and villages that constituted the front, between Lanzerath (also home to Bouck's I&R

Platoon), Merlscheid, Berterath, Krewinkel, Afst, Roth and Kobscheid. By sprinkling Damon's 18th Squadron across the front in this fashion, Devine ensured that none of them would have any superiority in firepower to repel an attack, and each, in turn, would be overwhelmed. His second squadron, the 32nd commanded by Lieutenant-Colonel Paul Ridge, was ready in reserve at Vielsalm. When the attack came in, the reserve squadron was undergoing maintenance, to the extent that engines had to be reassembled before units could move. Devine based himself at Manderfeld, in the centre of his sector.

Following the barrage on 16 December, Colonel Devine first ordered the 32nd Squadron forward to join him in Manderfeld and, at about 12.30 p.m., to retake Lanzerath. However, they were soon intercepted by *Fallschirmjägers* using captured US tank destroyers to fire on them. The Golden Lions' headquarters in St Vith heard the demise of the 18th Cavalry Squadron as it happened, including the exchange of insults between Lieutenant Farrens in Krewinkel and his attackers. What was left of the squadron withdrew at 1.00 p.m. on Devine's orders to the ridgeline at Manderfeld; soon outflanked again, they were obliged to withdraw a second time, as darkness fell at 4.00 p.m., although none of Devine's superiors had sanctioned this. During the day, the 18th Squadron lost 159 men and most of their vehicles. The situation had begun to overwhelm Devine, a disciplinarian who liked clean vehicles and smart uniforms. Having moved back from Manderfeld, he set off to confer with Major-General Jones of the 106th Division, to whose command he was attached. The latter, as we have seen, was himself being overtaken by the gradual encirclement of his division, and was about to have his game-changing conversation with General Middleton.

Jones was too busy to see Devine, but at St Josef's Convent in St Vith he did encounter Brigadier-General William M. Hoge, the stern-faced leader of Combat Command 'B' of the 4th Armored Division. 'What the devil's happening out there?' Hoge asked Devine, but the colonel was apparently too shattered to offer a coherent explanation, having witnessed both his beloved squadrons chewed up by panzers. The rock-like Hoge was as unimpressed by the combat-weary cavalry officer as he was by Major-General Jones. Both, he felt, were tired, reacting badly and hardly capable of rational decision-making. In fact, Jones may have been suffering from concussion after a near-miss from a shell. Meanwhile, Devine, who had gone to St Vith in search of orders, returned empty-handed to what was left of his 14th Cavalry Group.

On the 17th, Devine set up a new CP at Poteau, a few miles due west of St Vith (and shortly to become the centre of its own drama on 18 December), and at 5.00 p.m. again set off to see Jones in St Vith. This time, en route, at Kaiserbaracke crossroads, he ran straight into the vanguards of *Kampfgruppe Hansen* of 1st SS Division driving along their *Rollbahn* 'E'. His vehicle was shot up, and, managing to escape on foot, a clearly shaken Devine returned to Poteau, told Damon to take temporary command of the whole Cavalry Group and proceeded again for St Vith. On his arrival, to General Jones the cavalry commander seemed 'almost hysterical', talking of being 'chased by Tiger tanks' and suggesting they evacuate the division's headquarters in St Vith. Devine was certainly under a great deal of pressure and had clearly lost control of events. He never returned to the 14th Cavalry. Early the following day he was relieved of command, along with Lieutenant-Colonel Ridge, and what remained of the Group was merged into a provisional squadron under Lieutenant-Colonel Damon.[16] Theirs were the first of many heads to roll in the American military hierarchy during the Battle of the Bulge.

Up at Lanzerath, rather than lurk in the houses and stay warm the eighteen-strong I&R Platoon commanded by First Lieutenant Lyle J. Bouck occupied a series of foxholes and bunkers with overhead cover outside Lanzerath, giving them commanding views into Germany – when the weather permitted. The I&R's position was on the tree-lined crest of a small ridge overlooking Lanzerath, a straggle of stone-built houses in this frontier region that was neither Belgian nor German, but both. The settlement also contained a small US detachment of anti-tank guns from the 14th Cavalry Group, which underlined this was the inter-corps boundary. Bouck worked for V Corps, whereas the cavalry were owned by Middleton's VIII Corps. Like some of the other GIs along the front, Bouck had sensed something amiss, for all of the I&R Platoon had heard continuous sounds of German transport drifting across the front on the 15th, which had kept his men awake. Thus they commenced 16 December having had no sleep. It meant they were probably the first to see the Germans approach, but the shelling had cut their landline communications.

As the opening barrage, heralding *Herbstnebel*, ceased falling on Lanzerath, the cavalry detachment withdrew, leaving Bouck's men as the only Checkerboard unit along the inter-corps boundary guarding the key avenue of approach into their sector. Undaunted, he managed to call up his regiment by SCR-300 radio and was ordered to stay in place and send a patrol into Lanzerath. Observing an approaching formation of German infantry, recognisable as airborne forces by the camouflaged paratrooper smocks they wore, Bouck tried to call down artillery fire but discovered none was available, due to multiple attacks elsewhere within the divisional sector. As a column of *Fallschirmjäger* passed through Lanzerath in front of them, Bouck prepared to ambush the group by allowing a few to pass ahead unmolested.

As their commander arrived, a blonde teenage girl ran out of a house and pointed out Bouck's position, destroying his surprise. Whether the girl was a genuine sympathiser or was just trying to minimise the damage to her village, or prevent subsequent retribution from angry Germans, is difficult to tell, but her actions underlined the tensions of the local communities, caught between both camps and having nowhere to flee. Peeling off the road to their left, the *Fallschirmjäger* tried initially to assault uphill towards the I&R's position. The ground has changed little, about the length of a football field, then snow-covered and bisected by a fence. Whereas Bouck's positions were dug deep and camouflaged by recent falls of snow, the attacking paratroopers in their dark jump smocks were silhouetted against the white, making excellent targets.

Lieutenant Bouck's extra ammunition and machine guns wrought havoc with a whole battalion of the 9th *Fallschirmjäger* Regiment, all day. This is where the poor training of the ex-Luftwaffe, Kriegsmarine and conscript personnel revealed itself. They made no attempt to outmanoeuvre Bouck's position, as they could have done, but instead made at least three, costly, frontal assaults, being repulsed each time. After a pause to recover their wounded, the German paratroopers renewed their assault, though Bouck was again denied artillery support. Seconds after his last transmission, a bullet smashed the set he had been holding. By late afternoon the Platoon, who had been up all night, began to tire and run out of ammunition. As dusk arrived, about fifty paratroopers outflanked the I&R Platoon and began quickly to mop up each foxhole; each GI in the platoon became a prisoner, most were wounded, but astonishingly only one had been killed.

Bouck's action at Lanzerath has been much studied for its astonishing effect. His eighteen-man band appeared to have inflicted hundreds of casualties, effectively destroying a battalion of Generalmajor Walther Wadehn's 3rd Paratroopers. In fact, the *Fallschirmjäger* divisional records indicated thirty-three killed and eighty wounded, which was a very respectable rate of exchange for Bouck.[17] The effect, in terms of morale, on the rest of the German battalion would have been immense.

Unwittingly the platoon had halted not only the paratroopers but the 1st SS Panzer Division waiting behind for a corridor to be opened. Manteuffel's prediction of the likelihood of blockages along the narrow routes chosen by Sixth Army was entirely correct. Given that Dietrich's force was deemed Hitler's main effort, Bouck's tactical action had an operational effect in denying the advance of the panzers for a whole day.

In the confusion of the Ardennes battles, and because of the capture of Bouck's entire unit, the US Army initially overlooked their achievement. John D. Eisenhower's *The Bitter Woods* told their story in 1969, but it was not until October 1981 that the US Army belatedly awarded them a Presidential Unit Citation for Extraordinary Heroism (similar to a British 'battle honour'): Lieutenant Bouck and three others received the Distinguished Service Cross, five received the Silver Star and the nine remaining Bronze Stars. Although it took thirty-seven years for them to be recognised, the I&R Platoon of the 394th became the US Army's most decorated small unit of the Second World War.[18]

The action validated the infantry training of American divisions, for the 99th were new to combat themselves. In this sense, it suggests there was nothing at fault with the pre-battle preparation of the neighbouring Golden Lions Division either, or of any of the other units who were in the process of beginning to unravel further south. The stand of the platoon was down to Bouck's personal leadership and clear decision-making under stress. He not only made some excellent calls that day, but carried the platoon along with him, when one or two had thought withdrawal a better option. At the time, he considered his military action a failure and had no idea of the significance of the effect he achieved until long after the war. Bouck's platoon action was also representative of the legions of other, unrecognised American units who behaved similarly but did not survive. All along the front small groups of determined GIs were throwing grit into Hitler's machinery and slowing it down. *Herbstnebel* was already in trouble.

The action at Lanzerath also showed up the totally inadequate preparation of Hitler's infantry units for the Ardennes offensive. To label the unit that attacked Bouck as '*Fallschirmjäger*' constituted a slur on the fighting reputation of Germany's real parachute arm. Under other circumstances, well-trained German troops would have eliminated Bouck's position within minutes, but the hapless so-called paratroopers of December 1944, poorly led by inexperienced officers, allowed the I&R Platoon to badly damage the whole Ardennes plan.[19]

*

Meanwhile, what of the panzers supposed to be following the *Fallschirmjäger*? Wilhelm Mohnke, the commander of Dietrich's spearhead – the *Leibstandarte* Division – had issued orders to his *Kampfgruppen* (battle-group) commanders on 14 December from his HQ in the village of Tonsdorf. He had divided his formation into four all-arms combat commands, the most important of which took the name of its twenty-nine-year-old commander, *Kampfgruppe Peiper*, who usually led the division's panzer regiment. Max Hansen headed another, based on his 1st SS-*Panzergrenadier* Regiment, Rudolf Sandig a third, utilising his 2nd SS-*Panzergrenadiers*, and Gustav Knittel the fourth, built around his 1st SS Reconnaissance Battalion. There was even a *StrafGruppe* (penal unit) recorded in *Kampfgruppe Hansen*; its members had committed crimes and disciplinary breaches – which must have been extreme even by SS standards – and were put in Hansen's *Spitze* (literally the 'Point', or most forward echelon) in order to redeem themselves in combat; on occasion they also had to remove mines. They were always cold-shouldered and never allowed to eat or camp with the rest until deemed to have served their penance.[20]

Peiper assembled a formidable force with which to plough through American lines, to the Meuse and beyond, made his plans and briefed his subordinates the following day. His team numbered 117 tanks, 149 half-tracks, eighteen 105mm and six 150mm guns, around 30 anti-aircraft guns, all motorised, totalling 800 vehicles and 4,800 men: stretched end to end his column would tail back for sixteen miles. At twenty-nine, Peiper was almost the oldest in his *Kampfgruppe*; only his unit's medical officer, Sturmbannführer Kurt Sickel, aged thirty-seven, was older.[21]

The 1st SS-*Leibstandarte* Division and their twin, the 12th SS-*Hitlerjugend*, were to move on five roughly parallel routes, called *Rollbahn*. Those designated 'A', 'B' and 'C' were allocated to the 12th SS, while Mohnke was given 'D' and 'E'. Devised by Krämer, the Sixth Army's chief of staff, these were to keep snarl-ups to a minimum and ensure the smoothest possible flow of logistics. They were advisory and if divisional commanders wanted to take others, they were at liberty to do so.[22] Peiper's route was to be opened up by the *Fallschirmjägers* and Hansen's by the 12th *Volksgrenadiers*. Peiper, as did the others, organised his vanguard into a *Spitze* (point), commanded by Sturmbannführer (Major) Werner Pötschke, comprising a few Panthers and Panzer IVs, with a company of *Panzergrenadiers* and platoon of engineers, all mounted in half-tracks. Pötschke had a reputation for recklessness, and the role suited him perfectly.[23] So effective was this grouping, on roads or cross-country, that the Soviet army eventually incorporated it into their military doctrine as a 'Combat Reconnaissance Patrol', still practised today.

Various other groups followed at ten-minute intervals, Peiper himself followed another forward company, and bringing up the rear were his monster King Tigers, of which between fifteen and twenty were serviceable on *Null-Tag*. In Peiper's view, the Tiger II, often referred to unofficially as the *Königstiger* (King Tiger), or Royal Tiger, was more trouble than it was worth. At sixty-nine tons, twenty-two feet in length and over twelve feet wide, these tanks guzzled fuel (under half a mile per gallon, where a Sherman or Panzer IV achieved more than double that), were too heavy for most bridges, too wide for much of the twisting Ardennes road network and, above all, prone to mechanical breakdowns and broken tracks. In daylight hours they acted as a magnet for Allied aircraft. The magnitude of the German gasoline problem was illustrated by the fact that, logistically, *Kampfgruppe Peiper* required 52,000 gallons to move sixty miles, necessitating the frequent resupply, or the capture, of fuel stocks along their route.[24]

It was in *Kampfgruppe Peiper* that Obersturmführer Hans Hennecke served, leading a platoon of tanks in the 1st Panther Company. In a post-war interview, Peiper observed that his assigned *Rollbahn* 'D' was suitable for one-way traffic only, being too narrow and was 'not fit for tanks, only bicycles', possessing two unpaved sections which dissolved into muddy tracks, defeating their logistics tail. Peiper thought the terrain 'worse than Russia'.[25] Dietrich's chief of staff, Krämer, had been concerned about the Sixth Panzer Army's route ever since being briefed for the attack. Consequently, he had driven to the *Leibstandarte*'s training area and asked Peiper's advice. Krämer asked Peiper, as the expert in night-time tank advances, whether his column could manage a fifty-mile advance to Liège across the Eifel in the hours of darkness. Peiper said he'd drive the route personally and let him know. In fact, Hans Hennecke told me that he was the one who took his Panther over that distance on 11 December. 'I drove to Bad Munstereifel. It was a crazy exercise because it proved nothing,' he explained. 'Only that a tank could drive that distance at night along paved roads. Our actual route in the attack was through the mud in forests. But Peiper didn't ask me to do that. If he had, I'd have said it was not possible.'[26] However, Peiper assured Krämer that the move was feasible, with the qualification that the result might be different for a long column of armour.

Peiper's last minute orders to his *Kampfgruppe* commanders pulled no punches. 'Owing to the unfavourable terrain', he fully expected the leading panzers to be 'rubbed out'. He eyeballed them all: the task of his column would only be accomplished if and when one panzer reached the Meuse. 'You will go ahead at full speed on the assigned road. Your task will be fulfilled after you have been blown up.' When that happened, Peiper reminded them, their replacement 'is the tank right behind you. If shooting has to be done, it will be done while moving. There will be no stopping for anything. No booty will be taken, no confiscated enemy vehicles are to be examined . . . It is not the job of the spearhead to worry about prisoners of war. It is the job of the infantry following . . . Armed civilians will be treated as partisans.'[27]

The last few phrases would return to haunt Peiper.

It is clear his mission was all about speed, something the King Tigers couldn't achieve on the Belgian road network. He didn't like them and would have left them behind if he could have. Of this Hitler would have been unaware: he just looked naively at tank numbers and size: the bigger the better. Against this must be set the psychological value of these huge panzers when pitted against American infantry or even Shermans, with the latter's relatively thin armour and less powerful main gun. Although many troops reported the presence of King Tigers, only two battalions, or less than fifty, were actually used across the whole front, but who could blame a GI stuck in a foxhole about to be run down by a panzer for misidentification? To most American troops, any big tank trying to kill you was a Tiger. Admittedly, the sloping frontal armour of a King resembled that of a Panther Tiger, but a soldier in trouble doesn't stop to count the road wheels or turn to his recognition handbook. Similarly, many Allied memoirs talk of being under fire from 'eighty-eights', whereas most German field and anti-tank guns were of 75mm calibre. Thus, talk of 'Tiger tanks' and '88mm shellfire' needs to be interpreted as shorthand for tanks and artillery, rather than a specific descriptor.

Meanwhile Bouck's I&R Platoon, mostly wounded, had been brought down the hillside, which was littered with the bodies of dead paratroopers, and into the Café Scholzen in Lanzerath (these days a nightclub), where the injured were bandaged and those conscious then interrogated. The *Fallschirmjäger* officer quizzing the Americans at one point paused and observed, '*Ami*, you and your comrades are brave men'. The café contained a mixture of Americans and Germans, some wounded, all trying to doze; as the clock struck midnight, Bouck realised he had turned twenty-one. But shortly afterwards the door was flung open and in strode a furious figure dressed in black.

Peiper had experienced a bad day, to put it mildly. He had spent all of 16 December waiting for the *Fallschirmjäger*, or the 12th *Volksgrenadiers* to their north, to open up a route for his panzers, and was not best pleased. The roads were full of horse-drawn artillery belonging to *Volksgrenadier* and *Fallschirmjäger* units. Traffic moved forward at a crawl; eventually Peiper took the law into his own hands. Anything in his way would be run off the road by his panzers. Eventually he got going, moving cross-country when he needed. Reaching Losheim at 10.00 p.m. he heard the paratroopers had at last suppressed their opposition in Lanzerath and rushed forward to find them. The roads were still mined; ironically, these were not American devices: they had been laid by German engineers retreating in September.

Having lost two Panthers already, a third went up outside Merlscheid; its commander, Obersturmführer Werner Sternebeck, heard the explosion, felt the panzer jump and grind to a halt. Sternebeck had been given the unpleasant task of leading the *Spitze* by Peiper as a punishment for getting drunk in a *Gasthaus* just before the offensive. Fearing Peiper's wrath at another delay, he swiftly abandoned his mount and leapt on to another.[28] With his de-mining engineers too far back in the column to help, Peiper now used his half-tracks as mine detectors and lost some, with their crews, but that was his signature ruthlessness. At Lanzerath his temper hardly improved when he strode into their headquarters to find everyone asleep. Instead of fighting, the paratroopers appeared to have gone to bed. Where was the regimental commander? Oberst Helmuth von Hoffmann, new to ground combat, introduced himself. The SS officer unfolded his map. It was too big for the small table. He grabbed bayonets and crucified it to the wall. Peiper was ready for business.

Why were his men not advancing? – Hoffmann was waiting for artillery support. Why? – Because of American opposition. Where? The Oberst didn't know. He had heard from a battalion commander, who had heard from a company commander . . . 'Enough'. The shouting woke the American prisoners who feared the argument was over their fate. Nothing could have been further from the truth. Peiper's mind was fixed on roads, rivers and bridges. The Americans huddled in the corner didn't exist in his mind. 'My battlegroup will move out at 04.00 a.m.; one of your battalions will accompany me.' Oberst von Hoffmann, senior in rank to Obersturmbannführer Peiper, meekly acquiesced. *Kampfgruppe* Peiper was eighteen hours behind schedule.

20

'A 10 Per Cent Chance of Success'

JOCHEN PEIPER KNEW that ahead of him, and his colleagues of Hugo Kraas's 12th SS-*Hitlerjugend* Division, some 870 paratroopers under the command of Freiherr von der Heydte were due to have landed at the Baraque Michel (*Michelshütte*) crossroads, on *Rollbahn* 'A', today the N68, midway between Spa and Monschau. Baraque Michel was an old coaching inn on the *Hohen Venn* (High Fens), one of the highest points above sea level in Belgium, and an obvious position to seize. Heydte had experienced enormous trouble simply assembling enough trained jumpers. Some of his volunteers openly admitted they had never jumped out of an aeroplane before, which, as we have seen, prompted Heydte to complain to Model, who ordered him nevertheless to proceed 'even if the mission has only a 10 per cent chance of success'. Heydte could at least control the preparation of his men and equipment for Operation *Stösser*, but over the aircraft conveying him he had no authority. In the latter case, pilots had to identify the precise drop zone area and hold the plane steady and level at a fixed height while the jumpers exited.

This was extraordinarily difficult by day, without the threat of hostile aircraft, but even more challenging when conducted by planes flying at night, in formation, without lights, prior reconnaissance or possession of recent aerial photographs. In fact this was the only recorded night-time drop of the *Fallschirmjäger*. Furthermore, as navigation and piloting was done by the flying branch of the Luftwaffe, the *Fallschirmjäger*, though wearing the same swooping eagle as their flying brethren, took no part in the navigation. Thus great trust was required between jumpers, pilot and navigator to ensure the troops – and their equipment, which was dropped separately by parachute-canister – landed together and close to their objective. Despite Göring's personal assurances, in the chaotic state of the Third Reich of December 1944 initially not enough Junkers-52 tri-motors could be found, there was no spare fuel for practice jumps, few of their young pilots had ever flown in formation or combat, let alone at night, and none had ever worked with paratroopers.

The drop was initially delayed when some of the assigned aircraft failed to appear at the appointed aerodrome. A new drop time, as specified in the orders given to Dietrich, was set for 03.00 a.m. on 17 December. Due to 12th SS Panzer Division's lack of progress, the drop zone remained the Baraque Michel crossroads, seven miles north of Malmedy. Heydte's mission was to hold it for twenty-four hours until the arrival of the SS formation. Faced with potential investigations by the Gestapo as to why the drop had failed to materialise as originally planned, Heydte pushed hard to continue and eventually sixty-seven Junkers-52 transport planes were assembled (a tremendous achievement for the Luftwaffe in itself), and with around 870 *Fallschirmjäger* and their supply canisters on board, took off during a powerful snowstorm with strong winds and low cloud cover. Compared to the operations of the Allied airborne divisions on D-Day, who had trained hard for six months beforehand, the results were risible and demonstrated that Hitler's security paranoia once again compromised what had been a promising idea. Göring's assurances that he could deliver what he patently could not further exacerbated the problem.

Many planes flew off-course almost immediately; some conveyed 200 *Fallschirmjäger* to the vicinity of Bonn, where their passengers enthusiastically jumped into German-held terrain, over fifty miles from their objective, and to their chagrin, well behind their own lines; others returned, unable to find their drop zones with their troops still on board. Of those who exited their planes, many found the prevailing strong winds cast them far away from their colleagues. A substantial number made rough landings and were killed or crippled upon impact. Heydte himself, though landing on target, suffered a broken arm and by noon on 17 December had collected less than a quarter of his force, amounting to some 300 paratroops. With most of his supply containers also dispersed, his radios lost, and enough ammunition only for a brief engagement, his men lurked in woods near to their crossroads, waiting for the arrival of the 12th SS-*Hitlerjugend* Division, and planned to seize their designated road junction just before the latter's arrival. On the 20th, after three days of waiting for the panzers, with limited food, water and no medical support, the young colonel split his forces into three groups and bid them filter through the lines back to Germany as best they could. Eventually an exhausted Heydte, wounded, frostbitten and suffering from exposure, was forced to seek sanctuary from German civilians in Monschau and, making contact with some nearby GIs, surrendered the following day.

In fact Heydte had achieved more than he realised; because of the dispersal of the drop, *Fallschirmjäger* were reported all over the Ardennes, and the Allies believed a major division-sized jump had taken place. At the same time, inspired by the British tactic used in Normandy, German aircraft had 'a trick of dropping parachutes with straw dummies in them to terrorise the civilian population,' remembered Vincent Petringa of the 505th Military Police Battalion. His battalion recovered nineteen such dummies.[1] Real or phoney, the *Fallschirmjäger* threat diverted substantial numbers (an entire infantry regiment and a combat command totalling about 6,000 men), who spent several precious days on cordon and search duties looking for Heydte's men. Some paratroopers had died alone when they landed or succumbed to their landing injuries days later; several were found in the lonely Ardennes when the snow melted the following spring. A few continue to be found, and a small museum in Bastogne exhibits the webbing, helmet and weapons found on the remains of one poor soul who died alone and was discovered in the 1970s.

It was all such a far cry from the 1941 battle for Crete where the *Fallschirmjäger* had made their reputation, if at an excessively high cost in casualties and aircraft. So much more could have been achieved with proper training and rehearsal. Even Dietrich's refusal to countenance the issue of carrier pigeons had a consequence, for this denial prevented Heydte from sending back vital intelligence about American units, or his own unit's condition. Looking back at the mission, Heydte and his *Fallschirmjäger* were committed to support only Dietrich's Sixth Army. Much better use could have been made elsewhere of the distinguished colonel who had led his men with great ability in Tunisia and Normandy. In Manteuffel's sector, where the terrain was kinder, there were many more open meadows for drop zones, or landing zones for gliders (which the Americans used when they resupplied Bastogne from the air). After the war, Manteuffel revealed he had discussed the potential deployment of *Fallschirmjäger* in Fifth Army's sector at St Vith, Houffalize and Bastogne, but had felt that 'although the Wehrmacht still had several thousand airborne troops at its disposal, it was not able to commit them any longer with a certainty that they would achieve success'.[2] Heydte's deployment and capture neatly illustrated the consequences of Hitler's dogged refusal to change even minor details and his obsession in supporting only Dietrich's Sixth Army, which condemned his loyal *Fallschirmjäger* to impotence.

Some of the troops rounding up Heydte's *Fallschirmjäger* belonged to Colonel George W. Smythe's 47th Infantry Regiment, known as 'The Raiders'. On 17 December, as he moved towards the northern shoulder of the Bulge between Elsenborn and Monschau, Smythe, who was part of the US 9th Infantry Division, encountered streams of leaderless American troops from a wide variety of other outfits, including artillerymen, tankers, armoured infantrymen, tank-destroyer crews, cavalry reconnaissance units and service personnel, some with their guns and vehicles, others without and on foot, who had begun to drift to the rear, nervous, frightened, often assuming a panzer was just around the corner. From his jeep, Smythe began to rally the US Army flotsam and jetsam around the centre of his own 47th Regiment, restoring morale, eventually being given unqualified command of all whom he collected. A *Washington Star* columnist observed that 'Colonel Smythe in few hours organised what was essentially a complete new division from American units caught and smashed in the breakthrough, and used it to mop up groups of enemy paratroopers in the forest'. His actions, mirrored elsewhere along the front, brought him a Distinguished Service Cross. Smythe had been trained well; his divisional chief of staff was the highly capable Colonel William C. Westmoreland, the future (and controversial) commander of US forces in Vietnam.[3]

The *Fallschirmjäger* operation wasn't the only fiasco. There was another Luftwaffe mission that was to herald the Ardennes attack which also completely failed to materialise. Operation *Bodenplatte* (baseplate) was designed to coincide with the beginning of *Herbstnebel*, as a sudden thunderclap against nearby Allied airbases. This was the reason for the *Jägeraufmarsch* (fighter concentration) that Ultra had identified in November. An unprecedented number of Luftwaffe aircraft were to be deployed in a special mission against airfields in Belgium, hoping to destroy huge numbers of Allied aircraft on the ground, when pilots were off their guard. In the run-up to Christmas and in the generally poor weather, it was expected that USAAF and RAF intelligence would fail to anticipate such a raid. It was a brilliant concept, but the weather precluded the Luftwaffe from playing their part.

Jumping ahead a little, *Bodenplatte* was resurrected on the first day of January 1945, when it was completely pointless. Some 1,035 fighters were sent on their breakfast swoop against the Allied air forces. They achieved tactical success, destroying an estimated 305 Allied aircraft on the ground (including Monty's personal transport, a C-47 gifted from Eisenhower with an American crew) and damaging 200 more. However, this came at a heavy price, for 234 of the Luftwaffe's pilots were killed, wounded or captured – their largest single-day loss in the entire war. Moreover, eighteen of these were unit commanders and fifty-nine were flight leaders – the lifeblood of the Luftwaffe.[4] Some were the victims of fratricide on their return, poorly briefed German air-defence crews assuming that large formations of incoming aircraft could only be American.

Monday morning, 1 January 1945, found Flight Lieutenant Derek Lovell, usually flying RAF Typhoon fighters with 197 Squadron, sitting on a thunderbox surrounded by a hessian screen 'minding my own business. I could suddenly hear b-b-b-b-boom. I peered over the hessian and could see fighters going over the far end of the airfield, which I have to tell you is the most magnificent way of relieving any constipation.'[5] Meanwhile, the 403 (Royal Canadian Air Force) Squadron Operations Record Book for that same day noted, in the distinctive language of the period:

> The first day of the New Year and what a way to start it off. At about 0830 hours this morning we had a social call from Jerry in the form of about 30 aircraft which strafed the 'drome. They strafed everything in sight, the aircraft, hangars, dispersals and personnel and what a mess they made of things. They didn't get away that easy. Three of our kites, flown and led by P/O Steve Butte, P/O Mac Reeves and F/S Lindsay respectively were just taking off on a patrol when Jerry appeared over the 'drome. Within minutes of becoming airborne, Butte shot down and destroyed three enemy aircraft, two ME 109s and one FW 190. Mac Reeves shot down and destroyed two FW 190s and Lindsay destroyed one ME 109 and probably destroyed a further ME 109. Considering the odds against them, it was a damn good show.[6]

Observers on the ground later told Pilot Officer Butte, who was awarded a Distinguished Flying Cross for his triple victory, 'that I had started shooting before my undercarriage had been retracted, usually the first operation after take-off'.[7]

Had the Germans analysed their opponents more carefully, they would have realised they needed to target not Allied aircraft, which could be replaced quickly, but their pilots, who could not – only thirty-five Allied aircrew were lost.[8] Had they targeted aircrew living quarters instead of aircraft, the Luftwaffe could have irreparably damaged the Allied air effort, at least for a while, for the centre of gravity of any air force is its flying crew. As it was, Operation *Bodenplatte* weakened that of the Luftwaffe beyond hope of recovery. Its fighter boss, General Adolf Galland, later observed, 'We sacrificed our last substance'. The Allies replaced the aircraft lost on the ground, in some cases within the day, negating the effect, to the extent that the skies of 1 January 1945 still saw the second largest Allied sortie rate of the battle.[9] The RAF's Second Tactical Air Force, whose airbases had been attacked, nevertheless achieved 1,084 sorties the same day.

To put all this in context, by 16 December 1944 the Luftwaffe had assembled almost 2,400 tactical aircraft in the west, far more than the number dedicated to the May 1940 operation over the same terrain.[10] This air armada equated to eighteen fighter wings, a force the Luftwaffe had never possessed before, and could not be disregarded by the Allies, even though the latter had achieved both numerical and qualitative superiority in the air. Hitler, however, misled his Luftwaffe commanders in ordering them to assemble huge fighter forces in the west, without telling them *why*.

The Luftwaffe assumed it was for the overwhelming counter-air operation, *der Grosse Schlag* (the Great Blow), for which they had been preparing throughout the autumn – a crippling blow administered in a single day of mass air combat against the bomber fleets of US Eighth Air Force. Hitler, who neither understood air power, nor – as was amply clear – trusted the Luftwaffe's leadership, in fact needed his air force to support his armies in their advance through the Ardennes. However, the fighter forces defending the Reich in late 1944 were proficient only in air-to-air combat; tactical air-to-ground sorties supporting a blitzkrieg required different (and rehearsed) skills, which were only a dim memory for a few of the Luftwaffe's older pilots. Consequently, the Luftwaffe built the wrong structure for *Herbstnebel*, creating a command chain separate from the ground units they were required to support. Unlike the earlier blitzkrieg of 1940, there was no integrated air–land command structure, planning, or operations staff. The lowest level of any coordinated activity was in Model's Army Group 'B' headquarters.[11]

The Luftwaffe's training for the Ardennes wasted precious fuel and ammunition rehearsing air-to-air combat, neglecting to pay any attention to fighter–ground attack, with its different munitions and tactics, which they believed was not their remit. Their airfields were located far from the front, to enable the concentration of fighter units and their timely direction towards American bomber formations. No attempt was made to develop tactical forward airfields to support fast-moving ground operations, a skill they had perfected in North Africa in support of Rommel.

As each German division required logistical support amounting to around 500 tons per day, *Herbstnebel* needed at least 2,000 truckloads per day to sustain the advance. This was exactly the challenge the Allies had encountered in the autumn of 1944 and had overcome with the Red Ball Express. For security and deception reasons, Hitler had directed that much of the fuel and combat supplies for the Ardennes offensive be dumped east of the Rhine, more than sixty miles from the Eifel, so as not to draw unnecessary attention to the concentration areas. After *Null-Tag*, these stretched traffic routes, channelled by wintry conditions (where off-road progress was a muddy impossibility), with choke points over the Rhine, merely compounded German logistics problems. These factors served to constrict all logistics support to a few roads, exacerbating their vulnerability to Allied air interdiction.

During the early days of the Bulge the two air forces met in the skies over fog-shrouded Belgium between 16 and 19 December, when the Luftwaffe attempted to get under the low ceilings to support the panzers. Major-General Elwood R. 'Pete' Quesada's US Ninth Air Force's fighters engaged them, claiming 136 kills. Abysmal flying weather closed in on the entire battlespace from 19 to 23 December. Even so, Air Marshal Sir Arthur Coningham's Second Tactical Air Force (2nd TAF) still managed 316 sorties, though they were unable to observe their effect.[12] During this period, the German land advance enjoyed its greatest rate of penetration, extending to a maximum of fifty miles. Low clouds, snow-covered terrain and the fast-moving battle made navigation and ground target identification challenging for both sides, but Allied radar operators helped their fighters get under and through the weather both in the target areas and at their airfields.[13]

From the outset, Eisenhower's air commanders decided on three priorities: air supremacy to prevent the Luftwaffe from supporting the advancing German land forces; close air support to the Allied land units; and air interdiction against the German logistics tail and the facilities it required – the roads, railways, bridges, as well as the combat supplies themselves. A layered air defence policy was developed that Luftwaffe pilots had to negotiate just to get into the combat zone. From 24 December, Eighth Air Force heavy bombers bombed the German forward airbases, and their fighter escorts strafed them daily. Allied fighter sweeps were timed to coincide with returning Luftwaffe aircraft, typically low on fuel and ammunition; forced to engage while landing, many Luftwaffe pilots ran out of fuel.

During 23–27 December, when flying conditions had improved somewhat, the Allied air forces flew more than 16,000 sorties, many of these interdicting the flow of German logistics.[14] On the 23rd alone, Coningham's 2nd TAF and Quesada's Ninth Air Force managed 2,128 sorties, claiming 96 German aircraft, 220 vehicles and 17 panzers destroyed. Other aircraft resupplied Bastogne by airdropping supplies, IX Troop Carrier Command flying 962 sorties and dropping 850 tons of supplies to the defenders, and losing only 19 C-47 Dakotas.[15] In the hours of darkness, night fighters of the RAF's 85 Group harassed German bombers flying singly to disrupt Allied ground movement. Over the night of 23–24 December, for example, a Mosquito from 488 Squadron, Royal New Zealand Air Force (RNZAF), downed two Junkers-88s within minutes and three Kiwi crews from the squadron also claimed kills over Malmedy. The following day, Christmas Eve, Allied aircraft flew 7,380 sorties.[16]

It was on 23 December, when the skies cleared, that the Luftwaffe changed priorities, dividing their effort equally between ground attack and bomber intercept, executing neither well. The lack of coordinated air–land planning, the relative inexperience of most Luftwaffe pilots compared to their opponents, fuel shortages, the short operational range of their aircraft, and distance of airfields from the Ardennes crippled the German air force's effectiveness irreparably. To their credit, and against these odds, the Luftwaffe managed to fly as many as 1,200 sorties on some days, but Allied air supremacy was maintained and the Luftwaffe made little impact on Allied ground movement – though those GIs under air attack might disagree.

*

Underneath this battle, and mostly oblivious to it, lay Hitler's panzers. At their forefront, that first evening of 16–17 December, was Peiper. Although he was unaware of it, Heydte's *Fallschirmjäger* had yet to deploy with Operation *Stösser* when he was arguing with Oberst von Hoffmann in the café at Lanzerath. It would in any case prove a damp squib and contribute nothing to his tactical activities, or those of his colleagues. The impact of the other Special Forces mission, Operation *Greif*, conducted simultaneously by Obersturmbannführer Otto Skorzeny, was much greater. As we saw, Skorzeny had been ordered personally by Hitler to form a special unit, Panzer Brigade 150, to seize one or more of the bridges over the Meuse before they could be destroyed; they would wear US uniforms and travel in captured vehicles. Faced with shortages of American speakers, uniforms, equipment and vehicles, Skorzeny was forced to scale down his ambitions and recast Panzer Brigade 150 into two distinctly separate entities.

One was a commando unit innocuously named *Einheit* (Unit) *Stielau*, containing his best English-speakers: designed as a deep reconnaissance group, these would man captured jeeps and drive through the American lines to capture bridges, alter signposts and create general confusion. To polish their American English, some commandos were actually posted to POW camps to listen to and imitate the latest slang and news from the US – where at least one was rumbled and beaten unconscious. Skorzeny's other unit was a much larger body, which would travel with the panzer spearheads and, at the last moment, rush ahead to seize vital positions. Some of this latter group would travel in conventional German vehicles to support the commandos. Other crews operating Allied transport possessed an English speaker who was to buy enough time to negotiate a checkpoint, divert forces or issue false orders. They had some, but not enough US transport for their requirements, so various German vehicles had to be altered to look American, complete with phoney unit codes, and all were painted olive drab, with the five-pointed white star, the universal Allied air recognition symbol, prominently displayed.

As the brigade prepared for action, Skorzeny let the latrine rumours spread as to their purpose: most seemed to think they were to break through Allied lines, rendezvous at the Café de la Paix in central Paris, in order to capture General Eisenhower at SHAEF – which Skorzeny was content to let them believe. On 16 December Panzer Brigade 150 moved forward with the 1st and 12th SS Divisions and the 12th

Volksgrenadiers, but the slow progress of all three and consequentially fully alert American defenders negated much of the point of Skorzeny's unit and eventually they were re-employed as conventional combat troops. On the other hand, the deep penetration of US-occupied territory by *Einheit Stielau* commandos in jeeps was an entirely different matter. Skorzeny boasted later of the success of his four-man jeeps of saboteurs, possibly to boost his post-war credentials as a military 'consultant', but the damage done or confusion caused was not his most significant achievement.

Once the word was out that German commandos in US uniforms were prowling around, all vehicles were stopped routinely at every junction and headquarters. Checkpoints sprang up throughout the Allied rear, greatly slowing the movement of all soldiers and equipment. American troops began asking not for passwords, but questions they felt only other GIs would know, such as the identity of Mickey Mouse's girlfriend, or the capital of Illinois. For some this was an amusing way to hit back at senior officers, and this last question resulted in the brief detention of General Omar Bradley; although he gave the correct answer – Springfield – the GI who questioned him apparently believed the capital was Chicago.

One common thread of Allied memoirs from this time is the fear and confusion caused by not knowing passwords. However, as Bill Armstrong of the 263rd Field Artillery recalled, the right questions also had to be asked. Wearing 'everything he owned' but still freezing, Armstrong was on sentry duty in deep snow one night, when he heard a jeep crawling along in low gear, coming from the east – 'where the Germans were!' As he shouted, 'Halt! Who goes there?' the vehicle pulled over and he made out three shadowy forms. 'Give me the password,' he demanded. After a series of urgent whispers, the GI next to the driver announced, 'I don't know the password. (Pause) Do you?' 'No,' replied Armstrong, 'without thinking of the consequences.' He remembered his sports questions and tried again: 'Who won the 1940 World Series?' Again whispering in the jeep, 'Hell, I don't know. (Another pause) Do you?' 'No,' Armstrong responded – this was beginning to look ridiculous. In desperation he asked, 'Where are you from?' 'Oakland, California,' came the reply. Quick as a flash, Armstrong demanded, 'Where's the best place to get a hot dog in Oakland?' 'Caspar's on Telegraph Avenue across from the roller rink.' Armstrong was from Berkeley, the neighbouring city, and the two fell to reminiscing before a growl from the GI in the back seat reminded them this was the war. 'After they left I realised the driver had not said a word. Just sat looking straight ahead. To this day I'm not sure that they were Americans.'[17]

According to Skorzeny, forty-four German soldiers wearing US uniforms were sent through the lines, all but eight returning. A point of suspicion, of which the Germans were unaware, was that Skorzeny crewed each jeep with four of his men, whereas GI custom was three to a jeep. A great many innocent travellers were thus ensnared in overloaded jeeps. All American officers carried, in addition to their metal dog tags, a laminated identity card, containing a photo. Curiously, these genuine documents carried an uncorrected spelling error: '*Not a Pass. For Indentification Purposes Only*'. In creating phoney ID cards, the spelling error had been repeated, but echoing the bureaucracy for which the Prussians were famous, one of Skorzeny's quartermasters had hand-corrected each mistake by hand, in ink, thus drawing attention to what was otherwise a perfect fake. Unfortunately for Skorzeny's *Einheit Stielau* commandos, German 'correctness' meant that the false officer IDs were easy to spot.[18]

Tens of thousands of innocent Allied troops were delayed or detained by suspicious GIs as a result – the British were especially at risk for not knowing American towns, cities or the minutiae of Disney characters, Hollywood film stars or baseball. Montgomery in his staff car was detained by American guards who'd heard a rumour the British field marshal with his distinctive beret was being impersonated. When Monty told his potential captors to cease such nonsense and ordered his driver to continue, they shot out his tyres and arrested him. Eisenhower, Bradley and Patton were much amused for days afterwards, and Skorzeny's bravado instantly grew on them. Slips of language gave away one German team who pulled into an American supply base and asked for 'petrol', instead of 'gas'. 'The eyes of the GI manning the pump became as big as saucers' in alarm, the Germans recognised their error, drove off in haste but overturned their jeep and were captured.[19] This put every British serviceman in danger, for whom gasoline was indeed (and remains), petrol.

In Paris, Lieutenant-Colonel Baldwin B. Smith, who looked enough like Ike to make passers-by do a double-take, was promoted to five-star general and driven in Eisenhower's conspicuous staff car each day the thirty-minute route from his villa to SHAEF at Versailles.[20] The genuine article, meanwhile, was obliged – under protest – to abandon his sacred villa and move in behind the wire to SHAEF, surrounded by presidential quantities of personal security. Lieutenant Kay Summersby, his British driver and aide (and, some would have it, his mistress), noted, 'Security even asked General Eisenhower not to walk outside the office, for fear a sniper might have slipped through the toe-to-toe guard. We were prisoners, in every sense of the word. This new, personal tension, coupled with the flood of bad news and rumours from the Ardennes, left most of the headquarters frankly apprehensive and depressed. Ike, the one solely responsible for the success or failure of our counterattack and therefore the only one entitled to the luxury of depression, had to smother his own feelings and act as the eternal optimist.'[21] The SHAEF appointments diary reveals that Ike was obliged to stay at the Hôtel Trianon Palace, Versailles, throughout the crisis from 16 December until 26 January, with the exception of his Verdun strategy meeting on 19 December and a conference with Montgomery near Brussels on the 28th.[22]

Forrest C. Pogue, later the highly distinguished scholar of the Second World War, was a thirty-two-year-old military historian attached to V Corps, with whom he had landed on Omaha Beach on 7 June. For him the big news of 16 December was his promotion to master sergeant, although with a doctorate in history from Clark University in Worcester, Massachusetts, he was probably the most overqualified individual at that rank in the US Army. He remembered the First Army quickly issued instructions containing sample questions for sentries, including the pronunciation of 'wreath', 'with nothing' or 'hearth hollow' (all apparently impossible for the German tongue to pronounce without suspicion). 'We were particularly suspect because our bumper markings were those of Twelfth Army Group, we wore First Army shoulder patches, and we claimed to be with V Corps. Worse still, we claimed to be historians and went about asking questions about casualties, troop dispositions, and the like. I still wonder why they did not shoot us.'[23]

Among those with the British 'Phantom' Communications Regiment, acting as Montgomery's personal eyes and ears, was a real actor, David Niven. The son of a well-to-do British Army captain killed at Gallipoli in 1915, he had been commissioned at Sandhurst in 1930 before finding fame in Hollywood four years later. Niven re-entered the British Army in 1940 and as a lieutenant-colonel in December 1944 was a frequent traveller between military headquarters, sometimes accompanied by his batman (a military valet), another actor by the name of Private Peter

Ustinov. Niven was often pulled over at roadblocks by suspicious GIs, and rarely knew the right password because of the number of units he passed through, but claimed he was always able to respond with his clueless British charm, 'Simply haven't the foggiest idea . . . but I recall I made a picture with Ginger Rogers in 1939 called *Bachelor Mother*' – a technique which apparently never failed to work. 'On your way, Dave, and Good Luck!', they would motion him through, thinking of picture houses back home.[24]

However, many, less famous, personnel were shot and killed by nervous, trigger-happy young soldiers pulling their first guard, because of an accent – a huge proportion of GIs had Germanic surnames and many retained the accent with which they had first stepped off the boat at Ellis Island. The Norwegian Americans who served in the 99th Infantry Battalion (Separate), which was composed entirely of their fellow countrymen, known as The Viking Battalion, and deployed in the Malmedy–Stavelot areas, found the routine of justifying their guttural accents particularly trying, if life-saving. Soldiers of both sides routinely wore clothing items and boots taken from prisoners or the dead in an effort to defeat the cold. In the case of those under suspicion, such items merely contributed to 'the case for the prosecution' and in the chaos of battle, many innocent German prisoners who happened to be wearing a looted US overcoat or GIs who had liberated a set of German boots were undoubtedly the victims of summary execution. Certainly, the number of recorded deaths of 'saboteurs' exceeds the number of Skorzeny commandos deployed, and many diaries and memoirs discuss the demise of 'fifth columnists' that were not otherwise recorded – nor were Belgian civilians exempt from the whole process.

The number of such deaths ran into the hundreds, if not four figures. The experience of J.R. McIlroy, a 99th Division squad leader, underlined how close to the edge soldiers of both sides were. The Company 'F' soldier of the 393rd Infantry was taking two German prisoners to the rear when intercepted by a lieutenant of a different company. The officer challenged McIlroy and asked the password; the answer was correct and the soldier with his two prisoners approached. 'We've been on patrol and captured two Germans. I want to take them to the PW collecting point. Do you know where that is?' he asked. Why did McIlroy have a German rifle and sub-machine gun, the officer asked. 'I just took them from the prisoners' was the response. 'And where is your rifle?' the officer continued. 'One of the guards of the prisoners has it' came the answer. The guards were trailing behind, out of sight. All seemed fine until the lieutenant noticed the GI was wearing German boots. 'What company are you with?' the officer asked quickly and abruptly. Fortunately, McIlroy's answer came without hesitation, 'Company "F", Second Battalion, 393rd Infantry'. The interrogation continued, 'Your company commander's name?' The questioning carried on until the officer had relaxed enough to ask, 'Where did you get those boots?' The quick and honest answer, 'I got them off a dead German – the soles give better traction in the snow', satisfied the lieutenant who warned McIlroy that as soon as he'd seen the German boots 'he had almost killed him without further ado'. The shaken GI plodded on with his captives, 'never as close to death in the Ardennes as at that moment'.[25]

One of Skorzeny's teams in US uniforms known to have been captured comprised Oberfähnrich (Senior Cadet Officer) Günther Billing, Unteroffizier Manfred Pernass and Gefreiter Wilhelm Schmidt, detained at Aywaille on 17 December for not knowing a password. They had penetrated the American lines, thirty miles distant, less than an hour earlier, and were found to have £1,000 and $900 in bank notes, German paybooks, two British Sten guns, two Colt .45-inch pistols, a German sub-machine gun and six US hand grenades. Billing had documents identifying him as Charles W. Lawrence, Pernass was Clarence van der Wert, and Schmidt had assumed the identity of one George Sesenbach.[26] During his interrogation, Schmidt confirmed that one of their missions was to capture Eisenhower in Paris. Though this was never his assignment, Skorzeny, as we have seen, was content to let this rumour run, so that many of his own unit believed it.

As a result, all senior Allied commanders became virtual prisoners in their headquarters, which strangled their movements just when they desperately needed to be touring the troops, assessing morale and being seen by the jittery French, Belgian and Luxembourger populations. Billing, Pernass and Schmidt, though, were executed by a US firing squad on 23 December after a court-martial. The names of these three have been grafted into most histories of the Ardennes, but reflected the fate of hundreds of unknown Germans, as Patton's diary indicated on 30 December 1944: 'On this day four Germans in one of our peeps [jeeps], dressed in American uniforms, were killed, and another group of seventeen, also in American uniforms, were reported by the 35th Division as follows: "One sentinel, reinforced, saw seventeen Germans in American uniforms. Fifteen were killed and two died suddenly . . ."'[27] A euphemism for an execution if ever there was one. This German stratagem is one of the lasting associations with the Ardennes, but it is extraordinary to consider that such a tactic had not been used routinely by either side before December 1944.[28]

21

Stray Bullets Whined Through the Trees Around Us

IN THE SOUTH of the US 99th Division's sector, Lieutenant Lyle Bouck with his I&R Platoon, among others, had critically delayed the attack of the 3rd *Fallschirmjägers*, who in turn were meant to be carving an opening for Mohnke's *Leibstandarte* behind. By the end of the day, as we have seen, an angry Peiper had pushed forward, dragging the *Fallschirmjäger* along in his wake. Bouck's valiant action had allowed the rest of Colonel Riley's US 394th Infantry valuable time to counter other thrusts around Losheimergraben, being made by the experienced 12th *Volksgrenadiers* under Generalmajor Gerhardt Engel. They, too, were trying to assist Peiper and Kraas by drilling holes in the American lines, allowing access to *Rollbahn* 'C' – the march route that passed from Losheim (in German hands) north-west via Losheimergraben to Büllingen and Bütgenbach.

The woods along the road between Losheim and Losheimergraben were, and remain, dense swathes of fir trees that line either side of the International Highway. On the eastern (German) side, sharp eyes will pick out the rows of moss-covered dragon's teeth anti-tank obstacles that once heralded the defences of the Siegfried Line, now frequently engulfed by woodland and brush. Various elements of the 394th Regiment, and Lieutenant-Colonel Jean D. Scott's 393rd, had garrisoned the Belgian (western) side and today their foxholes remain within the wood line. These are usually deep, with squared-off edges and therefore cannot be mistaken for natural depressions in the ground. Apart from the loss of their overhead cover – the foresters retrieved their logs after the war – the dugouts are pretty much how the GIs of the 99th left them in December 1944.

Shallower, more irregular holes mark the impact craters of artillery and mortar rounds. The surrounding trees have mostly been felled and replanted, but the new growth looks very much like the 1944 crop of pine trees would have seemed to the combatants, rushing through. In exactly this sector, Lieutenant Robert K. Dettor, Third Platoon commander with Company 'K' in Colonel Scott's 393rd Infantry, survived to record his combat memories of 16 December. Later, in a prisoner-of-war camp, he wrote on hidden scraps of paper: '06:40 am: Communications to CP and outposts cut. No contact with men except those in foxholes in immediate vicinity. German troops to rear. [My] heavy machine-gun to front seen captured . . . Enemy closing to within 20 feet of foxhole . . . I had four rounds [left]. Burp-gun to left rear firing at my foxhole hitting Hunter. I believe Hunter was dead . . . Last American food (chocolate) at approximately 12:30 pm; position overrun.'[1]

Companies 'B' and 'C' were also overwhelmed and the only reserves available, led by twenty-three-year-old First Lieutenant Harry C. Parker, were sent to restore the situation at about 10.30 a.m.. Parker, who was from Vermont and knew cold weather, with his little force moved up the 393rd's main supply road towards the International Highway. Taking advantage of the dense forest, they crept towards the *Volksgrenadiers*, who opened fire. Parker rose to his feet. 'Hell, there's no use lying here and getting killed,' he addressed his cobbled together band of GIs from the Regimental Anti-tank Mine Platoon, Ammunition and Pioneer Platoon, as well as a handful of cooks, clerks and runners. Giving the order to fix bayonets, his force broke into a run, yelling like a band of wild and desperate men.

Completely surprised, the Germans couldn't see what was coming but they could hear it. They fled in the opposite direction in complete disorder; those who didn't move fast enough were bayoneted. Parker's bayonet charge relieved the pressure and allowed Company 'C' to reorganise. The young officer received a Silver Star for this action. On a rainy day in November 1994, exactly where the bayonet charge occurred, and fifty years later, a set of dog tags surfaced from among the pine needles, along with remnants of a musette bag. They belonged to Harry C. Parker, who had survived the war, but dropped the bag containing his dog tags during the charge.[2]

A stroll around the sector today is instructive. Everywhere, keen eyes will detect the remains of US-issue gas masks and overshoes, both rubberised, and often the first things to be discarded by withdrawing soldiers – perhaps from Dettor's or Parker's men. A mangled canteen here, an old mess tin there, slivers of rusting shrapnel, cartridge cases and the tail fins of long-dead mortar bombs protrude from between the pine needles and there is generally the forlorn air of a long-forgotten battlefield about the place. It was these woods around Losheimergraben that Oberstleutnant Wilhelm Osterhold's 48th Grenadier Regiment attacked in the early hours of 16 December. Osterhold, already the proud possessor of a *Ritterkreuz* swinging at his throat for leadership in Russia, and part of Gerhardt Engel's 12th *Volksgrenadier* Division, himself led the initial assault on part of Riley's US 394th Infantry Regiment.

Despite the 12th *Volksgrenadier's* excellent reputation, the spry lieutenant-colonel – he was thirty – found some of his less experienced grenadiers had cut telephone wires leading to their own guns, erroneously thinking them to be attached to US booby traps. This breakdown of communications led to German artillery rounds falling short, injuring some of his men and stalling their advance. One of their early US captives observed of the *Volksgrenadiers'* unimpressive performance, 'Germans do a great deal of yelling in battle. At least one in three had automatic weapons, carried a great deal of equipment, wore camouflaged suits . . . German soldiers all ages. German officer had dress uniform on . . . Could not understand German form of attack. Men came, line upon line, through open field on left making them an easy target for flanking fire.' [3]

Some of Osterhold's Germans, including Helmut Stiegeler, were seen off when the US 81mm mortar section of Company 'D', led by Sergeant Del Stumpff, elevated their weapons to 89 degrees (almost perpendicular to the ground, ensuring the mortar round would land at the shortest possible range). They repelled the *Volksgrenadiers'* attack and earned the respect of the commander who had attacked them; Osterhold later said Stumpff and others in his unit deserved the highest recognition for their success in defeating his assault, though felt of his own preparation and training for *Herbstnebel*, 'I never took part in an attack which was worse planned'. Nevertheless, the Wehrmacht would credit him with making one of the breakthroughs at Losheimergraben and decorate him again with Oak Leaves for his Knight's Cross.[4]

Each US infantry battalion contained a 166-man heavy weapons company of eight .30-inch heavy machine guns and six 81mm mortars, like this one. It was the largest weapon available to a battalion commander and could throw a 15-lb high explosive projectile from 100 to 3,200 yards. An assembled mortar weighed 136 pounds but could be broken down into lighter loads to be man-packed into secluded positions. In the woods around Losheim and Losheimergraben, mortars belonging to the US 99th Infantry Division repelled a *VolksGrenadier* attack by elevating their weapons to 89 degrees (almost perpendicular to the ground), ensuring the rounds would land at the shortest possible range. (NARA)

Not far away, in the same stretch of woods, Technical Sergeant Bob Walter had been drafted in 1942, aged twenty. December 1944 found him commanding a platoon with Company 'L' of the 393rd Infantry, who were deployed in the tree line along the International Highway. He remembered being unconcerned about the opening bombardment because something similar occurred most days: 'For a few minutes we didn't think much about the incoming rounds. We had already become familiar with the Germans' habit of repeating their barrage patterns with clocklike precision. After that, we wouldn't hear from them until the next day. We'd taken to calling this our "daily allowance" and figured they were finally breaking with tradition and getting things done a little early that morning.'[5]

Sergeant Rod Ingraham, who had been evacuated to his regimental HQ with trench foot, recalled the same morning barrage each breakfast-time. 'I had been on the front line a couple of days when I got a new partner. He was an Italian boy from Brooklyn, New York. He had just finished basic training and been shipped over. His first words were, "So this is lock and load?" He could not believe that this was the front line of an ongoing war. Everything was quiet and people were walking around. I told him that in an hour or two we would be getting an artillery barrage. It was right on time. Give the Germans credit for being able to keep a schedule. A few landed fairly close, and I suddenly realized that he was hugging me.' [6]

After two hours of shelling, Sergeant Walter and his colleagues were mystified. 'We couldn't figure out what the Germans were shooting at and concluded that they were trying to knock out our artillery'. Once the bombardment had finished he was ordered to clear a German squad who'd infiltrated the company kitchen behind the lines, but the enigma continued: 'Not yet halfway to our objective, we began running into Germans – a lot of them. Instead of simply hiking back to our kitchen, we ended up having to fight our way in.' When Walter arrived, he radioed into his company CP, 'Something's wrong, sir. There are more Germans back here than there are in front of us!' He noted that the Germans generally moved on at his appearance: 'It seemed they were more interested in continuing west than in fighting us.' A young PFC asked to stay close to Walter, whom he concluded was lucky; after about ten minutes Walter turned to ask him something. 'He didn't respond, so I glanced over at him. A bullet had caught him between the eyes and he was gone.' [7]

By this time, Lieutenant Dettor of the 393rd had been captured and was being marched back to Germany. As he was ushered back behind the *Westwall*, the view of his first moments of captivity was enlightening. 'Roads filled with . . . staff cars, horses and wagons . . . ammunition trucks draped with large red crosses to disguise them as ambulances . . . heavy equipment coming to the front. Felt extremely depressed after seeing size of the attack.' However, in a little while, Dettor was sufficiently aware to notice 'German motor vehicles very poor. Much larger than American trucks but not as well made. Many vehicles broken down.'[8] In a nutshell, Dettor had seized upon one of the factors that would ultimately bring *Herbstnebel* to a halt: logistics. Heavy traffic on the roads, as we have seen, slowed down Peiper, and would ultimately prevent enough combat supplies of fuel and ammunition from reaching their own forward troops.

Dettor wasn't the only one marching into Germany. Private Roger V. Foehringer had been a freshman at Xavier University in Cincinnati, Ohio, when he was drafted. Posted to the Service Battery of 924th Field Artillery, attached to the 99th Division, 16 December found him on duty in Büllingen. The first he knew of trouble was when one of the 14th Cavalry Group's M-8 armoured cars belted through the village, pausing long enough for a crewman to warn Foehringer 'The whole damned German army is just down the road!' There was little chance to mount a defence and, with no transport of their own in sight, Foehringer and his colleagues were swiftly overwhelmed by Panther tanks, including that of Hans Hennecke, and *Panzergrenadiers* in half-tracks from the 1st SS Division.

Being made to march east to Germany, Foehringer and his fellow prisoners saw many flattened corpses, where tanks and trucks had run over them: 'They were like pancakes. We tried to detour round, but the guards made us march over them,' he remembered. 'In Honsfeld there were frozen corpses behind headstones. You could see how they had fought, one guy at a headstone, another behind a headstone, and there they were, frozen as they had been shot.'[9] GI prisoners immediately noticed the difference between the *Volksgrenadier* first-wave grenadiers and the panzer troops following behind. 'SS troops very cocky, treated American prisoners very rough,' noted one. 'While walking SS troops looted American prisoners, beat and kicked them. Ordinary front line soldier not too bad . . . Excellent camouflage discipline [of SS], vehicles, personnel emplacements, weapons.'[10]

PFC Donald Wallace, with 3rd Battalion of 394th Infantry at Buchholz station, also commented on the state of two *Volksgrenadier* prisoners he encountered. He never forgot that morning's 'terrible artillery barrage east of our position that lighted the horizon over the trees and went on for over an hour. The shooting war began soon after the barrage. From the farmhouse yard we could hear popping sounds coming from near the station. German troops had come out of the woods and Company "L" had taken them on. I crept along the yard in the front of the farmhouse [and] watched some of the fire fight near the station until I drew fire from somewhere near my position. Twigs were snapping on the shrubs above my head. The yard was full of holes from artillery explosions. I remember three German prisoners brought back to the farmhouse during the battle. Two of them were old men that were frightened and almost in tears.'[11]

A couple of miles north, Hugo Kraas's 12th SS Panzer Division (the *Hitlerjugend*) were waiting impatiently while their attendant infantry division, Oberst Viebig's 277th *Volksgrenadiers*, attempted to punch through the lines opposite the twin villages of Krinkelt-Rocherath on the high ground of the Elsenborn Ridge. This would allow the panzers access to the northernmost *Rollbahn* 'A' (Rocherath to Elsenborn and beyond), and its close neighbour, *Rollbahn* 'B', which stretched via Krinkelt, Wirtzfeld and Nidrum. They were opposed by elements of Colonel Alexander J. Mackenzie's US 395th Regiment. Five miles further north, Generalmajor Kaschner's 326th *Volksgrenadiers* (with Unteroffizier Josef Reinartz and the pipe-smoking Gefreiter Alfred Becker) were attacking Höfen and Monschau.

German prisoners volunteered praise of the 395th's fighting skill at Höfen: an *Oberstleutnant* said the Checkerboard Division 'was the best American outfit he ever had faced', and later, in the divisional prisoner-of-war cage at Linz, a German *Leutnant* asked his interrogator the name of the elite American unit that had defended Höfen months earlier. It was the US 395th Regiment, who had allowed the *Leutnant*'s company to come within nine feet of its lines before opening up with such terrific small arms and machine-gun fire that the Germans couldn't even remove their dead and wounded in their rapid retreat.[12]

In this area, near the eastern end of the Elsenborn Ridge, it was artillery even more than the Checkerboard's infantry battalions that slowed the German attacks, then halted them. Initially it was General Walter Lauer's field artillery battalions who checked the 12th SS and *Volksgrenadiers*, until the close of the 17th, when Gerow's V Corps artillery took over the fight with such effectiveness that one infantry battalion recorded a defensive barrage of 11,500 rounds during the night of 17–18 December. This reflected the general importance of artillery in the Ardennes, where the US Army fired around 1,255,000 artillery rounds from over 4,155 artillery pieces – a capability the Germans simply could not match.[13] The new American proximity fuse, which detonated a warhead when near, but not on, the target was also felt to be a hugely important innovation. Prior to the Ardennes the device, known as a VT (Variable Time) fuse, had only been issued to anti-aircraft units for fear the Germans might retrieve one and learn its secrets. Devastating against unprotected infantry, where the fuse could be set to explode a shell as an airburst fifteen to twenty feet above ground, it soon became the US weapon of choice against the *Volksgrenadiers*.

The Germans had missed the fact that a veteran division had also moved into the vicinity of the Elsenborn Ridge in order to lead the attack on the Roer dams. This was the US 2nd Indianhead Division, whose 23rd Infantry Regiment had occupied the woods in front of Krinkelt – the Krinkelterwald – and acted as a backstop to the Checkerboard's 393rd and 395th Regiments. The inter-unit boundaries in this whole sector were messy, following firebreaks and forest tracks, and not always clear, hence the 'alphabet soup' of different American units occupying the same large chunk of woodland. This meant a thin line of nervous GIs freezing in half-dug foxholes, staring through the trees at hordes of indistinct figures rushing towards them.

To conclude our overview of the German attack all along the Ardennes front, we will stay with the 2nd Infantry Division into 17 December, when they were called forward after their Checkerboard colleagues of the 99th had fought themselves to a standstill on the preceding day. The mission of Oberst Wilhelm Viebig's 277th *Volksgrenadiers*, along with Generalmajor Gerhard Engel's 12th *Volksgrenadiers* to their south, had been to batter their way through the American front on 16 December, held in this sector by the US 99th Division. Such had been the unexpected resistance thrown up by the 99th – personified by Lieutenant Bouck's I&R Platoon, but mirrored elsewhere – that Krämer in Sixth Army's headquarters was forced to alter his plans. The Checkerboarders had few casualties prior to 16 December but, over the next four days, divisional records identified fourteen officers and men killed, 915 wounded and 1,394 missing in action. An additional 600 passed through the division clearing station before 20 December as non-battle casualties – injuries, fatigue, respiratory problems caused by exposure, and trench foot.[14]

Dietrich's chief of staff now ordered the 12th SS-*Hitlerjugend* Panzer Division forward to join the two *Volksgrenadier* formations in a combined assault on the Losheimergraben–Krinkelt–Rotherath sector. This was in recognition of the desperate need to open *Rollbahns* 'A', 'B' and 'C', without which the *Hitlerjugend* was going nowhere. Instead of the *Volksgrenadiers* clearing the way for the panzers, their roles had been reversed. We might pause and speculate that, had this been the case right across the front (river crossings permitting), putting the panzer divisions first would certainly have achieved many more, and deeper, break-ins sooner than was actually the case. The new attackers comprised II Battalion, 25th SS-*Panzergrenadiers*, under Obersturmbannführer (Lieutenant-Colonel) Richard Schulze-Kossens, a former personal aide to Hitler. They deployed on foot and in armoured half-tracks, supported by some anti-aircraft vehicles, using their 20mm guns in a deadly anti-personnel role, and a few *Jagdpanzer* IV tank destroyers.[15]

Untersturmführer (Second Lieutenant) Ernst Stuhr, a platoon commander in the 12th SS Division, remembered the attack by mechanised infantry into the American-held woods: 'The Kompanie moved forward . . . I spotted Battalion commander Schulze standing upright at the side of the lane. [This was *Rollbahn* 'A'.] He was looking through his binoculars. An armed reconnaissance vehicle had taken up position in front of him. Its commander, a holder of the Knight's Cross, stood in the turret, observing the terrain through his binoculars . . . When we entered the woods there was a loud bang. A mine had exploded. An *Unterscharführer* [sergeant] lost his right lower leg. The woods were mined, the mines connected by above-ground wires . . . All sorts of shells exploded around us, not only on the ground, but also in the treetops.'[16]

Later on in the same attack, another officer, Obersturmführer (Lieutenant) Helmut Zeiner in the divisional anti-tank battalion, was driving his half-track along a narrow, occasionally winding forest lane [the same *Rollbahn* 'A'], and at a track junction 'all hell broke loose. The Americans had armour piercing weapons, snipers in the trees, and a few Shermans in ambush positions. *Oberscharführer* [Company Sergeant-Major] Roy was driving behind me. He was killed by a shot to the head. Roy had been awarded the Knight's Cross during the invasion [of Normandy]. He was a likeable young lad with a lot of skill and courage. None of that helped! The death of our comrade surely provoked a rage in us all, and I drove ahead recklessly.' The loss of his right-hand man, the senior NCO in the unit, was a grave loss to Zeiner, and indicated to him that the Ardennes fighting was every bit as deadly as Normandy.[17]

The sides were evenly matched, with excessive acts of bravery recognised by both the opposing armies. As the German armoured column ground down the forest track that was *Rollbahn* 'A' (and found to be in no way suitable as the main supply route of a major tank advance), Sergeant Vernon McGarity, from Tennessee, serving with Company 'L' of the Checkerboard's 393rd Infantry, grabbed a bazooka and destroyed its leading armoured vehicle. Rescuing a wounded GI, he then brought up additional ammunition and directed fire which drove off the nearby

Panzergrenadiers for a while. However, a German machine-gun squad had managed to work its way to his rear, cutting off his escape route. In a rage, he leapt towards the machine-gunners, despatching them with a rifle, and prevented all attempts to re-man the weapon. Only when he and his squad had run out of ammunition were they overwhelmed and taken prisoner. McGarity's inspiring heroism later brought him a Medal of Honor.[18]

Schulze-Kossens, commander of the II Battalion, 25th SS-*Panzergrenadiers*, took up the story, highlighting the fact that so many of his unit were recent recruits. 'Since the men were largely without combat experience, only the deployment of the officers in the front lines could help. In the first hours, all Kompanie chiefs were lost, either killed or wounded . . . *Oberscharführers* took over the companies. I remember the very difficult crossing of the Jansbach creek so well, because almost at the creek, I came under fire from snipers in the trees. I pretended to have been killed and, after some considerable time, I suddenly leapt up and into cover.'[19]

In effect, Schulze-Kossens acknowledged his battalion was so green that it could only function efficiently if its senior leaders were at the front doing the job of junior officers and NCOs. This was in complete contrast to their American counterparts, where the GIs may have been new to combat but all had undertaken between twelve and eighteen months' training before reaching the Ardennes. Nevertheless, the vastly better resourced SS-*Panzergrenadiers* operating in half-tracks and on foot, working where possible with the support of their panzers, soon sliced through the remnants of the 99th, pushing them back on to positions held by the 23rd Infantry of the US Indianhead Division, a veteran outfit who were in no mood to yield terrain.

However, as a result of their First World War experiences in the Vosges and Ardennes, the Germans had studied the pitfalls of woodland fighting extensively. All their junior officers, Wehrmacht and SS, had to study forest combat techniques, as this textbook observed:

> Thick woods are very apt to make men feel lost and bewildered, particularly when shots from an invisible hand come whistling through the branches. Wood fighting, owing to the constant danger of missing one's way and losing direction, and the length of time a good sniper can carry on without being detected, is one of the least desirable forms of warfare, especially when troops unaccustomed to woods are pitted against trained sharpshooters.[20]

Among those who were contesting the same woods opposite Schulze-Kossens was Captain Charles B. MacDonald, commanding Company 'I' in the 23rd Infantry Regiment. MacDonald, all of twenty-one, had been called forward into the Krinkelterwald during the night of 16–17 December and remembered their slit trenches 'amounted to little more than the snow scraped from the ground and a few inches of frozen earth removed'.[21] His regimental commander was Colonel Jay B. Lovless, a Texan, who had taken over on 16 June after his outspoken predecessor had fallen out with the divisional commander and been sacked. We have already met the predecessor, for he was Colonel Hurley E. Fuller, who was at this moment fighting for his life further south on the Ardennes front, leading the 110th Infantry of Cota's Bloody Bucket Division.

MacDonald's experience of that first long, cold night in the Krinkelterwald was mirrored by his company. 'I would drift off for a few minutes, only to awaken sharply with the realisation that I was shaking violently from the cold. I would get up, walk in a small circle, stamp my feet, and return to try once again to sleep.' In the early light his men made their trenches and foxholes deeper and at around 10.00 a.m. 'stray bullets from the small-arms fight up ahead began to zing through the woods. That was enough to tell us the attacking Germans were not far away.' They gradually got closer, for a little later 'a fury of small-arms fire sounded to the front. Stray bullets whined through the trees around us.'

Shortly after that, MacDonald noticed a jeep packed with men from the 99th Division, who should have been to their front, clip down the highway 'toward the rear at breakneck speed'. Then, coming over the wooded ridge to his front, MacDonald counted about two hundred Checkerboard soldiers, the remnants of nine hundred who had been fighting for twenty-four hours since the Germans first attacked. They passed through his position, some handing their spare ammunition and hand grenades to his men as they stumbled back. 'Two enlisted men, carrying a badly wounded lieutenant, stopped exhausted with my 3rd Platoon. They could carry him no further,' MacDonald recalled.[22]

A five-minute walk into the Krinkelterwald from the nearby car park will take one straight to MacDonald's position today, recognisable by the bigger dugout that his company headquarters required. Ahead, the ground slopes downhill slightly into a bowl with shallow inclines to left and right, then rises a few hundred yards away to a dominating crest, all within the forest. MacDonald next remembered 'a hail of small-arms fire which sounded like the crack of thousands of rifles echoing through the forest. There was no doubt now. My men could see the billed caps of the approaching troops. They were Germans.'[23] MacDonald's frequent references to the small-arms fire leaves no doubt that these were MP-44 assault rifles, the *Sturmgewehr*, which fired at the same 500–600 rounds-per-minute rate as the Browning Automatic Rifles (BAR) with which Company 'I' was equipped. Another Second Division GI described the experience of being under fire: 'when bullets come close to your head, they split the air so fast the air coming back together pops like a hard clap of hands. It really pops; only ricochets will buzz or whine or whir – so much for movie phoniness.'[24]

MacDonald fought off the first attack with mortars and corrected artillery fire, but his supporting Field Artillery Battalion was so short of shells they would only fire three rounds at a time, which did pitifully little damage to the advancing waves. 'Another hail of small-arms fire told me the attackers had reorganised for a second assault . . . I lay on my back in the slit trench, the platoon phone in one ear, the receiver of the battalion radio to the other. The chill from the frozen earth seeped through my clothes and I shivered, but I was surprised at my own calmness . . . The small-arms fire reached another crackling crescendo.'[25] Many junior military commanders today have perfected the art of listening to two radio nets simultaneously, a receiver in each ear as MacDonald was doing here, but this was a luxury denied to the Germans in 1944, who were issued only with a bulky radio down to company level.

Meanwhile the US 9th and 38th Infantry Regiments (the rest of the 2nd Division) who, with the 78th Infantry Division and CCB of the Ninth Armored, had been engaged on the operation to seize the Roer dams, were recalled after 07.00 a.m. on the 17th to help stem the tide on the high ground of the Elsenborn Ridge, around Krinkelt–Rotherath. Sergeant Joseph Jan Kiss, Jr, of the 38th Infantry, remembered of the move: 'We pulled back in broad daylight, about seven or eight miles from near Wahlershied to the twin towns of Krinkelt and Rocherath in Belgium under artillery fire. I hit the ground near a German foxhole, afraid to get in it as it may be booby trapped. A machine gun burst over me, tearing black bark off trees, exposing the white wood underneath, causing me to dive in the foxhole anyway.'

Under fire, the sense of urgency, remembered Kiss, was palpable. 'Keep moving. The dead or wounded that fell on the road were mashed by trucks, tanks and jeeps, bumper to bumper trying to escape. I saw men smashed flat as a pancake. You could see outlines of helmets through bodies twice a normal size, smashed flat. I had to stare at some for awhile to figure out that it was once a human being. Some animals in a burning barn across the road were crying and it sounded like the crying of human babies.' While Kiss was still free, Private Foehringer of the 99th Division had witnessed much the same during his march to captivity. In moments of confusion and stress, demonstrations of good leadership were vital. Sergeant Kiss never forgot what happened next.

'At a crossroad someone tapped me on the shoulder and said, "What outfit, son?" I said, "Charlie Company, 38th Regiment, Second Division". I saw two stars on his helmet, but I knew from pictures that he was General Walter Robertson, our Division Commander. He said, "Down this road to the left about two blocks to a brown brick house on the end". I said "Yes, Sir", called to my squad and took off. I heard later that he was all over the area trying to build up a good strong line and gather up stragglers.'[26] Just as Sergeant Kiss admired his general's good leadership in a crisis, he also responded to humour: having decided to build himself a dugout as a German artillery shell destroyed his old one, 'I had the new hole pretty deep when the new CO, Lieutenant Mode, walked up. "If you go any deeper, I'll court martial you for desertion!"'[27]

Further south, back at Captain MacDonald's position in the woods, after seven attacks by 'suicidal waves of fanatical infantrymen, whooping and yelling and brandishing their rifles like men possessed', at 3.30 p.m. the Germans brought up tanks (MacDonald called them 'five giant Tigers', but they were clearly Schulze-Kossens' *Jagdpanzer* IVs), which prised his company out from their positions.[28] Private Richard Cowan, in MacDonald's company, remembered the Germans were close enough for him to hear the officers' shouts and whistle signals.[29] MacDonald thought, 'Shades of General Custer. Our last stand. Hell, what does it matter? You never expected to get out of this war alive anyway. Not really.'[30] Already out of ammunition, the presence of the panzers decided their next course of action and Company 'I' withdrew gradually, leapfrogging back into Rocherath, passing a couple of Company 'C' Shermans commanded by Lieutenant Victor L. Miller of the 741st Tank Battalion which had destroyed the leading *Hitlerjugend* panzer, to be in turn knocked out by the following *Jagdpanzer*; the area was soon dubbed *Sherman Ecke* (Sherman Corner) by the Germans.

The 741st experienced a trying day, having commenced it on an entirely different mission of supporting the 2nd Division's thrust towards the Roer dams. By late morning they were fully engaged in the woods surrounding Rocherath and Krinkelt. Sergeant Ray Wilson, a gunner in a Company 'B' Sherman, remembered firing at a panzer that had suddenly appeared a mere seventy-five yards away. The shell bounced off its sloping frontal armour; there was no time to get in a second shot. Later on at dusk, when spotlights began stabbing the dark in all directions and one beam fell on a Sherman, Company 'B' realised the Germans had mounted searchlights on their tanks.[31] A Second Division sergeant recalled the atmosphere as the daylight faded: 'the artillery and machine gun fire was awful. German tracers were yellow, ours a reddish pink; they looked like pretty – but deadly – fireflies at night.'[32]

The 741st would destroy an estimated twenty-seven panzers over the next few days, losing eleven of their own, though some disabled tanks, immobilised inside the American lines, carried on the fight. With them, fighting in the same sector, was the 644th Tank Destroyer Battalion, who had earlier accompanied the 2nd Division into the Hürtgen. There, they had experienced the attentions of both the Luftwaffe's Messerschmitt 109s, followed by the 'American Luftwaffe's' P-38 Lightnings, 'taking over where the Germans left off'. At Krinkelt, the 644th employed their thirty-six self-propelled M-10s with such effect as to claim twenty-one panzers destroyed or disabled, for the loss of thirty-eight casualties and two M-10s. The experience of the 801st Tank Destroyer (towed) Battalion in the same area was strikingly different. Dug in along the infantry line, their three-inch guns received intense shelling and could be moved only at night. During the attack, bogged down in mud and unable to shift firing positions, their anti-tank guns quickly fell prey to direct fire or infantry assault; during 17–19 December the 801st lost seventeen guns and sixteen of the half-tracks which towed them, and the greatest combat value of the battalion came from the use of gun crews as infantry.[33]

Behind MacDonald's Company 'I' in the woods was Company 'M', assigned to protect the regiment's right flank, and provide depth support with several Browning .30-inch heavy machine guns set up on their tripods in fortified foxholes. As the grenadiers tore through Company 'I', one of the machine-gunners, PFC José M. Lopez, of Brownsville, Texas, picked up his heavy gun and repositioned himself to prevent the Germans from breaking through. First he mounted one of the 741st's Company 'B' Shermans, which he thought was waiting for someone to direct its fire. 'I climbed up and asked if anyone was alive. There was no answer.' The crew were dead; Lopez then leapt into a shallow hole that exposed everything from his waist up to enemy fire, set up his gun five feet to MacDonald's rear, and started spraying the advancing *Landsers*, dropping several. Undeterred by the presence of panzers in his vicinity, Lopez carried on machine-gunning his opponents, all the while under tank, artillery and small-arms fire.

Nearby, MacDonald watched as 'An American Jeep with two aid men, their red Geneva crosses painted on their helmets, tore down the highway . . . I held my breath. The Tiger [sic] tank would surely blast them from the road. Couldn't they see that the Germans were here now? They did. With the Jeep spinning on two wheels they turned around and tore back up the road. The tank did not fire.'[34] Meanwhile, Lopez repositioned himself and his machine gun several times, only falling back when out of ammunition. More than anyone else, he had ensured Company 'M's survival, and later more than a hundred dead *Panzergrenadiers* were counted in an arc around his several positions. As late as 1993 it was still possible to trace Lopez's various positions from the piles of empty .30-inch cartridges just beneath the forest floor. For his actions in the Krinkelterwald, Lopez was promoted to sergeant and awarded a Medal of Honor for what were dubbed his several 'seemingly suicidal missions'.[35]

Meanwhile, Captain MacDonald arrived back at his battalion CP, distraught at having lost his company and, in his eyes, failed in his first combat. He was amazed to be told by his CO, Lieutenant-Colonel Paul V. Tuttle Jr, 'Nice work, Mac . . . You held out much longer than I expected.'[36]

22

The Conference

WE'VE CRAWLED THROUGH the snow-covered pine needles with GIs and grenadiers, experiencing their war through the first days, but how did the Allied high command react?

Saturday, 16 December, had begun for Eisenhower with receipt of a letter from Montgomery, formally requesting authority to travel home for Christmas, but also demanding settlement of a bet the two had made on 11 October 1943 that the war would *not* be over by Christmas 1944. Eisenhower had thought it would. 'For payment, I think at Christmas', Monty had written, in his own handwriting. Ike said he still had nine days. The former was playing a round of golf at Eindhoven, in Holland, when a messenger arrived with a note about 'a hell of a row' happening in the Ardennes. His own front, he knew, had not been attacked, so he alerted several of his personal liaison officers and the Phantom Regiment with David Niven to head for First Army's sector via Hodges' headquarters in Spa, and relay the true situation back to him. Meanwhile he abandoned the game and returned to his Twenty-First Army Group HQ (code-named 'Lion') in Zonhoven, in Belgium, where he had quit his famous caravans and wintered indoors for nearly three months, between 9 November 1944 and 7 February 1945.[1]

At the Hôtel Trianon Palace, in Versailles, Eisenhower was holding his usual mid-morning conference with Air Chief Marshal Sir Arthur Tedder (his British deputy), and Generals Walter Bedell Smith (SHAEF chief of staff), Harold R. Bull (his chief G-3) and Kenneth Strong (the British chief G-2), when Thomas J. Betts (the American deputy G-2) knocked and whispered the first, tentative stirrings of news from the Ardennes attack to Strong, who announced it to the wider audience. At this early stage, it was disregarded as a spoiling attack and the day proceeded smoothly.[2]

When news of a captured copy of Rundstedt's Order of the Day was transmitted to SHAEF via First Army at about 11.00 a.m., the mood began to alter, not enough, though, to put a dampener on the wedding of Ike's orderly, Sergeant Mickey McKeogh, to Pearlie Hargrave, a popular WAC at SHAEF, in the Palace's rococo royal chapel. That morning Ike had also received word of his promotion to the five-star rank of General of the Army, which had been passed by Act of Congress two days earlier. Ike's advancement removed the embarrassment of having a British five-star field marshal (Montgomery) serving under him. His new appointment coincided with the similar elevations of George C. Marshall, Douglas MacArthur and Henry 'Hap' Arnold to the old civil war title

The ring of five stars on Eisenhower's shoulder announce that he has just been promoted to General of the Army – a rank equal to that of Montgomery's Field Marshalcy. Ike received the rank on the same day the Bulge started, but his position here – seated between his two army group commanders, Bernard Montgomery and Omar Bradley – reflected the fact that his biggest challenge was keeping the peace between these two feisty subordinates. (Author's collection)

that had expired with the death of General of the Army Phil Sheridan in 1888. Marshall's surname was apparently one reason why the British equivalent rank was not considered: Field Marshal Marshall would be too . . . undignified. As Captain Harry Butcher, Ike's personal aide, observed, Eisenhower had been a major for sixteen years, but in three years, three months and sixteen days he had risen six grades from lieutenant-colonel to five-star general.[3]

In the afternoon, the Polish General Kopansky arrived to award his country's *Virtuti Militari* medals to Eisenhower and Bedell Smith, and toasted the pair with Piper-Hiedsieck champagne. As dusk settled over Europe, Ike's old friend General Omar Bradley – Brad (they had known each other since West Point) – arrived in time to join him for a glass of champagne after the Polish medal ceremony. Ostensibly the Twelfth Army Group commander had come up to discuss the shortage of infantry replacements in Europe, but it was not often the Supreme Commander could lower his guard with an old confidant. The weather had prevented flying – just as Hitler's meteorologists predicted – so Bradley had spent much of 16 December driving from Luxembourg, over 260 miles of icy roads to Paris, hence his late arrival. Regardless, Eisenhower planned for them to retire later to his villa at Saint-Germain-en-Laye, and relax with a bottle of his favourite Johnny Walker Black Label Scotch whisky and several rubbers of bridge.

The villa had been 'inherited' from Field Marshals Rundstedt and Kluge, the two successive commanders of OB West. While the actual OB West headquarters had been a few hundred yards away in the Pavillon Henri IV, Rundstedt's own quarters, which Ike used, was the Villa David.[4] The last German staff had decamped hurriedly on 24 August 1944, though when I visited it to find where Rundstedt and Eisenhower had once lived, I found the Wehrmacht's reinforced concrete bunkers still in place, discreetly hidden among the rhododendrons. This was the ultimate symbol of triumph: in occupying his opponent's house, Ike was merely following in the footsteps of what that other great warrior, the Duke of Wellington, had done after Waterloo, when the latter acquired Napoleon's residence in Paris.[5]

Major-General Strong interrupted the bridge-playing with a serious update on the military situation. 'There had been,' he announced with that gentle apologetic air all British exude when announcing bad news, 'five major German penetrations into Middleton's VIII Corps front during the day. Size and extent still as yet unknown, but they had started early in the morning.'[6] The news caused concern, but not enough to end the evening, which finished when the Black Label was consumed.[7]

At this moment Bradley no doubt recalled his defence to General Strong of his own G-2's relaxed intelligence assessment. This was the meeting at his Twelfth Army Group headquarters in Luxembourg, only two days earlier, when Bradley had exclaimed in exasperation, 'Let them come'. Now, it appeared, the Germans had come knocking on his door. Bradley, knowing there were no strategic objectives in the Ardennes or anywhere east of the Meuse, had been, as we've seen, inclined to dismiss the report as a series of spoiling attacks, designed to disrupt the obvious forthcoming offensives by his First and Third Armies. Eisenhower ruminated, and perhaps for the very reason he was able to distance himself, immediately disagreed, announcing, 'That's no spoiling attack'.

In retrospect, this was perhaps the most defining moment of his Supreme Command. Eisenhower's personal vulnerability was that he had never commanded troops in battle. He was a lucky desk warrior and he knew it. This was the moment of his own testing. Unlike Major-General Alan W. Jones at the 106th Division, faced with similar uncertainties at the same time, Eisenhower was confident of himself and his judgement. Hitler had assumed that Allied bureaucracy would require Ike to check with Roosevelt and Churchill, Marshall and Brooke (behaviour he would expect of his commanders before they made any such dispositions), but the thought never entered Eisenhower's head. That's how command worked in a democracy: authority was entrusted and delegated to the field commander.

At the very moment when immediate decisions were crucial, Ike rose to the occasion and overruled his friend. What was happening in the Ardennes was something more than a distraction. His conclusion, however, would begin to sow the seeds of dissent between the two old friends, and their friendship would never be the same again, or as strong, as it had been at the start of this night.

Eisenhower acted without hesitation even when the situation was shrouded, literally as well as metaphorically, in the fog of war. Rundstedt's intentions – everyone from SHAEF downwards assumed it was the elderly *Oberbefehlshaber West* who was running this operation – were still unclear in those initial hours. Nevertheless, from Strong's first briefing Eisenhower was convinced the German attack was a strategic attempt to split the Allied front, and started to react accordingly. He may have reasoned that there was no other point in attacking a region that contained nothing worth seizing. Looking at the map, the Germans weren't even after Aachen. Eisenhower also had history on his side, for he knew this was exactly what the Imperial German Army had done in March 1918, under similar conditions of surprise. They had mounted a series of attacks along the Western Front, aimed at pushing the British and French back in different directions, splitting the Great War allies in two. Ike hadn't, of course, served in the First World War, but the work he did in drafting *A Guide to the American Battlefields in Europe* was unexpectedly useful to him now. In some ways he knew more about that war than those who had served in it, and the parallels with 1918 must have struck him.

In the words of one historian, 'This was the first occasion since he had assumed command of Allied ground forces that Eisenhower was able to influence the outcome of a battle . . . Now, when it mattered most, he was at the centre of a seminal battle whose outcome would determine the final course of the war.'[8] However, at this time, partly because of his controversial broad-front strategy, which was, as we've seen, why Middleton's VIII Corps was so stretched, SHAEF had few theatre reserves. In fact the only combat-ready formations to hand were two tired American airborne divisions, the 82nd and 101st, still recovering and re-equipping in the Reims area after Operation Market Garden in September. Neither was ideal, for airborne divisions by their very nature were lightly armed (they possessed very few vehicles and relatively little artillery, for example) and not equipped for sustained ground combat.

SHAEF had another bugbear that December evening, and Bradley's long journey had emphasised it. The Allied intelligence picture of the German attack was extremely opaque and communicating any worthwhile conclusions or orders between the Allied headquarters – Ike in Paris, Bradley in Luxembourg (code-named 'Eagle'), or Hodges in Spa (with the name of 'Master') was challenging. The Twelfth US Army Group commander and First Army headquarters appeared to be on opposite sides of the battlefield, which, if events snowballed out of control, might sever communications between the two.

Patton's view of a command post was that 'you must always have a road net from which you can move forward to any portion of your line. A CP situated at a spot where it is necessary to move to the rear is disadvantageous. In this connection it is always best, where practicable, to drive to the front, so that soldiers can see you going in that direction, and to save time, fly back by [Piper] Cub so that you are never seen going to the rear.'[9] The Ardennes would provoke the greatest challenge to the Allied system of command and control throughout the war. In order to make reasoned decisions at the operational level of war, a commander needed to be reasonably close, with a sense of the terrain, a measure of his opponents – who in this case appeared infused with fresh spirit, numbers and equipment – and knowledge that his own forces and their commanders were able to undertake his wishes. Ike on 16 December possessed none of these.

Nor did he know very much about the situation. Perhaps Eisenhower inwardly regretted that Montgomery, that constant thorn in his side, was nevertheless the originator of some excellent military practices. One of these was the team of trusted liaison officers whom Monty despatched everywhere as his personal representatives, with secure links back to his HQ, to bridge exactly the kind of information void the Supreme Commander was now facing. Another Monty innovation was his specialist GHQ Signals Regiment (called 'Phantom'), staffed by bright, confident young officers like David Niven, among others, which also enabled direct communication with every headquarters. The first SHAEF had known of the German incursions was General Strong's mid-morning briefing. Even these sparse facts were at best fragmentary. On 16 December, Eisenhower was battling against an information blackout from his own side, never mind the Germans.

To add to this, Bradley and his subordinate, Hodges, as far as Eisenhower could see, were in denial. Bradley remained non-committal that first evening about the nature of the attack, despite the fact that by early afternoon the stand-in for First Army's G-2 (Colonel 'Monk' Dickson at this stage was actually nearer Eisenhower in Paris than Spa) had already received a captured copy of Rundstedt's Order of the Day. Jones's 106th Division had discovered the details of Operation *Greif*. Later that evening, Berlin Radio broadcast its news item about 'a present of Antwerp for the Führer', yet General Sibert, the G-2 chief in Bradley's HQ, seemed unable to accept he was witnessing a major offensive. Initially, Hodges refused even to contemplate calling off his Roer dams offensive. 'Monk' Dickson, meanwhile, had received word that very night from Sibert that something 'was up' and set off at dawn on the 17th to see him in Luxembourg.[10]

The three key players on Eisenhower's staff who would have a pivotal role in planning SHAEF's response to the Ardennes were its ubiquitous chief of staff, Walter Bedell Smith (known as 'Beetle' because of his nervous energy), and the British officers Kenneth Strong and Major-General J.F.M. 'Jock' Whiteley, its Deputy G-3. The latter had worked for Eisenhower since late 1942 at Allied Forces HQ in the Mediterranean and was one of the few British officers Ike positively insisted on taking with him to SHAEF in 1943. Although he was officially Deputy G-3, Whiteley's ability, trustworthiness and general likeability was such that 'the Beetle' also employed him as an unofficial deputy chief of staff. Whiteley was particularly valuable because of his close personal bond with Monty's chief of staff, the affable Major-General Francis 'Freddie' de Guingand, although the relationship between the two headquarters was tempestuous. Noel Annan, a British intelligence officer at SHAEF, noted how 'it became the mark of a good British SHAEF officer to express dismay at the behaviour of Montgomery. Had he not challenged Eisenhower's broad-front across France? Had he not then intrigued to be reinstated as Commander in Chief of land forces and usurp Eisenhower's position? Did he not treat Eisenhower with contempt, refusing to visit him at his headquarters?'[11] To prevail against this new threat, the Allies would need to put aside such personal differences – if they could.

That first evening, with maps spread out on the floor, Bedell Smith, Strong and Jock Whiteley reasoned the road network of the Ardennes led the eyes of even a casual observer straight to the two transportation hubs of St Vith and Bastogne. Control of both these towns would regulate the speed and extent of any German advance. Apparently using an ancient German sword (of all portentous items), tracing routes and pointing to towns, they went on to deduce correctly that the German attack was aimed at splitting the British and US army groups. It was equally clear to them that, to manage the German penetration, its flanks needed to be contained, preferably at the northern and southern shoulders; the corridor in between could then be controlled and eventually choked, like slowly sealing a breach in a dam. After Bedell Smith was assured that reinforcements could reach Bastogne in time by road, they recommended this course of action to Ike.

Thus, Eisenhower alerted his only strategic reserve available – the 17th, 82nd and 101st Airborne Divisions – for emergency deployment to the Ardennes. That was his function as the strategic commander. The 82nd and 101st were already in France and could move immediately; the 17th would have to fly from England when weather permitted. There are, however, certain rules in the management of a military command chain that make for smooth running; one of these is that the man at the top should never bypass several levels of command to issue direct orders to those at the bottom – principles that Montgomery and Patton often forgot, or ignored. In terms of operations, Eisenhower had no wish to bypass or overrule his friend Bradley in the latter's command of Twelfth US Army Group. Ike would advise, but not order.

While Ike had alerted his strategic reserves, with the 82nd Airborne eventually destined for Werbomont, on the northern flank, and the 101st for Bastogne, it was up to Bradley to deploy his operational reserves. Eisenhower felt he needed a nudge: 'I think you'd better send Middleton some help,' he advised. Fortunately, there were two newly arrived US armoured divisions, William H. Morris's Tenth, nicknamed 'the Tigers', with Patton's Third Army, and Robert W. Hasbrouck's 7th Armored in Simpson's Ninth Army sector, north of the Ardennes. Bradley was openly reluctant to order the effervescent Patton to surrender his newest armoured division which would, he knew, trigger howls of profane outrage and protest. 'Tell him that Ike is running this damn war,' Eisenhower told his friend.

Thus Patton was summoned to a secure telephone link in his 'Lucky Forward' headquarters at Nancy and ordered by Bradley's chief of staff, Major-General Leven C. Allen, to commit the 10th Armored straightaway, sending one of its Combat Commands immediately to join the 101st Airborne, also just directed to Bastogne. There was, as predicted, a heated debate. 'As the loss of this division would seriously affect the chances of my breaking through at Saarlautern, I protested strongly,' wrote Patton later, 'saying that we had paid a high price for that sector so far, and that to move the Tenth Armored to the north would be playing into the hands of the Germans.'

Bradley then had to make a personal telephone call after Allen to nudge Patton into compliance. 'General Bradley admitted my logic, but said that the situation was such that it could not be discussed over the telephone.' [12] The armoured division was to report to Troy Middleton at his VIII Corps headquarters in Bastogne, which both readily identified as a key intermediate objective for any force in transit through the Ardennes. Although from his command post at the Caserne Molifor Patton may have protested vigorously, he was also aware of the intelligence concerns of his own G-2, Colonel Oscar Koch, a man he trusted, and who had been part of his intimate command group since Tunisia, over eighteen months earlier. Koch had predicted a German attack, and there it was. Eventually, Patton fell into line because he saw the opportunities for an offensive, if different from the one he had planned.

The US Ninth Army commander, William Hood Simpson, was (in Bradley's words) 'big, bald and enthusiastic'. From his headquarters in Maastricht, code-named 'Conquer', he was altogether more gracious than Patton in surrendering his 7th Armored Division on 16 December and sending it to St Vith. This was the 'Workshop' formation that Middleton had told the beleaguered General Jones, of the Golden Lions, was on its way to help him. The professionalism of Simpson's Ninth Army was demonstrated by the speed with which the 7th Armored Division reacted to the order to move to St Vith. They were first warned on 16 December at 5.45 p.m. to move south as soon as possible, with an advance party leaving 105 minutes later: an impressive achievement even by the standards of today. Simpson was a West Point classmate of Patton's, and

'Big, bald and enthusiastic', General William H. Simpson confers with Churchill, Montgomery and Brooke, while surrounded by Allied war correspondents amidst the 'dragon's teeth' of the Siegfried Line. The likeable US Ninth Army commander sent his 7th Armored Division with alacrity to help Middleton's VIII Corps in the opening days, and worked well with Montgomery when placed under his command. (US National Archives)

regarded as extremely capable; his headquarters 'was in some respects superior to any in my command' thought Bradley, while possessing none of the defects of First Army's.[13] Eisenhower observed of his dependable and professional Ninth Army commander, 'If Simpson ever made a mistake as an Army commander, it never came to my attention. Alert, intelligent, and professionally capable, he was the type of leader that American soldiers deserve.'[14]

Simpson had served in France in 1918, latterly as a divisional chief of staff, and progressed through Leavenworth and War College to reach three-star rank by 1943. Simpson's own chief of staff was General James E. Moore and the two forged an unusually close relationship, where, in the words of Simpson's biographer, 'they understood, trusted and admired each other . . . Often while Simpson was in the field, Moore would issue orders in the Commander's name, then tell Simpson later. So closely did the two work together that in many instances it is impossible to sort out actions taken or ideas conceived.'[15] This in so many ways reflected the synergy needed for a successful campaign headquarters.

After D-Day, when Simpson sent his staff officers to study how First and Third Armies worked, the differences between the two were analysed thus: 'First Army, probably reflecting its Chief of Staff Kean's suspicion and resentment of outsiders, would allow only Simpson and his chief of staff to visit his headquarters and staff sections. On the other hand, Simpson's West Point classmate, Patton, allowed anyone from Simpson's staff to visit his army – all were welcome at Third Army headquarters.'[16] The amenable Simpson and his Ninth Army had also already served under Montgomery for a while, a development which Bradley felt would not have worked so well with Hodges, and certainly not Patton. As the winter set in, there are records that Simpson, with more foresight than his fellow army commanders, 'directed the initiation of a massive supply effort designed to issue winter clothing' to his troops. Eisenhower found an echo in Simpson, who was one of the most diplomatic of American commanders, having charmed Montgomery and hosted the important 7 December conference at his Maastricht headquarters.

Late on 16 December, as soon as Simpson's headquarters received the order to despatch the 7th Armored, its Combat Command 'B' under Brigadier-General Bruce C. Clarke went on ahead to liaise with Middleton in Bastogne, before moving on to St Vith, where Clarke arrived towards midday on 17 December. The rest of Clarke's formation battled against the flow of retreating traffic to arrive soon afterwards and deployed from their line of march straight into combat. Clarke's early arrival ensured that St Vith would be held until 23 December, and bought a valuable week for the Americans to stymie the Germans and reorganise themselves. In due course, Clarke would take over command of St Vith from the traumatised General Jones of the Golden Lions. While it may have been Clarke's personal drive that brought him to St Vith in time, it was Simpson's tutelage that prepared him for his starring role in the drama unfolding. From the beginning, it was Simpson, far more certainly than Bradley or Hodges, and less grudgingly than Patton, who identified the German attacks as a major offensive and offered what help he could, sending not only 7th Armored, but the 30th Infantry and 2nd Armored Divisions as well. Within ten days, Simpson's Ninth Army had committed seven of its divisions to battle in the Ardennes.

The way these decisions came about challenges the view that the Ardennes was all 'prearranged', from the American perspective; that Middleton's front was deliberately weak in order to lure the Germans out from the safety of their *Westwall* and attack with their remaining panzers; that two US armoured divisions had been stationed north and south for just such an eventuality; and that Eisenhower and Bradley were prepared to sacrifice the lives of tens of thousands of GIs to bring about an early end to the war. In *The Last Assault*, Charles Whiting had looked at the end result, then worked back to spin his speculative conspiracy. The circumstances of the two armoured divisions' arrivals in theatre, the timing of the German attack and Patton's protests serve to undermine his argument.

With the decisions to alert the airborne forces and move their armour finalised for the moment, there was little else the pair could do, so Eisenhower and Bradley returned to their five rubbers of bridge, accompanied by the Scotch whisky to celebrate Ike's promotion, an honour Bradley would one day receive himself.[17]

On the morning of 17 December, Eisenhower, in a demonstration of his true self-confidence, sent a letter to Marshall, his boss, shouldering the blame for the surprise, but concluding, 'If things go well, we should not only stop the thrust, but be able to profit from it'.[18] One might have thought Bradley sufficiently concerned to have raced back to his own headquarters in Luxembourg first thing on 17 December, as 'Monk' Dickson had done, but he lingered at the Trianon Palace, perhaps to get more of the picture. It was remarkably fortunate that Bradley was in

Paris with Eisenhower when the news first broke. Had the two commanders been in their own separate headquarters, Ike may well have deferred to Bradley's more sanguine views of the situation – being much closer to the Ardennes – and Hitler might have gained at least another day. Bradley, too, demonstrated that he needed a nudge from Ike to deploy the two armoured divisions, as well as some moral back-up from his boss to confront an angry George Patton, sore at having to surrender his 10th Armored Division.

Meanwhile, Eisenhower and his SHAEF staff, now energised by having a 'real' campaign to fight, rather than pursuing endless turf wars over logistics and civil affairs, developed a response to the Ardennes attack. In some ways, SHAEF could be its own worst enemy. Noel Annan, working on its intelligence staff, described the set-up:

> Supreme headquarters was gigantic. The forward echelon [at Versailles] to which I belonged was equivalent in numbers to a division; how large the rear echelon was I never discovered. Strong's [intelligence] staff alone numbered over a thousand men and women. It was not as if the vast staff helped Eisenhower to make strategic decisions: they had already been taken at meetings between Eisenhower, his army group commanders and General Patton . . . as a result the plans SHAEF produced were rarely clear or convincing, since they were a series of compromises; and the staff spent more of their time producing papers to justify these decisions to the Combined Chiefs of Staff than in producing the data on which plans could be made . . . intelligence at SHAEF had been governed by what one might call the 'Happy Hypothesis', that the German Army had now been so shattered in Normandy and battered in Russia that it was only a matter of two or three months before the war would end.[19]

Big modern military operations, such as those seen in Bosnia, Iraq and Afghanistan (in all of which I worked), are baffling assemblies of very senior staff officers of many nations writing reports and advancing national agendas; they can best be summed up by the term 'warehouse generalship', where colonels are more in abundance than corporals. Noel Annan's diaries prove that today's coalition headquarters are merely slimmed-down versions of SHAEF in 1944–5. The tens of thousands of personnel comprising SHAEF rear echelon had remained in London. SHAEF Forward (code-named 'Shellburst') moved twice in September

1944, first to Granville on the Cherbourg peninsula, thence to Paris. 'No one can compute the cost of that move in lost truck tonnage to the front,' Bradley lamented privately, at the height of the logistics squeeze.[20]

This shatterproof, semi-transparent balloon, of the sort in which modern politicians tend to live, is what Eisenhower had overcome with his clear thinking, unattended by distracting minions, on that December night with Bradley when the crisis was first apparent. Everyone realised that their most powerful weapon – the Allied air forces – would remain grounded for the foreseeable future as the bad weather made any aerial response impossible; they were going to have to learn how to craft a land campaign for the first time without the assumption of lavish aerial support. Initially their stratagem would be to contain the German counter-offensive east of the River Meuse, allowing the First and Third Armies breathing space to devise a coordinated plan to destroy it.

Having ordered the 82nd and 101st Airborne Divisions to the Ardennes by truck in great haste, Ike also called over the 17th Airborne Division from England, and summoned Major-General Matthew B. Ridgway's XVIII Airborne Corps headquarters to command the three divisions. Days earlier, Ridgway had accompanied senior commanders of the 101st (the 'Screaming Eagles', after their shoulder insignia) back to England to lecture on their experiences during Market Garden. He had already sent its commander, Major-General Maxwell D. Taylor, back to the US on 5 December for staff conferences in Washington, DC. Thus the commanding generals of both the XVIII Airborne Corps and 101st were out of country when the storm broke in the Ardennes. Major-General James M. Gavin and Brigadier-General Anthony C. McAuliffe, the latter normally in charge of 101st's artillery, were in temporary command of the corps and division, respectively. With so many of the senior leaders out of theatre, their airborne troopers reasoned, they were unlikely to be deployed in combat operations in the near future.

A West Pointer, class of 1917, Ridgway had taken over the 82nd Infantry Division from Omar Bradley in 1942 and converted it into an airborne force. In mid-training the 82nd lost a cadre, taken away to form the nascent 101st Airborne, and thereafter a fierce rivalry developed between the two divisions. At that time, Ridgway commanded the former, with Max Taylor leading the division's artillery and Gavin a regiment of its parachute infantry, and in due course they became arch-competitors. After Major-General Bill Lee, the 101st's commander, was incapacitated by a heart attack in 1943, Taylor left to lead it, and the rising star, Gavin, moved up to become Ridgway's number two and chief planner for airborne aspects of Normandy. Afterwards, when Ridgway rose to command the XVII Airborne Corps, Gavin replaced him as commander of the 82nd (known as the 'All American', as the original formation contained men from every state), mirroring Taylor's position at the 101st. Ridgway earned his spurs commanding a corps in Market Garden, and – reasoned Ike – a spare, battle-tested, higher-formation headquarters led by a reliable commander was always a handy asset to have in a fluid campaign.

Missouri-born Maxwell Taylor had graduated from West Point in 1922, and shot to notice in September 1943 when he operated, in uniform, behind enemy lines in Italy to coordinate the deployment of 82nd Airborne Division into Rome airport in conjunction with the Salerno landings. On realising the proximity of German forces he cancelled the mission on his own initiative, though the division was already airborne and en route. When Lee suffered his heart attack in late 1943, his two possible successors were Taylor or Gavin. On the grounds of his cool performance in Rome, as well as age and seniority (Taylor was forty-three, Gavin thirty-seven), Taylor took over the 101st which had been raised at Camp Claiborne, Louisiana, in August 1942, jumping with them into Normandy and Arnhem.

Taylor was, as noted above, in Washington, DC, when the Bulge erupted, and in great haste took a series of cargo planes from Washington to Paris, then flew to Luxembourg. War correspondent Walter Cronkite remembered sharing the farmhouse CP of Lieutenant-Colonel Creighton W. Abrams' 37th Tank Battalion on 27 December when in strode Taylor, 'still sporting the dress uniform he was wearing in Washington DC when word reached him that his men had been surrounded at Bastogne'.[21] He and Taylor were old friends, as the twenty-eight-year-old Cronkite, then star reporter for *United Press*, had landed in one of 101st's gliders during Market Garden. As he climbed into his jeep to run the gauntlet of German fire down the only road into the besieged town, Taylor had offered a lift to Cronkite, who refused, feeling sure the 101st's boss was on 'a certain suicide mission'. Taylor never forgave himself for missing the Ardennes fighting; Cronkite likewise for not taking up the general's offer of a brush with death – 'the story would have been great – first correspondent into Bastogne,' he mourned later.[22]

In December 1944, Jim Gavin was the US Army's most experienced airborne soldier and its youngest divisional commander. Illegitimate and adopted, he had joined the army underage, was largely self-educated, and fought hard to win a place at West Point, graduating in 1929. He worked his way up through sheer ability to command a regiment of the 82nd in Sicily, where he won a Distinguished Service Cross and promotion to brigadier-general. After Normandy he was the natural successor to command the 82nd when Ridgway was promoted to command the Airborne Corps. The rivalry between Taylor of the 101st and Gavin grew more intense as each rose to higher responsibilities, both vying to be 'Mister Airborne' in the public mind, with the youthful Gavin normally capturing – and conquering – an admiring female fan club.

After the liberation of Paris, Gavin had joined a distinguished table at the Ritz for lunch, where the other guests were Ernest Hemingway, *Collier's* war correspondent Martha Gellhorn (then Hemingway's wife), Hemingway's mistress Mary Welsh and Marlene Dietrich. Gavin's drive and youth were irresistible to Gellhorn, and the two swiftly embarked on an affair. Gellhorn would be reporting in Italy when the Bulge broke, but managed to reach Belgium to cover the closing stages in January. In the meantime, Gavin had become ensnared by the charms of the other unattached lunchtime guest, Marlene Dietrich, who was 'crazy about him' during her pre-Ardennes tour of France and Belgium. In between, he indulged with his pretty English WAC driver.[23]

Anthony C. McAuliffe, who would become the future 'star' of the Bulge, though he lacked some of Gavin's charm, had become assistant division commander of the 101st following the death of his predecessor on D-Day. He had just missed the First World War, graduating from West Point days after the Armistice in November 1918, then spending some of the inter-war period in the Supply Division of the US War Department overseeing the development of the 4 x 4 Willys Jeep and bazooka. He had already performed well during the thirty-three days of his division's deployment in Normandy, and another seventy-two days in Holland. Bastogne would later win him a division of his own.[24]

Eisenhower's instructions to move the two France-based airborne divisions translated into action immediately, recalled Eduardo A. Peniche, an anti-tank gunner with Company 'D' of the 502nd Parachute Infantry Regiment. In the early hours of 17 December, he remembered 'the US Army MPs out in force clearing bars, bistros and bordellos in the city of Reims in northern France . . . My buddies and I were among the first to heed the MP's orders. There was, of course, a lot of bitching and complaining, and some of the troopers, drunk or not, were using

McAuliffe's role in the Ardennes reflected the Allies' unpreparedness beforehand. With Matthew Ridgway, the XVIII Airborne Corps commander, away in England and the 101st's general, Max Taylor, in the United States, the youthful James M. Gavin was in temporary charge of the corps and Anthony C. McAuliffe (1898–1975), usually coordinating the 101st's artillery, was acting commander of the 'Screaming Eagles' Division. Taylor would not manage to return until 27 December, by which time McAuliffe had led his division to Bastogne, held the town, and rejected a German surrender summons with his famous reply. 'Nuts' McAuliffe was rewarded with his own division on 15 January 1945. (NARA)

profanity to express their dissatisfaction. And why not? We had just come to France for R & R barely two weeks before, after seventy-two days of continuous fighting in Holland, where we had participated in Operation Market-Garden.'[25] Peniche's division, the 101st, packed their gear through the 17th, and he 'went to the motor pool area to check our 1/4 ton prime-mover (jeep) and to the gun shed to clean and bore-sight our anti-tank gun, a 57 mm . . . This move to the front lines was going to be different from Normandy and Holland; in both of those operations we had landed behind enemy lines by parachute and glider, this forthcoming movement to Belgium was going to be by truck.'[26]

Packed and ready, at 5.00 p.m. on Monday, 18 December, Peniche's unit left by truck for Bastogne, 120 miles distant. 'We travelled all night with black-out lights. Sergeant Joe O'Toole and two others were travelling by jeep pulling the AT gun. The long convoy was moving rapidly, under the circumstances, yet we managed to get two or three pee calls; the night was pretty chilly and one could feel the cold air in those open trucks. Being packed like sardines helped a bit, but it was standing room only. As we approached the Bastogne area we were able to hear in the distance the sound of artillery, ours and theirs.' By early Tuesday morning, 19 December, they had arrived outside the village of Longchamps, three miles north of Bastogne.[27] Driver Bill Albright of the 146th QM Truck Company drove some of the Screaming Eagles from Soissons: 'I don't think those airborne boys really enjoyed their trip because they were standing up the whole time.'[28]

To move the airborne divisions into place and transport others, SHAEF was able to lean on the organisational framework created for the Red Ball Express, wound down only weeks earlier. Since the embarrassment of empty quartermasters' stores in the autumn, the Red Ball had worked hard to create a combat reserve in case of just such an emergency, running gasoline, ammunition, rations and clothing into depots at Liège, Charleroi and Verdun. The war had by now become one of trucks and fuel. The US First Army moved 48,000 vehicles into the battle zone between 17 and 26 December. At the same time, Patton at Third Army noted that, during the month-long battle, seventeen divisions were moved an average distance of 100 miles to various points in Luxembourg and Belgium.

The operation to move the entire 101st began as Peniche moved out, with 3,801 trucks being employed, the last airborne soldiers arriving by 8.00 p.m. on 19 December. Others in the 101st 'were loaded on to the cargo beds of "Jimmies" and onto semi-trailers with some standing the entire trip, and driven through the night into Bastogne'.[29] As a result of Eisenhower and Bradley's meeting, on 17 December alone, some 11,000 trucks were on the road moving 60,000 men plus their combat supplies into the Ardennes. Within a week, 250,000 Americans had been redirected into the threatened sector – this was a war of logistics that Hitler could not hope to win. It is the sheer quantity of military *matériel*, moved by the unseen logistical heroes, that makes victory in modern war possible.

John Axselle, also of the 146th QM Truck Company, recalled how tired the drivers were after delivering their cargoes of airborne personnel. 'The drivers were dead beat from hauling these guys in and they'd pull

Fifty years after it was fired, the author found this unexploded anti-tank shell in December 1994, in the vicinity of Buchholz station, along the route of Kampfgruppe Peiper. About eight inches long, in all probability it was fired on 17 December 1944 from an American 57mm anti-tank gun at oncoming German armour. A veteran anti-tank gunner told the author how these shot solid rounds tended to deflect if they failed to hit a panzer at or near an angle of 90 degrees to the armor plate. At Bastogne, paratrooper Ed Peniche of the 101st Airborne Division crewed a gun firing these shells. (Author's collection)

up on the side of the road to get a little sleep and an MP came along and butted a carbine on the cab door. "You'd better get this s**t wagon outa here. The Germans are coming", and they could hear the tanks, so they left.' John E. McAuliffe (no relation) remembered those long truck journeys, too. 'We stopped for nothing. Being on the tailgate, I was the one who emptied the urine from the steel helmets that were passed down. Along the way I saw many wrecked vehicles, disabled tanks and strewn equipment; the ravages of the initial German breakthrough. Houses were bombed out, gutted, the countryside was a very bleak sight, and covered by deep snow.'[30]

There were many divisions that had arrived in the ETO (European Theater of Operations) that autumn who would find themselves in the Ardennes. Amongst them was Brigadier-General Alexander R. Bolling's 84th Infantry (the 'Railsplitters'), who had begun arriving in France from 1 November. En route from Pier 58 in Manhattan, veterans remembered, they were given absentee ballots for the presidential election between Franklin Roosevelt and New York State governor Thomas E. Dewey.[31] With them, assigned to Company 'G' of the 335th Infantry Regiment, was Private Henry A. Kissinger. The onset of the Bulge would find him with the Divisional Intelligence squad, quartered in Marche (a few miles from Hotton), as a German-speaking translator-driver, and later he would move on to the Counter Intelligence Corps.[32]

Eisenhower knew he had the US 87th ('Golden Acorn') Infantry Division, who had arrived in Le Havre on 28 November, and the US 11th Armored had landed in France that very day; he was also aware that Lieutenant-General Sir Brian Horrocks' XXX Corps were out of the line, and available for deployment. Also loitering in England was the third US airborne division, Major-General William M. 'Bud' Miley's 17th; during Operation Market Garden they had been in training, but Eisenhower, assured they were ready, had ordered them forward on 16 December too. Delayed by poor flying weather, they arrived only between 23 and 25 December and were then trucked hastily into Belgium, where they were attached to Patton's Third Army and deployed along the Meuse. Other formations training in England had their instructional periods cut short and were hurriedly sent to build up a continental combat reserve for instant deployment.

Among these was Major-General Herman F. Kramer's 66th Infantry Division, 'the Black Panthers', newly arrived in England. On 26 November their 262nd and 264th Regiments were herded on to an 11,700-ton old Belgian Congo liner, SS *Leopoldville*, for the short trip across the Channel. She had nosed her way across the waters and was within sight of Cherbourg on 24 December when she was struck by a torpedo fired from *U-486*. The liner took three hours to sink, but a series of confusing signals misled shore agencies as to the gravity of the situation. The result was that more than 750 American servicemen drowned or died from hypothermia out of 2,235 GIs who had set sail. A completely avoidable tragedy, on a par with the *Titanic*, the episode was excised from official records until the details were uncovered in 1996 by Clive Cussler, best-selling author of *Raise the Titanic!*

The *Leopoldville* tragedy was a symptom of the extreme concern the Ardennes offensive had created at SHAEF, though, once he was back at Twelfth Army Group headquarters in Luxembourg, Bradley seemed still under Noel Annan's 'Happy Hypothesis'; when he studied his maps, he exclaimed as much to Sibert as to anyone, 'Pardon my French . . . but where in hell has this son of a bitch gotten all his strength?'

23

The Tortoise Has Thrust His Head Out Very Far

At this juncture we shall jump ahead to the second major crisis conference of the campaign – that of 19 December – so closely connected as it was with the first held between Bradley and Eisenhower in Versailles.

On 18 December, Bradley had summoned Patton to his own headquarters – although the front was only twenty-five miles away north-east, Bradley felt it important to stay put, demonstrating confidence not only to his own troops, but to the people of Luxembourg. Patton was shown the extent of the German penetrations, which were far greater than he had realised. He had been forewarned by his G-2 Colonel Oscar Koch, that the forthcoming Saar offensive would almost certainly be postponed and Third Army required to counter-attack the panzers in the Ardennes. When Bradley asked what Third Army could do, Patton was thus able to reply if necessary he could have two divisions (4th Armoured and 80th Infantry) on the move the next day, and a third (the 26th), 'although it had 4,000 green replacements from Headquarters units' within twenty-four hours.[1]

Later, at 11.00 p.m. on the evening of the 18th, Eisenhower instructed all his key subordinates to meet at Verdun on 19 December to coordinate their next operational moves. Bradley was already aware of the forthcoming assembly at Verdun when he ordered Patton to join him in Luxembourg. He may have realised by then that First Army was in difficulty and possibly primed Patton to put on a 'star' performance.

The following morning, Eisenhower and Colonel James F. Gaunt (his British Military Assistant), his deputy Tedder; Strong and Bull, his chiefs of G-2 and G-3; Bradley; Devers; and Patton, and 'a large number of staff officers' all travelling separately, converged on a 'cold, dreary barracks' in Verdun, the old Roman fortress town.[2] Bedell Smith, with flu, stayed behind at Versailles to hold the fort, and Hodges, whose First Army was fighting for its life, had just moved to Chaudfontaine – ironically, his old headquarters in Spa was the very same building from which Generals Hindenburg and Ludendorff had directed the Imperial German armies more twenty-five years earlier. Hodges was also incapacitated with flu, his chief of staff, Bill Kean, running the show in his stead, but their absence mattered less because the meeting was called to find overall ways of countering the threat. Containing it was First Army's task.[3]

Late on 16 December, First Army had alerted J. Lawton Collins of VII Corps to release his US 1st Infantry Division from the vicinity of Aachen, and two combat commands of the 3rd and 9th Armored Divisions, to assist in the Ardennes, but Hodges' initial response was lacklustre, with none of Patton's fire and aggression. The slow response was partly because the German opening artillery bombardment had knocked out most telephone lines to forward units (as it was designed to do), and reports from some sectors were initially tardy. It was also because Hodges misunderstood the situation; he simply did not believe the German attacks represented a major threat.

Throughout 16 December, First Army had persisted in continuing the Roer dams attack, although the formation responsible, 'Gee' Gerow's V Corps, was itself under attack elsewhere from the Sixth Panzer Army. Hodges' initial assessment, like Bradley's, was that *Herbstnebel* was a local spoiling attack designed to disrupt the attack on the dams – which he formally cancelled only at 07.00 am on the 17th, far later than was wise. In the absence of positive direction from his army commander, it was the V Corps commander, Gerow, who actually ordered US 2nd Division to cease their attack, and sent Colonel Lovless's 23rd Infantry Regiment (containing Captain Charles MacDonald) to assist the beleaguered 99th Division in the woods forward of Krinkelt on the Elsenborn Ridge. Similarly it was Gerow who directed his V Corps artillery assets towards Elsenborn, which ultimately held off the Germans.

Though his First Army headquarters War Diary has recently been published, Courtney Hicks Hodges remains the most enigmatic of the senior US commanders, and open to much retrospective criticism.[4] We have seen how his First Army headquarters was dysfunctional, with strong personalities, including 'Monk' Dickson, whom he failed to keep in check. To what extent the fifty-seven-year-old Georgian commanding general was physically under the weather on 16–18 December, or whether there was an additional element of psychological shock – 'this can't be happening' – which generated denial and inability to decide on rational courses of action, remains to be seen. He certainly retained an inferiority complex from years before, as a result of having to leave West Point after a year because of poor grades, which led to his joining the army as an enlisted man. Post-war historians were generally kind to Hodges for in the following months his First Army recovered their stride extremely well as they lanced into Germany. After the war, General Hasbrouck, of the 7th Armored Division, thought that 'Hodges was a poor excuse for an Army Commander. He was too old and too frail' – though it is worth remembering in this context that the fire-breathing Patton was two years older than Hodges. [5]

Nevertheless, some within his HQ had noted that over 16–18 December Hodges was 'sitting with his arms folded on his desk, his head in his arms'. This is not to say that he became a Paulus figure in Stalingrad, indifferent to the suffering of his men – more than any officer in the First Army Hodges understood the agony of front-line combat, having served as a battalion commander and winning a Distinguished Service Cross in the Meuse–Argonne in the First World War. Still, it was the domineering Major-General 'Bill' Kean, regarded as 'resolute and steady', who 'badgered the staff in Hodges' name', who kept First Army's headquarters functioning under the most trying of circumstances for the first couple of days.[6]

The Hodges leadership dilemma was compounded by the fact that on 18 December First Army headquarters removed itself in haste from the Hôtel Britannique in Spa to the Hôtel des Bains in Chaudfontaine, near Liège. The use of hotels, we might observe, was not pandering to luxury, but a reflection of the number of rooms they would have available to house all the staff sections of a big headquarters, and their staff. The day before, Colonel Dickson, returning from Paris via Sibert's G-2 Intelligence cell in Luxembourg, had driven across the Ardennes, witnessing the upheavals of troops, checkpoints at every junction, nervous military policemen, jittery refugees, wild rumours, defensive measures being made, and gasoline dumps being moved. On his arrival at First Army's Forward HQ in Spa, he recommended to Hodges that a move rearwards might be wise. During the morning of 18 December, when in conference with J. Lawton Collins of VII Corps, a report came through that 'German tanks were a couple of miles down the road'. Though false, Hodges's HQ reacted with alacrity and had started to vanish within the hour.

Major Tom Bigland, Monty's chief liaison officer at Bradley's Luxembourg headquarters, remembered 'early on the nineteenth we set off for First Army HQ. We found no Army MPs in Spa and walked into the HQ to find literally not one single person there except a German woman. Breakfast was laid and the Christmas tree decorated in the dining room, telephones were in all the offices, papers were all over the place, but there was no one left to tell visitors where they had gone to. Germans [friendly civilians] in the town said they had gone suddenly at 03.00 a.m.'[7] However conducted, there had been an air of panic about the removal, which failed to impress visitors to the now-empty building, including 7th Armored Division officers on their way to St Vith, and Montgomery's liaison officers. Apparently, sensitive papers, maps showing dispositions, the working telephone exchange and even unopened Christmas presents had been abandoned. Rumours soon circulated around Twenty-First Army Group that a state of paralysis existed in the American First Army's headquarters, which soon reached the ears of Jock Whiteley, the Deputy G-3 at SHAEF.[8]

The 19 December meeting at Verdun thus came hard on the heels of these First Army dramas, and reminded those present how easy it was to be overwhelmed by panic. The commanders striding in to Ike's crisis meeting were just the latest in a long list of generals whose footsteps had echoed off Verdun's walls. The modern battlements had been built by the finest military engineer of his time, Vauban, whose castle remains to this day the badge of the US Corps of Engineers. More ominously, within earshot and in the lifetimes of all those present, the bloody battle for Verdun had been fought, with its staggeringly awful death toll – some 300,000 in all – just twenty-eight years earlier. De Guingand represented Montgomery; those who wanted to saw the British field marshal's absence as spite; others felt it a diplomatic attempt to avoid being sucked into what was primarily an American affair. Before departing from Nancy, Patton had alerted his staff and two of his corps commanders that Third Army would be called on to come to the relief of First Army; where and when would be decided at Verdun.

By this time, Berlin's boasting about the Ardennes offensive had permeated around the world. On Monday, 18 December, General Sir Alan Brooke, Britain's Chief of the Imperial General Staff (CIGS), recorded in his private diary, 'Germans are delivering strong counter offensive against Americans, who have no immediate reserves to stem the attack with. They ought ultimately to hold it all right, and to have an opportunity of delivering serious counter blow which might well finish off Germans.' Surprisingly, Brooke then went on to demonstrate that he shared the somewhat unbalanced views of Montgomery about the US Army's professional skills. 'But I am not sure whether they have the skill required. I doubt it. It is a worrying situation, if I felt that the American divisional, corps, army commanders and staff were more efficient than they are, there is no doubt that this might turn out to be a heaven sent opportunity. However, if mishandled it may well put the defeat of Germany back for another six months.'[9]

Brooke, like the rest of the Allied world, was still nursing the illusion that this was Rundstedt's attack, and not Hitler's, for he continued, 'Perhaps as a "good German" he [Rundstedt] considers that there may be a definite advantage in bringing this war to an early conclusion, and consequently accepts all risks, great as they are, willingly?'[10] This was a worrying admission, that Britain's senior serviceman and Churchill's top military adviser had not the faintest idea of the nature of Hitler's dictatorship, that none of Germany's generals had ever possessed the freedom to act, as Brooke assumed Rundstedt was doing in December 1944.

This was a huge news story that echoed around the world; on 19 December, the banner headlines of the *Brisbane Courier-Mail* announced 'Hun Counter Makes Gains. Tanks and Infantry Behind American Lines. Paratroops Too'.[11] The same day, United Press war correspondent Jack Frankish, with the US First army, whose wires were picked up by many newspapers around the world, observed with much foresight, 'one immediate tactical aim of the Nazis was believed to be the capture of large American supply dumps to replenish their own thin reserves, particularly gasoline'.[12] 'Germans Sweep West Through Luxembourg', reported the *New York Times*; 'US Reveals Big Nazi Gains', said the *Detroit Free Press.* That all these organs of news could report a severe setback in the midst of the war underlined that the Allied coalition (which then referred to itself as 'The United Nations' on propaganda posters) was a collection of democracies battling against a repressive dictatorship. The well-connected British Member of Parliament Harold Nicolson confided in his diary on the same day, 'Rundstedt has staged a startling offensive in the Malmedy sector. It seems it started three days ago and that he has penetrated our lines by as much as twenty miles. The optimists say that this is the last suicide fling; the pessimists say that there is nothing to stop him getting to Paris or at least to Liège. But what most people seem to think is that it has the comparatively limited objective of forcing us to leave the sacred soil of the Fatherland. It may be that they will succeed, and then we shall have a peace-offer.'[13]

On the same day, *The Times* reported soberly from London, 'Nazi Push Seen as Greatest Gamble of War'. Its editorial intoned,

> The German army appeared today to have taken its greatest gamble of the war, staking everything on a single desperate offensive to halt the allied march on Berlin now. Decisive failure in this big push, observers believed, might lead to a German military collapse and the final defeat of the Wehrmacht west of the Rhine. The full scope and purpose of the enemy's winter offensive is still obscured by military censorship on both sides of the front, but field dispatches hinted strongly that the battle now swirling along the Belgian border may prove to be the last great action of the western war . . . All accounts indicated the Nazis have finally committed the cream of their armored reserves to this offensive, and the German home radio service boasted that the long-silent Adolf Hitler personally planned and ordered the attack.[14]

Ironically this last sentence in an open-source newspaper report was more accurate than Brooke's assessment that this was Rundstedt's attack. By 19 December, Brooke's views about the US Army were still harsh, but he seemed to trust Ike's judgement, writing, 'Very little more news of the war in France, Eisenhower seems quite confident and so do his staff, that they can deal with this situation. I only hope that this confidence is not based on ignorance!'[15] It seems there was an enormous gulf between his grudging acknowledgement of the US Army and its undoubted professionalism in the field. Given that Montgomery was Brooke's protégé, it is obvious whence Monty's own highly developed prejudices sprang.

Churchill, though, had every confidence, writing to Roosevelt, 'His Majesty's Government have complete confidence in General Eisenhower and feel acutely any attacks made on him', and went on to outline measures 'to bring another 250,000 [personnel] into or nearer the front line'. Churchill released the contents of the letter to the media and phoned Eisenhower beforehand to alert him to this public display of prime ministerial support. Ike's aide, Butcher, wrote that 'General Ike appreciated the gravity of the difficult decision the Prime Minister had made, and spoke of his gratitude for this additional evidence of the unshakeable resolution of the Prime Minister'. Churchill's remarks about confidence in Ike were designed to offset any derogatory comments Monty was in the habit of making.[16]

Similarly, Harold Nicolson wrote to friends from his medieval castle at Sissinghurst, in Kent, on 19 December, 'People are pretty glum about the Rundstedt offensive. "Is it serious?" I whispered to Anthony Eden [the British Foreign Secretary, during a House of Commons debate]. "Yes," he answered, "it's bad, very bad indeed" . . . It has created a gloom such as I have not seen for months.' Whereupon, in that baffling manner that gentle aristocrats possess, Nicolson concluded, 'And as we are such a sporting folk, it has also aroused some admiration for von Rundstedt's skill and enterprise.'[17] By contrast, Nicolson's Prime Minister, Churchill, was ever inclined to look for the silver lining, and wrote to his friend, Field Marshal Smuts, 'As usual I am optimistic: the tortoise has thrust his head out very far.'[18]

At this time, the British Embassy in Washington, DC, sent London the American view of *Herbstnebel*, as seen through British eyes. 'The reverses on the Western Front have had a profoundly sobering effect on American public opinion . . . Coming when it did, Rundstedt's breakthrough . . . had a steadying effect in forcing the average American to hesitate, if only for a moment, about the invincible might of his country, to reflect upon the still formidable dangers threatening him from east and west, and consequently upon the necessity for firmer understanding with, at any rate, his major Allies.'[19]

Thus, when Ike and his senior commanders assembled for their 19 December meeting, the spotlight of the free world's politicians and media was already focused on the early German successes, adding to the pressure on them. Of course the outside world had no knowledge of the gathering in the cold and dismal French barracks at Verdun, but when Eisenhower arrived at 11.00 a.m., he was determined to lighten the mood. 'The present situation is to be regarded as one of opportunity for us and not of disaster. There will be only cheerful faces at this conference table,' he beamed, mirroring the self-assurance of his earlier letter to Marshall. Eisenhower had overseen similar tense meetings, most notably in southern England before Overlord, at Southwick House outside Portsmouth, when he was forced to postpone D-Day by twenty-four hours. This meeting would be as crucial, he knew, although history would judge that he had already initiated the corrective steps necessary on 16 December. Yet, there was no denying Eisenhower was tense; his 200-mile journey from Paris in appalling weather, surrounded by a cohort of protective armoured vehicles, cannot have helped.

Patton immediately responded to Ike's opener: 'Hell, let's have the guts to let the sons of bitches go all the way to Paris. Then we'll really cut 'em up and chew 'em up.' The room apparently erupted in laughter, some of it forced, but not all, and the ice had been broken. Eisenhower replied, 'George, that's fine. But the enemy must never be allowed to cross the Meuse.' Those present agreed that all Allied offensive activity elsewhere must cease while the Ardennes threat was addressed. Eisenhower's strategy had already been worked out, as we have seen: use the Meuse as a stop line to contain the German assault, then throttle it. Devers' Sixth Army Group would move north to take over much of Third Army's sector, allowing Patton to counter-attack.

In order to do so, part of Third Army would have to reorientate its axis from facing east, to north. Such a manoeuvre would require his forces to be relieved in place, disengage, then pivot 90 degrees in mid-winter, with all their vehicles, equipment and logistics, and move over icy roads to concentrate at Arlon in less than seventy-two hours. Normally such an undertaking would require weeks of staff work, but Patton had in fact devised *three* alternative plans beforehand, each allocated a code word, and designed to meet any need he could foresee of Eisenhower's. This much Patton had anticipated; he didn't know exactly what Ike would request, but had put himself in a position to be able to agree immediately, simply by issuing the appropriate code word to his headquarters by phone.

Patton, with false modesty, wrote later, 'When it is considered that I left for Verdun at 09.15 a.m., and that between 08.00 a.m. and that hour we had had a staff meeting, planned three possible lines of attack, and made a simple code in which I could telephone which we were to use, it is evident that war is not so difficult as people think.'[20] It still required an outrageously confident commander with complete assurance of the professional skill of his subordinates even to contemplate the execution of such a breathtaking manoeuvre; there was little doubt that George Patton was the only one in the Allied camp capable of rising to the challenge. There is probably no military commander in the world today who would embrace such a course of action at such short notice.

'I felt as if I were walking with destiny, and that all my past life had been but a preparation for this hour and for this trial,' wrote Churchill of the moment he took over as Prime Minister on 10 May 1940. 'I thought I knew a good deal about it all, I was sure I should not fail.'[21] In the same way that history has judged Ike's supreme military achievement as coming on the night of 16 December, Patton's came at this conference. 'This was the sublime moment of his career,' according to Martin Blumenson, Patton's biographer and the distinguished author of seventeen works on the Second World War in North Africa and Europe. Patton, with his deep sense of military history and destiny, would certainly have felt that all his years of study and war-making were in preparation for this moment, a 'single, defining instant in which the fate of the war rested on the right decisions being made and carried out by the men in that dingy room,' thought Carlo D'Este, another biographer.

Constantly referring to the various maps propped on easels around the room, Eisenhower then addressed Patton: 'George, I want you to make a strong counterattack with at least six divisions. When can you start?' Patton, backed by the superb staff at his headquarters and the foresight of Koch, was ready to play his aces. 'As soon as you're through with me,' the Third Army commander replied. 'When can you attack?' Eisenhower persisted. 'The morning of 21 December, with three divisions.' In other words, in forty-eight hours: Patton had thrown down the gauntlet. 'It created a ripple of excitement. Some people thought I was boasting and others seemed to be pleased,' he observed.[22] A few were shaking heads and muttering at Patton's misplaced humour. The British contingent laughed, misunderstanding his seriousness.

Patton's aide, Lieutenant-Colonel Charles R. Codman, witnessed 'a stir, a shuffling of feet, as those present straightened up in their chairs'. 'Don't be fatuous, George,' Ike responded with obvious irritation. 'If you try to go that early, you won't have all three divisions ready and you'll go piecemeal. You will start on the twenty-second, and I want your initial blow to be a strong one! I'd even settle for the twenty-third if it takes that long to get three full divisions.' Waving his trademark cigar, Patton took the floor, illustrating his intentions on Eisenhower's maps. Two of his three corps would be employed for the counter-attack, with Patch's Seventh Army taking over most of Third Army's sector in the Saar – ironically the very region from which Hans Nikolaus Eisenhauer had emigrated to America, exactly 200 years before. Patton pointed to the German incursion and looked at the Twelfth Army Group commander, 'Brad, the Kraut's stuck his head in a meat-grinder . . . and this time I've got hold of the handle,' he boasted, all the while turning his fist in a grinding motion.

More ripples of appreciative laughter. Eisenhower and Bradley cannot have anticipated this turn of events, but Patton now held centre-stage and, what was more, had definitely eased the tension. Ike was acting more as a chairman, encouraging his Third Army commander – he had, after all, long been his protector. What is interesting about this meeting, which involved far more than these famous exchanges, was that Bradley, whose army group had been attacked, said very little, mostly observing. It would, perhaps, have been impossible for anyone to upstage Patton at this moment, but there may also have been a sense of guilt. Bradley's gamble of keeping the Ardennes weak, his defence to Eisenhower of that policy on 7 December after the Maastricht meeting with Montgomery; his further defence of his G-2 on 14 December, and his disregard of the evidence of a German build-up had critically endangered the Allied advance. He, more than anyone else, had looked in the mirror for Hitler's intentions, and seen only a reflection of his own. His own reputation was now on the line, the Twelfth Army Group commander knew.

It was in this light that Bradley acknowledged Third Army's performance denoted 'a greatly matured Patton . . . the Third Army staff had pulled off a brilliant effort'. In acknowledging the staff work behind Patton's performance, Bradley was perhaps hinting he had prepared the way with his 18 December briefing to the Third Army's commander. More telling was the interchange between Eisenhower and Patton as the meeting broke up. 'Funny thing, George,' the Supreme Commander observed, 'every time I get a new star I get attacked.' Ike was referring to the Afrika Korps attack on the Kasserine Pass, which had coincided with Eisenhower's last promotion. 'And every time you get attacked, Ike, I pull you out,' the quick-witted Third Army commander responded, at the top of his game, referring to his own successful defence in Tunisia just after Kasserine.

'Larger than life' is a sobriquet applied to several military figures, but, in the case of General George Smith Patton, Jr, the title was just. He came to the fore remarkably quickly in the Second World War, having become a household name only from 1943, much later than Montgomery or Rommel, and yet was better-known than either Eisenhower or Bradley. That the Patton legend has lingered is due in part to his early and unlikely death – not as he would have wished, clipped by a shell in the turret of his tank, but in a road traffic accident, just months after the war's end in 1945. Few great captains (neither Napoleon or Wellington, for example) in history have justified a film of their life, but Francis Ford Coppola's 1970 screenplay for *Patton* only added to the mystique; ironically the film's technical adviser was Patton's boss, and often his bitterest critic, Bradley.

George S. Patton (1885–1945) as he saw himself. Patton had joined the US cavalry from West Point in 1909 in the days when horses still dominated the battlefield. At heart a romantic and from childhood obsessed with war, he felt his entire career was spent in preparation for a fleeting opportunity to become one of the great captains of history. His military life witnessed the last of the boots-and-saddles era and the ushering in of the atomic age. Despite his affinity for the past, Patton embraced modern technology with outstanding rapidity and proficiency, becoming one of the supreme exponents of armoured warfare. (NARA)

As Carlo D'Este observed, 'Patton represented the individuality and passion for life of a man who was so thoroughly a product of America'. Only the United States could have produced a commander with his flamboyance, love of publicity, impeccable turnout, ostentatious accessories – the burnished helmet, jodhpurs, polished riding boots, whip and ivory-handled revolvers – as well as his flagrant insubordination, which is what Bradley feared on 16 December. Patton suffered from dyslexia, but wrote as he spoke, as he commanded – full of fire and exuding confidence ('he was grotesquely confident', according to one historian), which he inherited from a long line of soldiers. Schooling at the Virginia Military Institute (VMI) and West Point (class of 1909) provided the discipline, which he likewise, and ruthlessly, expected from all his subordinates, and his entry into the cavalry added the flair. He was a superb horseman and competed in the Modern Pentathlon at the 1912 Olympics – a sporting feat he could share with the German Fifth Army's commander, Manteuffel. Luck is also a vital ingredient of successful commanders, one that is often overlooked, and Patton was born at the right time to serve in both world wars.

From childhood his absorbing interest was military history, which equipped him with an extra ace for high command. He saw himself as an authentic military genius whose entire life was spent in preparation for a fleeting opportunity to become one of the great captains of history. Promoted to captain, Patton joined Pershing's American Expeditionary Force (AEF), seeing action in the Meuse–Argonne offensive of September–November 1918, and returning in 1919 as Colonel Patton with a Distinguished Service Cross. Reverting to his peacetime rank of captain, he would not regain his colonelcy until 1938. By the time America joined the war in 1941, Patton had more experience of handling armour than any other US soldier, taking the 2nd Armored Division to North Africa. He was happiest at the operational level; one criticism that can certainly be made of him was that he had little understanding of politics or strategy.

Few would disagree that he was unquestionably the outstanding exponent of armoured warfare produced by the Allies; Montgomery, for example, knew surprisingly little about the interior of a tank. Although Tunisia gave Patton little chance to demonstrate his flair, he was promoted to command II Corps on Bradley's recommendation, then lieutenant-general to lead the US Seventh Army in Sicily. There, the speed of his advance surprised his own colleagues (especially the British) as well as the Germans. His capture of Palermo justified Eisenhower's faith in him, but his arrival in Messina prior to Montgomery did nothing to improve relations between these two prima donnas. At this juncture, he slapped the face of two shell-shocked soldiers resting in field hospitals, accusing them of cowardice. An army surgeon complained and the newspapers got hold of the story. As a result, Marshall nearly sent him home, as many would have desired, but Eisenhower intervened and Patton moved from Seventh to Third Army, in England.

That his former subordinate Bradley, and not Patton, commanded the US First Army on D-Day was 'punishment' for the slapping incident. Yet, Dwight David Eisenhower (whom Patton referred to in private as 'Divine Destiny', after his initials) protected him because of his spectacular battlefield victories. Patton's vital contribution to Operation Overlord's success was to head up FUSAG, the fictional First US Army Group, supposedly planning an invasion from Dover. Though Patton found the role acutely frustrating, the Germans paid him the compliment of refusing to believe the Allies would land without Patton, and he cooled his heels in England until 1 August 1944, when his Third Army was activated.

Again, Patton's characteristic disregard for orders, demonstrated in Sicily, impounding of supplies (particularly fuel) destined for neighbouring friendly formations, and lack of protection for his flanks paid off. He made essentially the same reckless advances that Rommel had conducted four years earlier, in the opposite direction, with the same results, and there are many similarities between the two. A less confident commander might have paused, and the war could have lasted longer. Patton was willing to gamble his reputation on reckless tactical moves in a way many admired but few dared imitate, 'a soldier's soldier' according to one historian, 'fiery, romantic, unique'. The nineteenth of December 1944 surely belonged to George S. Patton, Jr

It was at this juncture that the British general Jock Whiteley returned to Paris on the night of 19 December, full of concern about First Army. The main German effort seemed to him to be aimed at Namur, with rumours of paratroops around Malmedy and Spa. Hodges' First Army by all accounts seemed to be struggling, and Bradley's HQ was much too far south, in Luxembourg. Whiteley became convinced privately that someone other than Hodges needed to be given temporary control of the northern sector of the German-held salient while First Army sorted themselves out. That could only mean Montgomery. The attraction for

Whiteley was probably less Montgomery *per se* (he was never a fan), than his seasoned staff and their seemingly crisis-proof HQ. He also sensed urgency, for at this stage the panzers were still rampant all over the Ardennes.[23] Whiteley called de Guingand to feel his way. 'If Ike asked Monty to take over First Army, how soon could you do it?' 'Tomorrow morning' came the reassuring response. Whiteley made it clear that this was purely a speculative enquiry and nothing had yet been decided, although he didn't go so far as to admit this was a private idea of his own that had no official backing whatsoever.

Whiteley found an ally in his fellow Briton, Kenneth Strong, whose own view was that the Allies were failing to match up to the situation, and that Bradley underestimated the crisis at Hodges' headquarters, now reunited with its rear echelon at Chaudfontaine. At about midnight, the SHAEF chief of staff in Paris, Bedell Smith, was woken by the two British major-generals who explained their concerns to him. Ailing with flu, in a cot placed next to his office, and his slumber interrupted, Bedell Smith, sensing a British plot, let rip at the pair, suggesting their behaviour was unacceptable. He was of the opinion that whenever there was any real trouble, the British had no faith in the Americans to handle it. Ironically, neither Strong nor Whiteley were pro-Montgomery, being two of SHAEF's most loyal and senior staff officers, but Bedell Smith in his temper fired them on the spot, labelling them 'sons of bitches' and 'limey bastards'. Even since Normandy, there had been sniping between the two nations within SHAEF as to the operational management of the war, despite Eisenhower's efforts, as the arch-conciliator, to outlaw such behaviour. Coalition warfare to him was a religion.

Bedell Smith couldn't get back to sleep. The more he brooded, the more he saw sense in what they had said, even if they were 'limey bastards'. Realising the unpopularity of such a move, and how it would play out back in the United States, Bedell Smith could also see that militarily it made sense, though it was not a solution he would have immediately worked out himself. Furthermore, he realised Whiteley and Strong had been right to come to him, because such a suggestion – appointing Montgomery – could only come from an American. Bedell Smith then consulted Bradley, knowing it would be a difficult matter to broach. In suggesting that his arch-rival Montgomery, and a Brit to boot, should control half of what had been his battlespace could be interpreted as a harsh judgement on his own generalship. Yet, as Bedell

Smith had come to realise, in the gravity of the situation it was a sensible solution.

At this stage, Eisenhower was not in the loop. The Bedell Smith–Bradley conversation was certainly difficult and both sides had different recollections of it, though in Bradley's later memoir, *A General's Life*, he regretted not standing up to Bedell Smith, observing, 'I made one of my biggest mistakes of the war' in agreeing to the proposal. He went on, 'instead of standing up to Smith, telling him that SHAEF was losing its head, that I had things under control, and reassuring him that Hodges was performing magnificently under the circumstances', Bradley caved in and accepted that it might become necessary for Monty to temporarily command the northern portion of the battlefield. Bradley could have done two things to ameliorate the situation: he could have gone to visit Hodges and assess his subordinate himself; and he should in any case have moved his HQ away from Luxembourg to a site where he could have commanded the entire Bulge. Instead, he elected to do neither, and history has not judged Bradley kindly in this regard.

The following morning Bedell Smith rehabilitated Whiteley and Strong straightaway, telling them that, after his morning conference of 20 December, he would present their proposal to Ike, but as his own, and framed as an American idea. What had finally brought Bedell Smith around was his discovery that Bradley's HQ in Luxembourg had been out of communication with Hodges' headquarters for more than forty-eight hours; admittedly this was during the latter's move, but to lose contact with a major headquarters for even an hour under any circumstances was, and remains, a major sin. It was an indicator that neither Bradley nor Hodges had the situation under control. In this light, it was easy for Eisenhower to accept Bedell Smith's recommendation to divide the Ardennes front into two as a temporary expedient. Montgomery would be given operational command of all Allied forces (the US First and Ninth Armies) in the northern half of the Bulge. Bradley retained control of its southern flank – essentially Patton's Third Army).

Ike then phoned his new orders through to Bradley in person. They were not well received. This was where their friendship, so strong on the evening of 16 December, began to unravel. Bradley protested loudly, attempting to play the national red card: 'By God, Ike, I cannot be responsible to the American people if you do this. I resign.' But

Ike, too, was an American as well as Bradley's superior, noting that as Supreme Commander it was he who was responsible: 'Your resignation therefore means absolutely nothing.' This carried on until Eisenhower ended the debate with 'Well, Brad, those are my orders'. Ever after, Bradley blamed Monty for this 'plot' against him, whereas in reality, as we have seen, there was none, and he would never acknowledge that SHAEF had some justice behind their action. In this sense, the Twelfth Army Group commander had been his own worst enemy.

By 20 December, Brooke, the CIGS in London, understood the situation in the Ardennes was more alarming than he had at first realised; this came via an exuberant communication from Twenty-First Army Group headquarters in the following terms: 'telegram from Monty which showed clearly that the situation in France was serious. American front penetrated, Germans advancing on Namur with little in front of them, north flank of First American Army in state of flux and disorganisation, etc. Also suggesting he should be given command of all forces north of the penetration [this was after the Whiteley–Strong intervention] . . . Got Winston to put the proposal to Ike . . . Ike agreed and had apparently already issued orders to that effect.'[24]

Under Monty were two American armies, Hodges' First and Simpson's Ninth. When Monty first visited First Army's HQ, now in the safety of Chaudfontaine, Hodges made such a poor impression on the field marshal that Monty lobbied Eisenhower for him to be relieved of command. It was not his call to make, of course, but Hodges knew he would have to improve his game radically, for – coalition stresses or not – there were no second chances in war. Bradley seems to have been overprotective of First Army's commander, perhaps for no other reason than Hodges was his successor when he rose to lead the Army Group. By contrast, we have already met the wholly professional attitude of General William H. Simpson and his Ninth Army during the battle. Fully aware of the tensions of coalition unity at such a moment of crisis in the Allied command chain, Simpson at Maastricht did much to ensure things ran smoothly with Montgomery.

During this period, Simpson reported to Ike, 'I and my Army are operating smoothly and cheerfully under the command of the Field Marshal. The most cordial relations and a very high spirit of cooperation have been established between him and myself personally and between our respective Staffs. You can depend on me to respond cheerfully, promptly and as efficiently as I possibly can to every instruction he gives . . . The Field Marshal paid me a visit and at his request I took him to the headquarters of my XIX Corps where I had all of my corps and division commanders assembled to meet him. After all had been introduced to him, he made us a splendid talk on the present situation.'[25] The Allies had resolved their high-level differences and could now focus on limiting and destroying the Bulge. In their eyes, this was a battle they would inevitably win: the only unknown was how long it would take.

PART THREE

24

A Pint of Sweat and a Gallon of Blood

WE MUST LEAVE the commanders and their conferences and return to the GIs and grenadiers fighting for their lives. We'll first revisit the terrain assaulted by Erich Brandenberger's Seventh Army in the south. Then, winding our way through the whitened woods and towns, via Manteuffel's Fifth Panzer Army around Bastogne, finish eighty-nine frozen miles further north, near Monschau and on the Elsenborn Ridge, in the landscape littered with Dietrich's SS troopers of the Sixth.

We last saw the men of the US 4th Ivy Infantry Division, 60th Armored Infantry Battalion (of the 9th Armored), and part of Norman 'Dutch' Cota's 28th Infantry, slugging it out with *Fallschirmjäger* and *Volksgrenadiers* west of the Sûre and Our rivers. As noted earlier, Brandenberger's four German infantry divisions in the south had been given very modest objectives: to seize the river line between Echternach and Vianden and, overcoming US forces in the vicinity, move westwards. It was envisaged that all of Brandenberger's battalions – each relying on around fifty horses for mobility – would advance south of Bastogne (a prize for Manteuffel's Fifth Panzer Army) and no further west than Martelange, about thirty miles from the river line and fifteen miles south of Bastogne. Their general mission was to block any unwelcome attention from Patton's widely anticipated Third Army counter-attack, from far to the south of Luxembourg.

On the American right flank, Colonel Robert H. Chance's 12th Infantry Regiment had taken the brunt of the German attack, spearheaded by the 212nd *Volksgrenadiers.* Chance's two forward battalions had been pushed back on 16 December, despite counter-attacks, because the rest of 4th Division (the 8th and 22nd Infantry Regiments) were initially holding another sector of the front further south. They were soon transferred north to join their comrades in the fray.

Jack Capell of Headquarters Company in the 8th Infantry, who had complained bitterly on being recalled from his rest camp, never forgot the arctic temperatures when fighting in this sector with the rest of 4th Division: 'Some of us still had no overcoats, and although we had the new longer and heavier field jackets, they were not sufficient against the cold. We had wool gloves and the new combat boots. They had leather tops, which replaced the old leggings, but they offered no greater protection from the cold and wet . . . We supplemented our clothing by cutting up burlap sacks found in farmhouses. We wrapped these around our heads, necks and legs. The Germans did the same thing, and some of the prisoners we took were so wrapped up they looked like mummies . . . More than once, after a seemingly endless session on sentry duty, I returned to my hole for shelter so cold and thoroughly fatigued that I was afraid to fall asleep for fear of freezing to death.'

Conrad (from Louisiana and therefore known as 'Frenchy') Adams was also with the 8th Infantry, in Company 'E'. He was manning a machine gun, miserable under his shelter-half in a snowstorm with a sore throat. Some of his buddies were drinking cognac or schnapps, but, not being a drinker, he found another use for the alcohol. 'We hadn't taken off our boots for a couple of months, so after removing the liner, I put some of the liquor in my helmet, took off my boots and soaked my feet in the helmet – boy did that feel good.' [1]

On 17 December, 'a gray, foggy day', when the situation was 'extremely vague', according to the 70th Tank Battalion's After Action Report, General Barton released a reserve infantry battalion, which was sent forward to aid Chance's 12th Regiment.[2] In support were two platoons (ten tanks) of the 70th's Shermans, some of which fought their way into Berdorf, each tank bearing five soldiers. Some of those infantry were the crews of disabled tanks and maintenance men, all serving as riflemen. They attacked a large building, formerly an American headquarters, pumped several rounds into its stone walls before seeing the Stars and Stripes being unfurled on the roof and realised it was still occupied by GIs, not grenadiers. Such 'friendly (which it certainly wasn't) fire' incidents marred the already difficult fighting for both sides. Driver Robert McEvoy remembered that up the road, defending Consdorf, was only one Sherman tank manned by two men, with a handful of cooks, MPs and stragglers who picked up rifles to contest the village.

In Osweiler, a commode and sink were blown intact from one house on to the rear decking of a 70th Battalion Sherman: the tankers jokingly complained about the lack of a bathtub, which remained in the stricken house.[3] Later, another tank was suddenly surrounded by Germans who opened fire from several directions. The hatches were shut but the driver's periscope was hit, obscuring his vision. In his eagerness to direct his Sherman to safety the commander yanked out the microphone cable, meaning the driver couldn't receive verbal instructions either. Somehow the driver turned his steed about, blindly rattled down a side road before crashing into a house from which German fire was coming. As the building collapsed on to the tank and the crew prepared to surrender, they were beaten to it by the *Volksgrenadier* squad inside the house, who emerged, hands held high, marvelling at the driver's resolve in ramming their house.[4]

Ed Gossler was a gunner in one of the 70th's Shermans: 'The fields were so wet that neither our tanks nor theirs could go cross-country,' he recalled. His tank was one of three counter-attacking eastwards towards Dickweiler near the Sûre river; they reached their destination, but a GI yelled to him, 'You guys got binoculars? I think they're sending us reinforcements!' A closer look revealed the opposite, 'Hell no, those are Krauts coming in!' *Volksgrenadiers* poured down a nearby hill from Osweiler, a village to their rear. His three tanks lined up to fire. 'The Germans heard our tanks . . . and dropped to the ground and started setting up their machine-guns . . . We had a pretty good defence but they had no protection, no place to hide. They were only a couple hundred yards away, so we had little trouble hitting them. The whole hillside was littered with dead Germans. We kept firing until those who were left surrendered.'

Oberst Kornprobst's 320th *Volksgrenadier* Regiment (belonging to Generalmajor Franz Sensfuss) had crossed open ground, bunched together in large groups, and paid the price for their inexperience. Sensfuss later observed his high casualties were partly due to a lack of artillery support 'because heavy weapons could not be ferried over, due to a lack of ferries . . . after forty-eight hours a bridge at Weilerbach was

German and American armoured divisions were predominantly equipped with the Panzer Mark IV (top) and US M-4 Sherman (bottom). Both weighed in at 29–35 tons, were around nine feet high, equipped with a 75mm gun and manned by a crew of five. The two tanks were under-protected by late 1944 standards and Panzer IV crews tended to attach armoured side-skirts, while Sherman tankers used spare tracks, sandbags and even wood to trigger warheads before they could penetrate their armour. The extra weight created additional strain on transmissions, engines and suspensions, making both types maintenance-heavy. The snow and ice of the Ardennes added to the clumsiness of these armoured vehicles, which often had to be chipped out of frozen mud in the mornings when plunging overnight temperatures left them welded to the ground. Both had relatively narrow tracks, and this Sherman has extensions added to its caterpillar tracks in order to give it better surface grip. (NARA)

established but lay under artillery fire and air attack'. He lamented his lack of tanks: 'the division was without any panzer support, while the enemy attacked with numerous tanks. Only four assault guns were assigned. None of the promised replacements arrived.'[5] Over 200 were killed, only one officer and thirty-seven other ranks surviving to surrender to Gossler and his buddies, who then watched helplessly as hungry, wild pigs attacked the frozen corpses for food.[6] This left Gossler, his three tanks, nearly forty prisoners and a few GIs caught in Dickweiler, behind the German high tide from 16 December until Christmas Eve. During this time German aircraft flew overhead dropping leaflets urging them to surrender.

By the winter of 1944–5, tank battalions like the 70th, in reaction to the requirements for a better gun, improved suspension and thicker armour, were equipped with upgraded M-4 Sherman tanks. Like the Panzer IV, the principal German tank in the Bulge, the Sherman (named after the civil war general, best known for his March to the Sea in 1864, breaking the back of the Confederacy) was crewed by five and weighed thirty tons, a significant issue when mobility in the Ardennes often rested on little bridges and the weight they could carry. Manoeuvre in the wintry months of 1944–5 was tricky, as the Sherman's narrow caterpillar tracks gave it poor traction on snow and ice (film footage exists of Allied tanks skating sideways down frozen highways). The VII Corps commander, J. Lawton Collins, remembered following a tank destroyer 'with its broad, steel caterpillar treads, just ahead of our Jeep, going slowly down a side-hill slope, and unable to check its massive momentum, slid off the icy road and tumbled downhill, carrying its helpless driver to his death'.[7] Panthers and King Tigers, by contrast, with their wider tracks which spread their weight more evenly, fared much better. Furthermore, German tanks could pivot on the spot, often giving them the edge in urban combat.

The effectiveness of German and American tanks lay in the professional bond between the three-man turret crew: commander, loader and gunner. The former from his cupola maintained a special awareness of the battlefield, by sight and radio, choosing targets before they chose him; the loader had to be quick off the mark with ammunition, and avoid losing his fingers as the breech closed and mechanism recoiled. The Sherman's gunner used a telescopic sight to confirm targets and aim; this was essentially a twenty-two-inch-long telescope with glass lenses of fixed magnification.

The panzers had the best: Zeiss optics with multiple magnification settings and an anti-glare filter. The same Sherman crewman also controlled the electric turret traverse, which operated far quicker than the manual equipment fitted in German tanks – a significant advantage over the Panzer IVs, Panthers and King Tigers encountered in the Ardennes. Firing the main armament was by a button on the turret traverse, or foot pedal. All US Shermans in Normandy had carried a 75mm gun, but by the time of the Ardennes a significant proportion mounted the newer high-velocity armour-piercing 76mm cannon, which increased the range at which a Panther or Tiger could be engaged, with the likelihood of a kill out to 1,000 yards.

However, Tiger tanks could still destroy Shermans from 2,000 yards and, after the heavy armour losses of the Bulge, Eisenhower asked that no more 75mm Shermans be sent to Europe. 'The infantrymen used to call the tanks steel coffins,' wrote 4th Armored Division veteran Nat Frankel. 'No statistic could ever dissuade them. I remember talking to a wounded infantryman . . . He had taken a glancing shot in the stomach, and a deeper slug in the thigh. "You still think it's better outside?" I asked him, in reference to a remark I had heard him make about what lunatics tankers have to be. "I don't give a sh*t if you double the lead," he answered. "Just give me oxygen and I'll die happy".'[8]

Whatever its shortcomings, the Sherman's production quantities had a quality of their own which the Third Reich could not match. By the time manufacture had finished at the American Locomotive Company, Baldwin Locomotive Works, Detroit Tank Arsenal, Lima Locomotive Works, Pressed Steel Car Company, Pacific Car and Foundry Company and the Pullman Standard Car Company, among others, a staggering 62,312 Sherman hulls had been assembled. The greatest proportion of these were tanks, though some were adapted into gun platforms for the armoured field artillery battalions, operating the M-7 Priest with its 105mm gun, or tank destroyers like the M-10 and M-36 (with their three-inch or 90mm cannon, respectively).

Often overlooked is the fact that the huge number of Sherman hulls was matched by a similar investment in tank recovery and repair equipment, which meant a high proportion of disabled armoured vehicles were repaired and returned to service. Although Panthers, Tigers and King Tigers were perceived to rule the battlefields in 1944–5, Shermans were not originally designed to engage the panzers. The US Army's 1941 Field Manual for Operations confirmed that though capable of engaging in all forms of combat, the primary function of medium armour (i.e. the Sherman) was 'offensive operations against hostile rear areas', therefore *not* infantry support or tank-versus-tank work. Early American doctrine held that all anti-armour operations were best done by tank destroyers, hence the TD battalions.

'We generally wore a crash helmet with goggles and carried a .45-inch calibre Browning pistol in a shoulder holster which fitted neatly under our armpits,' remembered Captain Horace R. Bennett, of the 4th Armored Division. 'Wearing one on the hip, like a gunslinger, or General Patton, may have looked mighty fine, but in a burning tank with seconds between life or death, none of us wanted to lose our lives because of a pistol getting caught in a hatch. We were slim in those days, but it was always a tight squeeze wriggling in and out of those hatches. I also got a "Grease Gun" from another knocked out tank. It was a small and cheap version of a Thompson sub-machine gun, like Al Capone and his gangsters used, and chambered for the same calibre as my pistol. We liked it because it was light, you could stow it anywhere, and its magazine held 30 rounds – enough to get you out of trouble. It was a copy of the German *Schmeisser*, and I took it everywhere I went at night, just in case,' Bennett added. [9]

Fighting 'buttoned up' with all hatches closed in the freezing Bulge weather against an opponent armed with machine guns and mortars made sense to tank crews, but Patton forbade it on the move in his formations. The young cavalry lieutenant (and future Pulitzer Prize-winner) Eugene Patterson recalled an outdoor pep talk that Third Army's commander gave to all officers of the newly arrived 10th Armored Division in a natural amphitheatre near the famous 1870 battle site of Mars La Tour on 4 November 1944. 'Six hundred officers, from second lieutenants like me to our major-general sat on our helmets in the mud, semi-circled before him. Every word whipped up clearly to the farthest anti-aircraft half-track watching with quad-50s on the rim of the bowl lest some stray Messerschmitt spot this inviting target in the rain.'

'Keep your head outside the hatch so you can see where the hell you're going and where the Krauts are shooting at you from,' Patton had intoned at parade-ground volume. 'Give the sons of bitches a target so you can see where they are and go kill them. Never button up a tank in Third Army and blind yourself . . . When you attack be fast and violent. The more violent you are, the fewer of your men get shot. Forget everything you learned at Fort Knox [the US armour school] about conserving ammunition. Shoot. Fire scares the *Heinies*. A mortar or an artillery piece that isn't firing is just junk. Shoot off your ammo. I'll get you some more . . . Remember I expect you to move forward rapidly. A pint of sweat will save you a gallon of blood.'

Controversial from the opening seconds, Patton's speech to his division had begun 'Welcome to Third Army, you Tenth Armored Tigers. You and I are going to kick some German ass . . . Don't ever let me find one of you platoon leaders riding three tanks back from the point, the way they taught you at Fort Knox, and putting your sergeant up front,' he admonished. 'I expect every platoon leader in Third Army to ride the lead vehicle. Men expect an officer to lead. Your basic goddam command in this army is "follow me". And don't ever let me find some cowardly bastard among you covering up the rank on his helmet with mud, the way some shitass armies let their officers hide. Let your men see you shine up that bar until the Krauts can use it for an aiming stake.'

Soldiering with Hodges' First rather than Patton's Third Army, David Skelly, a machine-gunner with the 109th Infantry Regiment, spoke for many when he recalled the days before the Bulge in his unit: 'At this point in time, almost all officers no longer wore insignia of rank, on helmets or the shoulder patches of their jackets; there had been several casualties among them caused by sharpshooters. Many lower-level officers had now followed their example and likewise removed their chevrons. Only a dull white stripe, painted horizontally (for an NCO) or vertically (for officers) on the back rim of the helmet let us know the rank.'[10] While practical, this created problems of morale, and challenged leadership, with the Germans being seen even to control aspects of officer-recognition amongst the GIs. It was, in fact, a counter-productive reaction to an age-old battlefield problem; hiding rank never solved the issue and created more confusion. Snipers knew that officers stayed close to radios, and even if they did not salute in combat, men treated their leaders deferentially, even in the field. No wonder Patton railed against this sort of practice.

The general went on: 'Your grandson will ask you someday, "What did you do in the war, Granddaddy?" You can tell the little bastard, "Son, your granddaddy fought with the Third United States Army and an old bitch named General George Patton". Then he highballed a salute to us, mounted his shiny Jeep, sped up the muddy aisle, and vanished over the hill rim while every officer in the Tenth Armored Division snapped to astounded attention and held a long hand salute until he was gone.' Patterson confided to his diary, 'For an instant I wondered if my general might not be mentally stable. I'd never seen or heard of general officers talking this way. They'd always been distant starchy figures personifying . . . dignity and rectitude – until now.'[11] Major Haynes W. Dugan, who served in the US 3rd Armored Division headquarters throughout the war, wrote to me in 1994, observing more generously, 'I am not sure that the press fully understood him, for he was a proud Virginia gentleman, and a cavalryman who believed in unrelenting pursuit; but when not obeyed he was known to mutter "we need some killing around here"'.[12]

Patton's insistence on commanders peering out of their turrets ceased when artillery fire rained down. In such circumstances, buttoning up was a necessity, though not to everyone's liking. In the Ardennes, many new crewmen experienced combat for the first time, as Jack Lovell, commanding an M5 Stuart tank in the 70th Tank Battalion, recalled of a green replacement: 'He couldn't take all the explosions so close to us, and he went off his beam. He wanted out of the tank, and I had a hell of a time – nearly had to knock him out – keeping him in. He would have been a goner from all the shrapnel coming off those tree bursts. I finally quieted him down and called the medics on the radio. I told them we had a man who had to get out of there. They came to get him when the artillery fire stopped. I helped him get out of the tank, and he was completely nuts by that time. During the Bulge we had put a lot of people in tanks who had never been in them before. People like cooks and clerks, who weren't trained or anything.'[13]

Other men showed their reluctance to soldier in different ways. Lieutenant Belton Cooper of the 3rd Armored Division remembered 'one oddball GI from the maintenance battalion got lost and wound up in Liège. When the MPs apprehended him six weeks later, he was wearing an Eisenhower jacket with captain's bars and both Air Force and ordnance lapel insignias.' Instead of charging him with desertion, carrying potentially the same penalty as meted out to Eddie Slovik, 'he was given a Section 8 (incompetent for military service) and a dishonourable discharge'.[14]

Instilled with the Patton doctrine, which required his combat soldiers to wear neckties while Courtney Hodges of the US First Army did not (Patton's MPs were quick to pick up any offenders), Shermans of the 70th Tank Battalion fought on in 4th Ivy Infantry Division's area from the 17th until relieved on 24 December. Although on the face of it the battalion escaped remarkably lightly, with thirty casualties, six tanks and one half-track lost, nearly all of its vehicles were in workshops on 16 December, with many personnel away, and these losses in fact represented a high proportion of those people and vehicles committed.

Elsewhere on the US 4th Division's front during 17 December, a company of seventeen more Shermans arrived from CCA of the 9th Armored Division, which was already defending Barton's left flank, a little to the north. Much attention focused initially on this sector, where a German regiment from the 276th *Volksgrenadier* Division started moving through the Schwarz Erntz gorge. This was a ravine into which ran many small streams from higher ground, and gave rise to the local nickname of 'Little Switzerland'; it also formed the boundary between 4th Infantry and 9th Armored Divisions. Inter-unit boundaries are always a favourite for an attacker to exploit, because in the confusion of combat, terrain can soon be surrendered or left unguarded without one or other defending unit being fully aware.

Barrelling to the rescue from down south, exactly as the Germans had feared, came Major-General William H. H. Morris's 10th Armored Division (the Tigers). This was the first of Patton's divisions sent to the Bulge when Eisenhower suggested to Bradley in Paris on the 16th that VIII Corps could use some help. With the Tigers rode Eugene Patterson, whose somewhat humiliating introduction to war had occurred shortly after Patton's astonishing speech in early November. The green young officer had halted his vehicles before Metz, crawled forward to a string of foxholes along a ridgeline and asked of the nearest GI, 'Soldier, where's the front line?' The infantryman 'examined me for a moment with bloodshot eyes as he pondered his response, which was eloquent. "Shit, Lieutenant, you're on it", he said disgustedly and spat.'[15]

Patterson commanded the thirty men of Troop 'C', part of the 90th Cavalry Reconnaissance Squadron (Mechanised) in the 10th, equipped with M-8 armoured cars and jeeps. Arriving in Normandy from 23 September 1944, his troop had prepared for combat by salvaging 'steel turret rings from knocked-out US armor and welded them to the turrets of our under-gunned M-8 armored cars on legs of angle iron we scrounged. We cannibalised crashed American bombers for 0.50-inch caliber machine-guns to mount on the turret rings. We stole lengths of angle iron and welded one upright on the front bumper of each jeep to snap the piano wire Germans liked to string tight across the road to decapitate jeep riders.'[16]

The cavalry officer, safe in a warm requisitioned house with his fellow officers, recalled the urgent summons to the Bulge on 16 December. 'The captain returned from squadron headquarters bringing word of a big German attack on Americans to the north. Somebody said he was glad they were getting it, not us. Then as the night drew on, someone rushed in and said it *is* us! Urgent orders had come to roll the whole Tenth Armored Division 75 miles north into immediate counter-attack . . . Not soon. *At Once! Now! Move!* We broke for our platoon billets at a run.'[17] Patterson joined Brigadier-General Edwin W. Piburn's Combat Command 'A' which had arrived in Colonel Chance's beleaguered 12th Infantry's area by the following afternoon, eighteen hours later – no mean feat for an armoured column under combat conditions. Piburn himself had only just taken command over CCA on 15 December, but led it into battle regardless at daybreak on the 18th. Their friends in Colonel William L. Roberts' Combat Command 'B' rolled straight on another thirty miles and into Bastogne, where we shall meet them later.

Securing key road junctions during the move north, Patterson remembered 'as dawn broke on 17 December, I witnessed the most thrilling sight I can remember in my life . . . a whole American armored division roaring to war'.[18] Lieutenant Belton Cooper told me of the overnight move of his 3rd Armored Division's 1,200-vehicle combat command into the Ardennes at roughly the same time. With each driver following the blackout lights (masking plates over the front- and rear-mounted lights which let out an inch-wide slit of light) of the vehicle in front, 'The movement was a pure nightmare. Despite a system of guides and sentries there was lots of confusion and a constant stop-start situation . . . The intervals were extremely erratic and often after prolonged stops the vehicles would get stretched out. When this happened, the vehicle in the rear would drive rapidly to catch up, but in the mist and darkness it often came upon another stopped vehicle and banged into the rear of it. If a two-and-a-half-ton GMC truck happened to hit a three-quarter-ton weapons carrier, it would simply knock it off the road. If a tank skidded into a Jeep, it would have squashed it flatter than a pancake. I made sure I didn't get in front of a tank that night.'[19]

Experience had taught Cooper to expect that his armoured column would normally experience 150 to 200 breakdowns during a night march of fifty to sixty miles. When this happened, the vehicles would be repaired on the shoulder of the road. If this could not be done quickly, crews were told to stay with the vehicles and maintenance units from the rear would get to them. Sixty per cent of the vehicles in Cooper's column had arrived in the assembly area by daybreak, but it was late afternoon before the rest had arrived.[20] These breakdowns were due to accidents and maintenance issues rather than combat, and illustrated how challenging just keeping vehicles on the road was throughout that winter. If this was true for the US Army, it was doubly so for the Germans whose armour had a higher tendency to malfunction, whose vehicle pool contained a myriad captured or impressed civilian trucks with few spare parts, and who had relatively little maintenance and recovery equipment.

In some instances, when a tank or truck had rolled on to its side, Cooper's maintenance crews found themselves working in the dark, crawling along rain-soaked ditches and under wrecked vehicles to hook up a towing cable, all the while not knowing exactly where the Germans were and listening out for the tell-tale signs of a fire-fight up the road. The rumours of German soldiers touring the rear areas in American jeeps steeled him against the arrival of unknown US Army vehicles and more than once led to (in retrospect, comic) confrontations with MPs, where each group thought the other were Germans in GI uniform.[21]

Throughout the Bulge, as we shall see, each US armoured combat command could break down into three temporary Task Forces, usually a battalion-sized combat grouping named after the senior commander, comprising elements of tank, armoured infantry and field artillery battalions, to establish blocking or offensive forces. They achieved varying degrees of success and emulated the German style of *ad hoc Kampfgruppen*, likewise named for their commanders. The Tigers' Combat Command 'A' was thus broken down into Task Forces, named for Lieutenant-Colonels Thomas C. Chamberlain of the 11th Tank Battalion, Miles L. Standish of the 61st Armored Infantry and John R. Riley of the 21st Tanks.

The fighting in support of the 4th Ivy Division took place between 18 and 21 December along three axes: on the American left, Task Force Chamberlain successfully denied the *Volksgrenadiers* use of the Schwarz Erntz gorge, which could have been exploited to push straight to the rear sectors of both Barton's 4th Infantry and Leonard's 9th Armored, and pose serious command and control problems. Task Force Standish in the centre cleared the area around Berdorf, but on 20 December a *Volksgrenadier* attack retook the bitterly contested village. Task Force Riley on the right recaptured Scheidgen, but at Lauterborn (where General Sensfuss had placed his divisional headquarters in a mill), the German resistance was ferocious, forcing the Task Force to withdraw. One of Riley's sub-units reached Echternach, but the company commander (Company 'E' of Chance's 12th Infantry) refused to withdraw, believing he was still under General Barton's orders forbidding 'any retrograde movement'.

According to the wonderfully titled *Terrify and Destroy*, the first post-war history of the 10th Armored Division, 'For three crucial days tankers, doughs and cannoneers lashed at the Germans, engaging superior forces, keeping them confused and occupied until III Corps could assemble sufficient strength for a counter-thrust to push the salient back across the Sauer river line.'[22] Actually, numbers and firepower were about equal for both sides, and though US reinforcements largely contained the break-in throughout 4th Infantry Division's sector, they weren't yet strong enough to destroy it. PFC James G. Lancaster's (61st Armored Infantry) memory of Task Force Standish, which consisted of a few tanks and M-10s, and some infantry in half-tracks, totalling about 250 men, was typical of these small unit actions. He remembered: 'We jumped off early in the morning and got to the centre of Berdorf with little trouble. Here we met the enemy head-on and fought for three days with little progress on either side. Artillery bombardment from the Germans with shells and rockets was continuous.' On 21 December, they were ordered to withdraw: 'We left Berdorf under a terrific artillery bombardment, leaving 350 enemy dead, seven tanks and three half-tracks knocked out. We lost four dead, twenty wounded, one tank and four half-tracks.' [23]

Another GI in the 61st, Corporal Joseph W. Bulkeley, remembered the loss of his friend, the platoon barber Andy Klein of Detroit. They had entered a wood without realising the Germans had passed its coordinates to their artillery – who then shelled the Americans. 'In less than an hour we had lost a lot of men killed and wounded. Later things quieted down and we found German foxholes to climb into. The night turned bitter cold but there was a great big full moon up there,' Bulkeley remembered. Then his friend Joe Stefanisko squatted down at the lip of his foxhole and whispered that a piece of metal from a tree-burst had penetrated Andy Klein's helmet, as well as the liner and wool-knit cap. 'I don't think Andy ever knew what happened. When we found him we thought he'd dropped off to sleep. When our second platoon commander heard Andy got it, he broke down and cried like a baby,' Bulkeley added.[24] The US units throughout the sector still took casualties and, although the 61st Armored Infantry did not suffer to the extent of some other battalions, they had still lost 27 killed, 119 wounded and 15 missing – 19 per cent – out of 830 by the end of the month.[25]

To the north of all these 4th Infantry Division dramas lay the battered US 60th Armored Infantry, part of the 9th Armored Division. On 16 December, we left Captain Roger Shinn of the 60th under severe shell-fire in Beaufort. After a day of combat, he remembered the night of the 16th when 'great gatherings of searchlight beams groped toward us from the opposite shore. Obviously the Germans were very confident, since they operated by artificial light without any means of shielding it.' Their opponents continued to use searchlights for most of the first week.

Shinn moved his CP (for the third time in twenty-four hours) to the Hôtel Meyer, still in Beaufort, and tried to follow orders from his battalion commander to attack at nightfall on the 17th. This proved impossible without communications to his own supporting artillery, and some *Volksgrenadiers* eventually drew close enough to hurl hand grenades through the windows, his men taking cover behind stacked-up pieces of furniture. Shinn recalled: 'Before the entrance to the hotel stood one of our Jeeps in flames. In the flickering light I spotted the outlines of several German soldiers, stuck the barrel of my M1 carbine through a broken window and fired. One fell to the ground immediately. Obviously I had hit him; he was the first human being I had directly and visibly killed . . . Meanwhile the Germans had blown up the main door and pushed into the lobby.'[26]

With bullets whistling all about, Shinn ushered his men out of the rear of the Beaufort hotel in twos and threes, inched past a burning half-track, whose fuel tank contained sixty gallons of gasoline, and crept through the ruins, making contact with withdrawing gunners of the 3rd Armored Field Artillery. He was safe for the time being. The artillerymen observed others from the 60th Armored Infantry who had made it through the lines. In their withdrawal they had donned blankets and German helmets and passed on foot through the flickering rubble of Beaufort, full of drunken German soldiers. 'When they were called to from afar and ordered to halt, they simply shouted *Heil Hitler* and kept on marching.'[27]

Meanwhile, on reporting to his own CO, Shinn was ordered to counter-attack on the 18th after he had got some sleep. Shinn went into action again an hour after first light, advancing with half-tracks and tanks, but several fell to *Panzerfaust* teams along the way: an indication of successful German penetrations. Supporting 105mm rounds from the M-7 Priests of Lieutenant-Colonel George Ruhlen's 3rd AFA dissuaded some grenadiers from persisting, Shinn recalling, 'German infantrymen stormed out of the woods, their hands over their heads, and ran towards us. They surrendered by the group, even by the platoon. More than a hundred of them were taken prisoner and guarded by some of our slightly injured soldiers. Most of the Germans were very young, dirty and hungry.'[28] Ruhlen recorded that these timid *Landser* were from the 986th *Volksgrenadier* Regiment, all young conscripts and medically discharged veterans who had crossed at Wallendorf and were under the command of Generalmajor Kurt Möhring, who within the day would be sacked and lose his life when driving to the rear.

Shinn withdrew with his remaining tanks back to his battalion HQ and returned on foot later that night with a trusted sergeant to rescue some trapped and wounded GIs he had left behind earlier. He went on to describe the experience of sleep deprivation suffered by many soldiers on both sides, particularly in the first few days of the Ardennes:

> While daylight remained, we pored over the map and picked our route. We ate a K ration meal. I was weak from lack of food, but excitement kept me from noticing it. We gulped a few Benzedrine pills and put chocolate rations in our pockets . . . I took off my heavy outer garments, and got everything bulky or noisy out of my pockets. I turned over my glasses and a few odds and ends to a headquarters sergeant . . . We were exhausted. Our eyes, halfway through the third night with no sleep (or

> half-an-hour, to be exact) refused to focus. The sky was cloudy, and in the dim moonlight we could see nothing. Sometimes the landscape seemed to swim. Any object, if we looked long enough at it, appeared to move.[29]

Benzedrine was the brand name of an early amphetamine drug, marketed from 1933. Issued by commanders on both sides in the Ardennes, it had the useful military qualities of acting as an appetite suppressant and a euphoric stimulant, which shook off the lethargy of tired soldiers. Even two Benzedrine tablets were not enough to keep Shinn and his sergeant properly alert, or from making reasoned combat judgements, for shortly afterwards, as he rushed forward too quickly in the dark, 'there was a grunt that sounded something like a "Halt". In the split second that I had to make a decision, I could not tell whether it was an American or a German voice. So I simply halted. My eyes struggled to see. There was a rifle barrel sticking out of a hole in the ground. Another grunt, and other men came running toward us. Closing in from the sides, they grabbed our weapons and searched us. Then they marched us off into the darkness. We were prisoners of war.'[30] In the early hours of the 19th, Shinn and Sergeant Ziringer were lucky not to have been shot out of hand, but their method of capture was similar to many lost and tired GIs and grenadiers throughout that December and January.

As Shinn and Ziringer were marched into captivity, Ruhlen's gunners spent 19 December aiding the escape of scattered 60th Armored Infantry units by breaking up German infantry attacks with 105mm shellfire, assisted by half-tracks of the 482nd AAA (Anti-Aircraft Artillery) Battalion armed with quadruple .50-inch Browning machine guns in the ground-defence role. With dark humour, the 'Quad-Fifty' machine-gun mounts were dubbed 'meat-choppers'. Wherever the 60th Armored Infantry had been obliged to abandon their vehicles and move on foot they had thoughtfully buried their equipment in the woods and booby-trapped their half-tracks. By 21 December, Ruhlen's unit had been reinforced by the 10th Armored Division, now arriving in the sector in force.

Meanwhile, General Franz Beyer's LXXX Corps was still feeding troops, artillery and a few assault guns over pontoon bridges. Some infantry units failed to cross until 18 December, some artillery never crossed at all. Finally, the 212th Fusilier Battalion, containing Grenadier

Peter Kelch, with General Sensfuss personally in the lead, and supported by a single assault gun, captured Echternach on 20 December – but four days behind schedule. The American company commander, along with 132 of his men, defending from an old factory, were overwhelmed and marched into captivity – somewhat needlessly, as they could have withdrawn when Task Force Riley reached them on 18 December. As Sensfuss stated proudly in his post-war debrief, 'I myself served in the battle at Echternach. The enemy defended himself with toughness.'[31]

Sensfuss, demonstrating the German tradition of leadership from the very front, was slightly wounded in the attack on Echternach but carried on in command. In neither the American nor British armies were commanding generals expected to be in the midst of the fighting, where they would instantly lose all situational awareness. In the Third Reich, with its inherited notions of personal sacrifice, of proving one's loyalty through bravery, such ideas were more deeply ingrained. Hitler had been injured in the First World War, gaining the Black V*erwundetenabzeichen*

The Achilles heel on 16 December for both Brandenberger and Manteuffel proved to be their ability to build bridges quickly and under fire. They failed to develop a metal assault bridge that could be deployed instantly, and instead were forced to use the Organisation Todt's civil engineers to custom-make wooden bridges of the type shown here, which were time-consuming to construct and not robust when under fire. (Author's collection)

(Wound Badge), which he wore proudly below his Iron Cross on his uniform tunic. It became the Führer's yardstick for judging the bravery of others. In August 1942 he had humiliated the army chief of staff Generaloberst Franz Halder in one of their frequent stand-up arguments when he bellowed, 'What can you tell me about the troops? You, who was sitting in the same chair in the Great War, and yet who failed even to earn the *Verwundetenabzeichen* for being wounded in combat?'[32] Thus Generalfeldmarschall Walther von Reichenau proudly wore the *Infanterie-Sturmabzeichen* (Infantry Assault Badge) normally awarded to riflemen for front-line attacks, but in his case it was honestly won for leading attacks under fire – though when serving in Russia as a field marshal. This, in turn, triggered an intense and competitive desire to win medals, probably far more so than in other armies, and very much in accordance with Hitler's Darwinian notions of 'survival of the fittest'.

Generalmajor Franz Sensfuss felt his division had 'fulfilled its mission. Further success was denied because the neighbours failed. The neighbouring division [Kurt Möhring's 276th *Volksgrenadiers*] paused even on the first day . . . My right flank, now exposed, was permanently menaced.'[33] History bears him out. Beyer's two *Volksgrenadier* divisions in LXXX Corps may have fallen short of Army Group 'B's expectations, but they had actually done rather well against better trained and equipped US units and probably exceeded their own aspirations. If Beyer's men had been more mobile and had had better bridging, they might have ranged much further – before Patton's inevitable and crushing counter-attacks.

The river crossings were always going to be General Brandenberger's weakness. In the end, he attempted to build eight bridges: two were constructed at Roth and Gentingen (both on 17 December); a damaged bridge at Weilerbach was repaired for use on 18 December; two were completed at Edingen and Bollendorf (19 December), though the latter was destroyed on Christmas Eve; one at Dillingen was ready on Christmas Day and another at Vianden on 28 December; a planned structure near Echternach was never completed due to US artillery fire. Every single bridge needed to be operational by the end of 16 December: that none were spelled doom to the entire Seventh Army timetable.

25

A Man Can Make a Difference

FOLLOWING PATTON'S CONFERENCE with Eisenhower and the other commanders at Verdun, he had phoned his code word back to his HQ in Nancy which alerted his staff that General Manton S. Eddy's XII Corps was to disengage at once and move its and Third Army's forward HQs into Luxembourg City. Major-General Willard S. Paul's 26th Infantry Division had been resting in Metz when it was rushed to the southern fringes of the Bulge on 20 December. Known as the 'Yankee Division', it had been raised from the Massachusetts Army National Guard and was formerly based in Boston. They had a long journey from Metz, standing up in open trucks and trailers, via Longwy and Arlon, Staff Sergeant Bruce E. Egger of Company 'G', 328th Infantry, remembering some areas 'seemed to be untouched by the war, with stores bedecked with decorations and Christmas trees'. His buddy, Lieutenant Lee Otts, of the same company, observed, 'Whenever we slowed up in a small town we would barter with the civilians for bread and wine'.[1]

At the same moment, General Eddy (and thus Patton) took over Barton's 4th Infantry Division, the 70th Tank Battalion, 10th Armored Division (including CCB which had gone to Bastogne), CCA of the 9th Armored Division (which included the much-battered 60th Armored Infantry Battalion), Rudder's 109th Infantry Regiment, and other scattered units of the 28th Bloody Bucket Infantry Division. Meanwhile, the weather conditions deteriorated; a howling blizzard blew straight into the faces of tank commanders riding in the exposed turrets of their tall

Shermans. They wrapped themselves in scarves and overcoats and downed mittens and goggles as they navigated their lumbering steeds over the icy cobbles of empty villages.

Ever alert for security laspses, German signals intelligence monitored a whole series of lazy messages emanating from American headquarters which indicated the movement of reinforcements in large numbers towards the Bulge. The first of these materialised on 21 December in the form of two fresh US infantry divisions, the 5th and the 80th, tasked to contain the southern edge of the German Bulge and prevent any further incursions to the west or south. In fact, the Germans were already spent, as we have seen and, forewarned of American reinforcements, Beyer's LXXX Corps (with the 212th and 276th *Volksgrenadier* Divisions) had actually drawn back slightly into better defensive positions, like a boxer anticipating an attack from his opponent. The 276th tried a final counter-attack in the late afternoon of 21 December, preceded by three 75mm *Sturmgeschütz* (StuG) assault guns.

The three StuGs were put out of action, but American intelligence officers became very concerned when they found one StuG bore SS markings – for no units of the Waffen-SS were known to be in the southern sector of the Bulge; the reason for this may have been a last-minute substitution at a depot, or replacement in a workshop, but the instance remains a minor puzzle to this day. 'Numerous Germans who surrendered after the 21 December attack had American jackets and equipment, many of them even wore the emblem of our division on their coats,' observed Lieutenant-Colonel Ruhlen. 'Those who were found with pieces of American uniforms had to remove them; this also applied to shoes. Thus they marched shivering toward the prison camp.' Regarded possibly as prisoner abuse in modern times – a bootless prisoner could die in such sub-zero temperatures – December 1944 was a different era. 'A certain ruthlessness came over us after we had found numerous dead American soldiers with head wounds or ripped-open bodies, with pieces of German equipment that had been stuck into them [whether ante-mortem torture or post-mortem abuse, Ruhlen didn't state]. In this area the Germans were making short work of American prisoners who were caught with German materials,' Ruhlen remembered of the tit-for-tat brutality that started to reign through the Ardennes.[2]

The opening salvoes of Patton's counter-attack against the southern shoulder came on the morning of 24 December – Christmas Eve – which dawned clear and cold, at 20 degrees Fahrenheit below, a bane to the infantrymen but a boon to gunners and fighter pilots who used the opportunity to drop fragmentation and napalm bombs at bridging points along the rivers, with strafing and bombing runs on targets of opportunity. Able to put only 300 bombers into the air on 19 and 23 December, the US Eighth Air Force ordered a maximum effort on this clearest of days since the offensive began, to bomb logistics dumps and bridges in support of the US Army. Among the 2,046 bombers and 853 fighters which took to the skies in the largest single operation mounted by the Eighth were the four-engined B-24 Liberators of the USAAF's 20th Bombardment Wing, flying out of Tibenham airbase, Norfolk, in eastern England.

Demonstrating his much-admired leadership qualities, the Wing's executive officer, with over twenty combat missions under his belt, would fly occasional uncredited sorties to keep his hand in. Airmen and GIs alike were surprised to find the modest, mild-mannered lieutenant-colonel was none other than James Stewart, whom they remembered starring with Cary Grant and Katharine Hepburn in *The Philadelphia Story*, released in 1940, for which he had received an Oscar nomination for Best Actor. Stewart's flying was no cakewalk; the commander of the 4th Bombardment Wing on 24 December, Brigadier-General Frederick W. Castle, was shot down in his B-17 and killed.[3] Stewart had traded his Hollywood career to fight in the forces and would retire eventually as a major-general. He would pick up his film career after the war, and another Best Actor nomination, with perhaps his best-known performance (ironically of a small-town banker unable to serve in the war) in *It's a Wonderful Life*, in 1946.

Tank driver Robert McEvoy, who had witnessed the fight in Consdorf days earlier, remembered 'Wall-to-wall American bombers and cargo planes. They dropped us supplies by parachute – red ones, green, yellow, white. Man, they were a welcome sight.'[4] The Allies colour-coded their silk canopies so ground troops could tell what was in a parachute container before it even hit the ground. Red meant weapons and ammunition; yellow was for medical supplies; blue signified containers of rations; white indicated miscellaneous equipment, and green (khaki) was reserved for personnel, such as medics, signallers and other specialists who jumped in to supplement beleaguered garrisons where necessary.

Among the new arrivals was Major-General S. Leroy Irwin's US 5th Division, whose badge was a red diamond. No strangers to combat, they had landed on Utah Beach during 9 July, and liberated Verdun with three tanks of the 7th Armored Division on 31 August. They had also been rushed up from Metz, which they had taken on 22 November. In support of their 24 December counter-attack, 5th Division's own artillery fired 5,813 rounds, adding to the corps artillery's effort amounting to 21,173 shells. Out of the line, Ruhlen reported that his own battalion had used over 26,000 rounds by Christmas Day: 'from 16 to 23 December, we had theoretically fired an average of one round every forty seconds. The highest shot cadence was achieved on 21 and 22 December. On each of these days we fired approximately 7,100 rounds. Day and night the ammunition vehicles of our Service Battery supplied the guns with urgently needed shells. The loaders and drivers ate while they drove; we ourselves, according to army orders, had absolute priority for ammunition since we were known to be the only artillery unit in this threatened sector for days.'[5]

At this stage, the 26th Division had decided to issue gas masks, solely, remembered Staff Sergeant Bruce Egger, 'because the Germans dressed in American uniforms who had infiltrated our lines had not captured any'. With the clear skies, the weather was depressingly cold too. Egger remembered a buddy who had left his boots outside his foxhole one night found them so frozen solid the next morning as to be unwearable.[6] Christmas Eve saw limited American gains, with the six attacking US battalions losing about two hundred casualties, thanks to the well-dug-in *Volksgrenadiers* and their effective counter-battery fire. The main achievement was that Barton's 4th Ivy Infantry Division had been relieved; some of them – including Colonel Chance's 12th Infantry – had been in combat for eight continuous days, fighting in sub-zero temperatures. Among those relieved on Christmas Eve was tanker Ed Gossler in Dickweiler, who had survived on K-ration crackers, honey from a beehive and a couple of pigs, caught, butchered and fried. The arrival of Irwin's 5th Infantry Division gave him 'the best Christmas I ever had'.[7]

Christmas Day saw Lieutenant Otts' platoon of the 75th Division pinned down by machine-gun fire attacking Eschdorf, 'stretched out prone in a frozen ditch, where we remained for 6½ hours. Every few minutes the bullets came zinging down the road and across the flat, snow-covered fields on both sides of us, so we were afraid to stand up. I made several trips up and down the length of my platoon on my stomach, trying to keep the men awake. As long as we kicked our feet and flexed our hands and fingers, I knew we wouldn't freeze.' Later, his men found comfort in the warmth of an old barn. Sitting on a log, 'I turned on my flashlight and discovered it was a dead German, frozen stiff with his mouth open and his eyes rolled back.'[8] Staff Sergeant Eggers would write home on 27 December, 'There was no Christmas for me this year; it will have to be postponed for another year or two. I just couldn't get that Christmas spirit, and who could when there is anything but peace and goodwill toward fellow men over here.' Perhaps his friend in the same company, Lieutenant Otts, was practising self-censorship when he wrote two days later, 'If it hadn't been for the fighting, it would have been one of the most beautiful Christmases I had ever spent. I had never seen such a white Christmas nor such beautiful country. The rolling hills, the snow-covered fields and mountains, and the tall, majestic pines and firs really made it a Christmas I'll never forget in spite of the fighting.' In his 'V'-mail letters home, there was no way that a GI could really convey the real mood and horrors of the front, and most never attempted to.[9]

In the immediate aftermath of battle, it is traditional for commanders to write and thank their colleagues – especially subordinates – for the military support they received which contributed to success. Such letters are designed to be read out to soldiers of the recipient unit, or repeated in their daily Orders. Copies are also held by the receiving Commanding Officer and influence his prospects of promotion. Thus, with appropriate hyperbole, on 26 December, Colonel Chance wrote to Lieutenant-Colonel Davidson of the 70th Tank Battalion that 'the highest praise is deserved by you and other officers and enlisted men of the 70th Tank Battalion for the most outstanding tank support that this infantry regiment has ever witnessed'.[10]

The US counter-offensive was sustained over three days, by which time the west bank of the Sûre had been reached at several points, and Beyer's corps were hastening to back-track eastwards across the river and regain the protection of the Siegfried Line. By the end of their December Ardennes counter-attack, Irwin's 5th Division 'Red Diamonds', whom the Germans came to know as *die Roten Teufel* (the 'Red Devils'), had recaptured great quantities of abandoned American equipment, acquired 830 prisoners and wiped out the enemy threat to the southern flank of the salient. However, they had also sustained 945 combat losses and 620 non-battle casualties – a ratio repeated throughout the Bulge, where the low temperatures, endless snowdrifts and countless icy streams contributed to all manner of sicknesses, from respiratory problems, to frostbite and trench foot.[11]

However, US commanders among Patton's counter-attacking divisions began to note the poor training that newly arrived reinforcements had received. When, on Christmas Day, a P-47 Thunderbolt flew low over American lines, some of the 75th Division's new men stood up and fired at it with their rifles. Another was killed, recalled Lieutenant Otts, 'standing up firing when he should have been lying flat in the snow. I yelled at him to get down, but he couldn't hear me above the noise, and before anyone could pull him down, a bullet hit him right in the forehead.'[12] Nevertheless, the Germans were suffering from exactly the same inexperience.

Exactly ten days after their initial assault, the 212th *Volksgrenadiers* had withdrawn, among them the Eastern Front veteran Grenadier Peter Kelch in the division's Fusilier Battalion; the 276th would follow them the following day, the 27th. Any pursuit was made more difficult by German artillery well hidden on the east bank and able to rain down defensive fire on US units that ventured too close. Those grenadiers trapped on the west bank fought stubbornly wherever they were attacked, the last formal resistance ending on 28 December. Of Beyer's two infantry divisions, Dempwolff's 276th *Volksgrenadiers*, whose first commander, Möhring, had died on 18 December, lost well over 2,000, with some of its companies reduced to ten men. The 988th Grenadier Regiment lost 1,162 killed, wounded and missing from the 1,868 on their rosters for 15 December, a loss rate of 62 per cent sustained over twelve days of fighting. Casualties among his 986th and 987th Regiments were not dissimilar.

Generalleutnant Franz Sensfuss's 212th *Volksgrenadier* Division had taken an even heavier pounding, suffering casualties of about 4,000 officers and men; among the survivors was Major Ernst Schrotberger of the 212th *VolksArtillerie* Regiment, who returned without his guns. This was his second retreat in such a landscape: he had already endured a Russian winter during which his horses died in the extreme cold. Due to traffic congestion and Allied air power, some of his gunner colleagues had never even managed to cross the Sauer, which ensured their ultimate safety. As Generalmajor Sensfuss reported, 'The enemy air raids were particularly efficient . . . The constant supremacy of fighter bombers on the road Trier–Bitburg was very disagreeable. The roads were not useable during the day.'[13]

After tracking the left-hand pair of Brandenburg's four divisions that were assaulting the Americans in Luxembourg, we need to turn our attention to the northern two formations of General Kniess's LXXXV Corps. These comprised Oberst Erich Schmidt's 352nd *Volksgrenadiers* and, adjacent to the Fifth Panzer Army, Generalmajor Ludwig Heilmann's 5th *Fallschirmjäger* Division, which was charged with protecting the left flank of Manteuffel's panzer thrust to Bastogne, the region's key route centre. Both formations were to cross the Our river, and the 352nd ordered to push west up the Sûre valley, capturing Diekirch and Ettelbrück. On the receiving end of both was the lone 109th Infantry Regiment, led by the legend of D-Day, who had scaled the heights of the Pointe du Hoc with his Rangers, Lieutenant-Colonel James Earl Rudder. As the American historian Trevor N. Dupuy has noted, the two German divisions possessed a combined combat strength of 32,730, as against Rudder's 4,985 including attached units, or a ratio of 6.5 to one. In terms of opposing infantry, the figures may have been as high as fifteen to one.[14]

German intelligence had compiled a detailed list of US units across the Ardennes, with names of commanders and strength gained from prisoner interrogations and wireless intercepts. They knew that Cota's Twenty-Eighth 'Bloody Bucket' Division had been decimated in the Hürtgen and convinced themselves that Rudder's 109th would therefore fold within the first couple of days. Initially their assessments seemed correct: on 16–17 December one regiment of *Fallschirmjägers* had surrounded and forced the surrender of the US battalion defending Weiler, and a second achieved the same, assisting the 352nd *Volksgrenadiers* at Foühren as well. Although Rudder lost his forward outposts and squad positions, they had turned the Hoesdorf plateau into a killing zone for their *Volksgrenadier* opponents.

Early on the 17th, Rudder found the Germans had penetrated the northern boundary between his 109th Regiment and the 110th Infantry at Hosheid, cutting him off from his parent 28th Division. Later that day, as the last of his anti-tank guns was destroyed, he discovered that German engineers had completed their first major bridge across the Our, enabling those StuGs of 11th Assault Gun Brigade not yet in action to slither across the river. Due to the low cloud and poor light, for the first time since landing in Normandy on D-Day, Rudder had no air support – a luxury he and his fellow Allied commanders had automatically counted on, whenever needed. By the end of 17 December, Rudder found he was isolated and about to be surrounded – Heilmann's 5th *Fallschirmjäger* Division had outflanked him to the north and the 60th Armored Infantry Battalion had pulled back, exposing his southern flank.

By the 18th Rudder was being attacked by 75mm StuG and *Hetzer* armoured assault guns, aiming for Diekirch. At the same moment

Volksgrenadier reinforcements rushed over a second wooden bridge. Of note was that neither German crossing in Rudder's sector was a metal combat engineer bridge, but, instead, a roughly constructed wooden affair which was surely an indication of the paucity of raw materials available, as well as an admission that the Panzer armies had first call on the best equipment. After midday on 18 December, Rudder withdrew westwards with Cota's reluctant permission, falling back towards the Herrenberg hill (or the Härebierg, today a military training ground where I have exercised), shadowing Diekirch to the north. His men dug into the 'dead' ground just behind the crest, which offered them cover from view and hostile fire, and thus invisibility from the advancing Germans.

Accompanying Rudder was Lieutenant-Colonel Jim Rosborough's 107th Field Artillery with towed 105mm guns, who had trained for six months at Porthcawl in South Wales before deploying to France with the rest of the 28th Division. They had slowly withdrawn alongside the rest of Rudder's regiment and dug in on the Herrenberg. When late in the afternoon of 18 December the order came to head into Diekirch and redeploy westwards, one of their gunners, Bob Davies with Battery 'C', remembered leaving behind 'numerous rounds of ammunition and fuses which there had been no time to destroy and heading for Diekirch followed by two other trucks towing the guns'. He noticed that the familiar road sign for Diekirch 'was not pointing in the right direction. Without giving much thought to the matter, we went on. Somewhat later we met twelve to fifteen military policemen in new-looking uniforms and armbands. They looked like soldiers ready for a parade, since their uniform trousers were neatly pressed.'

'The MPs all carried Thompson submachine-guns and were remarkably clean-shaven,' thought Davies. 'They stopped the convoy and a lieutenant stepped up to us. From inside the truck I heard how, in perfect English, he persuaded the driver to take a different route to Diekirch. The other MPs did not say a word during this conversation. Only now did I remember the road sign pointing the wrong way and I whispered to Staff Sergeant Phil Marino, who sat next to me, "I think these MPs are Krauts". Since the driver hesitated, the MP lieutenant drew his pistol and three of his men cocked their weapons and pointed them at me as I tried to load my M-1 carbine. Sergeant Marino growled at me: "Do you know what you're saying?" and ordered the driver to take the prescribed route.'[15] Although he never did get to Diekirch, Davies and his truck managed to reach safety.

Knowing he could trade space for time, in order for reinforcements to arrive, Cota had suggested Rudder fall back on Bastogne, the key town to his north-west, but the 109th's commander had enough situational awareness to realise he would be simply retreating into the path of Manteuffel's Panzer Army if he headed in that direction. Instead he argued wisely that he could guard the otherwise uncovered Diekirch–Ettelbrück road running east–west. By the end of 18 December, Rudder's third day of defence, his regiment had been whittled down to about 50 per cent, but had expended 280,000 rounds of small-arms ammunition, called down 10,000 artillery rounds and 5,000 mortar bombs, thrown 3,000 hand grenades and loosed off 300 bazooka rounds. This had slowed the advance of his opponents significantly, who by 19–20 December were still only completing their schedule for Day One in Rudder's sector.[16]

That evening he conferred with his immediate superiors, Cota of the Bloody Bucket Division, Leonard of the 9th Armored (to his south) and Middleton, commanding VIII Corps. By then, Rudder had three options: to fight and be annihilated *in situ*; to withdraw south and link up with CCA of the 9th Armored Division, whose battles we have just followed; or to continue to retire westwards, slowing his opponents and inflicting damage where he could. Middleton gave him complete freedom to 'use your own judgement as you are on the ground' – a refreshing contrast to his opposite numbers in the Wehrmacht who were firmly under Hitler's inexpert thumb at every level.[17]

Meanwhile, Captain Harry S. Kemp, executive officer of Rudder's 3rd Battalion, had found himself obliged to order the civilian evacuation of Diekirch by midnight, but they had to keep off the main road to Ettelbrück. Kemp knew this to be a hugely controversial and unpopular move, which was ill-received by the townsfolk who had welcomed the GIs with open arms weeks earlier.[18] (His observations would later find their way into a military study of controlling civilian refugees, written by Kemp in anticipation of ordering German townsfolk to flee a Soviet invasion of Cold War Europe.) By 19 December, Rudder had withdrawn his regiment from the Herrenberg and had the satisfaction of watching the Germans expend huge quantities of ammunition on a feature he no longer occupied. In the Dupuy study noted earlier, it was estimated that over the first four days of combat Rudder inflicted average daily losses on the Germans of 436, while suffering a similar average of 259 each day to his own command – an indication of the intensity of the fighting as well as Rudder's professionalism.[19]

At this stage, Rudder, at 50 per cent strength, realised he could not hope to compete with the 352nd *Volksgrenadier* Division, his principal antagonists, who would soon annihilate his command completely. He knew from captured maps that the Germans intended to continue westwards along the Diekirch–Ettelbrück–Arlon road, and accordingly divided his force into combat teams. Each all-arms force, comprising an infantry company with an array of anti-tank weapons, 105mm guns, engineers and the few remaining Shermans of the 707th Tank Battalion, permanently attached to Rudder's formation, which also towed his artillery pieces, was to ambush the *Volksgrenadiers* from a successive series of defensive positions along the route, in Feulen, Mertzig and Grosbous, then retire to avoid a head-on confrontation.

Captain Embert A. Fossum, whose Company 'L' had caused so much carnage at Hoesdorf, led the largest team to Grosbous, totalling about 180, although he had already lost more than that number in combat and through weather-related casualties. Fossum later wrote of his men's hunger and tiredness:

> [They] were so worn with loss of sleep and fatigue that orders did not arouse interest. They were almost too tired, cold and hungry to care. Incessant attacks by the enemy and the digging of three successive positions during the withdrawal had fatigued them almost beyond endurance . . . When they left their original position shortly after noon on the eighteenth, each man had carried one-third of a K-ration in his pocket. Another one-third had been issued as they left Diekirch on the night of the nineteenth . . . So it was a pretty badly beaten unit that headed for Grosbous. Morale was certainly at a low ebb.[20]

Cota encouraged Rudder to harry the Germans as much as possible, due to his knowledge that Bastogne, now completely encircled, was about to be counter-attacked by two fresh US infantry divisions assembling in his vicinity, the Massachusetts Guardsmen of the 26th and the 'Blue Ridge' 80th (so-named as they comprised draftees from Virginia, West Virginia, Pennsylvania and Maryland). Rudder's mission now became one of preventing the *Volksgrenadiers* from interfering with the concurrent attempts to relieve Bastogne. Guided through Ettelbrück and Grosbous by armband-wearing local resistance fighters, Rudder had Fossum's task force dig in on high ground near Grosbous, overlooking the Ettelbrück to Arlon road from where on 22 December they were able to ambush 'a column of men and vehicles, one-and-a-half miles long with towed artillery pieces and two tanks at its tail and no patrols for security on its flanks'.

The result was a massacre – a hackneyed phrase, but in this case accurate: with his artillery hitting the Germans' rear first to prevent escape, Fossum's men caused an estimated 2,000 casualties, 'the fire was kept up for twenty minutes on everything that moved, with not one shot received in return,' wrote Fossum, and Rudder laconically recorded, 'We stacked them [the dead Germans] in piles along that road from Ettelbrück'.[21] Fossum's performance, which brought him a Bronze Star and Croix de Guerre, had been outstanding.[22] Rudder knew his regiment's hard training and combat experience had been rewarded, for the ambush could have been spoiled easily by a single trigger-happy GI, but their fire discipline, despite extreme exhaustion, was superb. His 109th Regiment linked up with units of the US 10th Armored (the Tigers) on 24 December, when they continued to clear the villages of Gilsdorf and Moestroff of *Volksgrenadiers*, but their well-being was never again so perilous.

Thus ended nine astonishing days of combat, which saw Rudder's men, in the words of a Third Army G-2 Report, 'destroying the entire 915th *Volksgrenadier* Regiment, Major von Criegeren's 916th, and a major part of the 914th Regiment of the 352nd *Volksgrenadier* Division'. Much of the debris of these encounters has since found its way into Monsieur Roland Gaul's excellent and well-stocked National Museum of Military History in the heart of Diekirch. A stone's throw to the south-west lies the little town where in AD 451 Attila the Hun built a river bridge, in time giving his name to the settlement which developed subsequently – Ettelbrück, meaning 'Attila's Bridge'. Today, another important military commander, George Patton, guards the town in the form of a magnificent statue, complete with his binoculars and twin Colt revolvers, cast in bronze. A memorial museum to the general forms one of the town's main tourist attractions.

However, the battle had cost Rudder's 109th Regiment 875 combat and non-battle casualties, including missing and prisoners, which equated to a loss rate of 29 per cent.[23] Rudder's performance elevated his already considerable achievements far above the norm, bringing him a Silver Star in addition to the Distinguished Service Cross he had received on D-Day. He demonstrated that in modern war – and in the Ardennes in particular – the actions of the individual could still make a difference.

26

No More Zig-Zig in Paris

BASTOGNE. THE SMALL Walloon town of 14,000 lies in the Belgian province of Luxembourg, on a gentle ridge, 1,600 feet above sea level. The height brought it dominance over the surrounding terrain, and it was where several ancient, well-drained roads met. Ask a local the name of their town and you might get one of three answers, reflecting each of Belgium's official languages: in Flemish it is *Bastenaken*; Germans call it *Bastenach*; the French speakers, who make up 40 per cent of Belgium's population, have long known it as Bastogne (the end rhyming with 'coin'). During and since the 1944 battles, many adopted the American pronunciation, where the end rhymes with 'cone'. This ambiguity reflects Belgium itself, for both town and country were places that people passed through rather than stayed in. The first visitors were early nomadic Europeans searching for game or grazing. Later came armies heading east or west, spearheaded by the Romans; by then the region was inhabited by the Treveri, a tribe of Gauls.

The name described how the town appeared to the medieval traveller, emerging from the fog and forests of the Ardennes: a bastion. In 1332, John of Bohemia, Count of Luxembourg and son of the Holy Roman Emperor, had the settlement encircled by defensive walls. Its ramparts boasted fifteen turrets, of which only one remains today, named after the old Gallic tribe: the Porte de Trèves. Very little else survives from this era except the solid mass of the church of Saint-Pierre, which would play an important role as an aid station in the coming battle. John of

Bohemia, alas, lost his sight – and ten years later, aged fifty – his life, groping his way into battle against the English on the battlefield of Crécy in August 1346. An ally of King Philip VI of France in the Hundred Years War, his courtiers tied their horses to his, and led their monarch into battle. All were found later, slain around their disembowelled leader 'like the petals of a tulip, pluck'd': a gruesomely appropriate image to retain 600 years later, when other warriors stumbled through the murk of the Ardennes – similarly alerted more by sound than by sight.

Belgian independence brought the installation of Leopold I as the nation's first monarch on 21 July 1831 – Belgium's national day. One of the first handbooks of the new European state, *The Traveller's Guide Through Belgium*, published in Brussels in 1833, described Bastogne as a 'rich, handsome town – the Paris of the Ardennes – the town is celebrated for the excellence of its hams, and for its extensive corn-market', containing 'nearly 2,000 inhabitants who are principally engaged in woollen manufacture and leather-dressing'.[1] It was scarcely much larger when occupied, then pillaged by Imperial Germany during the First World War. Its experience from 1940 had been harsh, but it had not suffered the fate of nearby St Vith and Malmedy, both of which had been annexed into the Third Reich's *Rheinprovinz*, and whose male citizens were conscripted into German uniform.

All this was ancient history to the American soldiers who arrived at the noisy and congested Belgian crossroads town near the Luxembourg border in December 1944. Despite the fact that there are certainly more picturesque places in the Ardennes than Bastogne, its importance was that all roads within the region led to and through the town: whoever occupied it controlled the route network of the entire region. The same is still true today – and hence why Bastogne remains easily the busiest of places in the otherwise tranquil and quiet Ardennes. Bars and cafés line the rue du Sablon, Bastogne's main street that ends in the town square, now called the Place Général McAuliffe and graced with a Sherman tank. You can sip a beer in relative tranquillity, however, for the recently opened A26 highway to the west has siphoned much traffic out of the little town.

The sixteenth of December 1944 was a 'wet, soggy day' as PFC Don Addor of the 20th Armored Infantry made his way over to battalion headquarters. 'It had been raining almost every day since we had landed in France', Addor remembered thinking as he took over duty on his unit's telephone switchboard. He was enjoying 'how warm and comfortable my feet felt in my Christmas socks', just mailed from home, when he took a call for his CO, Major William R. Desobry. 'The calling voice with a strong note of authority said, "Major, how soon can you be ready to move out?" The major said, "In an hour or two". The voice said, "Make that 45 minutes!" The major's answer was "Yessir!" and the entire battalion began to haul ass in double time.'[2]

Just as Combat Command 'A' of the US 10th Armored Division had peeled off to aid the 4th Infantry Division in their defensive battles, Colonel William L. Roberts' Combat Command 'B' – a long column of Sherman tanks, tank-destroyers and half-tracks, including Desobry's 20th Armored Infantry – drove straight for Bastogne, arriving in the greying dusk of Monday afternoon, 18 December. These were the first combat soldiers to reach the vulnerable town, then home to Troy Middleton, the VIII Corps headquarters, quartered in the Heintz Barracks, and corps service troops, scattered in the vicinity. Combat Medic Robert Kinser of the 3rd Tank Battalion rolled into town at 9.00 p.m. 'It was pitch black and we could not even see the next vehicle . . . We stayed at a big church [Saint Pierre], where we found the MPs living. That night all were sitting by the phone waiting.'[3]

There had not been time to evacuate the civilian population of Bastogne, and an estimated 3,000 civilians – their numbers swelled by refugees – who could not flee westwards, retreated to their cellars in fear, to sit out the battle. By the end of the fighting, 127 had been killed or wounded. Another forty would die later from unexploded ordnance. Of Bastogne's 1,250 homes, 700 would be totally destroyed or made uninhabitable. These figures were eclipsed by the eventual death and destruction in the hamlets and villages within a six-mile radius of the town, where 350 civilians died, 3,556 homes, stables and stone barns were gutted and 1,300 seriously damaged. Few livestock, on which the farming communities relied, would make it through.

Nonetheless, most of these people also did whatever they could to help and provide shelter for their American liberators. A few, who felt they had already suffered enough, guarded their remaining possessions from the GIs, but under the guidance of the acting mayor, Léon Jacqmin, many inhabitants started offering up spare blankets to the Americans for warmth and bed linen for snow camouflage. Jacqmin was also responsible for centralising all the food stocks within the town – during the coming siege, the townsfolk would offer up countless pigs, cattle (and eventually horses) for slaughter, milk and sugar, and seven tons of flour and two tons of biscuits to ensure both defender and citizen had enough to eat.[4] This was all gratefully received, because the defenders soon ran short of rations.

With all his fighting units further east already battling for their lives, Middleton directed Roberts, a veteran of the First World War, to deploy his command in three roadblocks, named after their leaders, five miles from the town in a crescent-shaped arc facing eastwards. Middleton was then ordered by US First Army to shift his own headquarters south-west to Neufchâteau, remaining only to see that McAuliffe and Roberts understood their mission: defend Bastogne to the last round. From his HQ in the Hôtel LeBrun (today the White House Restaurant and Hotel), Roberts ordered Desobry north to block the N15 at Noville. He then put an avuncular arm around the shoulders of the twenty-six-year-old major: 'By tomorrow morning you'll probably be nervous. Then you'll probably want to pull out. When you begin thinking like that, remember I told you *not* to pull out.'[5] Desobry took with him fifteen Shermans, five light Stuart tanks, a company of armoured infantry in half-tracks, five M-10 tank destroyers, three armoured cars and six jeeps. Colonel Eugene A. Watts later argued these roadblocks were 'doomed to failure because we were ordered to use only one company of armoured infantry and one of tanks at each site'.[6]

Desobry recalled later being led to the edge of Bastogne by an MP. 'Noville is two towns up, straight down that road . . . So we went through Foy, which was the first, then we came to Noville. No Germans there. The town was deserted. It was a bit after midnight [the first minutes of 19 December] and we deployed around the town and set up outposts. Then we proceeded to try to get some sleep.'[7] PFC Don Addor didn't even know the town's name. 'Our detachment of men and vehicles had to creep through the night. The damn fog was so thick we couldn't go but a few miles per hour and ran off the road a couple of times. All of a sudden we stopped. A voice from up ahead declared we were here. I looked around and wondered where here was. As I got more used to the fog I could see stone buildings along each side of the road. It was a small crossroads town. The word was that we were to hold it and the intersection at any or all costs.'[8]

Some of Addor's buddies started to make foxholes, forming an outer cordon forward of the town. They heard other troops entrenching around them. When it got lighter they decided to make contact with the other diggers. Addor's friend stood up and looked out of his hole 'and was staring a damn Kraut in the face'. Both sides 'beat the Hell out of there. They ran back their way' and his friends ran into Noville.[9] All through the night, US stragglers drifted through; some Desobry drafted into his group, others 'were in such a state of shock that they were of no value to the defense and allowed to continue into Bastogne'.[10] Mercifully the fog shrouded such sights, which would have damaged Team Desobry's morale far more than they did.

At about 04.30 a.m. the flow of stragglers ceased. A period of unnatural silence followed, and Desobry's men tensed, waiting. It was better that Desobry and Addor remained in ignorance of their future opponents: they included Oberst Meinrad von Lauchert's entire 2nd Panzer Division, who had already ejected Colonel Hurley Fuller's 110th Regiment from Clervaux.

Under Colonel Roberts' orders, a second task force, commanded by Lieutenant-Colonel Henry T. Cherry, had wheeled east out of Bastogne, following the N12 to Neffe, Mageret and Longvilly; a third group, led by Lieutenant-Colonel James O'Hara, took the N34 south-east to Marvie and Wardin, to block the highway from Wiltz. By this time, two earlier roadblocks from CCR of the 9th Armored Division, ten miles out along the eastern route leading to St Vith and about halfway between Clervaux and Bastogne (Task Forces Rose and Harper), had both had been overcome, and their survivors were falling back down the N12 to Longvilly. Amongst those killed was Harper himself, a West Point-educated tanker and classmate of Hank Cherry's. By this point, Desobry, Cherry and O'Hara were the only real defence Bastogne would have until the arrival of 101st Airborne, under the temporary leadership of its artillery commander, Brigadier-General Anthony McAuliffe.

Middleton knew that time was against him. On his right flank, the US Fourth Ivy Infantry Division with the help of 10th Armored's CCA had successfully blocked the advance of Brandenberger's Seventh Army *Volksgrenadiers*. Colonel Rudder's 109th Regiment had folded south, like the hinge of a gate, and was contesting every mile. However, VIII Corps' left flank was dissolving before Middleton's very eyes, as Alan W. Jones's 106th Golden Lions Division was being overwhelmed on the Schnee Eifel, in front of St Vith. Colonel Gustin Nelson's 112th Regiment had hinged back north to join CCB of the 7th Armored Division with Bruce C. Clarke, and the sole surviving regiment of the Golden Lions, the 424th, in defending the town itself. Their efforts at St Vith would buy valuable time.

To Middleton's front, the situation was even more dire. During 17 December, Colonel Hurley Fuller's 110th Regiment had been virtually destroyed by Manteuffel's panzers along the west bank of the Our river in their defence of Marnach, Hosingen, Consthum and Holzthum. At Marnach, eight US tanks were destroyed in minutes. A mid-morning conversation on the 17th between Fuller and his commander, General 'Dutch' Cota, underlined the gravity of the situation. After responding to his subordinate's plea for more artillery, Cota reminded the pipe-smoking colonel, 'Remember your orders are to hold at all costs. No retreat, nobody comes back.' Silence settled on the conversation. 'Do you understand, Fuller?' Cota reiterated. 'Yes, sir', replied Fuller, 'nobody comes back.'[11]

Late on the 17th, at 6.25 p.m., Fuller phoned Cota to warn him that panzers were directly outside his own HQ, the Hôtel Claravallis in Clervaux. With that, he and his remaining staff escaped up the rock face to the rear from an upstairs room. At 6.39 p.m. a final message was received by Cota from 110th Regiment's switchboard sergeant. He was alone and was about to sabotage his equipment. Fuller and his staff were soon captured while trying to make their way out of town. In Clervaux Castle, Fuller's Headquarters Company of 102 officers and men fought on until early on 18 December, by which time five Shermans had engaged the panzers, destroying four Mark IVs for the loss of three of their own. (The Hôtel Claravallis is back in business, and a lifelike bronze figure of a GI, a restored Sherman tank and 88mm gun, plus a museum within the renovated castle, serve to remind the visitor to Clervaux of those dramatic moments of 17–18 December 1944.)

American aggressiveness on the 16th had been robust enough, but once the Germans had completed their bridges at Dasburg and Gemünd, nothing could stop the panzers from overwhelming or bypassing Fuller's village strongpoints. From his CP in the Hôtel Schmitz at Hosingen, Captain Frederick Feiker, commanding Company 'K' of the 110th, had soon realised from a captured map that the German aim was to reach Bastogne, which gave a sense of purpose to his all-round defence of the little town. With a garrison of about 270 GIs, including engineers, anti-tank-gunners and some tank crew, he set about holding up the Germans for as long as possible. They were soon surrounded by scores of enemy dead; however, the situation changed as soon as the panzers were able to join the *Volksgrenadiers* in attacking the town. On the 17th, they lost much of their friendly artillery support, as the American guns were forced back out of range. Gradually their ammunition and food was whittled away until, in the early hours of the 18th, a quick check revealed only two rounds of smoke for their 81mm mortars, their supporting Sherman tanks had been knocked out and most of his men were, if not wounded, down to their last cartridges, as a result of heavy hand-to-hand fighting over the preceding two days.

With a heavy heart, and no prospect of relief, Feiker decided to surrender what was left. All spare K-rations were issued, records burned and supplies destroyed. At 09.00 a.m., with white flags hanging from the few remaining buildings, Feiker with his brother officer, Captain William H. Jarrett, walked across the rubble-strewn town to discuss surrender arrangements with an officer from the 26th *Volksgrenadiers.* As they played for time, the last military equipment was smashed. The last radio message, at about 10.00 a.m., read: 'We're down to our last grenades. We've blown up everything there is to blown up except the radio and it goes next.' Then after a sob, the radio operator signed off: 'I don't mind dying and I don't mind taking a beating, but I'll be damned if we give up to these bastards.'[12]

Unteroffizier Ludwig Lindemann of the 26th *Volksgrenadiers* recalled that they had to 'fight for every cellar and every garden wall' in Hosingen, but destroyed seven tanks and captured 381 US officers and men.[13] As well as Hosingen, Consthum and Holzthum also fell on the 18th, but they had already served their purpose: Manteuffel's Fifth Panzer Army was way behind schedule.

By then Middleton knew that the remnants of Fuller's 110th Regiment – who had lost approximately 2,750 out of 3,200 – CCR of the US Ninth Armored Division and Cota's headquarters troops in Wiltz had nothing like enough combat power to prevent Manteuffel's Fifth Panzer Army from knifing its way through the terrain and reaching his headquarters within a few hours. Bastogne was doomed.

Or was it? As a result of Eisenhower's 16 December orders, from 5.00 p.m. on Monday, 18 December, all 11,000 men of the 101st Airborne Division, plus their heavy weapons, vehicles and equipment, were raced through the night in vast convoys of trucks, skating across the snow and ice, headlights blazing despite the black-out conditions of wartime, to reach Bastogne before the panzers. Some, like Ralph K. Manley of the 501st Parachute Infantry Regiment, had been on a twenty-four-hour pass in Paris, where he came across a loudspeaker van blasting out its urgent message on a repeated loop, 'All soldiers report to your units immediately! As quickly as possible! Any way possible!'[14] William R. Barrett of the 420th Armored Field Artillery remembered noticing one paratrooper who had come straight from leave still 'wearing his dress uniform and carrying a .45 pistol as he jumped from his truck into the snow'.[15]

Manley's mode of transportation to the front was a Port Battalion semi-trailer, used to haul bulk goods off merchant ships and into warehouses. He had no idea what was going on, but realised the seriousness of whatever it was when he saw a vehicle coming the other way laden with GI corpses and 'as it rounded a corner some of the bodies fell off the truck'.[16] Bill Druback was woken up and just told 'to take whatever equipment you could get your hands on, and you grabbed what was available and that's the way we went on these semis. Biggest truck I'd ever seen.'[17] Donald R. Burgett of the 506th Parachute Infantry Regiment (PIR), then nineteen, noted some of the trucks taking him to Bastogne 'had been intercepted on roads throughout the region – no matter who they belonged to or what their priority – unloaded on the spot, and redirected to collect the paratroopers'.[18] Manley and his colleagues began

German signals intelligence (SIGINT) was excellent throughout the campaign. Patient interception alerted them to the move of the US 82nd and 101st Airborne Divisions from the Reims area towards the Bulge, while they also monitored Patton's military policemen, who sent the numbers and identities of US vehicle columns to their own headquarters. (Author's collection)

to arrive in and around Bastogne, frozen to the marrow, most having stood like cattle for up to fourteen hours in an open-topped semi-trailer, protected from the elements only by its four-foot wooden sidewalls.

All the Screaming Eagles remember the same flow of panic-stricken GIs stumbling back that Team Desobry had also witnessed. Don Burgett observed, 'they shambled along in shock and fear, blocking the road completely, eyes staring straight ahead, mumbling to themselves . . . I had never before – or since – seen such terror in men. Their fear was so great, so consuming.'[19] Major Dick Winters of Company 'E' of the 506th PIR thought 'they were just babbling. It was pathetic. We felt ashamed.'[20] Burgett recalled the retreating hoards refused to hand over their weapons or ammunition but Dick Winters' Company 'E' persuaded others to part with bandoliers, clips and grenades, noting that in surrendering their arms and ammunition, the fleeing troops may have – in their own minds – 'relieved themselves of any further obligation to stand and fight'.[21]

Panic was expressed in another way. Burgett's truck convoy was blocked by 'some dumb son-of-a-bitch captain commanding a maintenance company that was retreating with heavy vehicles and refused to move'. It took the 101st's Assistant Divisional Commander, Brigadier-General Gerald J. Higgins, alternatively ordering and cajoling every driver in person, to clear the road, but not before Higgins had drawn his pistol in exasperation and several of Burgett's buddies had silently unsheathed their trench knives with another solution in mind.[22]

Eighteen of the US Army's European tented redeployment camps (dubbed 'repo-depos'), from where reinforcements (known as 'repple-depples') were sent to the front-line divisions, were based around Reims. The city hosted the US Assembly Area Command, whose communications the Germans routinely intercepted. After the war, Manteuffel would comment, 'our signals reconnaissance functioned efficiently and speedily'; wireless traffic from Reims revealed to General von Lüttwitz, commander of XLVII Panzer Corps, that the airborne troops were on their way.[23] He was ebullient, knowing who would be first in Bastogne. Earlier that day, the 26th *Volksgrenadiers* had secured bridgeheads over the Clerf river, easing the way for his twin tank divisions. Advancing on two roughly parallel axes, 2nd Panzer Division to the north with Panzer Lehr to the south, there seemed nothing to stop these two powerful formations from rapidly enveloping Bastogne. Lüttwitz also knew his panzers could make mincemeat of lightly armed paratroopers. He assessed the Screaming

Eagles were 120 miles distant, and that with the darkness, wintry conditions and logistical nightmare of moving vast numbers of troops quickly, his panzers, about twenty miles away, would be sure to reach Bastogne first, with horrific consequences for its defenders.

Along the way, Panzer Lehr's armoured reconnaissance battalion raced ahead to Wiltz, to where the remnants of Fuller's 110th Regiments had retreated. A reluctant Cota was ordered by Middleton to move his 28th Division's headquarters back to the Bastogne suburb of Sibret and leave the defence of Wiltz to Major Stickler, executive officer of Colonel Fuller's 110th. Robert W. Eichner worked in the T & T [Telephone and Telegraph] Section of the 28th's signal company in Wiltz, operating the division's telephone and telegraph service. He remembered how 'the headquarters was in danger of being captured, so we knew we would be infantrymen again, as we had been trained in the beginning. Our lieutenant picked me to detail five men to stay behind and man the switchboard. Others were told to do likewise in all sections of the headquarters, typewriter boys, police, medics, and engineers.' Everyone else, recalled Eichner, 'piled into the trucks, standing up only. I had only one leg in the truck body. The convoy started out into the dead of the night. How much noise that convoy made!' However, Eichner's group was ambushed. 'Silhouetted was a German tank in the middle of the road. It lowered its gun and let go. The jeep up front was a direct hit. Then machine-guns opened up. I didn't wait for any invitation to leave and headed for the forest.'[24]

Unteroffizier Eduard Job recollected the battle for Wiltz when acting as gunner in a Panzer Lehr *Jagdpanzer* tank destroyer. 'The commander [the old Afrika Korps and Normandy veteran Generalleutnant Fritz Bayerlein] moved at the head of the battlegroup in his command half-track . . . The driver picked up the pace since we were being engaged. Small-calibre rounds were smacking into the side-skirts. The fighting compartment was ringing like a bell. We then reached a defile, which offered us some cover and concealment. Our four fighting vehicles rolled through it. At the end of the defile, which led to a patch of woods, we turned back in the direction of Wiltz. "Guns 1 and 3: ten o'clock . . . Guns 2 and 4: two o'clock!" The tank destroyers pivoted in the designated directions. Our vehicle gave a jolt when it moved through a ditch.'[25]

Every small settlement that Bayerlein and the other panzer commanders encountered harboured a potential series of hazards, whether narrow stone buildings, ideal for defence, trees, engineer-made obstacles or infantry and anti-tank weapons. Through the surrounding woods, groups of GIs trudged, among them Signaller Robert Eichner. As he left his ambushed convoy outside Wiltz, he noted, 'the Germans sent a flare up. It lit the place like daylight. We were told during training if this ever occurred, to stand still. Movement is what they would see. When it burnt out I headed for the deepest part of the forest.'[26] The threat from armed, organised gangs, like Eichner's, also delayed Bayerlein's march considerably, the more so in the bad weather and poor light; factors which had not been taken into account in the Wolf's Lair or Berlin.

Job in his *Jagdpanzer* remembered seeing 'the trail of flames revealing the location of a bazooka that had just fired . . . When I fired back, the round tore a big chunk out of the masonry building showering the area where the bazooka had been with rubble and concrete dust. There was no more firing from that location . . . Off to the right, where the fourth Jagdpanzer was located, we heard a couple of muffled blows . . . We saw a squad of American infantry had knocked out our sister vehicle. We opened up with our machine gun, sending the infantry scurrying and giving the crew some breathing room to dismount before their vehicle went up in flames.'[27] Job's account underlined how armour and infantry best worked hand-in-hand to subdue their opponents in any urban setting – it was this sort of relentless grind from village to village that tired and held back Panzer Lehr.

Among the defenders was Sergeant Max L. Noe. The Texan worked in the Postal Section under command of a captain who was director of the 28th's divisional band. His squad dug in on a hillside outside Wiltz, armed with a machine gun that had no tripod, so they used an apple box for a gun rest instead. Sergeant Noe took charge, being the only one qualified on the weapon; as he recalled, 'the machine gun bounced all over the place and if I hit a tank it was like throwing rocks on a tin barn'. However, his squad held the Germans for about eighteen hours before Noe and two others escaped into the woods, the rest of his men being killed, wounded or captured.[28]

Wiltz fell finally to attacks by the 26th *Volksgrenadiers* and the 5th *Fallschirmjäger* Division; the latter should not have been there at all. Manteuffel and Lüttwitz recorded their displeasure at the appearance of the paratroopers who seem to have been attracted by loot and the warmth of a large town, a relief from the penetrating cold. The German airborne formation was the northern division of Brandenberger's Seventh Army, and though ordered to cooperate with Manteuffel's panzers as a flank guard, had strayed across the inter-army boundary, against orders.

A small group of *Fallschirmjäger* engineers under Oberleutnant Walther Sander were surprised by a US vehicle column of the 110th Infantry moving at speed westwards through the Schumann's Eck road junction three miles south-west of Wiltz. A quick-thinking paratrooper reduced the leading half-track to a flaming wreck with a *Panzerfaust*, and several US tanks shared the same fate before the GIs were overwhelmed. As they were led away, Sergeant Gene Fleury of the 687th Field Artillery remembered the 'brazen paratroopers yelling "No more zig-zig [sex] in Paris"'. Another GI observed, 'They slapped and banged you around, stripped you down, took your watch, wallet, penknives, even made me take off my shoes.' Sander's squad would later bring their several hundred prisoners, a large number of American vehicles and captured artillery back east at the end of the campaign, winning their commander a Knight's Cross.[29]

The Lehr, meanwhile, had quit Wiltz, leaving the infantry to mop up, and pressed on towards Bastogne. Unfortunately, some horse-drawn *Volksgrenadiers* then slowed their advance by getting themselves mixed up with the armoured troops. Nevertheless, by 10.00 p.m. on the 18th, Panzer Lehr's advance columns, pushing ahead through appalling conditions, had reached the hamlet of Niederwampach, just six miles east of Bastogne.

As they did so, the first scouts from the US 501st Parachute Infantry Regiment of the Screaming Eagles were pulling up in the Main Square at Bastogne: the race was still neck and neck.

Cota, meanwhile, obliged to quit Wiltz, sped down the foggy N34 with his driver and an aide to report to Middleton in Bastogne. Suddenly a challenge rang out. 'Halt!', a word that was the same in German and English. The jeep, displaying the two stars of Cota's rank on a plate attached to its bumper, slowed to a stop. In the dark was a well-concealed patrol who had heard its approach – but from which side?

As Corporal Edward J. Gerrity, Jr, attached to Team O'Hara, later recalled, 'Every rifle and my .30-inch machine-gun were trained on the vehicle. Its occupants could not see us. Cota asked us who we were. Sgt Tom Holmes the platoon leader asked him who he was. He told us. We were not sure if they were Americans or Germans in American uniforms. Holmes then said he was coming out to the edge of the highway and if they tried anything they would be cut down. You could have heard the proverbial pin drop. Cota started to get out of the Jeep. Holmes told him to stay where he was. A brief, taut dialogue then ensued. Cota mentioned he was in a hurry. I shouted "General, what's behind you?" He barked, "The whole damn German army", and with that he was allowed to proceed.'[30]

Following close behind in another jeep was a former New York City cop – the first to be drafted – Lieutenant John A. Foley Jr. As an MP, Foley had guarded Eddie Slovik for a while during the latter's court-martial, and subsequently shadowed Cota everywhere as a sort of bodyguard. He remembered of that journey, 'We had to weave our way through Germans most of the journey before we ended up in Bastogne. By that time, the 28th had been pretty much overrun and was scattered all over the place. Most of the guys left behind in Wiltz were taken prisoner. We travelled south along tracks and small roads and met up at the new CP in Sibret.'[31]

Nearby, Panzer Lehr's commander, Bayerlein, was in the leading vehicle, a half-track, of an armoured column, also heading towards Bastogne. This was exactly where his mentor, Erwin Rommel (to whom he was once chief of staff) had taught him to be. Bayerlein had spent a frustrating day trading shots with GIs, skirting Wiltz, and struggling along minor, muddy roads, delayed by the *Volksgrenadiers* and their horses. Acutely aware of time running out, he had just received orders from his superior, Lüttwitz, to be in Bastogne that night, without fail.

He paused at the tiny gaggle of cottages that comprised Niederwampach and took stock with his operations officer, Oberstleutnant Kurt Kauffmann. They had three choices by which to reach their objective, less than an hour away: the column could lunge north to the N12; second, they could head south to the N34, but both were paved roads, and most likely well-guarded by the Americans; or, thirdly, they could plough straight on westwards along the track marked clearly on his map, which avoided both main roads and led through Mageret and beyond to Bastogne, a mere six miles away. According to a local farmer, the going was good and this had the advantage of being the most direct route, and was least likely to be defended.

Hedging his bets, Bayerlein sent part of his force north to Longvilly with some of the following *Volksgrenadiers*. Followed by fifteen tanks and *Panzergrenadiers* in half-tracks, he himself charged down the trail to Mageret. After a short distance the paved surface gave out to a softer surface; later still the route had become a farm track, barely distinguishable from the surrounding mud. To the local farmer in Niederwampach the going may have been good, but the Belgian was thinking in terms of horses and cattle, not a column of heavy armoured vehicles. Bayerlein realised that each set of caterpillar tracks churned the ground some more. Too late to turn back, he pressed blindly on, leaving bogged and stalled vehicles behind. (The trail has not changed and in December 1989, thoughtlessly following Panzer Lehr's exact tank tracks, I had to pay a puzzled farmer to extract my car from the glutinous mud and use his tractor to tow me along Bayerlein's route to the safety of a hard-surfaced road.) Back in 1944, the general's tanks and half-tracks endured a four-hour nightmare before, exhausted, they trickled into the hamlet of Mageret, which they found packed full of trucks, jeeps and ambulances. Bayerlein was right in assuming the route was undefended, for he had stumbled on an American medical unit.

The panzer general summoned another local Belgian for information on US military movements and was told that an American force of 'at least fifty tanks and just as many other armoured vehicles' had earlier passed by, along the N12, heading eastwards. This was Combat Team Cherry from CCB of the 10th Armored, heading for Longvilly where they were to establish their roadblock. Bayerlein might have paused to consider the veracity of these details, given it was gone 02.00 a.m. and pitch black – Team Cherry had in fact driven past at 7.20 the previous evening and comprised thirty Shermans and Stuarts of the US 3rd Tank Battalion (which Cherry commanded), Company 'C' of the 20th Armored Infantry, and platoons of the 55th Engineers and 90th Cavalry Squadron.[32] But he himself was tired and starting to make errors of judgement.

After an inexplicable wait in Mageret, at 05.30 a.m. on the 19th the Germans recommenced their cautious advance westwards along the hard-topped road towards Neffe, the noise of their engines drawing fire from US stragglers, the rearguard of Team Cherry and some of the 101st Airborne, now just deploying. None of this was a threat to his armour, but soon the Lehr's lead tank ran over a mine and was disabled. As usual, Hauptmann Kunze and the men of the divisional engineer battalion hurried forward to remove the American explosives strewn across the road and either side, before the march resumed. By 07.00 a.m. Bayerlein's column had reached the rail station at Neffe, just outside Bastogne. However, they were shattered, cold and anxious. They had no idea of the forces arrayed against them, could not see anything through the pre-dawn pea-soup fog and knew there were Americans equipped with tanks to their rear.

Although Bastogne now lay only two miles away – had the fog lifted they would have been able to see it clearly – Panzer Lehr's attack had stalled and Bayerlein himself seems to have lost the initiative. By midday he had turned his back temporarily on Bastogne and returned to Mageret. Bayerlein himself wrote after the war how he had asked one of the captured nurses in Mageret to look after his wounded, noticing she was 'young, blonde and beautiful' and admitting he was 'spellbound' by her. Any meaningful movement by Panzer Lehr seems to have halted while the forty-five-year-old unmarried general, by his own admission, wasted valuable time flirting with his young captive. Many historians have repeated this astonishing tale, though few have attempted to validate it. Bayerlein's biographer, Pat Spayd, has narrowed the candidate down to one of several military nurses in a platoon of the US 42nd Field Hospital, based at the Château de Wiltz, who had withdrawn and were taken prisoner at Mageret.[33] One historian thought she should be given a medal for fatally delaying Panzer Lehr's advance into Bastogne![34]

The 107th Field Evacuation Hospital had already been obliged to leave Bastogne in a hurry as the fighting approached. 'We were awakened in the middle of the night and told we were moving out,' remembered Combat Nurse Ruth Puryear. 'We could not take anything with us except what we had on. Hearing tanks in the distance we left everything except our patients, loading them on trucks, twelve to fourteen each. It was a race against the Germans. It was very cold and snowing; we had on long johns, fatigues and combat boots; we worked in them, and slept in them. We wore our boots in bed to keep warm. Little did we know that we would be in them for two weeks.' Puryear's unit relocated to an old castle. 'The ballroom was used for surgery, where we did 380 operations in thirty hours, working round the clock. There was a trophy room with animal heads on the wall. That is where I hung the plasma bottles – on the horns and heads of dead animals.'[35]

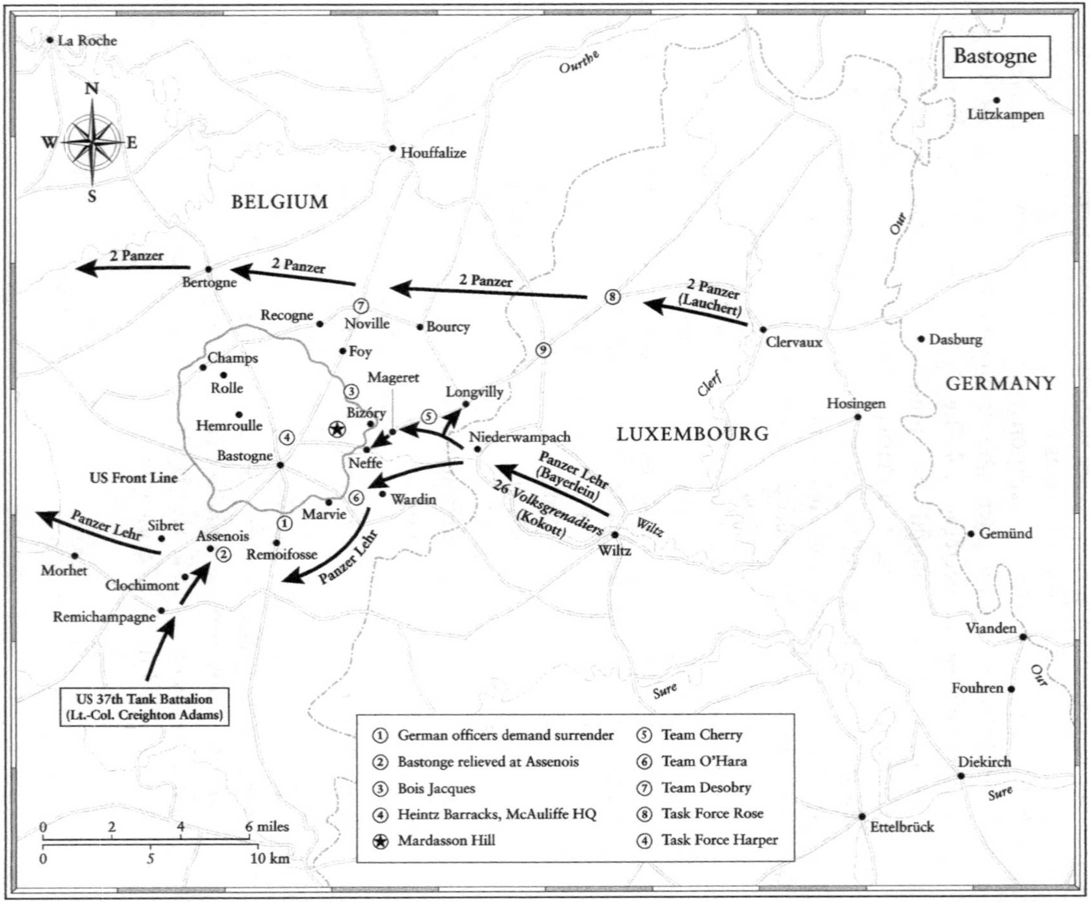
Bastogne
La Roche
N
W
E
S
Houffalize
BELGIUM
Ourthe
Lützkampen
Our
2 Panzer
Bertogne
2 Panzer
2 Panzer
2 Panzer
(Lauchert)
Clervaux
Dasburg
GERMANY
Recogne
Noville
Bourcy
Foy
Champs
Rolle
Hemroulle
Bastogne
Mageret
Bizóry
Longvilly
Niederwampach
Neffe
Wardin
Marvie
Clerf
Hosingen
LUXEMBOURG
US Front Line
Panzer Lehr
(Bayerlein)
26 Volksgrenadiers
(Kokott)
Wiltz
Wiltz
Gemünd
Panzer Lehr
Sibret
Assenois
Remoifosse
Morhet
Clochimont
Panzer Lehr
Remichampagne
Vianden
Our
Fouhren
Sure
US 37th Tank Battalion
(Lt.-Col. Creighton Adams)
① German officers demand surrender
② Bastonge relieved at Assenois
③ Bois Jacques
④ Heintz Barracks, McAuliffe HQ
Mardasson Hill
⑤ Team Cherry
⑥ Team O'Hara
⑦ Team Desobry
⑧ Task Force Rose
④ Task Force Harper
0 2 4 6 miles
0 5 10 km
Diekirch
Sure
Ettelbrück

27

The Hole in the Doughnut

On 19 December 1944, Generalleutnant Fritz Bayerlein still thought he had time on his side. Time enough for dalliance. He appears to have quit the company of his charming companion at around 2.00 p.m. on the 19th, when he suddenly became worried about the Americans to his rear, and elected to double-back and destroy the US force at Longvilly. Then he would return to take Bastogne. Moving swiftly, Bayerlein's force came upon a great line of stalled American vehicles, the remnants of Task Forces Rose and Harper (from the 9th Armored Division), with other stragglers from the 28th Division, packed bumper to bumper along the N12, retreating *towards* him. None of the Americans expected a German column to hit them from the west. At the first shots the GIs left their vehicles, fleeing across the terrain and making for the safety of Bastogne.

All rushed off except Team Cherry, now led by First Lieutenant Edward P. Hyduke, who were stationed one mile west of Longvilly by the roadside Grotto of St Michael. Hyduke's orders were to stand and fight. By now, Lieutenant-Colonel Cherry was separated from his command, having driven to liaise with Colonel Roberts in Bastogne, and found the N12 back to Longvilly blocked by Panzer Lehr. Undeterred, Cherry rounded up a miscellany of forces and created another roadblock at Neffe, commanding it from a nearby stone-built château. Lieutenant Hyduke, arrayed around the Grotto, would have to manage on his own. At the same time – and unplanned by Bayerlein – the 26th *Volksgrenadiers* also hit Longvilly from the south-east.

Private Joseph C. Syiek moving west from Longvilly with CCR, was caught in the battle around the Grotto, remembering, 'Our outfit pulled into the valley on Monday night [18 December]. The ground was soft and we were not able to pull the vehicles off the road for fear they would sink in . . . Early Tuesday morning we were surrounded and the Germans began to close in on us. As the day rolled on the enemy showered us with mortar, artillery and machine-gun fire. Men were going mad. There was no organisation, there was no way to go, we were all scared. Our tanks and trucks were the main targets; men ran to the slopes that formed the walls of Death Valley.' Syiek's story was typical of many GIs driving through the murky Ardennes, following the vehicle ahead, with little idea of where they or their opponents were.

Then, as now, once men are broken down into small groups morale plummets. Situations, such as the one Syiek found himself in, generally induce battlefield stress, an expression of the internal conflict in a soldier's mind. On one hand there is the desire to fight bravely and support one's comrades, so as not to let them down; on the other hand, there is a deep primeval survival instinct to turn and run. Stress narrows the span of attention, reduces the capacity for problem-solving and induces restlessness, irritability and jumpiness. Military historian S.L.A. Marshall observed that such strain was so common that 'less than twenty-five percent of US infantry in World War II employed hand weapons effectively'.[1] This is not post-traumatic stress disorder (PTSD), but a contributor to it.

Isolation can become, literally and metaphorically, a killer for soldiers in battle, but the effects can be reduced significantly by human interaction. Small groups, even pairs of soldiers, can act as an effective buffer against such combat stress, hence the importance of man-management and junior leadership at every level. Where direction is lacking, or troops became separated, lonely terrain such as that of the wintry Ardennes in 1944 greatly exacerbates these issues for all combatants.[2]

Stress could also express itself in soldiers looking for an easy exit from the battlefield in various ways. In the late afternoon of 19 December, during Team Cherry's battles with Panzer Lehr, twenty US half-tracks arrived, carrying 'about 200 stragglers from various units that had fallen back from other actions to the east. They were mostly tankers, and although they all dismounted from the half-tracks, only about forty of them, along with three captains and two lieutenants from CCR, moved toward the fighting. The others fled across fields.'[3] Elsewhere, PFC John Davis, a scout with the 106th Division, remembered resting when he heard a gunshot and found 'one of my friends had shot himself in the foot. My heart just sank to the ground. It seemed so unnecessary . . . This guy was one of the rocks of the company, solid and dependable, but he'd had enough . . . At one time or another, nearly everyone entertained the thought of getting out that way.'[4]

Lieutenant Otts of the 75th Division also recalled 'it was not unusual for someone to "accidentally" shoot himself in the hand or foot before almost every big push. These "accidents" became so frequent that an order came out requiring a court martial investigation of every such "accident".' Otts echoed John Davis's view that 'I'll bet there wasn't a man in the outfit who didn't thinking about shooting himself at some time or other'.[5] Meanwhile, 'Doc' M. Bedford Davis (no relation), a battalion surgeon attached to Colonel Rudder's 109th Regiment, arranged a three-day truce with his German opposite number over 17–19 December, transporting seriously wounded troops from a poorly equipped German aid station to better resourced US medical facilities. 'On the third day,' Davis related, 'the ambulance came in with the same German medical officer. This time he stated he was weary of fighting and wanted to be sent in as a POW. This I did reluctantly, a little envious at how easily he had extricated himself from the conflict.'[6] These three examples indicated different attempts to escape the 1944 battlefield – by flight, a self-inflicted wound, or surrender.

In his seminal *Anatomy of Courage*, Charles McMoran Wilson, later Winston Churchill's personal physician, observed that every person has a personal reserve of courage, which is used up in combat or stressful situations. However, each 'bank of courage' is different and the amount withdrawn also varies with the individual and circumstance. Thus it is impossible to measure how much courage has been used, or is left, in each individual – making it difficult to predict when and how ground troops, aircrew or naval personnel, for example, will collapse under the strain of continuous combat. Wilson argued that resilience can be helped by good leadership or the proximity of fellows undergoing the same stress. George W. Neill, with the 99th Checkerboard Division, remembered two men in the back seat of a jeep. 'They looked beaten. They showed no sign of recognition that I existed. They looked straight ahead with glazed, blank eyes. Their faces were covered with dirt and their beard four or five days old. Although physically uninjured, they resembled the living dead. I felt terribly sorry for them – a very different kind of war victim.'[7]

Some commanders realised that soldiers exhibiting excessive signs of breakdown also needed to be removed from their colleagues so as to prevent stress symptoms and panic from spreading. General Matthew Ridgway came across a sergeant in the Ardennes who had become hysterical, and thrown himself in a roadside ditch, crying and raving. 'I walked over and tried to talk to him, to help him get a hold of himself. But it had no effect. He was just crouched there in the ditch, cringing in utter terror. So I called my Jeep driver, Sergeant Farmer, and told him to take his carbine and march this man back to the nearest MP and if he started to escape, to shoot him without hesitation. He was an object of abject cowardice and the sight of him would have a terrible effect on any American soldier who might see him.'[8]

Ridgway's solution might seem brutal today, but fellow paratrooper Robert M. Bowen of the 101st Airborne Division recalled the drip-feed conditions of the Bulge that slowly broke men down, 'a biting wind blew over the chilling snow, piercing our inadequate clothing like a knife. We were hungry, cold, and depressed. Hungry because we had been living off of one or two K-rations a day for nearly a week. Cold because many of us did not have overcoats, overshoes, gloves or mufflers. And depressed because after fighting debilitating campaigns in Normandy and Holland with their high casualty rates, this one in Belgium threatened to be the last straw to push us over the edge.'[9]

Paratrooper Don Burgett noted how they had all been obliged to stack their heavy winter clothing by the roadside in order to be able to move fast in their attack on Noville. 'We stripped down to jumpsuits, jump boots, helmets and gloves.' His new company commander stated, 'there wouldn't be time to get cold, and we would come back and pick up our belongings the next day, after we'd whipped the Germans back to where they'd come from'.[10] They didn't believe him, and they were never able to return, adding to their misery. However, in the case of the 101st, strong *esprit de corps* and experience helped the paratroopers through their winter nightmare.

The excessive cold got to GIs of every arm of service, even tank troops. The US 6th Armored Division's history recorded, 'Snow, ice, and sub-freezing weather provided the setting for one of the most severe campaigns ever fought . . . Tank turrets froze, and had to be chipped free to regain traversing action. Iced breach blocks had to be manually operated. M-1 rifles refused to function until bolts were beaten back and forth with grenades. When escape hatches and tank doors stuck fast, they got "blow-torch" treatment. Ice formed in gas tanks and clogged lines. Feet froze. Men became so cold they "burned".'[11]

Most in the Ardennes were tested in this way, not just by the proximity of artillery but the relentless hunger, cold, general fatigue and sleep deprivation; newer units and those without combat experience suffered the most.[12] When George W. Neill, of the 99th, came under his first, prolonged artillery bombardment on 16 December, he recalled 'for the first time I could clearly hear shell fragments falling like a hailstorm, slicing into the hard, frozen ground outside my foxhole. They were everywhere. Anyone outside of a log-covered, deep hole would be dead in seconds, bleeding from numerous body wounds. At this point, I felt too tired and numb to be afraid.'[13]

Back at the Grotto of St Michael, Syiek wrote, 'There was one of three things to do. Fight a hopeless battle to the last man, surrender, or try an escape through the enemy in our rear. I chose the latter, and since my squad was disorganized and my company scattered, I asked for no one's permission. Other men went off to escape, but I took a different direction. I took a narrow path on the slope that led into a pine grove. Ten or fifteen yards in I noticed a stone stairway covered with pine needles, climbing and winding up a hill steeper and higher than Norfolk Street [back home in Worcester, Massachusetts]. At the first bend was the first Station of the Cross. It was carved from white rock mounted on a marble block. I blessed myself and went on up, and at each bend was another Station.' Syiek managed to overcome his battlefield stress, act logically and evade capture. He believed that his deep religious faith had shielded him from shells and deadly shrapnel as he moved through the religious statues on the hillside.[14]

The Americans fought tenaciously but by 3.30 p.m. the battle was over. Scores of dead GIs lay sprawled among the stone statues on the hillside around the Grotto, and the long column of 9th tanks, armoured cars, guns and jeeps burned – Panzer Lehr counted 200 US vehicles destroyed or captured. (In 1977, between the rocks on the hillside around the Grotto, I picked up a rusty bucket, only to realise it was a shell-damaged German steel helmet, left behind by a member of Panzer Lehr thirty-three years earlier who no longer needed it.) Edward Hyduke, though wounded, would survive to enjoy his well-earned Silver Star in retirement, despite many Bulge authors reporting his demise at the

Grotto.[15] Scores of Americans were taken prisoner, but some of CCR and Team Cherry managed to withdraw cross-country and link up with the 101st Airborne troops, who were now beginning to establish a continuous perimeter around Bastogne.

Lieutenant-Colonel Cherry himself, separated from his Team at the Grotto, nevertheless spent the 19th delaying Panzer Lehr and the 26th *Volksgrenadiers* from advancing beyond Neffe. By late afternoon the Germans had surrounded and set fire to his château, but he managed to slip away under cover of darkness, having tied down his attackers all day. As he did so, the 1st Battalion of Lieutenant-Colonel Julian Ewell's 501st Parachute Infantry Regiment had appeared in the vicinity, ensuring the Germans would get no closer to Bastogne. Cherry assessed with pride that, although his skirmishes had cost his force 175 officers and men (a quarter of his strength), seventeen tanks and the same number of half-tracks, they had inflicted at least the same losses on his enemy and more importantly had delayed the drive of an entire division on Bastogne by a day. The citation for Colonel Cherry's Silver Star read in part that for much of 19 December he had 'personally engaged the enemy with submachine-gun and pistol fire, dispersing an estimated twenty-five man group, in accordance with the highest standards of the military service'.

Fritz Bayerlein had paid a high price for his dalliance and subsequent diversion back to Team Cherry at Longvilly. Against the odds, Bastogne – which had been within Bayerlein's undoubted grasp twelve hours earlier – had since been secured by the paratroopers of the 101st Airborne, who had won the race to the town. By 09.00 a.m. on the 19th, all four of its regiments had deployed around it.

Ewell's 501st PIR were sited east, defending a sector from two to three o'clock, including Bizory and Neffe. Colonel Steve A. Chappius's 502nd PIR found themselves between Champs at eleven o'clock and Recogne at one o'clock in the north. With them was Ed Peniche, who dug in his anti-tank gun and made foxholes lined with straw in the grounds of an abandoned farmhouse at Longchamps. He first saw action on the 20th, attacking a pair of half-tracks belonging to a 2nd Panzer reconnaissance unit, and remembered the weather turning colder with some snow falling; on the 21st he woke up under a heavy blanket of snow with more falling until mid-afternoon, as it grew even colder. He could hear the sounds of a fire fight to his right throughout 19–20 December, which was where Colonel Sink's 506th PIR were battling against 2nd Panzer at Noville.[16] The Screaming Eagles' final unit, Colonel Joseph H. Harper's 327th Glider

Infantry Regiment, occupied two defensive sites at five and eight o'clock, to the south of Bastogne.

At the same time, the US 705th Tank Destroyer Battalion had arrived to join the 609th Tank Destroyers already in Bastogne; the former, released from the US Ninth Army up north, was equipped with M-18 Hellcats armed with 76mm guns – almost a match for a Tiger II with its 88mm cannon. Also present, or in the process of arriving, were the 755th and 969th Field Artillery Battalions, plus the highly mobile 420th Armoured Field Artillery with their self-propelled M-7 Priests, with 105mm guns mounted on a Sherman chassis. The latter proved invaluable, being able to reach all around the perimeter with their 12,000-yard range. They far outclassed the light 105mm guns of the airborne artillery, which had only a 4,500-yard range. Like father, like son: the 420th was very ably led by Major Willis D. Crittenberger, Jr, whose father was commanding US IV Corps in Italy at the time. All these outfits rapidly positioned themselves around the town, enabling Middleton and McAuliffe to feel a little more comfortable.

The other two teams establishing roadblocks had fought equally gallant delaying actions. Team O'Hara, with thirty tanks and 500 men, were positioned on the N34 near Wardin. Colonel O'Hara could hear the noise of battle and followed on his radio frequencies the skirmishes between the Germans and Teams Cherry and Desobry, but where, he wondered, were the Germans in his sector? He sent Captain Edward A. Carrigo and First Lieutenant John D. Devereaux on a jeep patrol to scout eastwards and find them. Locals flocked around their vehicle when they pulled up at the church of Saint Aubin in Wardin, and Devereaux stood up to practise his French. 'Have no fear, the US Army is here to stay. We will protect you,' he proclaimed, concluding with a theatrical bow which brought applause.

Continuing on their way, as the thick mist suddenly dissolved the pair came under fire when they spotted a column of half-tracks emblazoned with crosses rattling quickly towards them. 'My God, those are Krauts!' uttered Devereaux, slamming the jeep into reverse, spinning round and racing back to warn O'Hara, accelerator flat to the floor. Unfortunately they had to retrace their route through the crowd, still outside Wardin's little steepled church, and Devereaux, profoundly embarrassed, screamed, 'Get out of the way you morons, the Krauts are coming!'[17] Devereaux would win a Silver Star that day for his leadership in the defence of Wardin, but not for his thespian activities. At the end of the 19th, as

Panzer Lehr outflanked Wardin, moving cross-country, O'Hara was forced to withdraw a short distance west to Marvie. For the next month this area would be contested, with the Americans advancing several times before being beaten back. Not until 16 January was the village securely back in US hands, by which time it was 80 per cent destroyed.

Meanwhile, Major Desobry's team, with Don Addor, in Noville, had skirmished blindly with their opponents from 05.30 a.m. on the 19th, but it was only at 10.00 a.m. – when the dense cloud of fog lifted dramatically like a theatre curtain to reveal the whole area crawling with German tanks heading west to the Meuse – that their battle really commenced. By then, Addor had already met his opponents in the mist. 'I was walking down the main road through the fog when I heard someone approaching from behind. When he was alongside of me I looked over and saw he was a German rifleman. I can't tell you the sudden shock of seeing the enemy right there beside me! He ran one way and I the other.'[18]

The lifting of the fog surprised the Germans as well as the defenders, catching formations of troops and vehicles in the open. Fourteen panzers were spotted advancing along a ridge to the west of the N15, desperately looking for cover, of which ten were quickly despatched. Desobry was heartened by the arrival later that morning of the 1st Battalion of Colonel Robert L. Sink's 506th Parachute Infantry Regiment, who immediately counter-attacked the Germans, then dug in around Noville.

Artilleryman Barrett, who had noticed the paratrooper still wearing a dress uniform jumping out of a vehicle, joined his buddies in handing out any spare weapons, ammunition and blankets they had accumulated and squirrelled away in their vehicles, to the 101st boys, who in their haste to deploy were impossibly short of personal weapons. Also distributing ammo was Lieutenant George C. Rice, a 10th Armored Division officer, who had begged, stolen and borrowed all the spare .30-inch clips, .45-inch cartridges, grenades, mortar and bazooka rounds he could find in Bastogne. No one had told him to do this; he had simply realised how pitifully short the 101st were, and sat in his jeep by the roadside, handing ammo to the Screaming Eagles as they marched up to Noville with rifle and pack.[19]

Donald R. Burgett was with them as they dashed into Noville, hitting the Germans, throwing them off balance and pushing them back. Over the next forty-eight hours Desobry's armoured infantry, Sherman and tank-destroyer crews with the paratroopers, amounting to less than two battalions, managed to withstand attacks from the entire weight of 2nd Panzer Division. However, within minutes of their arrival a shell hit the command post in the village school opposite the church, killing the battalion's CO, Lieutenant-Colonel James L. LaPrade, who had fought through Normandy and Holland, and badly wounding Desobry, who was then swiftly evacuated to Bastogne. Addor discovered a German sniper active in Noville, who had secreted himself in the attic of one of the houses in the first few hours. His position was eventually discovered because he was using tracer rounds. Addor asked how they got him down. 'They didn't. They just riddled the whole length of the ceiling until blood started dripping through the bullet holes and they left his body up there.'[20]

Noville, a tiny cluster of stone houses and barns astride the N15, has changed little since the battle. German tanks crept repeatedly down the main road, duelling with Shermans, tank-destroyers and bazooka teams. Very soon the area became a wasteland of shattered houses, smoking vehicles, dust and rubble, with Germans and GIs thoroughly intermingled, occupying alternate houses. Shots rang out in every direction, tank guns fired through buildings, with both sides sustaining very high casualties. Dead animals and troopers littered the fields and lanes. Eventually the weight of 2nd Panzer against them proved too much for the remains of Team Desobry, and by late afternoon on 20 December the survivors had withdrawn south from Noville to Bois Jacques, woods which lay behind Foy.

Despite a thick fog which descended again, the departing vehicles were ambushed and the GIs became separated. Among them was Burgett, who managed to battle his way back to Foy, and Don Addor, who was struggling across a field when he 'heard a blast and I was blown into the air. I landed flat on my back. My helmet flew in one direction and my rifle went in another.'[21] He felt a large piece of mortar shrapnel in his back and within minutes he had also taken two bullets in his right leg. Fortunate to be rescued by his buddies, Addor's war was over and he began a long journey via Paris and Oxford to the Walter Reed Hospital in Washington, DC, which saw him lose his leg to gangrene.

Of the fifteen tanks that had first driven to Noville, four returned; two hundred of Desobry's men, including the major himself, had become casualties, as had 212 of the Colonel Sink's 506th (sometimes known as the 'Five-O-Sink' because of the longevity of his command). Lauchert's 2nd Panzer Division had lost twenty tanks destroyed at Noville, and twenty-five others needed repair. A whole *Panzergrenadier* battalion had been wiped out and 142 men taken prisoner. Worse still, Lauchert felt, was the lost time and precious spent fuel.[22]

Attached to Team Desobry was Dr John 'Jack' Prior, assigned to the 20th Armored Infantry Battalion to replace their medic, evacuated with pneumonia just before the battle began. He opened his aid station in Noville's bar, the Café Louis, from 06.00 a.m. on the 19th and had no shortage of business, though at one stage the half-track into which he had just loaded four patients received a direct hit as soon as it moved off. He managed to rescue his casualties under the gaze of the offending German tank commander. Eventually Prior evacuated all his patients into Bastogne by strapping them to salvaged doors, and tying these to the decks of Sherman tanks.

In the wake of the *Volksgrenadiers*, the security apparatus of the Third Reich quickly descended on each and every village. On 20 December, even while Team Desobry were contesting the area, a Gestapo unit arrived in Bourcy, a mile east of Noville. They spoke French fluently and questioned the villages, looking for Allied sympathisers and American stragglers. Two accompanied Marcel Roland to his cellar to plunder the best wine, but in their search uncovered a hidden American flag, used by the Rolands to welcome their liberators in September, and fabricated from lengths of dyed cloth. Roland was beaten badly by his captors, his screaming audible to all nearby, but it was only on 21 December that his body was discovered, dumped in the mud, his skull crushed by clubs. The Maquet family, who ran the village bar, had likewise been executed, but no one in Bourcy could think why. The Gestapo then moved into Noville, while the smoke of battle still hung over the town; there they executed eight men behind 'Doc' Prior's dressing station, the Café Louis, including the schoolmaster and the village priest.[23]

Following his hasty departure from Noville, 'Doc' Prior then set up a 10th Armored Division aid station on the rue Neufchâteau, where two Belgian nurses, Renée Lemaire and Augusta Chiwy, who was from the Belgian Congo, helped him care for the hundreds of badly wounded. On at least one occasion, Chiwy accompanied 'Doc' Prior to collect casualties from Mardasson Hill, north-east of Bastogne, wearing GI uniform because her own clothes had become saturated with blood. Prior said the bullets missed her because she was so small. Chiwy retorted, 'those Germans must be terrible marksmen – a black face in all that white snow was a pretty easy target'.

On 23 December a Luftwaffe bomb fell on the aid station, killing thirty wounded GIs and Lemaire. Chiwy was blown through a wall, but survived unscathed. The remainder were quickly moved into the Heintz Barracks and, by the time a second surgeon arrived by Piper Cub on 26 December to assist Prior and Chiwy, there were more than 600 serious cases. Today, a wall plaque commemorates Lemaire's death, but somehow Chiwy's bravery was overlooked. Happily this was remedied in June 2011, when King Albert II made her a Knight of the Order of the Belgian Crown for her work in 1944.[24]

As Bayerlein's men were battling with Team Cherry, Oberst von Lauchert realised his 2nd Panzer Division was running short of fuel. He knew that having to manoeuvre cross-country around Bastogne, instead of driving through it on surfaced roads, guzzled gasoline. So, too, did the battle for Noville. None of the US gasoline depots he had expected to capture had been discovered. Lüttwitz, XLVII Panzer Corps commander, requested permission on his behalf to fight his way into Bastogne, where he assumed there would be a large fuel dump. 'Forget Bastogne and head for the Meuse' came the terse reply from Manteuffel.

However, Bayerlein's Panzer Lehr was beginning to experience the same problem. After being held up by Team Cherry at Longvilly and Neffe, the division was ordered to bypass Bastogne to the south. Behind them, Oberst Kokott's 26th *Volksgrenadiers* had already been ordered to cease following the panzers and encircle and occupy Bastogne when the opportunity arose. Hitler's original plan was becoming unrecognisable. Gradually the villages around the perimeter were probed for weak spots by the grenadiers; Marvie, Bizory and Neffe all came under attack. Bastogne had been surrounded.

The view of the garrison was typified by the observation which circulated swiftly: 'They've got us surrounded – the poor bastards!' Later that night, 20 December, when US XVIII Airborne Corps called by radio to ask the situation, the 101st Division G-3, Lieutenant-Colonel Harry W.O. Kinnard, Jr, was wary of saying too much in case the Germans were monitoring the exchange. He replied simply, 'Visualise the hole in the doughnut. That's us!'[25]

28

Nuts!

MAJOR WILLIAM DESOBRY'S defence of Noville, the small town five miles north-east of Bastogne, over 19–20 December was achieved with the help of four M-18 Hellcat tank destroyers of the 705th Tank Destroyer Battalion. They were credited with an astonishing thirty kills against the 2nd Panzer Division over two days of intense combat.

The many dramatic accounts and after-action reports of the 101st and Team Desobry refer to the presence of 'Tigers' in Noville, but there were none fielded by 2nd Panzer or any other unit in the vicinity. The sloping front shared by the Tiger II and Panther explained this frequent misidentification. It was partly the Hellcat's efficacy that induced Oberst Meinrad von Lauchert, the division's commander, to conclude that the little town was held by a much stronger force that it was. Refused permission to fight his way into the Bastogne 'doughnut', and goaded by an impatient Manteuffel, he left off his attacks and headed west to the Meuse. Already, on the 21st, although the visibility was still limited, a few Allied fighter-bombers had made their presence felt along the roads leading back from Bastogne through Longvilly and Clervaux to Dasburg and the Our river. Henceforth the panzers would roll west, but with one eye cast heavenwards.

At dawn on Thursday, 21 December, as Bayerlein's troops from Panzer Lehr attacked the village of Morhet, those of the 26th *Volksgrenadiers* fighting alongside, took Sibret, both settlements to the south-west of Bastogne. There, the remains of the 110th Regiment and headquarters of the 28th Division were in place. Defending Sibret as an outpost of Bastogne's defence were the remnants of 28th Division – 200 GIs equipped with three howitzers and two bazookas. They were soon subdued. Panzer Lehr then recommenced its thrust west towards the Meuse, in tandem with the 2nd Panzer Division. Meanwhile, the *Volksgrenadiers* continued to probe their way around Bastogne's western perimeter, completing their encirclement of the town. The GIs within the 'doughnut' soon found the most effective remedy to German probes of their defences. A well-placed artillery concentration, fired indirectly from their several artillery battalions, and controlled by observers, rather than the use of direct-fire infantry weapons or tanks, would set the pattern for the next few days.

The cannoneers was soon reinforced by the arrival of a sister unit to the 969th Field (African American) Artillery Battalion. The 333rd were also an African American unit of the then racially segregated US Army, equipped with towed 155mm heavy guns. Despite the segregation of the era, some of its junior officers were black. They had landed at Normandy in July 1944 and seen continuous action since. The battalion had an impressive record, once firing 1,500 rounds in a twenty-four-hour period. They had also received recognition as *Yank Magazine* had published a laudatory article about them in the autumn of 1944. In the Ardennes, the 333rd had started out as part of Middleton's VIII Corps artillery based at Schönberg, covering the 106th Golden Lions divisional area. Two batteries had been overrun by the Germans on 17 December and most personnel killed or captured, including the CO, Lieutenant-Colonel Harmon Kelsey – a white officer – and 227 other officers and men. The remnants, about 300, withdrew into the Bastogne perimeter, but eleven black GI artillerymen evaded capture and were given shelter by a Belgian farmer in the hamlet of Wereth, north-east of St Vith.

Four SS men from *Kampfgruppe Knittel* (of the 1st SS-*Leibstandarte* Division) on a reconnaissance mission arrived shortly afterwards, discovered their presence and took them away. They were never seen again until the February thaw uncovered eleven frozen corpses nearby. By the time Captain William Everett examined the bodies, they had lain under the snow for nearly two months. 'On 15 February 1945, I personally examined the bodies of the American Negro soldiers listed below,' he wrote in a report. 'The perpetrators were undoubtedly SS enlisted men, but available testimony is insufficient to establish definite unit identification.' He then went on to detail how each had been killed by blows to the head, stabbed repeatedly with bayonets and shot multiple times. The investigation was closed and forgotten until local civilians who had witnessed the event researched further, identified the soldiers, though not their executioners, and in 1994 Hans Langer, son of the farmer who had sheltered the fugitives fifty years earlier, erected a memorial on the site of the massacre.[1]

Meanwhile, Field Marshal Model had realised that Bastogne's continued defiance was slowing the German advance considerably. The town lay on his Main Supply Route (MSR) and manoeuvring round it was time-consuming and fuel-inefficient. What the panzers needed was use of the town centre's road junctions, which would give them quick access to the rest of the Ardennes. He directed that Bastogne must fall on 22 December, leaving Manteuffel to devise a plan. Fifth Panzer Army headquarters did not consider offering Bastogne the chance to surrender – so far, the Americans appeared to be in bullish mode and not short of defiant aggression, particularly if their performance at Noville was anything to go by. However, the local corps commander, General von Lüttwitz, was impatient and decided to try and bluff the defenders into submission, neglecting to warn Manteuffel or his superiors of his intended actions. He had his staff compose and prepare a surrender ultimatum for delivery on the 22nd. After the war, Manteuffel was emphatic that he 'did not order either the writing or sending of a note of this kind'.[2] Heinz Kokott, commanding the 26th *Volksgrenadiers*, and Fritz Bayerlein of Panzer Lehr were both convinced the attempt would fail, and that they would have to crush the troublesome garrison.[3]

Shortly after 11.30 a.m. on Friday, 22 December, Sergeants Oswald Y. Butler and Carl E. Dickinson of the 327th Glider Regiment manning the Bastogne perimeter first noticed the four Germans walking up the road from Remoifosse, south-east of town. They were waving a white flag. PFC Ernest D. Premetz, who could speak German, motioned them forward and was addressed by Leutnant Helmuth Henke in English. 'We are parlementaires,' Henke announced. The four Germans – Henke, an officer with Panzer Lehr, Major Wagner, on Lüttwitz's XLVII Corps staff, and two enlisted men – were taken to a nearby platoon headquarters and, while the grenadiers waited, their officers were blindfolded and taken to the farmhouse which housed the HQ of Company 'F', where they presented their surrender ultimatum.

The document was brought to the 101st Division Headquarters at the

Heintz Barracks by Major Alvin Jones, the S-3, and Colonel Harper, the 327th's regimental commander. It was taken first to the division's acting chief of staff, Lieutenant Colonel Ned Moore. He and Harper then found General McAuliffe and told him he had a surrender ultimatum. McAuliffe first thought that the Germans were trying to surrender to *him*; he was disabused of the idea and shown the letter, typed in German and English, addressed 'to the U.S.A. Commander of the encircled town of Bastogne'. The English version read:

> The fortune of war is changing. This time the U.S.A. forces in and near Bastogne have been encircled by strong German armored units. More German armored units have crossed the river Our near Ortheuville, have taken Marche and reached St Hubert by passing through Hompré-Sibret-Tillet. Libramont is in German hands.
>
> There is only one possibility to save the encircled U.S.A. troops from total annihilation: that is the honourable surrender of the encircled town. In order to think it over, a term of two hours will be granted beginning with the presentation of this note.
>
> If this proposal should be rejected one German Artillery Corps and six heavy A. A. Battalions are ready to annihilate the U.S.A. troops in and near Bastogne. The order for firing will be given immediately after this two hours' term.
>
> All the serious civilian losses caused by this artillery fire would not correspond with the well known American humanity.
>
> The German Commander[4]

McAuliffe's reaction was to chuckle in disbelief – the Germans, with inferior numbers (from what he could make out) and shivering in the freezing countryside were demanding that he surrender the town. It made no sense: 'Us surrender? Aw, nuts!' was his comment to Moore, essentially meaning 'You've got to be kidding me'. He had just given the Germans, as he put it, 'one Hell of a beating at Noville, and all knew it'. He was annoyed, too, about the emotional blackmail contained in the reference to potential 'civilian losses'. McAuliffe treated the matter as some sort of sick joke on the Germans' part, then returned to other, more pressing business regarding the disposition of his troops and organising his defences; the 101st had not long arrived in Bastogne and there was much work to do. The German message was ignored. Sometime later the German delegation, hearing nothing, pressed for an answer. Only then did McAuliffe and Moore realise that some sort of official reply was needed.

The commander pondered a few minutes, stymied. 'Well I don't know what to tell them,' he told his headquarters staff. Lieutenant-Colonel Kinnard, who had grown up in Dallas and earlier coined the 'doughnut' metaphor, mused, 'That first remark of yours would be hard to beat'. McAuliffe responded, 'What do you mean?' Kinnard answered. 'Sir, you said *Nuts!*' This drew warm applause all round. McAuliffe grabbed a

It was on 22 December 1944 that, against the wishes of his superior Manteuffel, the commander of XLVII Panzer Corps, Heinrich von Lüttwitz (1896–1969), issued a surrender summons to Tony McAuliffe, defender of Bastogne. With his monocle, Knight's Cross and distinguished-sounding surname, the German was the very stereotype of a Nazi officer from central casting. The contrast between the lineages of the Barons von Lüttwitz and the Irish Catholic McAuliffe was emphasised by the American commander's reply – 'Nuts!' It was backwoods levity to counter Prussian pomposity. (Author's collection)

pencil and wrote down: 'To the German Commander, 'Nuts!' A.C. McAuliffe, Commanding'.

Such was the response to a request issued by the scion of an old and distinguished aristocratic family – Heinrich Diepold Georg Freiherr (Baron) von Lüttwitz, bearer of the Knight's Cross with Oak Leaves, formerly ensign in Uhlan Cavalry Regiment No. 1, and nephew of a First World War senior general. The Lüttwitz family traced their ancestry back to 1430, and among his relatives were the Barons von Richthofen and General Kurt von Hammerstein-Equord, a former Chief of the General Staff. The contrast between the lineages of the monocled Baron von Lüttwitz and the Irish Catholic McAuliffe – from West Virginia, though West Point-educated – couldn't have been greater. The 'Nuts!' reply was a little backwoods levity to counter Prussian pomposity.

Patton would, no doubt, have reached for some profanity, and a number of historians since have questioned whether McAuliffe's comment was a sanitised version of the past. It seems to rank with Eisenhower's 'OK Let's Go!' to launch D-Day, as one of the great understatements of history. I met Kinnard, then a retired lieutenant-general, at a Washington, DC, hotel in the late spring of 1984, just prior to the fortieth anniversary of D-Day. When McAuliffe's wife Helen first heard the story of the American reply to the German demand for surrender, the name of the commander who had sent the defiant message was not yet common knowledge. According to Kinnard, she knew instantly it was her husband, 'That was Tony all over,' she said, 'because "aw, nuts" was his special way of announcing extreme frustration.' Kinnard told me that after the war, in November and December 1945, the historian S.L.A. Marshall held ten debriefing conferences with some of the main players in the Bastogne story – Lüttwitz, Bayerlein and Kokott – which he also attended. At the first meeting, Kinnard's youth was a 'visible shock' to the German commanders, and Lüttwitz asked whether Marshall 'was certain he was chief of operations?' which Kinnard took as a great compliment.

Little thinking the word would carry into posterity, McAuliffe had his response typed out and given to Harper, who announced 'I will take it myself. It will be a real pleasure'. Harper drove to the farmhouse and told the waiting Germans that he had his commander's reply. The still-blindfolded Leutnant Henke asked, 'Is it written or verbal?' Harper placed it in his hand. The Germans were allowed to take off their blindfolds and read the message. They were understandably puzzled, trying to translate 'Nuts!' The major then asked, 'Is the reply negative or affirmative? If it is the latter I will negotiate further'. Harper started to lose his temper and retorted, 'The reply is decidedly not affirmative'.

Harper then took them back to where their men waited, saying to Henke, 'If you don't know what "Nuts" means, in plain English it is the same as '"Go to Hell". . . And I'll tell you something else, if you continue to attack we will kill every goddamn German that tries to break into this town.' Clearly surprised, the Germans saluted very formally. Henke responded philosophically, 'We will kill many Americans. This is war'. Harper then waved him off, 'On your way Bud', adding, 'and good luck to you'. By then it was 1.50 p.m.; Harper said later he always regretted wishing them good luck.[5]

Lüttwitz's bluff had been called and he had been made to look ridiculous. The Prussian had suffered a personal affront for making a threat on which he could not deliver. To his own superiors, Lüttwitz had demonstrated his total misunderstanding of the American soldier. Word of the unfolding drama spread around the GIs like wildfire, and many took the opportunity of the temporary ceasefire to shave, brew some coffee or walk around, stretching their legs. (Some observed the Germans doing the same.) Under these circumstances, word of their general's 'Nuts!' reply raised the morale of his defenders just when they needed it, for they were running desperately short of artillery ammunition. By the 23rd, one of the artillery battalions was down to 200 rounds. Determined to make every shell count, McAuliffe (usually in charge of the division's guns) rationed each request for support to two rounds per fire mission, however tempting the target.

The first heavy snowfalls had occurred the night before and Private Warren G. Maddox remembered arriving in a forest on the edge of town. 'For two hours I heard the clump of our picks and entrenching tools as we gnawed at rock-hard earth and tree roots. The night was clear. I remember the wind whistling past the trees, trunks ripped bare by the shelling. Our efforts were futile, but the exercise kept us from freezing. When we finally gave up chewing holes in the ground, we stomped up and down between the pines trying to stir up heat in our bodies. Any concerns about the freshly-turned earth identifying our positions disappeared with the fresh snowfalls of the twenty-second.'[6]

The air force promised to resupply when the weather cleared, and duly arrived overhead from 11.50 a.m. on 23 December. From wave after wave of C-47s, from the 53rd and 60th Troop Carrier Wings blossomed hundreds of parachutes, each in a different colour to indicate the nature of its burden. Many of the aircrew had flown the paratroopers below into Normandy on D-Day and wanted to help their buddies again. Kokott, commander of the 26th *Volksgrenadiers*, saw them from far away and thought the aircraft were dropping reinforcements of men, which caused confusion among the attackers. Although the US-built aircraft – known to Americans as the Skytrain and the British as a Dakota – had a formal capacity of 6,000 lbs, this was often exceeded.

Altogether 241 C-47s dropped 144 tons in 1,446 containers into a half-mile-square area around Bastogne, with such accuracy that ground troops were able to retrieve 95 per cent of the supplies. Even after the first drop, .30-inch calibre rounds, tank shells, penicillin, stretchers and blankets remained in short supply, but the air bridge had been opened and the formula was repeated on 24, 25 and 26 December. On the 20th, noted the 420th Armored Field Artillery's after-action report, 'Long awaited supplies dropped by parachute by several flights of C-47s. Battalion picked up 1,050 rounds of 105mm howitzer ammunition [but] no gas or rations. Ten gliders with gas and surgical team land.'[7] Clear weather enabled the Allies to attack German troop concentrations in the vicinity – '3,500 Allied Planes Pound Enemy; Thunderbolts Watch Over Tank Columns; Air Fleets Out for 3rd Day in Row' headlined the *Stars and Stripes* on 26 December. At night the Luftwaffe retaliated by bombing Bastogne.

By this time, Bastogne had become a symbol of American resistance, and, because of the publicity given to the (initially unnamed) defending general's stinging reply to the German surrender demand, the world's press was neglecting to report on most other aspects of the Ardennes campaign. Newspapers in the free world began wildly comparing the defenders of Bastogne to the Alamo, Verdun or Stalingrad. Although Bastogne was technically surrounded, at no time were the defenders outnumbered by their opponents. It was significant, too, that part of the defence was in the hands of airborne troops, who knew all about drop zones and the business of aerial resupply. Providing Roberts' 10th Armored and McAuliffe's Screaming Eagles could 'batten down the hatches', there was little doubt in Allied minds that Bastogne would survive.[8]

Thus Bastogne, rather than St Vith, was brought to the attention of the world. This, more than anything else, stirred Hitler to order that Bastogne be taken at all costs, a classic case of 'mission-creep', as considerable resources were redirected to achieving this new aim.

In addition to the surrender demand of 22 December, there were continuous probes around the now-continuous entire perimeter, but only two company-sized *Volksgrenadier* attacks developed in different sectors. On the 23rd, assaults were made in the west and south-east, but the clear weather attracted Allied air power which suppressed the German inclination to attack in daylight. However, patrolling, sniping and artillery fire brought a steady stream of casualties to both sides, as did the freezing weather. During the night of 24 December, combined tank and infantry attacks against the defenders were again launched and failed.

The attacks grew larger – up to regimental size – bolder, and more desperate on Christmas Day, but no more successful. Paratrooper Ed Peniche remembered the first hostile shells peppering his positions around 03.00 a.m. on Christmas morning, as a few Luftwaffe aircraft droned overhead dropping bombs. 'Minutes later, wearing snow suits, the first Grenadiers crept forward against our lines, supported by a few tanks . . . The snow-covered battlefield soon became a spectrum of bright

Pictured in Bastogne on 19 December, these two weary GIs had been in continuous action since escaping from Clervaux and fighting their way back, with the Germans snapping at their heels. Private Adam H. Davis of Philadelphia, Pa., and T/5 Milford A. Sillars, from Mooresville, Ind., were from Colonel Hurley Fuller's 110th Regiment of 'Dutch' Cota's 28th Infantry 'Bloody Bucket' Division. Both had become members of Team SNAFU, an *ad hoc* 'fire brigade' of stragglers, deployed to repulse German incursions of the perimeter. The prevailing view of the defending garrison was: 'They've got us surrounded – the poor bastards!' (NARA)

flares, deafening explosions and machine-gun tracers . . . Lying face down at the bottom of my foxhole, I remember praying both in English and Spanish.'[9] The American advantage of interior lines, whereby a 'fire brigade' reinforcement of troops and tanks, collected from a huge miscellany of units, could rush between threatened sectors, aided the defenders and hampered the Germans' efforts. They were known as Team SNAFU.[10]

As well as high explosives, German artillery also fired propaganda leaflets into the town, urging the defenders to surrender. Among the many different versions, one, decorated with crude drawings of angels, candles and festive pine sprigs, read:

> MERRY CHRISTMAS SOLDIER, and our deepest sympathy. It's tough being away from home at this time of year . . . especially when you're surrounded and out-numbered ten to one. Don't you feel your loved ones worrying about you, praying for you? Yes, old boy, praying and hoping you'll come back home again. Man, have you thought about it? What if you don't come back? Just remember this: where there's a will, there's a way. HOT CHOW AND SAFETY are waiting for you ONLY 300 YARDS AWAY

Bored GIs collected and swapped them like football cards, or used them to supplement their meagre supplies of K-ration toilet paper.

The Christmas Day attack was launched by Kokott's snow-suited *VolksGgrenadiers,* riding on eighteen white-painted Panzer IVs from the 15th *Panzergrenadier* Division, which attacked Bastogne from the north-west, between Champs and Hemroulle. The force, grinding forward in line abreast, broke through the outer lines of the 327th Glider Infantry, knocked out two American tank destroyers and wheeled towards two companies of the 502nd PIR. Directed by the regimental commander, Colonel Steve A. Chappuis in Rollé Château, the paratroopers responded by raking the tanks with machine-gun fire, killing many of the grenadiers. At the same time, US tank destroyers and bazooka teams accounted for several of the panzers as they re-formed into a column. Eventually American joint fires (from tanks, tank destroyers, bazookas and parachute field artillery) created such a storm of cross-fire that 'the German tanks were fired at from so many directions and with such a mixture of fire that it was not possible to see or say how each tank met its doom'.[11] This attack, however, showed that with more careful coordination and planning, the Germans still had the ability to penetrate the defences with near-catastrophic results. After the liberation of the traumatised ruins of Champs in January, the village schoolteacher found scrawled in chalk on the school's blackboard,

> May the world never again live through such a Christmas Night! Nothing is more horrible than meeting one's fate, far from mother, wife and children. Is it worthy of a man's destiny to bereave a mother of her son, a wife of her husband, or children of their father? Life was bequeathed us in order that we might love and be considerate to one another. From the ruins, out of blood and death shall come forth a brotherly world.
>
> [signed] a German Officer.[12]

Manteuffel's Fifth Panzer Army allocated more resources to crushing Bastogne, and on 26 December again attacked with battalion-size infantry and panzer teams. It was by then apparent that the defenders had perfected their infantry-armour-artillery (known as 'combined arms') defensive tactics, whereas the *Volksgrenadiers* and panzers rarely played to each other's strengths, and their combat efforts were clumsy by comparison.

Meanwhile, Patton had committed the US 4th Armored Division to break the German hold on Bastogne, with tank columns pushing from the south, from Martelange and Neufchâteau, through terrain held by 5th *Fallschirmjägers.* On the road was Sergeant Nat Frankel who had managed to get his tank bogged down in the mud. He stuck his head out of the turret and looked around. 'The first thing I saw was those two damn guns of his. Ivory-handled – ivory, not pearl, for, as he himself so famously said, only St Louis pimps wear pearl-tipped guns. They were strapped across his hips like a portable totem pole. Then I saw his eyes, glowering like two jewels planted in a Polynesian idol . . . His arms were waving, randomly but not fanatically. He was the very picture of total energy combined with godlike self-control . . . "What's wrong?" he bellowed. I told him. "Goddamn! This is no time to get stuck! Get this goddamn thing rolling!"'[13]

Finally, elements of Combat Command R, including Lieutenant-Colonel Creighton W. Abrams' 37th Tank Battalion, were poised at 3.00 p.m. on the 26th to close the final distance. Instead of a planned attack via Sibret, a late decision was made to dash along the less conspicuous Remichampagne–Clochimont–Assenois road, and into the perimeter. Abrams sent Captain William Dwight in his Sherman, leading seven others and a column of half-tracks from Company 'C', 53rd Armored Infantry Battalion, on ahead. With daylight fading, Abrams called for artillery support (four battalions were then available), directed by Lieutenant Bill Wood in a tiny spotter plane, on to Assenois, and such was his speed that when Dwight burst into the little village it was still under 'friendly' fire, which destroyed one of his half-tracks.

Covered by eight anti-tank guns, more than a hundred Germans emerged to tackle the column as it crashed through the settlement and the ensuing hand-to-hand fighting meant that only five Shermans and one half-track broke out of Assenois. In the confusion, nineteen-year-old Sergeant James R. Hendrix of the 53rd Armored Infantry, armed only with his rifle, forced the crew of an 88mm gun to surrender, destroyed two machine-gun nests before rescuing a burning GI from the flames of a half-track. His deeds would bring him a Medal of Honor. Guns blazing, the much-reduced column was stalled when the Germans spread Teller mines on the road, but these were cleared quickly by Dwight's tank crew and the advance resumed.

The last German position was an old Belgian concrete pillbox, which received three 75mm rounds from First Lieutenant Charles P. Boggess' tank, named 'Cobra King', then in the lead. As they cleared the surrounding woods, the relief column came upon an open field littered with blue, white and yellow parachutes from supply drops, and slowed down, reckoning they were approaching friendly lines. They saw foxholes with helmeted figures. Taking no chances, they called out. After several summons an officer emerged with a smile and said, 'I'm Lieutenant Webster, 326th Airborne Engineers, glad to see you guys!' It was 4.50 p.m. on 26 December and the siege had been lifted. Creighton Abrams in his tank 'Thunderbolt IV' joined them a few minutes later. All hope for German success to take Bastogne had died.[14]

McAuliffe had driven to the front line hoping Abrams' force would break through; by order, his greeting party were well-dressed and clean-shaven, to demonstrate that the 101st had everything under control. The following day saw Maxwell Taylor, hotfooted from Washington, finally reunited with his division. It was en route to

Bastogne that he offered four waiting journalists (Joseph Driscoll of the *New York Herald Tribune*, Norman Clark of the *London News Chronicle*, Cornelius Ryan of the *Daily Telegraph* and Walter Cronkite of *United Press*) a ride in his jeep down the still-contested road into Bastogne. They preferred to wait for a tank, knowing Taylor had no fear of acting as a 'bullet-magnet'.

Another individual hurrying towards Bastogne was Robert Capa, muffled in a looted German coat. He was the world's best-known war photographer by then; Hungarian-born, but a naturalised American, Capa's fame dated back to the combat images he had taken of the 'Falling Soldier' in the Spanish Civil War – a rifleman flung back by a bullet, caught in the moment of death. He had since waded ashore with the first wave at Omaha Beach on D-Day and now wanted to capture the Ardennes for *Life* magazine. First Lieutenant Kenneth Koyen, a pre-war newspaperman then on the 4th Armored Division's G-2 (intelligence) staff, was assigned to 'mind' him as he made pictures of the 4th on the road to Bastogne. Koyen suggested that for safety's sake Capa remove his greatcoat, but in the freezing temperatures the cameraman refused. So the pair drove forward by jeep until they found troops attacking across a frozen stubble field, and Capa dismounted and began to work. 'He was at some distance when I heard him shout and I then saw him running toward me with his arms upraised,' recalled Koyen. "Ken", he called, '"they're shooting at me! Tell them to stop!"' Some of the riflemen, advancing on foot behind us, had seen this strange figure on the snow-covered field and had fired. I signalled to the GIs and the desultory firing stopped. Capa and I exchanged a long glance. Without a word, he took off his coat and stowed it in the Jeep.' Capa had his photos, which duly appeared in the 15 January edition of *Life*.[15]

Hot on the heels of the 4th Armored came the 6th Armored Division, followed by elements of the 11th, with truckloads of ammunition, medical supplies and mail – the first for at least two weeks. Combat Medic Robert Kinser of the 3rd Tank Battalion accompanied the casualties back on 27 December: 'By then, there were over 2,000 wounded in Bastogne. I had an ambulance and went out with the first load . . . [in] a convoy of over 100 ambulances. We took them about forty miles back, transferred them, and went back to Bastogne.'[16] Meanwhile, 130 C-47s flew resupply missions, thirty-two more gliders landed with vital stores and personnel and trucks departed with civilians and prisoners. While the siege had cost the 101st alone just over 2,000 killed and wounded, they had killed 7,000 Germans, captured 697 prisoners and destroyed approximately 200 armoured vehicles. Panzer Lehr and 2nd Panzer Divisions reckoned that Bastogne cost them eighty-one tanks.[17]

The battle in the Ardennes was fought and won on the ground. However, the threat which slowed and ultimately stopped the 1944 blitzkrieg came from the air. According to Albert Speer, it was on 23 December that 'Model told me that the offensive had definitely failed – but Hitler had ordered it to continue'. As Reich Armaments Minister, Speer had set off for the front at the start of the campaign, having earlier pledged personally to Model that logistics for Army Group 'B' would flow unimpeded during the battle. Even on 16 December, his heart sank as he rode through the night 'in a Reichsbahn diesel car', when he saw the rail marshalling yards 'east of the Rhine jammed with freight cars. The enemy bombers had prevented the movement of supplies for the offensive.'

Thereafter Speer stayed with Model as 'a camp follower', remembering the chaotic states of the roads leading to the forward lines. 'Motor vehicles could move only a foot at a time along the three-lane highway. My car took an hour on average to move two miles, wedged in as it was by ammunition trucks. I kept fearing the weather might improve.' When it did so, the passage of supplies did, indeed, dry up 'when the foggy weather changed in a few days and the cloudless skies filled with innumerable enemy fighter planes and bombers. A drive by day became a problem even for a fast passenger car.' Then the supply services could operate only at night. In the end, Speer was forced to conclude the Wehrmacht had 'lost its erstwhile famous talent for organisation – surely one of the effects of Hitler's three years of [total] command'.[18]

Afterwards, Lieutenant-Colonel Ralph Ingersoll, then on Bradley's staff, drove over to see the famous battlefield. 'It was a hard, stark thing,' he wrote. 'The tanks were not much good there except as artillery. The dead lay frozen and stiff. When the men came to load them in trucks, they picked them up and put them in like big logs of wood. On the edges of town you could see where the German columns had broken through the perimeter from the burnt-out panzers the Germans had left behind. Mixed in with the wrecks of the tanks were the wrecks of the gliders – and here and there, black in the sun, were the little basketfuls of charred junk, that is all that's left of an aircraft when it goes into the ground at three or four hundred miles an hour.'[19]

To the north-east of Bastogne lies a very minor road, running from Bizory to Foy. When I first knew the region, everything to the right of the route was densely forested, but the terrain has since been levelled and become *Les Bois de la Paix* ('the Peace Woods'). Created on the Bulge's fiftieth anniversary, many trees are named in honour of the soldiers who fought there; from the air, I am told, the new trees are designed to form the emblem of UNICEF. A mile further ahead, on the left, is a little brick monument to Company 'E' of the 506th Parachute Infantry Regiment, made famous by the *Band of Brothers* TV series, though of course many other units fought here, before and after. Easy Company occupied foxholes in the Bois Jacques, on the left, another mile beyond, overlooking Foy.

On 13 January 1945, three companies of the Screaming Eagles attacked Foy, a drama depicted at length in *Band of Brothers*. The village had originally been seized on 18–19 December, as we have seen, by Lauchert's 2nd Panzer Division. They were relieved by *Volksgrenadiers*, and later still by the second-wave 9th Panzer Division, who were in occupation with a *Panzergrenadier* company including snipers, tanks and artillery support, when the Screaming Eagles attacked. After a stiff fight, the *Panzergrenadiers* were ousted, but returned the next morning, initially ejecting the 101st. Foy was finally secured by the paratroopers later that day, who then went on to seize Noville, the crossroads town they had first fought over on 19 December. Both settlements changed hands at least half a dozen times and were reduced to smoking rubble by the battle's end – incomprehensible today as both communities have recovered, with few traces left of the earlier destruction.

The pillbox on the rue de Fortin at Assenois remains, still bearing the shell-strikes from 26 December 1944, and is now a treasured landmark of the town. All around Bastogne, a ring of Sherman turrets on stone plinths marks the extent of the defensive perimeter along each of the seven main roads which radiated out in 1944. On the morning of 19 December a German patrol reached the Mardasson Hill, north-east of Bastogne; one member of the patrol was killed and is believed to be the grenadier who approached closest to the town. A huge star-shaped monument to the fallen was commenced on the spot in 1946, and the site has now been developed into a memorial complex and museum.

Chiselled into the monument are the names of each American state and every US unit that participated in the Bulge, with a dedication to the 'lasting friendship between the peoples of Belgium and the United States'. *Cobra King*, the first tank into Bastogne, is still in service with the US Army (when I saw her last, as the gate guard of Rose Barracks at Vilseck in Germany). The Kessler Farm, north of Remoifosse and west of Marvie, once the headquarters of Company 'F', where the German surrender delegates waited, still stands. So does McAuliffe's command post; the night before the 'Nuts!' drama, Colonel William L. Roberts of the 10th Armored relocated his CP from the Hôtel LeBrun, overlooking the town square, to join McAuliffe at the Heintz Barracks. Both men had also moved their operations room and communications centre to some dingy cellars underneath, from where they jointly conducted the battle for Bastogne.

National defence cuts announced in 2009 threatened to demolish this historic site, but the Belgian army countered with their own proposals and McAuliffe's CP is now 'The Nuts Cellar', a superb little museum, supplemented by exhibits loaned from the National Military Museum in Diekirch. It is run by a team of Belgian army volunteers who really care about this symbolic piece of American history. Their enthusiasm is tremendous.

In December 1944 Major John D. Hanlon, commanding the 1st Battalion of the 502nd PIR, appealed to the mayor of Hemroulle, north-west of Bastogne, for the loan of white bed linen for his men to wrap around themselves as camouflage against the snow. Monsieur Victor Gaspar rang the church bells to summon the villagers, explained the situation to them, and within no time more than 200 bedsheets had appeared, piled up in the little village square. All were gratefully received, with Hanlon promising to return them as soon as possible. His battalion – and the sheets – then disappeared into battle.

In 1947, a retired Lieutenant-Colonel Hanlon, by then the proud possessor of a Silver Star and two Bronze Stars, read an article on Bastogne in his local Boston newspaper, which mentioned, tongue in cheek, that Hemroulle was still waiting for the return of its sheets. He wrote to the Boston paper explaining that part of the story was his fault and, to his surprise, parcels of bed linen began to arrive in the mail from every corner of Massachusetts. When Hanlon returned to Hemroulle in February 1948, the church bells rang again, summoning the villagers. With much emotion on both sides, each received the same number of sheets they had 'loaned' him in 1944. Hemroulle then insisted on making Hanlon an honorary citizen and sending him home with paintings from the village church, which had survived the battle, and now hang on the walls of the churches of Winchester, Massachusetts, and its town hall.[20]

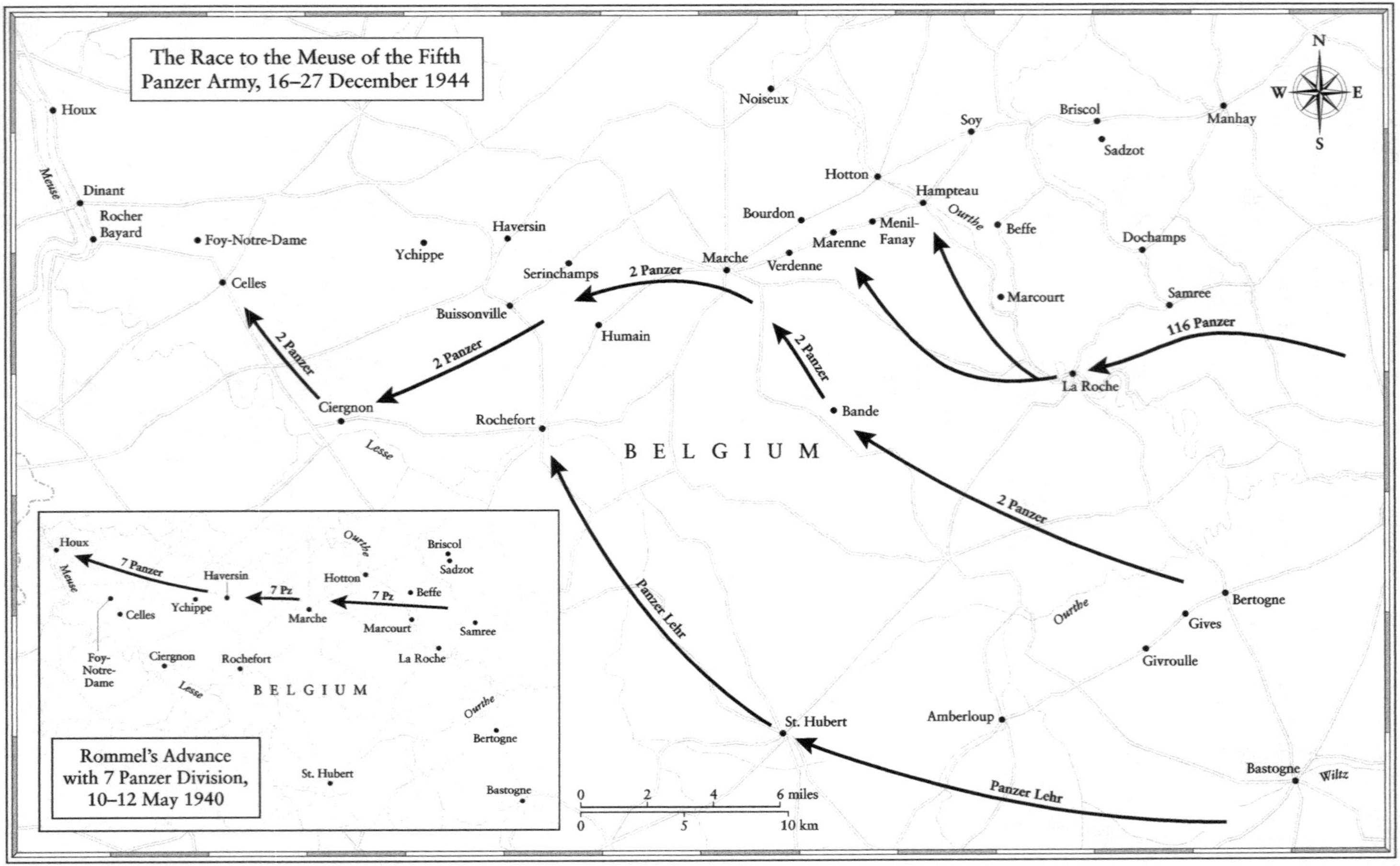
The Race to the Meuse of the Fifth Panzer Army, 16–27 December 1944
Houx
Meuse
Dinant
Rocher Bayard
Foy-Notre-Dame
Celles
Ychippe
Haversin
Serinchamps
Buissonville
Humain
Ciergnon
Rochefort
Lesse
Noiseux
Hotton
Bourdon
Marche
Verdenne
Marenne
Menil-Fanay
Hampteau
Ourthe
Soy
Beffe
Briscol
Sadzot
Manhay
Dochamps
Marcourt
Samree
La Roche
Bande
116 Panzer
2 Panzer
2 Panzer
2 Panzer
2 Panzer
2 Panzer
Panzer Lehr
Panzer Lehr
BELGIUM
St. Hubert
Amberloup
Givroulle
Gives
Bertogne
Ourthe
Bastogne
Wiltz
N
S
E
W
0 2 4 6 miles
0 5 10 km
Houx
Meuse
7 Panzer
Haversin
7 Pz
Hotton
7 Pz
Beffe
Briscol
Sadzot
Ourthe
Celles
Ychippe
Marche
Marcourt
Samree
Foy-Notre-Dame
Ciergnon
Rochefort
La Roche
Lesse
BELGIUM
Ourthe
Bertogne
St. Hubert
Bastogne
Rommel's Advance with 7 Panzer Division, 10–12 May 1940

29

Head for the Meuse!

General der Panzertruppe Hasso von Manteuffel was angry. Several matters irritated the baron on 20 December, but no more so than his subordinate's failure to take Bastogne on the evening of the 18th. He came over to Panzer Lehr's HQ in person and berated Fritz Bayerlein for his stupidity in choosing a muddy track to Mageret 'like an officer cadet who couldn't read a map'. He blamed him for undue caution throughout the 19th and a 'lack of fighting spirit' within the division – accusations which could get a commander shot in the Third Reich of late 1944. Lüttwitz had little doubt that, had Bayerlein chosen an alternative route, he would have broken through the roadblocks of Teams Desobry or O'Hara, neither of whom were fully deployed, and gained the town easily – the 101st being off-balance, in the process of arriving and short of ammunition. Kokott's *Volksgrenadiers* would have assisted in mopping up many of the straggling GIs in the vicinity. History suggests that Manteuffel and Lüttwitz were probably correct.

On the other hand, Heinz Kokott's 26th *Volksgrenadiers*, struggling through the mud on foot with wagons and artillery drawn by 3,000 horses, had done a magnificent job of keeping up with the tanks. Henceforth their task would be to stay and subdue Bastogne, in place of the panzers which had by then begun to hurry westwards. In fact, Lüttwitz and Manteuffel had already recommended Kokott for promotion to *Generalmajor*, which came through on 1 January. Meanwhile, Bayerlein was instructed to leave one of his *Panzergrenadier* Regiments,

Differential mobility between the panzer and *Volksgrenadier* divisions was a constant challenge throughout the campaign. In front of Bastogne, for example, the 3,000 horses towing the logistics and artillery of Heinz Kokott's 26th *Volksgrenadiers* struggled to keep up with the tanks and half-tracks of Panzer Lehr and 2nd Panzer Division. (Author's collection)

the 901st, to stay behind with Kokott, while the rest of the division moved on. Part of Heilmann's 5th *Fallschirmjäger* Division was also sent to Bastogne, but for the panzers – next stop, the Meuse!

The most northerly of Manteuffel's three panzer divisions was Siegfried von Waldenburg's 116th Panzer Division (the *Windhund*, or Greyhounds), which, accompanied by Oberst Rudolf Langhäuser's 560th *Volksgrenadiers*, belonged to Krüger's LVIII Panzer Corps. The *Windhund* Division had fought hard at Lützkampen to the north of the 2nd Panzer in the initial assault on the 16th. Despite attempts to build a bridge at Ouren, on the night of 16–17 December and throughout the 17th, they crossed the River Our using 2nd Panzer's bridge at Dasburg, captured Heinerscheid and Hupperdange on 17 December, destroying sixteen tanks and taking 373 prisoners (from Nelson's 112th Regiment), for similar losses of their own. They were under constant pressure from their superiors, Fifth Army and LVIII Corps, to get westwards as quickly as possible, using the opportunity of the 'German-friendly weather – fog and drizzle', but a heavy mortar shell exploded in the middle of a circle of commanders, the division's

War Diary noted, killing twelve including 'our excellent Division physician, Professor Bickert'.[1]

By late on 18 December the 116th Panzer's advance guard had entered Houffalize, capturing or destroying 'many trucks and vehicles and one Sherman' and seizing the Ourthe river bridges undamaged. Langhäuser's 560th *Volksgrenadiers* were making 'quite an effort' to keep pace with them, though at this stage, aware of the clock ticking, Army Group 'B' ordered the pace of advance accelerated. Manteuffel, meanwhile, was concerned about the division's order of march. 'Spearheads [are] too thin and narrow. When [you are] near the enemy, attack him from broader formations with fire. Heavy weapons throughout [are] much too far back. Armoured groups [must be] to the front everywhere, not just *Panzergrenadiers* by themselves.'[2] On this day the first complaints about fuel shortages surfaced in the war diary, 'No fuel', reported some of the artillery formations. 'All units that have arrived have enough for 20 kilometres, the advance battalion for 10 kilometres. Roads in the back jammed. [Which prevented trucks bearing fuel from moving forward.] Nothing coming in. Some tanks usable only by siphoning.'[3]

Just as Bayerlein was grinding down his atrociously muddy track into Mageret, Major Fritz Vogelsang, the 116th Division's IIa (Adjutant for officers), with supreme optimism, reflected their experience of Belgian roads. He noted, 'Now, everything is rolling smoothly in both directions, but above all, into the area of the breach . . . The weather is again misty, damp, cold and rainy. For our offensive it could not be any better! However, mud and dirt on the ruined roads and in the torn-up terrain almost remind one of Russian conditions! In most cases the grey of our uniforms show only in a few places between the layers of mud . . . The hole in the enemy front now finally seems to have been bored through. Merrily, the attack rolls west – hopefully for long!'

South of Houffalize, 116th Panzer came up against American units, where 'a large number of tanks and motor vehicles were captured or destroyed' along with 400 prisoners taken. There was, however, a cautionary note that 'the division attack on the morning of 19 December suffered considerable delays due to lack of fuel'. Fortunately that evening they overran Gives-Givroule, where a large fuel and supply depot was captured, enabling vehicles to top up – but petrol was becoming an ever-present concern for the 116th's commanders. By the evening of the 19th, Generalmajor Waldenburg had established his HQ near Bertogne, seven miles north-west of Bastogne, but the division was having to sideslip south-west to find intact bridges over the rivers. His formation was becoming dangerously spread out, a situation governed by centres of opposition, destroyed bridges and the road network.

The enthusiasm of the initial advance was caught in Adjutant Vogelsang's record for 20 December, which also reflected the deprivations all German soldiers had suffered during the preceding couple of years. 'The Americans are completely surprised and in constant turmoil. Long columns of prisoners march toward the east, many tanks were destroyed or captured. Our *Landsers* are loaded with cigarettes, chocolates, and canned food, and are smiling from ear to ear. The combat units were able to fill the gaps caused by missing vehicles in their convoys with captured ones. Along the roads are immense piles of artillery ammunition. I estimate the amount to be 25,000 rounds. How wonderful that this blessing will not fall on our heads!'[4]

Even though his advance looked promising, Waldenburg had already run out of intact bridges west and south of the Ourthe, with no time and few facilities to build replacements. Risking the loss of a whole day, he reluctantly ordered his division to turn around, retrace their steps to Houffalize and cross to the north and east bank of the Ourthe river, and thence head for La Roche and Noiseux.[5] These are journeys of a few minutes today, with scarcely a blink of the eye when a small local river is crossed. Back in 1944 the loss of a single bridge could send a whole division scurrying hither and thither, wasting their two most precious resources in short supply – time and fuel. This gave the Americans time to strengthen their defences, for example at La Roche, where twenty-four tanks were observed on the morning of 20 December, when before there had been none.

There was some compensation when at 4.00 p.m., in Samrée, when Waldenburg destroyed twelve tanks guarding a supply depot containing 26,400 gallons of fuel, neatly stacked in five-gallon jerrycans for ready use. The 16th Panzer Regiment's War Diary recorded, 'The successes of the last past days create great enthusiasm among our soldiers, especially since many prisoners were brought in . . .'[6] A beaming Manteuffel congratulated Waldenburg by radio on the 21st: 'Appreciation and gratitude to your magnificent men, your commanders and to you. Your successes adhere to proud tradition.' More succinctly, as the divisional adjutant put it, 'The faces of the prisoners are full of disbelief and amazement'.[7]

Yet the loss of time was crucial, for it allowed Major-General Maurice

Rose's 3rd Armored Division to deploy opposite the 116th on the 20th, followed by General Alex Bolling's 84th 'Railsplitters' Infantry Division (also known as the 'Hatchet Men') on the 21st – both units of J. Lawton Collins' US VII Corps. With the 84th were Harold P. 'Bud' Leinbaugh and John D. Campbell, both with Company 'K' of the 333rd Infantry Regiment (not connected with the artillery unit of the same number). As they arrived in Serinchamps, a hamlet due west of Marche, the local mayor told them, 'this was 1940 all over again; he seemed sure of it. He seemed to take perverse pride in explaining that Rommel had personally led his panzers through the region en route to the Meuse four years earlier'. Looking at Company 'K's weaponry, the mayor asked about American tanks, clearly anxious they had more than rifles to halt the German armour.[8] 'The local phones were working', the mayor told them, 'and he'd received calls an hour earlier reporting panzers rolling through villages ten miles away.' Behind them, along the west bank of the Meuse, Montgomery had started to position the British XXX Corps, with fifty tanks of the 29th Armoured Brigade defending the bridges at Namur, Dinant and Givet. Lieutenant D.H. Clark of the Royal Army Medical Corps remembered their Sherman tanks 'rumbling past, massive and effective-looking; the drivers were Hussars who had fought in them all the way up from Normandy. The tanks looked like tinkers' caravans, with cooking pots, wine flagons, bed rolls and miscellaneous loot dangling from the camouflage netting.'[9]

On the shortest day of the year, 21 December, the *Windhund* Division lunged for the little bridge over the Ourthe at Hotton, which is where this study of the Bulge campaign began. There, the mixed bag of defenders, numbering no more than 200, armed with one 57mm anti-tank and two 40mm anti-aircraft guns, were now wiser and perhaps the attackers over-confident. The Americans were fortunate to have present some combat engineers, who not only prepared the bridge for destruction but hastily laid mines and overturned vehicles to make roadblocks.

Using the cover of a forest that came close to the town, at 08.30 a.m. seven of the *Windhund*'s tanks and half-tracks suddenly hit Hotton after the briefest of artillery barrages. The 116th Division's War Diary noted that 'Nobody was expecting an attack, though the village, especially the bridge, was well secured by enemy tanks [in fact there were only two present to begin with], anti-tank guns and sharpshooters. A platoon was guarding a pedestrian footbridge upriver at Hampteau. Due to the loss of Oberleutnant Köhn's leading Panther and the wounding of several commanders by headshots, the attack, which was only escorted by weak infantry units, came to a halt. Köhn lost an eye and three men from his crew were killed. There was heavy fighting with enemy tanks, in which the opponent suffered heavy losses . . . our units in Hotton were under heavy fire all day.'[10]

Although the *Windhund* had the advantage of surprise, and the two US tanks were destroyed, the assault came to a halt because the Germans were too cocky. Had the attack been properly coordinated between tanks and *Panzergrenadiers*, Waldenburg would have got his bridge. However, his panzers went in without a proper reconnaissance and pretty much alone, and were picked off one by one. The town was not well defended at all, though the Germans perceived it to be. A strong, well-planned attack would have removed the defenders in a trice and one is left with the impression of a botched attempt to take Hotton on 21 December. Failure to take the town in the morning led to US reinforcements from 638th Tank Destroyer Battalion and Bolling's 84th Infantry Division arriving from Soy, to the north-east, at exactly the right moment in the afternoon, as the Germans tired, and eventually they began to outnumber the attackers.

The US defenders also dominated the terrain north-east of Hotton as far as Soy, and constantly threatened to outflank their attackers, who were compelled to use their armour in defence. Using up fuel by manoeuvring off-road remained a concern, although the almost empty panzer regiment had been able to refuel completely with the petrol captured at Samrée. Oberfeldwebel Pichler, commanding three Panthers, destroyed five Shermans at Soy, but the arrival of the 1st Battalion, 517th Parachute Infantry Regiment (to which the future Medal of Honor-winner Melvin E. Biddle was attached), and a company of tank destroyers on 22 December emphasised the fact that any further German advance by way of Hotton was out of the question.

By 22 December the 116th Division's attack at Hotton had culminated, although the Fifth Army orders received that night commanded 'Bypass resistance, only [lightly] cover the flanks, bulk [effort] remains the advance towards Maas [the Meuse]. Continue to confuse, split up, surround, reconnoitre in force, and deceive [the Americans]'. However, the reality of the campaign was already apparent. The assault was hopelessly behind schedule. The Hotton attack emphasised just how alert the US Army in the once-sleepy Ardennes had become.

To the 116th Division's north, the Sixth Panzer Army remained stuck on the Elsenborn Ridge, and General Lücht's LXVI Corps on their immediate right had just finished fighting for St Vith (it was captured on the night of 21–22 December). On their left, Panzer Lehr had reached Rochefort (south-west of Marche) and 2nd Panzer Division, Bande (between Marche and La Roche); part of Lüttwitz's XLVII Panzer Corps was still delayed at Bastogne. Behind them, Langhäuser's 560th *Volksgrenadiers* were attacking at Dochamps, midway between Manhay and Marche, while reinforcements in the form of the 2nd SS Panzer Division *Das Reich* were attacking the Baraque de Fraiture crossroads, north-east of La Roche.

At the same time, 2nd Panzer Division was pulling away on its dash to the Meuse, largely because it had managed to avoid American strongpoints after Bastogne. Viewed from the air (which was not yet possible), Lauchert's division would have looked like a finger, stretching for seven miles north-westwards, from Bastogne towards Dinant. However, there were no units to guard its flanks, for both Panzer Lehr to its left and 116th Panzer on its right had encountered tougher opposition and fallen behind. The 2nd Panzer was having to use some of its own combat power to protect its flanks, which inevitably slowed its advance. The further it lunged towards the Meuse, the weaker its spearhead became. The freezing weather took its toll on vehicles as well as people.

Hans Behrens, a wireless operator in a Panzer IV following behind with Generalleutnant Harald Freiherr von Elverfeldt's 9th Panzer Division, recalled of his opponents, 'The Americans came amiss as they had rubber pads on their tank tracks, and when the roads were icy, they just slid all over the place . . . Roads were just six inches of solid frozen gleaming ice . . . One saw an unending succession of lorries that had crashed out of control . . . On the camber of a road two men could slide one [panzer] sideways by merely pushing it.' Due to widespread American knowledge of the massacre of GIs by Waffen-SS soldiers at Malmedy on 17 December (which we shall examine shortly), panzer crewmen like Behrens also learned that US troops had taken to shooting SS men automatically on capture. This often extended to tank crews, whose black panzer uniform and death's head badge was frequently mistaken for membership of Himmler's legions. Behrens spent the Bulge dreading capture.[11] The reaction of Company 'K' of the 333rd Infantry was that 'the SS was going to have to pay, and pay heavily'. They 'just wanted to start killing Germans'.[12]

Already it was apparent that the Americans were reacting far quicker than expected, both in terms of delaying the advance but also in terms of flooding the area with reinforcements. The daily report from Army Group 'B', Model's headquarters, acknowledged that 'the continuous action of the 116th Panzer Division and the 2nd Panzer Division, under difficult terrain conditions and heavy enemy resistance, has caused combat effectiveness to drop heavily'.[13] In fact, the *Windhund* Division started 22 December with *no* battle-worthy tanks at all, but six replacement panzers arrived at midday, with twenty-seven soon following from the repair workshops. Some personnel began to trickle through to replace casualties, but shortages of fuel and ammunition still concerned the divisional staff.

Two last (and largely pointless) attempts were made to seize the bridge at Hotton at midnight on the 22nd and 02.15 a.m. on 23 December, using a battalion of *Panzergrenadiers* supported by tanks, after which responsibility for Hotton was handed to Oberst Rudolf Langhäuser's 560th *Volksgrenadiers* (in whose ranks sixteen-year-old Grenadier Werner Klippel was serving) and the 116th *Windhund* disengaged. The latter were now weak from casualties, equipment losses and lack of fuel, but some troops slipped south towards Marche, discovering that US blocking forces were in place, ready to meet them.

On Saturday, 23 December, Manteuffel had his three panzer divisions ready to strike for the Meuse; on the left, Panzer Lehr was about to attack Rochefort. In the centre, 2nd Panzer was closest to the Meuse, though strung out and not concentrated, with its advance guard four miles east of Celles and only eleven miles from the river line. The 116th Panzer was still fixed in the Hotton–Marche area. Behind these three panzer divisions, the second echelon of von Elverfeldt's 9th Panzer Division, in company with Remer's *Führer-Begleit-Brigade* and part of the 15th *Panzergrenadier* Division, were struggling forward, but all of these formations suffered from the same afflictions – superior Allied numbers, lack of fuel and ammunition and the crushing weight of hostile air power when the weather permitted.

Just as Manteuffel had skilfully rebalanced his forces and was poised to strike at the Meuse, the weather changed. The 23rd saw the first good flying conditions since the campaign began and the skies soon filled with Allied aircraft. The 116th War Diary lamented, 'continuous air raids on supply roads and towns of the rearward areas. *No Luftwaffe*.' They were there, but perhaps not visible to the 116th on the ground.

Men of the US 333rd Infantry Regiment recorded, 'Hundreds of planes,

German and American, but mostly American as far as we could tell, crisscrossed the sky, leaving long contrails from horizon to horizon. The dogfights were fascinating. Near noontime five smoking planes went down simultaneously. Flight after flight of low-flying Thunderbolts, Mustangs and Lightnings roared overhead toward the German lines. The planes gave a big boost to our morale . . . They were like geese in the sky.'[14] Lloyd Swenson was a twenty-year-old B-26 bomber pilot whose squadron had been getting ready to abandon its airbase on the Franco-Belgian border 'because the Germans were getting so close. We couldn't take anything with us, except our uniform and a toothbrush. Then on the twenty-third the fog lifted and it was a bright, clear day.' In the morning his squadron of twin-engined B-26 Marauders, 'a medium-range bomber, fast and very maneuvrable with a crew of five', was assigned a mission to destroy a vital rail bridge supplying the Bulge. Thirty-six aircraft from the 387th Bomb Group set out with Swenson, who remembered 'a few miles off Bastogne about twenty-five Messerschmitt 109s hurtled into our formation. As they did some of our P-51s [Mustang fighters] responded to our Mayday call. Over the intercom the tail gunner described the dogfight but I had to keep my eyes on flying the plane.'[15]

Down below, the *Windhund* Division noted, 'Across the entire western horizon the countless streaks of white vapour trails moved across the sky, an impressive, but scary show. The air was filled with uninterrupted humming. The number of bombers, fighter-bombers and fighters could not be counted!'[16] No sooner had Swenson returned from his bombing mission (in which five from his group of thirty-six were shot down) than he was assigned another in the afternoon to hit a communications centre at Prüm, just behind the German lines. *Flak* and fighters took a heavy toll of Allied aircraft that day and forty-one Ninth Air Force B-26s were shot down – 'by far the blackest day in Marauder history,' added Swenson. The following day, equally good for flying, he added another two missions over the Ardennes and eventually accumulated sixty-one before returning home.[17]

Despite air attacks, Bayerlein's Panzer Lehr ground forward through that Saturday and when darkness fell he and fifteen panzers had reached the outskirts of Rochefort, where Companies 'K' and 'I' of the US 335th Regiment (belonging to the Railsplitters' 84th Division) were waiting in defence. Few of the inhabitants had fled and numbers were swollen with refugees; none of the 4,000 civilians had anywhere to go but huddle in their cellars. The Lehr assaulted the town through the night of 23–24 December, as Obergefreiter Schüssler recalled: 'Dismount! The panzer we had been riding on rolled forward a bit, hit a low garden wall and knocked it over. The enemy machine-gun which had fired at us disappeared with a crunching impact . . . An arrow of tracers turned on us and threw us behind the cover of another wall. My machine-gun shuddered in my hands. The bolt ate the belt of ammo and spat out the empty cases. It fell quiet abruptly . . . We reached a back courtyard. As I was running I saw the brilliant flashes of bursting mortar rounds; I saw the "dark mice" [as he dubbed the mortar rounds] descend and impact on the roof. A hand grenade flew over our heads into the room where the Americans were. Its ear-deafening blast made us hit the deck. The enemy guns, set up on sandbags along the windows, fell silent.'[18]

The Americans in Rochefort put up a tough fight, but the town fell an hour after first light, with fewer than 150 of the two US infantry companies escaping. During the 24th, Panzer Lehr found themselves following the march route of 2nd Panzer Division; around Humain (north of Rochefort) they found the burned-out half-tracks of an entire *Panzergrenadier* company; 'the battle-group directed to Buissonville encountered ten knocked-out German tanks right outside the village,' recorded the Division.[19] Christmas Day found the headquarters of Panzer Lehr in St Hubert (south-east of Rochefort), a town of 3,500, where they received a concerted Allied bombing campaign from noon. 'The wrecks of divisional vehicles smouldered after the attacks . . . Through his binoculars the commander [Bayerlein] could see gliders heading in towards Bastogne, which was being supplied by air.'[20] Meanwhile, an American patrol watched a Panzer Lehr convoy heading towards Rochefort, which reflected a typical mix of German and impressed US vehicles, including 'one company of infantry, five German tanks, two Sherman tanks, fifteen half-tracks, two American Jeeps, one American 2½ ton truck, and three German ambulances'.[21]

By 24–25 December, the 116th Panzer Division was essentially fixed along the terrain between Hotton and Marche by General Alex Bolling's US 84th Infantry Division and its accompanying 771st Tank Battalion. In continuous skirmishes, the latter were able to split the panzer division into separate battlegroups and sub-units, around the villages of Verdenne, Marenne, Menil-Favay and Hampteau south of the Marche–Hotton road. The panzers were unable to fight as larger formations because of the strength of US troops in the vicinity, minefields and air support the GIs had on call. Early on 24 December the hamlet of Verdenne and its château were attacked and taken by Major Gerhardt Tebbe's 16th Panzer Regiment with a platoon (five) of Panzer IVs under Leutnant Grzonka, and another of four Panthers, led by Hauptmann Kuchenbach, supported by a weak battalion of *Panzergrenadiers.* Major Tebbe, an *Ostfront* veteran, who would be awarded a German Cross in Gold for his leadership in the Bulge and command panzers again in the future Bundeswehr, had already been obliged to abandon one of his Panthers along his line of march, in Houffalize. It is still there, mounted on a concrete plinth overlooking the right side of the road as you drive in from the direction of Bastogne and Noville.[22]

Company 'K' of the 84th Division was detailed to investigate the Verdenne area, for the German incursion threatened to sever the important Marche–Hotton road, running south-west to north-east, effectively the 84th's front line and crucial to their scheme of defence. Assured of support from Shermans of the 771st Tank Battalion, and under a clear Christmas Eve sky with 'the feel of snow in the air, the ground lightly frozen and covered with frost', they set off down a track which connected Verdenne with Bourdon, a mile to the north. 'Just ahead a tank loomed out of the darkness, its huge bulk filling the narrow road, branches pressing in on either side brushing its steel plates. Sergeant Don Phelps went forward to liaise with the tankers, pounding on the side of the hull with his rifle, "Hey, you guys, open up!" The hatch opened slowly, a creak of metal, and the head and shoulders of a man appeared. "*Was ist los?*" Machine-guns started to chatter, tracers lit up the sky, tank guns fired, mortar rounds exploded, and Company 'K' scattered – and leapt straight into the foxholes of the *Panzergrenadier* battalion protecting their tanks. Major Tebbe reckoned he may have had around forty panzers and half-tracks hidden in the woods at this point. The German salient near Verdenne "had been discovered in a curious way".'[23]

When this began, Major Gerhardt Tebbe, the panzer commander, recalled to me that on Christmas Eve he was in his *Befehlspanzer* (command tank), studying his maps. The radio relayed a programme from Cologne Cathedral where the bells were ringing in the festive season. Suddenly his reverie was broken by gunfire nearby, and he slammed shut his turret hatch.[24] On Christmas morning, some of the Railsplitters noticed 'Two German soldiers came stumbling forward toward our positions in the half-light, hands held high, yelling "*Nicht schiessen!*" ("don't shoot!"). We discovered that they actually understood very little German, and they finally made us understand they were Ukrainians, drafted into the German army.'[25]

Their appearance in this sector puzzled intelligence staff, but they turned out to be from Oberst Rudolf Langhäuser's 560th *Volksgrenadiers*, by far the weakest German formation in *Herbstnebel*, whose ranks included many older men from garrisons in Norway, with waif and strays from Russia and Ukraine. It is a sad reflection that many East European *Volksgrenadier* 'volunteers' never got the opportunity to surrender in this way. When suddenly faced with a figure in field grey waving his arms about and shouting incoherently (few *Volksdeutsche* had a good grasp of German, much less English), most nervous, trigger-happy GIs tended to shoot first and ask questions later.

At the end of Christmas Day, Verdenne had been cleared and 289 *Windhund* prisoners taken, though nine panzers counter-attacked in the afternoon, each one of which was destroyed by waiting Shermans. By then, many of the *Windhund*'s sub-units were scattered and encircled by stronger US forces in the Verdenne area. On 26 December, the 84th Hatchet Men went on to ambush an armoured column at Menil-Favay. The leading panzer ran over a pile of anti-tank mines which exploded with such force so as to blow the tank on to its side, ripping a hole in its belly armour, and killing the crew; this blocked the advance of the vehicles behind, leading to the destruction of twenty-six *Windhund* vehicles, including six tanks.

With US infantry and tank attacks proving too costly to subdue the 116th Panzer Division, the Americans used artillery instead. Their opponents noted, 'the deployment of American guns was overwhelming' – there were about 150 US cannon of varying calibres, including 155mm guns and eight-inch howitzers – which broke up every German attempt to break out. The 84th Division thought it 'the heaviest, most devastating bombardment we had ever witnessed. When the fire stopped, the cries for help from wounded and dying Germans carried clearly to our lines. We admitted to ourselves that we were sorry for the poor bastards up there.'[26] Eventually, on hearing that further reinforcement or relief of the *Windhund* was not possible, Waldenburg ordered the vehicles in the Verdenne pocket abandoned and the division went over to the defensive.[27] Remer's *Führer-Begleit-Brigade* had almost reached him and the Hotton area, with Elverfeldt's 9th Panzer trailing behind – both with a view to continuing the push westwards – when Berlin switched Remer back to Bastogne on Hitler's personal whim.[28]

There is nothing remarkable about the Verdenne woods today, except that they are full of the defensive trenches and foxholes dug by both sides, where old ammunition boxes, mortar fragments and shrapnel still litter the forest floor.

The 2nd Panzer Division, which had advanced further, was in a similar predicament, being spread out in scattered battlegroups between an area south-west of Marche and as far as Foy-Notre-Dame, near the Meuse, which Hauptmann von Böhm's Reconnaissance Battalion reached at midnight on 23 December. At the same moment a jeep manned by three Americans failed to stop at a joint Anglo-US manned checkpoint on the east bank of Meuse, at Dinant. When the vehicle careered through the Rocher Bayard feature – a narrow slit in the rock through which a Sherman could just squeeze – by a prearranged signal Sergeant Baldwin of the 8th Rifle Brigade (a British infantry battalion), a few hundred yards further on, pulled a necklace of anti-tank mines across the road, blowing up the jeep and killing its occupants. All three were found to be wearing US helmets and greatcoats over German uniforms; in their pockets were found very detailed plans of the Allied defences. These were almost certainly not Skorzeny commandos, but a scouting patrol of 2nd Panzer Division sent on ahead in an improvised disguise.[29]

Lauchert immediately pushed forward another battlegroup of *Panzergrenadiers*, tanks, artillery and engineers under Major Ernst von Cochenhausen, which reach Celles soon after. As with the *Windhund* along the Marche–Hotton line, 2nd Panzer was, in the words of its War Diary, 'hindered in its mobility through lack of fuel'. In other words, the Germans could advance no further. In two groups, Böhm at Foy and Cochenhausen at Celles, they dug in and virtually waited to be counter-attacked, but all the while hoping that 9th Panzer Division would break through behind them, or Panzer Lehr or the *Windhund* Division to their left and right flanks. The Germans' right flank was unguarded because 116th Panzer had not been able to move forward beyond Hotton, and the left was similarly unprotected because Panzer Lehr also lagged behind.

Thanks to intelligence gathered by two former Belgian army officers, Baron Capitaine Jacques de Villenfagne and his cousin, Lieutenant Philippe le Hardy de Beaulieu, who, dressed in white from head to toe and wearing white gloves, trekked through the crystal-clear night in minus 30 degrees of frost to map the panzers' positions, British troops in nearby Sorinnes were furnished with the exact locations and precise strengths of *Kampfgruppe von Böhm*.[30] During 24 December, Shermans of Lieutenant-Colonel Alan Brown's British 3rd Royal Tank Regiment (3 RTR) stationed on the east bank of the Meuse duelled cautiously with the forward tanks of Böhm's *Kampfgruppe*; at the same time rocket-firing Typhoons and P-51s harassed the Germans. Aerial observers also appeared in the skies, directing ground artillery onto targets with great accuracy. It was also obvious the latter were short of fuel as each Panther was seen to be towing up to three trucks.

Hitler spent Christmas Eve, *der Heilige Abend*, in the *Führerbunker* at the Ziegenberg *Adlerhorst* complex, elated that 2nd Panzer was so close to the Meuse. The flag noting their position was duly moved on the situations map. He disregarded the fact that they were out of fuel and under air attack. In the afternoon, his staff remembered, he had stood outside the command bunker, watching as thousands of tiny specks glittered in the winter sky overhead. They were American bombers, heading eastwards to bomb the heartland of the Reich.

Knowing that two battlegroups of his division were dangerously exposed, Lauchert asked for permission to withdraw his forward elements and regroup. His request did not get beyond Manteuffel, who knew that neither Model nor Hitler would permit it. Afterwards, Lauchert's chief of staff, Oberstleutnant Rüdiger Weitz, recorded, 'During the night the front line elements sent urgent calls for reinforcements and supplies of ammunition and fuel. More and more reports came in stating that the enemy was constantly reinforcing and was, in some cases, on our own supply road. The process of marching on Dinant had come to a halt.'[31]

On Christmas Day, Major-General Ernest N. Harmon's US 2nd Armored Division attacked Lauchert's exposed right flank at Foy-Notre-Dame, squeezing it between two task forces to the north and south. The US 82nd Armored Reconnaissance Battalion and 3 RTR also attacked from the west, forward of the Meuse. Major Noël Bell, serving with the British 8th Rifle Brigade, watched from a nearby vantage point. 'A squadron of P-38 Lightnings roared over us and circled low, determined to have a festive Christmas Day. Three Panthers, a certain amount of transport and a large number of entrenched infantry . . . were subjected to merciless and incessant attack from the Lightnings which soon began to dive to rooftop height with machine-guns blazing, dropping bombs at the same time.'[32]

The result was that *Kampfgruppe von Böhm* was surrounded, smashed and the survivors forced to surrender. After the Christmas Day battle,

General Harmon reported that he 'destroyed or captured eighty-two tanks, sixteen other armoured vehicles, eighty-three guns, and 280 motor vehicles. Twenty vehicles were captured and pressed into Allied service, including seven US trucks seized only days earlier. Harmon had taken the "panzer" out of the 2nd Panzer Division.'[33] The fact that only 148 men, including Böhm himself, were taken prisoner out of the thousand-plus personnel illustrated the crushing blow that had descended on the Reconnaissance Battalion of the 2nd Panzer Division. It had ceased to exist.

For the Führer's last Christmas, Oberscharführer Rochus Misch told me in 1993, Hitler's staff at the *Adlerhorst* conjured up a small *Weihnachtsbaum* (Christmas tree) complete with candles, under which lay modest gifts of cigarettes, of which the Führer disapproved, *Stollen* (fruit cake) and chocolates (he had a sweet tooth), wrapped in newsprint or bright paper. All present realised that any wistful references to the *Christkind* (Christ Child), a *Krippenspiel* (nativity play) or the *Weihnachtsmann* (St Nicholas or Santa Claus), who delivered a sack full of presents to good children, belonged to a different era, and were banned. The headquarters staff, secretaries and generals toasted one another with champagne; Hitler shared the intoxication of the moment, although he had not drunk alcohol: he was already high on the success of his armies. Yet the only Christmas present for which the Führer wished, victory in the Ardennes, was already unattainable.[34]

'That evening the Americans occupied the Farm Mayenne (formerly home to a Panther platoon)', wrote Noël Bell. 'Foy Notre Dame was a smouldering ruin in which half of "B" Squadron 3 RTR and the Americans leaguered for the night, after going round the village and getting Germans out of cellars, like ferrets after rats.'[35] Several Catholic GIs were recorded as lining up to confess their sins – with the aid of a pocket dictionary – to Father Coussin, a veteran of the Great War and the priest of Celles.[36]

Tactically, Lauchert had overstretched 2nd Panzer, which was in any case out of fuel. The unrelenting pressure for progress came from General von Lüttwitz, who hovered nearby, protective of the division he had commanded from February to September in 1944, and forever breathing down Lauchert's neck. Today, one of the 2nd Panzer Division's Panther tanks has survived the attentions of the post-war scrap dealers, and – minus its road wheels and tracks – stands guard outside the crossroads in Celles, where a series of signboards with maps explain the battle in detail, reminding passing motorists how close the Fifth Panzer Army came to their goal of reaching the Meuse.

Thus the spearhead of the entire *Herbstnebel* campaign had been halted and blunted. The Army Group War Diary noted, 'On 25 December, the attack by Army Group "B" was the target of strong enemy counter-attacks from the north and west against spearheads of the Fifth Panzer Army. The back-and-forth battles lasted the whole day.' Panzer Lehr observed that their divisional logistics elements suffered terribly over 24–25 December. Every drop of gasoline had to be brought forward by vehicle and the division lost thirty fuel trucks during their march to the front, not including those bogged down in the mud, broken down or caught in accidents. 'A *Flak* battery that attempted to reply to an attack of P-38 Lightnings simply disappeared under a hail of bombs. Hardly any men of the battery survived and the division's armoured maintenance workshops were swept up in a maelstrom of fire.'[37]

By the time Army Group 'B' ordered the Sixth Panzer Army to disengage from the Elsenborn Ridge and strengthen the effort of Fifth Army on 25 December, it was too late. On his own initiative, Bayerlein withdrew the forward elements of Panzer Lehr back into Rochefort during the night of 25–26 December. This was an acknowledgement that Hitler's original plan of putting most weight on the German right, favouring the Waffen-SS, had been a disaster, and that Manteuffel's Fifth Panzer Army sector had always shown the greatest promise.

This was not just because of Manteuffel's fighting qualities and judgement as a commander, but because the terrain was far better suited and offered more alternatives to fast-moving armoured troops. Surprise was the major advantage the Germans possessed and that had largely been thrown away by the length of time the panzer formations took to bridge their river lines during the first couple of days. Had the Fifth Army possessed Dietrich's bridging equipment, engineering assets and weight of artillery support, enabling it to bridge efficiently and effectively on 16–17 December, it might have made the Meuse, but even then would not have managed to get much beyond.

On 26 December, 116th Panzer Division was ordered 'onto the defensive', in theory to await the arrival of second echelon relief units, but in reality acknowledging that the offensive was over. The battle would thenceforth be to retain whatever gains had been made. 'The Other Fellow', as Bradley habitually referred to his opponents, 'reached his high-water mark today', he reported to Bedell Smith at Ike's headquarters. On this day

Major Fritz Vogelsang, the 116th's Divisional Adjutant, noted, 'This morning, fighter-bombers and bombers turned La Roche into a smoking pile of rubble. Our anti-aircraft guns were able to shoot down some of the attackers . . . if only the weather would turn bad again!' Vogelsang also assessed the accumulated personnel losses since the 16th, as at least 1,907 killed or wounded, 1,278 taken prisoner and an unspecified number missing; a total of 113 armoured vehicles of all types had been destroyed – only seven tanks and four tank destroyers were still battleworthy.

'The Division lost much of its combat value, inner strength, quality, speed and flexibility of leadership. It will be able to compensate for these losses through its reserves, but not for those valuable officers, including a large number of battalion commanders, adjutants and company commanders and most of the junior leaders . . . of special impact is the loss of fifteen radio and three other armoured communications vehicles . . . Losses are so high that the two *Panzergrenadier* regiments, where all four battalion commanders became casualties, have to be considered as nearly destroyed.' The combined battle strength on 29 December of the two *Panzergrenadier* regiments totalled 1,184 out of the nearly 5,000 who started the campaign.[38] Divisional headquarters came in for some harsh treatment on the same day; in despair, as Major Vogelsang recorded, 'Fighter-bombers appeared and took care of some of the few houses . . . Then artillery planes began to circle and directed well-controlled fire from heavy guns. Explosions everywhere! Finally it became too uncomfortable; nobody can conduct a paper war from a foxhole!'[39]

30

The River of Humiliation

THE 106TH INFANTRY Division, Alan Jones's Golden Lions, had experienced a frustrating first day of combat on 16 December. None of their training back in the USA or England had prepared them for the freezing conditions of the Christmas-card-pretty Schnee Eifel, with its narrow, winding roads, and mist-shrouded, snowy hills, interspersed with dense forests of fir and pine. Neither had they expected a total lack of situational awareness. The hostile bombardment had cleverly hit their artillery positions first, then headquarters, finally infantry units. Confusion reigned because the lines were out; even those who got through did not get any orders: nobody knew anything.

Pete House served the 105mm guns of Battery 'A' of the division's 590th Field Artillery Battalion, based in Oberlascheid, a tiny settlement midway on the Bleialf to Auw 'Skyline Drive', high on the Schnee Eifel. In 1994 he told me how his unit was hit hard on the 16th: 'The German army knew the location of every rock and stream and could drop a shell wherever they wanted with great precision,' he observed. 'Each time we moved into position and fired our guns the Germans quickly located us and would fire back. We soon learned when orders for a fire mission came in to have everything packed and our trucks brought right up to the guns. As soon as the firing was over it was "move like hell" because immediate German counter-battery fire would be incoming.'[1]

Sergeant John P. Kline, a former ASTP scholar, had been brought up in Indiana where his best subjects at high school were 'basketball and girls'. He remembered his first German artillery barrage: 'It was unbelievable in its magnitude. It seemed that every square yard of ground was being covered. The initial barrage slackened after forty-five minutes or an hour. The woods were raked throughout the day by a constant barrage of small arms and artillery fire. We were pinned down in the edge of the woods and could not move. I found some protection in a small trench, by a tree, as the shelling started. I heard a piece of metal hit the ground. It was a large jagged, hot, smoking piece of shrapnel, about eighteen inches long and four inches wide. It landed a foot or two from my head. After it cooled off I reached out and picked it up.'[2]

'Incoming mail', as veterans referred to hostile artillery fire, turns any greenhorn into a veteran. It was – and remains – the first test of a soldier in battle, for the violence is random. Much of a GI's ability to survive rested on skill and professionalism, but enduring shellfire was a mental test for those who could 'take it' and those could not. It was an exam that couldn't be prepared for in advance: a soldier only knew how he would react when the storm of steel started to land around him. Some prayed; others were wonderstruck, describing the ground reverberating like Jell-O; still others ran around screaming in terror. John A. Swett in Company 'H' of the 423rd remembered a German victim of shellfire: 'He appeared to be very young, perhaps fourteen or fifteen years old. He had a deep vertical slice in his back, perhaps twelve inches long and down to his rib cage. He had been given a cigarette and seemed to be unconcerned about his condition. Probably he was in a state of shock.'[3] Some GIs shot themselves in the hand or foot, to be swiftly evacuated out of the battle zone. Corporal Hal Richard Taylor in the 423rd Regiment's Anti-Tank Company saw a fellow GI reacting to fire for the first time 'crouched near the floor. He had dropped his rifle and had his arms crossed over his head' – *inside* a German bunker where he was perfectly safe.[4]

In the nearby 99th Division, William Bray recalled the post-shelling reaction of a pair of GIs 'who crouched for two days whimpering with their knees drawn up and blankets over their head. They had gone to the toilet in their pants', but he did not condemn them for the 'horror of that artillery would cause a breakdown in the best of us'.[5] John A. Swett remembered seeing 'a tall lean fellow digging himself a foxhole. When he finished his hole he got into it and nothing could prise him loose. He was still digging for more than an hour afterwards.'[6] Kline's observations of those first moments under fire continued: 'At one point, as I looked to the right along the edge of the woods, I saw six or eight ground bursts. They hit in a small area along the tree line where several soldiers were trying to find protection. One of those men was hurled through the air and his body was wrapped around a tree trunk several feet off the ground. There were continuous cries from the wounded screaming for Medics.'[7]

Perhaps the fact that the Golden Lions had the youngest average age of any division in the US Army decreased their resilience. Some were so young, green to combat and ill trained, they knew that they didn't stand a chance. Pete House told me of some new arrivals at his POW camp in fresh-looking uniforms. He asked them for their division and was astonished to find they didn't know. After basic training in the United States followed by ten weeks of training in one of the dreary redeployment camps (one of the infamous and much-hated 'repo-depos'), they'd been dropped off at night next to their foxholes by a sergeant they'd never seen before or since, and soon after had been captured. Such a lack of unit cohesion increased a sense of isolation and disinclination to do anything, especially under fire.[8] Some soldiers (British, German, as well as GIs) have admitted to me in interviews that they did not know the names of any towns or villages they passed through ('all looked the same after shelling'), and barely knew the names of their officers.

Many of the newly conscripted *Volksgrenadiers* were as poorly trained, but in the first flush of victory their high morale spurred them on, as one wrote home on 24 December: 'Yes, you are surprised that we are again in Belgium, but we advance every day. Well, what does father say to that? I had a conversation with him last time about the war and he was not very convinced then that we should be able to do such a thing. Everyone is enthusiastic as never before.'[9] Late in the night of the 16th, as many of Middleton's corps artillery units were ordered out of the sector, the Golden Lions hung on, in many cases unaware of the danger their forward units were in. They were determined to retain control of the Roth–Auw road, which would otherwise give the 18th *Volksgrenadiers* control of the northern sector of the 106th's front, abutting the Losheim Gap. Equally important was the southern town of Bleialf – which boasted a population of over 1,000 and a railway station – and the route that ran from it to Schönberg, for dominance of that area would determine whether any of the Golden Lions could receive reinforcements – or withdraw.

Defending Roth, a gaggle of two dozen fieldstone houses and barns, Captain Stanley E. Porche's Troop 'A' of the 18th Cavalry fought through the morning but were forced to surrender in the afternoon of the 16th. Bleialf, in the gap south of the Schnee Eifel hills, had, meanwhile, been surrounded and attacked since early on the 16th. It was a more significant town with several large mills and warehouses, for the area had prospered on lead mining for centuries (*Blei* meaning 'lead' and the *Alf* being the local stream). Corporal Hal Richard Taylor had been stationed there for a few days before the attacks came in, and remembered when the first barrage lifted: 'The whole damned German army, it seemed, came right at us, yelling and cheering as if it were a football game!'[10] The ill-disciplined young grenadiers belonged to Oberstleutnant Witte's 293rd *Volksgrenadier* Regiment.

During a lull in the struggle for Bleialf, the GIs called to some of the *Volksgrenadiers* to surrender; two stepped forward to obey, but were ordered back by their sergeant. The grenadiers stood there for a moment, undecided on what to do, eventually heading towards the American lines, whereupon their sergeant shot them dead. In clearing the town, Taylor remembered a driver 'a big man, about 200 pounds . . . could lift twice his weight' who worked his way through buildings in Bleialf, bayoneting Germans. As he did so, 'he also hoisted them through the windows on his bayonet as if he were spearing hay with a pitchfork. Then he would shake them loose and let them drop to the ground below . . . As he pitched the freshly-slain *Volksgrenadiers,* everyone – Germans included – ceased fire and watched, awe-struck.' Eventually the pitchforker fell, but Taylor 'counted more than thirty bayoneted Germans whom he had killed'.[11] Sadly, it seems, medals and recognition escaped this unnamed hero.

In a counter-attack at noon, Taylor's group in Bleialf had started to repel the Germans and under Captain Warren G. Stutler from the 423rd's Headquarters Company began to clear the town. They were joined by men from the 81st Combat Engineers, members of the Regiment's Cannon Company and cooks and clerks from Headquarters and Service Companies, none of whom were trained riflemen. This motley crew ousted the Germans from Bleialf and formed a 'provisional battalion' under Lieutenant-Colonel Frederick W. Nagle, executive officer of the 423rd – but at high cost. Of the 176 officers and enlisted men from the 81st Engineers who helped eject the *Volksgrenadiers* from Bleialf, only forty-six returned to their parent unit.[12]

Although the official histories suggest that Bleialf was taken on the 16th, Taylor's evidence is at odds with this. He recorded that his unit of the 423rd Infantry kept its foothold in the key village, supported by US artillery, into the next morning and withdrew only when ordered by radio just before dawn on the 17th. Early that morning, Coleman Estes of the division's 81st Combat Engineer Battalion remembered the frozen bodies of the dead, German and American, twisted in their final tortured moments of combat, 'looking like wax sculptures in the snow'.[13] John Kline saw Bleialf after the battle, too: 'There was much evidence that a large-scale battle had just taken place . . . a real shoot-out, with hand-to-hand fighting. Dead Americans and Germans lay in doors, ditches and hung out of windows.'[14] After the GIs departed, Bleialf was overrun, allowing German armour to make its way towards Schönberg virtually unopposed. Accounts of the Bulge suggest little or no activity in the air by either side on 17 December, but Taylor witnessed 'a roar and saw a P-47 [Thunderbolt] right on the tail of a Focke-Wulf. The P-47 scored a hit and the German plane crashed. A few seconds later another P-47 tailing a Messerschmitt shot it down about half a mile away. Those were the only Allied planes I saw in the battle.'[15]

Apart from General Jones's surreal conversation with his corps commander of 16 December, when Jones had thought Middleton was directing him to keep his two units on the Schnee Eifel, and Middleton thought he had ordered the opposite, poor communication between the 106th's regiments and St Vith led to even more confusion over what exactly to do during the night of the 16–17 December. It was becoming clear to all that the Golden Lions' 422nd (to the north) and 423rd Regiments, between Auw and Bleialf, were in danger of being bypassed. Incredibly, many in the two regiments had yet even to fire a shot, but already their only hope of survival lay in withdrawing from the Schnee Eifel and stopping the Germans at Schönberg, with its heavy stone bridge across the Our river. It did not happen: as we have seen, Jones had erroneously ordered them to stay in place, thinking that was Middleton's wish. Schönberg was overwhelmed swiftly on 17 December with its vital bridge intact (it had not even been prepared for demolition) and that night both Manteuffel and Model, who liked to be up front with the troops, met in its cobbled streets. 'I'm sending you the *Führer-Begleit-Brigade*', the élite unit of troops who had once guarded Hitler and had their own tanks, the field marshal told the Fifth Army's commander, amidst the chaos of the newly captured town, clogged with transport, prisoners and wounded. The Golden Lions' fate had been sealed.

With German armour controlling the Auw–Schönberg–St Vith road, as well as the route to Bleialf, the two US regiments withdrew to the higher ground of the Schnee Eifel to regroup. Their situation was not desperate: they had a day's supply of K-rations, ammunition, water, their own transport, but the swiftness of the German advance had meant they were unable to evacuate their casualties and were short of surgical supplies. They had the use of logging trails between their positions – which would soon turn to mud with frequent use – but the Germans controlled the road network below, which is what counted. Their biggest problem was that they were inexperienced and lacked dynamic leadership – both the regimental colonels, Cavender of the 423rd and the younger Descheneaux of the 422nd, tended to wait for orders rather than make their own decisions.

One thing was obvious, apart from the fact that the 422nd and 423rd were surrounded: they had to regain the initiative. The last message received from the Divisional HQ in St Vith at 8.00 p.m. on the 18th made it clear that it was imperative Schönberg be retaken. Overnight, the GIs moved out of their positions on the Schnee Eifel under cover of heavy fog, and prepared to seize the town, then move westwards towards St Vith. By this stage, the two regiments had separated, contact between them was lost and every unit had taken a few casualties. Artilleryman Pete House, with Lieutenant-Colonel Vanden Lackey's 590th Battalion, remembered that as the 18th ended, 'we were exhausted, hungry and cold. Cooks had not prepared any meals since the morning of the sixteenth. I received no emergency rations. Cold weather clothing and bedding was never issued. That night we moved to an open field. We only had four rounds for our 105 mm howitzers left. We received orders to destroy all the equipment and be prepared to hike back to our lines. It was with great pleasure that I destroyed two 610 FM communications radios with a pick as they had rarely worked.'[16]

Corporal Taylor noted that his Anti-Tank Company, usually numbering over a hundred men, had dwindled to about thirty.[17] On the evening of the 18th, Technical Sergeant Willard F. Nelson, with the 422nd Regiment, remembered having to shoot his way through a mob of advancing Germans, using the .30-inch calibre machine gun mounted on his jeep. He was the company clerk and had never fired the gun before; the vibrations broke the windshield. Loaded with all the company records, Nelson and his driver careered away to safety. 'About two miles later, we went around a corner too goddamned fast, tipped the Jeep over. It was upside down and I got thrown into a ditch. I remember spending the night in that ditch.'[18]

The battalions were moved into assembly areas before daylight on the 19th, and at 08.30 a.m. battalion commanders were given orders for their attack on Schönberg to begin at 10.00 a.m. However, caught between German positions in Auw and Bleialf, from 09.30 a.m. the 423rd Regiment started being subjected to heavy artillery concentrations, which killed one battalion CO and several company commanders.[19] John Kline of Company 'M', the 423rd's Heavy Weapons outfit, remembered the move towards his destination, 'a heavily wooded area (Linscheid Hill, marked as Hill 546 on the map) southeast of the town . . . I was with a .30-inch calibre machine-gun high on a hill, overlooking a slope leading into a valley. I could see, about 1,000 yards to the northwest, the house tops of Schönberg.' Kline assessed that the hostile artillery barrage came from German anti-aircraft units firing uphill from Schönberg. 'Those guns were a decisive factor in the outcome of the battle,' he felt. 'We had very little artillery support. I learned after the war that the 423rd's artillery support was overrun by the Germans troops.'[20]

The attacks went in, but the 1st and 3rd Battalions lost heavy casualties and became pinned down by artillery fire from the *Flak* guns. The *Volksgrenadiers* had massed these around Schönberg to protect the Our bridge and vehicle convoys on the main road to St Vith, but turned them instead on the GIs rushing down the tree-studded slopes above. The result was devastating: many of the companies were scattered and overwhelmed, or destroyed, piecemeal. The 2nd Battalion moved to the right and attached themselves to the 422nd Infantry Regiment. Gunner Pete House recalled to me: 'When it became daylight on the nineteenth we moved up a steep field to the left and went into firing position along the edge of the woods – with only four 105mm rounds left. I opened a can of pork and gravy that we had "borrowed" from the navy while on the LST crossing the English Channel and was heating it when the

Germans hit us with everything. Of course I should have dug a foxhole. One of the guys had borrowed my shovel so I ran into the woods looking for a stream bed for protection.'[21]

Corporal Taylor watched these attacks 'from a grandstand seat', thinking the sight 'a scene of pure hell. As hundreds of men surged down the hill, the German artillery fired on them and shells exploded in the pine trees overhead. With that the men panicked and ran back up the hill,' he remembered. 'Officers yelled and swore at the men to form into an organised body, again and again. Three times, maybe seven times, this happened until finally the exhausted men simply sat down to rest, despite the urgings of officers who obviously were also exhausted and frustrated at the turn of events.'[22] The attempt to retake Schönberg had been a disaster. The men were now scattered in small groups in the hills above the town, low on food and ammunition.

At 3.45 p.m., Colonel Cavender called a conference and several witnesses recalled his comments. '"There's no ammunition left", he began, "I was a GI in World War One and I try to see things from their standpoint. No man in this outfit has eaten all day and we haven't had water since early morning. Now, *what's your attitude to surrendering*?"' The answer was stupefied silence. Then hostility. Cavender, with uncharacteristic decisiveness, settled the matter: 'Gentlemen, we're surrendering at 4.00 p.m'. Corporal Taylor was flabbergasted at what happened next. 'Then small bodies of men began to hold up their hands. They were starting to surrender. We couldn't believe what we were seeing.'[23]

The fact that the regiment was *ordered* to surrender, against the better judgement of many, only made it worse, and created a deep rancour that endured for decades. Some GIs begged their officers and NCOs to be able to continue the fight. PFC Kurt Vonnegut, a regimental scout, wanted to slink off and carry on fighting, but instead raged at his own powerlessness, having no food and only a few rounds of ammunition. He found somewhere to lie down and wait. Several others collapsed in exhaustion beside him; someone suggested they fix bayonets and die fighting. From the forest surrounding them a German-accented voice, amplified by a loudspeaker, echoed through the late afternoon gloom. 'Come out!' ordered the voice. Vonnegut got to his feet, raised his hands and joined what he later termed 'the river of humiliation'.[24] A historian of the Golden Lions recorded that from about 4.00 p.m. on the 19th and throughout 20 December, a German loudspeaker van played 'American jazz intermingled with hearty invitations to come in for hot showers, warm beds and hot cakes for breakfast'. However, a few volunteers led by Staff Sergeant Richard A. Thomas eventually put an end to 'Berlin Betty's playful reference to the joys of playing baseball in a POW camp' with a 'well-directed hand grenade'.[25]

This sort of runaway success inspired one *Landser* to write home: 'We shall probably *not* have another Christmas here at the front, since it is absolutely certain that the American is going to get something he did not under any circumstances reckon with. For the "*Ami*", as we call him, expected he would celebrate Christmas in Berlin, as I gather from his letters. Even I, as a poor private, can easily tell that it won't take much longer until the Ami will throw away his weapons. For if he sees that everybody else is retreating, he runs away and cannot be stopped any more. He is also war-weary, as I myself learned from prisoners.'[26]

Colonel Descheneaux's 422nd Regiment to the north of Cavender's 423rd suffered similar setbacks. When tanks appeared on the Roth, Auw and Schönberg roads, they were initially misidentified as being from the US 7th Armored coming to their rescue. The let-down was cruel when the force, actually belonging to Otto Remer's *Führer-Begleit-Brigade*, raked the GIs with fire.[27] Descheneaux sensed he was surrounded and powerless to resist further. Corporal Stanley Wojtusik of the 422nd hadn't eaten for three days and remembered his regiment 'was short of bazookas. I don't know if they would have really stopped those tanks unless you hit them right in the bogey wheels – we surely couldn't stop them with our M-1 rifles. We were able to shoot most of the ground troops, but we had no defence against the tanks.'[28] From his ditch near the overturned jeep, Willard F. Nelson recalled 'someone shouted "the tanks are coming, we got help". See, [the caterpillar tracks of] tanks sound like a million mice screaming, they squeak. So, they came up over the hill and "Jesus Christ, that's good, here's the tanks" but they was German tanks. We surrendered.'[29]

Some troops, like PFC Leon Setter of Headquarters Company in the 422nd had no idea of the situation. He spent 16 and 17 December guarding the 2nd Battalion's HQ in a pillbox two miles east of Schlausenbach. Setter was in complete ignorance of the coming catastrophe, merely on a 'class-one alert because of enemy activity in the area'. His squad moved out through a fire-fight on the 19th and that afternoon to his amazement, 'My squad leader called us together and told us our situation looked bad. We were surrounded. He concluded by telling us to dig foxholes to protect ourselves from the shelling.'

Aware of Cavender's mood, Colonel Descheneaux called a conference of his own officers at his headquarters, which was situated next door to the regimental aid post. 'I don't believe in fighting for glory if it doesn't accomplish anything. It looks as if we'll have to pack it in.' His friend, Lieutenant-Colonel Thomas P. Kelly of the 589th Artillery, objected, 'Jesus, Desh, you can't surrender'. Descheneaux looked at the mounting pile of dead and wounded. 'As far as I'm concerned, I'm going to save the lives of as many as I can. And I don't give a damn if I am court-martialled!' Medical Sergeant Bud Santoro remembered the tree bursts from the German *Flak* guns – 'a tinkling rustling as the deadly shrapnel rained down'. After tending over twenty casualties, he climbed the hill to the regimental aid post. He saw Colonel Descheneaux and told him they needed to evacuate the casualties for better medical attention. Santoro remembered the tears in his colonel's eyes as he was told 'It's OK, there'll be evacuation, Sergeant. We are surrendering'.[30] Leon Setter was perplexed. 'As I finished digging my hole, the squad leader returned to tell me that Colonel Descheneaux had ordered the entire 422nd Regiment to surrender and destroy our weapons. Needless to say, I was confused. This had been my first day in actual combat. What was going to happen next?'[31]

Lieutenant Alan Jones, Jr, son of the division's commander, and Operations Officer of the regiment's 1st Battalion, stared dumbly in disbelief – then guilt. Technical Sergeant Edward L. Bohde, a platoon leader with Company 'L' of the 422nd, remembered the day's combat as *Volksgrenadiers* advanced with panzers. 'We lay there, firing away as the tanks came closer and closer firing their 88's in our midst. Then, above the roar of gunfire and commotion, I heard our Company Commander shout, "Stop firing, Stop firing!", and saw him stand up with a white cloth tied to the end of his rifle, raised high above his head. I, though, continued to fire at the enemy, either because I was in a state of disbelief or because that was the way I was trained. Kill the enemy! A number of men around me continued to do the same until we heard another order, "Cease firing, Cease firing, You're getting innocent men killed. At this last order I did stop firing my rifle and saw all of my comrades standing up with their hands held high above their heads.'[32]

One of Descheneaux's staff, Major William Cody Garlow, a grandson of 'Buffalo Bill' Cody, volunteered to fetch a German officer. Garlow fluttered a pair of white handkerchiefs and walked over to the *Volksgrenadier* artillery headquarters to arrange a ceasefire. In the wood line above the Schönberg–Andler road, thousands of GIs began destroying their weapons and equipment. A private fixed Descheneaux with a look of burning resentment, holding up his rifle. 'I've carried this goddamn thing for months. I've never even fired it once in anger!' he screamed as he broke it against a tree. Santoro, the medical sergeant, witnessed one lieutenant place his wristwatch on a rock and smash it, saying, 'Those bastards don't get this'.[33] Major Garlow returned with a German *Leutnant*, but hadn't the nerve to tell him of the thousands waiting to surrender. Garlow 'represented 400–500 men', he had stated. When the pair returned to Descheneaux, the German turned to Garlow. 'Major, you told me you had only 400–500 men here, but . . . I understand,' he said discreetly.

The *Leutnant*, who spoke French, and Descheneaux, a French Canadian, made the necessary arrangements. Corporal Wojtusik watched as the Germans approached his unit under the protection of a white banner. 'We all saw that white flag and we thought they were surrendering to us,' he recollected. 'Unfortunately that wasn't the case. They were there to let us know we were surrounded.'[34] John A. Swett, manning the regiment's 81mm mortars, recalled being out of ammunition: 'A loud speaker came up from the base of the hill, and a voice with no trace of German accent said, "Your officers have surrendered you. Come down off the hill and form up on the road". This was repeated a number of times and the lack of firing of any kind indicated this was probably the end of the war for us. When the truth of the situation sunk in, I had the immediate job of taking my weapons apart and throwing their parts as far as I could into the forest. I could see troops already forming up on the road as I came down the hill.'[35] Tears streaming down his face, the colonel encouraged those who wished to try and filter through the lines to St Vith – and led the rest into humiliating captivity. On hand was a German *Kriegsberichter* camera crew who recorded several famous clips of helmeted American prisoners stumbling along the roadside and in the fields as panzers rolled past. The look of dejection on their faces was remarkable. This wasn't how it was meant to be.[36]

Sergeant John Kline recalled, 'there were many wounded and dead in

GIs are marched towards Germany as a massive King Tiger tank fills the road; it is over 12 feet wide and 10 feet tall, but at 70 tons could cross very few bridges in the region and guzzled fuel. Such images, of large numbers of Americans being herded past the mighty panzers, made excellent propaganda for the Third Reich, but such dramas only occurred during the first three days – near St Vith, where two regiments of the 106th 'Golden Lions' Division were captured, and here in the Losheim gap, where prisoners from the 99th 'Checkerboard' Division are following the road back to Germany, between Lanzerath and Merlscheid. The both cases, GIs remembered that more primitive, horse-drawn transport followed the panzers, which the German cameras did not film. (NARA)

the ditches and fields as we were led out of the woods, and a German truck burning in the middle of the road. Behind the truck was an American infantryman lying in the middle of the road in his winter uniform, a heavy winter coat, ammo belt and canteen. He was lying on his back, as if he were resting. The body had no head or neck. It was as if somebody had sliced it off with a surgical instrument, leaving no sign of blood.' Swett remembered the headless corpse too. For Taylor, the imagery was different. He would never forget the 'German soldier sitting in a captured Jeep, not a day over sixteen. He had found a case of chocolate and had a bar in each hand. His mouth was smeared and he was eating with double time speed.'[37]

The elation of the Wehrmacht, which for years had experienced only defeat, knew no bounds. Hitherto, all had been fed on Goebbels' lies of successes. All of a sudden they were faced with the reality of victory rather than mere propaganda. With their own eyes they witnessed the impossible: the surrender and seeming collapse of many American units. Leutnant Behrman, an artillery officer attacking through the Schnee Eifel with the 18th *Volksgrenadiers*, recorded in his diary:

> 18 December: The infantry is before St Vith. The men hear the wildest rumours of success.
> 19 December: Endless columns of prisoners pass; at first about a hundred, then another group of about one thousand. Our car gets stuck on the road. I get out and walk. Generalfeldmarschall Model himself directs the traffic. (He's a little, undistinguished-looking man with a monocle.) Now the thing is going. The roads are littered with destroyed American vehicles, cars and tanks. Another column of prisoners passes.
> 20 December: The American soldiers have shown little spirit for fighting. Most of them often said, 'What do we want here? At home we can have everything much better'. That was the spirit of the common soldier. If their officers thought that way??? A rumour has been started that Eisenhower was taken prisoner. It will probably prove to be only a rumour.
> 21 December: Roads still clogged, but traffic continues. Vehicles are almost exclusively captured American equipment. It was a tremendous haul. St Vith has fallen.[38]

The first moments of capture are shocking for any soldier. Tension and a sense of failure mingle. Though combat soldiers share the brotherhood and understanding of the front, both sides remain tense – one false or misinterpreted move can result in death. There are usually a few seconds after the hands or a white flag go up before the surrender gesture is registered and firing stops. Men can go down in those split seconds. An invisible line is then crossed from the moment a soldier might be legitimately killing a combatant, to committing a war crime in killing a prisoner. The tension is on both sides. Weapons are thrown down, often helmets too. Coleman Estes remembered, 'we had to unbuckle our ammo belt holding our water bottle, medical package, gas mask, and everything down to our field jackets'.[39]

It is a sober reflection that the further back a captive soldier travels from the front line, the more likely he is to be abused. PFC Jim Forsythe was with Company 'A' of the 424th Regiment, defending Winterspelt in the southern sector of the 106th's front. His experience of the changing behaviour of his captors illustrates the point. They had been attacked by Leutnant Kurt Schwerdtfeger's 164th Grenadier Regiment, high on their stimulants. On the 17th, Forsythe's captain surrendered to the first German he saw (rather too enthusiastically, Forsythe felt). 'The one who searched me was polite. The first thing he did was to take two cigarettes from a pack of four in my coat pocket. He put one in his mouth and one in my mouth, lit them, and put the remaining two in my pocket. He spoke good English and told me to put my arms down and that if I behaved I would not be harmed.' A day later, however, the combat troops had moved on, leaving the POWs with many others, lying wounded or dead in a barn at Winterspelt. Other troops arrived to march them off to a POW camp, but before they left, 'the Germans went around the downed Americans, probing with bayonets, and any that flinched or moved were shot in the head with pistols . . . simply because they could not walk and keep up with the other prisoners'.[40]

Corporal Taylor was searched by a red-headed German youth, who 'demanded the glasses I was wearing, which happened to be gold rimmed. He took them, broke the lenses, and crushed the frame into a wad which he dropped into a small canvas bag. It contained several pieces of gold, some of which were crowns still attached to teeth . . . He did the same to a second pair, then spotted my ring – a high school class ring. My fingers were swollen and the ring wouldn't budge. He started to remedy that problem by whipping out a 6½ inch knife and motioning that he would cut off my finger. I shouted for an officer. That scared him, so he ran off and left me.'[41] He was lucky. When Pete House was escorted down the hill to the road by mostly teenage artillerymen, 'we carried three wounded men with us. I don't know how many dead or wounded were left in the woods. Of course we were searched. They let me keep my pocket knife, watch, and overshoes. Treated us good – but no food. Some of us were ordered to prepare their *Flak* guns for moving. One American refused saying that it was against the Geneva Convention. A German officer pulled his pistol and shot him in the head. That's when I learned to forget the Geneva Convention.'[42]

Far different was the case when II Battalion of the 293rd *Volksgrenadier* Regiment captured a group of 106th GIs on 20 December at Bleialf. In doing so, the grenadiers also freed some Germans who had earlier been taken prisoner. The Germans informed their liberators that they had been interrogated by 'two Jewish-American soldiers from Berlin', part of a six-man IPW (Interrogation of Prisoners of War) Team attached to the 106th. According to the documents of his trial, held on 20 April 1945, the German battalion commander, Hauptmann Kurt Bruns had the two GIs identified and, stating 'The Jews have no right to live in Germany', detailed Feldwebel Hoffmann to execute them immediately. On 13 February 1945 the remains of Staff Sergeant Kurt R. Jacobs and Technician 5th Grade Murray Zapler were discovered and identified outside Bleialf.[43] Despite protestations that he was 'only following orders', the judge at his trial sentenced Bruns to hang.

After the surrender of Bataan in the Philippines to Japan on 9 April 1942, where 15,000 American and 60,000 Filipino troops were marched into captivity, this was the largest mass surrender of US troops since the civil war, and most prisoners of the 106th shared John Kline's experience of being 'walked in columns to Bleialf and herded into a church yard. It had turned dark and the temperature was dropping. Most of us were without overcoats. We had only our field jackets and our winter issue of olive drab uniforms with long johns. We had to sleep on the ground. I remember how nervous I was. I wondered what was going to happen to us when day break came.'[44]

However, as Earl S. Parker, in Company 'E' of the 423rd, was marched back behind the panzers and self-propelled guns that had caused his regiment so much trouble, the old-fashioned nature of the Wehrmacht was revealed to him. He was 'surprised to see horse-drawn artillery, supply wagons and field kitchens – even some officers on horseback'.[45] Approximately 6,500 men went into captivity on 19 December, though word did not reach St Vith immediately of the surrender. By the 21st more were captured as isolated garrisons gave themselves up.

Others fought on. Several sub-units of the 18th Cavalry and 589th Artillery Battalion had separately battled their way into Schönberg, initially unaware it had been taken, or of the mass surrender taking place behind them. They came across rows of American 6 x 6 trucks lined up ahead of them and assumed the occupants to be GIs, but realised just in time from the shape of their helmets they were Germans.

Some GIs backed off, others stayed to fight until they were faced with German tanks. These may have belonged to Remer's *Führer-Begleit-Brigade*, but King Tigers from the 506th Heavy Tank Battalion were also beginning to use the route from Manderfeld via Andler and Schönberg, to reinforce their advance to Vielsalm. They belonged to the Sixth Panzer Army, but had trundled over their boundary into Manteuffel's territory in order to use the main road, more suitable for the massive Tiger IIs.

From one such panzer unit, Leutnant Rockhammer wrote home to his wife on 22 December, 'You cannot imagine what glorious hours and days we are experiencing now. It looks as if the Americans cannot withstand our important push. Today we overtook a fleeing column and finished it. We overtook it by a back road through the woods, just like on manoeuvres, with sixty Panthers. And then came the endless convoy, filled to the brim with American soldiers. It was a glorious bloodbath, vengeance for our destroyed homeland. Our soldiers still have the old zip, advancing and smashing everything. The snow must turn red with American blood. Victory was never as close as it is now.'[46]

All the GIs attacking Schönberg had eventually to abandon their vehicles and attempt to hike west towards St Vith and safety. Both Captain Arthur C. Brown and Lieutenant Eric Fisher Wood of the 589th Artillery shared similar experiences in Schönberg and escaped separately to the woods north-west of town. Brown and a small band of men were sheltered by a local farmer, Edmond Klein, near Stavelot. In his 1949 study of the 106th Division, *Lion in the Way*, Colonel Ernest Dupuy spent four pages describing the roving wolf-pack activities of Wood, who escaped into the trees just as the Germans were about to seize him and, possibly with other cut-off GIs, organised a guerrilla band which harassed German units from the woods around Meyerode. Charles Whiting in two of his books about the Bulge also wrote of Wood's lonely six-week war against the Germans, and of the locals finding his body surrounded by seven dead Germans, whom he had despatched. Nearby lay the remains of PFC Lehman M. Wilson of the 82nd Airborne Division.

Their remains were discovered in early February 1945 with a date of death fixed at late January. It seems a perfect story, except that US official military records state Wood's date of death as 17 December 1944 on the headstone bearing his name, in the Henri-Chapelle American Cemetery.[47] A forester certainly met and sheltered an

American fugitive at this time who answered to Wood's description, but no concrete evidence has ever surfaced as to Wood's activities, or demise. That his father, a general, later became a member of General Eisenhower's staff was perhaps instrumental in giving this tale of a latter-day Robin Hood some 'legs', and Belgians insist that Wood was buried where he fell; a stone cross stands where the local community in Meyerode commemorate him. Probably we shall never know whether an American dragon-slayer lurked in these woods, though most would wish it to be true.[48]

Post-war, Captain Alan Jones, Jr, the general's son, penned a staff paper for the Infantry School at Fort Benning on the Schnee Eifel operation. Among many robust criticisms, he concluded the defeat was the result of 'the combination of the weakest unit holding the least desirable defensive position, which controlled an important avenue of approach, and could have resulted only in success of the enemy's attack'. The problem was exacerbated by the lack of reserves, as all three regiments were committed in line. Communications throughout the period, he wrote, 'were erratic or non-existent' and no schemes had been made during planning for alternate methods of contact.

Jones felt that, had aerial resupply drops been initiated, as they were for Bastogne, they 'could have maintained the fighting strength of two surrounded infantry regiments and one field artillery battalion on the Schnee Eifel'. The two regimental staffs, he argued, should have made every effort to maintain the closest possible coordination, which they utterly failed to do. Lack of food and water (as Colonel Cavender had suggested) was no justification for organising the capitulation, he wrote, nor did he feel that a commander had the right to order his men to surrender in such circumstances. Finally, he insisted that a regimental command post should never be located next to the regimental aid post, for the sight of the 422nd's casualties piling up on 19 December 1944 had obviously unnerved the already fraught Colonel Descheneaux. In short, Jones suggested, both senior officers had 'lost the plot'.[49]

The Germans were even more critical, Oberstleutnant Dietrich Moll, chief of staff of the 18th *Volksgrenadiers*, observing, 'The 106th Division's failure must largely be blamed on the lack of initiative of its officers, NCOs and General Jones. There had been no combat reconnaissance even before the [German 16 December] attack began,' he asserted. 'A surprising fact, considering that bad weather had prevented air reconnaissance. Pushing eastward from the Schnee Eifel positions, a combat patrol would undoubtedly have discovered some indication of our preparations. No American preparations had been made to block the Our valley or blow up the bridge at Schönberg . . . Once their rear communications had been cut off, units surrendered too easily. Even after German units had penetrated deep into their positions, there was no evidence of coordinated leadership, nor was there any attempt to launch a counter attack.'[50]

But all was not in vain, for Manteuffel had expected to take St Vith on 17 December and the Golden Lions permanently damaged his precious timetable. It would take another week of brutal fighting before the Germans entered what would be the devastated remains. In 1970 Manteuffel wrote a letter to a retired 106th artillery officer, stating he could not understand why the division received so much criticism for the debacle of the Ardennes. As far as he was concerned, they held up an entire corps for four days, forcing many of his troops to manoeuvre north or south in their attempt to reach St Vith. That was a remarkable achievement by anyone's standards, the baron felt, and worthy of great pride, not blame. By the war's end the Golden Lions would have received the impressive tally of 325 Bronze Stars, sixty-four Silver Stars and one Distinguished Service Cross for their time in combat.

The little settlements that witnessed the hard fighting over 16–19 December 1944 have recovered and grown, to the extent that many of the 106th veterans I have met there display difficulty in orientating themselves. Builders in Bleialf still have to be careful with the legacy of unexploded wartime munitions – an earth-moving machine uncovered twenty large artillery shells in 2009 – all still assessed as lethal. Head north out of Bleialf and take a right at the first junction, to Auw. In 1944 this was called 'Purple Heart Corner', though some GIs dubbed it '88 Corner'. Either way, the nicknames indicated what would happen if a soldier lingered there.

On the left of the route to Auw – Skyline Drive – in the tree line, was where the 422nd and 423rd were ultimately surrounded and captured. In 1993, writer and historian Charles Whiting found a 1944 walkie-talkie from the drama, broken in two, in that very location. Ten years later I discovered a gas mask, a magazine for a Thompson sub-machine gun and a battered mess tin. Many of the old pillboxes inhabited by the Golden Lions were destroyed in March 1945 by the 315th Infantry Regiment of the US 90th Division, who 'filled many of the larger forts with tons of captured explosives and ammunition. Then it detonated the charges, which in a mighty blast, destroyed the fruits of years of German planning and the work of thousands of slave labourers who had died in the construction of the impregnable Siegfried Line.'[51] The former bunkers are now indicated by large lumps of moss-covered concrete. The area abounds with dugouts and the detritus of the battle, so much so that walking there is still hazardous, but the foxholes are now inhabited by, well – foxes.

31

Roadblocks

'THE SUCCESS OF the Fifth Panzer Army will rest on the early capture of St Vith,' Manteuffel had predicted before *Unternehmen Herbstnebel*. His offensive, which had fully engulfed the 422nd and 423rd Regiments, immediately threatened the crossroads town and its population of around 2,000. Only the timely arrival of the US 7th Armored Division, along with the 81st and 168th Combat Engineers and elements of 9th Armored, 28th and 106th Divisions, stood in their way. The engineers straightaway dug in to defend Prummerberg Hill, which dominates the Schönberg–St Vith road. From the afternoon of the 17th, they slowed the 18th *Volksgrenadiers,* who were advancing with their assault guns and armoured half-tracks, using well-directed artillery fire. Meanwhile, US tanks and tank destroyers were hurried forward to block the route, alongside the 38th Armored Infantry and a troop of cavalry.

The Prummerberg was soon dotted with foxholes dug by the engineers and infantrymen, giving them overwatch of the sector. During 18 December, the Germans tried three times to swamp the defenders on the hill, but they stayed in position until ordered to withdraw by Brigadier-General Bruce C. Clarke, originally commanding CCB of the 7th Armored, who had by then taken over command of St Vith from General Jones. (A stone memorial to the 168th Engineer Combat Battalion now stands at the top of the Prummerberg, and near to it remain several of their foxholes.) Clarke was soon joined by a fellow brigadier-general, William M. Hoge, who commanded CCB of the 9th

Armored and had been ordered to make contact with the 424th Regiment, to the south of St Vith. From then on, the two brigadiers, old friends, worked together to defend the town with their relatively meagre resources.

On 18 December the defenders' fears were heightened when the Germans ambushed an American convoy at the little road junction of Poteau, the midpoint on the road between Vielsalm and St Vith, and six miles *west* of Clarke's headquarters. General Hasbrouck, the 7th's commander, ordered an immediate counter-attack using CCA: 'Imperative you retake Poteau and hold it!' They managed, but only after they found their opponents were not *Volksgrenadiers*, but the superbly trained *Kampfgruppe Hansen* of the 1st SS-*Leibstandarte* Division. The initial attack had been made on a column of US vehicles, comprising a troop of M-5 light tanks and M-8 armoured cars from the 18th Cavalry and towed guns of the 820th Tank Destroyer Battalion (of the 7th Armored's CCA), commanded by Major J.L. Mayes, heading north out of Poteau. Taken by surprise, the GIs had little time to put up a defence and fled or were captured.

The best-known pictures from the Bulge – which appear in every book about the Ardennes (including an image on the jacket of this book) and show German troops rushing past blazing US vehicles – originate from this 18 December encounter. The Poteau location, with its burning half-tracks silhouetted against the snow-covered terrain, proved very photogenic, as at least one Waffen-SS ciné cameraman and a photographer discovered. They lingered to record much footage, and pose the attackers in a variety of staged assaults for the camera, which duly found their way back to the Propaganda Ministry in Berlin. Yet these are not the combat images they purport to be – there are no prisoners, dead or wounded, though the American column had clearly been ambushed only a short while earlier.

Heeding General Hasbrouck's orders, after dusk, the 48th Armored Infantry and Shermans from the 40th Tank Battalion fought their way into Poteau. In a furious battle lit by the flames from burning tanks, the GIs flushed the SS from the village. The day-long battle for Poteau has been carefully researched by several modern historians, some of the participants in the propaganda images identified, and in 1998 the Ardennen-Poteau '44 Museum was established in the old customs warehouse at the Poteau junction by Rob and Jacqueline de Ruyter. Their museum is packed with vehicles, military equipment, uniformed mannequins and well-presented dioramas about the battle. Recently they

A German soldier (identified as belonging to the Waffen-SS from his camouflaged jacket) urges his men past a burning American convoy. This picture was taken near the crossroads at Poteau, west of St Vith, on 18 December 1944, and is from the same sequence as the front cover image. A *Kriegsberichter* (war reporters) unit came across these flaming jeeps just after the fighting had finished. The cameramen marshalled passing SS troops to re-enact their assault on the US vehicles. After several takes, the soldiers, who belonged to *Kampfgruppe Hansen* of the 1st SS-*Leibstandarte* Division, moved on and the war reporters sent their iconic images, recorded both as newsreel and still photographs, back to Berlin. (NARA)

acquired a German armoured half-track, in which they drive visitors around the scene of the famous 18 December 1944 ambush.[1]

Back in St Vith, throughout the night of 18–19 December, the GI defenders could hear the movement of vehicles to their front and were twice attacked, as the *Volksgrenadiers* probed for a weak spot to attack on the 19th. The Germans tried through the entirety of the following day in the fog, but their assaults were driven back. The defenders now knew (from prisoners) they were facing at least a German corps, comprising the 18th and 62nd *Volksgrenadiers*, with the 1st SS-*Leibstandarte* Panzer Division identified to their north and 116th Panzer to the south.

A large defensive arc, known in time as the 'Fortified Goose Egg' was established using three armoured combat commands and the remnants of the 106th Division. To the north was Colonel Dwight Rosebaum's CCA of the 6th Armored; Clarke's CCB protected the front of St Vith, and Hoge's CCB was stationed to the south, contesting the Our crossing at Steinbrück – where Hoge's men eventually blew up the all-important bridge on the 18th. With these were as many other units as could be found: spare armoured infantry, field artillery, tank, tank destroyer and combat engineer battalions were rounded up and sent to the 'Goose Egg', along with stragglers, enlisted men and officers, collected by MPs and formed into provisional units, no matter what their original trade – whether cook, quartermaster or signaller.

The remaining fighting units of the 106th, Colonel Reid's 424th Regiment and the 591st Field Artillery Battalion, had fought on, slowly falling back towards St Vith. The 106th Division's heavy artillery battalion, the 592nd (equipped with 155mm howitzers) had moved back during the night of the 17th and been firing non-stop since the 18th. Initially Clarke and Hoge had to battle against a flow of US Army traffic heading in the opposite direction, as reporter Jack Belden, covering the war for *Time* and *Life* magazines, described: 'The road was jammed with every conceivable kind of vehicle. An enemy plane came down and strafed the column, knocking three trucks off the road, shattering trees and causing everyone to flee to ditches'. All recall that V-1 buzz bombs roaring overhead, and sometimes falling in their midst, added to the sense of terror.[2]

Clarke's own CCB had to clear a path forwards for their armour, to move into the Goose Egg: 'We started getting vehicles to move over to the sides. Slowly a path was beginning to open and the tanks began to roll along at a snail's pace, with halts every fifty to one hundred feet. [Coming from the opposite direction] several times senior officers in command cars attempted to pull out into a space which I was opening up, and each time I told them to get back, that I didn't care who they were, nothing was coming through except our tanks and anything else which was headed for the front.'[3] Belden also observed a sense of shame among those witnessing the retreat, if not in those doing the retreating: 'I noticed in myself a feeling that I had not had for some years. It was a feeling of guilt that seems to come over you whenever you retreat. You don't like to look anyone in the eyes. It seems as if you have done something wrong. I perceived this feeling in others also.'[4]

As the weight of the German attack on St Vith increased during the

20th, Clarke and Hoge shifted some of the weak flanks back to protect their exposed rear, turning the arc into a horseshoe. Morale dipped twice during the night of 20–21 December as Germans managed to penetrate part of the defence but were repelled, and sank further when a platoon of three officers and thirty-five men from the 423rd Regiment turned up at St Vith, having evaded capture since the Schnee Eifel surrender of the 19th. This was the first the defenders knew of the loss of two entire regiments of the 106th, whom they assumed were still out there fighting somewhere. Clarke called a meeting of unit commanders and heard that, though they were not surrounded, supply convoys were having to battle their way into St Vith; immediately he ordered reduced rations and a sparing use of artillery, heightening a sense of siege.

The chief ration and fuel depot used by the defenders was at Samrée, which, as we have seen, was seized by Waldenburg's 116th Panzer Division late on 20 December. So desperate were the 7th Armored, Golden Lions and Nelson's 112th Infantry for supplies that items were still being issued from the north end of the Samrée dump while the south side was under attack by Waldenburg's panzers. The last seven trucks to escape were loaded with fuel during the fighting, covered by tommy-gun toting guards recruited from General Clarke's kitchen crews back in St Vith. The convoy took two days, with a night spent hiding in the woods, to return, running the gauntlet of four German ambushes in which one GI was killed and three wounded.[5]

On 21 December huge attacks were launched around the perimeter, preceded by deadly artillery strikes. Manteuffel was now desperate to eliminate this obstacle to his plans. To the front, five major attacks, using the Schönberg road as an axis, were recorded at 11.00 a.m., 12.30 p.m., 2.00 p.m., 4.10 p.m. and 5.10 p.m. It was the same on the flanks. The front, facing east and manned by the 38th Armored Infantry, had sustained the worst and most concerted attacks. Major Boyer, S-3 of the 38th, recalled later:

> We were under assault by two battalions of enemy infantry, each attacking in a narrow front, with two companies abreast. The Krauts kept boring in, no matter how fast we decimated their assaults. As fast as we would repel one, another would return. All machine-guns were employing swinging traverse and taking a deadly toll. One, which heretofore had been dishing out a deadly hail of fire all along the front, was hit by a *Panzerfaust*, which struck the barrel halfway between the breach

> and the muzzle. The gunner fell forward on the gun with half his face torn off; the loader had his left arm torn off at the shoulder and was practically decapitated, while the gun commander was tossed about fifteen feet away from the gun to lie quite still.[6]

The 38th withstood all, reinforced by the remnants of Colonel Gustin M. Nelson's 112th Regiment of the Pennsylvania National Guard (the 'Bloody Bucket' Division), who were now scattered right across the front, with their commander holed up in Bastogne. Earlier, Nelson's men had so effectively resisted the attack of LVIII Panzer Corps as to prevent 116th Panzer Division and 560th *Volksgrenadiers* from crossing the River Our at Lützkampen, and forced them to use 2nd Panzer Division's bridge at Dasburg. After a magnificent four-day stand along the river line, forcing his opponents to outflank him, late on 19 December Nelson attached himself to the southern flank of the Golden Lions' 424th Regiment, and hence became wrapped up in the defence of St Vith.

'I established a mobile counter-attack force of part of a battalion of tanks, concealed near and behind St Vith,' remembered Clarke. 'It was used to counter-attack whenever the Germans established a dangerous situation, but only to sweep the enemy away, then I'd withdraw it for employment elsewhere. I was giving up maybe a mile a day, under enormous pressure. However, my German opponent needed to advance many miles, and quickly, to achieve his mission. The Seventh Armored prevented him from doing that.'[7] By 8.00 p.m., the American front had been penetrated in multiple places and was in danger of collapse, so at 10.00 p.m., Clarke issued the order to withdraw to the high ground west of St Vith. By then, the Goose Egg contained Hoge's CCB of the 9th Armored, the 112th and 424th Regiments, the 275th Armored Field Artillery and 965th Field Artillery Battalions; various engineer units, plus all the remaining elements of the 7th Armored Division – in all about 20,000 Americans. However, it rested on one very tenuous supply route, leading west from Vielsalm.

At noon on 20 December the much-debated plan for Field Marshal Montgomery to take charge of the northern half of the Bulge battlefield had come into effect. The mechanics of who commanded them initially did not matter much to Clarke and Hoge, still fighting for St Vith. In fact, they came under command of Matthew Ridgway's XVIII Airborne Corps, which controlled the rest of 7th Armored and 82nd Airborne Division who garrisoned the terrain just behind St Vith. (When the 101st

Screaming Eagles under Tony McAuliffe had been sent to Bastogne, Jim Gavin's 82nd All Americans had been deployed to the northern Ardennes at the same moment.)

On 22 December, Montgomery initially ordered that Clarke form a perimeter to be supplied from the air, as was being planned for Bastogne. Clarke demurred, and Hasbrouck argued on Clarke's behalf that the St Vith defenders had been almost destroyed the previous night. The remaining homesteaders simply hadn't the strength to circle the wagons: the Indians were too strong. After several radio conferences, the plan was amended. Accordingly, from his HQ in Vielsalm, Ridgway, commanding the XVIII Airborne Corps, ordered the withdrawal of the Goose Egg to positions behind Gavin's 82nd Airborne. Those in the Goose Egg thus received a gracious message from Montgomery (their new commander, though none were aware of it): 'You have accomplished your mission – a mission well done. It is time to withdraw, with all honour.'

General James Gavin, commanding the 82nd, visited the CP of the 106th at Renceveaux, west of Vielsalm, on 21 December. He felt sorry for General Jones, 'the picture of dejection', but was impressed and envious of the division's new trucks and trailers parked outside. 'There were two huge trailers containing doughnut-making machines and all kinds of vans and administrative vehicles' – which seemed to sum up the American way of war in late 1944 – doughnut-making machines at the front.[8] The following day Jones, who had just been appointed Ridgway's Assistant Corps Commander, suffered a heart attack and had to be hospitalised, having already been relieved of his division – the stress induced by the loss of his two regiments and his son becoming a prisoner of war can scarcely be imagined.

Gavin wrote later of his admiration 'for the way in which Montgomery congratulated all those who fought at St Vith for the fine job they did'. He was full of praise, too, for 'the ubiquitous British field officer and a "Phantom Regiment" Jeep and radio [which] stayed in close touch with us. Monty had a policy of stationing a young field officer at every division headquarters [whose] mission was to keep Montgomery's headquarters informed at once of everything that was taking place. I thought the system was excellent, since all too frequently information does not get to an army headquarters or higher for hours, until it is too late.'[9] Gavin did not go on to explore the difference one of Monty's liaison officers would have made at General Jones's HQ in St Vith on 16

December. Given one, the misunderstanding with Middleton, his superior in Bastogne, might never have happened.

It was on the 22nd that Eisenhower issued one of his very rare Orders of the Day (only two had preceded it, on 6 June and 14 August 1944, and six would follow it in 1945). The occurrence indicated the gravity of the moment. However, its tone was upbeat, not desperate, and a masterpiece of public relations:

> The enemy is making his supreme effort to break out of the desperate plight into which you forced him by your brilliant victories of the summer and fall. He is fighting savagely to take back all that you have won and is using every treacherous trick to deceive and kill you. He is gambling everything, but already, in this battle, your gallantry has done much to foil his plans. In the face of your proven bravery and fortitude, he will completely fail.
>
> But we cannot be content with his mere repulse.
>
> By rushing out from his fixed defenses the enemy may give us the chance to turn his great gamble into his worst defeat. So I call upon every man, of all the Allies, to rise now to new heights of courage, of resolution and of effort. Let everyone hold before him a single thought – to destroy the enemy on the ground, in the air, everywhere – destroy him! United in this determination and with unshakable faith in the cause for which we fight, we will, with God's help, go forward to our greatest victory.[10]

Ridgway had not approved of Monty's plan to withdraw the troops now in his XVIII Airborne Corps out of the Goose Egg. It went against his gut instinct. Though he understood the reason for pulling the armoured troops out from St Vith, he was also aware that the 101st Airborne in Bastogne were surrounded and about to be supplied from the air. It seemed as though one rule had been applied to St Vith and a second to Bastogne. Neither was he keen on pulling back Gavin's 82nd Airborne (his old command), as Monty later ordered on 24 December, adhering to the very British notion of a 'tidy battlefield'. If the 82nd had won terrain by spilling blood, they should not then have to relinquish it, Ridgway felt, especially on the command of a foreign general.

Gavin admitted the new orders 'shortened the sector allocated to the 82nd by about fifty percent, thus enabling us to do much better on the defensive', that it was 'far superior in terms of fields of fire and cover for the defenders' and he would be 'in a much better position to launch a counter-attack' from it, but it still went against his division's motto of 'No ground gained is ever relinquished'. Nevertheless they obeyed; some discipline was called for.[11] For all the much-vaunted efficiency of Gavin's division, the combat historian, Master Sergeant Forrest Pogue, remembered visiting a farmhouse where a detachment of the 82nd had set up a CP. 'We entered through the kitchen, where two GIs were sitting at a stove. They glanced at us as we went through a door into the next room. The room was empty of officers or men, but the wall had a map showing the division's dispositions and at one side were all the passwords and alternate challenges for the week. We made note of locations, noted some of the challenges, went back out, got into our Jeep, and drove away without ever being asked who we were or what we wanted.'[12]

In fact there was almost no withdrawal from St Vith, as Hoge and Clarke found their wheels and tracks were mired in thick Ardennes mud and any movement seemed a remote possibility. There was discussion of having to stay put in St Vith and fight it out. Clarke spent a restless night. By the morning of 23 December 'a miracle had happened', as he later put it. Even lower temperatures had frozen the mud solid, enabling his vehicles to be chopped out of the ice. At 06.00 a.m. they started rolling, with Clarke directing the traffic flow (much as he had done on first entering the beleaguered town). The day dawned clear and the arrival of the massed Allied air fleets did much to restore morale and protect the move of first Hoge's CCB and then Clarke's troops, bringing up the rear at 10.00 a.m., and following the armoured traffic along the road via Poteau to Vielsalm. As fighters patrolled overhead and C-47s in the distance headed towards Bastogne, for the first time in days Clarke allowed himself to fall asleep, roped to his seat, while his faithful driver, Sergeant Jendrewski, drove on. His column leapfrogged back, with Remer's *Führer-Begleit-Brigade* snapping at their heels; all had crossed the bridge at Vielsalm when it was blown at midday.

The artillery officer, Leutnant Behrman of the 18th *Volksgrenadiers*, whose diary we have already sampled, recorded the abrupt change of circumstances with the arrival of good flying weather:

> 24 December: Dive-bombers [most likely P-47s] attack and hit a house in front of me. Two metres more and it would have been me. We take

> our car and race towards St Vith. Here dive-bombers attack again and strafe all roads. During the night more bombs fall.
> 25 December: On the road to Hinderhausen [midway between Poteau and St Vith] a dive-bomber starts for us. We are able to stop the lorry in time to get off the road as the bullets start flying about us. Nothing is to be seen of our air force. Where is it? Our anti-aircraft guns knock down two bombers. The pilots parachute down but the dogs are lucky and the wind drives them toward the west.
> 26 December: During the afternoon we undergo the second large-scale air attack on St Vith. The house shakes and the windows break. The terrorised family seeks refuge in the cellar. Babies cry but the bombers keep coming. There's nothing left of St Vith.[13]

The defence of St Vith had bought the Americans seven working days and stopped cold one of the two main thrusts of *Herbstnebel*. However, it came at the cost of 3,400 casualties, eighty-eight tanks and twenty-five armoured cars from 7th Armored and the 14th Cavalry. In 1964 Clarke and Manteuffel met when the former had just stepped down as commander of the US Army in Europe (USAEUR). 'Why didn't you just overwhelm us with a powerful frontal assault on 17 December?' asked Clarke of the baron. 'We assessed that we were up against at least a division, if not a corps,' answered the Fifth Panzer Army's former commander. 'Every time we probed your defences we found tanks, but in our preliminary briefings we were led to believe there were no armoured formations in our way.'[14]

Clarke hadn't slept properly in days and, after Vielsalm, his surgeon ordered him to take a strong sleeping tablet, which knocked him out immediately. Sometime after midnight a staff officer tried to wake him with the news that he was to report immediately to General Ridgway, his corps commander. 'The hell with it,' the exhausted brigadier managed to say before he lapsed back into well-earned slumber. A mild rocket from Ridgway followed in the morning, upbraiding him for not reporting, but Clarke was past caring. He knew he'd done an outstanding job. 'In that case, I'd like your permission to leave and return to Third Army, where I know General Patton will be glad to see me,' he retorted. At that, Ridgway relented: 'Well, just don't let it happen again.'

On Christmas Eve, Manteuffel phoned Jodl at the Ziegenberg *Adlerhorst* to tell him the offensive had definitely failed. His tanks had run out of fuel near the Meuse, the Seventh Army had stalled in the south; the Sixth had made no progress on the Elsenborn Ridge and St Vith had only just fallen. Antwerp was, as he had always suspected, an impossible dream. However, he suggested he still might be able to envelop the US forces east of the Meuse. 'Give me reserves, and I will take Bastogne, reach the Meuse, swing north and help the Sixth Panzer Army to advance,' he countered. 'But I must have sufficient petrol and air support – and I need a reply tonight.' Despite the baron's urgings, Hitler refused to make a decision until 26 December, when he offered him the requested reserves – which by then could not move through lack of fuel. *Herbstnebel* was doomed to continue. After the war, Manteuffel told Basil Liddell Hart that, even on 24 December, 'I think a limited success would still have been possible – up to the Meuse. Afterwards, however, Hitler condemned us to a corporal's war. There were no big plans, only a multitude of piecemeal fights.' Rundstedt was even more forthright: 'I wanted to stop the offensive on 22 December, when it was plain we could not achieve the aim, but Hitler furiously insisted that it must go on. It was Stalingrad No. 2.'[15]

During Christmas week, Jim Gavin of the 82nd was invited to dinner with General Hodges at the First Army's HQ, when the conversation turned to Field Marshal Montgomery. Hodges' staff spoke of him with 'amusement and respect. Obviously they liked him, and they respected his thorough professionalism.' One officer thought Monty 'optimistic, meticulous, precise and cautious'. This goes some way to challenging the post-war view, led by General Omar Bradley and sustained in recent years by historian Stephen E. Ambrose, that all Americans detested Montgomery: many admired his military skills, if not his public utterances. By contrast, the First Army staff were less than amused by Patton and his Third Army, who seemed to be out to grab the headlines, especially in the army's daily, *Stars and Stripes.* What had particularly irked them was Patton's prayer. On 8 December, the exuberant general had phoned the Head Chaplain of his Third Army, Father James H. O'Neill, demanding, 'Do you have a good prayer for weather? We must do something about those rains if we are to win the war.' O'Neill composed one and sent it round within the hour. Patton read it, approved and directed him to have 250,000 copies printed for distribution to every man in the Third Army:

> Almighty and most merciful Father, we humbly beseech Thee, of Thy great goodness, to restrain these immoderate rains with which we have

> had to contend. Grant us fair weather for Battle. Graciously hearken to us as soldiers who call upon Thee that, armed with Thy power, we may advance from victory to victory, and crush the oppression and wickedness of our enemies and establish Thy justice among men and nations.

That was all very well, but when *Stars and Stripes* printed the prayer in a special box on the front page, Hodges felt the Patton publicity machine had gone too far. First Army demanded, and got, a separate edition of *Stars and Stripes* that printed their stories.[16]

Some of the 589th Field Artillery Battalion, mostly from Battery 'A' and Battalion HQ, with three 105mm howitzers, had managed to fight their way through Schönberg, and headed towards St Vith. The force of about one hundred, led by Major Arthur C. Parker III, represented all that was left of the twelve-gun battalion which supported the 422nd Infantry Regiment of the Golden Lions. On 19 December, Parker was directed to hold a crossroads north-east of St Vith, known as the Baraque de Fraiture. It consisted then, as it does today, of a few buildings on one of the highest summits in the Ardennes (over 2,000 feet), and a key intersection of the north–south road from Bastogne to Liège with a good east–west route running between Vielsalm and La Roche.

When Parker's men reached the crossroads, everyone was exhausted and numb from the bitter cold.[17] In addition to his own force, Parker enlisted the help of four passing half-tracks with quad .50 calibre machine guns, odd tanks and some towed anti-tank guns, a cavalry troop and, later, Company 'F' from the 325th Glider Infantry Regiment (of Gavin's 82nd Airborne): in all, fewer than 300 soldiers. On the same evening, seventeen-year-old Kanonier Josef Reusch, with the 560th *Volksgrenadiers* had arrived in the village of Montleban, between Houffalize and Parker's position. 'I spent the evening in a hayloft. Our guns stood in the courtyard of the farm when suddenly, in the middle of the night, an American convoy rolled through the village with tanks and trucks. The alarm was not sounded, simply because there was no point to it, since everything happened so fast!'[18] He went back to sleep.

The 20th was quiet for both sides at the Baraque de Fraiture, although a dozen *Volksgrenadier* cycle troops on a scouting mission were engaged and some killed. Over the following days, two company-sized probing attacks from the 560th *Volksgrenadiers* were repulsed. Among them was Josef Reusch, whose guns had just been destroyed and he had become a rifleman. His memories are of dense fog on 21–22 December and such thick snow that his tent, in the woods surrounding the Baraque de Fraiture, collapsed on top of him. Under mortar fire, in the pre-dawn darkness of 22 December, an officer patrol from the 2nd SS *Das Reich* Panzer Division was captured and identified. Low on fuel, the SS unit were scouting a move from Houffalize to turn right at the crossroads and attack Vielsalm. That evening, Parker was wounded by mortar shell fragments, lost consciousness and was evacuated. Major Elliot Goldstein, also of the 589th, stepped in to continue the defence. However, their defensive positions were clearly outlined against the newly fallen snow to the Germans, who thus worked out all their positions.

The following morning, the 23rd, Obersturmbannführer Otto Weidinger, commander of the SS-*Der Führer* Regiment, initially sent his II Battalion of *Panzergrenadiers* to take the crossroads. They succeeded in knocking out the towed anti-tank guns and advanced slightly before being forced back by a counter-attack from the glider infantry company and five Shermans from the 3rd Armored Division, recently arrived. Ingeniously, the SS then took radios from captured US vehicles and began to jam the frequencies used by the American forward observers when calling for fire support. Jim Gavin of the 82nd Airborne had gone up to the Baraque de Fraiture as the afternoon of the 23rd waned, increasingly concerned for its safety. 'I went to the town of Fraiture and proceeded from there toward the crossroads. I encountered such a tremendous volume of fire that it was suicide to go any further. Small-arms fire was ricocheting in all directions. Interspersed with this was artillery, mortar and tank fire.'[19]

At 4.00 that afternoon, preceded by effective German artillery, another attack was launched by Weidinger, this time with two panzer companies. Three of the Shermans were knocked out, the rest retreated, and the II and III Battalions of Weidinger's *Der Führer* Regiment then stormed the crossroads. Two US tanks and a few officers and men slipped through to friendly lines, but the rest were overwhelmed; of the 116-man glider rifle company, only forty-four rejoined their parent unit. Weidinger had wisely attacked at last light, when the Allied air support had turned for home and, earlier in the day, Josef Reusch remembered the 'fighter aircraft attacking with rockets. Additionally they dropped bombs and fired cannon. Every half hour they returned and started again. First they destroyed an anti-aircraft battery and then they turned on us!'[20]

One escapee was T/4 Randolph C. Pierson, who worked in the 589th's

Fire Direction Center and had just celebrated his twenty-first birthday on 19 December, the day they arrived. He managed to escape but was wounded and captured the same evening. Interrogated by an SS officer on the 24th, at the end Pierson was asked, 'Why did you fight so hard at Baraque de Fraiture? Do you hate the Germans so much?' 'My answer was very calculated, "I don't hate the Germans, but your men were trying to kill me". He smiled, and then replied in perfect English, "I hope you survive this ugly war. If you do, I advise you to finish your college education".'

Later, Pierson, in company with an 82nd paratrooper, was being taken to a POW collection centre by a wounded German corporal. 'To my surprise, the paratrooper suddenly bent over as if in pain, the guard approached him, and was dropped by a vicious right hand upper-cut. I caught the German's rifle as it flew into the air, out of his hands, and pinned him to the frozen ground with a vicious bayonet thrust through his chest. The paratrooper and I instantly broke into a fast run for the snowy Ardennes forest. He in one direction, and I in another. Later I was rescued.'[21]

Though the Baraque de Fraiture had been lost, its surviving defenders had withdrawn with 'high morale. They claimed that they had inflicted tremendous casualties on the Germans before withdrawing,' recorded Jim Gavin.[22] The battle then moved four miles north-west to another crossroads at Manhay, where the main north–south highway intersects with another, running from Stavelot via Trois-Ponts west to Grandmenil, Erezée and Hotton. As recently as 22 December, Manhay had been the CP of Major-General Maurice Rose, commanding the US 3rd Armored Division. A US tank company was hurried to Manhay, where an attack by the 2nd SS Division, flanked by the 560th *Volksgrenadiers*, developed on Christmas Eve.

During the German advance on Manhay from the Baraque de Fraiture via Odeigne on 24 December, an SS panzer column, preceded by a captured Sherman, tripped several US 7th Armored Division roadblocks, then raced ahead and overwhelmed the crossroads, engaging several American vehicles passing through at the time. In the lead by then was Panther 401, commanded by Oberscharführer Ernst Barkmann, a six-foot blond tank ace who had already chalked up twenty-eight victories in Normandy. His tank came to a halt opposite the Sherman of Frank Ostaszewski, which had stalled with engine failure. Barkmann acted quicker than the Sherman crew: 'In seconds the tank turret turned to the right and the long barrel slammed against the turret of the Sherman. Gunner to commander, "I cannot fire – the turret traverse is jammed!" The driver, *Rottenführer* Grundmeyer, moved back a few paces. Then *Unterscharführer* Poggendorff, the gunner, fired a shell into the middle of the enemy tank at a distance of a few yards. The explosion that followed wrecked the Sherman, but miraculously all of the crew, including Ostaszewski, survived.'[23]

Josef Reusch was still in the mêlée and recalled the confusion of intermingled forces: 'On one occasion, American first aid trucks with wounded drove through our position. Immediately we decided to change our position and followed the trucks to the next road intersection.'[24] Over Christmas Day, US counter-attacks by the 3rd Armored Division were frustrated when strafed in error by their own air force, which killed thirty-nine GIs, and Manhay remained in German hands.[25] On 26 December, panzer attacks to the north of Manhay and as far west as Grandmenil were countered by the density of US forces now flooding into the area – in addition to elements of the 3rd Armored and 82nd Airborne Divisions, the US 75th Division had also arrived. They possessed two luxuries the Germans did not: unlimited fuel and massive amounts of artillery on call, and these factors ensured that, by the evening of 26 December, Grandmenil had been retaken.

The stories of these three crossroads encounters – at Poteau, Baraque de Fraiture and Manhay (along with Hotton, where we began) – typify much of the winter fighting in the Ardennes. The weather and required speed of advance dictated there could be little off-road movement. An offensive in the summer months would have produced a very different result for the attackers, when they could have freely manoeuvred around the intersections. The Alamo-style defence at these locations required great bravery, as they were often encounters to the last man, the last bullet, but needed initiative also. They also represent many other defences where the heroes – a few GIs clustered around a machine gun – went unrecognised because all perished in their valour. Parker's actions at the Baraque de Fraiture are studied by soldiers for his resourcefulness in holding up much of a German division for several days. For this reason, the location had become known as 'Parker's Crossroads', even by the locals, though no doubt inspired by the 1862 encounter in Tennessee, between Confederate and Union forces, of the same name.

At Parker's Crossroads, a memorial plaque to the 106th Division and a wartime 105mm howitzer – facing east – now stand by the side of what is today a very busy intersection. In June 1945, the battered 106th Division was reconstituted, and Parker, recovered from his wounds, returned to command a new 589th. Another reminder of the Bulge is at Grandmenil, where the 2nd SS-*Das Reich* Panzer Division left behind one of their tanks on Christmas Day in 1944. The crew of Panther 407 had to leave their mount because of fuel shortage and abandoned it in a field. It survived the post-war scrapmen and today sits by the town's roundabout.

The *Das Reich* panzer attacks of 26 December constituted another high tide of the German push west, which had likewise culminated for the 2nd Panzer Division on 25–26 December at Foy-Notre-Dame and Celles, near the Meuse. The Waffen-SS did, however, make one last attempt to exploit a thousand-yard gap in the American defences, between the villages of Sadzot (a small settlement of about twenty houses, known as 'Sad-Sack' to the GIs, after a *Stars and Stripes* cartoon character) and Briscol, four miles west of Grandmenil. Really a local attack rather than a major attempt to break out to the west, it was launched by two battalions of the 25th SS *Panzergrenadier* Regiment of the *Hitlerjugend* Division. They had been withdrawn from the Elsenborn Ridge and sent to reinforce the *Das Reich* Division. The defenders of Sadzot included Company 'C' of the 87th Chemical Mortar Battalion, whose two platoons and company CP were all billeted inside the houses because of the extreme cold. (Every US infantry division had a chemical mortar battalion attached to it, which operated 4.2inch (107mm) mortars, capable of firing high-explosive and white phosphorus shells. The latter could shroud targets with smoke and cause casualties through burns.)

At 01.00 a.m., the SS storm troopers slipped into the village, slit the throats of the few sentries and began lobbing stick grenades through windows and raking each building with automatic fire. The mortarmen were completely surprised but recovered rapidly. Lieutenant Gordon Byers found an M-5 light tank and ordered its commander to come and help, but the tank crew refused. Byers was in no mood to listen. 'He issued the order to the crewman one more time and when the sergeant refused again the lieutenant calmly drew his .45 and pointed it at the soldier's head. That finally convinced him, with Byers manning the machine-gun on top of the vehicle, blazing away at every German he saw.' Somehow they survived, and caused such confusion in the German ranks that a number of his men were able to escape.

About thirty mortarmen escaped down a trail and were challenged for a password. They gave the correct one, but were attacked, several being killed. The shooters were part of a parachute infantry battalion of the 509th PIR (part of Gavin's 82nd Airborne Division) in the area who worked to different passwords and 'had been tricked before in Italy by Germans dressed as GIs'. The extremely confused series of fire-fights, fought with small arms, knives and fists, began in the early morning darkness of 28 December, continued through the day and into the 29th, before being finally repulsed.

Major-General Fay B. Prickett's 75th Infantry Division, in VII Corps reserve, were also in the vicinity, working with the battle-tested Maurice Rose's 3rd Armored to gain experience. Mortar Sergeant William E. Breuer was sent to rouse some help from a regiment of the 75th whose CP was known to be in the vicinity. 'Despite the sounds of battle that could be clearly heard from inside the house, the regimental commander and other officers were lounging around drinking coffee. There wasn't even a guard posted outside. Breuer explained to the colonel that the men of the 87th were under heavy attack in Sadzot just 800 yards away and needed immediate help.' None was forthcoming. 'It took just a moment for the incredulous mortar sergeant to realise that the regimental commander had no idea where his troops were.'[26]

It cost the mortarmen fifty-three killed, but 189 German dead were afterwards counted in and around the village. The battle of Sadzot represented the Germans' last major offensive activity in the Ardennes, for on 29 December Generalfeldmarschall Model ordered the Sixth Panzer Army over to the defensive and began stripping it of its armour.[27]

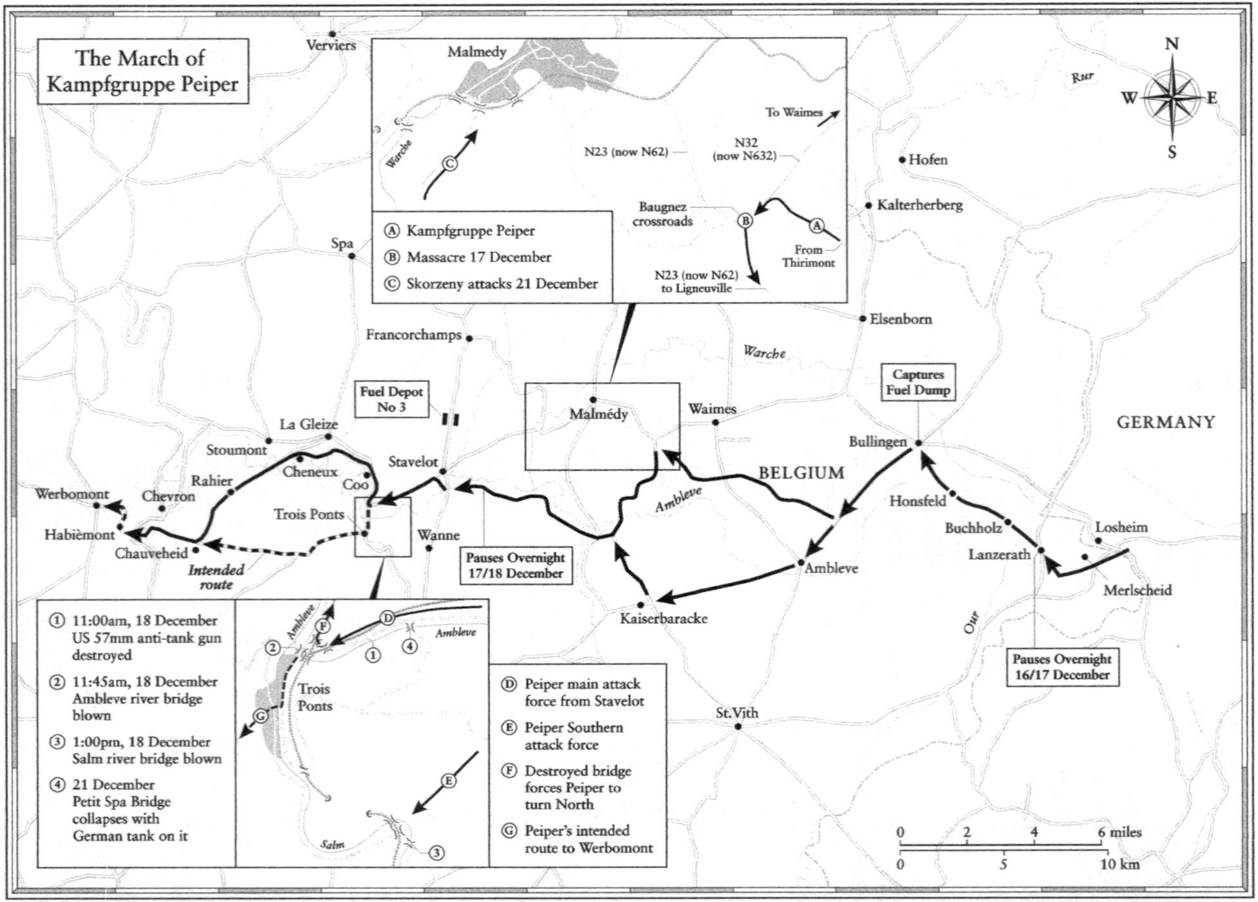
The March of
Kampfgruppe Peiper
Verviers
Malmedy
Warche
To Waimes
N23 (now N62)
N32
(now N632)
Baugnez
crossroads
From
Thirimont
N23 (now N62)
to Ligneuville
Ⓐ Kampfgruppe Peiper
Ⓑ Massacre 17 December
Ⓒ Skorzeny attacks 21 December
Spa
N
W
E
S
Rur
Hofen
Kalterherberg
Elsenborn
Francorchamps
Warche
Captures
Fuel Dump
Fuel Depot
No 3
La Gleize
Malmédy
Waimes
GERMANY
Bullingen
Stoumont
Stavelot
BELGIUM
Cheneux
Rahier
Coo
Werbomont
Chevron
Trois Ponts
Ambleve
Honsfeld
Buchholz
Losheim
Habièmont
Wanne
Chauveheid
Pauses Overnight
17/18 December
Ambleve
Lanzerath
Merlscheid
Intended
route
Kaiserbaracke
Our
① 11:00am, 18 December
US 57mm anti-tank gun
destroyed
② 11:45am, 18 December
Ambleve river bridge
blown
③ 1:00pm, 18 December
Salm river bridge blown
④ 21 December
Petit Spa Bridge
collapses with
German tank on it
Ambleve
Ambleve
Trois
Ponts
Salm
Ⓓ Peiper main attack
force from Stavelot
Ⓔ Peiper Southern
attack force
Ⓕ Destroyed bridge
forces Peiper to
turn North
Ⓖ Peiper's intended
route to Werbomont
Pauses Overnight
16/17 December
St.Vith
0
2
4
6 miles
0
5
10 km

32

Malmedy

We last visited the northern shoulder of the Bulge battlefield on the night of 16–17 December. There we encountered Obersturmbannführer Jochen Peiper, who had bayoneted his map to the wall in Lanzerath's Café Scholzen. He was angry and frustrated at the lack of progress made by the 3rd *Fallschirmjäger* and 12th *Volksgrenadier* Divisions, commanded by Generalmajors Walther Wadehn and Gerhardt Engel, both meant to be ahead of him.

As one of the spearheads of the Sixth Panzer Army, Peiper knew that every hour's delay translated into more coordinated American resistance. Having conferred with Oberst von Hoffmann, commander of the 9th *Fallschirmjäger* Regiment, Peiper pulled his *Kampfgruppe* out of Lanzerath as soon as he could, retaining one paratrooper battalion. He at least was now on *Rollbahn* 'D', where he was meant to be, if late. To his north, *Kampfgruppen* of the 12th SS-*Hitlerjugend* should have been advancing in parallel. Peiper's left flank (*Rollbahn* 'E') was being covered by another 1st SS-*Leibstandarte* Division battlegroup, that of his colleague, Standartenführer Max Hansen. The latter's route, which would take him to the crossroads at Poteau, was where the now-famous propaganda photographs were taken. A reconnaissance unit (*Kampfgruppe Knittel*), operating forward of Hansen, on *Rollbahn* 'E', would be responsible for executing the Wereth eleven.

Extremely aware of the likelihood of alert US units to his front, Peiper did not intend to let the darkness of the wintry night delay him further.

With two Panthers grinding forward in the lead, he instructed the *Fallschirmjäger* to walk by the side of each armoured vehicle guiding his drivers under combat conditions; some of the paratroopers displayed white handkerchiefs to indicate their presence, as Peiper was determined not to show any unnecessary lights. The remainder rode on his tanks. Fähnrich (Ensign) Rolf Odendahl was one of them. He remembered that many of his fellow *Fallschirmjäger* leaders were 'senior sergeants and sergeants of the Luftwaffe, who were used as riflemen without any infantry training'.[1] Peiper might have chanced charging ahead with blazing beadlights, for most American defenders were, in fact, asleep.

Buchholz, with its little station, was the next village Peiper reached – at about 05.00 a.m. – and was held by two platoons of the 99th Division's Company 'K' (of Colonel Don Riley's 394th Infantry Checkerboarders). Most of its sleepy-eyed American garrison were woken by the sounds of German voices on the roads outside, or pounding at the door. They were rounded up immediately, though a few resourceful individuals escaped. Soon, thousands of GIs would be on the run, cut off from their units but determined not to surrender, dodging German patrols when they could. These opening hours were chaotic and confused, with no such thing as a front line any more. The 394th Regiment (about 3,500 full-strength) would record 959 casualties over 16–17 December, including thirty-four killed, and an astounding 701 missing – many later confirmed as taken prisoner. In Buchholz the Germans overlooked at least one American soldier, a radio operator hidden in a cellar, who began to transmit back details of *Kampfgruppe Peiper*. Until capture, he counted thirty tanks, twenty-eight half-tracks; thirty captured American trucks and a long column of paratroopers moving through: in fact, it would take most of 17 December for Peiper's complete column of 800 vehicles to pass.[2]

PFC Don Wallace was with Company 'L' of the 3rd Battalion, 394th Infantry, in woods about 200 yards south-west of Buchholz station. He and the others were off the road and avoided the attentions of Peiper but were aware of the *Fallschirmjägers* moving about. During the night, Wallace had to take new passwords around the company. 'But the guys will shoot anything that moves!' he protested. Still, they had to be delivered. 'The forest was dark and very quiet. Every step I took during my search for the company I thought to myself "Gawd, I hope I don't step on a twig". I was scared and in the darkness I didn't want to make a sound. Suddenly I heard "Halt!" I remember my immediate response to this day. "Don't shoot, it's me, Wallace!" The guy knew me . . . I recognised his voice and he mine.'

Shortly afterwards they pulled back, Wallace remembering, 'We hit the ground as burp guns [German Schmeisser machine pistols] spat behind and bullets kissed the air around us.' Early on 17 December his squad 'spotted a large group of figures walking almost in formation along a road in front of us. They were only silhouettes, and we couldn't tell if they were friendly troops. We lay flat, being cautious, and waited till they had passed before we moved on.' He had made the right call, because the group were almost certainly *Fallschirmjäger*: the only Americans in the vicinity were by then moving cross-country, nervously, just as they were. Wallace's group eventually linked up with their company in Elsenborn, where he was 'so exhausted that I fell asleep on top of a pile of coal in a bin in the village'.[3]

While the *Fallschirmjäger* had been content to pause and wait for their artillery to catch up, Peiper insisted on pushing on, with his vehicles creeping forward in the pitch black. It was a hair-raising advance, tanks and half-tracks grinding through the snow, brushing past the densely packed pine trees, everyone tense and totally unaware as to the whereabouts of the next US roadblock. At some stage before 06.00 a.m., still in the dark, Peiper hit the next village – Honsfeld – a rest centre for the US 394th Regiment, his leading vehicles tagging on to a line of retreating American vehicles. This was to the complete surprise of its garrison who threw down their arms in panic as the panzers arrived. PFC Bill Hawkins from Company 'B' of the 612th Tank Destroyer Battalion, hauling towed anti-tank guns, had arrived the night before and was 'sleeping in the attic with three or four other buddies when I was awakened about daylight by one of our men and told to get up as the Germans had us completely surrounded. I kicked him downstairs and told him not to bother us anymore as I thought he was pulling a prank. Immediately one of our sergeants came up the stairs two at a time and informed us this was no prank but the real thing, at which we all jumped up and began looking out of the various windows and saw German soldiers everywhere we looked.'[4]

Honsfeld had been preparing for a completely different kind of visitor on 17 December – Marlene Dietrich – following her performance the night before to the 28th Division in Diekirch. Instead, it was Peiper's *Panzergrenadiers* who leaped off their tanks to round up bewildered Checkerboard GIs and those of the 14th Cavalry Group, who offered little trouble when cornered by Panthers clattering down the high street. A few Americans resisted and were cut down by automatic fire. Their bodies were still visible a few hours later, some crushed by passing tanks, clustered around the village water trough, when a war photographer passed through. He took a now-famous image of *Fallschirmjäger* troops stripping boots from the dead GIs, presumably to replace their own inferior footwear. The village was full of abandoned US equipment, and the *Kampfgruppe* captured fifteen three-inch, towed anti-tank guns, eighty trucks and some assorted reconnaissance vehicles – mostly jeeps, half-tracks and M-8 armoured cars. Although some paratroopers continued to ride on the tanks of Peiper's *Spitze*, the majority now returned to the command of their own division.

Peiper didn't have everything his own way in Honsfeld, losing several armoured vehicles; moreover, the *Fallschirmjäger* recorded thirty-eight killed in the vicinity. Among them was Leutnant Manfred Rottenberg, who had formerly served with a *Flak* battalion. Rottenberg had been transferred to 9th Parachute Regiment on the eve of the offensive, 15 December, and given a company of the regiment's II Battalion. With little experience, the young company commander – he was twenty-four – died in his first battle after less than twenty-four hours in combat.[5] Frances Hayes, Reconnaissance Sergeant of the 612th Tank Destroyer Battalion, remembered that a German 'jerked two 612th men out of the line of prisoners to carry a wounded SS officer to the aid station. They complied; however, the one at his head wrapped his hand around the German's throat and strangled him as they walked. They laid him on the floor, walked back, put their hands over their heads and merged back in line.'[6] During the mêlée, or afterwards, at least fifteen American prisoners and three Belgian civilians, including a sixteen-year-old girl, were mown down singly, or in small groups, in cold blood.[7] Nearby, German camera crews were active from first light recording hundreds of captured GIs, many wearing Checkerboard shoulder insignia, being herded down the road to Lanzerath and into the Fatherland. Tanks bearing happy panzermen rolled in the opposite direction: it made very good film footage for the Reich.

As it grew light, on leaving the village Peiper's column came under US fighter attack and several vehicles were lost, but not before the American aircraft were themselves ambushed by Messerschmitt 109s. Because of the atrociously slow going and with his fuel was running low, Peiper now left his assigned *Rollbahn* and headed for Büllingen and the hamlet of Dom Bütgenbach, where he had been alerted to a small American fuel dump. On the way, he captured eight American trucks which literally ran into his column, then attacked an airstrip at Morschneck, though eleven out of twelve tiny L-5 artillery-spotting aircraft managed to take off under fire. One was rescued by a sergeant who leaped into the cockpit, having only a few pre-war crop-dusting flying hours to his name. Büllingen, like Honsfeld, fell with little opposition at 08.00 a.m., though several of his tanks were damaged by American tank destroyers dug in west of the village. The Germans arrived so quickly that they captured a company of US 2nd Division soldiers lining up for breakfast. But others managed to hide all day and escape after dark. American prisoners were soon put to work filling the *Kampfgruppe*'s thirsty vehicles with some of the 50,000 gallons Peiper

The Ardennes sector was so quiet before the December offensive that soldiers amused themselves by shooting wild boar from spotter aircraft like this Piper L-4 Grasshopper. As Hitler hoped, appalling weather grounded Allied aircraft for significant periods just before and during the campaign, but it prevented Luftwaffe support too. The only US planes at risk of immediate capture were those of the liaison and observation squadrons, which greatly enhanced the work of US field artillery battalions. Early on 17 December, Kampfgruppe Peiper overran an airstrip where several of these aircraft managed to take off under fire, one piloted by a sergeant who leapt into the cockpit, having only a few pre-war crop-dusting flying hours to his name. (NARA)

seized in the market square. Here, at least one wounded American was executed personally by one of Peiper's battalion commanders, Sturmbannführer Josef 'Jupp' Diefenthal (who would later stand trial and be convicted of war crimes).[8]

In the vicinity, at 08.30 a.m., Staff Sergeant Herman M. Johnson was riding in a US 2nd Division jeep with Privates Smith and Wilson when in the morning mist they suddenly 'rounded a curve and there was a German tank,' remembered Johnson. 'They took us prisoner . . . They asked me what unit we were from, but we didn't tell them anything. At this point they turned the driver [Wilson, who was wearing a Red Cross brassard on his sleeve] and Smith [who was slightly wounded] loose, but kept me prisoner inside an armoured vehicle.'[9]

Now alerted to the presence of German forces far behind their own lines, an American artillery barrage from Bütgenbach, the next village north-west, hurried Peiper, riding up in one of his armoured half-tracks, out of Büllingen at around 10.00 a.m. At this stage all the Americans monitoring the progress of Peiper's armoured column expected him to continue north-west along the N32, the best road to Bütgenbach, then swing due north to Elsenborn and up on to the high ground of the Elsenborn Ridge. The Americans, of course, were unaware of the Sixth Panzer army's *Rollbahn*, and the German mindset of sticking to their assigned routes. Had Peiper been more cognisant of the tactical situation, and less slavishly following Rollbahn 'D' (even though his army chief of staff claimed the routes were only discretionary), he would no doubt have acted differently.

Up on the Elsenborn Ridge lay the twin villages of Krinkelt and Rocherath, forward of which were GIs of both the US 99th and 2nd Infantry Divisions. As we saw from the leadership of soldiers like Captain Charles MacDonald (in the 2nd), the Americans in the woods were putting up such a spirited defence against the units attacking on Peiper's right – the 277th *Volksgrenadiers* and 12th SS-*Hitlerjugend* Divisions – that neither German formation was able to make any progress whatsoever. The Elsenborn Ridge – where Heydte's paratroopers were due to land – would prove vital high ground for gun positions, which American artillery exploited to the full.

Before the attack the elevated terrain had been unoccupied: a tactical gift to the side that seized it first. Neither US division anticipated a threat from their rear and had nothing in place by way of meaningful defence, had Peiper determined to lance into their southern flank via Bütgenbach and Elsenborn. Behind the town that gave the ridge its name lay the huge military training area around Camp Elsenborn, built by the Prussians in 1895 and a ready-made logistical base for the US Army in 1944. All this could have been Peiper's. He could have surrounded and cut off both the northern US infantry divisions on the Elsenborn Ridge, and opened the way for the 12th SS-*Hitlerjugend* into the bargain, had he but known that all he needed to do was turn north.

Peiper was unaware of these potential easy victories – his intelligence was poor – and he seems to have been so obsessed with following his assigned *Rollbahn* that, on leaving the hard-surfaced N32 which ran through Büllingen, he instead turned south-west and took a series of minor roads that ran via Mödersheid, Schopen and Ondenval to Thirlmont, which his *Spitze* entered at noon. From there they should have carried straight on westwards to Ligneuville, still on *Rollbahn* 'D' and where he learned an important headquarters was located. That route, however, looked equally as poor as the route he'd just driven; part of his *Spitze* did indeed drive straight on and became hopelessly bogged down, so Peiper instead elected to head north-west again to rejoin the better surfaced N32 at the Baugnez crossroads, and immediately turn south once more to Ligneuville.

This meandering route of Peiper's makes little sense with hindsight. Jochen Peiper is often presented as a panzer commander *par excellence*, gifted with cunning and initiative, but in this instance it seems his initiative had left him. At a time when speed was essential, he was traversing perhaps thirteen miles of minor routes, making an average of under 4.5 miles per hour in appalling conditions, when he could have remained on the far superior N32, travelling a shorter distance in better conditions – and would have saved himself an hour, if not two, when every minute counted.[10]

The reason was partly his assigned route, to which he was adhering with unnecessary fixation (though he had deviated once already into Büllingen), but also his awareness that the N32 route was in fact *Rollbahn* 'C', which 'belonged' to the 12th SS-*Hitlerjugend* Division, whom he expected to see using it at any moment. It would make no sense for two *Kampfgruppen* to use the same road, and indeed cause logistical chaos, so he stuck to his original orders. Besides, he had been fired on from Bütgenbach and probably reasoned the Americans would be more alert along the N32, meaning he would have to fight for every mile. He was wrong: on 17 December there were almost no US defences along the N32 at all.

However, along the minor roads he captured two patrolling jeeps, whose crews revealed that no one knew exactly where Peiper's column was, the general view being that his *Kampfgruppe* was still on the outskirts of Büllingen. That soon changed: the long-drawn-out column was soon spotted by a jeep patrol and the neighbourhood alerted, which caused near panic in Ligneuville, where the headquarters of the 49th Anti-Aircraft Brigade were quartered in the Hôtel du Moulin. All left hurriedly apart from its commander, Brigadier-General Edward J. Timberlake, who stayed with his staff to finish lunch.

In nearby Malmedy, one of the largest towns in the Ardennes, with 5,000 souls and an importance on a par with St Vith and Bastogne, concern was widespread. Like St Vith (named after the early Christian saint St Vitus), Malmedy had religious origins, with an abbey dating back to AD 651.[11] This meant the town had a large number of old stone buildings, and was an important crossing point over the River Warchenne – its original, Old German, name had been *Malmünd* (*Malümund-arium* being 'a confluence of rough waters'), which had altered over time to Malmedy. On 17 December the US 30th ('Old Hickory') Infantry Division, formed from National Guard units from North and South Carolina and Tennessee, was transferred from Simpson's Ninth Army to V Corps of Hodges' First Army and rushed to the Malmedy–Stavelot area.

The town was well over double its usual population, including 6,000 refugees, and had already received long-range German shelling on 16 December, killing and wounding civilians. Passers-by remembered a teenage girl lying in a pool of blood next to her severed legs, still shod in pretty red laced shoes. Allied flags were hidden away and explosions echoed as GIs blew up stores; the local section of the Belgian Red Cross and US units there – including the 47th Field Hospital, 546th Ambulance and 575th Ambulance Companies, a GI reinforcement depot, the civil affairs section and a host of administrative staff – packed up, took to their vehicles and pulled out west, in the direction of Stavelot. The streets were jammed with queuing vehicles and over 4,000 civilians who'd decided to leave: the remaining inhabitants and soldiers were lucky that Peiper's *Kampfgruppe* was not interested in Malmedy but in the Meuse, for there would have been little with which to defend the town on that fateful Sunday, 17 December.[12]

Shortly after 12.45 p.m., Peiper's column reached the N32, turned west for a few yards and, before they reached the Baugnez crossroads, his *Spitze* spotted a small American convoy. It included about thirty 6 x 6 trucks, Dodge weapons carriers and jeeps driving up the hill from Malmedy and turning south at the junction. They belonged to Battery 'B' of the 285th Field Artillery Observation Battalion and were redeploying south to Luxembourg City. Peiper's men opened fire on the American column from the east – a range of about 800 yards across the fields – completely surprising their opponents. Some GIs at the front and rear escaped. A few were killed or wounded, but the majority abandoned their vehicles and took cover in roadside ditches. Peiper, close to his *Spitze*, arrived at the crossroads and gave the order to cease fire. He was in desperate need of undamaged American vehicles. There had been little resistance from the GIs. What happened next remains highly controversial and is the grimmest event connected with the Battle of the Bulge.

An unknown number of Americans were killed in the fire-fight and the remainder surrendered. They were searched and gradually herded into a field by the crossroads. Peiper sent a situation report, giving his location to his divisional commander, Mohnke, and had a few words with Pötschke. He may have rebuked him for the halt, for the destruction of useful American vehicles, or for wasting time. He may have ordered him to shoot the prisoners. We simply do not know for certain what passed between the pair. At this stage, Pötschke tried to recruit some American drivers for the undamaged US vehicles from among the prisoners, shouting 'Chauffeur? Chauffeur?' to the prisoners, who completely ignored him. This may have helped to seal their fate. Motioning Jupp Diefenthal to follow him, at about 1.30 p.m., Peiper set off to catch up his *Spitze*. It had just started heading south to Ligneuville, the location of the 'important' American HQ. Peiper knew that an American general (Timberlake) might be quartered there, was keen to capture him and therefore impatient to move on. Meanwhile, several other US vehicles, including ambulances, had also driven out of Malmedy. Some halted at the rear of the stationary convoy, and their crews were taken prisoner. In all, some 113 Americans, including medics and troops from other units, were left under guard in the field. Between 2.15 and 2.30 p.m., pistol shots rang out, followed shortly afterwards by fire from several machine guns. The prisoners were cut down in cold blood.

Those who were still alive were despatched by head shots at close range. All the while, the long armoured column of the *Kampfgruppe* drove past. Despite the killings, more than fifty GIs had survived, shamming death. Sometime between 3.00 and 4.00 p.m., they made an escape attempt but were spotted and more were killed.[13] In addition, the widowed owner of the Café Bodarwe, on the crossroads, was shot and her house burned to the ground. This was despite the fact that she had at first welcomed the Germans with gifts of cigarettes and liquor. She considered herself German, as did her neighbours (the local menfolk had fought for the Kaiser in the First World War). Madame Bodarwe's two sons were Wehrmacht soldiers. Other Belgians overheard passing SS men asking their officers if they could execute the civilians who had witnessed the shootings.[14] PFC Homer 'Bud' Ford, a military policeman on point duty at the Bodarwe Café, was rounded up with the rest and shot in the left arm when the firing began. He threw himself into the snow and lay still. 'I started to shiver from the cold. I was afraid they would see me shivering, but they didn't. I had my head down and couldn't see, but could hear them walking around. I heard them shoot pistols next to me. I could hear them pull the trigger then the click. I also heard their rifle butts hit the heads of the wounded.'[15]

At dusk, about 4.00 p.m., the CO of the 291st Engineer Combat Battalion, Lieutenant-Colonel Dave Pergrin, based in nearby Malmedy (which, surprisingly, never fell to the Germans), heard the firing and moved up on foot to investigate. He encountered three of the survivors, rushed them back into Malmedy and reported to First Army headquarters that there had been some kind of massacre of American prisoners. 'SS troops vicinity [map reference] L 8199 captured US soldier, traffic MP, with about two hundred US soldiers. American prisoners searched. When finished, Germans lined up Americans and shot them with machine pistols and machine guns. Wounded informant who escaped and more details follow later.'[16] One of Pergrin's men, watching the survivors coming down, recalled, 'It shocked us badly and we vowed that if the Krauts were taking no prisoners, we would take none ourselves.'[17]

Survivors trickled into Pergrin's headquarters through the night; in all, forty-six managed to escape from the field, of whom four died later.[18] Pergrin's message was received at Hodges' First Army HQ at 4.50 that afternoon, around two and a half hours after the event. By sheer coincidence a jeep containing Hal Boyle of Associated Press and *Time* magazine's Jack Belden had arrived in Malmedy almost as Pergrin submitted his report. Without reference to Eisenhower or Bradley, let alone Washington, First Army headquarters took the decision to give the story the very widest publicity, with an alacrity that would shame modern military-media operations personnel.[19] Hodges' chief of staff, Major-General Bill Kean, wrote in his diary that evening, 'There is absolutely no question as to its proof – immediate publicity is being given to the story. General Quesada has told every one of his pilots about it during their briefing.'[20]

Hal Boyle – fortuitously in the right place at the right time – set to work on his typewriter and his copy was transmitted to the United States the same night – passed, somewhat to his surprise, without censorship or delay. With Eisenhower's blessing, Boyle's material rose above this. By

American dead, mostly from Battery 'B' of the 285th Field Artillery Observation Battalion, lie where they were gunned down in cold blood by *Kampfgruppe Peiper* on 17 December 1944. The location was just south of the Baugnez crossroads, but the massacre has taken the name of the nearby town – Malmedy. The Germans made no attempt to conceal what they had done, suggesting this was the way they routinely operated on the Eastern Front, using terror as a weapon. The atrocity was immediately given maximum publicity by Hal Boyle of Associated Press and *Time* magazine's Jack Belden, who happened to be in the vicinity. It stiffened American resolve to resist. Note how the censor has concealed the face of the GI in the foreground. (NARA)

the following evening the story hit the American press. The *Abilene Reporter News*, for example, led with the headline 'Germans Mow Down Americans', the *Kansas City Star*, 'Kill GI Wounded'. Boyle's news story, from 'An American Front-Line Clearing Station, Belgium, Dec 17', began,

> 'Weeping with rage, a handful of doughboy survivors described today how a German tank force ruthlessly poured machine gun fire into a group of about 150 Americans who had been disarmed and herded into a field in the opening hours of the present Nazi counteroffensive. "We had to lie there and listen to German-non-coms kill with pistols every one of our wounded men who groaned or tried to move," said T-5 William B. Summers, of Glenville, W. Va., who escaped by playing dead . . . "We just hoped and prayed while we lay there listening to them shoot every man that moved," said T-5 Charles F. Appman, of Verona, Pa. The survivors lay in tense, rigid silence in the freezing mud . . . Jack Belden, of *Time* magazine, and I rode back to this clearing station with the first survivors picked up by our reconnaissance jeeps.'[21]

It was a master stroke of news management and galvanised the US Army into action in a way nothing else could have done.

The SHAEF Public Relations Division (PRD), which included over a hundred official news censors, had relocated gradually from London to Paris in the autumn of 1944. Initially, there were news blackouts and delays imposed by the PRD during the early stages of the Bulge. For example, no one was allowed to report the estimated 8,000 casualties and prisoners lost by the 106th Golden Lions Division on 17–20 December for at least a month. By 1 January 1945, there were 924 Allied war correspondents and photographers accredited to SHAEF Public Relations. Although most of these, like Lee Miller, Martha Gellhorn, Robert Capa, Hal Boyle or Ernest Hemingway, were attached to units in the field, who acted as their 'minders', the task of providing censorship guidance and onward communication of news copy filed through SHAEF was the responsibility of its Public Relations Department, commanded by a former intelligence officer, Brigadier-General Frank A. Allen, Jr.

By way of illustration of the volume of press material it processed, in February 1945 alone, SHAEF censors passed 13,075,600 words written by correspondents; its public relations officers wrote 9,529,345 words of 'good news' stories for domestic consumption; they analysed 44,221,377 words which appeared in Allied and Axis newspapers; and scrutinised 1,089,155 still pictures and 39,000 feet of film footage.[22]

Most GIs in the Ardennes were made aware of the Malmedy story within the following twenty-four hours, and reacted accordingly: typical was the Frago ('Fragmentary Order'), issued by the 328th Infantry of the 26th Division, for an attack in Luxembourg on 22 December: 'No SS troops or paratroopers will be taken prisoner, but will be shot on sight.'[23] Master Sergeant and combat historian Forrest C. Pogue, whom we have met already, recorded on 20 December: '[V] Corps is publicising killing of 200 [sic] prisoners taken first day by Germans. Are said to have stood them in a field. Killed them with [fire from] tanks as they came by.'

Pogue went on to note: 'Photographs were taken of the dead men and circulated to the lower commands with instructions that all units be made aware of the nature of the enemy they were now facing . . . An armored infantry lieutenant, noting my surprise [at his instructions to execute a troublesome sniper], said that his outfit had captured enemy soldiers on a recent occasion and, after saving two for questioning, disposed of the rest. His excuse was that, being tankers, they couldn't handle the others.' Ironically this may have been the exact same reason that Peiper's men committed their atrocity, and Pogue, for one, may have realised this. He certainly paused to muse on paper, 'A massacre like the one at Malmedy is brutal only because it is larger or calculated to provoke terror.'[24]

There are several interpretations of the atrocity. That all were victims of the initial fire-fight was immediately disproven, even by SS witnesses, who conceded foul play from the beginning. A premeditated massacre was considered unlikely – as many prisoners captured earlier in Honsfeld had already been sent to the rear. Staff Sergeant Johnson's two jeep companions, captured at 08.30 a.m., had been released unharmed almost immediately. There was a possibility that once the initial pistol shots were heard, the American prisoners panicked and tried to escape, unnerving the German guards and prompting them to open fire. Subsequent eyewitness testimony and forensic evidence contradicted this, because of the number executed at point-blank range. Alternatively, the need to keep the battle-group moving was at odds with keeping so many prisoners, and a snap decision was taken to shoot them. The fact that seven GIs survived – volunteering to drive the *Kampfgruppe*'s newly acquired US vehicles – also suggests a spontaneous German decision, rather than premeditation. None of this, however, obscures the fact that at the Baugnez crossroads on 17 December 1944, there were some who contravened all rules of war.

The area remained contested and US forces made no attempt to recover the bodies until the 30th Infantry Division retook the area. On 14–16 January 1945, seventy-one American bodies were recovered from under the deep snow of the Baugnez crossroads area, where they had lain for a month, frozen stiff and fully clothed. Photographers were on hand to record the crime scene, as each GI was removed from his snowy grave. Major Giacento Morrone and Captains Joseph Kurcz and John Snyder, all doctors with the nearby 44th Evacuation Hospital, carried out full autopsies. Most of the dead GIs still possessed watches, rings, money and valuables. Forty-three had died from gunshot wounds to the head, at least six had been clubbed to death and nine still had their arms raised above their heads. In other words, no attempt had been made to conceal the dead, or the nature of their deaths, in any way at all. A major crime had nonetheless been committed and from 16 May to 16 July 1946 the US Army held a special two-month trial in the former concentration camp at Dachau. Seventy-five defendants appeared before a military court. The trial was widened to include all those US victims executed along the route of *Kampfgruppe Peiper*.[25]

There was no doubt as to who had fired the first pistol shots at Baugnez – the 'hot-headed' Romanian volunteer, Georg Fleps, a panzer crewman, who admitted the deed. The Dachau trial was filmed, and watching the footage today is chilling. The blond-haired Fleps stands to attention, emotionless. When found guilty and sentenced to death, Fleps nods in full comprehension, like a loyal foot soldier accepting a minor admonition.[26] However, finding out who had ordered the killings was more problematical. Among those indicted was the Sixth Army's Dietrich and his chief of staff, Krämer, and Priess of the 1st SS Panzer Corps; the *Leibstandarte*'s commander, Mohnke, was at this stage a 'guest' of the NKVD in Moscow.

Attention focused on four officers, specifically: Peiper, as leader of the *Kampfgruppe* who perpetrated the massacre; Werner Pötschke, in charge of the 1st SS Panzer Battalion; Jupp Diefenthal, leader of the 3rd SS-*Panzergrenadier* Battalion (whom a GI had already witnessed executing a prisoner earlier that day in Büllingen); and Obersturmführer Erich Rumpf, leading the 9th SS-Pioneer Company. Pötschke had died in combat in March 1945, but the others were present at Dachau in May 1946.

It appears that Rumpf, who had dismounted from his half-track and was watching, gave the command to members of his pioneer company to 'bump off' the American prisoners. He had been ordered to do so by either Diefenthal or Pötschke. Fleps, the loader of a tank passing at the time and motioned to pull over, leaning out of his turret hatch, fired the opening shots. They were followed immediately by the crews of several armoured half-tracks parked by the side of the road, firing their machine guns. Several of Rumpf's men were then ordered into the field to 'finish off' any surviving GIs.

Whether Peiper had directed the massacre was never established, as he was well past the spot by the time the firing started. However, even if he didn't give the order, he certainly knew what would happen. The later GI testimony was hazy, because those clustered in the field were far more concerned for their lives than in remembering German faces. During interrogation the Waffen-SS closed ranks and several different versions of the events emerged, but generally adhered to the narrative here.[27] Obersturmführer Hans Hennecke, for one, never told me that he had seen the GIs lying dead or wounded in the field after the shooting, while driving past in his Panther, followed by the rest of the 1st Panzer Company.[28]

Apart from settling the scorecard for Allied bombing raids on German cities, such as Düren, as we have seen, it was clear that the *Leibstandarte* intended to fight in the Ardennes as they had done in Russia, with complete disregard for their opponents. In the Soviet Union, Peiper and other SS commanders had regarded it as a 'badge of honour' to burn down entire Russian villages, shooting every inhabitant.[29] Just before *Herbstnebel* began, Peiper – who had commanded *der Lötlampe Abteilung* (the 'Blowtorch Battalion') in the east – had briefed his men: 'In the coming operation, the regiment will have the duty to attack recklessly. No consideration will be paid to man or machine. The coming mission will be the last chance to win the war. The enemy must become totally crazed with fear that the SS is coming. That is our obligation.'[30]

It was never proven whether the decision to kill prisoners was made at the Baugnez crossing, or before *Herbstnebel* began, but the context was clear to all – Peiper's men were to treat GI prisoners as they had done surrendering Russians (few of whom ever survived) and use fear as a weapon in itself. There had been no consequences or reprisals from their behaviour in the east, and they assumed – because they would win – there would be none from such behaviour during *Herbstnebel*. Peiper and Mohnke, and their superiors, were guilty of encouraging this mentality.

This interpretation is confirmed by what happened next on the *Kampfgruppe*'s march. Peiper continued south from the Baugnez crossroads to Ligneuville, where they arrived at around 1.45 p.m. General

Timberlake's lunch in the Hôtel du Moulin had been interrupted by an American soldier running down the road from Baugnez, probably a survivor from Battery 'B', shouting that the Germans were just behind him. Lunch was abandoned. Peiper arrived minutes later and captured the village. Here he met up with his *Spitze*, which had halted at the small stone bridge over the Amblève river to check for demolitions. Machine-gun and anti-tank fire was exchanged with other GIs in Ligneuville – administrative troops including a mess sergeant named Lincoln Abraham. The Germans lost a Panther and a half-track, the Americans a couple of armoured vehicles under repair in the village.

More than twenty GIs, including Abraham, were captured in this encounter and placed under guard in the hotel.[31] Peiper's *Spitze* were angry because of the casualties they had just received in Ligneuville. After the war, Oberscharführer Paul Ochmann detailed how he and Sturmmann Suess lined up seven prisoners by the roadside at the top of a bank. 'Thereupon I shot the first American from a distance of about 20cm. I shot him in the neck from the rear . . . All told, I myself shot and killed with my pistol four or five. Sturmmann Suess shot the others in my presence.'[32] This was a very different kind of atrocity from that which was about to happen up the road at Baugnez in the forthcoming minutes. The motivation seems to have been revenge for those in the Panther and half-track who were killed or injured, and had nothing to do with the 'inconvenience' of holding prisoners of war – as the remaining GIs in the hotel were spared.

A memorial now details the seven Americans, one of whom was Abraham, murdered in Ligneuville, an event witnessed by at least one local civilian.[33] At this stage, the *Leibstandarte*'s commander, Mohnke (who would have by then been aware of the Baugnez massacre, having driven past it), came forward to the Hôtel du Moulin, where he set up his forward HQ. The *Spitze* of Peiper's *Kampfgruppe* had, meanwhile, pushed on at around 5.00 p.m. – well after dark – towards Stavelot. Along the way they ran into a jeep carrying the US 7th Armored Division's chief of staff, Colonel Church Matthews, who was killed, and further on, in the hamlet of Vau Richard, a memorial records where three local villagers and twelve GIs were murdered by the SS. Beyond Vau Richard, sometime after 7.30 p.m., the Germans encountered a twelve-man roadblock set up by Lieutenant Pergrin's 291st Engineer Combat Battalion on the eastern approaches to Stavelot. After an exchange of fire, the Americans escaped and Peiper ordered his column to pause for the night of 17–18 December. It had been a long day.

The *Leibstandarte*'s actions at the Baugnez crossroads thus needs to be seen in the wider context of the way *Kampfgruppe Peiper* treated their prisoners of war and civilians all along their line of march.

However, such excesses were not confined to Malmedy, or to the Waffen-SS; neither was there a coordinated German approach to terror. It was driven by personality and circumstances. In the later stages of the campaign, Sergeant Hobert Winebrenner, from Merriam, Indiana, of the 90th Division's 358th Infantry, was on a reconnaissance mission near Bras-Haut, on the outskirts of Libramont and fifteen miles south-west of Bastogne. He 'noticed several large lumps in the snow. I scooped and scraped to uncover a handful of dead GIs. Clearly they were not killed in action, but afterward, execution style. The enemy apparatus took issue with their carrying German sidearms as souvenirs. Although top brass warned us of the dangers, we all did it. The captors had stuck a pistol in each prisoner's mouth and fired, then left the weapon and horrible expression behind, both frozen in place and time on each murdered man's face . . . I advised my team to ditch any and all German paraphernalia.'[34] There were no Waffen-SS units recorded in the area, and it seems likely that these GIs were murdered by an ordinary *Volksgrenadier* unit. Hauptmann Kurt Bruns, who ordered the execution of the two Jewish GIs of the Golden Lions' IPW Team at Bleialf on 20 December, was similarly a *Volksgrenadier*, not a Waffen-SS, officer.

Thomas Hobbes famously wrote that in time of war, the life of man [was] 'solitary, poor, nasty, brutish, and short'.[35] It certainly was for the infantry of both sides during the Ardennes. Captain Charles MacDonald of the US 2nd Division recalled taking a German prisoner, who 'wore no cap or helmet, but a dirty, blood-stained bandage stretched across his forehead'. 'I have no gun. My comrades have left me when I am wounded', the German had told him. MacDonald detailed two men to take him back for interrogation. 'The two men . . . had made a quick trip. "Did you get him back OK?" MacDonald asked. "Yessir," they answered and turned quickly toward their platoons. "Wait a minute," I said. "Did you find Company 'A'? What did Lieutenant Smith say?" The men hesitated. One spoke out suddenly. "To tell you the truth, Cap'n, we didn't get to Company 'A'. The sonofabitch tried to make a run for it. Know what I mean?" "Oh, I see," I said slowly, nodding my head. "I see".'[36]

Prisoners in the Ardennes, particularly after the Malmedy massacre, held an ambiguous status. Sometimes they were seen purely in terms of their utility rather than as fellow warriors. On Christmas Eve in the woods around Verdenne, as a squad in Company 'K' of the US 335th Regiment (belonging to the Railsplitters' 84th Division) was 'herding its prisoners to the rear, one of the [American Sherman] tankers suddenly took out his .45 and shot two of the Germans . . . The men grabbed the tanker before he could fire again, but the GIs understood the man's rage. "Those tankers had just lost one of their friends," said one. Another barked at the tankers, "You dumb sons of bitches," he told their lieutenant. "Now we're going to get some more of our guys killed going out and trying to get more prisoners".'[37] A GI of the Checkerboard Division witnessed something similar when clearing the town of Höfen on 20 December. Seven Germans had emerged from a cellar with their hands up. 'Suddenly one of the Americans, a private, screamed, "You wounded my sergeant!" He started firing an automatic weapon and, before anyone could stop him, all seven Germans lay lifeless on the ground. There were no repercussions I know of for the private.'[38]

Injured opponents posed the greatest challenge – on logistical grounds, as well as humanitarian – as paratrooper Donald R. Burgett explored in his honest memoirs, *Seven Roads to Hell.* The Screaming Eagle remembered the aftermath of a brutal hand-to-hand fight in the Bois Jacques woods overlooking Foy, on 21 December, when he came across two wounded *Volksgrenadiers.* The first was 'an older German sitting in the snow with a torn pants leg and a blood-soaked bandage tied to his left thigh. He caught my eye and waved weakly. I motioned him to come forward, and he struggled to his feet and limped painfully over to me . . . he appeared to be a mature, distinguished man. He had graying hair at the temples, giving him the appearance of a businessman, a father or a grandfather, rather than that of a soldier.' Before Burgett could do anything, another paratrooper 'who must have been a 3rd Platoon replacement because I didn't recognise him as being one of their men' shot the old man. '"He was my prisoner", I snarled, turning to face the other man. I stared directly into his eyes, pressing a finger into his chest. "If you ever shoot another of *my* prisoners, I'll blow *your* f***ing head off".'[39]

Burgett's second German from the same engagement was also wounded, lying on his back in the bottom of a slit trench. 'He was unarmed . . . Tears streamed down his cheek "*Nicht schiessen!*", he babbled, "*Bitte, bitte! Nicht schiessen!*"' ('Don't shoot! Please, please! Don't shoot!'). Burgett was pointing his .45 pistol at the German, when he was asked by a buddy what he was doing. 'Just getting ready to kill the Kraut,' Burgett replied. 'Leave him here,' his friend replied. '"But we can't take him with us", I argued, "We have no guards for them; we can't feed them. Hell, we don't have enough food for ourselves. We don't have medics – they've all been killed or captured. We can't even take care of our own wounded properly. We just can't take any prisoners right now". "I know," he replied, "but the only Krauts left alive are the badly wounded and they'll die tonight." It was cruel. We had no choice. We had to leave them there. The temperature was well below zero. There would be no survivors. I holstered my forty-five, turned, and walked away from the man in the hole.'[40]

Reactions differed according to personalities, not units. Within a day or so of the massacre at Malmedy, George W. Neill of the 99th Division, up on the Elsenborn Ridge (and possibly fighting SS troops), recorded that a friend of his got lost in the dark and stumbled on a German position. 'I said I was an unarmed *Amerikanser* medic. The voice in the darkness replied in broken English: "You are lost. Go back the way you came".'[41] Meanwhile, Kurt Gabel, a paratrooper with the 17th Airborne Division, remembered his shock on hearing the command 'Fix Bayonets', with all its merciless implications for close fighting. 'I felt the shock of it jerk my body. Surely this was some kind of psychological game they played in Company 'F'! Fix bayonets? That's World War I stuff. Bayonets were for opening C-ration cans. Sometimes you threw them at trees while imitating Errol Flynn or John Wayne, and of course in basic training you had to pretend how fierce you were as you thrust them into sandbag dummies. But here?'[42] Though no GI realised it, ground combat had become far more extreme since Normandy, and troops on both sides were becoming inured to brutality.

Raymond Gantter, a graduate of Syracuse University, served as a private in the 1st US Infantry Division before being awarded a Silver Star and, later, a battlefield commission. When quartered in a requisitioned house near Waimes (very near Peiper's route), just after the massacre, he witnessed twenty-four German soldiers being 'questioned' in the alley next to his billet. 'It sickened me because I knew it was wrong and there was nothing I could do about it. Killing is clean . . . but torture is dirty . . . ugly, foul, twisted, debasing both the victim and the wielder of the whip . . . Some of the prisoners were beaten, slugged by hard American fists, kicked in the testicles by hard American boots, knocked to the ground and trampled upon. Most of them were young, seventeen, eighteen . . . some were crying, helplessly, like children. And their crime? The American cigarettes in their pockets, the small items of GI equipment they wore? Nine out of ten of us wore or carried some article of German issue . . . Brutality, however sweetened by the hot justice of the moment is brutality still.'[43]

33

The Northern Shoulder

THE DIVISIONS ON the northern flank of the attack were to make the shortest journey to the River Meuse. As we have seen, Hitler's prized 12th SS-*Hitlerjugend* and its accompanying *Volksgrenadiers* came to a grinding halt against the US 99th and 2nd Divisions of V Corps on the Elsenborn Ridge, preventing them from reaching the road network leading to the Meuse and Antwerp.

Despite the challenging terrain, the lure was that only twenty miles west of the front line lay Spa, a town of around 8,000. An attractive cluster of fine buildings, in a wooded valley surrounded by undulating hills and countless springs, Spa had long been renowned for its healing waters. In the eighteenth century many luxury hotels and casinos had sprung up to make it a fashionable resort. The abundance of comfortable rooms led the Kaiser's army to use it as a major headquarters in the First World War. Patient signals interception had told Berlin that in December 1944 Courtney H. Hodges' US First Army was doing the same. A dozen miles north of Spa was Verviers, a vital railhead. Liège, on the Meuse, the largest American supply centre in Europe, was another twenty-five miles north-west of Spa. Although crossings over the Meuse between Huy and Liège were the Sixth Army's real objective, had Oberstgruppenführer Sepp Dietrich's men managed to break through to any of these destinations they might have scored a major operational victory, delaying the Allied advance into Germany by several months.

With the stakes of the 'northern shoulder' so high, it was fortunate indeed that, from the Allied perspective, this was the only sector where the Germans had failed to advance. Between 16 and 19 December, Dietrich's Sixth Army – fronted by the 326th, 277th and 12th *Volksgrenadier* Divisions – battled for the terrain north and south of the twin villages of Krinkelt–Rocherath; subsequently they moved against the Elsenborn Ridge itself, where they were halted by massive American artillery strikes and air power. Dietrich battered away at the ridge for a week, reinforcing failure day after day, before Hitler conceded defeat, and (far too late) on the 23rd, redirected his SS panzer divisions south to reinforce Manteuffel's Fifth Army.

Krinkelt–Rocherath both dated from the eleventh century but had maintained their separate identities and never merged, though to the naked eye they seem as one. This corner of Belgium had experienced an unusually turbulent history long before 1944. Under Hapsburg domination from the fifteenth century, the area was, successively, under Spanish, Austrian and French rule before becoming part of the German Empire in 1871. After the First World War, Krinkelt–Rocherath became part of Belgium, but from May 1940 was annexed by the Third Reich, with 250 inhabitants conscripted into the Wehrmacht, of whom seventy-one would be killed by 1945.

The villagers found themselves trapped during the fighting. With the water mains ruptured, many houses burned down and most of their 3,000 head of cattle and pigs perished in agony in the flames, were felled by shrapnel or slaughtered by troops for meat. On 19 December some inhabitants managed to flee a mile west to Wirtzfeld, where they came upon some 2nd Division GIs who were standing around and drinking coffee. As the villagers begged for a hot drink, they were immediately surrounded by seven or eight Americans with outstretched cups. So shell-shocked were the refugees that their shaking hands could not lift the drinks to their mouths. Mrs Hedwig Drösch, wife of the US-appointed bürgermeister, remembered tearfully that the GIs instantly held their canteen cups to the villagers' lips to help them drink.[1] Krinkelt's church was so badly damaged in the fighting that it had to be replaced, but opposite it today are two polished memorial stones, commemorating the heroism of the US 2nd and 99th Divisions.

As we have seen, the 277th and 12th *Volksgrenadier* Divisions overran many forward US positions on 16 December, but their attack swiftly became bogged down under the heavy fire from prepared positions of Major-General Walter E. Lauer's 99th Infantry Division on their flanks.

They also drew a rapid response from American artillery, who had pre-registered the areas forward of their own infantry. Further north, the 3rd Battalion of the US 395th Regiment covered the town of Höfen and Troops 'B' and 'C' of the 38th Cavalry Reconnaissance Squadron, Monschau. Both were attacked by Generalmajor Kaschner's 326th *Volksgrenadiers*. The cavalry's defensive measures had included digging very good foxholes with plenty of overhead cover and laying eighty truckloads of barbed wire, trip flares, mines and booby traps. It paid off: they lost only fifteen killed.

The 38th Cavalry managed to hold the 751st *Volksgrenadier* Regiment at Monschau, and were eventually relieved by the US 9th Division, as Lieutenant Alfred H. M. Shehab, commanding 3rd Platoon of Troop 'B', recalled: 'One of my lads came running into the CP and said, "Lieutenant, there is someone out there!" Crouching behind a tree, I hollered, "Who's there?" A voice came back, "Well, who the hell are you?" So I replied, "Well, who the hell are you?" We finally made a deal, and met in an open space. They turned out to be the 47th Infantry Regiment, who had been told that we were wiped out.'[2] The cavalry's CO, Lieutenant-Colonel Robert O'Brien, observed afterwards, 'The whole action was an example not of any heroic action, but of what an efficient, active defense can do. There was no great leadership: the men didn't need it.'[3]

Further south, at Höfen, the German advance was stopped dead, even though the defenders lacked armoured support. Small-arms and mortar fire, as well as hand-to-hand combat, ejected those Germans who had penetrated into Höfen. Later, Lieutenant-Colonel McClernand Butler, a pre-war Illinois National Guardsman and the Third Battalion's CO, observed of his opponents at Höfen, 'The Germans made big mistakes when they committed their troops piecemeal. If they had used all three regiments of the 326th *Volksgrenadier* Division on that first day, they would have gone right through us.'[4] The Germans here were weaker, possessing no tanks of their own, as their attack was designed to act as a flank guard to Dietrich's panzers, in the same way that Brandenberger's armourless Seventh Army guarded the southern flank of Manteuffel's panzers.

On 17 December, the defending 99th Checkerboarders were joined by the US 2nd Infantry Division, including Charles B. MacDonald's Company 'I' of the 23rd Regiment. Fortunately Major-General Leonard T. Gerow, commander of US V Corps since D-Day, had immediately appreciated the magnitude of the 16 December attack and the importance of the Elsenborn Ridge. On his own initiative, with the headquarters of First Army at Spa in disarray, Gerow ordered the 2nd Division to abandon their attack on the Roer dams and pull back on to the high ground of Elsenborn Ridge. American tanks and tank destroyers quickly arrived to help stem the onslaught, opposed by the 12th SS-*Hitlerjugend* and their infantry; but the Germans still failed to clear a route for their panzers.

Major-General Walter M. Robertson, of the 2nd Division (the Indianheads, after their distinctive shoulder patch) moved his headquarters into Elsenborn, stating that he intended to hold the twin villages until the Checkerboarders and his own men had retreated back through them and onto the Elsenborn Ridge. This would then become the MLR (Main Line of Resistance). The headquarters of the stern-faced Major-General Walter E. Lauer was in a commandeered villa in nearby Bütgenbach.

As for the civilian population, they had to cope as best they could: only thirty-five people were allowed to stay in Elsenborn, to take care of their cattle. The rest were instructed, 'Take very few clothes and a little food; you will be back in a few days'. For most, those 'few days' would last four months. In late March 1945, they returned to find their livestock dead, their homes damaged or destroyed by artillery, from which nearly every piece of wood – doors, shutters, furniture, floorboards and stairways – had been removed by GIs, either for kindling or to provide overhead cover for their foxholes.

The seventeenth of December was the day of Charles MacDonald's defence of the *Krinkelterwald*, when he witnessed the acts of valour that led to the award of a Medal of Honor to Sergeant José M. Lopez. Two other such medals were won in the vicinity that day, indicating the severity of the fighting. During 17–18 December near Rocherath, PFC William A. Soderman, also of the 2nd Division, disabled three Panthers and killed several groups of Germans with his bazooka before being severely wounded and evacuated. Meanwhile, PFC Richard E. Cowan of MacDonald's Company 'I' fought off *Volksgrenadiers* all day from his machine-gun position, enabling his colleagues to withdraw.

On 18 December, German infantry and armour attacked the twin villages again, supported by *Nebelwerfer* (multi-barrelled mortar) units, and the 560th *Schwere-Panzerjäger-Abteilung* (Heavy Anti-tank Battalion), an army unit, equipped with *Jagdpanzer* IV and *Jagdpanther* (literally 'hunting Panther') tank destroyers. These were powerful armoured vehicles with an 88mm gun on a Panther chassis, but operated best in defence rather than attack. Their three-inch-thick, sloping frontal armour made them ideal for ambushes, but, being turretless, they were vulnerable in an advance without supporting infantry. *Jagdpanther* commanders liked to direct the vehicle standing up in their cupolas, for better battlefield awareness, but were frequently despatched by head shots.[5] An American tank crewman, Sergeant Otie T. Cook, agreed with the need for all-round visibility. Before the war he had been a Virginia National Guardsman who then transferred into the 745th Tank Battalion and was attached to the US 1st Infantry Division in the Bulge. He confided, 'You don't realise that being in a tank, all you know is what you see in front of you, and what's inside of the tank. Having to use the periscopes made that worse. You can't see behind. You can't see above. You don't know anything else that's going on.'[6]

In the event, the narrow streets of the twin villages proved the most unsuitable environment for the *Jagdpanthers*, where American bazooka rounds rained down from upper-storey windows. Operating conditions in the woodlands around the twin villages were not much better, where the SS armour was halted by artillery, anti-tank fire and mines. American tankers noted that the longer barrelled guns of the Panthers and Panzer IVs prevented their turrets from rotating between the trees, which was not a problem for the much shorter-barrelled 75mm Shermans.

As they loomed out of the fog, GIs had learned to let the panzers pass. Then they would emerge from their own foxholes to take on the following German infantry with any weapon to hand – rifles, grenades, bayonets, knives, sharpened shovels. One GI tried to stop a tank by jamming his rifle between the links of its tracks, recalled another. Defending Krinkelt, the 1st Battalion of the US 38th Infantry, under Lieutenant-Colonel Frank Mildren, came under huge pressure. He directed one of his staff to call the regimental CP for more armoured support. 'Sir, we're being overrun by Jerry tanks,' went the message. The 38th's commander replied, 'Tell me, son, how many tanks? And just how close are they to you?' As a German vehicle lumbered past, vibrating the whole building, the young officer then replied, 'Well, Colonel, if I went up to the second floor, I could piss out the window and hit at least six.'[7] Fearing an imminent breakthrough, it was that night, the evening of the 18th, when more than 2,000 First Army headquarters staff hurriedly packed up and left their comfortable billets in Spa.[8]

The mainstay of the American defence was the artillery they hastily assembled on the high ground of the Elsenborn Ridge. It was devastating in its intensity and accuracy: a total of 348 guns, including sixteen 105mm and 155mm battalions from the 1st, 2nd, 9th and 99th Divisions, plus heavier V Corps artillery, were quickly dug in, and able to respond instantly to requests from any quarter. By 21 December this figure had risen to twenty-three artillery battalions, and probably represented the 'greatest concentration of artillery firepower in the European Theatre, if not in American history'.[9] They were directed by Brigadier-General John H. Hinds (usually commander of the 2nd Division's artillery) who, on 19 December, reported firing 5,760 rounds on the twin villages of

The defence of the Northern Shoulder of the Bulge saw the 'greatest concentration of artillery firepower in the European Theatre, if not in American history'. This included twenty-three battalions of guns, plus mortars and rockets, directed by Brigadier-General John H. Hinds (usually commander of the 2nd Division's artillery). They were mostly 105mm howitzers like these, whose firepower defeated all German attempts to seize the Elsenborn Ridge. On 19 December, Hinds reported shooting 5,760 rounds at the twin villages of Krinkelt-Rocherath in one twenty-minute fire mission. (NARA)

Krinkelt–Rocherath in one twenty-minute fire mission.[10] To these must be added the six 105mm guns that each US infantry regiment possessed in its canon company, the six 81mm mortars in each battalion heavy weapons company, and a US chemical mortar battalion possessing forty-eight 4.2-inch mortars. The latter could hurl a high-explosive mortar bomb nearly 4,000 yards. Driving past, PFC Alvin R. Whitehead, with the 394th Infantry, remembered seeing 'more artillery in position than I thought existed in all of the Army'.[11]

Among the US artillery tactics employed were TOT ('time on target') concentrations, where rounds from different firing points and types of gun struck the target simultaneously, allowing the huge array of artillery available, close and distant, to concentrate firepower on the attackers. They were joined by eight-inch heavy guns firing from further back, and the 18th Field Artillery Battalion, who fired 4.5-inch rockets. 'We heard their trucks forming a line on the Monschau–Kalterherberg–Elsenborn road . . . In a few moments, they launched two salvos of screaming rockets over our heads, totalling 1,025 rounds. Before the Germans could return fire, the mobile rocket battery had packed up and left,' remembered one nearby GI.[12]

First Army's Lieutenant-General Courtney H. Hodges wrote later of the Bulge that 'all arms and services combined to inflict a disastrous defeat upon the enemy . . . Of the principal arms which could be brought to bear directly upon the enemy, infantry, armor, and air were seriously handicapped by weather and terrain. Through it all, however – day and night, good weather and bad – the flexibility and power of our artillery was applied unceasingly.'[13] Soldiers of the US 99th Division one night thought they could hear tanks forward of their positions on the Elsenborn Ridge and called for artillery support. 'It was awesome – the shells bursting in front of us and advancing toward the enemy like marching troops. In the morning we looked out and saw three German tanks and some half-tracks, all in ruins.'[14] The SS-*Hitlerjugend*'s historian recorded, 'In the final analysis, with infantry matched at 1:1, the American artillery superiority of 10:1 was the decisive factor'.[15]

One Checkerboard soldier manning a foxhole was detailed to help the artillery behind him register their guns. 'They fired. I can still see and feel what happened. The shell landed about three feet in front of my position. The gunner asked where it had landed. I told him, "I am picking hot metal out of the hole in front of me." Another round landed to my left. Two machine-gunners disappeared. We never found enough of them to have anything to bury. I was very upset, angry and disgusted. "Sorry," said the artilleryman over the field telephone. They fired another round which landed well forward of our position. With a few more rounds, they had their guns sighted in.'[16]

'Friendly' artillery had its own limitations, however; as Captain Harry R. Ostler, commander of a battery of towed 105mm howitzers, reported, 'Our battery displaces every day, sometimes for seven days in a row . . . When we drop trails in a new position, immediately the men begin the tedious task of digging. They never stop to rest until the gun is completely dug in, and their own trenches, with overhead cover, are complete. Issue sandbags are filled and used to form a parapet around the howitzer sections.'[17] Typically, in the hard winter conditions, GIs – whether infantry or artillerymen – found they needed explosives just to blow holes in the solid ground.

When 'Mac' McMurdie of the 394th Infantry tried to dig in on the Elsenborn Ridge at dusk on 20 December, he remembered, 'The ground was frozen. We took our turn digging and got a little warmed up from the work. With our entrenching tools, we could only chip out little pieces at a time. We were digging holes about fifty feet or so apart – digging as if our lives depended on it. We got down about eighteen inches through the frozen ground before we got to regular earth and could dig at a decent rate.'[18] In the white jungle of fir forests, another GI remembered his close encounter with some Germans doing the same. A platoon sergeant set off in the dark to contact a neighbouring company. He encountered some soldiers digging into the frozen ground. '"Company G?" he asked. Just as he spoke he realized they were Germans. "Nix" one of the German soldiers replied as he continued chipping at the ground. The sergeant pivoted slowly, and trudged off through the snow. He was well back to his company before some hostile fire followed in his direction.'[19]

Captain Richard Van Horne, of the 991st Field Artillery Battalion (attached to the 9th Division), bemoaned that 'muzzle flash and blast were two of our greatest headaches. No matter how cleverly concealed a gun might be, the tremendous muzzle flash and the billowing clouds of white smoke immediately compromised the position.'[20] Another artillery unit reported, 'This battalion has one man in four wearing a Purple Heart after four months of combat . . . One night we had seven killed and nine wounded in one battery by counter-battery fire.'[21]

In this respect the limitations of the horse-drawn *Volksgrenadier* artillery and *Nebelwerfer* units were a significant obstacle to effective German fire support. Their older guns, of varying calibres, had neither the range nor the mobility to take on their opponents efficiently, and they had only limited stocks of ammunition. Fähnrich Rolf Odendahl, of the 3rd *Fallschirmjäger* Division, recalled that, 'towards the end of the offensive, due to lack of ammunition, our forward artillery observer had only two rounds available to fix the locations of blocking barrages in case of an attack'. He remembered seeing the Americans walking around on the slopes opposite, 'but [we] were not allowed to [open] fire. Only in an emergency were we permitted to fire.'[22] These shortages extended even to the SS. Interrogation of an artilleryman in Obersturmbannführer Rudolf Sandig's 2nd *Panzergrenadier* Regiment of the *Leibstandarte* revealed that his 75mm self-propelled gun had only thirty rounds and, 'since he has had it, the gun has not been fired . . . Only enough fuel to make an ordered trip is issued. The SP now has five litres (about 1¼ gallons) in it.'[23]

American gun batteries preferred positions near hard-surfaced roads, for ease of ammunition resupply, but, unless strict camouflage discipline was enforced, their locations were soon compromised by the many German aircraft prowling around at night, dropping flares, 'which lit up the area and tended to bring out the unnatural from the natural'. On such occasions, carefully planned and well executed camouflage discipline 'was the difference between life and death . . . This meant no chow lines and no bunching of personnel into groups . . . At supper time we noted with alarm that mess kits glittered in the weak sun as the soldiers crowded close to the kitchen truck.' Everything had to be dug in below ground level and covered with logs and sandbags, including, 'Guns, oil, gas, water, kitchens, trucks, trailers, radios, everything – arms, projectiles, powder and fuzes'.[24]

Responding to orders issued at 1.45 p.m. on 19 December, the 393rd and 394th Infantry Regiments of the 99th began withdrawing from their positions in and around Krinkelt–Rocherath from about 5.30 p.m., and moved back the short distance north-west on to the Elsenborn Ridge. They were covered by a rearguard of the 741st Tank and 644th Tank Destroyer Battalions, with the last tank platoon leaving at 02.00 a.m. As they did, T/4 Truman Kimbro, who was serving with the 2nd Engineer Combat Battalion, laid a string of anti-tank mines under intense fire outside Rocherath. In doing so, he was riddled with bullets and died from his wounds, but for carrying out his mission under the greatest adversity he was awarded a posthumous Medal of Honor. William F. McMurdie, with Company 'A' of the 394th, remembered that the 1st Battalion in which he served could only muster 260 officers and men from the original 825 they started with three days earlier. Company 'C' had dwindled from 180 men to just eight. 'Lieutenant-Colonel Robert H. Douglas, our battalion commander, almost cried when he saw how many men had been lost, and said he felt personally responsible.'[25]

Robertson's US 2nd Division had reversed the direction of their attack (from the Roer dams to Elsenborn), reorientated instantly from assault to defensive mode, and then conducted a withdrawal from contact, all within three days. He later observed, 'Leavenworth [the Command and General Staff College] would say it couldn't be done – but I don't want to have to do it again!'[26] Today the high ground is a NATO training area, but in traversing the fifteen miles between Bütgenbach and Monschau it is possible to get a sense of the realigned American positions, after 19 December. Infantry foxholes 'were in the shape of an "L",' wrote a Checkerboard Division soldier. 'The longer part was about seven feet long, the other about five feet. We took timbers and logs to put across the long part of our hole, and then put all the dirt on top of the wood, or behind us, so our helmeted heads would blend in with the background. We put a blanket across the entrance to the covered area, where we would then sleep . . . Our lamp was a water canteen filled with gasoline, with a sock as a wick. We collected all the blankets we could to make our "bed" dry . . . I remember that at the sixteenth blanket, properly folded and put in place, we decided we were "dry".'[27]

The foxhole owner captured a German who commented on how surprised he was to find he had been fighting black troops. On being told there were no black troops in the line, he retorted, 'but black men just captured me'. A check revealed that the Americans' makeshift canteen lamps had covered their faces, necks, hair and hands with soot. The result was a twenty-four-hour pass to Verviers for a shower call.[28] In the snowy landscape, another rifleman, PFC James R. McIlroy with Company 'F', of the 393rd Regiment, remembered, 'We prayed, with shells falling all around us. Sometimes it seemed the shelling would never cease. There were so many hits by artillery that the landscape around us looked like a black and white checkerboard. We just held on and prayed the next one would be a dud.'[29]

Forward Artillery Observer James R. McGhee of the 334th Field Artillery later described the effect of a warhead that wasn't a dud on an orders group. 'Captain Nicolson, the company commander, called his platoon leaders and me together to give us our instructions. At that moment a horrendous explosion tore into us. In the instant before unconsciousness I saw a brilliant orange-yellow fireball with chunks of black in it, then nothing. Oblivion. When I started regaining my senses, I was still on my feet, reeling and staggering aimlessly about. The return of full consciousness was slow and labored, like struggling to wade through deep mud. Technical Sergeant Keith Mericle was dead with a gaping hole behind his right ear. Lieutenant Rerich was bleeding all over from multiple wounds. Lieutenant Lee Scott had been knocked out . . . We found the muzzle of a shattered carbine and verified that it ended in 6666, the last four digits of Captain Nicolson's weapon. His helmet was collapsed from back to front and flattened.' Of the captain himself, nothing was ever found.[30] In many cases, such oblivion through artillery fire was the true meaning of 'missing in action'. This was almost never communicated to next of kin, for whom the awfulness of being ripped apart and literally 'atomised' was too terrible to contemplate.

The intense cold made matters worse, as Lieutenant-Colonel McClernand Butler of the 395th Infantry remembered: 'The snow got up to twelve-feet deep in drifts. I think it was about three feet deep on the flat. A man who got hit in the open could die within fifteen minutes unless he was evacuated. It was bitterly cold and it was a miserable time.'[31] In summarising the medical effects on an infantry division in this sector, Lieutenant-Colonel Walter R. Cook, Chief Surgeon of the 2nd Infantry Division, reported in a 1 January 1945 secret document, 'the total battle casualties for December was 1,966, of which eighty were officers. Total non-battle casualties evacuated from the division was 1,971. Of these, 148 cases were returned to duty from the clearing station within twenty-four hours. Practically all of these were mild combat exhaustion cases.'

The medics treated civilian and German casualties too. Captain Alex G. Shulman was a neurosurgeon who remembered one German soldier brought in. 'He was fourteen, fifteen. Looked like a lost little boy . . . a sad, dirty looking kid with a terrible gash in his head . . . As I took him to the operating room, he started to cry . . . I could speak a little bit of German and a little bit of Yiddish helped. All I did was get a basin of hot water and some soap and washed his hair.' Shulman looked at the wound, which was healing nicely. The boy finally explained his tears. '"They told me I'd be killed. And here you are, an American officer, washing my hands and face and hair." I reminded him that I was a Jewish doctor, so he would get the full impact of it.'[32]

Lieutenant-Colonel Cook's 1 January 1945 report continued: 'Some 153 cases of trench foot (compared with thirty-eight last month) were admitted and 134 cases of respiratory disease (139 last Month). There were 651 cases of combat exhaustion as compared to fifty-nine cases in November . . . In all, 3,192 cases were evacuated from the division to the clearing station during the month of December, of which 352, or eleven percent, were returned to duty. During the recent counter-offensive, more than ninety percent of battle casualties were due to shell fragments.'[33] These were worrying figures, given that an infantry division's strength was supposed to number just over 14,000 men and replacements were drying up.

Cook also noted 'thirteen cases of acute gonorrhoea were incurred during the month, contracted in Paris while on pass'. On his R and R in Paris just before the Bulge, Sergeant Jay H. Stanley, with one of the division's field artillery battalions, confided to me in 1994 that, with his buddies, 'we hit a bar, and before we knew it we each had a girl on our laps. The girls were keen to show us they wore no underwear, "You buy me drink?" was how the conversation started. I was real tempted, but my girl walked off when I asked if she had treated German soldiers the same way.'[34]

One of Colonel Cook's deputies, his neuropsychiatrist, Major Gilbert Kelly, appended a brief study of the combat exhaustion cases, which were clearly a major concern. Kelly observed, 'When the men moved into the vicinity of Elsenborn they left heated shelters and slept in the cold, snow, mist and rain . . . in such conditions it was impossible to keep the men dry and warm. Many of the combat exhaustion cases were actually ones of exposure . . . Over ninety percent of the cases fell into one of three categories,' observed Kelly. 'In the first group were men who had been wounded and evacuated past the division level and had developed a conditioned fear complex. The second group comprised those who had previously been evacuated for exhaustion and returned to the division. The third group were men who had been fighting since the Division landed in Normandy and might be termed battle fatigue cases. There were very few who could be thought of as malingerers.'[35]

One of those sent back observed, 'You can't get any colder than in the back of a 2½-ton army truck in the Belgian winter . . . Finally, we arrived at our destination, which was an evacuation hospital consisting of large tents in a field . . . We were taken to one that had a stove and cots, so were able to get warm after our ride. They told us that the best they could do was to get hot water so we could wash, shave and change clothes. That was more than we had for a month. I can clearly remember how kind those men were to us.'

After the much-needed break, on the following morning he thought the abrupt change from warmth and safety back to the front line was almost unbearable. At the end of their return journey, 'the talk stopped; we had travelled far enough to hear our artillery firing. Our escape from reality was about to end. The existence and endurance ability of a truck-load of dogfaces was about to start once more . . . We left the truck and walked out of Elsenborn, past the shattered church and last houses, to the junction where the 4.2-inch mortar crew was set up, past the tank and company CP to the draw where the knocked-out ambulance was . . . But, as I went back to my hole dug into the deep snow and Belgian soil, my gut muscles hardened and my ears strained for any strange sound, I was thinking, "The break from combat was not worth it, because I had to come back".'[36]

Another GI found his stay in the divisional hospital confused his loyalties. It was in a converted schoolhouse behind the lines, full of GIs with minor wounds, trench foot and the like. 'I lingered as long as I could under the hot spray of the shower . . . I closed my eyes and let the heat from the steam put me into a brief stupor. As I returned from the shower, I passed a medical orderly munching on a Hershey bar. He nodded to me and asked if there was anything I would like. "Haven't had one of those since I left Fort Jackson," I answered, gesturing towards the candy bar. "Really? We get boxes of them. I'll get ya some. I know the companies get 'em all the time." "They probably never get past the command post and the mess hall," I replied . . . After two nights I had taken all I could stand, in spite of the comforts of clean sheets, showers, and hot food. I was tired of the shirkers and felt guilty about being away from my squad, and requested a return to my unit.'[37]

Major Kelly's study of combat exhaustion was an honest enquiry into a medical phenomenon that was then little understood (especially by Patton), and reflected similar figures for each American front-line division. No comparative German statistics have survived, but when fighting was of a similar intensity for the British and Canadians (for example in the Reichswald in February–March 1945), they suffered these rates too. Kelly went on to note that 'In a period of two days, over 500 men were interviewed at Camp Elsenborn and approximately 400 of these were returned to their units. Unquestionably, a great many rejoined because of a deep feeling of individual and unit pride, and that now – if ever – they were needed.'[38] Such 'band of brothers' loyalty in extreme adversity was a handy indicator of the efficacy of the American infantry's training and preparation for combat. At least one US airman realised that life for the 'Joes on the ground' was very different. Having just completed a mission over the Ardennes, the flyer exclaimed from the comfort of his armchair, 'I was just thinking. All of us guys flying planes are such lucky pr*cks. We go through hell, but then we come back to a bed and a hot meal and a good night's sleep . . . But those poor goddam bastards in the f**king infantry . . .'[39]

Another battalion surgeon, Dr John Kerner, with the 35th Division, thought 'In many ways, it was worse than Normandy. Although we had a better setup for our [aid] station, winter made the field conditions worse. It was extremely difficult to evacuate wounded men through the snow even with chains on jeeps and ambulances. There also was the problem of men literally freezing before the aid men could get to them with first aid and evacuation. I taught the medics to make sleds which had a low profile and moved through the snow easily.' Kerner then reflected an anxiety which was common through the whole army, and is often overlooked by historians. 'The worst thing about our situation was that we did not understand exactly what was going on' – something that frequently pertains even to modern warfare. With remarkable honesty Kerner then concluded, 'We were frightened and disheartened. We had thought the war was about over, and now we seemed to be fighting for survival.'[40]

Also attached to Cook's secret report was that of Lieutenant-Colonel Cecil F. Jorms, CO of the 2nd Medical Battalion, responsible for administration of the division's clearing stations and ambulances. He praised the staff of Collecting Station 'C', in Krinkelt, who on 17 December, when casualties had begun to accumulate in large numbers, transported them 'out of town in all available ambulances and trucks, including the Collecting Company kitchen truck. They were all volunteer drivers, who had no assurance that a back road, improvised by the 2nd Engineer Battalion, was yet open'.

Jorms went on to record the loss of three clearly marked ambulances, struck by panzers, and that on the same evening in Krinkelt, after air bursts had shattered all the windows of the collecting station, a 'German

Tiger tank had taken up position twenty-five yards from the station. Members could hear German commands in broken English ordering American soldiers driving [Red Cross-marked medical] Jeeps and trucks around the corner to "dismount and be recognised". These were shot in cold blood where they stood and two of them, still breathing, were brought into the Collecting Station where they died of their wounds, despite frantic efforts to save them . . . The experiences of the other two Collecting Companies [in Rocherath and Murringen] were equally unconventional and hazardous during the period 16 to 18 December 1944.'[41]

The troops who executed the drivers were from the 12th SS-*Hitlerjugend*, imbued with the same cold-blooded ruthlessness as their colleagues in the 1st SS-*Leibstandarte*, who had committed the Baugnez massacre only hours earlier, on the same day. Word soon spread throughout the 2nd Division of the brutality in the twin villages. 'That stiffened us,' remembered Vern B. Werst, from Oregon. 'We all felt we had to be tougher from now on, and give no quarter to those bastards of the SS.'[42] Some GIs taken prisoner in Krinkelt were interrogated by a German officer with a pistol held to their heads. At the end of each session the officer pulled the trigger, but the firing pin always struck an empty chamber. The German thought this hilarious, and would pat each of his victims on the shoulder, saying, 'You and your friends are good soldiers'.[43]

The American dispositions on the northern shoulder looked like this. To the right and left of the Bütgenbach–Elsenborn–Monschau road, the US 1st Infantry Division (specifically released from 'Lightning Joe' Collins' VII Corps due to the gravity of the situation) now occupied positions as far north as the village of Berg. An impressive obelisk on a traffic island south of Bütgenbach marks the presence here of the 'Big Red One' (as the 1st Division was called, after its shoulder badge) in 1944. The 2nd Infantry Division garrisoned the front beyond Berg up on to the crest of high ground, where the 99th Checkerboarders took over; Major-General Louis A. Craig's 9th Division was responsible for the line as far as Kalterherberg. A 9th Division GI, Technical Sergeant Peter J. Dalessandro, was with Company 'E' of the 39th Infantry, holding a road junction overlooking Kalterherberg. On 22 December when a German attack developed, which threatened to overwhelm his position, he defeated it by personally directing mortar fire and did the same thing during a later assault. This second proved more serious, and he successively manned a machine gun, hurled hand grenades and finally called for a barrage on his own position: 'OK, mortars, let me have it – right in this position!' Incredibly, he survived, though a prisoner, his bravery later being recognised with a Medal of Honor.

In 1944, the 9th Division's medical aid station was located between Höfen and Kalterherberg in a 'Hansel-and-Gretel-like retreat, hidden alone in a dark wood, sporting a big shell hole in its roof. Bodies of GIs were also brought here to await interment in the division's temporary burial ground.'[44] This was the Hôtel Perlenau, still in business (and where I tend to stay when visiting the northern shoulder of the Bulge). The surrounding hillsides were once riddled with the foxholes of the 99th Checkerboard Division, and subsequently their 9th Division replacements. Prior to 16 December, four and a half infantry divisions had covered most of the eighty-plus miles of the Ardennes front; now four divisions were covering less than fifteen miles. Most of the infantry regiments in these divisions would spend the next few weeks manning foxholes in freezing temperatures, but they had achieved their purpose – despite all attempts, the *Volksgrenadiers* would never manage to set foot on the high ground.

On 19 December the Germans decided to abandon their costly frontal assaults against Krinkelt–Rocherath and disengage. Ironically, this was just as the Americans had decided to leave. Generalmajor Walter Denkert's 3rd *Panzergrenadier* Division then took over responsibility for the twin villages and, at 02.25 a.m., long before first light, the SS-*Hitlerjugend* and 12th *Volksgrenadier* Divisions attacked the hamlet of Dom Bütgenbach, in an attempt to outflank the twin villages to the south.[45] As we have seen, this was something Jochen Peiper could have achieved easily in the early hours of the 17th – when there was precious little there – but instead he hurried along his assigned *Rollbahn*. By 19 December, Dom Bütgenbach was a completely different proposition, and the assault was met by a deluge of fire from units of the Big Red One, as was a second attack on the 20th.

During this first attack, Corporal Henry F. Warner of the 26th Infantry, 1st Division, risked being overrun as he stayed at the 57mm gun he was serving and disabled two *Hitlerjugend* tanks; however, a third approached to within five yards while he was attempting to clear a jammed breach block. Demonstrating great spirit, Warner jumped from his gun pit, fired his pistol at the tank commander standing in the turret, killed him and forced the tank to withdraw. This was confirmed by the records of the 12th SS-*Hitlerjugend* Division: 'The commander of the point *Jagdpanther* advancing on the road was shot in the head when the American positions were approached. The driver pulled his vehicle back to escape the fire, but rammed the vehicle behind. Against the ferocious defensive fire from anti-tank guns . . . a company of *Jagdpanthers* succeeded in breaking into the American positions . . . prisoners were brought back and identified as members of the 26th Regiment of the US First Infantry Division.'[46]

On the 21st, an even heavier attack by the *Hitlerjugend* followed, preceded by a three-hour artillery bombardment of such ferocious intensity that it tore great holes in the US 1st Division's lines. The Germans broke through the perimeter of Lieutenant-Colonel Derrill M. Daniel's 2nd Battalion, 26th Infantry, then manoeuvred down his line, destroying machine guns and anti-tank weapons. The battalion commander and his staff dropped their radios and maps, picked up weapons and joined the fray. Wireless communication was lost and just when it seemed they had been overrun, a platoon of the 613th Tank Destroyer Battalion arrived and stabilised the situation. Its M-36 Jackson self-propelled guns, equipped with 90mm cannon, were some of the few US armoured fighting vehicles that could destroy heavy German tanks at a distance. Corporal Warner, with his little anti-tank gun, was again in action. He despatched another panzer and was in the process of engaging a second when a burst of fire from its machine gun killed him. For his acts of valour over the two days, Warner was posthumously awarded the Medal of Honor.

The Germans saw their 21 December attack on Dom Bütgenbach like this: 'Some veils of fog were still spreading across the pasture, but they were dissolving quickly. A flash of flame, as if ignited by the hand of a ghost, shot up from the rear of *Untersturmführer* Schittenhelm's panzer. A thick, heavy mushroom cloud of smoke covered the vehicle, two men bailed out. *Hauptmann* Hils issued orders to take up position towards three o'clock. He stood in the turret of his panzer, studying the map. Then he fired a signal flare to mark the final direction. We awaited the [order to] "March!" Since nothing happened, I looked again at his panzer. The turret was burning! Hils could no longer be seen. The hull crew were leaving . . . It had to be assumed the turret crew had been killed. Abruptly, an almost indescribably devastating fire from the American artillery set in.'[47] By Christmas Eve, 782 German bodies had been counted in Lieutenant-Colonel Daniel's sector, but his battalion had suffered over 250 killed, wounded or missing.[48]

The 22nd saw the last tank attack on the south of the Elsenborn Ridge, beginning at 06.30 a.m., also defeated by American artillery, which had fired 10,000 rounds the previous day. The *Hitlerjugend* reported the loss of twenty-nine panzers on 21 December and five more the following day; these were losses they could not sustain. On the 23rd, they received orders to abandon the Elsenborn Ridge and reinforce the Vielsalm sector, where they eventually arrived at Sadzot, as we have seen. Their War Diary noted, 'movements will be possible only at dusk'.[49] This was because the Allied air forces returned to the skies on 23 December, which cheered the defenders. 'By the middle of the morning, the B-17's started coming over, and they came and they came and they came,' observed Staff Sergeant Richard H. Byers, with Battery 'C' of the 371st Field Artillery Battalion. 'We all stood out in the yard, awed by fine feathery white streams of vapor streaked across the sky, and the fighters scrawling wavy designs, as they try to murder each other . . . Every so often we would see a B-17 get hit and start falling, leaving a trail of smoke which would break up into two or three streamers. Then we could see the parachutes blossom out and count them, hoping that everyone got out of that plane alive.' Witnessing the perils of the airmen, Byers felt lucky to be on the ground where 'They had to hit you to get you, not simply hit your vehicle'.[50]

On Christmas morning, First Lieutenant Samuel L. Lombardo, of Company 'I' with the 394th Infantry remembered waking to 'the roar of hundreds of bombers filling the sky heading for the heart of Germany. I had been saving all the caramel candy bars from our rations and I decided to dump a few into my canteen cup full of coffee. What a discovery! The coffee turned out to be creamy and sweet. It's amazing that such a simple thing could raise my morale that much.'[51] More depressingly, others recalled their chaplain asking for a detail of men to 'open the individual mail packages of those lost in each company. We had to take out all the perishable foods to eat. Valuables were sent back to families in the States.' There were so many dead in Company 'B', remembered Technical Sergeant Bernard Nawrocki of the 393rd Infantry, that 'we had a lot of food which came in handy for our frozen soldiers'.[52] Life was radically different for their opponents. 'A sad Christmas and still no food,' wrote a *Landser* of Oberst Viebig's 277th *Volksgrenadier* Division on 25 December, 'The only water we have is from a foxhole. There are only a few men left in the battalion.'[53] The following day, 26 December, a final *Volksgrenadier* attempt was made on the ridge itself,

The reaction of this young *Fallschirmjäger Obergefreiter* to becoming a prisoner of war speaks volumes about his sense of unit pride and shame of capture. German paratroopers were highly indoctrinated, and regarded as 'true believers' in the Nazi creed, on a par with the SS. This youthful captive was a rarity in the Luftwaffe's 3rd Parachute Division, where few had ever jumped into combat. This was because he wears the diving eagle Parachutist's badge (*Fallschirmschützenabzeichen*), for making five qualifying jumps, which will no doubt shortly become a GI souvenir. Part of Oberst Helmut von Hoffmann's *Fallschirm Regiment* 9, this *Obergefreiter* had fought through Lanzerath attached to *Kampfgruppe Peiper* on 16 December, only to be captured by the US 1st Infantry Division at Weywertz, near Bütgenbach, on 15 January 1945. (NARA)

but artillery fire repeatedly broke up their attacks even as they were being formed.

Just before his death in 1990, Hugo Kraas, the former commander of the 12th SS-*Hitlerjugend*, revisited Dom Bütgenbach and recalled the fighting there 'had been the darkest days of his military life'.[54] North-east of Rotherath, a small portion of the line, once defended by the Checkerboard's 395th Regiment, has been preserved and was opened in 2000 as the Hasselpath Memorial Site. It contains map boards explaining the combat and the original foxholes, a command bunker and rebuilt aid post that were contested by the GIs and grenadiers. Some of the former battlefields north of Elsenborn are likewise untouched, being off-limits to the public as a military training area. In the vicinity in 2008 a researcher came across positions of the 277th *Volksgrenadier* Division. Amidst the evidence of hand-to-hand combat – a US Garand rifle with its bayonet, German canteens and ammunition boxes – he found the possessions (but not the remains) of Grenadier Joh Zander, identified from the remains of his rotting backpack.

In the same year, other researchers discovered the remains of two 3rd *Panzergrenadier* Division soldiers, Hubert Redecker and Wilhelm Schlömann, in a shell hole where they had lain since being cut down by American artillery fire on 22 December 1944. Both were 29th Grenadier Regiment men, from its 3rd Company, and still wearing helmets and all their equipment. They were identified by their dog tags and later interred with due ceremony at the German military cemetery at Lommel in Belgium, alongside four others who, despite the researchers' best efforts, eluded identification and were buried, alas, as '*Unbekannt*' – unknown.[55]

The defenders and inhabitants of Elsenborn and Krinkelt–Rocherath look askance at the attention that has been paid to Bastogne since the Battle of the Bulge. The siege – with the presence of war correspondents and photographers, the newsworthy parachute drops, gliders landing with supplies, McAuliffe's 'Nuts!' reply to the German surrender summons, and the arrival of Patton's relief forces – stole the newspaper headlines. These events soon became the narrative of the Bulge and, in time, shorthand in popular memory for the wider Ardennes campaign.

Those present at St Vith and Elsenborn have felt – with every justification – left out of the story. St Vith perhaps, quite unfairly, might have been regarded by the less well-informed as a setback, because it was relinquished – though its defence was conducted in the finest tradition of the Alamo by Bruce Clarke and William Hoge. However, on the northern shoulder, between Monschau and Elsenborn, the American divisions stood firm and repelled the Germans every time. The 'silence of northern shoulder' was partly because there were no war correspondents present. The static nature of the fighting on the Elsenborn Ridge, which simply required GIs to hold their ground in the miserable weather, where there were no rapid movements of troops and tanks, was not as exciting to reporters – 'stationary resistance' did not make headlines.

There is another reason as to why the fighting around Elsenborn is less well-known than it should be. The northern areas of the fighting, around St Vith and Elsenborn, are located in the German-speaking zone of Belgium, which, as we have noted, had experienced a turbulent history even before joining the *Kaiserreich* in 1871 and Third Reich in 1940. The uncertainties of war and peace in this region have left its population less inclined to celebrate the dramas of 1944 and to concentrate on its wild scenery instead. Today, the area's tourism is geared towards cycling and hiking, not war. Thus many of its visitors have no clue about its crucial importance to the defence of the Ardennes in December 1944.

34

Those Damned Engineers!

JUST TO THE south of the Elsenborn Ridge we left Obersturmbannführer Jochen Peiper camped just outside Stavelot on the night of 17–18 December. A town of about 5,000, Stavelot, like Malmedy and St Vith, had religious roots. Until the ravages of the French Revolution, the town had been linked with Malmedy as a tiny principality overseen by an abbot; the original monastic church had been built in 1090, but all was torn down in 1794.[1] An ancient, respectable town, it possessed many old stone buildings, some warehouses, a rebuilt abbey, and a network of cobbled streets.

However, the sight of American troops passing through from Malmedy, all heading west, on Sunday, 17 December, had triggered a general civilian exodus. There were dark memories of the former occupiers in Stavelot. During the German retreat of September, in nearby Werbomont, fanatical soldiers had executed twenty-two men and women in reprisal for resistance activity, and a further four, one a priest, outside the town itself.

Just to the north of the town was US Fuel Depot Number Three, containing up to three million gallons of gasoline, stacked in tens of thousands of jerrycans, piled under the trees along a five-mile stretch of road – exactly what Peiper needed – and guarded by sixty men of the 5th Belgian Fusiliers. They had been recruited from former soldiers and resistance members in Mons immediately after the liberation in late September. The 5th was the first unit of the Belgian army to be formed on national territory since 1940.

The commander of the 1st SS Panzer Regiment was Obersturmbannführer Joachim 'Jochen' Peiper (1915–76), whom some historians have elevated to godlike status because of his reputation as a warrior. In fact, he missed several good opportunities to penetrate quicker and further behind the American lines. In his post-war interrogation, Peiper cited a series of battles with the American defenders of Stavelot which prevented him from seizing the town. No such combat took place and the truth was that this expert in night-time tank movement spent the night of 17–18 December asleep outside his objective. A fanatical Nazi, Peiper was arrogant, devious and manipulative. (NARA)

Although Peiper's men had spent two long days on the road, he was under enormous pressure to reach the Meuse. The *Herbstnebel* plan called for his first panzers rolling up to the banks of the river at Huy on the evening of 17 December. However, by this hour, the *Kampfgruppe* had only reached the outskirts of Stavelot – barely one-third of the required distance. Peiper still had another forty miles to go along *Rollbahn* 'D'. Perhaps this underlined the impossibility of the original plan – nevertheless, at this juncture, Peiper paused overnight before attacking Stavelot, despite knowing that every hour he delayed would see a more alert American defence. Looking down on to the town that night was one of his Panther commanders, Eugen Zimmermann, who remembered, 'we could see the lights of many vehicles and hear them. I had the impression the *Amis* [Americans] were withdrawing.'[2] Peiper could have used the confusion of this night-time American retreat to cloak a swift seizure of Stavelot: tired though his *Kampfgruppe* were, there appears no excuse for Peiper halting in the dark.

The first major post-war historical interview with Peiper was conducted on 7 September 1945 by the US Army historian Major Ken Hechler. In it, Peiper offers a very specific reason why Stavelot was not taken on the 17th. What he says is most revealing about his character. The former *Obersturmbannführer* stated, 'At 4.00 p.m. we reached the area of Stavelot, which was heavily defended . . . We shelled Stavelot with heavy infantry howitzers and mortars . . . At 6.00 p.m. a counter-attack circled round a high hill and hit my column from the south . . . After the counter-attack was repulsed, I committed more infantry to attack Stavelot again. We approached the outskirts of the village [sic] but bogged down because of stubborn American resistance at the edge of Stavelot. We . . . launched no additional organised counter-attacks until the dawn of 18 December 1944.'[3]

It is an instructive lesson in the use of source documents – for here, Peiper demonstrably lied to Major Hechler. There was no SS assault on Stavelot that evening, nor were there any recorded American counter-attacks. We know he arrived much later because of the roadblock his *Spitze* encountered long after dark at about 7.30 p.m. Peiper invented a dramatic evening attack on Stavelot to conceal the fact that he was asleep. Veterans and historians also note that the Germans rarely attacked at night. Hechler's 1945 interview notes also point out that it was only halfway through the session that Peiper revealed he spoke 'perfect English'. As Hechler notes, 'This so astounded both the interpreter and myself that we sat with our jaws hanging open for a full half-minute . . . In addition, on several subsequent occasions he turned heatedly on the interpreter and corrected his interpretation with perfect English.'[4]

In short, Peiper was devious and manipulative, if on occasion charming. Hechler also notes, '*Oberst* Peiper is a very arrogant, typical SS man, thoroughly imbued with the Nazi philosophy. He is very proud of his regiment and division and is inclined to make derogatory remarks about other units. He is possibly frightened about his future disposition [the coming war crimes trial]. As soon as it became apparent that our conversation would be confined to military tactics and not his war crimes, he opened up.'[5]

In 1944, Peiper was not to know that almost every military unit in Stavelot was leaving town. The same had been true in Malmedy, where there were few troops able to defend the ancient town, apart from two companies, totalling 180 men, of Lieutenant-Colonel Pergrin's 291st Engineers (some of whom had also been despatched to Stavelot). Peiper had missed two good opportunities on Sunday, 17 December. Not only was Malmedy his for the taking that afternoon, but he could then have driven down a good main road for no more than five miles to seize Stavelot as well, also relatively undefended, before nightfall. Taking advantage of the chaos of the American withdrawal, nightfall on 17 December might even have seen his *Kampfgruppe* in Trois-Ponts or Werbomont, and halfway to his objective of the Meuse.

Due to their assigned routes and with no knowledge of the American dispositions ahead, *Kampfgruppe Peiper* was feeling its way down minor roads, usually proceeding at barely a walking pace. Several of the Belgians executed by Peiper's men were local people, plucked off the roadside, forced to act as guides and murdered when they were no longer considered useful. This was because the *Spitze* and Peiper had very few maps of the area. This was an omission suffered by most formations involved in *Herbstnebel*. Instead, captured American maps were prized, with their highly detailed scales of 1:25,000 and 1:50,000 (copied from the British), or US Army 1:200,000 route maps, copied from the French 1938 Michelin series. The standard German maps of Belgium, Luxembourg and France – as Generalmajor Friedrich Kittel, of the 62nd *Volksgrenadier* Division, observed – were also Michelin 1:200,000 scale tourist maps.[6] Throughout the war, the company was obliged to produce mapping for the occupiers in this standard scale, which had also been used for the earlier German invasion of May 1940. They are exactly the same as Michelin's equivalent modern maps (apart from larger settlements and new roads), and, of course, fail to show the minor roads and tracks the panzers needed to use to outflank American positions, detailing only major routes.[7]

We have a sense of how poorly defended the Malmedy–Stavelot area was on the 17th, because between midnight and dawn on 18 December large numbers of reinforcements were rushed to the threatened sector. The Vikings – Lieutenant-Colonel Harold D. Hansen's Norwegian American Battalion, whom we met earlier, and who found the routine of justifying their guttural accents at checkpoints particularly trying – were the first significant force to arrive in Malmedy, at about 03.00 a.m.[8] Following them were elements of the 526th Armored Infantry, under Major Paul Solis, the 825th Tank Destroyer Battalion, and on the 18th, the 120th Regiment of the 30th Division, released from the Ninth Army. The 30th was led by Major-General Leland J. 'Hollywood' Hobbs, a skilled and flamboyant commander, who had graduated from West Point with Eisenhower and Bradley, and taken over the 30th from Simpson, now his Ninth Army boss. Hobbs had led his formation through Normandy and imbued its ranks with his aggressive fighting qualities. It had a superb combat reputation.

With the advance of both the *Leibstandarte* and *Hitlerjugend* obviously slowing, Otto Skorzeny realised there was less need for his trained commando teams. There was no point in them driving ahead in their GI uniforms and jeeps if there were no panzer spearheads with which to link up. The Americans were also now on the alert and looking out for them. With his mission compromised, Skorzeny lobbied Sepp Dietrich and Fritz Krämer at Sixth Army headquarters to be allowed to deploy the considerable resources of his Panzer Brigade 150 as a normal combat unit. Peiper had bypassed the defenceless Malmedy on 17 December, instead massacring the GIs of 285th Field Artillery Observation Battalion at Baugnez, just out of town. Now Skorzeny was ordered to take Malmedy with his troops. Believing it to be only lightly defended, he attacked the town at 03.30 a.m. on 21 December.

Skorzeny's intelligence was incorrect: as we have seen, the Viking Battalion and the 120th Regiment (three battalions) were in occupation, alongside Pergrin's 291st Engineers. As no German artillery support was available, Skorzeny planned a two-pronged surprise attack from Baugnez (scene of the massacre on the 17th) in the east, and the south-west. The Baugnez attack was soon shredded by the defenders and rapidly abandoned. Moving from Ligneuville, through Bellevaux, and attacking along the Route de Falize, Skorzeny preceded his other attack with five Panthers disguised as American M-10 tank destroyers. However, they triggered trip flares, alerting the defenders who brought down such a weight of defensive artillery fire that this attack, too, was eventually abandoned with heavy casualties.

It was during this engagement that PFC Francis S. Currey of Company 'K', 120th Infantry, used a bazooka to destroy a tank with one round, suppressed a German-held house with other shots, drove off three panzers threatening his buddies with more anti-tank rounds and manned a machine gun to cover the withdrawal of colleagues. Such actions, and more besides, would win him the Medal of Honor. Skorzeny's attack had been defeated, and it had been a ridiculous waste of highly trained specialist troops – the commando leader's fighting instinct had overcome his common sense in sending such a valuable asset into battle. This underlined, too, the poor state of German tactical intelligence in December 1944: Skorzeny had no clue as to the strength of the defenders. After his abortive assault, the remnants of the Panzer Brigade were transported back to their training base at Grafenwöhr, their usefulness at an end.

Two days after Skorzeny's attack, on 23 December, the good weather brought out the Allied air forces, as we've seen. Six B-26 Marauders from the 322nd Bomber Group hit Malmedy in error, thinking it was the German town of Zülpich, further east. The tragedy was compounded with a much heavier raid by B-24s on Christmas Eve, and – incredibly – again on Christmas Day, when the centre was bombed by four B-26s, who had mistaken the town for St Vith, which had just fallen to the Germans. The appalling death toll from three days of 'friendly' fire was 225 civilians and 37 GIs killed and over 1,000 wounded, in addition to 1,160 houses rendered uninhabitable.[9] Worse was the scepticism that US Army personnel attached to any projected operations of the 'American Luftwaffe'. Some of the bombing may have been provoked by US anti-aircraft fire, for American aircraft recognition skills were notoriously bad. Sergeant Otie Cook from the 745th Tank Battalion was reprimanded for shooting down an aircraft with a .50-inch Browning machine gun. 'The trouble was it was a British one. The pilot was mad at me. "Bloody Yanks. You shoot at anything!" he said, right after I had shot him out of the air. Then he told me: "By the way, jolly good shooting!"'[10]

We now return to Peiper's attack on Stavelot of 18 December. The River Amblève flows through the small town, which then had a population of about 5,000, and was surrounded by densely wooded, high ground to the north and south. Those GIs in Stavelot who were not withdrawing overnight had begun to prepare defensive positions on the south-east side of the town, unaware of the actual threat facing them. All they knew was that a roadblock had been attacked the night before, though the offending Germans had not been identified. A company of engineers overlooked the southward-facing, multi-arched stone bridge over the river, built in 1576, and had laid mines to its front, but – possibly misunderstanding their orders – had not readied it for demolition.[11]

Most of Stavelot lay to the north of the crossing, but some of the town was on the southern side. Peiper was attacking from the south, and his route took him downhill, over that bridge and into town. At about 06.00 a.m. on the 18th US engineers removed the mines, allowing a patrol from Major Solis's 526th Armored Infantry to cross and climb the steep slope opposite in their half-tracks. They ran into fire from Peiper's *Spitze* which was descending the hill. The American vehicles were destroyed, their crews killed or wounded, though some managed to recross the bridge.

Peiper's troops, meanwhile, could see the structure was not prepared for demolition and waited for their panzers to support an attack over the river and into town. At 08.00 a.m. on the 18th, his artillery opened fire on Stavelot. In the leading Panther, Eugen Zimmermann had been briefed to race for the bridge, taking care of an American 57mm anti-tank gun in front of it. He remembered, 'Slowly it got light. We ran our engines to warm them. "Driver, march!" We met no resistance. The anti-tank gun was there. We rammed it out of the way. Onto the bridge. I saw another anti-tank gun behind the corner of a house. "Gunner, Open fire!" The 7.5 cm missed. "Driver accelerate!" We drove over the trail of the anti-tank gun. It broke and ended up on the driver's hatch. Heavy firing from all sides. Gradually it decreased, and we were through.'[12]

Hans Hennecke followed, and eventually the whole *Kampfgruppe* rolled down the long hill over the bridge at the bottom and into Stavelot. The first few German vehicles charged through the town, without any infantry strength to mop up their American opponents, but as more of the *Kampfgruppe* arrived the balance of forces tilted and the GIs started to withdraw. A few German tanks were hit, yet Peiper's men did not waste time subduing the town, and the *Spitze* turned left out of Stavelot toward Trois-Ponts at about 10.00 a.m. It was in Stavelot that Hennecke – commanding the charge downhill – had his Panther put out of action, but he transferred to another and continued on. Sheer momentum had carried Peiper's men into town. The arrival of some of his King Tigers further dispirited the defenders, as Lieutenant John V. Pehovic of the 526th Armored Infantry recalled: 'The Germans brought up a monstrously huge King Tiger tank . . . [against which] the anti-tank guns proved ineffective . . . By this time it was obvious that the Germans had overwhelming force and we had nothing that could stop the Tigers.'[13] Peiper was also lucky that the defenders, many of whom had not seen action before, had arrived at night, with no sense of the geography of the town they were to defend (though neither, admittedly, had Peiper).

The Americans in Stavelot were not well organised; had they destroyed the bridge, with the numbers and weapons at their disposal, they should have been able to hold off Peiper for the rest of the day, at least until more reinforcements arrived. The Amblève river would not have stopped Peiper's infantry from wading over, but as he had no combat bridging a sabotaged crossing would have amounted to a major impediment. With the bridge intact, however, the remainder of the *Leibstandarte* column (more than 800 vehicles) continued to pour into Stavelot throughout the day. Some convinced themselves that the townsfolk had taken up arms with the Americans against them and an orgy of destruction began. Belgians on the street were executed at random. An SS soldier in a moving half-track was observed laughing hysterically as he idly machine-gunned houses, killing and wounding families in their own homes.

Almost immediately squads of the US 117th Infantry, supported by M-10s from the 843rd Tank Destroyer Battalion, began to counter-attack Stavelot behind Peiper, and by the evening of the 18th had retaken a fair proportion of the town. The fighting spilled into the 19th, when other *Kampfgruppen* of the 1st SS-*Leibstandarte* launched attacks from the south to keep open supply routes to Peiper. On the night of the 19th, the old stone bridge was blown by GIs, something that should have been done on Peiper's first appearance. Captain Leland E. Cofer of Company 'A', 105th Engineer Battalion with the Old Hickory Division, remembered receiving orders about noon on 19 December to destroy the structure. Under cover of darkness, he and his men placed twenty 50lb boxes of TNT in one stack directly over the first span. As Cofer recalled, 'We pulled the fuse igniters and took off running, disregarding any noise we might make. Then a couple of short blocks away, we heard KA-BOOM!!! It was a terrific explosion. Stone masonry houses close to the ends of the bridge collapsed and any remaining windows near the bridge were blown out. The first span had disappeared, it was a good gap. As our company commander, Captain James Rice, told Hal Boyle, the Associated Press reporter, "No German tank can jump that."'[14]

The Germans were furious. Hand grenades were thrown into cellars; a group of twenty-two women and children were mown down along a hedgerow along the route to Trois-Ponts. The SS gave up trying to retake the northern part of Stavelot on 20 December, but would retain control of that part which lay to the south until 13 January. By the end of the Ardennes campaign, 920 out of Stavelot's 1,250 houses would be destroyed or damaged; memorials around the town record the names of 138 civilians murdered by the SS. It was noted that the majority of the perpetrators were between sixteen and nineteen years old, and had embarked on their orgy of mayhem with a sense of anarchy: they could do anything they wanted – and did.[15] Many of Stavelot's victims lie in a common grave in front of the abbey. (Last

To avoid the poor roads that *Kampfgruppe Peiper* had encountered, other vehicles from the 1st SS *Leibstandarte* Division detoured south to the crossroads at Recht, then and today still known as the *Kaiserbaracke*, (the 'Kaiser's junction', from the days when this was part of Imperial Germany). A sequence of cleverly composed images, recording King Tiger tanks and half-tracks racing past, and SS troopers pausing at the signpost pointing to Malmedy and St Vith, have become some of the iconic images of the Ardennes campaign. (NARA)

time I drove through the town, I noticed that the walls of some houses, such as Number 19, rue de Haut Rivage, still bore the bullet holes from December 1944.) Overlooking the replacement stone bridge on the Amblève is a 1944-era US half-track, commemorating those of the 30th Division who fought here, including the engineers who demolished the 368-year-old bridge.

Not all the German vehicles supporting *Kampfgruppe Peiper* continued along his *Rollbahn*. When word filtered back as to its atrocious state and slow going, especially between Büllingen and Ligneuville, other *Leibstandarte* vehicles took a much longer detour, south from Büllingen, via Amel (the German name for the town of Amblève), to a crossroads at Recht, where they turned north to rejoin Peiper at Stavelot. At the crossroads, then and today still known as the *Kaiserbaracke* (the 'Kaiser's junction', from the days when this was part of Imperial Germany), several Waffen-SS *Kriegsberichter* (war photographers) had gathered to record the might of the Third Reich as it trundled into battle. Taken on 18 December, their pictures – of cigar-smoking young SS troopers in their *Schwimmwagen* (amphibious jeep) pausing at a signpost pointing to Malmedy and St Vith, a King Tiger tank and half-tracks, loaded with German soldiers – like the others we have noted, have become some of the iconic images of the Ardennes campaign.

A mile north of Stavelot, on the road to Francorchamps, was the huge US gasoline dump, along a five-mile stretch of road. Ironically, Peiper – again desperately short of fuel – was unaware of this depot, and would certainly have deviated from his advance to capture fresh supplies. During the morning, Major Paul Solis, acting CO of the 526th Armoured Infantry Battalion, had stationed himself near a squad manning a 57mm anti-tank gun at the foot of the N622, the minor road leading north to Francorchamps. As the panzers moved through Stavelot, Major Solis retreated back up the Francorchamps road, convinced the Germans would follow him to the fuel. On reaching the dump, he immediately ordered the GI and Belgian guards to pour as much fuel as possible into a dip in the road and burn it. To Solis's thinking, this had the double effect of producing the perfect anti-tank barrier and denying Peiper his gasoline.[16]

The fuel started to burn, though Solis's orders were later countermanded when reinforcements arrived in the form of the US 117th Infantry Regiment, and it became apparent that Peiper was heading elsewhere – by which time 124,000 gallons had gone up in flames.

Jerrycans shot up into the air, propelled by the force of combustion. (At the site in the 1980s, I found one of them, expanded and burst open by the heat, discarded and forgotten in the undergrowth.) Peiper never knew how close he had been to the precious gasoline, the presence of which, fortuitously, had not been marked on any map captured by his *Kampfgruppe*. None of his men even ventured up the Francorchamps road (though the screenplay for the 1965 movie *Battle of the Bulge*, discussed later, climaxes with the character of a German panzer commander, modelled on Peiper, arriving at a US supply depot, based on this fuel dump, trying to seize its precious gasoline, and perishing in the attempt). In fact, the opposite was the case – the 117th Infantry ordered the flames put out so they could get past and into action against the SS in Stavelot.

In the September 1945 interview, Ken Hechler asked Peiper where he expected to capture gasoline. Peiper replied, 'Our divisional intelligence officer had a situation map purporting to show your supply installations. We believed from that map that we could capture gasoline at Büllingen and Stavelot.' Hechler went on, 'Did you realise that you came within 300 yards of a three-million gallon gasoline dump at Spa? [Hechler actually meant the big depot at Stavelot, not Spa.]' Hechler's interview notes then record, 'With a typical gesture *Oberst* Peiper shrugged his shoulders, smiled rather arrogantly, and said in English "I am sorry". He didn't know of the existence of the gasoline dump.'[17] Peiper had expected to find fuel in Stavelot piled in jerrycans in the town square, as he had done in Büllingen. Its absence, he assumed, was because the Americans had moved it – not because it still lay there, under his very nose, a mile north of Stavelot.

Here again, Peiper had been let down by faulty intelligence. Had he continued his advance through the night of 17–18 December, he would have had more time to discover and correct his error in overlooking the fuel, in undreamt-of quantities – as the Belgian fusiliers and Major Solis's small group of GIs would not have been able to prevent a determined German assault from overwhelming the gasoline dump. Now, without waiting for the rest of his *Kampfgruppe*, or the 3rd *Fallschirmjägers*, whom he hoped were following closely in his wake, he pressed on.

Peiper could sense the American defences stiffening and was aware that the next town, Trois-Ponts, was a crucial bottleneck. As its name suggested, the town contained three river bridges of tactical importance. It was at the confluence of the Amblève and Salm rivers. Through it, the main north-east–south-west road from Malmedy and Stavelot ran to Manhay, Hotton and Marche. In Trois-Ponts, it intersected with the north–south road from Liège to Vielsalm, Clervaux and Luxembourg. Here, too, was the junction of the Spa to Luxembourg line with the Amblève valley railway. Arriving from the east, in order to pursue his *Rollbahn* 'D', Peiper needed to pass through a pair of railway tunnels, turn left immediately and drive over the Amblève river bridge. Five hundred yards later, his *Kampfgruppe* would then need to execute a right turn over the Salm river. This would be a complicated series of manoeuvres for 800 armoured vehicles in peacetime, but under fire presented all manner of hazards and a perfect ambush spot. Peiper was convinced the sector would be defended, and feared the bridges were prepared for demolition: he would be right on both counts.

To be sure of seizing Trois-Ponts and its valuable bridges to continue his advance westwards, Peiper split his force in two. The main body approached the town from the north bank of the Amblève from Stavelot, but a smaller column moved along the south bank towards the high ground at Wanne, which led to another bridge over the Salm, south of Trois-Ponts. Shortly after 11.00 a.m., the slowly moving *Spitze* with the northern main body encountered a solitary American 57mm anti-tank gun, stationed forward of the railway tunnels, belonging to Major Solis's 526th Armored Infantry. It fired several rounds before it was destroyed and its crew of four killed.

The fighting slowed the *Kampfgruppe*'s progress right down, and during this exchange, at about 11.45 a.m. on 18 December, the river bridge over the Amblève was blown by Captain Sam Scheuber's Company 'C' of the 51st Engineer Combat Battalion, very audibly. This was a major blow to *Kampfgruppe Peiper*, who were for the moment unable to move any further along their assigned *Rollbahn*, which should have seen them progress beyond Trois-Ponts, out of the twisting Amblève valley and on to the fast highway that led, via Werbomont and Hamoir, to the Meuse at Huy. Although nearly forty miles away, travelling on the much better road might have seen them reach the Meuse that very night. With Peiper thus frustrated, Americans on the far bank, watching through binoculars, counted nineteen tanks of his *Spitze* exit the railway tunnels and turn right, for Coo and Stoumont. Engineers of the 51st and 291st Engineer Battalions defended Trois-Ponts until the arrival of the 505th Parachute Infantry, but could do little to prevent *Kampfgruppe Peiper* from venting their frustration on nearby civilians. One Engineer GI watched helplessly as SS troopers pursued and executed a teenage boy on the far side of the river. Memorials in town commemorate the 82nd Airborne and nineteen civilians, ranging in age from thirteen to seventy-one, murdered by the SS.

Peiper hoped for better news from his southern attack group, but the Lower Salm bridge was also blown on the 18th, at 1.00 p.m., virtually in their faces. This indicated that the defenders were now fully alert, which was likely to be the case all along Peiper's projected route. He possessed no bridging equipment: his superiors had gambled that his speed and audacity would win him intact bridges, and so far they had been right. Thereafter, Peiper would need combat bridging to cross the damaged spans, which he did not possess. This also underlined a logistics issue; for Peiper's southern attacking force reported their fuel tanks were dry. Although they had filled up with captured gasoline at Büllingen the day before, slow going in the appalling weather and the road network – Peiper's route was very hilly – had doubled his fuel consumption.

Thereafter his panzers could operate whenever gasoline (only his eight-wheeled Puma armoured cars worked on diesel) was brought forward, all the way down the line of march, from the Fatherland – but not otherwise. The millions of gallons sitting in American jerrycans five miles away would have made all the difference to his tactical mobility. Without realising it at the time, any chance of success that *Kampfgruppe Peiper* had disappeared with the destruction of the Trois-Ponts crossings. They had run out of time. Their situation was now that of a cornered animal, which would grow more vicious and unpredictable with every day. Peiper's main force of panzers, therefore, had no option but to turn right after the railway tunnels and follow the north bank of the Amblève, towards Coo and Stoumont, where they hoped to secure another bridge over the river at Cheneux, which would lead to a second crossing over the River Lienne – a tributary that flowed into the Amblève – at Hâbièmont. That could return the *Kampfgruppe* to their correct *Rollbahn*, still take them out of the Amblève valley, and would leave them with only one other bridge (over the Ourthe at Hamoir) between them and the Meuse. If they achieved this, the detour would constitute merely an extra loop in their march. But the real cost would be time.

Peiper's mood improved on hearing from his *Spitze* that the Cheneux bridge had been taken. It had been readied for demolition, but no orders to blow it were received by the American engineers guarding it. At around 1.30 p.m. on 18 December, as the column was crossing, the *Kampfgruppe* came under concerted air attack and lost a dozen vehicles, including two Panthers. '*Jabos* [Allied fighter-bombers] hung in the air like wasps,' reminisced one trooper. During the attack, Peiper and Gustav Knittel, one of his sub-unit commanders, had to take shelter in the old bunker which still overlooks the bridge, to the left of the road. They lost two precious hours until 4.00 p.m., when fog and bad light drove off the aircraft. Their final objective was the 180-foot timber trestle Neufmoulin bridge, over the Lienne at Hâbièmont, which his leading Panthers approached at 4.45 p.m. As daylight was fading, soldiers of Company 'A', with Lieutenant-Colonel Pergrin's 291st Combat Engineer Battalion, led by Lieutenant Alvin Edelstein, blew the Lienne bridge as the panzers rattled up to it. A commemorative plaque marks this spot, where the panzers ran out of steam – and bridges. Peiper apparently sat with a leaden heart, pounded his knees and swore bitterly, over and over, '*diese verdammten Ingenieure!*' ('Those damned engineers!')[18]

In the meantime, Major-General James Gavin's 82nd Airborne Division (alerted with the 101st which had gone to Bastogne with McAuliffe) had arrived in Werbomont, ten miles west of Trois-Ponts, transported standing up from Reims at high speed, in the usual mix of open-topped 6 × 6 trucks and semi-trailers. With them the 82nd brought a 'truck-load of *Panzerfausts* captured from the Germans in Holland', which were greatly preferred to their own bazookas.[19] At Werbomont they created a defensive perimeter, and immediately Colonel Reuben H. Tucker's 504th Parachute Infantry Regiment advanced on foot to Rahier, midway between the Lienne and Cheneux bridges. Tucker's 1st Battalion threw out a protective screen towards Cheneux, where they encountered Peiper's men.

With the Lienne bridge out, Peiper was forced to withdraw, leaving a rearguard and most of his anti-aircraft units at Cheneux, and concentrated around La Gleize. Some German half-tracks managed to find a way over the Lienne at Chauveheid, but the bridge could not support tanks. They crossed during the night of the 18th, and were ambushed by Gavin's men just short of Werbomont. The following morning Gavin recorded driving out by jeep to inspect his division's overnight handiwork. 'I came on five knocked-out German armored vehicles and self-propelled guns, with several dead Germans lying along the road.'[20] This would be the furthest western point reached by any of Peiper's men. The arrival of the 82nd Airborne was again an indication of Peiper's wasted time the previous night outside Stavelot. The intervening hours had enabled an entire airborne division to block his route westwards.

Although some reinforcements managed to get through to him, Peiper was now desperately short of fuel and in danger of being cut off. The following morning, 19 December, his *Kampfgruppe* attacked Stoumont, which was strongly held by the 30th Division's 119th Regiment, and soon joined by Tucker's paratroopers. The battle carried on through the day, but the Americans were stubborn and held out, the US 740th Tank Battalion accounting for several Panthers. Meanwhile, Tucker's 504th Parachute Infantry took the fight to the *Kampfgruppe*. They attacked Cheneux during the night of 20–21 December, capturing fourteen German half-tracks which they henceforth used as their own, but his First Battalion lost 225 dead and wounded in the extremely bloody close combat.

Colonel William E. Ekman's 505th Parachute Infantry Regiment, meanwhile, sealed the front from Trois-Ponts south to Vielsalm, to prevent any further incursions westwards and Colonel Roy E. Lindquist's 508th PIR did the same, occupying Chevron and the high ground south-east of Werbomont, around Bra, where the Germans had earlier executed seven young men. (This was just to the north of the crossroads battlesites of the Baraque de Fraiture and Manhay that we studied earlier.) Peiper could now make no further progress until resupplied, and conducted a gradual fighting withdrawal towards La Gleize. Further German reinforcements arrived during 20 December, for Mohnke – the divisional commander – had realised that his best chance of progress lay with Peiper. On 21 December, Mohnke concentrated the bulk of his division on the heights between Trois-Ponts and Wanne in an attempt to relieve Peiper. On the high ground, across the Salm river from Mohnke, Gavin placed his airborne artillery, covering Trois-Ponts from the south-west. From there he was able to give the *Leibstandarte* a severe mauling.

With the bridge over the Amblève in Stavelot destroyed, a *Jagdpanzer* IV was ordered to cross north, over the weak bridge over the Amblève at Petit-Spai, just east of Trois-Ponts. Reluctant to risk the flimsy structure, Hauptsturmführer Otto Hoist nevertheless drove his twenty-six-ton tank destroyer onto the bridge, both of which promptly ended up in the Amblève. The replacement bridge still spans the river just before the first Trois-Ponts railway tunnel. High water, a strong current and US artillery fire prevented any further bridging, and by 22 December Peiper's situation had deteriorated, with air drops of supplies – including gasoline, rations and ammunition – ending up in the hands of Tucker's 504th Parachute Infantry.

Nearby lay the old stone-built Château de Petit-Spai (today in ruins), a home for war-orphaned children, which was taken over by the *Leibstandarte.* When one toddler waddled up to an SS trooper, grabbed his hand and innocently welcomed him, '*Bonjour, Monsieur l'Américain*', the reaction was predictable – the resident priest was immediately sought out and shot in cold blood, and the young children and their guardians herded into the cellars, without food, water or any sanitary arrangements. Peiper's men stayed for two days, deliberately terrorising the children. When their place was taken by a *Volksgrenadier* unit, the atmosphere changed immediately. Food and water was arranged for the half-crazed waifs and their fearful attendants.[21] This incident, better than many others, illustrated the brutality that Dietrich (its first commander), Mohnke and Peiper – among others – had fostered in the 1st SS-*Leibstandarte* Division. Every German unit may have had its thugs, but the SS deliberately encouraged them.

Under intense artillery fire (the 30th Infantry Division recorded firing more than 57,000 shells into the area), on 23 December Peiper received orders to break out from his contracting perimeter at La Gleize. The 82nd Airborne and 30th Infantry Divisions, meanwhile, were doing their best to contain any movement of Peiper's and block other *Leibstandarte* support from reaching him. On the 23rd, between Trois-Ponts and Stoumont, at Petit-Coo, Company 'I' of the 120th Infantry (30th Division) was pinned down by extremely heavy automatic fire coming from a house. With a colleague, Staff Sergeant Paul L. Bolden crawled forward and hurled fragmentation, then phosphorous grenades into the building, opened the door and despatched twenty SS troopers, but was severely wounded by the remainder. In extreme pain he attacked again, killing the rest and survived to be decorated with the Medal of Honor. Meanwhile, up the road, Peiper began disabling his remaining 135 armoured vehicles; their fuel tanks were, in any case, empty. They sabotaged those they could, then about 800 men of the *Kampfgruppe* trekked on foot back to the divisional HQ at Wanne, overlooking Trois-Ponts. They arrived just before dawn on Christmas Eve; with them was Hans Hennecke. The airborne troops and 30th Division GIs thought at first of re-employing Peiper's remaining armour as their own, but 'the maintenance issues were insuperable', so they were sabotaged by American engineers – just in case the Germans were to return.

Among the many tanks left behind in La Gleize was King Tiger, No. 213, once commanded by Obersturmführer Wilhelm Dollinger. It is there still. Escaping the scrapman, and restored by the local community, the Tiger II is parked outside the town's 'December 44 Historical Museum', which contains an astonishing amount of memorabilia connected with Peiper (including his map case, left in the village), and his American opponents. A visit makes a fitting conclusion to any tour of the Ardennes battlefields.[22] The bloody march of *Kampfgruppe Peiper* had ended.[23]

35

End of the Bulge

CELEBRATING CHRISTMAS WAS hard for both sides in the Bulge. In Bastogne, a packed Midnight Mass was held in the fifteenth-century, shell-damaged Église de Saint Pierre. Brigadier-General Tony McAuliffe preferred to drive out to Savy, north-west of town, in his jeep and attend a field service with his old friends in Edward L. Carmichael's 321st Glider Airborne Artillery. Before he set off, McAuliffe heard German prisoners singing '*Stille Nacht*' and '*O Tannenbaum*' and stepped into their basement to wish them 'Merry Christmas'.[1] To boost morale, he also distributed this printed message to those under his command in Bastogne:

> Merry Christmas! What's merry about all this you ask? We're fighting – it's cold – we aren't home. All true, but what has the proud Eagle Division accomplished with its worthy comrades of the 10th Armored Division, the 705th Tank Destroyer Battalion and all the rest? Just this: We have stopped cold everything that has been thrown at us from the north, east, south and west.[2]

McAuliffe was doing what great commanders do – inspiring by example and sharing in the pain. He knew that help was on its way but that most of his GIs, taking huge casualties, freezing in their foxholes, had very little awareness of the bigger picture. McAuliffe was also anxious to make sure they realised the importance of their sacrifices, and continued:

> We have identifications from four German panzer divisions, two German infantry divisions and one German parachute division. These units, spearheading the last desperate German lunge, were heading straight west for key points when the Eagle Division was hurriedly ordered to stem the advance. How effectively this was done will be written in history; not alone in our Division's glorious history but in world history. The Germans actually did surround us, their radios blared our doom. Allied troops are counterattacking in force. We continue to hold Bastogne. By holding Bastogne we assure the success of the Allied armies. We know that our Division commander, General Taylor, will say: 'Well done!' We are giving our country, and our loved ones at home, a worthy Christmas present and, being privileged to take part in this gallant feat of arms, are truly making for ourselves a Merry Christmas.[3]

Christmas carols echoed from a hundred candlelit cellars in Bastogne and from thousands more, scattered throughout the Ardennes, sung by civilians, prisoners and soldiers. Others had no such refuge. Many of the Golden Lions, Checkerboarders and Bloody Bucket GIs found themselves in 'forty-by-eights' (box cars, designed for forty soldiers or eight horses), cold and hungry, in a railway siding, heading for prison camps deep in Germany. Some would be bombed en route by the Royal Air Force. No one could remember who first started singing 'Silent Night', but soon the whole train took up the refrain, heard by German passengers waiting on a nearby platform for their own train. Moved, they persuaded the Wehrmacht guards to bring water for the thirsty, captive Americans.

Lionel P. Adda, with Company 'D', of the 393rd Infantry, was digging himself a new foxhole, when he was visited by two GIs: 'One of them thrust a small, almost-cold turkey leg into my hand, the other handed me two slices of white bread and a couple of pieces of hard candy. This was my Christmas dinner.' This story was repeated across the Bulge, as men shared whatever they had, including delicacies sent from home. Adda then realised, 'As I crouched in my still fairly shallow hole and started to eat the turkey before it turned stone cold, "eighty-eight" shells began falling. Almost choking on that first bite, I realized that the Germans were watching those two poor soldiers and harassing them with artillery fire as they delivered our meals . . . It seemed almost criminal to me that the lives of soldiers could be jeopardised for such an almost meaningless gesture, perhaps so that some quartermaster could report to his superior that every man in his sector had turkey on Christmas Day.'[4]

Deep in the woods, fifty miles further north along the front, twelve-year-old Fritz Vincken reacted to the banging at the front of his family's lonely cottage. He quickly blew out the candles and opened the door. He found two lost GIs shivering on the doorstep, clutching a third, wounded comrade. His mother immediately took charge. There could be no question of turning them away, whatever the penalties – even though the Vincken's house was over the frontier, in Germany. Fritz was told to get some potatoes and Hermann, the family rooster they had been fattening for Christmas. As the meal took shape, there was more banging at the door. Other lost Americans, thought Fritz. He opened up to find four figures – dressed in shabby field grey – seeking shelter. Elisabeth Vincken also invited them in, wished them *fröhliche Weihnachten* – and offered to share the meal they could smell cooking. Then she warned them she had other 'guests', whom 'you might not think of as friends'. The *Unteroffizier* in charge tensed immediately, '*Amis*?' But before they could say another word, Frau Vincken warned them: 'This is Christmas Eve. There'll be no shooting here'. She went on, 'One of them is wounded and fighting for his life and all are exhausted, like you – and hungry. Any of you could be my sons. Let's forget about killing.' Two of the Germans were mere boys – about sixteen – and the young *Unteroffizier* could not decide what to do, so Frau Vincken decided for him. 'Put your rifles by the woodpile and come in, before you get any colder.' Elisabeth then collected the GIs' carbines also.

Fritz fetched more potatoes and his mother got on with preparing the meal. The *Unteroffizier*, who had been a medical student at Heidelberg, examined Herby, the wounded GI. Then Frau Vincken bade them all sit down to eat and said grace. 'There were tears in her eyes,' Fritz recalled later, 'and as I looked around the table, I saw that the battle-weary soldiers were filled with emotion. Their thoughts seemed to be many, many miles away.' As the tension melted, the *Unteroffizier* produced some wine. The GIs – who introduced themselves as Jim, Ralph and Herby – donated their instant coffee, the rest hunks of bread or other treats they had been saving. They somehow conversed in a mixture of German, French and English. After dinner they exchanged cigarettes and Elisabeth Vincken led them outside to look up at the Star of Bethlehem. Shortly afterwards they all fell asleep in their heavy coats on the Vincken's floor, enjoying the warmth and trust they put in each other. On Christmas morning, they exchanged greetings and all helped make a stretcher for Herby. Retrieving their weapons, they shook hands and departed in opposite directions. Elisabeth Vincken never saw any of them again, but always said, 'God was at our table that night'. In January 1996, Fritz – who had emigrated to America – traced one of the GIs, Ralph Blank, formerly with the 121st Infantry, and the two met shortly before their respective deaths.[5] In 2002 this moving story was used as the basis of the movie *Silent Night*.[6]

After it had fallen to the Germans, St Vith was bombed heavily by the RAF and USAAF on Christmas Day. Many perished, including a GI caught in the grounds of what had been the American HQ, St Josef's Convent. After the war, his remains were discovered near a lone tree in the precinct. Under a wooden cross marked '*Soldat Amerikanisch*' were discovered charred bones, strands of hair, vestiges of clothing, remnants of GI shoes and a small tin holding two American dog tags, numbered 36824575, later matched to John R. McLeod. He was buried in the Ardennes American Cemetery.

To their great surprise, in 1949 the authorities in Washington, DC, discovered that McLeod had survived the war, and wrote formally to ask how his identity discs had ended up in St Vith. The former GI, with Company 'B', 393rd Infantry, of the 99th Division replied that he had been taken prisoner on 16 December, and two days later his dog tags and all identification papers were removed from him by a German officer. He thought they had been taken to be used by a German commando to get through American lines. Today the US authorities are still not sure of the nationality of the soldier found in St Vith and who lies in the cemetery. His headstone reads: 'Here Rests in Honored Glory. A Comrade in Arms. Known but to God'.[6]

On 26 December, it was clear that the panzers of the Fifth and Sixth Armies had been halted short of their objectives along the River Meuse. In some sectors, such as the Elsenborn Ridge, there was hardly any progress at all. In the *Adlerhorst*, Hitler steadfastly refused to acknowledge the ruination of his dream. Sharing his fantasy world, and with the 2nd Panzer Division reporting their forward units almost on the Meuse, the OKW *Kriegstagebuch* (War Diary) suggested, 'The envisioned thrust across the Meuse to the northwest still appears possible'. However, at Model's headquarters, the Army Group 'B' chief of staff, Krebs, concluded, 'Today a certain culminating point has been reached'. The fanatically loyal Krebs could see what most acolytes could not, which was that *Herbstnebel* had reached its high tide, well short of its aspirations. Even

Jodl conceded, 'We cannot force the Meuse' – a fact that he had previously acknowledged in his covering note to Rundstedt, when issuing the final orders back on 1 November.

Yet the Führer – still keeping to his bizarre sleeping habits, generally retiring at 04.00 a.m. and rising at noon – having staked everything on this attempt, was not willing to give up. 'We have had unexpected setbacks – because my plan was not followed to the letter,' he ranted. 'We stand to lose everything. If the other side announces one day, "We've had enough!" No harm will come to them. If America says, "Enough! Stop! No more American boys to Europe!" It won't hurt them. New York remains New York. Nothing will change. But if we say, "We've had enough, we're packing up", then Germany will cease to exist.' He was echoing a theme he had first proposed in *Mein Kampf*, that Germany would either become a world power or cease to exist.[7]

At this stage, Generaloberst Heinz Guderian appeared at the *Adlerhorst* to warn that the Eastern Front would collapse when the Soviets invaded, an event he expected on a daily basis. Ignoring him completely, Hitler ordered Bastogne, whose siege had already been lifted that very day by Creighton Abrams' tanks, to be captured 'at all costs', though this no longer had any tactical relevance to the offensive. Meanwhile, from 21 December he had also been planning a further attack along the front, into Alsace, which duly materialised on 1 January as Operation *Nordwind*.

Even in such moments of crisis, Hitler was often able to carry his court with him on his surreal journey. He would go on to rave, 'If the *Vaterland* continues to do its duty and does still more; if the soldier at the front takes the valiant *Vaterland* as an example and stakes his life for his native land, then the whole world will be shattered in its assault against us. If the front and the *Vaterland* are jointly determined to destroy those who act like cowards or those who sabotage the fight, then they will save the nation. At the end of this struggle, a German victory must come and we will enjoy our proud good fortune. When this war comes to an end, we shall put victory into the hands of a young generation. This youth is the most precious thing that Germany possesses. It will be an example for all generations to come.'[8]

Imbued with this sort of spirit, one of his most loyal servants, Oberst Otto Remer and his *Führer-Begleit-Brigade* arrived in the Bastogne sector on 27 December and attacked immediately, and without prior reconnaissance. Their over-hasty attempt was disorganised and duly halted. The next day witnessed another attack, in an awful snowstorm, coordinated by the German XXXIX Corps of Generalleutnant Karl Decker. He used Remer's Brigade, the 115th Regiment (of the 15th *Panzergrenadier* Division), 901st *Panzergrenadier* Regiment (left behind by Bayerlein's Panzer Lehr), plus Kokott's 26th *Volksgrenadier* Division. Some of Kokott's grenadiers captured on 1 January complained that though not short of ammunition, 'their detachment had not been issued food for several days'.[9] Decker's assault failed, running up against the defenders, now reinforced by Brigadier-General Harrold's CCA of the 9th Armored Division, sent straight from their successful defence of the front further south.

Although a slim supply corridor was operating into Bastogne, the fighting around the perimeter remained deadly. Dr Henry Hills was a surgeon who landed by glider outside the town on 26 December; three of his colleagues were killed by German fire even before they landed. Hills went straight into a fifty-hour session of non-stop operations on the 400 serious cases that had accumulated – Jack Prior was working on them too. There were so few anaesthetists that Hills found himself obliged to teach a cook how to administer the required dose of sodium pentothal in order for him to set a facture. The cook beamed with pride, 'Now I've done everything in this army'.[10]

On 28 December, ever the optimist, Hitler warmed to the theme of attacking Alsace, stating that his new undertaking 'will automatically bring about the collapse of the threat to the left flank of our offensive in the Ardennes. We will then actually have knocked out half the enemy forces on the Western Front. Then we will see what happens. Then there will be 45 additional German divisions and I do not believe that in the long run he [Eisenhower] can stand up to those. We will yet be masters of our fate.'[11] To counter Hitler's forty-five 'ghost' divisions (which, in reality, no longer existed), the Allies were channelling all available formations to the Bulge.

The US 6th Armored, with the 35th, 87th and 90th Infantry Divisions, were deployed north from Patton's Third Army. The 83rd Infantry came south from Simpson's Ninth Army, and the 11th Armored and 17th Airborne, both newly arrived in Europe, were also hurried to the Ardennes. Montgomery had Horrocks' XXX Corps send the British 6th Airborne, 53rd Welsh, 43rd Wessex and 51st Highland Divisions, plus two armoured brigades (six battalions of tanks) to guard the north bank of the River Meuse between Givet and Liège. The field marshal, whom Eisenhower had charged on 20 December with commanding the northern half of the Bulge (the inter-army group boundary ran from five miles south of St Vith to Givet, on the Meuse), knew that Ultra decrypts were once again producing vital intelligence. His, and Patton's, complete faith in Ultra and Bletchley's SLU officers was in contrast to Brigadier-General Sibert at Twelfth Army Group and Dickson at US First Army. The latter would move their headquarters twice in the middle of the campaign, on 18 and 22 December, with all the disruptions to command and control that entailed.

Since the Germans had broken their radio silence, code-breakers at Bletchley Park knew which signals to decipher. They managed to unravel the evening situation reports of Brandenberger's Seventh Army, Sepp Dietrich's Sixth Panzer and Model's Army Group 'B' with delays of no more than six to twelve hours. Urgent signals bearing tactical information were sometimes cracked in three hours. Apart from the surprise of *Bodenplatte* on 1 January, most Luftwaffe operational and reconnaissance orders for the coming twenty-four hours were also decrypted in advance, Bletchley Park giving anything related to the Ardennes their maximum effort – in obvious atonement for their earlier failure to predict the offensive. Although Ultra was not decisive in the eventual Ardennes victory, it gave the cautious Montgomery – much criticised for delaying the start of his own counter-offensive – an enormous advantage, for he knew he could afford to wait.[12]

On the 29th, Patton's attempt to expand the corridor into Bastogne, using Hugh J. Gaffey's 4th Armored and the 35th Infantry Divisions, initially stalled when it encountered two battalions from Heilmann's 15th *Fallschirmjäger* Regiment, exhausted but still vicious. Gaffey was one of Patton's most trusted officers, having served as Third Army chief of staff until taking over the Fourth. Captain John Kerner, the surgeon with the 35th Division whom we met earlier, remembered the attack. He had just prepared a bunch of frostbite cases for evacuation when a full colonel came by to check on the wounded. He asked Kerner, 'What's wrong with these men?' When told, he ordered, 'Warm them up and send them back to duty. I need every man I can get.' Kerner countered, 'I'm sorry, sir. If these men go back to duty, there is a good chance they will lose a hand or a foot.' The colonel was unmoved: 'I'm ordering you to send these men back to duty.' Kerner refused, 'I'm sorry, sir, I can't do that.' The colonel was furious, 'I'll recommend you face a court-martial.' Nothing more was heard, the men were evacuated and received Purple Hearts.[13]

Undeterred and responding to a request for help with the wounded in Bastogne, Kerner then loaded a Sherman with medical supplies and scrambled aboard the outside with two NCOs. 'They put their other tanks in a position to protect us, one on either side of the supply tank onto which we climbed and got as low as possible, using the gear fastened to it as cover,' he remembered. The tankers carried their bedrolls, extra clothing and spare tracks on the outside of their vehicles. 'Much to our surprise, the commander had found a concealed route into Bastogne, and we encountered minimal hostile fire – what little there was had an overwhelming response from our group which consisted of four tanks, a tank destroyer and a jeep containing the scouts who had found the route.'[14]

On 30 December, Patton tried another assault to ease the situation around Bastogne with the 11th Armored and 87th Infantry Divisions, but they ran straight into Panzer Lehr and the 26th *Volksgrenadiers*, who were also attacking, west of town. At the same time, elements of the *Leibstandarte* and the newly arrived 167th *Volksgrenadier* Division, under Generalmajor Harald Schultz, hit positions of the US 35th and 26th Divisions. The horse-drawn 167th had only arrived on 28 December from Slovakia, where it had been formed. Captured grenadiers told their US interrogators they had had to fight Slovak partisans during their training. The 167th then travelled west by rail over seven days, moving at night for fear of Allied air attacks. They had originally been issued with First World War-vintage horse-drawn 75mm cannon, but these had been replaced by 81mm mortars. They were ordered where possible to capture American mortars of the same calibre, which were regarded as superior weapons.[15]

In their first battle, the 167th were massacred by Allied artillery and incessant air attacks, and the *Leibstandarte* lost fifty-five tanks and assault guns. Despite the best efforts of their tank workshops, the panzer units around Bastogne had become seriously depleted. By 1 January, the *Führer-Begleit-Brigade* possessed fifty-one armoured vehicles, the 3rd and 15th P*anzergrenadier* Divisions had forty-one and forty-eight respectively, the *Leibstandarte* reported fifty-eight and the 9th Panzer Division was operating with seventy-five. However, even though Eisenhower had now committed thirty-eight US divisions to the Ardennes, his formations were suffering too.

In the north, at this stage, Gerow's V Corps held excellent defensive positions at Elsenborn and could absorb all the blows Dietrich was able to give. To the west of Gerow, Ridgway's XVIII Airborne Corps had welcomed Hasbrouck's 7th Armored Division out of St Vith and into its fold, but were confronted with more open, challenging terrain to defend. They were blessed with the overall advantage of the Germans' fuel shortage, which – with the destruction of bridges – had brought Peiper's advance to an end. Beyond Ridgway lay Collins' VII Corps, designated as Monty's counter-thrust formation, which had blocked the 2nd Panzer Division's desperate thrust towards the Meuse.

In the west, forming a stop-gap, Brian Horrocks' British XXX Corps took over patrolling the far bank of the River Meuse and the demolition guards of every bridge. In the south, Middleton's VIII Corps had come under Patton's command on 20 December. Since then they had resisted all attempts to pinch out the Bastogne garrison. While Middleton stood firm, Major-General John B. Millikin's III Corps coordinated Patton's counter-attack towards Bastogne, clearing terrain as it went. To Millikin's east, Major-General Manton S. Eddy's XII Corps took over the defending units around Luxembourg and in the south of the Bulge, gradually winkling Brandenberger's Seventh Army out of its footholds.

At the tip of the Bulge, there was much confusion as to who occupied which village, as Captain Guy Radmore of the British 6th Airborne Division nearly found to his cost. Having just arrived in the Ardennes on New Year's Eve, 'after a difficult drive through cold, fog and snow', he and a colleague decided to celebrate, and went to the Château Royal d'Ardennes, a luxury country hotel (still in business), near the Meuse and midway between Dinant and Givet. 'We arrived and, to our astonishment, were greeted by a receptionist and a head waiter in a tail coat. Having organised a bath and a bottle of wine, we enquired as to how long ago the Germans had left, and were amazed to be told, "They left through the garden about ten minutes ago".'[16]

On 3 January, under Montgomery's guidance, Hodges' First Army attacked from the north and Patton's Third – under Bradley – continued to respond from the south. The two armies were at this stage about twenty-five miles apart. Eisenhower and Patton had been waiting impatiently since New Year's Day for the northern move, spearheaded by Collins' VII Corps, then comprising the US 2nd and 3rd Armored and 83rd and 84th Infantry Divisions. The call was Monty's, but he ensured that Collins (whom he requested specifically, as the most aggressive US corps commander) was supported by generous quantities of artillery and air support.

Prior to this, Monty had actually required Ridgway's XVIII Airborne Corps to draw back a little, shortening the northern perimeter of the Bulge, something that annoyed Gavin's 82nd Airborne Division, who – as we've seen – were reluctant to yield terrain they'd paid with blood to win. There was good military logic to the slight withdrawal, as Gavin later admitted, but it came at a cost. German troops in the area, including Mohnke's *Leibstandarte*, were able to occupy a few more villages and vent their frustrations on the inhabitants. The result was more civilians put to death, homes burned and livelihoods destroyed.

The Germans by this stage had very little strength left with which to oppose Collins' VII Corps attack. Their divisions had been written down so much that the 2nd SS *Das Reich* was only 6,000 strong, and the 560th *Volksgrenadiers* 2,500. Prisoners taken from the 560th at this time revealed that battalion strengths were down to around 150 men, though knew little of their unit. All were former members of the Luftwaffe, transferred to the infantry in November, and had arrived at the front as replacements only three days earlier.[17]

Otto Skorzeny wrote to a fellow officer in the 9th SS bemoaning the Ukrainian replacements reaching the SS, 'who do not even speak German. There is a shortage of everything, but here it is the men that count. I have learnt what it means, for instance, to attack without heavy weapons, because there is no transport to bring forward mortars and anti-tank guns. We have to lie out on frozen ground, a target for the *Jabos* . . . If only we had just one division here, trained and equipped and with the élan we both knew in 1939, so long ago . . . Heil Hitler!'[18]

Because Army Group 'B' had focused, as Hitler ordered, on Bastogne, Monty's northern thrust came as a surprise. The Germans, as well as Patton, Gerow of V Corps and Hodges at First Army, had expected an attack further east, aimed at the base of the Bulge, enveloping all the *Herbstnebel* troops, but Monty chose instead to flatten and push the Bulge back, working from west to east. He was worried – and with some justification – that a combination of hardened German units and the appalling wintry conditions might prove the undoing of his counter-thrust, for the weather had begun to deteriorate again and slowed US advances to less than a mile a day.

RAF Wing Commander Desmond Scott, usually in charge of a wing of RAF Typhoons, ground attack fighters, wrote of driving his jeep through the region to reconnoitre a new airbase, and described conditions with his pilot's eye: 'Sleet was falling, the roads were icy, and to add to the danger, we kept running into masses of super cooled fog. As soon as this fog hit anything it turned to "Rhine [i.e. very thick] ice", with which no windscreen wiper can cope. The glass became an ice shield and in order to stay on the road and keep going, we drove with our heads out of the side of the Jeep. Several times we slid off the road and had to be dragged back on, sometimes by a passing truck, once by a Sherman tank.'[19] This was the time when Brigadier Sugden of 158th Brigade died when his scout car skidded and overturned.[20]

Soon, Ridgway's XVIII Airborne Corps joined in the attack, and on 7 January the key road junction, the Baraque de Fraiture (Parker's Crossroads) was retaken. However, the Germans could still give a good account of themselves and Monty's anxieties proved justified on the same day, when the US 551st Parachute Infantry Battalion – an independent airborne unit – tangled with Generalmajor Friedrich Kittel's 62nd *Volksgrenadier* Division. Having fought their way up from southern France, the paratroopers had eventually arrived in Werbomont on 21 December 1944, with a strength of 643 officers and men. A near-continuous series of assaults had whittled their numbers down to 250 men by 7 January.

That day they attacked and took the village of Rochelinval (five miles downriver from Trois-Ponts) from an entire *Volksgrenadier* regiment, but lost more than one hundred in the snows before the village, including their CO, Lieutenant-Colonel Wood G. Joerg. Just fourteen officers and ninety-six men remained of the original 643. Since the 551st were a single-battalion entity and had no paratrooper replacements available, they were absorbed into Gavin's 82nd Airborne Division. With the survivors scattered and the battalion's records lost, nothing of the 551st's history was known until its veterans sought recognition for their sacrifices in the 1990s. The battalion was belatedly awarded a Presidential Unit Citation in 2001 and several plaques have recently been dedicated to the 551st in Rochelinval, where a visit provides a sobering study of a gruelling hand-to-hand battalion action.[21]

Popular history has the German attacks peaking at Christmas and the campaign slowly subsiding during the ensuing month. In fact, the battles around Bastogne between Christmas and the New Year were some of the most damaging to both sides. Even the unleashing of the Allied counter-thrust from 3 January was not easy, for the Americans (and a few of their British compatriots) were also fighting plunging temperatures, which were the lowest of the entire campaign. German and US vehicular movement was slow, their infantry were soon exhausted wading through the two- or three-foot snowdrifts, and the wounded rarely survived, if left unattended for more than fifteen minutes.

The weather story of the Bulge was not a simple one of continuous fog and snow, as is often portrayed. Although it had been snowing in late November, covering the higher parts of the Ardennes and Eifel regions – which impeded the concentration of attacking units, but hid them also – by 16 December most of the snow had disappeared. German propaganda film footage bears this out. The US 17th Field Artillery Observation Battalion, on the northern shoulder, noted the following temperatures on 16 December: at 01.40 a.m., 27 degrees Fahrenheit (–3°C); 11.40 a.m., 34 degrees (1°C); and at 11.35 p.m., 38 degrees (3°C). This was miserable weather for troops living in the open.[22]

The Ardennes has a quirky microclimate and conditions can vary rapidly over a few miles. Contrary to popular belief, not every day of the 1944–45 campaign witnessed snow, and the weather gods produced an unpredictable mixture of blizzards, fog, ice and rain, which hampered the attackers as much as the defenders. The very conditions Hitler sought to ground the Allied air forces played havoc with his own logistics, fatally delaying the arrival of fuel and ammunition. (NARA)

From *Null-Tag* until 20 December, the weather was generally damp and misty. Although this cloaked the Germans, it also momentarily worked against them: the slight thaw slowed the panzers and sudden openings in the thick fog occasionally revealed the attackers in dramatic fashion, as we saw at Noville. On 21–22 December, competing weather fronts then froze the higher ground, on the Elsenborn Ridge and elsewhere, leaving the lower highways slippery and muddy, as few were paved. Conditions were briefly an unpredictable mixture of snow, blizzards, fog and rain, all of which hampered the Fifth and Sixth Armies and their supply networks.

Snow brought German logistics traffic through the Eifel to a standstill, where there was no grit and few snowploughs. Snow fences were torn down by cold troops scrounging for firewood. Speer's civil engineers who might have solved these mobility problems were all employed further westwards at the front. By the time snowploughs reached the vital supply routes, the skies had cleared sufficiently for Allied fighters to pounce on them. *Volksgrenadier* Gefreiter Otto Gunkel told me how sparse his rations had become due to the supply shortages. When he entered a farmhouse containing American rations in early January, he found three cans: one of beans, another of cherries and a third of macaroni, emptied them into an abandoned GI helmet and ate the mess with his fingers. He rounded off his repast with a captured chocolate bar and lit up a Lucky Strike. 'Best meal I'd eaten for years,' he thought.[23]

Between 23 and 27 December, a high-pressure system brought cold, dry winds from the east, and the skies became crystal-clear for Allied aircraft, but temperatures on the ground dropped very low indeed, freezing the earth to stone and turning roads to glass. On the 27th, the 17th Artillery noted lower figures than before: 01.45 a.m., 14 degrees Fahrenheit (–10°C); 1.50 p.m., 25 degrees (–4°C); and at 11.40 p.m., 17 degrees (–8°C). As the temperature rose slightly around 29 December, arctic air from Scandinavia brought heavy snow, blizzards and greatly reduced visibility at ground level. GI 'Mac' McMurdie of the 99th Division remembered, 'Then it started snowing, snowing, snowing, until it was hip deep in every spot. All night long we took turns digging the snow out of the hole. We would sweat while working then just about freeze when we stopped. And it was no use trying to put on our greatcoats. They had all been frozen solid and were useless.'[24] The snow settled thickly on the frozen ground, creating treacherous conditions for man and vehicle – these were the conditions Desmond Scott encountered, and which killed Brigadier Sugden.

John Davis, a scout with the 424th Infantry, who somehow had escaped the Golden Lions' bruising encounters with the Wehrmacht on 17–21 December, recalled the day the cold got too extreme. He came across a soldier's corpse wrapped in a blanket. 'I kept going. Taking that blanket would have violated military etiquette, not to mention my own personal code of right and wrong. I walked another ten feet. Then I retraced my steps . . . "Sorry, buddy," I whispered, "but I need this more than you do." A deep sense of shame spread through me, but I kept the blanket and didn't look back.'[25]

On New Year's Day, 1945, First Lieutenant Kendall M. Ogilvie of the 17th Artillery recorded even lower temperatures: 03.40 a.m., 20 degrees Fahrenheit (–7°C); 11.45 a.m., 23 degrees (–5°C); while at 9.40 p.m., 13 degrees (–11°C).[26] These were conditions that Russian Front veterans would recognise, and both sides realised they greatly reduced the effectiveness of armoured troops, transportation and artillery units, never mind the infantry. Tanker J. Ted Hartman observed, 'never did I imagine at age nineteen I would be driving a tank in battle', but the thrill soon wore off. Moving through the Ardennes with the US 11th Armored Division, he declared, 'The weather was freezing and those tanks were cold, cold.' He remembered the 'frost forming over the interior of the thick steel walls' of his tank, and his crew suffering from frostbite and trench foot inside their vehicles.[27]

'You couldn't touch the tanks or your hands stuck to the metal,' agreed a crewman with the 761st Tank Battalion, an African American armoured unit known as the 'Black Panthers'. George 'E.G.' McConnell still remembered Patton's speech of welcome to his battalion. 'I would never have asked for you if you weren't good. I have nothing but the best in my Army,' thundered 'Old Blood and Guts', Third Army's affectionate nickname for their commander. 'I don't care what color you are as long as you go up there and kill those Kraut sonsofbitches. Everyone has their eyes on you and is expecting great things from you . . . Don't let them down, and damn you, don't let me down! They say it is patriotic to die for your country. Well, let's see how many patriots we can make out of those German sonsofbitches.' They all loved it, but the Bulge was less agreeable. 'The tracks were real quiet because of the snow. Beautiful country, but you couldn't really appreciate the beauty,' observed McConnell, 'every tree, snow-bank, could be deadly. But, boy was it cold, like living in a steel refrigerator turned to maximum.'[28]

Overall, figures recorded during *Herbstnebel* ranged from 43 degrees Fahrenheit (6°C), recorded on 19 December, to minus 7 degrees Fahrenheit (–22°C), noted at Wiltz on 1 January, with a gradual decline in average daily temperatures throughout the period. The unusually poor weather was stressed by SHAEF to journalists and reflected in the newspaper headlines. 'Yank Troops, Tanks Advance Two Miles Through 4-Foot Snow', read the *Baltimore News-Post* on 9 January.[29] The temperatures were much lower than the historic norm for December–January, when the thermometer generally hovers between 33 and 35 degrees Fahrenheit (1 and 2 °C). However, even today, a visitor to the Ardennes may be struck by the region's quirky microclimate: as anyone who has followed a race at the Spa-Francorchamps circuit (home to the Belgian Grand Prix) will remember, the start line can be bathed in brilliant sunshine, but torrential rain can be drenching the drivers only a short distance away.

Aware of the danger of losing his remaining panzers, Hitler authorised Model to withdraw some units on 8 January, followed by the whole of I and II SS Panzer Corps, plus the *Führer-Begleit-Brigade* – all his personal favourites – on the 9th. The same day, Patton began a drive against Manteuffel's Fifth Army in two feet of snow, when the mercury registered –6° Fahrenheit (–21°C), but his opponents gave ground only grudgingly – they were fighting to keep their escape routes open, not for their *Vaterland*. With morale, as well as the temperatures, plummeting, the Fifth and Sixth Panzer Armies extricated themselves from the Allied jaws as best they could, but the lack of fuel and rations, as well as hostile aircraft, hampered their efforts besides the snow – which served only to increase their fuel consumption.

On 11 January a link-up was made between British troops moving from the west and GIs advancing from the north, when the 1st Black Watch of Horrocks' XXX Corps entered La Roche, encountering Company 'C' of the 635th Tank Destroyer Battalion, attached to the US 4th Cavalry Group. One of the Scotsmen, Harris McAllister, remembered, 'we crossed over the wrecked Ourthe River bridge and met American soldiers in their armoured car. We sat down, round a fire of petrol and sand in a bucket, and shared coffee with them. Then a photographer with a reporter arrived in a jeep and we were made to rush down a street from opposite ends, meet and shake hands in the middle.' The posed photo made headline news, and is reproduced on a marble plaque at the same spot, the corner of rue de la Gare and Route de Cielle in La

Roche, today.[30] Monty's news management was quick off the mark, for by 12 January some papers were already running the story 'Montgomery's Men Capture Laroche' – which was news to the GIs they had met there, and others throughout the Bulge who were unaware of any British presence in what was principally an American campaign.[31]

If there were any lingering hopes in the *Adlerhorst* about the continued viability of *Herbstnebel*, they were dashed on 12 January when the Soviets launched their New Year's offensive, as Guderian had warned. We have noted how the original Ardennes plan, as argued by Hitler, had been to secure victory in the west, then transfer those victorious units back east to meet the Russians. The result was the worst of all possible worlds. On 15 January, Rundstedt received permission to withdraw his forces back to Cherain, near Houffalize, which was immediately broadcast in the following terms: 'A Berlin military spokesman announced to-day that the German counter-offensive was over. "The task given to Field Marshal Model's armies has been fulfilled," he said. "The aim of the German offensive was not so much to gain ground as to reduce pressure on other parts of the front. The German Command decided to attack in order to force the Allies to cease their offensive on the Roer and in the Saar and Alsace. This has happened, and the Germans have once more gained time."' Inevitably, western newspapers interpreted this in terms of: 'Von Rundstedt's Bulge Caving In. Berlin Admits Drive is Over', 'Bulge: Berlin Admits Defeat' or 'Germans Flee Bulge'.[32]

The previous day the two American armies in the Bulge had made contact for the first time. Beneath the battlements of the eleventh-century castle in La Roche (earlier liberated by the Black Watch), soldiers of the 24th Cavalry Reconnaissance Squadron, from Collins' VII Corps, met paratroopers of the 507th Parachute Infantry of the 17th Airborne Division, a newly committed formation of Patton's Third Army. Two days later, at 09.05 a.m., the jaws snapped shut at Houffalize, when Task Force Green of Patton's 11th Armored Division encountered the 41st Armored Infantry of Collins' Second Armored Division advancing from the north. Plaques located just out of town commemorate the event.

The American advance continued, taking St Vith on the 23rd – recaptured, appropriately, by Hasbrouck's Seventh Armored Division, which had defended it a month earlier. Only three houses remained habitable. By the end of the month, almost every German gain had been eliminated. Meanwhile the Führer had quit the *Adlerhorst* at 6.00 p.m. on 15 January (proof, if ever it was needed, that the offensive was over), boarded his personal train, the 'Brandenburg', and by ten o'clock the following morning was back in Berlin. Thereafter he retreated to the *Reichskanzlei* and his *Führerbunker* beneath.

Allied casualties included 8,607 dead, 21,144 missing and 47,139 wounded, totalling 76,890, to which must be added about 20,000 non-battle casualties (frostbite, trench foot and the like), plus aircrew losses. The cost to the Germans remains difficult to prove conclusively, and at best, is an estimate based on the casualty lists compiled every ten days by OKH, the '*Personelle blutige Verluste des Feldherres*'. This indicated 10,749 dead, 22,487 missing or captured and 34,225 wounded for the 10 December–30 January period, totalling 67,261. (OKW later released far higher figures of 15,652 killed, 27,582 missing or captured and 41,600 wounded, a total of 84,834.)[33] The true figure may lie between the two, making German and American casualties about even. However, in terms of matériel losses, very little of Hitler's divisions remained, compared with their strengths of twenty-four days earlier.[34] Eisenhower noted the loss of 733 Allied tanks, of which Berlin claimed to have captured ninety-one. Overall the Wehrmacht lost about 600 irreplaceable panzers in *Herbstnebel*: the 12th SS-*Hitlerjudgend* could muster only twenty-six tanks and assault guns, and its battalions averaged only 120 men. They suffered 9,870 men killed, wounded and captured, including 328 officers and 1,698 NCOs. If the elite, fanatical divisions were being hammered on such a scale, then this, if nothing else, surely underlined the end of the Reich.[35]

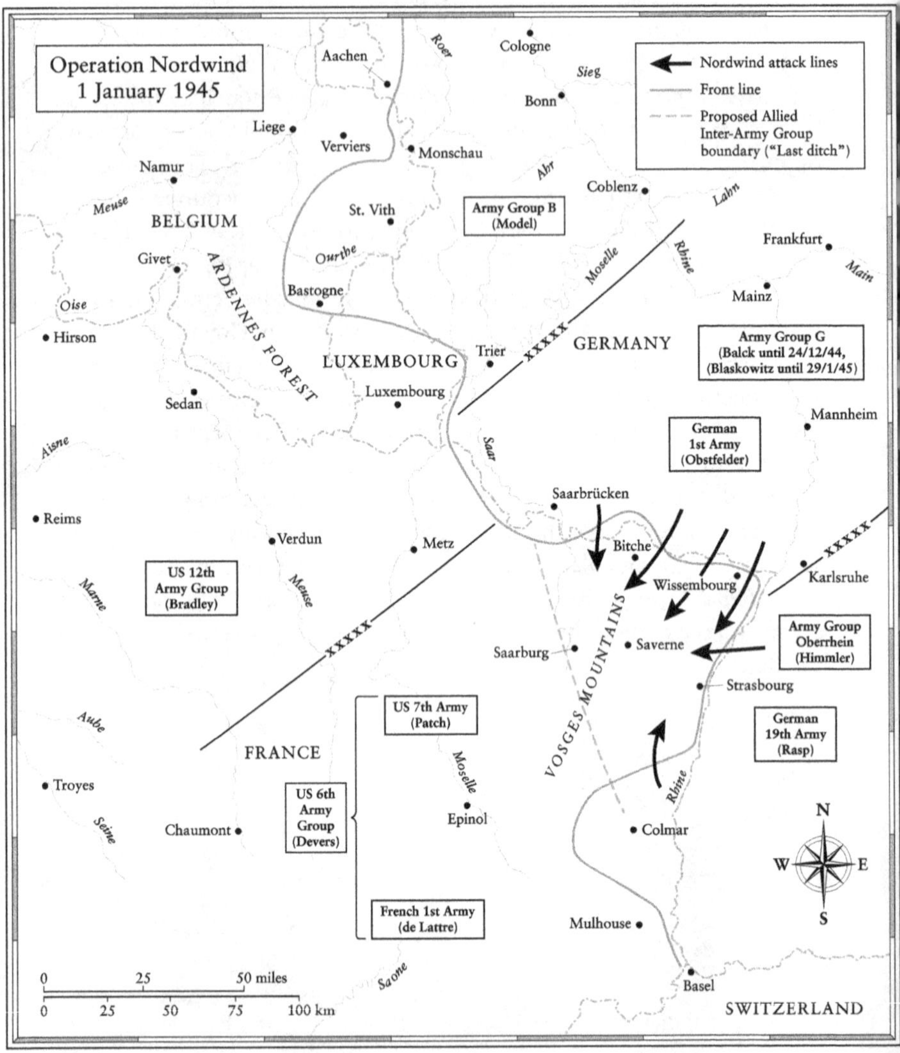

Operation Nordwind
1 January 1945
Nordwind attack lines
Front line
Proposed Allied
Inter-Army Group
boundary ("Last ditch")
Aachen
Cologne
Roer
Sieg
Bonn
Liege
Verviers
Monschau
Namur
Ahr
Coblenz
Lahn
Meuse
BELGIUM
St. Vith
Army Group B
(Model)
Frankfurt
Main
Rhine
Mosel
Mainz
Givet
ARDENNES FOREST
Ourthe
Bastogne
Oise
Hirson
GERMANY
Army Group G
(Balck until 24/12/44,
(Blaskowitz until 29/1/45)
Trier
LUXEMBOURG
Luxembourg
Sedan
Mannheim
Aisne
Saar
German
1st Army
(Obstfelder)
Saarbrücken
Reims
Verdun
Metz
Bitche
Karlsruhe
Wissembourg
US 12th
Army Group
(Bradley)
Marne
Meuse
VOSGES MOUNTAINS
Saarburg
Saverne
Army Group
Oberrhein
(Himmler)
Strasbourg
Aube
US 7th Army
(Patch)
German
19th Army
(Rasp)
FRANCE
Moselle
Troyes
US 6th
Army
Group
(Devers)
Rhine
Epinol
Seine
Chaumont
Colmar
N
W
E
S
French 1st Army
(de Lattre)
Mulhouse
Saone
Basel
0
25
50 miles
0
25
50
75
100 km
SWITZERLAND

36

The Performance of a Lifetime

On 1 January 1945, in an attempt to regain momentum, Berlin launched two new operations. One was the Luftwaffe's *Bodenplatte*, the aerial assault on Allied air bases which was originally intended to precede *Herbstnebel*. Montgomery was furious that it damaged his personal C-47, a gift from Eisenhower, who immediately replaced it.

On the same day, Hitler directed that Generaloberst Johannes Blaskowitz's Army Group 'G' (south of Model's troops) strike at the thinly stretched front of General Sandy Patch's US Seventh Army, who occupied the Alsace sector, south of Patton's troops. Patch's men had landed in southern France in August, and with the First French Army – the two forming Devers' Sixth Army Group – fought their way past the city of Strasbourg to the German frontier. This second brainchild of Hitler's, Operation *Nordwind* (North Wind) – which involved General Hans von Obstfelder's First and Friedrich Weise's Nineteenth Armies – was planned over ten days and designed to deflect American attacks away from the southern flank of the Bulge.

From wireless intercepts, the Germans were aware that Patch's formation was weaker than it had been, had gone over to the defensive and also occupied the fronts of two of Patton's corps, redirected to the Ardennes. In circumstances similar to Middleton's on 16 December, the eve of *Nordwind* found Patch covering 126 miles of front, from Saarbrücken to Strasbourg, with just six divisions. Ike had also withdrawn two of Patch's divisions into theatre reserve.

Thanks to Ultra, SHAEF was aware that *Nordwind* was on its way, though not the precise point of impact or its objectives, and simply ordered Patch to withdraw westwards. He was to shorten his lines, create a reserve and relinquish northern Alsace, including Strasbourg, to the Germans. But Ike and Patch had not reckoned with Charles de Gaulle, or the commander of the First French Army, Général Jean de Lattre de Tassigny, who, supported by Churchill, refused point-blank the proposal, on political grounds. De Gaulle, with one eye firmly fixed on the proximity of German forces in the Ardennes to France, was concerned about setting precedents, but more importantly felt that conceding territory back to the Germans would undermine his own political leadership. His power base was by no means secure in France, with many left-leaning or avowedly Communist groups seeking any means to discredit him. He could not let Strasbourg, which sat on the Franco-German frontier and symbolised the liberation of France, be reclaimed by the Reich.

Although Captain Harry Butcher, Eisenhower's personal aide, recorded that de Gaulle 'feared there would be such a reaction in France, that his government might fall', it was the loss of personal credibility that worried de Gaulle most. In fact, France was not legally governed at all by de Gaulle: he had simply arrived in Normandy and proclaimed himself head of state.[1] In the end, *Nordwind* was halted and Butcher noted that Ike had diplomatically 'modified his order because, from a purely military standpoint, he could not afford to have his lines of supply and his vast rear areas endangered by civil unrest, which would accompany a revolt against de Gaulle's government'.[2] Butcher's words smoothed over what promised to become a major diplomatic incident, with de Gaulle effectively blackmailing Eisenhower by threatening civil unrest. The aftershocks reverberated at the highest levels of Allied command and gave warning that de Gaulle would be a challenge to Western solidarity after the war.

In the event, *Nordwind* saw three German corps punch a hole in the American lines, aided by fog and thick forests, gain about ten miles, then stall. As in the Ardennes, the American 'shoulders' held, in this case Major-General Wade Haislip's XV Corps to the north and Major-General Edward H. Brooks' VI Corps in the south. Brooks was an unflappable warrior, having won a Distinguished Service Cross in 1918 and led the 2nd Armored Division through Normandy before his promotion to corps command in October. Later in 1945, it would be Brooks who accepted the personal surrender of General Erich

Brandenberger, erstwhile leader of the German Seventh Army in the Ardennes. On 5 January, Blaskowitz renewed his attacks against VI Corps and by the 15th of the month Brooks' formation was fighting for its survival, being assailed on three sides. This was no mere feint: at least seventeen German divisions participated, including the 6th SS-*Gebirgsjäger* (Mountain), 17th SS-*Panzergrenadier*, 21st Panzer and 25th *Panzergrenadier* Divisions. Some of these were reserve formations held by OKW, which might otherwise have been committed to *Herbstnebel*.

A counter-attack by the US 14th Armored Division temporarily halted the Germans, and on the 21st, with casualties mounting, and running out of replacements, armour, ammunition and combat supplies, Brooks, with French help, managed to break contact and withdraw to fresh defensive positions along the Zorn, Moder and Rothbach rivers. By 25 January the German offensive was spent and had drawn to a close, enabling the US Seventh and French First Armies to counter-attack, recapturing the ground lost north of Strasbourg. The *Nordwind* fighting was every bit as desperate and vicious as that in *Herbstnebel*, with the weather and ground worse. The terrain comprises high mountains ranging up to 4,000 feet, and plunging valleys, mostly wooded. The ground was known to several of the French and German commanders, who had contested the same area during 1914–18; the young Leutnant Erwin Rommel had cut his teeth in combat there, and the hillsides are littered with the detritus and trenches of both world wars.

Writing of the campaign, one of Himmler's National Socialist Guidance Officers sent a sympathetic report back to OKW about *Nordwind*. His words, which might also have encompassed any formation in the Ardennes, concluded:

> The longer one observes the Nineteenth Army in their hard battles in Alsace, the more one's esteem grows for a fighting community that, after all, is not really a trained army, but actually a thrown-together heap. It is fantastic that in spite of this, a cohesive organisation has grown out of that heap. To be sure, however, it is now an exhausted organisation. Even the strongest will is broken through uninterrupted combat. Many individuals are at the end of their rope. If one could give them just two days' sleep, it might be different. As a result of attrition, there are regiments [normally of 3,000] with a strength of 80–150 men; that such units can actually continue to attack is doubly impressive.

> Everywhere, the decisive difference comes down to the performance of individuals. Many officers are resigned that their lives are over, and they want to sell them dearly.[3]

Had *Nordwind* occurred in isolation it would no doubt have achieved the same status as the Battle of the Bulge for soldiers and historians, but in the event it was overshadowed by the latter and is consequently little known. The US Seventh Army suffered 11,609 battle casualties, not including substantial losses to sickness and frostbite, and the Germans 22,932.[4] In German minds *Nordwind* was linked to *Herbstnebel*, as we have seen from Hitler's comments during its planning, but the same is true also in American military history. After the war, the US Army issued the Ardennes–Alsace campaign streamer to the battle flags of units that took part in either struggle.

Notwithstanding the problems caused by de Gaulle, Anglo-American relations had been fraught with difficulties for most of 1944, largely due to the political failure to agree a 'broad' or 'narrow front' strategy against the Germans. The alliance had prospered largely on account of Eisenhower's efforts as the arch-conciliator. The arch-villain, as we have already noted, was Montgomery, who was unwilling to accept Ike's supremacy as leader, or that Eisenhower's 'broad front' strategy was correct. With Monty's appointment to command the northern half of the Bulge from 20 December, this seemed to the British field marshal a vindication of his view that American generalship was inferior.

A news blackout imposed on 16 December slowed the release of details to the outside world from the Ardennes; for example, it was announced only on 18 January by Secretary of War Henry L. Stimson that, several weeks earlier, 'the 106th Division had suffered 8,663 casualties, including 416 killed, 1,246 wounded and that most of the 7,001 missing were presumed to be prisoners'.[5] The news came only once victory in the Ardennes was assured.

Montgomery's assumption of command in the Bulge was not made public until announced by Bedell Smith in a press conference at SHAEF in Paris on 5 January. In the background, ever since Monty had taken command on 20 December, his boss – the British CIGS, Field Marshal Alan Brooke – while agreeing that SHAEF was a bureaucratic and inefficient organisation, warned Monty privately on numerous occasions, 'Events and enemy action have forced on Eisenhower the setting-up of a more satisfactory system of command . . . It is important that you should not, even in the slightest degree, appear to rub this unfortunate fact into anyone at SHAEF. Any remarks you make are bound to come to Eisenhower's ears sooner or later.'[6]

Two days later Monty brushed off this gentle admonition, for he responded to Brooke, 'I think I see daylight now on the northern front, and we have tidied up the mess and got two American armies properly organised. But I can see rocks ahead and no grounds for the optimism Ike seems to feel. Rundstedt is fighting a good battle.'[7] Six days after that, Monty penned another smug missive to his boss following a meeting with Eisenhower: 'Ike was definitely in a somewhat humbler frame of mind, and clearly realised that present trouble would not have occurred if he had accepted British advice and not that of American generals.'[8]

Clearly, Monty's attitude would lead to trouble in the Allied camp. It erupted after a press conference he held at his Twenty-First Army Group headquarters in Zonhoven (these days known as the 'Villa Monty'), Belgium, on Sunday, 7 January, two days after his command in the Bulge had been made public. Using maps to illustrate the campaign (which had not yet drawn to a close), he began with some prepared remarks before moving on to questions.[9] 'As soon as I saw what was happening in the Ardennes, I took certain steps myself to ensure that if the Germans got to the Meuse, they certainly would not get over that river,' he said. 'I employed the whole available power of the British group of armies: this power was brought into play very gradually and in such a way that it would not interfere with the American lines of communications. Finally it was put into battle with a bang and today British divisions are fighting hard on the right flank of the United States First Army. You thus have the picture of British troops fighting on both sides of American forces who have suffered a hard blow. The battle has been most interesting; I think possibly one of the most interesting and tricky battles I have ever handled.'[10]

At a distance of many decades, this text still oozes arrogance; at the time it was regarded as incendiary – and was portrayed as such in the Allied media. From London, the *Daily Mail* duly reported the next day, 'Montgomery Foresaw Attack. His Troops Were All Ready To March. Acted "On Own" To Save Day'.[11]

Montgomery and his supporters subsequently claimed he was misunderstood or misinterpreted, but the field marshal knew exactly what he was doing. The media event was held in Monty's villa, not at SHAEF or an American headquarters. He had cleared his proposed text – which did not remotely resemble the words he actually delivered – and the holding of the conference itself, in advance, with Eisenhower, Brooke and Churchill.

However, throughout the event he omitted to recognise the enormous sacrifices of American soldiers in the Bulge, failed to name a single US commander, vastly overstated the role of the British and cast himself as the strategic genius behind the defence, whereas it had been Eisenhower. It was so provocative that Major Tom Bigland, Monty's personal liaison officer attached to Bradley's headquarters, who had been present, noted on the same evening that 'shortly after the BBC Nine o'clock news had covered it, and on a wavelength close to that of the BBC', German radio also reported the conference in English, aware that it would 'stir up anti-British feelings among the Americans'.[12]

It is hard not to agree with Eisenhower, Bradley and most American commanders that Monty's version of events was a gross distortion of the truth of the Ardennes campaign. Monty was not clever with war correspondents, but even sympathetic ones, like the Australians Chester Wilmot and Alan Moorehead, were dismayed. His only guiding hand, his long-suffering chief of staff, Major-General Francis 'Freddie' de Guingand, was in England being treated for appendicitis. Even his headquarters staff agreed with Brigadier 'Bill' Williams, his intelligence chief, that 'the presentation was quite appalling'. Major Bigland, who knew both Bradley and Monty well, thought this incident caused more Anglo-American ill feeling 'than anything else in the war – even efforts to put things right in the press failed'.[13]

There was another motive for Monty's press conference. The field marshal continued to ignore Brooke's advice, and on 31 December had sent Eisenhower another missive about reforming the SHAEF command structure and giving him, Monty, greater prominence. As a result, Ike finally snapped and had drafted (but not sent) a letter to Marshall in Washington, DC, asking to be relieved – in fact it was a request to choose between Monty and himself. Eisenhower's British deputy, Air Chief Marshal Sir Arthur Tedder, supported his boss without hesitation. De Guingand had sensed trouble and warned Monty that he was not irreplaceable, for his great rival, Field Marshal Sir Harold Alexander, commanding Allied forces in Italy, was prepared to take over Twenty-First Army Group in his stead; moreover, 'Alex' and Eisenhower were old friends, having worked together in the Mediterranean in 1942–3.

At de Guingand's dictation, Monty had written a swift letter of apology to Ike ('Very distressed that my letter may have upset you and I would ask you to tear it up. Your devoted subordinate, Monty'). Thus Monty's 7 January press conference was also designed to send a coded apology to Eisenhower. He concluded, 'it is teamwork that pulls you through dangerous times; it is teamwork that wins battles . . . the captain of our team is General Eisenhower. I am devoted to Ike. We are the greatest of friends.' But these words went unheard, and the damage created a full-scale transatlantic gale. Churchill's own contribution to damage limitation was his historic 18 January 1945 House of Commons speech, where he graciously paid tribute to the American soldiers and warned, 'Care must be taken in telling our proud tale not to claim for the British Army an undue share of what is undoubtedly the greatest American battle of the war'.[14] The Prime Minister's words were a coded rebuke to Montgomery.

Eisenhower immediately sought to conciliate Bradley, who, with his staff, had 'exploded with indignation'. On 9 January, Ike awarded his friend a Bronze Star for his leadership of the Twelfth Army Group through the crisis, and the same day Bradley held a press conference of his own, to justify his role, which he felt had been impugned by Monty. He defended his own strategy and explained that 'in leaving the Ardennes lightly held, I took a calculated risk. Had we followed more cautious policies, we would still be fighting west of Paris', generously concluding that 'Field Marshal Montgomery has made a notable contribution to the battle'.[15] This led to the *New York Times* headline the next day, 'Our Risk May Win, Bradley Declares'.[16]

Other, pro-Montgomery papers criticised Bradley: 'Gen. Bradley Taken to Task', headlined the *Daily Mail*, suggesting, 'Some of his [Bradley's] statements will be regarded by the British as unnecessarily offensive. The statement that Field Marshal Montgomery's command on the northern flank is only temporary bears only one interpretation, namely, that Montgomery is good enough to be given a position of responsibility in an emergency, but when the danger is over his services are no longer required . . . The British will regard, with dismay, Montgomery's relegation to a somewhat unimportant part of the front held before von Rundstedt's break-through. The country will need convincing that his services could not be put to better use.'[17]

More than a month later, Churchill, Eisenhower, Brooke and Bedell Smith were still engaged in damage limitation. Eisenhower wrote to Marshall on 9 February that the conference 'is still rankling in Bradley's mind and I must say I cannot blame him'.[18] As he commented in his 1948 memoirs, *Crusade in Europe*, 'This incident caused me more distress and worry than did any similar one of the war. I doubt if Montgomery ever came to realize how resentful some American commanders were. They believed he had belittled them – and they were not slow to voice reciprocal scorn and contempt.'[19] Despite his protestations, Monty knew he had belittled them, and thereafter Anglo-American military relations were never quite the same.

For General Jim Gavin of the 82nd and other American commanders, the 7 January press conference came hard on the heels of Montgomery's decision to launch his counter-attack in the Bulge on 3 January. Bradley, Patton and their subordinates were highly critical of the late start, and shared the unanimous view that his counter-stroke should have begun much earlier, perhaps on 31 December or 1 January. In his memoirs, Gavin thought that, while 'British and American troops always fought well side by side', American leaders could not understand Monty's desire for a 'tidy battlefield', or why he wanted a 'very conservative, albeit costly, phase line by phase line counter-offensive'.[20]

To Gavin's mind, Monty's flaws were essentially cultural. The most sympathetic of American commanders towards Montgomery, he concluded that the field marshal simply did not understand America's 'national psychological make-up'. GIs liked a fast-moving, fluid battle, which meant that Monty's more formal 'set-piece' events were 'rarely to American liking'. Along with Simpson and Collins, he admired Montgomery's professionalism, but all were appalled by his lack of tact.[21] We have dwelt on the 7 January press conference and its consequences at length because it helped shape America's post-war view of the Ardennes and British generalship, right down to today.[22]

Perhaps the final military judgement should come from one of Monty's opponents. Much later on, Hasso von Manteuffel observed, 'The operations of the American First Army had developed into a series of individual holding actions. Montgomery's contribution to restoring the situation was that he turned that series of isolated actions into a coherent battle fought according to a clear and definite plan. It was his refusal to engage in premature and piecemeal counter-attacks which enabled the Americans to gather their reserves and frustrate the German attempts to extend their breakthrough.'[23] Manteuffel's interpretation was at odds with the conclusions of the late Stephen E. Ambrose, who in 1997 maintained, 'Putting Monty in command of the northern flank had no effect on the battle'.[24]

Could *Herbstnebel* have succeeded? Its operational aim was to reach the Allies' logistics base of Antwerp, which opened for maritime freight on 26 November, as the Red Ball Express and other road-based supply lines from Normandy wound down. Hitler's assessment, that Antwerp was the Allied 'centre of gravity' (their most vulnerable asset, without which they could not continue to prosecute the war), was basically correct. Yet *Herbstnebel*'s overarching strategic objective was different. It was to destroy the cohesion of the Western Allies. Again, in concluding that Nazi Germany might survive, or buy much-needed time, if the Western alliance somehow shattered, was logical.

However, in assuming the alliance was fragile, Hitler was fundamentally mistaken. He believed that the Americans and British were not 'natural bedfellows' and that a fundamental setback, such as the loss of Antwerp, would cause the Anglo-US common purpose to founder. His rationale was illustrated on 31 August 1944, shortly after the end in Normandy, when he remarked, 'They are stumbling to their ruin . . . The time will come when the tensions between the allies will become so great that the break will occur . . . Throughout history coalitions have always gone to pieces sooner or later. One has only to wait for the moment, no matter how hard the going.'[25] This statement was more a reflection on his personal view of the value of coalitions than the political reality of 1944.

How could this have happened? By what process would the vast political-military architecture of Roosevelt's and Churchill's war machine, carefully constructed since 1941, involving huge numbers of politicians, staff officers and civil servants supporting many high-level military committees, and Eisenhower's SHAEF, numbering 20,000 multinational personnel, suddenly collapse because of an unexpected German success, such as the loss of Antwerp? The wartime 'special relationship' was born of an unusually close bond between Churchill, whose mother was American, and Roosevelt. It was echoed by King George VI, and Brooke – if sorely tested by his protégé, Montgomery – Marshall and Eisenhower, for whom it was said to be a 'religion'. ('You can call me a sonofabitch', Ike is alleged to have said, 'but not an American sonofabitch.') Its immense strength was such that it grew into NATO after the war.

Apart from dividing the Allies, *Herbstnebel* had another purpose altogether, which was to buy time. With the Anglo-American armies divided or off-balance, all available reserves would then be rushed eastwards to meet the anticipated 1945 Soviet offensive – a strategic plan which recognised Germany's diminishing resources. By late 1944 the fronts were interconnected: one could only be reinforced at the expense of another, and the forces used in the Bulge were also desperately needed in the east, where, for example, twelve weak infantry divisions covered 725 miles from the Carpathians to the Baltic, with no reserves.

Generaloberst Heinz Guderian, as chief of OKH, and responsible for the Russian Front, was highly critical of the late start of *Herbstnebel*, originally planned for mid-November but delayed several times. He observed that the mid-December date, even if it resulted in a decisive victory in the west, left no time to switch reinforcements to the east to meet the expected Soviet New Year push, which duly materialised on 12 January. Three times, on 24 December, 1 and 9 January, Guderian warned Hitler of the fragility of the east, stating on the last occasion that the front was 'like a pack of cards'. When Marshal Koniev struck three days later, with his forty-two rifle divisions, six armoured corps and four mechanised brigades (numbers which dwarfed those employed in the Ardennes), there was little to check his advance. With forces ratios of 11:1 in infantry, 7:1 in tanks, 20:1 in artillery and 20:1 in the air, Warsaw fell on 17 January and by 5 February Zhukov had reached the River Oder, fifty miles from Berlin.[26]

It would have taken far more than bickering and apportioning blame for the loss of Antwerp to drive apart the British and Americans, who were – in any case – bound by a common pledge, which they took seriously, of demanding the 'unconditional surrender' of Germany and Japan. Hitler had no conception of the strength of the Anglo-American coalition and failed to realise he had no means of damaging it. Thus *Herbstnebel* was doomed from the start. Even if, by some unholy miracle, his troops had made it to Antwerp – what then? It is significant that there was no campaign plan to develop any military activity after the seizure of Antwerp.

Against all the odds, had Hitler succeeded, there is every reason to suppose the Western Allies in 1944–5 would have carried on fighting and eventually recaptured the port. At the very beginning of 1945, Eisenhower had seventy-three divisions under his command in North-West Europe, with almost unlimited fuel, vehicles and ammunition. Of these, forty-nine were infantry, twenty armoured and four airborne. Twelve were British, eight French, three Canadian, one Polish, but the vast majority (forty-nine) were American.

Additionally, there were numerous independent armoured and artillery battalions or brigades, and powerful Belgian, Dutch and Czechoslovak battlegroups. It would have been necessary to destroy a substantial chunk of these for the Reich to achieve a decisive result. Even though the Germans had the initial element of surprise, *Herbstnebel* employed a maximum of only twenty-eight divisions, with very limited fuel and ammunition. Having stunned their opponents into complete inactivity, some of these victorious German divisions were supposed afterwards to redeploy to the east and fight the Russians!

By occupying Antwerp, Hitler's armies would have been left at the end of a vastly overextended logistics tail, stretching from the Ardennes to the Belgian harbour. Such a line of communications would have been disastrously vulnerable to Allied air interdiction, about which Göring and his diminished Luftwaffe could do absolutely nothing. If Allied air power or snow didn't destroy the German advance, the arrival of mud would most certainly. There were very few adequate roads that led via the Ardennes, from the Meuse to Antwerp. Although Generalmajor Friedrich von Mellenthin had maintained, when attached to 9th Panzer Division, that his experiences in Russia 'stood me in good stead; I knew all about the problems of moving through snow and ice – a subject about which the Americans still had much to learn', only main roads were paved in 1944, and those soon broke down with the constant passage of wheels and tracks in traffic volumes for which they had not been designed.[27]

Germany's experience of Russia provided endless examples of the wear and tear to men, horses, vehicles and weapons caused by mud. Guy Sager, a German soldier in Russia, recalled how his truck, 'whose wheels by this time were balls of mud, was pulled forward while its engine rattled helplessly'.[28] Mud, like snow, increased fuel consumption and placed greater strain on engines and gears, plastered radiators, piled up under mudguards and tore off axles and other vehicle parts. This applied equally to weapons, where artillery became inaccurate and clogged rifles inoperable. Operating in mud physically drained soldiers far more than snow, and demoralised them also. In 1918, General Ludendorff (after whom the Remagen bridge was named) commented, 'You can't clean your rifle when your hands are covered an inch thick'.

The traditional German solution to moving huge numbers of men and amounts of *matériel* over long distances was to use railways, not trucks – Germany had plenty of coal but little gasoline. In the invasions of France and Russia, trains were very quickly sustaining the advance. Yet despite Germany's wealth in locomotives and rolling stock, the threat from the Allied air forces ensured that railways were of no immediate relevance in assisting a German advance to Antwerp. The Wehrmacht would have to rely on trucks, after all – all of which Hitler overlooked, or refused to acknowledge.

Hitler's dream of a massive assault reaching Antwerp in days was sabotaged by the reality that his army was scarcely more mobile than their predecessors who had entered Belgium in August 1914. In the earlier assault, using the Schlieffen Plan, it was the sheer inertia of hundreds of thousands of men and horses struggling on foot and hoof to keep up with an ambitious timetable in good weather that eventually led to the Kaiser's ambitions being dashed. The scenario in December 1944 was the same with three added complications: the weather was appalling, the Allies ruled the air and their first line of opponents, the US Army, were tactically savvy and well resourced.

Even the tactical aim for the Fifth and Sixth Panzer Armies of reaching the Meuse proved too difficult for the petrol-guzzling panzers. Utilising captured American vehicles and fuel might have been a short-term remedy (just as for Rommel in the North African desert) but was not a viable solution for a prolonged campaign. If the main panzer columns had reached the River Meuse – which none did – they would have been highly vulnerable crossing it, and certainly intercepted on the far bank, as the British 29th Armoured Brigade managed to do at Dinant to a German-crewed jeep on 23 December. *Herbstnebel* was thus thrice damned: tactically from getting to the Meuse, operationally from reaching Antwerp and strategically from fracturing the Anglo-American alliance.

Hitler failed to realise or refused to see that by 1944 the European war had become a *Materielschlacht*, a war of resources, where the unleashed economic might of the United States was outperforming that of Nazi Germany. He bamboozled his subordinates with promises of victory by secret weapons, yet failed to appreciate that the limited deployment of new tactical technologies could not alter the strategic balance in Germany's favour. Longer range U-boats, Tiger II tanks, MP-44 assault rifles, Messerschmitt 262 jet fighters, Me-163 rocket interceptors, V-1 doodlebugs and V-2 rockets could only nibble at the Allied superiority of numbers.

It was preordained that Hitler's army would not reach the Meuse; it was not strong enough. 'Consent and evade' seemed to be the tactic practised by most German commanders from late 1944. Consent to Hitler's wild plan, but evade responsibility for the consequences of its failure. At the end of the day, deep down Hitler's generals must have realised that the Bulge was likely to bog down into fighting for the possession of a few small Belgian towns or village crossroads. Even the loyal hatchet man Sepp Dietrich could not conceive of its success; only a few 'true believers' like Jochen Peiper thought it might work.

When Major Ken Hechler asked the tank commander in September 1945, 'Did you honestly expect to reach the Meuse in one day?' according to the interview transcripts, Peiper 'paused for a brief period before answering, wrinkled his brow and said, "if our own infantry had broken through by 07.00 a.m. as originally planned, my answer is 'yes', I think we might have reached the Meuse in one day"'.[29] Very few German field commanders seemed to have shared his view. These minor tactical flourishes sidestepped the operational certainty that the Allies were going to squeeze the Bulge flat after the panzers had run out of fuel.

It would not matter that around 800 American tanks, nearly 2,000 trucks and 800 aircraft were lost in the Ardennes for they could be replaced immediately, and many were repaired. Every German piece of armour, truck or plane destroyed was unrecoverable and irreplaceable. Eisenhower concluded after the war that the Ardennes campaign set Allied plans back by between two and three months at the most, and actually hastened the end of the war by destroying German reserves that would have been encountered on the other side of the Rhine later on. In fact, the Russians were the real beneficiaries of *Herbstnebel*, for the Fifth and Sixth Panzer Armies would have done very serious damage to the Red Army's advance on Berlin, and would have consumed less gasoline fighting in its defence. Even then, they would not have altered the operational outcome. With minor variations, it is difficult to conceive of any other outcome to the Ardennes offensive other than a German defeat.

If shattering the Anglo-US coalition was Hitler's strategic objective, he chose the wrong methods – to reach for Antwerp via the Ardennes – by which to achieve it. The only way in 1944 he might have influenced, or tested, the Allied strategic alliance would be by his own strategic diplomatic overtures – putting out peace feelers. But in the Führer's world such a concept was *verboten*. As we have seen, Hitler's own understanding of international coalitions was naïve in the extreme. He rarely travelled abroad in his life, spoke no foreign languages and understood very little of other cultures or races. Instead he preferred to believe in his own pseudo-Wagnerian nonsense of pan-European Aryan peoples.

Germany's alliance with Italy, whose soldiers were always regarded as inferior, was never equal. Similarly, Nazi relations with Japan represented a series of lost opportunities as the Axis partners never coordinated their military activities to mutual advantage.

The most beneficial alliance, that with the Soviet Union between August 1939 and June 1941, bought peace on Germany's eastern frontier when she most needed it, but was unilaterally sabotaged by Hitler's invasion of Russia. Even there, the opportunities to be gained by liberating millions of Ukrainians from the oppressive yoke of Communism were thrown away by Nazi brutality. Likewise, many Frenchmen, led by Pétain, might have done more to help Germany, but found the Vichy regime was merely a front by which to plunder France of her assets; so, too, with other occupied nations. Similarly in the First World War, the Führer would have witnessed the unequal way the *Kaiserreich* treated its Austro-Hungarian, Turkish and Bulgarian partners.

The strengths and weaknesses of international alliances and coalitions were simply beyond Hitler's comprehension: he never interpreted the world in terms of forging friendships and sharing ideals. Ironically his own party, the National Socialist German Worker's Party (NSDAP), had been an amalgamation of many small political organisations with divergent views. Hitler gobbled them up for their Deputies in the Reichstag and their members, like a corporate giant today greedily acquiring a market share. For all the rhetoric, Adolf Hitler only ever thought in terms of seizing and maintaining power for its own sake, not of building consensus. Thus he could not understand the nature and strength of the Allied alliance against him. On many levels, then, his Ardennes adventure was predestined to be nothing more than an irrelevant and hopeless dream.

The triumph of the US Army was that it had been surprised by Hitler's war machine in the most unfavourable circumstances imaginable, had taken a very bloody hit, struck back and ultimately had not been found wanting. The truest test of an army is not when everything is going according to plan, but when it can prevail despite the Clausewitzian fog of war. In the public mind, the Ardennes was principally a land battle, but in the degradation of the German logistics 'tail' and destruction of their forces on the battlefield, the Allied air forces played a key role. The triumph was essentially one of a team – infantry, armour, artillery and air power working in harmony, as typified by the little battle for Hotton. Each arm, integrated with the others, was necessary to triumph in the Ardennes.

The Third Reich's convoluted and competitive command chains, with Hitler's cronies and favourites interfering, meant the Fatherland could never match the Allied professionalism and skill in making war. Hitler's forces were destined always to achieve a poor second place. They had their moments of dazzling bravura, but were to shine briefly only with the effect of a solo instrument among a mediocre ensemble, which looked better than it was, led by an ill-tempered bandmaster.

Although defeat lay four months away, the men and *matériel* thrown away in the Ardennes meant that Germany had already lost the Second World War in Europe by the end of the Bulge.

The man responsible more than any other was Eisenhower. He had seen the need for decisive action immediately on 16 December. Like the conductor of a professional symphony orchestra, he had overseen the preparations of the assembled groups of woodwind, brass, percussion, strings and keyboards, all skilled on their own instruments, each section led by their principals. They were well-rehearsed and had already given several virtuoso concerts before they came to their greatest challenge. The conductor sought to resolve personality clashes and rivalries, and worked the artistes hard. The result was the performance of a lifetime.

PART FOUR

37

Beyond the Bulge

'The failure of the Ardennes offensive meant that the war was over. What followed was only the occupation of Germany, delayed somewhat by a confused and impotent resistance.'

Albert Speer[1]

ON 30 DECEMBER 1944, Larry Newman stomped through the freezing snow and mud of Bastogne. 'It was cold as hell,' he recalled. The journalist had just talked with the Third Army's commander: he and Patton had become friends. The general had driven into the beleaguered town to decorate Brigadier-General McAuliffe and Lieutenant-Colonel Chappuis, CO of the 502nd Airborne Infantry, with the Distinguished Service Cross for their leadership in the defence of the town. Newman wore a helmet and was dressed in olive-drab combat gear, but he carried no weapons other than those of his trade – a pencil, notepad and portable typewriter.

Newman had followed Patton's war as a United Press International and International News Service war correspondent ever since the battlefields of North Africa and Sicily. He was in Bastogne to cover the Ardennes campaign, and began by interviewing the general. 'Patton was calm, cool, collected,' Newman recalled. 'It was war to him. What he had been brought up to expect – he had served in World War I, his father graduated from VMI and his grandfather and great uncle had been killed in the Civil War, one in Pickett's Charge, back in 1863 [at Gettysburg].'

Using his maps and reports, Patton described to Newman how the Germans had penetrated deep into Belgium, tearing open a huge dent in the Allied lines, threatening to break through to the north Belgian plain and seize Antwerp. Several papers had already referred to the salient in the Allied lines, but no one knew exactly what to call it.[2] Although the battle was exactly two weeks old, Newman, new on the scene, was about to file his first despatch about it. He needed a new angle. He began to toy with the words Patton had given him on his notepad, etched with his memories of battlegrounds, stories of heroism and sacrifice, flecked with grime and blood from other conflicts.

The phenomenon had been around for as long as military history itself. A precedent had been set already during the First World War when the German front lines had curved in a giant arc around the Belgian city of Ypres throughout 1914–18, leaving an eastwards-facing fist, protruding from the British lines. In that war the Ypres area had been known as 'The Salient'. Newman wanted something different, less formal, and more . . . American. 'I named it the Battle of the Bulge', he remembered modestly.[3]

Within a short space of time, Newman's term had become widely accepted shorthand for the battle. The very next day the US Army's newspaper, *Stars and Stripes*, echoed Newman's UPI report with its own banner headline 'Retake ⅓ of Bulge'. No papers had named the battle in such bold terms before; for example the *Topeka Daily Capital* in Kansas had earlier spoken of the 'Nazi's Salient Into Belgium'. After Newman's story, the entire media seized on the new word and turned it against the Germans. By 15 January the *Baltimore News-Post* proclaimed 'Germans Flee Bulge', without having to qualify the headline in any way. Larry Newman had made his enduring contribution to military history.

'On the seventeenth [of January 1945], I personally congratulated Milliken and Middleton on the successful termination of the Bulge,' wrote Patton at the time, incorporating Newman's vocabulary into his memoirs. 'Although we had not driven the Germans back to the line from which they started, we had on that date begun this final operation.'[4] This was the day after the First and Third Armies finally met outside Houffalize and sealed the Bulge. After that the German defeat was, if it had ever been in doubt, certain. 'Autumn Mist' thus lasted for exactly a month, from 16 December to 16 January.

Some writers have suggested 25 January, though the US Army's official historians cite 28 January as the final day, when the last German detachments still fighting inside the Bulge were eliminated.[5] 'Lightning

Joe' Collins in his autobiography took the view that with Hasbrouck's recapture of St Vith on 23 January, 'While some fighting, chiefly by the Third Army in the southern shoulder, continued until January 28, the Battle of the Bulge was over'.[6] Eisenhower thought it even more abbreviated; in his own 1948 memoir, *Crusade in Europe*, the campaign peters out after the link-up of the First and Third, Ike concluding, 'The losses on both sides in the Battle of the Ardennes were considerable. Field commanders estimated in the month ending 16 January . . .' Eisenhower's son, who wrote an account, entitled *The Bitter Woods*, agreed, stating that on 16 January 'The Bulge had been closed, although the battle was not considered officially over until twelve days later, when the lines were restored to those held before the morning of 16 December.'[7]

However, the young captain and US Army Historian who had witnessed it all, Robert E. Merriam, ended his 1947 account, 'Still fighting the weather as much as the tough German resistance, the two armies moved forward relentlessly, and by early February the Germans were back to the West Wall, along nearly the entire length of the Ardennes front.'[8] At least one military history magazine has discussed the battle being fought between 16 December to 8 February.[9]

A 90th Infantry Division GI, Corporal Edward A. Bennett, of Company 'B', 358th Infantry, is usually reckoned to be the last soldier awarded a Medal of Honor in the Ardennes offensive. When his company was pinned down by machine-gun fire coming from a house in Heckhuscheid, Bennett crawled round the back, killed a German sentry with his trench knife, entered the building and despatched three grenadiers with rifle fire, another three with his .45 pistol and clubbed to death an eighth, allowing the company's advance to continue. However, Bennett's act of valour took place in Heckhuscheid, a village in the Bulge battlefield, defended by the 106th Golden Lions on 16–19 December. His deed took place on 1 February 1945, long after the official closure date of the campaign.

Does ascertaining the real end-date of the Ardennes campaign matter? In terms of arriving at a true figure of the American and German dead, then, yes it should. There will be a small number of personnel from both sides who died after the US Army's closing date of 28 January, whose sacrifices sit outside the official parameters. Apart from the estimated 3,000 Belgian and Luxembourger civilians who perished, hundreds more continued to die from unexploded ordnance in the region, and as late as 1972 a ten-year-old boy fell victim to a wartime hand grenade.[10]

As importantly, in today's era, when the term 'victory' has become more elusive to define, how should we define victory in the Ardennes in 1945? Military tradition has it that the end of a battle occurs when the enemy is driven back to where he started. Yet local historians have assessed that after 25 January some eighty-three towns in the Ardennes region had yet to be liberated by American forces, the last of which – Leithum in northern Luxembourg and Wahlerscheid in Belgium – fell to the US 90th and 9th Divisions respectively on Thursday, 1 February.[11] So perhaps Merriam was closer to the mark in suggesting that the Battle of the Bulge, to use Newman's handy phrase, ended not on 28 January, but on 1 February, if not later.

At the beginning of 1945, Roosevelt and Churchill had shifted their strategic gaze to the Eastern Front and, as an indication of their shared concern over the Ardennes, the latter had cabled Stalin on 6 January: 'The battle in the West is very heavy . . . I shall be grateful to know if you can tell me whether we can count on a major Russian offensive on the Vistula front, or elsewhere, during January . . . I regard this matter as urgent.' The two Western leaders were anxious to see if Stalin was willing to take any pressure off the Ardennes with an attack in the east. The Russian leader replied the following day, 'We are preparing an offensive, but the weather is at present unfavourable. Nevertheless, taking into account the position of our allies on the Western Front, GHQ of the Supreme Command [i.e. Stalin himself] has decided to accelerate the completion of our preparation . . . You may rest assured that we shall do everything possible to render assistance to the glorious forces of our allies.'[12]

Whether or not Stalin actually accelerated anything, the Russian New Year offensive opened with intense fury on 12 January, just as OKH Chief Heinz Guderian had warned. In this sense Stalin was a decided beneficiary of the Battle of the Bulge, with many of the Wehrmacht's best divisions, fresh equipment and most of its armour deployed in the west. Yet there was a sting in the tail for the Western leaders, as there was for anyone negotiating with Stalin. The following month the 'Argonaut' Conference took place between Churchill, Roosevelt and Stalin in the unlikely splendour of the Tsar's former summer residence, later the HQ of Field Marshal von Manstein, the Livadia Palace, at Yalta in the Crimea.

This hugely controversial meeting was held between 4 and 11 February principally to discuss the post-war map of Europe and sparked fierce debate over the future of Poland. Stalin and his team emerged as the clear 'winners', due to a very frail Roosevelt and their constant reminders to the Western leaders of how the Soviet Union had rescued America and Britain militarily in their hour of need. Before this last gathering of the wartime 'Big Three', Churchill had, alas, overplayed his hand in requesting help, when the Bulge had already been won.[13]

Panic, meanwhile, gripped those Germans caught in the east, nearest Stalin's military steamroller. Pushed back, they tried to evacuate as many personnel trapped in East Prussia and occupied Poland as possible. On 30 January 1945, the 25,000-ton *Wilhelm Gustloff*, a German liner packed with German civilians, officials and military personnel, was sunk by a Soviet submarine in the Baltic Sea while evacuating from Gdynia (Gotenhafen). Due to the sheer terror of falling into Soviet hands, the ship was grossly overloaded, with around 10,600 people on board. Most, including 5,000 children, perished, making it the most tragic loss of life in maritime history. Under similar circumstances, a month later the same Russian submarine sank the liner *General von Steuben* on 10 February, sending to their deaths another 4,000 people fleeing the Russians.

Even as Hodges' First and Patton's Third were busy clearing the area of the Bulge, further north Montgomery launched Operation Blackcock on 14 January along the German–Dutch border. Named after the Scottish black male grouse, the concept was to remove General Gustav-Adolf von Zangen's German Fifteenth Army from the eastern banks of the Maas (still the Meuse in various tongues) and out of their bridgehead south-west of the Roer. Miles Dempsey's XII Corps advanced into the so-called Roer Triangle, formed by the Dutch towns of Roermond and Sittard and Heinsberg in Germany, and over twelve days pushed Zangen's forces back further into Germany.

The Fifteenth had been slated for the Ardennes operation, but been forbidden on Hitler's orders from participating; now it was on the receiving end of Allied military activity, regardless. Had it been committed, Zangen's formation would surely have been shredded already in *Herbstnebel*, and it is difficult to see what other German forces could have been summoned to resist Blackcock. In the event, the British 7th Armoured, 43rd (Wessex) and 52nd (Lowland) Divisions and 1st Commando Brigade had completed the operation by 26 January, killing or capturing 2,500 Germans in conditions that mirrored those of the Ardennes, eighty miles to the south.

By this time, Hodges' US First Army, which had been under

Montgomery's control since 19 December, reverted to Bradley's Twelfth Army Group on 17 January, although Simpson's Ninth stayed, for the time being, with Monty. This left Montgomery free to dust off his original plans to reach and cross the northern stretches of the Rhine, as his American colleagues attempted the same further south. In order to clear the western banks in preparation for an assault crossing of the great river, Crerar's First Canadian Army, supported by Horrocks' British XXX Corps, launched Operation Veritable on 8 February. This was designed to start from the area of Groesbeek, south of Nijmegen, which had been in Allied hands since the Market Garden operation of September 1944. Veritable was to break through the Reichswald, a densely wooded area sandwiched between the Meuse and Rhine rivers, some forty miles north of the Roer Triangle.

Apart from a thick tangle of undergrowth – no forestry had been undertaken since 1939 – the huge German state woodland was dominated by artillery, sewn with obstacles and booby traps, and was extremely muddy, which made progress almost as tough and miserable as it had been in the Hürtgen Forest. Veritable had been planned originally for early January, when the ground would have been frozen, thus offering better going for the Allies. There was also a hope that the northern end of the Siegfried Line was less well prepared than elsewhere, offering perhaps a chance to outflank defenders, but the Ardennes campaign delayed Monty's plan by at least a month. By the time of Veritable the terrain had thawed and become a quagmire with the consistency of treacle, and the Germans were fully alert, aware of what was about to happen.

Having studied and walked part of the Veritable operation with a British military staff ride in early December 2000, I can confirm that at that time of year conditions in the Reichswald – as in all the forests of the region – are awful. In 1945 snow covered the Wehrmacht's mines sewn the previous autumn. In 2000, armed with period combat maps on which the German positions were fully annotated, I encountered a hard forest floor which immediately gave way when I applied my whole body weight. Within seconds I was up to my knees in freezing mud, and would have sunk further had I been carrying a full battle load. Fortunately I had friends on hand to haul me out and strong, hot coffee to revive me, but in 1945 the Canadians, with supporting British troops, were also under direct threat from machine guns and indirect fire from mortars, never mind artillery shells, which burst among the tree tops, raining down red-hot needles of shrapnel everywhere.

Decades later, the undergrowth still contained the contours of anti-tank ditches, coils of rusty barbed wire which threatened nasty wounds, an unexploded mortar bomb and, deeper into the woods, one former German gun position yielded a couple of shellcases poking out of the loam. Nearby in an old foxhole was a battered mess tin of the pattern supplied to British or Canadian troops. Made of aluminium, its date of manufacture was clearly visible – 1944. Alongside was a decaying GI-issued pocket heater known as the M-42 Coleman stove after the company headquartered in Wichita, Kansas, which produced millions for US military use from 1942. The forerunner of most modern camping stoves, this one no doubt had been traded by a GI and subsequently abandoned or lost by its new owner. It made the point as graphically as my adventure with the mud that soldiers needed hot food and drinks to keep going in those wintry conditions.

Among the several accompanying veterans, Captain Ian C. Hammerton of the 22nd Dragoons was awarded a Military Cross for his command of a troop of five Sherman flail (demining) tanks. Although very effective and capable of detonating anti-personnel mines and booby traps ('which went off like firecrackers'), and Teller (anti-tank) mines buried up to six inches underground, Hammerton recalled his tanks were 'useless in thick forests. They broke their tracks on the numerous felled trees,' he remembered, and were more vulnerable to sinking into the muddy floor of the Reichswald – as I had done – than to German fire. Flail tanks (which incorporated a rotating drum of chains, forward of the vehicle, which beat the ground to detonate mines) were used by the British, but much less so by the US Army.

Operation Veritable was the northern part of a pincer movement, with Operation Grenade, its southern jaw, designed to be launched simultaneously. The actors in this latter drama were Simpson's US Ninth Army, but the Germans, meanwhile, had released the waters retained by the Roer dams and floods prevented any military activity until the levels subsided, forcing Simpson to attack late, on 23 February. Nevertheless the speed with which he attained his objectives illustrated the exhausted nature of the Wehrmacht, its energy spent earlier in the Bulge. Simpson's GIs soon made up for lost time, erecting over a dozen bridges across the Roer, south of Heinsberg, with sixteen battalions on the far bank by nightfall of the first day. This was exactly the kind of operation Brandenberger's German Seventh Army had been trying to achieve two months earlier, but were hampered by the lack of air cover or bridging units.

Before Veritable was complete the Allied air forces left their mark on German soil in a way that has never been forgotten. Dresden, medieval capital of Saxony, was attacked by four air raids between 13 and 15 February, when 1,250 RAF and USAAF bombers dropped more than 3,900 tons of high-explosives and incendiaries on the city. The resultant firestorm destroyed over 1,600 acres of urban landscape and killed around 25,000 civilians. Other raids followed, but subsequent commentators have noted that the city, about the size of Manchester, England, had at the time been the largest remaining unbombed city left in Germany. 'The intentions of the attack are to hit the enemy where he will feel it most, behind an already partially collapsed front . . . and incidentally to show the Russians when they arrive what Bomber Command can do,' observed a contemporary RAF briefing document.[14]

Unbeknownst to the Allied airmen, below in the city were many US prisoners of war, captured in the Ardennes, on work details; among them was PFC Kurt Vonnegut from the 423rd Infantry Regiment of the Golden Lions Division, taken captive on the Schnee Eifel during 19 December. His experience of being locked in a concrete abattoir during the raids and of retrieving the remains of German civilian victims afterwards gave rise to his surreal 1969 novel, *Slaughterhouse Five.* Endlessly discussed in college classes the world over, Vonnegut's literary offering ensures that Dresden will always remain a disturbing footnote to the Allies' prosecution of the war.

Even though it was obvious that the Canadians, British, French and Americans would shortly reach the west bank of the Rhine, Hitler insisted that his troops fight their corner in a series of pointless delaying actions rather than bolster the defences east of the Rhine. Veritable took two weeks to emerge from the Reichswald, just as Simpson was launching Grenade, whereupon the northern offensive was renewed as Operation Blockbuster and finally linked up with the US Ninth Army near Geldern on 4 March. The day before, the town of Krefeld, a port lying on the west bank of the Rhine and north-west of Düsseldorf, had fallen to the US 84th (Railsplitters) Division, part of Simpson's Ninth Army. Order needed to be restored to the town's 200,000 inhabitants quickly, so the only GI in Divisional Intelligence who spoke German (the rest knew French) was promoted to become Administrator of Krefeld, in charge of everything from gas, water, power and transportation to garbage and hunting war criminals. The fact that he was a mere private mattered not; within eight days he had rebuilt Krefeld's civilian government: the name of this multi-talented individual was Henry A. Kissinger.[15]

Eisenhower and Montgomery acknowledged the Rhineland as 'some of the fiercest fighting of the whole war', as they approached Germany's traditional western barrier, where those *Fallschirmjäger* left from the Bulge and elsewhere 'fought with a fanaticism un-excelled at any time in the war', thought Captain Hammerton, who had served at the front since D-Day. Fighting continued as the Germans retained a bridgehead at Wesel to evacuate men and as much equipment as possible, but on 10 March the German withdrawal ended and the last bridges over the northern Rhine were destroyed. The three-month 1945 battles for the Rhineland, incorporating Blackcock, Veritable, Grenade and Blockbuster, had cost the Germans dear; their total losses may have been as high as 400,000 men, of whom 280,000 were prisoners.

Various crossings of the Rhine followed rapidly and inevitably. To a certain extent, ever since the formation of SHAEF Eisenhower had anticipated two massive battles for his Allied forces. First was the invasion of France, followed by a crossing of the Rhine. No one had anticipated the events would be separated by as much as nine months. As Montgomery established his men along the west bank of the Rhine, he put the finishing touches to Operation Plunder, his plan to propel the Twenty-First Army Group across the river and into northern Germany. Bradley, meanwhile – still smarting from criticism of his handling of the Ardennes – prepared to execute his own scheme to cross and advance beyond the Rhine: Operation Lumberjack, starting on 1 March.

Far bolder in concept, Bradley's concept was for his armies to forge across the Rhine and seize the industrial towns along the river, surrounding the large number of Germans known to be defending the industrial heartland of the Ruhr – the remnants of Field Marshal Model's Army Group 'B'. To Bradley's mind, this presented an alternative strategy which would seize territory and immobilise most of the remaining Wehrmacht forces in the west, in contrast to Monty's plan of thrusting deep into north-eastern Germany. Despite Eisenhower's warnings that Berlin was not an objective of the Western Allies, Bradley and Monty may still have interpreted what had become a personal rivalry in terms of an American-British race towards the German capital. In the event, Lumberjack became a starting pistol which saw US VII Corps reach the banks of the Rhine opposite Cologne on 5 March, while, to the south, US III Corps advanced to Bonn and Remagen.

The Allies anticipated a huge setpiece river crossing, but an unforeseen opportunity arrived when the defenders failed to destroy the Ludendorff railway bridge at Remagen. The crossing, as its name implied, dated back to 1916, and was built to enhance the flow of personnel and logistics to the Western Front, a role it also fulfilled during the Ardennes offensive, with one track planked over to allow vehicular traffic. By early March it remained the last intact bridge across the Rhine, necessary because of the 75,000 troops from Zangen's Fifteenth and Manteuffel's Fifth Panzer Armies who were defending the western banks. Hitler ordered that the bridge be readied for demolition but blown at the last possible moment. Such an action is a complicated military manoeuvre known as a 'reserve demolition', whereby destruction is achieved when the opponent is approaching, or on, the object concerned, usually a crossing. Blown too early, friendly troops can be left on the wrong side; destroyed too late and the opposing force might have a chance to rush across.

Such was the case at 3.40 p.m. on 7 March, when, seeing American troops on the Ludendorff bridge, Hauptmann Bratge, the engineer officer with the defenders, detonated the explosive charges attached to the structure. There was a tremendous explosion as witnesses saw the bridge physically lift into the air before smoke and dust obscured the site. When the air cleared, the Ludendorff bridge remained standing, much to the Germans' consternation: the explosives supplied had not been powerful enough to destroy it. Minutes afterwards, GIs of the US 9th Armored Division – whom we met in the Ardennes – led by Lieutenant Karl H. Timmermann, had fought their way across the still-smoking bridge. Despite efforts to contest the area, the structure had fallen into the hands of the 27th Armored Infantry Battalion, and the defence surrendered at 5.15 p.m. Within twenty-four hours most of the 9th Armored had been rushed across with other formations following. The initiative to try and storm the Ludendorff came from Timmermann's superior, Brigadier-General William Hoge, leading Combat Command 'B', whom we met defending St Vith, with Bruce C. Clarke of the 4th Armored Division.

The first of Timmermann's men across the bridge – and thus the first Allied soldier to reach the eastern bank of the Rhine – was Sergeant Alexander A. Drabik. His background and that of his company commander, Timmermann, neatly illustrated the chaotic story of some European migrants to America, for Drabik's parents had been born in Poland, and Timmermann, raised in Nebraska, was the son of a US soldier of German ancestry on post-war occupation duty, and his German war bride. Both GIs had been wounded in the defence of St Vith, but since returned to duty. Some of Timmermann's colleagues had been captured by Peiper's *Kampfgruppe* and executed at Malmedy. Three months later, these two former Europeans were able to turn the tables on their tormentors in spectacular fashion at Remagen, which brought both men Distinguished Service Crosses. Eisenhower called their act 'worth its weight in gold . . . one of those bright opportunities of war which, when quickly and firmly grasped, produce incalculable effects on future operations'.[16]

Meanwhile, persuaded he was surrounded by traitors, a vengeful Hitler ordered loyal Nazis to court-martial the local German commanders at Remagen; five were condemned to death. The Wehrmacht engineer responsible for blowing the bridge, Bratge, escaped because he was a prisoner in American hands, but the area's defenders, Majors Scheller, Kraft and Strobel, and Leutnant Peters, were executed for no more than being in the wrong place at the wrong time. In 1967 a legal review exonerated the officers.[17] Although the bridge is now gone – weakened by the failed detonation and subsequent German bombing to destroy it, including raids by V-2 rockets, it collapsed into the river exactly ten days later, killing or wounding 121 US engineers in the vicinity; a very good museum at the site tells the drama of its capture and subsequent demise.

I have often visited this stretch of the Rhine, and enjoyed the company of a former Bundeswehr colonel, Hans-Joachim Krug, commissioned into the Wehrmacht in 1944, who lives in Linz, opposite Remagen on the east bank. His father was a resourceful and distinguished Wehrmacht colonel who had commanded a bunker behind a British beach on D-Day. Krug junior has built his delightful retirement home amidst some of the former gun positions overlooking the river and knows the story of the bridge in intimate detail. 'It's all about leadership,' he mused one day to me when discussing Timmermann, surrounded by military history books and hunting trophies. 'The junior leader can still make a difference in a big war. You call such a man "the strategic corporal". It is good that individuals can still make a difference.'[18] He is right. Soldiers need to know they can influence events by their determination and professionalism.

Field Marshal Gerd von Rundstedt has threaded his way through our story several times as *Oberbefehlshaber West*, but, following the loss of the Ludendorff railway bridge, the Führer was looking for scapegoats.

On 9 March Hitler phoned Rundstedt from Berlin to reveal he had assigned Albert Kesselring, formerly supreme commander in Italy, to replace him. This was little more than shuffling the deckchairs on the *Titanic*, but Rundstedt was probably happy enough to hang up his field marshal's baton after a military career of fifty-two years. There was a final audience with Hitler on 11 March, whereupon he turned his back on the 'Bohemian Corporal' whom he loathed so much and retreated to a sanatorium in Bad Tölz, becoming a prisoner of the 36th Texas Division on 1 May. Generalfeldmarschall 'Smiling Albert' Kesselring inherited three army groups ('H' under Blaskowitz in the north, in the centre and the most numerous was Model's 'B', and to the south, SS-Gruppenführer Paul Hausser's Army Group 'G'), all three amounting to no more than twenty-six divisions. At the same time there were an estimated 214 German divisions fighting the Russians, though many were divisions in name only.

Perhaps the US Army was the appropriate force to deal with the spontaneous gift of a bridge across the Rhine. On 19 March, Patton, who had been fighting through the Palatinate, received a directive from Bradley to take the water barrier 'on the run'. His Third Army obliged on the night of 22 March, crossing by hasty assault south of Mainz at Oppenheim, just before midnight; Patton had just beaten his old sparring partner Monty across the great river. On 24 March, Patton recorded how he drove to the Rhine and went across the pontoon bridge just completed by the 540th Combat Engineers, in the middle 'stopping to spit in the river'.

This was an expression of his unbridled joy at finally crossing the iconic waterway, but what he meant (and was corrected in later editions of his posthumous memoirs) was that the Third Army commander halted to take a piss in the fast-flowing waters, a much-photographed event. Ever the dramatist, when Patton reached the far side '[I] deliberately stubbed my toe and fell, picking up a handful of German soil in emulation of Scipio Africanus and William the Conqueror, who both stumbled and both made a joke of it, saying, "I see in my hands the soil of Africa", or ". . . the soil of England". I saw in my hands the soil of Germany.'[19] Opposition had been light and within twenty-four hours the entire US 5th Division had crossed. The following day, Patton's men made another Rhine crossing near Worms.

Montgomery preferred his setpiece, carefully rehearsed attacks and was personally far less inclined to be flexible. His Twenty-First Army

Group, including the Canadian First, British Second and US Ninth Armies, began its offensive nearly two weeks after the Remagen drama, with Operation Plunder. This was his assault crossing of the Rhine at Rees and Wesel, where the river was twice as wide and holding a far higher volume of water than at Remagen. Plunder began at 9.00 p.m. on 23 March, and soon had over 16,000 British and American troops across in bridgeheads on the eastern bank. The troops used landing craft, US-manufactured Buffalos (also known as Alligators), DD tanks and other amphibious craft.[20]

Monty's preparations were extensive: for the crossing, 8,000 Royal Engineers deployed with 22,000 tons of assault bridging, including 25,000 wooden pontoons, 2,650 assault boats of varying types, 120 river tugs, 80 miles of balloon cable and 260 miles of steel wire rope. Number 159 Wing of the RAF deployed balloon barrage personnel to operate winches that hauled ferries and rafts; even the Royal Navy provided teams to construct anti-mine booms to prevent floating mines from destroying Monty's pontoon bridges. The comparatively light casualty rate experienced by the 153rd and 154th Brigades of 51st Highland Division, the first troops across, supported by Staffordshire Yeomanry swimming Shermans, may have justified the field marshal's caution, but German strength and morale had largely evaporated already.[21]

In addition, the largest Special Forces deployment of the war was mounted by the British Special Air Service (SAS) in Operation Archway. This consisted of two reinforced SAS squadrons, 300 personnel mounted in seventy-five armed jeeps and trucks, who slid across the Rhine on 25 March. Their mission was deep reconnaissance of the German rear, seeking out centres of resistance; one group stumbled on the Bergen-Belsen concentration camp, and their remit widened to hunting down war criminals.

There are several interesting parallels between the planned river crossings of the opening phase of *Herbstnebel* and Montgomery's later crossings of the Rhine, as executed in Operation Plunder. Both were assault river crossings against an opponent in prepared defensive positions, launched under conditions of surprise. Both employed Special Forces units operating behind the lines, though in the case of Archway the SAS wore their own uniforms. Though Hitler's obsessions with operational security preserved the secret but compromised any meaningful training or build-up of logistics and reserves, Monty managed the opposite. His forces trained extensively and were well-resourced. One may draw the inevitable conclusion that Hitler in December 1944, with weather on his side and a complacent opponent, could have risked trading some of his secrecy for training, giving his armies more of a fighting chance than they had.

Plunder was complemented early the following morning by Operation Varsity, which saw the US 17th and British 6th Airborne Divisions – both veterans of the Bulge – dropped simultaneously from a single aerial lift, unlike deployments in Normandy and Arnhem which constituted several waves, hours or even days apart. The huge airborne effort consisted of 1,696 transport planes – mainly C-47 Dakotas and C-46 Curtiss Commandos, towing 1,348 gliders, protected by 1,000 escorting fighters – a total of no fewer that 4,000 aircraft. In addition, 120 Liberators overflew the area dropping supplies shortly after the landings.

Churchill insisted on being present (on the small knoll where he stationed himself with Brooke, the CIGS) and watched the aerial armada, which stretched for more than 200 miles and took over two and a half hours to pass. It inspired those attacking and demoralised the German defenders, as it was designed to do. Altogether, in the four days of Plunder and Varsity, Montgomery suffered 7,000 casualties including 1,000 dead – not far removed from the losses of D-Day; tragic figures so close to the end of the war, but far less than he had any right to expect.

It also conveyed a message to the Russian liaison officers attached to the various Allied headquarters. The sight was even more impressive than Normandy (where the weather obscured the aerial armada); it was a fantastic display of Anglo-Canadian-American raw military muscle, never since as numerous as it was then, and staged – reading between the lines – simply because the Allies could. (I witnessed something similar during the closing days of Operation Iraqi Freedom in 2003, when there were many attempts to deploy hitherto uncommitted forces or introduce new weapons, not necessarily because they were needed but because of a general sense that the war-fighting phase of the invasion was about to end.)

Later that evening, Churchill recorded how Montgomery controlled his battle, via his liaison officers, just as he had done in the Ardennes.

> At 8.00 p.m., we repaired to the map wagon . . . for nearly two hours a succession of young officers, of about the rank of major, presented themselves. Each had come back from a different sector of the front. They were the direct personal representatives of the Commander-in-Chief, and

> could go anywhere and see anything and ask any questions they liked of any commander, whether at divisional headquarters or with the forward troops. As in turn they made their reports and were searchingly questioned by their chief the whole story of the day's battle was unfolded. This gave Monty a complete account of what had happened by highly competent men whom he knew well and whose eyes he trusted.[22]

Churchill's account is not only illuminating about Montgomery's style of command, but full of wistfulness; these were exactly the kind of duties he had performed as a very junior officer in 1897 on the North West Frontier (of modern Pakistan), a year later at Omdurman and subsequently in the Boer War. The whiff of cordite was part of the British Prime Minister's very being, and, having been banned from witnessing D-Day from a warship, he had fought hard to be present for the Rhine crossing.

To the surprise of all, the crossings had not been greatly contested by General Alfred Schlemm's First Parachute Army, perhaps reflecting the state of German morale. 'My dear General', Churchill is said to have observed to Eisenhower when the pair conferred on the morning of 25 March, 'the German is whipped. We've got him. He is all through.' The moment Ike departed, Churchill crossed the Rhine with Monty in a landing craft. His setting foot on the eastern bank of the river symbolised the arrival of Britain's senior politician across the traditional border of Germany – an obstacle no hostile army since Napoleon's had managed to traverse in war.

There was a second symbolic act Churchill felt obliged to perform, conveniently overlooked in his memoirs but attested to by those present. When he had reached the Rhine's eastern bank, Churchill, like Patton the day before, also urinated into the waters, an act that seems to have been pretty universal from the lowest private to general or prime minister (excepting, so far as we know, Montgomery). Later in the day the Prime Minister started to clamber across the tangled railway bridge at Wesel under German artillery enemy fire. Churchill, aged seventy, greatly enjoyed the thrill of being under fire again, but for Eisenhower this adventure was too daring. The latter noted that had he been present he would never have permitted Churchill to cross the river, just as he had banned Churchill from the D-Day beaches.[23]

Meanwhile, further south at Remagen, the US 9th Armored Division and other units had been striving to break out of the bridgehead they had forged earlier in the month. Four panzer formations were sent there by a furious Hitler and led by the erstwhile commander of Panzer Lehr in the Ardennes, Fritz Bayerlein. By this time, the Lehr numbered a pathetic 300 men and fifteen tanks; it was accompanied by the 9th Panzer Division of 600 men and fifteen tanks, 106th Panzer Brigade with just five panzers, while the most numerous was the 11th Panzer Division with 4,000 men, twenty-five tanks and eighteen artillery pieces. They had managed to bottle up the intrepid GIs at Remagen, but had no gasoline to counter-attack.[24] On 25 March the US forces finally broke out of Remagen, just as the Dempsey's British Second Army subdued all resistance at Wesel, eighty miles north. Events moved on at a huge pace, and on the following day Patton's Third Army captured Darmstadt and Main, allowing a link-up with General Alexander M. Patch's US Seventh Army, who had also crossed the Rhine near Worms.

The following evening witnessed an extraordinary attempt to infiltrate an American armoured column fifty miles behind German lines, and to reach and liberate US Army captives incarcerated in a prison camp. The purpose was to free Patton's son-in-law, Lieutenant-Colonel John K. Waters, being held near Hammelburg. Patton personally assigned the mission, which is said to have inspired the equally bizarre 1970 movie *Kelly's Heroes* (starring Clint Eastwood and Telly Savalas), to Lieutenant-Colonel Creighton Abrams' Combat Command 'B' of the 4th Armored Division, whom we last met at Bastogne. Led by Captain Abraham Baum, the task force of 300 men and fifty-seven tanks, jeeps and half-tracks reached the camp, but were surrounded on the return journey; most were captured and very few returned unwounded. A furious Eisenhower reprimanded Patton and the failed raid was thereafter shrouded in secrecy. The mission nevertheless reveals much about Patton's sheer boldness as well as his humanity.

A final humiliation for Germany was the arrival on 31 March of Général Jean de Lattre de Tassigny's US-equipped French First Army, who had landed in Provence during August 1944 as part of Operation Dragoon, and fought their way through France, liberating the country as they went. Operation Undertone was General Jacob Devers' Sixth Army Group (comprising the US Seventh and French First Armies) plan to occupy Germany up to the west bank of the Rhine, largely fought against Hausser's Army Group 'G' and the southern equivalent of Bradley's Operation Lumberjack. Assisted by Patton's Third Army on their left who outflanked the German defenders, Undertone reached the area of Karlsruhe within ten days; then, on the last day of March, de Tassigny's Frenchmen crossed the Rhine near Speyer, the first to do so since Napoleon's *Grande Armée.*

For all but the most fanatic of Nazis, the Reich's main effort now became to hold the Russians in the east for as long as possible in order to get as many soldiers and civilians to the west. Since the opening of the New Year's Russian offensive on 12 January, the Red Army had advanced almost unchecked through eastern Poland and up to the German border itself. By 28 March, Dempsey's British Second Army had begun their offensive eastwards towards the River Elbe, as Simpson's Ninth, which had remained under British command since the battle of the Bulge, moved on as the upper arm of the Ruhr encirclement.

It was immediately obvious to all outside the *Führerbunker* in Berlin that the end was near, though for how much longer the fighting would last no one could tell.

38

On to Berlin!

At the end of the Yalta conference Churchill and Roosevelt left for the Middle East. On 15 February Churchill again met the US President aboard the heavy cruiser USS *Quincy*. As Churchill observed, 'The President seemed placid and frail. I felt that he had a slender contract with life.'[1] He was right. Exhausted by the war, but with the end in sight, Roosevelt was in need of a rest. He travelled to the 'Little White House', his cottage in Warm Springs, Georgia, for a fortnight of relaxation before the founding conference of the United Nations. At 1.00 p.m. on 12 April Roosevelt was in the living room of his cottage surrounded by friends and family, having his portrait painted. The conversation was lively, the atmosphere congenial.

The president turned to the artist, and having reminded her that they had only fifteen minutes left, suddenly announced, 'I have a terrific pain in the back of my head'. He slumped forward unconscious, and died very shortly afterwards of a massive cerebral haemorrhage. Despite the fact that most Americans knew he was not a well man, suffering from polio since 1921, the president's death was met with great shock and grief around the world – particularly among the GIs serving in Europe, whom he had brought through the Great Depression; they had barely known another president within their lifetimes. Many, hardened in combat, nevertheless broke down in tears.

The extent of FDR's paralysis had been kept secret – he was never seen in a wheelchair in public, for example – but his declining health had not been obvious. His relative youth made the event more tragic – he was only sixty-three. He had been elected to the White House in November 1932, two months before Hitler came to power in Germany, when thirteen million Americans were unemployed. After twelve years in office, several of them under the added stress of steering his nation through a world conflict, Roosevelt was simply worn out. Harry Truman immediately acceded to the White House, but had only become vice-president on 20 January, replacing Henry A. Wallace, who thus missed being the thirty-third President of the United States by eighty-two days.

The day after Roosevelt's death, the Red Army captured Vienna. Bradley's Twelfth Army Group had fanned out, with Hodges' US First Army advancing as the southern limb creeping around the Ruhr pocket. On 4 April, the encirclement was completed, with Hodges' and Simpson's armies linking up, whereupon Simpson and his army reverted to Bradley's command. Field Marshal Model had placed the bulk of his Army Group 'B' in the Ruhr because he was convinced the Allies would aim straight for this important manufacturing heartland. Instead, his army group, which had given the Western Allies so much trouble since Normandy, was trapped in the Ruhr pocket and its 325,000 remaining soldiers became prisoners. Among the defenders of the Rhine pushed back towards the Ruhr was Hauptmann Otto Carius, who had received his Knight's Cross from Himmler the previous year. Commanding a company of massive *Jagdtigers* (seventy-ton assault guns armed with a 128mm cannon), he surrendered his unit to US forces on 15 April.

Blind to military logic, Hitler had blamed Model for the failure in the Ardennes, and on 21 January issued an order overriding the field marshal's authority, and asserting that in future all the divisions of Army Group 'B' would be personally responsible to him. By then, Hitler was making insane pronouncements. The capture of the Remagen bridge compounded Model's 'guilt', and when, in early April, Model's formation was surrounded in the Ruhr, Hitler's malevolent response was to forbid surrender or attempts to break out, and order the destruction of the area's economic infrastructure. Model saw this for what it was – a death sentence to future German generations – and for the first time in his life he deliberately disobeyed his Führer.

Instead of fighting on, he disbanded his army group, discharging from military service the oldest and youngest and granting the remainder permission to surrender or break out, which caused the ultra-loyal Goebbels to denounce the entire formation, Model included, as traitors to the Reich. This left any defence in the west up to *ad hoc* garrisons consisting of a few Wehrmacht professionals, armed police, roving SS squads, Luftwaffe *Flak* units, *Volkssturm*, Hitler Youth and a miscellany of menacing Nazi Party auxiliaries. Most coordinated resistance had broken down – some towns and cities resisted, many did not. Everything Model had stood for was in tatters, and the regime he had fought for disowned him. His conflicts of loyalty and fears of war crimes trials in Russia led him to shoot himself on 21 April. Ten years later, as his son Brigadier-General Hans-Georg Model, a retired Bundeswehr officer related to me, the field marshal's remains were recovered from his lonely woodland grave and he now shares a military headstone with the anonymous Hermann Henschke in the Vossenack Soldiers' Cemetery near to the Hürtgen Forest.[2]

At this stage SHAEF feared a large-scale last stand by SS fanatics from an 'Alpine Redoubt' in the mountains of Bavaria and Austria. This was National Socialist propaganda – the fruit of Himmler's and Goebbels' overactive imagination – but SHAEF's G-2 Department, led by General Kenneth Strong, was determined not to be caught out a second time as they had been by the Ardennes attack. Noel Annan, the intelligence officer at SHAEF, recalled the rumours that 'desperadoes in disguise, called werewolves, were said to be planning sabotage and assassinations; a werewolf headquarters was said to have been captured. Strong excused himself for taking these phantoms seriously by saying that after the Ardennes he would not risk another miscalculation of German resistance.'[3] It gave the Russians an excuse – if one was needed – to execute or deport around 10,000 young German males, who may or may not have been complicit, but much (unnecessary as it turned out) Allied attention was thus shifted towards southern Germany.

Stores, currency and weapons were certainly secreted away and no doubt impressive quantities still lie concealed in salt mines and other hidden venues, providing plots for future novelists, but the werewolves amounted to little more than angry Hitler Youth scattering nails and glass on German roads. In reality, they were a distant echo of Churchill's Auxiliary Units, set up in 1940 to sabotage and cause mayhem in a German-occupied Britain. Colonel-General Nikolai Berzarin, Soviet commandant of Berlin, died in suspicious circumstances, and Bremen's US Military Police HQ blew up, which may have been an accident; a few unfortunate jeep crews were decapitated by wires stretched across country roads; the Allied governor of Aachen was assassinated; and one of Montgomery's liaison officers, Major John Poston, was ambushed and killed on 21 April 1945, but these were isolated incidents rather than a coordinated national movement. In truth, German citizens were sick of war.

Meanwhile, another formation had arrived in Europe, the US Fifteenth Army, and Lieutenant-General Leonard Gerow was promoted from V Corps to command it. Its task from mid-January 1945 was rehabilitating, re-equipping and training various units of Bradley's army group that had suffered heavy losses during the Ardennes campaign. The Fifteenth also processed all new units arriving into theatre and on 15 March it assumed command of the forces that were bottling up the German forces left behind in the French Atlantic ports. Later on, with Simpson's Ninth, it contained and then helped capture the 325,000 Army Group 'B' soldiers trapped in the Ruhr pocket, later taking on responsibility for processing many displaced persons (DPs), the forced civilian labourers roaming the Reich, often armed, sometimes disease-ridden and frequently dangerous.

Most Wehrmacht prisoners were interned in nineteen *Rheinwiesenlager* (Rhine meadow camps), overseen by the US Army. These eventually held between one and two million German troops, until demobilised by September 1945. Controversially, they were not designated Prisoners of War (PW), but Disarmed Enemy Forces (DEF) and thus not subject to protection by the Geneva Convention. The huge numbers defeated US attempts at administration and prisoners were left to run their own camps, with maybe as many as 10,000 (one historian has alleged a million, which cannot be right) dying from starvation, disease, dehydration and exposure because of poor sanitation and the lack of buildings – most lived in Wehrmacht or GI-issued tentage.[4]

This may seem shocking in the twenty-first century (a 1969 US military review would admit grave shortcomings), but in the context of the concentration camps, personally witnessed by many GIs – when Patton toured the Ohrdruf prison camp, near Weimar with Bradley and Ike on 12 April, the tough-as-nails general allegedly vomited – 'factories of murder' as one still-distressed GI tried to explain to me, the vengeful mood was understandable.

On 18 April, war photographer Lee Miller had followed the US 2nd Infantry Division into Leipzig, where she came across a young infantry captain who had taken the surrender of the entire metropolis. This caused huge problems as his tiny force could not cope with the number of prisoners, or the daunting prospect of temporarily running a major city. He was Charles MacDonald, whom we first met dodging German bullets on 16 December.[5] Ironically, the last Nazi diehards had dug in around the giant 300-foot memorial commemorating an earlier battle for Leipzig – the 'Battle of the Nations' which saw an earlier coalition of Russia, Prussia, Austria and Sweden beat Napoleon around the city in October 1813.

Nearby at the same time was Lieutenant-Colonel J. Strom Thurmond, the Civil Affairs officer who had landed by glider on D-Day with the 82nd Airborne Division. Recently awarded a Bronze Star, the former judge was totally unprepared for the scenes of horror when he entered Buchenwald concentration camp south-west of the city: 'I had never seen such inhumane acts in my life. I couldn't dream of treating men in such a manner,' he recollected. The future Senator from South Carolina thought, 'It was awful. It was very difficult to say what effect it has on anybody, but it's an experience you never would forget'.[6]

Later on in April, the US First and Ninth Armies came level with the Elbe river, the demarcation zone between the Western and Russian forces agreed at Yalta, and Patton's Third Army had stretched into western Czechoslovakia, Bavaria and northern Austria. Devers' Sixth Army Group headed south-west, into Austria and northern Italy; the Black Forest and Baden were overrun by the French First Army. Meanwhile, the British and Canadians had moved north-east towards Hamburg, crossing the River Elbe and on towards Denmark and the Baltic. Much controversy exists as to whether American forces should have strayed beyond the Elbe, but this was never Eisenhower's call to make.

Ike had formally communicated to Stalin on 28 March that he was not interested in taking Berlin. He and Bradley were subsequently much criticised by their fellow countrymen for holding off an attack on the German capital, but his many critics were (and remain) only vocal because of the gift of hindsight: in April 1945 the Cold War was still distant, and neither general wanted to be held responsible for the tens of thousands of GI casualties Berlin would have cost. Stalin's 1 April response to Eisenhower was that he was not interested in Berlin either, stating, 'Berlin has lost its strategic importance. Only secondary forces will be allotted to its capture . . . The main thrust by Soviet forces will begin in the second half of May.' He lied, and on the same day, in what some historians have termed the world's largest 'April Fool', the Russian leader immediately tasked Koniev and Zhukov, his two most competitive and aggressive field commanders, to seize the city, now knowing he had a free hand.

However, Eisenhower was not alone in failing to see the writing on the wall in terms of future East–West relations. At the end of April, with idle US forces on the Czech frontier, Ike proposed liberating Prague, alone of all the capitals of central Europe yet to be freed. Despite the fact that there were no Soviet troops within seventy miles of the Czech capital, Ike's suggestion was met by violent protest from Stalin – Czechoslovakia was to be in the Soviet sphere of interest and Czech gratitude to America for its liberation would not be welcome in Moscow.[7] When asked on 8 May by journalists, 'General, why didn't we take Prague?' Patton observed without further comment, 'I can tell you exactly why . . . Because we were ordered not to', which told the world all it needed to know.[8]

Stalin was amazed that American incursions into southern Germany and up to the Czech border hadn't met more resistance; in fact there was precious little German will, or the means with which to oppose the US Army – but the ever-paranoid Stalin thought otherwise. He assumed the Nazis and Americans were doing 'some kind of a deal' together at his expense. In one of the small patrols from the Russian and US armies that eventually made contact around noon on 25 April on the Elbe was PFC Igor Belousovitch of the US Sixty-Ninth Division, who could so easily have been one of the Russian Cossack detachment he met. His parents were Russians who had fled the Revolution, first to Shanghai, where Igor was born in 1922, then to America.[9]

The Russian troops, wearing fur hats and sporting their medals, glinting in the sun, on their combat tunics, marvelled at the American armour. Unaware that the Sherman tanks operated by many Red Army units had been built in the United States and shipped in convoys to the USSR, the Russians wondered why the US Army were using tanks manufactured by the Soviet people. Their leaders never told them about Lend-Lease.

The union of the armies meant that Germany was a Reich no longer. It had been sliced in two. The following day, 26 April, Major-Generals Emil Reinhardt and Vladimir Rusakov, commanders of the US 69th Infantry Division of Hodges' First Army and the 58th Guards Rifle Division of General Aleksei Zhadov's Russian Fifth Guards Army respectively, met formally at Torgau, south-west of Berlin. This was an important propaganda event for both sides, Soviet and American, and rare

35mm colour footage exists of the iconic moment 'when East met West', as the specially painted signboards proclaimed. The movie cameraman was Lieutenant-Colonel George Stevens, a Hollywood professional who had left the world of movies in 1942 to serve overseas. He formed SPECOU (the Special Coverage Unit of the US Army Signal Corps), better known as the Hollywood Irregulars, and his six hours of spectacular Second World War colour (not colourised) footage is unique, only seeing the light of day after his death in 1975.[10]

Adolf Hitler had celebrated his fifty-sixth birthday in the Berlin Reich Chancellery – where the final details of *Herbstnebel* had been decided – on 20 April, the last occasion that most of the old guard turned up to congratulate him. Earlier, on 16 April, Russian troops had forced their way across the River Oder and started punching their way through the final Wehrmacht positions protecting Berlin on the Seelow Heights. To take Berlin – ever since Stalingrad a Russian dream, whatever the US and British aspirations were – the Soviets had some 2.5 million troops available, equivalent to all the Western armies put together, 6,250 tanks and 7,500 aircraft. This was a prize to be attained regardless of human lives or material destruction.

By the 19th the defenders were streaming back and, on Hitler's birthday, for the first time Russian guns could be heard bombarding the capital. The following day the first Soviet tanks began poking through the city's outskirts. An unwelcome birthday present was the news that Nuremberg, symbolic cradle of the Third Reich and defended by 7,000 fanatics, had fallen to the US Seventh Army, with the Stars and Stripes flying over Adolf Hitler Platz that very day. Photographer Lee Miller stopped by its remains, levelled by the Allied air forces, where she felt, 'This is the first German city or possession of any kind I feel sorry for having wrecked' – but that was before she encountered Dachau.[11]

On 25 April, Zhukov had closed his ring of steel around the capital: there was no way out. For many German and Russian soldiers this would be a fight to the death. There are many conspiracy theories as to what finally happened to the German leader, but it appears that, as the security situation deteriorated, Hitler and his entourage withdrew into the *Führerbunker* complex beneath the Chancellery. With the nearest Russian troops about two hundred yards away, after midnight on 29 April, Hitler married his long-term mistress Eva Braun in a small civil ceremony and the following day at about 3.30 p.m. the pair committed suicide, Hitler by gunshot, his new wife by poison. His death coincided with the capture by three US divisions of the birthplace of Nazism, Munich.

One of the few witnesses to Hitler's last days was Hans Krebs, Model's chief of staff at Army Group 'B' throughout the Ardennes; by April he had succeeded Guderian as Chief of the Army General Staff (OKH), the last of a long line of generals dating back to Gerhard von Scharnhorst, first appointed in 1808. Krebs later observed the suicide of the Goebbels family on 1 May, and blew out his own brains in the garden of the *Führerbunker* the following morning. Another individual skulking around Hitler's headquarters was the odious Brigadeführer Wilhelm Mohnke, who had commanded the 1st SS Division in the Ardennes and thus bore some responsibility for Malmedy and other massacres.

Mohnke had been wounded in an air raid and once recovered was charged with the defence of the *Führerbunker*. After his leader's death, Mohnke tried to lead a group of headquarters staff to safety, but, finding Russian soldiers everywhere, surrendered on 2 May 1945.[12] The day also saw Soviet war photographer Yevgeny Khaldei taking his iconic images of Russian soldiers unfurling a huge Red Army flag from the roof of the Reichstag. Below lay a smoking city of dead cars and tanks, gun barrels split like celery, arranged on a canvas of corpses and rubble. Berlin had fallen.

To the north, Miles Dempsey's Second Army captured Bremen on 26 April after a week of combat, and British and Canadian paratroopers reached the Baltic city of Wismar just ahead of Soviet forces on 2 May. Two days later Montgomery took the military surrender of all German forces in Holland, north-west Germany and Denmark on Lüneburg Heath, an area between the cities of Hamburg, Hanover and Bremen, taking effect on the 5th. On this day occurred one of the most bizarre incidents of the war, underlining the chaotic nature of the dying days of the Reich.

Sherman tanks of the US 12th Armored Division's 23rd Tank Battalion liberated the idyllic Austrian castle, Schloss Itter, in the Tyrol. Its inhabitants were hostages of the Reich, including former French prime ministers Paul Reynaud and Eduard Daladier, a sister of de Gaulle and Generals Weygand and Gamelin. Their reverie of freedom was soon interrupted when diehard fanatics of the 17th SS *Panzergrenadier* Division arrived to execute the prisoners. As the Frenchmen and GIs prepared to fight for their lives, they were *joined* by a squad of Wehrmacht guards, led by two German officers, Major Gangl of the Wehrmacht and Hauptsturmführer Schrader of the SS, who took up arms with the Allies against their former colleagues. The motley coalition only narrowly prevailed against their would-be executioners with the help of local Austrian partisans.[13]

On 7 May at his headquarters in the Technical College of Reims, Eisenhower accepted the unconditional surrender of all German forces to the Western Allies and the Soviet Union; it was signed for SHAEF by Bedell Smith and for the Third Reich by General Alfred Jodl, with Russian and French witnesses, effective the following day, which was designated VE (Victory in Europe) Day. Susan Hibbert, a British sergeant working in SHAEF, then signalled the War Office in London: 'The mission of this Allied Force was fulfilled at 02.41 a.m. local time, 7 May 1945'. The building, at 12 rue Franklin Roosevelt, now houses a fine little museum recording the event. As the Russians wanted their own surrender ceremony, Field Marshal Wilhelm Keitel, as head of OKW and Jodl's superior, signed an identical document to the one agreed at Reims, at Karlshorst, near Berlin, on 8 May, with Tedder acting for Eisenhower, witnessed by Carl Spaatz and de Lattre de Tassigny. It was 143 days after the Battle of the Bulge had begun.

In his last will and testament, Hitler appointed Grand Admiral Dönitz as his successor, who broadcast the news of his predecessor's demise to the world on 1 May and set up a new German government in the Fatherland's most northern city, Flensburg. It ran a mere sliver of territory (in reality no more than a Nazi theme park centred on the Naval Officers' Academy at nearby Mürwik) until 23 May. Dönitz and company spent most of their three-week existence moving soldiers and civilians out of Russian clutches. With their arrest a brief power vacuum ensued until the dissolution of the Third Reich on 5 June, when the United States, Russia, Great Britain and France assumed direct control of the administration of Germany, with absolute powers. Only on 30 August did the Allied Control Commission, then running Germany (yet to be sub-divided into occupation zones), prohibit the wearing of German military uniform. The Nazi Party was formally disbanded on 10 October and on 12 November, the German Armed Forces. Thus, like the Bulge, it is perhaps difficult to state definitively when the Third Reich disappeared for good.

For some, the anxieties of war and peace continued for weeks. It was only on 29 May, twenty-one days after the surrender, that a letter reached Indianapolis, where Kurt Vonnegut, Sr, learned that his son, who had been listed as missing in action since 22 December, was alive; the younger Vonnegut had been liberated earlier by the Red Army. Meanwhile, Otto

Skorzeny, the SS commando leader, had become 'the most wanted man in Europe', when identified as the brains behind the supposed December plan to kill Eisenhower. The six-foot-two-inch, scar-faced Austrian had become a mythical bogeyman to Allied troops but his capture descended into farce. When he presented himself at an American command post on 15 May, the sergeant at the desk shook his head, being too busy to book in prisoners. Nevertheless he provided a jeep to take the guest, in the full dress uniform of a Waffen-SS *Obersturmbannführer*, to divisional headquarters in Salzburg.

The driver of the jeep knew the name, pulled into a tavern and ordered a bottle of wine. 'Skorzeny is it? If you are Skorzeny, you'd better take a drink. Tonight you'll hang.' Yet on reaching Salzburg, the GI left Skorzeny, still armed, outside a hotel and drove off to take lunch. The SS officer spent the rest of the day being passed between unsuspecting officers before it suddenly dawned on someone that Europe's most wanted man was in their midst, whereupon he was arrested, disarmed, handcuffed and taken in a convoy of armoured cars, an automatic pressed against his heart throughout, to a higher HQ where he was paraded before the exploding flashlights of the world's press. 'It was thought best to keep Skorzeny with his hands manacled behind his back,' reported the *Daily Express*. 'When he was given a cigarette, it was lit for him and he had to have the ash shaken off him. A glass of water was held to his lips.'[14] The war correspondents cowered in his presence; according to the *New York Times*, 'Skorzeny certainly looks the part. He is striking in a tough way; a huge powerful figure. The Beast of Belsen [Josef Kramer, its Commandant, just arrested] is something out of a nursery in comparison.'[15]

Of the other attackers in the Bulge, the diminutive Hasso von Manteuffel had afterwards been given command of the Third Panzer Army on the Eastern Front, but managed to move his formation westwards before capitulating to British troops at Hagenow, south of Schwerin, on 3 May. Erich Brandenberger had gone on to lead the German Nineteenth Army, which he surrendered to General Edward H. Brooks of the US VI Corps, at Innsbruck on 5 May. After their unsuccessful defence of Vienna, the bulk of the 1st SS Panzer Division – minus their panzers – headed for the US–Soviet demarcation line at Enns in upper Austria.

Among those who crossed westwards before a 01.00 a.m. curfew on 9 May was Hans Hennecke, then Training Company commander, overseeing sixteen- and seventeen-year-old recruits. 'We threw away our weapons, officers retained their pistols. It was night, we were anxious we would not cross in time. Some of my recruits had become children again in their fear. We knew what the Russians would do to us. At the checkpoint the Americans removed many of our decorations for souvenirs, which greatly offended us. They regarded us as walking Christmas trees, thinking our hard-won decorations were as festive baubles to be had for the taking,' he remembered. Hennecke remained in American hands. His colleagues caught in the Soviet zone were never seen again.[16] With him was his *Kampfgruppe* commander in the Bulge, Jochen Peiper, who kept his identity secret and subsequently escaped captivity. He was rearrested on 28 May, but not identified until 21 August. His army commander, Sepp Dietrich, turned himself over to Master Sergeant Herbert Kraus of the US 36th Infantry Division at Berchtesgaden on 8 May.

Another master sergeant, Forrest C. Pogue, remembered the last day of the European War, D+336, in the Czech city of Pilsen. As he recorded in his diary: 'heard the official announcement of VE Day. Was glad I heard it in Czechoslovakia; one of the first of Germany's victims . . . No blackouts: to many of the fellows, that was the best thing they had ever seen.'[17]

39

Punctuation Marks of History

WINSTON CHURCHILL THOUGHT that battles were the grammatical devices which regulated history. If so, the terrain of the Bulge must rank as one of the most important pages of the Second World War story on which such marks were written. The Ardennes was also one of the most recognisable 'triumphs' of American military history. The fact that the campaign had started with a setback, and the US Army had rallied and thrashed their opponents, merely enlarged the nature of the victory. There was no doubt who won, nor any debate about the extent and decisive nature of the US achievement. Subsequent wars, from Korea and Vietnam (the first two overseen by senior officers who had served in the Ardennes) to Iraq and Afghanistan, mired with armistices or hostile public opinion, have proven less easy to define as Churchillian 'punctuation marks'.

As soon as the fighting had ended, the Allies began to examine the circumstances of the battle. They were shocked that, despite their own superiority in men, machines, technology and intelligence, their opponents, who were mostly ill-trained *Volksgenadiers*, had still managed to conceal vast numbers of attacking formations, capture 23,554 Allied soldiers and advance almost sixty miles within a few days.[1] This concern was exacerbated by the ever-chillier relations between Anglo-American forces in western Germany and their Soviet counterparts, which soon manifested itself as the Cold War.

Among the first to note the worsening nature of the East–West alliance was George Patton. On 7 May, shortly after Hitler's death and as Germany surrendered, he met the US Under-Secretary of War, Judge Robert P. Patterson, in Austria. The two men got on extremely well together, Patton recording of his political boss, 'he has a most remarkable memory for names, and could tell the officers to whom he was introduced where he had last seen them. He is also exceptionally well informed on history, particularly that of the Civil War, so we had a very enjoyable talk together.' Patton was gravely concerned over the Soviet failure to respect the demarcation lines separating the Soviet and American occupation zones.

He was also alarmed by plans in Washington for the immediate partial demobilisation of the US Army, saying to Patterson, 'Let's keep our boots polished, bayonets sharpened, and present a picture of force and strength to the Red Army. This is the only language they understand and respect.' Patterson, a robust supporter of the armed forces, who had won a Distinguished Service Cross for valour in 1918 and had mobilised the US Army in 1940, nevertheless responded with a brush-off, typical of the immediate post-war optimism of politicians: 'George, you have been so close to this thing so long, you have lost sight of the big picture.'[2]

There was an understanding among many Western military commanders, led by Patton, that Russia remained overtly aggressive and a wise course of action would be to confront Stalin's brand of Communism while the chance existed. Attending meetings and social functions with senior Red Army officers, Patton noted in his diary on 14 May, 'I have never seen in any army at any time, including the German Imperial Army of 1912, as severe discipline as exists in the Russian army. The officers, with few exceptions, give the appearance of recently civilized Mongolian bandits.' Four days later, he again observed, 'If it should be necessary to fight the Russians, the sooner we do it the better.' On 20 May, he reiterated his concern in a letter to his wife, 'If we have to fight them, now is the time. From now on we will get weaker and they stronger.'

Patton's anxieties were reflected by some Western politicians such as Churchill, who in May 1945 had ordered plans to be drawn up for a possible war against Stalin's Soviet Union. The objective would be 'to impose upon Russia the will of the United States and the British Empire. Even though the will of these two countries may be defined as no more than a square deal for Poland, this does not necessarily limit the military commitment.' The Chief of the Imperial General Staff (Brooke) and his planners responded with outlines for a surprise attack by up to forty-seven British and American divisions (around a million personnel) initiated from the area of Dresden, also using Polish forces and up to 100,000 former Wehrmacht soldiers, including men and their leaders who had fought in the Ardennes.

Brooke's team observed that (as with the German attack in the Bulge), any quick success would be due to surprise alone. Reflecting on the failure of Operation Barbarossa in 1941, they warned that if a rapid victory was not forthcoming before winter, the Allies would be committed to a total war which would be protracted. Due to a Soviet numerical superiority over the West in Europe of 4:1 in men and 2:1 in tanks, in the official British report submitted to Churchill of 22 May 1945, Brooke's team deemed the offensive operation 'hazardous' – surely an understatement, but one which reflected in every way the strategic situation that OKW faced in November–December 1944.[3]

Accepting this, albeit reluctantly, Churchill, fearing that the relocation of US forces to the Pacific for the invasion of Japan might tempt Stalin to take offensive action in Western Europe, on 10 June 1945 instructed Brooke to ascertain 'what measures would be required to ensure the security of the British Isles in the event of war with Russia in the near future'. After further research, staff work and war games, Brooke's planners concluded that if the United States focused on the Pacific Theatre, Great Britain's odds against a Soviet drive through Western Europe would be 'fanciful'. In light of this, the Joint Planning Staff named both plans, for offensive and defensive activities, 'Operation Unthinkable', reflecting their view of Britain's chances of success. Certainly, we know the Wehrmacht's planners for *Wacht am Rhein* harboured privately the exact same doubts for success in December 1944.

On 19 May 1946, President Truman invited Churchill to speak in the former's home state of Missouri, at Westminster College in Fulton. Churchill – now acting as prophet and not Prime Minister, for Clement Atlee had defeated him in the General Election on 26 July the previous year – brought with him one of the most famous speeches of all time, which subsequently became shorthand for East–West relations of nearly half a century.

In speaking of an 'Iron Curtain' that had descended from 'Stettin in the Baltic to Trieste in the Adriatic', Churchill acknowledged the truth of Russian duplicity which many leaders in the West were still refusing to face. As his daughter-in-law Pamela Harriman later observed in 1987, 'So powerful was the phrase, it cut like a thunderbolt through the public dialogue; so pronounced was the turning point marked by this speech, so wise does it seem at least in retrospect, that leaders since then return to it and quote it repeatedly to validate their own policies.'[4]

Ten months later, President Harry Truman himself echoed Churchill's erudition in an address to the US Congress, amid the crisis of the 1946–9 Greek Civil War. On 12 March 1947, Truman argued that if Greece and Turkey did not receive Western aid badly needed, both countries would fall inevitably under Communist domination, with consequences throughout the region. This became the Truman Doctrine, and historians have come to consider this a convenient date to signal the start of the Cold War, and the birth of a containment policy to stop Soviet expansion.

If anyone harboured lingering doubts, Churchill's warnings seemed vindicated in 1948. By then the United States had, along with Great Britain and France, combined their occupation zones in West Germany into one military province, hoping to bring security and economic stability to its inhabitants. In February 1948, the three Western powers proposed to the Soviets that a new four-power German currency be created. Stalin refused to accept the idea, intent on triggering a Communist uprising in West Germany through economic unrest. The Western powers went ahead anyway and established their own tripartite currency in June.

The temperature rose rapidly as the Soviets, trying to push the Allies out of West Berlin, suddenly announced that all vehicles and trains travelling through East Germany to the German capital were to be searched. The West refused to permit such interference, whereupon Stalin raised the stakes by blocking the movement of all surface traffic to West Berlin on 27 June, threatening the western portion of the city with starvation. An order to begin supplying West Berlin by air was signed by General Lucius Clay (who had succeeded Eisenhower as Military Governor of occupied Germany in March) the same day. The American ambassador to Britain, John G. Winant, enunciated the West's view that 'the right to be in Berlin carried with it the right of access', and a Top Secret CIA memorandum to Truman stressed the importance of Berlin as a base for intelligence operations, sanctuary for refugees and anti-Communist propaganda missions.[5]

The ten-month airlift carried over two million tons of supplies in 270,000 flights until the Soviets finally lifted the blockade on 12 May 1949, by which time Berlin had become a symbol of Western resolve to stand up to the Soviet threat, without being forced into a direct conflict. German veterans shook their heads, wondering what might have been had the Luftwaffe been able to mount a similar airlift into Stalingrad over the winter of 1942–3 – or supported *Herbstnebel* in December 1944.

The Berlin blockade heightened the tensions of the Cold War, greatly increasing concerns about the vulnerability of Western Europe to an attack by the Soviet Army (as the Russian force was officially known from 25 February 1946). Predating the blockade, in the Brussels Treaty of March 1948, Britain, France, the Netherlands, Belgium and Luxembourg had already agreed mutual assistance in the event of such an attack. On its own this treaty was too weak to deter the Soviet Union from aggression, but the drama of the blockade and airlift served only to persuade America that Russia was an increasingly serious military threat. The Vandenberg Resolution of June 1948 enabled the US to enter into military treaties with foreign states, and on 4 April 1949 the United States, Canada, the Brussels powers and most of the other Western European nations signed the North Atlantic Treaty, agreeing to mutual defence in the event of an attack by the Soviet Union.

The cornerstone of NATO doctrine was, and remains, Article 5, in which its signatories agreed that 'an armed attack against one or more of them . . . shall be considered an attack against them all'. The NATO nations began immediately to study ways of countering Soviet military aggression and of (in the words of Article 3) laying the foundations for 'cooperation in military preparedness'. Thus by 1948–9, in the minds of all Western military commanders, the Wehrmacht had been replaced as the principal military aggressor by Stalin's forces, and Western fear throughout the Cold War era was of a sudden surprise attack, of the kind achieved by the Germans, albeit with a smaller force, in December 1944. Against this backdrop, interest in the Battle of the Bulge was heightened not only in terms of US Army history for its own sake, but for the potential lessons it offered for fighting World War Three.

Doctrine for offensive activity in any potential NATO–Warsaw Pact encounter emphasised, as had been learned in the Battle of the Bulge, vast numbers of tanks and mechanised infantry, employed under conditions of surprise, shock and moving at high speed, advancing as far as possible before a reaction was triggered. From the late 1940s, strategists of both sides focused on the terrain of the Fulda Gap, an area between the East German border and Frankfurt am Main that was the most obvious route for any Soviet tank attack on West Germany from Soviet-occupied Europe. Attacking forces instinctively search for geological 'gaps' which lead to objectives such as river lines, good manoeuvre terrain, cities or ports. It is no coincidence that Napoleon withdrew along the Fulda Gap after the Battle of Leipzig in 1813, and US XII Corps advanced eastwards through it in March–April 1945.

The region around the village of Fulda is very similar to the Ardennes, and characterised by deeply scoured glacial valleys, separated by steep-sided hills, surmounted by forests. The valleys often have a stream or river running through them, and frequently a road as well. Where valleys meet, roads intersect, and there is normally a village or town; generally the terrain consists of impassable hillsides, wooded hilltops (often with fire breaks through them), narrow valleys with frequent bridges and river crossings. Off-road the 'going' for armour is almost impossible. As a consequence, the US and West German forces in the area envisaged a defence by holding road junctions and towns, stationing guns and armour on the hilltops.

Soviet doctrine foresaw combined arms assaults, the frequent use of chemical weapons against built-up areas, and attempts to bypass NATO roadblocks wherever possible. The concept of a major tank battle in the vicinity of the Fulda Gap was a predominant element of NATO war planning throughout the Cold War, and weapons (such as Apache attack helicopters and A-10 tank-busters) were developed specifically to counter it.

Thus, in preparing for a third world war, the template that both East and West used was the German breakthrough into the Ardennes of both 1940 and 1944 via the smaller Losheim Gap. This relatively narrow (five-mile-wide) terrain in the Ardennes did not offer perfect going for tanks, but was better than most of the surrounding ground, and closely resembled the Fulda. Throughout the Cold War, NATO drilled its troops in the Losheim Gap, in rehearsal for what might occur in the Fulda. My personal experience of this was in the mid-1980s with the British Army of the Rhine (BAOR), which had been the main peacetime element of

UK land forces from the end of the Second World War, where the bulk of the army was based in Germany, prepared to counter aggressive Soviet armoured attacks.

The teeth of BAOR were the three or four divisions – the numbers varied – of I British Corps, subordinated to NORTHAG (NATO's Northern Army Group). Altogether, BAOR varied between 25,000 and 60,000 troops (which reflected British government defence spending rather than the nature of the threat), commanded by a four-star general in Rheindahlen, which also housed the headquarters of RAF Germany. While the British Corps area of responsibility extended from the West German border near Hanover, in the event of war BAOR would become British Support Command, which would supply the fighting troops of 1 British Corps and guard the rear areas right back to the Antwerp. Then – just as in 1944 – the same port was the logistics centre for the British.

In these years NATO was regularly tested by vast exercises; part of a series called REFORGER (REturn of FORces to GERmany), when the whole of the British (and other) corps deployed on exercise, supported by huge reinforcements arriving from the UK and US. I took part in two of these, Crusader in 1980 and Lionheart in 1984, and during the latter put my humble platoon headquarters in a shallow depression in the ground by a railway bridge. The feature turned out to be a Second World War headquarters location, along the line of the old Stavelot–Malmedy railway line, which my platoon realised when we dug to expand our position, unearthing all manner of cartridges, radio batteries, ammunition boxes and other GI debris. I had unwittingly made the same choice for a command post as my unknown predecessor in 1944, and his unit had left behind the archaeological evidence to prove it. Perhaps supporting my own belief that the Russians might one day attack was the fact that we discovered only shrapnel, empty cartridges, mangled mess tins and incoming bullet heads under the pine needles, suggesting that the position had seen combat action.

West Germany would not join NATO until 1955, but former German officers were already cooperating with official US Army official historians in piecing together their recollections. Their observations were vital to early NATO doctrine, for they had successfully engaged the Soviet army in tactical battles on the Eastern Front, and had also fought over terrain that might feature in any future war with Russia.

*

The first voice in print about the Ardennes belonged to a Texan veteran of the First World War who had pursued a career as a reporter with the *Detroit News* in the interwar years. By 1941, aged forty-one, Samuel Lyman Atwood Marshall had been commissioned as a major and was assigned to the US Army Historical Section. Known as 'Slam' (after his initials) to his friends, Marshall started after-action interviews with combat veterans first in the Pacific, and subsequently Europe, becoming chief historian of the European Theater of Operations. He came to know many of the best-known Allied commanders, including Patton and Bradley, conducted hundreds of interviews of all ranks, and was an early proponent of oral history techniques. In particular, Slam favoured group interviews, where he would gather surviving members of a front-line unit and debrief them collectively. Rising eventually to brigadier-general, his writings carried great weight and sometimes caused controversy within the US Army establishment.

With Marshall's *Bastogne: The First Eight Days*, published in 1946, the floodgates opened to a great wave of literature on the harsh winter campaign, which continues to this day. Although dealing with only the early days of the Bulge and the activities of the 101st Airborne Division, *Bastogne* offered immediate impressions of soldiers who had fought in these encounters just a year earlier. Slam's message was how decisive leadership and incidents of individual heroism overcame both the weather and the Germans.[6]

Other writers immediately went to work interviewing those they could, Americans and Germans, and it helped that most early authors were veterans of the Bulge campaign itself. Aware that as many as 600,000 Americans had fought in the battle, with the commercial opportunities that offered, the next was Robert E. Merriam, whom we first met motoring along the Skyline Drive in October 1944. He had joined the US Army as a private and after Infantry Officers Candidate School became a second lieutenant in 1943, aged twenty-five. In late 1944, shortly after he was sent to the European Theatre, Captain Merriam found himself attached to a Historical Service Team at 7th Armored Division during the Battle of the Bulge.

Merriam remained in Europe after the end of the war as an official US Army Historian, interviewing hundreds of participants and planners of the battle for the Ardennes. As no official public history of the Ardennes campaign was planned for some while (in fact it would be twenty years), on his release from the military Merriam used the interviews he had made, together with his own combat experience to write *Dark December*, published in 1947. Written so close to the events, Merriam's account was surprisingly objective, because he had interviewed many German commanders as well as Americans, avoiding the one-sided nature of many contemporary accounts. Praised by Eisenhower, Merriam's book sold extremely well and he became much sought after as a Bulge expert and book reviewer. Importantly, he concluded that Allied intelligence had failed catastrophically – there was no plan to lure the Germans into attacking, with Middleton's Corps as bait – and that Montgomery's generalship was sound: a view that many Americans still find unpalatable today.[7]

We have also met Captain Charles B. MacDonald, five years younger than Merriam, who fought the battle with US 2nd Division and published his combat memoirs, *Company Commander*, in the same year of 1947. These three, Marshall, Merriam and MacDonald – all witnesses of the battle – became the mainstay of initial interpretations of the campaign. All saw the Bulge as a reaffirmation of American military greatness. Despite the intelligence failure and early setbacks, within days US troops had recovered from the shock of the attack very quickly, formulated a strategy and counter-attacked with determination and skill.

Many GIs, who were relatively green, had taken on some of Nazi Germany's best and won, something the French and Belgians in 1940 had failed to achieve over the same terrain against the same enemy. As such, argued Slam, Merriam and MacDonald, the events in the Ardennes were an affirmation of George C. Marshall's vision and training, and a triumph of American manhood. Despite the dominance of Allied air power, not present in 1940, and lack of fuel – which might lessen, but not degrade America's enhanced military reputation – this is an interpretation which has endured over time and remains prevalent today.

Merriam saw events unfold at the higher echelons. MacDonald's brilliant combat memoir covered three major phases of the American effort in north-west Europe at unit level: stalemate along the Siegfried Line, the Battle of the Bulge, and the final drive into Germany. Although *Company Commander* covered only the initial phases of the Bulge, it remains in print because of the author's remarkably honest self-analysis of his evolution as a combat leader, for which he would win a Silver Star and Purple Heart.

In 1945 MacDonald joined the staff of the US Army Center of Military History, serving as chief of the European section, writing several official histories on the war in Europe. He came to be seen very much as the official US voice on the Ardennes offensive, in retirement writing a further volume of personal Bulge memoirs, the much-lauded *A Time for Trumpets: The Untold Story of the Battle of the Bulge.*[8] By contrast Merriam, who had been a US Army Historian, pursued a career post-war as a public official, running as the Republican nominee for Mayor of Chicago in 1955, and serving as deputy assistant to President Eisenhower from 1958 to 1961.[9]

The next major narrative appeared in 1959, fifteen years after the fighting, when John W. Toland, a professional writer who had not fought in the Ardennes, published *Battle: The Story of the Bulge*, the first account by a non-official historian. His approach was very different from the wide perspective of Merriam or professional depth of Marshall and MacDonald. *Battle* could have been a literary disaster, but Toland did a great job of making sense of the confusing and chaotic manoeuvres in the winter forests by focusing on personal stories of ordinary soldiers. Toland's journalistic, anecdotal writing style told the campaign story through the eyes of many eyewitnesses: this was a good approach and acknowledged that the war years were long passed, that some of his readership had no military experience, and many were 'tactically illiterate'. With Toland, combat history was no longer 'owned' by generals and professional officers, but by all ranks, who once had been soldiers and were again civilians.

Unlike Toland, the trio of Marshall, Merriam and MacDonald had worked as official historians. In response to a presidential directive in August 1943 the US Army had established a Historical Branch which deployed Information and Historical Service Teams, to which Merriam and Forrest C. Pogue belonged, to collect documents, interviews and impressions direct from the combat zone. (This was a task similar to the one I performed for NATO and the UK in Bosnia and Iraq.)

Another prominent historian in the branch was Major Kenneth W. Hechler who was attached to the US 9th Armored Division in 1945 when its units captured the Ludendorff Bridge at Remagen.[10] In September 1945 he conducted the first Historical Branch interview with Jochen Peiper and the following year interviewed many of the defendants prior to the Nuremberg Trials, including Hermann Göring. Approaching his hundredth birthday as I write, Ken Hechler was a Truman aide and went on to serve as a Congressman from 1959 to 1977 but maintained a writing career periodically publishing books and articles connected with the Bulge and Remagen.

The collection of information and narrative writing of unit operations would, in time, become the American Forces in Action Series, of which the US Army had published fourteen studies by 1947, of which Marshall's *Bastogne* was one.[11] A second, longer task was to write a comprehensive history of the war. This evolved as the U.S. Army in World War II Series, and was produced by a separate Historical Division, established in November 1945, which MacDonald joined.

Redesignated later as the Office of the Chief of Military History (OCMH), its authors received open access to all documents and were instructed to present triumphs and failures in a fair and unbiased way. Written at some chronological distance from the events, these histories were generally praised as comprehensive and analytical. Pogue's masterful portrait of Ike's military leadership, *The Supreme Command*, was one OCMH volume which appeared in 1954. Hugh M. Cole, who had been a historian with Patton's Third Army at the time of the Bulge, and was a professional colleague of Marshall and MacDonald, was the eventual author of the OCMH volume, *The Ardennes: Battle of the Bulge*, published in 1965.

Cole's official US history was published in 1965, but far more influential was a movie released in the same year, director Ken Annakin's *Battle of the Bulge*. It brought the campaign to an audience too young to remember the war. This was not the first film dealing with the Bulge, and has been succeeded by several others, but remains the most ambitious and memorable.[12] William A. Wellman (himself a First World War veteran) had earlier directed the black and white movie *Battleground*, released in 1949, which focused on a squad of 101st Airborne Division in the woods around Bastogne. In complete contrast to the broad perspective of *Battle of the Bulge*, the Wellman movie dwelt on the psychology and morale of a very small group of soldiers, with very little action footage or heroics.

Wellman's film was based on a diary kept by the screenwriter Robert Pirosh, formerly a master sergeant, who had won a Bronze Star when serving with the 320th Infantry Regiment (Thirty-Fifth Division) in the Ardennes, and was anxious to preserve accuracy. Regarded as 'the best of the war movies made during the immediate post-war period',

Battleground received five Academy Award nominations, winning two, including one for Pirosh.[13] Despite its age, it still holds up extremely well and captures the atmosphere of fear and isolation in the foggy and sub-zero conditions of 1944. Released at the height of the Cold War, it contained an uncompromising message about the contemporary Russian menace; when an army chaplain was asked if the war was really necessary, the character responds, 'We must never let any kind of force dedicated to a super race or a super idea or a super anything get strong enough to impose itself on a free world.'[14]

On the other hand, *Battle of the Bulge*, which premiered on 16 December 1965 (the twenty-first anniversary of the battle), suffered from being shot in the bright sunlight of 1960s Spain, which hardly resembled the wintry, freezing forests of Germany, Belgium and Luxembourg. The reason for this was that President Franco's Spanish army offered a battalion of fully equipped soldiers plus many wartime-era tanks and vehicles, mostly US surplus, for a knock-down fee. Another problem was that out of a rich cast of real personalities, Annakin chose to keep all his characters fictional: not a single one depicted an actual historical figure, and none were associated with any real units. This is curious, given that the British-born Annakin had earlier directed a very successful D-Day movie, *The Longest Day*, and his senior military adviser, General Meinrad von Lauchert, was the commander of 2nd Panzer Division during the real Battle of the Bulge.

Several of the film's themes reflected reality: the US false sense of security before the battle, Germans disguised as American troops, the Wehrmacht's shortage of fuel and the ruthless march of a panzer column (led by the fictional Colonel Hessler, played by Robert Shaw), inspired obviously by Jochen Peiper and his *Kampfgruppe*. Although 1960s Spain was still awash with Second World War-era German armoured vehicles, there was no effort to use armour authentic to the period. Purists have noted the irony of the film using US-produced M-47 'Patton' tanks to depict Tiger IIs.

The film therefore implied that *every* German tank was a King Tiger, whereas we know very few were actually used compared with other models (and those deployed were notorious for mechanical breakdowns). It is perhaps significant that neither of its two screenwriters, Philip Yordan and Milton Sperling, had seen any military service but were Hollywood professionals. Though it remains a television staple, with hindsight the movie represented a low point in post-Second World War cinematography: 'the worst of the large-scale war epics' remains the critics' collective view.[15] *The Saturday Review* accused the screenwriters of 'going out of their way to avoid historical fact', and Eisenhower himself felt the historical inaccuracies were such that he emerged from retirement to denounce the film.[16]

Despite its shortcomings, the most important interpretation of Annakin's movie was that it reaffirmed in US minds that the Battle of the Bulge was a purely American struggle, representative of that mighty continent's involvement in the European Theatre. That thirty-two US divisions fought in the Ardennes, where the daily battle strength of US Army units averaged twenty-six divisions and 610,000 men, proves that the Battle of the Bulge was a bigger commitment for the US Army than Normandy, where nineteen divisions fought, and far larger than the Pacific.[17] Altogether, the US Army Ground Forces activated ninety-one divisions during the Second World War: of which all but three entered combat. The vast majority of these deployed to Europe (sixty-one divisions), as opposed to the remainder, which deployed to the Pacific, to which should be added six US Marine divisions.[18]

Far more important in the Ardennes were the endless non-divisional units, independent tank destroyer, artillery, tank and anti-aircraft battalions, who played their role alongside the badged divisional units, swelling US numbers and firepower greatly. The legacy of these statistics, the early authors such as Marshall, Merriam, Hechler, Pogue and MacDonald, and Annakin's *Battle of the Bulge* movie, was that the Ardennes has since become American shorthand for the whole ground campaign in Europe. The Bulge represented the US achievement in the Second World War in a way no other single battle ever could.

Ike himself had already returned to the Bulge battlefields with a camera crew to star in one of the first made-for-television documentaries, a grainy, black and white, twenty-six-part series made by ABC-TV and released in 1949. It had the same title as his memoirs, *Crusade in Europe*, published the year before, and proved such a hit on the small screen that other networks imitated the successful formula.[19] Ike narrated personally from key locations that had dominated the fighting in North-West Europe, including the Ardennes, then little changed from the dramatic events of the previous war-torn decade.

Four years after Ken Annakin's movie, the next significant contribution to understanding the Bulge was John Eisenhower's *The Bitter Woods*, which appeared in 1969.[20] Perhaps motivated by his father's stinging criticism of the earlier film, *The Bitter Woods* was outstandingly well researched, incorporating many fresh interviews with participants, of high and low rank. Whereas the earlier writers – Marshall, Merriam and MacDonald – had only limited access to German commanders, who were often still captive and cautious in their responses because of potential war crimes trials, John Eisenhower's status brought him access to almost anyone he wanted. West Germany had joined NATO in 1955, the same year its new army, the Bundeswehr, was established and led by former, moderate, Wehrmacht officers: the former enemy was now a staunch ally.

Thus, in the more benign atmosphere of the 1960s, he was able to meet and charm former opponents such as Manteuffel and von der Heydte as well as Allied commanders such as Bruce C. Clarke and Montgomery. The younger Eisenhower had graduated from West Point on D-Day, 6 June 1944, and was trained as a soldier; his book therefore, conceived as a study of command, offered much tactical analysis and new insights. Although his father died just before its publication, the volume was well received and has dated only because of the 1974 revelation of the Allied code-breaking effort at Bletchley Park, and our knowledge of the extensive contribution that Ultra made to Allied victory – or, in the case of the Bulge, to the Allies' intelligence failure. Nevertheless, *The Bitter Woods* remains a fine case study of a major Second World War campaign.

Another good account of the campaign, by Second World War veteran Gerald Astor, appeared in 1992. However, *A Blood-Dimmed Tide* neatly illustrates the prevailing bias of many accounts. Astor skilfully wove his narrative around the stories of forty-seven American soldiers, but only *seven* Germans. The vast majority of histories of the Ardennes campaign have – perhaps understandably – concentrated on the US side of the campaign, where the more numerous GI veterans proved more accessible and easier to interview in English. Furthermore, of those few Germans who feature in the many Bulge books, Jochen Peiper and Otto Skorzeny inevitably steal the reader's attention, leaving little voice for the 300,000 other Germans who participated, an imbalance this present book attempts to correct.

As noted above, thirty years after the events of the Bulge, the last great secret of the Second World War, the use of strategic intelligence derived from the German Enigma enciphering machine, was revealed in 1974. The medium was Group Captain Fred Winterbotham's ground-breaking book, *The Ultra Secret*, which immediately challenged the intelligence picture painted by all Bulge authors writing previously. Few were aware of (or were forbidden from unveiling) the knowledge gleaned from Enigma decrypts – so valuable, they were given the special classification Top Secret Ultra, or simply Ultra. Winterbotham, who was in charge of the secure delivery of Ultra to field commanders, via the Special Liaison Units (SLUs) whom he recruited and trained, included a special chapter on Hitler's Ardennes Offensive in his book. He demonstrated Ultra's weakness: that when OKW and its associated headquarters relied on telephone rather than radio communications, many lives were lost because the Allies could learn nothing of the Germans' plans and intentions.

It was easy to dismiss Ultra's failure to anticipate the German tactical surprises in the Ardennes of May 1940 because the system, working out of Bletchley Park, now a suburb of Milton Keynes, was not then fully functioning. Not so in December 1944; Winterbotham acknowledged there had been a genuine intelligence failure, caused by an over-reliance on high-grade Ultra signals intelligence. There was no evidence that Ultra had been compromised, and Hitler's decision to maintain radio silence during the build-up to the attack had been simply good operational security; the Germans in any case went back to the use of Enigma after the beginning of the Bulge attack. Winterbotham recalled of the German precautions, 'prisoners of war later revealed how all the troop and tank movements up to the front had been done at night and that signals had been delivered by hand by motorcyclists'.

Charles Whiting challenged this view of Ultra in his 1994 book, *Last Assault*, alleging that the Bletchley Park code-breakers *had* identified and warned the Allied High Command in advance of the impending attack. He concluded that the result at Ike's headquarters was not complacency, but a devious plan to let the assault come, even weakening the front to be attacked, in order to surround and destroy the last German panzer reserves. Whiting argued that with his foreknowledge of *Herbstnebel*, 'Eisenhower had been prepared to sacrifice a whole US corps [Middleton's VIII] to get the Germans to come out of their prepared defences and fight in the open'.[21]

A prolific author of military histories and veteran of the Second World War himself who disdained generals, always writing from a private's point of view, Whiting built his 1994 book around the accusation that Middleton's corps was 'purposefully weakened' during the weeks prior to the Ardennes assault, as Eisenhower 'had to force [the Germans] out . . . into an area of his own choice – the Ardennes'. Whiting went on to assert 'But what of the bait? What of the young soldiers of Middleton's corps . . . How could Eisenhower explain away their sacrifice?' Hinting that Ike immediately instituted a cover-up at the highest levels to conceal his strategy, Whiting concluded, 'Now I think the time has come to reveal how thousands of young American lives were sacrificed for such a strategy – deceit in high places, sacrifices in lower ones. It is not a pretty tale.'[22]

Whiting's book ignores the success of German operational security and deception, which played a big part in blinding American military vision. The concepts of deception and surprise have been advocated by every military theorist from Sun Tzu to Clausewitz and were first recorded at Troy in Homer's *Iliad.* As with most military setbacks, the answer lies not with one big conspiracy but a series of avoidable institutional failures. Whiting's book sits in the same category as the debate about precisely what the US knew in advance of Pearl Harbor or the 9/11 attacks: he failed to provide any hard evidence, merely extreme conjecture.[23]

Many more official archives in the US and UK have been released since Whiting's 1994 book and, despite assiduous scrutiny, none of them provide the slightest hint of a cover-up. The complicity of a huge number of senior officers would have been required to initiate and conceal such a strategy in 1944, and no memoirs have surfaced to date supporting Whiting's view. As an official historian serving at the highest levels in the Balkans and Iraq, supported by the most advanced array of intelligence sources and devices, I have personally witnessed senior commanders and intelligence personnel misappreciate enemy intentions and capabilities in the Clausewitzian fog and friction of operations. In these pages I have tried to lay Whiting's assertions to rest. If anything, the Ardennes proved the resilience of the US soldier, and his ability to improvise, rather than the wisdom and insight of his commanders. Such mistakes happen, and would recur, as history soon proved.

Three Americans throughout the 1980s and 1990s also helped return the Battle of the Bulge to wider US consciousness. The first was the radio journalist and interviewer Studs Terkel, who died, aged ninety-six, in 2008. His contribution to understanding the Second World War, '*The Good War': An Oral History of World War II*, won the 1985 Pulitzer Prize for Nonfiction. Terkel was discharged after a year in the US Army Air

Force because of perforated eardrums, a condition resulting from childhood operations and making him unfit for overseas duty. However, he found a way to serve by celebrating the service of others in *The Good War*. It was his most popular work, in which he demonstrated how the efforts of ordinary Americans at home were as important as those of the combat troops, sailors, fighter pilots or generals at the front. Among his chapters, *The Good War* recorded the Battle of the Bulge through the eyes of doctors and nurses as well as infantrymen, his strength – in the words of one British reviewer – was that his work was 'completely free of sociological claptrap, armchair revisionism and academic moralising'.[24]

A few years later, author and television presenter Tom Brokaw followed the same path with his 1999 book *The Greatest Generation*. As he put it, when standing on the Normandy beaches in 1994, 'by then I had come to understand what this generation of Americans meant to history. It is, I believe, the greatest generation any society has ever produced.'[25] Brokaw argued, as many have done but few as persuasively, that, following the careless Jazz Age of F. Scott Fitzgerald's *The Great Gatsby*, it was the Great Depression of the later 1920s and 1930s that toughened the Americans who went to war in December 1941. (Ironically, Second Lieutenant Fitzgerald's training officer at Fort Leavenworth in 1917 was Captain Dwight Eisenhower.)[26]

Their experiences of poverty, hunger and unemployment, pushed to the edge in John Steinbeck's 1939 novel *The Grapes of Wrath*, made them far more resilient than the Third Reich and Japan ever expected, and so better able to overcome the adversities of war and death. Thus, this argument runs, without the necessary pain of the Depression years, the miseries of the Hürtgen and Ardennes might not have been overcome; it certainly magnifies the achievement of the GI Generation in 1941–5. Brokaw's title has endured alongside the methods of Terkel, who was credited with transforming oral history into popular literature and a valid historical discipline, now studied and practised by universities the world over.

The third major influence was Professor Stephen E. Ambrose, founder of the National World War II Museum in New Orleans, Louisiana. As a military historian, Ambrose's earliest studies were on the civil war, though he became the official biographer of Eisenhower and later Nixon. However, he was most associated with his works on the Second World War, including *Band of Brothers*, which followed Major Dick Winters'

Company 'E', 506th Parachute Infantry Regiment of Maxwell Taylor's 101st Airborne Division from their training in the USA and southern England (on the very doorstep of my home) through D-Day to their war in the Ardennes and beyond. Ambrose's achievement with *Band of Brothers* was to link the very well-known story of D-Day to that of the Ardennes, the twin high-water marks of America's European War, through a single unit that fought in both battles.

Later works included *D-Day* and *Citizen Soldiers*, leading to his appointment as adviser for Steven Spielberg's 1998 seminal movie *Saving Private Ryan*.[27] This in turn gave rise to the highly popular 2001 HBO mini-series, *Band of Brothers*, based on his earlier book, all of which helped sustain the wide interest in the Second World War brought about by the fiftieth anniversary of D-Day and the Bulge.[28] The executive producers, Spielberg and Tom Hanks (respectively director and star of *Saving Private Ryan*), set the emphasis firmly on the winter of 1944–5; whereas two of the ten episodes are set in Normandy, four portray aspects of the Bulge, usually dwelling on the freezing woods around Bastogne.[29]

It was after his first book on the Normandy campaign, *Pegasus Bridge*, that I first met Ambrose, who demonstrated his deft, forensic touch in bringing together Major John Howard, whose glider troops seized the bridge of the title in the dying minutes of 5 June 1944, Oberst Hans von Luck, senior surviving officer of the 21st Panzer Division, and Madame Arlette Gondrée who as a young girl had witnessed the June 1944 drama.[30] Ambrose was the first to reassemble these three at the Pegasus Bridge, getting them to tell essentially the same story, but from three widely differing points of view. I owe him an enormous personal debt of gratitude, for all three became friends.

Meanwhile, in every state in the United States the flame of remembrance has been kept alight for soldiers of the campaign and their relatives at local level by the influential Veterans of the Battle of the Bulge, formed in 1981 at the Arlington County Courthouse, Virginia. Their worthy aims suggest an outward-looking organisation that will stand the test of time: memory of the sacrifices involved; preservation of historical data and battle sites; fostering international peace and goodwill, as well as the promotion of friendship among the survivors and their descendants. The few full members left are those who received a battle star for the Ardennes Campaign, though their descendants now keep the numbers and interest as high as ever. The readership of their sixty-nine chapters, spread throughout the US and Belgium, eagerly await each edition of their very professional quarterly newsletter, *The Bulge Bugle.* Since 1982, this journal has produced an unrivalled source of veterans' stories of inestimable value to present and future historians, such as Charles B. MacDonald's former aide and researcher, Danny S. Parker, who has emerged as a sage on the Ardennes, with four books on different aspects of the campaign to his credit.[31] I am equally grateful to them.

40

Reputations

MILITARY STUDIES OF the Bulge abound, particularly among the world's military communities because of the events of twenty-nine years later, when Egypt and Syria jointly launched a near-fatal surprise attack on Israel, heralding the Yom Kippur War of 6–25 October 1973. The circumstances were remarkably similar. Just as the Allies were lured into a false sense of security by the anticipated celebration of Christmas, and an assumption that the German army was exhausted and demoralised by December 1944, the IDF (Israel Defense Forces), its secret service counterpart, Mossad, and the CIA, were off their guard as Yom Kippur, the holiest day in Judaism, occurring that year during the Muslim holy month of Ramadan, approached in 1973.

The prevalent Israeli assumption was that the Egyptian and Syrian armies (which had been so devastated a few years earlier in the Six-Day War of 1967) were inferior and 'spent'. Yet the Arab armies had recovered, carefully rehearsed, and incorporated new technologies into their plans. Israel received many warnings beforehand, from intelligence sources, satellite imagery, the monitoring of Arab troop movements and those of their Soviet advisers; even King Hussein of Jordan flew secretly to Tel Aviv to warn Israeli Prime Minister Golda Meir on 25 September, all of which fell on deaf ears until the last moment. Similarly, in 1944, aerial photography, prisoner-of-war interrogations and indicators from Ultra decrypts were ignored in favour of the prevailing mindset that there would be no attack.

As in 1944, both the Syrians and Egyptians preceded their massed tank attacks with the deployment of commandos to seize key positions and disrupt the movement of reserves to the Golan and Sinai. Defending their southern frontier, the Israelis were strung along the Bar-Lev Line in thinly held outposts, in a similar fashion to Middleton's VIII Corps holding the Ardennes. With many troops occupying fixed defences along a wide front, in both cases the defenders found that enemy attacks against a narrow sector of their lines meant that those units in positions elsewhere could initially contribute little to the decisive action: this also happened to the French in 1940. Although, in 1973 the Egyptians crossed the Suez Canal with more imagination and competence than German engineers managed in 1944, it was the IDF, like the US Army in 1944, which managed to hang on, marshal their resources and ultimately prevail.

When the Israelis finally understood an attack was imminent just before war commenced, their reaction was sluggish, with precious hours wasted, and the initial counter-attacks were poorly coordinated, committed piecemeal and destroyed with heavy loss. The fog and friction of war, along with uncertainty, false or ambiguous intelligence reports, and difficult terrain, all combined to degrade Israel's military picture before and during the first few hours of combat. Just as the Germans had concealed their intentions in 1944 using elaborate security and deception measures, the Egyptians and Syrians did likewise in 1973, blinding or confusing Israel's array of human and mechanical sensors. They rehearsed the mobilisation of reserves and mounted exercises near the Israeli borders so many times, which created an impenetrable 'background noise', that the real intelligence picture for their opponents was soon distorted.

There was some important German influence in Egypt and Syria, which dated back to the war, and had its roots in the anti-British and pro-Nazi attitudes of Vichy Syria, Rashid Ali in Iraq, King Farouk of Egypt and the Grand Mufti of Jerusalem. Post-war these states immediately became a safe haven for those fleeing justice and retribution from the Allies in Europe. Many Egyptian nationalists had been disappointed when Rommel failed to break through at Alamein in 1942 and liberate them from British rule. Later King Farouk had been 'impressed' by his garage mechanics recruited from Afrika Korps POWs, and 'wondered what he might achieve with officers from elite units of the Gestapo and SS who had fought so hard against the hated British'.[1]

Perhaps it is just an amazing coincidence that none other than Otto Skorzeny acted as a senior military consultant to Egypt's first president, General Mohammed Naguib, who seized power from Farouk in 1952 with Gamal Abdel Nasser. For several years, Skorzeny recruited a staff made up of former German officers to train the Egyptian armed forces. These included at least two other senior Ardennes veterans: Generalmajor Otto-Ernst Remer, who (along with Skorzeny) played a decisive role in foiling the 20 July Plot and led to his command of the *Führer-Begleit-Brigade* in December 1944, and Skorzeny's business partner, *Fallschirmjäger* Major Gerhard Mertens, whom we met leading his pioneer battalion at Vianden in the Bulge, and with Skorzeny and Remer held the Knight's Cross. With Skorzeny in 1943, Mertens had liberated Mussolini, and was employed to raise and train Egypt's elite Parachute Battalion.

The drain of ex-Wehrmacht and SS figures trickling away to Egypt and Syria was first broken as a story by the German magazine *Der Spiegel* in April 1952 under the headline 'Heil Rommel'.[2] It noted that other senior figures mentoring the Egyptians included General der Artillerie Wilhelm Fahrmbacher, who held corps commands in the Wehrmacht and tutored the central planning staff in Cairo, Generalmajor Oskar Munzel, an ex-commander of the 2nd and 14th Panzer Divisions, Generalmajor Max von Prittwitz und Gaffron, Generalleutnant von Ravenstein, who had commanded the 21st Panzer Division under Rommel, and Luftwaffe Stuka ace Oberst Hans-Ulrich Rudel. The latter had flown 2,500 combat missions over Russia, claimed 202 Soviet tanks destroyed and emerged as the most highly decorated German serviceman of the war.

Additionally, *Der Spiegel* mentioned 'hundreds of former regimental and battalion commanders, staff officers and air force officers' as well as other SS and Gestapo officers who demonstrated their pro-Arab loyalties by their wartime anti-Jewish credentials.[3] For example, the sinister Sudeten German SS-Gruppenführer Alois Moser, together with his assistant, SS-Gruppenführer Friedrich Buble, were in charge of training Egyptian youth along the lines of the *Hitlerjugend*, while in 1972 the Jewish Telegraphic Agency revealed that SS-Standartenführer Erich Weinmann, former Gestapo chief of Prague, had long been residing in Alexandria as consultant to its police force.[4]

These ex-Nazis were true believers, not just guns for hire. Skorzeny was one of the main figures behind ODESSA (*Organisation der ehemaligen SS-Angehörigen*), the organisation created to spirit away former SS members to refuges in South America and the Middle East (though at least one historian, Guy Walters, argues that ODESSA never actually existed). Remer was active in German politics, founding two neo-Nazi parties which were banned before he fled to Spain and died in exile. Mertens was active in Remer's political organisations and Skorzeny's arms-dealing and consultancy ventures, working with authoritarian regimes in several countries, including Persia and Chile as well as Egypt. Equally unrepentant was Hans-Ulrich Rudel, who advised right-wing governments in Argentina and Paraguay, and was later active in Remer's Socialist Reich Party.

Their collective legacy to Egypt was both political and military; for example, among the several Palestinian refugees who received commando training from Skorzeny was Yasser Arafat. When Naguib was replaced by Nasser in 1953, Skorzeny was appointed the new Egyptian president's chief military adviser for several years, becoming a multi-millionaire from arms deals in the process. He had formally departed by the time Egypt united with Syria, creating the United Arab Republic (1956–62), but it is impossible not to believe he and his *Herbstnebel* colleagues left a profound military influence behind them.[5]

Skorzeny was also very close to Franco's Spain, holding a Spanish passport until his death in 1975, where he acted as an intermediary in Bonn's negotiations for possible bases in Spain for the Bundeswehr, in the event of fighting an unsuccessful war with Russia for possession of West Germany. A Canadian journalist reported in 1960 that 'aggrieved German diplomats in Madrid have complained to the Foreign Office here that Skorzeny enjoys something akin to celebrity status with the Spanish government'.

Throughout the 1950s and 1960s, he was prominent in right-wing regimes across the world, where there were genuine fears of Communist world domination. Documents recently released by the Madrid and Bonn governments outlined Skorzeny's plans to establish a German-recruited formation, numbering up to 200,000 former soldiers, willing to fight under Spanish command, to be known as the Legion Carlos V, in the event of the then widely anticipated Third World War. These plans were made with the connivance of US and German authorities (ironically Eisenhower then being president), and their various secret services.[6]

Skorzeny also placed Rainer Kriebel, a former Afrika Korps staff officer, who had transferred to the Waffen-SS in 1944, as head of a military mission to retrain Syria's army with ex-Luftwaffe Oberst Heinz Heigl (one-time CO of *Kampfgeschwader* 200, the German air force's special operations unit), to mentor its military air service.[7] In the late 1940s, Kriebel, Remer and Skorzeny had already had to collect their thoughts about their wartime experiences and write reports for the US Army Intelligence Service. They would have also been very familiar with some of the Arab weapons: between 1951 and 1954, Syria bought around 150 refurbished ex-Wehrmacht panzers from France, Czechoslovakia and Spain, some of which were later captured by Israel in the 1967 Six-Day War.[8]

In 1973, thousands of hand-held Rocket-Propelled Grenades (RPGs), a weapon developed from the 1944 *Panzerfaust*, annihilated IDF counter-attacks, where the recipients were frequently Israeli half-tracks and up-gunned Sherman tanks, acquired from the US as surplus after the Second World War, some of them conceivably veteran machines from the Ardennes campaign. To counter the threat of Allied air power in 1944, the Germans developed very effective mobile air defences based on tanks and trucks; the Arabs similarly used Soviet-designed surface-to-air missile (SAM) batteries to negate some of the danger posed by the Israeli Air Force. The Soviet ZSU 23-4 used by the Egyptians (quadruple-mounted anti-defence cannon built on to a tank) was actually a direct copy of the *Wirbelwind* anti-aircraft panzer used in December 1944.

The Egyptians also preceded their attacks with air attacks on radar installations, airfields and command posts, but these were remarkably ineffective, as in the manner that *Bodenplatte* (the Luftwaffe air attack originally conceived to herald *Herbstnebel*) failed for the Germans. Although by 1973 the military influence in Egypt and Syria was emphatically Russian, the Soviet approach had been developed from studying and improving upon German blitzkrieg doctrine and its component equipment. Skorzeny's chief legacy to Egypt was the surprise attack and deception template first used in 1944 in the Ardennes, and developed by Nasser's successor, Anwar el-Sadat, when the latter became president of Egypt in 1970. This was the same Lieutenant Sadat of the Egyptian Signal Corps who in 1942 had relayed secret messages of support from his army colleagues to Rommel.[9]

The Yom Kippur War for Israel exactly reinforced the lessons learned after 1944: that bias, self-deception, overconfidence and careless considerations of enemy capabilities can lead to an unpleasant military surprise. As in 1944, faulty intelligence analysis, swayed by preconceptions, obscured the real intentions and capabilities of Israel's opponents. Both attacks indicate that, despite cutting-edge intelligence technology, operational surprise was still – and remains – possible. The unanticipated events of September 11 2001 serve to reinforce this lesson: a devious and clever opponent is always capable of outwitting even a technologically advanced power.[10]

As we saw when discussing the events and consequences of the Malmedy massacre, the 1946 trial of its perpetrators, held in the former Dachau concentration camp, also thrust the Bulge into the post-war limelight. The crime had outraged the American military, and after the war the US Army sought to bring those responsible to justice. Eventually, as noted, seventy-five former Waffen-SS men were assembled and tried en masse before a military court of senior US Officers between May and July. The accused included Sepp Dietrich, Fritz Krämer, his chief of staff, Hermann Priess, of the I SS Panzer Corps and seventy-two other members of *Kampfgruppe Peiper*, including its commander. The verdicts ranged from forty-three, including Peiper and Hans Hennecke, sentenced to death; twenty-two (including Sepp Dietrich) to life imprisonment; Priess and one other were given twenty years; one was sentenced to fifteen years and five to ten years. Despite the overwhelming desire for justice, it started to emerge that, in their enthusiasm, investigators and prosecutors had overstepped the mark by conducting mock trials, using false death sentences, beatings and abuse to extort confessions.

When a subcommittee of the US Senate began to investigate the trial in 1949, the ambitious Senator Joseph McCarthy whose state, Wisconsin, contained a large American German population, started challenging the verdicts. Using the aggressive questioning and bullying tactics which later made him famous, even towards the survivors of the massacre, he interpreted the trial as an attempt by left-wing German Jewish intelligentsia in the US Army to attack the anti-Communist German defendants. He left the proceedings before the year was through, but many felt at the time his motivation to intervene was pure self-interest. His star waned quickly after formal censure by his colleagues in 1954.

The Malmedy massacre trial had, nevertheless, become well and truly mired in controversy, and the international situation had moved on. Although NATO had been formed originally, in the words of its first Secretary-General, Lord Ismay, 'to keep the Americans in, the Russians out and the Germans down', the Cold War had grown more intense, requiring the help of West Germany and putting pressure on the US Army to commute the death sentences to life imprisonment and shorten the prison terms. Eventually all seventy-three of the convicted were released; among the last were Dietrich, released in October 1955, and Peiper, freed in December 1956.

Less fortunate were those of both sides who died and were listed as missing in action (MIA), their combat graves never being identified. Throughout the 1950s and 1960s reports would hit the newspapers of human remains being recovered in the battlefield areas. Modern military researchers using metal detectors, ground-penetrating radar and DNA techniques have increased the rate of finds and greatly improved the probability of positive identification. This was prompted by the Bosnian wars of the 1990s and the needs of the United Nations to analyse, interpret and identify the mass graves of various ethnic factions, a grisly reality I witnessed in person, and which gave birth to the whole new science of forensic archaeology.

The efforts of local enthusiasts in the Ardennes have been supplemented by specialised investigation and recovery teams from the US Joint Prisoner of War/Missing in Action Accounting Command (JPAC), whose heart-warming mission is 'never to leave a fallen comrade behind'. Author Bill Warnock has written movingly in *The Dead of Winter: How Battlefield Investigators, WWII Veterans, and Forensic Scientists Solved the Mystery of the Bulge's Lost Soldiers*, of the meticulous research involved in the recovery and identification of twelve missing GIs in the Ardennes over recent years, often helped by my colleague William C. C. Cavanagh, while others have managed similar feats for the young *Volksgrenadiers* and *Fallschirmjäger* who lie in their lonely graves.[11] From the amount of battlefield detritus I have stumbled on over the years, it is evident there are many more soldiers yet to be 'brought home'.

And what of their commanders? Courtney H. Hodges, who succeeded Bradley at the US First Army, witnessed a unique double, being present at the surrenders of both Germany at SHAEF headquarters in Reims and the Japanese Empire in Tokyo Bay on 2 September 1945; he retired as commander of First Army in 1949. George Patton of the Third became the military governor of Bavaria. Frequently careless with the media and inclined to controversy, on 28 September Ike felt obliged to relieve him of his governorship and on 7 October of his beloved Third Army. A token was offered to him in the form of the tiny US Fifteenth Army, then a small headquarters staff tasked to compile a history of the war in Europe. But peacetime was not for Patton and he had decided to leave this last position and not return to Europe after his Christmas 1945 leave, before fate intervened in the form of a traffic accident on 8 December.

This left him with a broken neck and a spinal cord injury, paralysing him from the neck down. He died in his sleep of a heart attack on 21 December 1945. There was no evidence of foul play (as many conspiracy theorists have suggested) and although he did not die as he might have wished, in combat, he lies buried at the head of his men in the American Military Cemetery in Luxembourg. Simpson of the Ninth undertook a mission to China in July 1945 and subsequently commanded the US Second Army in Tennessee. Very much the unsung hero in the USA, he retired in November 1946. Troy Middleton led his superb VIII Corps through to the end, accumulating 480 days of combat from 1943 to 1945, more than any other American general officer. He retired a second time in 1945, returning to take up a series of distinguished positions at Louisiana State University.

A staggering number of America's post-war leaders had served in the Ardennes, in many cases it being their performance on that winter battlefield that pushed them to the very top: they would influence their armed forces for decades to come. The Bulge experience not only dominated the Cold War in Europe but stretched as far forward as Korea and Vietnam, where during 1964–8 General William Westmoreland harked back to the days when he had served as chief of staff of the 9th Infantry Division on the northern shoulder of the Bulge. His deputy in that theatre was the tank battalion commander who had broken into Bastogne, Creighton Adams, who would serve as Army Chief of Staff from 1972 before cancer killed him two years later. Another Korean War general was Oscar Koch, Patton's G-2, who became commander of the 25th Infantry Division, retiring from military service in 1954.[12]

Eisenhower succeeded George C. Marshall as Army Chief of Staff at the war's end to be followed in 1948 by Omar Bradley. His next three successors were all Bulge veterans: J. Lawton Collins, Matthew Ridgway and Maxwell Taylor. Eisenhower went on to head Columbia University briefly before returning to Europe as the Supreme Allied Commander, Europe (SACEUR), from 1950 until 1952, when he was followed by Matthew Ridgway. Although President Truman had approached Ike to run as his successor, in the event Ike ran as a Republican, marking the

Grand Old Party's first incumbent of the Oval Office in twenty years, serving for two terms as the thirty-fourth President.

After a year as Army Chief of Staff in August 1949, Bradley was appointed as the United States' first Chairman of the Joint Chiefs of Staff. Maxwell Taylor would later serve in the same office between 1962 and 1964. Eisenhower was briefly the first Commander-in-Chief of the United States Army Europe (USAEUR); among his successors in that post was Clarence R. Huebner, who had commanded the US 1st Infantry Division on Omaha Beach and taken over V Corps when his predecessor left to command the Fifteenth Army. Manton Eddy, one of Patton's corps commanders, William M. Hoge, who made his name at St Vith, and Anthony McAuliffe, author of the 'Nuts!' note at Bastogne and eventually Bruce C. Clarke all followed Huebner, the latter from 1960 to 1962. The flamboyant Leland S. 'Hollywood' Hobbs, commander of the 30th Division, retired as Deputy Commander of the US First Army in 1953. Harry Kinnard, who suggested the 'Nuts!' response to McAuliffe, later led the 1st Cavalry Division (Airmobile) in Vietnam. His 1965 battle in the Ia Drang valley was recounted in the 1992 book *We Were Soldiers Once . . . And Young*.

James Gavin played a central role desegregating the US Army, beginning with the incorporation of the all-black 555th Parachute Infantry Battalion into his 82nd Airborne Division. Retiring as a lieutenant-general, he was called out of retirement in 1961 to serve as a highly successful US Ambassador to France. After the war, the Office of Strategic Services (OSS) became the CIA, whose second director had formerly commanded the US Ninth Air Force, the tactical formation based in England and France, which supported the Allied armies over the Ardennes – Hoyt S. Vandenberg; he was followed later by Walter Bedell Smith, from 1950 to 1953. One of his departmental chiefs, the Head of Covert Operations, was Edwin L. Sibert, Bradley's former G-2 at Twelfth Army Group. On 30 March 1945 the 3rd Armored Division's popular commander, Maurice Rose, had the unfortunate distinction of becoming the highest ranking American killed by enemy fire in the European Theatre during the war, caught in a German tank ambush near the city of Paderborn. Most felt he would have gone to much higher office after the war.

'Dutch' Cota's reputation had already been tainted by the Hürtgen Forest. Though not his fault, the battering his division received in the Ardennes didn't help. He was unfortunate that, after such a fine performance on Omaha Beach, he twice ended up in the lion's jaws, and left the US Army in 1946. One of his subordinates, James Earl Rudder, on the other hand, flourished. From a lieutenant in the National Guard before the war, Rudder rose eventually to become a major-general and president of his alma mater, Texas A & M University. In many ways his achievements there during the 1960s, of turning an ultra-conservative, all-white male military school of 7,500 students into a 14,000-strong, co-educational, multi-ethnic college, where membership of the Corps of Cadets was voluntary, were as brave as taking on the Germans twenty years earlier.

In the United Kingdom, Field Marshal Montgomery stepped into Brooke's shoes as Chief of the Imperial General Staff (CIGS) in June 1946, which was universally regarded as a disastrous move, as he antagonised both his superiors and subordinates. Monty may have been a robust commander in war but proved no peacetime warrior, insulting all and sundry – particularly his American contemporaries – through ill-judged post-war lectures and memoirs. With his elevation, the career prospects of any officers, however talented, who had served at SHAEF, were limited on account of Monty's prejudices against that organisation. Major-General Strong retired, eventually becoming the first Director of the Joint Intelligence Bureau and latterly first Director-General of Intelligence at the UK Ministry of Defence. His 1968 memoirs, *Intelligence at the Top*, did their best to whitewash SHAEF's failure to predict the Ardennes. Monty's own G-2, Edgar 'Bill' Williams, returned to academic life, being elected a Fellow of Balliol College, Oxford, in 1945; by then he had received several decorations and would be knighted in 1973.

The influence of the Ardennes lingered in Germany too. Many senior commanders perished in 1945, were hanged at Nuremberg, like Jodl and Keitel, or died of natural causes – Rundstedt in 1953, Brandenberger in 1955 and Dietrich in 1966 – Hasso von Manteuffel was released from Allied captivity in 1947, served in the Bundestag from 1953 to 1957 and advised on the redevelopment of the Bundeswehr. Fritz Bayerlein, too, was released from detention in 1947 and, like Manteuffel and Brandenberger, took part in the US Army Historical Division's Foreign Military Studies Program.

This amounted to nearly 2,500 papers, devoid of politics and purely military in scope, written from 1945 to 1959 by former senior officers, which covered most aspects of the Reich's war effort. They were influential because at the operational level they concentrated on German successes, in logistics, the handling of armour, command and control, security, deception and surprise. They helped to rebuild German military self-confidence – vital to NATO – and forge the reputation of the new Bundeswehr.

Some studies – in the era of the Cold War – examined the methodology of defeating the Soviets in battle, but many focused on Germany's last big campaign in the west – the Battle of the Bulge. The program, devised with considerable forethought, included the invaluable 'ETHINT' (European Theater Historical Interrogations) series of interviews with senior commanders, conducted immediately after the war. It also covered narrative histories of units on the Western Front and campaign analyses, written by committees of former officers. Just about every senior *Herbstnebel* commander alive after the war, and in western custody, took part. As many were conducted within a year of the events of the Bulge, they provide a particularly rich seam of primary source material, which I and countless others have found profitable to mine.

Friedrich von der Heydte became head of the Institute for Military Law at the University of Würzburg, a Brigadier-General in the Bundeswehr Reserves, and an influential figure in post-war Catholic circles. Heinz Guderian's son, Heinz-Günther, stayed with the Greyhound (*Windhund*) Panzer Division until the war's end. Joining the Bundeswehr at its creation, he rose to become Inspector-General of Panzer Troops, fittingly the same post his father had held in the Wehrmacht, retiring in 1974. Guderian's former commander of the Greyhounds, Gerhard, Graf von Schwerin, was appointed as chief adviser on military issues and security policy to Chancellor Konrad Adenauer. The odious Wilhelm Mohnke, whose wartime career was characterised by his proximity to executions and massacres, was captured in Berlin and handed over to the NKVD and, curiously, released in 1955. Despite several attempts in Britain and Germany to indict him for war crimes, he constantly denied any complicity and, rather unjustly, died of natural causes in August 2001.

Perhaps the most curious story of all was that of Jochen Peiper, who in 1972 built himself a retirement home near Traves in eastern France. Leading a quiet and discreet life, translating books and writing articles about the war and motor sport, he made no attempt to conceal his identity. In 1974 he was identified by a former Communist partisan and by 1976 the left-wing newspaper *L'Humanité* had drawn attention to his whereabouts. Sending his family away to safety, the former *Kampfgruppe* commander was last seen alive the night before Bastille Day in 1976. The following day, Gendarmes were called to the charred remains of his house, gutted by fire, which contained the badly burned body of the late SS-*Obersturmbannführer*, a bullet in his chest and still clutching a rifle and pistol. The brazen manner of his execution caused Communist Party offices to be attacked throughout France, but, as his biographer pointed out, Peiper could have begun a new life anywhere in the world, simply by buying a plane ticket.[13] Perhaps he knew his own history compelled him to stay in Europe: Malmedy had finally caught up with him.

At the other end of the command chain, the Second World War ended for most GIs in some small town in Germany. Captain B. MacDonald was actually over the border in Czechoslovakia, at Radčice, near Pilsen. He attended a gathering put on by the village population to celebrate the war's end. At the close, those present prepared to sing their national anthem, the first time they had been permitted to perform it in public for seven years. It was a poignant moment. 'The people rose as one, and every boy, girl, man and woman joined in the singing with clear, lusty voices that made goose-pimples rise on my arms. Some of the older people cried, and it was all I could do to keep the tears from my eyes.' Afterwards MacDonald walked on to the terrace and saw 'light streaming from the windows and Army vehicles driving on the highway with their headlights on . . . I suddenly realised that I could light a cigarette once again in the open without fear of drawing enemy fire, and I did. It was a simple thing, but it gave me a wonderful feeling that life was worth living again.'[14]

Acknowledgements

IT WAS THE long shadow of the First World War that dominated the news media as I researched and wrote *Snow and Steel*. The centenary of its outbreak fell in the summer of 2014 and it was while travelling in the footsteps of Eisenhower that I realised how much the ghosts of 1914-18 haunted all the senior commanders in the Bulge. Ike's headquarters in Paris – where he and Bradley first heard of the German attacks on 16 December 1944 – was the Trianon Palace Hotel at Versailles. I learned when staying there that during 1918 it housed the Inter-Allied Military Council, the Great War predecessor of SHAEF, and the following year the terms of the Versailles Treaty were agreed in the hotel's salon. The famous document itself was signed later in the Hall of Mirrors of Louis XIV's nearby Palace.

Naturally, I also felt obliged to stay in the Hotel Britannique in Spa, the headquarters of Courtney Hodges' US First Army. Here, too, the shadows of 1914–18 abounded. In March 1918 the German General Staff, led by Hindenburg and Ludendorff, installed themselves in the Britannique, in preparation for their Spring Offensive – the last major foray by an earlier German army, and not unlike *Herbstnebel*. November of that year saw the Kaiser take the decision to abdicate in Hindenburg's office on the first floor. In December 1944, the staff told me, Hodges – consciously or unconsciously – actually occupied the very same office that had witnessed the dramas of 26 years earlier. The Hotel Claravallis in Clervaux provided a different echo of the past. Although the present structure is modern, it was rebuilt on the site of the old hotel which witnessed Colonel Hurley Fuller's heroic defence of 17 December 1944 and is a good point from which to consider the battles of the 'northern shoulder' of the Bulge. To the managers and staff of all three hotels, who looked after me sumptuously, I owe a debt of gratitude for their time and help.

I have been fortunate that several colleagues, including Dr Roger Cirillo of the Association of the US Army (ausa.org), Major General David T. Zabecki, US Army, Dr Steve Prince, and Toby Macleod, were kind enough to read through early drafts, correct and challenge some of my wilder conclusions. Roger Cirillo also loaned or gave me many helpful volumes. So too did my fellow historian and close friend James Holland (www.griffonmerlin.com), author of many sound books on military history and in whose company I have found much enlightenment and wisdom. James is the co-founder of the Chalke Valley History Festival (cvhf.org.uk) which for a week each July fields many erudite speakers on a wide range of historical topics, several of whom – wittingly or unwittingly – opened up new lines of thought for this book. Thanks you to James, and all who have served on the Chalke Valley Front.

I am fortunate to work at the UK Defence Academy, Shrivenham, where officers sleep contentedly through my lectures on aspects of military history and current defence analysis. Nevertheless my long-suffering bosses, Dr. Laura Cleary, head of the Centre for International Security and Resilience, and Dr. Sylvie Jackson, generously gave me valuable time to research and write about the Battle of the Bulge, whilst my secretary, Anne Harbour, was kind enough to fend off visitors at crucial moments. I also lecture on air power to other somnolent military personnel at RAF Halton, Buckinghamshire, where the staff of the Airman's Command Squadron, led by Squadron Leader Matt Cornish, and latterly Squadron Leader Rachel Portlock, and Flight Lieutenants Mark Adams and Matt Copson, have been especially tolerant of my all-hours writing activities.

I have visited the Ardennes and associated locations countless times, often in the company of my friend, colleague and mentor, the late, great, Professor Richard Holmes, under whom I worked for nearly fifteen years. It was he who first taught me how to 'read' an old battlefield, and together we interviewed many a veteran or clambered over a disused trench. Richard died far too young, departing to join the Great Muster Beyond in 2011, and daily I still miss his sparkle. Another departed friend was Colonel Emile Engels of the Belgian Army who took much trouble to guide me over 'his' battlefields. Over the years, NATO forces, and particularly the British Army, have invited me to guide them around the Ardennes region I have come to know so well, but there is always a trade. I offer historical knowledge in exchange for their military insights: it is a barter that works wonderfully, and on every battlefield tour or staff ride I have never failed to expand my understanding of the 1944–45 winter campaign, as seen through the eyes of serving soldiers.

Ideas shared with friends and colleagues from the UK-based International Guild of Battlefield Guides (www.gbg-international.com) have increased my comprehension further. I have also greatly enjoyed exploring the area with Sam Doss of OSS and Colonel Peter Herrly, former US Defense Attaché in Paris. To Major General Mike Reynolds I owe a special debt of gratitude for sharing with me the results of his many years of study on *Kampfgruppe* Peiper; likewise, Major General Mungo Melvin, author of the definitive biography of Erich von Manstein, has mentored me over the years on the Wehrmacht, whilst Major General Graham Hollands, based in his hospitable Normandy mansion (www.lebocage-bedandbreakfast.com), has been an equally supportive friend with no end of advice on the Allied forces of 1944–45. My enthusiasm for the Battle of the Bulge grew partly out of my studies of the Normandy campaign, for so many US units fought in both areas, while the Red Ball Express linked the two. I often begin a tour of the 1944 battlefields to follow the GIs from Normandy to the Bulge by staying at the wonderful Château de Saint-Maclou (www.chateaudesaintmaclou.com), a beautiful 17th century house lovingly restored by an English couple, Robin and Nicola Gage, and tucked away in the countryside near Honfleur and Le Havre. It is an appropriate start point, for nearby were the vast US transit camps (named after cigarette brands, Pall Mall, Phillip Morris, Lucky Strike), where most GIs began and many German prisoners ended their war in Europe.

Amongst my professional colleagues, Professors Chris Bellamy, John Buckley, Gary Sheffield, Sir Hew Strachan, and Trevor Taylor have all suggested lines of research or useful insights, as have Drs Ed Flint, Dale Clark and Bryan Watters. Dr. David Turns has given me invaluable advice on matters of international law, Dr David Chuter has steered me through the delicate issues of Second World War French politics and advised on the figure of Charles de Gaulle. Air Commodore Nick Randle and Group Captain Chris Finn have likewise guided me on aspects of aerial warfare, as has Colonel Paul Beaver. Lieutenant-Colonel John Starling has, as always, been most helpful on all aspects of Allied and German infantry weaponry. Thank you also to Cristina de Santiago, who researched Otto Skorzeny and German armoured vehicles for me, Rob and Jacqueline de Ruyter of the fantastic Ardennes '44 Museum at Poteau (www.museum-poteau44.be); Monsieur Roland Gaul and the staff of his National Museum of Military History in Diekirch (www.mnhm.lu); the staff of Museum of the Battle of the Bulge in Clervaux Castle; and those of the December '44 Museum at La Gleize (www.december44.com). Major John Thomas of the 1940s Swansea Bay Museum (www.1940sswanseabay.co.uk) kindly traced the history of some US units stationed in England for me. Many other friends have been helpful in collecting or collating memoirs, and supportive with suggestions, including Nataliya Kreminska, Rachel Daniels and Iain McKay of Cranfield University's Barrington Library, Guy Leaning and the British Overseas Chums (BOCs), Mike St Maur Sheil, Angeliki Vasilopoulou and Guy Walters.

Other institutions, including the 101st Airborne Museum in Bastogne (www.101airbornemuseumbastogne.com); the Bastogne Historical Center on the Mardasson Hill (now renamed the Bastogne War Museum, www.bastognewarmuseum.be); the Truschbaum Museum at Camp Elsenborn; the Baugnez 44 Historical Center outside Malmedy; the Bastogne Barracks, with its Nuts Cellar at 40 Rue de la Roche; the Bastogne Ardennes '44 Museum, located on the N84 (www.bastogneardennes44.com); and the *Musée de la Bataille des Ardennes* in La Roche (www.batarden.be) have all been most kind in opening their archives and explaining their exhibits. The staff of three American war cemeteries, wonderfully maintained by the American Battle Monuments Commission (abmc.gov), have also been most helpful. The Henri-Chapelle Cemetery is one of the largest in Europe, with nearly 8,000 US soldier and airmen graves. In the Ardennes Military Cemetery at Neuville-en-Condroz, southwest of Liège, lie 5,000 more war dead, many from the capture of Aachen before the Ardennes battles. A mile from Luxembourg Airport another 5,000 are buried: at their head rests General George Patton, still facing his troops. My thanks, too, for helping to trace various soldiers, go to the *Volksbund Deutsche Kriegsgräberfürsorge* (German War Graves Commission), who maintain their cemetery at Recogne, containing 6,800 German soldiers, and the Commonwealth War Graves Commission (cwgc.org), who likewise look after the cemetery at Hotton, where this book begins, and where 666 warriors slumber on.

This book would not have been possible without access to the extensive archives of the US National Archives and Records Administration (NARA) at College Park, Maryland, where Dr Mitchell (Mitch) A. Yockelson, who teaches at the US Naval Academy and is a military history specialist for NARA, was instrumental in tracking down many records and interviews, including that of Ken Hechler with Jochen Peiper. Similarly invaluable, the staff at the National Defense University Library, Washington DC (for the Maxwell D. Taylor papers), and those at the US Army Heritage and Education Center (USAHEC) in Ridgway Hall, US Army Military History Institute (USAMHI), who hold the Creighton Adams, James M. Gavin and Matthew B. Ridgway papers, and US Army War College Library in Root Hall, all located at the US Army War College complex, Carlisle, Pennsylvania, have been hugely helpful.

My thanks to staff or colleagues at the following: the British Commission for Military History (www.bcmh.org.uk); British Newspaper Archive (BNA) of the British Library; Churchill Archives Centre, Churchill College, Cambridge (www.chu.cam.ac.uk/archives); *Das Bundesarchiv*, Freiburg, Germany (www.bundesarchiv.de); the Combined Arms Research Library (CARL) of the US Army Command and General Staff College, Fort Leavenworth, Kansas (www.cgsc.edu); the Development, Concepts and Doctrine Centre, Watchfield (www.gov.uk/government/groups/development-concepts-and-doctrine-centre); Imperial War Museum, Lambeth (www.iwm.org.uk); Joint Services Command and Staff College, Watchfield (www.da.mod.uk/colleges/jscsc); Land Warfare Centre; Liddell Hart Centre for Military Archives, King's College, London (www.kingscollections.org/catalogues/lhcma); Royal College of Defence Studies, London (www.da.mod.uk/colleges/rcds); Royal Military Academy Sandhurst (www.sandhurstcollection.co.uk); and other museums, archives and websites who have kindly made available their exhibits, records and scholarly research.

These also include *After the Battle* magazine and its Editor-in-Chief, Winston Ramsey (www.afterthebattle.com), who pioneered the 'then-and-now' format of military history photographic interpretation; the Battle of the Bulge Memories website (www.battleofthebulgememories.be); the *Stadtarchiv und Landesgeschichtliche Bibliothek* (State City Archives and Historical Library) of Bielefeld, Germany (www.bielefeld.de); CEBA (*Cercle d'Études sur la Bataille des Ardennes* – Study Group on the Battle of the Bulge, www.ceba.lu); CIBRA (*Centre de Recherche et d'Information sur la Bataille des Ardennes* – Centre of Research and

Information on the Battle of the Bulge, www. criba.be); *Deutsches Panzer Museum*, Munster (www.panzermuseum-munster.de); Eisenhower's and Bradley's papers in the US Library of Congress (www.loc.gov); the Bedell Smith, J. Lawton Collins, Eisenhower and Hodges papers, Eisenhower Presidential Library, Abilene, Kansas (www.eisenhower.archives.gov); *Landesarchiv Baden-Württemberg*, Stuttgart, Germany (www.landesarchiv-bw.de); Troy H. Middleton Personal Papers and Middleton Room Memorabilia, Louisiana State University Archives, Baton Rouge, (www.lib.lsu.edu); The National Archives, Kew (www.nationalarchives.gov.uk); National Infantry Museum and Soldier Center, Columbus, Georgia (www.nationalinfantrymuseum.org); National WWII Museum, New Orleans (www.nationalww2museum.org); General George Patton Museum and Centre of Leadership, Fort Knox, Kentucky (www.generalpatton.org); Peace Museum, Bridge at Remagen (www.bruecke-remagen.de); RAF Museum, Hendon (www.rafmuseum.org.uk); James Earl Rudder Papers, Cushing Memorial Library and Archives, Texas A&M University (www.library.tamu.edu); Tank Museum, Bovington, Dorset (www.tankmuseum.org); Harry S. Truman Library, Independence, Missouri (www.trumanlibrary.org); US Army Quartermaster Museum, Fort Lee, Virginia (www.qmmuseum.lee.army.mil); United States Military Academy West Point Museum (www.usma.edu); Veterans of the Battle of the Bulge (www.veteransofthebattleofthebulge.org); and the Virginia Military Institute Museum (www.vmi.edu).

Visiting the Belgian Grand Prix circuit just down the road from Hodges' First Army headquarters at Spa reminds one that researching and writing a work like this is not unlike entering a car for a Formula One race. The writer is like the driver, but there are many behind the scenes keeping the author and his work 'on the road'. It was Tim Bent, History Editor at Oxford University Press in New York who first encouraged me to re-examine the Battle of the Bulge as Father Time dragged the campaign past its 70th anniversary. I am grateful to him for steering me in the direction of the Ardennes and away from other projects. Tim also provided invaluable editing and advice, culturally fine-tuning my more obscure Briticisms, where necessary, into solid American, and challenging some of my poorly argued assertions. This volume would be nowhere without my agents, Patrick Walsh and Alex Christofi at Conville & Walsh, who have worked hard, mentoring me through this project. That this is the third book I have written for Preface publisher Trevor Dolby is a measure I hope of his confidence in me, and a tribute to his forbearance, for he has long learned how challenging I find the publishing equivalent of D-Days and H-Hours. Trevor, your patience is truly humbling. Trevor's team at Preface, this time including Katherine Murphy, Phil Brown and Philippa Cotton have worked their professional magic to get this mass of pages and illustrations into order and production under the tightest of deadlines. This author is overwhelmed by your efforts on his behalf.

Many individuals who lived through the events of 1944–5, soldiers and civilians, have contributed to this book. I wish I could have included every anecdote, but in the interests of painting as wide a panorama as possible, I found I was obliged to omit some stories and reminiscences. On some occasions, such as the fiftieth and sixtieth anniversaries of 16 December 1944, I was swamped with too many veterans to interview. I apologise to the individuals concerned if I have misspelled names, misreported or omitted their stories. It is you, who served and witnessed these events, who have made this book possible: *Snow and Steel* is my salute and gratitude for your service.

Notes

Foreword

1. Today the figure is 15 per cent. See Ancestry 2000, *Census 2000 Brief* (June 2004), at: http://www.census.gov/prod/2004pubs/c2kbr-35.pdf
2. Military Vehicle Conservation Group Liberty Highway Tour of the Ardennes, 13–27 August 1978, reported in many Belgian and Luxembourg (*Le Soir, L'Avenir du Luxembourg, Le Jour, Tageblatt für Lëtzebuerg, Le Courier, La Meuse*) newspapers at the time.

Introduction

1. In 1944 it numbered about 800. The wider Hotton municipality, including outlying hamlets and villages, today totals 5,400.
2. Ken Hechler, *Holding the Line: The 51st Combat Engineer Battalion and the Battle of the Bulge, December 1944–January 1945* (Studies in Military Engineering, Number 4, Office of History, US Army Corps of Engineers, Fort Belvoir, Virginia, 1988), p. 38.
3. These US uniforms were more probably worn against the cold, than to deceive, as German winter clothing was in short supply and generally inferior. Interview at http://home.earthlink.net/~crcorbin/LeRoy2.html
4. Hechler, *Holding the Line*, op. cit., p. 41.
5. The commander of 116th Panzer, Siegfried von Waldenburg, later regarded the reverse suffered in and around Hotton as the turning point for his division during the battle. He observed after the war, 'Our own casualties for the battle of Hotton were heavy; several of our tanks were lost through enemy artillery, others were damaged. Gradually the troops came to realise that what was to have been the deciding blow must have failed, or that victory could not be won; with that, morale

and then efficiency began to suffer.' For a fuller account of the battle, see: http://www.batarden.be/site/en/histoire-de-la-roche-dans-la-bataille-des-ardennes.html

6. T. Rees Shapiro, 'Melvin E. Biddle, Honored for Heroism in Battle of the Bulge, dies at 87', article in *Washington Post*, Tuesday, 21 December 2010.
7. http://cualumni.clemson.edu/page.aspx?pid=1737. For a fuller account of this engagement, see Lt-Col. Alfred S. Roxburgh, CO 289th Infantry Regt, 75th Infantry Division, '*Brief Paper Examining the Facts and Drawing a Conclusion as to Who was in Command of the Augmented Attack and Defense on the Hill, La Roumière, 24, 25 and 26 Dec 44 and Why a 23:30 24 Dec 44 Night Attack was Critical*', Command Paper at: http://75thdivisiondad.com/75th_division_command_paper.htm
8. Generalmajor Rudolf Bader (PW 352173), 560th *Volksgrenadier* Division: Ardennes Campaign, 16 December 1944–25 January 1945, MS #B-024, 30 May 1946, NARA. Klippel lies at Block 15, grave 245 of the Recogne Cemetery, Bastogne.
9. The square names him as lieutenant, whereas Zulli was a captain, and has him dying on 21 December, whereas official US records suggest he died on 22 December.
10. Peter Schrijvers, *The Unknown Dead. Civilians in the Battle of the Bulge* (University Press of Kentucky, 2005), pp. 213–23; Robert K. McDonald, *The Hotton Report* (Finbar Press, 2006).
11. Major Loring went on to serve in the Korean War with the 8th Fighter Bomber Group. He was killed while leading a flight of four F-80 Shooting Star jets in a close-support mission on 22 November 1952. After being hit repeatedly by ground fire, he deliberately crashed his plane into the enemy missile sites, destroying all of them, for which he was posthumously awarded the Medal of Honor.
12. Interviews by Charles R. Corbin Jr with 3rd Armored Division combat veterans: Jack B. Warden, at http://home.earthlink.net/~crcorbin/Hotton.html
13. Major Peter Henry Lawless, MC, War Correspondent, *Daily Telegraph*, killed 9 March 1945, aged fifty-three (Plot VII, Row A, Grave 8). My thanks to Guy Leaning and his 'British Overseas Chums – the BOCs', with whom I last visited the cemetery.
14. Robert Rhodes James (ed.), *Winston S. Churchill: His Complete Speeches, 1897–1963*, Vol. VII, *1943–1949* (Chelsea House Publishers, 1974), pp. 7095–8.
15. This superseded the much-quoted US War Department General Order No. 114 of 7 December 1945. See Department of the Army, General Order No. 63, *Units Entitled to Battle Credits: Ardennes–Alsace* (HQ Department of the Army, 20 September 1948); Department of the Army Pamphlet 672–1, *Unit Citation and Campaign Participation Credit Register* (HQ, Department of the Army, July 1961).

1. In the Eagle's Nest

1. Helmut Heiber (ed.), *Hitlers Lagebesprechungen* (Institut für Zeitgeschichte, 1962), p. 721, and Felix Gilbert, *Hitler Directs His War* (Oxford University Press, 1951).
2. 427 Squadron, based at RAF Leeming, operating Halifaxes, 11 December 1944, TNA Kew.

3. Albert Speer, *Inside the Third Reich* (Macmillan, 1970), p. 440.
4. The fundamentals of Hitler's speech to his commanders is taken from General Hasso von Manteuffel's chapter 'The Battle of the Ardennes 1944–5', in H.A. Jacobsen and J. Rohwer, *Decisive Battle of World War II: The German View* (André Deutsch, 1965), pp. 401–2.
5. Percy Schramm, *Hitler: The Man and the Military Leader* (Allen Lane, 1972), p. 108.
6. Peter H. Merkl, *The Making of a Stormtrooper* (Princeton University Press, 1980).
7. This was a conscious move by the Reichswehr in the aftermath of the revolutions of 1918–20 throughout Germany to make sure that middle- and lower-class revolutionaries did not enter the ranks of the German officer class, particularly the infantry and cavalry. Hence the disproportionate number of officers bearing the titles of 'von', '*Ritter*' (knight), '*Freiherr*' (baron), and '*Graf*' (count). Logically, aristocrats tended to be better-educated and thus proficient in the many examinations needed for promotion and entry into the General Staff. Nevertheless there were fewer nobles than in the pre-1918 Kaiser's army. Men from humbler backgrounds gravitated towards Nazi organisations where background was not a barrier to advancement, though there were many nobles in both the Luftwaffe and SS.
8. Heinz Linge, *With Hitler to the End* (Frontline, 2009), p. 164.
9. The idea, apparently, was Göring's. On 2 August 1944 in East Prussia, he proposed that as 'an outward token of gratitude for Hitler's miraculous escape on 20 July the entire Wehrmacht (army, navy and air force) should adopt the Hitler salute forthwith'. It was signed into law the same day. Göring had learned the key link man in the conspiracy, shuttling between the main players, was Luftwaffe Lieutenant-Colonel Caesar von Hofacker, a cousin to Stauffenberg. Perhaps Göring's offer to change the salute was to deflect any stain from his service. David Irving, *Hitler's War* (Hodder & Stoughton, 1977), p. 677.
10. This was altered by statute on 24 September 1944, when Wehrmacht members were allowed to join the Nazi Party.
11. Martin Blumenson, *United States Army in World War II, European Theater of Operations, Breakout and Pursuit* (Center of Military History, US Army, 1961), p. 213.
12. Irving, *Hitler's War*, op. cit., p. 684.
13. Führer Directive No. 51, issued on 3 November 1943 in East Prussia, copy at: http://www.alternatewars.com/WW2/WW2_Documents/Fuhrer_Directives/FD_51.htm
14. Percy Schramm (ed.), *Kriegstagebuch Des Oberkommando Der Wehrmacht 1944–45, Band IV/7: 1.Januar 1944–22.Mai 1945* (Bernard & Graefe Verlag, 1982), p. 463.

2. The Machinery of Command

1. A 60,000-acre site, the *Maybach* bunker complexes were constructed in 1934–5, with subterranean communication links to the military commands in central Berlin. Fast-moving Soviet forces occupied the virtually intact Zossen bunker

facilities on 20 April 1945. When a telephone suddenly rang, one of the Russian soldiers answered it. The caller was a senior German officer asking what was happening. 'Ivan is here,' the soldier replied in Russian. The two *Maybach* bunkers were destroyed in 1946, but the communications centre, code-named *Zeppelin*, remains, being used by the Warsaw Pact during the Cold War. It was manned for more than three decades, abandoned only when Russian troops pulled out in 1994, and is now open to the public as a museum.

2. The best modern account is Oberst Karl-Heinz Frieser, *The Blitzkrieg Legend: The 1940 Campaign in the West* (Naval Institute Press, 2005). Consequently historians now view blitzkrieg as the consequence of victory in May 1940, rather than its cause.
3. The controversial David Irving has written that 'Percy Schramm was himself a mediocre historian, and the published volume of the *Kriegstagebuch des Oberkommandos der Wehrmacht for 1942–3*, written by his colleague Helmuth Greiner, is largely faked. I obtained Greiner's real diary and handwritten notes and private letters from his widow and you can see from them the post-war fakery that went into the published edition.' Irving's admonition is an undeserved insult to the highly distinguished Schramm. While not disputing that the OKW *Kriegstagebuch*, from which I quote throughout this book, was pieced together after the war, and occasionally embellished, there is no indication it was a fake. Rather, because the original was burned in 1945, it is a reconstruction from the surviving fragments and the memories of Schramm and Greiner, and stands as a perfectly legitimate historical document. As an Official Historian of UK and NATO military operations in Bosnia and Iraq, I have experienced similar moments where speeches, conversations and documents have had to be reconstructed in the absence of the originals, lost or destroyed. Irving's unfair attack on Schramm is at: http://www.fpp.co.uk/Letters/Hitler/McMahon_030209.html
4. See David Stone, *First Reich. Inside the German Army During the War with France 1870–71* (Brassey's, 2002) and Terence Zuber, *The Battle of the Frontiers. Ardennes 1914* (The History Press, 2007).
5. The Germans employed 75 Pz IV, 70 Pz V and 32 StuG for the attack towards Avranches. Irving, *Hitler's War*, op. cit., pp. 684–5.
6. See Mark J. Reardon, *Victory at Mortain: Stopping Hitler's Panzer Counteroffensive* (University Press of Kansas, 2002) and Robert Weiss, *Fire Mission!: The Siege at Mortain, Normandy, August 1944* (Burd Street Press, 2002).
7. Linge, *With Hitler to the End*, op. cit., p. 164.
8. Joachim Ludewig, *Ruckzüg: The German Retreat from France, 1944* (MGFA/University Press of Kentucky, 2012), p. 283.
9. B. H. Liddell Hart, *The Other Side of the Hill* (Cassell, 1948), p. 445.
10. Schramm, *Kriegstagebuch*, p. 359.
11. John D. Heyl, 'The Construction of the Westwall, 1938: An Exemplar for National Socialist Policymaking', article in *Central European History*, Vol. 14/1 (March 1981), pp. 63–78.
12. John S. D. Eisenhower, *The Bitter Woods: The Battle of the Bulge* (G. P. Putnam's Sons, 1969), p. 112; Irving, *Hitler's War*, pp. 689–90.

13. Joseph F. McCloskey, 'British Operational Research in World War II', article in *Operations Research*, Vol. 35/3, pp. 453–70.
14. Becker memoir courtesy of *Der Erste Zug* website, at: http://dererstezug.com/VetBecker.htm
15. Blumenson, *United States Army in World War II*, op. cit., p. 208.
16. Ian Gooderson, 'Allied Fighter-Bombers Versus German Armour in North West Europe 1944–1945: Myths and Realities', article in *Journal of Strategic Studies*, 14/2 (June 1991), p. 221.
17. Speer, *Inside the Third Reich*, op. cit., pp. 405–6; Irving, *Hitler's War*, op. cit., pp. 700 & 751; Hugh M. Cole, *The Ardennes: Battle of the Bulge* (US Army Center of Military History, 1965; new edn 1993), p. 5.
18. H. R. Trevor-Roper, *Hitler's War Directives* (Sidgwick & Jackson, 1964), pp. 262–78.
19. Percy Schramm, *Ardennes Offensive*, MS-A-862, p. 119.
20. General der Infanterie Hans Krebs (1898–1945) served in the 78th Infantry Regiment from September 1914 to July 1919, and held staff positions from 1929. Krebs, who spoke fluent Russian, became an assistant to the military attaché in Moscow, 1933–4. His subsequent career was that of chief of staff of various formations, rising to Generalmajor when Chief of Staff of Model's Ninth Army in February 1942. In March 1943, he was made Chief of Staff of Army Group Centre and promoted to Generalleutnant, for which he received a Knight's Cross, and followed his old boss to Army Group 'B' from September 1944 until February 1945 when he was appointed Deputy Chief of the Army General Staff. In succession to Heinz Guderian, on 1 April 1945, Krebs was appointed last Chief of the Army General Staff (OKH) and remained in the *Führerbunker* below the Reich Chancellery during Hitler's final moments. With the Russians yards away, he and General Wilhelm Burgdorf committed suicide in the early morning hours of 2 May 1945.
21. Speer, *Inside the Third Reich*, p. 395.
22. John Toland, *Adolf Hitler* (Doubleday, 1976), pp. 1124–5 and William L. Shirer, *The Rise and Fall of the Third Reich* (Simon & Schuster, 1960), pp. 1086–7.
23. OKW War Diary, Operations Order No. 795, 3 September 1944.

3. I Have Made a Momentous Decision!

1. Milton Shulman, *Defeat in the West*, (Secker & Warburg, 1947), p. 228.
2. Schramm, *Kriegstagebuch Des OKW*, 6 September 1944, op. cit., p. 431.
3. Eisenhower, *The Bitter Woods: The Battle of the Bulge*, op. cit., pp. 112–13.
4. Schramm, *Kriegstagebuch*, op. cit., p. 380.
5. OKW War Diary, 6 September; OB West War Diary 7 September 1944.
6. War Diary LXXX Army Corps, 8–10 September 1944.
7. Shulman, *Defeat in the West*, op. cit., p. 268.
8. Ibid., p. 228.
9. The earlier V-1 (doodlebug) flying bomb attack on Britain started during the night of 13–14 June 1944; a total of 10,500 missiles would be launched; 3,957 were destroyed by anti-aircraft defences and fighters, but 3,531 reached England

and 2,353 fell on London. The death toll from this last blitz was 6,184 killed and 17,981 seriously injured. Of the 1,115 V-2 rockets launched against England, 517 fell on London, killing 2,754 people and injuring 6,523. The last V-1 was destroyed over Sittingbourne in Kent on 27 March 1945. Two days later the last V-2 fell on Orpington in Kent.

10. Speer, *Inside the Third Reich*, op. cit., pp. 409–10.
11. Irving, *Hitler's War*, op. cit., p. 729.
12. Douglas E. Nash, *Victory Was Beyond Their Grasp. With the 272nd Volksgrenadier Division from the Hürtgen Forest to the Heart of the Reich* (Aberjona Press, 2008), p. 12.
13. Forrest C. Pogue, *Pogue's War: Diaries of a WWII Combat Historian* (University Press of Kentucky, 2001), pp. 263–4. Entry for Monday, 27 November (D+174).
14. Irving, *Hitler's War*, op. cit., p. 704.
15. Technically, it was *not* known as the Sixth SS Panzer Army until 2 April 1945. It is frequently referred to as the Sixth SS Army by historians of the Bulge, but did not receive the SS designation until after the Ardennes offensive.
16. Schramm, *Kriegstagebuch Des OKW*, 14 September 1944, op. cit., p. 372.
17. *Kriegstagebuch Des 6. Panzer Armee*, MSS A-924, ETHINT-15. NARA.
18. Irving, *Hitler's War*, op. cit., p. 705.
19. *Personal Diary of General Kreipe during the period 22 July–2 November 1944* (MS # P-069, D739.F6713, MHI Library, Carlisle, Pennsylvania), p. 24.
20. Toland, *Adolf Hitler*, pp. 1128–9; Heinz Günther Guderian, *From Normandy to the Ruhr: With the 116th Panzer Division in World War II* (The Aberjona Press, 2001), p. 283; Cole, *The Ardennes*, p. 17; Charles B. MacDonald, *The Battle of the Bulge* (Weidenfeld & Nicolson, 1984), pp. 10–11.
21. In series 2, Episode 12 (Killing Hitler) of the *Unsolved History* TV documentary series, first aired in February 2004, Hitler's conference room and the heavy map table it contained were rebuilt several times to the exact same dimensions. A briefcase left under the table, which held a like amount of explosive of the same destructive power, was similarly detonated and the results recorded, measured and analysed. They prove, to my satisfaction, that Hitler's life was saved on 20 July 1944 only by an adjutant casually moving the briefcase to the far side of a thick table leg. Two identical rooms and tables were built and destroyed in these experiments, with the briefcase on different sides of the table leg, near to a mannequin of Hitler and away from him. The briefcase bomb nearest Hitler would undoubtedly have killed him. The one furthest from him had the destructive force of the blast contained and deflected by the table leg, mimicking what happened on the day. Stauffenberg's bomb, unluckily, was an incredibly near-miss.
22. Courtesy of Professor Theodore Hesburgh, President of the University of Notre Dame, Indiana. The communication of a vision is a vital aspect of leadership. John F. Kennedy, Martin Luther King, Nelson Mandela, Margaret Thatcher and Barack Obama are all examples of political leaders with a vision. Their vision does not necessarily have to be popular, but a vision brings a far-sighted strategic sense of direction and purpose, which is often preferable to the short-term, tactical leader who is reactive.

23. Unlike many of the early Nazis who were descended from Bavarian, southern German or Austrian Catholic families, the Bormann brothers were born into a devout Lutheran family. Albert Bormann (1902–89) was to become an arch-rival of his more famous elder brother, Martin (1900–1945). Both were early Party members, Martin being a great friend of Rudolf Hess and joining the Party in 1927, Albert shortly after. By October 1931, Albert had joined the *Kanzlei des Führers* (Hitler's Chancellery, not a state institution, but Hitler's personal office), responsible for the Nazi Party administration. In 1938, Albert became Chief of the *Persönliche Angelegenheiten des Führers* (Personal Affairs of the Führer) office, not under the jurisdiction of his brother, and handled much of Hitler's routine correspondence. Martin meanwhile became personal secretary to Hess, and when in May 1941 Hess fled to Britain, Martin Bormann immediately succeeded him as head of the Party Chancellery, and built his power as a master of political intrigue. Both brothers worked in the *Führerhauptquartier*, but remained distant. Traudl Junge, Hitler's last secretary, worked for Albert before moving on to Hitler. Albert is much less well known than his sibling because he consciously avoided the limelight, and seems to have been genuinely liked by most of Hitler's inner circle. He remained in the *Führerbunker* in Berlin until ordered to fly out on 20 April 1945, hence he managed to survive, unlike Martin (despite numerous claims to the contrary), whose remains were found by construction workers in West Berlin in December 1972. Martin Bormann had been tried *in absentia* at Nuremberg in October 1946 and sentenced to death for his participation in crimes against humanity. This put an end to much speculation that Martin Bormann had somehow escaped in the confusion of the Russian capture of Berlin and reached South America. Albert Bormann, by contrast, was merely sentenced by a Munich de-nazification court to six months of hard labour and released in October 1949. Refusing to write his memoirs, Albert Bormann died in 1989.
24. Transcript of 1973 Thames Television interview with Albert Speer, Reel 4, Imperial War Museum sound archive.
25. Edwin P. Hoyt, *Goering's War* (Robert Hale, 1990), p. 186.
26. Roger Manvell and Heinrich Fraenkel, *Hermann Göring* (William Heinemann, 1962), p. 223.

4. Adolf Hitler

1. Adolf Hitler, *Mein Kampf* (Hutchinson, 1969, English edition), p. 183.
2. For sources, see David *Lewis, The Man Who Invented Hitler* (Headline, 2003) and John F. Williams, *Corporal Hitler and the Great War 1914–1918* (Frank Cass, 2005).
3. Williams, *Corporal Hitler and the Great War*, op. cit., p. 191.
4. Hugo Gutmann (1880–1962) was a Nuremberger by birth and member of the German Jewish population which numbered about 500,000 in 1914, of whom 100,000 served in the Kaiser's forces during the First World War and 12,000 lost their lives. (Anne Frank's father and uncle were also officers in the WWI German army.) During the 1920s, Gutmann owned and ran an office furniture shop in

Nuremberg, and during the Third Reich era was protected from arrest and continued to receive a war pension, as a result of the influence of both SS personnel who knew his history, anti-Nazi elements in the German Police, and probably Hitler himself. In 1939, Gutmann and his family escaped to Belgium, migrating to the USA the following year; he settled in the city of St Louis, Missouri, where he changed his name to Henry G. Grant and went back into the furniture trade, dying in 1962.

5. Williams, *Corporal Hitler and the Great War*, op. cit., p. 191; Werner Maser, *Hitler*, (Allen Lane, 1973) op. cit., pp. 92–3.
6. Joachim C. Fest, *Hitler* (Weidenfeld & Nicolson, 1974), p. 118 and note 10, p. 1144.
7. Hitler, *Mein Kampf*, op. cit., pp. 184–5.
8. Fest, *Hitler*, op. cit., p. 118.
9. Lewis, *The Man Who Invented Hitler*, pp. 21 and 215–16; Toland, *Adolf Hitler*, op. cit., pp. xvi–xviii.
10. My italics. Ibid, pp. 215–17. The exchange is from a thinly veiled story called *Der Augenzeuge* (The Eyewitness), written in 1938 by the Czech novelist Ernst Weiss, to whom Forster passed the medical notes of Hitler's remarkable case in the 1930s. In Weiss's novel, the patient, known simply as A.H., was 'a corporal of the Bavarian regiment, an orderly in the regimental staff', who had been 'gassed by a grenade' fired by the English on his last patrol, and suffered symptoms so that his 'eyes had burned like glowing coals' and, 'being emotionally disturbed', had been sent to a special clinic, known simply as 'P'. David Lewis's book *The Man Who Invented Hitler* is a compelling thesis that this is the true story of what happened to Adolf Hitler in October–November 1918, and to my mind it rings true. The details surrounding the case were only revealed in 1943 to US agents by one of Edmund Forster's fellow doctors, and the novel published without acclaim or notice in 1963, long after the deaths of Forster and Weiss. Forster's life was in danger after revealing this knowledge, and he committed suicide as the Germans marched into Paris (where he was living in exile) in June 1940.
11. Hitler, *Mein Kampf*, op. cit., pp. 185–8.
12. See also Ian Kershaw, *Hitler 1889–1936: Hubris* (Allen Lane, 1998), pp. 96–105.
13. Winston S. Churchill, *The Gathering Storm* (Cassell, 1948), p. 41.
14. *Churchill* was fascinated by willpower and wrote about T. E. Lawrence ('of Arabia') in similar terms in his mini-biography of the latter in *Great Contemporaries* (Thornton Butterworth, 1937, revised 1939). Full of unrepentant admiration for this enigmatic figure, Churchill wrote 'Solitary, austere, inexorable, he moved upon a plane apart from and above our common lot . . . he reigned over those with whom he came in contact. They felt themselves in the presence of an extraordinary being. They felt that his latent reserves of force and willpower were beyond measurement.' He might have been a German writing about Hitler in the 1930s. Coming from Churchill, this underlines his understanding of the importance of willpower, whose admiration and exercise of it were very much hallmarks of his own long and distinguished life. See also Paul A. Alkon, *Winston Churchill's Imagination* (Bucknell University Press, 2006), Chapter One, pp. 1–40.

15. Carl von Clausewitz, *On War*, Chapter One, second and thirteenth paragraphs.
16. Alan Bullock, *Hitler. A Study in Tyranny* (Odhams, 1952), p. 56.
17. Major-General F.W. von Mellenthin, *Panzer Battles. A Study of the Employment of Armour in the Second World War* (Cassell, 1955), p. 424.
18. Schramm, *Hitler: The Man and the Military Leader*, op. cit., p. 110.
19. Speer, *Inside the Third Reich*, op. cit., p. 367.
20. Toland, *Adolf Hitler*, op. cit., p. 1124.
21. Transcript of 1973 Thames Television interview with General Walter Warlimont, Reel 6 [13.00], Imperial War Museum sound archive.
22. Speer, *Inside the Third Reich*, op. cit., p. 104.
23. Heinz Linge, 'I was Hitler's Valet: Memoirs of the Manservant Whose Final Act of Devotion was to Burn his Master's Body', article in *Daily Mail*, 6 August 2009; at http://www.dailymail.co.uk/news/article-1204388
24. Letter home to Frau Bormann, 9 September 1944. Roger Manvell and Heinrich Fraenkel, *Heinrich Himmler* (William Heinemann, 1965), p. 216.
25. I interviewed Misch in 1993 at his home in Rudow, south Berlin. He was an important eyewitness of Hitler's last days in the Berlin *Führerbunker* during April 1945. Born in 1917, he spent nine years in Soviet captivity until 1953 and died in September 2013, while this book was being written.
26. Maser, *Hitler*, op. cit., pp. 308–10.
27. Toland, *Adolf Hitler*, p. 1120.
28. Toland, *Adolf Hitler*, pp. 1114–18; Linge, 'I was Hitler's Valet', op. cit.
29. Irving, *Hitler's War*, op. cit., p. 750.
30. Walter C. Langer, *The Mind of Adolf Hitler* (Secker & Warburg, 1973), pp. 28–39.
31. Speer, *Inside the Third Reich*, op. cit., p. 411.
32. See David Irving's *The Secret Diaries of Hitler's Doctor* (Sidgwick & Jackson, 1983), for Dr Morell's account of Hitler's medical conditions.
33. 'Hair sprouted from his ears and cuffs. On his thick fingers he wore exotic rings obtained during overseas voyages, on which he had also picked up some foreign eating habits. For example, he would not peel an orange but bit into it until the juice squirted out,' said Christa Schroeder in *Er War Mein Chef* (1985); translated as *He Was My Chief: The Memoirs of Adolf Hitler's Secretary* (Frontline, 2009).
34. Speer, *Inside the Third Reich*, op. cit., p. 105.
35. Ibid.
36. Irving, *Hitler's War*, op. cit., p. 710.
37. Fest, *Hitler*, op. cit., pp. 1067–71.
38. Toland, *Adolf Hitler*, p. 1131.
39. Irving, *Hitler's War*, op. cit., pp. 733–6.
40. Allan Hall, 'As He Took Over Europe and Slaughtered Millions, There was Only One Thing Hitler Feared . . . Going to the Dentist', article in *Daily Mail*, 11 December 2009; at http://www.dailymail.co.uk/news/article-1234784
41. Hall, 'As He Took Over Europe', op. cit.; Linge, 'I was Hitler's Valet', op. cit.
42. Transcript of 1973 Thames Television interview with General Walter Warlimont (1894–1976), Reel 7, Imperial War Museum sound archive.
43. See Marcia Lynn Whicker, *Toxic leaders: When Organizations Go Bad* (Quorum

Books, 1996) and Jean Lipman-Blumen, *The Allure of Toxic Leaders: Why We Follow Destructive Bosses and Corrupt Politicians – and How We Can Survive Them* (Oxford University Press, 2004).

44. Speer, *Inside the Third Reich*, op. cit., pp. 407–8.
45. See the helpful site on these matters, at: http://www.autism.org.uk/about-autism/related-conditions/pda-pathological-demand-avoidance-syndrome.aspx
46. Schramm, *Hitler: The Man and the Military Leader*, op. cit., p. 118.
47. Speer, *Inside the Third Reich*, op. cit., p. 423.
48. Roger Manvell and Heinrich Fraenkel, *Doctor Goebbels* (William Heinemann, 1960), p. 223.
49. Heinz Guderian, *Panzer Leader* (Michael Joseph, 1952), p. 378.

5. Unconditional Surrender

1. Personal Diary of General Kreipe during the period 22 July–2 November 1944 (MS # P-069, D739.F6713, MHI Library, Carlisle, Pennsylvania), p. 24.
2. Ibid., pp. 20–21.
3. Ibid.
4. Speer, *Inside the Third Reich*, op. cit., pp. 407–8.
5. This was on 26 July 1944, when Leutnant Alfred Schreiber damaged a Photo Reconnaissance Mosquito of No. 540 Squadron RAF PR Squadron, which subsequently crashed.
6. http://forum.axishistory.com/viewtopic.php?f=66&t=119848
7. Fritz Hahn, *Waffen und Geheimwaffen des Deutschen Heeres: 1933–1945* (Bernard & Graefe, 1986); Bernhard R. Kroener, Rolf-Dieter Müller and Hans Umbreit, *Das deutsche Reich und der Zweite Weltkrieg*. Vol. 5/2: *Organisation und Mobilisierung des deutschen Machtbereichs 1942–45* (Militarygeschichtlichen Forschungsamt/ Deutsche Verlags, 2003); aircraft figures from: http://www.ww2aircraft.net/forum/aviation/german-c-production-26147.html. *Flak* barrel totals calculated from http://www.sturmvogel.orbat.com/GermWeapProd.html
8. Speer, *Inside the Third Reich*. While Speer's memoirs provide fascinating insights into the workings of the Third Reich, they are also problematic in relation to the Holocaust, about which he claimed he knew very little. In 1995, Gitta Sereny's book *Albert Speer: His Battle with Truth* (Macmillan) challenged Speer's version of events, claiming that his omissions and denials of knowledge were based on efforts to avoid execution at Nuremberg and that some of his later writings actually contradicted his court testimony. Sereny's understanding of Speer as a crafty and intelligent witness who spent his remaining years trying to justify his actions both to himself and the public ring true. Thus his memoirs need to be read with a cautionary warning and may be only partly reliable.
9. H. R. Trevor-Roper, *Hitler's Table Talk, 1941–1944* (Weidenfeld & Nicolson, 1953), p. 279.
10. Audie Murphy, *To Hell and Back* (Transworld, 1949), p. 197.
11. These are hotly debated figures. I have used data from an objective online debate, here: http://forum.axishistory.com/viewtopic.php?f=66&t=150084, and Lutz

Budraß, Jonas Scherner and Jochen Streb, 'Demystifying the German "Armament Miracle" During World War II: New Insights from the Annual Audits of German Aircraft Producers' (Discussion Paper No. 905, Economic Growth Center, Yale University, January 2005).

12. Steven Zaloga, *Panther vs. Sherman: Battle of the Bulge 1944* (Osprey, 2008), pp. 12–14, and the very comprehensive US Air Force Strategic Bombing Survey German Tank Production Report at http://www.sturmvogel.orbat.com/tankrep.html. These overall figures hide the fact that Panzer IV production declined from 334 in June 1944 to only 207 in December. Panther tank production never reached its expected peak of 600 units per month and declined from a high of 400 in July to 308 in December.
13. Charles B. MacDonald, *The Siegfried Line Campaign. United States Army in World War II. European Theater of Operations* (Office of the Chief of Military History, Department of the Army, Washington, DC 1963), p. 71.
14. Noel Annan, *Changing Enemies* (HarperCollins, 1995), pp. 124–5.
15. Heinz Günther Guderian (1914–2004) was Inspector of Panzer Troops in the Bundeswehr, the position his father had held in the Third Reich. He retained his position as Operations Officer of 116th Panzer Division from May 1942 until the end of the War. Retiring in 1974 – I met him when serving in Germany in 1980 – he wrote the divisional history of his unit, *From Normandy to the Ruhr: With the 116th Panzer Division in WWII.*
16. 'Balck has strong claims to be regarded as our finest field commander,' wrote Major-General Friedrich-Wilhelm von Mellenthin. General Hermann Balck (1897–1982) came from a military family. His great-grandfather served in the King's German Legion under the Duke of Wellington; his grandfather was an officer in the British Army's Argyll and Sutherland Highlanders. His father, William Balck, was a Generalleutnant in the German army and a Knight of the Order Pour le Mérite; Hermann Balck was nominated for the Pour le Mérite in October 1918, but the war ended before his citation could be processed. In the Second World War, he received the Knight's Cross of the Iron Cross with Oak Leaves, Swords and Diamonds, ending in command of the Sixth Army. Sadly, his autobiography, *Ordnung im Chaos: Erinnerungen, 1893–1948*, has yet to appear in English. See David T. Zabecki, 'The Greatest German General No One Ever Heard Of', article in *World War II* magazine (April/May 2008).
17. Georg Grossjohan, *Five Years, Four Fronts* (Aegis, 1999), pp. 202–203.
18. Schramm, OKW War Diary; Shulman, *Defeat in the West*, op. cit., p. 276; Irving, *Hitler's War*, op. cit., p. 706.
19. Shulman, *Defeat in the West*, op. cit., p. 278.
20. Author's lectures on Psyops, delivered to the NATO School, Oberammergau, Germany.
21. Shulman, *Defeat in the West*, op. cit., p. 280.
22. The bunker in Aachen from where Wilck commanded and which witnessed his surrender has been preserved, but is currently under threat of demolition for apartments. The anti-Wilck leaflet is at http://www.bunkertours.be/nein_zum_abriss-1.html
23. Winston Churchill, *The Hinge of Fate* (Cassell, 1951), p. 615. Churchill's memoirs

state that in his 20 January 1943 cable to the War Cabinet in London the matter was discussed: 'We propose to draw up a statement of the work of the conference for communication to the Press at the proper time. I should be glad to know what the War Cabinet would think of our including in this statement a declaration of the firm intention of the United States and the British Empire to continue the war relentlessly until we have brought about the "unconditional surrender" of Germany and Japan. The omission of Italy would be to encourage a break-up there. The President liked this idea, and it would stimulate our friends in every country.' The War Cabinet responded the same day, stating that they did not think Italy should be excluded. Churchill seems to have believed that the matter would be further discussed but both he and Roosevelt became very occupied while dealing with General de Gaulle. His memoirs continued, 'It seems probable that as I did not like applying unconditional surrender to Italy I did not raise the point again with the President, and we had certainly both agreed to the communiqué we had settled with our advisers. There is no mention in it of "unconditional surrender". It was submitted to the War Cabinet, who approved it in this form' (pp. 614–15). So the matter had been under discussion but it had not been part of the joint communique that the two leaders agreed in advance.

24. Agostino von Hassell and Sigrid MacRae, *Alliance of Enemies: The Untold Story of the Secret American and German Collaboration to End World War II* (St Martin's Griffin, 2008).
25. Chester Wilmot, *The Struggle for Europe* (Collins, 1952), p. 570.
26. *Time*, 2 October 1944. http://content.time.com/time/magazine/article/0,9171,933072,00.html
27. Speer, *Inside the Third Reich*, op. cit., p. 433.

6. A Bridge Too Far

1. MacDonald, *The Siegfried Line Campaign*, op. cit., p. 471.
2. Pogue, *Pogue's War*, op. cit., pp. 271–2.
3. Charles Whiting, *'44: In Combat From Normandy to the Ardennes* (Spellmount, 1984), pp. 168–72.
4. Günther Schmidt, 'The 272 VGD In Action In The Eifel, 1944–45', courtesy of *Der Erste Zug* website, at: http://www.dererstezug.com/272ndInAction/272ndInAction(1).htm
5. Generalmajors Rudolf Freiherr von Gersdorff and Siegfried von Waldenburg, *116 Panzer Division in the Hürtgen Forest*, 2–14 Nov. 1944 (ETHINT 56), pp. 1–8.
6. Reuters, 9 September 1944.
7. *The Papers of Dwight David Eisenhower: The War Years*, edited by Alfred D. Chandler, Jr (Johns Hopkins Press, 1970), Vol. IV, pp. 2124.
8. It is an interesting reflection on democracy that during the Second World War, Britain suspended political elections 'for the duration', while the USA continued with them. Roosevelt's policy here was right, and in the 7 November elections he won easily over the Republican contender, Governor Thomas E. Dewey of New York, taking thirty-six states to Dewey's twelve.

9. SHAEF – Supreme Headquarters of the Allied Expeditionary Force.
10. Carlo D'Este, *Bitter Victory: The Battle for Sicily July–August 1943* (Collins, 1988), p. 106.
11. US 3rd Armored Division report 18 Sept. 44, MacDonald, *The Siegfried Line Campaign*, op. cit., p. 68.
12. *US Army Battle Casualties and Non Battle Deaths in World War II, Final Report, 7 December 1941–31 December 1946* (Prepared by Statistical and Accounting Branch, Office of the Adjutant General, Washington DC, 1947) p. 32. See http://www.ibiblio.org/hyperwar/USA/ref/Casualties/Casualties-1.html#theater
13. Stephen A. Hart, *Colossal Cracks: Montgomery's 21st Army Group in Northwest Europe, 1944–45* (Stackpole, 2007), p. 47.
14. Eisenhower's personnel numbers *excluded* Devers' Army Group until December 1944, which came under the Mediterranean Theatre. See Forrest C. Pogue, *The Supreme Command, The US Army in World War II, European Theater of Operations* (Office of the Chief of Military History, Department of the Army, Washington, DC, 1954) pp. 542–4. See http://www.ibiblio.org/hyperwar/USA/USA-E-Supreme/USA-E-Supreme-E.html
15. Roland G. Ruppenthal, *Logistical Support of the Armies*, Volume II: *September 1944–May 1945* (US Army in World War II, European Theater of Operations series, US Army Center of Military History, 1995), p. 6.
16. Blumenson, *United States Army in World War II*, op. cit., pp. 681 and 694; MacDonald, *The Siegfried Line Campaign*, op. cit., p. 10.
17. US Army Transportation Museum website, at http://www.transchool.lee.army.mil/museum/transportation%20museum/redballintro.htm
18. Bart H. Vanderveen, *The Observer's Fighting Vehicles Directory* (Frederick Warne, 1972), p. 57; *War Machine* magazine, No. 125, pp. 2495–9; Donald E. Meyer (comp.), The First Century of GMC Truck History, at: http://www.gmheritagecenter.com/docs/gm-heritage-archive/historical-brochures/GMC/100_YR_GMC_HISTORY_MAR09.pdf
19. John A. Adams, *The Battle for Western Europe, Fall 1944: An Operational Assessment* (Indiana University Press, 2010), pp. 23–7.
20. The Group were originally the 801st, renumbered to 492nd on 13 August 1944. The nickname came from the agent-dropping mission title, Operation Carpetbagger. The Bomb group actually moved 822,791 gallons of gasoline to Patton's Third Army.
21. Alfred M. Beck, *Technical Services, the Corps of Engineers, the War Against Germany, The US Army in World War II* (US Army Center of Military History, Government Printing Office, Washington, DC, 1985), pp. 257–60.
22. Rudi Williams, 'African Americans Gain Fame as World War II Red Ball Express Drivers', *US Department of Defense News Story* (American Forces Press Service, Washington, DC, 15 February 2002) and Dr Steven E. Anders, 'POL on the Red Ball Express', article in *Quartermaster Professional Bulletin* (Spring 1989). John R. Houston's account courtesy of the US Army Transportation Museum, http://www.transchool.lee.army.mil/museum/transportation%20museum/personalstories.htm. Houston's daughter became the famous singer Whitney Houston.

23. *Eisenhower Papers*, Vol. IV, pp. 2143.
24. Charles B. MacDonald, *A Time for Trumpets*, (William Morrow & Co., 1985), p. 51.
25. Ibid., p. 2120.
26. *Personal Diary of General Kreipe*, 16 September 1944, op. cit., p. 24.
27. Field Marshal the Viscount Montgomery of Alamein, *Normandy to the Baltic* (BAOR, 1946), p. 198.
28. OB West Operations Report, 24 September 1944, No. 8547.

7. A Port Too Far

1. Peter H. Merkl, *Political Violence under the Swastika* (Princeton University Press, 1992), p. 539.
2. Speer, *Inside the Third Reich*, op. cit., p. 415.
3. John Lukacs, *The Hitler of History* (Random House, 1997), p. 166.
4. Toland, *Adolf Hitler*, op. cit., p. 829.
5. See my earlier book, *Monty and Rommel: Parallel Lives* (2011). Also Toland, *Adolf Hitler*, op. cit., p. 1136; Russell H. S. Stolfi, *A Bias For Action: The German 7th Panzer Division in France & Russia 1940–1941* (Perspectives on Warfighting No. 1, Marine Corps University, 1991); and *Blitzkrieg: The German Army at War, 7th Panzer Division 'The Ghost Division'* (Panzertruppen Publications, 2013), pp. 103–12.
6. William B. Breuer, *Bloody Clash at Sadzot* (Zeus, 1981), p. 40.
7. David Jordan, *Battle of the Bulge. The First 24 hours* (Greenhill, 2003), p. 102.
8. Charles *Foley*, *Commando Extraordinary: Otto Skorzeny* (Longmans, Green & Co., 1954), p. 131.
9. Eisenhower, *The Bitter Woods*, op. cit., pp. 122–6, 138–9 and 164–5; Jean-Paul Pallud, *Battle of the Bulge: Then and Now* (After the Battle, 1984), pp. 106–128.
10. Otto Skorzeny, *Skorzeny's Special Missions: The Memoirs of the Most Dangerous Man in Europe* (Robert Hale, 1957), pp. 145–50; Foley, *Commando Extraordinary*, op. cit.; and Charles Whiting, *Skorzeny: The Most Dangerous Man in Europe* (Pen & Sword, 1998).
11. Kershaw, *Hitler*, Vol. 1: *1889–1936: Hubris*, op. cit., p. 77.
12. Shulman, *Defeat in the West*, op. cit., p. 277.
13. Charles B. MacDonald, *The Last Offensive: United States Army in World War II, European Theater of Operations* (Office of the Chief of Military History, Department of the Army, Washington, DC, 1973), p. 22.
14. Transcript of 1973 Thames Television interview with General Siegfried Westphal, Reels 3 & 4, Imperial War Museum sound archive.
15. Guderian, *From Normandy to the Ruhr*, op. cit., p. 283.
16. Shulman, *Defeat in the West*, op. cit., pp. 289–90.
17. Shulman's post-war, October 1945 interview with Rundstedt, widely cited, but originally in *Defeat in the West*, op. cit., p. 290.
18. As Model and Krebs died separately in May 1945, descriptions of his relations with Rundstedt and of his view of *Wacht am Rhein* are taken from an interview

with one of his staff officers. See Charles V. P. von Luttichau, Report on the Interview with Mr Thuisko von Metzch, 14–19 March 1952, on Operations of Army Group 'B' and Its Role in the German Ardennes Offensive, 1944 (Office of the Chief of Military History/ NARA RG 319, R-series, #10), pp. 25–6.
19. Shulman, *Defeat in the West*, op. cit., p. 290.
20. General Siegfried Westphal, *The German Army in the West* (Cassell, 1951), pp. 179–80.
21. Rundstedt Testimony, *Trial of the Major War Criminals before the International Military Tribunal*, Vol. XXXI (Nuremberg, 12 August 1946).
22. Letter, Jodl to Westphal, 1 November 1944, *Kriegstagebuch Des Oberbefehlshaber West.*
23. Operation Directive, 10 November 1944, ibid.
24. On 1 November 1944 Zangen's Fifteenth Army was combined with General der Fallschirmtruppe Alfred Schlemm's First Parachute Army to form Army Group 'H' (for Holland), under Generaloberst Kurt Student.
25. Hitler, *Mein Kampf*, op. cit., pp. 180–81.
26. Oberstleutnant Freiherr von der Heyte, *Kampfgruppe von der Heyte* (25 Oct.–22 Dec. 1944), 33pp. interview of 1948, Foreign Military Studies, B-823, NARA.
27. Patrick Leigh Fermor, *A Time of Gifts* (John Murray, 1977), p. 197.
28. Westphal, *The German Army in the West*, op. cit., p. 172.
29. Author's interview with Hauptmann Otto Carius, Knight's Cross with Oak Leaves, Royal Military College of Science, UK, 2000.
30. Westphal, *The German Army in the West*, op. cit., p. 189.
31. Sometimes written as *O-Tag*, *Null* being German for zero.
32. Franz *Kurowski, Elite Panzer Strike Force: Germany's Panzer Lehr Division in World War II* (Stackpole, 2011), p. 170.

8. Heroes of the Woods

1. Cole, *The Ardennes*, op. cit., footnote 1, p. 19.
2. Besides the scene of his 1940 breakthrough, Hitler had some personal experience of the area, for in May 1940, General (as he then was) von Rundstedt set up the headquarters of his Army Group 'A' in Bastogne, where the Führer visited him.
3. Ludewig, *Rückzug. The German Retreat from France, 1944*, op. cit., p. 206.
4. Steve R. *Waddell, United States Army Logistics: The Normandy Campaign, 1944* (Praeger, 1994), p. 99.
5. Benjamin King and Timothy J. Kutta, *Impact: The History of Germany's V-weapons in World War II* (Da Capo Press, 1998), alt. title: *Hammer of the Reich*, Chapter 10. 'Antwerp and the German Attack on Allies Supply Lines 1944–1945'.
6. Ibid.
7. Trevor-Roper, *Hitler's Table Talk*, op. cit., p. 188.
8. BBC News broadcast, 11 December 1941.
9. Trevor-Roper, *Hitler's Table Talk*, p. 279.

10. Ibid., p. 188.
11. Klaus P. Fischer, *Hitler and America* (University of Pennsylvania Press, 2011).
12. Another of Wedemeyer's classmates at the Kriegsakademie was Wessel Freytag von Loringhoven, a fellow 20 July 1944 plotter with Stauffenberg.
13. John J. McLaughlin, *General Albert C. Wedemeyer: America's Unsung Strategist in World War II* (Casemate, 2012); Albert C. Wedemeyer, *Wedemeyer Reports!* (Henry Holt, 1958).
14. Trevor-Roper, *Hitler's Table Talk*, op. cit., p. 181.
15. Thomas Sowell, *Ethnic America: A History* (Basic Books, 1981), pp. 43–68; Benjamin J. Patterson, *Ethnic Groups USA* (Xlibris, 2008), pp. 59–84.
16. General der Infanterie Friedrich Wiese, *Nineteenth Army (1 Jul.–15 Sep. 1944)*, interview in 1949, WWII Foreign Military Studies, MS-B-787, p. 30; and Generalleutnant Walter Botsch, *Operations in Lorraine, Nineteenth Army (16 Sep.–17 Nov. 1944)*, WWII Foreign Military Studies, interview in 1948, MS-B-515, p. 63, both NARA.
17. Shirer, *The Rise and Fall of the Third Reich*, op. cit., p. 101.
18. Fest, *Hitler*, op. cit., p. 37.
19. http://www.wagneropera.net/Themes/Wagner-In-Movies-Stukas-1941.htm
20. See http://www.youtube.com/watch?v=FoU-iCT21fc
21. See M.H. Kater, *The Twisted Muse: Musicians and their Music in the Third Reich* (Oxford University Press, 1997); R.A. Etlin (ed.), *Art, Culture and Media under the Third Reich* (University of Chicago Press, 2002).
22. Matthew Boyden, *Opera. The Rough Guide* (Rough Guides, 1999), pp. 251–79.
23. Robert G. Lee and Sabine Wilke, 'Forest as Volk: Ewiger Wald and the Religion of Nature in the Third Reich', paper in *Journal of Social and Ecological Boundaries* (Spring 2005), pp. 21–46.
24. The significance of trees and forests to Nazi mythology was explained as early as 1929 by Walther Schoenichen, in *Der Umgang mit Mutter Grün: Ein Sünden- und Sittenbuch für Jedermann* (In the Company of Mother Earth: An Everyman's Book of Vice and Virtue). Schoenichen was a German biologist and environmentalist, and an early member of the NSDAP. Göring appointed him in 1942 as Director of the Reich Forest Ministry.
25. Leni Riefenstahl, *Triumph des Willens* (1935), at 0:49:00.
26. Kershaw, *Hitler*, Vol. 1: *1889–1936: Hubris*, op. cit., p. 239.
27. Bill Yenne, *Hitler's Master of the Dark Arts. Himmler's Black Knights and the Occult Origins of the SS* (Zenith Press, 2010).
28. In 1945, seized SS records were found to include lists of names with the initials NN (*Nacht und Nebel*).
29. Ian Fleming, the Second World War British intelligence officer who planned assassination attempts against the Führer, would locate all the opponents of his eponymous hero, James Bond, in secret lairs based on Hitler's various headquarters.
30. See Tony Clunn, *The Quest for the Lost Legions* (Savas Beatie, 2005), and Adrian Murdoch, *Rome's Greatest Defeat. Massacre in the Teutoburg Forest* (Sutton, 2006).
31. Fergus M. Bordewich, 'The Ambush That Changed History', article in *The Smithsonian Magazine* (September 2005).

32. The massive free-standing victory statue standing on Mamayev Kurgan hill overlooking Volgograd (formerly Stalingrad) in southern Russia is remarkably similar, and this may contain a political message to the *Hermannsdenkmal*, and all it represents.
33. Kershaw, *Hitler*, Vol. I: *1889–1936: Hubris*, op. cit., p. 77.
34. *Völkischer Beobachter*, 5 January 1933.
35. Murdoch, *Rome's Greatest Defeat*, op. cit., p. 175.
36. Karl Richard Ganzer, *Das deutsche Führergesicht; 200 Bildnisse deutscher Kämpfer und Wegsucher aus zwei Jahrtausenden* (J. F. Lehmann, München, 1937). Ganzer was a Nazi hack who produced dozens of books in a similar vein.
37. *Der Spiegel*, 28 August 2009.
38. Murdoch, *Rome's Greatest Defeat*, op. cit., p. 178; David B. *Cuff, The Clades Variana and the Third Reich*, academic paper, the University of Toronto, May 2010.
39. Trevor-Roper, *Hitler's Table Talk*, op. cit., p. 78.
40. Murdoch, *Rome's Greatest Defeat*, op. cit., p. 436.
41. Fest, *Hitler*, op. cit., p. 988.
42. Trevor-Roper, *Hitler's Table Talk*, op. cit., p. 486–7. Hitler, of course, was incorrect in stating that Arminius commanded the Third Legion, when he was only a senior auxiliary, and the legions concerned were the 17th, 18th and 19th.

9. Who Knew What?

1. Omar N. Bradley and Clair Blair, *A General's Life: An Autobiography by General of the Army Omar N. Bradley* (Simon & Schuster, 1983), p. 351.
2. Carlo D'Este, *Eisenhower: A Soldier's Life* (Henry Holt and Company, 2002); obituaries, *Guardian*, 22 February 2000, *New York Times*, 9 March 2000.
3. Ralph Bennett, *Ultra in the West: The Normandy Campaign of 1944–45* (Hutchinson, 1979).
4. See Group Captain F.W. Winterbotham, *The Ultra Secret* (Weidenfeld & Nicolson, 1974); *The History of the Special Liaison Units under the Control of Special Liaison Unit 1 (SLU 1)*, 1 January 1940–31 December 1945, HW 49/1 UK National Archives, Kew.
5. Under SHAEF, Allied staff branches were organised as follows: G[eneral staff branch] 1 = Personnel matters; G-2 = Intelligence; G-3 = Planning and Operations; G-4 = Supply issues; G-5 = Civil Affairs; G-6 = Publicity and Psychological Warfare Division, which was later split into two, unnumbered staff divisions, Psychological Warfare and Public Relations. Each usually had a US head and British deputy or vice versa. The British system of General Staff appointments put operations, training and intelligence under the 'G'[eneral Staff] branch, while personnel and supply were part of the 'A'[djutant General's] and 'Q'[uartermaster General's] staff. The German equivalents were I-a (chief of staff or chief G-3 operations); I-b (chief G-4 supply and movement); I-c (chief G-2 intelligence); I-d (chief G-3 training); II-a (G-1 personnel – officers); II-c (G-1 Personnel – other ranks).
6. Forrest C. Pogue, *The Ardennes Campaign: The Impact of Intelligence* (edited

transcript of remarks to the NSA Communications Analysis Association, 16 December 1980), pp. 28–9. Available online at: http://www.nsa.gov/public_info/_files/cryptologic_spectrum/ardennes_campaign.pdf

7. Lieutenant-Colonels Charles R. Murnane and Samuel M. Orr.
8. Tom Bigland, *Bigland's War* (Privately printed, 1990).
9. David W. Hogan, Jr, *A Command Post at War. First Army Headquarters in Europe 1943–45* (US Army Center of Military History, Washington, DC, 2000), p. 291. Bradley remained hugely popular among his old headquarters staff at First Army, the veterans among them seeing 'Twelfth Army Group staff as interlopers in assuming their role as the main American field headquarters on the Continent', and some 'did not hesitate to bypass their army group counterparts to deal direct with Bradley'.
10. Diane T. Putney, *Ultra and the Army Air Forces in World War II. An Interview with Associate Justice of the US Supreme Court Lewis F. Powell, Jr* (Office of Air Force History, US Air Force, Washington, DC, 1987), p. 22.
11. This was Lieutenant-Colonel James D. Fellers. See MacDonald, *A Time for Trumpets*, op. cit., p. 61.
12. Memorandum For Colonel. Taylor, Office of the Military Attaché, US Embassy, London, from Lieutenant-Colonel Rosengarten, Subject: Report on ULTRA Intelligence at the First US Army, 21 May 1945; and Rosenthal, Subject: Notes on ULTRA Traffic, First US Army, 27 May 1945, both RG 457, SRH-023, NARA; Rosengarten, pp. 6–7.
13. MacDonald, *A Time for Trumpets*, op. cit., p. 55.
14. Patrick Delaforce, *The Battle of the Bulge: Hitler's Final Gamble* (Longmans, 2006) pp. 82–4; Gerald Astor, *Terrible Terry Allen: Combat General of World War II. The Life of an American Soldier* (Presidio Press, 2003), pp. 83–4.
15. Pogue, *The Ardennes Campaign*, op. cit.
16. Hogan, *A Command Post at War*, op. cit., p. 291. While regarded as 'a fine intelligence officer, a dedicated, careful craftsman in an army that valued his field all too lightly', Dickson was his own worst enemy in picking fights with Sibert, Thorson and Kean.
17. Ibid., p. 288.
18. Ibid., pp. 288–9.
19. Major Daniel P. Bolger, 'Zero Defects: Command Climate in First US Army, 1944–45', article in *Military Review* (May 1991), pp. 61–73. Available at http://www.foreignpolicy.com/images/090716_zero-defects-(May_1991_MR)-Bolger.pdf
20. Hogan, *A Command Post at War*, op. cit., p. 289.
21. Lieutenant-Colonel Melvin C. Helfers.
22. Major Kevin Dougherty, 'Oscar Koch: An Unsung Hero Behind Patton's Battles', article in *Military Intelligence Professional Bulletin* (April–June 2002), p. 64.
23. Hogan, *A Command Post at War*, op. cit., p. 290.
24. MacDonald, *A Time for Trumpets*, op. cit., pp. 52–3.
25. E.g., Forrest C. Pogue, *The Ardennes Campaign*, op. cit.
26. James L. *Gilbert* and John P. *Finnegan* (eds), *US Army Signals Intelligence in World*

War II. A Documentary History (Center of Military History, United States Army, Washington, DC, 1993), pp. 179–201.

27. Jay von Werlhof, 'One Man's Decision: Why SHAEF Failed to Halt the Battle of the Bulge', article in *The Bulge Bugle* (August 2003), pp. 11–16.
28. 'Eisenhower knew Battle of Bulge was coming – 1st Lt. Ray Walker of Punta Gorda gave him the word', story in the *Charlotte Sun* newspaper, Port Charlotte, Florida, 16 December 2002; also http://donmooreswartales.com/tag/battle-of-the-bulge/
29. Ibid.
30. MacDonald, *A Time for Trumpets*, op. cit., p. 57.
31. The Office of Strategic Services (OSS) was the US intelligence agency formed when Roosevelt ordered Colonel William J. Donovan to create an organisation based on the British Secret Intelligence Service (MI6) and Special Operations Executive (SOE); it became the predecessor of the Central Intelligence Agency (CIA). OSS was established on 11 July 1941 with Donovan as the 'Co-ordinator of Information', and it was designed initially to coordinate espionage activities behind enemy lines for all branches of the US armed forces. Prior to this, America had no overseas intelligence service.
32. William J. Casey, *The Secret War Against Hitler* (Regnery, 1988). See also Robert Sherrod's review of Casey's book, 'A Spook When Young', in the *New York Times*, 25 September 1988.
33. Colonels Robert A. Schow, John H. Claybrook, Lieutenant-Colonel Howard B. St Clair, John K. Montgomery, Jr, Paul S. Reinecke, Jr, and 1st Lieutenant John S. D. Eisenhower, Infantry Report of the General Board, United States Forces, European Theater, Organization and Operation of the Theater Intelligence Services in the European Theater of Operations, Study #14, File: 320.2/57, n.d., but c.1946. Available at http://usacac.army.mil/cac2/cgsc/carl/eto/eto-014.pdf
34. Interview in 1999 with my second cousin, George Stephen Clive Sowry, RNVR, who worked at RAF Medmenham and his wife, Section Officer Jeanne Sowry, WAAF, who also worked at Medmenham.
35. Constance Babington Smith, *Evidence in Camera* (Chatto & Windus, 1957), pp. 222–3; Taylor Downing, *Spies in the Sky. The Secret Battle for Aerial Intelligence During World War II* (Little, Brown, 2011), pp. 321–3.
36. John F. Kreis (ed.), *Piercing the Fog: Intelligence and Army Air Forces Operations in World War II* (US Air Force Historical Studies Office, Washington, DC, 1996), p. 88.
37. Peter Calvocoressi, *Top Secret Ultra* (Cassell, 1980) p. 48; Asa Briggs, *Secret Days: Code-breaking in Bletchley Park* (Frontline, 2011), pp. 122–3.
38. Obituary: 'Peter Calvocoressi: Political Writer Who Served at Bletchley Park and Assisted at the Nuremberg trials', *Independent*, 20 February 2010.

10. The Cloak of Invisibility

1. Bennett, *Ultra in the West*, op. cit., pp. 192 and 199.
2. Ibid., p. 195.

3. Ibid., p. 194.
4. Ibid., pp. 195–6.
5. Ibid., p. 197.
6. Ibid., p. 197.
7. Ibid., p. 201.
8. Ibid., pp. 197–8 and 202–3.
9. Ibid., pp. 178–9.
10. Ibid., pp. 196, 197 and 202.
11. Paul H. Van Doren, 'A Historic Failure in the Social Domain (Social Domain case study using the 16 December 1944 surprise attack in the Ardennes Forest)', paper given at the Decision making and Cognitive Analysis Track, 10th International Command and Control Research and Technology Symposium, McLean, Virginia, 13–16 June 2005, p. 13. Paper at http://www.dodccrp.org/events/10th_ICCRTS/CD/papers/035.pdf
12. MAGIC decode SRS 1419 of Baron Oshima's 6 September report on his 4 September conference with Hitler, and Van Doren, 'A Historic Failure', op. cit., p. 28.
13. MAGIC SRS 1492 decode of Baron Oshima's 20 November report on his 15 November meeting with German Foreign Minister Ribbentrop, and Van Doren, 'A Historic Failure', op. cit., p. 30.
14. MacDonald, *The Battle of the Bulge*, op. cit., pp. 24–5; Robert E. Lester (Project Editor) and Blair D. Hydrick (Compiler), *A Guide to the Microfilm Edition of World War II Research Collections. Top Secret Studies on U.S. Communications Intelligence during World War II*, Part 2: *The European Theater* (University Publications of America, 1989); Eisenhower, *The Bitter Woods*, p. 173.
15. MacDonald, *A Time For Trumpets*, op. cit., p. 64.
16. Rosengarten Report, on ULTRA Intelligence at the First US Army, op. cit., p. 5.
17. MacDonald, *The Siegfried Line Campaign*, op. cit., pp. 243–6.
18. 12th Army Group G-2 Periodic Report #165, 17 November 1944, Annex 2, file 99/12–2.1, RG407, NARA.
19. 12th Army Group G-2 Periodic Reports, Weekly Periodic Summary No. 15, period ending 18 Nov. 44, file 99/12–2.1, RG407, NARA.
20. Trevor N. Dupuy, David L. Bongard and Richard C. Anderson, Jr, *Hitler's Last Gamble: The Battle of the Bulge, December 1944–January 1945* (HarperCollins, 1994), p. 4.
21. Oscar W. *Koch* and Robert G. Hays, *G-2 Intelligence for Patton* (Schiffer Publishing, 1999), p. 94; MacDonald, *A Time For Trumpets*, op. cit., p. 69.
22. MacDonald, *A Time for Trumpets*, op. cit., p. 70.
23. Ibid., pp. 70–71.
24. Cole, *The Ardennes*, op. cit., p. 57.
25. Dupuy et al., *Hitler's Last Gamble*, op. cit., pp. 4 and 40–1; Bradley and Blair, *A General's Life*, op. cit., p. 354.
26. Eisenhower, *The Bitter Woods*, op. cit., p. 165
27. Eisenhower, *The Bitter Woods*, op. cit., p. 212; Pogue, *The Ardennes Campaign*, op. cit., p. 31; Harry Yeide, *Steel Victory* (Presidio, 2003), p. 191.
28. Major Jade E. Hinman, *When the Japanese Bombed the Huertgen Forest. How the*

Army's Investigation of Pearl Harbor Influenced the Outcome of the Huertgen Forest, Major General Leonard T. Gerow and His Command of V Corps from 1943–1945, A Monograph for the School of Advanced Military Studies US Army Command and General Staff College, Fort Leavenworth, Kansas, 2011. Also, http://www.battleofthebulgememories.be/en/stories/us-army/345-the-battle-of-elsenborn-december-44-part-i-of-v.html

29. Charles Whiting, *The Last Assault* (Leo Cooper, 1994), p. 55.
30. Memoir of Cecil R. Palmer (1922–2010) at: http://www.99thinfantrydivision.com/cecilpalmer.php
31. Stephen E. Ambrose, *Citizen Soldiers* (Simon & Schuster, 1997), p. 187.
32. Memoir of Cecil R. Palmer, op. cit.
33. Jerry C. Hrbek, 'They're Our Prisoners', article in *The Bulge Bugle* (May 1994), pp. 16–18. Obituary at http://obits.masslive.com/obituaries/masslive/obituary.aspx?pid=154819594
34. Of specific relevance to the Ardennes, Charles B. MacDonald wrote *Company Commander* (Infantry Journal Press, 1947); *The Battle of the Bulge* (Weidenfeld & Nicolson, 1984), published in the USA as *A Time for Trumpets* (William Morrow, 1985) in addition to official histories and other works. Also useful is Charles D. *Curley, How a Ninety-Day Wonder Survived the War* (Ashcraft Enterprises, 1991).
35. Ambrose, *Citizen Soldiers*, op. cit., p. 181.
36. Charles Roland Memoir, Eisenhower Center, University of New Orleans. Amongst others, George W. Neill, *Infantry Soldier: Holding the Line at the Battle of the Bulge* (University of Oklahoma Press, 2002) is another useful 99th Division memoir.

11. This is a Quiet Area

1. Wilmot, *The Struggle for Europe*, pp. 573–4.
2. For the perfectly justifiable reason that no American officer had ever commanded an army group before.
3. See Chapter 5 on Middleton in J.D. Morelock's *Generals of the Ardennes. American Leadership in the Battle of the Bulge* (National Defense University Press, 1994).
4. Ibid., p. 235.
5. Eisenhower, *The Bitter Woods*, op. cit., p. 175.
6. Ambrose, *Citizen Soldiers*, op. cit., p. 187.
7. Roland Gaul, *The Battle of the Bulge in Luxembourge*, Vol. I: *The Germans* (Schiffer Publishing, 1994) p. 130.
8. Bradley R. McDuffie, 'For Ernest, With Love and Squalor: the Influence of Ernest Hemingway on J.D. Salinger', article in *The Hemingway Review* (22 March 2011).
9. Robert O. Babcock, *War Stories: Utah Beach to Pleiku. 4th Infantry Division* (Saint John's Press, 2001), p. 292.
10. Ernest Hemingway, *Across the River and into the Trees* (Charles Scribner's Sons, 1950).
11. William Walton, 'The Battle of the Hürtgen Forest. A Gloomy German Wood Takes Its Place in US History Beside the Wilderness and the Argonne', article in *Life* magazine, 1 January 1945.

12. George Wilson, *If You Survive* (Presidio Press, 1987), p. 193.
13. Carolyn Burke, *Lee Miller. On Both Sides of the Camera* (Bloomsbury, 2005), pp. 236–7.
14. Babcock, *War Stories*, op. cit., p. 335.
15. Ibid., pp. 334–5.
16. Charles Whiting, *Papa Goes to War. Ernest Hemingway in Europe 1944–45* (Crowood Press, 1990), p. 159.
17. Major Frederick T. Kent, 'The Operations of 22nd Infantry Regiment (4th Infantry Division) in the Hürtgen Forest, Germany, 16 November–3 December 1944' (Rhineland Campaign, Personal Experience of a Regimental S-4), Research Paper for the Advanced Infantry Officer's Course No.1, 1946–1947, The Infantry School, Fort Benning, Georgia. At http://1–22infantry.org/history2/hurtgenpageone.htm. Also see Wilson, *If You Survive*, op. cit.
18. Major John T. Litchfield, and ten other officers, *The Ardennes: The Battle of the Bulge: Winter Defense and Counterattack* (Student Research Paper, Combat Studies Institute, US Army Command and General Staff College, Fort Leavenworth, Kansas, 1984), p. 44.
19. Due to the proximity of German land forces to the transmitter during the Bulge campaign, Luxembourg went off-air between 19 and 23 December. See *The Psychological Warfare Division, Supreme Headquarters Allied Expeditionary Force. An Account of Its Operations in the Western European Campaign 1944–45* (1951), pp. 41 and 89; David *Garnett, The Secret History of the Political Warfare Executive 1939–1945* (St Ermin's Press, 2002), pp. 426–7.
20. 1115th AAA Gun Battalion memoir courtesy of their website: http://www.115th-aaa-gun-bn.com/Story/luxembourg.php
21. The PX was an abbreviation of 'Post Exchange', the US equivalent of the British NAAFI, where minor non-issue luxuries and comforts could be purchased by troops just behind the combat zone. It was not open to civilians. See David Colley, *The Road to Victory. The Untold Story of Race and World War II's Red Ball Express* (Brassey's, 2000), Chapter 16, pp. 123–31.
22. *Newsweek*, 8 January 1945.
23. *Life* magazine, 26 March 1945.
24. *Yank* newspaper, 4 May 1945.
25. Paul F. Jenkins (1916–2007), oral interview; OH-146, Wisconsin Veterans Museum Research Center, 2000.
26. Gaul, *The Battle of the Bulge in Luxembourg*, Vol. I: *The Germans*, op. cit., pp. 13–15.
27. Ambrose, *Citizen Soldiers*, op. cit., p. 181.
28. Eisenhower, *The Bitter Woods*, op. cit., p. 176.
29. Roland Gaul, *The Battle of the Bulge in Luxembourg*, Vol. II: *The Americans* (Schiffer Publishing, 1995), pp. 129–130.
30. Donald Bein interview, March 2011. http://www.battleofthebulgememories.be/index.php?option=com_content&view=article&id=594%3Athe-weather-on-16-december-1944&catid=1%3Abattle-of-the-bulge-us-army&Itemid=6&lang=en
31. M. Bedford Davis, *Frozen Rainbows*, (Meadowlark Publishing, 2003), p. 211.

32. Danny S. Parker, *Battle of the Bulge: Hitler's Ardennes Offensive, 1944–1945* (Combined Books, 1991), p. 39.
33. MacDonald, *A Time for Trumpets*, op. cit., p. 94.
34. Marguerite Linden-Meier Report, M 1232–1/R-1232–1, Military Archives, US Army Command and General Staff College, Fort Leavenworth, Kansas. I am grateful to Mr Roland Gaul for alerting me to this file.
35. Marlene Dietrich became a naturalised US citizen in 1939. Gaul, *The Battle of the Bulge in Luxembourg*, Vol. II: *The Americans*, op. cit., pp. 105–6; John C. McManus, *Alamo in the Ardennes: The Untold Story of the American Soldiers Who Made the Defense of Bastogne Possible* (John Wiley, 2007), p. 33.
36. MacDonald, *A Time for Trumpets*, op. cit., pp. 11–14.
37. Missing Air Crew Report for Flying Officer John R.S. Morgan, Major Glenn Miller and Lieutenant-Colonel Norman F. Baessell, 01/08/1945, Missing Air Crew Report number 10770, 12/1944, Record Group 92: Records of the Office of the Quartermaster General, 1774–1985, NARA. Of numerous theories advanced over the years, from a story which first appeared in December 2001, it seems most likely that Miller's plane wandered into an area where returning Allied aircraft could jettison their unused bomb loads. See http://www.theguardian.com/uk/2001/dec/15/humanities.research
38. Eisenhower, *The Bitter Woods*, op. cit., p. 205.
39. Robert E. Merriam, *Dark December: The Full Account of the Battle of the Bulge* (Ziff-Davis Publishing Co., 1947), p. 65.
40. http://www.lerenfort.fsnet.co.uk/page24N.htm
41. Whiting, *The Last Assault*, op. cit., p. 13.
42. Colonel Daniel B. Strickler, *After Action Report of the German Ardennes Breakthrough As I Saw It from 16 Dec 1944–2 Jan 1945*, Record Group 407, 110th Infantry Regiment, 28th Infantry Division, Box 8596, NARA.
43. Cole, *The Ardennes*, op. cit., p. 193.
44. Gerald Astor, *A Blood-Dimmed Tide: The Battle of the Bulge by the Men Who Fought It* (Dell Publishing, 1992), p. 44.
45. Whiting, *Papa Goes to War*, op. cit., p. 173.
46. Major Jeffrey P. Holt, *Operational Performance of the U.S. 28th Infantry Division, September to December 1944* (Master's Thesis, U.S. Army Command and General Staff College, Fort Leavenworth, Kansas, 2004), p. 44. Available at: http://www.dtic.mil/dtic/tr/fulltext/u2/a284499.pdf
47. Lt. Thomas J. Flynn interview 1–2 May 1945, Company 'K', 110th Infantry Regiment, 28th Infantry Division, Record Group #407, NARA; McManus, *Alamo in the Ardennes*, op. cit., p. 36.
48. Oral interview Lieutenant-Colonel (ret.) Joe Soya, 1982, Paul Van Doren Collection, Small Manuscript Collection, George C. Marshall Library, Lexington, Virginia.

12. Brandenberger's Grenadiers

1. Harry Yeide, *Fighting Patton. George S. Patton Jr Through the Eyes of His Opponents* (Zenith Press, 2011), p. 360.

2. Bruce Quarrie, Order of Battle (12): *The Ardennes Offensive. I Armee & VII Armee. Southern Sector* (Osprey, 2001), pp. 10–12.
3. Yeide, *Fighting Patton*, op. cit., pp. 359–60.
4. The recorded strength of 2nd *Flak* Division on 8 November was 20 heavy batteries (80 × 88mm towed guns) and 21 light/medium batteries (84 × 37mm and 20mm towed guns) on towed mountings. The 15th *Flak* Regiment nominally comprised 9 heavy batteries (36 × 88mm towed guns) and 6 light/medium batteries (24 × 37mm and 20mm towed guns), but the precise allocation of weapons seems to have varied. See http://www.ww2.dk/ground/flak/2fladiv.htm
5. Samuel W. Mitcham, Jr *Panzers in Winter. Hitler's Army and the Battle of the Bulge* (Stackpole, 2008), p. 20
6. *Völkisher Beobachter*, 3 August 1944.
7. *Volksgrenadiers* and *Volksgrenadier* divisions should not be confused with the *Volkssturm*, raised at the same time, as we have seen.
8. The 257th *Volksgrenadier* Division comprised 40 per cent returning convalescent soldiers, for example.
9. Gunter K. Koschorrek, *Blood Red Snow* (Greenhill, 2002), p. 290.
10. Irving, *Hitler's War*, op. cit., p. 682.
11. Headquarters Fifth Panzer Army, Directive on Tactics, 20 November 1944.
12. Wolfgang Fleischer, *Das letzte Jahr des deutschen Heeres 1944–1945* (Dörfler, 2007), p. 129.
13. Edgar Christoffel, *Krieg am Westwall 1944/45* (Helios, 2011), p. 242.
14. As NATO Historian for IFOR and SFOR during 1996–7, I encountered large numbers of WW2-era weapons and ammunition used by the various Croat, Serb and Bosnian factions, including PO-8 Luger pistols, MG-34 and MG-42 machine guns, MP-40 machine-pistols, M-1911 semi-automatic pistols, Thompson sub-machine guns and Sten guns. Sealed cans of ammunitions bearing dates from 1941 to 1944 also surfaced and were still being issued to the local militias.
15. Kiss memoir, *The Bulge Bugle*, Vol. XII/1 (February 1993), p. 17.
16. Kiss memoir, ibid. Although the carrying of rubber hoses by *Volksgrenadiers* featured prominently in the 1965 movie *Battle of the Bulge*, I have not encountered this in other memoirs of the Ardennes campaign.
17. These included guns of 75, 100, 105, 120, 122, 128, 150 and 152mm calibres. The figures vary in different sources; these are from Cole, *Battle of the Bulge*, op. cit., p. 213.
18. Karl G. Larew, 'From Pigeons to Crystals: The Development of Radio Communication in US Army Tanks in World War II', article in *The Historian*, Vol. 67/4 (Winter 2005).
19. The archives vary as to the number of *Nebelwerfer* projectors deployed with Seventh Army. This is the figure cited in Cole, *The Ardennes* op. cit., p. 213.
20. Gaul, *The Battle of the Bulge in Luxembourg*, Vol. I: *The Germans*, op. cit., pp. 239–42.
21. There seems to have been little uniformity or standardisation in *Volksgrenadier* divisions. The *Sturmgeschütz* (StuG) assault gun was Germany's most common

AFV of the Second World War. Built on the chassis of the Panzer III tank, but without a turret, it was initially intended as a mobile, armoured light gun for infantry support. Gradually the StuG was employed as a tank destroyer and eventually used to replace tanks in armoured formations. They weighed twenty-four tons, carried a crew of four and a 75mm gun; more than 11,500 were built, plus an additional 1,000 modelled on the Panzer IV chassis. Collectively, they destroyed more enemy tanks than panzers, and by 1944 *Sturmgeschütz* units *claimed* to have knocked out 20,000 tanks. They were far more cost-effective than tanks and, because of their low silhouette, StuGs were easy to camouflage and harder to hit than a conventional tank. However, their lack of a traversable turret gave them a severe disadvantage in an offensive, so they were better suited to defensive scenarios. The *Hetzer* ('Baiter'), of which nearly 3,000 were manufactured, was smaller, built on to the Czech Pz 38(t) chassis, weighing in at fifteen tons, also carrying a crew of four with a 75mm gun. It was one of the most common of late-war German AFVs, and popular with crews on account of its mechanical reliability and the fact that its small size made it easy to hide. Many nations used StuGs and Hetzers for decades after the war, a tribute to their practicality and durability.

22. Nat Frankel and Larry Smith, *Patton's Best: An Informal History of the 4th Armored Division* (Hawthorn Books, 1978) pp. 135–6.
23. The archives are at variance, citing between twenty-one and twenty-seven vehicles.
24. After captivity, Schmidt wrote several papers for the US Army Military History Programme, including *B067 – 352nd Volksgrenadier Division, 16 December 1944–25 January 1945* (1946) and *P-032G – Ardennes Project*; both in Foreign Military Studies, NARA.
25. Courtesy of Grenadier Regiment 916 research website at: http://www.gr916.co.uk
26. Yeide, *Fighting Patton*, op. cit., p. 363.
27. Gaul, *The Battle of the Bulge*, Vol. I: *The Germans*, op. cit., pp. 132–3.

13. The Baron

1. Germà Bel, 'Against the Mainstream: Nazi Privatization in 1930s Germany', article in *Economic History Review* (2009); Winfried Wolf, *Car Mania: A Critical History of Transport, 1770–1990* (Pluto Press, 1996), pp. 94–5.
2. Arvo L. Vecamer, 'Deutsche Reichsbahn – The German State Railway in WWII', online article at: http://www.feldgrau.com/dreichsbahn.html
3. Patton also competed in Olympic Pentathlon at the 1912 Olympics in Stockholm.
4. Liddell Hart, *The Other Side of the Hill*, op. cit., p. 452.
5. Ibid.
6. Ibid., pp. 450–51.
7. The sixty-two-year-old Lucht had seen service in the First World War, the Spanish Civil War, when he commanded the artillery of the German Condor Legion supporting Franco, and in France and Russia, where he had shone as a divisional and corps commander. In October 1943 the old warhorse was given LXVI Corps in Russia, which he took to southern France in August 1944 to oppose the

Operation Dragoon landings; thereafter his formations were pulled back to Germany in preparation for *Herbstnebel*.

8. Manteuffel's post-war recollections to the US Army Historical Programme are B-151 and B-151a, *Fifth Panzer Army, Ardennes Offensive*. Others in the series of immense value are B-321, *LVIII Panzer Corps in the Ardennes Offensive, 16 December 1944–11 January 1945* (General der Panzertruppen Walter Krueger); A-939, *The Assignment of the XLVII Panzer Corps in the Ardennes, 1944–45* (General der Panzertruppen Heinrich von Luettwitz); B040, *26th Volks Grenadier Division in the Ardennes Offensive* (Generalmajor Heinz Kokott); A-955, *Report on the Campaign in Northern France, the Rhineland, and the Ardennes* (Oberst Hans-Juergen Dingler); B-506, *LVIII Panzer Corps Artillery, 1 November 1944–1 February 1945* (Generalmajor Gerhard Triepel); A-941 and A942, *Panzer Lehr Division, 1 December 1944–26 January 1945 and 15–22 December 1944* (both Generalleutnant Fritz Bayerlein), all Foreign Military Studies, NARA.
9. Pallud, *Battle of the Bulge: Then and Now*, op. cit., p. 48.
10. Shulman, *Defeat in the West*, op. cit., pp. 279–80.
11. The fifty-two-year-old chain-smoking Walter Krüger was a highly decorated veteran panzer commander with service in France and two and a half years in Russia, by which time he had won a Knight's Cross and Oak Leaves. In January 1944 he was rested and given LVIII Panzer Corps in France, whom he would eventually take to the Ardennes.
12. Waldenburg's 1973 obituary is at: http://www.116thpanzer.com/forum/m/836079/viewthread/4409928-generalmajor-siegfried-von-waldenburg
13. On 7 June 1944, the division possessed 78 Panthers, 66 Panzer IV and 13 PzIII.
14. Generalmajor Rudolf Bader, *560th Volks Grenadier Division – Ardennes Campaign (16 December 1944–25 January 1945)*, B-0024, RG-338 Foreign Military Studies, NARA.
15. David Stone, *Hitler's Army: The Men, Machines, and Organization: 1939–1945* (Zenith Press, 2009), pp. 204–07.
16. Shuling Tang, 'History of the Automobile: Ownership per Household in the United States', chapter in *Transportation Deployment Casebook. History of the Automobile: Ownership per Household in the United States*. E-book at: http://en.wikibooks.org/wiki/Transportation_Deployment_Casebook/History_of_the_Automobile:_Ownership_per_Household_in_U.S. Americans possessed 22,500,000 vehicles in 1935 and a population of 127,250,000. This equated to one vehicle per 0.7 per cent of American households at the time. Apart from a population rise, the household ownership percentage and individual ownership percentage remained broadly similar through the war years. See also: Richard J. Evans, *The Third Reich in Power: 1933–1939* (Penguin, 2006).
17. James J. Weingartner, *A Peculiar Crusade: Willis M. Everett and the Malmedy Massacre* (New York University Press, 2000), p. 61.
18. Hasso von Manteuffel, MS #B-151a, and ETHINT-46, *Fifth Panzer Army, Mission of November 1944–January 1945*, Foreign Military Studies, NARA.
19. Generalmajor Heinz Kokott, B-040, *26th Volks Grenadier Division in the Ardennes Offensive*, Foreign Military Studies, NARA.

20. Colonel S. L. A. Marshall, *Bastogne. The Story of the First Eight Days, in Which the 101st Airborne Division Was Closed Within the Ring of German Forces* (Infantry Journal Press, 1946), pp. 174–6.
21. *Jabo*=abbreviation of *Jagdbomber* (light bomber or ground attack aircraft).
22. Every source seems to cite slightly different figures. As an average these will be broadly correct. Cole (p. 177) cites 27 Panzer IVs, 58 Panthers, and 48 StuGs.
23. In the 2nd Panzer Division, the battlegroups, large organisations of 2,000–3,000 personnel, were known as *Kampfgruppe* (KG) Cochenhausen, KG von Bohm, KG Gutmann and KG Holtmeyer.
24. Lauchert was well regarded by Heinz Guderian and had been an observer of the Normandy battles, where he encountered Sepp Dietrich, who also had a favourable opinion of him.
25. P.A. Spayd, *Bayerlein: From Afrika Korps to Panzer Lehr. The Life of Rommel's Chief-of-staff Generalleutnant Fritz Bayerlein* (Schiffer Publishing, 2003).
26. Bayerlein became an articulate commentator on the WW2 German army and wrote extensively, was involved in the reformation of the Bundeswehr and worked with film companies; Bayerlein died in his home town of Würzburg in 1970.
27. Pallud, *Battle of the Bulge: Then and Now*, op. cit., pp. 50–51; Samuel W. Mitcham, *Panzer Legions: A Guide to the German Army Tank Divisions of World War II and Their Commanders* (Stackpole, 2007), pp. 201–4. On 12 December, Panzer Lehr reported 23 Panthers, 30 Panzer IVs, 15 Jagdpanzers and StuGs and 14 Jagdpanzers IVs. Due to its excellent and uncontroversial reputation, Panzer Lehr remains in the Bundeswehr's Order of Battle today, its only named division.
28. Colonels Paul Freiherr von Hauser and Joachim Ritter von Poschinger led 901st and 902nd *Panzergrenadier* Regiments respectively. Panzer Lehr deployed in three *Kampfgruppen*, named after the Reconnaissance Battalion commander, Major Gerd von Fallois, Hauser's KG (*Kampfgruppe*) 901 and KG 902, commanded by Poschinger.
29. Steven J. Zaloga, *Battle of the Bulge 1944 (2): Bastogne* (Osprey, 2004), p. 23.
30. Generalmajor Otto-Ernst Remer, *The Führer-Begleit-Brigade in the Ardennes*, MS #B-592 and MS #B-383 (1954), NARA.
31. Author's translation from Hans Hejny, *Der letzte Vormarsch: Ardennenschlacht 1944* (Europäischer Verlag, 1983), a rare published account of the battle from a German soldier's point of view.

14. We Accept Death, We Hand Out Death

1. John A. McCarthy, Walter Grunzweig and Thomas Koebner (eds), *The Many Faces of Germany* (Berghahn, 2004), pp. 214–15. I met Graf von Einsiedel (b. 1921) in Berlin in 1983. He died in 2007.
2. Based on several author interviews with Herr Hans Hennecke, February–April 1981.
3. April 1945 found him promoted to Training Company commander, overseeing sixteen- and seventeen-year-old recruits, when he was captured.
4. Josef 'Sepp' Dietrich, who was born in that decade of years (1885–95) that

furnished most senior commanders of the Second World War – in his case, in 1892, making him fifty-two at the Battle of the Bulge. Born into the poorest of backgrounds, he volunteered in 1914 for the Bavarian artillery and served in some of the same battles as Hitler, who was a Bavarian infantryman. In February 1918 he was assigned to a tank unit, seeing action as gunner in a unit of captured British tanks, winning an Iron Cross and promotion to sergeant-major. A pre-war drifter, he returned home a decorated hero with an ability to lead and command, which was Hitler's story too. Although he first came across his future Führer in 1921, it was not until 1928 that Dietrich actually joined the NSDAP (Party Member 89,015) and the *Schutzstaffel.* His SS number was 1,177 of an organisation that eventually numbered thirty-eight divisions and 950,000 men, and had been founded in 1921 as bruisers and brawlers to protect Hitler's person at his first political meetings.

Hitler immediately took to his chief bodyguard, whom he considered rough but straight as a die, with a proven war record and sense of humour that cheered even the darkest moments of the nascent Nazi Party. On Hitler's election as Chancellor in January 1933, Dietrich was tasked to create the SS Watch-Battalion-Berlin (*Stabswache Berlin*), a display unit to guard the Reich Chancellery, which later became the SS-*Leibstandarte* (Life Guard) Adolf Hitler, with a strength of nearly 1,000. Dietrich's lack of education showed when he took the *Leibstandarte* to Poland in September 1939 – then a brigadier, Dietrich's prior military experience was as an NCO, twenty-one years earlier. Fortunately, his 1a (chief of staff) was an ex-regular army colonel and Kriegsakademie graduate, Willi Bittrich, who provided the brains, while Dietrich rose to the role of leader. The regiment was one of the few fully motorised units in the German army and participated in the campaigns against Poland and France, where it performed adequately, rather than brilliantly.

By the end of 1940, the Waffen-SS (or fighting-SS) was confirmed as a regular unit of the German military, with Dietrich at its head in the rank of General der Waffen-SS. The *Leibstandarte* was further expanded and in April–May 1941 invaded Yugoslavia and Greece, where it shone in combat. In 1941, Dietrich's regiment was expanded into a division of 13,000 officers and men and arrived in Russia. During the 1941–2 winter campaign Dietrich himself suffered severe frostbite, indicating that he was not tucked up safe and warm in his HQ, and won admiration for getting to know many of the men under his command by name. Hitler personally followed Dietrich's achievements in Russia on his situation map, the *Leibstandarte's* movements indicated by a flag annotated 'Sepp'. In 1942 Dietrich's command was again in Russia with some of the first Tiger tanks, and a divisional strength of 21,000 – significantly more than army divisions and surely a mark of favouritism. Hitler awarded him Diamonds to his Knight's Cross for his outstanding leadership in Normandy and promoted him to *Oberstgrüppenführer*, a rank below Himmler, assessing him as 'unique . . . a man who is simultaneously cunning, energetic and brutal. Under his swashbuckling appearance, Dietrich is a serious, conscientious, scrupulous character. And what care he takes of his troops!' As a reaction to 20 July, and in what was widely interpreted throughout Germany as a reward for the wider loyalty of the Waffen-SS, Hitler entrusted him with the Sixth Panzer Army. On hearing this, the ever-loyal Krämer, knowing his old boss would need help in his new assignment, resigned his own command of the 12th SS-*Hitlerjugend* Division to accompany 'Sepp' into battle yet again as his chief of staff.

5. Close to Rommel, Dietrich had just waved the latter off from his own HQ on 17 July 1944 when Rommel's staff car was attacked by Allied fighters in Normandy. Rommel's alleged parting words to Dietrich were, 'Something has to happen! The war in the West has to be ended!' To which Dietrich was supposed to have responded, 'You, *Herr Generalfeldmarschall*, are my commander-in-chief, and I shall obey only you, whatever the order!' This is frequently interpreted as Rommel sounding out Dietrich's likely response to a change of leadership (i.e. Hitler's assassination, which was attempted on 20 July). Dietrich's ambivalence reflected his growing (and widely known) disillusionment with Hitler's command style, and a refusal to countenance retreat from Normandy – if true, an abrupt change of heart for Hitler's loyal henchman of sixteen years.
6. Dietrich surrendered to Patton's men on 8 May 1945. After the war, he was found guilty of complicity in the massacre of American soldiers near Malmedy, though his responsibility for the deed was never proven. Sentenced to life for contradicting 'the customs and ethics of war', several anti-Nazi former colleagues, among them Guderian and Speidel, testified on his behalf and the sentence was commuted to twenty-five years. Released in October 1955, he was later sentenced by a German court for murder during the June 1934 massacre of the SA leadership. He enjoyed seven years of liberty before dying of a heart attack in April 1966, aged seventy-tree – an unlikely end for a soldier who, at several moments, should have met death on the battlefield. Despite a bloody reputation, his biographer Charles Messenger argues convincingly that Dietrich was not an ideologically committed Nazi, just a rather good leader of men, who was never afraid to roll up his sleeves and muck in. In his last years he helped found the *Hilfsorganisation auf Gegenseitigkeit der Waffen SS* (Waffen-SS Self Help Organisation) or HIAG, which lobbied successfully for Waffen-SS soldiers to be paid a war pension like their Wehrmacht colleagues. At what was probably the last big gathering of the Waffen-SS, 7,000 wartime comrades, as well as former adversaries, came to his funeral, where Wilhelm Bittrich, his first chief of staff, gave the address.
7. Freytag von Loringhoven (1914–2007) obituaries, *Guardian*, 28 March 2007; *New York Times*, 1 April 2007.
8. Philipp Freiherr von Boeselanger (1917–2008) obituaries, *Daily Telegraph*, 2 May 2008; *New York Times*, 3 May 2008; online interview at: http://operationvalkyrie.wordpress.com/primary-sources/
9. Pallud, *The Battle of the Bulge: Then and Now*, op. cit., pp. 30–33.
10. Shulman, *Defeat in the West*, op. cit., pp. 290–91.
11. Bruce Quarrie, *The Ardennes Offensive: VI Panzer Armee: Northern Sector* (Osprey, 1999), p. 20.
12. During the fighting, Oberst Kosmalla was seriously wounded and Generalmajor Eugen König of 12th *Volksgrenadier* Division took command.

13. Schmidt memoir, op. cit.
14. Otto Gunkel, 'The Reestablishment of the 272nd VGD at Döberitz', courtesy of *Der Erste Zug* website, at: http://www.dererstezug.com/272ndInAction/272ndInAction(3).htm
15. Schmidt memoir, op. cit.
16. Gunkel memoir, op. cit.
17. Ibid.
18. Wego died in an attack on 4 January 1945, his *Soldbuch* evidencing his death retained a small steel splinter piercing it. He is buried in the VDK military cemetery at Gemünd.
19. Reinartz details courtesy of http://aufhimmelzuhause.com/id33.htm website.
20. Becker memoir courtesy of *Der Erste Zug* website, at: http://dererstezug.com/VetBecker.htm
21. Ibid.
22. Philip Howard Grey, 'The True North Shoulder and How It Upset Hitler's Schedule', article in *The Bulge Bugle*, Vol. XXVIII/4 (November 2009), pp. 6–10.
23. Max Hastings, *Armageddon, The Battle for Germany 1944–45* (Macmillan, 2004), p. 232.
24. Richter details courtesy of http://www.wehrmacht-awards.com/Forums/showthread.php?t=532514 website.
25. Colonel C.P. Stacey, *Official History of the Canadian Army in the Second World War*, Vol. III, *The Victory Campaign, The Operations in North-West Europe, 1944–1945* (Ottawa, 1966), p. 270; Timm Haasler, Roddy MacDougall, Simon Vosters and Hans Weber, *Duel in the Mist*, vol. 2, *The Leibstandarte during the Ardennes Offensive* (Panzerwrecks 2012), p. 208.
26. Major-General Michael Reynolds, *The Devil's Adjutant* (Spellmount, 1995), p. 49.
27. Author's interview with Hennecke, 1991, op. cit.
28. Hans Bernard (1920–2010) interview, Robert Kershaw, *Tank Men: The Human Story of Tanks at War* (Hodder & Stoughton, 2008).
29. Kershaw, *Tank Men*, op. cit.
30. Freytag von Loringhoven obituaries, op. cit.
31. Whiting, *The Last Assault*, op. cit., p. 173; Paul Eisen, 'From the people who brought you The Destruction of Dresden . . . The Flattening of Düren', online article (20 February 2012) at: http://www.deliberation.info/from-the-people-who-brought-you-the-destruction-of-dresden-the-flattening-of-duren/
32. Kershaw, *Tank Men*, op. cit.
33. Peter von der Osten-Sacken (1909–2008) and Edouard Jahnke interviews, Kershaw, *Tank Men*, op. cit.
34. Stacey, *Official History of the Canadian Army*, Vol. III, *The Victory Campaign*, op. cit., p. 270.
35. Sources differ only slightly on these numbers, which are nevertheless broadly correct for 16 December 1944.
36. Kressmann (b. 1918) interview, Kershaw, *Tank Men*, op. cit.
37. Werner Kinnett (1927–89) interview by Bill Medland for *Military Magazine*, 1985.

38. Hans Baumann (b.1925) interview, Kershaw, *Tank Men*, op. cit.
39. Bernhard Heisig, later an artist (1925–2011) interview, Kershaw, *Tank Men*, op. cit.
40. Stacey, *The Victory Campaign*, op. cit., p. 270.
41. Fritz Langanke (1919–2012) interview, Kershaw, *Tank Men*, op. cit.
42. Stacey, *The Victory Campaign*, op. cit., p. 270.
43. He was captured by the 106th Division. MacDonald, *A Time for Trumpets*, op. cit., pp. 93–4; Whiting, *The Last Assault*, op. cit., pp. 28–9.
44. Haasler, et al. *Duel in the Mist*, vol. 2, op. cit., p. 209.
45. Ibid., p. 208.
46. Cole, *The Ardennes*, op. cit., p. 260.
47. Philipp von Boeselanger obituaries, op. cit.; Jürgen Girgensohn, later an SPD politician (1924–2004) interview, Kershaw, *Tank Men*, op. cit.

Interlude

1. J. Neumann and H. Flohn, 'Great Historical Events That Were Significantly Affected by the Weather: Part 8, Germany's War on the Soviet Union, 1941–45; II. Some Important Weather Forecasts, 1942–45', article in the *Journal of the American Meteorological Society*, Vol. 69/7 (July 1988), pp. 734–5.
2. Royce L. Thompson, *Study of Weather of the Ardennes Campaign* (CMH, 2 October 1953), p. 7.
3. James Arnold, *Ardennes 1944: Hitler's Last Gamble in the West* (Osprey, 1990), p. 24.
4. Schroeder, *He Was My Chief*, op. cit., p. 125.
5. These were *U-810*, *U-1053* and *U-1228*. See: *Battle of the Atlantic: U-Boat Operations, December 1942–May 1945*, Central Security Service, National Security Agency, Publication SRH-008, pp. 171–3. Online at: http://www.ibiblio.org/hyperwar/ETO/Ultra/SRH-008/SRH008-12.html
6. Eisenhower, *Crusade in Europe*, op. cit., p. 345.
7. POW website at: http://www.radiomarconi.com/marconi/monumento/pow/pows.html

15. Null-Tag

1. Shulman, *Defeat in the West*, op. cit., p. 283. Leuthen was the 1757 battle which saw Frederick the Great at his peak. He used terrain and decisive manoeuvre to destroy the much larger Austrian army in the Seven Years' War, thus establishing Prussia's military reputation. The association of smashing a much larger rival would have been known to most of Model's audience.
2. Arthur Wellesley, 1st Duke of Wellington – letter to John Croker, 8 August 1815.
3. Author's interview, William S. Blaher, 106th Division, Hotel Zur Post, St Vith, 17 December 1994.
4. The number of artillery tubes and rocket projectors is reported variously as 1,600

and 1,900. Some were from detachments of the neighbouring Army Groups, and took no further part in *Herbstnebel*, other than to contribute to the opening surprise.

5. Michael Green and James D. Brown, *War Stories of the Battle of the Bulge* (Zenith Press, 2010), p. 41.
6. Details in his *Wehrmacht Soldbuch* courtesy of Swayne Martin. Peter Kelch died on 21 May 1945, aged twenty-one, fourteen days after the war ended, and lies in the Heidelberg-Friedhof Cemetery.
7. In captivity, Generalleutnant Franz Sensfuss wrote several papers on the history of 212nd *Volksgrenadiers* for the US Army Historical Division, including VGD: MSS # A-930, A-931, und B-073.A-930, A-931, and B-073.
8. The main sources for German Seventh Army are the US post-war interviews and debriefs now in Foreign Military Studies at NARA. They include: A876, *Ardennes Offensive of Seventh Army, 16 December 1944–25 January 1945* (General der Panzertruppen Erich Brandenberger); B-030, *LXXXV Corps, 1 December 1944–10 January 1945* (General der Infanterie Baptist Kniess) and B-081, *LXXX Corps, 13 September 1944–23 March 1945, Part Two* (General der Infanterie Dr Franz Beyer); the divisions are recorded in A-930, A-931, *212th Volksgrenadier Division-Ardennes, 16 December 1944–25 January 1945* (Generalleutnant Franz Sensfuss); B-023 (Heilmann); B-067, *352nd Volksgrenadier Division, 16 December 1944–25 January 1945* (Generalmajor Erich Schmidt); B-073 *212th Volksgrenadier Division, Ardennes* (Sensfuss); and P-032f, *Ardennes Project* (Generalmajor Hugo Dempwolff).
9. Gaul, *The Battle of the Bulge in Luxembourg*, Vol. II: *The Americans*, op. cit., p. 129.
10. William J. Gaynor, 'Did They Fool Us?', article in *The Bulge Bugle* (November 2010), p. 23.
11. Whiting, *Papa Goes to War*, op. cit., p. 167.
12. Ibid., p. 178.
13. Illustrative of the morale-boosting information about the war contained in US newspapers (but forbidden in the United Kingdom), on 23 March 1945, the *Le Mars* [Plymouth County, Iowa] *Semi-Weekly Sentinel* repeated a US Fourth Division Order of the Day, which read, 'Over four months ago after advancing through the Ardennes, the Fourth Infantry Division broke through the Siegfried Line and occupied the Schnee Eifel. Relieved by another division, the Fourth moved north and attacked through the Huertgen Forest, moved south again and successfully defended the city of Luxembourg against the German counter-offensive in December, attacked across the Sure and Our Rivers and advanced against continuous opposition until it was again opposite the Schnee Eifel. In spite of almost incredible weather conditions and the long period of continuous contact with the enemy, the division then recaptured the Siegfried Line defenses on the Schnee Eifel and captured the fortified town of Brandscheid which had heretofore successfully withstood all attacks made against it. The 70th Tank Battalion contributed aggressive and invaluable support throughout this entire operation.' The *Le Mars Sentinel* went on to report, 'The 70th Tank Battalion is

commanded by Lieutenant-Colonel Henry E. Davidson Jr, of Uniontown, Pennsylvania. Company 'A', which supports the 8th Infantry, is led by Captain Gordon A. Brodie of Le Mars. Capt. Francis E. Songer commands Company 'B' in support of the 12th Infantry, and First Lieutenant Preston E. Yoeman of Crystal Lake, Illinois, commands Company 'C' in support of the 22nd Infantry. Captain Herman Finkelstein of Philadelphia is commanding officer of Company 'D' which is used in general support.'

14. Zaloga, *Panther vs. Sherman: Battle of the Bulge 1944.*
15. Yeide, *Steel Victory,* op. cit., pp. 201–4; Belton Y. Cooper, *Death Traps: The Survival of an American Armoured Division in World War II* (Presidio, 2003), pp. 156–63.
16. Babcock, *War Stories,* op. cit., pp. 341–2.
17. Ibid., p. 336.
18. Cecil E. Roberts, *A Soldier from Texas* (Branch-Smith Inc., Texas, 1978), p. 54.
19. Gaul, *The Battle of the Bulge in Luxembourg,* Vol. II: *The Americans,* op. cit., p. 117.
20. Ibid., pp. 119–20.
21. Lieutenant-Col George Ruhlen's 3rd Armored Field Artillery Battalion, equipped with 105mm howitzers mounted on the M-7 tracked Sherman chassis.
22. AAR, 60th Armored Infantry Battalion, 9th Armored Division, Oct 44 Thru Mar 45, AAR #361-U, Ref. 8609-AIB-131, NARA.
23. AAR, 60th Armored Infantry Battalion, op. cit.
24. Gaul, *The Battle of the Bulge in Luxembourg,* Vol. II: *The Americans,* op. cit., p. 130.
25. Ibid., p. 131.
26. Möhring's cap, ear muffs and map case are now in the Diekirch Historical Museum.
27. Whiting, *Papa Goes to War,* op. cit., p. 182.

16. The Bloody Bucket

1. One of many distinguished tactical leaders on 6 June 1944, Rudder's activities in particular have been lionised by Americans not least because of his portrayal in *The Longest Day,* but also because of his subsequent achievements at Texas A & M University, of which he was later President. He died in 1970.
2. Reporting for duty six weeks later, Slovik informed his company commander that he was 'too scared' to serve in a rifle company and asked to be reassigned to a rear area unit, adding he would run away if he were assigned to a rifle unit. As the 109th had been hard hit in Normandy and were heading for the Hürtgen and needed every spare man, he was sent to a rifle platoon. Slovik wrote a series of notes to his superiors, stating his intention to run away if sent into combat, and refused to withdraw them. Slovik was buried in the Oise-Aisne American Cemetery, alongside ninety-six other American soldiers executed for crimes such as murder and rape, an unhappy reminder of another problem the US Army was experiencing as well as fighting the Germans.
3. Gaul, *The Battle of the Bulge in Luxembourg,* Vol. II: *The Americans,* op. cit., pp. 41–2.

4. Cole, *The Ardennes*, op. cit., p. 214.
5. Gaul, *The Battle of the Bulge in Luxembourg*, Vol. I: *The Germans*, op. cit., pp. 58.
6. Special Report [German] Army (SRA), 1148 31 December 1944, National Archives (Kew, UK), Ref. WO 208/4140.
7. Gaul, *The Battle of the Bulge in Luxembourg*, Vol. II: *The Americans*, op. cit., p. 87.
8. MacDonald, *A Time for Trumpets*, op. cit., p. 151.
9. Ibid. Emphasis (*complete*) in original transcript.
10. See Sönke Neitzel and Harald Welzer, *Soldaten on Fighting, Killing and Dying. The Secret Second World War Tapes of German POWs* (Simon & Shuster, 2012).
11. Gaul, *The Battle of the Bulge*, Vol. II, op. cit., p. 88.
12. Gaul, *The Battle of the Bulge*, Vol. I, op. cit., pp. 37–8.
13. Ibid.
14. Gaul, *The Battle of the Bulge*, Vol. I, op. cit., pp. 35–6.
15. Ibid., p. 35.
16. Gaul, *The Battle of the Bulge*, Vol. I, op. cit., pp. 63.
17. Ibid.
18. Ibid., pp. 104–5.
19. Ibid., p. 81.
20. Ibid., p. 84.
21. Author's interview, Hubert 'Bill' Cavins, 28th Division, Hotel Zur Post, St Vith, 17 December 1994.
22. Ibid., p. 60.
23. Ibid.
24. Davis, *Frozen Rainbows*, op. cit., pp. 211–12.
25. Eisenhower, *The Bitter Woods*, op. cit., p. 208.
26. Macdonald, *A Time for Trumpets*, op. cit., p. 151.
27. See the excellent Hoesdorf Plateau Guided Walk website at: http://www.mnhm.lu/www/france/downloads/the-u.s.-side.pdf
28. Letter home, 30 January 1945 from Lieutenant John J. Perkins. He seems to echo a very similar description of the First World War Western Front. See *The Western Front*, Introduction by Sir Douglas Haig, illustrations by Muirhead Bone (The War Office /*Country Life*, 1917).
29. Lieutenant-Colonel James E. Rudder, *Unit Report No.6, From 1 Dec 44–31 Dec 44, 109th Infantry Regiment* (4 January 1944), NARA.
30. Whiting, *'44: In Combat From Normandy to the Ardennes*, op. cit., pp. 167–8; Jeff Johannes and Doug Nash, *German Rations at the Front: A snapshot of what the German Soldier consumed during the Battle of the Bulge*, at http://gr914.webs.com/rations.htm
31. Bruce E. Egger and Lee MacMillan Otts, *G Company's War* (University of Alabama Press, 1992), p. 113.
32. Author's interview with T/Sergeant Gilbert T. Gouveia, Company 'G', 333 Infantry Regiment, Hotel Zur Post, St Vith, 17 December 1994.
33. Richard D. Courtney, *Normandy to The Bulge* (Southern Illinois University Press, 1997), p. 54.

34. Johannes and Nash, *German Rations at the Front*, op. cit.
35. IPW (Prisoner of War) Interrogation Reports, IPW Team 60, 134th Infantry Regiment, 35th Infantry Division, 2 January 1945, NARA.
36. Ibid.
37. See A-931, Generalleutnant Franz Sensfuss, *212th Volksgrenadier Division*, op. cit.

17. The Baron's Blitzkrieg

1. Shulman, *Defeat in the West*, op. cit., p. 283.
2. 106th Division, S-3 (Operations) Signals Log, 16 December 1944, NARA.
3. Author's translation from Hejny, *Der letzte Vormarsch*, op. cit.
4. Liddell Hart, *The Other Side of the Hill*, op. cit., p. 459.
5. *An Interview with Generalmajor Heinz Kokott*, ETHINT-44, 29 November 1944; *Ardennes Offensive, Battle of Bastogne*, Part 1, Ms. No. B-040, not dated, both NARA.
6. Liddell Hart, *The Other Side of the Hill*, op. cit., p. 459.
7. Jenkins, Oral Interview, Wisconsin Veterans Museum Research Center, op. cit.
8. Ibid.
9. Wilfrid R. Riley, '188th Combat Engineers in Belgium', article in *The Bulge Bugle*, Vol. XXXIII/1 (February 2014), p. 8.
10. Lieutenant-Colonel Charles R. Shrader, *Amicicide: The Problem of Friendly Fire in Modern War* (University Press of the Pacific, 1982).
11. Yeide, *Steel Victory*, op. cit., pp. 199–201.
12. William C. C. Cavanagh, *A Tour of the Bulge Battlefield* (Leo Cooper, 2001), p. 160; Mike Tolhurst, *Battleground Europe. Bastogne* (Leo Cooper, 2001), p. 39; McManus, *Alamo in the Ardennes*, op. cit., p. 75.
13. Interview by Hugh Ambrose in the Eisenhower Center, University of New Orleans; Ambrose, *Citizen Soldiers*, op. cit., p. 190.
14. Ibid.
15. Frank A. LoVuolo memoir, *The Bulge Bugle*, Vol. IX/1 (February 1990), pp. 12–13.
16. Ibid.
17. 'Colonel With Cane Led the Attack', *New York Sun*, 9 January 1945, p. 4.
18. Shoemaker memoir, courtesy of his grandson, at: http://www.327gir.com/28thInfantry.html
19. Reusch memoir, courtesy of http://www.stengerhistorica.com/History/WarArchive/VeteranVoices/Reusch.htm
20. Chamness memoir, *Bulge Bugle*, May 2001; http://www.battleofthebulgememories.be/stories26/32-battle-of-the-bulge-us-army/725-hq-company-112th-infantry-regiment-28th-id.html
21. Clarence Blakeslee, 'The Battle Started on 16 December 1944', article in *The Bulge Bugle*, Vol. XXXIII/1 (February 2014), p. 29.
22. Charles Haug memoir from Green and Brown, *War Stories of the Battle of the Bulge*, op. cit., p. 43.
23. Shoemaker memoir, op. cit.
24. Sergeant (later Colonel) Olsen memoir courtesy of http://www.justinmuseum.com/oralbio/lolsenbio.html

25. Haug memoir in Green and Brown, *War Stories of the Battle of the Bulge*, op. cit., p. 45.
26. Ibid., pp. 46–7; McManus, *Alamo in the Ardennes*, op. cit., pp. 77–8.
27. Schober memoir, courtesy of http://www.veteransofthebattleofthebulge.org/2012/06/21/milton-j-schober-106th-id-a-collection-of-memories/
28. Reusch memoir, op. cit.
29. Chamness memoir, op. cit.
30. Major Thomas Michael McGinnis, *Unit Collapse: A Historical Analysis of Two Divisional Battles in 1918 and 1944*, Master Degree Thesis, US Command and General Staff College, Fort Leavenworth, Kansas, 1987.

18. Golden Lions

1. For example, at http://lions44.hubpages.com/hub/Ardennes106th
2. Morelock, *Generals of the Ardennes. American Leadership in the Battle of the Bulge*, op. cit., p. 280.
3. Smallwood memoir, courtesy of CRIBA (*Centre de Recherches et d'Informations sur la Bataille des Ardennes*) website, at: http://www.criba.be/index.php?option=com_content&view=article&id=308:my-war&catid=1:battle-of-the-bulge-us-army&Itemid=6
4. Mike Tolhurst, *St Vith. US 106th Infantry Division* (Leo Cooper, 1999), p. 40.
5. Charles B. MacDonald, *A Time for Trumpets*, op. cit., p. 114. MacDonald was making a personal observation here, as a former captain in 2nd Division.
6. Smallwood memoir, op. cit.
7. Kester memoir, courtesy of CRIBA (*Centre de Recherches et d'Informations sur la Bataille des Ardennes*) website, at: http://www.criba.be/index.php?option=com_content&view=article&id=467:give-me-the-jeep&catid=1:battle-of-the-bulge-us-army&Itemid=6
8. Kline memoir, courtesy of: http://www.indianamilitary.org/German%20PW%20Camps/Prisoner%20of%20War/PW%20Camps/Stalag%20VIII-A%20Gorlitz/John%20Kline/Kline-John.pdf
9. Berninghaus memoir, courtesy of Traces website, at: http://www.traces.org/USPOW.berninghaus.html
10. Kline memoir, op. cit.
11. MacDonald, *A Time for Trumpets*, op. cit., p. 115.
12. Berninghaus memoir, op. cit.
13. Smallwood memoir, op. cit.
14. Colonel R. Ernest Dupuy, *St. Vith. Lion in the Way* (Infantry Journal Press, 1949), Chapter 4, pp. 21–62. There are no complete records for the division, as those of 422nd and 423rd Infantry Regiments, and other divisional units were destroyed before capture.
15. Ibid.
16. Ibid.
17. Smallwood memoir, op. cit.
18. Dupuy, *St. Vith. Lion in the Way*, op. cit.

19. *The Cub of the Golden Lion*, Newsletter of the Veterans of the 106th Infantry Division.
20. Howard Peterson memoir, *The Bulge Bugle*, Vol. XII/1 (February 1993), p. 20.
21. Interview, ex-Leutnant Kurt Schwerdtfeger (1919–2007), at Biedenkopf, 10 December 1994. Schwerdtfeger turned twenty-five on 22 December, in the middle of the fighting. Jüttner (1908–2003) was later awarded the rare distinction of Swords to his Knight's Cross with Oak Leaves, served as a colonel in the post-war Bundeswehr and died in 2003, aged ninety-five.
22. Martin memoir, courtesy of *The Bulge Bugle*, August 1991, pp. 15–16.
23. Allan Hall, 'Junkies in Jackboots: Nazi Soldiers Given Highly Addictive Crystal Meth to Help Them Fight Harder and Longer', story in the *Daily Mail*, 31 March 2011.
24. Dupuy, *St Vith. Lion in the Way*, op. cit.
25. Ibid.
26. Ibid.
27. Ibid.
28. US Army Corp of Engineers, EP No. 870-1-25 'Interview with General William M. Hoge', article in *Engineer Memoirs* (Published by US Army 1993), p. 130.
29. Dupuy, *St. Vith. Lion in the Way*, op. cit.
30. Ibid.
31. John Toland, *Battle. The Story of the Bulge* (Random House, 1959), p. 35. Charles B. MacDonald gives a slightly longer version of this conversation, though essentially the same details, from an interview with the US Signals officer, Captain Ralph G. Hill Jr, responsible for connecting the Jones–Middleton call. See *A Time for Trumpets*, op. cit., pp. 128–9.
32. Dupuy, *St. Vith. Lion in the Way*, op. cit.
33. Morelock, *Generals of the Ardennes*, op. cit., pp. 294–5.
34. Dupuy, *St. Vith. Lion in the Way*, op. cit.
35. Lieutenant David Millman, *Unit History of Company 'C' of the 331st Medical Battalion, 106th Infantry Division* (1945), NARA; unit history also courtesy of CRIBA (*Centre de Recherches et d'Informations sur la Bataille des Ardennes*) website, at: http://www.criba.be/index.php?option=com_content&view=article&id=347:co-qcq-331st-medical-battalion-106th-infantry-division-unit-history&catid=1:battle-of-the-bulge-us-army&Itemid=6
36. Christianson memoir courtesy of CRIBA (*Centre de Recherches et d'Informations sur la Bataille des Ardennes*) website, at: http://www.criba.be/index.php?option=com_content&view=article&id=289:my-two-years-six-months-and-twenty-eight-days-in-world-war-ii&catid=1:battle-of-the-bulge-us-army&Itemid=6
37. 106th Division, S-3 (Operations) Signals Log, 16 December 1944, NARA.
38. Dupuy, *St. Vith. Lion in the Way*, op. cit.
39. Ibid.

19. They Sure Worked Those Two Horses to Death

1. Whiting, *The Last Assault*, op. cit., p. 55.

2. Robert E. Humphrey, *Once Upon a Time in War* (University of Oklahoma Press, 2008), p. 25.
3. Ibid., pp. 44, 48.
4. So was I, and it is an awesome responsibility when all your soldiers are older than you are, and you have to try and shield your immaturity and inexperience of life from them.
5. Humphrey, *Once Upon A Time in War*, op. cit., p. 60.
6. 'Overseas with the 99th Division', Wallace memoir courtesy of CRIBA (*Centre de Recherches et d'Informations sur la Bataille des Ardennes*) website at: http://www.criba.be/index.php?option=com_content&view=article&id=98:overseas-with-the-99th-division&catid=1:battle-of-the-bulge-us-army&Itemid=6
7. Haas memoir, courtesy of http://www.memoriesofwar.com/veterans/haas.asp
8. Humphrey, *Once Upon a Time in War*, op. cit., p. 60.
9. John E. McAuliffe memoir, *The Bulge Bugle*, Vol. XII/1 (February 1993), p. 18.
10. Howard P. Davies, *United States Infantry, Europe 1942–45, Key Uniform Guide* (Arms & Armour Press, 1974).
11. Humphrey, *Once Upon a Time in War*, op. cit., p. 63.
12. Michael Lawrence, 'Alhambra Man Recalls Battle of the Bulge', article in the *Alhambra Source*, 12 December 2013.
13. Humphrey, *Once Upon a Time in War*, op. cit., p. 65.
14. Ibid., p. 82.
15. Charles Roland Memoir Eisenhower Center, University of New Orleans. Among others, Neill, *Infantry Soldier: Holding the Line at the Battle of the Bulge*, op. cit., is another useful 99th Division memoir.
16. Pallud, *Battle of the Bulge: Then and Now*, op. cit., p. 133.
17. Reynolds, *The Devil's Adjutant*, op. cit., p. 70.
18. Harry Levins, 'New book gives WWII platoon its due finally', article in *St Louis Post-Dispatch*, 18 December 2004. Alex Kershaw's extremely readable *The Longest Winter* (Da Capo Press, 2004) is devoted to this entire episode.
19. Lieutenant-Colonel John R. Finch and Major-George J. Mordica II, 'Miracles: A Platoon's Heroic Stand at Lanzerath', article in *Combined Arms in Battle Since 1939* (US Army Command and General Staff College Press, 1992), p. 179; MacDonald, *A Time for Trumpets*, op. cit., p. 177; Eisenhower, *The Bitter Woods*, op. cit., pp. 182–93; Astor, *A Blood-Dimmed Tide*, op. cit., pp. 479–86.
20. Haasler, MacDougall, Vosters and Weber, *Duel in the Mist*, vol. 2, *The Leibstandarte during the Ardennes Offensive*, op. cit., p. 213.
21. Reynolds, *The Devil's Adjutant*, op. cit., p. 50.
22. Ibid., p. 40.
23. Ibid., p. 52; The 12th SS operated in exactly the same fashion, being subdivided into four all-arms *Kampfgruppen*, named after their commanders, Kuhlmann, Müller, Krause and Bremer.
24. VIII Corps, G-2 Periodic Report No. 196, 30 December 1944. Box 3965, 208-2.1/ RG-407, NARA.
25. See 'An Interview with Joachim Peiper', 7 September 1945, Foreign Military Studies, ETHINT-10/ RG-338, NARA.

26. Author's interview with Hans Hennecke, 1981, op. cit.
27. See Case Number: 6-24 (*US* vs. *Valentin Bersin et al.*), pp. 1906–8, File Number: US011/NARA. Also cited in Danny S. *Parker, Fatal Crossroads* (Da Capo Press, 2012), p. 29; James J. Weingartner, *Crossroads of Death* (University of California Press, 1979), and the same author's *Americans, Germans, and War Crimes Justice: Law, Memory, and 'The Good War'* (Greenwood, 2011).
28. Reynolds, *The Devil's Adjutant*, op. cit., p. 72.

20. 'A 10 Per Cent Chance of Success'

1. Petrina memoir, *Bulge Bugle*, Vol. XIII/4 (November 1994), p. 27.
2. *An Interview with Gen. Pz. Hasso von Manteuffel: Fifth Panzer Army, Nov 44–Jan 45*, ETHINT-46, 29 and 31 October 1945; *Answers to Questionnaire of 9 April 1946*, both NARA.
3. Joseph S. Kennedy, 'Norristown Fielded Winning WWII General George Smythe & his 47th Infantry Fought in Two Major Battles in The European Theater', article in *Philadelphia Inquirer*, 5 November 1995; Lewis Sorley, *Westmoreland. The General Who Lost Vietnam* (Houghton Mifflin, 2011), p. 21; and US 9th Division history website, at: http://9thinfantrydivision.net/battle-history/ardennes-alsace/
4. Colonel William R. Carter USAF, 'Air Power in the Battle of the Bulge: A Theater Campaign Perspective', article in *Airpower Journal* (Winter 1989).
5. Stephen Darlow, *Victory Fighters: The Veterans' Story* (Grub Street, 2005), p. 219.
6. No. 403 Squadron RCAF (Royal Canadian Air Force): Operations Record Book, AIR 27/1781, The National Archives, Kew.
7. Darlow, *Victory Fighters*, op. cit., p. 221.
8. Sources inevitably provide different figures, but these are broadly correct.
9. Carter, 'Air Power in the Battle of the Bulge', op. cit.
10. Jet aircraft: 40; bombers: 55; ground-attack: 390; single-engine fighters: 1,770; twin-engine fighters: 140; Reconnaissance: 65; Total: 2,460. Frank Craven and James L. Cate (eds), *The Army Air Forces in World War II*, Vol. 3, *Europe: Argument to V-E Day, January 1944 to May 1945* (University of Chicago Press, 1948), p. 673.
11. Harold R. Winton, 'Air Power in the Battle of the Bulge: A Case for Effects-Based Operations?', article in *Journal of Military & Strategic Studies*, Vol. 14/1 (Fall 2011).
12. Darlow, *Victory Fighters*, op. cit., p. 215.
13. Major Donna C. Nicholas, USAF and Major Albert H. Whitley, USAFR, *The Role of Air Power in the Battle of the Bulge*, Research Report, Air Command and Staff College Air University, Maxwell Air Force Base, Alabama (April 1999); John F. Fuller, *Thor's Legions: Weather Support to the US Air Force and Army, 1937–1987* (American Meteorological Society, 1990).
14. Approximately 8,500 sorties were flown by the Ninth Air Force between 23 and 27 December 1944. The British Second Tactical Air Force, the Eighth Air Force and RAF Bomber Command accounted for the remainder of the 16,000 sorties.
15. MacDonald, *A Time for Trumpets*, op. cit., p. 522.

16. Darlow, *Victory Fighters*, op. cit., pp. 214–16.
17. 'Memoires of the Battle of the Bulge', article by W. C. Bill Armstrong, Service Battery, 263rd Field Artillery Battalion, in *The Bulge Bugle*, Vol. XXIII/1 (February 2004), p. 23.
18. Paul Fussell, *The Boys' Crusade* (Weidenfeld & Nicolson, 2003), p. 137; Michael Schadewitz, *The Meuse First and Then Antwerp: Some Aspects of Hitler's Offensive in the Ardennes* (J. J. Fedorowicz, 1999).
19. Schadewitz, *The Meuse First*, op. cit., p. 210.
20. Foley, *Commando Extraordinary*, op. cit., p. 144.
21. Kay Summersby [ghost-written Frank Kearns], *Eisenhower Was My Boss* (Prentice-Hall, 1948).
22. Alfred D. Chandler and Stephen E. Ambrose (eds), *The Papers of Dwight David Eisenhower, The War Years*: Vol. V (Johns Hopkins Press, 1970), pp. 175–180.
23. Pogue, *Pogue's War: Diaries of a WWII Combat Historian*, op. cit., pp. 301–302.
24. After the war, Eisenhower would present Niven with a Legion of Merit for setting up the BBC Allied Expeditionary Forces Programme, a radio news and entertainment station.
25. Memoir: George Lehr, Company 'F'/ 393rd Infantry, 'Odyssey: A personal view of World War II', courtesy of 99th Infantry Division Association website, at: http://99div.com/direct/odyssey_a_personal_view_of_world_war_ii+312lehr+4f6479737365793a204120706572736f6e616c2076696577206f6620576f726c6420576172204949
26. Pallud, *Battle of the Bulge: Then and Now*, op. cit., pp. 108–109.
27. George S. Patton Jr, *War As I Knew It* (Houghton Mifflin, 1947), p. 207.
28. Skorzeny was tried as a war criminal in 1947 for this *ruse de guerre*. He and nine officers of the Panzerbrigade 150 were charged with 'improperly using American uniforms by entering into combat disguised therewith and treacherously firing upon and killing members of the US forces'. Acquitting all defendants, the military tribunal drew a distinction between using enemy uniforms during combat and for other purposes including deception. A surprise defence witness was RAF Wing Commander Yeo-Thomas, a former SOE agent, who testified that he and his operatives also wore German uniforms behind the lines.

21. Stray Bullets Whined Through the Trees Around Us

1. Dettor memoir, *The Bulge Bugle*, Vol. XIII/4 (November 1994), pp. 19–20.
2. Parker survived the war, retired to Florida and died aged eighty-five in September 2006; Major-General Walter E. Lauer (intro.), *Battle Babies: The Story of the 99th Infantry Division* (Stars and Stripes, 1945); and courtesy of MIA Project website at: http://www.miaproject.net/battlefield-relics-memorabilia/battlefield-relics/bayonet-charge/
3. Ibid.
4. Hastings, *Armageddon*, op. cit., p. 232; 'Oberst Osterhold: Noble Foe, Good Friend Dies' (11 June 2002), 99th Infantry Division Association website at: http://99div.com/olddirect/oberst_osterhold_noble_foe_good_friend_dies+03osterhold+4f6

265727374204f73746572686f6c643a204e6f626c6520666f652c20676f6f64206672696 56e642064696573

5. Walter memoir, courtesy of Historynet.com website, at: http://www.historynet.com/robert-walter-recalls-his-baptism-of-fire-during-the-battle-of-the-bulge.htm
6. Ingraham memoir, op. cit.
7. Walter memoir, op. cit.
8. Dettor memoir, op. cit.
9. Roger V. Foehringer (1924–2006) memoir courtesy of http://www.faehrtensucher.com/ardennen-1944-1945/persönliche-geschichten/roger-foehringer/; obituary at: http://articles.chicagotribune.com/2006-12-17/news/0612170145_1_roger-prospect-heights-late
10. Ibid.
11. Wallace memoir, courtesy of CRIBA(*Centre de Recherches et d'Informations sur la Bataille des Ardennes*) website, op. cit.
12. Lauer, *Battle Babies: The Story of the 99th Infantry Division*, op. cit.
13. Cole, *The Ardennes*, op. cit., pp. 658–9. The figure of 1,250,000 American rounds fired during the Battle of the Bulge sounds suspiciously low. Allied artillery was capable of firing this quantity over a week in 1916 and during a twenty-four-hour period by 1918.
14. Cole, *The Ardennes*, op. cit., Chapter VI: 'The German Northern Shoulder Is Jammed'.
15. William C. C. Cavanagh, *The Battle East of Elsenborn: The First US Army at the Battle of the Bulge, December 1944* (Pen and Sword, 2004) pp. 87–8; Hubert Meyer, *The 12th SS: The History of the Hitler Youth Panzer Division*, Vol. 2 (Stackpole, 2005), p. 252.
16. Meyer, *The 12th SS: History of the Hitler Youth Panzer Division*, Vol. 2, op. cit., pp. 253–4.
17. Ibid., p. 254.
18. Douglas Martin, 'Vernon McGarity, Dies at 91, War Hero; Fought in the Battle of the Bulge', article in *New York Times*, 23 May 2013.
19. Ibid., p. 255.
20. Cited in Brigadier Sir James Edmonds, *Official History of the [First World] War, Operations in Italy 1915–1919* (HMSO, 1949), p. 218.
21. MacDonald, *Company Commander*, op. cit., p. 97.
22. Ibid., p. 101.
23. Ibid.
24. Memoir, *The Bulge Bugle*, Vol. XII/1 (February 1993), p. 17.
25. MacDonald, *Company Commander*, op. cit., p. 102.
26. Kiss memoir, *The Bulge Bugle*, Vol. XII/1 (February 1993), p. 17.
27. Ibid., p. 18.
28. MacDonald, *Company Commander*, op. cit., p. 104.
29. Cavanagh, *The Battle East of Elsenborn*, op. cit., p. 95.
30. MacDonald, *Company Commander*, op. cit., p. 105.
31. Yeide, *Steel Victory*, op. cit., pp. 195–7.

32. Kiss memoir, op. cit.
33. Cole, *The Ardennes*, op. cit., Chapter VI: 'The German Northern Shoulder Is Jammed'.
34. MacDonald, *Company Commander*, op. cit., p. 111.
35. Adam Bernstein, 'Medal of Honor Winner Jose M. Lopez Dies at 94', article in *Washington Post*, 18 May 2005.
36. MacDonald, *Company Commander*, op. cit., p. 113.

22. The Conference

1. *Not* Zondhoven (there is no such place), as is often inaccurately reported; Bigland, *Bigland's War*, op. cit., p. 80.
2. D. K. R. Crosswell, *Beetle. The Life of General Walter Bedell Smith* (University Press of Kentucky, 2010), p. 807.
3. Captain Harry C. Butcher, *My Three Years With Eisenhower* (William Heinemann, 1946), p. 611.
4. The Pavillon Henri IV, built on the ruins of the Château Neuf of King Henri IV, was a historic place, where Louis XIV was born and had spent his youth and where his father, Louis XIII, had died.
5. And one of Napoleon's mistresses.
6. G. E. Patrick Murray, 'Eisenhower as Ground-Forces Commander: The British Viewpoint', article in *Transactions of the American Philosophical Society*, Vol. 97/4.
7. Crosswell, *Beetle. The Life of General Walter Bedell Smith*, op. cit., p. 808.
8. D'Este, *Eisenhower: A Soldier's Life*, op. cit.
9. Patton, *War As I Knew It*, op. cit., p. 178.
10. Eisenhower, *The Bitter Woods*, op. cit., p. 240.
11. Annan, *Changing Enemies*, op. cit., pp. 115–16.
12. Eisenhower, *The Bitter Woods*, op. cit., pp. 188–9.
13. Bradley and Blair, *A General's Life*, op. cit., p. 395.
14. Cole C. Kingseed, *Old Glory Stories: American Combat Leadership in World War II* (Naval Institute Press, 2006), p. 89; Morelock, *Generals of the Ardennes*, op. cit., p. 154.
15. Thomas R. Stone, 'General William Hood Simpson: Unsung Commander of the US Ninth Army', article in *Parameters* Vol. XII/2 (February 1980).
16. Ibid.
17. On 22 September 1950, Bradley was promoted to General of the Army, to date the last US commander to achieve that rank.
18. Stephen E. Ambrose, *Eisenhower: Soldier and President* (Simon & Schuster, 1991), p. 172.
19. Annan, *Changing Enemies*, op. cit., pp. 116–17.
20. Crosswell, *Beetle*, op. cit., p. 740.
21. Timothy M. Gay, *Assignment to Hell. The War Against Nazi Germany with Correspondents Walter Cronkite, Andy Rooney, A.J. Liebling, Homer Bigart and Hal Boyle* (NAL Caibre, 2012), pp. 421–2; Walter Cronkite, *A Reporter's Life* (Knopf, 1996), p. 121.
22. Cronkite, ibid.

23. T. Michael Booth and Duncan Spencer, *Paratrooper. The Life of Gen. James M. Gavin* (Simon & Schuster 1994).
24. Major-General Anthony McAuliffe assumed command of the 103rd Infantry Division on 15 January 1945.
25. Eduardo Peniche (retired Professor of Spanish at Lone Star College, Kingwood, Texas) memoir courtesy of Lone Star College System website, at: http://www.lonestar.edu/library/kin_Peniche.htm
26. Ibid.
27. Ibid.
28. Colley, *The Road to Victory*, op. cit., pp. 190–92.
29. Ibid., pp. 190–91.
30. McAuliffe memoir, *The Bulge Bugle*, Vol. XII/1 (February 1993), p. 19.
31. Author's interview with T/Sergeant Gilbert T. Gouveia, Company 'G', 333rd Infantry Regiment, Hotel Zur Post, St Vith, 17 December 1994.
32. Walter Isaacson, *Kissinger: A Biography* (Simon & Schuster, 1992), pp. 47–8.

23. The Tortoise Has Thrust His Head Out Very Far

1. Patton, *War As I Knew It*, op. cit., p. 190.
2. Ibid., pp. 190–191; Chandler and Ambrose (eds), *The Papers of Dwight David Eisenhower*, Vol. V, op. cit., pp. 175–6.
3. Crosswell, *Beetle*, op. cit., pp. 810–14.
4. Major William C. Sylvan and Captain Francis G. Smith Jr (eds), *Normandy to Victory: The War Diary of General Courtney H. Hodges and the First US Army* (University Press of Kentucky, 2008),
5. Morelock, *Generals of the Ardennes*, op. cit., p. 180.
6. John A. Adams, *The Battle for Western Europe, Fall 1944: An Operational Assessment* (Indiana University Press, 2010), p. 159.
7. Bigland, *Bigland's War*, op. cit., p. 81.
8. Eisenhower, *The Bitter Woods*, op. cit., p. 245.
9. Field Marshal Lord Alanbrooke (eds Danchev and Todman), *War Diaries 1939–1945* (Weidenfeld & Nicolson, 2001), p. 636.
10. Ibid.
11. Front page, *Courier-Mail*, Brisbane, Tuesday, 19 December 1944.
12. *Daily Telegraph*, Tuesday, 19 December 1944.
13. Harold Nicolson, *Diaries and Letters 1939–45* (Collins, 1967), p. 423.
14. *The Times*, Tuesday, 19 December 1944.
15. Winston S. Churchill, *The Second World War*, Vol. VI, *Triumph and Tragedy* (Cassell, 1954), p. 240. Alanbrooke, *War Diaries*, op. cit., p. 636.
16. Churchill, *The Second World War*, Vol. VI, op. cit., p. 241; Butcher, *My Three Years with Eisenhower*, op. cit., p. 621.
17. Nicolson, *Diaries and Letters*, p. 424.
18. Churchill, *The Second World War*, Vol. VI, op. cit., p. 240.
19. H. G. Nicholas (ed.) *Washington Weekly Despatches 1941–1945. Weekly Political Reports from the British Embassy* (Weidenfeld & Nicolson, 1981), pp. 486–7.

20. Patton, *War As I Knew It*, op. cit., p. 190.
21. Churchill, *The Second World War*, Vol. I: *The Gathering Storm* (Cassell, 1948).
22. Patton, *War As I Knew It*, op. cit., p. 191.
23. Butcher, *My Three Years with Eisenhower*, op. cit., pp. 618–19.
24. Alanbrooke, *War Diaries*, op. cit., p. 637.
25. Russell F. Weighley, *Eisenhower's Lieutenants* (Indiana University Press, 1981), p. 615.

24. A Pint of Sweat and a Gallon of Blood

1. Babcock, *War Stories: Utah Beach to Plieku*, op. cit., pp. 341–7.
2. 70th Tank Battalion AAR – Yeide, *Steel Victory*, op. cit., p. 202.
3. Ibid., pp. 202–203.
4. Gaul, *Battle of the Bulge in Luxembourg*, Vol. II: *The Americans*, op. cit., p. 140.
5. Interview with Generalmajor Franz Sensfuss, 10 April 1946, MS A-930, NARA, pp. 4 and 6.
6. Marvin Jensen, *Strike Swiftly. The 70th Tank Battalion from North Africa to Normandy to Germany* (Presidio, 1997), pp. 266–7.
7. General J. Lawton Collins, *Lightning Joe: An Autobiography* (Louisiana State University Press, 1979), p. 294.
8. Frankel and Smith, *Patton's Best*, op. cit., pp. 133–4.
9. Author's interview Horace R. Bennett, 17 December 1994, St Vith, Belgium.
10. Gaul, *Battle of the Bulge in Luxembourg*, Vol. II, op. cit., p. 81.
11. Eugene Patterson, *Patton's Unsung Armour of the Ardennes. The Tenth Armored Division's Secret Dash to Bastogne* (Xlibris, 2008), pp. 24–5.
12. Correspondence in 1994 with Lieutenant-Colonel Haynes W. Dugan (1913–2007) of Shreveport, Louisiana, Assistant G-2 and Publicity Officer at US 3rd Armored Division 1941–5. See also website at: http://3ad.com/history/wwll/dugan.pages/articles.pages/patton.htm
13. Jensen, *Strike Swiftly*, op. cit., pp. 270–71.
14. Cooper, *Death Traps*, op. cit., p. 166.
15. Patterson, *Patton's Unsung Armour*, op. cit., p. 35.
16. Ibid., p. 28.
17. Ibid., p. 39.
18. Ibid., p. 53.
19. Correspondence with Mr Belton Y. Cooper (1917–2007) of Birmingham, Alabama, in October–December 1994 and his book, *Death Traps*, op. cit., p. 165.
20. Ibid., p. 166.
21. Correspondence with Mr Belton Y. Cooper, op. cit.
22. Ray Moore, *Terrify and Destroy. The Story of the 10th Armored Division* (printed in Paris, 1945), p. 3.
23. Patterson, *Patton's Unsung Armour*, op. cit., pp. 55–6.
24. *The Bulge Bugle*, Vol. XIV/2 (May 1995), p. 18.
25. After Action Report, 61st Armored Infantry Battalion, 10th Armored Divison,

Nov 44 thru May 45 (US Army Combined Arms Research Library (CARL), Fort Leavenworth, Kansas).

26. Gaul, *Battle of the Bulge in Luxembourg,* Vol. II, op. cit., pp. 123–4; Roger Shinn, *Wars and Rumours of Wars* (Abingdon Press, 1972), p. 30.
27. Gaul, *Battle of the Bulge in Luxembourg,* Vol. II, op. cit., p. 133.
28. Ibid., pp. 125–6.
29. Shinn, *Wars and Rumours of Wars,* op. cit., pp. 43–4.
30. Ibid., p. 44.
31. Interview with Generalmajor Franz Sensfuss, op. cit., p. 6.
32. Christian Hartmann, *Halder: Generalstabschef Hitlers, 1938–1942* (Schöningh, 2010), p. 331. Cited in Neitzel and Welzer, *Soldaten,* op. cit., p. 280.
33. Interview with Generalmajor Franz Sensfuss, op. cit., p. 5.

25. A Man Can Make a Difference

1. Egger and Otts, *G Company's War,* op. cit., p. 99.
2. Gaul, *Battle of the Bulge in Luxembourg,* Vol. II, op. cit., p. 136.
3. Graham Smith, *The Mighty Eighth in the Second World War* (Countryside Books, 2001), pp. 237–40.
4. Jensen, *Strike Swiftly,* op. cit., pp. 273–4.
5. Gaul, *Battle of the Bulge in Luxembourg,* Vol. II, op. cit., p. 137.
6. Egger and Otts, *G Company's War* op. cit., pp. 102–3.
7. Jensen, *Strike Swiftly,* op. cit., p. 268.
8. Egger and Otts, *G Company's War,* op. cit., pp. 108–9.
9. I have found the same. Inevitably I found my own letters home from Sarajevo or Iraq could never reflect the reality of military operations, and I practised self-censorship.
10. Jensen, *Strike Swiftly,* op. cit., p. 284.
11. The US 75th Infantry Division also reported cases of dysentery, jaundice and pneumonia.
12. Egger and Otts, *G Company's War,* op. cit., p. 110.
13. Interview with Generalmajor Franz Sensfuss, op. cit., p. 6.
14. Thomas M. Hatfield, *Rudder: From Leader to Legend* (Texas A & M University Press, 2011), p. 225.
15. Gaul, *Battle of the Bulge in Luxembourg,* Vol. II, op. cit., pp. 107–8.
16. Ibid., Chapter 12.
17. Michael Weaver, *Guard Wars: The 28th Infantry Division in World War II* (Indiana University Press, 2010), pp. 235–6.
18. Captain Harry M. Kemp, *The Operations of the 3rd Battalion, 109th Infantry (28th Infantry Division) in the vicinity of Diekirch, Luxembourg, 16 December–23 December 1944* (Personal Experience of a Battalion Executive Officer, Advanced Infantry Officers Course, The Infantry School, Fort Benning, Georgia, 1949–50).
19. Dupuy, Bongard, and Anderson, *Hitler's Last Gamble, op. cit.,* Chapter 7.
20. Major Embert A. Fossum, *The Operations of Task Force 'L', 109th Infantry (28th Infantry Division) near Grosbous, Luxembourg, 20–23 December 1944* (Personal

Experience of a Task Force Commander, Advanced Infantry Officers Course, Fort Benning, Georgia, 1948–9); Hatfield, *Rudder: From Leader to Legend*, op. cit., p. 233.

21. Ibid., pp. 236–7.
22. Fossum (1917–77) went on to fight in Korea, retired as a colonel, and become Professor of Military Science at the University of Oregon.
23. Weaver, *Guard Wars*, op. cit., p. 240.

26. No More Zig-Zig in Paris

1. *The Traveller's Guide Through Belgium, Or [A] New and Complete Geographical, Historical, and Picturesque Account of That Country With Information on Its Curiosities, Antiquities and Customs, Best Hotels, Etc. Etc., A Detailed Description of All Objects Worthy of Notice, And Principal Roads To Holland* (Wahlen, 1833), pp. 213–14.
2. Don Addor, *Noville Outpost to Bastogne: My Last Battle* (Trafford, 2004), pp. 5–7.
3. Michael Collins and Martin King, *The Tigers of Bastogne: Voices of the 10th Armored Division in the Battle of the Bulge* (Casemate, 2013), p. 65.
4. Schrijvers, *The Unknown Dead*, op. cit., pp. 189–91; 335 and 367.
5. Tolhurst, *Battleground Europe: Bastogne*, op. cit., p. 70.
6. Ibid., p. 64.
7. Collins and King, *The Tigers of Bastogne*, op. cit., p. 64.
8. Addor, *Noville Outpost to Bastogne*, op. cit., pp. 10–11.
9. Ibid., p. 18.
10. F. Phillips, *To Save Bastogne* (Stein and Day, 1983), p. 160.
11. Tolhurst, *Battleground Europe: Bastogne*, op. cit., p. 44.
12. Alice M. Flynn, *Unforgettable: The Biography of Captain Thomas J. Flynn* (Blue Sky Publishing, 2011), pp. 90–108.
13. Tolhurst, *Battleground Europe: Bastogne*, op. cit., p. 46.
14. Collins and King, *The Tigers of Bastogne*, op. cit., p. 67.
15. Ibid., p. 83.
16. Ibid., p. 67.
17. Courtesy of Skylighters (website of the 225th AAA Searchlight Battalion from Omaha Beach to V-E Day), at http://www.skylighters.org/xmas2002/index3.html
18. Donald R. Burgett, *Seven Roads to Hell: A Screaming Eagle at Bastogne* (Presidio Press, 1999).
19. Ibid., p. 47.
20. Stephen E. Ambrose, *Band of Brothers: From Normandy to Hitler's Eagle's Nest* (Simon & Schuster, 1992), p. 179.
21. Ibid., p. 180.
22. Burgett, *Seven Roads to Hell*, op. cit., pp. 44–6.
23. An Interview with Gen. Pz. Hasso von Manteuffel: Fifth Panzer Army, Nov 44–Jan 45, ETHINT-46, 29 and 31 October 1945; *Answers to Questionnaire of 9 April 1946*, both NARA.

24. '28th Signal Company in the Bulge', Robert W. Eichner memoir, courtesy of *Battle of the Bulge Memories* website, at http://webcache.googleusercontent.com/search?q=cache:5F1NKKLGgCQJ:www.battleofthebulgememories.be/stories26/32-battle-of-the-bulge-us-army/737–28th-signal-company-in-the-bulge.html+&cd=40&hl=en&ct=clnk&gl=uk
25. Kurowski, *Elite Panzer Strike Force*, op. cit., pp. 173–4.
26. Eichner memoir, op. cit.
27. Ibid.
28. Max L. Noe memoir, courtesy of The Military Order of the Purple Heart, Texas Capital Chapter 1919, Austin, Texas. Webpage at: http://webcache.googleusercontent.com/search?q=cache:wnCetuyBwE0J:www.purpleheartaustin.org/noe.htm+&cd=34&hl=en&ct=clnk&gl=uk
29. Christer Bergström, *The Ardennes 1944–1945: Hitler's Winter Offensive* (Bergstrom, 2014).
30. Patterson, *Patton's Unsung Armour of the Ardennes*, op. cit., pp. 58–9.
31. John A. Foley (1915–2001) memoir, courtesy of his son Jack and the bloody-bucket.be website, at: http://webcache.googleusercontent.com/search?q=cache:gWrdm6GXIZAJ:www.bloodybucket.be/johnafoleybis.htm+&cd=32&hl=en&ct=clnk&gl=uk
32. Kurowski, *Elite Panzer Strike Force*, op. cit., pp. 176–7.
33. A US Army Field Hospital was a small, mobile unit of just over 200 personnel, which included 13 physicians, 3 dental officers, 5 medical administrative officers, 18 nurses, 183 enlisted men, a chaplain and two Red Cross workers. Specialised surgeons, nurses and technicians were assigned as necessary. The outfit was subdivided into a headquarters and three smaller units, known as platoons or detachments, each equipped to serve as an independent mini-hospital. Most patients were those who were too severely wounded to withstand an ambulance ride further back. Much time was spent in moving, usually at night under blackout conditions, and field hospitals were based where possible in large stone buildings, such as schools or factories.
34. The Château de Wiltz is today a wonderful luxury hotel, where a stay is highly recommended. Wiltz was also headquarters of the 103rd Medical Battalion, which supported Cota's 28th Infantry Division.
35. Dr John W. Fague, 'A Combat Nurse in the Bulge', article in the *News Chronicle* of Shippensburg, Pennsylvania, 12 July 2002; article in *The Bulge Bugle*, Vol. XXIII/1 (February 2004), p. 10.

27. The Hole In The Doughnut

1. Colonel S. L. A. Marshall, *Men Against Fire: The Problem of Battle Command in Future War* (original edition 1947; new edition, University of Oklahoma Press, 2000), p. 9.
2. Majors D. N. Charles, T. J. Camp, I. R. Fielder, W. H. Moore and G. W. C. Waddell, *The Effects of Isolation on Small, Dispersed Groups of Men on the Battlefield* (Group Research Project, 24 Army Command & Staff Course, 1990).

3. Phillips, *To Save Bastogne*, op. cit., p. 148.
4. John Davis with Anne Riffenburgh, *Up Close: A Scout's Story From the Battle of the Bulge to the Siegfried Line* (Merriam Press, 2008), p. 86.
5. Egger and Otts, *G Company's War*, op. cit., p. 101.
6. Davis, *Frozen Rainbows*, op. cit., p. 213.
7. Neill, *Infantry Soldier. Holding the Line at the Battle of the Bulge*, op. cit., pp. 251–2.
8. General Matthew B. Ridgway and Harold H. Martin, *Soldier: The Memoirs of Matthew B. Ridgway as told to Harold H. Martin* (Harper, 1956); and see Ralph Storm, 'Medics in the Bulge', article in *The Bulge Bugle*, Vol. XXIII/1 (February 2004), p. 9.
9. Robert M. Bowen served in the 1st Battalion of the 401st Glider Infantry Regiment, which acted as a divisional reserve battalion from D-Day onwards. Courtesy of Skylighters website, op. cit., at http://www.skylighters.org/xmas2002/index7.html
10. Burgett, *Seven Roads to Hell*, op. cit., pp. 64–5.
11. Major General R. W. Grow (Intro.), *Brest to Bastogne: The Story of the 6th Armored Division* (Stars & Stripes, Information and Education Division, Special and Information Services, ETOUSA, Paris, *c.* 1945), p. 1.
12. Charles McMoran Wilson (Lord Moran), *The Anatomy of Courage* (Constable, 1945).
13. Neill, *Infantry Soldier*, op. cit., p. 237.
14. Courtesy of Syiek family archives at http://www.syiek.com/bastogne/
15. Including Hugh Cole, Charles B. MacDonald and John S. D. Eisenhower.
16. Courtesy of http://www.lonestar.edu/library/kin_Peniche.htm
17. Collins and King, *The Tigers of Bastogne*, op. cit., pp. 89–90; personal interviews in Wardin, December 1989.
18. Addor, *Noville Outpost to Bastogne*, op. cit., p. 19.
19. Ambrose, *Band of Brothers*, op. cit., p. 180; Burgett, *Seven Roads to Hell*, op. cit., p. 60.
20. Addor, *Noville Outpost to Bastogne*, op. cit., p. 24.
21. Ibid., p. 49.
22. Guy Franz Arend, *Bastogne: A Chronology of the Battle for Bastogne with Comments* (Bastogne Historical Center, 1987), pp. 125–33.
23. Schrijvers, *The Unknown Dead*, op. cit., pp. 101–103.
24. Courtesy of Colonel Emile Engels; the Bastogne Historical Center; and website at: http://www.blackfive.net/main/2013/12/band-of-brothers-nurse-augusta-chiwy-someone-you-should-know.html
25. Arend, *Bastogne*, op. cit., p. 139.

28. Nuts!

1. Torsten Ove, 'The Next Page: Soldiers' Honor Restored: The Wereth 11 of WWII', article in *Pittsburgh Post-Gazette*, 7 November 2010; Rodney Cress, 'Remembering the Wereth 11 and Black GIs', article in *Salisbury Post* (North Carolina), 10 November 2013; Jim Michaels, 'Emerging from History: Massacre of 11 Black

Soldiers', article in *USA Today*, 8 November 2013. In 2010, Robert Child directed a documentary, *The Wereth Eleven*, narrating the story of the eleven African American soldiers murdered by SS during the Battle of the Bulge.

2. An Interview with Gen. Pz. Hasso von Manteuffel: Fifth Panzer Army, Nov 44–Jan 45, ETHINT-46, 29 and 31 October 1945, NARA.
3. Arend, *Bastogne*, op. cit., pp. 152–5.
4. Ibid., pp. 159–60.
5. McAuliffe's whole life became defined by the 'Nuts!' comment. His performance in the Bulge earned him a Distinguished Service Cross and command of the 103rd Infantry Division. He was a later commander in Europe and Korea and retired from the US Army as a full general in 1956, dying in 1975. Kinnard commanded the 1st Cavalry Division (Airmobile) in Vietnam and died in 2009. See his obituary in the *New York Times*, 10 January 2009. My interview with General Kinnard was in May 1984, just before the fortieth anniversary of D-Day. See transcript of interview with Lieutenant-General (retired) H. W. O. Kinnard on PBS documentary *The American Experience: 'Vets Remember: A colonel in the 101st airborne, H.W.O. Kinnard, discusses surrender'*, at website: http://www.pbs.org/wgbh/americanexperience/features/bonus-video/bulge-vets-kinnard/
6. Interview by author, St Vith, December 1994.
7. 420th Armored Field Artillery AAR, 26 December 1944, NARA.
8. Colonel Ralph M. Mitchell, *The 101st Airborne Division's Defense of Bastogne* (Combat Studies Institute, 1986).
9. Ibid.
10. Standing for 'Situation Normal, All F****d Up.'
11. Cole, *The Ardennes*, op. cit., p. 479.
12. Pallud, *Battle of the Bulge: Then and Now*, op. cit., p. 345; Arend, *Bastogne*, op. cit., p. 215.
13. Frankel and Smith, *Patton's Best*, op. cit., p. 41.
14. Professor A. Harding Ganz, 'Breakthrough to Bastogne', article in *Leadership Handbook for the Armor Officer: Thoughts on Leadership* (US Armor School, Fort Knox, Kentucky, 1986), pp. 2–44 to 2–58; Cavanagh, *A Tour of the Bulge Battlefield*, op. cit., pp. 151–5.
15. Courtesy of Kenneth Koyen, 'Combat Photographer Robert Capa and the Battle of the Bulge', article in *History of Photography*, Vol. 25/4 (Winter 2001). Capa was killed on 25 May 1954 covering the war in Indochina.
16. Collins and King, *The Tigers of Bastogne*, op. cit., p. 212.
17. Mitchell, *The 101st Airborne Division's Defense of Bastogne*, op. cit.; Arend, *Bastogne*, op. cit., p. 244.
18. Speer, *Inside the Third Reich*, op. cit., pp. 416–17.
19. Ralph Ingersoll, *Top Secret* (Harcourt, Brace, 1946).
20. Cavanagh, *A Tour of the Bulge Battlefield*, op. cit., pp. 147–8; Schrijvers, *The Unknown Dead*, op. cit., pp. 372–3.

29. Head For the Meuse!

1. Guderian, *From Normandy to the Ruhr*, op. cit., pp. 302–10.
2. Ibid., p. 310.
3. Ibid.
4. Ibid., p. 317.
5. Ibid., pp. 317–18; 321.
6. Ibid., p. 320.
7. Ibid., pp. 321 and 317.
8. Harold P. Limbaugh and John D. Campbell, *The Men of Company K* (William Morrow and Co., 1985), p. 130.
9. Nigel de Lee, *Voices From the Battle of the Bulge* (David & Charles, 2004), p. 202.
10. Guderian, *From Normandy to the Ruhr*, op. cit. p. 323.
11. Behrens survived being taken prisoner in late February 1945. Interview courtesy of Imperial War Museum Sound Archive, Catalogue #14228, interviewed 10 June 1994.
12. Limbaugh and Campbell, *The Men of Company K*, op. cit., pp. 131–2.
13. Guderian, *From Normandy to the Ruhr*, op. cit., p. 325.
14. Limbaugh and Campbell, *The Men of Company K*, op. cit., pp. 133–4.
15. Denise Goolsby, 'Bomber Kept Busy in Battle of the Bulge', article in the *Desert Sun*, California, 17 December 2010, courtesy of website at: http://archive.desertsun.com/article/20101218/NEWS13/12180304/Bomber-kept-busy-Battle-Bulge
16. Guderian, *From Normandy to the Ruhr*, op. cit., p. 330.
17. Goolsby, 'Bomber Kept Busy in Battle of the Bulge', op. cit.
18. Kurowski, *Elite Panzer Strike Force*, op. cit., pp. 183–5.
19. Ibid., p. 186.
20. Ibid., p. 187.
21. Lieutenant Leonard R. Carpenter, *On the Counter-Reconnaissance Screen, 23–24 December 1944: The Defense of Marche's area* (Statement to T/5 Jack Shank, Historical Section 84th Infantry Division) NARA.
22. Author's interview with Oberst (retd) Gerhardt Tebbe, Münster, Germany, May 1984.
23. Limbaugh and Campbell, *The Men of Company K*, op. cit., pp. 135–41. Also see *Railsplitters*, a small booklet, introduced by Major-General Bolling, covering the history of the 84th Infantry Division, published (*Stars & Stripes*, Paris, 1945).
24. Author's interview with Oberst (retd) Gerhardt Tebbe, op. cit.
25. Limbaugh and Campbell, *The Men of Company K*, op. cit., p. 143.
26. Ibid., pp. 148–9.
27. Cavanagh, *A Tour of the Bulge Battlefield*, op. cit., pp. 191–4.
28. An Interview with Gen. Pz. Hasso von Manteuffel: Fifth Panzer Army, Nov 44–Jan 45, ETHINT-46, 29 and 31 October 1945, NARA.
29. Noël Bell, *From the Beaches to the Baltic: The Story of the G Company, 8th Battalion, the Rifle Brigade During the Campaign in North-west Europe* (Gale & Polden, 1947).
30. Pallud, *Battle of the Bulge: Then and Now*, op. cit., p. 352.

31. MSS # A-939 (General der Panzertruppen Heinrich von Lüttwitz), *The Assignment of the XLVII Panzer Corps in the Ardennes 1944–1945* and B-456 (Oberstleutnant Rüdiger Weiz), *2nd Panzer Division, 21–26 December 1944*, both at NARA.
32. Bell, *From the Beaches to the Baltic*, op. cit.
33. General James Gavin, *On to Berlin* (Viking, 1978), p. 249.
34. Author's interview with Misch in 1993 at his home in Rudow, south Berlin.
35. Bell, *From the Beaches to the Baltic*, op. cit.
36. Schrijvers, *The Unknown Dead*, op. cit., p. 254.
37. Kurowski, *Elite Panzer Strike Force*, op. cit., p. 188.
38. Guderian, *From Normandy to the Ruhr*, op. cit., pp. 337–8.
39. Ibid., pp. 337–9.

30. The River of Humiliation

1. Author interview with Pete House, St Vith, 17 December, 1994. Also: 'My experiences during the Battle of the Bulge', memoir courtesy of website at: http://www.indianamilitary.org/German%20PW%20Camps/Prisoner%20of%20War/PW%20Camps/Stalag%20IX-B%20Bad%20Orb/Pete%20House/Experiences/Experiences.htm
2. Kline memoir, courtesy of website at: http://home.planet.nl/~wijer037/bulge/forms/the%20106th%20infantry/John%20Kline.htm
3. Author interview with John A. Swett, St Vith, 17 December 1994. Also: memoir, courtesy of Veterans of the Battle of the Bulge website, at http://www.veteransofthebattleofthebulge.org/2012/04/17/john-a-swett-106th-infantry-division-army-history/
4. Hal Richard Taylor, *A Teen's War . . . Training, Combat, Capture* (1st Books Library, 1999), p. 112. Taylor (1925–2010) retired as Director of Public Affairs from the US Department of Agriculture in 1980 after a career that included work at four universities and for a special project in communication. Then he became an international consultant and secretary-treasurer of the Agricultural Communicators in Education (ACE).
5. Humphrey, *Once Upon a Time in War*, op. cit., p. 122.
6. Swett interview and memoir, op. cit.
7. Kline memoir, op. cit.
8. Pete House interview and memoir, op. cit.
9. Captured German letter home, dated 24 December 1944, quoted in *Twenty-First Army Group Psychological Warfare Summary*, January 1945. Cited in Shulman, *Defeat in the West*, op. cit., p. 313.
10. Taylor, *A Teen's War*, op. cit., p. 115.
11. Ibid., pp. 117–18.
12. Marilyn Estes Quigley, *Hell Frozen Over: The Battle of the Bulge* (AuthorHouse, 2004), p. 90.
13. Ibid., pp. 87–8.
14. Kline memoir, op. cit.
15. Ibid., p. 121.

16. Pete House interview and memoir, op. cit.
17. Taylor, *A Teen's War*, op. cit., p. 123.
18. Nelson memoir, courtesy of website at: http://www.battleofthebulgememories.be/en/stories/us-army/698-interview-with-willard-nelson-422nd-inf-regt.html
19. Colonel Charles C. 'Moe' Cavender, 'The 423rd in The Bulge', article in *The Cub* (newsletter of the 106th Division), Vol. 3, No. 4 (November 1946). See also http://www.106thinfdivassn.org/the423.html
20. Kline memoir, op. cit.
21. Pete House interview and memoir, op. cit.
22. Taylor, *A Teen's War*, op. cit., p. 124
23. Ibid.
24. Charles J. Shields, *And So It Goes: Kurt Vonnegut: A Life* (Henry Holt, 2011), pp. 57–9; Ervin E. Szpek and Frank J. Idzikowski, *Shadows of Slaughterhouse Five. Recollections and Reflections of the American Ex-POWs of Schlachthof Fünf* (iUniverse, 2008), Chapter 4, pp. 78–138.
25. Dupuy, *St. Vith: Lion in the Way*, op. cit., pp. 148–9.
26. Captured letter home, dated 24 December 1944, quoted in *Twenty-First Army Group Psychological Warfare Summary*, January 1945. Cited in Shulman, *Defeat in the West*, op. cit., p. 314.
27. Bruce Watson, *When Soldiers Quit: Studies in Military Disintegration* (Praeger, 1997), Chapter 6: Surrender: Disintegration of a Division, December 1944, pp. 90–110.
28. Wojtusik memoir: Joseph Andrew Lee, 'POW Recalls Battle of the Bulge', article in *On Patrol* (Magazine of the USO – United Service Organizations), 7 January 2011.
29. Nelson memoir, op. cit.
30. Quigley, *Hell Frozen Over*, op. cit., pp. 101–102.
31. Setter memoir, courtesy of *The Bulge Bugle*, Vol. X/4 (November 1991), p. 10.
32. Edward L. Bohde memoir 'The Way It Was', courtesy of Pegasus Archive website at: http://www.pegasusarchive.org/pow/edward_bohde.htm
33. Quigley, *Hell Frozen Over*, op. cit., p. 102.
34. Wojtusik memoir, op. cit.
35. Swett interview and memoir, op. cit.
36. Eisenhower, *The Bitter Woods*, op. cit., pp. 291–4; Pallud, *Battle of the Bulge: Then and Now*, op. cit., pp. 197–200; Cavanagh, *A Tour of the Bulge Battlefield*, op. cit., pp. 119–22; Whiting, *The Last Assault*, op. cit., pp. 133–9; Colonel Thomas P. Kelly, Jr, *The Fightin' 589th* (1st Book Library, 2001); Dupuy, *St. Vith: Lion in the Way*, op. cit., pp. 133–7; Joseph Martin Giarrusso, *Against All Odds. The Story of the 106th Infantry Division in the Battle of the Bulge* (Master of Arts Thesis, San Jose State University, December 1998); Major P. J. St Laurent, Major C. L. Crow, Major J. S. Everette, Major G. Fontenot and Major R. V. Hester, *The Battle of St Vith, Defense and Withdrawal by Encircled Forces. German 5th & 6th Panzer Armies versus US 7th Armored Division and Attachments, 17–23 December 1944* (Report, US Army Command and General Staff College, Fort Leavenworth, Kansas, 1984); Quigley, *Hell Frozen Over*, op. cit., Chapter 5, pp. 87–105; Frank L. Andrews, *The*

Defense of St Vith in the Battle of the Ardennes December, 1944 (Master of Arts Dissertation New York University, February 1964). Andrews fought and was captured at St Vith as a member of the 168th Engineer Combat Battalion.

37. Taylor, *A Teen's War*, op. cit., p. 127.
38. Captured German diary quoted in *First Canadian Army Intelligence Summary*, 30 January 1945. Cited in Shulman, *Defeat in the West*, op. cit., p. 316; William Donohue Ellis and Thomas J. Cunningham, Jr, *Clarke of St. Vith. The Sergeants' General* (Dillon/Liederbach, 1974), p. 113.
39. Quigley, *Hell Frozen Over*, op. cit., p. 105.
40. Green and Brown, *War Stories of the Battle of the Bulge*, op. cit., pp. 87–8.
41. Taylor, *A Teen's War*, op. cit., p. 127.
42. Pete House interview and memoir, op. cit.
43. Bruns was sentenced to death on 20 April 1945. Headquarters, First US Army, Case Notes of *United States* v. *Hauptmann Kurt Bruns*, Office of the Staff Judge Advocate, 20 April 1945, declassified 1 March 1948, NARA.
44. Kline memoir, op. cit.
45. Earl S. Parker, *Memoirs of a Tour of Duty: WWII in Europe* (1stBooks, 2001), p. 33.
46. Captured letter home dated 22 December 1944, quoted in *US 101st Airborne Division G-2 Report*, January 1945, cited in Shulman, *Defeat in the West*, op. cit., pp. 313–14.
47. PFC Lehman Malone Wilson of the 82nd Airborne lies in the Springfield National Cemetery, Missouri, with a date of death recorded as 29 January 1945.
48. Dupuy, *St. Vith. Lion in the Way*, op. cit., pp. 150–54.
49. Captain Alan W. Jones, Jr, *Operations of the 423rd Infantry Regiment, 106th Infantry Division, in the vicinity of Schönberg, Germany, during the Battle of the Ardennes, 16–19 December 1944* (Personal Experiences of a Battalion Operations Officer, Advanced Infantry Officer's Class No. 1, 1949–1950, The Infantry School, Fort Benning, Georgia). Jones's father, commanding the 106th, was felled by a heart attack in the first week of battle, his stress being compounded by the news that Alan, Jr, was listed as missing in action; it was some time before news arrived that he was a POW. The Divisional XO, Brigadier-General Perrin, took over until 7 February, when he was replaced by Major-General Donald Stroh. After St Vith was retaken, the 424th Infantry and 591st and 592nd Field Artillery Battalions saw combat for another two months, fighting their way back into Germany.
50. Oberstleutnant Dietrich Moll, *18th Volksgrenadier Division* (1 Sept. 1944–25 Jan 1945), Foreign Military Study B-688, Historical Division, USAEUR, now at NARA.
51. US 90th Divisional History, January–March 1945, 'The Ardennes'.

31. Roadblocks

1. Jacqueline and Bob de Ruyter, *Ardennen Poteau '44 Battlefield Guide*. The museum's website is at: www.museum-poteau44.be
2. Jack Belden 'Retreat in Belgium', in Samuel Hynes, Anne Matthews and Nancy

Caldwell Sorel, *Reporting World War II: American Journalism 1938–1946* (Library of America, 2001), pp. 596–9.
3. Ellis, *Clarke of St. Vith*, op. cit., pp. 96–7.
4. Belden, 'Retreat in Belgium', op. cit.
5 Andrews, *The Defense of St Vith*, op cit., pp. 77–8.
6. Major Donald P. Boyer, Jr, *Narrative Account of the Action of the 38th Armored Infantry Battalion at St Vith, 17–22 December, 1944*, NARA.
7. Bruce C. Clarke memoir, Combined Arms Research Library.
8. Gavin, *On to Berlin*, op. cit., p. 229.
9. Ibid., pp. 232–3; 237.
10. Pogue, *The Supreme Command*, op, cit., Appendix 'F', Orders of the Day, p. 547.
11. Gavin, *On to Berlin*, op. cit., pp. 238–9.
12. Pogue, *Pogue's War*, op. cit., p. 303.
13. Captured German diary quoted in *First Canadian Army Intelligence Summary*, 30 January 1945, op. cit.
14. Ellis, *Clarke of St Vith*, op. cit., p. 135.
15. Liddell Hart, *The Other Side of the Hill*, op. cit., pp. 462–5.
16. Gavin, *On to Berlin*, op. cit., pp. 243–4.
17. Sergeant First Class (retired) Richard Raymond III, 'Parker's Crossroads: The Alamo Defence', article in *Field Artillery* (August 1993).
18. Reusch memoir, op. cit.
19. Gavin, *On to Berlin*, op. cit., p. 235.
20. Reusch memoir, op. cit.
21. Pierson memoir, courtesy of Battle of the Bulge memories website, at: http://www.battleofthebulgememories.be/en/stories/us-army/659-parkers-crossroads.html
22. Gavin, *On to Berlin*, p. 235.
23. George Winter, *Manhay. The Ardennes. Christmas 1944* (Fedorwicz, 1989), p. 17.
24. Reusch memoir, op. cit.
25. George Winter, *Manhay*, op. cit.
26. Michael Connelly, *The Mortarmen* (Trafford, 2005), p. 150.
27. Connelly, *The Mortarmen*, op. cit., pp. 143–53; William B. Breuer, *Bloody Clash at Sadzot*, op. cit.

32. Malmedy

This chapter was inspired by the series of battlefield staff rides (named 'Exercise Pied Peiper') researched by Major-General Mike Reynolds in the 1970s, when he was a battalion commander with British forces stationed in Germany. The result of General Reynolds' work has been several books and the battlefield tours, still practised by the British Army today, which not only investigate US and German tactics but leadership issues as well.

1. Courtesy of Hans Wijers. http://home.planet.nl/~wijer037/bulge/forms/Fallschirmjager.htm
2. Pallud, *Battle of the Bulge: Then and Now*, op. cit., p. 135.

3. Wallace memoir, courtesy of CRIBA (*Centre de Recherches et d'Informations sur la Bataille des Ardennes*) website, op. cit.
4. Reynolds, *The Devil's Adjutant*, op. cit., p. 77.
5 Leutnant Manfred Rottenberg is buried at the *Volksbund Deutsche Kriegsgräberfürsorge* (VDK-German War Graves Commission Cemetery) at Lommel, Belgium, among 32,331 identified and 6,221 unidentified other graves from the Second World War.
6. Don Smart, *Company 'B', 612th Tank Destroyer Battalion: Action at Honsfeld, Belgium, During the Battle of the Bulge* (e-book at http://www.microrap.biz/612th-tdb/_adobe/company_b_history.pdf), p. 8
7. MacDonald, *A Time for Trumpets*, op. cit., pp. 203–4.
8. Ibid., p. 207.
9. Parker, *Fatal Crossroads*, op. cit., p. 182.
10. Reynolds, *The Devil's Adjutant*, op. cit., p. 83.
11. Lying in a much-contested part of Belgium, Malmedy was annexed by France in 1795 and by Prussia in 1815, and was often spelt in the French way, Malmédy (with the accent), to define it as French, though today the accent has been dropped.
12. Schrijvers, *The Unknown Dead*, op. cit., pp. 63–4; Reynolds, *The Devil's Adjutant*, op. cit., pp. 86–7.
13. In 1946, a US War Crimes Trial identified a total of 308 US soldiers and 111 Belgian civilians, including those killed at the Baugnez crossroads, who had been murdered by *Kampfgruppe Peiper*.
14. Parker, *Fatal Crossroads*, op. cit., pp. 205–20.
15. Bob Wyatt, *Leeton in World War II. A Small Town's Sacrifices* (AuthorHouse, 2011), p. 319.
16. Whiting, *'44: In Combat from Normandy to the Ardennes*, op. cit., p. 191.
17. Parker, *Fatal Crossroads* op. cit., p. 184.
18. Reynolds, *The Devil's Adjutant*, op. cit., pp. 88–93.
19. Gay, *Assignment to Hell*, op. cit., pp. 409–12.
20. Eisenhower, *The Bitter Woods*, op. cit., p. 237.
21. *Abilene Reporter News*, 18 December 1944; *Kansas City Star*, 18 December 1944. Charles F. Appman (1919–2013) died in August 2013. See his obituary, *Pittsburgh Post-Gazette*, 30 August 2013.
22. Pogue, *The Supreme Command*, op. cit., Appendix A: SHAEF and the Press, June 1944–May 1945, pp. 519–28.
23. Cole, *The Ardennes*, op. cit., Chapter XI, note 5.
24. Pogue, *Pogue's War*, op. cit., pp. 296–8.
25. Reynolds, *The Devil's Adjutant*, op. cit., pp. 93–7; Record Group 153: Records of the Office of the Judge Advocate General (Army), 1792–2010, NARA.
26. See: http://www.youtube.com/watch?v=u5X0VyAJUOo
27. Reynolds, *The Devil's Adjutant*, op. cit., pp. 252–9; Parker, *Fatal Crossroads*, op. cit., pp. 127–54
28. See Parker, *Fatal Crossroads*, op. cit., p. 267. To be fair, I never asked Hennecke about the events at Baugnez on the occasions we met. Being a British Army

officer in the Cold War era, I was more interested in his life fighting the Russians.

29. Parker, *Fatal Crossroads*, op. cit., p. 130.
30. Ibid., p. 27.
31. Reynolds, *The Devil's Adjutant*, pp. 98–100.
32. Cavanagh, *A Tour of the Bulge Battlefield*, op. cit., pp. 85–7.
33. They are: Sergeants Lincoln Abraham and Joseph F. Collins, T/4 Caspar S. Johnston, T/5 John M. Borcina and Privates Clifford H. Pitts, Nick C. Sulliven and Gerald R. Carter. After the war, the families of three men had them returned to the States for burial. Nick Sullivan is buried in Kentucky, Gerald Carter in Kansas, and Lincoln Abraham in Minnesota; the rest remain buried in Belgium.
34. Hobart Winebrenner and Michael McCoy, *Bootprints* (Camp Comamajo Press, 2005), pp. 181–2.
35. Thomas Hobbes, *Leviathan* (1651), Chapter 12.
36. MacDonald, *Company Commander*, op. cit., p. 142.
37. Leinbaugh and Campbell, *The Men of Company 'K'*, op. cit., p. 143.
38. Neill, *Infantry Soldier*, op. cit., p. 247.
39. Burgett, *Seven Roads to Hell*, op. cit., pp. 162–3.
40. Ibid., pp. 165–6.
41. Neill, *Infantry Soldier*, op. cit., pp. 243–4.
42. Kurt Gabel, *The Making of a Paratrooper: Airborne Training and Combat in World War II* (University Press of Kansas, 1990), p. 173.
43. Raymond Gantter, *Roll Me Over: An Infantryman's World War II* (Presidio, 1997), pp. 129–130. Gantter was thirty when he entered the army and began to keep a journal in September 1944. He completed the manuscript in 1949; he died in 1985 and his book was published posthumously in 1997.

33. The Northern Shoulder

1. Schrijvers, *The Unknown Dead*, op. cit., p. 20.
2. Shehab memoir, courtesy of: http://www.veteransofthebattleofthebulge.org/vbob/wp-content/uploads/2010/12/shehab-story.pdf
3. Pogue, *Pogue's War*, op. cit., p. 322.
4. Neill, *Infantry Soldier*, op. cit., pp. 247–8.
5. Also equipped with *Jagdpanthers* and fighting in the Ardennes were the 519th Heavy Panzer Battalion and 559th.
6. Author interview with Otie T. Cook (1920–2013), North Carolina, 1994; and 'Wineka column: A Veteran's Memories', article in the *Salisbury Post* (NC), 1 December 2009.
7. Ralph E. Hersko, 'US Troops Fight at Elsenborn Ridge', article in *The Bulge Bugle*, Volume XXIX/2 (May 2010), p. 9.
8. The 1942 TOE (table of establishment) for a US Army headquarters was 759. It is likely, with protective troops and war establishments, that figure had reached at least 2,000 by December 1944 when all its elements, including the supply and rear echelons (not previously co-located), were lodged in Spa. See Hogan, *A*

Command Post at War, op. cit., p. 298. They moved on 18 December to the Hôtel des Bains in Chaudfontaine, then on 22 December, behind the Meuse to a Belgian army barracks at Tongres, eleven miles north of Liège.

9. Michael D. Doubler, *Closing With the Enemy. How GIs Fought the War in Europe, 1944–1945* (University Press of Kansas, 1994), p. 225.
10. Cavanagh, *The Battle for the Twin Villages*, op. cit.
11. Alvin R. Whitehead, 'Shower Time', online article, courtesy of the MIA Project website.
12. Neill, *Infantry Soldier*, op. cit., p. 234.
13. Lieutenant-Colonel James M. Gleckler, 'Neglected, Hard-Learned Lessons: Looking back at Field Artillery Tactics, Techniques and Procedures in Major Combat Operations', article in *Fires* magazine (September–October 2012), pp. 53–62.
14. William F. McMurdie, *Hey, Mac! A Combat Infantryman's Story* (Red Apple Publishing, 2000), p. 89.
15. Meyer, *The 12th SS: The History of the Hitler Youth Panzer Division*, Vol. 2, op. cit., p. 296.
16. McMurdie, *Hey, Mac!*, op. cit., p. 89.
17. Captain Harry R. Ostler, *Field Artillery Journal* (March 1945).
18. McMurdie, *Hey, Mac!*, op. cit., p. 87.
19. December 2006 interview with Dr John Kerner, who was originally born John Kapstein, changing his name later in life. In 1939 he attended medical school in Berkeley, California, where he joined the ROTC, and served as a battalion surgeon in both the 10th Mountain Division and 35th Infantry Divisions. Courtesy of Dr John Kerner, Telling Their Stories, Oral History Archives Project, Urban School of San Francisco, California.
20. Captain Richard Van Horne, *Field Artillery Journal* (February 1945).
21. Major Donovan Yeuell, *Field Artillery Journal* (February 1945).
22. Courtesy of Hans Wijers, at http://home.planet.nl/~wijer037/bulge/forms/Fallschirmjager.htm
23. 'Interrogation Report, 134th Regiment, 1 Jan 45 [of] 1 PW from 8th Co, 2nd Regt, 1st SS Armd Div'. IPW [Team] 60, US 35 Infantry Division, NARA.
24. Gleckler, 'Neglected, Hard-Learned Lessons', op. cit., pp. 59–60.
25. McMurdie, *Hey, Mac!*, op. cit., p. 84.
26. Combat Interview No. 20: 2nd Division, Commanding General (Combat Interviews, Adjutant General's Office, World War II Operations Reports), 407/427, NARA.
27. McMurdie, *Hey, Mac!*, op. cit., pp. 87–8 and 91.
28. Ibid., p. 107.
29. James R. McIlroy, 'Foxhole Monotony', online article courtesy of the MIA Project website, at: http://www.miaproject.net/war-stories/jr-mcilroy-foxhole-monotony/
30. James R. McGhee, 'Personal Account', courtesy of the 87th Division Legacy Association website, at: http:/www.87thinfantrydivision.com/History/334FA/Personal/000003.html

31. 'World War II: Interview with Lieutenant-Colonel McClernand Butler', article courtesy of *Military History* magazine (June 1996).
32. Lawrence van Gelder, 'Alexander G. Shulman, 81; Used Ice for Burn Treatment', obituary in the *New York Times*, 12 July 1996; Studs Terkel, '*The Good War': An Oral History of World War II* (The New Press, 1984), pp. 282–3.
33. Walter R. Cook, Lieutenant-Colonel, Surgeon, *Medical Bulletin*, Office of the Surgeon, HQ Second Infantry Division, December 1944, NARA.
34. Author interview with former Sergeant Jay H. Stanley, St Vith, 17 December 1994.
35. Cook, *Medical Bulletin*, op. cit.
36. Whitehead, 'Shower Time', online article, op. cit.
37. Gene Garrison, *Unless Victory Comes. Combat With a Machine Gunner in Patton's Third Army* (Casemate, 2004), pp. 124–5.
38. Cook, *Medical Bulletin*, op. cit.
39. Ralph G. Martin, *The GI War, 1941–1945* (Little, Brown, 1967), p. 206.
40. December 2006 interview with Dr John Kerner, op. cit.
41. Cook, *Medical Bulletin*, op. cit.
42. Author interview with Vern B. Werst, 17 December 1994, St Vith.
43. Cavanagh, *The Battle East of Elsenborn and the Twin Villages* (Pen & Sword, 2004), p. 164.
44. Neill, *Infantry Soldier*, op. cit., pp. 251–2.
45. Dom is an abbreviation for the French word 'domaine', meaning that Dom Bütgenbach was an old landed estate.
46. Meyer, *The 12th SS*, op. cit., p. 293.
47. Ibid., pp. 298–9.
48. Doubler, *Closing With the Enemy*, op. cit., pp. 211–14.
49. Ibid., p. 307.
50. Richard H. Byers, 'Christmas on the Ridge', online article courtesy of the MIA Project website, at: http://www.miaproject.net/war-stories/elsenborn-christmas-day-on-the-ridge/
51. Samuel L. Lombardo, 'Christmas on the Ridge', op. cit.
52. Bernard Nawrocki, 'Christmas on the Ridge', op. cit.
53. Parker, *Battle of the Bulge*, op. cit., p. 197.
54. Meyer, *The 12th SS*, op. cit., pp. 302–3.
55. My thanks to the MIA project for alerting me to this story at: http://www.miaproject.net/mia-search-recoveries/slaughter-on-a-remote-hill/

34. Those Damned Engineers!

1. *Handbook To Belgium* (Ward Lock, 1921), p. 282.
2. Reynolds, *The Devil's Adjutant*, op. cit., p. 108.
3. Major Ken Hechler, An Interview with Obst. Joachim Peiper (NARA/ETHINT 10, 7 September 1945), pp. 18–20.
4. Ibid. I am most grateful to Major-General Mike Reynolds for drawing the inconsistencies in Peiper's testimony to my attention.
5. Hechler interview, op. cit., cover note and p. (i).

6. Cavanagh, *A Tour of the Bulge Battlefield*, op. cit., p. 15.
7. The best modern map, which covers the entire battlefield, is Michelin Sheet No. 214 (1:200,000 scale), the exact successor of those used by the Germans in 1944. In more detail, the following 1:100,000 scales maps are also most helpful: 115: Ciney–Houffalize; 116: Esneux–St Vith; 118: St Hubert–St Vith.
8. Officially the 99th Infantry Battalion (Separate). This was an independent unit, part of the Twelfth Army Group's special troops, and had no connection with the 99th (Checkerboard) Division.
9. Schrijvers, *The Unknown Dead*, op. cit., pp. 64–8.
10. Cook memoir, op. cit.
11. A German prisoner later claimed to have 'fixed' the explosives on the Stavelot bridge so that it couldn't be blown, but this was an idle boast. The bridge was never even prepared for demolition. See Gavin, *On to Berlin*, op. cit., p. 214.
12. Reynolds, *The Devil's Adjutant*, op. cit., pp. 120–21; Hans Wijers, *Battle of the Bulge*, Vol. Two, *Hell at Bütgenbach/ Seize the Bridges* (Stackpole, 2010), pp. 184–5; Ralf Tiemann, *Die Leibstandarte, Band IV/2* (Munich Verlag, 1987), pp. 81–2.
13. Wijers, *Battle of the Bulge*, Vol. Two, op. cit., p. 185.
14. Captain Leland E. Cofer, 'The bridge at Stavelot', article in *The Bulge Bugle*, Volume XIX (February 2000), pp. 12–14.
15. Schrijvers, *The Unknown Dead*, op. cit., pp. 40–49.
16. Cole, *The Ardennes*, op. cit., Chapter XI 'The 1st SS Panzer Division's Dash Westward, and Operation Greif', pp. 266–7.
17. Hechler interview, op. cit., p. 8.
18. Janice Holt Giles, *The Damned Engineers* (Houghton Mifflin, 1970), Introduction.
19. Gavin, *On to Berlin*, op. cit., p. 223.
20. Ibid., p. 219.
21. Schrijvers, *The Unknown Dead*, op. cit., pp. 49–51.
22. I am most grateful to the director and staff of the December 44 Historical Museum at La Gleize. Their website is at: http://www.december44.com/en/history_battle_of_the_bulgela_gleize.htm. Another of Peiper's King Tigers has also survived. This tank, with turret number 332, was abandoned, out of fuel, near Trois-Ponts, and captured on 24 December 1944. It was then moved to Spa and eventually shipped to the Aberdeen Proving Grounds in Maryland, USA.
23. Cole, *The Ardennes*, op. cit., pp. 259–71.

35. End of the Bulge

1. Arend, *Bastogne*, op. cit., pp. 199–200.
2. Original in Bastogne Historical Center, reproduced in Arend, *Bastogne*, op. cit., pp. 198–9.
3. Ibid.
4. Lionel P. Adda, 'Grateful for Small Things', article in *The Bulge Bugle*, Volume XII/4 (November 1993), p. 26.
5. 'Hier wird nicht geschossen', article in *Der Spiegel* magazine, 13 May 1985; article

by Fritz Vincken in *The Frederick Post*, 22 January 1996; Rod Ohira, 'Fritz Vincken, Bakery Owner, Dead at 69', article in *Honolulu Advertiser*, 11 January 2002; Rod Ohira, 'The Night God Came to Dinner', online article, courtesy of the Divine Mercy Center of Hawaii, webpage at: http://www.divinemercyhawaii.org/index.cfm?load=page&page=302.

6. Courtesy of the MIA Project, http://www.miaproject.net/x-files/x-4013-unknown-or-unbekannt/. The US Army recovery team later found the remains had been transported from elsewhere and buried in St Vith, deepening the mystery. Known from his files as X-4013, the unidentified soldier, who is as likely to be German as American, lies at Plot A, Row 17, Grave 3, in the Ardennes American Cemetery, Neuville-en-Condroz, Neupré, Belgium.
7. Hitler, *Mein Kampf*, op. cit., p. 741. He repeated these ideas at length in the last major public speech before his death, on the 25th Anniversary of the Announcement of the National Socialist Party's Programme, 24 February 1945.
8. Ibid.
9. Interrogation Report, 134th Inf Regt, IPW [Team] 60, 1 Jan. 45, NARA.
10. Hills memoir, Stephen Ambrose Manuscript Collection, National D-Day Museum, New Orleans, Louisiana.
11. General Walther Warlimont, *Inside Hitler's Headquarters* (Weidenfeld & Nicolson, 1964), p. 493.
12. F. H. Hinsley, *Official History of the Second World War: British Intelligence in the Second World War* (HMSO, 1993), p. 566.
13. Kerner interview, op. cit.
14. Ibid.
15. Interrogation Report, 134th Regt, IPW [Team] 60, 2 Jan. 45, NARA.
16. Peter Harclerode, *'Go To It': The Illustrated History of the 6th Airborne Division* (Caxton, 1990), p. 113.
17. Interrogation Report, 134th Inf Regt, IPW [Team] 60, 23 Jan. 45, NARA.
18. Max Hastings, *Armageddon* (Macmillan, 2004), p. 268.
19. Desmond Scott, *Typhoon Pilot* (Secker & Warburg, 1982), p. 157.
20. Brigadier Sugden died at 7.15 p.m. on 4 January 1945.
21. See: Gary Orfalea, *Messengers of the Lost Battalion* (The Free Press, 1997).
22. Weather observations of First Lieutenant Kendall M. Ogilvie, Battery 'A', 17th Field Artillery Observation Battalion, NARA.
23. Author's interview with former Gefreiter Otto Gunkel, 981st *Volksgrenadier* Regiment, Monschau, September 1992.
24. McMurdie, *Hey Mac!*, op. cit., p. 109.
25. John Davis, *Up Close: A Scout's Story* (Merriam Press, 2012), p. 66.
26. Ogilvie, 17th Field Artillery Observation Battalion, op. cit.
27. J. Ted. Hartman, *Tank Driver* (Indiana University Press, 2003), pp. 47, 54 and 58.
28. Joe W. Wilson Jr, *The 761st Black Panther Tank Division in World War II: An Illustrated History of the First African Armoured Unit to See Combat* (McFarland & Co., 1999), p. 53.
29. Front page, *Baltimore News-Post*, 9 January 1945
30. Cavanagh, *A Tour of the Bulge Battlefield*, op. cit., p. 166.

31. 'Allied Progress Continues in Belgium: Montgomery's Men Capture Laroche', *Daily Telegraph*, Friday, 12 January 1945.
32. *The Advocate* (Tasmania), Friday 12 January 1945, front page; *Daily Mail*, Tuesday, 16 January 1945, front page; *Baltimore News-Post*, Monday, 15 January 1945, front page.
33. Pallud, *The Battle of the Bulge: Then and Now*, op cit., p. 481. It must be stressed, however, that though every source quotes a different figure, somewhere in the 75,000–80,000 range is likely to be broadly accurate.
34 Though critically low on fuel (with not enough even to reach Antwerp), the Germans were also dangerously short of vehicles before *Herbstnebel* began, with little ability to recover or repair those battle-damaged or broken down, and certainly possessed too few to reach the Belgian port under combat conditions in mid-winter. For example, on 10 December, 116th Panzer Division (at 75 per cent strength) reported they were deficient of 432 trucks, 111 *Maultier* tracked transports and thirty-two prime movers for artillery. Failing even to reach the Meuse had cost them (by 27 December) an additional 128 half-tracks and motorcycles, 112 trucks, five *Maultier* and five prime movers. All the attacking divisions reported similar or greater deficiencies. The majority of the infantry and artillery units, including all the *Volksgrenadier* divisions, had limited mobility, relying completely on horses for all their transportation and resupply needs. Horses and their four-wheeled wagons were slow and more vulnerable to winter weather than vehicles. Most of the Wehrmacht's trucks were destroyed or abandoned during the latter stages of *Herbstnebel*. See Guderian, *From Normandy to the Ruhr*, op cit., pp. 291 and 525.
35. Mitcham, *Panzers in Winter*, op. cit., p. 160.

36. The Performance of a Lifetime

1. Butcher, *My Three Years With Eisenhower*, op. cit., p. 625.
2. Ibid.
3. Schramm (ed.), *Kriegstagebuch Des Oberkommando Der Wehrmacht 1944–45*, op. cit., p. 30.
4. Dr Roger Cirillo, *Ardennes-Alsace* (US Army Center for Military History, 2006), pp. 37–43 and 48–53.
5. '106th Division Has Heavy Loss: More than 7,000 Men Believed Prisoners', *Tuscaloosa News*, Tuesday, 23 January 1945, p. 6.
6. CAB106/1069, TNA, Kew, UK.
7. CAB106/1071, TNA, Kew, UK.
8. Ibid.
9. One of Monty's personal liaison officers, Major Tom Bigland, has left a record of Monty's words. See *Bigland's War*, op. cit., pp. 84–6.
10. See my earlier work, *Monty and Rommel: Parallel Lives* (Preface, 2011), pp. 448–50.
11. *Daily Mail*, Monday, 8 January 1945, p. 1.
12. Bigland, *Bigland's War*, op. cit., p. 84.
13. Ibid.

14. Caddick-Adams, *Monty and Rommel: Parallel Lives*, op. cit., pp. 448–50.
15. Bradley, *A General's Life*, op. cit., pp. 384–5.
16. *New York Times*, Wednesday, 10 January 1945, p. 1.
17. *Daily Mail*, Wednesday, 10 January 1945, p. 1.
18. Eisenhower Papers #2276. See Crosswell, *Beetle, The Life of General Walter Bedell Smith*, op. cit., p. 1035.
19. Dwight D. Eisenhower, *Crusade in Europe*, op. cit., p. 389.
20. Gavin, *On to Berlin*, op. cit., pp. 258–9.
21. Ibid.
22. Wilmot, *The Struggle for Europe*, op. cit., pp. 610–14.
23. Delaforce, *The Battle of the Bulge: Hitler's Final Gamble*, op. cit., p. 318.
24. Ambrose, *Citizen Soldiers*, op. cit., p. 218.
25. Schramm, *Hitler: The Man and the Military Leader*, op. cit., pp. 169–70, and Fest, *Hitler*, op. cit., pp. 1066–7.
26. Guderian, *Panzer Leader*, op. cit., pp. 382–7; Mellenthin, *Panzer Battles. A Study of the Employment of Armour in the Second World War*, op. cit., p. 411.
27. Mellenthin, *Panzer Battles*, op. cit., p. 409.
28. Guy Sager, *The Forgotten Soldier* (Weidenfeld & Nicolson, 1971), p. 87.
29. Hechler, Interview with Peiper, op. cit., p. 9.

37. Beyond the Bulge

1. Speer, *Inside the Third Reich*, op. cit., p. 420.
2. Britain's *Daily Mail* published a banner headline on 29 December 1944, stating 'Patton's 3rd Army Strikes at "Bulge" from South', but the prissy *Daily Mail* put the word 'Bulge' in inverted commas, thinking it indecorous and rude.
3. Patton, *War As I Knew It*, op. cit., p. 208; Sean M. Walsh, 'It Was Newman's Call at The Battle of the Bulge', article in *Cape Cod News* (Hyannis, Massachusetts), 5 January 1995; *The Bulge Bugle*, Volume XV/4 (November 1996), p. 15.
4. Patton, *War As I Knew It*, op. cit., p. 221.
5. MacDonald, *A Time for Trumpets*, op. cit., p. 617.
6. Collins, *Lightning Joe: An Autobiography*, op. cit., p. 294.
7. Eisenhower, *The Bitter Woods*, op. cit., p. 429.
8. Merriam, *Dark December*, op. cit., p. 174.
9. Map issued with *Images of War Magazine*, Vol. 3/No. 38 (Marshall Cavendish, 1990).
10. Schrijvers, *The Unknown Dead*, op. cit., pp. 359–73.
11. Mitchell Kaidy, 'Battle of the Bulge Was Longer, Bloodier than Army Admits', article in *The Bulge Bugle*, May 2000.
12. Churchill, *The Second World War*, Vol. VI, op. cit., p. 243.
13. Churchill and Roosevelt (who was quartered on the ground floor of the Livadia itself) went there at the most drab time of the Crimean year. I can vouch for the fact it looks its best in the summer months with spectacular views on to the cobalt-blue Black Sea. These days its upper rooms house exhibitions about the Russian royal families who lived there, while downstairs is devoted to the Yalta conference.

14. Stewart Halsey Ross, *Strategic Bombing by the United States in World War II: The Myths and the Facts* (McFarland, 2003), p. 180; Norman Longmate, *The Bombers* (Hutchinson, 1983), p. 333.
15. Isaacson, *Kissinger: A Biography*, op. cit., p. 48.
16. Eisenhower, *Crusade in Europe*, op. cit., p. 418.
17. 'German Court Reviews Execution Over Failure To Blast Remagen Bridge', article in *Park City Daily News* (Bowling Green, Kentucky), 1 February, 1967, p. 25.
18. Author interview with Oberst Krug, October 2000.
19. Patton, *War As I Knew It*, op. cit., pp. 273–4.
20. When used with great success in the Pacific by US Marines, they were known as LVTs – Landing Vehicles Tracked, or Amtracs; in Italy they were labelled Fantails.
21. Lieutenant-General Sir Brian Horrocks, *Corps Commander* (Sidgwick & Jackson, 1977)
22. Churchill, *The Second World War*, Vol. VI, op. cit., pp. 363–4.
23. Ibid., p. 365.
24. Charles B. MacDonald, *US Army in World War II, The Last Offensive* (Office of the Chief of Military History, Department of the Army, 1973), p. 221.

38. On to Berlin!

1. Churchill, *The Second World War*, Vol. VI, op. cit., p. 348.
2. Interview with Brigadier-General (retd) Hans-Georg Model, Steigenberger Hotel, Bad Neuenahr-Ahrweiler, October 2000.
3. Annan, *Changing Enemies*, op. cit., pp. 125–6.
4. This era of post-WW2 German history is not easy reading, as Giles MacDonogh in his *After the Reich: From the Liberation of Vienna to the Berlin Airlift* (John Murray, 2008) suggests. Equally uncomfortable, though almost certainly wrong, is James Bacque's *Other Losses, an Investigation into the Mass Deaths of German Prisoners at the Hands of French and Americans After World War II* (MacDonald, 1989). He asserts that 'over 800,000, almost certainly over 900,000 and quite likely over a million' German prisoners were killed in US prison camps after the war. US academics have noted that Bacque is a Canadian novelist with no previous historical research or writing experience, who has made a lot of money from his allegations, which are popular with the Holocaust Denial community. He certainly treats historical evidence and documentation in a cavalier fashion, and when a panel of distinguished American academics was convened to discuss Bacque's allegations, the late Stephen Ambrose spoke for them in noting that his charges were 'demonstrably absurd'. Abuse certainly took place, but it was neither institutional nor widespread.
5. Burke, *Lee Miller*, op. cit., p. 253.
6. Jack Bass and Marilyn W. Thompson, *Ol' Strom: An Unauthorized Biography of Strom Thurmond* (University of South Carolina Press, 2002), p. 76.
7. Wilmot, *The Struggle for Europe*, op. cit., p. 705.
8. Patton, *War As I Knew It*, op. cit., p. 330.
9. Harold Evans, *The American Century* (Jonathan Cape, 1998), p. 344.

10. Max Hastings, *Victory in Europe* (Weidenfeld & Nicolson, 1985), pp. 137–63.
11. Burke, *Lee Miller*, op. cit., p. 258.
12. Mohnke managed to survive his Soviet captivity and, perversely, avoided all charges of war crimes, dying in his bed, aged ninety.
13. Stephen Harding, *The Last Battle: When US and German Soldiers Joined Forces in the Waning Hours of World War II in Europe* (Da Capo Press, 2013).
14. *Daily Express*, 18 May 1945.
15. *New York Times*, 18 May 1945.
16. Based on several author's interviews with Herr Hans Hennecke, February–April 1981.
17. Pogue, *Pogue's War*, op. cit., p. 377.

39. Punctuation Marks of History

1. These figures are much disputed and relate to the fact that US casualty returns were collected by a variety of sources (e.g. division, corps, army, hospitals) and assessed over time periods, not regions, thus some casualties were not related to the Bulge. The killed and wounded figure of 76,890 is that inscribed on the solemn and imposing Mardasson Memorial, dedicated in 1950, and situated just outside Bastogne. The stone structure was built in the shape of an enormous five-pointed pentagram, and contains the names of all the US states; its twelve-metre-high roof offers excellent panoramic views of the battle ground around Bastogne. POW statistics from the report by the Office of the Assistant Secretary for Policy, Planning, and Preparedness (OPP&P), *Former American Prisoners of War* (US Department of Veterans Affairs, April 2005), p. 5. The US non-battle casualties may have been as high as 20,000; to these totals should be added British losses of 200 killed and 1400 wounded.
2. Patton, *War As I Knew It*, op. cit., pp. 328–30.
3. British War Cabinet, Joint Planning Staff, *Russia: Threat to Western Civilization (Operation Unthinkable)*, [Draft and Final Reports: 22 May, 8 June and 11 July 1945], Public Record Office, CAB 120/691/109040/002.
4. Pamela C. Harriman, 'The True Meaning of the Iron Curtain Speech', article in *Finest Hour*, Vol. 58 (Winter 1987–1988), at: http://www.winstonchurchill.org/learn/biography/in-opposition/qiron-curtainq-fulton-missouri-1946/174-the-true-meaning-of-the-iron-curtain-speech
5. Central Intelligence Agency, *Effect of Soviet Restrictions on the US Position in Berlin* (Top Secret Report for President Truman, 14 June 1948) at the Harry S. Truman Library and Museum, Berlin Airlift Study Collection.
6. Originally published by the Infantry Journal Press, Washington, DC, in 1946, Marshall's *Bastogne* is available as a free download at http://www.history.army.mil/books/wwii/Bastogne/bast-fm.htm. He shared the credit for *Bastogne* with his assistants, Captain John G. Westover and Lieutenant A. Joseph Webber.
7. Later editions of *Dark December* were titled *The Battle of the Ardennes*, and an edition published to tie in with the 1965 movie *Battle of the Bulge*.

8. Published in the United Kingdom as *The Battle of the Bulge.*
9. Robert Edward Merriam died aged sixty-nine in 1988. The Robert E. Merriam Papers 1918–1984 are housed in the University of Chicago Library.
10. Hechler interviewed several of the US and German soldiers involved, in 1957 publishing the *The Bridge at Remagen: The Amazing Story of March 7, 1945* (new edition, Presidio Press, 2005), which was adapted into a successful film in 1969.
11. US Army Field Manual FM 1–20, *Military History Operations* (February 2003), pp. 1–2/1–3.
12. Other movies depicting the Battle of the Bulge include: *Attack!* (Robert Aldrich, 1956); *The Last Blitzkrieg* (Arthur Dreifuss, 1959); *Ski Troop Attack* (Roger Corman, 1960); *Counterpoint* (Ralph Nelson, 1968); *Castle Keep* (Sydney Pollack, 1969); *A Midnight Clear* (Keith Gordon, 1992); *Silent Night* (Rodney Gibbons, 2002); *Saints and Soldiers* (Ryan Little, 2003) and *Everyman's War* (Thad Smith, 2009)
13. Jay Hyams, *War Movies* (Gallery Books, 1984), p. 114.
14. Ibid.
15. Ibid., p. 158
16. *Saturday Review*, review of *Battle of the Bulge* (1966, Volume 49/1, p. 43).
17. Cirillo, *Ardennes-Alsace*, op. cit., p. 53. The nineteen US divisions in Normandy were the 1st, 2nd, 4th, 5th, 8th, 9th, 28th, 29th, 30th, 35th, 79th and 83rd, 90th Infantry; 2nd, 3rd, 4th and 6th Armored; and 82nd and 101st Airborne.
18. Some fifteen divisions fought in the third major US theatre, the Mediterranean, of which seven later also redeployed to fight in Europe.
19. *Crusade in Europe* was acknowledged as inspiring the twenty-six-episode documentary series, *The Great War* (about the First World War), shown on UK, Canadian and Australian television from 1964. Its main narrator was Michael Redgrave, with additional readings by Ralph Richardson. The formula was also repeated with outstanding success in another twenty-six-part documentary, Thames Television's *The World at War* of 1973–4, produced by Jeremy Isaacs and narrated by Laurence Olivier. All three were critically acclaimed and received huge viewer figures.
20. John Eisenhower had also been in talks with film producer Tony Lazzarino about writing a screenplay for a Battle of the Bulge movie, reportedly titled *The 16th of December* or *The Final Guns.* Scheduled for release in December 1969, it was never made, and Eisenhower's research was instead more profitably directed to his book, *The Bitter Woods.*
21. Whiting, *The Last Assault*, op. cit., p. 225.
22. Ibid., p. xvii.
23. Whiting (1926–2007) joined the British Army aged sixteen, lying about his age. By 1945 he had reached the rank of sergeant in the 52nd Reconnaissance Regiment (52nd Lowland Division), operating in armoured cars and serving in France, Holland, Belgium and Germany in the last months of the Second World War.
24. Terkel, '*The Good War*': *An Oral History of World War II*, op. cit.
25. Tom Brokaw, *The Greatest Generation* (Random House, 1999), Introduction.
26. Mary Jo Tate, *The Critical Companion to F. Scott Fitzgerald: A Literary Reference to His Life and Work* (Infobase, 1998), pp. 306–7.

27. Ambrose, *Band of Brothers*, op. cit.; *D-Day, June 6, 1944: The Climactic Battle of World War II* (Simon & Schuster, 1994); *Citizen Soldiers*, op. cit.
28. As an indication of this new interest, annual visitor numbers at the Omaha Beach cemetery, run by the American Battlefields Monuments Commission, where *Saving Private Ryan* begins, have reached almost two million per year, since the premiere of the film, making Ambrose (albeit indirectly) one of the most influential military historians of modern times.
29. The TV series also used David Kenyon Webster's *Parachute Infantry: An American Paratrooper's Memoir of D-Day and the Fall of the Third Reich* (Louisiana State University Press 1994), which was based on his wartime diaries, but only published forty years later, long after the author's death in 1961.
30. Stephen E. Ambrose, *Pegasus Bridge: June 6, 1944* (Simon & Schuster, 1984).
31. See their website at: http://www.veteransofthebattleofthebulge.org/

40. Reputations

1. Nicholas Goodrick-Clarke, *Hitler's Priestess: Savitri Devi, the Hindu-Aryan myth, and Neo-Nazism* (New York University Press, 1998), p. 174.
2. *Der Spiegel*, 9 April 1952, 'Heil Rommel'.
3. *Der Spiegel*, ibid. Also, David Patterson, *A Genealogy of Evil: Anti-Semitism from Nazism to Islamic Jihad* (Cambridge University Press, 2010), pp. 93–5, and Nicholas Goodrick-Clarke, *Black Sun: Aryan Cults, Esoteric Nazism and the Politics of Identity* (New York University Press, 2001), Chapter 5.
4. Jewish Telegraph Agency, 4 February 1972, 'Names of 13 High-ranking Nazis Disclosed; One of Them Now in Egypt'.
5. Skorzeny died in 1975, Remer in 1997, Martins in 1993 and Rudel in 1982.
6. Rafael Poch, ' El jefe de comandos de Hitler quiso formar un ejercito alemán en la España de los cincuenta', and 'Un nazi en la España de Franco', articles in *La Vanguardia*, 4 and 8 December 2011. I am most grateful to Cristina de Santiago for her research in Spain into Otto Skorzeny.
7. Ken Silverstein, *Private Warriors* (Verso Books, 2000), p. 112.
8. These included about 120 Panzer IV, the balance being *Jagdpanzer* IV and StuG III.
9. See Dani Asher's *The Egyptian Strategy for the Yom Kippur War: An Analysis* (McFarland & Co., 2009)
10. See General Avraham (Bren) Adan, *On the Banks of the Suez* (Presidio Press, 1980).
11. Bill Warnock, *The Dead of Winter: How Battlefield Investigators, WWII Veterans, and Forensic Scientists Solved the Mystery of the Bulge's Lost Soldiers* (Chamberlain, 2005).
12. Brigadier-General Oscar W. Koch (1897–1970)
13. Reynolds, *The Devil's Adjutant*, op. cit., pp. 264–9.
14. MacDonald, *Company Commander*, op. cit., pp. 302–3.

Bibliography

Unpublished Sources:

Libraries and Archives

Bielefeld State Historical Library and City Archives: details of Nazi party election poster for Lippe state election, 1933, featuring Hitler with the Hermannsdenkmal

Harry S. Truman Library, Independence, Missouri: Oral History Interview with Gen. Bruce C. Clarke by Jerry N. Hess, 14 January, 1970; see: http://www.trumanlibrary.org/oralhist/clarkeb.htm

Landesarchiv Baden-Württemberg, Eugenstraße 7, D-70182 Stuttgart, Germany. Wacht am Rhein postcards and images.

West Point Center for Oral History: Interview with Paul Andert, a platoon sergeant who served under Patton at the Bulge; see: http://www.westpointcoh.org/westpointcoh/interview/a-platoon-sergeant-who-served-under-patton-at-the-bulge

UK National Archives, Kew: WO 219–2246 (Papers of the Supreme Headquarters Allied Expeditionary Force, 1944 to 1945, Intelligence and Security Services, November 1944)

US National Archives and Records Administration (NARA): US Army Europe [USAEUR], Historical Division, Headquarters, Foreign Military Studies Branch, transcripts of original interviews (with date of interrogation), all now at NARA, Series M1035, as follows: ETHINT is a contraction of 'European Theater Historical Interrogations'. These manuscripts record the first American historical interviews with German officers, including some of very high rank, in the immediate post-war period. A few of these officers have made more complete and accurate reports at a later date. Most of the interrogations were conducted at Bad Mondorf, Luxembourg, in the summer and autumn of 1945.

Personal Records

Bader, Generalmajor Rudolf, '560th Volks Grenadier Division: 11 Nov 44–25 Jan 45' (1946)
Bayerlein, Generalleutnant Fritz, '26 VG Div, Ardennes and Panzer Lehr Division, Ardennes' (Oct. 1945); 'Additional questions – Ardennes Offensive' (1945); 'Panzer Lehr Division, 15–22 December 1944' (1946); 'Panzer Lehr Division, 12–30 Jan. 45' (1946); 'Panzer Lehr Division, 1 December 1944–26 January 1945' (1946)
Blumentritt, General der Infanterie Günther, 'The Ardennes Offensive' (1948)
Bodenstein, Oberst Werner, 'Report of My Activities during the American's Campaign on the West Front – Ardennes: LIII Corps, 16 December 1944–25 January 1945' (1946)
Brandenberger, General der Panzertruppe Erich, 'Seventh Army: 1 Sep. 44–25 Jan. 45' (1946); 'My attitude to the Report of Lieutenant General Wirtz' (1946)
Buechs, Major Herbert, 'OKW – Ardennes Offensive' (31 Aug 1945)
Denkert, Generalleutnant Walter, 'Commitment of the 3rd Panzer Grenadier Division during the Ardennes Offensive' (21 Nov. 1945); '3rd Panzer Grenadier Division: 16–28 Dec. 44' (1947); '3rd Panzer Grenadier Division: 28 Dec. 44 to 25 Jan. 45' (1945)
Dietrich, Generaloberst (Waffen-SS) Joseph ('Sepp'), 'Sixth Panzer Army, Ardennes' (8–9 Aug. 1945); 'Sixth Panzer Army in the Ardennes' (10 Jul. 1945)
Dingler, Oberst Hans-Jürgen, 'Report on the Campaign in Northern France, the Rhineland, and the Ardennes' (1946)
Engel, Generalleutnant Gerhard, '12th Volks Grenadier Division: 3–29 Dec. 44' (1947)
Felber, General der Infanterie Hans-Gustav, 'XIII Corps: 1–25 Jan. 45' (1946)
Fieger, Oberst Georg, '989th Grenadier Regiment: 14 Dec. 44–17 Dec. 44' (1946)
Gersdorff, Generalmajor Rudolf Christoph Freiherr von, 'The Ardennes Offensive' (1945)
Greiffenberg, General der Infanterie Hans von, 'Initial Preparations for the Ardennes Offensive' (1952)
Hausser, Generaloberst der Waffen-SS Paul, 'Effect of Ardennes Offensive on Army Group 'G', 25 January–21 March 1945' (1946)
Heilmann, Generalmajor Ludwig, 5th Parachute Division: 1 December 1944–12 January 1945' (1 Mar. 1946)
Hentschel, Generalleutnant der Luftwaffe Karl, '5th Fighter Division: 16 Dec. 1944–25 Jan. 1945' (1946)
Heydte, Oberst Friedrich Freiherr August von der, 'Kampfgruppe von der Heydte: 25 Oct.–22 Dec. 1944' (31 Oct. 1945)
Hitzfeld, General der Infanterie Otto Maximilian, 'The Ardennes Offensive' (1954)
Hoecker, Generalleutnant Hans-Kurt, '167th Volks Grenadier Division: 24 December 1944–February 1945, Corps Hoecker: 2–10 March 1945 and 59th Infantry Division: 20 March–24 April 1945' (1946)
Hummel, Oberst Kurt, '79th Volks Grenadier Division: 30 Dec. 44–31 Jan. 45' (1946)
Jodl, Generaloberst Alfred, 'OKW Planning, Ardennes' (26 Jul. 1945); 'OKW, Ardennes Offensive' (31 Jul. 1945)
Kaschner, Generalmajor Dr Erwin, '326th Volks Grenadier Division: 16 Dec. 44–25 Jan. 45' (1945); 'Ardennes Offensive, right wing, 326th Volks Grenadier Division: 10 December 1944–16 December 1944' (1946)
Keitel, Generalfeldmarschall Wilhelm, 'Questionnaire on the Ardennes Offensive' (1945)
Kittel, Generalleutnant Friedrich, 'Report on the Ardennes Offensive: The 62nd Volks Grenadier Division' (1946)

Kniess, General der Infanterie Baptist, 'LXXXV Corps: 1 Dec. 44–10 Jan. 45' (11 Aug 1945)
Kokott, Generalmajor Heinz, '26th Volks Grenadier Division breakthrough to Bastogne, 24–28 Dec. 1944, in the Ardennes Offensive' (29 Nov. 1945)
Kolb, Generalmajor Werner, '9th Volks Grenadier Division: 1 Nov. 44–5 Feb. 45' (1947)
Kraemer, Generalmajor (Waffen-SS) Fritz, 'Sixth Panzer Army in the Ardennes Offensive' (14–15 Aug 1945); 'Sixth Panzer Army in the Ardennes Offensive' (11 Oct. 1945); 'Sixth Panzer Army in the Ardennes Offensive' (7 Nov. 1945); 'LXVII Infantry Corps in the Ardennes Offensive' (17 Nov. 1945); 'LXVII Infantry Corps in the Ardennes Offensive' (20 Nov. 1945)
Krüger, General der Panzertruppe Walter, 'LVIII Panzer Corps' (1945); 'Offensive in the Ardennes from 16 Dec. 44–2 Feb. 45' (1947)
Langhaeuser, Generalmajor Rudolf, '560th and 12th Volks Grenadier Divisions: The Attack and Defense Battle in the Ardennes: 16 December 1944–17 January 1945' (1946)
Lucht, General der Artillerie Walter, 'Ardennes Campaign' (1945); 'LXVI Army Corps in the Ardennes Offensive' (1945); 'LXVI Army Corps, Continuation of the Ardennes Offensive' (1948)
Lüttwitz, General der Panzertruppen Heinrich von, 'The Assignment of the XLVII Panzer Corps in the Ardennes 1944–1945' (1954); 'XLVII Panzer Corps Investment of Bastogne' (13 Oct. 1945); 'XLVII Panzer Corps – The Break through to Bastogne' (1 Nov. 1945); 'XLVII Panzer Corps, Mission 24 Oct–5 Dec 1944' (24 Nov. 1945)
Manteuffel, General der Panzertruppe Hasso-Eccard von, 'Mission of Fifth Panzer Army, 11 Sep. 1944–Jan. 1945' (21 June 1945); 'Mission of Fifth Panzer Army, Nov. 1944–Jan. 1945 (29 and 31 Oct 1945)
Mellenthin, Generalmajor Friedrich von, 'Comments on Patton and the U.S. Third Army, Sep. 1944 (16 May 1946)
Metz, Generalleutnant Richard, 'Fifth Panzer Army Artillery in the Ardennes Offensive 1944' (1946)
Peiper, Oberst (Waffen-SS) Joachim, '1st SS Panzer Regiment in the Ardennes, 11– 24 Dec. 1944 (7 Sep. 1945); '1st SS Panzer Regiment in the Ardennes, 16–19 Dec. 1944' (18 Sep. 1945)
Püchler, General der Infanterie Karl, 'LXXIV Corps, Ardennes' (1946)
Remer, Generalmajor Otto Ernst, 'Führer Begleit Brigade, Ardennes' (15 Aug. 1945); 'Führer Begleit Brigade: Nov. 44–12 Jan. 45' (1947); 'The Führer Escort Brigade in the Ardennes Offensive' (1954)
Rothkirch und Trach, General der Kavallerie Edwin von, 'LIII Corps: 8 Dec. 44–21 Jan. 1945' (1946)
Rundstedt, Generalfeldmarschall Gerd von, 'OB West, Ardennes Offensive' (3 Aug. 1945)
Schimpf, Generalleutnant Richard, '3d Parachute Division, Ardennes Campaign: 16 December 1944–25 January 1945' (1946)
Schramm, Major Percy Ernst, 'The Preparations for the German Offensive in the Ardennes: Sep. to 16 Dec. 1944' (1945); 'The Course of Events of the German Offensive in the Ardennes: 16 Dec. 44 to 14 Jan. 45' (1945); 'Answers to the questions of 15 Feb. 1946' (1946). Schramm kept the war diary of the Wehrmacht Operations Staff.
Sensfuss, Generalleutnant Franz, '212th Volks Grenadier Division, Ardennes: 16 Dec. 1944–25 Jan. 1945' (1945)
Skorzeny, Oberstleutnant (Waffen-SS) Otto, 'Ardennes Offensive: Role of Commandos and 150th Panzer Brigade' (12 Aug. 1945)

Staudinger, Generalleutnant der Waffen-SS Walter, 'The Artillery Command of the Sixth Panzer Army during the Ardennes Offensive, 1944–1945' (11 Aug. 1945)

Stumpff, General der Panzertruppen Horst, 'Tank Maintenance, Ardennes' (11 Aug. 1945)

Thoholte, General der Artillerie Karl Philipp, 'Army Group 'B' Artillery, Ardennes' (1946)

Triepel, Generalmajor Gerhard, 'LVIII Panzer Corps Artillery: Ardennes Offensive: 1 Nov. 44 to 1 Feb. 45' (1947)

Viebig, Generalmajor Wilhelm, '277th Volks Grenadier Division: Nov. 44–Jan. 45' (1946)

Voigt, Generalmajor Hans-Hubert, '340th Volks Grenadier Division at Bastogne, Clervaux and the West Wall: 25 Dec. 44–30 Jan. 45' (1954)

Wagener, Generalmajor Carl, 'Fifth Panzer Army, Ardennes: 2 Nov. 44–16 Jan. 45' (1945); 'Main reasons for the Failure of the Ardennes Offensive' (1945)

Waldenburg, Generalleutnant Siegfried von, '116th Panzer Division, Ardennes' (1946)

Westphal, General de Kavallerie Siegfried, 'Ardennes Planning' (7 Sep. 1945)

Wirtz, Generalleutnant Richard, 'Army Group 'B' Engineers: 1–25 Jan. 1945' (1945)

Zanssen, Generalmajor Leo, 'Ardennes: 16 December 1944–25 January 1945' (1946)

Other Unpublished Sources:

After Action Report, Third US Army, 1 August 1944–9 May 1945, Vol. 1 Operations (published by 652d Engineer Battalion, 1945), from the Digital Combined Arms Research Library (DCARL)

After Action Report, 36th Cavalry Reconnaissance Squadron, Period 1–31 December 44 DCARL

Army Air Forces Evaluation Board in the European Theater of Operations, *The Effectiveness of Third Phase Tactical Air Operations in the European Theater, 5 May 1944–8 May 1945* (published August 1945) DCARL

British Army 5 Airborne Brigade, *Battlefield Tour to Eben-Emael and the Route of Kampfgruppe Peiper, October 1988* (UK Joint Services Command and Staff College, Watchfield, 16–20 October 1988)

Commanding General, US Army Europe (USAEUR), *Senior Leader Staff Ride Battlebook: The Battle of the Bulge* (USAEUR, n.d.). Available at: http://www.eur.army.mil/pdf/botb-staff-ride.pdf

Gallagher, Lt.-Col. William J., (Intro.), *Victory TD: The History of the 628th Tank Destroyer Battalion in Training and Combat, Prepared by and For the Men Who Saw Action with the Battalion in France, Belgium, Luxembourg, Holland and Germany* (628th TD Battalion, 1945) DCARL

Kean, Maj.-Gen. W.B., (Foreword), *Combat Operations Data, First Army Europe, 1944–1945* (HQ, First US Army, 1946) DCARL

Harding, J. J., *The German Operation in the Ardennes 1944, A Short Study* (Non-Technical Research Paper 3, UK Army Historical Branch, MOD, n.d.)

Headquarters, 1st British Corps, *Exercise Pied Peiper Battlefield Tour 1987* (HQ 1st British Corps, Bielefeld 16–17 July 1987)

Headquarters, Northern Army Group (NORTHAG), *Battlefield Tour 1985: Offensives in the Ardennes, December 1944–January 1945* (NATO, 17 & 18 September 1985)

Headquarters Third United States Army, Notes on the Bastogne Operation (HQ Third US Army, 16 January 1945 – NARA, Record Group No. 407)

Headquarters, Twelfth Army Group, Weekly Intelligence Summary No. 18 for Week Ending 9 Dec. 44 (DCARL)

Headquarters United Kingdom Support Command Germany, *Battlefield Tour 14–15 April 2005 Ardennes 1944 Staff Reader* (UKSC (G), 2005)

Higher Command and Staff Course, *Wacht am Rhein Staff Ride 1988* (UK Joint Services Command and Staff College, Watchfield, 1988)

Junior Division, The Staff College, *Exercise Snowy Owl Ardennes Battlefield Tour, 21–25 November 1994* (UK Joint Services Command and Staff College, Watchfield, 1994)

Marshall, Col. S. L. A., *The Siege of Bastogne* (Historical Section European Theater of Operations, 1945) DCARL

Academic and Military Research Papers:

23rd Hussars (Members of the Regiment), *The Story of the Twenty-Third Hussars 1940–1946* (Privately Printed by the Regiment, 1946)

Adams, Capt. James F., *Operations of Company 'F', 327th Glider Infantry (101st Airborne Division) in the defense of Bastogne, Belgium, 19–26 December 1944* (Personal Experience of a Company Commander, Advanced Infantry Officers Course, Fort Benning, Georgia, 1946–7)

Adams, Maj. Jonathan E., Jr., *Operations of 'A' Company, 508th Parachute Infantry, 82nd Airborne Division, Near Rencheaux, Belgium, 22–25 December 1944* (Personal Experience of a Company Commander, Advanced Infantry Officers Course, Fort Benning, Georgia, 1947–8)

Andrews, Frank L., *The Defense of St. Vith in the Battle of the Ardennes, December, 1944* (MA Thesis, Department of American Civilization, New York University, 1964)

Baily, Charles M.; Boykin, Joyce B.; Karamales, Lloyd J., and Young, Victoria I., *Anti-Armor Defense Data Study for the US Army Concepts Analysis Agency: US Anti-Tank Defense at Dom Butgenbach, Belgium, December 1944* (Science Applications International Corporation, 1990)

Barber, Maj. Keith H., *German Ardennes Counter Offensive 16 December 1944 to 2 January 1945* (Report, Advanced Infantry Officers Course, Fort Benning, Georgia, 1947–8)

Barber, Maj. Wilfred, *Operations of Company 'A', 331st Infantry, 83rd Infantry Division, at Langlir, Belgium, 11–12 January 1945* (Personal Experience of a Rifle Company Commander, Advanced Infantry Officers Course, Fort Benning, Georgia, 1949–50)

Barth, William M., *Battle of the Bulge: Intelligence Lessons for Today* (US Army War College Military Studies Program paper, Carlisle, Pennsylvania, 1993)

Beeson, Maj. John J., III, *Operations of Company 'D', 104th Infantry, 26th Infantry Division, in the attack from Bettborn to Buschrodt, Luxembourg, 22–24 December 1944* (Personal Experience of a Heavy Weapons Company Commander, Advanced Infantry Officers Course, Fort Benning, Georgia, 1949–50)

Benson, Kevin C. M., *Educating the Army's Jedi, The School of Advanced Military Studies and the Introduction of Operational Art into U.S. Army Doctrine 1983–1994* (PhD Thesis, University of Kansas, 2010)

Bogardus, Maj. Allan L., *Operations of Company 'C', 291st Infantry, 75th Infantry Division, in the attack on the High Ground Outside Grand Halleux, Belgium, 15–16 January 1945* (Personal Experience of a Company Commander, Advanced Infantry Officers Course, Fort Benning, Georgia, 1949–50)

Booth, Brian, *Sources of North Atlantic Data Used by German Meteorologists, 1940–1945* (History of Meteorology and Physical Oceanography Special Interest Group, Royal Meteorological Society, Newsletter 3, 2010, pp. 6–8)

Borows, Stephen Dominic, *Clarke of St. Vith: Brigadier-General Bruce C. Clarke's Combat Command 'B' of the Seventh Armoured Division at the Battle of St. Vith, Belgium, Ardennes Campaign, 16 December–23 December 1944* (Ph.D. Thesis, University of Louisville, 1989)

Bouwmeester, Maj. Han, *Beginning of the End: The Leadership of SS-Obersturmbannführer Jochen Peiper* (MA Thesis, US Army Command and General Staff College, Fort Leavenworth, Kansas, 2004)

Brant, Maj. Bruce A., *Retrograde at the Operational Level of War* (Monograph, US Army Command and General Staff College, Fort Leavenworth, Kansas, 1987)

Bressler, Capt. Howard E., *2nd Armored Division in the Ardennes* (Monograph, Advanced Officers Class, The Armored School, Fort Knox, Kentucky, 1948)

Broadus, Maj. Wendell M., *15th Cavalry Reconnaissance Squadron in the Ardennes Offensive, 16 December 1944 to 1 January 1945* (Monograph, Advanced Officers Class, The Armored School, Fort Knox, Kentucky, 1947)

Brown, Maj. John S., *Winning Teams: Mobilization-Related Correlates of Success in American World War II Infantry Divisions* (MA Thesis, US Army Command and General Staff College, Fort Leavenworth, Kansas, 1985)

Bruley, Capt. Henry L., *Operations of Company B, 289th Infantry (75th Infantry Division) in the crossing of the Salm River, 14 –20 January 1945* (Personal experience of a Company Executive Officer, Advanced Infantry Officers Course, Fort Benning, Georgia, 1948–9)

Buckhout, Maj. Laurie G. Moe, *Signal Security in the Ardennes Offensive: 1944–1945* (MA Thesis, US Army Command and General Staff College, Fort Leavenworth, Kansas, 1997)

Budraß, Lutz, Scherner, Jonas and Streb, Jochen, *Demystifying the German 'Armament Miracle' During World War II. New Insights from the Annual Audits of German Aircraft Producers* (Economic Growth Center, Yale University, Center Discussion Paper No. 905, January 2005)

Cain, Maj. Francis M., III, *The 1111th Engineer Group in the Bulge: The Role of Engineers as Infantry in AirLand Battle* (Monograph, US Army Command and General Staff College, Fort Leavenworth, Kansas, 1985)

——— *The Ardennes – 1944: An Analysis of the Operational Defense* (Monograph, US Army Command and General Staff College, Fort Leavenworth, Kansas, 1986)

Campana, Capt. Victor W., *Operations of the 2nd Battalion, 504th Parachute Infantry, 82nd Airborne Division, in the German Counter-Offensive, 18 December 1944–10 January 1945* (Personal Experience of a Battalion S-3, Advanced Infantry Officers Course, Fort Benning, Georgia, 1946–7)

Campbell, Capt. John, Jr., *Operations of the 3rd Battalion, 134th Infantry (35th Infantry Division) in the battle of Lutrebois, Belgium, 28 December 1944–4 January 1945* (Personal Experience of a Company Commander, Advanced Infantry Officers Course, Fort Benning, Georgia, 1947–8)

Charles, Major D. N.; Camp, Major T. J.; Fielder, Major I. R.; Moore, Major W. H.; and Waddell, Major G. W. C., *The Effects of Isolation on Small, Dispersed Groups of Men on the Battlefield* (Group Research Project, 24 UK Army Command & Staff Course, 1990)

Claflin, Lt.-Col. Robert C., *The Operational Art as Practised by General George S. Patton, Jr., During the Battle of the Bulge* (Research Paper, US Naval War College, Rhode Island, 1994)

Clark, Maj. Robert L., IV, *The Essential Elements of Operational Surprise* (Monograph, US Army Command and General Staff College, Fort Leavenworth, Kansas, 1987)

Clayton, Maj. George A., *Operations of the 3rd Battalion, 394th Infantry Regiment (99th Division) in the German Ardennes counteroffensive, 16 December 1944–1 January 1945* (Personal experience of a Battalion Executive Officer, Advanced Infantry Officers Course, Fort Benning, Georgia, 1947–8)

Cockrell, Philip Carlton, *Brown Shoes and Mortar Boards: U.S. Army Officer Professional Education at the Command and General Staff School, Fort Leavenworth, Kansas 1919–1940* (Ph.D. Thesis, University of South Carolina, 1991)

Creighton, Capt. James R., *Operations of Company 'F', 101st Infantry, 26th Infantry Division, in the Attack on the Mon Schumann Crossroads, Luxembourg, 27 December 1944–3 January 1945* (Personal Experience of a Company Commander, Advanced Infantry Officers Course, Fort Benning, Georgia, 1949–50)

Croft, Capt. Lucian C., *Operations of the 2nd Battalion, 104th Infantry, 26th Infantry Division, in the Attack from Grosbous to Wiltz, Luxembourg, 22–29 December 1944* (Personal Experience of a Heavy Weapons Company Commander, Advanced Infantry Officers Course, Fort Benning, Georgia, 1947–8)

Curran, Capt. Charles E., Jr., *Operations of the VIII Corps in the German Ardennes counteroffensive, 16–26 December 1944* (Personal experience of a Corps Liaison Officer and Assistant G-3, Advanced Infantry Officers Course, Fort Benning, Georgia, 1947–8)

Dadisman, Capt. Chester E., *Operations of the 1st Battalion, 376th Infantry Regiment, 94th Infantry Division, in the SAAR-Moselle Triangle at Tettingen, Butzdorf, Southwest of Trier, Germany, 14–18 January 1945* (Personal Experience of a Battalion Intelligence Officer, Advanced Infantry Officers Course, Fort Benning, Georgia, 1949–50)

Dale, Maj. Matthew B., *The Professional Military Development of Major General Ernest N. Harmon* (MA Thesis, US Army Command and General Staff College, Fort Leavenworth, Kansas, 2008)

Davis, Floyd J., *The Staff: Another Dimension of the Operational Level of War* (Study Project, US Army War College, Carlisle, Pennsylvania, 1988)

Daykin, Maj. Albert, *Operations of the 1st Battalion, 119th Infantry, 30th Division, in the Attack on Stoumont, 19–22 December 1944* (Personal Experience of an Artillery Liaison Officer, Advanced Infantry Officers Course, Fort Benning, Georgia, 1949–50)

Deming, Lt.-Col. Dennis C., *German Deception in the Ardennes: Lessons for the Senior Leader* (US Army War College Military Studies Program paper, Carlisle, Pennsylvania, 1989)

Dominique, Dean James, *The Attack Will Go On. The 317th Infantry Regiment in World War II* (MA Thesis, Louisiana State University, 2003)

Dressler, Maj. William E., and six other officers, *Armor under Adverse Conditions: 2nd and 3rd Armored Divisions in the Ardennes Campaign, 16 December 1944–16 January 1945* (Research Report, Committee No. 3, Officers Advance Course, The Armored School, Fort Knox, Kentucky, June 1949)

Dull, Lt.-Col. Harry L., Jr, *Communications Intelligence (COMINT) in the Prelude to the Battle of the Bulge* (US Army War College Paper, Carlisle, Pennsylvania, 1977)

Dunham, Capt. Leland Rockwood, *Operations of Company 'K', 101st Infantry Regiment (26th Division) in the vicinity of Kaundorf, Luxembourg, 25– 30 December 1944* (Personal Experience of a Company Commanding Officer, Advanced Infantry Officers Course, Fort Benning, Georgia, 1947–8)

Fabianich, Maj. Keith P., *Operations of the 3rd Battalion, 395th Infantry Regiment (99th Division) prior to and during the German counteroffensive, 10 November–24 December 1944* (Personal experience of a Company Commander and Battalion S-3, Advanced Infantry Officers Course, Fort Benning, Georgia, 1947–8; *Infantry School Quarterly*, July 1948)

Ferguson, Reuben D., *An Investigation Into the Effects of the Music of Richard Wagner on the Pseudo-Mysticism of Adolf Hitler and the Third Reich* (Academic paper at http://www.arkrat.net/hitwag.htm)

Finley, James P., (ed.), *US Army Military Intelligence History: A Sourcebook* (US Army Intelligence Center & Fort Huachuca, Arizona, 1995)

Flowers, Maj. Jack D., *Patton, Third Army and Operational Manuever* (Monograph, US Army Command and General Staff College, Fort Leavenworth, Kansas, 1998)

Fontenot, Maj. Gregory, *The Lucky Seventh in the Bulge: A Case Study for the AirLand Battle* (MA Thesis, US Army Command and General Staff College, Fort Leavenworth, Kansas, 1985)

Fossum, Maj. Embert A., *The Operations of Task Force 'L', 109th Infantry (85th Infantry Division) near Grosbous, Luxembourg, 20–23 December 1944* (Personal Experience of a Task Force Commander, Advanced Infantry Officers Course, Fort Benning, Georgia, 1948–9)

Frandsen, Maj. Herbert L., *Counterblitz: Conditions for a Successful Counteroffensive* (Monograph, US Army Command and General Staff College, Fort Leavenworth, Kansas, 1990)

Galbreaith, Maj. Robert B., *Operations of the 2nd Battalion, 327th Glider Infantry, 101st Airborne Division, in the Defense of Bastogne, Belgium, 20–26 December 1944* (Personal Experience of a Battalion Commander, Advanced Infantry Officers Course, Fort Benning, Georgia, 1947–8)

Gendron, Maj. Thomas J., *The Operations of the 2nd Battalion, 26th Infantry (1st US Infantry Division) at Dom Bütgenbach, Belgium, 18–21 December 1944* (Personal Experience of a Battalion S-3, Advanced Infantry Officers Course, Fort Benning, Georgia, 1949–50)

Giarrusso, Joseph Martin, *Against All Odds: The Story of the 106th Infantry Division in the Battle of the Bulge* (MA Thesis, San Jose State University, 1998)

Gibson, Maj. David J., *Shock and Awe: A Sufficient Condition for Victory?* (Research Paper, US Naval War College, Rhode Island, 2001)

Greene, Maj. Michael J. L., *Contact at Houffalize, Belgium: Contact of the 1st and 3rd Armies* (Monograph, Officers Advance Course, The Armored School, Fort Knox, Kentucky, May 1948)

Gribble, Lt.-Col. G. D., Jr, *ULTRA: Its Operational Use in the European Theater of Operations, 1943–1945* (US Army War College Strategy Research Paper, Carlisle, Pennsylvania, 1991)

Hamilton, Maj., William W., *Defensive Culmination – When Does the Tactical Commander Counterattack?* (Monograph, US Army Command and General Staff College, Fort Leavenworth, Kansas, 1991)

Hancock, Maj. William F., Jr, *Operations of 1st Battalion, 9th Infantry (2nd Infantry Division) in a Hasty Defense against Armored Attack, 17–18 December 1944* (Personal Experience of a Battalion XO, Advanced Infantry Officers Course, Fort Benning, Georgia, 1949–50)

Hankel, Capt. Halland W., *Operations of Company 'M', 38th Infantry, 2nd Infantry Division, in the vicinity of Krinkelt, Belgium, 17–20 December 1944* (Personal Experience of a Company Commander, Advanced Infantry Officers Course, Fort Benning, Georgia, 1948–9)

Harvey, Maj. Murray L., *Operations of the 3rd Battalion, 507th Parachute Infantry, 17th Airborne Division, 'The Battle of Dead Man's Ridge', vicinity of Laval-Chisogne, Belgium, 7–8 January 1945* (Personal Experience of a Battalion Liaison Officer, Advanced Infantry Officers Course, Fort Benning, Georgia, 1948–9)

Hayes, Dr. Richard E., and Sugarman, Kristi, *The State of the Art and the State of the Practice: Battle of the Bulge: The Impact of Information Age Command and Control on Conflict – Lessons Learned* (Command and Control Research and Technology Symposium, Evidence Based Research Inc., 2006)

Higgins, Maj. George A., *The Operational Tenets of Generals Heinz Guderian and George S. Patton, Jr.* (MA Thesis, US Army Command and General Staff College, Fort Leavenworth, Kansas, 1985)

Hilton, Capt. Wilbur S., *Operations of the 3rd Battalion, 289th Infantry, 75th Infantry Division, at Grandmenil, Belgium, 25 December 1944–7 January 1945* (Personal Experience of a Battalion Operations Officer, Advanced Infantry Officers Course, Fort Benning, Georgia, 1947–8)

Hinman, Major Jade E., *When the Japanese Bombed the Huertgen Forest. How the Army's Investigation of Pearl Harbor Influenced the Outcome of the Huertgen Forest, Major General Leonard T. Gerow and His Command of V Corps from 1943–1945* (A Monograph for the School of Advanced Military Studies US Army Command and General Staff College, Fort Leavenworth, Kansas, 2011)

Hoffmann, Lt.-Cmdr. Richard J., USN, *Painting Victory: A Discussion of Leadership and Its Fundamental Principles* (MA Thesis, US Army Command and General Staff College, Fort Leavenworth, Kansas, 1987)

Hollinger, Maj. John C., *Operations of 433d Infantry (106th Division) at Schlassenback, Germany, 15–20 December 1944* (Personal Experience of a Regiment Assistant S-3, Advanced Infantry Officers Course, Fort Benning, Georgia, 1949–50)

Hollstein, Capt. Jean W., *Operations of 506th Parachute Infantry (101st Airborne Division) in The Defense of Bastogne, 19–20 December 1944* (Advanced Infantry Officers Course, Fort Benning, Georgia, 1949–50)

Holt, Maj. Jeffrey P., *Operational Performance of the US 28th Infantry Division, September to December 1944* (MA Thesis, US Army Command and General Staff College, Fort Leavenworth, Kansas, 1994)

Horton, Maj. James E., *Operations of the 920th Tank Destroyer Battalion in a Retrograde Movement during the German counteroffensive in the Ardennes-Alsace Campaign, 14–25 December 1944* (Personal Experience of a Battalion Supply Officer, Advanced Infantry Officers Course, Fort Benning, Georgia, 1949–50)

Hutchinson, Capt. Robert C., Jr, *Operations of Company 'B', 630th Tank Destroyer Battalion supporting the 110th Infantry in vicinity of Clervaux, Luxembourg, 16–31 December 1944* (Personal Experience of a Company Commander, Advanced Infantry Officers Course, Fort Benning, Georgia, 1947–8)

Hyle, Capt., Archie R., *Operations of 3rd Battalion, 291st Infantry (75th Infantry Division) north of Aldringen, Belgium, 22 January 1945* (Personal Experience of a Battalion Intelligence Officer, Advanced Infantry Officers Course, Fort Benning, Georgia, 1947–8)

Jackson, Maj. William F., and eight others, *The Employment of Four Tank Destroyer Battalions in the ETO* (Research Report by Committee 24, Officers Advanced Course, US Armor School, Fort Knox, Kentucky, 1950)

James, Capt. Alan W., *Operations of the 423rd Infantry (106th Infantry Division) in the vicinity of Schonberg during the battle of the Ardennes, 16–19 December 1944* (Personal experience of a Battalion Operations Officer, Advanced Infantry Officers Course, Fort Benning, Georgia, 1947–8)

Jarkowsky, Maj. Jeffrey, *German Special Operations in the 1944 Ardennes Offensive* (MA Thesis, US Army Command and General Staff College, Fort Leavenworth, Kansas, 1994)

Jenkins, Capt., Joseph E., *Supply Operations in the 1st Battalion, 501st Parachute Infantry Regiment, 101st Airborne Division, in the Battle of Bastogne, 18–26 December 1944* (Personal Experience of a Battalion S-4, Advanced Infantry Officers Course, Fort Benning, Georgia, 1948–9)

Johnson, Maj. Kevin D., *Intelligence Preparation of the Theatre* (Monograph, US Army Command and General Staff College, Fort Leavenworth, Kansas, 1991)

Jones, Capt. Alan W., *The Operations of the 423rd Infantry (106th Infantry Division) in the Vicinity of Schonberg during the Battle of the Ardennes, 16–19 December 1944* (Personal Experience of a Battalion Operations Officer, Advanced Infantry Officers Course, Fort Benning, Georgia, 1949–50)

Kaune, Lt.-Col. Patrick N., *General Troy H. Middleton: Steadfast in Command* (Monograph, US Army Command and General Staff College, Fort Leavenworth, Kansas, 2011)

Kays, Marvin D., *Weather Effects During the Battle of the Bulge and the Normandy Invasion* (Atmospheric Sciences Laboratory, US Army Electronics Research and Development Command, White Sands Missile Range, New Mexico, 1982)

Keller, Major Brian A., *Avoiding Surprise: The Role of Intelligence Collection and Analysis at the operational Level of War* (Monograph, US Army Command and General Staff College, Fort Leavenworth, Kansas, 1992)

Kemp, Capt. Harry M., *The Operations of the 3rd Battalion, 109th Infantry (28th Infantry Division) in the vicinity of Diekirch, Luxembourg, 16 December–23 December 1944* (Personal Experience of a Battalion Executive Officer, Advanced Infantry Officers Course, The Infantry School, Fort Benning, Georgia, 1949–50)

Kemp, Maj. James B., *Operations of the 612th Tank Destroyer Battalion (T), Second Infantry Division, in the Battle of the Bulge, Vicinity of Elsenborn Corner, 16–31 December 1944* (Personal Experience of a Battalion Executive Officer, Advanced Infantry Officers Course, The Infantry School, Fort Benning, Georgia, 1949–50)

Kennedy, Maj. James L., Jr, *The Failure of German Logistics during the Ardennes Offensive of 1944* (MA Thesis, US Army Command and General Staff College, Fort Leavenworth, Kansas, 2000)

Kent, Maj. Frederick T., 'The Operations of 22nd Infantry Regiment (4th Infantry Division) in the Hürtgen Forest, Germany, 16 November–3 December 1944' (Personal Experience of a Regimental S-4, Advanced Infantry Officers Course, The Infantry School, Fort Benning, Georgia, 1946–7)

Keyes, Maj. Lewis H., *Operation of 106th Infantry Division, 15–22 December 1944* (Advanced Infantry Officers Course, The Infantry School, Fort Benning, Georgia, 1949–50)

Kievit, Maj. James O., *Operational Art in the 1944 Ardennes Campaign* (Monograph, US Army Command and General Staff College, Fort Leavenworth, Kansas, 1987)

Kindsvatter, Maj. Peter S., *An Appreciation for Moving the Heavy Corps – The First Step in Learning the Art of Operational Maneuver* (Monograph, US Army Command and General Staff College, Fort Leavenworth, Kansas, 1986)

Krainik, Capt. Edward B., *The Allied Counterattack, 26 December 1944–27 January 1945*

(Report, Advanced Infantry Officers Course, The Infantry School, Fort Benning, Georgia, 1948–9)

LeFebvre, Capt. Henry E., *Operations of the 2nd Battalion, 508th Parachute Infantry Regiment, 82nd Airborne Division, in the withdrawal from and recapture of Thier-du-Mont Ridge, Belgium, 22 December 1944–7 January 1945* (Personal Experience of a Battalion Operations Officer, Advanced Infantry Officers Course, The Infantry School, Fort Benning, Georgia, 1948–9)

LeGare, Maj. Ben W., *Operations of 2nd Battalion, 394th Infantry (99th Infantry Division) in the German Counteroffensive, Vicinity of Losheimergraben, Germany, 16–19 December 1944* (Personal Experience of a Battalion XO, Advanced Infantry Officers Course, The Infantry School, Fort Benning, Georgia, 1949–50)

Litchfield, Maj. John T. and ten other officers, *The Ardennes: The Battle of the Bulge: Winter Defense and Counterattack* (Student Research Paper, Combat Studies Institute, US Army Command and General Staff College, Fort Leavenworth, Kansas, 1984)

MacDonald, Maj. Robert J., *Another von Rundstedt Blunder – Bastogne: 3rd Battalion, 327th Glider Infantry in the Defense of Bastogne, December 1944* (Monograph, Advanced Infantry Officers Course, The Infantry School, Fort Benning, Georgia, May 1948)

McCrorey, Maj. James L., *Combat Operations of Combat Team 9, Combat Command 'A', (6th Armored Division) in fighting near Wardin, Belgium, 3–5 January 1945* (Personal Experience of a Battalion S-3, Advanced Infantry Officers Course, Fort Benning, Georgia, 1948–9)

McDonald, Maj. Eugene O., *Operations of the 3rd Battalion, 289th Infantry Regiment (75th Division) in the Salm Offensive, vicinity of Salm Chateau, Belgium, 15–21 January 1945* (Personal Experience of a Battalion Executive Officer, Advanced Infantry Officers Course, Fort Benning, Georgia, 1948–9)

McGinnis, Maj. Thomas M., *Unit Collapse: A Historical Analysis of Two Divisional Battles in 1918 and 1944* (Master Degree Thesis, US Command and General Staff College, Fort Leavenworth, Kansas, 1987)

——— *Jomini and the Ardennes: An Analysis of Lines of Operation and Decisive Points* (Monograph, US Army Command and General Staff College, Fort Leavenworth, Kansas, 1988)

Marks, Capt. Sidney M., *Operations of the First Battalion 517th Parachute Infantry Regiment at Soy Belgium, 22–24 December 1944* (Personal Experience of a Battalion Liaison Officer, Advanced Infantry Officers Course, The Infantry School, Fort Benning, Georgia, 1948–9)

Meyers, Capt. Francis J., Jr, *Operations of 3rd Platoon, Company 'G', 505th Parachute Infantry (82nd Airborne Division) on the Salm River in the vicinity of Petite Halleux, Belgium, 25 December 1944* (Personal Experience of a Platoon Leader, Advanced Infantry Officers Course, Fort Benning, Georgia, 1948–9)

Mobley, Capt. Dan A., *Operations of the 1st Battalion, 417th Infantry (76th Infantry Division) in the crossing of the Saur River and attack against Siegfried Line, Echternach, Luxembourg, 1–15 February 1945* (Personal experience of the Division Commander's Aide-de-Camp, Advanced Infantry Officers Course, Fort Benning, Georgia, 1948–9)

Mocello, Lt.-Col. Gerald A., *The Battle of the Ardennes: Analysis of Strategic Leadership and Decisions* (US Army War College Strategy Research Paper, Carlisle, Pennsylvania, 1999)

Moon, Maj. William P., Jr, *Operations of the 1st Battalion, 422nd Infantry, 106th Infantry Division, in the Battle of the Bulge, in the vicinity of Schlausenbach, Germany, 10–19*

December 1944 (Personal Experience of a Battalion Executive Officer, Advanced Infantry Officers Course, The Infantry School, Fort Benning, Georgia, 1949–50)

Moore, Lt.-Col. Theo K., *'The Crux of the Fight': General Joseph Lawton Collins' Command Style* (Monograph, US Army Command and General Staff College, Fort Leavenworth, Kansas, 2011)

Morton, Maj. Gregory, *Field Artillery Support for III Corps Attack, 18–26 December 1944* (MA Thesis, US Army Command and General Staff College, Fort Leavenworth, Kansas, 1985)

Musick, Capt., L. A., *Operations of the 3rd Battalion, 513th Parachute Infantry (17th Airborne Division) in the Battle of the Bulge, 25 December 1944–9 January 1945* (Personal Experience of a Battalion S-2, Advanced Infantry Officers Course, Fort Benning, Georgia, 1946–7)

Myers, Capt. Francis J., Jr, *Operations of 3rd Platoon, Company G, 505th Parachute Infantry (82nd Airborne Division), at Salm River, vicinity of Petite Halleux, Belgium, 25 December 1944* (Personal Experience of a Platoon Leader, Advanced Infantry Officers Course, Fort Benning, Georgia, 1946–47)

Nicholas, Maj. Donna C., USAF, and Whitley, Maj. Albert H., USAFR, *The Role of Air Power in the Battle of the Bulge* (Research Report, Air Command and Staff College, Maxwell Air Force Base, Alabama, 1999)

O'Halloran, Capt. John T., *Operations of the 1st Platoon, Company 'B', 401st Glider Infantry, 101st Airborne Division, in the Battle of Bastogne, Belgium, 25 December 1944* (Personal Experience of a Platoon Leader, Advanced Infantry Officers Course, Fort Benning, Georgia, 1948–9)

Page, Lt.-Col. Leander, III, *Weather Support to the Modern Army* (US Army War College Essay, Carlisle, Pennsylvania, 1982)

Phillips, Maj. Ivan G., *Operations of the 502nd Parachute Infantry Regiment, 101st Airborne Division, in the Defense of Bastogne, 24–25 December 1944* (Personal Experience of a Regimental Communications Officer, Advanced Infantry Officers Course, The Infantry School, Fort Benning, Georgia, 1947–8)

Powe, Maj. N. B. and Wilson, Maj. E. E. *The Evolution of American Military Intelligence* (US Army Intelligence Center and School, Fort Huachuca, Arizona, 1973)

Read, Maj. Steven N., *Planning for the Unplannable: Branches, Sequels and Reserves* (Monograph, US Army Command and General Staff College, Fort Leavenworth, Kansas, 1990)

Reeves, Lt. Cmdr. Brian, USN, *General Matthew B. Ridgway: Attributes of Battle Command and Decision-Making* (Research Paper, US Naval War College, Rhode Island, 1998)

Rivette, Capt. Donald E., *Operations of the 2nd Battalion, 26th Infantry, 1st Infantry Division, at Dom Bütgenbach, Belgium, 16–21 December 1944* (Personal Experience of an Anti-Tank Company Commander, Advanced Infantry Officers Course, The Infantry School, Fort Benning, Georgia, 1948–9)

Roberts, Maj. Elvy B., *Operations of the 501st Parachute Infantry (101st Airborne Division) at Bastogne, Belgium 19–20 December 1944* (Personal Experience of a Regimental S-3, Advanced Infantry Officers Course, Fort Benning, Georgia, 1947–8)

Roberts, Jonathan P., *How Has the Representation of World War II on Film Changed From 1939–2009* (BA Honours Dissertation, University of Wales, 2010)

Rosenbaum, Lt.-Col. Michael D., *The Battle of the Bulge: Intelligence Lessons for the Army After Next* (US Army War College Strategy Research Paper, Carlisle, Pennsylvania, 1999)

Rowe, Maj. Richard J., Jr, *Counterattack: A Study of Operational Priority* (Monograph, US Army Command and General Staff College, Fort Leavenworth, Kansas, 1987)

St. Laurent, Maj. P. J.; Crow, Maj. C. L.; Everette, Maj. J. S.; Fontenot, Maj. G., and Hester, Maj. R. V., *The Battle of St. Vith, Defense and Withdrawal by Encircled Forces. German 5th & 6th Panzer Armies versus US 7th Armored Division and Attachments, 17–23 December 1944* (Report, US Army Command and General Staff College, Fort Leavenworth, Kansas, 1984)

Sanderson, Maj. Jeffrey R., *General George S. Patton, Jr.: Master of Operational Battle Command. What Lasting Battle Command Lessons Can We Learn From Him?* (Monograph, US Army Command and General Staff College, Fort Leavenworth, Kansas, 1997)

Scanlon, Maj. John H., *Operations of Company 'B', 318th Infantry Regiment (80th Division) during the German Ardennes counteroffensive, 19–24 December 1944* (Personal Experience of a Company Commander, Advanced Infantry Officers Course, Fort Benning, Georgia, 1947–8)

Schopper, Maj. Jared B., *The Collection and Processing of Combat Intelligence as Performed by the US Army during Operations in Northern Europe* (MA Thesis, US Army Command and General Staff College, Fort Leavenworth, Kansas, 1964)

Schumacher, Capt. Fred W., *Employment of the 2nd Platoon, Company 'M', 333rd Infantry Regiment (84th Division), 24–26 December 1944* (Personal Experience of a Platoon Leader, Advanced Infantry Officers Course, Fort Benning, Georgia, 1947–8)

Shaifer, Capt. Edward F., Jr, *Operations of Company 'B', 504th Parachute Infantry (82nd Airborne Division) in piercing the Siegfried Line near Losheimergraben, Germany, 2–4 February 1945* (Personal experience of a Platoon Leader, Advanced Infantry Officers Course, Fort Benning, Georgia, 1948–9)

Simmons, Capt. Wesley J., *Operations of Company 'K', 394th Infantry, 99th Infantry Division, in Defensive Action, near Elsenborn, Belgium, 16–21 December 1944* (Personal Experience of a Company Commander, Advanced Infantry Officers Course, The Infantry School, Fort Benning, Georgia, 1949–50)

Sinesi, Michael P., *Wacht am Rhein, Hollywood Style. A comparison and contrast of Hollywood's version of the Ardennes Offensive in the film Battle of the Bulge to the earlier film Battleground and the Historical Event* (Research Paper, 1996–7 George C. Marshall Undergraduate Scholars Program, Bridgewater College, Virginia, 1997)

Siska, 1st Lt. John R., *Operations of Company 'A', 1st Battalion, 424th Infantry (106th Infantry Division) at Winterspelt, Germany, 12–18 December 1944* (Personal Experience of a Rifle Platoon Leader, Advanced Infantry Officers Course, Fort Benning, Georgia, 1948–9)

Slaughter, S. D., *The Cavalry Group as an Economy Force: 4th Cavalry Group, 19–30 December 1944* (Research Report, Officers Advanced Course, The Armored School, Fort Knox, Kentucky, 1950)

Smith, Capt. Bill G., *Operations of the 551st Parachute Infantry Battalion, attached to the 82nd Airborne Division and the 517th Parachute Infantry Regiment, in the attack in the vicinity of Trois Ponts, Belgium, 2–7 January 1945* (Personal Experience of a Headquarters Company Commander, Advanced Infantry Officers Course, Fort Benning, Georgia, 1949–50)

Smylie, John Hubbard, *US Army VIII Corps Under General Troy H. Middleton in the Ardennes Offensive, December 16–December 31, 1944* (Ph.D. Thesis, Tulane University, 1979)

Solomon, Capt. Edward M., *Operations of the 18th Infantry (1st Infantry Division) in the counter-attack of the Bulge, 15–30 January 1945* (Personal experience of an Antitank

Company Commander, Advanced Infantry Officers Course, Fort Benning, Georgia, 1948–9)

Stark, Capt. Marshall W., *Operations of the 1st Platoon, Battery 'C', 80th Airborne Anti-Aircraft Battalion, 82nd Airborne Division, in the Battle of the Bulge, 17 December 1944–3 January 1945* (Personal Experience of a Platoon Leader, Advanced Infantry Officers Course, The Infantry School, Fort Benning, Georgia, 1947–8)

Stephens, Capt. John M., Jr, *Operations of Company 'G', 23rd Infantry Regiment (2nd Infantry Division) in securing Ondenval Pass in the vicinity of Ondenval, Belgium, 15–20 January 1945* (Personal experience of a Company Commander, Advanced Infantry Officers Course, Fort Benning, Georgia, 1948–9)

Stone, Thomas Richardson, *He Had the Guts to Say No. A Military Biography of William Hood Simpson* (Ph.D. Thesis, Rice University, Houston, Texas, 1974)

Sullers, Lt.-Col. Robert R., and seven others, *Armor at Bastogne* (Report Prepared by Committee 4, Officers' Advanced Course, The Armored School, Fort Knox, Kentucky, 1949)

Thaden, Maj. Russell H., *Intelligence Preparation of the Battlefield and Predictive Intelligence* (Monograph, US Army Command and General Staff College, Fort Leavenworth, Kansas, 1986)

Thompson, Capt. Clarence A. Jr, *Operations of the 1st Battalion, 502rd Parachute Infantry (101st Airborne Division) at Champs, Belgium, 25 December 1944* (Personal Experience of a Company Commander, Advanced Infantry Officers Course, Fort Benning, Georgia, 1947–8)

Townsend, Capt. James M., *Operations of the 81-mm Mortar Platoon, Headquarters Company, 1st Battalion, 517th Parachute Infantry Regimental Combat Team at Soy, Belgium, 21–26 December 1944* (Personal Experience of an 81mm Mortar Platoon Leader, Advanced Infantry Officers Course, The Infantry School, Fort Benning, Georgia, 1948–9)

Tully, Capt. John N., Doctrine, *Organization and Employment of the 4th Cavalry Group during World War II* (MA Thesis, US Army Command and General Staff College, Fort Leavenworth, Kansas, 1994)

Van Doren, Paul H., *Decision Making and Cognitive Analysis Track: A Historic Failure in the Social Domain using the December 16 1944 surprise attack in the Ardennes Forest as a Social Domain Case Study* (Research Paper to the 10th International Command and Control Research and Technology Symposium [ICCRTS] on the Future of C2, McLean, Virginia, 13–16 June, 2005)

Warden, Maj. Irving P., *Operations of Cannon Company, 110th Infantry (28th Infantry Division) in the Defense of Munchausen, Luxembourg, 16–19 December 1944* (Personal Experience of a Company Commander, Advanced Infantry Officers Course, Fort Benning, Georgia, 1948–9)

Waters, Lonn Augustine, *Secrecy, Deception and Intelligence Failure: Explaining Operational Surprise in War* (MSc Thesis, Massachusetts Institute of Technology, 2005)

Way, Capt. Everet C., *Operations of the 289th Infantry (75th Infantry Division) at Grandmenil, Belgium, 21 December 1944–2 January 1945* (Personal Experience of an Antitank Company Commander, Advanced Infantry Officers Course, Fort Benning, Georgia, 1946–7)

Weigel, Capt. Levene J., *Operations of the 1st Platoon, Company 'H', 422nd Infantry (106th Infantry Division) in the German Ardennes counteroffensive, 12–19 December 1944* (Personal Experience of a Platoon Leader, Advanced Infantry Officers Course, Fort Benning, Georgia, 1948–9)

Whitehead, Lt.-Col. Gary W., *Missed Opportunity: Reducing the Bulge* (US Army War College Strategy Research Project, Carlisle, Pennsylvania, 2001)

Wilbeck, Maj. Christopher W., *Swinging the Sledgehammer: The Combat Effectiveness of German Heavy Tank Battalions in World War II* (MA Thesis, US Army Command and General Staff College, Fort Leavenworth, Kansas, 2002)

Willis, Bob E., Jr, *The Measure of Battle: A Study of Combat Effectiveness in the US 4th Armored Division and the German Panzer Lehr Division in the ETO, July 1944 to December 1944* (MA Thesis, Hawaii Pacific University, 2003)

Wirtz, James J., *Explaining an Instance of Intrawar Intelligence failure: the American Military's Response to the 1968 Tet offensive* (Ph.D. Thesis, Columbia University, 1989)

Wright, Capt., David B., *Operations of the 1st Battalion, 110th Infantry (28th Infantry Division) in the vicinity of Hinercheid and Marnach, Luxembourg, 16–18 December 1944* (Personal Experience of a Battalion Operations Officer, Advanced Infantry Officers Course, Fort Benning, Georgia, 1948–9)

Published Sources:

Adams, John A., *The Battle for Western Europe, Fall 1944: An Operational Assessment* (Indiana University Press, 2010)

Adan, Gen. Avraham (Bren), *On the Banks of the Suez* (Presidio Press, 1980)

Addison, Col. John K., 'The Making of a World War II Battalion Commander', article in *Army Magazine*, Vol. 56/3 (Mar. 2006)

Addor, Don, *Noville, Outpost of Bastogne: My Last Battle* (Trafford Publishing, 2006)

Adkins, A. Z., Jr, *You Can't Get Much Closer Than This: Combat with Company 'H', 317th Infantry Regiment, 80th Division* (Casemate, 2005)

Agte, Patrick, *Jochen Peiper: Commander Panzer Regiment Leibstandarte* (J. J. Fedorowicz, 1999)

Alanbrooke, Field Marshal Lord, (ed. Alex Danchev and Daniel Todman), *War Diaries 1939–1945* (Weidenfeld and Nicolson, 2001)

Aldrich, Richard J., *Witness To War: Diaries of the Second World War in Europe and the Middle East* (Doubleday, 2004)

Alexander, Larry, *In the Footsteps of the Band of Brothers: A Return to Easy Company's Battlefields with Sgt. Forrest Guth* (New American Library, 2010)

Alkon, Paul K., *Winston Churchill's Imagination* (Bucknell University Press, 2006)

Allen, George R. and Peggy, *To Bastogne for the Christmas Holidays, 1944* (Published by the authors, 1994)

Allen, Col. Robert S., *Lucky Forward: The History of General George Patton's Third US Army* (Vanguard Press, 1947)

Allen, William Rodney, *Conversations with Kurt Vonnegut* (University Press of Mississippi, 1988)

Ambrose, Stephen E., *The Supreme Commander: The War Years of Dwight D. Eisenhower* (University Press of Mississippi, 1970)

——— 'Eisenhower and the Intelligence Community in World War II', article in the *Journal of Contemporary History*, Vol. 16/1 (Jan., 1981)

——— *Eisenhower: Soldier and President* (Simon & Schuster, 1991)

——— *Band of Brothers, E Company, 506th Regiment, 101st Airborne: From Normandy to Hitler's Eagle's Nest* (Simon & Schuster, 1992)

——— *D-Day, June 6, 1944: The Climactic Battle of World War II* (Simon & Schuster, 1994)

——— *Citizen Soldiers: The US Army from the Normandy Beaches to the Bulge to the Surrender of Germany, June 7, 1944–May 7, 1945* (Simon & Schuster, 1997)

——— *The Victors. The Men of World War II* (Simon & Schuster, 1998)

Anders, Dr Steven E., 'POL on the Red Ball Express', article in *Quartermaster Professional Bulletin* (Spring 1989)

Annan, Noel, *Changing Enemies* (HarperCollins, 1995)

Anon, *The Traveller's Guide Through Belgium, Or [A] New and Complete Geographical, Historical, and Picturesque Account of That Country With Information on Its Curiosities, Antiquities and Customs, Best Hotels, Etc. Etc., A Detailed Description of All Objects Worthy of Notice, And Principal Roads To Holland* (Wahlen, 1833)

——— *US Army Battle Casualties and Non Battle Deaths in World War II, Final Report, 7 December 1941–31 December 1946* (Prepared by Statistical and Accounting Branch, Office of the Adjutant General, Washington DC, 1947)

——— *The Psychological Warfare Division, Supreme Headquarters Allied Expeditionary Force. An Account of Its Operations in the Western European Campaign 1944–45* (SHAEF, Bad Homburg, October 1945)

Antal, John F., 'Decisive Leadership: Brigadier-General Bruce C. Clarke and the Battle of St. Vith', article in *Armor*, Vol. 102 (November–December 1993)

Arend, Guy Franz, *L'Offensive des Ardennes et la Bataille de Bastogne* (Bastogne Historical Center, 1985)

——— *The Battle for Bastogne, 'If You Don't Know What Nuts Means': A Chronology of the Battle for Bastogne with Comments* (Bastogne Historical Center, 1987)

Arn, Edward C., and Mushkat, Jerome (Editor), *Memoirs of a World War II Infantryman, 1940–1946* (University of Akron Press, 2006)

Arnold, James R., 'Battle of the Bulge', article in *Infantry*, No. 74 (Nov.–Dec. 1984)

——— *Ardennes 1944: Hitler's Last Gamble in the West* (Osprey, 1990)

Arnold-Foster, Mark, *The World at War* (Collins, 1973)

Arrington, Grady P., *Infantryman at the Front* (Vantage Press, 1959)

Asher, Dani, *The Egyptian Strategy for the Yom Kippur War: An Analysis* (McFarland & Co., 2009)

Astor, Gerald, *A Blood-Dimmed Tide: The Battle of the Bulge by the Men Who Fought It* (Dell Publishing, 1992)

——— *Terrible Terry Allen: Combat General of World War II. The Life of an American Soldier* (Presidio Press, 2003)

——— *Battling Buzzards: The Odyssey of the 517th Parachute Regimental Combat Team 1943–1945* (Random House, 2009)

Atkinson, Rick, *The Guns at Last Light: The War in Western Europe, 1944–1945* (Henry Holt and Co., 2013)

Austra, Kevin R., 'The Battle of the Bulge: The Secret Offensive', article in *Military Intelligence* (Jan.–Mar., 1991)

Axelrod, Alan, *Patton: A Biography* (Palgrave Macmillan, 2006)

Babcock, John B., *Taught to Kill: An American Boy's War from the Ardennes to Berlin* (Potomac Books, 2005)

Babcock, Robert O., *War Stories: Utah Beach to Pleiku: 4th Infantry Division* (St John's Press, Louisiana, 2001)

Babington Smith, Constance, *Evidence in Camera* (Chatto & Windus, 1957)

Baldridge, Robert C., *Victory Road. The World War II Memoir of an Artilleryman in the ETO* (Merriam Press, 1995)

Baldwin, William C., 'Engineers in the Battle of the Bulge' article in *Engineer* (1994); at: http://www.6thcorpscombatengineers.com/docs/Engineers/Engineers%20At%20The%20Bulge.pdf

Barron, Leo and Cygan, Don, *No Silent Night: The Christmas Battle for Bastogne* (New American Library, 2012)

Barnett, Corelli (ed.), *Hitler's Generals* (Weidenfeld & Nicolson, 1989)

Basden, Barry, *Crack! and Thump; With a Combat Infantry Officer in World War II* (Camroc Press, 2007)

Bauserman, John, *The Malmédy Massacre* (White Mane Publishers, 1995)

Beck, Alfred M., Bortz, Abe, Lynch, Charles W., Mayo, Lida, and Weld, Ralph F., *US Army in World War II: The Corps of Engineers: The War against Germany* (US Army Center of Military History, 1985)

Belchem, Maj.-Gen. David, *All in a Day's March* (Collins, 1978)

Bel, Germà, 'Against the Mainstream: Nazi Privatization in 1930s Germany', article in *Economic History Review* (2009)

Bell, Noël, *From the Beaches to the Baltic: The Story of the G Company, 8th Battalion, the Rifle Brigade During the Campaign in North-west Europe* (Gale & Polden, 1947)

Bennett, Ralph, *Ultra in the West* (Hutchinson, 1979)

Bergström, Christer, *The Ardennes 1944–1945: Hitler's Winter Offensive* (Bergstrom, 2014)

Berlin, Dr Robert H., *US Army World War II Corps Commanders: A Composite Biography* (Combat Studies Institute, Fort Leavenworth, 1989)

Beschloss, Michael, *The Conquerors: Roosevelt, Truman and the Destruction of Hitler's Germany 1941–1945* (Simon & Schuster, 2002)

Bied, Dan, *Dan Bied's 1945: A Remembrance* (Craftsman Press, Iowa, 1995)

Bietenholz, Peter G., *Historia and Fabula: Myths and Legends in Historical Thought from Antiquity to the Modern Age* (Brill, 1994)

Bigelow, Michael E., 'Big Business: Intelligence in Patton's Third Army', article in *Military Intelligence*, Vol. 18/2 (April–June 1992)

Bigland, Lt.-Col. T., *Bigland's War: War Letters of Tom Bigland 1941–5* (Published by the author, 1990)

Bilder, Michael, *A Foot Soldier for Patton: The Story of a 'Red Diamond' Infantryman with the U.S. Third Army* (Casemate, 2008)

Bishop, Chris, *German Infantry in WWII* (Zenith, 2008)

Blades, Brooke S., 'European Military Sites as Ideological Landscapes', article in *Historical Archaeology*, Vol. 37/3, *Remembering Landscapes of Conflict* (2003)

Blakeslee, Clarence, *A Personal Account of WWII by Draftee #35887149* (Self-published, 1998)

Blumberg, Corporal Nathan, *Charlie of 666: A Memoir of World War II: the Story of an Artillery Battery from Camp Bowie to Boston, Britain, the Battle of the Bulge, Bavaria and Beyond* (Wood Fire Ashes Press, 2000)

Blumenson, Martin, *United States Army in World War II, European Theater of Operations, Breakout and Pursuit* (Center of Military History, US Army, 1961)

——— 'Patton and Montgomery: Alike or Different?', article in *Army*, No. 22 (Jun. 1972)

——— *The Patton Papers: 1940–1945* (Houghton Mifflin, 1974)

——— *Patton: The Man behind the Legend, 1885–1945* (William Morrow & Co., 1985)

——— 'Bradley-Patton: World War II's "Odd Couple"', article in *Army* magazine, No. 35 (December 1985)

Blumentritt, Gen. Gunther, *Von Rundstedt: The Soldier and the Man* (Odhams Press, 1952)

Blunt, Roscoe C., Jr, *Inside the Battle of the Bulge: A Private Comes of Age* (Praeger, 1994)

——— *Foot Soldier: A Combat Infantryman's War in Europe* (Da Capo Press, 2001)

Bodden, Henry, *In the Footsteps of Valor* (H. E. B. Enterprises, 2011)

Bodnar, John, *The "Good War" in American Memory* (Johns Hopkins University Press, 2010)

Bolger, Maj. Daniel P., 'Zero Defects: Command Climate in First US Army, 1944–45', article in *Military Review* (May, 1991), pp.61–73

Bolling, Maj.-Gen. A.R. (Introduction), *Railsplitters: History of the 84th Infantry Division* (Stars & Stripes newspaper, 1945)

Boog, Horst, Krebs, Gerhard, and Vogel, Detlef, *Germany and the Second World War, Vol. VII: The Strategic Air War in Europe and the War in the West and East Asia, 1943–1944/5* (Oxford University Press, 2006)

Bookman, John T. and Powers, Stephen T., *March to Victory: Guide to World War II Battles and Battlefields from London to the Rhine* (Atlantic Books, rev. edn, 1994)

Booth, T. Michael and Spencer, Duncan, *Paratrooper. The Life of Gen. James M. Gavin* (Simon & Schuster, 1994)

Borch, Fred L., III, 'The Malmedy Massacre Trial: The Military Government Court Proceedings and the Controversial Legal Aftermath', article in *The Army Lawyer* (March 2012), pp.22–27

Bordewich, Fergus M., 'The Ambush That Changed History', article in *The Smithsonian Magazine* (September 2005)

Boritt, Gabor S., (ed.), *War Comes Again: Comparative Essays on the US Civil War and World War II* (Oxford University Press, 1995)

Bovy, Marcel, *La bataille de l'Amblève: les combats sur le front nord du saillant des Ardennes 16 décembre 1944–28 janvier 1945* (Les Amitiés Mosanes, 1950)

Bowen, Robert, *Fighting With the Screaming Eagles: With the 101st Airborne from Normandy to Bastogne* (Greenhill, 2001)

Boyden, Matthew, *Opera. The Rough Guide* (Rough Guides, 1999)

Bradley, Gen. Omar N., *A Soldier's Story* (Henry Holt, 1951)

——— and Blair, Clay, *A General's Life* (Simon & Schuster, 1983)

Bradlin, James W., 'The Forgotten Pennsylvanians', article in *Army* magazine, Vol. 37 (August 1987)

Braim, Paul F., *The Will to Win: the Life of General James A. Van Fleet* (Naval Institute Press, 2001)

Bredbenner, Edgar E. Jr., *80th 'Blue Ridge' Infantry Division* (Turner Publishing, 1999)

Brett-Smith, Richard, *Hitler's Generals* (Osprey, 1976)

Breuer, William B., *Bloody Clash at Sadzot: Hitler's Final Strike for Antwerp* (Berkley, 1990)

——— *Unexplained Mysteries of World War II* (J. Wiley, 1997)

Brian, Denis, *The Faces of Ernest Hemingway. Intimate Portraits of Ernest Hemingway by Those Who Knew Him* (Grafton, 1988)

Briggs, Asa, *Secret Days: Code-breaking in Bletchley Park* (Frontline, 2011)
Brinkley, Douglas, *Cronkite* (Harper, 2012)
Brokaw, Tom, *The Greatest Generation* (Random House, 1999)
Brotherton, Marcus, *A Company of Heroes: Personal Memories about the Real Band of Brothers and the Legacy They Left Us* (Berkley, 2010)
——— *Shifty's War: The Authorized Biography of Sergeant Darrell 'Shifty' Powers, the Legendary Sharpshooter from the Band of Brothers* (Berkley, 2011)
Brown, Anthony Cave, *Bodyguard of Lies* (Harper & Row, 1975)
Brown, James D. and Green, Michael, *War Stories of the Battle of the Bulge* (Zenith Press, 2010)
Brownlow, Donald Grey, *Panzer Baron: the Military Exploits of General Hasso von Manteuffel* (Christopher Publishing, 1975)
Bruce, David K. E., *OSS Against the Reich: The World War II Diaries of Colonel David K. E. Bruce*, (ed.) Nelson D. Lankford (Kent State University Press, 1991)
Bruning, John R., *The Battle of the Bulge: The Photographic History of an American Triumph* (Zenith Press, 2011)
Budraß, Lutz, Scherner, Jonas and Streb, Jochen, *Demystifying the German "Armament Miracle" During World War II: New Insights from the Annual Audits of German Aircraft Producers* (Discussion Paper No. 905, Economic Growth Center, Yale University, January 2005)
Buffetaut, Yves, *La bataille des Ardennes* (Militaria Magazine No. 39, Histoire et Collection, 2000)
——— *Le siège de Bastogne* (*Militaria* Magazine No. 42, Histoire et Collection, 2001)
——— *Ardennes 1944, Hitler peut-il encore gagner la guerre?* (*Bataille* Magazine No. 5, Histoire et Collection, 2004)
Bullock, Alan, *Hitler, A Study in Tyranny* (Odhams, 1952)
Buntin, Robert 'Bob' W., *A Long Way Home* (Alexander Books, 2008)
Burgett, Donald R., *Seven Roads to Hell: A Screaming Eagle at Bastogne* (Presidio Press, 1999)
Burke, Carolyn, *Lee Miller. On Both Sides of the Camera* (Bloomsbury, 2005)
Butcher, Capt. Harry C., USNR, *My Three Years with Eisenhower* (William Heinemann, 1946)
Butler, Ivan, *The War Film* (A. S. Barnes, 1974)
Bykofsky, Joseph, and Larson, Harold, *US Army in World War II: The Transportation Corps: Operations Overseas* (US Army Office of Chief of Military History, 1961)
Caddick-Adams, Peter, *Monty and Rommel: Parallel Lives* (Preface, 2011)
Cailloux, Lucien, Ardennes *1944: Pearl Harbor en Europe*, Vols. 1 and 2 (Lemaire, 1969–70)
Calvocoressi, Peter, *Top Secret Ultra* (Cassell, 1980)
Campbell, David R., *Fighting Encircled: A Study in Leadership* (US Army Center of Military History, 1987)
Campion, Martin C., 'War Games: World War II in the West', article in *The History Teacher*, Vol. 10/4 (August, 1977)
Carter, Col. William R., USAF, 'Air Power in the Battle of the Bulge: A Theater Campaign Perspective', article in *Airpower Journal* (Winter 1989)
Casey, William J., *The Secret War Against Hitler* (Regnery, 1988)
Cavanagh, William C. C., *Dauntless: a History of the 99th Infantry Division* (Taylor Publishing, 1994)

——— *Krinkelt-Rocherath: The Battle for the Twin Villages* (Christopher Publishing, Norwell, Mass., 1985); published in the UK as *The Battle East of Elsenborn and the Twin Villages* (Pen & Sword 2004)

——— *A Tour of the Bulge Battlefields* (Pen & Sword, 2001)

Cerami, Joseph R., 'Kasserine, the Bulge and AirLand Battle: Changes in the Tactical Role of Corps Artillery', article in *Field Artillery* (October 1989)

Chamberlain, Peter, and Doyle, Hilary, *Encyclopedia of German Tanks of World War Two: A Complete Illustrated Directory of German Battle Tanks, Armoured Cars, Self-Propelled Guns and Semi-Tracked Vehicles, 1933–1945* (Arms and Armour Press, 1978)

Chandler, Alfred D., and Ambrose, Stephen E., *The Papers of Dwight David Eisenhower: The War Years*, Volumes I-V (John Hopkins University Press, 1970)

Chernitsky, Dorothy, *Voices from the Foxholes: Men of the 110th Infantry relate personal accounts of what they experienced during World War II* (Chernitsky, 1991)

Christoffel, Edgar, *Krieg am Westwall 1944/45* (Helios, 2011)

Churchill, Rt. Hon. Winston S., *Great Contemporaries* (Thornton Butterworth, 1937; revised 1939)

——— *The Second World War, Vol I: The Gathering Storm* (Cassell, 1948)

——— *The Second World War, Vol. IV: The Hinge of Fate* (Cassell, 1951)

——— *The Second World War, Vol. VI: Triumph and Tragedy* (Cassell, 1954)

Cirillo, Dr Roger, *Ardennes-Alsace 1944–1945* (US Army Center of Military History, 1994)

Clark, Lloyd, *The Silent Battle: The British and the Ardennes Offensive, December 1944–January 1945* (Sutton Publishing, 2007)

Clarke, Gen. Bruce C., 'The Battle for St.-Vith: Armor in the Defense and Delay', article in *Armor*, Vol. 83 (November–December 1974)

Clausewitz, Carl von, *On War*, translated and edited Michael Howard and Peter Paret (Princeton University Press, 1989)

Clunn, Tony, *The Quest for the Lost Legions* (Savas Beatie, 2005)

Codman, Col. Charles R., *Drive* (Little, Brown, 1957)

Colbaugh, Jack, *The Bloody Patch: a True Story of the Daring 28th Infantry Division* (Vantage Press, 1973)

Colby, John, *War from the Ground Up: The Ninetieth Division in WWII* (Eakin Press, 1991)

Cole, Hugh M., *US Army in World War II: The European Theater of Operations. The Ardennes: The Battle of the Bulge* (US Army Center of Military History, 1965; new edn, 1993)

Colley, David P., *The Road to Victory: The Untold Story of Race and World War II's Red Ball Express* (Brassey's, 2000)

Collins, J. Lawton, *Lightning Joe: An Autobiography* (Louisiana State University Press, 1979)

Collins, Michael, and King, Martin, *Voices of the Bulge: Untold Stories from Veterans of the Battle of the Bulge* (Zenith Press, 2011)

——— *The Tigers of Bastogne: Voices of the 10th Armored Division in the Battle of the Bulge* (Casemate, 2013)

Compton, Lt. Lynn, and Brotherton, Marcus, *Call of Duty: My Life Before, During and After the Band of Brothers* (Berkley, 2008)

Conekin, Prof. Becky E., 'Lee Miller: Model, Photographer, and War Correspondent in Vogue, 1927–1953', article in *Fashion Theory: The Journal of Dress, Body & Culture*, Vol. 10/1 (Mar./Jun. 2006)

Connell, J. Mark, *Ardennes: The Battle of the Bulge – 1944–45* (Brassey's UK, 2003)

Connelly, Lt.-Col. Donald B., 'Harmon and Collins at the Bulge: Commiting the 2nd Armored Division, 22–28 December 1944', Chapter XVII in Combat Studies Institute Faculty, *Studies in Battle Command* (US Army Command and General Staff College, Fort Leavenworth, Kansas, 1996)

Connelly, Michael, *The Mortarmen* (Trafford Publishing, 2006)

Cooke, David, and Evans, Wayne, *Kampfgruppe Peiper at the Battle of the Bulge* (Stackpole, 2008)

Cooling, Benjamin Franklin (ed.), *Case Studies in the Development of Close Air Support* (Office of Air Force History, USAF, 1990)

Cooper, Belton Y., *Death Traps: The Survival of an American Armored Division in World War II* (Presidio Press, 2003)

Cosmas, Graham A., and Cowdrey, Albert E., *US Army in World War II: The Medical Service in the European Theater of Operations* (US Army Center of Military History, 1992)

Costley, Bill, *Oberscharführer, 6. SS-Gebirgs Division Nord: Pictorial Guide: Clothing, Arms, Gear, Personal Items, Vol. 1* (Costley, 1989)

——— *Platoon Sergeant, 80th Blue Ridge Infantry Division, Third US Army: Pictorial Guide: Clothing, Arms, Gear, Personal Items, Vol. 2* (Costley, 1990)

——— *Obergefreiter, Jäger Battalion Light Infantry Division, Pictorial Guide: Clothing, Arms, Gear, Personal Items, Vol. 3* (Costley, 1993)

——— *Gefreiter, 5th Parachute Division (Fallschirmjager), Pictorial Guide: Clothing, Arms, Gear, Personal Items, Vol. 4* (Costley, 1995)

Courtney, PFC Richard D., *Normandy to the Bulge: An American Infantry GI in Europe during World War II* (Southern Illinois University Press, 1996)

Cox, Edgar 'Ted', and Adams, Scott, *The Men of Fox Company: History and Recollections of Company 'F', 291st Infantry Regiment, Seventy-Fifth Infantry Division* (iUniverse, 2012)

Crain, Col. Charles L., *Stories from Three Wars: One Soldier's Memories* (Reprint Company, 2005)

Craven, Wesley Frank, and Cate, Maj. James Lea, *The Army Air Forces in World War II, Vol. 3, Europe: Argument to V-E Day, January 1944 to May 1945* (University of Chicago Press, 1951)

Creveld, Martin Van, *Supplying War: Logistics from Wallenstein to Patton* (Cambridge University Press, 1977)

——— *Fighting power: German and US Army Performance, 1939–1945* (Greenwood Press, 1982)

——— *Command in War* (Harvard University Press, 1985)

——— *The Art of War: War and Military Thought* (Orion Publishing, 2000)

Crookenden, Gen. Sir Napier, *The Battle of the Bulge 1944* (Ian Allen, 1980)

Cross, Robin, *The Battle of the Bulge 1944: Hitler's Last Hope* (Spellmount, 2002)

Crosswell, D. K. R., *Beetle: The Life of General Walter Bedell Smith* (The University Press of Kentucky, 2010)

Culver, Bruce, *Sdkfz 251 Half-Track 1939–45* (Osprey, 1998)

Cuppens, Gerd, *Massacre à Malmédy? Ardennes – 17 Décembre 1944: Le Kampfgruppe Peiper dans les Ardennes* (Editions Heimdal, 2001)

Curley, Charles D., *How a Ninety-day Wonder Survived the War: The Story of a Rifle Platoon Leader in the Second Indianhead Division during World War II* (Ashcraft Enterprises, 1991)

Currey, Cecil B., *Follow Me and Die. The Destruction of an American Division in World War II* (Military Heritage Press, 1984)

Daddis, Maj. Gregory A., 'Understanding Fear's Effect on Unit Effectiveness', article in *Military Review* (July–August 2004)

Darlow, Stephen, *Victory Fighters: The Veterans' Story* (Grub Street, 2005)

Davidson, William, *Cut Off. Behind Enemy Lines in the Battle of the Bulge with Two Small Children, Ernest Hemingway, and Other Assorted Misanthropes* (Stein & Day, 1972)

Davies, Howard P., *United States Infantry, Europe 1942–45, Key Uniform Guide* (Arms & Armour Press, 1974)

Davis, John, and Riffenburgh, Anne, *Up Close – A Scout's Story: From the Battle of the Bulge to the Siegfried Line* (Merriam Press, 2008)

Davis, M. Bedford, *Frozen Rainbows: The World War II Adventures of a Combat Medical Officer* (Meadowlark, 2003)

Decker, Maj. Jeffrey W., 'Logistics and Patton's Third Army: Lessons for Today's Logisticians', article in *US Air & Space Power Chronicles online journal*, March 2003

D'Este, Carlo, *Bitter Victory: The Battle for Sicily July–August 1943* (Collins, 1988)

——— *Patton: A Genius for War* (HarperCollins, 1995)

——— *Eisenhower: A Soldier's Life* (Henry Holt and Co., 2002)

——— *Dec 16 1944: Ardennes Offensive Begins, an "Abysmal Failure of Allied Intelligence"* online article at www.commandposts.com, 16 December 2012

DeFelice, Jim, *Omar Bradley: General at War* (Regnery History, 2011)

'World War II Intelligence: The Last 10 Years' Work Reviewed', article in *Defense Analysis*, Vol. 3/2 (1987) Special Issue: Intelligence

De Guingand, Gen. Sir Francis, *Operation Victory* (Hodder and Stoughton, 1947)

Delaforce, Patrick, *The Battle of the Bulge: Hitler's Final Gamble* (Longman, 2006)

De Lee, Nigel, *Voices From the Battle of the Bulge* (David & Charles, 2004)

Delvaux, Jean-Michel, *La bataille des Ardennes autour de Celles* (Delvaux, 2004)

——— *La bataille des Ardennes autour de Rochefort, Vols. 1 and 2* (Delvaux, 2004)

De Meyer, Stefan, Haasler, Timm, MacDougall, Roddy, Weber, Hans, and Vosters, Simon, *Duel in the Mist: Kampfgruppe Peiper, Stourmont, December 19th, 1944. Vol. 1: The Leibstandarte during the Ardennes Offensive* (AFV Modeller, 2007)

Dermience, Victor, *Bataille des Ardennes, 1944–1945: Le Carrefour Sanglant: Libramont-Chevigny, Saint-Hubert, Sainte-Ode* (Dermience, Bruxelles, 1995)

De Ruyter, Jacqueline and Rob, *Ardennen Poteau '44 Battlefield Guide* (Ardennen Poteau '44 Museum, 2000)

Devers, General Jacob L., *Report on Army Ground Forces Activities, World War II* (Office of the Commanding General, Army Ground Forces, 1946)

Dieckhoff, Gerhard, *3. Infanterie-Division (mot.), 3. Panzergrenadier-Division 1939–1945* (E. Börries Druck und Verlag, 1960)

Dietrich, Steve E., 'The Professional Reading of General George S. Patton, Jr.', article in *Journal of Military History*, Vol. 53 (October 1989)

Dipietro, Francis, *Veteran of the Ardennes: The World War II Letters Home of PFC Francis Charles DiPietro* (iUniverse, 2006)

Doherty, Joseph C., *The Shock of War: Unknown Battles that Ruined Adolph Hitler's Plan for a Second Blitzkrieg in the West, December–January, 1944–45* (Vert Milon Press, 1995)

Dorman, Angelia Hardy, *Reflections on the Human Legacy of War: Martha Gellhorn in Europe 1943–1945*, essay at http://home.nwi.net/~dorman/angie/gell2.htm

Doren, Paul H. Van, 'A Historic Failure in the Social Domain (Social Domain case study using the 16 December 1944 surprise attack in the Ardennes Forest)', paper given at the Decision Making and Cognitive Analysis Track, 10th International Command and Control Research and Technology Symposium, McLean, Virginia, 13–16 June 2005.

Doubler, Michael D., *Closing with the Enemy: How GIs Fought the War in Europe, 1944–1945* (University Press of Kansas, 1994)

Doughty, Robert Allan, *The Breaking Point: Sedan and the Fall of France, 1940* (Archon, 1990)

Dougherty, Maj. Kevin, 'Oscar Koch: An Unsung Hero Behind Patton's Battles', article in *Military Intelligence Professional Bulletin* (April–June 2002), pp. 64–6.

Downing, David, *The Devil's Virtuosos: German Generals at War, 1940–5* (St Martins Press, 1977)

Downing, Taylor, *Spies in the Sky. The Secret Battle for Aerial Intelligence During World War II* (Little, Brown, 2011)

Doyle, Hilary L., and Jentz, Thomas L., *Panzerkampfwagen IV Ausf. G, H and J 1942–45* (Osprey, 2001)

Draper, Sgt. Theodore, *The 84th Infantry Division in The Battle of the Ardennes, December 1944–January 1945* (Historical Section, 84th Infantry Division, 1945)

Dugdale, Jeff, *Panzer Divisions, Panzergrenadier Divisions, Panzer Brigades of the Army and the Waffen SS in the West: Autumn 1944–February 1945, Ardennes and Nordwind, Their Detailed and Precise Strengths and Organisations* (Military Press, 2003)

Dupuy, Colonel R. Ernest, *Lion in the Way: The 106th St. Vith Infantry Division in World War II* (Infantry Journal Press, Washington DC, 1949)

Dupuy, Col. Trevor N., Bongard, David L., and Anderson, Richard C., *Hitler's Last Gamble: The Battle of the Bulge, December 1944–January 1945* (HarperCollins, 1994)

Dworschak, Thomas W., *Hitler's Watch on the Rhine: The Battle of the Bulge* (Land Warfare Papers No. 12, Institute of Land Warfare/Association of the US Army, 1992)

Egger, Bruce E., and Otts, Lee McMillian, *'G' Company's War: Two Personal Accounts of the Campaigns in Europe, 1944–1945* (University of Alabama Press, 1992)

Ehrman, John, *Grand Strategy, Volume 6: October 1944–August 1945* (HMSO, 1956)

Eisenhower, Gen. Dwight D., *Report by Supreme Commander to the Combined Chiefs of Staff on Operations in Europe of the Allied Expeditionary Force, 6 June 1944 to 8 May 1945* (Government Printing Office, 1946)

——— *Crusade in Europe* (Doubleday, 1948)

——— (ed. Alfred D. Chandler, Jr), *The Papers of Dwight David Eisenhower. The War Years*, Vols. IV and V (Johns Hopkins University Press, both 1970)

Eisenhower, John S. D., *The Bitter Woods: The Battle of the Bulge* (G. P. Putnam's Sons, 1969)

——— *Strictly Personal* (Doubleday, 1974)

Ellis, Maj. L.F., and Warhurst, Lt.-Col. A.E., *History of the Second World War: Victory in the West, Vol. II: The Defeat of Germany* (HMSO, 1968)

Ellis, William Donohue, and Cunningham, Jr., Thomas J., *Clarke of St. Vith: The Sergeants' General* (Dillon/Liederbach, 1974)

Elmhirst, Air Marshal Sir Thomas, 'Air Reconnaissance – its Purpose and Value', article in the *Royal United Services Institution Journal*, Vol. 97/585 (1952)

Elstob, Peter, *Bastogne: the Road Block* (Ballantine Books, 1968)

——— *Hitler's Last Offensive* (Macmillan, 1971)

Engels, Col. Emile, *Ardennes 1944–1945: Guide du Champ de Bataille* (Racine, 1994)

——— *Bastogne: Trente Jours sous la Neige et le Feu* (Racine, 1994)

English, John A., *Patton's Peers: The Forgotten Allied Field Army Commanders of the Western Front, 1944–45* (Stackpole, 2009)

Essame, Maj.-Gen. Hubert, *Patton: A Study in Command* (Batsford, 1973)

Etlin, R.A. (ed.), *Art, Culture and Media under the Third Reich* (University of Chicago Press, 2002)

Evans, Harold, *The American Century* (Jonathan Cape, 1998)

Evans, Richard J., *The Third Reich in Power: 1933–1939* (Penguin, 2006)

Farago, Ladislas, *Patton: Ordeal and Triumph* (Astor-Honor Inc., 1963)

Featherstone, Fred E., *118th Infantry Regiment: World War II* (Privately printed, 1996)

Felix, Charles Reis, *Crossing the Sauer: A Memoir of World War II* (Burford Books, 2002)

Ferguson, Carl E., Sr, *Ardennes-Alsace: One Soldier's Story* (Privately printed, 1999)

Fessler, Diane Burke, *No Time for Fear: Voices of American Military Nurses in World War II* (Michigan State University Press, 1997)

Fest, Joachim C., *Hitler* (Weidenfeld & Nicolson, 1974)

Fey, Will, *Armor Battles of the Waffen SS 1943–45* (Stackpole Books, 2003)

Finch, Lieutenant-Colonel John R., and Mordica, Major George J., 'Miracles: A Platoon's Heroic Stand at Lanzerath', article in *Combined Arms in Battle Since 1939* (US Army Command and General Staff College Press, 1992)

Fischer, Thomas, *Soldiers of the Leibstandarte: SS-Brigadeführer Wilhelm Mohnke and 62 Soldiers of Hitler's Elite Division* (J. J. Fedorowicz, 2008)

Fischer, Klaus P., *Hitler and America* (University of Pennsylvania Press, 2011)

Fitzharris, Joseph C., *Patton's Fighting Bridge Builders: Company 'B', 1303rd Engineer General Service Regiment* (Texas A & M University Press, 2007)

Fleischer, Wolfgang, *Das letzte Jahr des deutschen Heeres 1944–1945* (Dörfler, 2007)

Fleig, Raymond E., *707th Tank Battalion in World War II: Northern France, Rhineland, Ardennes, Central Europe* (Privately printed, 1993)

Flynn, Alice M., *Unforgettable: The Biography of Captain Thomas J. Flynn* (Sky Blue Publishing, 2011)

Foley, Charles, *Commando Extraordinary: Otto Skorzeny* (Longmans, Green, 1954)

Foley, William, *Visions from a Foxhole: A Rifleman in Patton's Ghost Corps* (Presidio Press, 2004)

Folkestad, William B., *The View from the Turret: The 743rd Tank Battalion during World War II* (White Mane, 1996)

Forty, Lt.-Col. George, *Patton's Third Army at War* (Ian Allan, 1978)

——— *The Armies of George S. Patton* (Arms and Armour, 1996)

——— *Tank Commanders: Knights of the Modern Age* (Firebird, 1998)

——— *The Reich's Last Gamble: The Ardennes Offensive, December 1944* (Cassell, 2000)

Fox, Don M., *Patton's Vanguard: The United States Army Fourth Armored Division* (McFarland & Co., 2007)

Francard, Michel et Moërynck, Robert, *Le Mémorial du Mardasson à Bastogne* (Musée de la Parole en Ardenne, 2005)

Francois, Dominique, *507th Parachute Infantry Regiment: A Forgotten Regiment: Normandie, Ardennes, Allemagne* (Heimdal, 2002)

——— *508th Parachute Infantry Regiment: Red Devils: Normandy – Ardennes – Germany* (Heimdal, 2003)

Frankel, Nat, and Smith, Larry, *Patton's Best: An Informal History of the 4th Armored Division* (Hawthorn Books, 1978)
Franks, Norman L. R., *The Battle of the Airfields: 1st January 1945* (William Kimber, 1982)
Frieser, Oberst Karl-Heinz, *The Blitzkrieg Legend: The 1940 Campaign in the West* (Naval Institute Press, 2005)
Fuller, John F., *Thor's Legions: Weather Support to the US Air Force and Army, 1937–1987* (American Meteorological Society, 1990)
Furbringer, Herbert, *9. SS-Panzer-Division Hohenstaufen* (Editions Heimdal, 1984)
Fussell, Paul, *Wartime: Understanding and Behavior in the Second World War* (Oxford University Press, 1989)
——— *The Boys' Crusade: The American Infantry in Northwestern Europe, 1944–1945* (Modern Library, 2003)
Gabel, Dr Christopher R., *Seek, Strike, and Destroy: US Army Tank Destroyer Doctrine in World War II* (Leavenworth Papers No. 12, Combat Studies Institute, 1985)
Gabel, Kurt, *The Making of a Paratrooper: Airborne Training and Combat in World War* II (University Press of Kansas, 1990)
Gaffey, Maj.-Gen. Hugh J. (Introduction), *The 4th Armored: From the Beach to Bastogne* (Divisional History booklet, *Star & Stripes* newspaper, 1945)
Gantter, Raymond, *Roll Me Over: An Infantryman's World War II* (Presidio Press, 1997)
Ganz, A. Harding, 'Breakthrough to Bastogne', article in *Leadership Handbook for the Armor Officer: Thoughts on Leadership* (US Armor School, Fort Knox, Kentucky, 1986)
——— 'Patton's Relief of General Wood', article in *Journal of Military History*, Vol. 53 (July 1989)
Ganzer, Karl Richard, *Das deutsche Führergesicht; 200 Bildnisse deutscher Kämpfer und Wegsucher aus zwei Jahrtausenden* (J. F. Lehmann, München, 1937)
Garnett, David, *The Secret History of the Political Warfare Executive 1939–1945* (St Ermin's Press, 2002)
Garrison, Gene, *Unless Victory Comes: Combat with a Machine Gunner in Patton's Third Army* (Casemate, 2004)
Gaul, Roland, and Force, Edward, *The Battle of the Bulge in Luxembourg: The Southern Flank, 1: December 1944–January 1945*, Vol. I: *The Germans* (Schiffer Publishing, 1994)
——— *The Battle of the Bulge in Luxembourg: The Southern Flank December 1944–January 1945*, Vol. II: *The Americans* (Schiffer Publishing, 1995)
Gavin, Gen. James M., *On to Berlin: Battles of an Airborne Commander 1943–1946* (Viking Press, 1978)
Gay, Timothy M., *Assignment to Hell: The War Against Nazi Germany with Correspondents Walter Cronkite, Andy Rooney, A.J. Liebling, Homer Bigart, and Hal Boyle* (New American Library, 2012)
Gellhorn, Martha, *The Face of War* (Rupert Hart-Davis, 1967)
Geocart, *1:100,000 Atlas of Belgium & Luxembourg* (Geocart, 1998)
Gersdorff, Generalmajor Rudolf Christoph Freiherr von, *Soldat im Untergang* [Soldier during the Downfall] (Ullstein, 1982)
Giambroni, Sergeant Andy, *Odor of War* (Trafford Publishing, 2006)
Gilbert, Felix, *Hitler Directs His War* (Oxford University Press, 1951)
Gilbert, James L., and Finnegan, John P. (eds.), *US Army Signals Intelligence in World War II. A Documentary History* (Center of Military History, United States Army, Washington, DC, 1993)

Gilbert, Sir Martin, *Winston S. Churchill, Vol. VII: The Road to Victory 1941–1945* (Heinemann, 1986)

Giles, Janice Holt, *The GI Journal of Sergeant Giles* (Houghton Mifflin, 1965)

——— *The Damned Engineers* (US Army Corps of Engineers Historical Division, 1985)

Girbig, Werner, *Six Months to Oblivion: the Defeat of the Luftwaffe Fighter Force over the Western Front, 1944/1945* (Schiffer Publishing, 1989)

Goldstein, Donald M., Dillon, Katherine V., and Wenger, J. Michael, *Nuts! The Battle of the Bulge* (Brassey's, 2003)

Gooderson, Ian, 'Allied Fighter-Bombers Versus German Armour in North West Europe 1944–1945: Myths and Realities', article in *Journal of Strategic Studies*, 14/2 (June 1991)

Goolrick, William K., and Tanner, Ogden, *Battle of the Bulge* (Time/Life Books, 1979)

Goodrick-Clarke, Nicholas, *Hitler's Priestess: Savitri Devi, the Hindu-Aryan myth, and Neo-Nazism* (New York University Press, 1998)

——— *Black Sun: Aryan Cults, Esoteric Nazism and the Politics of Identity* (New York University Press, 2001)

Gordon, John, 'The Gunners of Bastogne', article in the *Field Artillery Journal*, No. 54 (September–October, 1986)

Gould, Jonathan S., *The OSS and the London 'Free Germans': Strange Bedfellows*, historical essay at CIA website, https://www.cia.gov/library/center-for-the-study-of-intelligence/csi-publications/csi-studies/studies/vol46no1/article03.html

Greelen, Lothar van, *Verkauft und verraten: Westfront 1944* [*Sold and Betrayed: Western Front, 1944*] (Welsermühl, 1963)

Green, Michael and Gladys, *Patton and the Battle of the Bulge* (Zenith Press, 1999)

——— and Brown, James D., *War Stories of the Battle of the Bulge* (Zenith Press, 2010)

Green, Roger G., and four other authors, *Human Factors for Aircrew* (Avebury Aviation, 1996)

Greenfield, Kent Roberts, *US Army in World War II: The Organization of the Ground Combat Troops* (Office of the Chief of Military History, Department of the Army, 1947)

——— (ed.), *US Army in World War II, Pictorial Record: The War Against Germany: Europe and Adjacent Areas* (Center for Military History, 1951)

Grégoire, Gérard, *Les Panzers de Peiper Face à L'U.S. Army* (Published by the author, 1986)

Greil, Lothar, *Oberst der Waffen-SS Joachim Peiper und der Malmedy-Prozess* (Schild, 1980)

Greinal, Renee, *Christmas 1944 at Isle-la-Hesse, Bastogne* (Ceuterick/Louvain, 1965)

Grossjohann, Maj. Georg, *Five Years, Four Fronts: The War Years of Georg Grossjohann - Memoir of a German Soldier 1939–45* (Aberjona Press, 2001)

Grow, Major General R. W. (Introduction), *Brest to Bastogne: The Story of the 6th Armored Division* (Stars & Stripes, Information and Education Division, Special and Information Services, ETOUSA Paris, *c.* 1945)

Guarnere, William, Heffron, Edward, and Post, Robyn, *Brothers in Battle, Best of Friends* (Berkley, 2008)

Guderian, Heinz, *Panzer Leader* (Michael Joseph, 1952)

Guderian, Heinz Günther, *From Normandy to the Ruhr: With the 116th Panzer Division in World War II* (Aberjona Press, 2001)

Gurley, Franklin Louis, 'Policy Versus Strategy: The Defense of Strasbourg in Winter 1944–5', article in *The Journal of Military History*, Vol. 58/3 (July 1994)

Haasler, Timm, *Hold the Westwall: The History of Panzer Brigade 105, September 1944* (Stackpole, 2011)

——— and MacDougall, Roddy, Weber, Hans, and Vosters, Simon, *Duel in the Mist, Vol. 2: The Leibstandarte during the Ardennes Offensive* (Panzerwrecks, 2012)

Hadden, Alexander H., *Not Me! The World War II Memoir of a Reluctant Rifleman* (Merriam Press, 1997)

Hahn, Fritz, *Waffen und Geheimwaffen des Deutschen Heeres: 1933–1945* (Bernard & Graefe, 1986)

Hamilton, Nigel, *Monty: The Field-Marshal, 1944–1976* (Hamish Hamilton, 1986)

Handel, Michael I. (ed.), *Leaders and Intelligence* (Frank Cass, 1989)

Hanford, William B., *A Dangerous Assignment: An Artillery Forward Observer in World War II* (Stackpole Books, 2008)

Harclerode, Peter, *'Go To It': The Illustrated History of the 6th Airborne Division* (Caxton, 1990)

Harmon, Gen. Ernest N., MacKaye, Milton, and MacKaye, William Ross, *Combat Commander: Autobiography of a Soldier* (Prentice Hall, 1970)

Harrison, Allie Cleveland, *Unsung Valor: A GI's Story of World War II* (University Press of Mississippi, 2000)

Hart, Stephen A., *Colossal Cracks: Montgomery's 21st Army Group in Northwest Europe, 1944–45* (Stackpole, 2007)

Hartman, J. Ted, *Tank Driver: With the 11th Armored from the Battle of the Bulge to VE Day* (Indiana University Press, 2003)

Hartmann, Christian, *Halder: Generalstabschef Hitlers, 1938–1942* (Schöningh, 2010)

Hassell, Agostino von, and MacRae, Sigrid, *Alliance of Enemies: The Untold Story of the Secret American and German Collaboration to End World War II* (St Martin's Griffin, 2008)

Hastings, Max, (with pictures by George Stevens), *Victory in Europe* (Weindefeld and Nicolson, 1985)

——— *Armageddon: The Battle for Germany 1944–45* (Macmillan, 2004)

Hatfield, Thomas M., *Rudder: From Leader to Legend* (Texas A & M University, 2011)

Hays, Robert, *Patton's Oracle: Gen. Oscar Koch, as I Knew Him* (CreateSpace, 2013)

Hechler, Maj. Kenneth W., *The Enemy Side of the Hill: The 1945 Background on the Interrogation of German Commanders* (Historical Division, Special Staff, US Army, 1949)

——— *Holding the Line: The 51st Engineer Combat Battalion and the Battle of the Bulge, December 1944–January 1945* (US Army Corps of Engineers Historical Division, 1988)

——— *The Bridge at Remagen: The Amazing Story of March 7, 1945* (new edition Presidio Press, 2005)

Heefner, Wilson Allen, *Patton's Bulldog: the Life and Service of General Walton H. Walker* (White Mane, 2002)

Heiber, Helmut (ed.), *Hitlers Lagebesprechungen* (Institut für Zeitgeschichte, 1962)

Heintz, Joss, *In the Perimeter of Bastogne* (Omnia, 1965)

Hemingway, Ernest, *Across the River and into the Trees* (Charles Scribner's Sons, 1950)

Herman, Arthur, *Freedom's Forge: How American Business Produced Victory in World War II* (Random House, 2012)

Hérubel, Michel, *La Bataille des Ardennes* (Presses de la Cité, 1979)

——— *La bataille des Ardennes 1944–1945* (Gazette des Uniformes, No. 18, 2004)

Heyl, John D., 'The Construction of the Westwall, 1938: An Exemplar for National Socialist Policymaking', article in *Central European History*, Vol. 14/1 (March 1981)

Hewitt, Robert L., *Workhorse of the Western Front: The Story of the 30th Infantry Division* (Infantry Journal Press, 1946)

Higdon, Thomas J., and (ed.), Quintana, J. T., *Personal Diary of SSgt. Thomas J. Higdon, Jr.* (Amazon Digital, 2011)

Higgins, Maj. George A., 'German and US Operational Art: A Contrast in Maneuver', article in *Military Review*, Vol. LXV/10 (October 1985)

Hinsley, F. H. Thomas, E. E. Simkins, C. A. G., and Ransom, C. F. G., *British Intelligence in the Second World War: Its Influence on Strategy and Operations, Vol. 3 Part II* (Cambridge University Press, 1988)

Hinsley, F. H., *Official History of the Second World War: British Intelligence in the Second World War* (HMSO, 1993)

Hirshson, Stanley P., *General Patton: A Soldier's Life* (HarperCollins, 2003)

Hitler, Adolf, *Mein Kampf* (Hutchinson, 1969 English edition)

Hobar, Basil J., 'The Ardennes 1944: Intelligence Failure or Deception Success?', article in *Military Intelligence*, No. 10 (October–December, 1984)

Hogan, Jr., David W., *A Command Post at War: First Army Headquarters in Europe, 1943–1945* (US Army Center of Military History, Washington, DC, 2000)

Hoffa, Harlan, *The Myth of Memory* (Privately printed, 1979)

Hofmann, Dr George F., *Super Sixth: The History of the 6th Armored Division in World War II* (Sixth Armored Division Association, 1975)

——— *Through Mobility We Conquer: The Mechanization of U.S. Cavalry* (University Press of Kentucky, 2006)

Holmes, Richard, *The World at War: The Landmark Oral History from the Previously Unpublished Archives* (Ebury Press, 2007)

Horrocks, General Sir Brian, *A Full Life* (Collins, 1960)

——— *Corps Commander* (Sidgwick and Jackson, 1977)

Horstmann, Harry, *Die Ardennenoffensive 1944 – Kampfkraft, Organisation und militärische Leistung* (GRIN Verlag, 2007)

——— *In den Ardennen 1944: Die letzte Offensive der Wehrmacht* (Books on Demand, 2008)

Houston, Donald E., *Hell on Wheels: The 2nd Armored Division* (Presidio Press, 1977)

Houston, Robert J., *D-Day to Bastogne: A Paratrooper Recalls World War II* (Exposition Press, 1980)

Michael Howard, *British Intelligence in the Second World War*, Vol. 5 (HMSO, 1990)

Hoyt, Edwin P., *The GI's War. American Soldiers in Europe during World War II* (Da Capo, 1988)

——— *Goering's War* (Robert Hale, 1990)

Hughes, Howard, *When Eagles Dared: The Filmgoers' History of World War II* (I. B. Taurus, 2012)

Hughes, Thomas Alexander, *Overlord: General Pete Quesada and the Triumph of Tactical Air Power in World War II* (Free Press, 1995)

Humphrey, Robert E., *Once Upon a Time in War: The 99th Division in World War II* (University of Oklahoma Press, 2008)

Hunnicutt, R. P., *Sherman: A History of the American Medium Tank* (Presidio Press, 1976)

——— *Stuart: A History of the American Light Tank* (Presidio Press, 1992)

——— *Half-Track: A History of American Semi-Tracked Vehicles* (Presidio Press, 2001)

Hyams, Jay, *War Movies* (Gallery Books, 1984)

Hynes, Samuel, Matthews, Anne, and Sorel, Nancy Caldwell, *Reporting World War II: American Journalism 1938–1946* (Library of America, 2001)

Idzikowski, Frank J., *Shadows of Slaughterhouse Five. Recollections and Reflections of the American Ex-POWs of Schlachthof Fünf* (iUniverse, 2008)

Ingersoll, Ralph, *Top Secret* (Harcourt, Brace, 1946)

Irgang, Frank, *Etched in Purple: One Soldier's War in Europe* (Caxton Press, Idaho, 1949; Potomac Books, 2008)

Irving, David, *Hitler's War* (Hodder & Stoughton, 1977),

——— *The Secret Diaries of Hitler's Doctor* (Sidgwick & Jackson, 1983)

Irwin, John P., *Another River, Another Town: A Teenage Tank Gunner Comes of Age in Combat, 1945* (Random House, 2003)

Irzyk, Brig.-Gen. Albin F., *He Rode up Front for Patton* (Ivy House Publishing, 1996)

——— *Gasoline to Patton* (Elderberry Press, 2004)

Isaacson, Walter, *Kissinger: A Biography* (Simon & Schuster, 1992)

Jackson, Kathi, *They Called Them Angels: American Military Nurses of World War II* (Bison Books, 2006)

Jacobsen, H. A., and Rohwer, J., *Decisive Battle of World War II: The German View* (André Deutsch, 1965)

James, D. Clayton, *A Time for Giants: Politics of the American High Command in World War II* (Franklin Watts, 1987)

James, Robert Rhodes (ed.), *Winston S. Churchill: His Complete Speeches, 1897–1963*, Vol. VII, *1943–1949* (Chelsea House Publishers, 1974)

Janes, Terry D., *Patton's Troubleshooters* (Opinicus Publishing, 1988)

Jeffers, Harry Paul, *Taking Command: General J. Lawton Collins from Guadalcanal to Utah Beach and Victory in Europe* (New American Library, 2009)

Jensen, Marvin, *Strike Swiftly! The 70th Tank Battalion from North Africa to Normandy to Germany* (Presidio Press, 1997)

Jewett, Dean F., *Hinder forward: The 168th Engineer Combat Battalion in ZI and ETO from May 1943 through November 1945* (Penobscot Press, 2001)

Johnson, Maj. Gerald K., 'Black Soldiers of the Ardennes', article in *Soldiers* magazine, (February 1981)

Jones, Grant, 'Education of the Supreme Commander: The Theoretical Underpinnings of Eisenhower's Strategy in Europe, 1944–45', article in *War & Society*, Vol. 30/2 (August 2011)

Jordan, David, *Battle of the Bulge. The First 24 hours* (Greenhill, 2003)

Jordan, Jonathan W., 'Battle Command: Bradley and Ridgway in the Battle of the Bulge', article in *Military Review*, Vol. 80/2 (Mar/Apr. 2000)

——— *Brothers, Rivals, Victors: Eisenhower, Patton, Bradley and the Partnership that Drove the Allied Conquest in Europe* (New American Library, 2011)

Joy, Dean P., *Sixty Days in Combat: An Infantryman's Memoir of World War II in Europe* (Presidio Press, 2004)

Jung, Hermann, *Die Ardennen-Offensive 1944/45: Ein Beispiel für die Kriegführung Hitlers* (Musterschmidt, 1971)

Kane, Steve, *The 1st SS Panzer Division in the Battle of the Bulge* (International Graphics Corporation, 1982)

Kater, M. H., *The Twisted Muse: Musicians and their Music in the Third Reich* (Oxford University Press, 1997)

Keane, Michael, *Patton: Blood, Guts, and Prayer* (Regnery History, 2012)

Keefer, Louis E., *Scholars in Foxholes: The Story of the Army Specialized Training Programme in World War Two* (McFarland & Co., 1988)

Kelly, Jr., Col. Thomas P., and Goldstein, Lt.-Col. Elliott, *The Fightin' 589th* (1st Books, 2001)

Kemp, Col. Harry M., *The Regiment: Let the Citizens Bear Arms! A Narrative History of the 109th Infantry Regiment during WWII* (Nortex Press, 1990)

Kershaw, Alex, *The Longest Winter: The Battle of the Bulge and the Epic Story of World War II's Most Decorated Platoon* (Da Capo Press, 2004)

Kershaw, Ian, *Hitler, Vol. 1: 1889–1936: Hubris* (Allen Lane, 1998)

——— *The End: The Defiance and Destruction of Hitler's Germany, 1944–1945* (Penguin Press, 2011)

Kershaw, Robert, *Tank Men: The Human Story of Tanks at War* (Hodder & Stoughton, 2008)

King, Benjamin, and Kutta, Timothy J., *Impact: The History of Germany's V-weapons in World War II* (Da Capo Press, 1998); alternative title: *Hammer of the Reich*

Kingseed, Cole C., *Old Glory Stories: American Combat Leadership in World War II* (Naval Institute Press, 2006)

Kirkpatrick, Lyman B., *Combat Intelligence: A Comparative Evaluation: A former G-2 Officer at Army Group Level Analyzes Sources of Battlefield Intelligence*, historical essay at CIA website, https://www.cia.gov/library/center-for-the-study-of-intelligence/kent-csi/vol5no4/html/v05i4a05p_0001.htm

Knightley, Phillip, *The First Casualty – From the Crimea to Vietnam: The War Correspondent as Hero, Propagandist and Mythmaker* (André Deutsch, 1975)

Koch, Brig.-Gen. Oscar W., and Hays, Robert G., *G-2: Intelligence for Patton* (Schiffer Publishing, 2004)

Koessler, Maximilian, 'International Law on Use of Enemy Uniforms as a Stratagem and the Acquittal in the Skorzeny Case', article in the *Missouri Law Review*, Vol. 16 (1959)

Koschorrek, Gunter K., *Blood Red Snow* (Greenhill, 2002)

Koskimaki, George, *The Battered Bastards of Bastogne: The 101st Airborne and the Battle of the Bulge, December 19, 1944–January 17, 1945* (One Hundred First Airborne Division Association, 1994)

Koyen, Kenneth, 'Combat Photographer Robert Capa and the Battle of the Bulge', article in *History of Photography*, Vol. 25/4 (Winter 2001)

Krehbiel, Bill J., *The Pride of Willing and Able: a Chronology of Company 'L', Third Battalion, 319th Infantry, 80th Infantry Division in World War II* (Krehbiel, 1992)

Kreis, John F. (ed.), *Piercing the Fog: Intelligence and Army Air Forces Operations in World War II* (US Air Force Historical Studies Office, Washington, DC, 1996)

Kreisle, James E., *Forty Years After, 1944–1984* (Published by the author, 1992)

Kroener, Bernhard R., Müller, Rolf-Dieter, and Umbreit, Hans, *Das deutsche Reich und der Zweite Weltkrieg*. Vol. 5/2: *Organisation und Mobilisierung des deutschen Machtbereichs 1942–45* (Militarygeschichtlichen Forschungsamt/ Deutsche Verlags 2003)

Kunz, William J., *Third and Ten: A Field Artillery Forward Observer's Account of Actions with the US Army's 3rd Infantry Division during WWII in North Africa, Sicily, Italy, France, Germany and Austria* (BookSurge Publishing, 2009)

Kurowski, Franz, *Elite Panzer Strike Force: Germany's Panzer Lehr Division in World War II* (Stackpole, 2011)

La Longue Vue, *Bataille des Ardennes: Itineraires du Souvenir* (La Longue Vue, Bruxelles, 1994)

Lamb, Richard, *Montgomery in Europe 1943–45: Success or Failure?* (Buchan & Enright, 1983)

Lande, D. A., *I Was with Patton: First-Person Accounts of WWII in George S. Patton's Command* (Zenith Press, 2002)

Langer, Walter C., *The Mind of Adolf Hitler* (Secker & Warburg, 1973)

Larew, Karl G., 'From Pigeons to Crystals: The Development of Radio Communication in US Army Tanks in World War II', article in *The Historian*, Vol. 67/4 (Winter 2005)

Larrabee, Eric, *Commander in Chief. Franklin Delano Roosevelt, His Lieutenants & Their War* (Harper & Row, 1987)

Lauer, Maj.-Gen. Walter E., *Battle Babies: the Story of the 99th Infantry Division in World War II* (*Stars and Stripes* newspaper, 1945)

Leadbetter, Wyland F., 'Engineer Combat Battalions in Their Secondary Role as Infantry during the Battle of the Bulge', in *Military History Anthology* (Combat Studies Institute, Fort Leavenworth, Kansas, 1984)

Lee, Robert G, and Wilke, Sabine, 'Forest as Volk: Ewiger Wald and the Religion of Nature in the Third Reich', paper in *Journal of Social and Ecological Boundaries* (Spring 2005)

Lee, Ulysses, *The Employment of Negro Troops. The United States Army in World War II, Special Studies* (US Army Center of Military History, 1966)

Leff, Murray, *Lens of an Infantryman: A World War II Memoir with Photographs from a Hidden Camera* (McFarland, 2006)

Legge Jr., Jerome S., 'Resisting a War Crimes Trial: The Malmédy Massacre, the German Churches, and the U.S. Army Counterintelligence Corp', article in *Holocaust and Genocide Studies*, Volume 26/2 (Fall 2012)

Leigh Fermor, Patrick, *A Time of Gifts* (John Murray, 1977)

Leinbaugh, Harold P., and Campbell, John D., *The Men of Company 'K'* (William Morrow, 1985)

Lewin, Ronald, *Ultra Goes to War* (Hutchinson, 1978)

Lewis, David, *The Man Who Invented Hitler: The Making of the Führer* (Headline, 2003)

Liddell Hart, Capt. Basil H., *The Other Side of the Hill. Germany's Generals: their Rise and Fall, with their own Account of Military Events 1939–1945* (Cassell, 1948); US edition: *The German Generals Talk*

——— *History of the Second World War* (Weidenfeld & Nicolson, 1970)

Light, John H., *An Infantryman Remembers World War II* (Beidel Printing House, 1997)

Linderman, Gerald F., *The World Within War: America's Combat Experience in World War II* (Free Press, 1997)

Lindsay, Lt.-Col. Sir Martin, *So Few Got Through* (Collins, 1946)

Linge, Heinz, *With Hitler to the End* (Frontline, 2009)

Lipman-Blumen, Jean, *The Allure of Toxic Leaders: Why We Follow Destructive Bosses and Corrupt Politicians – and How We Can Survive Them* (Oxford University Press, 2004)

Litwak, Leo, *The Medic: Life and Death in the Last Days of World War Two* (Algonquin Books, 2001)

Lombardo, Samuel, *O'er the Land of the Free* (Beidel Printing House, 2000)

Longmate, Norman, *The Bombers* (Hutchinson, 1983)

Longue, Mathieu, *Massacres en Ardenne – Hiver 1944–1945* (Editions Racine, 2006)

——— *Kampfgruppe Knittel* (Heimdal, 2011)

Looney, Michael, *Battle of the Bulge: The Untold Story of Hofen* (Victory Publishing, 2010)
Lowry, Col. Montecue, J., 'Troy Houston Middleton: Military Educator and Combat Commander', article in *Military Review*, Vol. LXV/10 (October 1985)
Lucas, James, *Das Reich* (Cassell, 1991)
Ludewig, Joachim, *Rückzug. The German Retreat from France, 1944* (University Press of Kentucky, 2012)
Lukacs, John, *The Hitler of History* (Random House, 1997)
Lüttichau, Charles V. P., Graf von, 'The German Counteroffensive in the Ardennes', Chapter 17 in Kent Roberts Greenfield and Martin Blumenson, *Command Decisions* (Harcourt, Brace and Co., 1959/US Center of Military History, 1960)
Lynch, Dan, and Rutherford, Paul, *Into the Dragon's Teeth, Warrior's Tales of the Battle of the Bulge* (Whitston Publishing, 2005)
MacDonald, Charles B., *Company Commander* (Infantry Journal Press, 1947)
——— *US Army in World War II: The Siegfried Line Campaign* (Government Printing Office, 1963)
——— 'The Neglected Ardennes', article in *Military Review*, No. 43 (Apr. 1963)
——— *The Mighty Endeavour: American Armed Forces in the European Theater in World War II* (Oxford University Press, 1969)
——— *US Army in World War II: The Last Offensive* (Government Printing Office, 1973)
——— *The Battle of the Bulge* (Weidenfeld & Nicolson, 1984), published in the USA as *A Time for Trumpets: The Untold Story of the Battle of the Bulge* (William Morrow & Co., 1985)
MacKenzie, Fred, *The Men of Bastogne* (McKay, 1968)
MacLean, French, *Quiet Flows the Rhine: German General Officer Casualties in World War Two* (Fedorowicz, 1996)
McCarthy, John A., Grunzweig, Walter, and Koebner, Thomas (eds), *The Many Faces of Germany* (Berghahn, 2004)
McCloskey, Joseph F., 'British Operational Research in World War II', article in *Operations Research*, Vol. 35/3 (May–June 1987)
McDonald, Robert K., *The Hotton Report* (Finbar Press, 2006)
McDuffie, Bradley R. 'For Ernest, With Love and Squalor: the Influence of Ernest Hemingway on J.D. Salinger', article in *The Hemingway Review* (22 March 2011)
McLaughlin, John J., *General Albert C. Wedemeyer: America's Unsung Strategist in World War II* (Casemate, 2012)
McManus, John C., *Alamo in the Ardennes: The Untold Story of the American Soldiers Who Made the Defense of Bastogne Possible* (Wiley Press, 2007)
McMillan, Richard, 'I Was There! – British Fought Like Tigers at the Ardennes Tip', article in *The War Illustrated*, Volume 8/199 (2 February 1945), p. 601
McMurdie, William F., *Hey, Mac! A Combat Infantryman's Story* (Red Apple Publishing, 2000)
McNab, Chris, *MG 34 and MG 42 Machine Guns* (Osprey, 2012)
McNiece, Jake, and Killblane, Richard, *The Filthy Thirteen – from the Dustbowl to Hitler's Eagle's Nest – the 101st Airborne's Most Legendary Squad of Combat Paratroopers* (Casemate, 2007)
Mace, Paul, *Forrard: The Story of the East Riding Yeomanry* (Pen & Sword, 2001)
Mahe, Yann, *La Bataille des Ardennes* (Batailles & Blindés, No. 17, 2011)

Malarkey, Don, and Welch, Bob, *Easy Company Soldier: The Legendary Battles of a Sergeant from World War II's 'Band of Brothers'* (St Martin's Griffin, 2009)

Mansoor, Peter R., *The GI Offensive in Europe: The Triumph of American Infantry Divisions, 1941–45* (University of Kansas Press, 1999)

Manteuffel, Gen. Hasso von, 'The Ardennes', Chapter in Seymour Freidin and William Richardson (eds), *The Fatal Decisions* (Berkley, 1958)

——— 'The Battle of The Ardennes 1944–5', Chronicle XI in Dr Hans-Adolf Jacobsen and Dr Jürgen Rohwer, *Decisive Battles of World War II: The German View* (André Deutsch, 1965)

Manvell, Roger, and Fraenkel, Heinrich, *Doctor Goebbels* (William Heinemann, 1960)

——— *Hermann Göring* (William Heinemann, 1962)

——— *Heinrich Himmler* (William Heinemann, 1965)

Marinello, Edward A., *Battle of the Bulge: A Soldier's Commentary* (Nova Science Publishers, 2005)

Marshall, S. L. A., *Bastogne. The Story of the First Eight Days, in Which the 101st Airborne Division Was Closed Within the Ring of German Forces* (Infantry journal Press, 1946/ Archive Media Publishing, 2012)

——— *Men against Fire: The Problem of Battle Command* (William Morrow, 1947)

Martin, Frank 'Pepper', and Ernestine L., *My Time in the Army – 1943 – 1946* (Amazon Kindle, 2000)

Martin, Frank Wayne, *Patton's Lucky Scout – The Adventures of a Forward Observer for General Patton and the Third Army in Europe* (Crickhollow Books, 2009)

Martin, Gerhard, *Letzter Lorbeer: Fallschirmpioniere in der Ardennenschlacht 1944, 1945; im Rahmen der 5. Fallschirmjägerdivision* [Last Laurel: Parachute Pioneers in the Battle of the Bulge 1944–1945, in the 5th Parachute Division] (Nation Europa, 2002)

Martin, Ralph G., *The GI War, 1941–1945* (Little, Brown, 1967)

Maser, Werner, *Hitler* (Allen Lane, 1973)

Matheny, Michael R., *Carrying the War to the Enemy: American Operational Art to 1945* (University of Oklahoma Press, 2011)

Mather, Sir Carol, *When the Grass Stops Growing: A Memoir of the Second World War* (Pen & Sword, 1997)

Mattson, Gregory L., *SS-Das Reich: The History of the Second SS Division, 1941–1945* (Zenith Press, 2002)

Mauch, Christof, *The Shadow War Against Hitler* (Columbia University Press, 2003)

Maudlin, Bill, *Up Front* (Henry Holt, 1945)

Megargee, Geoffrey P., *Inside Hitler's High Command* (University Press of Kansas, 2002)

Mellenthin, General F. W., *Panzer Battles. A Study of the Employment of Armour in the Second World War* (Cassell, 1955)

Meller, William F., *Bloody Roads to Germany: At Huertgen Forest and the Bulge: an American Soldier's Courageous Story of World War II* (Berkley, 2012)

Merkl, Peter H., *The Making of a Stormtrooper* (Princeton University Press, 1980)

——— *Political Violence under the Swastika* (Princeton University Press, 1992)

Merriam, Ray (ed.), *The Battle of the Bulge* (World War II Journal No. 3, Merriam Press, 2003)

Merriam, Robert E., *Dark December: The Full Account of the Battle of the Bulge* (Ziff-Davis Publishing Co., 1947); republished by Ballantine in 1957 as *The Battle of the Bulge.*

Messenger, Charles, *Hitler's Gladiator: The Life and Times of Oberstgruppenführer and Panzergeneral-Oberst Der Waffen-SS Sepp Dietrich* (Brassey's, 1988)

——— *The Last Prussian: A Biography of Field Marshal Gerd Von Rundstedt, 1875–1953* (Brassey's, 1991)

Meyer, Hubert, *The 12th SS: The History of the Hitler Youth Panzer Division*, Vol. 2 (Stackpole, 2005)

Meyers, Col. James J., *Proud to be: Memoir of Colonel James J. Meyers* (82nd Airborne Division War Memorial Museum, 2001)

Mierzejewski, Alfred C., 'When did Albert Speer give up?', article in *The Historical Journal*, Volume 31/2 (June 1988)

Miller, Donald L., *Eighth Air Force. The American Bomber Crews in Britain* (Aurum, 2007)

Miller, Robert A., *Division Commander: a Biography of Major General Norman D. Cota* (Reprint Company, 1989)

Mitcham, Samuel W., *Hitler's Field Marshals and Their Battles* (Leo Cooper, 1988)

——— *Panzers in Winter: Hitler's Army and the Battle of the Bulge* (Praeger, 2006)

——— *Panzer Legions: A Guide to the German Army Tank Divisions of World War II and Their Commanders* (Stackpole, 2007)

Mitchell, Col. Ralph M., *101st Airborne Division's Defense of Bastogne* (Combat Studies Institute, 1986)

Monahan, Evelyn, and Neidel-Greenlee, Rosemary, *And If I Perish: Frontline US Army Nurses in World War II* (Anchor, 2004)

Montgomery of Alamein, Field Marshal the Viscount, *Normandy to the Baltic* (BAOR, 1946)

——— *Memoirs* (Collins, 1958)

Moore, Ray, *Terrify and Destroy. The Story of the 10th Armored Division* (printed in Paris, 1945)

Moorhead, Alan, *Eclipse* (Hamish Hamilton, 1946)

Moranda, George P., and George E., *Two Wars and One Love: Front-Line Soldiers Remember World War II through the Battle of the Bulge and the Korean Conflict* (iUniverse, 2009)

Morelock, Jerry D., 'Death in the Forest', article in the *Field Artillery Journal*, No. 54 (September–October 1986)

——— *Generals of the Ardennes: American Leadership in the Battle of the Bulge* (National Defense University Press, 1994)

——— 'General Omar Bradley's Battle of the Bulge', article in *Armchair General*, Vol. 3/6, January 2007

Motley, Mary Penick, *The Invisible Soldier: Experience of the Black Soldier, World War II* (Wayne State University Press, 1975)

Mrozek, Steven J., *82nd Airborne Division* (Turner Publishing, 1997)

Mudd, Capt. J. L., 'Development of the American Tank-Infantry Team During World War II in Africa and Europe', article in *Armor* (September/October 1999)

Munch, Paul G., 'Patton's Staff and the Battle of the Bulge', article in *Military Review*, No. 70 (May 1990)

Murdoch, Adrian, *Rome's Greatest Defeat: Massacre in the Teutoburg Forest* (Sutton Publishing, 2006)

Murphy, Audie, *To Hell and Back* (Transworld, 1949)

Murray, G. E. Patrick, *Eisenhower versus Montgomery: the Continuing Debate* (Praeger, 1996)

Murray, Williamson, 'War, Theory, Clausewitz, and Thucydides: The Game May Change but the Rules Remain', article in *Marine Corps Gazette*, Vol. 81 (January 1997)

——— *War, Strategy, and Military Effectiveness* (Cambridge University Press, 2011)

Murrell, Robert T., *Operational History of the 80th Infantry Division: August 1944 to May 1945* (Murrell, 2001)

'Musketeer' [pseudonym], 'The Campaign in North-West Europe—III: June, 1944–February, 1945: Some Aspects of Administration', article in the *Royal United Services Institution Journal*, Vol. 103/609 (1958)

Muth, Jörg, *Command Culture: Officer Education in the U.S. Army and the German Armed Forces, 1901–1940, and the Consequences for World War II* (University of North Texas Press, 2011)

Nafziger, George F., *The German Order of Battle: Vol. 1, Panzers and Artillery in World War II* (Greenhill Books, London, 1999)

Nash, Douglas E., *Victory Was Beyond Their Grasp: With the 272nd Volks-Grenadier Division from the Hürtgen Forest to the Heart of the Reich* (Helion, 2008)

Neill, George W., *Infantry Soldier: Holding the Line at the Battle of the Bulge* (University of Oklahoma Press, 2002)

Neillands, Robin, *The Battle for the Rhine: The Battle of the Bulge and the Ardennes Campaign, 1944* (Overlook Press, 2007)

Neitzel, Sönke and Welzer, Harald, *Soldaten: On Fighting, Killing and Dying. The Secret Second World War Tapes of German POWs* (Simon & Schuster, 2012)

Neumann, J., and Flohn, H., 'Great Historical Events That Were Significantly Affected by the Weather: Part 8, Germany's War on the Soviet Union, 1941–45; II. Some Important Weather Forecasts, 1942–45', article in the *Journal of the American Meteorological Society*, Vol. 69/7 (July 1988)

Neysen, Joseph, *Gouvy-Beho, Dans Les Pas Des 3e DB, 83e DI, 84e DI* (Weyrich, 2011)

Nicholas, H.G. (ed.), *Washington Despatches, 1941 to 1945: Weekly Political Reports from the British Embassy* (University of Chicago Press, 1981)

Nicholls, Lester M., *Impact: The Battle Story of the Tenth Armored Division* (Bradbury, Sayles, 1954)

Nicolson, Harold (ed. Nigel Nicolson), *Diaries and Letters 1939–45* (Collins, 1967)

Niemi, Prof. Robert, *Film and Television History in the Media* (ABC-CLIO, 2006)

Nobécourt, Prof. Jacques, *Hitler's Last Gamble: The Battle of the Bulge* (Chatto & Windus, 1967)

Nordyke, Phil, *Four Stars of Valour: The Combat History of the 505th Parachute Infantry Regiment in World War II* (Motorbooks International, 2006)

——— *More Than Courage: Sicily, Naples-Foggia, Anzio, Rhineland, Ardennes-Alsace, Central Europe: The Combat History of the 504th Parachute Infantry Regiment in World War II* (Zenith Press, 2008)

——— *All American, All the Way. A Combat History of the 82nd Airborne Division in World War II: From Market Garden to Berlin* (Zenith Press, 2010)

Nye, Roger H., 'Whence Patton's Military Genius?', article in *Parameters*, No. 21 (Winter 1991–92)

——— *The Patton Mind: The Professional Development of an Extraordinary Leader* (Avery Publishing, 1993)

——— *The Challenge of Command* (Perigee, 2001)

O'Donnell, Patrick K., *Operatives, Spies and Saboteurs: The Unknown Story of the Men and Women of World War II's OSS* (Free Press, 2004)

Orange, Vincent, *Tedder. Quietly in Command* (Frank Cass, 2004)
Orfalea, Gregory, *Messengers of the Lost Battalion: Heroic 551st and the Turning of the Tide at the Battle of the Bulge* (Simon & Schuster, 1997)
Ossad, Stephen L., and Marsh, Don R., *Major General Maurice Rose: World War II's Greatest Forgotten Commander* (Taylor, 2003)
Overy, Richard, *Why the Allies Won* (Jonathan Cape, 1995)
Pallud, Jean-Paul, *Ardennes 1944 Peiper & Skorzeny* (Osprey, 1987)
——— and Ramsey, Winston G., *Battle of the Bulge: Then and Now* (After the Battle; 2nd revised edition, 1986)
Palmer, Robert R., Wiley, Bell I., and Keast, William R., *US Army in World War II: The Procurement and Training of Ground Combat Troops* (Historical Department of the US Army, 1948)
Parker, Danny S., 'German Tiger Tanks were at the Battle of the Bulge, but Not in the Numbers Usually Cited for Them', article in *World War II Magazine* (March 1990)
——— *Battle of the Bulge: Hitler's Ardennes Offensive, 1944–1945* (Combined Books, 1991)
——— *To Win the Winter Sky: Air War over the Ardennes* (Combined Publishing, 1994)
——— (ed.) *Battle of the Bulge: The German View – Perspectives from Hitler's High Command* (Greenhill, 1997)
——— *Fatal Crossroads: The Untold Story of the Malmedy Massacre at the Battle of the Bulge* (Da Capo, 2011)
Parker, Earl S., *Memories of a Tour of Duty: WWII in Europe* (AuthorHouse, 2001)
Passmore, David, and Harrison, Stephan, 'Landscapes of the Battle of the Bulge: WW2 Field Fortifications in the Ardennes Forests of Belgium', article in the *Journal of Conflict Archaeology*, Vol. 4/ Numbers 1–2 (2008)
Patrick, Murray, G. E., *Eisenhower vs. Montgomery: The Continuing Debate* (Praeger, 1996)
Patterson, David, *A Genealogy of Evil: Anti-Semitism from Nazism to Islamic Jihad* (Cambridge University Press, 2010)
Patterson, Eugene, *Patton's Unsung Armor of the Ardennes: The Tenth Armored Division's Secret Dash to Bastogne* (Xlibris, 2008)
Patton, Jr, George S., *War As I Knew It* (Houghton Mifflin, 1947)
Pearlman, Dr Michael D., 'The US Third Army at the Battle of the Bulge, 1944', Chapter 17 in Roger J. Spiller (ed.), *Combined Arms in Battle Since 1939* (US Army Command and General Staff College Press, 1992)
Penrose, Antony, and Scherman, David E., *Lee Miller's War: Photographer and Correspondent with the Allies in Europe 1944–45* (Thames & Hudson, 2005)
Pergrin, Col. David E., *Engineering the Victory: The Battle of the Bulge, a History* (Schiffer Publishing, 1996)
——— and Hammel, Eric, *First Across the Rhine: The 291st Engineer Combat Battalion in France, Belgium and Germany* (Zenith Press, 1989)
Perry, Mark, *Partners in Command. George Marshal and Dwight Eisenhower in War and Peace* (Penguin USA, 2007)
Persico, Joseph E., *Piercing the Reich: The Penetration of Nazi Germany by American Secret Agents During World War II* (Viking, 1979)
Peterson, Harry M., Jr, *Our Days Are a Shadow: A Diary of Escape, Capture, and Imprisonment in German Stalags* (Lee Brooke, 2006)

Peterson, Richard W., *Healing The Child Warrior: A Search for Inner Peace* (Published by the author, 1992)
Phillips, Henry Gerard, *The Making of a Professional: Manton S. Eddy, USA* (Greenwood Press, 2000)
Phillips, Robert E., *To Save Bastogne* (Stein and Day, 1983)
Pimlott, John, *The Battle of the Bulge* (Prentice-Hall, 1983)
Pirnie, Thomas B., *We Thought We Were Going Home: As Told by Rhode Island WWII Battle of the Bulge Veterans* (Westerly Printing Co., 2000)
Pogue, Forrest C., *US Army in World War II: European Theater of Operations, Part III: The Supreme Command Washington* (Government Printing Office, 1954)
——— *George C. Marshall: Organizer of Victory, 1943–1945* (Viking Press, 1973)
——— *The Ardennes Campaign: The Impact of Intelligence* (edited transcript of remarks to the NSA Communications Analysis Association, 16 December 1980)
——— *Pogue's War: Diaries of a WWII Combat Historian* (University Press of Kentucky, 2001)
Porter, Maj.-Gen. Ray E., (Introduction), *The 75th Division in Combat: Ardennes-Colmar-Ruhr* (*c.*1946)
Price, Frank, *Troy H. Middleton: A Biography* (Louisiana State University Press, 1974)
Province, Charles M., *Patton's Third Army: A Chronicle of the Third Army Advance, August, 1944–May, 1945* (Hippocrene Books, 1992)
Puryear, Edgar F., Jr, *Nineteen Stars: A Study in Military Character and Leadership* (Presidio Press, 1981),
——— *American Generalship: Character Is Everything: The Art of Command* (Presidio Press, 2001)
Putney, Diane T., *Ultra and the Army Air Forces in World War II. An Interview with Associate Justice of the US Supreme Court Lewis F. Powell, Jr* (Office of Air Force History, US Air Force, Washington, DC, 1987)
Quarrie, Bruce, *The Ardennes Offensive: VI Panzer Armee: Northern Sector* (Osprey, 1999)
——— *The Ardennes Offensive: V US Corps & XVIII US Airborne Corps: Northern Sector* (Osprey, 1999)
——— *The Ardennes Offensive: V Panzer Armee: Central Sector* (Osprey, 2000)
——— *The Ardennes Offensive: VII US Corps and VIII US Corps and British XXX Corps: Central Sector* (Osprey, 2000)
——— *The Ardennes Offensive: 1 Armee & VII Armee: Southern Sector* (Osprey, 2001)
——— *The Ardennes Offensive: US III & XII Corps: Southern Sector* (Osprey, 2001)
Quigley, Marilyn Estes, *Hell Frozen Over: The Battle of the Bulge* (AuthorHouse, 2004)
Ramsay, Winston G. (ed.), *After the Battle Magazine, No. 4: The Battle of the Bulge* (Battle of Britain Press, 1975)
——— *After the Battle Magazine, No. 73: With the Company Commander; American historian Charles B. MacDonald returns to the battlefields in the Ardennes* (Battle of Britain Press, 1991)
Rapport, Leonard, and Northwood, Arthur, Jr, *Rendezvous With Destiny. History of the 101st Airborne Division* (Konecky & Konecky, 2001)
Rass, Christoph, and Lohmeier, Jens, 'Transformations: Post-Battle Processes on the Hürtgenwald', article in *Journal of Conflict Archaeology*, Vol. 6/3 (2011)
Ravenhill, Brigadier C., OBE, 'The Influence of Logistics on Operations in North-West Europe, 1944–1945', article in the *Royal United Services Institution Journal*, Vol. 91/564 (1946)

Rawson, Andrew, *Images of War: Battle of the Bulge* (Pen & Sword, 2005)

Ray, Sgt. Marion, and Brannon, Dan, *Damn Cold and Starving – A Soldier's Reflection as a World War II Prisoner* (Brannan-Ray Publishing, 2006)

Raymond, Sergeant First Class (retired) Richard, 'Parker's Crossroads: The Alamo Defence', article in *Field Artillery* (August 1993)

Reardon, Mark J., *Victory at Mortain: Stopping Hitler's Panzer Counteroffensive* (University Press of Kansas, 2002)

Redmann, Kerry P., *Unfinished Journey: A World War II Remembrance* (Lyons Press, 2006)

Reeves, Lt.-Col. Joseph R., 'Artillery in the Ardennes', article in *Field Artillery Journal*, No. 36 (March 1946)

Reichelt, Dr Walter E., *Phantom Nine: The 9th Armored (Remagen) Division, 1942–1945* (Presidential Press, 1987)

Reid, Robert 'Bob', *Never Tell an Infantryman to Have a Nice Day* (Xlibris Corporation, 2010)

Renouf, Tom, *Black Watch: Liberating Europe and Catching Himmler – My Extraordinary WW2 with the Highland Division* (Little, Brown, 2011)

Reynolds, Maj.-Gen. Michael, *The Devil's Adjutant: Jochen Peiper, Panzer Leader* (Spellmount, 1995)

——— *Men of Steel: 1st SS Panzer Corps, 1944–45 – The Ardennes and Eastern Front* (Spellmount, 1998)

——— *Sons of the Reich: The History of II SS Panzer Corps* (Spellmount, 2001)

Rice, Douglas, *Through Our Eyes: Eyewitness Accounts of World War II* (iUniverse, 2008)

Rickard, John Nelson, *Advance and Destroy: Patton as Commander in the Bulge* (University Press of Kentucky, 2011)

Ridgway, Gen. Matthew B., and Martin, Harold H., *Soldier: The Memories of Matthew B. Ridgway* (Harper, 1956)

Rieth, John K., *Patton's Forward Observers: History of the 7th Field Artillery Observation Battalion, XX Corps, Third Army* (Brandylane Publishers, 2004)

Ritgen, Helmut, *Die Geschichte Der Panzer-Lehr-Division Im Westen 1944–1945* (Motorbuch Verlag, 1979)

——— *The Western Front 1944: Memoirs of a Panzer Lehr Officer* (J.J. Fedorowicz, 1995)

Riva, Maria, *Marlene Dietrich: by Her Daughter* (Alfred A. Knopf, 1992)

Rivette, Capt. Donald E., 'The Hot Corner at Dom Butgenbach', article in *The Infantry Journal*, Vol. LVII/4 (October 1945)

Roberts, Andrew, *Masters and Commanders: How Four Titans Won the War in the West, 1941–1945* (Harper Perennial, 2010)

——— *The Storm of War: A New History of the Second World War* (Harper, 2011)

Roberts, Cecil E., *A Soldier from Texas* (Branch-Smith, 1978)

Roberts, John M. 'Jack', *Escape! The True Story of a World War II POW the Germans Couldn't Hold* (Brundage Publishing, 2003)

Ronningen, Thor, *Butler's Battlin' Blue Bastards* (Brunswick, 1993)

Roosevelt, Kermit, *The War Report of the OSS*, 2 vols. (Walker, 1976)

Ross, Stewart Halsey, *Strategic Bombing by the United States in World War II: The Myths and the Facts* (McFarland, 2003)

Ross, William F., and Romanus, Charles F., *US Army in World War II: The Quartermaster Corps: Operations in the War Against Germany* (US Army Center of Military History, 1965)

Rottman, Gordon, *World War II US Cavalry Units: European Theater* (Osprey, 2012)
Royle, Trevor, *Patton: Old Blood and Guts* (Casemate, 2005)
Rubin, Steven Jay, *Combat Films: American Realism, 1945–2010* (McFarland & Co., 2nd revised edn., 2011)
Ruppenthal, Roland, *US Army in World War II: The European Theater of Operations, Logistical Support of the Armies, Vol. 2 September 1944–May 1945* (US Army Center of Military History, Washington DC, 1995)
Rush, Robert S., 'A Different Perspective: Cohesion, Morale, and Operational Effectiveness in the German Army, Fall 1944', article in *Armed Forces & Society*, Vol. 25/3 (Spring 1999)
Rusiecki, Stephen M., *The Key to the Bulge: The Battle for Losheimergraben* (Stackpole, 2009)
Rust, Kurt Albert, *Der Weg der 15. Panzergrenadier-Division von Sizilien bis Wesermünde, Teil 2: Frankreich - Wesermünde 1944–1945* (Selbstverlag, 1990)
Sager, Guy, *The Forgotten Soldier* (Weidenfeld & Nicolson, 1971)
Sanders, Jim, *Saving Lives, Saving Memories* (Kindle/IF Books, 2009)
Sas, Anthony, 'The War Game: An Indispensable Tool in the Study of Military Geography', article in *Journal of Geography*, Vol. 78/3 (1979)
Sasser, Charles W., *Patton's Panthers: The African-American 761st Tank Battalion in World War II* (Simon & Schuster, 2005)
Saunders, Hrowe H., *Die Wacht am Rhein: Hitlers letzte Schlacht in den Ardennen 1944/45* (K. Vowinckel-Verlag, 1984)
Sayer, Ian, and Botting, Douglas, *Hitler's Last General: The Case against Wilhelm Mohnke* (Bantam Transworld, 1989)
Schadewitz, Michael, *First the Meuse, Then Antwerp* (J. J. Fedorowicz, 1999)
——— *Zwischen Ritterkreuz und Galgen: Skorzenys Geheimunternehmen Greif in Hitlers Ardennenoffensive 1944/45* (Helios Verlag, 2007)
Scherer, Wingolf, *Die letzte Schlacht* (Helios Verlag, 2004)
——— and Broch, Ernst-Detlef, *Untergang: Kampf und Vernichtung der 277. Division in der Normandie und in der Eifel* (Helios, 2005)
Schifferle, Peter J., *America's School for War: Fort Leavenworth, Officer Education, and Victory in World War II* (University Press of Kansas, 2010)
Schiller, Bill, and Thompson, Lisa, *75th Infantry Division: Ardennes, Central Europe, Rhineland* (Turner Publishing, 2002)
Schramm, Percy (ed.), *Kriegstagebuch Des Oberkommando Der Wehrmacht 1944–45, Band IV/1: 1.Januar 1944–22.Mai 1945* (Bernard & Graefe Verlag, 1982)
——— *Hitler: The Man and the Military Leader* (Allen Lane, 1972)
Schrijvers, Peter, *The Unknown Dead: Civilians in the Battle of the Bulge* (The University Press of Kentucky, 2005)
——— *Liberators: The Allies and Belgian Society, 1944–1945* (Cambridge University Press, 2009)
Schroeder, Christa, *He Was My Chief: The Memoirs of Adolf Hitler's Secretary* (Frontline, 2009)
Scott, Desmond, *Typhoon Pilot* (Secker & Warburg, 1982)
Semmler, Helmut, *SS-Flak: Memoir of SS-Sturmmann Helmut Semmler, SS-Flak-Abteilung 9, 9th SS-Panzer-Division Hohenstauffen, Ardennes, 1944–45* (Shelf Books, 1999)
Sereny, Gitta, *Albert Speer: His Battle with Truth* (Macmillan, 1995)

Shapiro, Milton J., *Tank Command: General George S. Patton's 4th Armored Division* (McKay, 1979)
Sheaner, Herb, *Prisoner's Odyssey* (Xlibris, 2009)
Shields, Charles J., *And So It Goes: Kurt Vonnegut: A Life* (Henry Holt, 2011)
Shinn, Roger L., *Wars and Rumours of Wars* (Abingdon Press, 1972)
Shirer, William L., *The Rise and Fall of the Third Reich* (Simon & Schuster, 1960)
Shomon, Lt.-Col. Joseph James, *Crosses in the Wind* (Stratford House, 1947)
Shrader, Lieutenant-Colonel Charles R., *Amicicide: The Problem of Friendly Fire in Modern War* (University Press of the Pacific, 1982)
Shulman, Milton, *Defeat in the West* (Secker & Warburg, 1947)
Silverstein, Ken, *Private Warriors* (Verso Books, 2000)
Sinal, Chris A., 'Sic Semper Fidelis and Tempus Fugit: American Military Nationalism and the European Theatre of the Second World War', article in *Past Imperfect*, Vol. 12 (2006)
Sixsmith, Maj.-Gen. Eric Keir Gilborne, *Eisenhower as Military Commander* (Batsford, 1973)
Skorzeny, Otto, *Skorzeny's Special Missions* (Robert Hale, 1957)
Smallwood, Frederick, *My War: in the Battle of the Bulge* (Privately printed, 2002)
Smith, Bradley F., *The Shadow Warriors: OSS and the Origins of the CIA* (Basic Books, 1983)
Smith, Col. C. Cabanne, *My War Years, 1940–46: Service on Gen. Patton's Third Army Staff* (Rosenblatt Publishing, 1989)
Smith, Graham, *The Mighty Eighth in the Second World War* (Countryside Books, 2001)
Smith, R. Harris, *OSS: The Secret History of America's First Central Intelligence Agency* (University of California Press, 1972)
Smith, Gen. Walter Bedell, *Eisenhower's Six Great Decisions: Europe 1944–1945* (Longmans, Green, 1956)
Smith, Robert L., *"Medic!" A World War II Combat Medic Remembers* (Creative Arts Book Co., 2001)
Sorley, Lewis, *Thunderbolt. From the Battle of the Bulge to Vietnam and Beyond: General Creighton Abrams and the Army of His Time* (Simon & Schuster, 1992)
——— *Westmoreland: The General Who Lost Vietnam* (Houghton Mifflin, 2011)
Sowell, Thomas, *Ethnic America: A History* (Basic Books, 1981)
Spanos, William V., *In the Neighborhood of Zero: A World War II Memoir* (University of Nebraska Press, 2010)
Sparrow, Lt.-Col. J. H. A., *The Second World War, 1939–1945: Army Morale* (The War Office, 1949)
Spayd, Pat A., *Bayerlein: From Afrika Korps to Panzer Lehr. The Life of Rommel's Chief-of-staff Generalleutnant Fritz Bayerlein* (Schiffer Publishing, 2003)
Speer, Albert, *Inside the Third Reich* (Macmillan, 1970)
Spielberger, Walter J., *Panther and its Variants* (Schiffer Publishing, 1997)
——— and Doyle, Hilary L., *Tigers I and II and their Variants* (Schiffer Publishing, 2007)
Spiller, Roger J., 'S. L. A. Marshall and the Ratio of Fire', article in *The RUSI Journal*, Vol. 133/4 (1988)
Stacey, Colonel C. P., *Official History of the Canadian Army in the Second World War*, Vol. III, *The Victory Campaign, The Operations in North-West Europe, 1944–1945* (Ottawa, 1966)

Stahlberg, Alexander, *Bounden Duty: Memoirs of a German Officer, 1932–45* (Brassey's, 1990)

Stein, Marcel, *A Flawed Genius: Field-Marshal Walter Model, A Critical Biography* (Helion, 2010)

Steinhardt, Dr Frederick P., *Panzer Lehr Division 1944–45* (Helion, 2010)

Stephany, *Ardennes 44 – La Dernière Offensive Allemande* (Ixelles Editions, 2010)

Stoler, Mark A., *Allies and Adversaries: The Joint Chiefs of Staff, the Grand Alliance, and U.S. Strategy in World War II* (University of North Carolina Press, 2006)

Stolfi, Russell H. S., *A Bias For Action: The German 7th Panzer Division in France & Russia 1940–1941* (Perspectives on Warfighting, No. 1, Marine Corps University, 1991)

Stone, David, *Hitler's Army: The Men, Machines, and Organization: 1939–1945* (Zenith Press, 2009)

——— *Shattered Genius: The Decline and Fall of the German General Staff in World War II* (Casemate, 2012)

Stone, Lt.-Col. Thomas R., 'General William Hood Simpson: Unsung Commander of US Ninth Army', article in *Parameters*, Vol. XI, No.2 (June 1981)

Strauss, Franz Josef, *Die Geschichte der 2. (Wiener) Panzer-Division* (Nebel Verlag, 2005)

Strawson, Maj.-Gen. John, *The Battle for the Ardennes* (Batsford, 1972)

Strong, Gen. Sir Kenneth, *Intelligence at the Top: the Recollections of an Intelligence Officer* (Cassell, 1968)

Suid, Lawrence H., *Guts and Glory: The Making of the American Military Image in Film* (University Press of Kentucky, 2002)

Summersby, Captain Kay, *Eisenhower Was My Boss* (Prentice Hall, 1948)

Suri, Jeremi, *Henry Kissinger and the American Century* (Harvard University Press, 2007)

Swaab, Jack, *Field of Fire: Diary of a Gunner Officer* (The History Press, 2005)

Swanson, Vernon E., *Upfront with Charlie Company: A Combat History of Company 'C', 395th Infantry Regiment 99th Infantry Division* (Red Danube Publishing, 1997)

Sydnor, Charles W., Jr, *Soldiers of Destruction: The SS-Death's Head Division 1933–45* (Princeton University Press, 1977)

Sylan, Maj. William C., and Smith, Capt. Francis G., Jr, *Normandy to Victory. The War Diary of General Courtney H. Hodges and the First US Army* (The University Press of Kentucky, 2008)

Szpek, Jr, Ervin E., Idzikowski, Frank J., and Szpek, Heidi M., *Shadows of Slaughterhouse Five: Reflections and Recollections of the Ex-POWs of Schlachthof Fünf, Dresden, Germany* (iUniverse, 2008)

Taaffe, Stephen R., *Marshall and His Generals: U.S. Army Commanders in World War II* (University Press of Kansas, 2011)

Tate, Mary Jo, *The Critical Companion to F. Scott Fitzgerald: A Literary Reference to His Life and Work* (Infobase, 1998)

Taylor, Gen. Maxwell D., *Swords and Plowshares* (W. W. Norton, 1972)

Taylor, Hal Richard, *A Teen's War: Training, Combat, Capture* (AuthorHouse, 1999)

Taylor, Zane S., *Lesser Heroes* (Tate Publishing, 2008)

Tedder, Lord, *With Prejudice: The War Memoirs of Marshal of the Royal Air Force, Lord Tedder* (Cassell, 1966)

Terkel, Studs, *The Good War – An Oral History of World War II* (New Press, 1997)

Thompson, George R., and Harris, Dixie R., *US Army in World War II: The Signal Corps: The Outcome, Mid-1943 through 1945* (US Army Center of Military History, 1965)

Thompson, Royce L., *Study of Weather of the Ardennes Campaign* (US Army Center for Military History, 1953)

Thompson, Timothy J., *The Ardennes on Fire, Vol. One: December 16, 1944. The First Day of the German Assault* (XLibris, 2010)

Tieke, Wilhelm, *In the Firestorm of the Last Year of the War* (J. J. Fedorowicz, 1999)

Tiemann, Ralf, 'Der Endkampf der Panzergruppe Peiper in den Ardennen – 25.12.1944' ('The Final Battle of Kampfgruppe Peiper in the Ardennes'), article in *Der Freiwillige*, Vol. 31/12 (December 1985), pp. 29–32.

——— *Die Leibstandarte, Band IV/2* (Munin Verlag 1987)

Toland, John, *Battle: The Story of the Bulge* (Random House, 1959)

——— *Adolf Hitler* (Doubleday, 1976)

Tolhurst, Mike, *Battle of the Bulge: St Vith: 18 Volks-Grenadier Division v. US 106 Division* (Battleground Europe/Pen & Sword, 1999)

——— *Bastogne* (Battleground Europe/Pen & Sword, 2000)

Tomblin, Barbara Brooks, *G.I. Nightingales: The Army Nurse Corps in World War II* (University Press of Kentucky, 2003)

Tory, Peter, *Giles at War* (Headline, 1994)

Trevor-Roper, H. R., *Hitler's Table Talk, 1941–1944* (Weidenfeld & Nicolson, 1953)

——— *Hitler's War Directives* (Sidgwick & Jackson, 1964)

Truscott, Gen. Lucian K. Jr, *Command Missions: A Personal Story* (E. P. Dutton, 1954)

Tsouras, Peter G., *Battle of the Bulge: Hitler's Alternate Scenarios* (Greenhill Books, 2006)

Turner, John Frayn, and Jackson, Robert, *Destination Berchtesgaden. The Story of the United States Seventh Army in World War II* (Ian Allan, 1973)

Turner, Barry, *Countdown To Victory. The Final European Campaigns of World War II* (Hodder & Stoughton, 2004)

Urbain, Eric, *Little Known Front: Battle of the Bulge in the Communes of Libramont, St. Hubert & Ste, Ode, 21 December 1944–14 January 1945* (Odyssey Press, 2004)

US Army Armor School, *The Battle of St. Vith, 17–23 December 1944. An Historical Example of Armour in the Defense* (Merriam Press, 1995)

Vanderveen, Bart H., *The Observer's Fighting Vehicles Directory* (Frederick Warne, 1972)

Vannoy, Allyn R., and Karamales, Jay, *Against the Panzers: United States Infantry versus German Tanks, 1944–1945 – A History of Eight Battles Told Through Diaries, Unit Histories and Interviews* (McFarland & Co., 1996)

Vorwald, Philip, *Battle of the Bulge through the Lens* (After the Battle, 2000)

Votaw, John, *Blue Spaders: The 26th Infantry Regiment, 1917–1967* (Cantigny First Division Foundation, 1996)

Waddell, Steve R., *United States Army Logistics: The Normandy Campaign, 1944* (Praeger, 1994)

Wade, Maj. Gary, *Conversations with General Lawton J. Collins* (Leavenworth Papers No. 5, Combat Studies Institute, 1983)

——— *World War II Division Commanders* (Leavenworth Papers No. 7, Combat Studies Institute, 1983)

Wagner, Sharon Wells, *Red Wells: An American Soldier in World War II* (BookSurge Publishing, 2006)

Walden, Greg, *Tigers in the Ardennes: Schwere SS-PanzerAbteilung 501 in the Battle of the Bulge*; essay at: http://www.ss501panzer.com/index.htm

Wallace, Col. Brenton Greene, *Patton and his Third Army* (Military Service Publishing Co., 1946)

Walther, Herbert, *The 1st SS Panzer Division: A Pictorial History* (Schiffer Publishing, 1989)
Walton, William, 'The Battle of the Hürtgen Forest. A Gloomy German Wood Takes Its Place in US History Beside the Wilderness and the Argonne', article in *Life magazine*, 1 January 1945
Wandrey, June, *Bedpan Commando: The Story of a Combat Nurse during World War II* (Elmore Publishing, 1990)
Ward, Geoffrey C., and Burns, Ken, *The War: An Intimate History, 1941–1945* (A.A. Knopf, 2007)
Ward Lock, *Handbook to Belgium* (Ward Lock, 1921)
Warden, Jack B., *Battle for Hotton: 3d Platoon, B Company, 36th A.I. Regt., 3rd Armored Division* (Privately printed, 1994)
Warlimont, Gen. Walter, *Inside Hitler's Headquarters, 1939–45* (Weidenfeld & Nicolson, 1964)
Warnock, Bill, *The Dead of Winter: How Battlefield Investigators, WWII Veterans, and Forensic Scientists Solved the Mystery of the Bulge's Lost Soldiers* (Chamberlain Bros., 2005)
Watson, Bruce Allen, *When Soldiers Quit: Studies in Military Disintegration* (Praeger, 1997)
Weaver, Michael, *Guard Wars: The 28th Infantry Division in World War II* (Indiana University Press, 2010)
Webster, David Kenyon, *Parachute Infantry: An American Paratrooper's Memoir of D-Day and the Fall of the Third Reich* (Louisiana State University Press, 1994)
Wedemeyer, Albert C., *Wedemeyer Reports!* (Henry Holt, 1958)
Weidinger, SS-*Obersturmbannführer* Otto, *History of 2 SS Panzer Division Das Reich, Volume V: 1943–1945* (J. J. Fedorowicz, 2012)
Weighley, Russell, *Eisenhower's Lieutenants: The Campaign of France and Germany 1944–1945* (Indiana University Press, 1981)
Weingartner, James J., *Crossroads of Death: The Story of the Malmédy Massacre and Trial* (University of California Press, 1979)
——— 'Unconventional Allies: Colonel Willis Everett and SS-Obersturmbannführer Joachim Peiper', article in *The Historian*, Vol. 62/1 (September 1999)
——— *A Peculiar Crusade: Willis M. Everett and the Malmédy Massacre Trial* (New York University Press, 2000)
——— *Americans, Germans, and War Crimes Justice: Law, Memory, and 'The Good War'* (Greenwood, 2011)
Weintraub, Stanley, *11 Days in December: Christmas at the Bulge, 1944* (New American Library, 2007)
Weiss, Robert, *Fire Mission!: The Siege at Mortain, Normandy, August 1944* (Burd Street Press, 2002)
Weiss, Wilhelm, *Ardennen '44: Der Einsatz der 26. Volks-Grenadier-Division. Ehemalige Rheinisch-Westfälische 26. Inf. Div. bei den Kämpfen um Bastogne* (Helios Verlag, 2011)
Werlhof, Jay von, *One Man's Decision: Why SHAEF Failed to Halt the Battle of the Bulge, 114th Signal Radio Intelligence Company on 16 December 1944*; essay at http://www.asa-alpiners.com/decision.htm
Westmoreland, William C., *A Soldier Reports* (Doubleday, 1976)
Westphal, Gen. Siegfried, *The German Army in the West* (Cassell & Co., 1951)
Wharton, Patricia Yearout, *Reading between the Lines: A World War II Correspondence, May 1944 – March 1945* (Privately printed, 1999)

Wheeler, James Scott, *The Big Red One: America's Legendary First Infantry Division from World War 1 to Desert Storm* (University Press of Kansas, 2007)
Whicker, Marcia Lynn, *Toxic leaders: When Organizations Go Bad* (Quorum Books, 1996)
Whipple, Colonel William, 'Logistical Problems during the German Ardennes Offensive' article in *Military Review*, Vol. 28/2 (May 1948)
Whiting, Charles, *Massacre at Malmédy* (Leo Cooper, 1971)
——— *Death of a Division: The True Story of the 16,000 Troops of the U.S. 106th Inf. Div., Destroyed in the Battle of the Bulge* (Arrow, 1979)
——— *West Wall: The Battle for Hitler's Siegfried Line, September 1944–March 1945* (Secker and Warburg, 1983)
——— *'44 : In Combat from Normandy to the Ardennes* (Spellmount, 1984)
——— *Ardennes: The Secret War* (Century, 1984)
——— *Papa Goes to War: Ernest Hemingway in Europe 1944–45* (Crowood Press, 1990)
——— *The Last Assault: 1944–The Battle of the Bulge Reassessed* (Leo Cooper, 1994)
——— *Skorzeny: the Most Dangerous Man in Europe* (Pen & Sword, 1998)
——— *The Battle of the Bulge, Britain's Untold Story* (Sutton, 1999)
——— *The Ghost Front: The Ardennes Before the Battle of the Bulge* (Da Capo Press, 2002)
Whitlock, Flint, *Given Up for Dead: American GI's in the Nazi Concentration Camp at Berga* (Westview/Perseus, 2005)
Whitman, George P., *Memoirs of a Rifle Company Commander in Patton's Third US Army* (Battleground Books, 1993)
Wijers, Hans J., *Battle of the Bulge, Vol. One: The Losheim Gap / Holding the Line* (Stackpole, 2009)
——— *Vol. Two: Hell at Bütgenbach/ Seize the Bridges* (Stackpole, 2010)
——— *The Battle of the Bulge* [earlier edition], *Vol. 1, The Losheim Gap: Doorway to the Meuse* (Wijers, 2006)
——— *Vol. 2, Holding the Line: US V Corps stops the 1st SS Panzer Corps* (Wijers, 2006)
——— *Vol. 3, Hell at Bütgenbach: We Fight and Die Here* (Wijers, 2006)
——— *Vol. 4, Seize the Bridges: Spearhead to Antwerp* (Wijers, 2006)
——— *Vol. 5, Desperate Stand: The Bitter Defense of the Schnee Eifel (VIII Corps at St. Vith 106th Inf. Div.)* (Wijers, 2006)
——— *Vol. 6, The Battle for St. Vith: 17th–23rd December 1944 (VIII Corps at St. Vith – 7th Armd. Div.)* (Wijers, 2006)
——— *Vol. 7, Operations of the 3rd Fallschirmjäger-Division: Defense of the North Sector between December 1944 and January 1945* (Wijers, 2006)
Williams, Capt. F. D. G., 'The Labors of Sisyphus: The Writings of S. L. A. Marshall', article in *Defense & Security Analysis*, Volume 2/2 (1986), pp. 167–172
Williams, John F., *Corporal Hitler and the Great War 1914–1918: The List Regiment* (Frank Cass, 2005)
Wilmot, Chester, *The Struggle for Europe* (Collins, 1952)
Wilson, Charles McMoran (Lord Moran), *The Anatomy of Courage* (Constable, 1945)
Wilson, George, *If You Survive: From Normandy to the Battle of the Bulge to the End of World War II, One American Officer's Riveting True Story* (Ballantine Books, 1987)
Wilson, Jr, Joe W., *The 761st Black Panther Tank Division in World War II: An Illustrated History of the First African Armoured Unit to See Combat* (McFarland & Co., 1999)
Winebrenner, Hobert, and McCoy, Michael, *Bootprints* (Camp Comamajo Press, 2005)

Winter, George, *Manhay: the Ardennes Christmas 1944* (J. J. Fedorowicz, 1990)

Winterbotham, Gp. Capt. F. W., *The Ultra Secret* (Weidenfeld & Nicolson, 1974)

Winters, Maj. Dick, and Kingseed, Cole C., *Beyond Band of Brothers: The War Memoirs of Major Dick Winters* (Berkley, 2006)

Winters, Harold A., *Battling the Elements: Weather and Terrain in the Conduct of War* (Johns Hopkins University Press, 1998)

Winton, Harold R., *Corps Commanders of the Bulge: Six American Generals and Victory in the Ardennes* (University Press of Kansas, 2007)

——— 'Normandy to Victory: The War Diary of General Courtney H. Hodges and the First U.S. Army. Diary maintained for Hodges by his aides Major William C. Sylvan and Captain Francis G. Smith, Jr.,' review in the *Journal of Military History* 73/3 (2009)

——— 'Airpower in the Battle of the Bulge: A Case for Effects-Based Operations?', article in the *Journal of Military and Strategic Studies*, Vol. 14/1 (2011)

Wishnevsky, Stephan T., *Courtney Hicks Hodges: From Private to Four-Star General in the United States Army* (McFarland & Co., 2006)

Wiwjorra, Ingo, 'German archaeology and its relation to nationalism and racism', Chapter 9 in Díaz-Andreu, Margarita, and Champion, Timothy, *Nationalism and Archaeology in Europe* (UCL Press, 1996)

Wolf, Winfried, *Car Mania: A Critical History of Transport, 1770–1990* (Pluto Press, 1996)

Wood, C. E., *Mud. A Military History* (Potomac Books, 2006)

Wood, James A., 'Captive Historians, Captivated Audience: The German Military History Program, 1945–1961', article in *The Journal of Military History*, Vol. 69/1 (January 2005)

Wortmann, Karl, 'Parole: Frohe Weihnachten', ('Password: Merry Christmas'), article in *Der Freiwillige*, Vol. 24/12 (December 1978), pp. 4–6

Wurst, Spencer Free, and Wurst, Gayle, *Descending From the Clouds: a Memoir of Combat in the 505 Parachute Infantry Regiment, 82nd Airborne Division* (Casemate, 2004)

Wyatt, Bob, *Leeton in World War II. A Small Town's Sacrifices* (AuthorHouse, 2011)

Yeide, Harry, *Steel Victory. The Heroic Story of America's Independent Tank Battalions at War in Europe* (Presidio Press, 2003)

——— *The Longest Battle: September 1944 to February 1945 – From Aachen to the Roer and Across* (Motorbooks International, 2005)

——— *The Tank Killers: A History of America's World War II Tank Destroyer Force* (Casemate, 2010)

——— *The Infantry's Armor: The U.S. Army's Separate Tank Battalions in WWII* (Stackpole, 2010)

——— *Fighting Patton: George S. Patton Jr. Through the Eyes of His Enemies* (Zenith Press, 2011)

Yenne, Bill, *Hitler's Master of the Dark Arts. Himmler's Black Knights and the Occult Origins of the SS* (Zenith Press, 2010)

Zabecki, Maj.-Gen. David T., *The German 1918 Offensives: A Case Study in the Operational Level of War* (Routledge, 2006)

——— 'The Untold Story of Patton at Bastogne', article in *World War II Magazine*, Vol. 22/7 (November 2007)

Zak, George K., *Soldier Boy* (Vantage Press, 1998)

Zaloga, Steven J., *Battle of the Bulge 1944 (1): St Vith and the Northern Shoulder* (Osprey, 2003)

——— *Battle of the Bulge 1944 (2): Bastogne* (Osprey, 2004)
——— *US Armored Divisions: The European Theater of Operations, 1944–45* (Osprey, 2004)
——— *Panther vs. Sherman: Battle of the Bulge 1944* (Osprey, 2008)
——— *Armored Attack 1944: U.S. Army Tank Combat in the European Theater from D-Day to the Battle of Bulge* (Stackpole, 2011)
——— *Armored Victory 1945: U.S. Army Tank Combat in the European Theater from the Battle of the Bulge to Germany's Surrender* (Stackpole, 2012)
Ziemssen, Dietrich, *The Malmédy Trial: A Report Based on Documents and Personal Experiences* (Merriam Press, 1988)
Zuber, Terence, *The Battle of the Frontiers: Ardennes 1914* (The History Press, 2008)

Other Media:

Blue Ridge – Newsletter of the 80th Division Veterans Association
The Bulge Bugle – Newsletter of the Veterans of the Battle of the Bulge
Checkerboard – 99th Infantry Division Association Newsletter
The Cub – Newsletter of the 106th Division
Daily Mail newspaper
Der Spiegel, 9 April 1952, 'Heil Rommel'
Images of War Magazine, Vol.3/No. 38, 'The Last Blitzkrieg. Antwerp or Bust!' (1990)
Life, 'Bulge Air Battle: Planes Mark Clear Christmas Sky' (22 January 1945)
Newsweek, reviews of *Battleground* (14 November 1949) and *Battle of the Bulge* (10 January 1966)
New York Times, review of *Battle of the Bulge* (18 December 1965)
The Railsplitter – Newsletter of the 84th Division Veterans Association
The Saturday Review, critique of *Battle of the Bulge* (1966, Volume 49/1, p. 43)
Stars and Stripes newspaper
Time, review of *Battle of the Bulge* (31 December 1965)
Toronto Globe and Mail newspaper
Völkischer Beobachter newspaper

Film, TV & Radio:

Battleground (movie, dir. William A. Wellman, 1949)
Crusade in Europe, Part 20: The Battle of the Bulge (documentary, based on Eisenhower's book, ABC TV, 1949)
Attack! (movie, dir. Robert Aldrich, 1956)
The Last Blitzkrieg (movie, dir. Arthur Dreifuss, 1959)
Ski Troop Attack (movie, dir. Roger Corman, 1960)
Battleline, Episode 31: Battle Of The Bulge: Battle at Bastogne (documentary, prod./dir. Frank De Felitta and narrated by Chet Huntley, NBC TV, 1963)
Battle of the Bulge (movie, dir. Ken Annakin, 1965)
The Battle of the Bulge... The Brave Rifles (documentary, prod. Laurence E. Mascott and narrated by Arthur Kennedy, Mascott Productions, 1965)

The Big Picture: The Battle at St. Vith, Parts I & II (documentary, prod. US Army Pictorial Center, Department of Defense and narrated by Robert Taylor, 1965)

Counterpoint (movie, dir. Ralph Nelson, 1968)

Castle Keep (movie, dir. Sydney Pollack, 1969)

World at War, Episode 19: 'Pincers', August 1944 – March 1945 (documentary, prod. Jeremy Issacs and narrated by Laurence Olivier, Thames TV, 1974)

G. I. Diary, Episode 8: *The Bulge* (documentary, exec. prod. Arthur Holch; narrated by Lloyd Bridges, 1978)

World War II with Walter Cronkite, Episode 1: *Battle of the Bulge* (documentary, narrated by Walter Cronkite, CBS, 1982)

V for Victory, Episode 8: *The Battle of the Bulge* (documentary, Acorn Media, 1989)

A Midnight Clear (movie, dir. Keith Gordon, 1992)

American Experience: The Battle of the Bulge: World War II's Deadliest Battle (documentary, dir. Thomas Lennon; written by Lennon and Mark Zwonitzer, and narrated by David McCullough, PBS, 1994); transcript at http://www.pbs.org/wgbh/americanexperience/features/transcript/bulge-transcript/

Secrets of World War II, Season 1, Episode 13: *The Secrets of the Battle of the Bulge* (documentary, prod. Jonathan Martin and narrated by Robert Powell, Nugus/Martin Productions, 1998)

Great Blunders of WWII, Season 1, Episode 5: *The Battle of the Bulge* (documentary, prod. Jonathan Martin and narrated by Stan Watt, History Channel, 1998)

Band of Brothers, Episodes 6 *'Bastogne'* and 7 *'The Breaking Point'* (movie, dirs. Steven Spielberg and Tom Hanks, HBO, 2001)

The War in Colour, Episode 18: *The Battle of the Ardennes* (documentary; alternative title: *Battlefront – the Historical Battles of WWII in Color*; dir. Tracy Pearce, National Geographic, 2001)

Silent Night (movie, dir. Rodney Gibbons, 2002), based on the true Christmas story of Elisabeth and Fritz Vincken

Saints and Soldiers (movie, dir. Ryan Little, 2003)

War Stories with Oliver North, Season 3, Episode 29: *Battle of the Bulge* (documentary, prod. Pamela K. Browne and Jim Gaffey, 2003)

The Battle of the Bulge Remembered by Walter Cronkite (NPR broadcast, 27 December 2004) at: http://www.npr.org/templates/story/story.php?storyId=4246503

Marching Once More: 60 Years after the Battle of the Bulge (documentary, prod. Brenda Hughes, ed. Adam Alphin, Wetbird Productions, 2004)

Al Murray's Road To Berlin, Episode 7: *The Battle of the Bulge* (documentary, prod. Ludo Graham and narrated by Al Murray, Discovery Channel, 2004)

Transcending Bonds: The 75th Infantry Division Revisits the Battle of the Bulge (documentary, dir. Ian Denny, Kaos Films, 2005)

Battleground: The Art of War – Battle of the Bulge (documentary, Season 1, Episode 2, dir. Dean Alioto; prod. Gary Tarpinian, 2005)

BattleField Detectives, Season 3, Episode 1: *The Battle of the Bulge* (documentary, dir. James Millar/David Wright; prod. Keith Farrell/James Millar, History Channel, 2005)

Shootout! Season 2, Episode 2: *The Battle of the Bulge* (documentary, dir. and writer Laura Verklan, prod. Sam Dolan, History Channel, 2006)

The Lost Evidence: Battle of the Bulge (documentary, prod. Taylor Downing and dir. Steve Baker, Flashback Productions, 2007)

The War File: Tanks! The Ardennes Offensive (alternative title: *Line of Fire*; documentary, Cromwell Productions, 2008)

Everyman's War (movie, dir. Thad Smith, 2009)

Patton 360, Episode 9: *Battle of the Bulge* (documentary, prod. Rob Beemer and dir. Tony Long, 2009)

Generals at War, Episode 3: *The Battle of the Bulge* (documentary, prod. and dir. Robert Hartel, ed. Rick Alpin, National Geographic, 2009)

The American Road to Victory, Episode 3: *The Americans in the Bulge* (documentary, dir. Richard Lanni/Heidi Mehltretter and presented by Ellwood von Seibold, Living Battlefield/Labyrinth Media, 2010)

The Wereth Eleven (documentary, dir. Robert Child; narrated by Corey Reynolds, Ardennes Group, 2010) The story of the eleven African-American soldiers murdered by SS during the Battle of the Bulge.

Greatest Tank Battles, Season 1, Episode 6: *The Battle of the Bulge: Race to Bastogne* (documentary, prod. Ira Levy and Peter Williamson; dir. Paul Kilback; narrated by Robin Ward, History Channel Canada, 2010)

World War II in Color, Episode 10: *Closing the Ring* (documentary, prod. Philip Nugus and narrated by Robert Powell, Nugus Martin Productions, 2010)

World War II: The Last Heroes, Season 1, Episode 5: *Battle of the Bulge* (documentary, prod. and narrated by Jeremy Llewellyn-Jones, 2011)

Season of Valor – The Battle of the Bulge (documentary, prod. Rod Gragg, Coastal Carolina University, 2011)

Lectures:

Ose, Dr Dieter, *German Preparations for the Ardennes offensive* (Diekirch, 15 December, 2004)

Zabecki, Maj.-Gen. David T., *Failure of Allied Intelligence and American Reaction Following the First Days of the German Surprise Attack* (Diekirch, 15 December, 2004)

Index

Page numbers in *italics* refer to images. Towns and villages are listed under countries.

www.ingramcontent.com/pod-product-compliance
Lightning Source LLC
LaVergne TN
LVHW090428230725
816804LV00022B/759
9780190627799